Shooter's Bible

101ST EDITION

BLISH

Skyhorse Publishing books may be purchased in bulk at special discounts for sales promotion, corporate gifts, fund-raising, or educational purposes. Special editions can also be created to specifications. For details, contact the Special Sales Department, Skyhorse Publishing, 555 Eighth Avenue, Suite 903, New York, NY 10018 or info@skyhorsepublishing.com.

www.skyhorsepublishing.com

10 9 8 7 6 5 4 3 2 1

ISBN-13: 978-1-60239-801-6
ISSN: 0080-9365

Printed in the United States of America

Note: Every effort has been made to record specifications and descriptions of guns, ammunition, and accessories accurately, but the Publisher can take no responsibility for errors or omissions. The prices shown for guns, ammunition, and accessories are manufacturers' suggested retail prices (unless otherwise noted) and are furnished for information only. These were in effect at press time and are subject to change without notice. Purchasers of the book have complete freedom of choice in pricing for resale.

Special thanks to the National Rifle Association, for access to their image archives.

CONTENTS

FOREWORD

This year's *Shooter's Bible*, the 101st edition, begins a new chapter in the eighty-six-year-old reference book's history. Yes, this new edition covers all of the new guns, ammo, and optics, as always, but now, for the first time, it's being produced by a different publisher. Let me explain . . .

First, a bit of history. *Shooter's Bible* began as the mail-order catalog of the Stoeger Arms Corporation back in 1923. The first numbered edition of *Shooter's Bible* was published in 1925; it's been published annually, and in some cases bi-annually, ever since. More than 7 million copies were sold in that time, and it continues to be the ultimate reference book for millions of people who want information on new guns, ammunition, optics, and other accessories, as well as up-to-date prices and specifications for thousands and thousands of firearms.

Until this year, *Shooter's Bible* had been published by Stoeger Arms which, since 2000, has been a division of the Benelli Corporation. In 2008, and for reasons known only to them, Benelli decided to stop publishing not only *Shooters Bible*, but all Stoeger books, and to shut down that division entirely.

While this was transpiring, the editors at Stoeger published the 100th anniversary edition of *Shooter's Bible*. It was distributed in 2008, but due to the impending closure of the company, only a very small number of copies were sold. This was in sharp contrast to the average of 100,000 copies sold each previous year. With Stoeger closing up shop, an institution was on the verge of dying, until . . .

Earlier this year, Skyhorse Publishing, a new publishing house run by Tony Lyons, formerly the publisher of the Lyons Press, acquired the rights to a number of Stoeger titles, including *Shooter's Bible*, and will publish the popular reference book every year going forward.

Recognizing that most people had been unable to find copies of the 100th anniversary edition, Skyhorse has included the 2008–2009 new products section, which was assembled by the Stoeger staff, as well as the 100th anniversary edition retrospective, which traces the history of *Shooter's Bible* from its first issue through 2008. Also included in this edition is the regular yearly New Products section for firearms, ammunition, and optics manufactured in 2009 and/or planned for 2010. This section was assembled by Wayne van Zwoll, no stranger to any of you who like to read about firearms, shooting, and hunting.

To further enhance the 101st edition, Skyhorse has also bought the rights to republish the popular feature, "The 50 Best Guns Ever Made," by long-time *Field & Stream* shooting columnist, David E. Petzal. That piece, which appeared in the February 2005 issue of *Field & Stream*, generated a tremendous response at the time, as readers of the popular magazine debated the merits of each of the 50 guns, while others questioned why their favorite guns were not included.

When asked if he would add any guns to the 50 Best, Petzal replied that the Barrett Model 99 deserves a place in that list: "The idea of chambering a sporting rifle for the monster .50 Browning cartridges goes back fifty years or more, but only within the past ten years or so have we seen the proliferation of sporting rifles built to handle the Big .50. Barrett was the leader from the start in this idea, and its Model 99 is typical of the breed. It's a bullpup single-shot bolt-action that weighs 25 pounds, has a 30-inch barrel, and is equipped with a huge clamshell muzzle brake that makes the beast shootable. The Barrett 99—and rifles like it—redefine what is possible with a shoulder-fired arm. People hunt with them, and shoot in benchrest matches, and just blaze away at distant boulders in the desert for the sheer hell of it. Just shooting one—never mind if you hit anything—is a memorable experience of itself."

Tough to argue with that, although I'm thinking that the new Benelli Vinci might deserve a spot in the 50 Best as well. And which gun would you drop if you had to make room for a Barrett or Benelli? Such is the grist for long debates.

Skyhorse Publishing is extremely proud to be the new publisher of *Shooter's Bible*. It is a job the whole staff takes seriously, and readers can rest assured that every step will be taken to ensure that each annual edition will be as accurate, up-to-date, and useful as is humanly possible.

—*Jay Cassell*

INTRODUCTION

Shooter's Bible dates way back. Before Eugene Stoner designed what became the AR-15. Before Elmer Keith lobbied for a .44 Magnum. Before Remington announced its most successful pump shotgun, 10 million 870s ago. Shooter's Bible came before James Bond and color television, Sputnik, power steering and the GI Bill. It was well established long before McDonald's slid its first burger off the grill. Actually, Shooter's Bible predates World War II and the Great Depression. Since 1923, when firearms importer A. F. Stoeger assembled his first price list, his publication has grown. It saw the debut of the .357 Magnum, the .257 Roberts, even the .270 Winchester. Shooter's Bible became the standard reference for hunters and competitive marksmen, for handloaders, collectors, and everyone interested in the history, manufacture, and performance of sporting arms.

Now, 7 million copies later, it still is. Today, Shooter's Bible is packed with even more guns, ammunition, and optics; more ballistics data; more shooting tips; more background and technical savvy on the firearms you like best. The most important change this year is the extensive New Products section. There you'll find the latest, most innovative guns, loads, and sights. In photos and specifications, you'll be up-to-date on hardware that defines the shooting industry—all in a format that invites comparisons and helps you sift the best from the rest. Reading Shooter's Bible, you'll join the most accomplished of shotgunners, handgunners, and rifle enthusiasts. Many of these men and women got their start in, and stay abreast of the shooting world with Shooter's Bible.

A personal note: I'm fascinated by the history of the firearms industry, and have written about it often. A lot of that history has passed through the pages of Shooter's Bible. Eighty-seven years ago, A. F. Stoeger published its first price list of imported guns and accoutrements. You could have bought an original Luger for as little as $27.50, a full-stocked Mauser Sporting Rifle for $65, a first-quality German boxlock double shotgun for $80. The Broomhandle Mauser pistol with buttstock would have set you back $45—about what you'll spend these days to fill your sedan's gas tank. In the grim decade that followed, prices inched down to court a cash-strapped public. At one point, Parker's beautiful A1 Special double shotgun sold for $750.

Stoeger's catalog trundled into war to emerge as "The Shooter's Bible". A loyal customer evidently coined the name, first used on the cover in 1944. A year later, A. F. Stoeger died. He was succeeded by his son, A. F. Stoeger, Jr. By the time I was toddling about in the early 1950s, Shooter's Bible had become one of the country's premier gun publications, running to nearly 600 pages. The catalog grew, joined now by a series of feature articles, ballistics tables, and technical charts. As it passed from family hands, the Stoeger firm changed its corporate face but kept Shooter's Bible alive. Stoeger Publishing Company produced the book; then, as Stoeger Publishing, Inc., it was acquired by Sako Oy, the Swedish rifle manufacturer. Mostly Sako wanted the firearms importing and distribution part of the business: Stoeger Industries, Inc. In 2000, the Beretta group of Italian gunmakers bought Sako and its Stoeger companies. Shooter's Bible stayed on under new management.

This edition of Shooter's Bible marks another change. The book is now in the capable hands of veteran publishers Tony Lyons and Jay Cassell. They're both committed to preserving the rich history of Stoeger while delivering taut, lively, informative text and crisp images on the hundreds of pages that make each Shooter's Bible a browser's delight. You'll want this book in your hands. Two decades ago, I had the privilege of editing Shooter's Bible. It's been my pleasure to update this one. I suspect in years to come that successive editions of Shooter's Bible will more than earn their place on your bookshelves. It's what real shooters read.

—Wayne van Zwoll

NEW PRODUCTS, 2009–2010

The salesman laughed. "We could stop taking orders now and keep the lines busy through most of 2010." Oh, that the auto industry were so pressed! But this fellow worked for an ammunition company. His colleagues at gun firms have felt the surge too. "We can't keep enough 1911s to parse out for review," one told me. "Demand for autoloading pistols has never been stronger." Another allowed that "Black guns are selling to the walls. If it's an AR-15, somebody wants it. If it's one of the top-end models, they're willing to wait months."

Elections that put Democrats in charge in D.C. commonly draw gun enthusiasts to store counters. But in 2009, even the most committed defenders of the Second Amendment had to admit that any threats of tighter gun restrictions were trumped by concerns of the economy. After a rush to stock up on ammo and primers, and to snatch that last carbine from the rack, shooters confronted the restricted cash flow that had begun to affect almost every other American. Manufacturers running overtime shifts could see that sales would eventually fall off. Some invested in plant equipment and hired additional staff to take advantage of the spike in demand. Others hewed to a more conservative approach. "If you can parlay investments into more market share during a pull-back," said one sage executive, "those expenditures can pay off. But you also need innovative new products to keep customers interested. And you can't dispense with advertising. When sales dip in the wake of a buying binge, you must maintain or grow your piece of the market pie."

Not all segments of the firearms industry have participated equally in the recent boom. Expensive shotguns "have been a bit soft, compared to the tactical hardware," observed a wholesaler. "But even those of us who qualify as dinosaurs in the business have been astounded at the sales of ordinary sporting ammo—not just .223, .308, and .45, but deer cartridges and magnums, even loads for heavy African game." In an economic climate that has outfitters scrambling for clients, it's obvious gun enthusiasts aren't just planning for the next safari.

"We sell dreams," an executive confided to me years ago. It's still true. Much of the ammunition purchased over the last months will be a long time getting shot. It will go to enthusiasts who will never kill a brown bear or an elephant or fire a 1,000-yard match or engage multiple hostiles in a fire-fight—but who relish their association with men who do. Guns and ammo provide a tangible link. Cowboy Action shooters use their hardware to travel back in time, where imagination brings them face-to-face with outlaws and the rough edge of the western frontier. Yes, dreams matter to the market.

Some firearms are still built as tools, with scant emphasis on cosmetics and more attention given to durability and reliability. Other guns qualify as art, their walnut too lovely to risk in a saddle scabbard or on alpine rock, their engraving unappreciated by the great unwashed. Collectibles comprise not only historical firearms made long ago, but current models with that elusive combination of features and feel that will one day make it a coveted classic. Most rifles, shotguns, and handguns comprise elements of tool and art. Fast-changing markets and increasing competition—especially in the areas of tactical guns and optics— 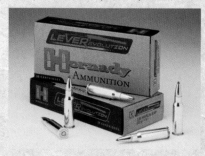 demand that new products also offer something different. A tall order, and one that often leads to gimmickry. Long-term profits depend on lasting appeal. In the New Products section of this 101st edition of *Shooter's Bible*, you'll find guns and sights across a range of prices, with all the data you need to sift and compare, to assess the utility of new features and select what will give you the most fun—and better shooting.

Nearly all developments in centerfire rifles have built on the turn-bolt mechanism designed and then refined by Peter Paul Mauser. The powerful, flat-shooting cartridges that get most attention these days match up well with bolt guns. But strong lever mechanisms have grabbed headlines too—partly due to the Cowboy Action game. Cowboy Action compels participants and spectators to live out real and imagined Old West gun-play, with period hardware. Costumes and aliases add spice. Hunters enamored with the lever action now have deadlier loads in Hornady LeverEvolution cartridges. The pointed FlexTip bullet, safe in tube magazines, gives shooters taut bullet arcs, greater accuracy, and more down-range power. LeverEvolution ammo has breathed new life into the likes of the .30-30, .32 Special, .35 Remington, and .45-70. It's also available in more modern loads. Legacy Sports International offers some of the best-finished, smoothest-flicking lever guns for the Cowboy game, in its Chiappa-built M92. Marlin, now owned by Remington, still builds the best-selling lever guns for big game hunters. The new .338 Marlin Express cartridge gives them .30-06 reach.

The lever gun is fast, but no faster than Blaser's R93: a straight-pull, collet-locking rifle with a telescoping bolt. It cycles like a Ferrari shifter; the trigger pull is crisp as the snap of a glass rod. Accuracy matches that of the best traditional bolt-action sporters. And the 2010 field is chock full of variations on that theme. Browning's X-Bolt has a much better stock than its predecessor, the A-Bolt—plus a clever tab on the bolt knob that lets you unlock the action and shuck cartridges with the safety on. Kimber's trim 84M now comes in Classic Stainless form, and the long-action 8400 has been chambered in .280 Remington Improved. If you want an outstanding bolt rifle with understated class, look at the McMillan line, including the Prodigy, with Jewell trigger. Hewing to a tight budget this year? Consider the new Mossberg ATR and 4x4 rifles, both now with LBA (Lightning Bolt Action) trigger, adjustable to 2 pounds.

Remington sells more bolt rifles than any other maker these days. For 2010, several new versions of the 700 include barrels triangular in cross-section. No magic here, but these barrels are shooting small groups! Digital camo distinguishes the stock of the 700 VTR Desert Recon. A new chambering is available in Remington's R-15 rifle (an AR-15 by

Bushmaster). The .30 Remington AR pushes 125-grain bullets at 2,800 fps, about the speed you'll get from 150s in a .308. But the stubby round fits an AR-15 mechanism.

Sako's flagship Model 85 has been joined by the A7 in two action lengths and 12 chamberings. A polymer box magazine reflects trends at the Finnish rifle-maker, responsible for the Tikka line as well. Both the 85 and the A7 feature three-lug bolts and hammer-forged barrels. There's a fresh stable of rifles at Ruger, too. The Hawkeye profile announced last year replaces the old 77 Mark II in more sub-models. The .300 and .338 Ruger Compact Magnum rounds deliver high velocities from the 20-inch barrels of Hawkeye carbines. The No. 1 single-shot now chambers the .475 Linebaugh and .460 S&W. BPI's CVA rifle line, initially for muzzle-loading enthusiasts, includes for 2010 an Apex switch-barrel gun that accepts black-powder tubes, plus modern centerfire rifle barrels.

Innovator and CEO Ron Coburn and engineer Scott Warburton developed AccuTrigger for Savage rifles. Now they've patented AccuStock, a molded polymer stock with an action cradle that straddles the magazine well. The cradle acts like a V-block. When you draw the action down, the sides spring apart as much as .048. The receiver bottoms on a machined shelf, so the cradle walls and base bear tightly against the receiver. A small wedge-shaped block in front of the recoil lug engages a tapered mating face in the forend rib, pushing the action back as you tighten an additional screw, and pressing the recoil lug against its abutment. "The block, spine, and cradle make stock and metal function as a unit," claims Ron. Plans are to phase AccuStock into Savage's first-tier rifles quickly as a standard feature.

Smith & Wesson's big news for 2010 is a small rifle—a rimfire version of its M&P 15. The rifle features polymer upper and lower components, a quad rail, a six-position stock and a 25-round magazine. Handgun offerings include new entries in the Classic series: Model 15 .22, Model 14 .38 Special, Models 57 and 58, .41 Magnum. If S&W dominates in the field of revolvers, Taurus has succeeded in marketing a long line of look-alikes and some innovative new models. A howling success recently has been The Judge, a five-shot revolver that accepts both .45 Long Colt and .410 shotshell ammo. There's a new version this year. Ruger has added to its roster of single-actions and listed a follow-up to its popular LCP (Lightweight Compact Pistol). The LCR has a cleverly designed alloy and polymer frame with a stainless cylinder that holds five .38 Special +P rounds. It wears a 2-inch barrel, Hogue grips. Ruger has also announced a SASS revolver in .357 for Cowboy Action shooters—and sells it in pairs. The SR9 autoloading pistol, a 4-inch 10-shot 9mm, now comes in two configurations.

Among the 79 (count 'em!) 1911s in Kimber's 2009 catalog, you'll find a Team Match II in 9mm. The Stainless Ultra Raptor has an alloy frame, the Stainless Pro Raptor a stainless frame. Both come from the Custom Shop with night sights, ambidextrous safety, and zebra-wood grips. The Tactical Entry II and Tactical Custom HD have carbon-steel slides and stainless frames with checkered front straps, night sights, ambidextrous safeties, extended magazine wells. Competition in the 1911 field continues to ratchet up in response to an apparently insatiable appetite for John Browning's classic pistol. Para Ordnance, formerly a Canadian company, will be supplying its 1911, LDA, and P-series autoloaders from a new home in the Carolinas. Recently it announced a G.I.-style 1911. No frills—though refinements aren't totally lacking. Affordably priced, the gun should prove a hit among shooters put off by four-figure prices for 1911s.

Shotgunners will recognize many old numbers in the new product offerings this year. Remington has produced 10 million 870 pump-guns, but it has just unveiled an 870 Express Tactical, with seven-shot magazine under an 18-inch barrel and XS Ghost Ring sights. The new 870 SureShot Superslug is designed for deer hunting. It has an extra-heavy, fluted, 25-inch rifled barrel and a Weaver scope rail on the receiver. The firm's 11-87 line has grown, with its Compact Sportsman Supercell EXT, a 20-bore with an adjustable stock intended to fit youngsters through their growth stages. Remington

has also come up with a Model 887 pump gun; its ArmorLokt jacket seals off the weather.

Weatherby's lightweight, fast-handling over/under guns have been joined recently by autoloaders with a surprisingly lively feel, and the pump-action Upland PA-08. Walnut-stocked, with interchangeable chokes, the PA-08 comes with a 26- or 28-inch ribbed barrel—at a list price that will take you back years!

Mossberg's 535 ATS pump is wallet-friendly too. This thumbhole turkey gun has a ported barrel tube and synthetic stock. So does the new 939 Magnum Turkey Gun, an autoloader on an action proven in rigorous tests in the dove fields of South America. Browning's new Maxus Stalker and Maxus Duck Blind 12-gauge self-loaders come in both 3-inch and 3 ½-inch chamberings. They're heavy guns, for extended shooting with stiff loads at big birds. Camo-finished synthetic stocks are standard. Vent ribs of course.

If you're more enamored with little guns that handle like wands, Blaser's newest F3 is worth a look. A worthy addition to this line of carefully fitted over/unders, the 28-gauge is built on an appropriately slim frame. Pick it up, and you'll think of a top-grade Merkel sub-bore, or a Perazzi. Another name to remember: Fausti. This mid-price Italian shotgun, in all its many forms, combines the aesthetic appeal of the finest smoothbores with a pick-me-up-and-shoot-me quality that compels you to forget the pretty wood and call the shorthair. Fausti builds the excellent Weatherby line of stack-barrel guns but also sells under its own label.

Shotgun ammunition, like centerfire and now even rimfire rifle and pistol ammo and black powder projectiles, changes so fast that the word "evolves" no longer applies. While refinements in pellet materials, wad design, and powders may be incremental, the new products and packaging that result fill catalogs every year. Federal's Flight Control wad and Black Cloud waterfowl loads, and its V-Shok Heavyweight Coyote charges (1 ½ ounce of BBs) are headliners for 2010. So is the company's Trophy Bonded Tip bullet—as a component now, as well as in factory centerfire rifle loads. Federal catalogs more bullet choices than any other major ammunition firm. But Winchester and Remington have kept their labs busy too. Both now offer lead-free hunting bullets, and Remington has come up with Disintegrator Varmint Ammunition, featuring a bullet with an iron/tin core. Winchester's .22 Xpediter fires a 32-grain plated hollow-point bullet at 1,640 fps from a nickel-plated case. The company also has tin rimfire bullets: a 30-grain in the .22 WMR at 2,200 fps, and a 28-grain Long Rifle at 1,650. E-Tip and Power Max Bonded rank as most recent in Winchester's line of big game bullets. The company lists PDX1 and DualBond bullets in defense loads for handguns.

Speer Gold Dot, Remington Golden Saber, and Hornady's new Personal Defense loads make every handgun more effective than it was with traditional bullets. Hunting ammo for revolvers has likewise put on muscle, with bullets like the Nosler Partition, Barnes Expander, and CastCore offered in Federal ammo. Bullet companies like Swift, with its new 25-caliber Scirocco, have been so busy that as components and in loaded cartridges, new bullets number in the dozens.

The Swedish firm of Norma has not only grown its ammunition line substantially, with the PH line of 12 big-bore cartridges; it has also come up with new mid-caliber rounds. The .300 and .338 Norma Magnums are based on the .338 Lapua hull trimmed to fit actions designed for common belted short magnums like the 7mm Remington and .338 Winchester—and the potent .308 and .358 Norma Magnums. Head size of these new beltless Norma rounds is the same as that of the Lapua, so bolt faces for the .532 belted heads will not accept them without machine work. What you get for the extra trouble is a very efficient round with more horsepower than you expect. The Norma team is developing a .375 on the same case.

You can't shoot a rifle or a handgun accurately without sights. Optical sights have all but replaced "irons" in the field—except on African stopping rifles and on traditional whitetail guns used where thickets keep most shots inside spitball range. No narrative could quickly condense the long list of new rifle-scopes for 2010. It's easier to explain why so many are so similar: they're made at the same factory. Importing a line of optics from Japan, China, or the Philippines has become a popular pastime, it seems, for people who couldn't possibly raise the capital or find the talent to start an optics firm Stateside. In truth, though, most of these scopes are very, very good. The mid-priced models out-perform the most expensive scopes of just a few years ago. After all, the technology to make top-quality lenses and coatings is available just about everywhere. The most useful improvements have come in the way of coatings to better transmit light, and in new adjustments that are easier to use and more precisely repeatable. Wider power ranges in variables have arrived; now instead of a "three times" 3-9x magnification range, you can get a "six times" 3-18x. In reticles, Trijicon has brought its military-proven combination of tritium and fiber optic illumination to new hunting scopes. Zeiss has developed a scope with a magnetic switch that works with the cocking tab on a Blaser rifle to illuminate the reticle when you thumb the tab forward for a shot.

Well, you get the picture. There's too much glass to cover in text. Leupold alone has enough news to merit a feature article. The next pages, starting on page 35, will give you a graphic review. They're stuffed with the newest guns, ammunition, and optics—just what you expect from *Shooter's Bible*. It's what real shooters read. Before you go there, though, check out David E. Petzal's piece on the 50 best guns ever made, reprinted with permission of *Field & Stream* magazine. It will get you thinking.

—*Wayne van Zwoll*

The 50

Best Guns
Ever Made

BY DAVID E. PETZAL

People love lists. We have lists of the best and worst dressed, the scariest movies, the most beautiful celebrities, the most talented athletes, the dumbest politicians, and just about every other category a magazine editor can dream up. I love lists and am occasionally asked to rattle off my list of what I think are the best guns ever made. However, I've never done so in public. Until now. ¶ This is a subjective ranking in order, but all the firearms here have several things in common: All are superlative designs; all were chosen without regard to price; all were commercial successes to a greater or lesser degree; and almost all were influential on the design of other guns. You'll notice that there are no military or target arms here (with a few exceptions, for reasons explained). We decided to limit the list to hunting firearms, which is what F&S is about. In making my selection, I've limited myself to the past 100 years or so, going back to the introduction of smokeless powder, so these are guns of the modern era. In many ways, firearms have changed very little over the past century. That doesn't mean they haven't progressed; it means they were pretty good to begin with—and these are the best.

[1]
Winchester Model 70
(pre-1964)

It was not even an original design. The Model 70 was an improvement of Winchester's Model 54, which in turn was based on the Mauser Model 98. But upon its birth in 1936, it kindled a love affair that has never died. Winchester advertised it as "the rifleman's rifle," and the slogan stuck. This was the big-game rifle by which all others were measured, and it is still, in my opinion, the best factory bolt action ever made. ¶ The gun borrowed the best features from both the Mauser 98 and the Model 54. It retained the Mauser's massive extractor and controlled-feed system but utilized a cone-shaped breech like the Model 54's, which guided cartridges into the chamber even if they

TOP GUN: A pre-1964 Featherweight version of the Model 70.

weren't perfectly aligned. In place of the Mauser's slow, jarring firing-pin fall, the Model 70's was very fast and smooth. The trigger was the best ever designed for a hunting rifle, period—a three-piece miracle of simplicity that gave an excellent pull, would never fail, and once adjusted was adjusted forever. ¶ But the Model 70 has had a rocky road. Pre–World War II examples were fine, but after the war quality steadily declined, and the ones turned out before the old model's demise in 1963 were shoddy indeed. Winchester's then-president decreed that it must die because it was too costly to produce. ¶ In 1964, Winchester announced a new Model 70 that was cheaper and basically a good gun, but it was big-time, serious Ugly. Shooters beheld it and were outraged. Their fury did not abate until 1994, when Winchester reintroduced the traditional design under the name Model 70 Classic. ¶ Many of the original Model 70s are now collector's pieces, particularly in the scarcer calibers, and some people will pay very fancy prices for them. Its luster remains undimmed. Never before and probably never again will we see such a combination of accuracy, reliability, grace, and mystique. ▶

[2]
Mauser Model 98

Imagine someone building an automobile two years before the end of the 19th century, five years before the Wright brothers flew. Now imagine that this same automobile is still very much in use, still regarded by many as the best car around, and still in production. That is exactly what Peter Paul Mauser did when he designed his Model 98 rifle in Germany.

One of two military arms on this list, the 98 is here because it also comes in sporting versions, and because its action has been the basis for almost every bolt action made since 1900.

The Model 98 was the culmination of five preceding models and is, to quote *The Encyclopedia of Small Arms,* "the most successful bolt-action design ever produced." Made in the millions, it was used by most of the world's armies throughout the 20th century. If there is such a thing as an unstoppable machine, the Model 98 comes as close as anything.

New Mauser-actioned rifles are being crafted in Europe, and the military actions that date back 60 years or more remain sought after by gunsmiths and lovers of custom rifles. In some circles, if you mention that you have a short-action (G33/40) Mauser for sale, people will begin weeping and licking your shoes.

There is a reason for this: Come hell, high water, sand, ice, snow, mud, dirty ammo, rusty chambers, burst cases, or anything else, the Mauser 98 will function.

[3]
Winchester Model 12

It is well known among the snobbier of shotgun enthusiasts that no repeating shotgun can handle as well as an over/under or a side-by-side. But there is one repeater that points like the Finger of Doom itself—the Model 12 pump.

Introduced in 1914, the Model 12 lasted until 1976, when production costs drove it out of the

---

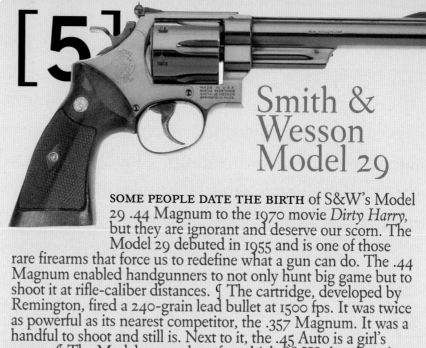

[5]
Smith & Wesson Model 29

SOME PEOPLE DATE THE BIRTH of S&W's Model 29 .44 Magnum to the 1970 movie *Dirty Harry,* but they are ignorant and deserve our scorn. The Model 29 debuted in 1955 and is one of those rare firearms that force us to redefine what a gun can do. The .44 Magnum enabled handgunners to not only hunt big game but to shoot it at rifle-caliber distances. ¶ The cartridge, developed by Remington, fired a 240-grain lead bullet at 1500 fps. It was twice as powerful as its nearest competitor, the .357 Magnum. It was a handful to shoot and still is. Next to it, the .45 Auto is a girl's caress. ¶ The Model 29 revolver, for which S&W chambered the new cartridge, was as fine a gun as Smith—or anyone else—knew how to make. Selling for the then astronomical sum of $240, Model 29s were beautifully fitted and finished, and each one came in its own handsome wooden case. ¶ Both powerful and beautiful to look upon, the Model 29 was very accurate as well. If you didn't care to break your hand with .44 Magnums, you could shoot .44 Specials in your Model 29, making it as docile and accurate a revolver as you could want. ¶ *Dirty Harry* was a vulgar sideshow. The S&W Model 29 is a masterpiece that changed the sport of shooting.

Winchester lineup. It came in every shape and form—from field models to riot guns to heavy waterfowl models—and in all gauges, but it was as a competition gun that the Model 12 was perhaps most dominant.

For decade after decade, if you did not shoot trap and skeet with a Model 12, you were an odd fellow. The Model 12 seemed to lock on a target and stay there, and you could not wear it out. Serious shooters would put several hundred thousand rounds through their guns, have some minor rebuilding done, and repeat the process. I've handled one Model 12 trap gun that had had a million shells shucked through it, and it was in much better health than its owner.

And it shot fast. Well-broken-in Model 12s had a slickety-slack smoothness that let you shoot them as quickly as an auto. Winchester's great exhibition shooter Herb Parsons used to hold five clay targets in his left hand, throw them into the air, and break them all before they hit the ground, pumping his Model 12 faster than the eye could follow.

The Model 12 has faded now, overshadowed by more modern guns, but in its time it was the repeater—indeed, the *shotgun*—against which all others were measured.

[4]
Remington Model 1100

Autoloading shotguns had been around for a long time by 1963, but the new Model 1100 was different. Previous self-loaders were heavy and handled like sledgehammers. If they were recoil operated, they kicked like mules. People

---

FIREARMS OF THE FUTURE

Scott Warburton, **DESIGN ENGINEER, SAVAGE ARMS**
"In the future, we need to create more accurate guns that can multi-task and be converted for different kinds of shooting. Their overall appearance should also change to fit the high-tech look of the future."

tolerated them only because they offered three or more fast shots. The 1100, on the other hand, was sleek, moderate in weight, and handled splendidly. Most important, it had softened recoil.

Its gas-operated action spread the rearward thrust of the gun over a long period of time and took the sting out of shooting. Trap and skeet competitors bought 1100s by the carload. New shooters, and people who otherwise would not be shooters, took to the 1100 as the one gun that would not beat the daylights out of them.

The 1100 was not perfect. It would jam if you didn't keep its gas system clean, and it wouldn't digest every kind of shell you fed it. Once you really began to pour the rounds through, an 1100 would break, but it was easy to fix. Not a "fine" gun like the Model 12, no marvel of fit and finish, the 1100 made extensive use of stamped parts. But it was, and is, a revolutionary gun.

[6]
Winchester Model 94

It is useful only at comparatively short range; it does not take to scope mounting; it is not accurate by today's standards. Every attempt to torture it into something else has failed. But if you say "deer rifle," you mean the Model 94 lever action. Short and light, it kicks hardly at all, gets on target fast, is ultrareliable, and carries comfortably in the hand.

Although the 94 has been chambered for half a dozen cartridges over the years, the overwhelming favorite is the .30/30. In fact, "thutty-thutty" and "deer rifle" are more or less synonymous. It's hard to imagine now, but the .30/30 was considered a red-hot high-velocity round when it first appeared in 1895. It was the first small-bore big-game load to utilize smokeless powder, and it fired 170-grain bullets at the then sensational velocity of 1970 fps.

A relic the 94 may be, but as hundreds of thousands of whitetails would testify, it's a very effective one.

[7]
Remington Model 700

In the years after World War II, Remington hired a pair of brilliant designers named Mike

Walker and Wayne Leek. The two men realized that if the company was to survive, it could not make guns the way it had before 1941. The new generation of Remingtons would have to be far simpler and cheaper to make. And so they came out with a horrible-looking rifle called the Model 721. It was cheap to make and looked it, but it was more accurate than any other factory rifle at the time.

In 1962, after an intermediate generation, the 721 morphed into the Model 700, which, although still a cinch to make, was a good-looking gun that retained all of its accuracy. The first minute-of-angle group I ever saw from a sport-

Benelli Autoloader

[8]

NEWTON'S FIRST LAW OF MOTION—an object at rest tends to remain at rest—drives the ultradependable Benelli action, which redefined autoloading reliability in the 1990s.

The Benelli system consists of nothing more than a three-part bolt assembly—a bolt body, a rotary bolt head, and a short, stout spring between the two. As the rest of the gun moves backward under recoil, the unfixed free-floating bolt body remains in place, butting against the bolt head, solidly locking the action, and compressing the spring. When the rearward movement of the gun slows, the spring throws the bolt backward, ejecting the spent shell.

This inertia system functions with a wide range of loads, and by beefing up the action, Benelli was able to turn the original 3-inch Black Eagle into the 3½-inch Super Black Eagle with relative ease. The company's lineup today consists of well over 100 model variations, from lightweight bird guns to magnum turkey-getters, all built around the same simple action.

Since the system doesn't bleed off expanding gases to operate, the gases and fouling blast out the barrel with the rest of the payload, leaving the inside of the gun clean. Benellis, therefore, keep on shooting under conditions that strangle most gas guns. They make the very short list of models South American outfitters keep as "house guns" that will cycle more rounds in a season than most guns shoot in their owner's lifetime.

Hunters praise their Benellis for reliable performance, but slick handling qualities may be the guns' best feature. Because it has no springs or pistons around the magazine tube, a Benelli auto is lighter and slimmer up front than any gas gun.

Finally, Benellis are *fast,* spitting out empties and chambering fresh rounds more quickly than any other auto. For average hunters, however, speed isn't a critical issue; function is. And the Benelli keeps on plugging long after other guns fall by the wayside.

THE RELIABLE AUTO

EJECTION CYCLE

[E]

[D]

The Benelli recoil system is simplicity itself, consisting of a bolt body (A), a bolt spring (B), and a rotary bolt head (C). As the gun recoils, the bolt body remains in place, compressing the spring and locking the bolt head. As recoil eases (D), the spring releases and ejects the empty shell (E). There's no gas system to worry about or clean, and Benellis will handle any kind of shell you feed them.

ACTION WHEN LOADED BEFORE FIRING

[A]   [B]   [C]

ing rifle came courtesy of a Model 700 7mm Remington Magnum.

Since its inception, the Model 700 has been the foundation for more superaccurate rifles than anything else. Its sheer simplicity of design and wonderful trigger make it the first choice of anyone who wants to shoot small groups.

[10]
Remington Model 870

Think of it as a Winchester Model 12 that is easy

which are used for plinking and small-game hunting, the normal task of a .22 auto.

But at some point it was discovered that if you installed a heavy target barrel and a custom trigger and replaced the factory stock with a high-combed target model, you'd have a rifle of uncanny accuracy that you could compete with and

[11] Browning Superposed

UNLESS YOU ARE AN ADVANCED GEEZER, you are unaware that over/unders were once a rarity in the United States. Then came the Browning Superposed, and all that changed. A John M. Browning design, the Superposed was made in Belgium and was introduced in 1931, two years into the Great Depression. This should have killed the costly Superposed, but it was so superior an arm that it survived and thrived. ¶ It was made in all gauges and in four grades and became a mainstay of hunters and competitive shooters alike. More important, for decades on end it was the definition of a "fine" gun. If you shot a Browning Superposed, you were shooting something special.

[9]
Remington XP-100

The development of handguns has progressed in a series of seismic jolts. One came in 1963, when Remington announced the XP-100, which looked like a prop from a Buck Rogers movie. It was not so much a handgun as a one-handed rifle. To make the gun, Remington utilized the bolt action from its Model 600 carbine, a Zytel stock borrowed from the Model 66 .22 autoloader, and a barrel rib and sights from the Model 660 magnum carbine. Designers didn't stop there, though. They also cooked up a red-hot varmint cartridge called the .221 Fireball to chamber in the new gun. The result was historic: For the first time, varmint hunters could pound pasture poodles without a rifle, and handgunning had taken on a whole new dimension.

to manufacture. The Model 870 made its debut in 1950 as one of the first of Remington's "new generation" of guns that did away with the complex machining of the past. And it may be sacrilege to say so, but the plebian 870 is probably as good a gun as the aristocratic Model 12. It pumps just as fast, points as well, is just as reliable, and is unbelievably long-lived. The late shotgunning great Rudy Etchen put 4 million rounds through his 870 with just some minor parts replacement to keep it going. The 870 is still with us, made in every configuration known to man, and it will probably be around for many years more.

[12]
Ruger 10/22

This may well be the most popular rimfire rifle in the world, and it is probably the most cobbled on. Arriving in 1964, the 10/22 has been made in half a dozen configurations, most of

win. The reliable, affordable 10/22 regularly morphs into a supergun, but millions of them are still being used to shoot squirrels and tin cans.

[13]
Browning Auto-5 Standard

It is called the Humpback and gets this unlovely name from its unlovely receiver, which forms an abrupt angle where it joins the stock. John M. Browning designed this recoil-operated autoloading shotgun, which debuted in the United States in 1903, was discontinued that same year, and then was reintroduced in 1923, this time to stay for 50 years. The Humpback had one glaring fault: It kicked. Its bolt came crashing back with enthusiasm. But it had one great virtue: It worked. Waterfowlers loved it. In an era of swollen cardboard shells that would stop any other gun, the Humpback kept shooting.

[14]
Springfield Model 1903

Besides the Model 98 Mauser, this is the only military arm to make my list. The '03 Spring-

FIREARMS OF THE FUTURE

Melvin Forbes, PRESIDENT, NEW ULTRA LIGHT ARMS
"It's not going to change. It's going to be all Model 70 Winchesters and nostalgia. You can't sell a gun unless it looks like granddaddy's gun."

field is a slavish copy of the Model 98; Mauser sued the Springfield Armory for patent infringement and won. This aside, the '03 is the most graceful military rifle ever made, and one of the most accurate.

It earns its place here because it changed us from a nation of lever-action shooters to a nation of bolt-action shooters. The Doughboys who were issued Springfields during World War I decided that the '03 was the way to go. Thousands upon thousands of the rifles were converted to sporting use, or their actions were used as the basis for custom rifles. The very first Springfield sporter was made in 1909 for President Theodore Roosevelt. As a military and a sporting arm alike, the '03 was an aristocrat.

[16]
Mossberg 500

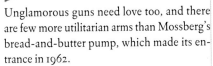

Unglamorous guns need love too, and there are few more utilitarian arms than Mossberg's bread-and-butter pump, which made its entrance in 1962.

It figures not in verse and song, but it's affordable, and it works, and that is enough for thousands and thousands of shooters who swear by the 500. Like all hugely successful designs, it has been produced in many configurations and is in current use by the U.S. military, which is a sure sign that the thing is tough. When your Purdey balks and your Parker doubles, turn to the Mossberg 500, for it will not fail you.

[17]
Remington Nylon 66

It's quite possible that our acceptance of synthetic stocks is due to a .22 rimfire autoloader that Remington first offered in 1959. It was called the Nylon 66 and had a stock made of a high-strength DuPont material called Zytel. It weighed only 4 pounds, held 14 rounds in a tubular magazine in the butt, and was offered in brown, black, or green. And it was unstoppable. I never cleaned mine and used it in 20-below temperatures, and it never failed me.

In 1959, over a period of 14 days, Remington's exhibition shooter Tom Frye shot at

Smith & Wesson Model 500

[15]

INTRODUCED IN 2003, this $4\frac{1}{2}$-pound monster of a double-action revolver is as much of a quantum leap over existing handguns as the Model 29 was 50 years ago. The .50 S&W cartridge fires a 400-grain bullet at over 1600 fps, leaving the .44 Magnum—and just about everything else—far in the dust. But the immensely strong, very expensive Model 500 revolver is surprisingly easy to shoot, considering how powerful it is. You want it, the Model 500 can drop it for you, from deer to Cape buffalo.

[A]

THE .50-CALIBER REVOLVER

[B]   [C]

The $10\frac{1}{2}$-inch-barrel model comes with a sling.

The 500's cylinder (A) holds five shots rather than six and employs an unusual ball detent that actually uses the force of recoil to hold the cylinder in alignment. This version of the revolver comes with a $10\frac{1}{2}$-inch barrel equipped with a muzzle brake (B) and an integral rail (C) for scope mounting. In size (D) and weight the Model 500 dwarfs a Model 629 .44 Magnum with a 4-inch barrel: 18 inches overall compared to $9\frac{5}{8}$; 82 ounces to 41.5.

SIZE COMPARISON

18"

$9\frac{5}{8}$"

The S&W Model 500 dwarfs the Model 629, itself a sizable revolver.

[D]

100,010 wood blocks thrown into the air, using two Model 66s. He hit all but six and had no malfunctions.

The Nylon 66 had a 41-year production run, and over a million were made.

[18]
New Ultra Light Arms Model 20

Prior to 1985, all light bolt-action hunting rifles began as heavy factory guns that were chopped, gouged, and hacked into svelteness. The first bolt gun that was born truly light was a .308 that weighed $5\frac{1}{2}$ pounds with a scope.

Melvin Forbes, a West Virginia gunsmith, enlisted the help of two friends to create a Kevlar stock that weighed only a pound, and then he designed a barreled action that did not have an extra ounce in it. The result was so light it seemed like a toy, and it was as accurate as much heavier guns. As for durability, a NULA action, used for testing by Nosler Bullets, had 4 million rounds cycled through it over $12\frac{1}{2}$ years before it was finally retired. That is probably more than you will shoot through one.

[20]
Smith & Wesson Triple Lock

Officially, it is called the .44 Hand Ejector First Model or the .44 Hand Ejector New Century, but to handgun fanciers it will forever be the Triple Lock, so called because its cylinder locks at three points instead of the usual two.

The Triple Lock is a big, heavy, strong revolver that was revealed to the world in 1908. Terribly expensive to produce, even in those days of cheap labor, it sold for $21 at a time when the average American worker made $5 a week.

The standard chambering for the Triple Lock was the .44 Special, although it was also offered in .38/40 and .45 Long Colt. Decades before the advent of the .44 Magnum, venturesome handloaders found that they could stuff .44 Special shells with far more powder than was ever intended, and that the results were interesting to say the least. You could not do this with just any revolver, but the Triple Lock could take it and not shoot loose or blow up.

Sadly, Smith & Wesson could not afford to make the gun past 1917. The Triple Lock was discontinued with only 15,000 produced. Today, it is regarded as a treasure, one of our finest American handguns, and a Triple Lock in prime condition will command $3,000 instead of $21.

[21]
Savage Model 110

Debuting in 1958—the same year as the Mark V—the Savage Model 110 was the polar opposite of the Weatherby. A cheap bolt-action rifle put together out of inexpensive parts, it had a rotten trigger, and its barrel was screwed

Weatherby
Mark V Deluxe

[19]

ROY WEATHERBY DESIGNED the cartridges that bear his name in the 1940s and built custom rifles around them, using whatever actions he could find. In 1958, he announced his own action, the Mark V, and it was as radical as his cartridges. Employing a massive bolt with nine, rather than two, locking lugs, it slid like a piston in the Mark V's receiver. The stocks were claro walnut, often very fancy, and as unlike other stocks as a California hot rod was unlike a showroom Buick.

On special order, Weatherby would build you a rifle that was fancier than anything else in any gun rack. Profuse engraving, gold and silver or contrasting wood inlays, carving, and elaborate checkering patterns were yours for the asking. At its dandified peak, the Mark V was not so much a firearm as an original American art form.

THE RADICAL ACTION

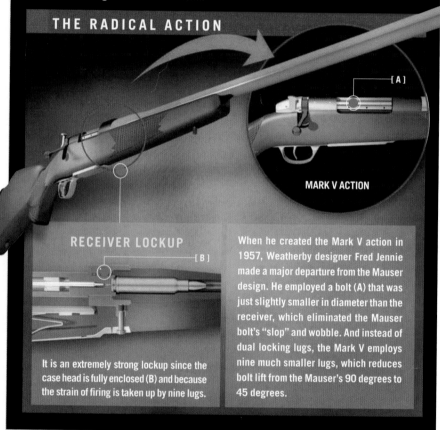

[A]

MARK V ACTION

RECEIVER LOCKUP

[B]

It is an extremely strong lockup since the case head is fully enclosed (B) and because the strain of firing is taken up by nine lugs.

When he created the Mark V action in 1957, Weatherby designer Fred Jennie made a major departure from the Mauser design. He employed a bolt (A) that was just slightly smaller in diameter than the receiver, which eliminated the Mauser bolt's "slop" and wobble. And instead of dual locking lugs, the Mark V employs nine much smaller lugs, which reduces bolt lift from the Mauser's 90 degrees to 45 degrees.

to the receiver by a slotted collar that added to the gun's ugliness. But the 110 functioned, and it didn't cost much, and it shot very, very accurately. And nearly 40 years later, this unassuming rifle would save Savage Arms from oblivion.

In the mid-1990s, when Savage had fallen on hard times and was about to close its doors, the company's new president, Ron Coburn, asked which gun they could still produce. The answer was the Model 110. And so it was all Savage made for a while, but the company put everything it had left into that one gun. Gradually, shooters caught on that the homely rifle would outshoot just about anything else out there, and the company prospered. Savage 110s (and its variants, the Models 111 and 116) will still win no prizes for beauty, but they are probably the most accurate factory rifles on the market.

FIREARMS OF THE FUTURE

Ward Dobler, DIR. OF MANUFACTURING, DAKOTA ARMS
"We'll have guns that use a practical caseless cartridge, and we'll see the development of a laser-rangefinding scope that automatically adjusts the reticle for the distance you're shooting at."

[22]
Ruger Mark I

William B. Ruger's first venture into the gun business failed, but he knew what he had done wrong, and his second attempt is the stuff of legends. He went into partnership with the artist Alexander Sturm, and Sturm, Ruger & Co. began selling a .22 semiauto pistol that looked a little like a German Luger and sold for the low (even for 1949) price of $37.50. This delightful little gun was rugged, accurate, and simple to manufacture. It was a huge and instant success. In 1951, Alexander Sturm died, and the red Ruger eagle on the Mark I grip was changed to black in mourning, but the pistol has remained intact.

[24]
Browning Gold

How do you replace a legend? Browning answered that question in 1994 with the Gold, the successor to the great but outdated A-5 autoloader. In 1997, Browning debuted the 3½-inch version. As the first "all-load" gas auto, the 3½-inch Gold broadened our idea of versatility; with one gun, you could interchangeably shoot anything from light 2¾-inch target loads to 3½-inch, 2-ounce turkey magnums or 1550 fps steel screamers, all with the significant recoil reduction of a gas-operated action.

The Gold has matured into a wonderfully shootable, reliable gun. The sporting clays version is one of just two autos (the Beretta 391 is the other) that you see in the winner's circle at sporting clays tournaments.

[25]
Marlin Model 336

Marlin's 336 is not as famous as the Winchester 94, but that is about the only way in which it falls short. It is the other Deer Rifle Supreme, and I believe it is a considerably better gun. It first went on sale in 1948. Like the Model 94, it is short, light, quick to point, and dead reliable. I have found it to be considerably more accurate

[23]
Parker

THERE IS MAGIC to that one word: It's shorthand for the Golden Age of American shotgunning, or simply for the finest American shotgun. Parkers were produced from 1866 to 1934 and spanned the transition from black to smokeless powder. They were crafted in a stupefying number of grades, gauges, and frame sizes. The Trojan was the plain working gun of the line, and ascending grades led to the sumptuous A-1 Special and the fabulous Invincible, of which only three were made. ¶ The Parker is a beautiful, fine-handling, and distinctive gun that is treasured above all others of its time. I can even put numbers to the esteem in which it is held: In perfect condition, the plain-vanilla Trojan is worth $2,000, and some versions of the A-1 Special will fetch $100,000. The three Invincibles are now regarded as priceless.

than the 94, and because it was designed with side ejection it takes very well to a scope. Finally, it is chambered for the .35 Remington, which is a better cartridge than the .30/30.

[26]
Marlin Model 39A

This is the other great Marlin—a .22 rimfire lever action that has been in continuous production in one form or another since 1939. I doubt if there is an experienced shooter who has never owned one of these rifles.

If the 39A has a fault, it is the takedown feature that has been part of the gun for just about forever. Turn a big knurled screw on the receiver, and the rifle becomes two pieces. Other people must like it, but I do not. When I owned one, I never saw a compelling reason to take the gun apart, and the feature added a needless complication to a design of otherwise sublime simplicity. That said, it is a marvelous gun that everyone has lusted after at one point or another.

[27]
Ruger Single-Six

In 1953, America was entering a TV Western craze; it was impossible to turn on your set and not see some horse's ass—literally. With all these small-screen cowpokes waving around Colt Peacemakers, Bill Ruger reasoned that an inexpensive version of the Peacemaker might sell well. And so was born the Single-Six, a .22 rimfire clone of the Colt Model 1873 Single Action Army revolver.

This was at a time when the single-action was thought by the gun industry to be deader than Billy the Kid. Ruger proved them wrong and resurrected the thumb-buster from oblivion.

[28]
H&R Topper

It's a basic, single-shot, exposed-hammer shotgun that dates back to 1946. Even today, when

[HOW IT WORKS]

Perazzi MX Series

[29]

THE PERAZZI OVER/UNDER is on this list even though it is used almost entirely for competition. It got here by virtue of its excellence, because it is the first modular shotgun, and because it has had a profound effect on the design of other shotguns. You can swap chokes, barrels, trigger groups, and stocks in the twinkling of an eye.

The Perazzi company has been around since the 1950s, but its guns did not make their presence felt here until the late 1960s. "Fifteen hundred dollars for a plain gun?" people bellowed. Then they got in line to buy one.

Perazzis are expensive, incredibly durable, and supremely successful. It is quite possible that, in the last 30 years, more clay-bird championships have been won with them than with anything else.

THE MODULAR SHOTGUN

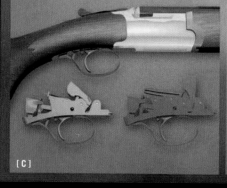

[A] ADJUSTABLE COMB

[B] INTERCHANGEABLE CHOKE TUBES

[D]

TRIGGER GROUP CHANGEOUT

[C]

Perazzi has perfected the modular shotgun. The comb (A) can be raised or lowered, adjusting the point of impact higher or lower. Choke tubes (B) can be interchanged. Trigger groups (C) can be swapped in a couple of seconds, giving you a choice of coil or V springs and/or barrel-firing sequence. The buttstock itself (D) can be removed and replaced in a minute or two via a bolt that's accessible through the recoil pad.

---

shooters are willing to pay any amount for guns, it's only $150. There is no counting how many Toppers over the years have enabled people to hunt who would not otherwise be able to do so.

[30]
Ithaca Model 4E

This single-barrel trap gun was the last survivor of the Golden Age of shotgunning. Introduced in 1926, it did not breathe its last until 1991, 50 years after Parker, L.C. Smith, A.H. Fox, and LeFever had all become history. Ithaca single-barrels came in eight grades and were prized during the early days of American trapshooting. It was a very simple gun, and very, very strong. Renowned composer and conductor John Philip Sousa used an Ithaca to break clay birds, and the company named its top-grade trap gun after him.

At the very end, 4Es were made exactly as they always had been, by hand, with pride.

[31]
Thompson/Center Contender Pistol

The T/C Contender was first marketed in 1967. It's a simple, single-shot, short-barreled firearm that offers almost unlimited versatility by virtue of interchangeable barrels. You can get it in a startling variety of calibers, from .22 LR up through centerfire rifle cartridges, and it will shoot with great accuracy.

Ironically, the T/C Contender is now available as a full-size rifle, which utilizes the same action but employs a 23-inch barrel, a full-size fore-end, and a buttstock. So this one-hand rifle is now a two-hand rifle.

[32]
Winchester Model 52 Sporter

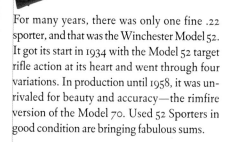

For many years, there was only one fine .22 sporter, and that was the Winchester Model 52. It got its start in 1934 with the Model 52 target rifle action at its heart and went through four variations. In production until 1958, it was unrivaled for beauty and accuracy—the rimfire version of the Model 70. Used 52 Sporters in good condition are bringing fabulous sums.

[33]
Ruger Number One

Part of Bill Ruger's genius lay in the fact that he did not believe in market research. He built what he liked, for his own reasons. In 1966, he literally raised the dead by bringing out a single-shot falling-block rifle. It was like reintroducing the matchlock or the snaphaunce, but Ruger doted on the single-shot, and that was that.

It would have cost a fortune to make, except that Ruger had conveniently reinvented a process called investment casting (last used in ancient Egypt). This enabled him to avoid the machining that would have been necessary to make the Number One's receiver.

Bill Ruger's baby was a solid success from the start, and it single-handedly resurrected the single-shot rifle.

[34]
Tar-Hunt RSG-12

Here is another gun that redefined firearms performance. During the 1970s and 1980s, rifled slug guns grew increasingly important, but for the most part, a slug gun was a 50-yard machine. A few could hack it at 75 yards, and a very few at 100 or more. Enter Tar-Hunt Custom Rifles, which in 1990 unveiled a bolt-action slug gun that was built like a rifle and shot like a rifle. It cost a lot of money, but it would put those big lumps of lead through the same hole at 100 yards and beyond with deadly certainty. Fourteen years later, it still has no serious rivals.

FIREARMS OF THE FUTURE

John C. Trull, PRODUCT MANAGER, REMINGTON ARMS CO.
"The biggest change you're going to see is the way in which we launch a projectile from a barrel. The old system of primer and gunpowder is going to be replaced by something entirely different—maybe along the lines of the electronic rail gun that NASA is experimenting with."

[36]
Dakota Model 76

The Dakota 76 was introduced in the year of America's Bicentennial and makes this list for one simple reason, best put by the dean of

American custom gunmakers, Jerry Fisher: "It's a perfect action that comes off an assembly line. No matter how fussy you are, you can't find anything wrong with it."

The 76 is the ultimate refinement of the Model 98 Mauser, combining the 98's best features with those of the Winchester Model 70. Only about 100 are made a year, and they start at $3,600. Nonetheless, Dakota is hard put to keep up with the demand.

[37]
Knight MK-85

Tony Knight is another country gunsmith who changed the way things are done. In 1985, he built a muzzleloader with the nipple at the rear of the barrel, directly behind the powder charge instead of alongside. This made ignition far more reliable and began the Great Blackpowder Revolution, which has resulted in muzzleloaders that are practically as accurate, reliable, and fast to load as cartridge-firing arms.

All this drives traditionalists mad. But ordinary hunters love it.

[38]
Ruger Blackhawk

With the Single-Six a success, Sturm, Ruger announced the Blackhawk single-action revolver. It was a much improved version of the Colt Peacemaker, chambered in .357 magnum, and was simple, extremely strong, and affordable. It marked the return of the single-action centerfire revolver as a viable firearm.

The Blackhawk was yet another Ruger triumph and enabled untold thousands of shooters to pretend that they were Wyatt Earp—except that their revolvers were better than his.

[HOW IT WORKS]

Savage Model 99

[35]

ITS STREAMLINED FORM first graced the shooting world a year before the 20th century, and it stayed in production for nearly all of that century. I think it is the greatest lever action, period, and at the least, it was far, far ahead of any other lever gun. The 99 was strong and sleek. It could handle pointed bullets because it used a rotary magazine rather than a tubular one, and thus could be chambered in .250/3000, .300 Savage, and other calibers more inherently accurate and powerful than those the Winchester Model 94 was chambered for at that time. It had a good trigger, and its accuracy was, for the most part, excellent. Sadly, it is a gun that cannot be produced without a good deal of hand labor, which makes it impossible to manufacture at a competitive price. The good news is that there are still plenty of 99s around, and they are just as effective in the 21st century as they were in the 20th.

THE ROTARY MAGAZINE

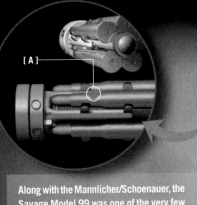

The 99 action looks simple but the rotary magazine must be fitted by hand.

Along with the Mannlicher/Schoenauer, the Savage Model 99 was one of the very few rifles to employ a rotary magazine (A). It held five cartridges in a spool that rotated into battery with each stroke of the lever. This enabled the 99 to employ spitzer bullets, which other, tube-magazine lever actions couldn't. The 99's bolt (B) locked at the rear, with the lever (C) camming into place behind it. It was a very strong system and allowed the use of high-intensity cartridges such as the .250/3000.

[39]
Ithaca Model 37

It's hard to please everyone, but the Model 37 has come pretty close. The 37—introduced in that year—loads and ejects from the bottom. This protects its innards from the weather and makes for an unusually reliable gun. Duck hunters loved it for that reason, as did cops and the military. It is also light for a pump gun, and so upland hunters took to it. The smoothbore slug version of the Model 37 was among the most accurate you could get in the era before slug guns were built like rifles, so add deer hunters to the list. All in all, there were 2 million Model 37s produced.

[41]
Winchester Model 71

You could argue that this is a failed design. Only 47,000 were made between 1935 and 1957, and it was chambered for an obscure cartridge called the .348. But that would be only part of the truth. The Model 71 is about the fastest-handling, slickest-operating lever action you can get your hands on. All of them are wonderful examples of pre-64 Winchester craftsmanship, and they pack a wallop. Elk hunters still go dippy over the Model 71, which now costs $800 to over $1,000.

[42]
Remington Model 32

The 32 was a hard-luck gun. To be an over/under in 1931 was to be marked as odd, to have split barrels was really strange, and to be expensive in the third year of the Great Depression was almost fatal. The 32 was made in very small numbers from 1941 to 1947, when it was abandoned. Probably only 7,000 or so were made. But it was a wonderful de-sign, far ahead of its time, and today lives on in the form of the Kreighoff K-80, which is essentially the same gun and is beloved by competitive shooters everywhere.

[43]
A.H. Fox

If I had left Parker off this list, or ranked it be-hind the Fox, I would be expelled from the Gun Writers' Union. But forgive me; I believe that the A.H. Fox is better. Made in Philadelphia from 1903 to 1930 and in Utica, New York, until 1946, the Fox was produced in a dizzying variety of grades and gauges, and all of them shared a wonderful simplicity that made them durable and trouble-free. Fox even had a single trigger design that worked reliably, which was rare indeed in those times.

Foxes do not bring the same kind of money that L.C. Smiths and Parkers command, but these guns live on today whereas the others don't—the Connecticut Manufacturing Co. of New Britain, Connecticut, is making high-grade Fox shotguns that are, if anything, better than the originals.

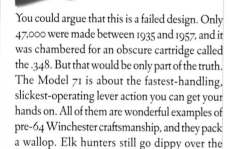

[40]
Remington Model 600 Magnum

IN 1965, I owned a brand-new Model 600 in .350 Remington Magnum. It was short and light, and it kicked very sincerely. The 600 Magnum lasted only three years, and then a funny thing happened: People recognized that this gun with the odd laminated stock and the nonfunctional nylon rib was sensationally effective. Nearly 40 years later, it has come to life again as the Model 673 Guide Rifle—a gun whose time has come round at last.

[44]
Freedom Arms Model 83

This company was founded in 1983 to produce a superstrong, ultra-high-quality single-action revolver chambered (most notably) for the hand-shattering .454 Casull cartridge. The Model 83 is a continuation of the tradition that began with the Smith & Wesson Triple Lock, and like the Triple Lock, it is a very expensive firearm, starting at more than $1,500. But I've never heard anyone who owns a Model 83 complain about the price.

[45]
Jarrett Signature Rifle

This bolt action's antecedent is the Kentucky rifle. Like the Kentucky, it comes from a small shop run by a self-taught gunsmith and designer, Kenny Jarrett. Similarly, it can be had plain or ornate, and the fancy versions are something to behold. It is very expensive, like the Kentucky, even the modestly appointed ones. And like the Kentucky, it is more accurate than anything else available, and not just more than the job requires but more than even the most crazed perfectionist could expect.

An African professional hunter once told me that the very best American rifle shots were in a league by themselves. And so is the Jarrett Signature.

FIREARMS OF THE FUTURE

Kenny Jarrett, PRESIDENT, JARRETT RIFLES
"Caseless ammunition. Self-adjusting laser-rangefinding scopes. Exotic materials in the barrels and actions." (And no, Jarrett and Ward Dobler of Dakota Arms did not consult with each other.)

Winchester Model 21

[46]

YOU CAN ARGUE until your teeth fall out about the merits of the great American doubles, but this fact stands beyond dispute: The Model 21 is the strongest of the lot. John Olin, president of Winchester, wanted it that way, and he put the Model 21 through hell before he put it on the market. There have been two incarnations: From 1931 until 1960 it was a mass-produced gun; from 1960 until 1982, the so-called round-frame 21s were made in the Winchester Custom Shop on a to-order basis only. ¶ While the Model 21 is not ranked with the Parker et al, there are a lot of people who are fanatics about it and pay high prices for even the plain field models. The money required for a custom-grade 21 would give you a myocardial infarction.

[47]
Westley Richards Droplock Double Rifle

One does not need a double rifle, but they are beautiful firearms, and romantic artifacts. There are at least half a dozen makers of fine doubles practicing the art, but I like the Westley, probably because I once seriously considered taking out a second mortgage to buy one. I didn't and still wonder if I did the right thing. You can have a Westley Richards Droplock for $69,000 in most of the standard elephant-bashing calibers.

[48]
Beretta SO6 EL Over/Under Shotgun

Beretta is the oldest manufacturer in the world, period, and produces, for the most part, very good guns that range in price from moderate to fairly expensive. At the top of the line, however, is something else altogether. The SO6 is a true sidelock, made in 12-gauge only to customer specs. It employs gorgeous wood, first-rate engraving, and the kind of metal-to-metal fit that you normally find only in fine watches. The reason it's here among the 50 best is because even priced at around $18,000 it's a bargain. For guns in this class, it's easy to spend two or three or four times what the SO6 costs, and the odds are that what you get won't work half as well. If I ever hit the lottery, the first words out of my mouth will not be "Oh boy," but "SO6, please."

[49]
Tikka T3 Hunter

If you will forgive the blasphemy, this is the modern version of the Winchester Model 70—a rifle that is just about flawless in every respect. T3s have been around since 2003, and they are as modern as it is possible to make sporting rifles while still retaining traditional lines. It's light, slick-handling, very tough, and far more accurate than all but the best Model 70s.

[50]
Merkel Model 2001EL

When the Germans build a shotgun, they expect it to breech up just as tightly after 200 years of hard use as it did on the day it was made, and they like it ornate in a Teutonic way, and as complex as it can be made, just to show how good they are as machinists. This over/under will not be shot loose by your unborn progeny 10 generations removed, but it is not overly fancy, and it is not overly complex. Some German shotguns tend to be overweight and don't handle as well as other fine guns, but the Merkel is a fine-handling, lively gun with distinctive lines and the life expectancy of a redwood tree. Ⓕⓢ

...AND THE WORST

Just as there are best guns, there are some on the other end of the scale. Here they are, in their varying degrees of ignominy.

1 MBA GYROJET MARK I MODEL B

From 1960 to 1969, MBAssociates of San Ramon, California, produced a rocket-firing handgun they called the Gyrojet (shown). It resembled an automatic pistol but instead held six .50-caliber miniature rockets, each one powered through four angled ports in its base. The firing pin was fixed, and the hammer was located in front of the rocket.

When you pulled the trigger, the hammer fell rearward, smacking the rocket on its nose and driving its primer against the firing pin. The rocket would ignite, pushing the hammer forward and down, and go spinning on its way to wherever it pleased.

The Gyrojet set standards of inaccuracy that have yet to be equaled, and in addition, if you shot at something from close range, the rocket would not have enough velocity to do any damage.

2 THE ORIGINAL KIMBER RIFLES

From 1980 to 1991, Kimber of Oregon (not to be confused with Kimber Manufacturing Inc. of Yonkers, New York, whose guns operate with relentless perfection) produced rimfire and centerfire rifles that often failed to work or shoot—sometimes both. These elegant guns were assembled from parts that were produced by a variety of sources, and said parts seldom worked in harmony. In the mid-1980s I owned the third left-hand Kimber .22 ever made and was spellbound by its beauty. Then I shot it, and I sold it the next day.

3 WINCHESTER MODEL 1400

When Winchester designed this sleek-looking auto in 1964, it tried to save money by adapting one frame size to several different gauges and thought to take up the slack space in the receiver with plastic inserts, which usually cracked and fell out. That is part one of this story. In 1965, the company embarked on an ambitious program of establishing Winchester-franchised trap and skeet ranges. These ranges were stocked with Model 1400s, and soon the inevitable took place. Operators and shooters alike were driven to a frenzy by the antics of the 1400. I once phoned such a range about something perfectly innocent, and the first sentence out of the owner's mouth was: "IF YOU SAY ONE WORD ABOUT THAT !#@&*% 1400, I'LL KILL YOU!"

That seemed to sum it up quite nicely.   —D.E.P.

The History of the Shooter's Bible

It is the dream of most entrepreneurs to succeed not only within their lifetime but beyond their time on earth.

Austrian immigrant, Alexander F. Stoeger (above) opened his first firearms sales and import business in a building on East 42nd Street in New York City as the exclusive agent for German Luger pistols and other European firearms in the United States and Canada. By 1928, Stoeger moved his operation to a more upscale location on 5th Avenue. His "gun room" (below) displayed a wide variety of high quality imported and domestic arms.

A SPECIAL MESSAGE FROM THE STOEGER ARMS CORPORATION

SHOW THIS CATALOG to your friends and neighbors. Ask them to send one dollar bill, stamps, check or money order for the latest copy of STOEGER'S Complete Catalog of Guns and other shooting equipment.

is the largest organization in America that is entirely devoted to guns and shooting equipment.

Our main display and sales room holds the most complete assortment of American and Imported guns and equipment known to us anywhere.

We aim to supply everything in the line of guns. If you want shooting equipment, we have it. That is our entire line.

That is why every person in the Stoeger organization devotes all of his time to guns. Our specialists know every problem of the hunter and marksman.

Experts do all of our buying both at home and abroad. Master craftsmen do all of our manufacturing and gun repairing.

SEE PAGE 8, "HOW TO ORDER"

Our gun catalog has long been a standard for shooters and gun dealers everywhere. This catalog, like our store, is the place where you may compare all leading makes of guns, and inspect an endless variety of accessories.

Every item sold by us must measure up to the standards of Stoeger Arms Corporation. That is why the name Stoeger has always meant something better than ordinary guns.

Your best assurance of satisfaction is our nation-wide reputation for quality merchandise, fair dealing and helpful service.

YOUR ORDER will receive the promptest attention possible. Shipments are made direct from our store at 507 Fifth Avenue, New York City.

EVERYTHING IN GUNS UNDER ONE COVER

SHOW THIS CATALOG to your friends and neighbors. Ask them to send one dollar bill, stamps, check or money order for the latest copy of STOEGER'S Complete Catalog of Guns and other shooting equipment.

On September 1, 1923, A. F. Stoeger published what is believed to be his first formal price list. This slender document advertised that Stoeger was the "Sole authorized importer for the United States and Canada of the genuine Mauser and Luger Arms and Ammunition." The document also advertised sale of Stoegerol, a trade secret proprietary solvent developed by A. F. Stoeger himself described in advertisements as a combination oil that not only lubricates, but also dissolves nitro powder, cleans firearms and acts as "a wound sterilizer." In 1923 Stoeger imported and sold German-made genuine original factory Luger pistols at a wholesale price as low as $15.00 each, as well as Anson & Deeley System self-cocking German-made double barrel shotguns, A.F.S. (named after A. F. Stoeger) trap guns, Luger holsters, shell belts and a variety of field binoculars, compasses and telescopes.

Stoeger's business took off and in 1925 A. F. Stoeger, Inc. printed its first numbered edition catalog. The catalog showed similarity to the price sheets previously printed and distributed by the company, but the information in the catalog had expanded to include a wider variety of information about the shooting sports, including illustrations of the dimensional specifications for buckshot and lead balls, and a listing of the hunting seasons for various types of game in each state throughout the United States. Although it lacked the title at the time, the first edition of The Shooter's Bible was born.

From its earliest days, The Shooter's Bible was more than just a source of advertisement for products sold by A. F. Stoeger. The 1931 edition of the publication touted Stoeger's company as "the only exclusive gun house in America" and provided customers with information not only relating to the services Stoeger rendered in repairing firearms of all makes and models, but

1926 Alexander Stoeger chose the European Auhrhun (Wood Grouse) as the logo for his firearms retail house. The logo appeared on the covers of his earliest mail order catalogs.

1927 By the mid '20s Stoeger Inc. billed itself as "The Only Exclusive Arms and Ammunition Importers — Jobbers in the United States." Items for sale included Merkel shotguns.

1939 New York World's fair opens in April. The cover of the "World's Fair Jubilee" catalog featured the Fair's symbols, the Trylon and Perisphere, flanked by the Stoeger eagles.

also advertised sale of firearm repair equipment, targets of various types for use by shooters and included an article entitled "The Fine Shotgun as an Investment" written by Captain Paul A. Curtis, shooting editor of *Field & Stream*. Stoeger's use of its commercial catalog as a go-to source for information about the shooting sports had begun. The 1931 edition also included, in pages adjacent to its sale of Parker A1 special side-by-side shotguns (for $750 each), descriptions of standardized skeet and trap stations with construction cost estimates provided for each and a recommendation of guns to be used.

Despite the Great Depression, A. F. Stoeger Inc. distributed the catalog at 50 cents per copy, and expanded to offer firearms from most major American and foreign makers. There were handguns from Colt, Smith & Wesson, Mauser, Walther, and Webley. The hunting rifle lines available through mail order included Winchester,

Remington, Savage, Stevens, Mossburg, Mauser, and Mannlicher-Schoenaur. In addition, Stoeger offered an extensive listing of shotguns from Parker, A. H. Fox, L. C. Smith, Winchester, Remington, Ithaca, Iver Johnson, Greener and their own line of German-made A. F. Stoeger guns.

In 1939, Stoeger published its "New York World's Fair 1939 issue" under the copyrighted title *Stoeger's Catalog and Handbook*, with the subtitle *Arms & Ammunition, Gun Accessories & Parts, Gunsmith Tools*. The Stoeger Company was now called Stoeger Arms Corp. and styled itself as "America's Great Gun House." In fact, the company had grown to such size that it had relocated to a spacious store at 507 5th Avenue in New York.

As it did with so many companies, World War II threatened the existence of Stoeger but here again, A. F. Stoeger proved an adept business man, converting his company from one that

1944 The 35th edition of the Stoeger catalog is one of the first to bear the "Shooter's Bible" label. The name was coined by a grateful customer writing to Stoeger during the late 1930s.

1946 After World War II, the *Shooter's Bible* expanded to more than 500 pages and included such items as Kaywoodie pipes and barbecue grills as well as the usual guns.

1956 The 47th Edition of *The Shooter's Bible* proclaimed itself the "World's Greatest Gun Book." That year Stoeger offered custom Mannlicher-Schoenaur rifles for $345.

1957

1967

$3.95

The SHOOTER'S BIBLE
48th EDITION 1957
World's Greatest GUN BOOK

The SHOOTER'S BIBLE
49th EDITION 1958
World's Greatest GUN BOOK

1958

Shooter's Bible
NEW
NO. 58
1967
EDITION

FEATURING:
COMPLETE REVIEWS BY THE NATION'S
FOREMOST GUN EXPERTS, COVERING EVERY
NEW DEVELOPMENT IN THE WORLD OF FIREARMS

BIG-BORE RIFLES by Jack O'Connor   SHOTGUNS by Pete Brown
SMALL-BORE RIFLES by Pete Kuhlhoff   HANDGUNS by Col. Charles Askins
RIFLE SCOPES & SIGHTS by Larry Koller AMMUNITION by Roger Barlow
TARGET & VARMINT RIFLES by Warren Page RELOADING TOOLS by R. A. Steindler

primarily sold firearms, ammunition and related products (then in limited supply because of the war effort) to one that also sold ping-pong tables, smoking pipes, chess and backgammon sets, ski clothing and skis, books and other publications. The Stoeger Company survived wartime shortages and throughout the war, copies of the catalog were shipped to fighting servicemen worldwide.

After World War II, Stoeger's business flourished and by 1948, the catalog had expanded to 544 pages. What had started as a sales catalog had grown to such an extent and included such a comprehensive listing of firearms, ammunition and shooting sports-related products that the Stoeger catalog was christened with the new name *The Shooter's Bible*. Sold in that year at a price of $1.50 each, *The Shooter's Bible* became not only the most comprehensive single volume review of hunting and shooting sports-related

products in the United States, but also became an important source of revenue for the Stoeger Arms Corporation. Unfortunately, although Stoeger Arms Corporation not only survived World War II but flourished in the years after, A. F. Stoeger did not live to see the post-war success of the company he had founded. In 1945, A.F. Stoeger died, to be succeeded as President of the company by his son A. F. Stoeger, Jr., and it was left to A. F. Stoeger, Jr. to note, in a letter printed in the inside cover of that year's edition of *The Shooter's Bible*, that "in spite of the continuing shortages of the most popular types of firearms and ammunition, the year just passed has by far exceeded in sales that of any previous year."

In the 1950s and 60s, publication of *The Shooter's Bible* became a substantial business in its own right, during a time when management of the Stoeger company had passed out of the

1957 With the wartime system of firearm and ammunition allotments ended, Stoeger promised "a full line of foreign and domestic guns" sold with "the assurance of prompt delivery."

1958 First formal price list was published advertising that Stoeger was the "Sole authorized importer for U.S. and Canada of the genuine Mauser and Luger Arms and Ammunition."

1967 In the 58th edition, editor John Olson warned readers to "be more watchful than ever" for "legislation that is designed to restrict your ability to purchase, own or use firearms."

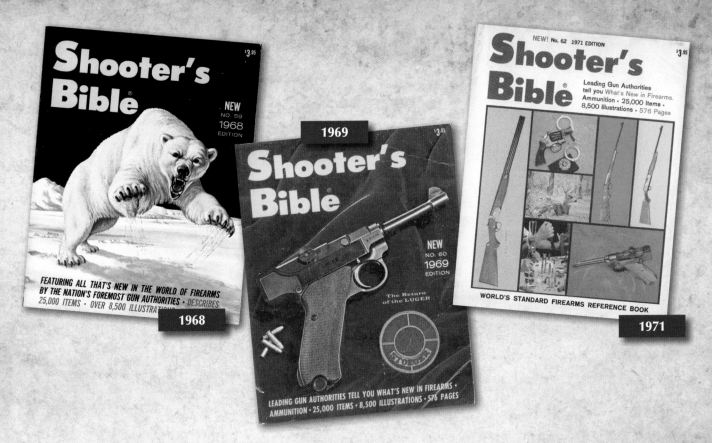

hands of Stoeger family. The 1961 edition ran to 576 pages and continued to include an amazing variety of products, from shotguns and rifles to air guns and ammunition, and included articles about the technical features of firearms, charts showing shotgun bores and chamber sizes, and such how-to articles as "How to Sight In" written by Jack O'Conner, Gun Editor for *Outdoor Life Magazine*. The 1961 edition included advertisements for duck decoys, targets, and firearm artwork, and sold sleeping bags, compasses and the continued availability of Stoegerol. The Stoegerol ads themselves increased dramatically in the claims made for that proprietary product, now being touted as a source of "rust insurance," "unexcelled nitro solvent," "dissolves metal fouling," "an excellent cleaning and lubricating oil," "gunstock polish," "leather preserver," and for use as "an emergency antiseptic." Stoeger also

sold target barrel polishes, barrel grease, oil finishes, browning and bluing solutions, and *The Shooter's Bible* faithfully cataloged the availability of each item.

By the 1970s, *The Shooter's Bible* (now simply called *Shooter's Bible*) had changed in nature but continued in prominence and success. In fact, the book was now being published by Stoeger Publishing Company located in South Hackensack, New Jersey and Stoeger's United States operations had been moved from New York City to the New Jersey location. Staying true to its role as a compendium of shooting sports related products, the new editions of the *Shooter's Bible* included the newest products available from various firearm and ammunition manufacturers, and for the first time included products that the Stoeger Arms Corporation did not sell directly. The publication focused more and more on

1968 The preface of this edition warned of the increasing shortage of commercial small arms and ammunition on the market due to military requirements for the war in Vietnam.

1969 The cover proclaims "The Return of the Luger." Stoeger Arms, which held the trademark on the "Luger" name, produced new P 08-style pistols in .22 caliber.

1971 George Nonte's article: "What's New in Muzzleloading" comments on new reproduction black powder arms from firms such as Navy Arms (Uberti) and Hopkins & Allen.

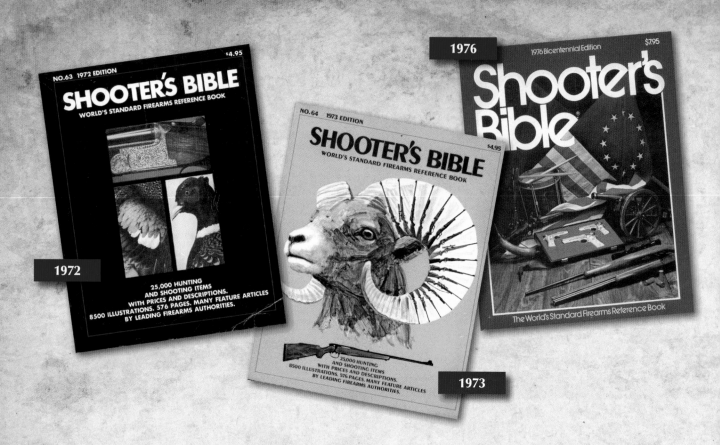

informative articles about the shooting sports and about various collectible types of firearms, as well as ballistics charts and general reference information that made the publication a must-have for gun owners.

In the 1990s, Stoeger was purchased by Sako Oy, the famous rifle manufacturer located in Finland. Sako's interest had primarily been in acquiring the firearm import and distribution portion of the Stoeger business (now known as Stoeger Industries, Inc.). Publication of the *Shooter's Bible*, as well as other publications such as *Gun Trader's Guide* and a miscellany of hunting and fishing related publications released by Stoeger Publishing Inc. came as part of that corporate acquisition.

It was because of Sako that the Stoeger company and, with it, the *Shooter's Bible*, became part of the Beretta group of companies in 2000. In that year, Beretta Holding S.p.A., the Italian company that owns such venerable firearms manufacturers as Fabbrica d'Armi Pietro Beretta S.p.A., Beretta U.S.A. Corp., Benelli Armi S.p.A., Benelli U.S.A. Corporation, Uberti S.p.A., and Franchi S.p.A. acquired Sako Oy. U.S. distribution and sale of Sako products became the responsibility of Beretta U.S.A. Corp. and Stoeger Industries, Inc. was placed under the ownership of Benelli U.S.A., where it continued to import and sell field grade sporting shotguns. Stoeger Publishing continued as well, not only with the *Shooter's Bible* but with an improved line-up of high quality publications dedicated primarily to the shooting sports, fishing and other outdoor pursuits.

I was asked by the patriarch of the Beretta companies, Cav. Ugo Gussalli Beretta, to serve as president for Stoeger when the company was acquired in 2000. Honored by the remarkable history and success of the *Shooter's Bible* and other

1972 A special feature by Tom McNally warns the "world's sportsmen" about dangers threatening wildlife with concerns ranging from DDT to the daming of free-flowing rivers.

1973 A close look at the cover of this *Shooter's Bible* reveals that the segments on the ram's horns are actually a selection of high-powered rifles that appear in the book.

1976 The "1976 Bicentennial Editon" contained a special reference section with listings ranging from North American arms museums to books and endangered species.

Stoeger Publications—books that I had read for decades—I quickly agreed. I am now privileged to possess in my office what is believed to be the only comprehensive collection of the *Shooter's Bible*, dating back to the original sales sheet published by A. F. Stoeger in 1923. Headquarters for Stoeger's activities were moved to the Beretta U.S.A. and Benelli U.S.A. offices in Accokeek, Maryland, and renewed life was breathed into all of the Stoeger publications through the dedicated team of publishers, editors and staff who serve on behalf of Stoeger Publishing at its new location.

The *Shooter's Bible* is a strong cord woven through the seam of America's shooting sports tradition. Annual publications are not eligible for listing in the *New York Times* bestseller list, but if they were, the *Shooter's Bible* would have listed in the *New York Times* bestseller list every year of its publication for the past several decades.

[Last year marked] the 100th edition of the *Shooter's Bible* since publication of the first numbered catalog issued by A. F. Stoeger in 1925. My task and that of the Stoeger Publishing staff has been to enhance the quality and availability of this fine publication while maintaining its time-proven and valuable mission as a source book for new shooting sports product information and for articles of interest to hunters and target shooters throughout the world.

With publication of [this] edition, we hope that our readers will agree that we have achieved this objective, honoring the legacy that A. F. Stoeger left to us all.

Jeffrey K. Reh
President

1981 Among the now-vanished product lines displayed in the 72nd Edition were American-made Winslow rifles, Mannlicher shotguns and Philippine Kassnar rifles.

1994 For the cover of the 85th Edition, the editors chose two Browning limited edition shotguns, the Auto-5 gold Classic and a 20-gauge Gold Classic Superposed.

2001 This set of Express Double Rifles (.30-06, .375H&H, .470 NR, .600 NE), were created for Beretta's 750th Anniversary. The lockplates depict lion, rhino, buffalo and elephant.

Stoeger's First Catalog

Alexander Stoeger chose the European capercaillie grouse or Auerhuhn (below) for the cover of his earliest retail catalogs. Although the inaugural sales sheet was issued in 1923, the first catalog was issued in 1925.

The following are facsimile pages from Stoeger's first sales sheet released in 1923. At the time, A. F. Stoeger, Inc. sold imported European firearms and accesories and police equipment.

A. F. STOEGER
Wholesale Price List
This Price List Cancels All Previous Quotations

The following prices are strictly wholesale and correspond with the numbers illustrated and described on catalog sheets. Our merchandise is of the highest possible quality and we aim to give exceptional values on all goods quoted. These Arms, Ammunition and Hunters' Supplies satisfy the most exacting requirements of shooters and lovers of rifles and guns.

Shot Guns

No.	Price
100	$ 19.50
200	75.00
201	80.00
202	125.00
203	145.00
250	175.00
330	150.00
350	170.00
360	11.50
370	75.00
400	22.00

Rifles

No.	Price
600	50.00
601	45.00
602	45.00
610	60.00
615	65.00
620	75.00
621	77.50
900	6.50

Pistols

No.	Price
700	9.00
701	9.00
702	10.00
710	22.50
715	25.00
750	17.50
751	17.50
752	22.50
753	22.50
775	1.50
776	2.50
900	6.50

Holsters

No.	Price	
1200	$ 7.20	Per Doz.
1210	7.20	" "
1220	9.00	" "
1250	18.00	" "
1251	30.00	" "
1252	3.70	Each
1253	2.75	"
1254	3.00	"
1255	3.30	"
1256	3.75	"
1260	2.50	"
1261	2.60	"
1262	3.60	"
1275	1.75	"

Holsters
(Continued from preceding column)

No.	Price	
1276	$ 3.00	Each
1277	3.00	"
1280	7.20	Per Doz.
1285	11.20	" "
1286	10.00	" "
1287	16.00	" "
1288	11.00	" "
1289	17.00	" "
1293	4.50	" "
1294	7.00	" "
1295	5.00	" "

Shell Bag

No.	Price	
1310	$13.80	Per Doz.

Shell Belts

No.	Price	
1320	$12.00	Per Doz.
1321	17.50	" "
1326	21.25	" "
1328	30.00	" "

Sling Strap

No.	Price	
1350	$ 9.00	Per Doz.

Canvas Gun Cases

No.	Price	
1400	$13.50	Per Doz.
1401	16.00	" "
1405	17.50	" "
1406	19.00	" "
1407	20.00	" "
1408	37.20	" "
1415	16.50	" "
1417	33.80	" "
1420	60.00	" "

All Leather Gun Cases

No.	Price	
1425	$10.00	Each
1430	14.25	"
1431	17.00	"
1445	18.50	"

Recoil Pads

No.	Price	
1600	$1.25	Each
1601	1.25	"

Field Glasses

No.	Price	
2000	$ 3.50	Each
2001	4.00	"
2002	5.00	"
2003	5.25	"
2004	4.25	"
2010	4.50	"

Field Glasses
(Continued from preceding column)

No.	Price	Each
2011	5.00	"
2012	5.00	"
2020	4.25	"
2021	4.75	"

Folding Telescopes

No.	Price	
2050	$ 3.25	Each
2051	4.25	"
2052	5.50	"

Binoculars

No.	Price	
2100	$17.00	Each
2101	18.50	"
2102	25.65	"
2103	28.15	"
2104	17.80	"

Imported Compasses per doz.

No.		Price
2200	40 mm.	$3.95
"	45 mm.	4.35
"	50 mm.	4.75
2201	40 mm.	4.95
"	45 mm.	5.40
"	50 mm.	5.75
2202	40 mm.	5.60
"	45 mm.	5.95
"	50 mm.	6.30
2203	40 mm.	4.90
"	45 mm.	5.15
"	50 mm.	5.60
2204	40 mm.	5.80
"	45 mm.	6.15
"	50 mm.	6.60
2205	40 mm.	6.30
"	45 mm.	6.75
"	50 mm.	7.15
2208	40 mm.	7.90
"	45 mm.	8.30
"	50 mm.	8.90
2270	25 mm.	1.00
"	30 mm.	1.10
"	35 mm.	1.20
"	40 mm.	1.40
"	45 mm.	1.70
"	50 mm.	1.80
2271	25 mm.	1.10
"	30 mm.	1.40
"	35 mm.	1.80
"	40 mm.	2.00
"	45 mm.	2.40
"	50 mm.	3.00

3000—Stoegerol—$7.20 per dozen 3 oz. cans—$5. per quart—$15. per gallon

All wholesale prices listed are net, except ammunition where we show gross prices with discount.
Prices subject to change without notice.

SOLE AUTHORIZED IMPORTER FOR THE UNITED STATES AND CANADA OF THE GENUINE MAUSER AND LUGER ARMS AND AMMUNITION

A. F. STOEGER, 224 EAST 42ND STREET NEW YORK
"Within a block of Grand Central Station"

"Stoegerol" the Wonderful Combination Gun Oil — nitro-solvent, rust-preventing, lubricating, antiseptic.

(OVER)

Highest Grade German Shot Guns

Leaders in Anson & Deeley System Self-Cocking Double-Barrel Shot Guns

These imported German Shot Guns are most carefully selected

No. 200—A First Quality German Safety Hammerless Shot Gun

The barrels are Krupp-Essen steel, suitable for nitro powder; dark blue finish, choked bored and targered, about 28-30 in. lengths, Greener breech; the rib is finely matted. The locks are the celebrated Anson & Deeley system, cocking indicator pins at sides, hand-engraved, stock with pistol grip and cheek piece, heel plate, plain and smooth finish, 12 or 16 gauge.

WEIGHT IN 16 BORE ABOUT 6½ POUNDS.
" " 12 " " 6¾ "

No. 201—As above, but in better finish, horn heel plate, pretty English engraving, superior stock, 12 or 16 gauge, same weight.

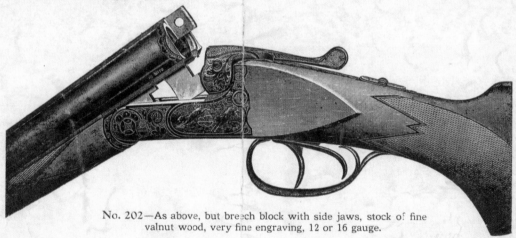

No. 202—As above, but breech block with side jaws, stock of fine valnut wood, very fine engraving, 12 or 16 gauge.

WEIGHT IN 16 BORE ABOUT 6½ POUNDS.
" " 12 " " 6¾ "

No. 203—As No. 202, but de Luxe pattern, finest possible finish of all parts, very elegant English style engraving showing chased shells or embossed hunting scenes, selected veined wood for stock, 12 or 16 gauge, same weight.

Highest Quality Ball and Shot Guns

The Leading Anson & Deeley System Self-Cocking Three-Barrelled Gun

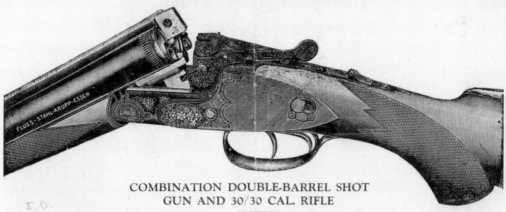

COMBINATION DOUBLE-BARREL SHOT GUN AND 30/30 CAL. RIFLE

No. 250—Genuine German Drilling Anson & Deeley System Self-Cocking Three-Barrelled Gun

This Gun has two shot barrels gauge 12 and one rifle barrel gauge 30-30, double catch and Greener locking gear, barrels genuine Krupp-Essen steel, suitable nitro powder, left barrel choke, right modified choke, rifle barrel with express boring, matted extension rib, automatic adjustable rear sight, Greener side and automatic safety, commutation on neck of stock, signal pins, side jaws on breech block, checkered patent snap for end, checkered pistol grip, walnut stock with cheek piece, very elegant English style engraving, excellent quality, high-grade finish. *WEIGHT ABOUT 7¼ POUNDS.*

The Best Anson & Deeley System Hammerless Ball and Shot Gun

No. 330—Anson & Deeley system HAMMERLESS self-cocking, best grade German Ball and Shot Gun, single-shot barrel choke, 12 or 16 gauge, rifle barrel underneath with express boring for 30-30 or 25-35 gauge, barrels genuine Krupp-Essen steel, suitable nitro powder, matted extension rib, Greener cross bolt action, side clips, safety on neck of stock, signal pins to show if Gun is cocked, side jaws on breech block, checkered patent snap for end, checkered pistol grip, walnut stock, very elegant engraving, excellent quality, high-grade finish.

WEIGHT ABOUT 7 POUNDS.

SOLE AUTHORIZED IMPORTER FOR THE UNITED STATES AND CANADA OF THE GENUINE MAUSER AND LUGER ARMS AND AMMUNITION

A. F. STOEGER, 224 EAST 42ND STREET NEW YORK
Within a block of Grand Central Station

"Stoegerol" the Wonderful Combination Gun Oil—nitro-solvent, rust-preventing, lubricating, antiseptic.

Mauser Automatics and Rifles — *Luger* Pistols

Mauser .25 and .32 Caliber
Automatic Pocket Pistols

Ten Shots, Using American Ammunition

List Prices { .25 Caliber **$16.00***
.32 Caliber **18.00***

A true weapon of defense.

Caliber	6.35 (.25)	7.65 (.32)
Magazine Capacity	9	8
Length of Pistol	5.4 inches	6.1 inches
Length of Line of Sight	4.6 inches	5.0 inches
Weight of Pistol	15 ounces	21 ounces
Muzzle Velocity f. s.	750	1142
Muzzle Energy f. lb.	61	148

Penetration		
in pine at 10 yards	2.75 inches	4.5 inches
in pine at 25 yards	2.25 inches	4.4 inches
in pine at 50 yards	2.1 inches	4.25 inches

Guaranteed at 10 yds. to shoot in 2-in. circle.

Guaranteed at 25 yds. to shoot in 6-in. circle.

WAFFENFABRIK MAUSER A.-G. OBERNDORFA.N. MAUSER'S PATENT

MAUSER

List Price **$80.00***

Genuine *Mauser* Sporting Rifle
All Calibers
Above cut shows the famous 1906 *Mauser* Sporting Rifle for U. S. Gov. Cartridge.

The *Luger* Automatic Repeating Pistol (Cal. 7.65$^{M}/_{M}$)
The Safest, Simplest, Most Accurate and Most Powerful

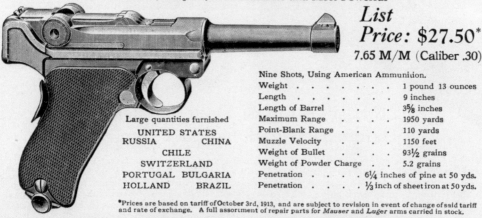

List Price: **$27.50***

7.65 M/M (Caliber .30)

Large quantities furnished

UNITED STATES
RUSSIA   CHINA
   CHILE
   SWITZERLAND
PORTUGAL   BULGARIA
HOLLAND   BRAZIL

Nine Shots, Using American Ammunition.

Weight	1 pound 13 ounces
Length	9 inches
Length of Barrel	3⅝ inches
Maximum Range	1950 yards
Point-Blank Range	110 yards
Muzzle Velocity	1150 feet
Weight of Bullet	93½ grains
Weight of Powder Charge	5.2 grains
Penetration	6¼ inches of pine at 50 yds.
Penetration	⅓ inch of sheet iron at 50 yds.

*Prices are based on tariff of October 3rd, 1913, and are subject to revision in event of change of said tariff and rate of exchange. A full assortment of repair parts for *Mauser* and *Luger* arms carried in stock.

SOLE AUTHORIZED IMPORTER FOR THE UNITED STATES

A. F. STOEGER   NEW YORK
606 WEST FORTY-NINTH STREET

American and German Ammunition always carried in stock.

Genuine Mauser Magazine Sporting Rifles
Chambered for 1906/30 U. S. Government Cartridge

No. 615. Mannlicher Type. Finest walnut stock to end of muzzle, with cheek piece, 20 inch round barrel, flat bolt, fish skin pistol grip, sling swivels, silver bead, steel butt plate with cleaning kit in butt. Front sight and sight protector; rear sight graduated to 1000 yards. Weight about 7 pounds.
Both the 1906/30 U. S. Government Service or Sporting cartridges can be used in this rifle.

Special Mauser Range Rifle
Chambered for the 1906/30 U. S. Government Service or Sporting Ammunition.

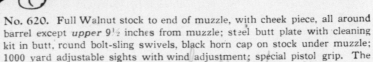

No. 620. Full Walnut stock to end of muzzle, with cheek piece, all around barrel except *upper* 9½ inches from muzzle; steel butt plate with cleaning kit in butt, round bolt-sling swivels, black horn cap on stock under muzzle; 1000 yard adjustable sights with wind adjustment; special pistol grip. The longer barrel gives it greater power and range. Weight 8¼ pounds.

No. 621. Same as above with collapsible peepsight.

No. 1100. Select water-proofed soft leather case for rifles with Sport stock.

No. 1120. Select water-proofed soft leather case for Mannlicher Style Rifles.

No. 1300. Best soft leather sling straps for Mauser rifles.

No. 1310. Imported leather butt plate pads.

DIAGRAM
of targets obtained with Mauser Magazine
Sporting Rifle

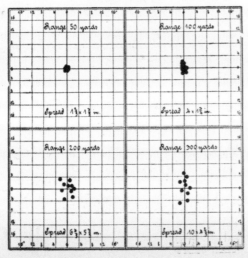

"STOEGEROL"
The Wonder Combination Oil. Worth its weight
in gold to every lover of a gun.

Nitro-solvent

Prevents corrosion

Prevents rust even in water

An ideal cleanser

Cleans pus germs in wounds of man or beast

No Hunter

No Soldier

No Ranchman

No Farmer

can afford to be without

STOEGEROL

the true wonder oil

Police, Shoulder and Flap Holsters

*Leaders in Leather and Canvas Gun Cases, Holsters,
Shell Belts, Slings, Recoil Pads, etc., etc.*

No. 1275

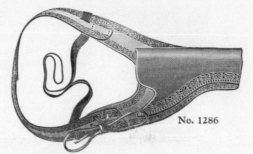

No. 1286

No. 1275—This holster has been officially adopted by the N. Y. City police department. Pocket and belt combination holster fitted with square leather back, to keep revolver in upright position; the back of this holster is made from 6-oz. best grade cowhide and the front is made of 4½-oz. hand bordered leather. Made for pocket revolvers 32 or 38 cal. having up to 4 inch barrels.

No. 1276—Made for Mauser or Colt 25 and 32, or Savage 32 cal. automatic.

No. 1277—Made for Colt 38 cal. automatic, pocket model.

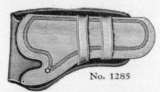

No. 1285

No. 1285—Made from 6″ cowhide embossed with beautiful designs in the following cal.: 32 cal. having barrel up to 6″ in length; 38 cal. having barrel up to 6″ in length. Military and police 5 and 6″, large frame revolvers 44 and 45 cal. up to 7½ inch barrels.

SHOULDER HOLSTERS

No. 1286—A holster made for the convenience of the pistol carrying public; made of 4-oz. leather with breast and shoulder strap handsomely engraved. Made to carry any type pistol.

No. 1287—Same as above, but made of 6″ leather, and finer quality.

No. 1288—Same as 1286, but made for persons of smaller frame.

No. 1289—Same as No. 1287, but made for persons of smaller frame.

FLAP HOLSTERS

No. 1293

No. 1293—Russet holsters. Made of 6″ leather with belt loops in the following cal.: 32 cal. having barrel up to 6″ in length; 38 cal. having barrel up to 6″ in length.

Military and police 4″ to 6″ barrels, also large frame revolvers 44 and 45 cal. having up to 7½ inch barrels.

No. 1294—Same as above, but made of 7 ounce high grade russet cowhide leather.

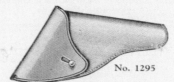

No. 1295

No. 1295—Made from 6″ russet leather cowhide with belt loops and brass flap button. 32 cal. having barrels from 3½ to 6″ in length; 38 cal. having barrels from 3½ to 6″ in length. Military and police revolvers having up to 6″ barrels. Other large frame revolvers 44 and 45 cal. having up to 7 inch barrels.

All leather used in the manufacture of these goods is carefully selected.

SOLE AUTHORIZED IMPORTER FOR THE UNITED STATES AND CANADA OF THE
GENUINE MAUSER AND LUGER ARMS AND AMMUNITION

A. F. STOEGER, 224 EAST 42ND STREET NEW YORK
"Within a block of Grand Central Station"

"Stoegerol" the Wonderful Combination Gun Oil—nitro-solvent, rust-preventing, lubricating, antiseptic.

Field Glasses and Binoculars

(Continued)

No. 2000

No. 2000—Sportiere—Paris—Field Glass
—covered with black morocco leather; black thumb-screw, nickeled tubes, cross-bars and mounting.
Object lens—19 lignes or $1\frac{3}{4}$ inches.
Height — $3\frac{1}{4}$ inches.

No. 2001—Sportiere—Paris—Field Glass
—covered with tan leather; black thumb-screw and nickeled tubes, cross-bars and mounting. Equipped with nickeled eye-cups eliminating side-lights.
Object lens—19 lignes or $1\frac{3}{4}$ inches.
Height — $3\frac{1}{4}$ inches.

No. 2002—Marchand Field Glass—
cone shaped, achromatic, 6 lenses; body covered with black morocco leather; japanned mounting. Scale on center tube. Equipped with carrying case and leather shoulder strap.
Object lens—19 lignes or $1\frac{3}{4}$ inches.
Height — $3\frac{3}{8}$ inches.

No. 2003—"Marchand" Field Glass—
a longer glass—achromatic, 6 lenses; body covered with black morocco leather; japanned mounting and oxidized tubes and rings. Provided with loops, carrying cord, case and leather shoulder strap.
Object lens—19 lignes or $1\frac{3}{4}$ inches.
Height — $4\frac{1}{8}$ inches.

No. 2004—Sportiere—Paris—Field Glass
—covered with black morocco leather; nickeled mounting. Equipped with nickeled eye-cups, eliminating side-lights. Extended nickeled sun-shades.
Object lens—19 lignes or $1\frac{3}{4}$ inches.
Height — $3\frac{3}{4}$ inches.

No. 2010—Sportiere—Paris—Field and Marine Glass—Covered with black morocco
leather; japanned mounting and with sun-shades. Tubes engraved "FIELD EXTRA POWERFUL," "MARINE EXTRA POWERFUL,"—illustrated on following page.
Object lens—19 lignes or $1\frac{3}{4}$ inches.
Height — 7 inches closed. $10\frac{3}{4}$ inches extended.

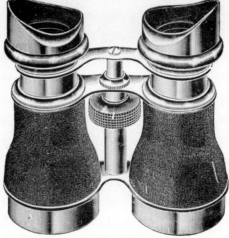

No. 2001

All glasses have cases and straps.

MAUSER

The World Famous Automatic Pocket Pistols

No. 700—Calibre .25, 10-shot Pocket
     Automatic.

No. 701—Calibre .25, 8-shot Vest-Pocket
     Automatic.

No. 702—Calibre .32, 9-shot Pocket
     Automatic.

These genuine Mauser Automatics are
the best, simplest and most reliable made
—not only so cheap, but so *dependable.*

Principal Features of Mauser Automatic

1. Ten and nine shots respectively.
2. Solidity and simplicity of construction.
3. Perfect workmanship.
4. Great accuracy, increased by special length of barrel.
5. Reliability and safety.
6. The state of the pistol, viz. cocked or not, is apparent externally.
7. Considerable penetrative power.
8. Subtantial grip and good balance.
9. Ease of taking to pieces for cleaning.
10. Attractive appearance, absence of projecting parts flat shape and consequent absence of bulge when carried in the pocket.

Genuine Mauser Combination Automatic and Wood Stock-Holster

A *wonderful firearm of
great power and range—
a Carbine and Pistol combined.*

No. 710—7.63 calibre (.300 bore) 10 shots;
3⅝-in. barrel sighted to 500 yards; factory new—a great weapon.

No. 715—7.63 calibre, renovated and mechanically perfect,
with 5⅝-in. barrel. This length pistol can no longer be made
under peace treaty, really good ones getting very scarce.
For efficiency, perfectly reliable working accuracy and safety, this well-known weapon stands in a class by itself.

Genuine Luger Pistols

No. 750—7.63 calibre, new, 3⅝-inch barrel.
          9 m/m calibre, used, but mechanically perfect, in these
          barrel lengths:

No. 751—6-inch.

No. 752—6-inch with squeezer grip.

No. 753—8-inch.

No. 1275—Wooden stock, plain to make Carbine of Luger Pistol.

No. 1276—Wooden stock with leather holster straps and magazine
        holder.

Manufacture of these
pistols now forbidden;
almost impossible to
obtain.

Fine Leather Holsters for Mauser and Luger Automatics

No. 1200—for Calibre .32

No. 1210—for Calibre .25

No. 1220—for Vest Pocket Calibre

No. 1230—Leather Belt Holster with Extra Magazine Pouch for Mauser Combination Pistols No. 710 and No. 715

No. 1231—Shoulder Straps for Carrying Pistols

No. 710 and 715

No. 1250—Luger Holster for 7.65 or 9 m/m up
to 6-inch Barrel.

No. 1251—Luger Holster for 9 m/m or with 8-
inch Barrel.

No. 1252—Quick Reach Patent Spring Holster for
Luger up to 4-inch Barrel

Genuine Mauser and Luger Ammunition

Smokeless Automatic Pistol Ammunition, Mauser Calibre 25-32-7.65
Smokeless Automatic Luger Ammunition, Luger Calibre 7.65; 9 m/m Carbine 7.65
Smokeless Rifle Ammunition, Calibre 6.5 K. P. Short; 6.5 P. P. Long; 7 m/m; 8 m/m Short; 8 m/m Long;
9 m/m; 9.3 m/m; 10.75 m/m.

U. S. 30 Calibre Springfield (U. S. Government Model 1906) *for Mauser Sporting Rifle*

1. Full Metal Jacketed Pointed Bullet.   2. Soft Pointed Round Nose Bullet.   3. Hollow Copperpoint, Pointed Bullet.

A FULL LINE OF REPAIR PARTS FOR ALL MAUSER AND LUGER ARMS ALWAYS IN STOCK

Genuine *Mauser* Self Loading Combination Pistol and Carbine

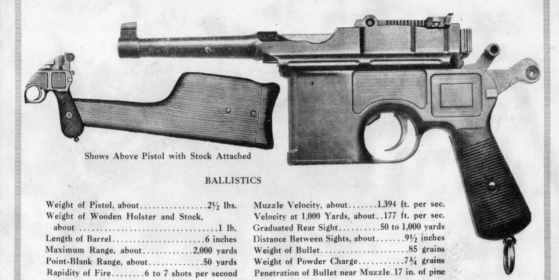

Shows Above Pistol with Stock Attached

BALLISTICS

Weight of Pistol, about................2½ lbs.	Muzzle Velocity, about.......1,394 ft. per sec.
Weight of Wooden Holster and Stock, about ....1 lb.	Velocity at 1,000 Yards, about..177 ft. per sec.
Length of Barrel......................6 inches	Graduated Rear Sight.........50 to 1,000 yards
Maximum Range, about...........2,000 yards	Distance Between Sights, about......9½ inches
Point-Blank Range, about............50 yards	Weight of Bullet.....................85 grains
Rapidity of Fire........6 to 7 shots per second	Weight of Powder Charge........7¾ grains
	Penetration of Bullet near Muzzle.17 in. of pine

THIS powerful arm stands in a class by itself, adapted for target work as well as for a hunting arm. The operation of extracting the empty fired shells, the cocking of the hammer, the reloading and closing of the action is done automatically, not by force of any part of the gases generated by the powder, but *mechanically by the recoil*. The barrel of this arm rests and slides on a track, and the recoil of the fired cartridge utilized to automatically perform the functions of discharging the empty shells, and reloading the weapon, is hardly felt. This arm is as accurate as a rifle, sighted up to 1,000 yards, and has a very low trajectory. The arm can either be loaded with or without a clip of *ten cartridges*. All parts are strong and simple and not liable to break or get out of order. There is not a screw in this arm and it can be taken apart for the purpose of cleaning, without the aid of any tools.

	List Price
Pistol complete, with wood Holster, 3⅝-inch Barrel (Cal. 7.63 M/M), new..........	$35.00
Pistol complete, with wood Holster, 6-inch Barrel (Cal. 7.63 M/M), perfectly renovated	45.00

(Peace Treaty does not permit the Mauser factory to manufacture 6-inch barrel, 7.63 M/M Pistols.)

Leather Holster to attach to belt and to fit over wood holster of pistol..............	4.50
Genuine imported Mauser 7.63 M/M full steel jacket or hollow point Cartridges for above pistols	60.00 per M.

It is of the greatest importance to use this Genuine Mauser Ammunition to insure proper working of this automatic pistol.

The above List Prices includes War Tax

German and American Ammunition for These Pistols Always Carried in Stock

SOLE AUTHORIZED IMPORTER FOR THE UNITED STATES AND CANADA

A. F. STOEGER   NEW YORK
606 WEST FORTY-NINTH STREET

A Look Inside Earlier Editions

For 85 years and more than 100 editions, Stoeger's catalog, handbook and reference guide, the Shooter's Bible, has showcased or offered for sale firearms, sporting goods and accessories that provide an extraordinary insight into the outdoor sports and activities that have been, and remain, so much a part of the American experience in the 20th century. The following facsimiles of page spreads from Shooter's Bibles of the past contain a small selection of the thousands of pages of items carried or showcased by the company over the years. These range from the "Thompson Anti-Bandit Sub-Machine Gun" sold legally for $200 in 1929 to high-grade Anschutz "Free rifles" in the 1990s. These and the hundreds of thousands of other items confirm Alexander Stoeger's claim that the Shooter's Bible was "The Worlds Greatest Gun Book."

A. F. STOEGER, Inc., 509 Fifth Avenue, NEW YORK, N. Y. — 46

Thompson Anti-Bandit Sub-Machine Gun

Model No. 21 (With Cutts Compensator)

Specifications: Caliber .45 Weight 9 pounds, 11 ounces. Length 33 inches. Length of Barrel 12½ inches. Equipped with Lyman sights and wind gauge. 20 cartridge capacity magazine. Ammunition caliber .45 Colt Automatic Pistol Ball Cartridges. Rate of Fire—600 shots per minute full automatically, or up to 100 aimed shots per minute semi-automatically firing single shots. Gun also with CUTTS COMPENSATOR (extra). This device stabilizes the gun when fired rapidly and reduces recoil to practically nothing. For Thompson Sub-machine Guns Model 1921, Cutts Compensators control the tendency of muzzle rising in full automatic machine gun fire.

The Thompson Anti-Bandit Gun is a new type of firearm combining the portability of a rifle with the effectiveness of a machine gun and was especially designed as an auxiliary to police departments and for the protection of Banks, Payrolls, Plants, Warehouses, Mines, Ranches, Railroads and Business Property of all kinds. Adopted and used by the U. S. Marine Corps, U. S. Navy Landing Forces, New York, Chicago, Detroit, Philadelphia, San Francisco, etc. Police Departments—Guaranty Trust Co., N. Y., and many Federal Reserve Banks, State Police, Texas Rangers, Northwest Mounted Police, National Guards and many other law enforcement bodies or business.

TAC Thompson Sub-machine gun complete with Cutts Compensator and one 20 Cartridge capacity box magazine.
Price .... $200.00 Each

TACC Thompson Sub-machine gun complete with 20 capacity box magazine but without Cutts Compensator.
Price .... $175.00 Each

TAC 1 20 shot magazine, ball cartridges, box model	$3.00 Each
TAC 2 18 shot magazine for shot cartridges (special)	$3.00 Each
TAC 3 50 shot magazine, ball cartridges, drum model	$21.00 Each
TAC 4 Discontinued	
TAC 5 Canvas web gun case (specify for TAC or TACC gun)	$16.50 Each
TAC 6 Canvas web belt only for carrying magazines	$2.00 Each
TAC 7 Canvas web base for 50 drum magazine	$5.00 Each
TAC 8 Discontinued	
TAC 9 Four pocket web case for four 20 shot box magazine	$5.00 Each

Same prices for Carbine Model, shooting semi-automatically only.
All sales subject to State and Federal Laws.

SEND YOUR GUN TO STOEGER'S FOR REPAIRS

A. F. STOEGER, Inc., 509 Fifth Avenue, NEW YORK, N. Y. — 47

Pearl, Ivory, Stag and Arthorn Pistol Grips

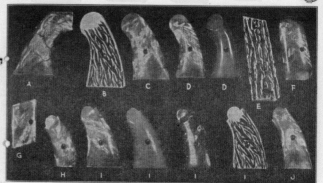

FOR COLT	Pearl or Extra Full Ivory	Ivory	Stag	Arthorn
S. A. Army (A)	$10.00	$6.50	$5.00	$4.00
New Service (b)	10.00	6.00	5.00	4.00
Army Special (c)	6.30	5.30	5.00	3.50
Officers' Model (c)	6.30	5.30	5.00	3.50
Pocket Positive	2.50	2.10	3.00	1.60
Police Positive (d)	4.20	3.90	4.00	3.00
Police Positive Special (d)	4.20	3.90	4.00	3.00
Auto. Military .45 (e)	10.00	7.40	4.00	4.00
Auto. Military or Pocket .38	5.30	5.00	4.40	3.00
Auto Pocket .32 or .380	5.00	4.10	3.50	2.50
Auto Pocket .25 (g)	2.50	2.10	2.50	2.00
Auto. Target .22	9.80	8.50	5.50	4.00
Bisley Model	14.20	10.00	6.00	4.00
FOR SMITH & WESSON				
N. D. .32 or .38 cal.	$1.60	$1.60	$3.00	$1.70
H. E. .32 cal. Mod. 1903 (h)	1.60	1.80	3.50	1.70
H. E. .44 cal. Mod. 1908	5.20	5.00	4.50	3.50
M. & P. .38 cal. Mod. 1902	4.00	3.00	4.20	2.50
M. & P. .38 cal. Mod. 1905 (i)	5.00	5.00	4.50	3.00
Regulation Police (j)	5.00	5.10	5.00	4.00
H. E. .45 cal. Mod. 1917	5.20	5.00	4.50	3.00
Heavy Frame .22/32	20.00	20.00	7.50	6.00
FOR MISCELLANEOUS				
Mauser .25 cal.	$6.00	$5.00	$5.00	$3.50
Mauser .32 cal.	7.00	5.50	5.50	3.50
Luger	......	14.00	11.00	8.00
Webley Air Pistol	5.00	5.00	4.50	3.00
Webley .25 cal.	5.00	4.50	3.50	2.00
Savage .380	5.50	5.00	4.00	2.50
Derringer	2.00	2.00	3.50	1.20
Baby Hammerless	1.20	1.20		1.20
H. & R. or I. J. D. A.	1.60	1.60	3.00	1.40

NOTE: Also that All Our Ivory Grips are of First Quality, Genuine Elephant Tusk.

Steer, Eagle or Buffalo Head Carved on one grip, on Ivory or Pearl Extra $5.50
Full Mexican Eagle, Full Firing Eagle or Full Buffalo Carved on one grip, on Ivory or Pearl, Extra $9.00
Initials carved on one grip each, Extra $2.00 .... Initials carved on one grip and filled in with blue or black lacquer, each, Extra $1.00

We call particular attention to our special Arthorn stocks which may be had in very beautiful imitation Ivory, amber, or tortoise shell, and which are unaffected by heat or cold. *Because of size, Luger grips cannot be made of Pearl.

SEND YOUR GUN TO STOEGER'S FOR REPAIRS

1929

1929

Original A. F. S. Model

"MERKEL BROTHERS"

3-BARRELED COMBINATION GUNS

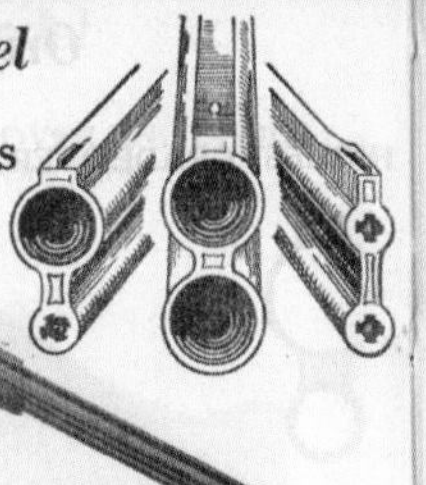

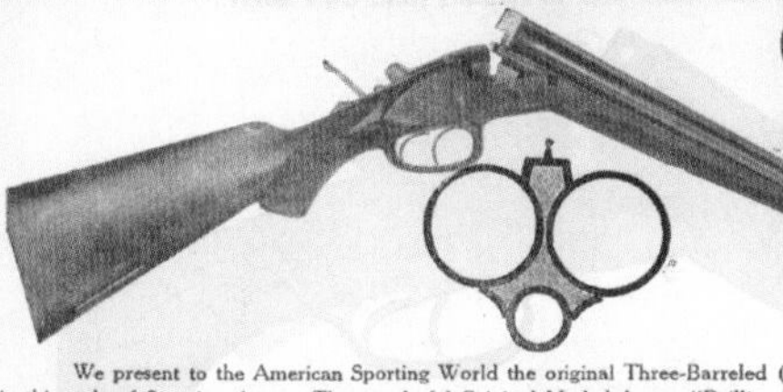

We present to the American Sporting World the original Three-Barreled ("Drilling") Guns which are the best in this style of Sporting Arms. The wonderful Original Merkel-Anson "Drillings"—2 shot barrels, any calibre, with rifle barrel preferably for calibre 30-30 Winchester underneath—are perfect in construction, safe, dependable and well balanced. These Three-Barrel Guns are far superior to anything offered, especially to those where the actions are located above the trigger plates, thereby unbalancing the gun as the action is too far in the rear. In our Genuine Merkel Bros. Anson & Deeley Three-Barreled guns, the action is nearly above the hand, which gives perfect balance.

Please remember this difference when competitors offer you cheaper three-barreled guns. In the Merkel-Anson "Drilling" the firing pins are non integral with the hammer securing thereby quick and safe action, also preventing rusting or breaking of inside mechanism or stock, due to "blowbacks", as the lock construction is place in the system and not in the stock as in cheaper drillings. Merkel stock sides are stronger and possess a much stronger connection between stock and action, a quality much to be desired in this kind of gun.

The barrels are of the celebrated Krupp fluid steel. Every barrel bears the proof marks that it has been tested and passed at the Merkel as well as the Government Proof-House.

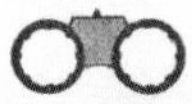

Double Barrel Rifles.

Double Barrel Rifles for Small or Big Game are also made with Barrels placed Over and Under.

We make a specialty of hand made Big Game Express Rifles of any specification and caliber to be built to order by the famous Merkel Brothers. Delivery time 3 to 4 months. It will pay you to call on us or to give us specifications before reaching a decision regarding the purchase of Big Game Rifles.

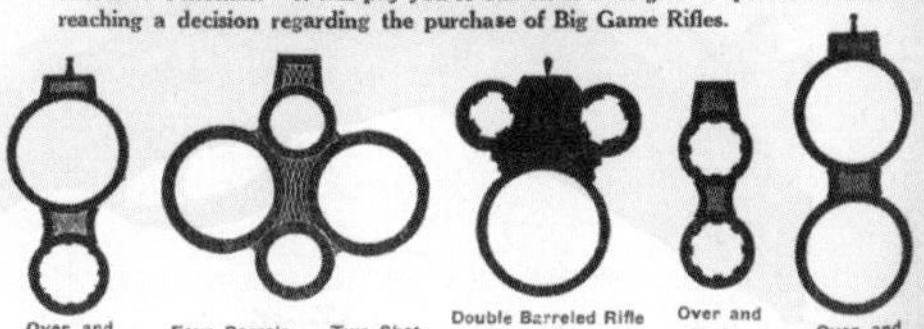

Over and Under Shot and Rifle Barrel — Four Barrels — Two Shot and Two Rifle — Double Barreled Rifle with Shotgun Barrel — Over and Under Rifle — Over and Under Trap or Field Gun

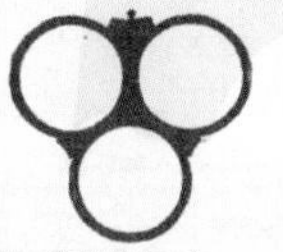

Three Shotgun Barrels

Any of above shown types in any desired calibre may be had on special order at no additional charge. Delivery time, about 4 months.

SEND YOUR GUN TO STOEGER FOR REPAIRS

Original A. F. S. Model

"MERKEL BROTHERS"

HIGHEST GRADE HAND MADE HAMMERLESS THREE - BARRELED GUNS

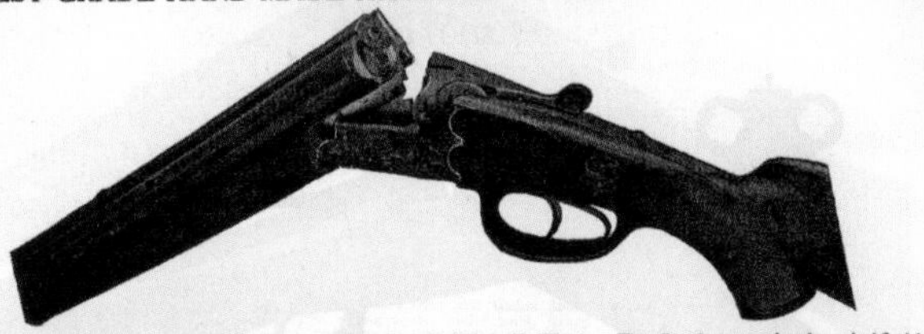

No. 275. BLITZ System Hammerless Three-Barreled Gun (Drilling). This Gun has two shot barrels 12, 16 or 20 gauge and one rifle barrel 30-30 or 25-35 caliber. Barrels are genuine Krupp fluid steel, suitable for nitro powder, right barrel modified, left full choke, rifle barrel with express boring, matted extension rib, automatic adjustable rear sight, Greener cross bolt and double underbolt, side clips, Geener side safety, also a special safety upon neck of stock which by pushing forward releases the safety and automatically adjusts back sight for rifle barrel, fine checkered pistol grip and patent snap fore-end, finest figured walnut stock, horn butt plate, fine English style or hunting scenes engraving. Weight 6½ to 7¼ pounds. .... **Price $265.00**

No. 276. Same as above, but with magazine for rifle cartridges in stock. .... **Price $275.00**

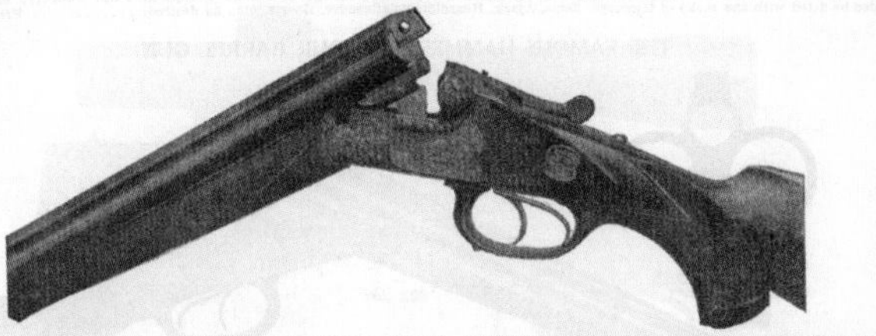

No. 280. Same as above but with ANSON & DEELEY or MERKEL ANSON system. .... **Price $307.50**

No. 281. Same as No. 280, but with magazine for rifle cartridges in stock. .... **Price $317.50**

No. 282. Same as No. 280, but with peep sight, automatic safety for the three barrels, special safety for rifle barrel on neck of stock. .... **Price $375.00**

These Three-Barreled Guns could be made with

Automatic Ejector	extra charge	$188.50	Krupp-Special Steel	extra charge	60.00
Horn Trigger Guard	extra charge	7.50	Boehler Antinitsteel	extra charge	72.50
Roechling-Electro-Steel	extra charge	47.50	Rifle Barrel for 30-06 Govt. or Other Rimless cartridges	extra charge	12.50

The Above Guns can also be made with Three SHOT Barrels.

SEND YOUR GUN TO STOEGER FOR REPAIRS

GENUINE MAUSER TWENTY SHOT 7.63 M/M PISTOL

THE PERFECT POLICE ANTI-BANDIT GUN WITH INTERCHANGEABLE 10 AND 20 SHOT MAGAZINES

ACCURATE RANGE 1100 YARDS

MODEL 712

Illustration shows pistol with twenty shot magazine inserted. Shown outside is the ten shot magazine.

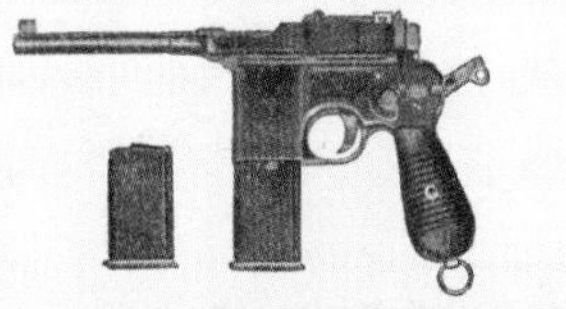

The Mauser Works now present their new autoloading pistol, Caliber 7.63 m/m (.30 Caliber) which permits *twenty consecutive shots* to be fired with one loading. It possesses the further novelty of uniting in the same weapon the Mauser "Clip" and "Detachable Magazine" systems of loading.

This arm occupies a very prominent part in the pistol world, being used for various purposes, such as a military arm used by Germany, Russia, Italy, Turkey, Finland, China, etc., as an efficient police weapon (regulation German police gun), as a target pistol and hunting arm. Special attention is called to its light weight, compactness, high degree of reliability and safety in handling. The weight of the pistol is only 2.79 pounds, and the length of the pistol is only 11.3 inches. This makes an ideal weapon to carry around for hunting, being slipped into the coat pocket. It is used by many sportsmen all over the world for hunting game such as deer, wild boar, wolves, bear, moose, etc. The Mauser is world famed for its great accuracy, hitting power and long range. It is considered the STRONGEST HITTING *and* FARTHEST SHOOTING pistol in the world with a maximum range of about 2,200 yards. Supplied with ten and twenty shot magazines.

In its essential structural features the new arm is identical with the universally known and reputed Standard Mauser auto-pistol Cal. 7.63 m/m, whose absolutely characteristic points of superiority have assured its sweeping success and unique reputation in all parts of the world.

GENERAL.—The new arm integrally embodies the salient characteristics of the Standard Mauser Pistol, namely:

1.—Total avoidance of pins and screws in working parts.
2.—Complete enclosure of mechanism in body.
3.—Grouping of working parts in self-contained assemblies.

thereby not only affording the most complete protection against corrosive gases, dust, snow and foreign bodies generally, but greatly facilitating cleaning, stripping and maintenance.

The chief parts subjected to severe stress have been considerably reinforced, enabling the arm to stand up without reserve to the racking stresses set up in quick fire.

MAGAZINE.—The arm is regularly equipped with a detachable 10-round magazine, which can be interchanged at will with a "long" magazine holding 20 rounds.

MAGAZINE CHANGING is exceedingly simple and certain. The empty magazine is released by pressing a stud on the right hand side of body, then inserting and securing the full one in place by a single motion. Any number of spare magazines can be carried in leather cases on the belt.

LOADING—Cock hammer and fully retract bolt, in which position it is then held by hammer. Smartly insert full magazine into arm, so that it snaps into place. Ease hammer, releasing bolt, which flies forward, carrying the topmost cartridge into chamber. The arm is now ready to fire.

On firing last cartridge, bolt is held back in its rearmost ("open") position by a projecting stud on carrier, leaving arm ready to reload, and giving the firer unmistakable warning that this is necessary.

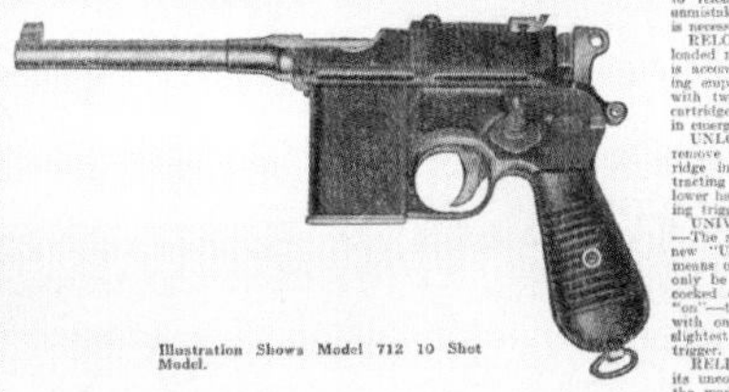

Illustration Shows Model 712 10 Shot Model.

RELOADING.—when a fresh loaded magazine is not available, is accomplished—without removing empty magazine—by refilling with two successive clips of 10 cartridges, a valuable advantage in emergency.

UNLOADING — Release and remove magazine and eject cartridge in chamber by gently retracting bolt. Release bolt and lower hammer, if cocked, by pulling trigger.

UNIVERSAL SAFETY LOCK —The arm is provided with the new "Universal" safety lock by means of which the arm can not only be rendered "safe" whether cocked or uncocked, but—safety "on"—the hammer is lowered with one hand and without the slightest risk by simply pulling trigger.

RELIABILITY — Apart from its unconditional reliability under the worst service conditions, the Original Mauser Quickfiring Pistol has been fully tried out by the severest possible tests with a large number of rounds, without loss of accuracy, malfunction of any kind or ascertainable wear. It is offered in complete confidence as an absolutely first rate automatic arm, fulfilling to the last iota the most exacting demands which a responsible War, Gendarmerie, Police or Customs Department can require in a weapon for the equipment of its officers and subordinates.

The original Mauser Auto-pistol Caliber 7.63 m/m alone combines unique structural superiority with the extreme accuracy of workmanship necessary to meet without reserve the most difficult and refined arms-technical problems arising in the functioning of automatic arms. It can be recognized by the Mauser trade-mark on left side of frame and marking on top of barrel and right side of frame: Waffenfabrik Mauser, Oberndorf a. Necker.

Mauser Pistol with interchangeable 10 and 20 shot magazines.... **$110.00**
Extra 10 Shot Magazine.......... **5.00**
Extra 20 Shot Magazine.......... **10.00**

NUMERICAL DATA OF MODEL 712

Caliber .... 0.300 in.
Total length .... 11.3 in.
Length of barrel with chamber .... 5.20 in.
Length of line of sight .... 9.05 in.
Weight of pistol with 10 shot magazine .... 2.79 lbs.
Ditto with 20 shot magazine .... 2.90 lbs.
Muzzle velocity (vo) .... 1392 f.s.

Muzzle energy (Vo) .... 366 ft. lbs.
Spread of 10 shots:
at 50 m. .... vertical 5.9 in. — horizontal 4.3 in.
at 100 m. .... vertical 9.8 in. — horizontal 7.9 in.
at 200 m. .... vertical 17.7 in. — horizontal 14.2 in.
at 500 m. .... vertical 59 in. — horizontal 49 in.

Rear sight graduated to .... 1000 m; 1100 yds.
Extreme range .... 2000 m; 2200 yds.
Penetration in pine:
at 50 m. .... 8 to 9 in.
at 100 m. .... 6.3 in.
at 200 m. .... 4.9 in.

NOTE: Shown on the left of the pistols illustrated is a small lever, which serves to convert the pistol into full automatic (machine gun). The model we offer does not have this feature due to Federal regulations nor can the model we offer, be converted.

© **A NEW GUN CARRIES A FACTORY GUARANTEE**

MAUSER AUTOMATIC POCKET PISTOLS

THE ORIGINAL MAUSER SELF LOADING AUTOMATIC POCKET PISTOL

COMPACT, ACCURATE, SAFE, AND TRUE WEAPONS OF DEFENSE
Pocket Models—25 cal. (6.35 MM), 10 shot; 32 cal. (765 MM), 9 shots

PRINCIPAL FEATURES

1. Ten, nine and eight shots respectively.
2. Solidity and simplicity of construction.
3. Perfect workmanship.
4. Great accuracy, increased by special length of barrel.
5. Reliability and safety.
6. The state of the pistol, viz., cocked or not, is apparent externally.
7. Considerable penetrative power.
8. Substantial grip and good balance.
9. Ease of taking apart for cleaning.
10. Attractive appearance, absence of projecting parts, flat shape and consequent absence of bulge when carried in the pocket.

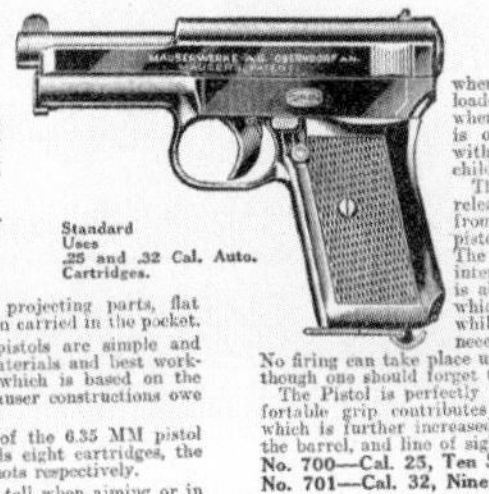

Standard Uses .25 and .32 Cal. Auto. Cartridges.

The component parts of the Mauser pistols are simple and strong and only the highest quality of materials and best workmanship are used in their manufacture which is based on the same methods and principles to which Mauser constructions owe their world wide reputation.

Magazine Capacity. As the magazine of the 6.35 MM pistol holds nine and that of the 7.65 MM holds eight cartridges, the pistol can be made to hold ten and nine shots respectively.

Security in Handling. The shooter can tell when aiming or in the dark by touch, whether the pistol is cocked or not—when cocked, the rear end of the striker is visible at the back of the breech. This is a most valuable feature, as the absence on other pistols of devices clearly showing the state of the weapon, has led to fatal accidents.

The pistol cannot be fired when the magazine is wholly or partly withdrawn. Accidents due to presumption that there was no cartridge in the barrel after withdrawing the magazine are thus made impossible.

The breech remains open after firing the last cartridge, but closes automatically as long as there is a cartridge in the magazine. This gives greater security in handling.

The Safety, which can be operated with ease by the thumb of the right hand when aiming, allows the weapon to be made safe when cocked or not cocked, loaded or not loaded, and as the breech cannot be opened when the pistol is safe, danger in carrying is obviated, nor can those unacquainted with the mechanism, such as servants or children, make the pistol ready for fire.

The system employed for unlocking, i. e., releasing the safety, prevents the safety from being unlocked while carrying the pistol in, or drawing it out of, the pocket. The involuntary firing of more shots than intended, commonly known as "Maximing" is absolutely prevented by the interceptor which disconnects the trigger from the sear while the breech is in motion and makes it necessary to pull the trigger for each shot. No firing can take place unless the breech is entirely closed, even though one should forget to release the trigger after firing.

The Pistol is perfectly balanced, and its substantial and comfortable grip contributes greatly to the accuracy of shooting which is further increased by the comparatively great length of the barrel, and line of sight.

No. 700—Cal. 25, Ten Shot.......... Price $25.00
No. 701—Cal. 32, Nine Shot.......... Price $28.00

THE NEW MAUSER VEST POCKET PISTOL

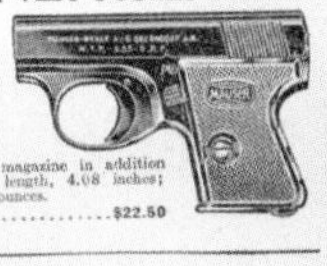

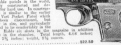

This is one of the smallest serviceable pistols in the world, ruggedly constructed and designed for hard use. In construction it is similar to the earlier model Vest Pocket Pistol which has been discontinued, but smaller in size, and particularly designed to lie comfortably in the hand. Holds six shots in the magazine in addition to one in the chamber. Total length, 4.08 inches; depth, 2⅝ inches; weight, 9½ ounces.
Price $22.50

COMPONENT PARTS LIST OF MAUSER POCKET MODEL

No.	Article	Price
1.	Barrel	$6.00
2.	Barrel Holder	2.25
3.	Barrel Holder Catch	1.25
4.	Striker (Firing Pin)	2.75
5.	Striker Spring	1.25
6.	Barrel Holder Guide	1.25
7.	Interceptor	1.00
8.	Rear Sight	1.25
9.	Extractor	2.50
10.	Breech	7.50
11.	Recoil Spring	1.25
12.	Ejector	3.00
13.	Double Action Spring	.75
14.	Grip Cover Plate	2.75
15.	Frame	7.50
16.	Magazine	3.50
17.	Trigger Complete	3.00
18.	Trigger Spring	.75
19.	Grip Cover Plate Screw, left	.50
20.	Grip Cover Plate Screw, right	.50
21.	Safety Locking Spring	1.50
22.	Trigger Catch Spring	.65
23.	Trigger Catch Pin	.50
24.	Trigger Catch	1.50
25.	Magazine Platform	.75
26.	Safety	3.00
27.	Sear	3.00
28.	Magazine Bottom Plate	.50
29.	Magazine Holder	2.50
30.	Magazine Spring	1.25
31.	Side Plate	3.00

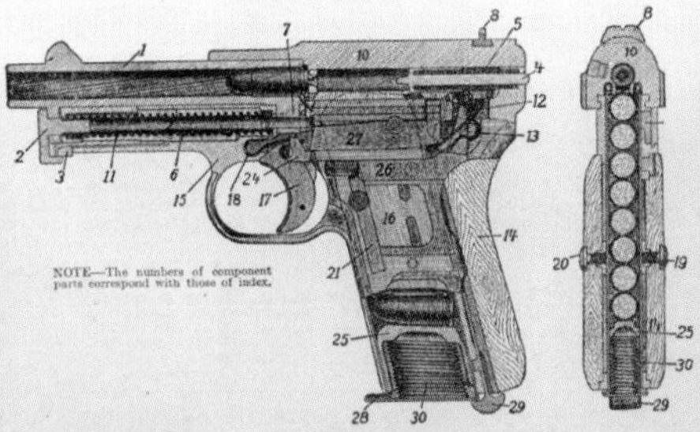

NOTE—The numbers of component parts correspond with those of index.

© **ALL SHIPMENTS ARE INSURED**

1935

1939

1943

1946

DRYBAK WOOD AND FIELD CLOTHING

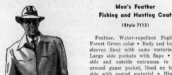

Men's Super-Twill Two-Length Hunting Coat

(Style 7434)

Attractive Forest Green, high count, high tensile strength Drybak Super-twill, permanently water repellent • Top sleeves and body lined with same material • Entire lower half of coat, forming bloodproof-coated Game Pocket, is new one-piece construction • Game Pocket unhooks on inside and zips down to form Trench coat length, and waterproof Drop Seat • Drybak Storm-flap Collar for complete head and neck protection • Hinge sleeves, action back • Patented hand-warmers cover 9 shell loops on each side of coat • Button flap breast pocket • Chest sizes 37, 40, 43, 46, 49, 52.

Price $19.95

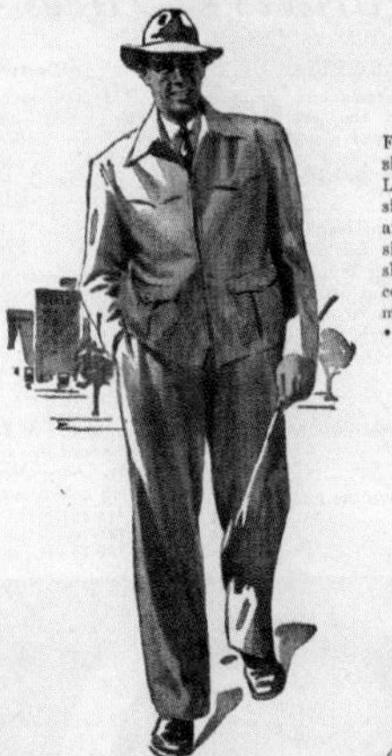

Men's Feather Fishing and Hunting Coat

(Style 7113)

Feather, Water-repellent Poplin—Forest Green color • Body and top of sleeves lined with same material • Large side pockets with flaps • Inside and outside entrances to all-around game pocket, lined on inner side with coated material • Hinged sleeves and pleated shoulders give complete freedom of shoulder and arm movement • Length about 30 inches • Chest sizes 37, 40, 43, 46, 49.

Price $12.50

Men's Feather Boot Pants

(Style 7362)

Price $7.85

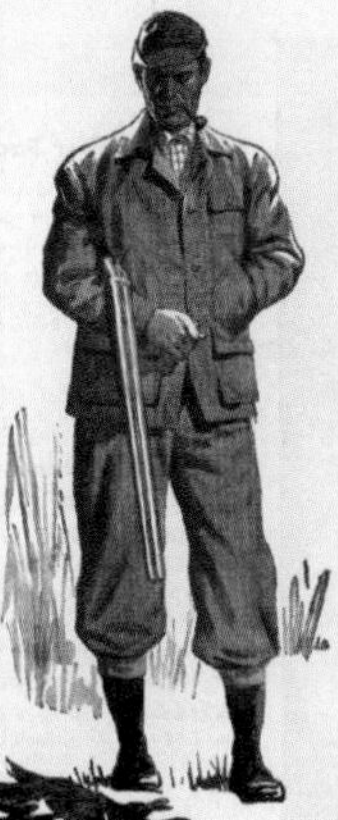

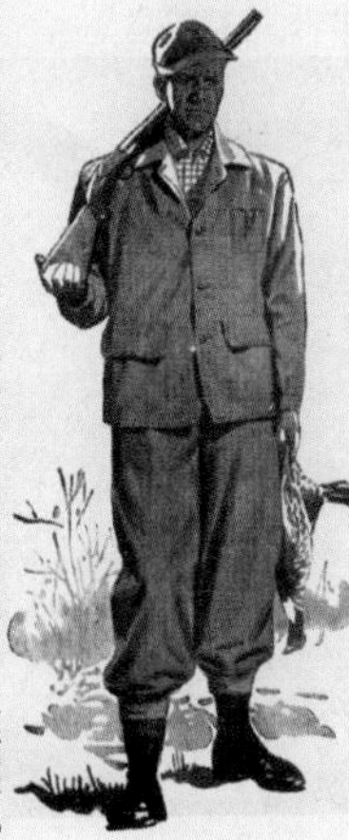

Cruiser Style Wood-Field Jacket Virgin Wool-lined

(Style 6190)

Sand color, vat dyed, wind and rain resistant Super-Twill outer material • Full lined with 9½ ounce all virgin wool, matching color • Cruiser style yoke with double thickness over shoulders, upper back and chest, zipper front • Seamless shoulder yoke gives special protection against rain or snow • 2 inside breast pockets with button closure formed by shoulder yoke • 2 pleated lower pockets with button flap closure • Nicely designed back with concealed utility pocket in lower section with zipper entrance • 2-button, adjustable cuffs, pleated • Weighs about 40 ounces; length about 28 inches • Chest sizes 37, 40, 43, 46, 49 inches.

Price **$18.50**

Woodfield Hat

(Style 9000)

Outdoor style with pinch-front crown • Light weight tan twill treated water-repellent • Wide, flexible stitched and bound, 2¾ inch brim can be worn turned up or down • Shaped, steam blocked, fiber-mesh lined crown with taped seams • Sweat band • Crown banded at brim with self-material • Sizes 6⅝ to 7½.

Price **$12.50**

©

CORRECT OUTDOOR WEAR

DRYBAK FEATHER FISHING CLOTHES

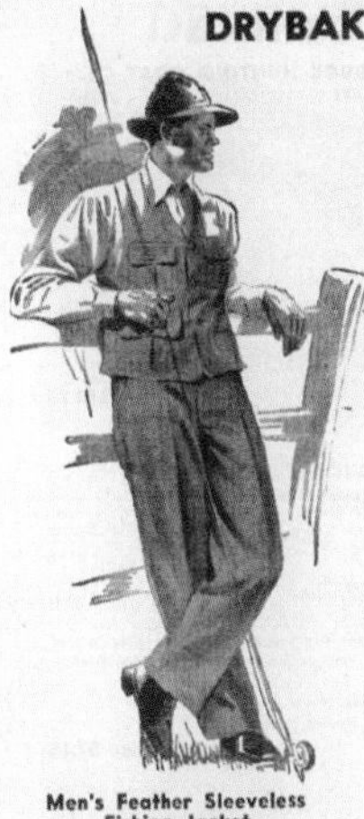

Men's Feather Fishing Coat

(Style 7111)

Forest Green, medium-weight, Water-repellent Poplin • 2 large, 2 small pleated front pockets; one on left sleeve; button closure • Shearling-wool fly pad built in left breast pocket • 1 large bellows pocket on back for game or utility use; button-flap entrance at each side • 2 large inside front pockets, button closure • Pleated shoulders for complete freedom of action • 2-button adustable cuffs, shirt style • Rod loop and keeper • Bar tacked at strain points • Cut full for comfortable fit and freedom of action • Length about 21 inches; weight about 13 ounces • for either wading or boat fishing • Chest sizes 37, 40, 43, 46, 49. **PRICE $8.25**

Fishing and Hunting Boot-Pants

(Style 7062)

Medium-weight Forest Green, Water-repellent Drybak Feather Poplin • Front of legs and seat lined • Button fly • 5 pockets, 2 hip pockets have button flap • Patented Drybak Edg-Bound Pockets are reinforced with tape binding around edges • Cut full for comfortable, roomy fit • Weight about 17 ounces • Light-weight water-repellent, will make excellent hiking, fishing or hunting pants • Knitted-bottoms tuck in top of boots • Even waist sizes 30-44, 33-inch inseam. **PRICE $7.85**

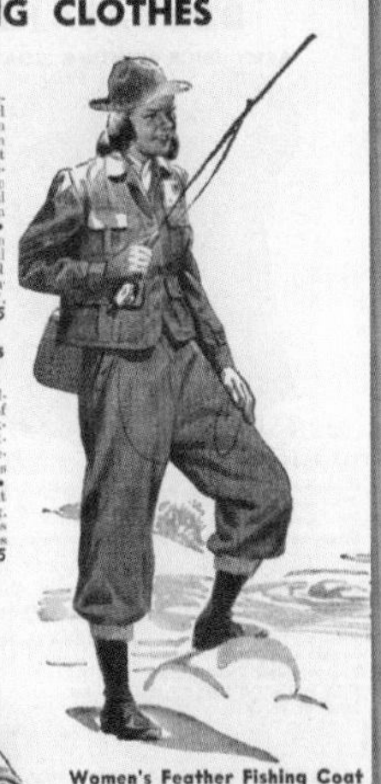

Men's Feather Sleeveless Fishing Jacket

(Style 7110)

Medium weight Forest Green Water-repellent Poplin • 2 large, pleated front pockets • 2 pleated breast pockets, left pocket with new design shearling-wool fly pad which folds in pocket when not in use • 1 large rear utility or game pocket with 4" bellows • Rod loop and keeper • Bar-tacked at all points of strain • Length—about 24 inches • Weight about 10 ounces • Excellent for wading, boat fishing or small bird shooting • Chest sizes 34, 37, 40, 43, 46. **PRICE $5.00**

Men's Feather and Hunting Pants

(Style 7363)

Medium-weight Forest Green, Water-repellent Feather Poplin • Front of legs and seat lined • Button fly • 5 pockets, 2 hip pockets have button flap • Patented Drybak Edg-Bound Pockets are reinforced with tape binding around edges • Cut full for comfortable, roomy fit • Weight about 17 ounces • Lightweight water-repellent, will make excellent hiking, fishing or hunting pants • Hemmed bottoms • Even waist sizes 30 to 44; 30, 32, 34-inch inseam. **PRICE $7.50**

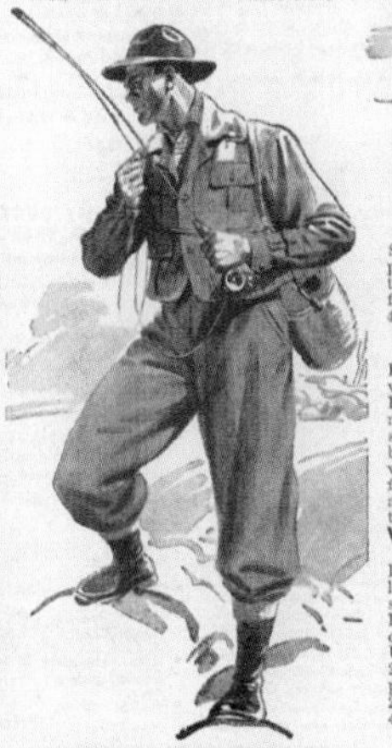

Women's Feather Fishing Coat

(Style 7112)

Similar to 7111 at left but with utility pocket about 4 by 5 inches with 2-button flap concealed in left lower pocket for keys, etc. Bust sizes 31, 34, 37, 40, 43 inches. **PRICE $8.25**

Women's Feather Trousers

(Style 7161)

Knitted Bottoms, Drybak Feather, water-repellent Poplin—Forest Green. Front of legs and seat lined with same material. Made in button, side opening style. 2 Front pockets. Patented Dryback Edg-Bound Pockets are reinforced with tape binding around edges. Cut full for comfortable, roomy fit. Weight about 17 ounces. Even waist sizes 24 to 36. 31-inch inseam. **PRICE $7.00**

Women's Feather Hunting Coat

(Style 7131)

Drybak Feather Water-repellent Poplin • Body and top sleeves lined with same material—Forest green color • Inner side of game pocket bloodproof coated, with two rear entrances • Utility pocket about 4 by 5 inches with 2-button flap concealed in left, lower pocket for keys, etc. • Weighs about 24 ounces • Bust sizes 31, 34, 37, 40, 43 inches. Similar to style 7330. **PRICE $10.50**

©

IT PAYS TO BUY THE BEST

GUN CARE

By CHARLES EDWARD CHAPEL

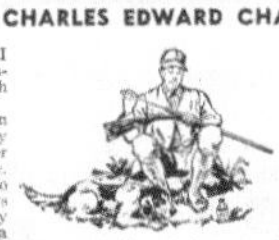

When I have plenty of spare time, which is seldom, I compound my own preparations for gun care, but I principally rely upon the Stoeger products which are much better than anyone can make at home.

I have been using Stoeger products for more than thirty years and I have been recommending them to my acquaintances for most of that time. To me, the Stoeger Arms Corporation is not merely a business house. Instead, it is a family of friends that has helped me to keep my guns in good condition. For example, I always keep a bottle of Stoegerol handy. This is a specially compounded oil that combines the functions of a cleaner, a solvent and a lubricant. It dissolves or prevents rust and corrosion, neutralizes nitro gases, dissolves metal fouling and is an excellent cleaning and lubricating agent. When rubbed into leather, it softens and preserves it. Mixed with about five volumes of water and well shaken, it serves as a good gunstock polish.

If guns receive the correct care, rust should not appear, but sometimes I find that one of my firearms has a little rust on the outside. I rub on some Stoeger Rust-Off with a strong cloth, work it back and forth vigorously, and then apply Stoeger Barrel Grease before storing the gun. This preparation will not hurt the hands or corrode the gun, even if it is not entirely removed. It can be used in the bore in a case of bad rusting and pitting, but I like some of the other Stoeger products better for this purpose.

Stoeger Barrel Grease is based upon a specially selected, acid-free petrolatum combined with rust-inhibiting elements to provide protection against moisture. Before applying the Barrel Grease, I swab the gun with Stoegerol to neutralize all deposits of acid and moisture. However, it should be emphasized that Barrel Grease is primarily intended for protecting arms during storage and shipment.

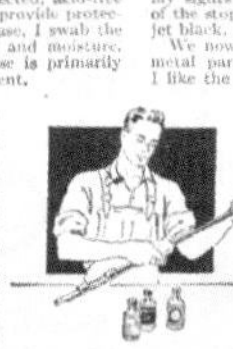

Stoeger Barrel Restorer No. 1 is a heavy-duty, abrasive lead-and-nickel solvent preparation which I use on rifles, shotguns and pistols, regardless of caliber or bore, if they have been subjected to hard use. Most experts use a leather buffer, but I prefer to apply this preparation with ordinary cloth patches and complete the treatment with clean patches soaked in Stoegerol. I have found that Barrel Restorer No. 1 is particularly effective in treating guns in which I have fired black powder with old-style primers, especially my muzzle-loading rifles and pistols.

Stoeger Barrel Restorer No. 2 is somewhat milder in its action than Barrel Restorer No. 1 but I advise using it promptly if an examination of the bore shows the presence of metal fouling. Like Barrel Restorer No. 1, it is applied with either a leather buffer or cotton patches and then followed with Stoegerol on cloth patches.

The Stoeger X-Ring Paste is a bore-cleaning preparation which is applied with a patch after the barrel has been treated with Barrel Restorer No. 2. The barrel is then wiped clean and dry. If the gun is to be stored or shipped, follow by swabbing with Stoegerol. This preparation is recommended for .22, .30, .38 and .45 caliber rifles and pistols, especially where the shooter wants a smooth bore for firing in matches.

In cleaning guns, the Stoeger one-piece, air-dried, all-hickory cleaning rods with their integral knurled tips provide insurance against damaging the bore. These rods are available for various calibers and bores, and in various lengths, for cleaning pistols, rifles and shotguns. I keep several on hand, one of them being a rod 72 inches long for cleaning muzzle-loading rifles. In addition, I use aluminum alloy, duraluminum, and steel cleaning rods, but the hickory rods are my treasured "pets".

When I go on short hunting or target-shooting trips, I carry with me a Stoeger Cleaning Kit. It contains a liberal supply of cleaning patches, a bottle of Stoegerol and a bottle of Noshine, the latter being used to darken sights. On longer trips, I carry the Stoeger Carry-All Kit Box. It is made of red cedar and divided into six compartments, one of which has a false bottom to provide two layers. Into this box, I pack cleaning rods, patches, oil cans, and various preparations for taking care of my weapons.

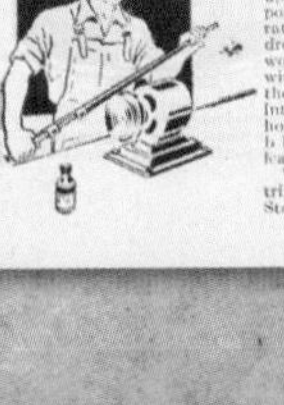

I mentioned above that Stoegerol softens and preserves leather, but that is only an incidental property of that amazing oil. A far better preparation for preserving leather is Stoeger Rejuvoline, which is not based upon oil and hence does not fill the pores or permit sub-surface deterioration. Instead, it is based upon anhydrous lanolin, obtained from sheep wool. I wash my leather goods first with saddle soap, dry slowly and thoroughly, and then rub Rejuvoline into the leather. I use it on rifle slings holsters, scabbards, shoes, puttees, belts and even on my old and rare leather-bound gun books.

When I get home from a hunting trip, or from the target range, I apply Stoeger Stock Polisher and Cleaner to the stocks of my guns, using a flannel rag and rubbing briskly. Ordinarily, one application is enough, but if there is a stubborn film of dirt, two applications may be needed to do a really good job of cleaning and polishing.

The Stoeger London Oil Finish is used on my gunstocks for preserving, darkening and excluding moisture. In finishing a new stock, I sandpaper the wood, dampen with water or vinegar, resandpaper until I can raise the grain no more, and then either rub the London Oil Finish in with my hands or apply it with a woolen rag. When I want to give a new, unfinished stock a superb, dull English finish, I scour the wood with rottenstone after the last sandpapering operation and before applying the London Oil Finish.

Although the Stock Polisher and Cleaner is adequate for ordinary care of wooden gun parts, the use of Stoeger Stock Wax is recommended after each use of a gun, particularly if it has a fine finish. This is very important if the stock or forearm has been in contact with sweaty hands, salt air or ordinary dampness.

Stoeger Noshine has been mentioned already as a sight blackener. In my various gun books and articles I have mentioned the fact that I like to blacken my sights in the smoke of burning camphor. Unfortunately, I am limited in this by the many laws against building fires in the woods and find that I can obey the law and still blacken my sights by applying Noshine with the brush attached to the top of the stopper in the bottle. It dries immediately into a non-reflecting jet black, but it can be wiped off easily with a rag.

We now come to the problem of blueing (also spelled *bluing*) the metal parts of firearms, particularly the barrel. For a quick job, I like the Stoeger Tutchup Bluer. It comes in two bottles. A cotton swab is used to apply Solution No. 1. It dries instantly and then Solution 2 is applied with a cotton swab and the blue appears.

The Stoeger S-75 Oxidizer, so named because it was the 75th and last of a series of experiments in compounding blueing preparations, requires the use of only one bottle. It gives a nearly instantaneous, genuine, acid blue with one application of a swab. However, it contains selenium, which is highly injurious to the skin and nails and should be handled only with rubber gloves. Therefore, it is recommended only for touching up worn surfaces and not for blueing a whole gun.

Stoeger Spray Blue is a special type of metal lacquer which may be applied through a sprayer and is especially recommended for nickel, and for stainless steel barrels, because these metals cannot be blued by the ordinary and usual oxidizing (rusting) process.

The Stoeger Lightning Bluer produces a permanent, chemical, blue-black finish in about fifteen minutes and is recommended for all parts and guns except soldered shotgun barrels. It consists of salts which are dissolved to form a solution in a tank into which the barrel or other part is lowered.

The Stoeger Old Connecticut Gun Bluer is probably the most popular of the fast-acting preparations. It is a liquid which can be applied to obtain a factory-like blue finish in less than an hour, without special equipment, such as tanks.

The Stoeger Gunsmith's Bluer is the preparation which the Stoeger people have always used in their own shops and on their finest guns. Only about 25 drops of the preparation are needed for blueing two barrels, but the process requires from three to four days to obtain a professional finish. Personally, I like it the best of all the Stoeger blueing preparations.

The Stoeger Peerless Blueing Kit consists of two Peerless blueing solutions, 4 tapered dowels for use as barrel plugs and handles, 1 pair of gloves, 1 package of steel wool, emery and crocus cloth, 1 package of oilfree cotton, and 1 bottle of finishing oil, complete with directions. Both amateurs and professionals use this kit.

The Stoeger Damascus Browner is not a bluer. It is used on the obsolete, Damascus or "Twist" laminated gun barrels which were popular before 1900. I warn everyone to not fire modern loads in guns having Damascus barrels, but for those who insist upon firing such guns and for collectors, I do recommend the use of the Damascus Browner to give the barrels a color or shade between brown-black and copper-red.

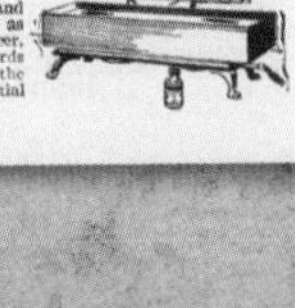

Finally, these are my own comments. They do not necessarily reflect the opinions of the Navy Department or the naval service at large and they are not to be construed as official. As a retired, regular officer, I am required to insert these words in all my writings or suffer the pains and penalties of court martial by my peers.

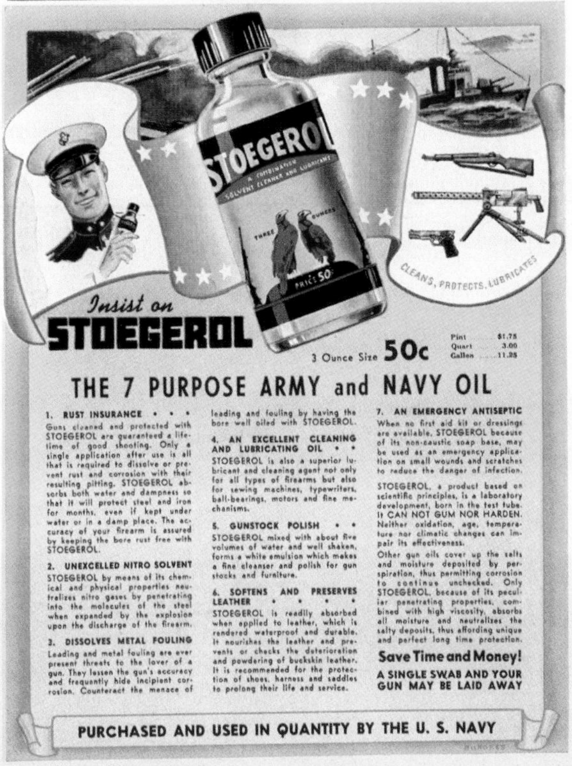

3 Ounce Size **50c**

Pint	$1.75
Quart	3.00
Gallon	11.25

THE 7 PURPOSE ARMY and NAVY OIL

1. RUST INSURANCE • • •
Guns cleaned and protected with STOEGEROL are guaranteed a lifetime of good shooting. Only a single application after use is all that is required to dissolve or prevent rust and corrosion with their resulting pitting. STOEGEROL absorbs both water and dampness so that it will protect steel and iron for months, even if kept under water or in a damp place. The accuracy of your firearm is assured by keeping the bore rust free with STOEGEROL.

2. UNEXCELLED NITRO SOLVENT
STOEGEROL by means of its chemical and physical properties neutralizes nitro gases by penetrating into the molecules of the steel when expanded by the explosion upon the discharge of the firearm.

3. DISSOLVES METAL FOULING
Leading and metal fouling are ever present threats to the lover of a gun. They lessen the gun's accuracy and frequently hide incipient corrosion. Counteract the menace of leading and fouling by having the bore well oiled with STOEGEROL.

4. AN EXCELLENT CLEANING AND LUBRICATING OIL • •
STOEGEROL is also a superior lubricant and cleaning agent not only for all types of firearms but also for sewing machines, typewriters, ball-bearings, motors and fine mechanisms.

5. GUNSTOCK POLISH • •
STOEGEROL mixed with about five volumes of water and well shaken, forms a white emulsion which makes a fine cleanser and polish for gun stocks and furniture.

6. SOFTENS AND PRESERVES LEATHER • • • •
STOEGEROL is readily absorbed when applied to leather, which is rendered waterproof and durable. It nourishes the leather and prevents or checks the deterioration and powdering of buckskin leather. It is recommended for the protection of shoes, harness and saddles to prolong their life and service.

7. AN EMERGENCY ANTISEPTIC
When no first aid kit or dressings are available, STOEGEROL because of its non-caustic soap base, may be used as an emergency application on small wounds and scratches to reduce the danger of infection.

STOEGEROL, a product based on scientific principles, is a laboratory development, born in the test tube. It CAN NOT GUM NOR HARDEN. Neither oxidation, age, temperature nor climatic changes can impair its effectiveness.

Other gun oils cover up the salts and moisture deposited by perspiration, thus permitting corrosion to continue unchecked. Only STOEGEROL, because of its peculiar penetrating properties, combined with high viscosity, absorbs all moisture and neutralizes the salty deposits, thus affording unique and perfect long time protection.

Save Time and Money!

A SINGLE SWAB AND YOUR GUN MAY BE LAID AWAY

PURCHASED AND USED IN QUANTITY BY THE U. S. NAVY

©

1949

1954

20 STOEGER ARMS CORPORATION, 45-18 COURT SQ., LONG ISLAND CITY 1, N. Y.

STEYR CUSTOM .22 CALIBER SMALL BORE CARBINE

A completely new replica of the world famous Mannlicher Schoenauer Carbine has now been developed by the Steyr factory chambered for the .22 long rifle cartridge.
The appearance of this new rifle is very similar to that of its big brother, the difference being in the new specially designed action which accommodates a five shot clip completely flush with the magazine floor plate. The new action has been built as short as possible with speed lock and opens and closes with the same smoothness as the larger gun. The trigger is similar to the regular M. S. single trigger and fully adjustable, allowing a crisp fast pull at any desired tension.

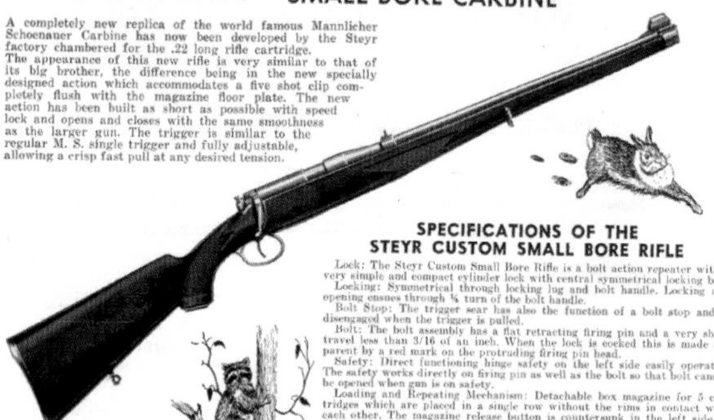

SPECIFICATIONS OF THE STEYR CUSTOM SMALL BORE RIFLE

Lock: The Steyr Custom Small Bore Rifle is a bolt action repeater with a very simple and compact cylinder lock with central symmetrical locking bolt.

Locking: Symmetrical through locking lug and bolt handle. Locking and opening ensues through ¼ turn of the bolt handle.

Bolt Stop: The trigger sear has also the function of a bolt stop and is disengaged when the trigger is pulled.

Bolt: The bolt assembly has a flat retracting firing pin and a very short travel less than 3/16 of an inch. When the lock is cocked this is made apparent by a red mark on the protruding firing pin head.

Safety: Direct functioning hinge safety on the left side easily operated. The safety works directly on firing pin as well as the bolt so that bolt cannot be opened when gun is on safety.

Loading and Repeating Mechanism: Detachable box magazine for 5 cartridges which are placed in a single row without the rims in contact with each other. The magazine release button is countersunk in the left side of the stock. Upon drawing back the release button the magazine drops out. The extraction and ejection of the cartridge case takes place by means of hinged forged extractor and a fixed ejector.

Trigger: Adjustable single two stage trigger.

Sights: Fixed leaf for 50 meters for the standard model. Fixed rear sight with hinged leaf for 100 meters as well as silver bead front sight.

Stock: Genuine walnut is used. The gun has a pistol grip with horn cap, checkered forend and pistol grip, and accessories such as forend cap, front and rear swivels and butt plate.

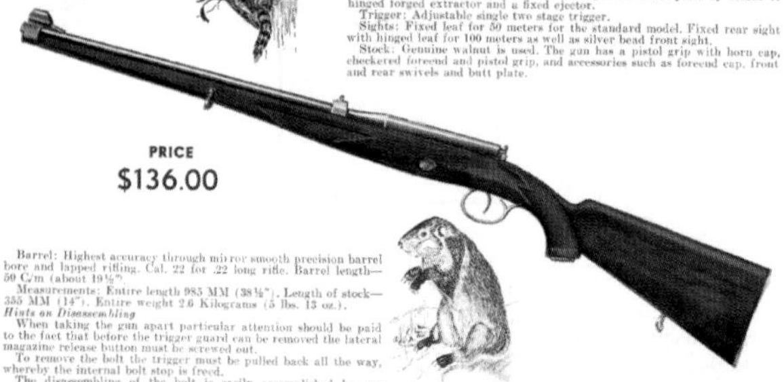

PRICE
$136.00

Barrel: Highest accuracy through mirror smooth precision barrel bore and lapped rifling. Cal. 22 for .22 long rifle. Barrel length—50 C/m (about 19½").

Measurements: Entire length 985 MM (38½"). Length of stock—355 MM (14"). Entire weight 2.6 Kilograms (5 lbs. 13 oz.).

Hints on Disassembling

When taking the gun apart particular attention should be paid to the fact that before the trigger guard can be removed the lateral magazine release button must be screwed out.

To remove the bolt the trigger must be pulled back all the way, whereby the internal bolt stop is freed.

The disassembling of the bolt is easily accomplished by unscrewing the rear bolt nut to the right since this part has a left hand thread. After the bolt handle and the firing pin spring have been removed the firing pin may be drawn out to the rear. The lateral safety lug together with the spring should be left in the bolt.

Assembly takes place in the reverse order but one should be careful to see that the end of the safety spring is properly placed in the internal rim recess of the bolt handle.

When putting the bolt into the action the bolt handle should be turned left relative to the chamber as far as the end of the safety spring. Then the bolt with the handle turned up is pushed into the receiver. In this connection the safety sear must be in the front or firing position and the trigger pulled back.

CLOSE-UP VIEW OF ACTION

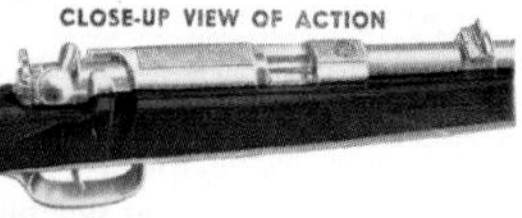

SMALL, LIGHT AND ACCURATE

AMERICA'S GREAT GUN HOUSE 21

SARASQUETA DOUBLE BARREL RIFLES

MODEL 13 DELUXE
PRICE
$750.00

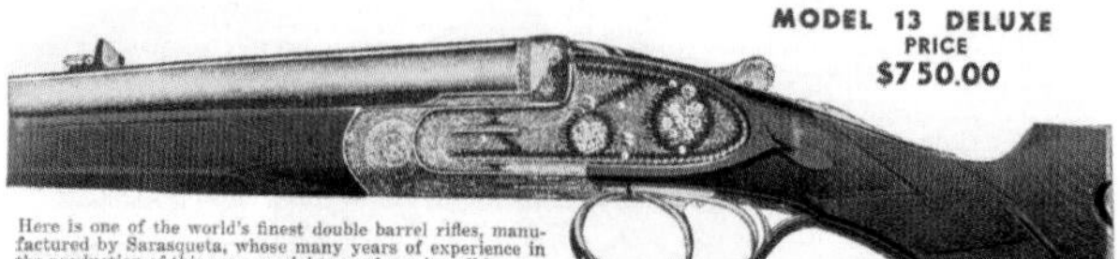

Here is one of the world's finest double barrel rifles, manufactured by Sarasqueta, whose many years of experience in the production of this very special type of gun is well known. The manufacture of double rifles is a specialty which requires more knowledge, patience and skill than any other type of two barrel gun. The barrels must be carefully brazed and soldered together and a regulating wedge placed between the barrels at the muzzle. The gun must then be repeatedly targeted and adjusted to bring the center of impact of both barrels at 100 yards to the same point.
In a double barrel rifle the principal feature must be extreme reliability, which is achieved thru the fact that this is really two independent single barrel rifles locked together. Failure of one side does not affect the other. To further assure safety the side lock is employed which practically guarantees against accidental discharge and is also very easy to remove and repair, since all lock parts lie on the plates and may be quickly replaced by the shooter himself. This model is unusually strong and suitable for the heaviest express cartridges. To withstand the pressure of these large shells the entire action has been especially reinforced and the treble lock is hand fitted with exceedingly great care to assure absolute rigidity even after several thousand rounds. Usually supplied with 24" barrel of finest steel. Available on special order only in practically any caliber. Deluxe engraving and finest walnut.

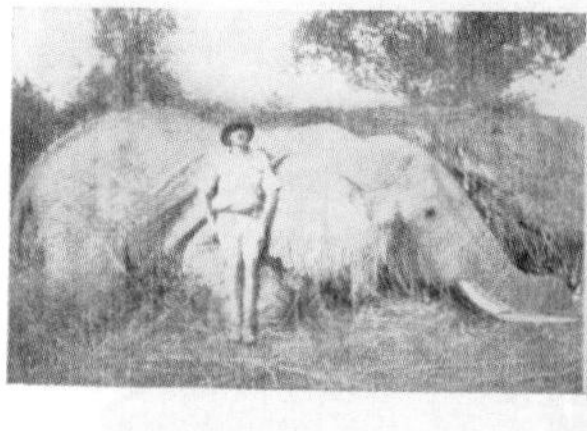

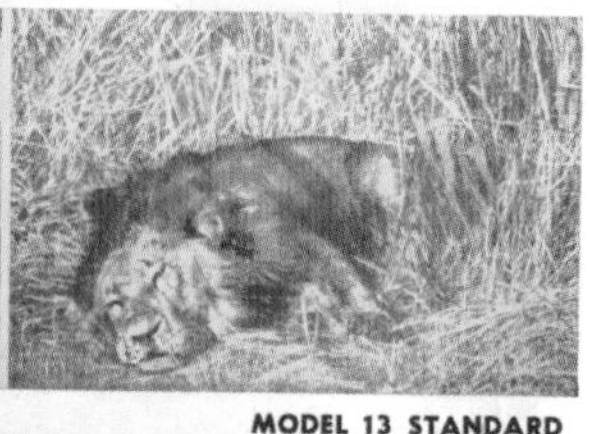

MODEL 13 STANDARD
PRICE
$450.00

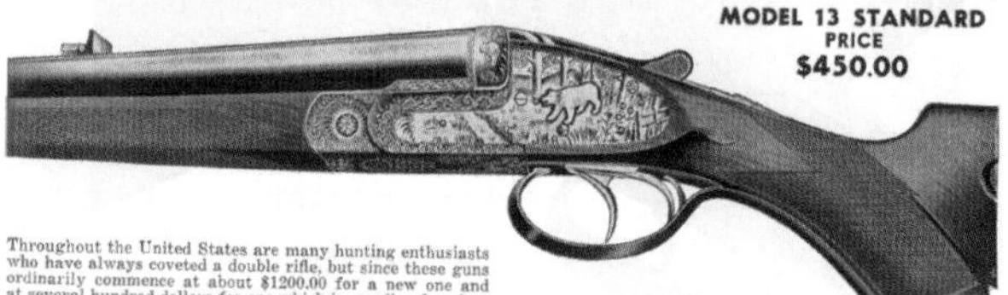

Throughout the United States are many hunting enthusiasts who have always coveted a double rifle, but since these guns ordinarily commence at about $1200.00 for a new one and at several hundred dollars for one which is usually of ancient vintage and chambered for some unavailable freak or proprietary cartridge together with a completely unsuitable stock, this aspiration is seldom realized. With the above thoughts in mind we have induced the factory to build such a gun, of identical quality to the Model 13, but with simple relief engraving of hunting scenes and walnut stock of good quality carefully finished and checkered. This gun may be had on special order, delivery in about six months, for any rimmed cartridge to and including .375 Magnum. It may also be had in 30/06 or .270

QUALITY DOUBLE RIFLES AT POPULAR PRICES

58 SHOOTER'S BIBLE, 55 RUTA COURT, SOUTH HACKENSACK, NEW JERSEY

MANNLICHER-SCHOENAUER CUSTOM MODELS

HAND-CARVING, ENGRAVING; MONOGRAMS & INLAYS

Any Mannlicher-Schoenauer Rifle or Carbine may be ordered with special custom decorations as outlined on this page. Prices for this custom work must be added to the basic cost of the gun itself.

The buyer is assured of the faithful reproduction of his specifications as the manufacturer executes every detail with meticulous care.

Prices shown on this page are uncommonly reasonable by today's standards for hand labor by skilled master-craftsmen. Should you desire a feature not covered by our listings here, write us outlining all details and we will obtain a special quotation from the manufacturer.

Custom carving & engraving prices must be added to cost of gun!

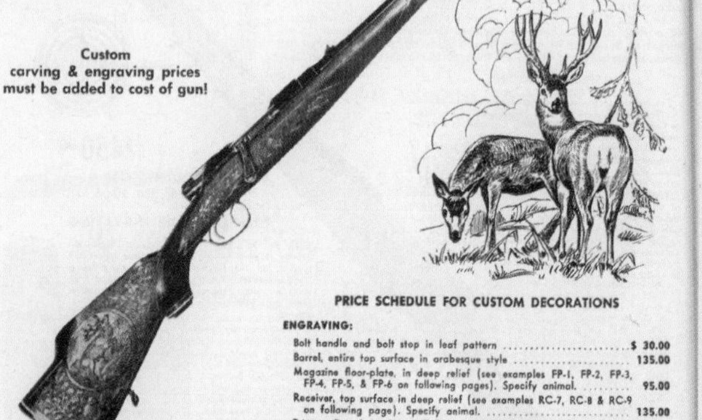

PRICE SCHEDULE FOR CUSTOM DECORATIONS

ENGRAVING:

Bolt handle and bolt stop in leaf pattern	$ 30.00
Barrel, entire top surface in arabesque style	135.00
Magazine floor-plate, in deep relief (see examples FP-1, FP-2, FP-3, FP-4, FP-5, & FP-6 on following pages). Specify animal.	95.00
Receiver, top surface in deep relief (see examples RC-7, RC-8 & RC-9 on following page). Specify animal.	135.00
Trigger Guard, in deep relief (see examples TG-10, TG-11 & TG-12 on following page). Specify animal.	45.00
Steyr Mount, Bases engraved	12.00

WOOD-CARVING:

Buttstock only, from butt to pistol grip, both sides, with acorn pattern.	$90.00
Buttstock Panel (as illustrated) with game animal. Specify animal.	90.00
Pistol Grip, carved with oak leaves & acorns in place of checkering	15.00
Forend Grip, carved with oak leaves and acorns in place of checkering	15.00

SPECIAL MATERIALS:

Custom or Premier Model rifle or carbine, furnished with Boehler Antinit Steel Barrel (famous for resistance to wear, rust erosion, etc.)	$40.00
Custom or Premier Model, rifle or carbine, furnished with selected walnut stock	47.50

TERMS AND DELIVERY

Orders for custom guns must be submitted with a down payment of at least 50% of the total cost, balance to be paid upon delivery. Once entered, such orders are non-cancellable. Delivery, from the time your order is entered may take from 90 to 120 days.

MONOGRAMS & GOLD INLAYS

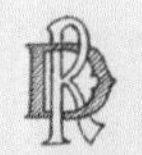

Monogrammed pistol-grip cap with two or three initials, engraved on inlaid silverplate $15.00

Monogrammed pistol-grip cap with two or three initials, engraved on inlaid 14-Karat goldplate $90.00

Genuine solid-gold game animal figure, recessed in floor-plate, receiver, or trigger guard. Your choice of game animal: deer, moose, bear, sheep, or antelope. All engraving in deep relief.

Gold game-animal inlay in floor-plate	$250.00
Gold game-animal inlay in receiver	285.00
Gold game-animal inlay in trigger-guard	120.00

OVER 50 YEARS OF SERVICE TO THE SHOOTER 59

EXAMPLES OF PREMIER ENGRAVING

We illustrate here samples of the deep-relief engraving that may be had on our Custom Grade Mannlicher-Schoenauers. The letters "FP" means floor-plate, "RC"—receiver, and "TG"—trigger guard. On special order purchaser may select any combinations. All custom guns are sold only on special order.

See preceding page.

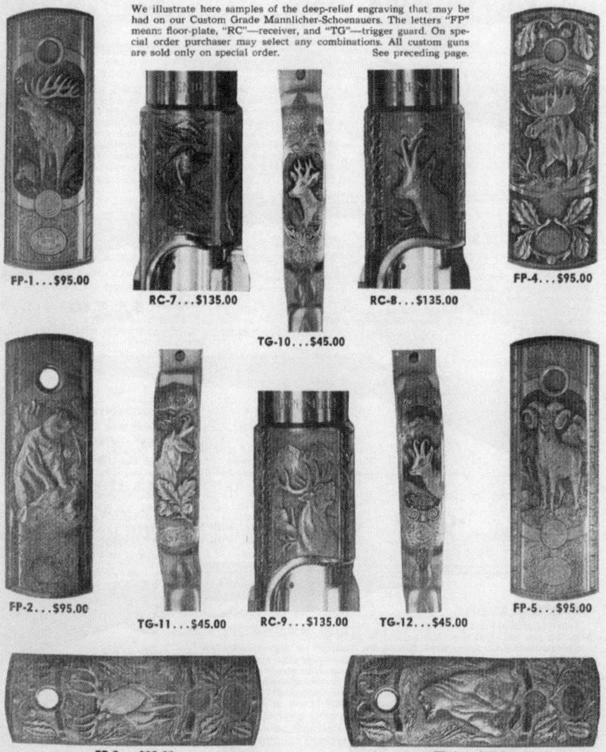

FP-1...$95.00 RC-7...$135.00 TG-10...$45.00 RC-8...$135.00 FP-4...$95.00

FP-2...$95.00 TG-11...$45.00 RC-9...$135.00 TG-12...$45.00 FP-5...$95.00

FP-3 $95.00 FP-6...$95.00

THE ART OF MASTER ENGRAVERS

1963

1969

48 SHOOTER'S BIBLE, 55 RUTA COURT, S. HACKENSACK, N.J.

LUGER .22 L. R. AUTOMATIC PISTOL

In this edition Stoeger Arms Corporation is announcing their new Luger pistol in .22 Long Rifle caliber (illustrated in full color on the cover).

A registered trade name owned by Stoeger Arms Corporation since 1929, the name "Luger" has been conspicuously absent from the commercial firearms market since the late 1930's. Designed and manufactured in the United States, it will handle all standard and high velocity .22 Long Rifle cartridges. Grip angle and balance of this model are identical to that of the original German Parabellum pistol. Even in weight the new version differs only by one ounce.

Features, specifications, models and prices are described below:

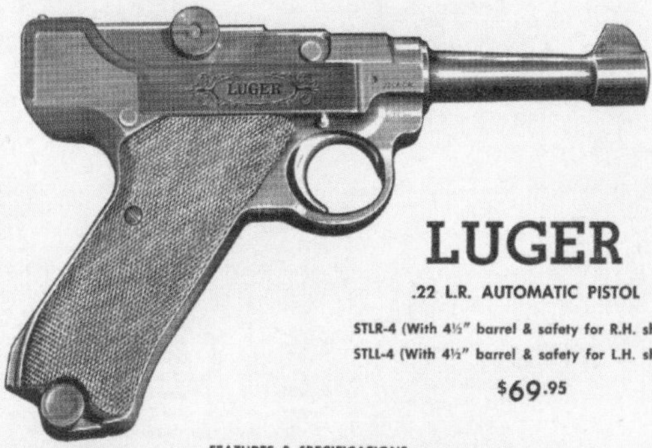

LUGER

.22 L.R. AUTOMATIC PISTOL

STLR-4 (With 4½" barrel & safety for R.H. shooter)

STLL-4 (With 4½" barrel & safety for L.H. shooter)

$69.95

FEATURES & SPECIFICATIONS

The Luger .22 caliber pistol is made with a toggle action, stationary sights and a target-quality trigger. It is equipped with an eleven-shot magazine which is housed in the grip portion of the frame. Cartridges feeding from the magazine are positioned in a straight line behind the chamber for smooth loading and trouble free performance.

The barrel is all steel and is hammer rifled for maximum accuracy. Sighting equipment includes a square-bladed front sight in combination with a fixed, square-notch rear sight.

All moving parts result in surfaces that are steel against steel. Cleaning and maintenance is greatly simplified by the simple takedown procedure. A takedown plunger hole, located in the rear of the frame, is aligned with the bore to facilitate cleaning of the barrel from the chamber end.

Available with choice left or right hand safety at no difference in price.

SPECIFICATIONS

Frame: one piece lightweight forged frame, machined to finished dimensions.

Trigger: light, crisp trigger pull of target quality.

Action: Hinged toggle action with fast lock design for instantaneous ignition.

Magazine: Eleven-shot capacity clip type magazine contained in grip area of the frame.

Grips: Genuine wooden grips checkered in fine line pattern.

Sights: Square bladed front sight with square-notch, stationary, rear sight.

Safety: Positive side lever safety. (The Luger is generally supplied with the safety on the left side for right handed shooters, however, it may also be had with a right hand safety for left handed shooters at no additional cost).

Barrel: Chambered for all .22 Long Rifle cartridges, standard or high-velocity. With hammer rifled bore the Luger barrel is solidly fixed to the frame. (Though not recommended for use with B-B Caps, C-B Caps, shorts, longs and shot cartridges, these shells may be fired in the Luger IF singly loaded into the chamber.)

MODEL STLR-4 (with 4½" barrel & safety for R.H. shooter) **$69.95**

MODEL STLL-4 (with 4½" barrel & safety for L.H. shooter) **$69.95**

OVER 50 YEARS OF SERVICE TO THE SHOOTER 49

LUGER .22 L.R. AUTOMATIC PISTOL

DETAILS OF CONSTRUCTION:

The Stoeger Luger is made with a fixed barrel-solid frame design. The barrel is fastened to the frame with an interference fit; i.e.—an oversize cross pin of novel design is used to lock the barrel to the frame.

The frame is a 7075 T6 aluminum forging (not a casting). This material was originally designed for aircraft fuselages and landing gears.

Typical values are:

Tensile strength, psi: 82,000
Yield strength, psi: 75,000

An uninterrupted band (approximately 2/10ths of an inch thick) encloses the action on all 4 sides. All sharp corners have been avoided and inside cuts have 3/32" fillets.

For wear resistance, however, the bolt moves on SAE 1050 (medium carbon steel) boltways. These boltways also support the sear and hammer pin and the magazine guide, which in turn holds the hammer strut plate. The entire action can easily be removed from the frame by withdrawing the main frame pin and pushing in the takedown plunger (in the rear of the gun). The sear bar retaining screw must also be removed before the action can be lifted from the frame.

The hammer and sear are heat treated to file hardness for greatest wear resistance.

The sear bar engages the sear *between* its supports, not on one side as in other autoloaders. This results in a smooth, unvarying trigger pull.

The take down plunger hole, in the rear of the frame, is exactly in line with the bore and, after the action has been removed forms an ideal support for any standard size cleaning rod. Thus, it is easy to clean the barrel from the chamber end. By properly guiding the cleaning rod, it is possible to avoid damage to the rifling.

The positioning of the in-line holes (barrel hole and take down plunger hole) permits "piano hinge" fixturing during manufacture. What this means is that the frame can be held by these holes and rotated around them against a stop. All important operations can be performed with the frame in this position, eliminating 75% of normal production tolerances since the width of the frame becomes unimportant as far as fixturing is concerned. A higher quality product is the result.

The most outstanding single feature of the gun is its smooth toggle action, which permits trouble free operation with all .22 L.R. cartridges, standard as well as high velocity.

The combination of the tough lightweight frame and the steel action components gives the gun its unsurpassed balance. The finest materials have been selected for each part. Thirty thousand rounds have been fired without a single malfunction and without a single broken part!

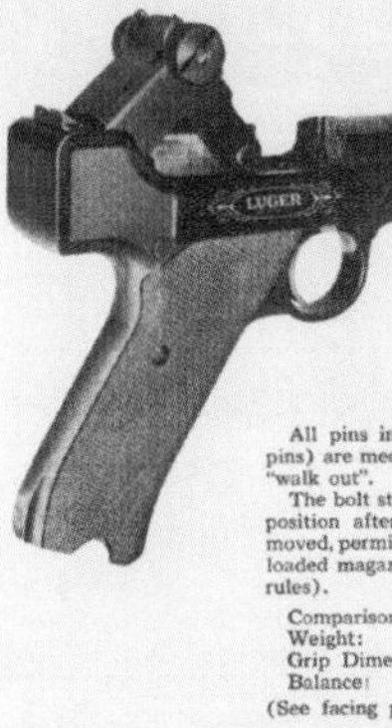

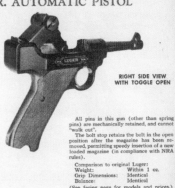

RIGHT SIDE VIEW WITH TOGGLE OPEN

All pins in this gun (other than spring pins) are mechanically retained, and cannot "walk out".

The bolt stop retains the bolt in the open position after the magazine has been removed, permitting speedy insertion of a new loaded magazine (in compliance with NRA rules).

Comparison to original Luger:

Weight:	Within 1 oz.
Grip Dimensions:	Identical
Balance:	Identical

(See facing page for models and prices.)

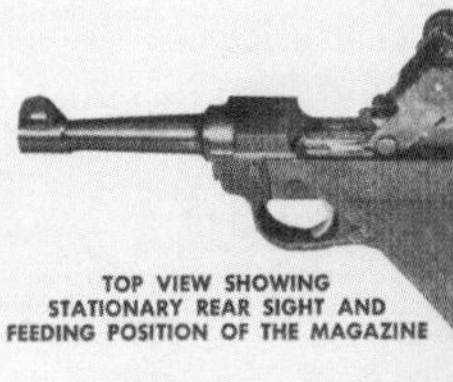

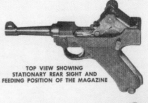

TOP VIEW SHOWING STATIONARY REAR SIGHT AND FEEDING POSITION OF THE MAGAZINE

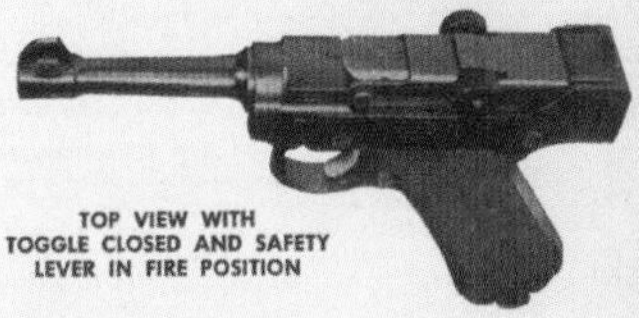

TOP VIEW WITH TOGGLE CLOSED AND SAFETY LEVER IN FIRE POSITION

FRANCHI FALCONET O&U SHOTGUN

IN 20 GAUGE

(WITH BUCKSKIN-COLORED OR EBONY-COLORED RECEIVER)

The Falconet shotgun is a superb new *lightweight* over & under equipped with selective single trigger, automatic ejectors, chrome-lined barrels, high ventilated rib, automatic safety and epoxy-finished, checkered, walnut stock and forend. These custom features, combined with a popular retail price and Franchi's new overhead-sear trigger mechanism, have propelled this model to the top of the over & under market.

For quail, pheasant, dove, grouse, turkey, rabbit or ducks, it's the lightest and fastest twin-tubed shotgun that a hunter could ever hope to handle. Yet, in spite of its lightweight, it is ruggedly built with chrome-molybdenum steel barrels, and an exclusive, rugged, light alloy receiver. Entirely forged and machined first quality components are used throughout.

The beautiful engraving of the receiver surfaces is particularly enhanced by the light background of the buckskin model.

The Ebony and Buckskin models are identical except for the color of the receiver and the fact that Buckskin models are priced slightly higher.

One of the most important features of all Falconet shotguns is the unique design of the selective trigger and sear mechanism which provides for a light, uniform and crisp trigger pull. This new patented design is exceptionally reliable; it has virtually eliminated faults such as mis-firing or doubling.

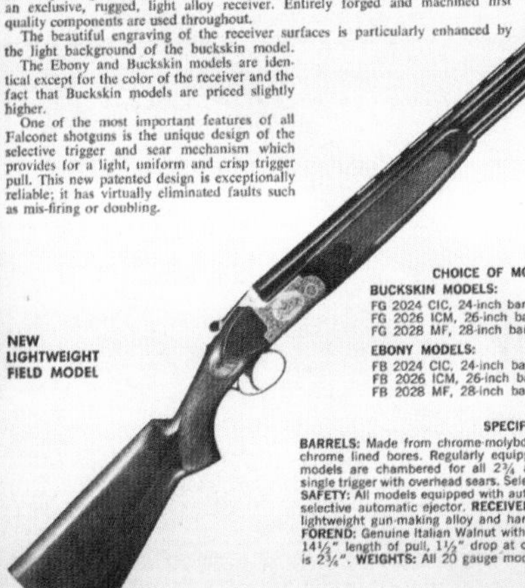

NEW LIGHTWEIGHT FIELD MODEL

FALCONET

20 GAUGE BUCKSKIN $305.95
20 GAUGE EBONY $295.95

CHOICE OF MODELS, BARRELS & CHOKES

BUCKSKIN MODELS:
FG 2024 CIC, 24-inch barrels, Cylinder & Imp. Cylinder chokes
FG 2026 ICM, 26-inch barrels, Imp. Cylinder & Modified chokes
FG 2028 MF, 28-inch barrels, Modified & Full chokes

EBONY MODELS:
FB 2024 CIC, 24-inch barrels, Cylinder & Imp. Cylinder chokes
FB 2026 ICM, 26-inch barrels, Imp. Cylinder & Modified chokes
FB 2028 MF, 28-inch barrels, Modified & Full chokes

SPECIFICATIONS

BARRELS: Made from chrome-molybdenum steel with cold-forged chokes and chrome lined bores. Regularly equipped with high, ventilated rib, 20 gauge models are chambered for all 2¾ and 3 inch shells. **TRIGGERS:** Selective single trigger with overhead sears. Selector is operated by safety button on tang. **SAFETY:** All models equipped with automatic safety. **EJECTORS:** Equipped with selective automatic ejector. **RECEIVER:** Forged and machined from a special lightweight gun-making alloy and hardened for maximum strength. **STOCK & FOREND:** Genuine Italian Walnut with checkered grip surfaces, epoxy finished. 14½" length of pull, 1½" drop at comb and 2¼" drop at heel. Pitch down is 2¾". **WEIGHTS:** All 20 gauge models about six pounds.

WEIGHT
20 Gauge . . . . 6 lbs.
Overall weight may vary slightly, depending upon barrel length and density of wood components.

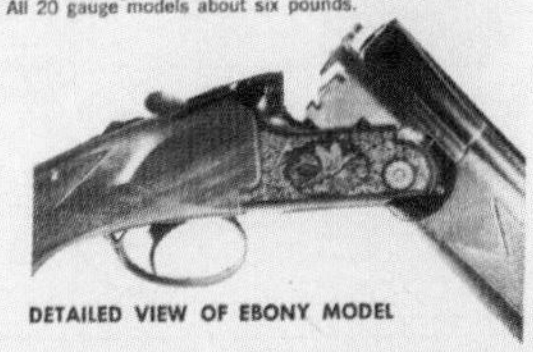

DETAILED VIEW OF EBONY MODEL

132 THE SHOOTER'S BIBLE

FRANCHI FALCONET O & U SHOTGUN

IN 28 GAUGE

(WITH BUCKSKIN-COLORED OR EBONY-COLORED RECEIVER)

The Falconet shotgun is a superb new *lightweight* over & under equipped with selective single trigger, automatic ejectors, chrome-lined barrels, high ventilated rib, automatic safety and epoxy-finished, checkered, walnut stock and forend. These custom features, combined with a popular retail price and Franchi's new overhead-sear trigger mechanism, have propelled this model to the top of the over & under market.

For quail, pheasant, dove, grouse, turkey, rabbit or ducks, it's the lightest and fastest twin-tubed shotgun that a hunter could ever hope to handle. Yet, in spite of its lightweight, it is ruggedly built with chrome-molybdenum steel barrels, and an exclusive, rugged, light alloy receiver. Entirely forged and machined first quality components are used throughout.

The beautiful engraving of the receiver surfaces is particularly enhanced by the light background of the buckskin model.

The Ebony and Buckskin models are identical except for the color of the receiver and the fact that Buckskin models are priced slightly higher.

One of the most important features of all Falconet shotguns is the unique design of the selective trigger and sear mechanism which provides for a light, uniform and crisp trigger pull. This new patented design is exceptionally reliable; it has virtually eliminated faults such as mis-firing or doubling.

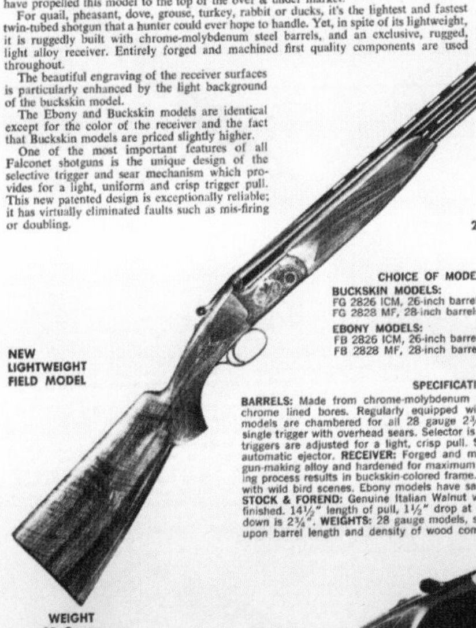

NEW LIGHTWEIGHT FIELD MODEL

FALCONET

28 GAUGE BUCKSKIN $335.00
28 GAUGE EBONY $325.00

CHOICE OF MODELS, BARRELS & CHOKES

BUCKSKIN MODELS:
FG 2826 ICM, 26-inch barrels, Imp. Cylinder & Modified chokes
FG 2828 MF, 28-inch barrels, Modified & Full chokes

EBONY MODELS:
FB 2826 ICM, 26-inch barrels, Imp. Cylinder & Modified chokes
FB 2828 MF, 28-inch barrels, Modified & Full chokes

SPECIFICATIONS

BARRELS: Made from chrome-molybdenum steel with cold-forged chokes and chrome lined bores. Regularly equipped with high, ventilated rib, 28 gauge models are chambered for all 28 gauge 2¾-inch shells. **TRIGGERS:** Selective single trigger with overhead sears. Selector is operated by safety button on tang; triggers are adjusted for a light, crisp pull. **SAFETY:** All models equipped with automatic ejector. **RECEIVER:** Forged and machined from a special lightweight gun-making alloy and hardened for maximum strength and wear. Unique hardening process results in buckskin-colored frame. Side surfaces attractively engraved with wild bird scenes. Ebony models have same frame but with gun blue finish. **STOCK & FOREND:** Genuine Italian Walnut with checkered grip surfaces, epoxy finished. 14½" length of pull, 1½" drop at comb and 2¼" drop at heel. Pitch down is 2¾". **WEIGHTS:** 28 gauge models, slightly under six pounds depending upon barrel length and density of wood components.

WEIGHT
28 Gauge
slightly under 6 lbs.
Overall weight may vary slightly, depending upon barrel length and density of wood components.

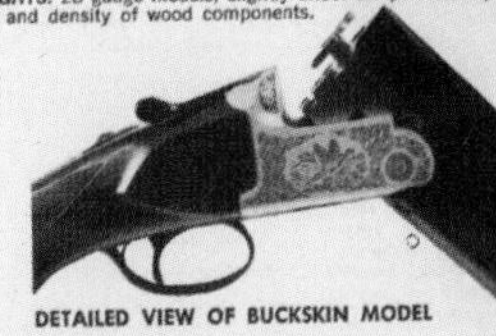

DETAILED VIEW OF BUCKSKIN MODEL

No. 63, 1972 EDITION 133

1972

1981

SAVAGE/ANSCHUTZ 22 SPORTERS

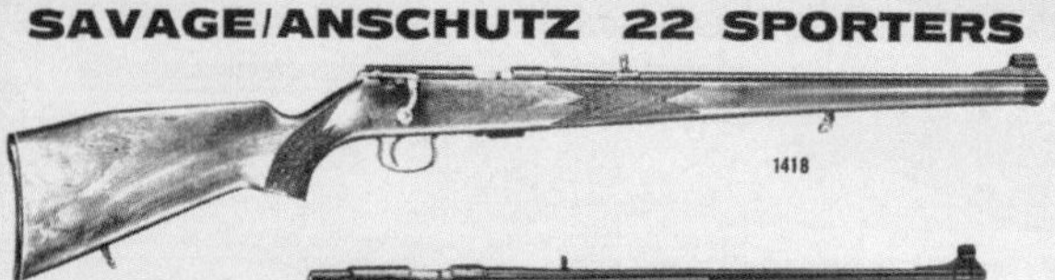

1418

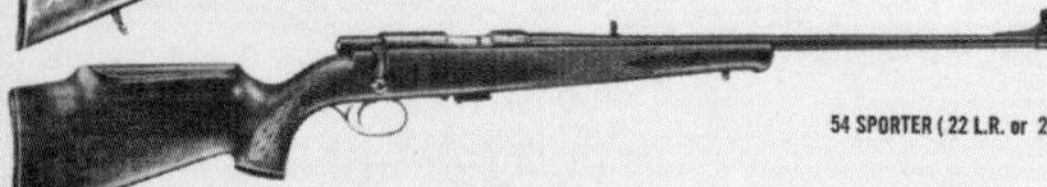

54 SPORTER (22 L.R. or 22 Mag.)

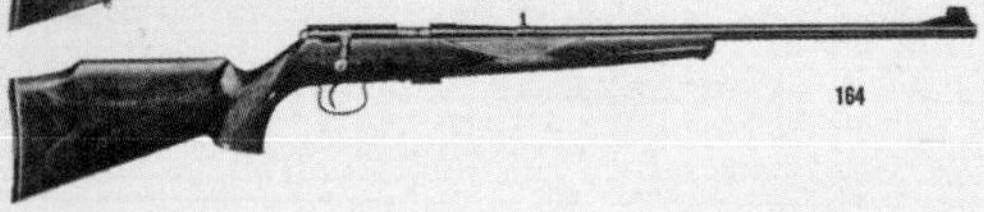

164

CUSTOM GRADE 22 SPORTERS

164 22 long rifle, 164-M 22 magnum. The action of the 164—is the same one used on the Savage/Anschutz model 64 target rifle. The barrel is precision bored for pinpoint accuracy. Receiver is grooved for instant scope mounting. The select European walnut stock has all the custom grade features,—Monte Carlo with cheek-piece, Wundhammer swell pistol grip, schnabel fore-end and checkering. **$326.40**

The 164-M is chambered for the 22 magnum cartridge for those longer range shots. **$333.50**

54 Sporter 22 long rifle, 54-M 22 Magnum. The model 54 Sporter combines the smallbore action with a handsome sporting Monte Carlo stock of fine French walnut. Strictly custom grade from the hand-carved roll-over cheek-piece and contoured pistol grip to the graceful schnabel fore-end. Both fore-end and pistol grip are hand checkered in a skip-line pattern.

The action is the Anschutz Match 54 that has dominated smallbore rifle shooting in recent years. Receiver is grooved for scope mount and drilled and tapped for scope bases. 54 Sporter, 22 L. R. **$576.10**

The 54-M magnum offers Anschutz - accurate shooting up to 100-125 yards for the varmint and small game hunter. 54-M, 22 Magnum. **$590.40**

Anschutz 1418 22 Long Rifle, 1518 22 Win. Mag. The action is the same as the model164but the stock is completely European. This compact Mannlicher sporter has features such as a choice of double-set or single-stage triggers, hand-cut skip-line checkering, stock inlays and European-style Monte Carlo stock with cheek piece.

1418 22 L.R. **$462.65**
1518 22 Mag. **471.10**

SPECIFICATIONS — FEATURES

MODEL	Barrel Length	Grooved for Scope	Tapped For Scope Mount	Sights		Trigger Factory set for crisp trigger pull.	Clip Magazine	Capacity	Safety	Checkered Stock			Fluted Comb.	White Liner	Butt Plate	Length Overall	Average Weight (Lbs.)
				Front	Rear					Cheekpiece	Monte Carlo	Walnut					
54, 54-M	24"	X	X	Hooded Ramp	Folding Leaf	X	X	6*, 5†	Wing	X	X	X	X	X	Hard Rubber	43"	6¾
164, 164-M	23"	X		Hooded Ramp	Folding Leaf	X	X	6*, 5†	Slide	X	X	X	X	X	Hard Rubber	40¾"	6
1418 1518	19¾"	X		Hooded Ramp	Folding Leaf	X	X	6*, 5†	Slide	X	X	X	X	X	Hard Rubber	37¾"	5½

Models 54, 164 and 1418 are chambered for 22 long rifle ONLY. **†Models:** 1518, 164-M and 54-M chambered for 22 W.M.R. ONLY. Clip capacity 4.
MODELS 164 Stock: Length 14"; drop 1½" at comb, 1⅜" at Monte Carlo, 2¼" at heel.
54 Stock: Length 14"; drop 1¼" at comb, 1¼" at Monte Carlo, 1½" at heel. RATE OF TWIST (R.H.) 1 turn in 16" for 22 L.R., 22 Mag. -
1418, 1518 Stock: Length 13½"; drop 1½" at comb, 2½" at Monte Carlo, 2½" at heel.

ANSCHUTZ & SAVAGE/ANSCHUTZ TARGET RIFLES

With Adjustable Cheek Piece, Combination Hand Stop / Sling Swivel and Variable Angle Hook Butt Plate

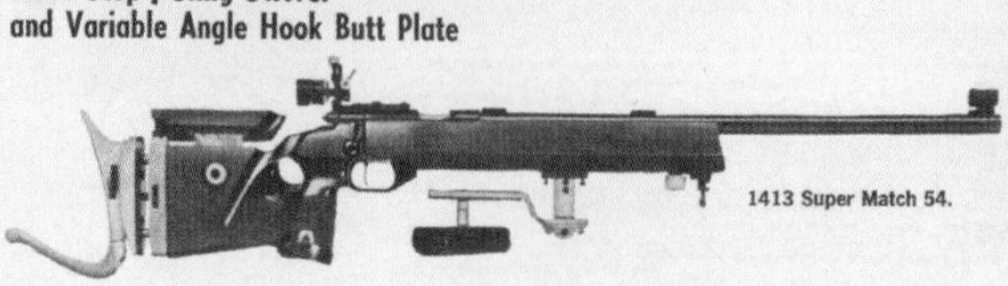

1413 Super Match 54.

You can have the Super Match 54 in three models (1413, 1407, 1411).

Model 1413 Super Match 54. The free-style international target rifle that dominates international competition for these reasons: a new superb Match 54 bolt design that is satin smooth; very short firing pin travel for extremely fast lock time; new conveniently located side safety. The new model 5071 Match Two-Stage Triggers are faster, more precise and more reliable. The mechanism reaction time is reduced. Other features include combination hand-stop/sling swivel, hook butt plate for right- and left-hand use, adjustable palm-rest, butt plate and cheek piece. **1413 Super Match 54 $1006.85. 1813-L,** left-hand stock **$1107.95.**

Model 1407 Match 54. Meets all International Shooting Union requirements and is suitable for all N.R.A. matches. Has new satin smooth Match 54 bolt design, new Match Two-Stage for precise and reliable adjustments and new convenient side safety. The whole stock and pistol grip are sculptured to fit the shooter in either a prone or standing position match. Hand-stop/sling swivel is included. **1407 ISU Match 54 $616.60 1807-L,** left-hand stock **$678.75.**

Model 1411 Match 54. The famous Anschutz prone rifle with the new Match 54 bolt design. Very short firing pin travel for extremely fast lock time. New conveniently located side safety, new single stage triggers are even faster, even more precise and reliable. The mechanism reaction time is reduced. Other features include adjustable cheek piece, combination hand-stop/sling swivel and adjutable butt plate. **1411 Match 54,** prone stock **$575.75 1411-L,** left-hand stock **$593.94**

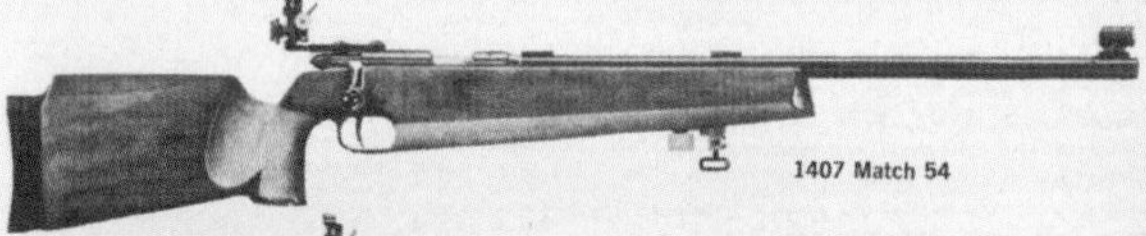

1407 Match 54

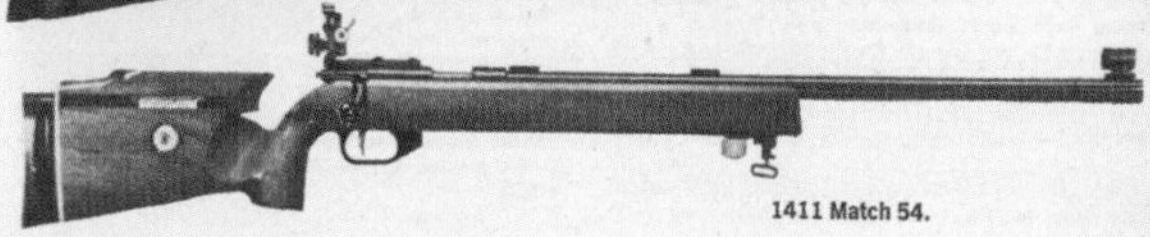

1411 Match 54.

TIKKA RIFLES

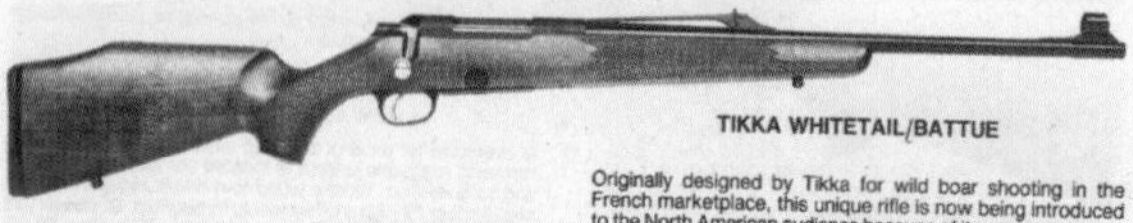

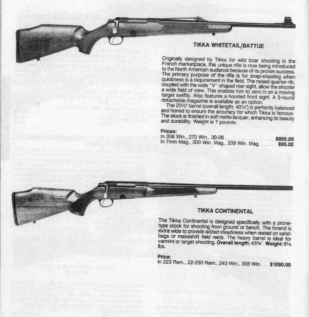

TIKKA WHITETAIL/BATTUE

Originally designed by Tikka for wild boar shooting in the French marketplace, this unique rifle is now being introduced to the North American audience because of its proven success. The primary purpose of the rifle is for snap-shooting when quickness is a requirement in the field. The raised quarter-rib, coupled with the wide "V"-shaped rear sight, allow the shooter a wide field of view. This enables him to zero in on a moving target swiftly. Also features a hooded front sight. A 3-round detachable magazine is available as an option.

The 20½" barrel (overall length: 40½") is perfectly balanced and honed to ensure the accuracy for which Tikka is famous. The stock is finished in soft matte lacquer, enhancing its beauty and durability. Weight is 7 pounds.

Prices:
In 308 Win., 270 Win., 30-06 .... **$860.00**
In 7mm Mag., 300 Win. Mag., 338 Win. Mag. **895.00**

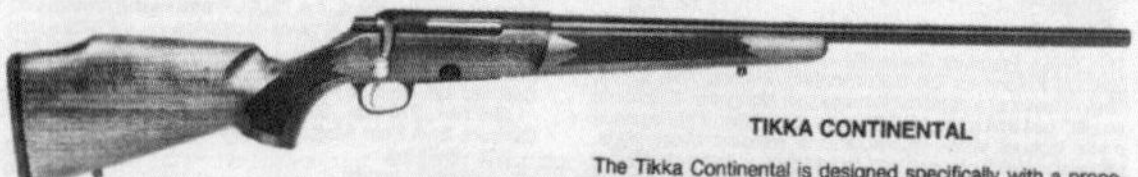

TIKKA CONTINENTAL

The Tikka Continental is designed specifically with a prone-type stock for shooting from ground or bench. The forend is extra wide to provide added steadiness when rested on sandbags or makeshift field rests. The heavy barrel is ideal for varmint or target shooting. **Overall length:** 43¾". **Weight:** 8½ lbs.

Price:
In 223 Rem., 22-250 Rem., 243 Win., 308 Win. . . **$1090.00**

A. UBERTI REPLICA RIFLES & CARBINES

ALL UBERTI FIREARMS AVAILABLE IN SUPER GRADE, PRESTIGE AND ENGRAVED FINISHES

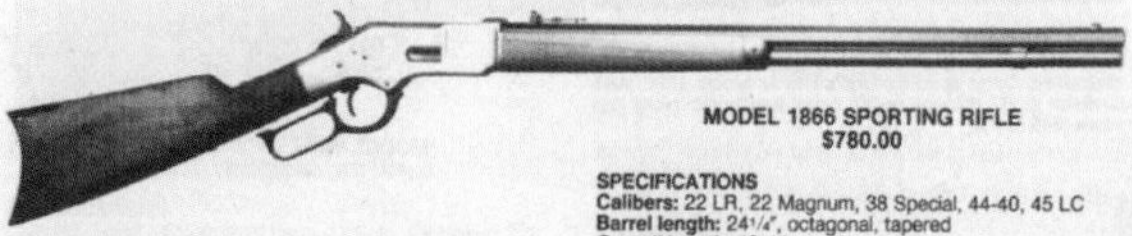

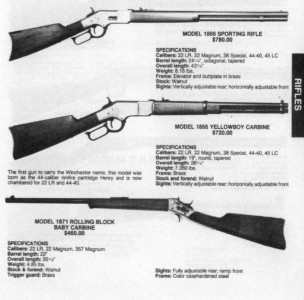

MODEL 1866 SPORTING RIFLE
$780.00

SPECIFICATIONS
Calibers: 22 LR, 22 Magnum, 38 Special, 44-40, 45 LC
Barrel length: 24¼", octagonal, tapered
Overall length: 43¼"
Weight: 8.16 lbs.
Frame: Elevator and buttplate in brass
Stock: Walnut
Sights: Vertically adjustable rear; horizontally adjustable front

RIFLES

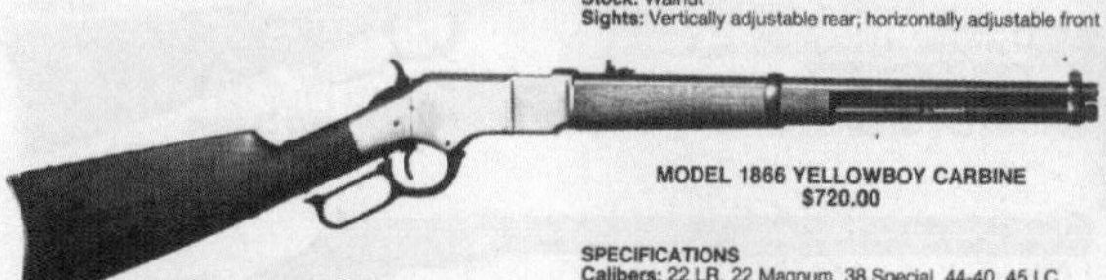

MODEL 1866 YELLOWBOY CARBINE
$720.00

SPECIFICATIONS
Calibers: 22 LR, 22 Magnum, 38 Special, 44-40, 45 LC
Barrel length: 19", round, tapered
Overall length: 38¼"
Weight: 7.380 lbs.
Frame: Brass
Stock and forend: Walnut
Sights: Vertically adjustable rear; horizontally adjustable front

The first gun to carry the Winchester name, this model was born as the 44-caliber rimfire cartridge Henry and is now chambered for 22 LR and 44-40.

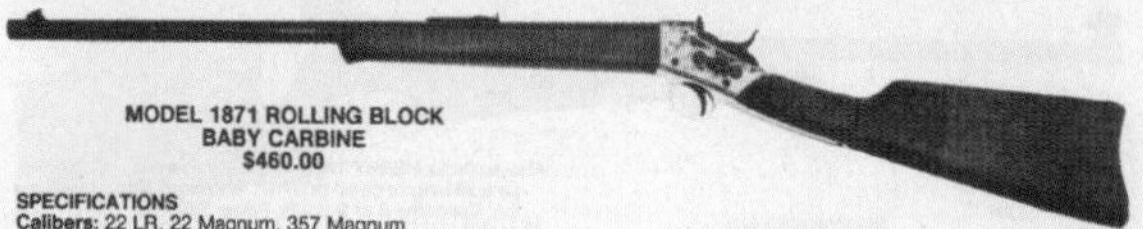

MODEL 1871 ROLLING BLOCK BABY CARBINE
$460.00

SPECIFICATIONS
Calibers: 22 LR, 22 Magnum, 357 Magnum
Barrel length: 22"
Overall length: 35½"
Weight: 4.85 lbs.
Stock & forend: Walnut
Trigger guard: Brass
Sights: Fully adjustable rear; ramp front
Frame: Color casehardened steel

1993

NEW Products: **Blaser Rifles**

BLASER K95 BARONESSE STUTZEN

Action: tilting-block single-shot
Stock: checkered Turkish walnut
Barrel: 19 ¾"
Sights: open rear, bead front on ramp
Weight: 5 lbs. 12 oz.
Caliber: .222 Rem, 5.6x50 RM, 5.6x52 R, .243 Win., 6.5x57 R, 7x57 R, .308 Win., .30-06, 8x57 IRS
Magazine: none
Features: Full-length stock, engraved receiver with side-plates, strong action that's safe to carry with a chambered cartridge before thumb-cocking.
Price: $15,500

BLASER R93 PRESTIGE

Action: straight-pull, collet-locking bolt
Stock: Grade 3 walnut
Barrel: 22 ¾" or 25 ½"
Sights: none (open sights standard on some models)
Weight: 6 lbs. 13 oz.
Caliber: choice of many popular chamberings
Magazine: single-stack, top-loading
Features: sideplates with English scroll on an action with smooth-feeding straight-up magazine, optional recoil reducer in stock. R93 action allows quick change of barrels/chamberings within cartridge groups.
Price: $3,275 (other grades, styles available in different price ranges)

K95 BARONESSE STUTZEN

R93 PRESTIGE

NEW Products: **BPI Rifles**

BPI APEX

Action: hinged-breech single-shot
Stock: synthetic, black or camo, ambidextrous design, configured for scope use, Crush-Zone recoil pad
Barrel: 25" (centerfire) and 27" (muzzleloader)
Sights: none
Weight: 7 ½ lbs.
Caliber: 10 popular centerfire chamberings, .222 to .300 Win. Mag and .45-70; barrels interchangeable with black powder, .22 rimfire barrels.
Magazine: none
Features: Bergara barrel and adjustable (3-5 pounds) trigger on this exposed-hammer, switch-barrel rifle enhance accuracy
Price: $577 (black, stainless) and $652 (Realtree camo, stainless) for muzzleloader, $611 (black, stainless) and $686 (Realtree camo, stainless) for centerfire or .22 rimfire chamberings.

NEW Products: **Browning Rifles**

BROWNING X-BOLT MICRO HUNTER

Action: three-lug bolt
Stock: satin finish walnut, sized for smaller shooters
Barrel: 20 or 22", low-luster blued finish
Sights: none
Weight: 6 to 6 ½ lbs.
Caliber: .223, .22-250, .243, 7mm-08, .308 Win, .270 WSM, 7mm WSM, .300 WSM, .325 WSM
Magazine: detachable rotary box
Features: adjustable "Feather" trigger, top-tang safety, bolt-unlock button, sling swivel studs. Also: new .223 and .22-250 chamberings in other X-Bolt versions, some in stainless/synthetic form.
Price: $839-$869 (magnums)

BROWNING A-BOLT TARGET

Action: three-lug bolt
Stock: checkered gray laminate with adjustable comb
Barrel: heavy contour, 28"
Sights: none
Weight: 13 lbs.
Caliber: .223, .308, .300 WSM
Magazine: detachable box
Features: the latest of an extensive line of long- and short-action A-Bolt rifles. Target-style beavertail forend, floating barrel, glass-bedded receiver, single-set trigger, top-tang safety. Stainless and carbon-steel versions are available.
Price: $1269 (.223, .308 carbon steel) to $1519 (.300 WSM stainless)

NEW Products: **Cooper Rifles**

COOPER 52

Action: three-lug bolt
Stock: checkered walnut
Barrel: 24"
Sights: none
Weight: 7 ¾ lbs.
Caliber: .25-06, .270, .280, .280 Imp., .30-06, .338-06, .35 Whelen
Magazine: detachable box, single stack
Features: semi-controlled feed, match-dimension chamber in air-gauged barrel, glass-bedded action, Remington-style recoil lug,
Price: from $1450

NEW Products: **Howa Rifles**

HOWA M-1500 RANCHLAND CAMO

Action: two-lug bolt
Stock: composite King's Desert Shadow pattern
Barrel: 20"
Sights: scope included
Weight: 8 ¼ lbs.
Caliber: .204, .223, .22-250, .243, 7mm-08, .308
Magazine: internal box
Features: Full camo combo packages includes Nikko Stirling 3-10x42 camo scope mounted to a one-piece base.
Price: $699

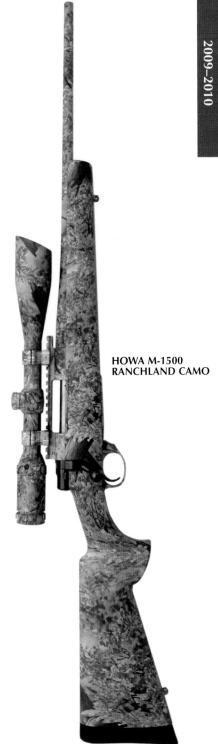

HOWA M-1500
RANCHLAND CAMO

NEW Products: Kimber Rifles

KIMBER M 8400 POLICE TACTICAL

KIMBER M 8400 POLICE TACTICAL

Action: two-lug bolt, extended handle
Stock: black, laminated with beavertail forend and three swivel studs (extra for bipod)

Barrel: match grade, 26" fluted
Sights: none, 20 MOA rail installed
Weight: 8 lbs. 11 oz.
Caliber: .300 Win Mag
Magazine: internal box
Features: fourth in a series of tactical rifles from Kimber, the new Police Tactical is a more powerful version of the Light Police Tactical in .308.
Price: $1476

NEW Products: Marlin Rifles

1895 SBL

338MX

MARLIN 1895 SBL

Action: lever
Stock: black/gray laminated, pistol grip with fluted comb, cut checkering, deluxe recoil pad
Barrel: stainless steel, 18 ½"
Sights: XS Ghost ring sights, attached Weaver-style rail
Weight: 8 lbs.
Caliber: .45-70 Govt.
Magazine: full-length tube
Features: big loop lever, length: 37 inches
Price: $806

MARLIN XL7W

Action: two-lug fluted bolt
Stock: checkered walnut (synthetic and brown laminate stocks also available)
Barrel: 22"
Sights: none, one-piece scope mount included
Weight: 6 ½ lbs.
Caliber: .270 or .30-06 (also new this year: short-action XS7 in .243, 7mm-08 and .308)
Magazine: internal box
Features: Pro-Fire Trigger System, Soft-Touch recoil pad, button rifling.
Price: $506

MARLIN 338MX AND 338MXLR

Action: lever
Stock: walnut (MX) or black-gray laminate (MXLR)
Barrel: 22 or 24 inch blue or stainless
Sights: adjustable semi-buckhorn folding rear, ramp front with brass bead
Weight: 7 ¼ and 7 ½ lbs.
Caliber: .338 Marlin Express (also in .308 Marlin Express)
Magazine: 2/3 tube
Features: delivers 180-grain .30-06 ballistics with a 200-grain bullet at 2,565 fps., 1-in-12 twist
Price: $806 laminated $610 walnut

NEW Products: **McMillan Rifles**

MCMILLAN PRODIGY
Action: Two-lug bolt
Stock: McMillan hand-laid synthetic; slim open grip with straight comb; Pachmayr recoil pad
Barrel: 24" Shilen stainless
Sights: none; drilled & tapped, Talley bases supplied
Weight: 7 lbs.
Caliber: popular standard and magnum chamberings
Magazine: internal box
Features: Glass bedding and alloy pillars, Jewell trigger, stainless receivers, washer-type recoil lug and MP-3 nickel two-lug bolts (spiral fluted). Bolt-face extractor and plunger ejector.
Price: $4295

NEW Products: **Mossberg Rifles**

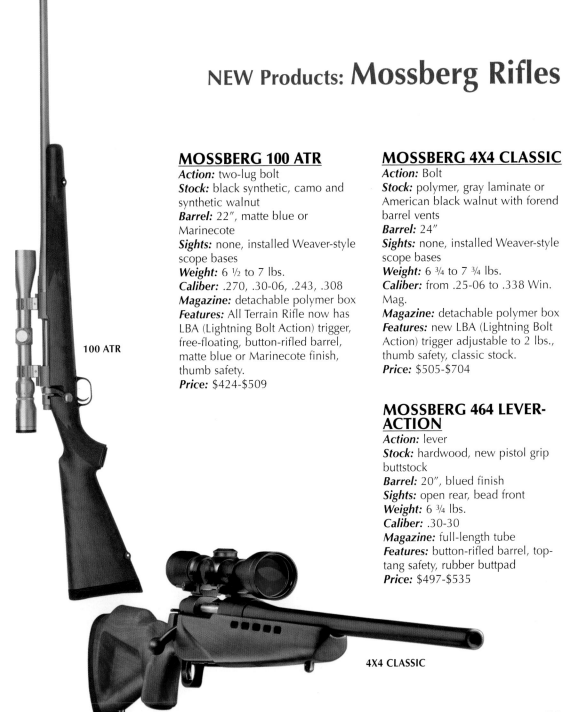

100 ATR

4X4 CLASSIC

MOSSBERG 100 ATR
Action: two-lug bolt
Stock: black synthetic, camo and synthetic walnut
Barrel: 22", matte blue or Marinecote
Sights: none, installed Weaver-style scope bases
Weight: 6 ½ to 7 lbs.
Caliber: .270, .30-06, .243, .308
Magazine: detachable polymer box
Features: All Terrain Rifle now has LBA (Lightning Bolt Action) trigger, free-floating, button-rifled barrel, matte blue or Marinecote finish, thumb safety.
Price: $424-$509

MOSSBERG 4X4 CLASSIC
Action: Bolt
Stock: polymer, gray laminate or American black walnut with forend barrel vents
Barrel: 24"
Sights: none, installed Weaver-style scope bases
Weight: 6 ¾ to 7 ¾ lbs.
Caliber: from .25-06 to .338 Win. Mag.
Magazine: detachable polymer box
Features: new LBA (Lightning Bolt Action) trigger adjustable to 2 lbs., thumb safety, classic stock.
Price: $505-$704

MOSSBERG 464 LEVER-ACTION
Action: lever
Stock: hardwood, new pistol grip buttstock
Barrel: 20", blued finish
Sights: open rear, bead front
Weight: 6 ¾ lbs.
Caliber: .30-30
Magazine: full-length tube
Features: button-rifled barrel, top-tang safety, rubber buttpad
Price: $497-$535

NEW Products: **Puma Rifles**

PUMA CHUCK CONNORS COMMEMORATIVE

Action: lever
Stock: walnut
Barrel: 20"
Sights: open
Weight: 6 ½ lbs.
Caliber: .44-40
Magazine: full-length tube
Features: limited edition of 1000

made in Italy by Chiappa Firearms, imported by Legacy Sports. This rifle commemorates the popular 1950's TV show, "The Rifleman." Large loop with set screw in trigger guard, Chuck Connors' signature etched on receiver and laser engraved on stock.
Price: $1299

NEW Products: **Remington Rifles**

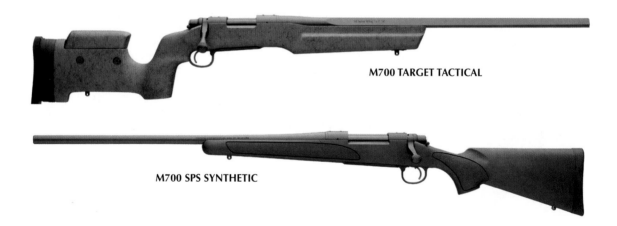

M700 TARGET TACTICAL

M700 SPS SYNTHETIC

REMINGTON M700 TARGET TACTICAL

Action: two-lug bolt
Stock: Bell & Carlson Medalist Varmint/Tactical stock with adjustable comb and length of pull
Barrel: 26" triangular VTR Barrel Profile with muzzle counter-bore
Sights: none
Weight: 9 lbs.
Caliber: .308 Win.
Magazine: internal box
Features: tactical extended bolt knob, all-steel hinged floorplate, 5-R hammer-forged target rifling, X-Mark-Pro externally adjustable trigger, thumb safety.
Price: $1972

REMINGTON M700 SPS SYNTHETIC, LEFT-HAND (ALSO VARMINT VERSION)

Action: two-lug bolt
Stock: black synthetic
Barrel: 24" or 26"
Sights: none
Weight: 7 ½ to 7 ¾ lbs (9 lbs in Varmint)
Caliber: .270 Win., .30-06, 7mm-08 Rem., .300 Win. Mag. (.17 Rem. to .308 in Varmint)
Magazine: internal box
Features: affordable left-hand version of most popular American bolt rifle.
Price: $639

REMINGTON M700 XHR XTREME HUNTING RIFLE

Action: two-lug bolt
Stock: synthetic in camo with Hogue overmolded accents on grip and fore-end
Barrel: 24" or 26" triangular contoured barrel, hammer forged, matte finish
Sights: none
Weight: 7 ¼ to 7 ¾
Caliber: .243 Win to .300 Rem Ultra Mag

Magazine: internal box
Features: X-Mark-Pro adjustable trigger, hinged floorplate, SuperCell recoil pad, polished jewel bolt.
Price: $879-$509

REMINGTON M597 FLX

Action: autoloading, recoil operated
Stock: Next Digital FLX camo
Barrel: 20" carbon steel matte
Sights: TruGlo fiber optic
Weight: 5 ½ lbs.
Caliber: .22 LR
Magazine: detachable 10-round box
Features: bolt-guidance system with twin tool-steel guide rails, last-shot, hold-open bolt for added safety.
Price: $260

R-25   M597 FLX   R-15

REMINGTON R-25 MODULAR REPEATING RIFLE

Action: autoloading, gas operated
Stock: synthetic camo (Mossy Oak Treestand)
Barrel: 20" carbon steel, matte blue
Sights: none, receiver-length Picatinny rail and gas block rail furnished
Weight: 7 ¾ lbs.
Caliber: .243 Win., 7mm-08 Rem., .308 Win.
Magazine: detachable 4-round box
Features: AR-style hunting rifle, single-stage hunting trigger, free-floated ChroMoly barrel.
Price: $1567

REMINGTON R-15 HUNTER

Action: autoloading, gas operated
Stock: synthetic camo
Barrel: 22"
Sights: receiver-length Pitcatinny rail for adding optics
Weight: 7 ¾ lbs.
Caliber: .30 Rem (also .223)
Magazine: detachable 4-round box
Features: New for 2009: .30 Remington addition to R-15 line that includes carbine and predator versions and new Thumbhole and Stainless Steel Varmint versions in .223.
Price: $1225

ROCK RIVER .308 MID-LENGTH

Action: autoloading, gas operated
Stock: Hogue rubber pistol grip, 6-position Tactical CAR Stock
Barrel: 16"
Sights: none on flattop verison, with front and rear rails (or A2 front and adjustable battle rear)
Weight: 8 to 8 ½ lbs.
Caliber: .308
Magazine: detachable box
Features: 1.5 MOA accuracy standard at 100 yards, RRA two-stage trigger
Price: $1135-$1185

NEW Products: **Rossi Rifles**

ROSSI TRIFECTA MATCHED SET IN LAMINATED STOCK

Action: hinged-breech single-shot
Stock: synthetic laminate available in 3 colors
Barrel: set of 3; 22" 20 gauge, 18 ½" .22LR; 22" .243 Win. Youth
Sights: shotgun barrel has brass bead front, .243 and .22 LR have fiber-optic open sights
Weight: 6 ½ to 7 lbs.
Caliber: 20 ga. Shotgun, .22 LR, .243 Win.
Magazine: none
Features: Three guns in one! Carrying case included, removable cheekpiece.
Price: $299-$329

RUGER ATI MINI-14

Action: autoloading, gas operated
Stock: 6-position collapsible/side folding buttstock, adjustable cheekrest, rubber butt, black nylon
Barrel: 16"
Sights: adjustable "ghost ring" aperture rear sight and non-glare post front sight; Ruger scope bases machined into receiver. (Ruger scope rings included).
Weight: 8 lbs.
Caliber: .223 Rem.

Magazine: detachable 20-round box (new)
Features: collapsible stock with under-guard pistol grip, quad rail up front, 1-in-9 rifling
Price: $872

RUGER MINI-14 TACTICAL

Action: autoloading, gas operated
Stock: black synthetic with pistol grip
Barrel: 16" with flash suppressor
Sights: adjustable "ghost ring" aperture rear sight and non-glare post front sight; Ruger scope bases machined

into receiver. (Ruger scope rings included)
Weight: 6 ¾ lbs.
Caliber: .223 Rem.
Magazine: detachable 20-round box (new)
Features: tactical variation of popular Mini-14, with 1-in-9 rifling. Also available: Target Hogue and Target Laminate rifles with heavy stainless barrels, Ranch Rifles and ATI, now all with 20-round boxes.
Price: $894

ATI MINI-14

MINI-14 TACTICAL

NEW Products: **Ruger Rifles**

RUGER M77 HAWKEYE PREDATOR

Action: two-lug bolt
Stock: Green Mountain Laminate
Barrel: stainless 22″ or 24″
Sights: none
Weight: 7 ¾ to 8 lbs.
Caliber: .223 Rem, .22-250 Rem. or .204 Ruger

Magazine: internal box (.223 Rem and .204 Ruger)
Features: lightweight varminter, trim version of M77, two-stage trigger, 3-position safety.
Price: $935

M77 HAWKEYE PREDATOR

NO. 1 IN .300 RCM

RUGER NO. 1 IN .300 RCM

Action: dropping-block single-shot
Stock: American walnut
Barrel: 22″
Sights: adjustable open rear sight on quarter-rib, blade front sight
Weight: 7 ¼ lbs.
Caliber: .300 RCM
Magazine: none
Features: lightweight hunting rifle with Alexander Henry-style forend
Price: $1147

RUGER SR-556

Action: autoloading, gas-operated
Stock: 6-position telescoping M4-style buttstock
Barrel: 16″ chrome-lined, cold hammer-forged
Sights: Troy Industries folding battle sights (provided standard)
Weight: 8 lbs.
Caliber: 5.56 Nato/.223 Rem.
Magazine: detachable 30-round box (3 included)
Features: chrome-plated, two-stage piston driven operating system, 4-position gas regulator, Hogue Monogrip pistol grip, Troy Industries quad rail, handguard and rail covers.
Price: $1995

SR-556

NEW Products: Savage Rifles

SAVAGE 10XP PREDATOR HUNTER IN SNOW

Action: two-lug bolt
Stock: composite in Snow camo
Barrel: 22"
Sights: none
Weight: 7 ¼ lbs.
Caliber: .204 Ruger, .223 Rem., .22-250 Rem., .243 Win.
Magazine: detachable box
Features: AccuTrigger, also available as a "package" rifle with scope.
Price: $806

NEW Products: Smith & Wesson Rifles

SMITH & WESSON M&P 15-22

Action: autoloading, recoil activated
Stock: polymer, collapsible 6-position
Barrel: 16"
Sights: AR-style adjustable
Weight: 6 lbs.
Caliber: .22 LR
Magazine: 25 round detachable box
Features: Upper and lower of high-strength polymer, front quad rail, accessories interchangeable with standard AR-15 5.56mm rifles.
Price: approximately $400

NEW Products: Thompson/Center Rifles

THOMPSON/CENTER TRIUMPH BONE COLLECTOR MUZZLELOADER

Action: muzzleloading with Toggle Lock breech
Stock: Composite camo and black
Barrel: 28" fluted, Weather Shield finish
Sights: open, fiber-optic
Weight: 8 lbs.
Caliber: .50 caliber
Magazine: none
Features: short Flex Tech stock. Reversible hammer extension, QLA muzzle system, Toggle Lock Action, Power Rod for easy field loading.
Price: $550-$650

NEW Products: **Traditions Rifles**

TRADITIONS VORTEK MUZZLELOADER

Action: hinged-breech muzzleloader
Stock: synthetic black or Soft Touch camo (thumbhole option)
Barrel: 28" blued or stainless
Sights: Williams fiber-optic
Weight: 12 ½ lbs.
Caliber: .50
Magazine: none
Features: aluminum ramrod, Accelerator Breech Plug, quick-release drop-out trigger, 209 shotgun primer ignition, over-molded stock and forend, recoil pad
Price: $390-$470; $411-$455 (Thumbhole)

TRADITIONS OUTFITTER

Action: hinged-breech centerfire
Stock: synthetic black or Soft Touch camo (thumbhole option)
Barrel: 24" blued fluted Wilson
Sights: Williams fiber optic
Weight: 7 ¼ lbs.
Caliber: .243, .270, .308, .30-06, .444
Magazine: none
Features: This model uses a true drop-in design that requires no factory fitting for replacement barrels and can be quickly converted from centerfire rifle to muzzleloader to shotgun. Rifle barrel drilled and tapped for scope mounting.
Price: $543-599; $565-$621 (Thumbhole)

VORTEK MUZZLELOADER

OUTFITTER

LT ACCELERATOR MUZZLELOADER

TRADITIONS LT ACCELERATOR MUZZLELOADER

Action: hinged-breech muzzleloader
Stock: synthetic black or Soft Touch camo (thumbhole option)
Barrel: 26" blued or nickel
Sights: TruGlo fiber-optic
Weight: 6 ¾ lbs.

Caliber: .50
Magazine: none
Features: aluminum ramrod, accelerator breech plug, lightweight, 1:28 twist rifling, 209 shotgun primer ignition, Fast Action release button, drilled and tapped for scope
Price: $278-$367; $300-$390 Thumbhole

WEATHERBY VANGUARD AXIOM

Action: two-lug bolt
Stock: synthetic Knoxx adjustable, with pistol grip and recoil-absorbing mechanism
Barrel: 22″ or 24″
Sights: none
Weight: 8 ½ to 8 ¾ lbs.
Caliber: .25-06, .270, .30-06, .257 Wby. Mag., 7mm Rem. Mag., .330 Win. Mag., .300 Wby. Mag. (Varmint version: .223 Rem., .22-250 Rem., .308 Win.)
Magazine: internal box
Features: new Vanguard from Weatherby's Custom Shop. 4″ of buttstock adjustment to fit any shooter, vertical pistol grip. Also: new

Vanguard Thumbhole Laminate with varmint-style forend, 22″ mid-weight barrel in .204, .223, .22-250, .308.
Price: starting from $879 (Varmint) $965 (Big Game)

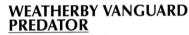

VANGUARD PREDATOR

WEATHERBY VANGUARD PREDATOR

Action: two-lug bolt
Stock: injection-molded composite in Natural Gear camo pattern
Barrel: 22″, camo
Sights: none
Weight: 8 lbs.
Caliber: .223 Rem., .22-250 Rem., .308 Win.
Magazine: internal
Features: factory-tuned adjustable trigger on Howa action, low-density recoil pad.
Price: $789

WEATHERBY MARK XXII SA

Action: semi-automatic rimfire
Stock: high gloss walnut with diamond inlay
Barrel: 20″
Sights: none, tip-off rail available
Weight: 6 ½ lbs.
Caliber: .22LR, .17 HMR

Magazine: detachable 10-round rotary box (.22 LR), 9-round (.17 HMR)
Features: CNC-machined bolt, Monte Carlo stock with cut checkering, hand-tuned trigger, guard-button safety, port at rear of receiver for easy cleaning.
Discontinued

WINCHESTER M70 COYOTE LIGHT

Action: two-lug bolt
Stock: black composite
Barrel: 22 or 24" stainless
Sights: none
Weight: 7 ½ lbs.
Caliber: .22-250, .243 Win, .308 Win, .270 WSM, .300 WSM, .325 WSM
Magazine: internal box
Features: Bell & Carlson carbon fiber stock with Pachmayr Decelerator recoil pad, flow-through vents on forend to reduce weight and help cool barrel. Skeletonized aluminum bedding block.
Price: $1069-$1099

WINCHESTER M70 ULTIMATE SHADOW

Action: two-lug bolt
Stock: black synthetic
Barrel: 22", 24", or 26"
Sights: none
Weight: 6 ½ to 7 lbs.
Caliber: .243, .308, .270, .30-06; 7mm Mag and .300 Win. Mag.; .270 .300 and .325 WSM.
Magazine: internal box
Features: WinSorb recoil pad, MOA trigger system, controlled round feed with external claw extractor.
Price: $739-$769

M70 COYOTE LIGHT

SUPER X RIFLE

WINCHESTER 1895 SAFARI CENTENNIAL 1909-2009

Action: Model 1895 lever
Stock: High Grade and Custom Grade, both finely checkered fancy walnut
Barrel: 24"
Sights: buckhorn rear sight, Marble's gold bead front sight
Weight: 8 lbs.
Caliber: .405 Win.
Magazine: detachable 4-round box
Features: receiver engraved with African big game animals, commemorating the 100th anniversary of Theodore Roosevelt's safari. Only 1,000 Custom Grade rifles to be built, and sold in sets with 1,000 High Grade rifles. An additional 500 High Grade rifles will be sold separately.
Price: $1749 and $3649

WINCHESTER SUPER X RIFLE

Action: autoloading, gas operated
Stock: checkered walnut
Barrel: 22 or 24" barrel
Sights: none
Weight: 7 ½ lbs.
Caliber: 270 WSM, 300 WSM, .30-06, .300 Win Mag.
Magazine: detachable box
Features: bolt-action accuracy from a combination of multi-lug rotating bolt and hammer-forged free-floating barrel. Hinged floorplate. Easily removable trigger assembly. Crossbolt safety. Low felt recoil.
Price: $979

NEW Products: **Benelli Shotguns**

BENELLI VINCI MAX4

Action: autoloading, inertia operated
Stock: black synthetic or camo (including new Max-4 HD)
Barrel: 26" or 28"
Chokes: set of 5 included
Weight: 6.8 to 6.9 lbs.

Bore/Gauge: 12 ga., 3"
Magazine: 3 + 1
Features: in-line inertial driven system, oversize lugs, Red Bar front sight, recoil reduction system
MSRP: $1379-$1479 (camo)

NEW Products: **Blaser Shotguns**

BLASER F3 28-GAUGE

Action: over/under, hinged breech
Stock: European walnut
Barrel: 28", 30" or 32"
Chokes: Briley Spectrum
Weight: 7 lbs.
Bore/Gauge: 28 gauge

Magazine: none
Features: Blaser introduces a 28-gauge to their F3 over/under shotgun line, including 12-bores (shown above) offered in Competition and Game models.
MSRP: starting at $6197

NEW Products: **Browning Shotguns**

BROWNING MAXUS STALKER AND MAXUS DUCK BLIND

Action: autoloading, gas operated
Stock: matte black composite (Duck blind camo composite)
Barrel: 26" or 28"
Chokes: interchangeable
Weight: 6 lbs. 14 oz.
Bore/Gauge: 12 gauge

Magazine: tube
Features: Flat, ventilated rib. 3" and 3 ½" chamber models.
MSRP: $1199-$1379 (Maxus Stalker) $1339-$1499 (Maxus Duck Blind)

L.C. SMITH .410, 28-GAUGE

Action: side-by-side, hinged breech
Stock: checkered walnut, pistol grip, semi-beavertail
Barrels: 26", solid rib

Chokes: 3 tubes supplied
Weight: 6 ½ lbs.
Bore/Gauge: .410, 3" or 28 ga.
Magazine: none
Features: box-lock action with engraved, case-colored side-plates, European manufacture, single selective trigger, automatic ejectors. Also: 12- and 20-gauge 3" models, and 12- and 20-gauge 3" over/under models.
Price: TBA

MOSSBERG 535 ATS THUMBHOLE TURKEY

Action: pump
Stock: synthetic black or camo
Barrel: 28″ matte blue or camo
Chokes: interchangeable
Weight: 7 lbs.
Bore/Gauge: 12 ga.
Magazine: tube
Features: 3 ½″, length: 40.5″, X-Factor Ported Tube.
MSRP: $429-$493

MOSSBERG 535 ATS THUMBHOLE TURKEY

MOSSBERG 935 MAGNUM TURKEY GUN

MOSSBERG 935 MAGNUM TURKEY GUN

Action: autoloading, gas operated
Stock: synthetic camo
Barrel: 22″ overbored
Chokes: interchangeable
Weight: 7.5 lbs.
Bore/Gauge: 12 ga. 3″ or 3 ½″
Magazine: tube
Features: magnum autoloading shotgun with X-Factor Ported Tube, drilled and tapped for bases and optics. Front and rear fiber optic sights. Overall length: 41.5″
MSRP: $732-$831

REMINGTON M105 CTI II

Action: autoloading, gas operated
Stock: American walnut
Barrel: 26" or 28", vent rib
Chokes: interchangeable Rem Chokes
Weight: 7 lbs.
Bore/Gauge: 12 ga. 3"
Magazine: tube
Features: Remington's lightest, softest-recoiling shotgun with 48% reduction in recoil. Autoloading 12 gauge with 3" chamber. Made from aircraft-grade titanium with carbon-fiber shell. "Double-down" bottom feed and ejection mechanism. CTi II improvements ensure performance with light 2 ¾-inch loads.
MSRP: $1548

M105 CTI II

**M11-87 COMPACT
SPORTSMAN SUPERCELL
EXT**

**M870 EXPRESS
TACTICAL**

REMINGTON M 11-87 COMPACT SPORTSMAN SUPERCELL EXT

Action: autoloading, gas operated
Stock: synthetic, black or camo
Barrel: 21" with vent rib
Chokes: modified
Weight: 6.5 lbs.
Bore/Gauge: 20 ga. 3"
Magazine: tube
Features: adjustable length of pull (LOP) system to fit young shooters as they grow. Supercell recoil pad.
MSRP: $772–$878 (camo)

REMINGTON M870 EXPRESS TACTICAL

Action: pump
Stock: synthetic, gray powder coat finish
Barrel: 18.5"
Chokes: Extended Tactical Rem choke tube
Weight: 7.5 lbs.
Bore/Gauge: 12 ga. 3"
Magazine: extended tube
Features: XS Ghost Ring Sights, ribbed forend. Overall length: 38 ½".
MSRP: $465-$505

NEW PRODUCTS 2009–2010

REMINGTON M870 SPS SURESHOT SUPERSLUG

Action: pump
Stock: synthetic, Mossy Oak Treestand camo
Barrel: extra-heavy, fluted, fully rifled, 25 ½"
Chokes: none
Weight: 7 7/8 lbs.
Bore/Gauge: 12 ga. 3"
Magazine: tube
Features: sights: drilled and tapped receiver with Weaver 429M rail. Finish: matte black, 47" long.
MSRP: $772

REMINGTON M887 NITRO MAG

Action: pump
Stock: synthetic, black or Waterfowl camo, built-in swivel studs
Barrel: 28", solid rib, H-Viz bead
Chokes: interchangeable Rem Chokes
Weight: 7 1/ 2 lbs.
Bore/Gauge: 12 ga. 3 ½"
Magazine: tube
Features: steel receiver, hammer-forged barrel, ArmorLokt polymer coating on all exposed steel, twin action bars, 48" long.
MSRP: $772

M870 SPS SURESHOT
SUPERSLUG

M887 NITRO MAG

NEW Products: **Rossi Shotguns**

TUFFY .410

ROSSI TUFFY .410

Action: single-shot, hinged breech
Stock: synthetic, black thumbhole
Barrel: 18.5 inches, matte blue or stainless
Chokes: full
Weight: 3 lbs.

Bore/Gauge: .410, 3"
Magazine: none
Features: single-shot youth shotgun. Buttstock holds five shells with a visible shell capacity window.
MSRP: $164-$172

NEW Products: **Verona Shotguns**

VERONA 401, 405, 406 SHOTGUN

Action: autoloading, inertia operated
Stock: Oil finished walnut with forend checkering
Barrel: 26″
Chokes: interchangeable
Weight: 7 lbs.
Bore/Gauge: 12 ga, 3″ or 3 ½″, or 20 ga., 3″
Magazine: tube
Features: Legacy Sports offers the Semi-automatic Verona shotgun (made by Pietta in Italy). Brass sight on standard model; fiber optic on deluxe. Pivoting bolt with integral double-charging lever and sleeve. Black nylon recoil pad. Silver, blue or pewter finish. 401 and 405 with 3″ chambering and the 406 series in 3 ½″.
MSRP: $1199-$1299

VERONA 501 SHOTGUN OVER/UNDER

Action: hinged breech
Stock: Oil finished walnut with round pistol grip and rounded forend
Barrel: 28 inches
Chokes: interchangeable
Weight: 7 lbs
Bore/Gauge: 20 and 28 ga.
Magazine: none
Features: Made by Fausti in Italy and imported by Legacy Sports. Two barrel sets in 20 and 28 gauge. 3″ magnum in 20 ga. Receiver has gold inlay of quail. Action features automatic safety and single, selective gold trigger. Black recoil pad.
MSRP: $2599

NEW Products: **Weatherby Shotguns**

WEATHERBY UPLAND PA-08

Action: pump
Stock: checkered walnut
Barrel: 26 or 28″ with vent rib
Chokes: 3 screw-in choke tubes
Weight: 6 ½ to 7 lbs.
Bore/Gauge: 12 ga. 3″
Magazine: tube
Features: Ventilated top rib and brass bead front sight. 3″ chamber.
MSRP: $389

UPLAND PA-08

NEW Products: **Winchester Shotguns**

WINCHESTER SUPER X3 GRAY SHADOW

Action: autoloading, gas operated
Stock: synthetic, gray with Dura-Touch armor
Barrel: 26″ or 28″ with vent rib
Chokes: 3 Invector Plus tubes supplied
Weight: 7 lbs.
Bore/Gauge: 12 ga. 3 ½″
Magazine: tube
Features: newest of several SX3 shotguns, spacers for drop, cast, length of pull.
MSRP: $1299

NEW Products: **Citadel Handguns**

CITADEL 1911 PISTOLS

Action: SA autoloading, recoil operated
Grips: checkered walnut
Barrel: 5" or 3 ½" (small frame)
Sights: Novak combat
Weight: 38 (5") or 30 ounces
Caliber: .45 ACP
Capacity: 8 or 6
Features: forged all-steel 1911 made for Legacy Sports Int'l, with skeleton loop hammer, lowered ejection port, full-length guide rod. Full-size model has extended ambidextrous thumb safety, front slide serrations.
MSRP: $575

NEW Products: **Kimber Handguns**

KIMBER STAINLESS PRO RAPTOR II

Action: SA autoloading, recoil operated
Grips: rosewood, scaled surface
Barrel: 4"
Sights: Tactical Wedge three dot (green) fixed night
Weight: 35 oz.
Caliber: .45 ACP
Capacity: 8
Features: Full size 1911 chambered in .45 ACP. Stainless steel slide and frame with hand-polished flat surfaces, satin finish over curves. Flat top slides with back-cut row of scales in gripping area and beavertail grip safety, ambidextrous thumb safety.
MSRP: $1248

STAINLESS PRO RAPTOR II

KIMBER TACTICAL ENTRY II

Action: SA autoloading, recoil operated
Grips: checkerd gray laminate
Barrel: 5" match grade
Sights: Kimber Tactical Rail for mounting; night sights
Weight: 40 oz.
Caliber: .45 ACP
Capacity: 7
Features: Stainless steel frame with front-strap checkering, extended magazine well. Also new: Tactical Custom HD
MSRP: $1428

KIMBER ULTRA CRIMSON CARRY II

Action: SA autoloading, recoil operated
Grips: Crimson Trace laser grips, checkered rosewood
Barrel: 3" bushingless match grade
Sights: combat iron sights
Weight: 25 oz.
Caliber: .45 ACP
Capacity: 7
Features: satin silver alloy frame, matte black steel slide, one of three new Crimson Carry pistols with laser grips.
MSRP: approximately $1400, depending on model

NEW Products: **ParaUSA Handguns**

PARAUSA GI EXPERT

Action: SA autoloading, recoil operated
Grips: checkered composite
Barrel: 5″
Sights: fixed white-dot combat
Weight: 39 oz.

Caliber: .45 ACP
Capacity: 8
Features: a plain-jane military-style 1911 with some refinements—skeleton loop hammer, stainless barrel, white dot sights and grooved, drilled trigger.
MSRP: $599

NEW Products: **Puma Handguns**

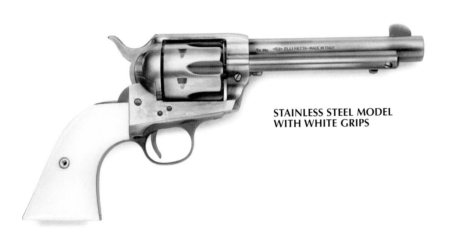

STAINLESS STEEL MODEL
WITH WHITE GRIPS

PUMA WESTERNER SA REVOLVERS

Action: SA revolver
Grips: white or walnut
Barrel: 4.75, 5.5 or 7.5 inch
Sights: strap groove and fixed blade
Weight: 36-40 oz.
Caliber: .45 LC, .357 Mag., .44-40
Capacity: 6
Features: Made in Italy by Pietta, imported by Legacy Sports Int'l. Stainless steel or color case hardened or nickeled carbon steel frame
MSRP: $529-$750

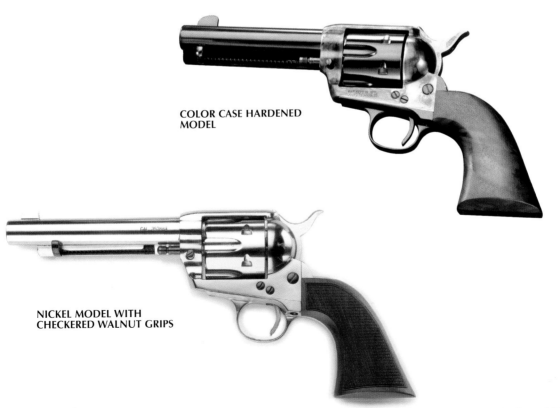

COLOR CASE HARDENED
MODEL

NICKEL MODEL WITH
CHECKERED WALNUT GRIPS

RUGER MARK III HUNTER

Action: SA autoloading, recoil operated
Grips: checkered cocobolo
Barrel: 4.5" target-crowned, fluted bull
Sights: HiViz front sight with 6 interchangeable LitePipes
Weight: 38 oz.
Caliber: .22
Capacity: 10
Features: Stainless steel frame. V-notch rear sight blade. Length: 8 ¾". Visible loaded chamber indicator.
MSRP: $620-$787

RUGER LCR

RUGER LCR (LIGHTWEIGHT COMPACT REVOLVER)

Action: DA revolver
Grips: Hogue
Barrel: 2"
Sights: fixed U-notch and ramp
Weight: 13 ½ oz.

Caliber: .38 Spl. +P
Capacity: 5
Features: synthetic fire-control housing, alloy frame, stainless steel cylinder, titanium front latch
MSRP: NA

NEW Products: **Sig Sauer Handguns**

SIG SAUER P238 NITRON

Action: SA autoloading, recoil operated
Grips: aluminum
Barrel: 2 ½"
Sights: SIGLITE night sights
Weight: 15 oz.
Caliber: .380
Capacity: 6
Features: Small frame. Overall length: 5.5", 3.96" high. Anodized alloy beavertail style frame with fluted aluminum grips. Stainless serrated slide. Available in black or two-tone with corrosion resistant Nitron slide.
MSRP: $515-$543

SMITH & WESSON CLASSIC M57 AND M58

Action: DA N-frame revolver
Grips: checkered square-butt walnut (target style on M57, standard on M58)
Barrel: 4" or 6"
Sights: Pinned red ramp front, micro-adjustable white outline rear (M57) or strap-groove rear (M58)
Weight: 45 or 48 oz.
Caliber: .41 Magnum
Capacity: 6
Features: This Classic Series six-shot revolver is available in bright blue or nickel. M57 has target hammer and trigger, M58 has lanyard fixture.
MSRP: approximately $925-$1100

CLASSIC M57

M14 NICKEL

SMITH & WESSON M14 NICKEL

Action: DA K-frame revolver
Grips: checkered square-butt walnut
Barrel: 6"
Sights: partridge-style front sight and micro-adjustable rear
Weight: 40 oz.
Caliber: .38 Special
Capacity: 6
Features: This Classic Series six-shot revolver is available in bright blue or nickel.
MSRP: approximately $800

SMITH & WESSON M18

Action: DA K-frame revolver
Grips: checkered square-butt walnut
Barrel: 4"
Sights: ramp front sight and micro-adjustable rear
Weight: 33 oz.
Caliber: .22 Long Rifle
Capacity: 6
Features: This Classic Series six-shot revolver is finished in bright blue.
MSRP: approximately $750

NEW Products: **Springfield Handguns**

SPRINGFIELD ARMORY EMP

Action: SA autoloading, recoil operated
Grips: checkered cocobolo or composite
Barrel: 3"
Sights: fixed combat tritium
Weight: 26 or 30 oz.
Caliber: 9mm or .40 S&W
Capacity: 9 or 8
Features: true short-action 1911 with 15 re-engineered parts. Stainless slide; matte black frame, extended grip safety, ambidextrous thumb safety.
MSRP: NA

NEW Products: **Taurus Handguns**

TAURUS 22 PLY/25PLY

Action: DAO autoloading, recoil operated
Grips: polymer
Barrel: 2 1/3″
Sights: fixed
Weight: 11 oz.
Caliber: .22 LR or .25 ACP
Capacity: 8 or 9
Features: ultra-light, polymer frame with tip-up barrel for safety and convenience during loading. Extended magazine for added grip.
MSRP: NA

TAURUS M709 SLIM

Action: SA/DA autoloading, recoil operated
Grips: polymer
Barrel: 3 ¼″
Sights: low-profile for easy concealment

Weight: 19 oz
Caliber: 9mm
Capacity: 7 (9 with extended magazine)
Features: blued, stainless or titanium versions.
MSRP: NA

TAURUS M738 TCP

Action: SA/DA autoloading, recoil operated
Grips: polymer
Barrel: blued or stainless
Sights: low-profile fixed
Weight: 8 ½ oz. titanium, 10 oz. blue or stainless
Caliber: .380 ACP
Capacity: 6, 8 with extended magazine
Features: the lightest Taurus available, but with a lethal chambering for self defense.
MSRP: NA

TAURUS JUDGE PUBLIC DEFENDER

Action: DA revolver
Grips: Ribber
Barrel: 3″ or 6 ½″ stainless or blue
Sights: fixed rear and fiber optic front
Weight: 22 oz. (3″ UltraLight), 29 oz. (3″ std), 32 oz. (6 ½″ std), 37 oz. (3″ magnum for 3″ .410 shells)
Caliber: .45 Colt and .410 shotgun, interchangeably
Capacity: 5 shot
Features: The new compact frame of alloy trims weight by half a pound. Available in stainless, blue steel or blue steel frame with titanium cylinder.
MSRP: NA

M738 TCP

M709 SLIM

22PLY

JUDGE PUBLIC DEFENDER

BRUNTON LITE-TECH 1.5-6X40

Features: Fully Broadband Multi-Coated lenses, waterproof/fogproof/shockproof. Available in 1.5-6x40 to 6-24x50 with Mil Dot or duplex reticle.
MSRP: $104-$194

BRUNTON ECHO 6-24X50

Features: Fully Broadband Multi-Coated lenses, waterproof/fogproof/shockproof. Available in 1.5-5x20 to 6-24x50 with glass-etched Mil Dot, Duplex or Ballistic reticle.
MSRP: $148-$448

NEW Products: **Burris Scopes**

BURRIS AR-332 PRISM SIGHT

Features: 3x tactical prism sight, waterproof to 5m, compact with Ballistic/CQ (close quarters) reticle, 1/3 MOA clicks, multicoated lenses and Picatinny rail mounting bracket, length: 5 inches, weight: 14 oz., matte black.
MSRP: $456

BURRIS AR TRIPLER

Features: 3x magnification with dot sight (or flip it away when you don't need it).

Mounts with AR-Pivot Ring or other 30mm fixed mount. Wire tethers prevent loss of caps. Waterproof to 5 meters.
MSRP: $304

BURRIS SIXX 2-12X50

Features: 6x magnification range, 4.5 inches eye relief, fixed position eye piece, 30mm tube, tactile rubber coated power ring, rapid-adjust diopter setting, HiLume StormCoat lens finish, waterproof/shockproof/fogproof, matte finish, 2-12x50 or

2-12x40.
MSRP: $1051-$1201

BURRIS XTR 3-12X50 (ALSO 1.5-6X40, 6-24X50)

Features: Fully multi-coated, Ballistic Mil-Dot reticle calibrated for 7.62-175MK and 5.56-77MK loads, turret parallax dial, tactical adjustment knobs, coyote brown finish on 30mm tube with walls 25% thicker for greater strength.
MSRP: $1466

AR TRIPLER

AR-322 PRISM SIGHT

SIXX 2-12X50

XTR 3-12X50

NEW Products: **Bushnell Scopes**

BUSHNELL ELITE 3200 WITH DOA 600

Features: Fully multi-coated lenses with Rainguard coating for a clear image in wet weather. One-piece, 1-inch aluminum tube, waterproof/fogproof/shockproof, ¼ MOA. Available with DOA 600 (Dead On Accuracy) reticle in 3-9x40 and 4-12x40 in matte finish. Extended-yardage aiming points reach to 600 yards with most rounds.
MSRP: $328-$440

NEW Products: **Insight Scopes**

INSIGHT MINI RED DOT SIGHT

Features: 1 MOA click adjustable for elevation and windage, manual control with 4 settings, impact-resistant polymer lens, waterproof up to 66 feet for 2 hours, weight: .85 oz.
MSRP: $650

NEW Products: **Leupold Scopes**

LEUPOLD ULTIMATESLAM

Features: Leupold's new 1-inch scope for black powder or slug guns. New SABR reticle, waterproof/fogproof, available in 2-7x33 and 3-9x40 in silver or black matte.
MSRP: $259-$269

LEUPOLD VX-3 5-10X50

Features: New Xtended Twilight Lens System giving brighter, sharper images in low-light, high-strength aluminum adjustment dials, dual spring erector. The VX-3L offers Leupold's Light Optimization Profile – the cut crescent shape delivering maximum light with a lower mount.

Waterproof/fogproof/shockproof, Argon/Krypton gas blend. Blackened lens edges maximizes clarity. Available in power ranges from 1.5-5x20 to 8.5-25x50 with 1-inch tube (30mm on Long Range versions) and ¼ MOA adjustments.
MSRP: $580-$660 (5-10x50); VX-3 line from $430 to $1049

VX-3 5-10X50

NEW Products: **Meopta Scopes**

MEOPTA MEOSTAR R1 4-16X44 TACTIC

Features: Adjustable objective setting zero from 3m to infinity, low-profile target knobs, ¼ MOA, Mil Dot reticle, waterproof/fogproof.
MSRP: $698-$1299

MEOPTA ARTEMIS 3000 3-9X42

Features: Solid steel tube, shock resistant, Nitrogen purged for fog and waterproof performance, ¼ MOA.
MSRP: $474-$1117

ARTEMIS 3000
3-9X42

R1 4-16X44

NEW Products: **Nightforce Scopes**

NIGHTFORCE 2.5-10X32 NXS

Features: Slim design with larger exit pupil allows fast target acquisition and improved light. Length: 12 inches. Weight: 19 ounces, with ¼ MOA adjustments in fully-enclosed hunting-style dials or exposed target knobs. ZeroStop technology with windage limiter. Three ballistic reticles offered in 2.5-10x32 and 2.5-10x24 compact versions.
MSRP: $1345-$1613

NIGHTFORCE F1 3.5-15X50

Features: Tactical scope with 30mm tube, turret parallax dial, reticle in the first focal plane. Offered in choice of three windage/elevation adjustments: ¼ MOA, .1 Mil Radian, or 1.0 MOA elevation/.5 MOA windage (optional turret caps available). Several long-range reticles,
MSRP: $2410

NIGHTFORCE TOP OF RING BUBBLE LEVEL

Features: Nightforce's new built-in bubble level replaces the top half of a ring mount, helping the shooter eliminate cant – critical at long range.
MSRP: $160

NEW Products: **Nikon Scopes**

NIKON COYOTE SPECIAL 3-9X40

Features: Nikon's new BDC Predator Hunting Reticle with circle design, Anti reflective, multicoated lenses, ¼ MOA click adjustments, generous eye relief and quick-focus eyepiece, 1-inch tube, waterproof/fogproof, two camo finishes available, 3-9x40 or 4.5-14x40.
MSRP: $350

NIKON AFRICAN 1-4X20

Features: Monarch African series offers Ultra ClearCoat lens systems, German #4 reticle, one-piece main body tubes, ½ MOA click adjustments (¼ MOA in 1.1-4x24), quick-focus eyepiece, waterproof/fogproof/shockproof, matte finish. Offered in 1-4x20 with 1-inch tube and 1.1-4x24 with 30mm tube (two versions).
MSRP: 1-4x20 $280, 1-4x24 $770-$860

**COYOTE SPECIAL
3-9X40**

**AFRICAN
1-4X20**

NIKON EDG 65 AND 85 FIELDSCOPE SPOTTING SCOPES

Features: ED (Extra-low Dispersion) fully multi-coated lenses, 65mm or 85mm objective lenses, zoom eyepiece, sliding sunshade, straight and angled body versions, waterproof/fogproof.
MSRP: 65MM $2700 85MM $3300

NIKON OMEGA MUZZLELOADER 1.65-5X36

Features: Nikon's BDC 250 reticle with easy-to-see "ballistic circles," 1-inch alloy tube, 5 inches eye relief, ¼ MOA click adjustments, 100-yard parallax setting, multi-coated lenses, waterproof/fogproof/shockproof, matte or camo finish.
MSRP: $240-$300

EDG 65

NITREX TR TWO SERIES RIFLE-SCOPES

Features: Available in EBX (Enhanced Ballistic-X), Fine-X with dot, and illuminated reticles. 2-10x42, 3-15x42, 3-15x50 and 4-20x50mm versions. TruCoat multi-coated lenses, pull-up resettable turrets, power selector ring and argon-filled 1-inch tubes, matte or silver, shockproof/fogproof/waterproof.
MSRP: $556-$870

PENTAX PIONEER II 4.5-14X42

Features: Available in 3-9x40 and 4.5-14x42. One-piece, 1-inch tube, waterproof, nitrogen-filled with fully multi-coated PentaBright lenses, ¼ MOA adjustments, quick-focus eyepiece, PentaPlex reticle.
MSRP: $199-$219

PENTAX GAMESEEKER 5X

Features: 3-15x magnification and 50mm objective for maximum light transmission. Waterproof, nitrogen-filled 1-inch tube, fully multi-coated lenses. ¼ MOA finger-adjustable dials.
MSRP: $239

PIONEER II 4.5-14X42

GAMESEEKER 5X

NEW Products: **Schmidt & Bender Scopes**

SCHMIDT & BENDER 2.5-10X40 SUMMIT

Features: S&B's first 1-inch scope for the American market, with A7 or A8 reticle in second focal plane. 3 ½ inches eye relief, fully multi-coated, first-quality S&B optics, ¼-minute clicks, quick-focus eyepiece
MSRP: $1,400

SCHMIDT & BENDER ZENITH 1.1-4X24

Features: A great choice for dangerous or fast-moving game at close quarters. Reticle is located in the second focal plane, so size remains constant throughout the magnification range. At lower magnification a wide field of view (36 yds/100 yds).
MSRP: $1730-$2289

ZENITH 1.1-4X24

NEW Products: **Sightron Scopes**

SIGHTRON HIGH-POWER SII SCOPES

Features: variable 3-12x42, 4.5-14x50, 6-24x42 and fixed 6x42 and 36x42 scopes with fully multi-coated optics, 1/8 and ¼ minutes per click, depending on magnification, AO and target knobs on target versions.
MSRP: $320-$650, approximately

NEW Products: **Swarovski Scopes**

SWAROVSKI Z6 5-30X50

Features: 30mm tube, fully multi-coated lenses, ¼-minute clicks, six-times magnification, Ballistic Turret for long shooting, wide choice of reticles. Other magnification ranges available. Z6i, or illuminated-reticle versions, have new top-side controls, day/night modes, 64 brightness levels, automatic shut-off.
MSRP: $2532-$3443

NEW Products: Swarovski Scopes

Z5 5-25X52

SWAROVSKI Z5 3.5-18X44, 5-25X52 P

Features: compact 1-inch tube with five-times power range, fully multi-coated optics, quick-focus eyepiece, available with long-range reticles, ballistic turret.
MSRP: $1532-$1776

SWAROVSKI Z3 SCOPE LINE

Features: Low-profile 1-inch tube, available in 3-9x36, 3-10x42, and 4-12x50 with fully multi-coated optics, standard and long-range second-plane reticles, quick-focus eyepiece and Ballistic Turret.
MSRP: $1087-$1410

SWAROVSKI Z3

NEW Products: Trijicon Scopes

TRIJICON ACCUPOINT 5-20X50

Features: Trijicon's long-range scope for varmint hunters and tactical shooters has fully multi-coated optics, fiber-optic and tritium aiming point illumination, 30mm hard-anodized aluminum tube, choice of post, duplex or Mil Dot reticles, external turret controls and side parallax adjustment.
MSRP: $1200

TRIJICON RMR SIGHT

Features: Trijicon's new red-dot sight can be teamed up with the ACOG or AccuPoint for fast target acquisition or precise aim at long range. Available with adjustable LED insert or dual-illuminated, battery-free fiber optics.
MSRP: LED $650, Dual Illuminated $475

ACCUPOINT
5-20X50

ACOG

RMR SIGHT

NEW Products: **Vortex Scopes**

VORTEX VIPER RIFLE-SCOPE

Features: Fully multi-coated optics with XR anti-reflective coating on XD premium glass, waterproof/fogproof with argon gas, one-piece 1-inch alloy tube. Fast-focus eyepiece and resettable ¼-minute adjustment dials. Magnification ranges from 2-7x32 to 6.5-20x50.
MSRP: $349-$489

NEW Products: **Weaver Scopes**

WEAVER TACTICAL 3-15X50, 4-20X50

Features: five-times magnification, first-plane reticle, 30mm tube, turret parallax adjustment, Mil Dot reticle. Available in 4-20x50 or 3-15x50 in matte finish.
MSRP: $514-$574

WEAVER SUPER SLAM 2-10X42

Features: One-piece 1-inch tubes, five times power range, SHR fully multi-coated lenses, EBX ballistic reticle, ¼-minute adjustments, 3-position, pull-up turrets (no caps), Argon-purged tubes, 3-point erector assembly, waterproof/fogproof/shockproof, in 2-10x42 to 4-20x50 power ranges in matte or silver.
MSRP: $555-$869

TACTICAL 4-20X50

SUPER SLAM
2-10X42

ZEISS COMPACT POINT REFLEX SIGHT

Features: Bright illuminated red dot sight for rifles, handguns, shotguns. Button adjusts illumination, which has automatic shut-off. Uses two Lithium 3V batteries. Three versions available: standard, Zeiss Plate and Blaser R93.
MSRP: $611 ($889 for Blaser R93 version)

COMPACT POINT
REFLEX SIGHT

ZEISS VICTORY VARIPOINT 1.1-4X24T AND 1.5-6X42T RETICLE #60

Features: These 30mm Victory scopes have a crosshair in the first plane, an illuminated dot in the second plane. (Reticle #60 is also available in 2.5-10x42, 2.5-10x50 and 3-12x56 Victory scopes). Best-quality Zeiss optics, LotuTec water-repellent coatings, 3.5 inches eye relief. Weight: 16 and 18.5 ounces.
MSRP: $2444

ZEISS VICTORY DIAVARI 2.5-10X50T AND 3-12X56T, SECOND-PLANE RET.

Features: These two 30mm Victory rifle-scopes now have second-plane reticle options, including the Rapid-Z 800 Ballistic Reticle for long-range shooting. LotuTec water-repellent lens coatings are standard. Four other Victory scopes offer second-plane reticles: the Diarange 2.5-10x50 and 3-12x56 laser range-finding scopes and the 6-24x72 and 6-24x72 FL variables.
MSRP: $2111 to $2556

NEW Products: **Barnes Ammunition**

BARNES BUSTER BULLETS

Features: full-jacketed lead-core handgun bullets for use on thick-skinned game – 300-gr. .429 (.44 Magnum), 325-gr. .451 (.454 Casull), 400-gr. .458 (.45-70 rifle), 400-gr. .500 (.500 S&W)

BARNES M/LE TAC-X

Features: All copper rifle bullets in .223, 6.8mm, .308, .50 BMG. Straight tracking through barriers and better weight retention than lead-core bullets.

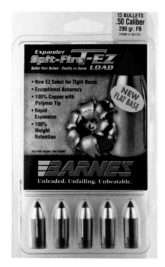

SPIT-FIRE T-EZ MUZZELOADER BULLETS

BARNES SPIT-FIRE T-EZ MUZZLELOADER BULLETS

Features: poly-tipped .451-diameter 250 or 290-grain all-copper for 50-caliber muzzle-loaders

BARNES BANDED SOLID BULLETS

Features: 400-grain .410 solids for .450/400 for heavy African game, in a line that includes 13 other bullets, from .375 to .600.

BARNES TRIPLE-SHOCK X BULLET

Features: new 80-grain .243, 80- and 100-grain .257, 120-grain 6.5mm bullets for centerfire rifles, sleek boat-tail bullets with three belt grooves, polymer tip

BARNES LOADED AMMO

Features: Barnes now markets ammo in boxes by Weatherby, Black Hills, DPX Corbon and other known firms that load Barnes bullets. Same ammo as from those sources, but now direct from Barnes.

NEW Products: **Black Hills Ammunition**

BLACK HILLS TAC-XP PISTOL AMMO

Features: 9mm, .40 S&W and .45 ACP with Barnes Tac-XP copper HP bullets

BLACK HILLS TSX BULLETS AND MPG BULLETS IN RIFLE AMMO

Features: 55-grain Barnes TSX bullets in .223, 85-grain TSX in .243 cartridges Also: 55-grain Hornady FMJ bullets in new-manufacture .223, and Multi-Purpose-Green lead-free bullets in .223. MPGs are frangible in soft targets.

FEDERAL V-SHOK HEAVYWEIGHT COYOTE

Features: 12 gauge, BB shot, 1 ½ oz.

FEDERAL VITAL-SHOK TROPHY BONDED TIP

Features: Built on the Trophy Bonded Bear Claw platform to provide deep penetration and high weight retention. Sleek profile, with tapered heel and translucent polymer tip. Nickel-plated. Available as component and in Federal loaded ammunition.

FEDERAL NYCLAD BULLETS

Features: in Federal Premium Personal Defense handgun ammunition, 125-grain .38 Special HP.

FEDERAL ULTRAMATCH RIMFIRE TARGET

Features: 40-grain, 1080 fps match load for .22 rimfire competition.

FEDERAL BLACK CLOUD SS WATERFOWL

Features: FLIGHTCONTROL wad tightens patterns, FLIGHTSTOPPER steel shot pellets, 10, 20 and 12 gauge.

NEW Products: **Fiocchi Ammunition**

FIOCCHI CENTERFIRE RIFLE LINE
Features: new loads for .22 Hornet, .223, 6.5x55, .308, including lead-free designs.

FIOCCHI CENTERFIRE HANDGUN LINE
Features: new Expanding Mono-block bullet load in 9x19 pistol ammo. XTP loads in 9mm, .38 Special, .357 SIG, .44 Special (Cowboy Action), .44 Magnum and .45 ACP.

NEW Products: **Hornady Ammunition**

DANGEROUS GAME LOADS

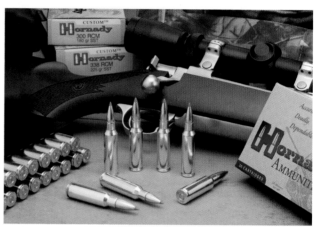

RUGER COMPACT MAGNUMS

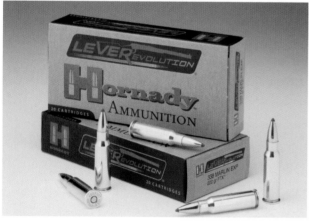

.338 MARLIN EXPRESS

CRITICAL DEFENSE PISTOL AMMO

HORNADY DANGEROUS GAME LOADS
Features: .404 Jeffery, .416 Ruger, .470 Nitro Express, .500 Nitro Express with Hornady DGS solid bullets for heavy African game. The line includes nine other cartridges.

HORNADY .300 AND .338 RUGER COMPACT MAGNUMS
Features: Developed by Hornady, the .300 and .338 RCMs are rimless magnums designed to deliver high velocities from short-action, short-barrel rifles. A 150-grain GMX .300 RCM load is new this year.

HORNADY .338 MARLIN EXPRESS
Features: A new case with a 200-grain FTX bullet loaded to 2565 fps gives Marlin's 1895 rifle the reach and power of a .30-06 to 300 yards.

HORNADY CRITICAL DEFENSE PISTOL AMMO
Features: Jacketed hollowpoint FTX bullets with polymer inserts make expansion reliable and consistent in varied media. First CD ammunition includes 90-grain .380, 110-grain .38 Special (and +P), 115-grain 9mm.

HORNADY GMX (LEAD-FREE) AND MATCH LOADS
Features: New GMX loads available in .270, 7mm Rem. Mag., .308, .30-06, .300 RCM, .300 Win. Mag. The .308 gets a new 155 Palma load, the .30-06 a 168-grain A-Max Match for the Garand.

NEW Products: Lapua Ammunition

LAPUA NATURALIS AND MEGA BULLETS

Features: Polymer-tipped Naturalis bullets with solid-copper design are designed for near-100% weight retention. The bonded, lead-core Mega bullet is an option. Lapua offers two target bullets as well, and cases that include the .220 Russian, 6mm BR Norma, 6.5 Grendel and 6.5/284. Loaded cartridges range from the .22 Long Rifle Match to sniper loads for the .338 Lapua.

NEW Products: Norma Ammunition

NORMA AFRICAN PH AMMO

Features: loaded cartridges with Woodleigh softnose and solid bullets, in chamberings popular for dangerous game, including .375 H&H, .404 Jeffery, .416 Rem. Mag., .416 Rigby, .450 Rigby, .458 Lott, .470 NE, .500 NE, .505 Gibbs.

NORMA ORYX BULLETS IN SMALL-BORE LOADS, OTHER ADDITIONS

Features: Norma's 55-grain Oryx softnose is now available in Norma ammo -- .222, .223, .22-250, .220 Swift. Also, Norma now loads the 6XC with the 95-grain Nosler BST and 100-grain Oryx, the .270 and .270 WSM with 156-grain Vulcan bullets. The 8x68 gets a 200-grain Swift A-Frame.

NEW Products: Nosler Ammunition

NOSLER BULLETS GROW HUNTING LINES

Features: 286-grain 9.3mm and 500-grain .470 solids for dangerous game, new .243, .270, 7mm and .338 lead-free E-Tips, 140-grain 7mm AccuBond, 150-grain .308 Ballistic Silvertip round-nose, 105-grain 6mm HPBT and 175-grain .308 HPBT match bullets. Also, .25-06 and 7mm-08 loads in the Nosler Custom ammunition line.

NEW Products: **Remington Ammunition**

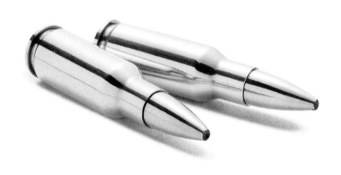

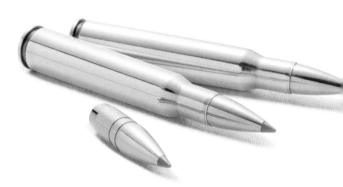

REMINGTON PREMIER .30 REM AR

Features: A short, 30-caliber round whose 125-grain bullets match the speed of .308 150s, for hunting deer-size game with the AR-15 modular repeating rifle. Ammo comes with Core-Lokt and AccuTip bullets (125 grains) and, in UMC loads, with full metal case (123 grains) bullets.

REMINGTON PREMIER COPPER SOLID

Features: This polymer-tipped copper bullet is of boat-tail design, and available in .243 Win (80 grains) to .300 Rem Ultra Mag (180 grains).

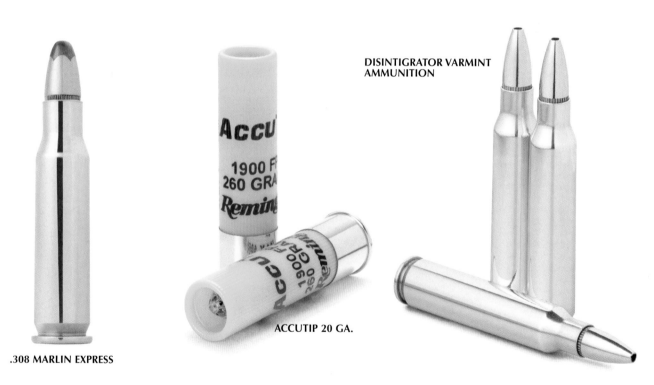

DISINTIGRATOR VARMINT AMMUNITION

ACCUTIP 20 GA.

.308 MARLIN EXPRESS

REMINGTON .308 MARLIN EXPRESS

Features: 150-grain Core-Lokt soft-point bullet at 2725 fps.

REMINGTON ACCUTIP 20 GA.

Features: Bonded Sabot 260-grain slug now comes in 20 gauge, in 2 ¾- and 3-inch loads,(385 grains in 12 gauge, also in 2 ¾- and 3-inch).

REMINGTON DISINTEGRATOR VARMINT AMMUNITION

Features: Fragible bullet design with iron/tin bullet core (no lead), designed to disintegrate upon impact on varmints. These 45-grain JHP bullets are offered in .223 and .22-250.

SIERRA PALMA AND LONG-RANGE BULLETS

Features: A 155-grain Palma Match bullet joins Sierra's MatchKing series that dominates high-power competition. The long-range line now includes 77-, 80-, and 90-grain .224s, 210- and 240-grain .308s and 300-grain .338s.

NEW Products: **Swift Ammunition**

SWIFT SCIROCCO 100-GRAIN .257

Features: Newest of sleek, polymer-tipped bullets for long shooting at big game, the 100-grain .25 is one of 10 Sciroccos, .224 to .338.

NEW Products: **Weatherby Ammunition**

WEATHERBY AMMO FOR DEER HUNTERS

Features: Weatherby now offers Barnes Tipped TSX bullets in Norma-loaded ammo for the .257, .270, 7mm, .300 and .30-378 Weatherby rounds. These lead-free bullets range in weight from 80 to 130 grains.

WINCHESTER PDX1 PISTOL AMMO

Features: Bonded jacketed hollowpoint loads in .38 Special, 9mm, .40 S&W and .45 ACP upset to 1 ½ times diameter in six-petal mushroom. Available in nickel-plated Personal Protection Ammunition

WINCHESTER POWERMAX BONDED

Features: Loads for the .270, .270 WSM, .30-30, .308, .30-06, .300 WSM and .300 Win. Mag. include PHP bullets with bonded lead core. Designed expressly for deer hunters.

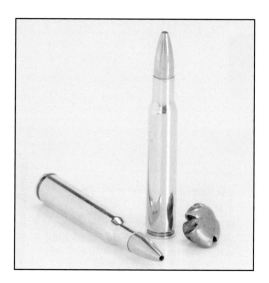

22 XPEDITER

WINCHESTER 22 XPEDITER

Features: 32-grain, plated hollowpoint bullets in nickel-plated cases distinguish this fastest of Winchester .22 Long Rifle rounds. Muzzle velocity: 1640 fps.

WINCHESTER DUAL BOND HANDGUN AMMO

Features: Hunting ammunition for the .454 Casull, .460 S&W and .500 S&W includes this "bullet within a bullet" with inner and outer jackets, mechanically bonded. Hollowpoint design delivers 12-petal upset.

NEW Products: **Browning Rifles**

X-BOLT

Action: bolt
Stock: composite, gloss finish walnut or satin finish walnut
Barrel: 22, 23, 24, 26 in.
Weight: 6.3-7 lbs.
Caliber: variety of calibers from 243 Win. to 375 H & H Mag
Magazine: detachable rotary
Features: available in several models: Stainless Stalker and Composite Stalker with composite stocks; Medallion and Hunter with wood stocks; all with adjustable three-lever Feather Trigger, bolt unlock button allows bolt to be unlocked and opened with safety on, X-Lock scope mounting system. Blued, stainless steel, low luster blued or matte blued barrels.

Composite Stalker: $879–909
Hunter: $879–909
Medallion: $989–1019
Stainless Stalker: $1099–1129

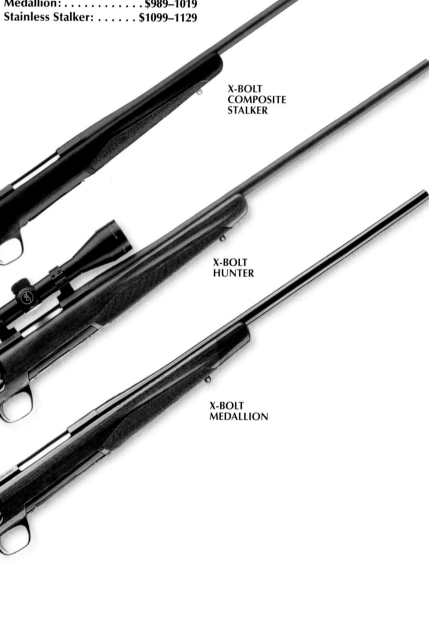

X-BOLT
COMPOSITE
STALKER

X-BOLT
HUNTER

X-BOLT
MEDALLION

NEW Products: **Harrington & Richardson Rifles**

HANDI-MAG
Action: single-shot centerfire
Stock: Monte Carlo synthetic
Barrel: 26 in., stainless steel
Sights: none
Weight: 7-8 lbs.

Caliber: 7mm Rem. Mag, 300 Win. Mag.
Magazine: none
Features: heat-treated blued carbon
steel receiver; transfer bar safety
Discontinued

SYNTHETIC HANDI-MAG

NEW Products: **Henry Repeating Arms Rifles**

LEVER .30-30
Action: lever
Stock: Straight grip American Walnut
with buttplate
Barrel: 20-in. round bull (steel version), 20-in. octagonal (brass version)
Sights: Marbles adjustable Semi-Buckhorn rear and brass beaded front

Weight: 8.3 lbs.
Caliber: .30-30
Magazine: 6 rounds
Features: drilled and tapped for scope;
tubular feed design
Steel: $749
Brass: $970

LEVER .30-30 BRASS
WITH OCTAGONAL BARREL

NEW Products: **Knight Rifles**

KP1 WURFFLEIN

KP1 WURFFLEIN

Action: centerfire
Stock: black composite, brown sand-stone laminate or Next G-1 Camo
Barrel: blued or stainless steel Green Mountain

Sights: fully adjustable, metallic fiber-optic
Weight: 7 lbs. 13 oz.
Caliber: .45-70
Magazine: single shot
Features: features barrel interchange-

ability, allowing users to go from .45/70 to various other calibers, plus muzzleloader, rimfire and shotgun barrels; recoil pad; sling swivel studs
Discontinued

NEW Products: **Marlin Rifles**

917VT

XL7

XL7C

Magazine: 4-shot and 7-shot clips
Features: blued carbon steel; sling swivel studs; rubber butt pad; grooved, drilled and tapped for scope bases (2 included)
Discontinued

Magazine: 4-shot and 7-shot clips
Features: nickel receiver; sling swivel studs; rubber butt pad; grooved, drilled and tapped for scope bases (2 included); thumb safety; red cocking indicator
Discontinued

917VST

Action: bolt
Stock: gray and black laminate, thumbhole pistol grip
Barrel: heavy 22 in. with microgroove rifling, stainless steel
Sights: none
Weight: 7 lbs.
Caliber: .17 HMR

917VT

Action: bolt
Stock: brown laminate, thumbhole pistol grip
Barrel: heavy 22 in. with microgroove rifling
Sights: none
Weight: 7 lbs.
Caliber: .17 HMR

XL7

Action: centerfire bolt
Stock: black synthetic or RealTree APG-HD camo
Barrel: 22 in.
Sights: none; 1-piece Weaver-style scope base included
Weight: 6.5 lbs.
Caliber: .30-06 Spg., .270 Win., .25-06 Rem.
Magazine: 4+1
Features: Fluted bolt; Pro-Fire trigger; Soft-Tech recoil pad; steel swivel studs; Weaver-style 1-piece scope base
Discontinued

464 LEVER-ACTION

Action: lever
Stock: wood
Barrel: 20 in.
Weight: 6.7 lb. (.30-30), 5.6 lb. (.22 LR)
Caliber: .30-30 Win., .22 LR
Magazine: 6+1 (.30-30), 13+1 (.22LR) rounds
Features: button-rifled barrel, recessed muzzle crown, top-tang safety, recoil softening rubber buttpad
MSRP: **$497**

4x4 .300 WIN. MAG. LAMINATE

Action: bolt
Stock: synthetic with laminate finish
Barrel: 24 in., matte blue
Weight: 6.7 lb.
Caliber: .300 Win. Mag.

Magazine: 3+1 rounds, drop box
Features: free-floating, button-rifled barrel, recessed muzzle crown, two-piece factory installed Weaver scope bases
MSRP: **$654**

464 22LR

464 30-30

4X4 300 WIN. MAG.

NEW Products: **Mossberg Rifles**

802 BLACK SYNTHETIC CHROME

802 PINK MARBLE SYNTHETIC

802 SCOPED COMBO

802 THUMBHOLE TIPDOWN

702 & 802 PLINKSTER BOLT-ACTIONS

Action: bolt
Stock: synthetic (black, pink, pink marble) or wood
Barrel: 18, 21 in., blue or brushed chrome
Sights: Adjustable rifle
Weight: 4.1-5.2 lb.

Caliber: .22 LR
Magazine: 10 rounds, detachable
Features: 702 Plinkster Bantam models feature a shortened 12-¼-in. LOP and 18-in. barrel for young shooters or smaller stature adults; offered in factory-mounted 4X scoped combo sets.
MSRP: . . . . from $162

NEW Products: **Legacy Sports International Rifles**

PUMA SCOUT

Action: lever
Stock: wood
Barrel: 20 in. blued
Sights: 2.5-32 Nikko Stirling riflescope
Weight: unavailable
Caliber: .17 Rem., .38 Spl./.357 Mag., .44 Mag., .45 Colt, .454 Casull
Magazine: 10+1

Features: .454 model fitted with shotgun-style recoil pad; crescent steel buttplates on other models.
MSRP: . . . . **$739-$849**

PUMA SCOUT

NEW Products: **Remington Rifles**

MODEL R-15 VTR

Action: semi-auto
Stock: synthetic; Advantage MAX-1 HD finish
Barrel: 22 in. (Predator); 18 in. (Carbine and Carbine CS)
Weight: 7.75 lbs. (Predator); 6.75 lbs. (Carbine and Carbine CS)
Caliber: .223 Rem., .204 Ruger
Magazine: 5 rounds
Features: free-floating button-rifled

chrome-moly fluted barrels with recessed hunting crown; single-stage hunting trigger; receiver-length Picatinny rail; ergonomic pistol grip; fore-end tube

drilled and tapped for accessory rails; compatible with aftermarket AR-15 magazines; lockable hard case included.
MSRP: **$1225**

R-15VTR
PREDATOR CARBINE

R-15VTR
PREDATOR CARBINE CS

MODEL 798 SAFARI GRADE

Action: bolt/long
Stock: synthetic, matte black finish
Barrel: 22 in.
Weight: 8.25 lbs.
Caliber: .375 H&H Mag, .458 Win Mag
Magazine: capacity 3
Features: Mauser 98 action with claw extractor; hammer-forged, blued carbon steel barrel; one-piece steel trigger guard/magazine assembly with hinged floorplate and steel magazine follower; rubber recoil pad; sporter-style, single-stage trigger with side mounted 2-position safety; sling swivel studs; receivers drilled and tapped for standard Mauser 98 scope mounts
Discontinued

MODEL 798 SATIN WALNUT STOCK

Action: bolt/long
Stock: synthetic, matte black finish
Barrel: 22 in. (Short); 24 in. (Long); 26 in. (Magnum)
Weight: 7.75 lbs. (Short); 8.25 lbs. (Long); 8.5 lbs. (Magnum)

Caliber: .243 Win, .270 Win, .308 Win, .30-06 Sprg. with shorter 22-in. barrels; 7mm Rem Mag and .300 Win Mag with standard 24-in. barrels; .375 H&H Mag and .458 Win Mag with 26-in. barrels
Magazine: capacity 3 or 4
Features: Mauser 98 action with claw extractor; hammer-forged, blued carbon steel barrels; one-piece solid steel trigger guard/magazine assembly with hinged floorplate and steel magazine follower; sporter-style, single-stage trigger with side mounted 2-position safety; receivers drilled and tapped for standard Mauser 98 scope mounts; rubber recoil pad; sling swivel studs
Discontinued

MODEL 798 SAFARI

MODEL 798 SPS (SPECIAL PURPOSE SYNTHETIC)

Action: bolt/long
Stock: synthetic, matte black finish
Barrel: 22 in. (Short and Long); 24 in. (Magnum)
Weight: 7.75 lbs. (Short and Long); 8.25 (Magnum)
Caliber: .243 Win, .270 Win, .308 Win, .30-06 Sprg, 7mm Rem Mag, .300 Win Mag

Magazine: capacity 3 or 4
Features: Mauser 98 action with claw extractor; blued hammer-forged, carbon steel barrel; one-piece steel trigger guard/magazine assembly with hinged floorplate and steel magazine follower; sporter-style, single-stage trigger with side mounted 2-position safety; receivers drilled and tapped for standard Mauser 98 scope mounts; sling swivel studs; rubber recoil pad
Discontinued

YOUTH MATCHED PAIR

Action: break-open single shot
Stock: black synthetic
Barrel: 22 in./18.5 in.
Sights: adjustable fiber optic front (rifle barrels), brass bead front (shotgun)

Weight: 3.75 lbs./5.6 lbs.
Caliber: .17 HMR or .22 LR rifle barrel and .410 gauge shotgun barrel
Features: quick-interchange rifle and shotgun barrels; matte nickel finish; rifle barrel drilled and tapped to hold

included scope mount base and hammer extension; Taurus Security System lock; carrying case and dual purpose strap included

.410/.17 HMR: **$219**
.410/.22 LR: **$239**

NRA MINI-14

Action: autoloader
Stock: Hogue OverMolded
Barrel: 16 in.
Sights: protected blade front, ghost ring adjustable aperture rear
Weight: 6.75 lbs.
Caliber: .233 Rem.

Magazine: 20-round detachable
Features: special edition rifle to raise money for NRA Institute for Legislative Action; special serial number sequence; blued finish; NRA metal gold-tone logo on grip cap
Discontinued

NEW Products: **Sako Rifles**

A7

MODEL 85 DELUXE

MODEL 85 KODIAK

A7
Action: bolt
Stock: synthetic
Barrel: 22.4-24.4 in.
Sights: none
Weight: 6.3-6.6 lbs.
Caliber: .243 Win., .22-250 Rem., 7mm-08 Rem., .308 Win., .338 Federal, .270 WSM, .300 WSM, .25-06 Rem., .270 Win., .30-06 Sprg., 7mm Rem. Mag., .300 Win. Mag.
Magazine: 3-round detachable
Features: match-grade hammer-forged-barrel in blued or no-glare stainless steel finish; forged steel bolt; adjustable single-stage trigger; "Total Control" magazine latch; comes with Weaver-style scope mounting blocks
MSRP: **$1000**

MODEL 85, DELUXE & KODIAK
Action: bolt
Stock: walnut (Deluxe); laminated (Kodiak)
Barrel: 22.5 in. (Deluxe); 21.25 (Kodiak)
Sights: none (Deluxe); adjustable (Kodiak)
Weight: 7.25 lbs. (Deluxe); 8 lbs. (Kodiak)
Caliber: .25-06, .270 Win., .30-06, .370 Sako Mag. (Deluxe); .338 Win. Mag, .375 H&H, (Kodiak)
Magazine: fixed, 4+1 rounds
Features: cold-hammer-forged, match grade barrel; Sako claw extractor; controlled round feed; single stage trigger; double cross bolts; integral tapered scope mounting rail; Deluxe with high-grade walnut stock with palm swell and raised cheek piece, rosewood fore-end & grip caps; Kodiak with laminated hardwood stock
Discontinued

NEW Products: **Savage Rifles**

64 BTV

Action: semi-auto rimfire
Stock: synthetic thumbhole laminate
Barrel: 20.5 in.
Sights: Adjustable notched rear, bead post front
Weight: 5 lbs.
Caliber: .22 LR
Magazine: detachable 10 round
Features: side ejecting
MSRP: **$347**

CUB T PINK

Action: single shot bolt
Stock: pink thumbhole laminate
Barrel: 16.1 in.

Sights: post bead front, rear peep
Weight: 3.5 lbs.
Caliber: .22 S, L, LR
Magazine: single shot
Features: Accutrigger; recoil pad
MSRP: **$280**

64 BTV 22LR

CUB T PINK

MODEL 25 CLASSIC

MODEL 25 LIGHT-WEIGHT VARMINTER THUMB

MODEL 25 LIGHT-WEIGHT VARMINTER

MODEL 25

Action: centerfire bolt
Stock: laminated
Barrel: 22 or 24 in. satin blue
Sights: none, Weaver-style scope bases installed

Weight: 8.35 lbs.
Caliber: .223 Rem., .204 Ruger
Magazine: 4-round detachable box
Features: available in Classic, Lightweight Varminter and Lightweight Varminter Thumbhole models; brown laminated or brown laminated thumbhole stocks
Lightweight Varminter: **$641**
Thumbhole: **$691**
Classic: **$672**

NEW Products: **Sig Sauer Rifles**

SIG 556 SWAT

Action: semi-automatic
Stock: adjustable MAGPUL CTR
Carbine buttstock
Barrel: 16 in.
Sights: flip up combat front and rear
Weight: 8.7 lbs.

Caliber: 5.56mm NATO
Magazine: 30 rounds
Features: alloy Quad Rail forearm;
Nitron X durable, corrosion resistant finish; two position adjustable gas piston operating rod system; flash suppressor
MSRP: $2000

556 SWAT
WITH STOCK EXTENDED

NEW Products: **Smith & Wesson Rifles**

I-BOLT CAMO SS2

I-BOLT STAINLESS STEEL REALTREE AP

Action: bolt
Stock: composite
Barrel: 23, 25-in.
Sights: none

Weight: 6.8 lbs.
Caliber: .25-06, .270, .30-06, 7mm
Mag, .300 Win.
Magazine: 3+1 or 4+1
Features: free-floated Thompson/
Center stainless steel, match grade

barrel; adjustable trigger; three-position, semi-lineal safety; receiver drilled and tapped, Weaver rail provided; checkered Monte Carlo stock in RealTree AP; flush sling swivel mounts
MSRP: $637

MODEL 70

Action: bolt
Stock: walnut or composite
Barrel: cold hammer-forged steel
Sights: none
Weight: not available
Caliber: available in popular calibers
Magazine: 3+1 to 5+1
Features: M.O.A. Trigger System;
Pre-64 Controlled Round Feeding,
3-position safety; blade-type ejector

Super Grade: **$1139–1169**
Featherweight Deluxe: **$799–839**
Sporter Deluxe: **$799–839**
Extreme Weather SS: . . . **$1069–1099**

**MODEL 70
SUPER GRADE**

**MODEL 70
FEATHERWEIGHT DELUXE**

**MODEL 70
SPORTER DELUXE**

**MODEL 70
EXTREME WEATHER SS**

NEW Products: **Airforce Air Rifles**

THE EDGE

Power: precharged pneumatic
Stock: composite
Sights: precision peep sight
Weight: 6.75 lb.
Caliber: .177
Features: ambidextrous cocking knob; adjustable forend; 100 shots per fill; stock adjustable for 35-42 in. length of pull; approved by the Civilian Marksmanship Program for Sporter Class competition
MSRP: **$466–600**

NEW Products: **Crosman Air Rifles**

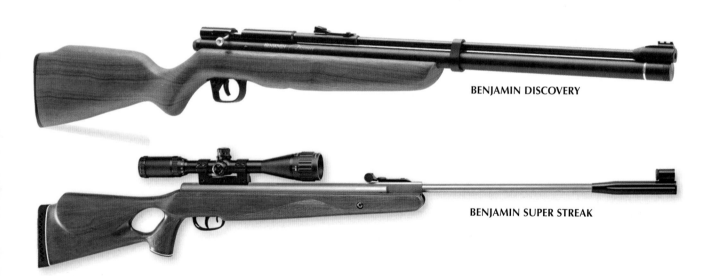

BENJAMIN DISCOVERY

BENJAMIN SUPER STREAK

BENJAMIN DISCOVERY

Power: compressed air or CO2
Stock: walnut
Barrel: 39 in. rifled steel
Sights: open
Weight: 5 lb. 2 oz.
Caliber: .177 or .22
Features: built-in pressure gauge; quick-disconnect fittings; receiver grooved to accept 11mm scope mounts; comes with three-stage hand pump; optional CO2 adapter; Williams Firesight fiber optic front and rear sights
MSRP: **$259–285**

BENJAMIN SUPER STREAK

Power: break barrel/spring piston
Stock: hardwood
Barrel: rifled steel, silver or black
Sights: micro-adjustable rear sight, hooded front sight
Weight: 8.5 lb.
Caliber: .177 or .22
Features: two-stage adjustable trigger; factory mounted CenterPoint Precision Optics 4-16x40mm scope with red/green illuminated Mil Dot reticle; ambidextrous thumbhole stock
Black: **$289–320**
Silver: **$289–320**

POWERLINE 500

POWERLINE 800

POWERLINE 1000

POWERLINE 500 BREAK BARREL
Power: break barrel/spring air
Stock: hardwood
Barrel: rifled steel
Sights: adjustable open
Weight: 6.6 lb.
Caliber: .177
Features: single shot; hooded front and micro-adjustable rear sights; variable 4x32 air rifle scope included
MSRP: $185

POWERLINE 800 BREAK BARREL
Power: break barrel/spring air
Stock: black composite
Barrel: rifled steel
Sights: adjustable open
Weight: 6.6 lb.
Caliber: .177
Features: single shot; hooded front and micro-adjustable rear sights; variable 4x32 air rifle scope included
MSRP: $121

POWERLINE 1000 BREAK BARREL
Power: break barrel/spring air
Stock: sporter-style black composite
Barrel: rifled steel
Sights: adjustable open
Weight: 6.6 lb.
Caliber: .177
Features: single shot; hooded front and micro-adjustable rear sights; variable 3-9x32 air rifle scope included
MSRP: $135

NEW Products: **Gamo Air Rifles**

BIG CAT 1200

WHISPER

BIG CAT 1200

Power: break barrel/spring piston
Stock: synthetic
Sights: 4x32 Air Rifle Scope with rings
Weight: 6.1 lb.
Caliber: .177
Features: 1200 fps with PBA ammunition; all-weather molded synthetic stock
MSRP: $170

WHISPER

Power: break barrel/spring piston
Stock: synthetic
Sights:open adjustable
Weight: 5.3 lb.
Caliber: .177
Features: single shot; integrated noise dampener; second stage adjustable trigger; 1200 fps with PBA or 1000fps with standard lead; all-weather molded synthetic stock; fiber optic front sight with sight guard; fiber optic adjustable rear sight
MSRP: $300

LEGACY SPORTING

Action: inertia operated semi-auto
Stock: walnut
Barrel: 28 in., 30 in.
Chokes: screw-in tubes
Weight: 7.5 lbs.
Bore/Gauge: 12
Magazine: 4+1 rounds
Features: vent target rib; Crio polished blue barrel; chambered for 2-¾ and 3-in. shells, Extended Chrome Crio Choke tubes (C, IC, IM, M, F); AA grade walnut stock; contoured gel recoil pad; black titanium insert with game scene on receiver.
MSRP: $1689–2269

LEGACY SPORTING
12-GAUGE

ULTRA LIGHT
20-GAUGE

ULTRA LIGHT 20-GAUGE

Action: inertia operated semi-auto
Stock: walnut
Barrel: 24 in.
Chokes: screw-in tube
Weight: 5.2 lbs.
Bore/Gauge: 20
Magazine: 2+1 rounds
Features: carbon-fiber vent rib; Crio barrel; chambered for 2-¾ and 3-in. shells; Crio tube chokes - IC, M, F; WeatherCoat finished stock; lightest 20-gauge auto made!
MSRP: $1539

NEW Products: **Beretta Shotguns**

SV10 PERENNIA

SV10 PERENNIA

Action: over/under
Stock: walnut
Barrel: 26 or 28 in.
Chokes: screw-in tubes
Weight: 7.3 lbs.
Bore/Gauge: 12
Magazine: none
Features: Optima-Bore high-performance cold, hammer-forged barrels; long guided extractors; chrome-lined bore and chamber; manual or automatic shell extraction; single selective trigger group; automatic safety; Optimachoke choke tubes; available with or without Kick-Off technology; semi-beavertail fore-end with constant fit fore-end iron; 3rd generation Beretta Over/Under to be launched
MSRP (with Kick-Off): **$3650**
(without Kick-Off): **$3250**

UGB25 XCEL

Action: break-open semi-auto
Stock: walnut
Barrel: 30 in.
Chokes: screw-in tubes
Weight: 8.1-9 lbs.
Bore/Gauge: 12
Magazine: 1 (in side carrier)
Features: short barrel recoil system; light alloy receiver; Optima-Bore barrel with lengthened forcing cone; locking system with break-open action for safe

operation — second round is visible in side cartridge carrier; 2¾ in. chambers; select walnut stock with water-resistant finish; adjustable drop, cast-on and cast-off; fore-end with extended checkered configuration; comes in case with accesories
MSRP: **$3500–3650**

UGB25 XCEL

NEW Products: **Browning Shotguns**

Weight: 8 lbs. 13 ozs., 8 lbs. 15 ozs.
Bore/Gauge: 12
Magazine: none
Features: barrel set: single barrel with adjustable Unsingle Rib and over/under barrel; Monolock hinge low-profile receiver; Reverse Striker ignition system; 4 Invector Plus Midas Grade choke tubes; HiViz Pro-Comp fiber optic sights; gloss-finish Monte Carlo grade III/IV walnut stocks; aluminum case
MSRP: **$3999**

CYNERGY CLASSIC TRAP UNSINGLE COMBO

Action: single-shot and over/under
Stock: walnut
Barrel: 32/34, 32/32, 30/34 and 30/3-in. combinations
Chokes: interchangable tubes

AS YOUTH SELECT

Action: semi-auto
Stock: walnut
Barrel: 22 in.
Chokes: M, IC, F
Weight: 6.7 lbs.
Bore/Gauge: 20
Magazine: 4
Features: 3-in. chamber; blued finish; magazine cut-off for single shot loading; extra O rings in box; Trio recoil pad with shims
MSRP: **$479**

NEW Products: **Franchi Shotguns**

HIGHLANDER - COLOR CASE HARDENED

Action: side-by-side
Stock: walnut
Barrel: 26 in.
Chokes: IC, M
Weight: 6 lbs.
Bore/Gauge: 20
Features: box-lock action; automatic safety and ejectors; single trigger; fine scroll engraving; A-grade walnut stock
MSRP: **$2799**

NEW Products: Franchi Shotguns

I-12 SPORTING

Action: inertia operated semi-auto
Stock: walnut
Barrel: 30 in.
Chokes: screw-in tubes
Weight: 6.5 lbs.
Bore/Gauge: 12
Magazine: 4+1 rounds
Features: ported, polished blue barrel; lengthened forcing cone; chambered for 2-¾ and 3-in. shells; screw-in extended choke tubes (C, IC, IM, M, F); 10-mm target rib; Twin Shock Absorber recoil reducing system; WeatherCoat walnut stock
MSRP: **$1379**

I-12 SPORTING
12-GAUGE 30

I-12 UPLAND HUNTER
12-GAUGE 26

I-12 UPLAND HUNTER

Action: inertia operated semi-auto
Stock: walnut
Barrel: 26 in.
Chokes: 5 tubes - C, IC, IM, M, F
Weight: 6.3 lbs.
Bore/Gauge: 12
Magazine: 4+1 rounds
Features: vent rib; polished blue barrel; chambered for 2-¾ and 3-in. shells; Twin Shock Absorber recoil reducing system.
MSRP: **$1169**

PARDNER WATERFOWL GUN

Action: break-open single shot
Stock: walnut
Barrel: 30 in.
Chokes: screw-in tubes
Weight: 9 lbs.
Bore/Gauge: 10
Magazine: none
Features: blued carbon steel action and barrel; transfer bar safety; modified WinChoke tubes; bead front sight; ventilated recoil pad; pistol grip stock; sling swivel studs.
MSRP: **$228**

**PARDNER
WATERFOWL GUN**

**TOPPER
TRAP GUN**

**ULTRA LIGHT
SLUG HUNTER**

TOPPER TRAP GUN

Action: break-open single shot
Stock: walnut
Barrel: 30 in.
Chokes: screw-in tube
Weight: 7 lbs.
Bore/Gauge: 12 ga.
Magazine: none
Features: blued carbon steel barrel with ventilated rib; electroless nickel coated carbon steel receiver; stainless steel IM extended choke tube; double

white bead sighting system; select walnut checkered Monte Carlo stock Pachmayr trap recoil pad
MSRP: **$362**

ULTRA LIGHT SLUG HUNTER

Action: break-open single shot
Stock: hardwood
Barrel: 24-in.
Chokes: none
Weight: 5.25 lbs.
Bore/Gauge: 12, 20
Magazine: none
Features: blued, polished carbon steel action and barrel; 24-in. Ultragon rifling; transfer bar safety; hammer extension; barrel with installed scope base; ventilated recoil pad; walnut-stained, Monte Carlo pistol-grip stock
MSRP: **$194**

NEW Products: **Mossberg Shotguns**

500 J.I.C. (JUST IN CASE) MARINER

Action: pump
Stock: black synthetic
Barrel: 18.5 in.

Chokes: cylinder bore
Weight: 5.5 lb.
Bore/Gauge: 12 ga.
Magazine: 4+1 capacity
Features: Marinecoat finish barrel;

3-inch chamber; pistol grip; impact-resistant tube with strap, multi-tool and knife; 28.75-in. overall length
MSRP: **$547**

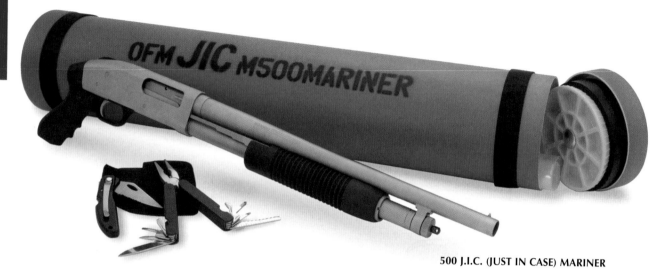

500 J.I.C. (JUST IN CASE) MARINER

500 ROLLING THUNDER

500 SUPER BANTAM SLUGSTER

500 ROLLING THUNDER 6-SHOT

Action: pump
Stock: black synthetic
Barrel: 23 in.
Chokes: cylinder bore
Weight: 5.75 lb.
Bore/Gauge: 12 ga.
Magazine: 4+1 capacity
Features: barrel with heat shield and barrel stabilizer; 3-inch chamber; pistol grip; 33.5-in. overall length
MSRP: **$471**

500 SUPER BANTAM SLUGSTER

Action: pump
Stock: synthetic
Barrel: 24 in.
Chokes: none
Weight: 5.25 lb.
Bore/Gauge: 20 ga.
Magazine: 4+1 capacity
Features: fully rifled bore; 3-in. chamber; ISB sights; blue or RealTree AP finish; stock with 12-13-in. adjustable LOP; gun lock
MSRP: . . . . **from $354**

NEW Products: **Mossberg Shotguns**

500 SUPER BANTAM TURKEY

Action: pump
Stock: synthetic
Barrel: 22 in.
Chokes: X-Full
Weight: 5.25 lb.
Bore/Gauge: 20 ga.

Magazine: 4+1 capacity
Features: 3-inch chamber; adjustable FO sights; adjustable synthetic stock with 12-13-in. adjustable LOP, available in Mossy Oak Obsession or RealTree Hardwoods HD green finish; gun lock
MSRP: **$410**

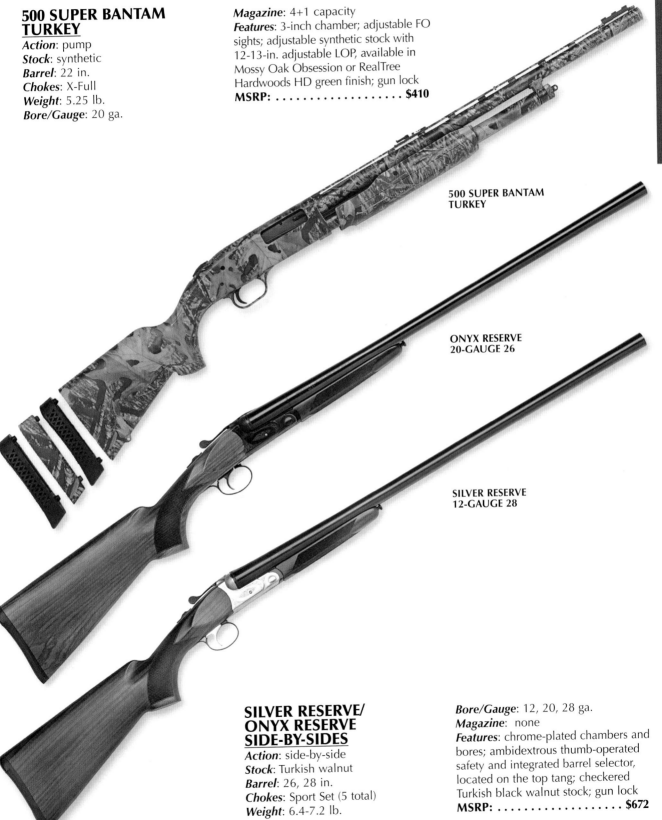

500 SUPER BANTAM TURKEY

ONYX RESERVE 20-GAUGE 26

SILVER RESERVE 12-GAUGE 28

SILVER RESERVE/ ONYX RESERVE SIDE-BY-SIDES

Action: side-by-side
Stock: Turkish walnut
Barrel: 26, 28 in.
Chokes: Sport Set (5 total)
Weight: 6.4-7.2 lb.

Bore/Gauge: 12, 20, 28 ga.
Magazine: none
Features: chrome-plated chambers and bores; ambidextrous thumb-operated safety and integrated barrel selector, located on the top tang; checkered Turkish black walnut stock; gun lock
MSRP: **$672**

NEW Products: **Remington Shotguns**

MODEL 870 WINGMASTER 100TH ANNIVERSARY COMMEMORATIVE EDITION

Action: pump
Stock: American walnut
Barrel: 28 in.
Chokes: screw-in tubes
Weight: 7 lbs.
Bore/Gauge: 12
Magazine: 3+1
Features: hammer-forged, carbon steel barrel with vent rib; limited edition, one-year issue with fine-line embellishments on receiver, left side with gold-inlayed centennial logo banner — "100 Years of Remington Pump Shotguns" flushing pheasant with anniversary years 1908–2008; high polish blued finish; gold-plated trigger; 3 RemChoke tubes: IC, M, F; high-gloss, B-grade American walnut stock
MSRP: **$1035**

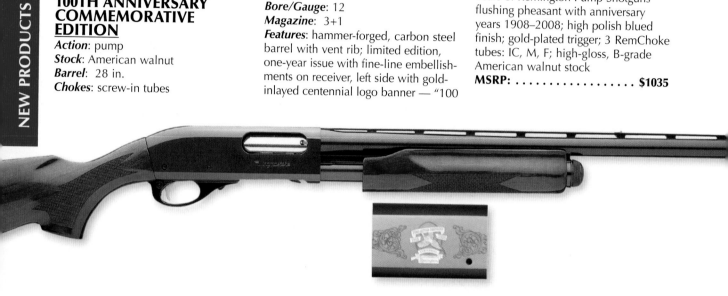

NEW Products: **Rossi Shotguns**

TURKEY GUN

Action: break-open single shot
Stock: hardwood
Barrel: 24 in.
Chokes: screw-in tube
Weight: 6.25 lbs.
Bore/Gauge: 12 ga.
Magazine: none
Features: 3.5-in. chamber; button rifled; matte blue finish; fiber optic sights; drilled and tapped barrel with included scope mount base; ambidextrous operation; removable Briley Extended Turkey Choke; installed sling swivels; satin oil-finished exotic wood, pistol grip stock; Taurus Security System
MSRP: **$187**

NEW Products: **Tristar Sporting Arms Shotguns**

**BRITTANY CLASSIC
SIDE BY SIDE**

COBRA PUMP

COBRA TACTICAL PUMP

BRITTANY CLASSIC SIDE BY SIDE

Action: side-by-side
Stock: hardwood
Barrel: 27 in.
Chokes: screw-in tubes
Weight: 6.3-6.7 lbs.
Bore/Gauge: 12, 16, 20, 28, .410 ga.
Magazine: none
Features: chrome lined barrels; solid raised barrel rib; engraved, case-colored one piece frame; auto selective ejectors; single selective trigger; top tang safety; 3 Beretta-style choke tubes (IC, M, F); satin oil finished, rounded pistol grip stock
Discontinued

COBRA PUMP

Action: pump
Stock: black synthetic
Barrel: 28 in.
Chokes: screw-in tubes
Weight: 6.7 lbs.
Bore/Gauge: 12 ga.
Magazine: 5+1
Features: 3-in. chamber; single unit receiver to keep out dirt and weather; vent rib with matted sight plane; 3 Beretta-style tubes (IC, M, F)
Discontinued

COBRA TACTICAL PUMP

Action: pump
Stock: black synthetic
Barrel: 20 in.
Chokes: screw-in tubes
Weight: 6.9 lbs.
Bore/Gauge: 12 ga.
Magazine: 5+1 rounds
Features: return spring in forearm, allows user to pull back on the forearm to eject the shell, spring returns the forearm back to position and shucks another shell into the chamber; 3 Beretta-style tubes (IC, M, F); matte black, separate pistol grip folding stock
MSRP: **$349**

PA-08 KNOXX HD

Action: pump
Stock: black synthetic
Barrel: 18 in.
Chokes: fixed cylinder
Weight: 7 lbs.
Bore/Gauge: 12 ga.
Magazine: 4+1 rounds
Features: aircraft-grade alloy receiver; recoil reducing, 4 in. adjustable Knoxx SpecOps pistol grip stock; designed for home protection
Discontinued

PA-08 KNOXX HD

PA-08 KNOXX
STRUTTER X CAMO

PA-08 KNOXX STRUTTER X CAMO

Action: pump
Stock: synthetic
Barrel: 24 in.
Chokes: adjustable integral
Weight: 7 lbs.
Bore/Gauge: 12 ga.
Magazine: 4+1 rounds
Features: aircraft-grade alloy receiver; heavy-duty dual bar slide action; vented top rib with fiber optic front sight; recoil reducing, adjustable Knoxx SpecOps pistol grip stock in Apparition Excel camo; integral Multi-choke System (M, F, XF)
Discontinued

SA-08 UPLAND

Action: autoloader
Stock: walnut
Barrel: 26 or 28 in.
Chokes: adjustable integral
Weight: 6 or 6.75 lbs.
Bore/Gauge: 20, 12 ga.
Magazine: 4+1 rounds
Features: adjustable gas system; screw on valve caps; chambers $7/8$ oz. to 3-in. loads; integral Multi-choke System (IC, M, F); oil-finish walnut stock
MSRP: **$669**

SA-08 UPLAND

SA-08 YOUTH

SA-08 YOUTH

Action: autoloader
Stock: walnut
Barrel: 26 in.
Chokes: adjustable integral
Weight: 5.75 lbs.
Bore/Gauge: 20 ga.
Magazine: 4+1 rounds
Features: vented top rib; dual valve system; matte black metal finish; integral Multi-choke System (IC, M, F); oil-finish walnut stock with 12 $1/2$-in. length of pull to fit women and younger shooters
MSRP: **$669**

SPEED PUMP BLACK SHADOW FIELD

Action: pump
Stock: composite
Barrel: 26, 28 in.
Chokes: screw-in tubes
Weight: 7 lbs., 7.25 lbs.
Bore/Gauge: 12
Magazine: 5+1
Features: 4-lug rotary bolt design; chrome plated barrels; fires all factory 2¾ in. and 3 in. steel, tungsten, bismuth and lead loads; Invector-Plus choke system
MSRP: **$359**

SPEED PUMP BLACK SHADOW FIELD

SPEED PUMP DEFENDER

SPEED PUMP WALNUT FIELD

SPEED PUMP DEFENDER

Action: pump
Stock: composite
Barrel: 18 in.
Chokes: open
Weight: 6.5 lbs.
Bore/Gauge: 12
Magazine: 5+1
Features: 4-lug rotary bolt design; chrome plated barrels; handles buckshot or rifled slugs; non-glare metal surfaces; deeply grooved forearm
MSRP: **$319**

SPEED PUMP WALNUT FIELD

Action: pump
Stock: walnut
Barrel: 26, 28 in.
Chokes: Invector-Plus system (I, M, F)
Weight: 7 lbs., 7.25 lbs.
Bore/Gauge: 12
Magazine: 4+1
Features: 4-lug rotary bolt design; chrome plated barrels for steel or tungsten shot; forearm with cut checkering; gloss-finished walnut stock
Discontinued

CW .45 ACP

Action: autoloader
Grips: textured polymer
Barrel: 3.64 in.
Sights: adjustable
Weight: 19.7 oz.
Caliber: .45 ACP
Capacity: 6+1 rounds
Features: DAO; lock breech; Browning
-type recoil lug; passive striker block;
no magazine disconnect; drift adjust-
able white bar-dot combat rear sight,
pinned-in polymer front sight
MSRP: **$606**

PM .45 ACP

Action: autoloader
Grips: polymer
Barrel: 3.14 in.
Sights: adjustable
Weight: 17.3 oz.
Caliber: .45 ACP
Capacity: 5+1 rounds
Features: DAO; lock breech;
Browning-type recoil lug; passive
striker block; no magazine disconnect;
drift adjustable, white bar-dot combat
sights (tritium night sights optional)
MSRP: **$855–974**

CW .45 ACP

PM .45 ACP

NEW Products: **North American Arms Handguns**

PUG MINI-REVOLVER
Action: revolver
Grips: rubber
Barrel: 1 in.
Sights: Tritium or white dot
Weight: 6.4 oz.
Caliber: .22 Mag
Capacity: 5 rounds
Features: XS sighting system
MSRP: $299–319

NEW Products: **Para USA Handguns**

1911 LIMITED

P14-45

1911 LIMITED
Action: autoloader
Barrel: 5 in. ramped, match, stainless
Sights: fiber optic front, adjustable rear
Weight: 40 oz.
Caliber: .45 ACP
Capacity: 8+1 rounds
Features: SA; stainless steel receiver; ambidextrous slide-lock safety; sterling stainless finish; two 8-round magazines included
MSRP: $1249

P14-45
Action: autoloader
Grips: Ultra Slim polymer
Barrel: 5 in. ramped, match, stainless
Sights: 3-white dot fixed
Weight: 40 oz.
Caliber: .45 ACP
Capacity: 14+1 rounds
Features: SA; carbon steel receiver; Para Triple Safety System (slide lock, firing pin and grip); Covert Black Para Kote finish; two 14-round magazines included (10-round magazines available in those states with restricted capacity)
MSRP: $919

P14-45 GUN RIGHTS

Action: autoloader
Grips: polymer
Barrel: 5 in.
Sights: fixed rear, fiber optic front
Weight: 40 oz.
Caliber: .45 ACP
Capacity: 14+1 rounds (10-round magazine available)
Features: SA; ramped, match, stainless barrel; stainless Classic Satin finish; specially made to support the N.R.A.'s Institute for Legislative Action
MSRP: **$1149**

PDA (PERSONAL DEFENSE ASSISTANT)

Action: autoloader
Grips: cocobolo wood
Barrel: 3 in. ramped, match, stainless
Sights: 3-dot tritium night sights
Weight: 24 oz.
Caliber: .45, 9mm
Capacity: 6+1 rounds
Features: DA; stainless slide; Covert Black frame; Para Triple Safety System (slide lock, firing pin and grip); two 6-round (.45) or 8-round (9mm) magazines; PDA logo on grips
PDA 9MM: **$1219**

P14-45
GUN RIGHTS

PDA .45

PDA 9MM

NEW Products: **Para USA Handguns**

PXT SSP

**SUPER HAWG
HIGH CAPACITY**

**SUPER HAWG
SINGLE STACK**

PXT SSP

Action: autoloader
Grips: rubber
Barrel: 5 in.
Sights: 3-dot white fixed
Weight: 39 oz.
Caliber: .45 ACP
Capacity: 8+1 rounds
Features: SA; ramped, match, stainless barrrel; Para Triple Safety System (slide lock, firing pin and grip); Covert Black Para Kote finish; two 8-round magazines
MSRP: **$899**

SUPER HAWG HIGH CAPACITY

Action: autoloader
Grips: polymer
Barrel: 6 in.
Sights: fiber optic front, adjustable rear
Weight: 41 oz.
Caliber: .45 ACP
Capacity: 14+1 rounds
Features: SA; ramped, match, stainless barrel; Classic Stainless finish; ambidextrous Para Triple Safety System (slide lock, firing pin and grip); two 14-round magazines included (10-round magazines available in those states with restricted capacity)
MSRP: **$1369**

SUPER HAWG SINGLE STACK

Action: autoloader
Grips: Double Diamond Checkered Cocobolo
Barrel: 6 in.
Sights: adjustable
Weight: 40 oz.
Caliber: .45 ACP
Capacity: 8+1 rounds
Features: SA; ramped, match, stainless barrel; Classic Stainless finish; ambidextrous Para Triple Safety System (slide lock, firing pin and grip); fiber optic front, adjustable rear sights; two 8-round magazines
MSRP: **$1369**

.22 CHARGER

Action: autoloader
Grips: black laminate
Barrel: 10 in.
Sights: N/A
Weight: 56 oz.
Caliber: .22 LR
Capacity: 10 rounds
Features: cross bolt safety; extended magazine release; combination Weaver-style and "tip-off" sight mount; bipod and gun rug with Ruger logo included
MSRP: **$380**

LCP (LIGHTWEIGHT COMPACT PISTOL)

Action: autoloader
Grips: integral
Barrel: 2.75 in.
Sights: none
Weight: 9.4 oz.
Caliber: .380
Capacity: 6+1 rounds
Features: through-hardened blued steel slide; glass-filled nylon frame height 3.6 in., width .82 in.; includes soft case
MSRP: **$347**

.22 CHARGER

LCP

NEW Products: **Sig Sauer Handguns**

P250

Action: locked breech DAO semiauto
Grips: polymer
Barrel: variable length
Sights: SIGLITE® Three Dot Night Sights
Weight: 24.6-30.8 oz.
Caliber: .45ACP, .40 S&W, .357 SIG, 9mm
Capacity: variable
Features: steel receiver with Nitron or two-tone finish; reversible magazine release; ambidextrous slide release; interchangable mechanism allows immediate change in caliber and size (subcompact, compact and full); integral accessory rail; interchangeable grips
MSRP: **$570–870**

M&P9L

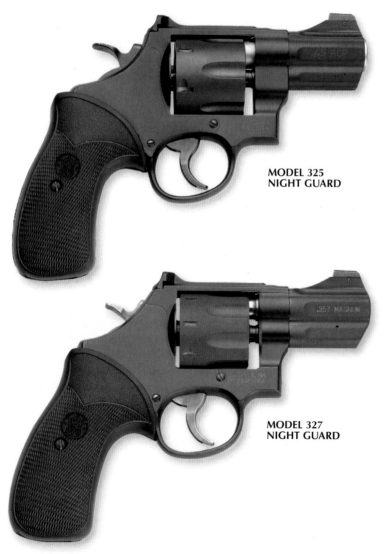

MODEL 325
NIGHT GUARD

MODEL 327
NIGHT GUARD

M&P9L

Action: striker fire action
Grips: synthetic
Barrel: 5 in.
Sights: open
Weight: 25.2 oz.
Caliber: 9mm
Capacity: 17 rounds
Features: through-hardened black Melonite stainless steel barrel; Zytel polymer frame reinforced with steel chassis; loaded chamber indicator on top of slide; ambidextrous slide stop; reversible magazine release; steel white-dot dovetail front, steel Novak Lo-Mount carry rear sights, (tritium sights available); enlarged trigger guard; 3 interchangeable grip sizes
MSRP: **$758**

MODEL 325 NIGHT GUARD

Action: single/double action revolver
Grips: synthetic
Barrel: 2.5 in.
Sights: open
Weight: 28 oz.
Caliber: .45 ACP
Capacity: 6 rounds
Features: scandium alloy frame; stainless PVD cylinder; matte black finish; XS Sight 24/7 Standard Dot Tritium front, Cylinder & Slide Extreme Duty Fixed back sights; Pachmayr Compac Custom grips
MSRP: **$1153**

MODEL 327 NIGHT GUARD

Action: single/double action revolver
Grips: synthetic
Barrel: 2.5 in.
Sights: open
Weight: 27.6 oz.
Caliber: .357 Magnum, .38 S&W Special
Capacity: 8 rounds
Features: scandium alloy frame; stainless PVD cylinder; matte black finish; XS Sight 24/7 Standard Dot Tritium front, Cylinder & Slide Extreme Duty Fixed back sights; Pachmayr Compac Custom grips
MSRP: **$1153**

MODEL 329 NIGHT GUARD

Action: single/double action revolver
Grips: synthetic
Barrel: 2.5 in.
Sights: XS Sight 24/7 Standard Dot Tritium front, Cylinder & Slide Extreme Duty Fixed back
Weight: 29.3 oz.
Caliber: .44 Magnum, .44 Special
Capacity: 6 rounds
Features: scandium alloy frame; stainless PVD cylinder; matte black finish
MSRP: **$1153**

MODEL 386 NIGHT GUARD

Action: single/double action revolver
Grips: Pachmayr Compac Custom
Barrel: 2.5 in.
Sights: XS Sight 24/7 Standard Dot Tritium front, Cylinder & Slide Extreme Duty Fixed back
Weight: 24.5 oz.
Caliber: .357 Magnum, .38 Special +P
Capacity: 7 rounds
Features: scandium alloy frame; stainless PVD cylinder; matte black finish
MSRP: **$1074**

MODEL 396 NIGHT GUARD

Action: single/double action revolver
Grips: Pachmayr Compac Custom
Barrel: 2.5 in.
Sights: XS Sight 24/7 Standard Dot Tritium front, Cylinder & Slide Extreme Duty Fixed back
Weight: 24.5 oz.
Caliber: .44 Special
Capacity: 5 rounds
Features: scandium alloy frame; stainless PVD cylinder; matte black finish
MSRP: **$1074**

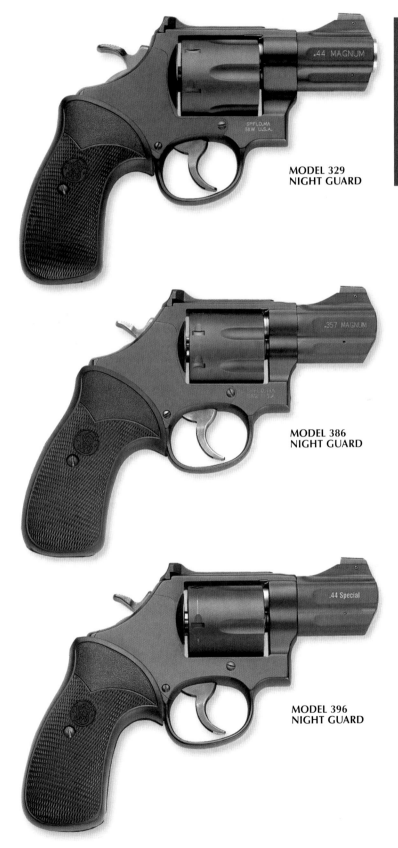

MODEL 329
NIGHT GUARD

MODEL 386
NIGHT GUARD

MODEL 396
NIGHT GUARD

NEW Products: **Smith & Wesson Handguns**

**MODEL 27
CLASSIC**

MODEL 327PD

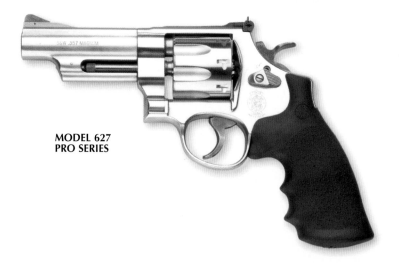

**MODEL 627
PRO SERIES**

MODEL 27 CLASSIC

Action: single/double action revolver
Grips: checkered square butt walnut
Barrel: 6.5 in.
Sights: pinned partridge front, micro adjustable rear with cross serrations
Caliber: .357 Magnum, .38 S&W Special
Capacity: 6 rounds
Features: carbon steel; classic style thumbpiece; color case wide spur hammer; color case serrated target trigger; High Bright Blue or Bright Nickel finish
MSRP: **$1090**

MODEL 327PD

Action: single/double action revolver
Grips: slip-resistant synthetic rubber
Barrel: 4 in.
Sights: red Hi-Viz pinned front, fully adjustable V-notch rear
Weight: 24.3 oz.
Caliber: 357 Magnum, .38 S&W Special + P
Capacity: 8 rounds
Features: lightweight scandium alloy frame; titanium cylinder; black matte finish
MSRP: **$1264**

MODEL 627 PRO SERIES

Action: single/double action revolver
Grips: synthetic
Barrel: 4 in.
Sights: interchangeable front, adjustable rear
Weight: 41.2 oz.
Caliber: .357 Magnum, .38 S&W Special
Capacity: 8 rounds
Features: precision crowned muzzle, chamfered charge holes, bossed mainspring, internal lock, cable lock
MSRP: **$1059**

NEW Products: **Springfield Handguns**

9MM ENHANCED MICRO PISTOL (EMP)

Action: autoloader
Grips: thinline cocobolo hardwood
Barrel: 3-in. stainless steel match grade, fully supported ramp
Sights: fixed low profile combat rear; dovetail front, tritium 3-dot
Weight: 33 oz.
Caliber: .40
Capacity: two 9-round, stainless steel magazines
Features: dual-spring recoil system with full-length guide rod; long aluminum match-grade trigger; forged steel slide with satin finish
MSRP: $1060–1400

NEW Products: **Taurus Handguns**

24/7 OSS STAINLESS STEEL

Action: single/double action autoloader
Grips: checkered polymer with Ambidextrous Indexed Memory Pads
Barrel: 5.25 in. Match Grade steel
Sights: Novak rear night sight option
Weight: 29.1 oz.
Caliber: .45 ACP, .40 S&W., 9mm
Capacity: 10+1, 12+1, 15+1 or 17+1 rounds
Features: integral Picatinny rail system accommodates slide-on lights or laser sights; SA/DA indicator on the rear of the slide that shows whether the pistol is in "cocked" or "decocked" mode, front slide serrations and reversible magazine release combine for increased versatility; Taurus Security System allows users to securely lock the gun
MSRP: . . . . $623-$686

MODEL 709B

MODEL 709

Action: double action autoloader
Grips: checkered polymer
Barrel: 6 in., stainless steel or black matte finish
Sights: fixed
Weight: 19 oz.
Caliber: 9mm
Capacity: 8+1 rounds
Features: 6 in. long and less than 1 in. thick; visual loaded chamber indicator; Taurus Security System allows users to securely lock the gun
MSRP: **$459–475**

MODEL 709SS

MODEL 856

Action: revolver
Grips: soft rubber
Barrel: 2 in.
Sights: fixed
Weight: 13.2 oz.
(Hy-Lite magnesium frame)
Caliber: .38 Special, .38 Special +P
Capacity: 6 rounds
Features: offered in several configurations, including a Hy-Lite magnesium model in .38 Special and standard version (.38 Special +P) in blue or matte stainless; Taurus Security System allows users to securely lock the gun
MSRP: **$441–488**

MODEL
856B2

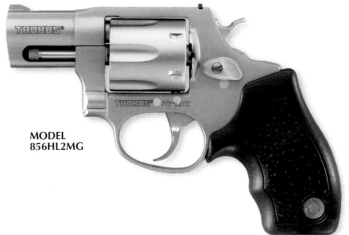

MODEL
856HL2MG

MODEL
856SS2

NEW Products: **Taylor's & Company Handguns**

SMOKE WAGON

Action: single-action revolver
Grips: checkered wood
Barrel: 4.75 or 5.5 in.
Sights: open rear sight groove, wide angle front sight blade
Weight: unavailable
Caliber: .38 Special, .357 Mag., .45 LC, .44-40
Capacity: 6 rounds
Features: low profile hammer; deluxe edition model includes custom tuning, custom hammer and base pin springs, trigger-spring at 3 pounds, jig-cut positive angles on trigger and sears, wire bolt and trigger springs
MSRP: . . . .(standard) **$485**
. . . . (deluxe) **$620**

NEW Products: **Walther Handguns**

PPS (POLICE PISTOL SLIM)

Action: Striker Fire Action autoloader,
Grips: black polymer
Barrel: 3.2 in.
Sights: 3-dot low profile contoured
Weight: 19.4 oz. (9mm), 20.8 oz (.40)
Caliber: 9mm, .40 S&W
Capacity: 6 and 7 round magazines (9mm), 5 and 6 round magazines (.40)
Features: Striker Fire Action pre-cocked; flat slide stop lever; Picatinny-style accessory; adjustable grip length and size; Walther QuickSafe technology; loaded chamber indicator on top of slide; cocking indicator on rear of slide; optional 8-round magazine available for 9mm and 7-round magazine for .40 S&W; Pachmayr Compac Custom grips
MSRP: **$713**

SHADOW

Lock: in-line
Stock: black reinforced synthetic
Barrel: 26 in.
Sights: open
Weight: 7.8 lbs.
Bore/Caliber: .50
Features: Green Mountain barrel, drilled and tapped for scope mounting; break-open action; black anodized receiver; stainless steel internal parts; 209 ignition; installed sling studs; rebound hammer; Monte Carlo-style stock with checkered grip and checkered Beartail forearm
Discontinued

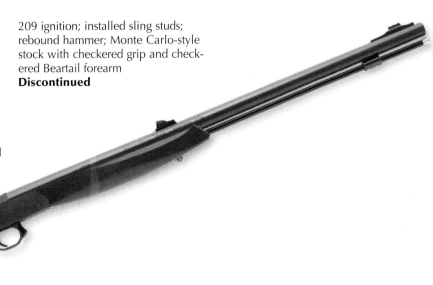

NEW Products: **Lyman Black Powder**

MUSTANG BREAKAWAY

Lock: in-line
Stock: hardwood
Barrel: 26 in.
Sights: fiber optic front and rear
Weight: 7.5 lbs.
Bore/Caliber: .50
Features: ½8-in. twist rifling; tang mounted shotgun-style safety; magnetized primer retention system; drilled and tapped for scope; Pachmayr "decelerator" recoil pad
MSRP: **$500**

NEW Products: **Pedersoli Black Powder**

GIBBS SHOTGUN
Lock: standard percussion
Stock: walnut
Barrel: 30.7 in.
Weight: 8.38 lbs.
Bore/Caliber: 12 ga.
Features: octagonal to round barrel; case hardened color-finished lock; grip and forend caps with ebony inserts; pistol grip stock
MSRP: **$1214**

SWISS MATCH STANDARD FLINTLOCK
Lock: flint
Stock: walnut
Barrel: 29.5 in.
Sights: adjustable

Weight: 16.9 lbs.
Bore/Caliber: .4
Features: octagonal; rust-brown finished 1:47 twist barrel; case-hardened color lock; double set trigger; steel ramrod; hook-shaped steel buttplate; moveable rear sight with windage and elevation adjustments
MSRP: **$2559**

GIBBS SHOTGUN

SWISS MATCH FLINTLOCK

HOWDAH HUNTER PISTOL

HOWDAH HUNTER PISTOL
Lock: standard percussion
Stock: walnut
Barrel: 11.25 in. double
Weight: 4.41-5.07 lbs.

Bore/Caliber: 20 ga. or .50 cal.
Features: engraved locks with wild animals scenes; case-hardened color finish; checkered walnut pistol grip with steel butt cap
MSRP: **$649**

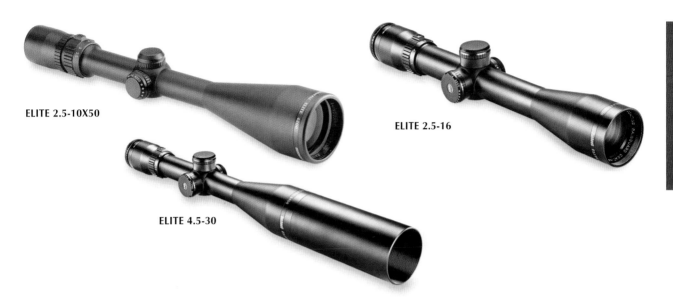

ELITE 2.5-10X50

ELITE 2.5-16

ELITE 4.5-30

ELITE 6500 SERIES

Features: a 6.5x magnification range (1:6.5 ratio from low to high power); push/pull turrets with resettable zero for easy sighting-in.; extended range of windage and elevation travel (60 inches on the 2.5-16x models), with .25 MOA quick adjust clicks, suitable for a broad range of game and distances; all models have a one-piece, 30mm tube to deliver plenty of light, and up to 4 inches of eye relief and a finer Multi-X reticle (Mil Dot versions of each model are also available); each model has side parallax adjustment; the 2.5x models can be adjusted from 10 yards to infinity and the 4.5 x models adjusts from 25 yards to infinity

Model	Field of View @100 yds.	Eye Relief (in.)	Click Value @ 100 yds.	Length (in.)	Weight (oz.)	Reticle	MSRP
2.5-16x42	41 ft @ 2.5 x 6.55 ft. @ 16x	3.9	0.25 in.	13.5	17.3	Multi-X or Mil-Dot	$718
2.5-16x50	42 ft @ 2.5 x 7 ft. @ 16x	3.9	0.25 in.	13.5	21.0	Multi-X or Mil-Dot	$807
4.5-30x50	21.6 ft @ 4.5 x 3.4 ft. @ 30x	4.0	0.25 in.	13.5	21.0	Multi-X or Mil-Dot	$936

VIDEOSCOPE

This compact, lightweight video camera with a 1.5-in. color display for preview and playback is designed to mount on top of a riflescope so users can digitally record images and activity.

Size: weight under 8 ounces, and less than 7 inches long.

Features: records up to 30 minutes of VGA quality digital video with its 1GB internal memory and rechargeable lithium-ion battery; the camera is waterproof and designed to withstand the recoil of .375 H&H rifles and 12 gauge shotguns; it can be quickly attached or removed from the riflescope; the 5x lens and 5-way button pad for easy operation; the VideoScope comes with a USB cable and no special software is required for downloading; includes AC and DC adaptors for recharging the battery, and 1-in. mounting rings for attachment to most riflescopes

MSRP: $315

VIDEOSCOPE ON SCOPE

NEW Products: **CenterPoint Precision Optics Scopes**

ADVENTURE 2-7x32

POWER CLASS 1TL 3-9x42 MM

ADVENTURE CLASS 2-7x32MM

Adventure Class 2-7x32mm combination scope for shotgun and muzzle-loader hunting. 2x to 7x magnification allows the shooter to dial in the target at closer distances; the 5.2 inches of eye relief allows for a comfortable shooting position for heavy recoil rifles. The 2-7x32mm is designed for all light conditions.
Features: Mil-Dot reticle illuminates red or green at various brightness settings;

angled front objective for built-in sun or rain protection; true hunter windage and elevation dials; flip open lens covers; medium-profile Weaver-style rings; CenterPoint limited lifetime warranty
MSRP: **$160**

POWER CLASS 1TL SERIES

Power Class 1TL Series scopes include 3-9x42mm and 1.5-6x44mm scopes.
Features: dual illuminated reticles; One Touch Lightning (1TL) technology with +/- brightness control; low profile

design; completely sealed base; nitrogen filled, European-style sealed 30mm, one-piece waterproof, shockproof and fog-proof tube; multi-coated lens surfaces; angled objective and integral windage and elevation housing with dual-sealed o-rings; target adjustable windage and elevation dials with zero locking and resetting capability; side focus parallax adjustment; etched glass floating duplex reticle; flip open lens covers; sunshade
MSRP: **$253**

NEW Products: **Columbia Sportswear Co. Scopes**

TIMBERLINE PHG 3-12x40

TIMBERLINE PHG 3-12x50

TIMBERLINE PHG

Performance Hunting Gear (PHG) riflescopes (manufactured by Kruger Optics).
Features: one-piece aircraft grade aluminum dry nitrogen filled body construction; fully-coated optics; water tested for reliable, fog-free performance; re-settable windage and elevation adjustments in accurate ¼ –minute clicks; armored power selector rings with ribbed surfaces
3-12x40: **$200**
4-16x40SF: **$250**

KONUSPRO M-30 SERIES

Features: black matte finish 30mm nitrogen-purged, fogproof and water-proof tubes; lockable tactical turrets, $1/8$ minute audible tactical adjustments; lockable fast-focus eyeball; greater windage/elevation and resolution; illuminated Blue Mil. Dot. Reticle; laser-etched glass reticle system; flip-up eye covers and detachable sunshade

4.5-16x40mm:	**$470–550**
6.5-25x44mm:	**$530–580**
8.5-32x52mm:	**$600–640**

ILLUMINATED VX-L 3.5-10x50 MM

PRISMATIC 1x14 MM

ILLUMINATED VX-L SERIES

The Illuminated VX-Ls feature Leupold 11-setting illumination system with variable intensity rheostat. The illuminated reticle and Light Optimization Profile provide low-light performance with reduced weight. Available with German#4 Dot and Boone & Crockett illuminated reticle options.

Features: Leupold Index Matched Lens System; DiamondCoat lens coatings; Leupold Second Generation waterproofing; dual-spring titanium nitride coated stainless steel adjustment system.

3.5-10x50mm:	**$1085**
4.5-14x50mm:	**$1185**
3.5-10x56mm:	**$1310**
4.5-14x56mm LR:	**$1310**

PRISMATIC 1x14 MM HUNTING

The Prismatic 1x14mm Hunting scope has an etched glass reticle that remains functional even if the batteries die.

Available in Illuminated Circle Plex or Illuminated Duplex.

Features: removable illumination module; 1x true power magnification; waterproof, shockproof and fog proof; Leupold Dark Earth finish easily adjusted focusing eyepiece; $1/2$-MOA click windage and elevation adjustment dials; compact 4.5-inch length

MSRP:	**$600**

QD MANAGER

VX-7L 4.5-18x56 MM
LONG RANGE

QD MANAGER SERIES

Developed by Leupold in association with the Quality Deer Management Association (QDMA). Based on Leupold's VX-L riflescope models. *Features:* Light Optimization Profile (a concave crescent in the bottom of the objective lens and bell that allows large objective riflescopes to be mounted low); 11 brightness setting illumination system with variable intensity rheostat; matte black finish; QDMA identity on the Leupold Golden Ring and QDMA logo medallion

3.5-10x50mm:	$1085
4.5-14x50mm:	$1185
3.5-10x56mm:	$1310
4.5-14x56mm LR:	$1475

VX-7 LONG RANGE MODELS

Features: Leupold's Xtended Twilight Lens System and Light Optimization Profile (a concave crescent in the bottom of the objective lens and bell that allows large objective riflescopes to be mounted low); 34mm main tube; SpeeDial adjustment system; Leupold Ballistics Aiming System reticles; dual erector springs; 34mm PRW rings; the VX-7L 3.5-14x56mm Long Range is available with XT Duplex, Boone & Crockett Big Game and Varmint Hunter's reticles; VX-7L 4.5-18x56mm Long Range reticle options include Fine Duplex, Boone & Crockett Big Game and Varmint Hunter

VX-7L 3.5-14x56mm LR:	$2375
VX-7L 4.5-18x56mm LR:	$2499

ENCORE HANDGUN 2.5-8x28 EER

MONARCH 2-8x32

MONARCH 4-16x50

MONARCH 8-32x50

SLUGHUNTER REALTREE 3-9x40

ENCORE HANDGUN 2.5-8x28 EER

The Encore 2.5-8x28 is designed to work with single shot handguns or revolvers and integrates the Nikon BDC reticle.

Features: waterproof, fogproof and shockproof; 2.5-8 variable zoom 1-inch tube; 28-inch objective; hand-turn adjustments and positive clicks; available in a matte or silver finish

Matte: **$455**
Silver: **$465**

MONARCH 2-8x32, 4-16x50SF, 8-32x50ED SF

The Monarch 2-8x32 features a large objective and superior low light performance.

Features: Nikon ED glass; Nikon BDC reticle; lead-and-arsenic-free Eco-Glass lenses; Ultra ClearCoat anti-reflective multicoatings; locking side-focus parallax adjustment; hand-turn reticle adjustment, Monarch Eye Box design with 4-time zoom range; constant 4 inches of eye relief; rear-facing magnification indicators on zoom control; quick-focus eyepiece

2-8X32: **$290–300**
4-16X50SF: **$440–450**
8-32X50ED SF: **$690–700**

SLUGHUNTER REALTREE APG HD

The Nikon 3-9x40 SlugHunter BDC 200 riflescope in RealTree APG HD (All-Purpose Green) camo.

Features: Nikon BDC (Bullet Drop Compensating) 200 reticle system (a trajectory compensating reticle with aiming points for various shot distances; calibrated to be sighted-in on the crosshair at 50 yards with two ballistic circles that represent 100-yard and 150-yard aiming points — lower reticle post becomes a 200-yard aiming point); 5 inches of eye relief; Nikon multicoated optics; ¼-MOA click adjustments; 100-yard parallax setting; waterproof, fogproof and shock proof; 11.3 inches long, weighs 13.7 oz

MSRP: **$260–270**

NEW Products: **Sightmark Scopes**

TACTICAL 8.5-25x50

TACTICAL 3-9x40

TACTICAL 3-9X
Features: multicoated lenses; over-sized windage, elevation and focusing adjustment knobs; 30mm nitrogen filled and purged tube; waterproof and fog-proof
MSRP: $130

TACTICAL 8.25-25x50
Features: multicoated lenses; oversize windage, elevation and focusing adjustment knobs; internally-illuminated mil-dot reticle; 1/8-in. locking MOA;

front diopter adjustment; nitrogen filled and purged tube; waterproof and fog-proof; comes with two 30mm mounting rings
MSRP: $250

NEW Products: **Sightron Scopes**

SII 6.5-20x42 TARGET

SII BIG SKY 6-24x42

Exactrack no-drift windage and elevation adjustment system; fully coated precision ground lenses with Sightron ZACT-7 Revcoat seven layer multicoating; nitrogen filled tube
Duplex: $510
Dot: $570
Mil Dot: $600

SII BIG SKY 6-24x42
Designed for small bore and high power silhouette competitive shooters. *Features:* 1/4 MOA click target knobs with 20 MOA per revolution, 60 MOA of windage and elevation adjustment; 1/2 inch MOA Target Dot reticle; one piece, aircraft quality nitrogen filled aluminum tube; waterproof and fog proof with climate control coating on exterior lens surfaces; Sightron no-drift windage and elevation adjustment Exactrack system; fully coated precision ground lenses with ZACT-7 Revcoat seven layer multi-coating; 3-inch sun shade
MSRP: $735–765

SII 6.5-20x42 TARGET
The Sightron SII variable-power target scope is available with dot, mil-dot or duplex reticles.

Features: low-profile target knobs; 720-degree adjustable objective; 3-in. detachable sun shade; one piece, air-craft quality aluminum tube; Sightron

Z6

Swarovski's Z6 scopes offer 50% more magnification, field of view, and eye relief.

Features: Swarovski lenses with Swarotop lens coating; waterproof and fog-proof; 6x zoom; low-design reticle illumination unit; High Grid technology eyepiece; watertight forged aluminum housing; microstructure grooves in tube to reduce reflection; 4-point coil sighting system; ergonomically designed operating elements; two separate memory locations for day and night settings; large choice of reticles

Z6 1-6x24:	**$1888**
Z6 1-6x24 EE:	**$1888**
Z6 1.7-10x42:	**$2032**
Z6 2-12x50:	**$2187–2257**
Z6i 1-6x24:	**$2443**
Z6i 1-6x24EE:	**$2443**
Z6i 1.7-10x42:	**$2732**
Z6i 2-12x50:	**$2807**

Z6

Z6 7-10x42

ACCUPOINT WITH CROSSHAIR RETICLE

Trijicon's AccuPoint riflescopes now come with a crosshair reticle. The AccuPoint with illuminated crosshair reticle does not require batteries for operation. Battery-free tritium technology provides amber illumination where the crosshairs intersect.

Features: Trijicon Manual Brightness Adjustment Override (allows the user to shade the tritium and fiber-optics during daylight to decrease the brightness of the illuminated reticle during increased light situations); aircraft quality, hard black matte finish anodized aluminum weather-resistant, nitrogen-filled scope body

MSRP: . . . . **$700-$950**

NEW Products: **Vortex Scopes**

CROSSFIRE 4-12x40

STRIKEFIRE

CROSSFIRE SERIES

Reticle styles include V-Plex (on most models), V-Brite (on select models), Fine Crosshair (on target model) and Mil Dot (on long-range target & varmint model). *Features:* fully multi-coated optics; solid, one-piece turned aircraft-grade aluminum alloy tube; waterproof/fog-proof construction; dry nitrogen purging to prevent internal fogging and corrosion; variable-zoom

1.5-4x32:	$129
2-7x32:	$129
2.5-10x50:	$179
3-9x40:	$139
3.5-10x44:	$150
4-12x40:	$150
6-24x50 AO:	$249

STRIKEFIRE RED DOT

Vortex's StrikeFire red dot scopes are compact, waterproof and shockproof.

Battery life ranges from 2,000 hours (83 days) to 3,000 hours (125 days), depending on power setting. *Features:* nitrogen-purged non-glare, black matte 30mm aluminum alloy tube; easily switches between intensity adjustable red and green dots; parallax free past 50 yards; unlimited eye relief; fully multi-coated lenses; flip-up lens caps; choice of rings for shotgun or AR mount
MSRP: $159

NEW Products: **Yukon Scopes**

HUNTER 3-9x40

The Yukon Hunter's variable lower power 3-9x magnification range is intended for shorter distance, rapid fire shooting in light to dense cover and the higher power for longer distances and more open terrain.

Features: multicoated optics; long eye relief; oversized windage and elevation knobs; ¼-inch MOA; front diopter adjustment; nitrogen filled tube; waterproof and fog-proof; comes with two 30mm mounting rings
MSRP: $80–100

NEW Products: **Zeiss Scopes**

ENHANCED VICTORY DIAVARI 6-24x72 T* FL

Features: Zeiss FL (fluoride-ion) glass; Rapid-Z Ballistic Reticle systems; 90 mm eye relief; parallax free adjustable from 55 yds to infinite; choice of illuminated reticles 34 mm centre tube (objective tube: 80 mm; eyepiece tube: 45 mm); length 14.9 inches; weight without rail 37.4 oz
MSRP: $4444

NEW Products: **Browning Sights**

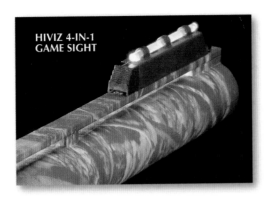

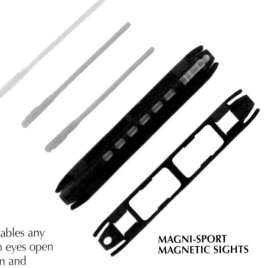

**MAGNI-SPORT
MAGNETIC SIGHTS**

HIVIZ 4-IN-1 GAME SIGHT

Includes both front and rear sights, making the 4-in-1 perfect for deer, turkey, waterfowl and upland hunting.
Features: injection-molded optical-grade resin sight construction; rear sight fully adjustable for windage and elevation; light-gathering LitePipes for low-light shooting; easily mounted
MSRP: **$40**

MAGNI-SPORT MAGNETIC SIGHT

Patent pending technology enables any shotgunner to shoot with both eyes open for improved target acquisition and better hand/eye coordination, refines shooting form, head-to-rib alignment and correct head position on the stock.
Features: one green and one red LitePipe; two sizes of magnetic base
MSRP: **$25**

NEW Products: **Bushnell Sights**

CAMO HOLOSIGHT

New model available in RealTree AP camo or matte black. Reticles available — standard, 65 MOA ring and 1 MOA dot.
Features: illuminated crosshairs; dedicated on/off button; reticle intensity memory; low-battery warning and auto shut-off; unlimited (½-in. to 10 feet) eye relief; waterproof, fog-proof, shock-proof; standard AAA battery operation; XLP model with Rainguard lens coating; fits on handguns, shotguns and rifles with a Weaver-style mount
MSRP: **$229**

NEW Products: **Lyman Sights**

NO. 2 TANG SIGHT FOR UBERTI '66 & '73

Number 2 Tang Sights now includes two of the most popular lever-action rifles, Uberti Winchester Models '66 and '73. Sights are designed to fold down to allow use of the rifle's mid-sight for close work and then be flipped up for the long range rifle events or hunting. *Features:* all steel construction, faithful to the original design; height index marks on the elevation post; two aperture sighting discs — .040 Target aperture and .093 diameter hunting aperture

MSRP: **$86**
MSRP: **$86**

NEW Products: **Sightmark Sights**

LASER DUAL SHOT

The Sightmark Dual Shot incorporates a laser that is in perfect parallel precision for shooting at fast moving targets. *Features:* 0 to infinity usage capabilities; removable for separate use; parallax corrected with adjustable reticle brightness control; low power consumption; built-in Weaver mount; wide field of view

MSRP: **$100**

4 x 32 ACOG

ACOG 6 x 48

R x 30 REFLEX

4x32 ACOG

Trijicon introduces the 4x32 ACOG to the consumer market for varmint or big game hunting.
Weight: 16.2 ounces
Size: 7.3″ L x 2.1″ W x 2.5″ H
Features: Bindon Aiming Concept (BAC); reticle with red chevron aiming point and incorporated bullet drop compensator (additional aiming points out to 800 meters); mounts to any MIL-STD-1913 rail with supplied mount; spacer system allows sight to be configured properly for varying weapon systems
MSRP: **$1275–1350**

ACOG 6x48

The ACOG 6x48 was designed and developed specifically for hunters.
Weight: 32.5 ounces
Size: 9″ L x 2.9″ W x 3″ H; mounts to any MIL-STD-1913 rail with supplied mount
Features: battery free, powered by Trijicon's fiber optics and tritium-based technology; reticle with either a red or amber chevron aiming point; incorporated bullet drop compensator (additional aiming points estimated for trajectory of the 5.56mm M855 out to 800 meters or the 7.62mm M80 round out to 1200 meters); manual brightness adjustment override; Bindon Aiming Concept; spacer system allows sight to be configured properly for varying weapon systems
MSRP: **$2000–2100**

Rx30 REFLEX SIGHT

The RX30 is a non-magnified, self-luminous sight providing increased field-of-view capabilities for fast target acquisition for the military, law enforcement and hunters.
Weight: 12.5 ounces
Size: 4.87″ L x 2.07″ W x 2.22″ H
Features: large objective and field of view; 42mm clear aperture lens; no batteries required; dual-illuminated sight with both fluorescent fiber optics and a tritium lamp; +/- 30 MOA (one click per inch at 100 yards)
MSRP: **$475**

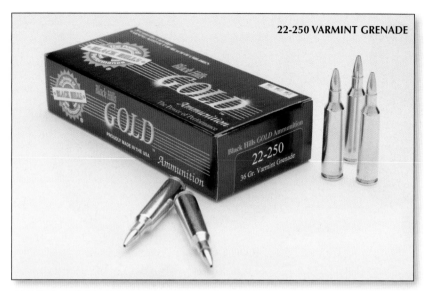

22-250 VARMINT GRENADE

.22-250 AND .243 WIN. VARMINT GRENADE

The Black Hills Varmint Grenade projectile contains no lead but has a core composed of a compressed copper/tin mixture, which disintegrates upon striking the target. This load, designed for varmint shooters, is now available with a 36-grain bullet in the .22-250 cartridge (4250 fps), and 62-grain bullet in .243 Winchester (3700 fps.).
MSRP: . . . . $27 (per box of 20)

6.5-284 NORMA

Black Hills has reintroduced the 6.5-284 caliber in cooperation with Savage Arms, which is offering factory chambered rifles in this caliber. Features: 142-grain Sierra MatchKing bullet (2950 fps.).
MSRP: . . . . $51 (per box of 20)

243 WIN VARMINT GRENADE

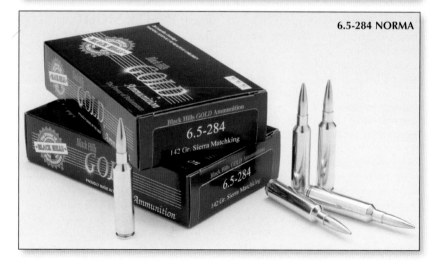

6.5-284 NORMA

NEW Products: **Federal Fusion Ammunition**

200-GRAIN .338 FEDERAL

Fusion has added a 200-grain, .338 Federal offering to its deer-focused rifle ammo lineup. This round (currently chambered by six major rifle manufacturers) will have a 200-grain (2660 fps.) load. The round is built on the .308 case and features a .338 diameter projectile.

MSRP: . . . . . $25–27 (per box of 10)

NEW Products: **Federal Premium Ammunition**

.327 FEDERAL MAGNUM

VITAL SHOK TROPHY BONDED TIP

TNT GREEN

.327 FEDERAL MAGNUM

Federal Premium has partnered with Ruger to introduce a new personal defense revolver cartridge designed to deliver .357 Magnum ballistics from a .32-caliber diameter platform. The .327 Federal Magnum is designed for use in lightweight, small-frame revolvers like the Ruger SP101. The ammunition will be available in three loads: Federal Premium 85-gr Hydra-Shok JHP, American Eagle 100-gr SP and Speer 115-gr Gold Dot HP.

MSRP: . . . . $25 (per box of 20)

TNT GREEN

TNT Green brings non-tox technology to the Federal Premium V-Shok varmint hunting line. This is a totally lead-free bullet that couples explosive expansion with match-grade accuracy. Initial offerings will include .222, .22-250 and .223 options.

MSRP: . . . . $25 (per box of 20)

VITAL-SHOK TROPHY BONDED TIP

The Vital-Shok Trophy Bonded Tip is built on the Trophy Bonded Bear Claw platform with numerous added features. A neon, translucent polymer tip and boat-tail design for flat trajectory and improved accuracy are combined with a solid copper shank to crush bone. Exterior skiving on the nickel-plated bullet provides optimum expansion at all ranges. The load also features a nickel plated case and bullet. Available in a full-line of offerings.

MSRP: . . . . $51 (per box of 20)

NEW Products: Fiocchi Ammunition

GOLDEN PHEASANT

45 AUTO XTPHP

GOLDEN WATERFOWL

.308

NICKEL TURKEY

.308 LOADS

Fiocchi Ammunition has engineered two new .308 Win. cartridges: the 308HSA .308 Win. cartridge loaded with the 150-grain SST bullet, and the 308HSC loaded with the 180-grain SST bullet. Each SST bullet has a premium polymer tip, a secant ogive, boattail spire point profile and the InterLock ring. The .308 HSA leaves the muzzle at 2,820 fps (from a 24-inch barrel). The .308 HSC leaves a 24-inch barrel at 2,620 fps.
Discontinued

.45 AUTO XTP-HP

A .45 Auto XTPHP, 230-grain round is a new addition to Fiocchi's Extrema Pistol X.T.P. ammunition line. Fiocchi has chosen the Hornady XTP 230-grain bullet to top off the round's nickel-plated brass case loaded with a careful choice of reliable powder. At the muzzle, Fiocchi's .45 Auto XTPHP 230-grain cartridge is rated at 900 fps velocity with an energy of 355 ft./lbs.
Discontinued

GOLDEN PHEASANT SHOT SHELLS

Golden Pheasant shot shells utilize a special hard, nickel-plated lead shot, based on Fiocchi's strict ballistic tolerances that ensure proven shot consistency — resulting in deeper penetration, longer ranges and much tighter patterns. Available in 12, 16, 20 and 28 gauge.
MSRP: . . . . . $16–20 (per box of 25)

GOLDEN WATERFOWL SHOT SHELLS

The Fiocchi Golden Waterfowl shot shells are 3-inch, 12 gauge shells loaded with 1-¼ ounces of steel shot in the hunter's choice of shot sizes BBB, BB, 1, 2, 3 or 4. Rated at 1,400 fps muzzle velocity.
MSRP: . . . . . $19–22 (per box of 25)

NICKEL-PLATED TURKEY SHOT SHELLS

Fiocchi's nickel-plated lead shot in its Turkey loads gives hunters the benefit of a denser, more consistent pattern with fewer stray pellets and increased range and penetration. Nickel-plating allows the pellets to retain their aerodynamic spherical shape as they pass through the shotgun's barrel and choke, providing truer flight characteristics, less wind resistance and a higher retained velocity at impact. Fiocchi Nickel-Plated Turkey loads also provide deeper tissue penetration. Available in 12 gauge, 2-¾, 3 and 3-½-in. shells. Shot sizes of 4, 5 and 6.
Discontinued

NEW Products: **Harvester Muzzleloading Ammunition**

SCORPION PT GOLD

Scorpion PT Gold Ballistic Tip Bullets are electroplated with copper plating that does not separate from lead core. The PT Gold offers greater accuracy at longer ranges than a hollow point. The 3% antimony makes the bullet harder than pure lead. Available in 50 caliber, 260- and 300-grain sizes.

MSRP: . $11–22 (per box of 12 or 50)

NEW Products: **Hornady Ammunition**

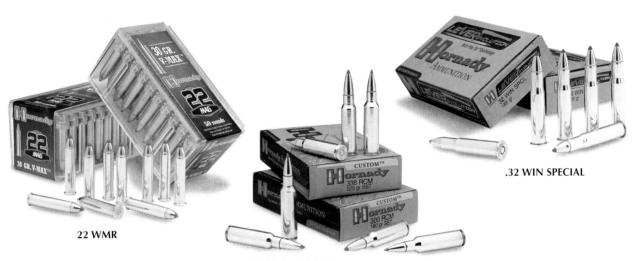

22 WMR

.300 RCM & .338 RCM

.32 WIN SPECIAL

.22 WMR

Hornady .22 WMR rimfire ammunition features a 30-grain V-MAX bullet that leaves the muzzle at 2,200 feet per second with excellent terminal performance out to 125 yards. Hornady's .22 WMR improves the accuracy of any .22 WMR rifle.

MSRP: . . . . . $15 (per dry box of 50)

.300 RCM AND .338 RCM

Most magnum cartridges require 24- to 26-inch-long barrels to achieve advertised performance. Hornady Ruger Compact Magnum cartridges achieve true magnum levels of velocity, accuracy and terminal performance in short action guns featuring a compact 20-inch barrel. Based on the beltless .375 Ruger case, the .300 and .338 RCMs feature cartridge geometry that provides for an extremely efficient cartridge case.

MSRP: . . . . . $40–50 (per box of 20)

.32 WIN SPECIAL

Hornady's .32 Winchester Special LEVERevolution cartridge features a 165-grain Flex Tip eXpanding (FTX) bullet that delivers a muzzle velocity of 2410 fps. This velocity combined with an impressive ballistic coefficient allows the .32 Winchester Special LEVERevolution to be effective out to 300 yards.

MSRP: . . . . $29 (per box of 20)

NEW Products: **Hornady Ammunition**

.357 MAG - 44 MAG

.450 NITRO EXPRESS

6.5 CREEDMOOR

SST-ML HIGH SPEED LOW DRAG SABOT

.357 MAG / .44 MAG

The .357 and .44 Magnum LEVERevolution cartridges feature 140- and 225-grain FTX bullets, launching at 850 to 1,900 fps. respectively. Now hunters who use both handguns and lever guns no longer have to use two different cartridges to get results.
MSRP: . . . . . $24–26 (per box of 20)

.450 NITRO EXPRESS 3¼-INCH

Hornady's .450 Nitro Express 3¼-in. ammunition features a 480-grain bullet with a muzzle velocity of 2,150 fps. Hornady's .450 NE offers two bullet styles — the Dangerous Game Solid (DGS), a non-expanding solid for deep penetration and the 480-grain Dangerous Game eXpanding (DGX) that expands to allow more energy to be transferred upon impact.
MSRP: . . . . $120 (per box of 20)

6.5 CREEDMOOR

The 6.5 Creedmoor was built for match rifles, including the Tubb 2000 and DPMS LR Series, with a case slightly shorter than the .260 Remington, eliminating any "Cartridge Overall Length" issues when using .308 Winchester length magazines.

Sharper 30-degree shoulder and aggressive body taper allow the 6.5 Creedmoor to deliver higher velocities than other 6mm and 6.5mm cartridges, and yet it operates at standard .308 Winchester pressures, thus increasing barrel and case life.
MSRP: . . . . $33 (per box of 20)

SST-ML HIGH SPEED LOW DRAG SABOT

Hornady's Low Drag Sabot reduces loading effort while preserving terminal performance. The SST-ML High Speed Low Drag Sabot fully engages the rifling to deliver pinpoint accuracy at 200 yards and beyond.
MSRP: . . . . $16 (per box of 20)

NEW Products: MDM Muzzleloaders Ammunition

DYNO-CORE MAGNUM

DYNO-CORE PREMIUM

DYNO-CORE MAGNUM MUZZLELOADING BULLETS

The Dyno-Core Magnum uses a polymer tip and base that is surrounded by a grooved lead cylinder. Upon impact, the tip is driven back into the bullet causing tremendous expansion. This full-bore, conical bullet is pre-lubricated with Dyno-Kote, a dry lube finish with no greasy, wax-based lubricants, for easy loading and quick follow-up shots.

MSRP: . . . .
   **(per pkg. of 8 Tri-Petal Quick
   Load saboted bullets). $13**

DYNO-CORE PREMIUM MUZZLELOADING BULLETS

The Dyno-Core Premium, a non-lead muzzleloading bullet that uses dual core tungsten technology to enhance performance. Terminal ballistics resemble those found in centerfire rifle bullets. This is a saboted non-lead bullet with a copper jacket, offered in an easy-to-load Tri-Petal sabot. Available in 50 caliber, 222 grains and 285 grains.

MSRP: . . . .
   **(per pkg. of 8 Tri-Petal Quick
   Load saboted bullets). . . . $18–25**

NEW Products: Remington Ammunition

7MM REM. ULTRA MAG POWER LEVEL AMMUNITION

The .300 Remington Ultra Mag Power Level ammunition introduced in 2007 is now available in 7mm Remington. Power Level III is the Full Power 7mm Remington Ultra Mag for big, tough game at extreme ranges. Power Level II is designed to take medium and large big game animals at extended ranges, offering reduced velocity, energy and recoil levels when the extreme performance of Power Level III ammunition is not required. Power Level I offers 270 Win./280 Rem. caliber performance for medium-sized big game animals at long range. It offers reduced velocity, energy and recoil levels when the magnum performance of Power Level III or Power Level II ammunition is not required.

MSRP: . . . . **$28 (per box of 20)**

NEW Products: Remington Ammunition

PREMIER ACCUTIP BONDED SABOT SLUG

Premier AccuTip is designed with a patent-pending Power Port Tip composed of high strength polycarbonate, which controls aerodynamic properties, balancing the slug and enhancing accuracy. Precision spiral nose cuts combined with the bonded brass-jacket construction of the 58 caliber, 385-grain bullet provides superior controlled-expansion characteristics.

The Premier AccuTip consistently expands to near 1 inch diameter at all ranges from 5 to 200 yards with over 95% weight retention for tremendous energy transfer and penetration. Offered in 12 gauge, 2-¾- and 3-in. loads. **Discontinued**

NEW Products: RWS Ammunition

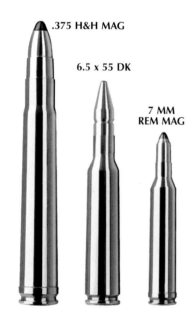

.375 H&H MAG

6.5 x 55 DK

7 MM REM MAG

.375 H&H MAG. UNI

This cartridge is loaded with a 301-grain RWS UNI bullet. It leaves the muzzle at 2,590 fps and produces 4,468 ft./lbs. of muzzle energy. It has a softer lead tip core united to a harder and heavier tail core section. The harder rear core is blended to join with the softer front to retard its mushrooming ability and to increase its penetration force. Deep penetration, followed by delayed shock, is a very effective and reliable technique for taking large, dangerous game. The RWS UNI bullet contains a hard nickel-plated jacket with a deep groove cut into its mid-section to initiate the delayed fragmentation effect. The torpedo-shaped tail, with its large base area, improves the external-ballistic performance by giving the projectile precise flight stability. After deeply penetrating and fragmenting, the residual body of the projectile is designed to continue through the animal's body making a clean exit after transferring its high amount of energy. MSRP: . . . . . $75–78 (per box of 20)

6.5x55 DK 140-GRAIN

The load is a twin-core projectile consisting of two lead cores of different hardness (a softer tip core backed by a harder tail core) surrounded by a jacket of tombac (an alloy of copper and zinc). For the separation from the softer tip core, the harder tail core is provided with an additional tough tombac jacket, and the weight ratio of the cores is 50:50 to ensure stability in flight. A groove in the rear section of the bullet bonds the tail core to the outer and inner jackets, and a groove in the front section (just above the inner jacket) serves as the breaking point for the front jacket. In use, the harder rear section of the bullet drives the softer front into the game animal, causing the front core to burst and deliver a high shock effect to the animal's nervous system while limiting fragmentation to the bullet's front section. The rear section travels through the animal and makes a clean exit, thereby increasing the knockdown power. The RWS 6.5x55 DK launches its 140-grain bullet at 2,855 fps and generates 2,534 ft./lbs. of energy from the muzzle. At 100 yards, it continues at a swift 2,557 fps with 2,032 ft./lbs. energy. MSRP: . . . . $39 (per box of 20)

7MM REM. MAG. ID

Specifically developed using RWS' patented "Quick Knock Down" ID Classic bullet concept, the RWS 7mm Remington Magnum ID is engineered with a soft lead tip plug that quickly and more effectively mushrooms against a harder, heavier rear lead base on impact, swiftly expanding to transfer the bullet's more than 2000 foot-pounds of energy to the body of the animal. This two-lead core is "married" inside specially designed nickel-plated jacket. Engineered with a precision increase in thickness toward its tail, the bullet has a torpedo shaped tail to provide optimum ballistic characteristics and higher flight stability for the cartridge's 2920 foot per second muzzle velocity. MSRP: . . . . $59 (per box of 20)

E-TIP

The E-Tip lead-free bullet from Winchester Ammunition is one of the latest products developed for big-game hunters and complies with current state non-toxic regulations. Co-developed with Nosler, this bullet features an E2 energy expansion cavity, which promotes consistent upset at a variety of impact ranges. The bullet is made of gilding metal instead of pure copper, which helps prevent barrel fouling and provides for a high performance sporting bullet that is lead-free. The polycarbonate tip prevents deformation in the magazine, boosts aerodynamic efficiency and initiates expansion. The E-Tip will initially be available in 180-grain bullets in .30-06 Springfield, .300 WSM, .300 Win-Mag and .308 Winchester.

MSRP: . . . . . **$53–67 (per box of 20)**

RACKMASTER SLUG, 3-IN.

The 1¹/₈ oz., 3-in. Rackmaster 12-ga. Slug provides increased velocity and greater lethal range. With a velocity of 1,700 feet per second (fps), this high-accuracy shotgun slug features the innovative Winglide stabilizer, which was specifically engineered to improve in-bore alignment and enhance downrange accuracy. Can be used in smooth bore or fully-rifled slug barrels, or a rifled choke tube.

MSRP: . . . . **$18 (per box of 5)**

SAFARI AMMUNITION

Offered in .375 H&H Magnum, .416 Rigby, .458 Winchester Magnum and .416 Remington Magnum cartridges, Winchester's Safari line pairs these popular African cartridges with Nosler Partition and Nosler Solid bullets. Nosler Partition bullets—with copper alloy jackets and lead-alloy cores—have long been favored for accuracy and terminal performance on game. Nosler Solids, with lead-free alloy construction, provide spectacular penetration and an impressively straight wound channel on large, thick-skinned game. Features nickel-plated cartridge cases and is packaged in reusable 20-round plastic boxes.

Discontinued

THEODORE ROOSEVELT COMMEMORATIVE AMMUNITION

Celebrating 150 years of Roosevelt's influence and achievement as arguably the greatest conservation hero North America has ever produced, the Theodore Roosevelt cartridges feature a nickel-plated shell casing bearing a special Roosevelt head-stamp in three popular calibers: .30-30 Win., .45 Colt and Roosevelt's favorite big bore lever-gun round, the .405 Winchester. The .30-30 Win. rounds are loaded with 150-grain Power-Point bullets and the .405 Winchester with 300-grain jacketed flat point bullets: both are boxed in 20-round packages. The .45 Colt is loaded with a 250-grain flat nose lead bullet and comes in a 50-count box. All Theodore Roosevelt cartridges are packaged in foil-embossed boxes.

MSRP: . . . . **$42-$56**

NEW Products: **Winchester Ammunition**

XP3 3-IN SLUG

XP3 3-IN. SHOTGUN SLUG

The Supreme Elite XP3 3-inch Slug features a one-piece, 300-grain sabot designed to deliver high energy and deep penetration on big game. Winchester developed the accurate lead-free-alloy projectile to extend consistent, ethical and lethal big game hunting ranges beyond 175 yards in 12-gauge rifled barrel slug guns.
MSRP: . . . . $23 (per box of 5)

NEW Products: **Alliant Powder Handloading**

20/28 SMOKELESS SHOTSHELL POWDER

20/28 is a powder designed to deliver competition-grade performance to 20 and 28 gauge clay target shooters. 20/28 has a density formulated for use in all modern reloading components. Available in 1-lb., 4-lb. and 8-lb. canisters.
MSRP:
(1 lb.) $18
(4 lb.) $66
(8 lb.) $123

NEW Products: **Lyman Reloading Handloading**

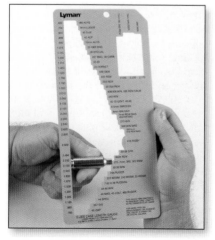

E-ZEE CASE GAUGE II

The E-Zee Case Gauge II measures over 70 popular American and metric rifle and pistol cases. New cartridges include the Winchester Short Magnums, the .204 Ruger and the .500 S&W. The simple slide-through design allows fast, easy and precise sorting of fired or resized cases based on SAAMI recommended maximum case length. Each E-Zee Case Gauge II is carefully crafted and CNC-finish machined. The gauge displays the maximum length dimension for each case in inches and has both inch and metric measuring scales.
E-ZEE Case Gauge II: $12–18

MINI DIGITAL RELOADING SCALE

The pocket-sized DS-1200 scale features an extended, 3-minute auto shut-off; powder pan, custom designed to facilitate bullet, powder and arrow weighing; easy to read, backlit LCD display; plus\minus .1 grain accuracy; up to 1200 grain capacity; measures in grains, grams, carats and ounces; stainless steel sensory platform; high-impact, plastic sensory cover that doubles as large powder pan. Uses two standard AAA batteries. Calibration weight and detailed instructions included, along with a foam lined case for storage and travel.

Mini Digital Reloading Scale: $37–42

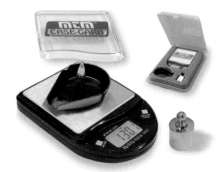

NEW Products: Nosler Bullets Handloading

30 CAL BALLISTIC TIP

.458

E-TIP

SOLIDS

30-CALIBER, 168-GRAIN BALLISTIC TIP

Nosler has added a 30-caliber, 168-grain Ballistic Tip bullet to its lineup for deer and antelope hunters. The bullet's polycarbonate tip resists deformation in the magazine and initiates expansion upon impact. The fully tapered jacket and special lead alloy core allows controlled expansion and optimum weight retention at all practical velocity levels. A heavy jacket base acts as a platform for a large diameter mushroom. The Ballistic Tip is a ballistically engineered Solid Base boat tail configuration that combines with the streamlined polycarbonate tip for long-range performance in the popular .30 caliber hunting cartridge. Color-coded by caliber, the green polycarbonate tip is nestled in the jacket mouth and streamlined. The heavy jacketed base prevents bullet deformation during firing.

MSRP: . . . . $21 (per box of 50)

.458 PARTITION

Nosler now offers the largest Partition bullet to date. Designed for .458 Winchester Magnum and .460 Weatherby Magnum, the .458 Partition is ideal for dangerous game like Cape buffalo. It provides excellent accuracy, controlled expansion and weight retention. When the front lead is released it causes tissue damage by fragmentation, while the mushroomed bullet penetrates enough to exit the animal or stop under the skin on the off-side hide.

MSRP: . . . . $110 (per box of 25)

E-TIP

The Nosler E-Tip is a lead-free bullet built on a highly concentric gilding metal frame. The polycarbonate tip prevents deformation in the magazine, boosts aerodynamic efficiency, and initiates expansion. Nosler's exclusive Energy Expansion Cavity allows for immediate and uniform expansion yet retains 95%+ weight for improved penetration. E-Tip also features a precisely formed boat tail that serves to reduce drag and provides a more efficient flight profile for higher retained energy at long range. The E-Tip's alloy provides less fouling. Available in 30 cal. 180-grain and 150-grain.

MSRP: . . . . . $29–36 (per box of 50)

SOLIDS

Nosler Solid Bullets feature a unique design and homogenous lead-free alloy construction to provide an impressively straight wound channel. Engineered with multiple seating grooves, Solids provide optimal load versatility with minimal fouling. Nosler Solids are designed to match the ballistic performance of the Nosler Partition bullets in the same caliber and weight, resulting in near identical points of impact for both bullets at typical hunting ranges. For dangerous game, hunters can use a Partition load on the first shot, followed by Solids and have confidence in shot placement and bullet performance. Available in .375 cal. (260 and 300 gr.), .416 cal. (400 gr.) and .458 (500 gr.).

MSRP: . . . . . $60–76 (per box of 25)

.22 CAL., 77 GR. HPBT MATCHKING CANNELURED

Sierra now offers its .22 caliber, 77 grain HPBT MatchKing in a cannelured version for the civilian market. Due to the fact that the 77-grain bullet is the heaviest magazine length tolerant .22 caliber bullet Sierra makes, it is a big favorite with the AR crowd. For years, many have requested a cannelured version for civilian use.

Cannelured: . . . $18 (per box of 50)
. . . .$137 (per box of 500)

6MM 95 GR. HPBT MATCHKING

Sierra's 6mm, 95 grain HPBT bullet was designed to fill the need for a lighter weight alternative to the Sierra 6mm 107 MatchKing. The bullet is built off the 6mm 107 HPBT MatchKing design with a long ogive, small meplat and improved boat tail to preserve downrange efficiency, enhance accuracy and reduce wind-drift. Sierra recommends a 9 in. twist rate or faster.

Matchking: . . . $30 (per box of 100)
. . . . $140–170 (per box of 500)

NEW Products: **Swift Bullets Handloading**

.243 SCIROCCO, 90-GRAIN

Swift's 90-gr. Scirocco bullet makes 6mm or .243 diameter shooters more effective than ever with a bonded core and state-of-the-art shape that delivers buck-bagging energy clear to the county line. The computer-designed shape includes a boat tail base, long frontal profile and pointed tip that pierces the atmosphere at high velocity. Wind deflection is hardly a factor because the bullet gets downrange with a shorter flight time due to its high ballistic coefficient. The plastic tip drives in for expansion at just the right instant. A thick jacket and bonded core combine to assure 80%+ weight retention and game-taking penetration.

MSRP: . . . . $51 (per box of 100)

Anschütz Rifles

RIFLES

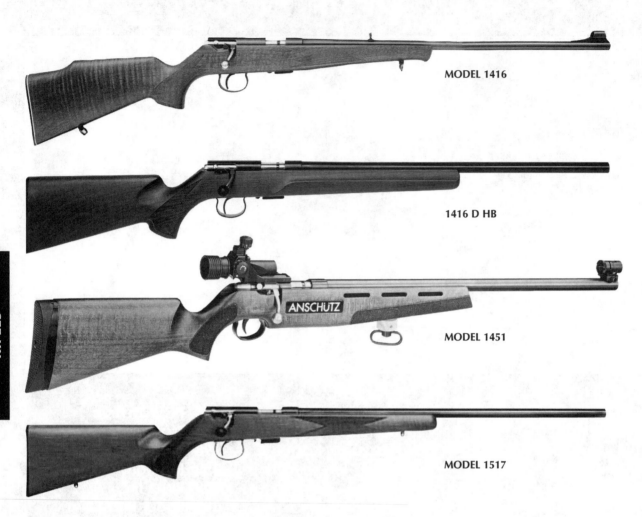

MODEL 1416

1416 D HB

MODEL 1451

MODEL 1517

MODEL 1416
Action: bolt
Stock: walnut
Barrel: 22 in.
Sights: open
Weight: 5.5 lbs.
Caliber: .22LR, .22 WMR
Magazine: detachable box, 5 rounds
.22 LR, 4-round .22 WMR
Features: M64 action; 2-stage match
trigger; checkered stock available in
classic or Monte Carlo
Classic: **$718–766**
Monte Carlo: **$718–746**

1416 D HB,
1502 D HB, 1517 D HB
Action: bolt
Stock: walnut
Barrel: 23 in.
Sights: none
Weight: 6.2 lbs.
Caliber: .22 LR, .17 Mach 2 and
.17 HMR, respectively
Magazine: detachable box, 5 rounds
   1416 D HB, 1507 D HB,
   1517 D HB:. **$800–989**

MODEL 1451
Action: bolt
Stock: Sporter Target, hardwood
Barrel: heavy 22 in.
Sights: open
Weight: 6.3 lbs.
Caliber: .22 LR
Magazine: detachable box, 10 rounds
Features: M64 action
1451: **$288–310**

MODEL 1517
Action: bolt
Stock: walnut
Barrel: target-grade sporter, 22 in.
Sights: none
Weight: 6.0 lbs.
Caliber: .17 HMR
Magazine: 4 rounds
Features: M64 action, heavy and
sporter barrels; Monte Carlo and
Classic stocks available; target-grade
barrel; adjustable trigger (2.5 lbs.)
Classic: **$949–1009**
Monte Carlo: **$967**

Anschütz Rifles

1702 D HB

MODEL 1903

MODEL 1827 FORTNER

1702 D HB
Action: bolt
Stock: walnut
Barrel: 23 in.
Sights: none
Weight: 8 lbs.
Caliber: .17 Mach 2
Magazine: detachable box, 5 rounds
MSRP: **$1512**

MODEL 1710
Action: bolt
Stock: walnut
Barrel: target-grade sporter, 22 in.
Sights: none
Weight: 6.7 lbs
Caliber: .22 LR
Magazine: 5 rounds
Features: M54 action; two-stage trigger; Monte Carlo stock; silhouette stock available
Model 1710: $1459–2079
With fancy wood: $1459–2079
Silhouette Model 1712: **$1759**

MODEL 1730 AND 1740 CLASSIC SPORTER
Action: bolt
Stock: sporter, walnut
Barrel: 23 in.
Sights: none
Weight: 7.3 lbs.
Caliber: .22 Hornet and .222
Magazine: detachable box, 5 rounds
Features: M54 action; Meister grade about $250 additional
1730 .22 Hornet,
    Monte Carlo: **$1979**
1730 .22 Hornet with
    heavy barrel: **$1869**
1740 .222
    with heavy barrel: . . . **$1050–1341**
1740 .222, Monte Carlo: . **$1500–1598**

MODEL 1827 FORTNER
Action: bolt
Stock: Biathlon, walnut
Barrel: medium 22 in.
Sights: none
Weight: 8.8 lbs.
Caliber: .22 LR
Magazine: detachable box, 5 rounds
Features: M54 action
1827: **$3089–3597**
With thumbhole stock: . **$3189–3697**

MODEL 1903
Action: bolt
Stock: Standard Rifle, hardwood
Barrel: heavy 26 in.
Sights: none
Weight: 10.5 lbs
Caliber: .22 LR
Magazine: none
Features: M64 action; adjustable cheekpiece; forend rail
1903: $900–1100
Left-hand: $950–1050

Anschütz Rifles

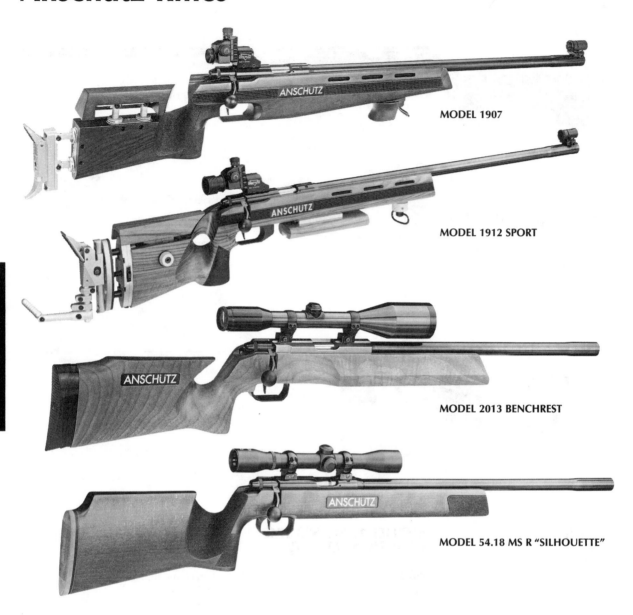

MODEL 1907

MODEL 1912 SPORT

MODEL 2013 BENCHREST

MODEL 54.18 MS R "SILHOUETTE"

MODEL 1907
Action: bolt
Stock: standard rifle, walnut
Barrel: heavy 26 in.
Sights: none
Weight: 10.5 lbs.
Caliber: .22 LR
Magazine: none
Features: M54 action; adjustable cheekpiece and butt; forend rail
1907: **$1599–1875**
Left-hand: **$1975–2025**

MODEL 1912 SPORT
Action: bolt
Stock: International, laminated
Barrel: heavy 26 in.
Sights: none
Weight: 11.4 lbs.
Caliber: .22 LR
Magazine: none
Features: M54 action; adjustable cheekpiece and butt; forend rail
1912: **$2400–2600**
Left-hand: **$2500–2700**

MODEL 2013 BENCHREST
Action: bolt
Stock: Benchrest (BR-50) walnut
Barrel: heavy 20 in.
Sights: none
Weight: 10.3 lbs.

Caliber: .22 LR
Magazine: none
Features: M54 action
2013: **$2460–3000**

MODEL 54.18 MS
Action: bolt
Stock: Silhouette, walnut
Barrel: heavy 22 in.
Sights: none
Weight: 8.1 lbs.
Caliber: .22 LR
Magazine: none
Features: M54 action
Discontinued

AR-10A2 CARBINE

AR-10B

AR-10T

RIFLES

AR-10A2 CARBINE

Action: autoloading
Stock: synthetic
Barrel: 16 in.
Sights: open
Weight: 9.0 lbs.
Caliber: .308
Magazine: detachable box, 10 rounds
Features: forged A2 receiver; NM two stage trigger; chrome-lined barrel; recoil check muzzle device; green or black synthetic stock
MSRP: **$1561**

AR-10A4 SPR (SPECIAL PURPOSE RIFLE)

Action: autoloading
Stock: synthetic
Barrel: 20 in.
Sights: none
Weight: 9.6 lbs.

Caliber: .308, .243 WIN
Magazine: detachable box, 10 rounds
Features: forged flattop receiver; chrome-lined heavy barrel; optional recoil-check muzzle device; green or black synthetic stock; Picatinny rail sight base
MSRP: **$1300–1500**

AR-10B

Action: autoloading
Stock: synthetic
Barrel: 20 in.
Sights: open
Weight: 9.5 lbs.
Caliber: .308
Magazine: detachable box, 20 rounds
Features: multi-slot recoil-check muzzle device; M-16 style front sight base, single stage trigger (two stage NM optional); chrome-lined barrel; forged

aluminum upper receiver; M-16 style tapered handguards; AR-10 SOF with M4 type fixed stock
MSRP: **$1729**

AR-10T AND AR-10A4 CARBINE

Action: autoloading
Stock: synthetic
Barrel: 24 in.; (Carbine: 16 in.)
Sights: open; (Carbine: none)
Weight: 10.4 lbs.; (Carbine: 9 lbs.)
Caliber: .308
Magazine: detachable box, 10 rounds
Features: forged flattop receiver; stainless T heavy barrel; carbine with chrome-lined barrel and recoil check muzzle device; two stage NM trigger
AR-10T: **$2155**
AR-10A4 Carbine: **$1465**

Armalite Rifles

AR-30M

AR-50

M-15 A2 CARBINE

M-15 A4 SPRII

AR-10 SUPERSASS

Action: semiautomatic
Stock: composite
Barrel: 24 in. SST T Heavy
Sights: Leupold 3.5 X 10 tactical telescopic sight
Weight: 11.97 lbs.
Caliber: .308 and 7.62mm
Magazine: 10-round box
Features: selectable gas valve; sound suppressor; full-length rail mounting system; adjustable buttstock; main accessories: flip up rear and front sights, high power throw lever rings, Harris bipod and ARMS throw lever adapter; complete rifle system: flip up front and rear sights, Leupold Vari X III 3.5-10X40 scope, high power throw lever rings, Harris bipod and ARMS throw lever adapter, Starlight case, Sniper Cleaning Kit; dummy sound suppressor available for display
MSRP: **$3078**

AR-30M RIFLE

Action: bolt
Stock: synthetic
Barrel: 26 in.
Sights: none   *Weight*: 12.0 lbs.
Caliber: .300 Win Mag, .308 Win, .338 Lapua
Magazine: detachable box

Features: Triple lapped match grade barrel; manganese phosphated steel and hard anodized aluminum finish; forged and machined removable buttstock; available with bipod adapter, scope rail and muzzle brake; receiver drilled and slotted for scope rail
.308 Win & .300 Win Mag: . . . **$1742**
.338 Lapua: **$1882**

AR-50

Action: bolt
Stock: synthetic   *Barrel*: 31 in.
Sights: none   *Weight*: 35.0 lbs.
Caliber: .50BMG   *Magazine*: none
Features: receiver drilled and slotted for scope rail; Schillen standard single stage trigger; vertically adjustable buttplate; vertical pistol grip; manganese phosphated steel and hard anodized aluminum finish; available in right- or left-handed version
MSRP: **$3359**

M-15 A2, M-15 A2 CARBINE AND M-15 A2 NATIONAL MATCH RIFLE

Action: autoloading
Stock: synthetic
Barrel: 16 in., (M-15A2), 20 in.
Sights: open

Weight: 7.0 lbs. (Carbine); 8.27 lbs.
Caliber: .223 REM
Magazine: detachable box, 10 rounds; 7 rounds (Carbine)
Features: forged A2 receiver; heavy, stainless, chrome-lined floating match barrel; recoil check muzzle device; green or black synthetic stock; Carbine with M-16 style front sight base; National Match Rifle with NM two stage trigger and NM sleeved floating barrel; M-15 A4 (T) with flattop receiver and tubular handguard
M-15A2: **$1150**
Carbine: **$1150**
National Match Rifle: **$1388**

M-15 A4 SPR II (SPECIAL PURPOSE RIFLE)

Action: autoloading
Stock: synthetic
Barrel: 20 in.
Sights: none
Weight: 9.0 lbs.
Caliber: .308, .243 WIN
Magazine: detachable box, 10 rounds
Features: forged flattop receiver; NM sleeved floating stainless barrel; Picatinny rail; two stage trigger; green or black synthetic stock; Picatinny gas block front sight base
M-15 A4 SPR 11: **$1413**

MODEL 1927 A1

**MODEL 1927 A1
COMMANDO**

This veteran design, the Thompson Submachine Gun, became famous during the "Roaring Twenties" and World War II. These replicas are legal autoloaders, not machine guns.

MODEL 1927 A1

Action: autoloading
Stock: walnut, vertical foregrip
Barrel: 16 in.
Sights: open
Weight: 13.0 lbs.
Caliber: .45 ACP
Magazine: detachable box, 20-rounds
Features: top-cocking, autoloading blowback; lightweight version 9.5 lbs.
Standard: **$1420–2000**
Lightweight: **$1220–1600**

MODEL 1927 A1 COMMANDO

Action: autoloading
Stock: walnut, horizontal fore-grip
Barrel: 16 in.
Sights: open
Weight: 13.0 lbs.
Caliber: .45 ACP
Magazine: detachable box, 20-rounds
Features: top-cocking, autoloading blowback; carbine version with side-cocking lever, 11.5 lbs.
1927: **$1393**
Carbine: **$1393**

It is not as essential for your rifle to shoot quarter-inch, half-inch or even one-inch groups as it is to really know what you and your rifle are capable of under ideal conditions. This builds confidence and lets you know what you can and cannot attempt in the field. Spend as much time shooting across a solid bench rest with good ammo as you can and really get to know your rifle.

Barrett Rifles

MODEL 82A1

MODEL 95

MODEL 99

MODEL 468

MODEL 82A1
Action: autoloading
Stock: synthetic
Barrel: 29 in.
Sights: target
Weight: 28.5 lbs.
Caliber: .50 BMG
Magazine: 10 rounds
Features: Picatinny rail and scope mount; fluted barrel, detachable bipod and carrying case
MSRP: $8900

MODEL 95, MODEL 99
Action: bolt
Stock: synthetic
Barrel: 29 in. or 33 in. (M99)
Sights: none
Weight: 25.0 lbs.

Caliber: .50 BMG
Magazine: 5 (M95) or none (M99)
Features: Picatinny rail; detachable bipod; M95 has fluted barrel and weighs 22 lbs.
M95: $6500
M99: $4000–4200

MODEL 468
Action: semi-automatic
Stock: synthetic
Barrel: 16 in.
Sights: target
Weight: 7.3 lbs.
Caliber: 6.8 Rem SPC
Magazine: 5, 10, 30 rounds available
Features: two-stage trigger; muzzle brake
Discontinued

Benelli Rifles

R-1 RIFLE

R-1 RIFLE COMFORTECH

R1 REALTREE APG HD

R1 SYNTHETIC

R-1 RIFLE

Action: autoloading
Stock: walnut
Barrel: 22 in. (Standard Rifle);
20 in. (Standard Carbine);
24 in. (Magnum Rifle)
Sights: none (option for riflesights available)
Weight: 7.1 lbs. (Standard Rifle); 7.0 lbs. (Standard Carbine); 7.2 lbs. (Magnum Rifle); 7.0 lbs. (Magnum Carbine)
Caliber: .30-06; .300 Win. Mag., .308 Win., .270 WSM, .300 WSM
Magazine: detachable box, 3-4 rounds (optional 10 rounds in 30-06)
Features: auto-regulating gas-operated system; three lugged rotary bolt; select satin walnut stock; receiver drilled and tapped for scope mount; base included
Standard Rifle: **$1379**

R1 RIFLE-COMFORTECH

Action: autoloader
Stock: synthetic
Barrel: 24 in. (.270 WSM, 300 WSM & .300 Win.); 22, 22 in. (.30-06) .308
Sights: None
Weight: 7.3 lbs.
Caliber: .270 WSM, .30-06 Springfield, .300 WSM, .300 WM
Magazine: 3 rounds
Features: ComforTech recoil absorbing stock system; optional interchangeable barrels; GripTight stock and fore-end; receiver is drilled and tapped for scope mount; Picatinny rail scope base included; open sights available
MSRP: **$1549**

R-1 RIFLE COMORTECH, .30-06 SPRINGFIELD, REALTREE APG HD

Action: autoloading
Stock: synthetic (Realtree APG HD)
Barrel: 22 in.
Sights: none
Weight: 7.2 lbs.
Caliber: .30-06 Springfield
Magazine: detachable box, 4 + 1 rounds
Features: Comfortech recoil dampening stock; auto-regulating gas-operated system; three lugged rotary bolt; receiver drilled and tapped for scope; optional extra-high gel comb
MSRP: **$1689**

Beretta Rifles

1873 RENEGADE SHORT-STROKE LEVER ACTION RIFLE

C X 4 STORM

STAMPEDE, BUNTLINE CARBINE

RIFLES

1873 RENEGADE SHORT-STROKE LEVER ACTION RIFLE

Action: lever
Stock: walnut
Barrel: 20 in.
Sights: open, adjustable
Weight: 7.1 lbs.
Caliber: .357 Mag., .45 Colt
Magazine: under-barrel tube, 10 rounds
Features: tapered, octagon barrel; color case-hardened frame with blued hammer, lever and barrel; gold bead front sight; straight, walnut stock with checkered fore-end; rubber butplate
MSRP: **$1350**

CX4 STORM

Action: autoloader
Stock: synthetic
Barrel: 16.6 in.
Weight: 5.75 lbs.
Caliber: 9mm, .40 S&W, .45 ACP
Magazine: removable box, 10-17 rounds
Features: cold hammer-forged chrome-lined barrel; blued finish; optional 30-round magazine; accepts full-size Beretta magazines from the 92/96 and Cougar series pistols
MSRP: **$900**

STAMPEDE, BUNTLINE CARBINE

Action: revolver
Stock: checkered walnut, inlaid gold Beretta medallion on both sides.
Barrel: 18 in.
Sights: open, fixed
Caliber: .45 LC
Capacity: 6 rounds
Features: working replica of the famous Buntline; transfer bar safety allows the revolver to be safely loaded with six cartridges rather than five and an open chamber; hooked trigger guard; brass crescent buttplate
MSRP: **$925**

Blaser Rifles

R93 PRESTIGE

R93

Action: bolt
Stock: walnut or synthetic
Barrel: 22 in.
Sights: none
Weight: 6.5 lbs., 7.0 lbs. (Magnum)
Caliber: .22-250, .243, .25-06, 6.5x55, .270, 7x57, 7mm/08, .308, .30-06; Magnums: .257 Wby. Mag., 7mm Rem. Mag., .300 Win. Mag., .300 Wby. Mag., .300 Rem. UM, .338 Win. Mag., .375 H&H, .416 Rem. Mag.
Magazine: in-line box, 5 rounds
Features: straight-pull bolt with expanding collar lockup
Left-hand versions: . . . . . .**add $141**
Synthetic: **$2000**
Prestige: **$3275**
Luxus: **$4460**
Attache: **$6175**

Blaser Rifles

R93 LRS2 TACTICAL

R93 LONG RANGE SPORTER 2

Action: bolt
Stock: tactical composite
Barrel: heavy, fluted 26 in.
Sights: none
Weight: 8.0 lbs.
Caliber: .223 Rem., .243, .22-250, 6mm Norma, 6.5x55, .308, .300 Win. Mag., .338 Lapua Mag.
Magazine: in-line box, 5 rounds
Features: straight-pull bolt; fully adjustable trigger; optional folding bipod, muzzle brake and hand rest
Long Range Sporter: $3848
.338 Lapua: $3300

R93 LRS2 TACTICAL RIFLE PACKAGE

Action: bolt
Stock: synthetic tactical with adjustments
Barrel: heavy, fluted 26 in.
Sights: none
Weight: 10.0 lbs.
Caliber: .308, .300 Win. Mag., .338 Lapua
Magazine: in-line box, 5 rounds
Features: package includes bipod, sling, Leupold Tactical scope, mirage band, muzzle brake
Long Range Tactical: $4200
.338 Lapua: $5000

S2 SAFARI

Action: tilting block, double-barrel
Stock: select Turkish walnut, checkered
Barrels: 24 in., gas-nitrated, sand-blasted, independent
Sights: open rear, blade front on solid rib
Weight: 10.1-11.2 lbs., depending on caliber
Caliber: .375 H&H, .500/.416 NE, .470 NE, .500 NE
Magazine: none
Features: selective ejectors; Pachmayr Decelerator pad; snap caps; leather sling; Americase wheeled travel case; scope mount of choice
MSRP (standard grade): $8500
(extra barrel set): $5300
   **Also available: S2 double rifle
   in standard chamberings,
   from .222 to 9.3x74R, 7.7 lbs.**

Brown Precision Rifles

CUSTOM HIGH COUNTRY

CUSTOM HIGH COUNTRY

Action: bolt
Stock: composite classic stock
Barrel: choice of contours, lengths
Sights: none
Weight: 6.0 lbs.
Caliber: any popular standard caliber
Magazine: box, 5 rounds
Features: Remington 700 barreled action; tuned trigger; choice of stock colors and dimensions
MSRP: $4895

CUSTOM HIGH COUNTRY YOUTH

Action: bolt
Stock: composite sporter, scaled for youth
Barrel: length and contour to order
Sights: none
Weight: 5.0 lbs.
Caliber: any popular standard short action
Magazine: box, 5 rounds
Features: Remington Model 700 or

Model 7 barreled action; optional muzzle brake, scopes, stock colors and dimensions; included: package of shooting, reloading and hunting accessories
MSRP: $1895

RIFLES

Brown Precision Rifles

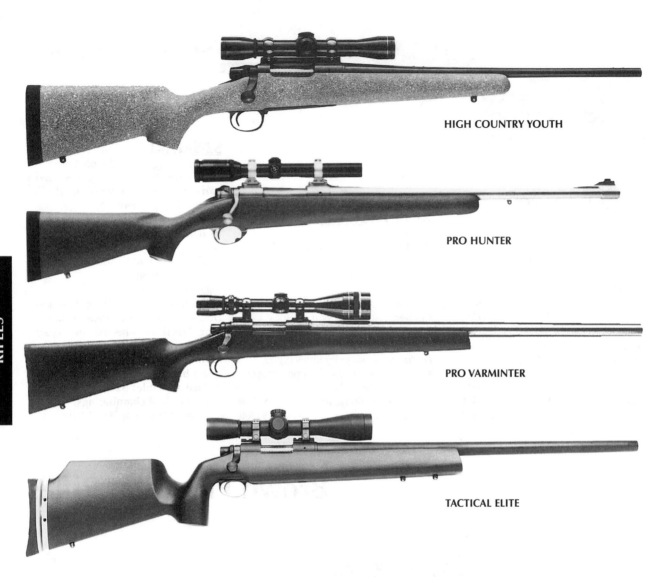

HIGH COUNTRY YOUTH

PRO HUNTER

PRO VARMINTER

TACTICAL ELITE

PRO HUNTER

Action: bolt
Stock: composite sporter
Barrel: Shilen match grade stainless
Sights: none
Weight: 8.0 lbs.
Caliber: any standard and belted
Magnum caliber up to: .375 H&H
Magazine: box, 3-5 rounds
Features: Model 70 action with Mauser extractor; tuned trigger; optional Talley peep sight and banded ramp front sight or Talley mounts with 8-40 screws; optional muzzle brake, Mag-Na-Porting; Americase aluminum hard case
Pro Hunter: **$6595**
Left-hand: **$6695**

PRO VARMINTER

Action: bolt
Stock: composite, varmint or bench rest
Barrel: heavy stainless match
Grade: 26 in.
Sights: none
Weight: 9.0 lbs.
Caliber: all popular calibers
Magazine: box (or single shot)
Features: Remington 40X or 700 action (right or left-hand); bright or bead-blasted finish; optional muzzle brake; after-market trigger; scope and mounts optional
Model 700, right-hand: **$3995**
Model 700, left-hand: **$4295**
Rem. 40X
    (with target trigger): **$4595**

TACTICAL ELITE

Action: bolt
Stock: composite tactical
Barrel: Shilen match-grade, heavy stainless
Sights: none
Weight: 9.0 lbs.
Caliber: .223, .308, .300 Win. Mag., (others on special order)
Magazine: box, 3 or 5 rounds
Features: Remington 700 action; Teflon metal finish; adjustable buttplate; tuned trigger; optional muzzle brakes, scopes
MSRP: **$4895**

Browning Rifles

.22 SEMI-AUTOMATIC

A-BOLT HUNTER

A-BOLT ECLIPSE HUNTER

A-BOLT HUNTER MEDALLION BOSS

A-BOLT WSSM MEDALLION

RIFLES

.22 SEMI-AUTOMATIC

Action: autoloading
Stock: walnut
Barrel: 19 in.
Sights: open
Weight: 5.2 lbs.
Caliber: .22 LR
Magazine: tube in stock, 11 rounds
Features: Grade VI has high grade walnut, finer checkering, engraved receiver
Grade I: **$639**
Grade VI: **$1389**

A-BOLT HUNTER

Action: bolt
Stock: walnut
Barrel: 20-26 in.
Sights: none
Weight: 7.0 lbs.
Caliber: all popular cartridges from .22 Hornet to .30-06, including WSMs and WSSMs.
Magazine: detachable box, 4-6 rounds
Features: BOSS (Ballistic Optimizing Shooting System) available; Micro Hunters weigh 6.3 lbs. with 20 in. barrel and shorter stock; left-hand Medallion available; Eclipse thumbhole stock available with light or heavy barrel (9.8 lbs.) and BOSS
Micro Hunter: **$799**
Eclipse Hunter: **$1229–1319**
Hunter: **$939**
Medallion: **$949**
Medallion BOSS: **$1029–1059**
Medallion,
    white gold: **$1349–1379**
Medallion,
    white gold BOSS: **Discontinued**

A-BOLT HUNTER MAGNUM

Action: bolt
Stock: walnut
Barrel: 23 in. and 26 in.
Sights: none   *Weight*: 7.5 lbs.
Caliber: popular magnums from 7mm Rem. to .375 H&H, including .270, 7mm and .300 WSM plus .25, .223 and .243 WSSMs
Magazine: detachable box, 3 rounds
Features: rifles in WSM calibers have 23 in. barrels and weigh 6.5 lbs.; WSSM have 22 in. barrels; BOSS (Ballistic Optimizing Shooting System) available; left-hand available
Magnum: . . . . **Discontinued**
Medallion Magnum: **Discontinued**
Medallion Magnum BOSS: . . **$1050**
Eclipse Magnum: **$1359**

Browning Rifles

A-BOLT STALKER

BAR LIGHTWEIGHT STALKER

BAR SAFARI, BOSS, WALNUT

BAR LONGTRAC STALKER

A-BOLT STALKER
Action: bolt
Stock: synthetic
Barrel: 22, 23 and 26 in.
Sights: none
Weight: 7.5 lbs.
Caliber: most popular calibers and magnums, including .270, 7mm and .300 WSMs; .25, .223 and .243 WSSMs
Magazine: detachable box, 3-6 rounds
Features: BOSS (Ballistic Optimizing Shooting System) available; stainless option; rifles in WSM calibers have 23 in. barrels and weigh 6.5 lbs.
Stalker: $919
Stainless: $1059–1169
Stainless, left-hand: $1079
BOSS: $919

Stainless, BOSS: $1139
**Stainless,
left-hand, Boss: $1169**
Varmint Stalker: $919

BAR
Action: autoloading
Stock: walnut or synthetic
Barrel: 20, 23, and 24 in.
Sights: open   *Weight:* 7.5 lbs.
Caliber: .243, .25-06, .270, .308, .30-06, 7mm Rem. Mag., .300 Win. Mag., .270 WSM, 7mm WSM, .300 WSM, .338 Win. Mag.
Magazine: detachable box, 3-5 rounds
Features: gas operated; lightweight model with alloy receiver and 20 in. barrel weighs 7.2 lbs.; magnum with 24 in. barrel weighs 8.6 lbs.; BOSS

(Ballistic Optimizing Shooting System) available; higher grades also available
Lightweight Stalker: $1099
Safari (no sights): $1099
WSMs: $900–1000
Safari, BOSS: $1229–1329
WSM & Mag: $1119

BAR LONGTRAC STALKER
Action: autoloader
Stock: composite
Barrel: 22 and 24 in.
Weight: 6.9 lbs. and 7.5 lbs.
Caliber: .270 Win, .30-06, 7mm Rem Mag, .300 Win Mag
Magazine: detachable box, 3-4-rounds
Features: matte black finish; recoil pad
MSRP: $1119

RIFLES

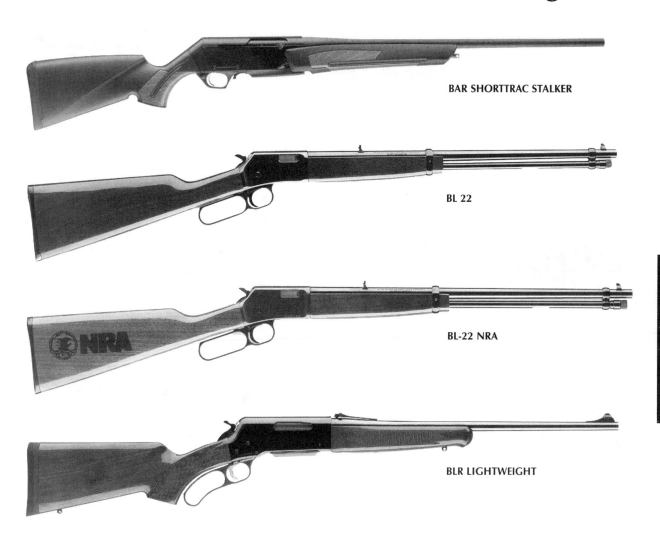

BAR SHORTTRAC STALKER

BL 22

BL-22 NRA

BLR LIGHTWEIGHT

BAR SHORTTRAC STALKER

Action: autoloader
Stock: composite
Barrel: 22 and 23 in.
Weight: 6.9 lbs. and 7.5 lbs.
Caliber: .243 Win, .308 Win, .270 WSM, 7mm WSM, .300 WSM
Magazine: detachable box, 3-4-round
Features: matte blued finish; recoil pad
MSRP: **$1119**

BL 22

Action: lever
Stock: walnut
Barrel: 20 or 24 in.
Sights: open
Weight: 5.0 lbs.
Caliber: .22 LR or .17 MACH2
Magazine: under-barrel tube, 15 rounds
Features: short stroke, exposed hammer, lever-action; straight grip;

also available in Grade II with fine checkered walnut
Grade I: **$549**
    .17 MACH2: . . . . . . **Discontinued**
Grade II: **$629**
    .17 MACH2: . . . . . . **Discontinued**
With 24" octagon bbl.: **$869**
    .17 MACH2: . . . . . . **Discontinued**
FLD Series
    (nickel receiver): **$589–669**

BL-22 NRA GRADE I

Action: lever, short 33-degree throw
Stock: gloss finish American walnut
Barrel: 20 in.
Sights: adjustable
Weight: 5.0 lbs.
Caliber: .22 S, L and LR
Magazine: tube, 15 rounds
Features: NRA mark on buttstock; steel, blue finish receiver and barrel
MSRP: **$504**

BLR LIGHTWEIGHT

Action: lever
Stock: checkered walnut
Barrel: 18 or 20 in.
Sights: open
Weight: 6.5-7.75 lbs.
Caliber: .22-250, .243, 7mm-08, .308, .358, .450, .270 WSM, 7mm WSM, .300 WSM, .325 WSM, .270, .30-06, 7mm Rem. Mag., .300 Win. Mag.
Magazine: detachable box, 3-5 rounds
Features: Long- and short-actions; rotating bolt heads; sporter barrel; stock with pistol grip and Schnabel forend
MSRP: **$889**

Browning Rifles

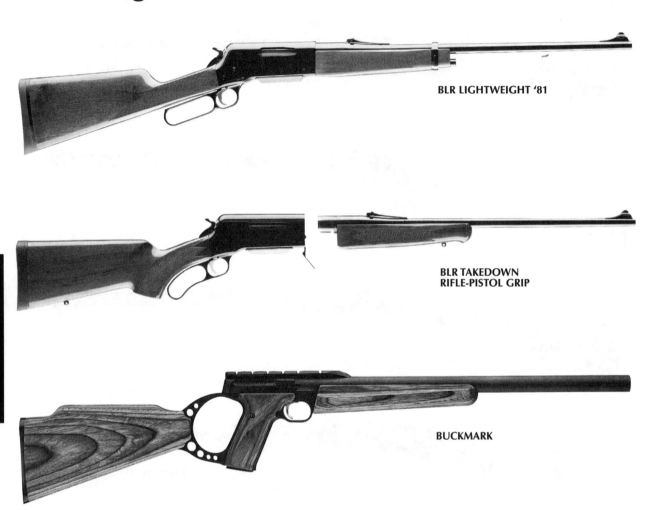

BLR LIGHTWEIGHT '81

BLR TAKEDOWN RIFLE-PISTOL GRIP

BUCKMARK

BLR LIGHTWEIGHT '81

Action: lever
Stock: straight-grip walnut
Barrel: 20, 22 or 24 in.
Sights: open
Weight: 6.5 or 7.3 lbs.
Caliber: .22-250, .243, 7mm-08,.308, .358, .450 Marlin, .270,.30-06 (22 in.), 7mm Rem. Mag.,.300 Win. Mag. (24 in.)
Magazine: 5 and 4 rounds (magnums)
Features: short action; alloy receiver; front-locking bolt; rack-and-pinion action
MSRP: **$859**

BLR TAKEDOWN RIFLE

Action: lever
Stock: gloss finish walnut
Barrel: 20, 22 and 24 in.
Sights: adjustable
Weight: 6.5-7.7 lbs.
Caliber: .22-250 Rem., .243 Win., 7mm-08 Rem., .308 Win., .358 Win., .270 Win., .30-06 Splfd., 7mm Rem. Mag., .300 Win. Mag., .300 WSM, .270 WSM, 7mm WSM, .450 Marlin, .325 WSM
Magazine: detachable box
Features: separates for storage or transportation; aircraft-grade alloy receiver; blued finish; drilled and tapped for scope mounts; scout-style scope mount available as accessory; sling swivel studs installed; recoil pad
MSRP: . . . .**starting at $939**

BUCKMARK

Action: autoloading
Stock: laminate
Sights: open
Weight: 5.2 lbs.
Caliber: .22 LR
Magazine: detachable box, 10 rounds
Features: also in target model with heavy barrel
Buckmark: **$639**

RMEF A-BOLT
SPECIAL HUNTER

T-BOLT

T-BOLT
TARGET/VARMINT 22

ROCKY MOUNTAIN ELK FOUNDATION A-BOLT SPECIAL HUNTER

Action: bolt
Stock: satin finish walnut; inset with RMEF logo
Barrel: 23 in.
Sights: none; drilled and tapped for scope mounts
Weight: 7.7 lbs.
Caliber: 325 WSM
Magazine: detachable box
Features: sling swivels; recoil pad; hinged floorplate
MSRP: $850–1200

T-BOLT

Action: bolt
Stock: checkered walnut
Barrel: 22 in.
Sights: none
Weight: 4.25 lbs. (average)
Caliber: .22 LR
Magazine: rotary box, 10-round
Features: straight-pull T-Bolt; receiver drilled and tapped for scope mounts; Double HelixT rotary box magazine; overall length 401/8 in.
MSRP: $699

T-BOLT TARGET/VARMINT 22

Action: bolt
Stock: satin finish walnut
Barrel: 22 in.
Sights: none; drilled and tapped for scope mounts
Weight: 5.7 lbs.
Caliber: .22 L.R.
Magazine: Double Helix magazine
Features: blued steel receiver and barrel; free-floating, heavy target barrel with semi-match chamber; straight pull bolt; gold-colored trigger; sling swivel studs installed
MSRP: $729

Bushmaster Rifles

16-INCH MODULAR CARBINE

A2 .308 20-INCH RIFLE

A2 CARBINE

A3 20-INCH RIFLE

16-INCH MODULAR CARBINE

Action: autoloader
Stock: synthetic
Barrel: 16 in.
Sights: open adjustable
Weight: 7.3 lbs.
Caliber: .223 Rem. (5.56mm)
Magazine: detachable box, 10 rounds (accepts all M16 types)
Features: forged aluminum A3 type flat-top upper receiver; chrome-lined moly steel fluted barrel with milled gas block; A. B.M.A.S. four rail free-floater tubular forend with Picatinny rails; skeleton stock; ambidextrous pistol grip; overall length 34.5 in.
MSRP: **$1780**

A2 .308 20-INCH RIFLE

Action: autoloader
Stock: polymer
Barrel: 20 in.
Sights: open

Weight: 9.57 lbs.
Caliber: .308 Winchester
Magazine: detachable box, 20 rounds (accepts all FN-FAL types)
Features: heavy alloy steel barrel with Bushmaster's Izzy muzzle brake; forged aluminum receiver; integral solid carrying handle with M16 A2 rear sight; overall length 42.75 in.
A2 .308 20-inch Rifle: . . . **$1725–1755**
A2 .308 w/AK brake: . . **Discontinued**

A2 CARBINE

Action: auto loader
Stock: polymer
Barrel: 16 in.
Sights: open, adjustable
Weight: 7.22 lbs.
Caliber: 223 Rem. (5.56mm)
Magazine: detachable box, 10 rounds
Features: lightweight forged aluminum receiver with M16 A2 design improvements; heavy profile barrel with

chrome-lined bore and chamber; M16 A2 sight system; overall length 34.74 inches; manganese phosphate finish
MSRP: **$985**

A2 AND A3 20-INCH RIFLES

Action: autoloader
Stock: polymer
Barrel: 20 in.
Sights: open, adjustable
Weight: 8.27 lbs.
Caliber: 223 Rem. (5.56mm)
Magazine: detachable box, 10 rounds
Features: forged aluminum receivers; A3 upper receiver with slotted rail; optional removable carry handle; military spec. heavy barrel with chrome-lined bore and chamber; ribbed front handguard; M16 A2 rear sight system; overall length 38.25 in.; manganese phosphate finish
A2 20 inch Rifle: **$1095**
A3 20 inch Rifle: **$1195**
Realtree gray camo: . . **Discontinued**

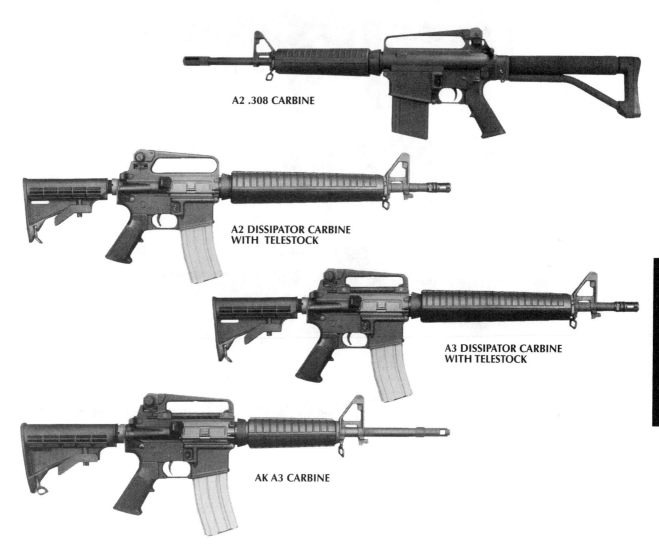

A2 .308 CARBINE

A2 DISSIPATOR CARBINE
WITH TELESTOCK

A3 DISSIPATOR CARBINE
WITH TELESTOCK

AK A3 CARBINE

A2 AND A3 .308 CALIBER CARBINES W/ SKELETON STOCK & IZZY BRAKE

Action: autoloader
Stock: polymer
Barrel: 16 in.
Sights: none
Weight: 8.5 lbs.
Caliber: .308 Winchester
Magazine: detachable box, 20 rounds (accepts all FN-FAL types)
Features: flat top forged aluminum upper receiver with Picatinny rail and ambidextrous controls for bolt and magazine release; heavy alloy steel barrel with Izzy muzzle brake; manganese phosphate finish
A2 Carbine: **$1715**
A3 Carbine: **$1770**

A2 AND A3 DISSIPATOR CARBINES

Action: autoloader
Stock: polymer
Barrel: 16 in.
Sights: adjustable
Weight: 7.68 lbs.
Caliber: .223 Rem. (5.56mm)
Magazine: detachable box, 10 rounds
Features: lightweight forged aluminum receivers; manganese phosphate finished heavy profile barrel with chrome lined bore and chamber; ribbed full length Dissipator handguards; M16 A2 sight system; removable carry handle; overall length 34.74 inches
A2 Dissipator: **$1105**
With Telestock: **$1130**
A3 Dissipator: **$1205**
With Telestock: **$1230**

A3 CARBINE, AK A3 CARBINE AND AK A2 RIFLE

Action: autoloader   **Stock:** polymer
Barrel: 16 in., 14.5 in, (AK A3 Carbine and Rifle)
Sights: open, adjustable
Weight: 6.7 lbs., 7.33 lbs. (AK A3 Carbine and Rifle)
Caliber: .223 Rem. (5.56mm)
Magazine: detachable box, 10 rounds
Features: forged upper and lower receivers with M16 A2 design improvements; heavy-profile barrel with chrome-lined bore and chamber; M16 A2 sight system; overall length 34.75 inches; manganese phosphate finish; AK muzzle brake permanently attached
AK A2 Rifle: **$1165**
A3 Carbine: . . . . **Discontinued**
AK A3 Carbine: **$1265**

Bushmaster Rifles

CARBON 15 TYPE 21

CARBON 15 TYPE 97

M4 A2 CARBINE

VARMINTER

CARBON 15 TYPE 21 RIFLE

Action: autoloader
Stock: synthetic
Barrel: 16 in.
Sights: none
Weight: 4.0 lbs.
Caliber: .223 Rem. (5.56mm)
Magazine: detachable box, 10 rounds (accepts all M16 types)
Features: carbon fiber upper and lower receivers; anodized aluminum Picatinny rail; stainless match grade barrel; quick-detach compensator; overall length 35 inches
MSRP: $916

CARBON 15 TYPE 97 RIFLE

Action: autoloader
Stock: synthetic
Barrel: 16 in.
Sights: none
Weight: 3.9 lbs.
Caliber: 5.56mm., 223 Rem.
Magazine: detachable box, 10 rounds (accepts all M16 types)
Features: fluted, stainless steel match grade barrel with Quick-Detach compensator; upper receiver mounted with anodized aluminum Picatinny rail; overall length 35 in.
Discontinued

M4 TYPE CARBINE

Action: autoloader
Stock: polymer
Barrel: 16 in.
Sights: open adjustable
Weight: 6.59 lbs.
Caliber: .223 Rem. (5.56 mm)
Magazine: detachable box, 10 rounds
Features: forged aluminum receivers with M16 A2 design improvements; M4 profile chrome-lined barrel with permanently attached Mini Y Comp muzzle brake; M16 A2 rear sight system; BATF approved, fixed position tele-style buttstock; manganese phosphate finish
MSRP: $1160

VARMINTER RIFLE

Action: autoloader
Stock: synthetic
Barrel: 24 in.
Sights: none
Weight: 8.75 lbs.
Caliber: .223 Remington (5.56 mm)
Magazine: detachable box, 5 rounds (accepts all M16 types)
Features: free-floating fluted heavy DCM competition barrel; V Match tubular forend with special cooling vents and bipod stud; Bushmaster competition trigger; overall length 42.25 in.
MSRP: $1325

Bushmaster Rifles

VARMINT SPECIAL

V MATCH RIFLE

XM15 E2S A2 20-INCH
STAINLESS STEEL

VARMINT SPECIAL RIFLE
Action: autoloader
Stock: synthetic
Barrel: 24 in.
Sights: none
Weight: 8.75 lbs.
Caliber: .223 Rem. (5.56 mm)
Magazine: detachable box, 5 rounds
Features: flat-top upper receiver with
B.M.A.S. scope risers; lower receiver
includes two stage competition trigger
and tactical pistol grip; polished stain-
less steel barrel
MSRP: **$1325**

V MATCH RIFLE AND CARBINE
Action: autoloader
Stock: synthetic
Barrel: 16 in. (Carbine),
20 in. or 24 in. (Rifle)
Sights: none
Weight: 6.9 lbs. (Carbine),
8.05 lbs. (Rifle)
Caliber: .223 Rem. (5.56mm)
Magazine: detachable box, 10 rounds
Features: forged aluminum V Match
flat-top upper receiver with M16 A2
design improvements and Picatinny
rail; heavy, chrome-lined free-floating
barrel; front sight bases available in
full sight or no sight versions; overall
length 34.75 in.
Carbine: **$1105**
Rifle: **$1115**

XM15 E2S A2 20-INCH STAINLESS STEEL RIFLE
Action: autoloader
Stock: synthetic
Barrel: 20 in.
Sights: open
Weight: 8.27 lbs.
Caliber: .223 Rem. (5.56 mm)
Magazine: detachable box, 5 rounds
(accepts all M16 types)
Features: heavy configuration, match
grade stainless barrel; available in
either A2 or A3 (with removable carry
handle) configurations
MSRP: **$1200–1250**

Chey-Tac Rifles

M-200

M-2OOC

M-310

M-200
Action: bolt
Stock: synthetic; retractable
Barrel: 30 in.
Sights: none
Weight: 27 lbs., 24 lbs.
(carbon fiber barrel)
Caliber: .408 CheyTac
Magazine: detachable box, 7 rounds
Features: heavy, free floated detachable fluted barrel; rear of barrel enclosed by shroud mount for bipod and handle; muzzle brake; receiver fitted with fixed MilStd Picatinny rail; fully collapsible, retractable buttstock containing integral hinged monopod.
MSRP: $11495

M-200C
Action: bolt
Stock: synthetic; retractable
Barrel: 25-29 in.
Sights: none
Weight: 26 lbs., 24.5 lbs.
(carbon fiber barrel)
Caliber: .408 CheyTac
Magazine: detachable box, 7 rounds
Features: heavy, free floated fluted barrel; rear part of barrel enclosed by tubular shroud as a mount for integral folding bipod and carrying handle; muzzle brake; manually operated, rotating bolt; top of receiver fitted with permanent MilStd Picatinny rail; fully collapsible retractable buttstock containing integral hinged monopod.
Discontinued

M-310
Action: bolt
Stock: synthetic
Barrel: 29 in.
Sights: none
Weight: 16.5 lbs.
Caliber: .408 CheyTac
Magazine: single-shot or detachable box available.
Features: stainless steel match barrel — choice of fluted or non-fluted; match grade trigger; muzzle break; McMillan A-5 stock w/ adjustable cheek piece.
Discontinued

Christensen Arms Rifles

CARBON CHALLENGE THUMBHOLE

CARBON ONE CUSTOM

CARBON ONE HUNTER

CARBON RANGER

CARBON TACTICAL

CARBON CHALLENGE
Action: autoloading
Stock: synthetic or wood thumbhole
Barrel: graphite sleeved 20 in.
Sights: none
Weight: 4.0 lbs.
Caliber: .22 LR
Magazine: rotary, 10 rounds
Features: 10/22 Ruger action; custom trigger and bedding
Challenge: . . . . Discontinued
.22 Mag.: . . . . Discontinued

CARBON ONE CUSTOM
Action: bolt
Stock: synthetic or wood sporter
Barrel: graphite sleeved 26 in.
Sights: none
Weight: 6.0 lbs.
Caliber: all popular magnums

Magazine: box, 3 rounds
Features: Remington 700 action; optional custom trigger
Discontinued

CARBON ONE HUNTER
Action: bolt
Stock: synthetic
Barrel: graphite sleeved 26 in.
Sights: none
Weight: 7.0
Caliber: any popular
Magazine: box, 3 or 5 rounds
Features: Remington 700 action
Discontinued

CARBON RANGER
Action: bolt
Stock: retractable tactical skeleton
Barrel: graphite sleeved, up to 36 in.
Sights: none

Weight: 18.0 lbs.
Caliber: .50 BMG
Magazine: box, 5 rounds
Features: Omni Wind Runner action; custom trigger; guaranteed 5 shots in 8 in. at 1000 yds.
Discontinued

CARBON TACTICAL
Action: bolt
Stock: synthetic
Barrel: graphite sleeved, 26 in.
Sights: none
Weight: 7.0 lbs.
Caliber: most popular calibers
Magazine: box, 3 or 5 rounds
Features: guaranteed accuracy ½ in. at 100 yards; optional custom trigger, muzzle brake
Discontinued

Cimarron Rifles

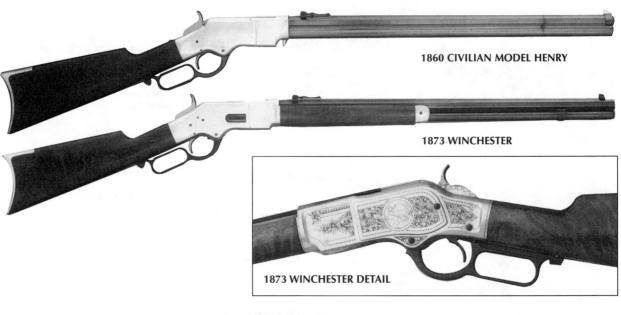

1860 CIVILIAN MODEL HENRY

1873 WINCHESTER

1873 WINCHESTER DETAIL

1873 DELUXE SPORTING RIFLE

1885 HIGH WALL

1860 CIVILIAN MODEL HENRY

Action: lever
Stock: walnut, straight grip
Barrel: 24 in.
Sights: open
Weight: 7.5 lbs.
Caliber: .44 WCF, .45 LC
Magazine: under-barrel tube, 11 rounds
Features: replica of the most famous American rifle of the Old West
MSRP: . . . . starting at $1338

1873 WINCHESTER

Action: lever
Stock: walnut, straight grip
Barrel: 24 in.
Sights: open
Weight: 7.5 lbs.
Caliber: .45 Colt, .44 WCF, .357, .32 WCF, .38 WCF, .44 Special
Magazine: under-barrel tube, 11 rounds
Features: Available: "Sporting" model, "Deluxe" model, "Long Range" model (30 in. barrel), and carbine (19 in. barrel); Deluxe model has pistol grip
Sporting: $1204
Deluxe: $1338
Long Range: $1284
Long Range Deluxe: $1405
Carbine: $1231

1885 HIGH WALL

Action: dropping block
Stock: walnut, straight grip
Barrel: octagon 30 in.
Sights: open
Weight: 9.5 lbs.
Caliber: .45-70, .45-90, .45/120, .40-65, .38-55, .348 Win., .30-40 Krag
Magazine: none
Features: reproduction of the Winchester single-shot hunting rifle popular in the 1880s
1885: $922–1270

Cimarron Rifles

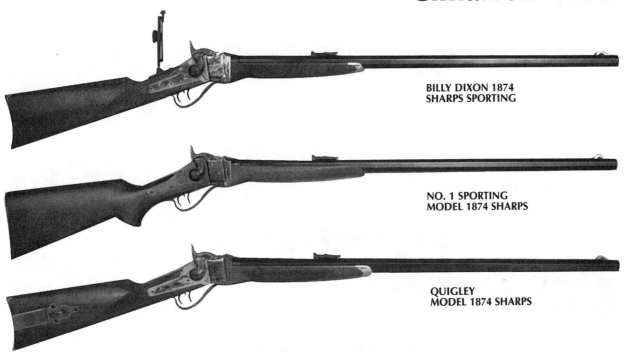

BILLY DIXON 1874 SHARPS SPORTING

NO. 1 SPORTING MODEL 1874 SHARPS

QUIGLEY MODEL 1874 SHARPS

BILLY DIXON 1874 SHARPS SPORTING

Action: dropping block
Stock: walnut, straight grip
Barrel: octagon 32 in.
Sights: open
Weight: 10.5 lbs.
Caliber: .45-70, .45-90, .45-110, .50-90
Magazine: none
Features: single-shot reproduction
MSRP: **1247**

NO. 1 SPORTING MODEL 1874 SHARPS

Action: dropping block
Stock: walnut, pistol grip
Barrel: 32 in. octagon
Sights: open   *Weight:* 10.5 lbs.
Caliber: .45-70, .50-70
Magazine: none
Features: single-shot reproduction; shotgun style buttplate; barrel features cut rifling, lapped and polished
MSRP: **$1598**

QUIGLEY MODEL 1874 SHARPS

Action: dropping block
Stock: walnut, straight grip
Barrel: octagon 34 in.
Sights: open
Weight: 10.5 lbs.
Caliber: .45-70, .45-90, .45-120
Magazine: none
Features: single-shot reproduction
MSRP: **$1416**

Colt Rifles

MATCH TARGET RIFLE

Action: autoloading
Stock: combat-style, synthetic
Barrel: 16 or 20 in.

Sights: open
Weight: 8.0 lbs.
Caliber: .223
Magazine: detachable box, 9 rounds

Features: suppressed recoil; accepts optics; 2-position safety; available with heavy barrel, compensator
Match Target: **$1119–1218**

Cooper Arms Rifles

CLASSIC

JACKSON SQUIRREL RIFLE

PHOENIX

VARMINTER

LIGHT VARMINT TARGET

CLASSIC SERIES
Action: bolt
Stock: checkered, Claro walnut
Barrel: match grade 22 in.
Sights: none
Weight: 6.5 lbs.
Caliber: .22 LR, .22 WMR, .17 HMR, .38 Hornet, .223, .308
Magazine: none
Features: single-shot; 3-lug bolt; also available in Custom Classic and Western Classic with upgraded wood
Classic: **$1400–1595**
Custom Classic:. **$2395–3195**
Western Classic: **$3295–3895**

JACKSON SQUIRREL RIFLE
Action: bolt
Stock: walnut
Barrel: 22 in.
Sights: none (fitted with scope bases)
Weight: 6.5 lbs.

Caliber: .22LR, .22WMR, .17HMR, .17 Mach 2
Magazine: detachable box, 4 or 5 rounds
Features: Stainless match grade barrel; Pachmayr butt pad; matte finished
MSRP: **$1595**

PHOENIX
Action: bolt
Stock: synthetic (Kevlar)
Barrel: 24 in.
Sights: none (fitted with scope bases)
Weight: 7.5 lbs.
Caliber: .17 Rem, .17 Mach IV, .223 Tactical, .204 Ruger, . 221 Fireball, .222 Rem, .222 Rem Mag, .223 Rem, .223 Rem AI, .22 PPC, 6mm PPC, 6x45, 6x47, 6.8 SPC
Magazine: single shot
Features: matte stainless barrel; aircraft-grade aluminum bedding block;

stock: hand-laid synthetics with Kevlar reinforcing surround; Model 21 and 22, right-hand option only
MSRP: **$1495–1595**

VARMINT SERIES
Action: bolt
Stock: checkered, Claro walnut
Barrel: stainless steel match, 24 in.
Sights: none
Weight: 7.5 lbs.
Caliber: .223, .38 Hornet, .308
Magazine: none
Features: 3-lug action in 4 sizes;
Also available: Montana Varminter, Varminter Extreme and Lightweight LVT
Varminter: **$1395–1495**
Montana Varminter:. . . . **$1595–1695**
Varminter Extreme: **$1995–2195**
Light Varmint Target: **$1595**

CZ (Ceska Zbrojovka Uhersky Brod) Rifles

MODEL 452 AMERICAN

MODEL 527 LUX

MODEL 527 PRESTIGE

MODEL 550

RIFLES

MODEL 452 AMERICAN

Action: bolt
Stock: checkered walnut sporter
Barrel: 22 in.
Sights: none
Weight: 7.0 lbs.
Caliber: .22 LR, .17 HMR, .22 WMR
Magazine: detachable box, 5 rounds
Features: adjustable trigger; European-style stock and open sights; Varmint version has heavy 22 in. barrel; Youth Scout rifle has shortened stock, 16 in. barrel

American, .22 LR:	$463
Lux, .22 LR:	$463
.22 WMR:	$497
.17 HMR:	$504
.17 MACH2:	Discontinued

MODEL 527

Action: bolt
Stock: checkered, walnut sporter
Barrel: 24 in.
Sights: open
Weight: 6.2 lbs.
Caliber: .22 Hornet, .222, .223
Magazine: detachable box, 5 rounds
Features: CZ 527 Carbine in .223, 7.62x39, CZ 527 full stock (FS) in .22 Hornet, .222 and .223 with 20 in. barrel and 527 Prestige in .22 Hornet and .223 with 22 in. barrel

Varmint:	$718
Lux:	$718
American:	$757
Carbine:	$727
FS:	$827
Varmint Kevlar:	$955
Prestige:	$1022

MODEL 550

Action: bolt
Stock: checkered walnut sporter
Barrel: 24 in.
Sights: open
Weight: 7.3 lbs.
Caliber: .243, 6.5x55, .270, 7x57, 7x64, .308, .30-06, 9.3x62
Magazine: box, 5 rounds
Features: adjustable single set trigger; detachable magazine optional; full-stocked model (FS) available; CZ 550 Safari Magnum has magnum length action, express sights in calibers .375 H&H, .416 Rigby, .458 Win.

American:	$623
Medium Magnum:	$690
FS:	$705
Prestige:	$854
Safari Magnum:	$875

MODEL 550 ULTIMATE HUNTING RIFLE

Action: bolt
Stock: walnut
Barrel: 23.6 in.
Sights: iron, adjustable
Weight: 7.7 lbs.
Caliber: .300 Win Mag
Magazine: box, 3 rounds
Features: broke-in hammer forged blued barrel; boresighted 5.5-22 x 50 Nightforce scope w/ R2 reticle mounted on 1 piece rings; aluminum hard case; minute of angle accuracy guarantee to 1000 yards

MSRP:	$3450

MODEL 550 VARMINT

Action: bolt   **Stock:** walnut
Barrel: heavy varmint 24 in.
Sights: open   **Weight:** 8.5 lbs.
Caliber: .308 Win., 22-250
Magazine: box, 5 rounds
Features: adjustable single set trigger; laminated stock optional; detachable magazine optional; also available: CZ 550 medium magnum in .7mm Rem. Mag. and .300 Win. Mag.

Varmint:	$841
Varmint Laminate:	$966
Medium Magnum:	$950

Dakota Arms Rifles

MODEL 10 SINGLE-SHOT

MODEL 76

MODEL 97 HUNTER

DOUBLE RIFLE

MODEL 10 SINGLE-SHOT
Action: dropping block
Stock: select walnut
Barrel: 23 in.
Sights: none
Weight: 5.5 lbs.
Caliber: from .22 LR to .375 H&H; magnum: .338 Win. to .416 Dakota
Magazine: none
Features: receiver and rear of breech block are solid steel; removable trigger plate
Action only: **$1875**
Standard or Magnum: **$4695**

MODEL 76
Action: bolt
Stock: select walnut
Barrel: 23-24 in.
Sights: none
Weight: 6.5 lbs.

Caliber: Safari: from .257 Roberts to .458 Win. Mag.; Classic: from .22-250 through .458 Win. Mag.(inc. WSM); African: .404 Jeffery, .416 Dakota, .416 Rigby, .450 Dakota
Magazine: box, 3-5 rounds
Features: three-position striker-blocking safety allows bolt operation with safety on; stock in oil-finished English, Bastogne or Claro walnut; African model weighs 9.5 lbs. and the Safari is 8.5 lbs.
Classic: **$4595**
Safari: **$6495**
African: **$7995**

MODEL 97 HUNTER SERIES
Action: bolt
Stock: walnut or composite
Barrel: 24 in.
Sights: open
Weight: 7.0 lbs.

Caliber: .25-06 through .375 Dakota
Magazine: blind box, 3-5 rounds
Features: 1 in. black recoil pad, 2 sling swivel studs
**Long Range Hunter
   (composite stock): Close-out deal
Deluxe Hunter
   (walnut stock):** . . . . **Discontinued**

DOUBLE RIFLE
Action: hinged breech
Stock: exhibition walnut, pistol grip
Barrel: 25 in.
Sights: open
Weight: 9.5 lbs.
Caliber: most common calibers
Magazine: none
Features: round action; elective ejectors; recoil pad; Americase
MSRP: . . . .**Price on request**

Dakota Arms Rifles

LONG BOW TACTICAL E.R.

PREDATOR

SHARPS RIFLE

TRAVELER

LONG BOW TACTICAL E.R.
Action: bolt
Stock: McMillan fiberglass, matte finish
Barrel: stainless, 28 in.
Sights: open
Weight: 13.7 lbs.
Caliber: .338 Lapua, .300 Dakota and .330 Dakota
Magazine: blind, 3 rounds
Features: adjustable cheekpiece; 3 sling swivel studs; bipod spike in forend; controlled round feeding; one-piece optical rail; 3-position firing pin block safety; deployment kit; muzzle brake
MSRP: **$4795**

PREDATOR
Action: bolt
Stock: checkered walnut
Barrel: match-grade stainless
Sights: none   *Weight*: 9.0 lbs.
Caliber: .17 VarTarg, .17 Rem., .17 Tactical, .20 VarTarg, .20 Tactical, .20 PPC, .204 Ruger, .221 Fireball, .222 Rem., .222 Rem. Mag., .223 Rem., .22 BR, 6 PPC, 6 BR
Magazine: none
Features: many options, including fancy walnut
MSRP: **$1995–4295**

SHARPS RIFLE
Action: dropping block
Stock: walnut, straight grip
Barrel: octagon 26 in.
Sights: open   *Weight:* 8.0 lbs.
Caliber: .17 HRM to .30-40 Krag
Magazine: none
Features: small frame version of 1874 Sharps
MSRP: **$4295**

TRAVELER
Action: bolt
Stock: take-down, checkered walnut
Barrel: choice of contours, lengths
Sights: none
Weight: 8.5 lbs.
Caliber: all popular cartridges
Magazine: box, 3-5 rounds
Features: the Dakota Traveler is based on the Dakota 76 design. It features threadless disassembly. Weight and barrel length depend on caliber and version.
Classic: **$6095**
Safari: **$7895**
African: **$9495**

Dixie Rifles

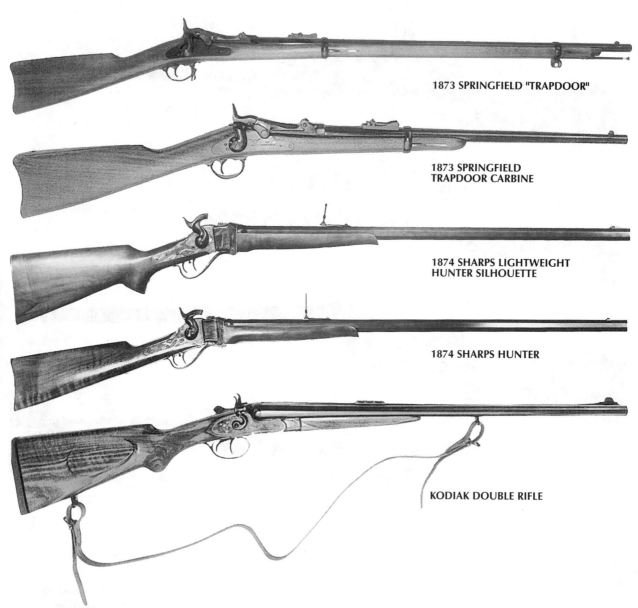

1873 SPRINGFIELD "TRAPDOOR"

1873 SPRINGFIELD TRAPDOOR CARBINE

1874 SHARPS LIGHTWEIGHT HUNTER SILHOUETTE

1874 SHARPS HUNTER

KODIAK DOUBLE RIFLE

1873 SPRINGFIELD "TRAPDOOR"

Action: hinged breech
Stock: walnut
Barrel: 26 or 32 in. (22 in carbine)
Sights: adjustable
Weight: 8.0 lbs.
Caliber: .45-70
Magazine: none
Features: single-shot rifle; first cartridge rifle of U.S. Army; Officer's Model (26 in.) has checkered stock; weight with 32 in. Barrel: 8.5 lbs. and 7.5 lbs. for carbine
1873 Springfield "Trapdoor": . **$1175**
Officer's Model: **$1500**
Carbine: **$1150**

1874 SHARPS LIGHTWEIGHT HUNTER

Action: dropping block
Stock: walnut
Barrel: 30 in.
Sights: adjustable
Weight: 10.0 lbs.
Caliber: .45-70
Magazine: none
Features: case-colored receiver, drilled for tang sights; also 1874 Sharps Silhouette Hunter in .40-65 or .45-70
Hunter: **$1150**
Silhouette:............... **$1250**

KODIAK DOUBLE RIFLE BY PEDERSOLI

Action: hinged breech
Stock: walnut
Barrel: 24 in.
Sights: open, folding leaf
Weight: 10.0 lbs.
Caliber: .45-70
Magazine: none
Features: double-barrel rifle with exposed hammers
MSRP: **$4500**

DPMS Panther Rifles

16-INCH AP4

.22 LR

A2 TACTICAL 16-INCH

AP4 CARBINE

RIFLES

16-INCH AP4 POST BAN W/MICULEK COMP.

Action: autoloader
Stock: synthetic
Barrel: 16 in.
Sights: open
Weight: 7.25 lbs.
Caliber: 5.56 x 45mm
Magazine: detachable box, 30 rounds
Features: forged aluminum alloy A3 flattop upper receiver with detachable carry handle; forged aluminum alloy lower receiver with semi-auto trigger group; AP4 contour chrome-moly steel barrel with fixed Miculek compensator; length: 34 in.
MSRP: **$944**

.22LR & DCM .22LR

Action: autoloader
Stock: synthetic
Barrel: 16 in., 20 in. (DCM)
Sights: open
Weight: 7.8 lbs., 8.7 lbs. (DCM)

Caliber: .22 LR
Magazine: detachable box, 10 rounds
Features: extruded aluminum alloy Lo-Pro flattop upper receiver; cast aluminum alloy lower receiver with semi-auto trigger group; DCM has A2 fixed carry handle; forged aluminum alloy lower receiver with semi-auto trigger group; chrome-moly steel bull barrel; heavy stainless barrel (DCM); length: 34.5 in., 38.25 in. (DCM)
Discontinued

A2 TACTICAL 16-INCH

Action: autoloader
Stock: synthetic
Barrel: 16 in.
Sights: open
Weight: 9.75 lbs.
Caliber: 5.56 x 45mm
Magazine: detachable box, 30 rounds
Features: forged aluminum alloy upper

receiver with A2 fixed carry handle; forged aluminum alloy lower receiver with semi-auto trigger group; heavy chrome-moly steel barrel with A2 flash hider; length: 34.75 inches
MSRP: **$814**

AP4 CARBINE

Action: autoloader
Stock: synthetic
Barrel: 16 in.
Sights: none
Weight: 6.7 lbs.
Caliber: 5.56 x 45mm
Magazine: detachable box, 30 rounds
Features: forged aluminum alloy A3 flattop upper receiver with detachable carry handle and adjustable rear sight; forged aluminum alloy lower receiver with semi-auto trigger group; chrome-moly steel barrel; telescoping stock: 36.24 in. extended, 32.5 collapsed
MSRP: **$904**

DPMS Panther Rifles

ARCTIC

SUPER BULL 24

BULL CLASSIC

BULL TWENTY

ARCTIC

Action: autoloader
Stock: synthetic
Barrel: 20 in.
Sights: none
Weight: 9.0 lbs.
Caliber: .223 Rem.
Magazine: detachable box, 30 rounds
Features: forged aluminum alloy A3 flattop upper receiver; forged aluminum alloy lower receiver with semi-auto trigger group; stainless steel fluted bull barrel; white coated, vented aluminum free float handguards
MSRP: **$1099**

BULL 24 SPECIAL & SUPER BULL 24

Action: autoloader
Stock: synthetic
Barrel: 24 in.
Sights: none
Weight: 10.25 lbs. (Bull 24 Special), 11.75 lbs.
Caliber: .223 Rem.
Magazine: detachable box, 30 rounds
Features: forged aircraft aluminum alloy A3 flattop upper receiver; forged aluminum alloy lower receiver with semi-auto trigger group; stainless steel fluted bull barrel; length: 43 inches (Bull 24 Special)
Bull 24 Special: **$1189**
Super Bull 24: . . . . . . **Discontinued**

BULL CLASSIC

Action: autoloader
Stock: synthetic
Barrel: 20 in.
Sights: open
Weight: 9.75 lbs.
Caliber: .223 Rem.
Magazine: detachable box, 30 rounds
Features: forged aluminum alloy upper receiver with A2 fixed carry handle; forged aluminum alloy lower receiver with semi-auto trigger group; stainless steel bull barrel; length: 38.5 inches
Discontinued

BULL SWEET SIXTEEN, TWENTY AND TWENTY-FOUR

Action: autoloader
Stock: synthetic
Barrel: 16, 20, or 24 in.
Sights: none
Weight: 7.75 lbs. (16 in.), 9.5 lbs. (20 in.), 9.8 lbs. (24 in.)
Caliber: .223 Rem.
Magazine: detachable box, 30 rounds
Features: forged aircraft aluminum alloy A3 flattop upper receiver; forged aluminum alloy lower receiver with semi-auto trigger group; stainless steel bull barrel
Bull Sweet Sixteen: **$899**
Bull Twenty: **$920**
Bull Twenty-Four: **$949**

RIFLES

DPMS Panther Rifles

16-INCH CARBINE

CLASSIC

DCM

LITE 16

CARBINE
Action: autoloader
Stock: synthetic
Barrel: 11.5 in. and 16 in.
Sights: none
Weight: 6.9 lbs. (11.5 in.), 7.06 lbs. (16 in.)
Caliber: 5.56 x 45mm
Magazine: detachable box, 30 rounds
Features: forged aluminum alloy upper receiver with A2 fixed carry handle and adjustable rear sight; forged aluminum alloy lower receiver with semi-auto trigger group; chrome-moly steel barrel flash hider; telescoping AP4 (6 position) stock: 35.5 in. extended, 31.75 collapsed (11.5 in.), 36.26 in. extended, 32.75 collapsed (16 in.)
11.5-inch Carbine: **$799**
16-Inch Carbine: **$799**

CLASSIC
Action: autoloader
Stock: synthetic
Barrel: 16 in., 20 in. (Classic)
Sights: open
Weight: 7.06 lbs. (Classic Sixteen), 9 lbs. (Classic)
Caliber: 5.56 x 45mm
Magazine: detachable box, 30 rounds
Features: forged aircraft aluminum alloy upper receiver with A2 fixed carry handle; forged aluminum alloy lower receiver with semi-auto trigger group; heavy chrome-moly steel barrel with A2 flash hider; chrome-plated steel bolt carrier with phosphated steel bolt
Classic Sixteen: **$799**
Classic: **$799**

DCM
Action: autoloader
Stock: synthetic
Barrel: 20 in.
Sights: none
Weight: 9.0 lbs.
Caliber: .223 Rem.
Magazine: detachable box, 30 rounds
Features: forged aluminum alloy upper receiver with A2 fixed carry handle and adjustable NM rear sight; forged aluminum alloy lower receiver with two stage semi-auto trigger group; stainless steel heavy barrel; length: 38.5 inches
MSRP: **$1099**

LITE 16
Action: autoloader
Stock: synthetic
Barrel: 16 in.
Sights: open
Weight: 5.7 lbs.
Caliber: 5.56 x 45mm
Magazine: detachable box, 30 rounds
Features: forged aluminum alloy upper receiver with A1 fixed carry handle; forged aluminum alloy lower receiver with semi-auto trigger group; chrome-moly steel lite-contour barrel with A2 flash hider; chrome plated steel bolt carrier with phosphated steel bolt; A1 rear and front sights
MSRP: **$730**

DPMS Panther Rifles

LONG RANGE .308

LO-PRO CLASSIC

RACE GUN

TUBER

LONG RANGE .308
Action: autoloader
Stock: synthetic
Barrel: 24 in.
Sights: none
Weight: 11.28 lbs.
Caliber: .308 Winchester
Magazine: detachable box, 9 rounds
Features: extruded aluminum upper receiver; milled aluminum lower receiver; Picatinny rail; stainless steel bull barrel; A-15 trigger group; length 43.6 in.
MSRP: **$1169**

LO-PRO CLASSIC
Action: autoloader
Stock: synthetic
Barrel: 16 in.
Sights: none
Weight: 7.75 lbs.
Caliber: .223 Rem.
Magazine: detachable box, 30 rounds
Features: extruded aluminum alloy flattop Lo-Pro upper receiver; forged aluminum alloy lower receiver with semi-auto trigger group; chrome-moly steel bull barrel; length: 34.75 in.
MSRP: **$725**

RACE GUN
Action: autoloader
Stock: synthetic
Barrel: 24 in.
Sights: open
Weight: 16.0 lbs.
Caliber: .223 Rem.
Magazine: detachable box, 30 rounds
Features: extruded aluminum alloy flattop lo-pro upper receiver; forged aluminum alloy lower receiver with JP adjustable trigger group; high polish stainless steel fluted bull barrel; chrome plated steel bolt carrier with phosphated steel bolt; Hot Rod free float handguard with bipod stud installed; Badger Ordnance Tac Latch included on charge handle; JP micro adjustable rear and front sights; length: 40 in.
Discontinued

SINGLE-SHOT AR RIFLE
Action: bolt
Stock: synthetic   *Barrel*: 20 in.
Sights: open   *Weight*: 9 lbs.
Caliber: 5.56 x 45mm
Magazine: none
Features: forged aluminum alloy upper receiver with A2 fixed carry handle and adjustable rear sight; single-shot forged aluminum alloy lower receiver with standard trigger group; chrome-moly steel barrel; length: 38.25 in.
Discontinued

TUBER
Action: autoloader
Stock: synthetic
Barrel: 16 in.   *Sights*: none
Weight: 7.64 lbs.   *Caliber*: .223 Rem.
Magazine: detachable box, 30 rounds
Features: forged aluminum alloy A3 flattop upper receiver; forged aircraft aluminum alloy lower receiver with semi-auto trigger group; chrome-moly steel heavy barrel; aluminum free-float 2-inch tube handguard with M-203 handgrip; length: 34.75 in.
Discontinued

RIFLES

BUSHVELD

DAMARA

SAVANNAH

TACTICAL

VARMINT

BUSHVELD

Action: bolt
Stock: McMillan composite
Barrel: 24 in., match-grade Shilen
Sights: open　　　　**Weight:** 8.5 lbs.
Caliber: .375 H&H, .416 Rem. Mag.,
.458 Win. Mag., .458 Lott
Magazine: deep box, 4 rounds
Features: lapped barrel, 3 position
safety, steel bottom metal, Talley scope
mounts with 8-40 screws; optional QD
scope; barrel-mounted swivel
Discontinued

DAMARA

Action: bolt
Stock: McMillan composite
Barrel: #1.5, 22 in.
Sights: none　　　　**Weight:** 6.1 lbs.
Caliber: .22-250, .243, 6mm, .260,
7mm/08, .308, .270 WSM, 7mm
WSM, .300 WSM

Magazine: box, 5 rounds (WSM: 3)
Features: lapped barrel, 3 position
safety, steel bottom metal; Talley scope
mounts with 8-40 screws; also available in long-action: .25/06, .270, .280,
7mm Rem. Mag., 7mm Wby., .300
Win. Mag., .300 Wby. Mag.
MSRP: **$3995–4095**

SAVANNAH

Action: bolt
Stock: McMillan composite
Barrel: #3 lightweight, 24 in.
Sights: open　　　　**Weight:** 7.5 lbs.
Caliber: .270 WSM, 7mm WSM, .308,
.300 WSM
Magazine: box, 3 or 5 rounds
Features: short-action; lapped barrel, 3
position safety, steel bottom metal;
long-action model in .270, .280,
7mm Rem. Mag., .30-06, 7mm Wby.
Mag., .340 Wby. Mag., .300 Win. Mag.,
.300 Wby. Mag., .338 Win. Mag. with
26 in.; #4 barrel in magnums: 8.0 lbs.
MSRP: **$3895–3995**

TACTICAL A5

Action: bolt
Stock: McMillan composite tactical
Barrel: heavy 26 in.
Sights: none　　　　**Weight:** 11.3 lbs.
Caliber: .308, .300 Win. Mag.
Magazine: box, 3 or 5 rounds
Features: Jewell trigger; Talley scope
mounts with 8-40 screws
MSRP: **$4495**

VARMINT

Action: bolt
Stock: McMillan composite varmint
Barrel: medium 24 in. or heavy 24 in.
Sights: none　　　　**Weight:** 9.0 lbs.
Caliber: .22-250
Magazine: none
Features: lapped barrel, 3 position
safety, steel bottom metal; optional 2
oz. trigger
Varmint: **$3895**

EMF Replica Rifles

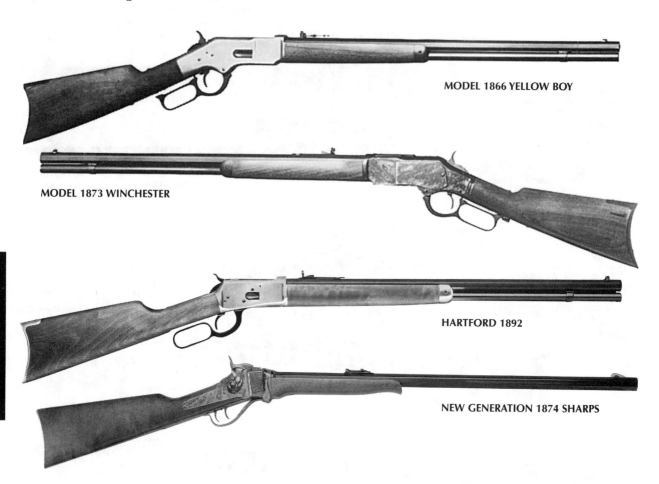

MODEL 1866 YELLOW BOY

MODEL 1873 WINCHESTER

HARTFORD 1892

NEW GENERATION 1874 SHARPS

MODEL 1860 HENRY

Action: lever
Stock: walnut
Barrel: 24 in.
Sights: open
Weight: 9.3 lbs.
Caliber: .44-40 and .45 LC
Magazine: under-barrel tube, 11 rounds
Features: blued barrel; brass frame
Discontinued

MODEL 1866 YELLOW BOY

Action: lever
Stock: walnut
Barrel: 24 in.
Sights: open
Weight: 8.0 lbs.
Caliber: .45 LC, .38 Special and .44-40
Magazine: under-barrel tube, 11 rounds
Features: blued barrel; brass frame
Discontinued

MODEL 1873 WINCHESTER

Action: lever
Stock: walnut
Barrel: octagon 24 in.
Sights: open
Weight: 8.1 lbs.
Caliber: .32-20, .357, .38-40, .44-40, .45 LC; carbine: .32-30, .357, .45LC
Magazine: under-barrel tube, 11 rounds
Features: magazine tube in blued steel; frame is casehardened; carbine has 20 in. barrel
Discontinued

HARTFORD 1892

Action: lever
Stock: walnut
Barrel: octagon or round 24 in.
Sights: open
Weight: 7.5 lbs.
Caliber: .357 and .45 LC
Magazine: under-barrel tube, 11 rounds
Features: blued, casehardened or stainless steel; carbine has 20 in. barrel
Case-hardened: **$610**

Blued: **$610**
Stainless: **$610**
Carbine, blued,
 round barrel: **$540**
Carbine, case-hardened,
 round barrel: **$550**
Carbine, stainless,
 round barrel: **$580**

NEW GENERATION 1874 SHARPS

Action: dropping block
Stock: walnut
Barrel: octagon 28 in.
Sights: open
Weight: 9.0 lbs.
Caliber: .45-70
Magazine: none
Features: single-shot, double-set triggers; Schnabel forearm, barrel in blue, white or brown patina
Discontinued

Excel Industries Rifles

ACCELERATOR

Action: autoloading
Stock: synthetic
Barrel: 18 in.
Sights: none

Weight: 8.0 lbs.
Caliber: .17 HMR, .22 WMR
Magazine: detachable box, 9 rounds
Features: fluted stainless steel bull barrel; pistol grip stock; aluminum shroud with integral Weaver scope and sight rail; manual safety and firing pin block; last round bolt hold-open feature
MSRP: **$488**

Harrington & Richardson Rifles

BUFFALO CLASSIC

CR CARBINE

ULTRA HUNTER

BUFFALO CLASSIC

Action: hinged breech
Stock: checkered walnut
Barrel: 32 in.
Sights: target
Weight: 8.0 lbs.
Caliber: .45-70
Magazine: none
Features: single-shot, break-open action; steel buttplate; Williams receiver sight; Lyman target front sight; antique color case-hardened frame
MSRP: **$407**

CR CARBINE

Action: hinged breech
Stock: checkered American black walnut
Barrel: 20 in.
Sights: carbine-style open sights
Weight: 6.2 lbs.
Caliber: .45 Long colt
Magazine: none
Features: case-colored receiver; case-colored crescent steel buttplate
MSRP: **$407**

ULTRA HUNTER

Action: hinged breech
Stock: hand-checkered, laminate
Barrel: 22, 24, and 26 in.
Sights: none
Weight: 7.0 lbs.
Caliber: .22 WMR, .223 Rem. and .243 (Varmint), .25-06, .30-06, .270, .308 Win
Magazine: none
Features: single-shot with break-open action and side lever release; Monte Carlo stock with sling swivels on stock and forend; scope mount included; weight varies to 8 lbs. with bull barrel
Ultra: **$324–386**
Ultra in .22 WMR: **$439**

Heckler & Koch Rifles

SL8

PSG1 MARKSMAN'S RIFLE

HK 94
Action: autoloading
Stock: synthetic
Barrel: 16.54 in.
Sights: none
Weight: 6.43 lbs. (A2 fixed stock),
7.18 lbs. (A3 collapsible stock)
Caliber: 9x19mm Parabellum
Magazine: detachable box,
15 or 30 rounds
Features: delayed roller-locked bolt system; Stoner-style rotating bolt; A2 fixed stock or A3 collapsible stock; HK claw-lock sight mounts; sold with tool kit
Discontinued

SL8
Action: autoloading
Stock: synthetic
Barrel: 20.80 in.
Sights: open
Weight: 8.60 lbs.
Caliber: 5.56x45mm
Magazine: detachable box, 10 rounds
Features: delayed roller-locked bolt system; match grade barrel with external fluting; available with Weaver type scope/sight rail or 13-inch Picitinny rail
MSRP: **$2449**

SP89
Action: autoloading
Stock/grip: synthetic
Barrel: 4.5 in.
Sights: open
Weight: 4.4 lbs.
Caliber: 9mm
Magazine: detachable box,
15 or 30 rounds
Features: delayed roller-locked bolt system; overall length 13 in.; 10.25 in. sight radius
Discontinued

SR9 (T) & PSG1 MARKSMAN'S RIFLE
Action: autoloading
Stock: synthetic
Barrel: 19.7 in.
Sights: open
Weight: 10.9 lbs.
Caliber: 7.62x51mm
Magazine: detachable box,
5 or 20 rounds
Features: delayed roller-locked bolt system; polygonal rifling; low-recoil buffer system; Kevlar reinforced fiberglass thumbhole stock; adjustable buttstock (SR9 target version); overall length 42.5 in.
Discontinued

Henry Repeating Arms Rifles

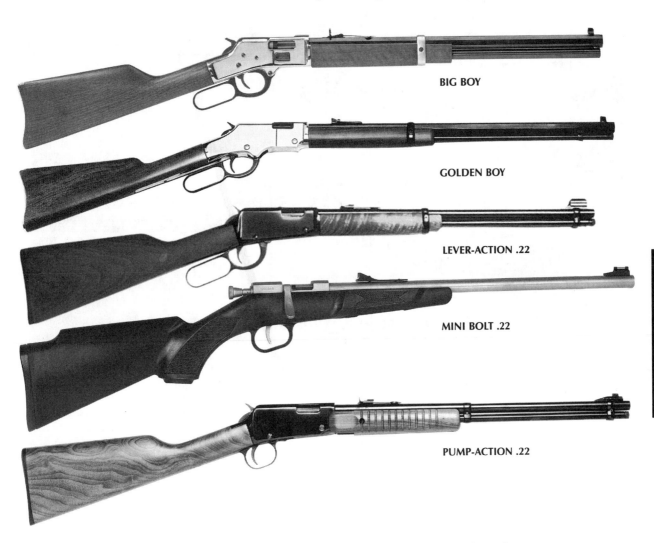

BIG BOY

GOLDEN BOY

LEVER-ACTION .22

MINI BOLT .22

PUMP-ACTION .22

BIG BOY

Action: lever
Stock: walnut
Barrel: 20 in. octagon
Sights: open
Weight: 8.7 lbs.
Caliber: .44 Mag., .45 LC
Magazine: 10 rounds
Features: brass receiver, barrel band, buttplate
MSRP: $900

GOLDEN BOY

Action: lever
Stock: walnut, straight-grip
Barrel: octagon 20 in.
Sights: open   **Weight**: 6.8 lbs.
Caliber: .22 LR, .22 WMR, .17 HMR
Magazine: under-barrel tube, 16-22 rounds
Features: brass receiver and buttplate per Winchester 66

Golden Boy (.22 LR): $515
.22 Mag:. $595
.17 HMR: $615

LEVER-ACTION .22

Action: lever
Stock: American walnut
Barrel: 18 in.
Sights: open
Weight: 5.5 lbs.
Caliber: .22 S, .22 L, .22 LR
Magazine: under-barrel tube, 15-21 rounds
Features: also available: carbine and youth model; .22 WMR with checkered stock, 19 in. barrel
Rifle, carbine or youth: . . . $325-340
Magnum:. $475

MINI BOLT .22

Action: bolt
Stock: synthetic

Barrel: stainless 16 in.
Sights: illuminated
Weight: 3.3 lbs.
Caliber: .22 S, .22 L, .22 LR
Magazine: none
Features: single-shot; designed for beginners
Mini Bolt:. $250
Acu-Bolt (20 in. bbl. &
    4x scope included): $400

PUMP-ACTION .22

Action: pump
Stock: walnut
Barrel: 18 in.
Sights: open
Weight: 5.5 lbs.
Caliber: .22 LR
Magazine: under-barrel tube, 15 rounds
Features: alloy receiver
MSRP: $515

Henry Repeating Arms Rifles

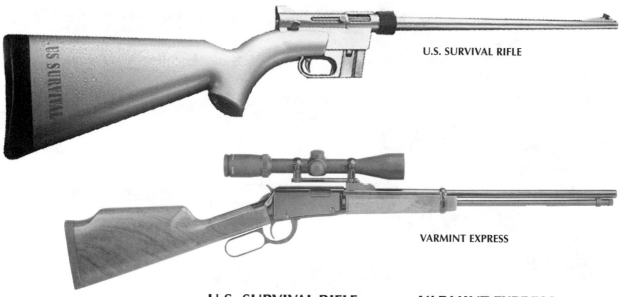

U.S. SURVIVAL RIFLE

VARMINT EXPRESS

U.S. SURVIVAL RIFLE
Action: Autoloading
Stock: synthetic butt stock
Barrel: 16 in.
Sights: open
Weight: 4.5 lbs.
Caliber: .22 LR
Magazine: detachable box, 8 rounds
Features: barrel and action stow in water-proof, floating stock
**Survival Rifle
   (black or silver):. $245
Camo: $310**

VARMINT EXPRESS
Action: lever
Stock: walnut
Barrel: 20 in.
Sights: none
Weight: 5.8 lbs.
Caliber: .17 HMR
Magazine: 11 rounds
Features: Monte Carlo stock; scope mount included
MSRP: $550

HOWA Rifles

MODEL 1500 HUNTER-STAINLESS

MODEL 1500 HUNTER
Action: bolt
Stock: American black walnut with cheekpiece
Barrel: 22 in.
Sights: none
Weight: 7.6 lbs.
Caliber: popular standard and magnum calibers from .223 Rem. to .300 WSM

Magazine: box, 5 rounds
Features: choice of blue or stainless; 22 in. (standard) or 24 in. (magnum) barrels; varmint model in .223, .22-50 and .308; checkered grips and forend
Discontinued

RIFLES

MODEL 1500 LIGHTNING-BLUE FINISH

MODEL 1500 SUPREME JRS CLASSIC

MODEL 1500 THUMBHOLE VARMINTER

MODEL 1500 ULTRALIGHT

MODEL 1500 LIGHTNING

Action: bolt
Stock: Black Polymer with cheekpiece or camo
Barrel: 22 in.
Sights: none   *Weight*: 7.6 lbs.
Caliber: popular standard and magnum calibers from .223 Rem. to .300 WSM
Magazine: box, 5 rounds
Features: choice of blue or stainless; 22 in. (standard) or 24 in. (magnum) barrels; new, modern checkered grips, palm swell and forend; barreled actions are available; 3-position safety
Discontinued

MODEL 1500 SUPREME SERIES

Action: bolt
Stock: laminated or black matte
Barrel: 22 or 24 in.
Sights: none   *Weight*: 7.6 lbs.
Caliber: .223, .25-06, .22-250, .243, 6.5x55, .270, .308, .30-06, 7mm Rem. Mag., .300 Win. Mag., .338 Win. Mag., .270 WSM, 7mm WSM, .300 WSM
Magazine: 3 or 5 rounds
Features: stainless or blue, nutmeg or pepper stock; also: Hunter rifles with walnut stock
Discontinued

MODEL 1500 THUMBHOLE VARMINTER

Action: bolt
Stock: laminated
Barrel: heavy 22 in.
Sights: none   *Weight*: 9.9 lbs.
Caliber: .223, .22-250, .243 Win., .308
Magazine: 5 rounds
Features: nutmeg, pepper or black stock color, blued or stainless; also: Sporter thumbhole version (7.6 lbs.) in 19 calibers including WSMs

Blued sporter:	**$649**
Magnum:	**$669**
Blue:	**$679**
Stainless:	**$779**
Stainless Sporter:	**$749**
Magnum:	**$769**

MODEL 1500 ULTRALIGHT

Action: bolt
Stock: Black texture wood
Barrel: 20 in.
Sights: none   *Weight*: 6.4 lbs.
Caliber: .243 Win., .308, 7mm-08
Magazine: box, 5 rounds
Features: mill-cut lightweight receiver; wood stock with textured flat black finish, blue finish; Youth model available

Ultralight "Mountain Rifle":	**Discontinued**
Stainless (.308 only):	**Discontinued**

Ultralight "Youth Model":	**$539**
Stainless (.308):	**Discontinued**

MODEL 1500 VARMINT

Action: bolt
Stock: blk polymer or American walnut
Barrel: 22 in.
Sights: none   *Weight*: 9.3 lbs.
Caliber: .223, .22-50 and .308
Magazine: box, 5 rounds
Features: choice of blue or stainless; 24 in. barrels; wood stocks with weather-resistant finish and laser-stippled grip and forearm panels
Discontinued

RIFLES

H-S Precision Rifles

PHR (PROFESSIONAL HUNTER RIFLE)

VTD (VARMINT TAKE-DOWN SYSTEM)

VAR (VARMINT RIFLE)

3-POSITION SAFETY WITH SAFETY INDICATOR AND COCKING INDICATOR

ONE PIECE BOLT BODY MACHINED FROM HEAT-TREATED 4142, 42-45 RC

TANG-MOUNTED BOLT RELEASE LEVER

STAINLESS STEEL FLOORPLATE AND SS DETACHABE MAGAZINE BOX WITH CENTER FEED DESIGN FOR POSITIVE CARTRIDGE FEEDING

BOLT HANDLE MACHINED WITH A 360° RING, SILVER-SOLDERED TO THE BOLT BODY

HARDENED STEEL-TIPPED FIRING PIN WITH SPEED LOCK SPRING

PHR (PROFESSIONAL HUNTER RIFLE)

Action: bolt
Stock: composite
Barrel: 24-26 in.
Sights: none
Weight: 8.0 lbs.
Caliber: all popular magnum calibers up to .375 H&H and .338 Lapua
Magazine: detachable box, 3 rounds
Features: Pro series 2000 action: full-length bedding block, optional 10x Model with match-grade stainless, fluted barrel, muzzle brake, built-in recoil reducer; Lightweight SPR rifle is chambered in standard calibers
MSRP: **$3045**

TAKE-DOWN RIFLES

Action: bolt
Stock: 2-piece composite
Barrel: any contour and weight 22-26 in.
Sights: none
Weight: 8.0 lbs.
Caliber: any popular standard or magnum chambering
Magazine: detachable box, 3 or 4 rounds
Features: rifle disassembles in front of action and reassembles to deliver identical point of impact; price includes carrying case, TD versions with sporter or tactical stocks; customer's choice of barrels and chambering
Left-hand model: **$4700–5200**
MSRP: **$4500–5000**

VAR (VARMINT)

Action: bolt
Stock: composite
Barrel: heavy 24 in.
Sights: none
Weight: 11.0 lbs.
Caliber: all popular varmint calibers
Magazine: detachable box, 4 rounds
Features: Pro-series 2000 action; full-length bedding block; also 10x version with fluted, stainless barrel, optional muzzle
MSRP: **$2910**

Jarrett Custom Rifles

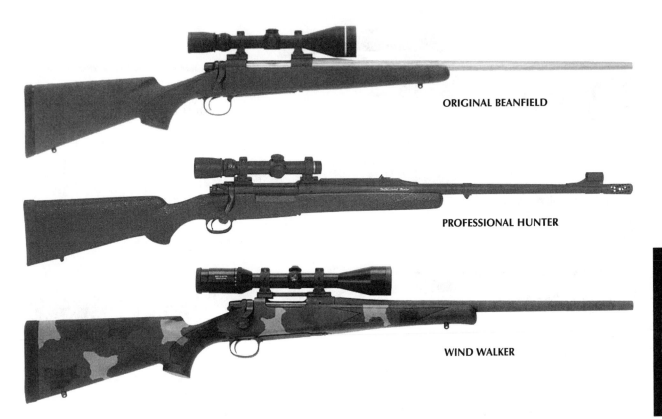

ORIGINAL BEANFIELD

PROFESSIONAL HUNTER

WIND WALKER

ORIGINAL BEANFIELD
Action: bolt
Stock: McMillan synthetic
Barrel: #4 match grade, 24 in.
Sights: none
Weight: 8.5 lbs.
Caliber: any popular standard or magnum
Magazine: box, 3 or 5 rounds
Features: Shilen trigger; Remington 700 or Winchester 70 action; Talley scope mounts, case, sling, load data and 20 rounds of ammunition; Wind Walker has skeletonized 700 action (7.3 lbs.); muzzle brake
MSRP: . . . . starting at $5380

PROFESSIONAL HUNTER
Action: bolt
Stock: synthetic
Barrel: 24 in.
Sights: open
Weight: 9.0 lbs.
Caliber: any popular standard or wildcat chambering
Magazine: 3 or 5 rounds
Features: muzzle brake; also two Leupold 1.5-5x scopes zeroed in Talley QD rings
MSRP: . . . . starting at $10400

WIND WALKER
Action: bolt
Stock: synthetic
Barrel: 20 in.
Sights: none
Weight: 7.5 lbs.
Caliber: any popular short-action
Magazine: box, 3 or 5 rounds
Features: Remington Model 700 short-action; includes Talley scope mounts, choice of scope plus case, sling, load data and 20 rounds of ammunition
MSRP: . . . . starting at $7380

Do you jerk the trigger when shooting a rifle? Adjust the grip of your shooting hand so your thumb doesn't wrap around the wrist of the stock. Sometimes eliminating your ability to "grip" the stock will solve the problem.

Kimber Rifles

MODEL 84M CLASSIC

MODEL 84M MONTANA

MODEL 84M SUPER AMERICA

MODEL 8400 CLASSIC

MODEL 84M

Action: bolt
Stock: checkered, Claro walnut
Barrel: light sporter, 22 in.
Sights: none
Weight: 5.6 lbs.
Caliber: .243, .22-250, .260, 7mm-08, .308
Magazine: box, 5 rounds
Features: Varmint model (7.4 lbs.) in .22-250 & .204 Ruger with 26 in. stainless, fluted barrel; Long Master Classic (7.4 lbs) in .223, .243 and .308 with 24 in. stainless, fluted barrel; Long Master VT (10 lbs.) in .22-250 with stainless, bull barrel, laminated target stock; Pro Varmint with 22 in. barrel in .204 Ruger and .223 Rem., 24 in. barrel in .22-250; Short Varmint/ Target (SVT) with 18.25 in. barrel in .223 Rem.
Classic: $1114
Varmint: $1224
Long Master Classic: $1224
Long Master VT: $1357
Pro Varmint: $1302
SVT: $1357

MODEL 84M MONTANA

Action: bolt
Stock: synthetic
Barrel: 22 in.
Sights: none
Weight: 5.3 lbs.
Caliber: .308, .243, .260, 7mm-08
Magazine: 5 rounds
Features: stainless steel 84M Montana, standard
MSRP: $1276

MODEL 84M SUPER AMERICA

Action: bolt
Stock: AAA walnut
Barrel: 22 in.
Sights: none
Weight: 5.3 lbs.
Caliber: .308, .243, .260, 7mm-08, .223 Rem.
Magazine: 5 rounds
Features: 24 LPI wrap checkering on select wood
MSRP: $2124

MODEL 8400 CLASSIC

Action: bolt
Stock: walnut
Barrel: 24 in.
Sights: none
Weight: 6.6 lbs.
Caliber: .270, 7mm, .325 WSM and .300 WSM
Magazine: 3 rounds
Features: 3-position safety
8400 Classic: $1172
8400 Montana, WSMs: $1312
8400 Super America: $2240

RIFLES

Kimber Rifles

SHORT VARMINT TARGET

HS (HUNTER SILHOUETTE)
Action: bolt
Stock: high-comb walnut
Barrel: medium-heavy, half-fluted 24 in.
Sights: none
Weight: 7.0 lbs.
Caliber: .22 LR
Magazine: detachable box, 5 rounds
Features: designed for NRA rimfire silhouette competition
Discontinued

KIMBER 22
Action: bolt
Stock: checkered, AA walnut
Barrel: 22 in. match grade
Sights: none
Weight: 6.5 lbs.
Caliber: .22 LR

Magazine: detachable box, 5 rounds
Features: Model 70-type, 3-position safety; bead blasted finish; deluxe checkering, hand-rubbed finish; 50-yard groups less than .4 in.; also available: no-frills Hunter model; Super America with fancy AA walnut stock with wrap-around checkering; Classic Varmint with walnut stock & 20 in. fluted barrel; Pro Varmint with laminated stock; Custom Classic with AAA walnut, matte finish and ebony forend
Discontinued

KIMBER 22 SVT (SHORT VARMINT TARGET)
Action: bolt
Stock: heavy, competition style laminate
Barrel: extra heavy, fluted, stainless 18.25 in.
Sights: none
Weight: 7.5 lbs.
Caliber: .22 LR
Magazine: detachable box, 5 rounds
Features: bead-blasted blue; gray laminated stock
Discontinued

Knight Rifles

KP1 VARMINT
Action: single shot
Stock: synthetic
Length: 39.5 in.
Sights: adjustable
Weight: 7.8 lbs.
Caliber: .17 HMR, .223 Rem.
Magazine: none

Features: Interchangable stainless steel barrel combination package with rimfire/centerfire caliber option; removable and non-adjustable trigger; synthetic Next G-1 Camo stock; recoil pad; sling swivel studs
Discontinued

Krieghoff Rifles

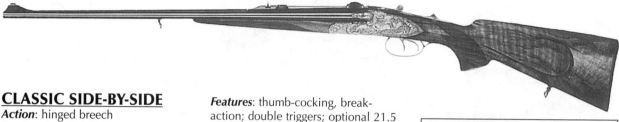

CLASSIC SIDE-BY-SIDE
Action: hinged breech
Stock: select walnut
Barrel: 23.5 in.
Sights: open
Weight: 8.0 lbs.
Caliber: 7x65R, .308, .30-06, .30R Blaser, 8x57, 9.3x74, .375 H&H, .416 Rigby, .458 Win., .470 N.E., .500 N.E.
Magazine: none

Features: thumb-cocking, break-action; double triggers; optional 21.5 in. barrel; engraved side plates; weight depends on chambering and barrel contour
Standard calibers: $9795
Magnum calibers: $12795
Extra barrels
   with forearm (fitted): . $4200–8950
Magnum barrels: $8950

L.A.R. Rifles

GRIZZLY BIG BOAR
Action: bolt
Stock: all steel sleeve with rubber butt pad
Barrel: 36 in.

Sights: none
Weight: 30.4 lbs.
Caliber: .50 BMG
Magazine: none
Features: Bull Pup single-shot; descending pistol grip; bi-pod; finish options
Grizzly: $2350
Parkerized: $2450
Nickel-frame: $2600
Full nickel: $2700
Stainless. $2600

Lazzeroni Rifles

MODEL 2005 GLOBAL HUNTER
Action: bolt
Stock: synthetic
Barrel: 22 or 26 in.
Sights: none
Weight: 6.1 lbs. (short-action) or 7.4 lbs. (long-action)

Caliber: nine Lazzeroni chamberings, from 6.53 Scramjet to 10.57 Meteor
Magazine: internal box, 3 rounds
Features: fluted stainless sporter barrel; long- or short-action; lightweight graphite composite stock and alloy bottom metal
MSRP: $6881–7999

Legacy Sports Rifles

PUMA M-92 RIFLES AND CARBINE

Action: lever
Stock: walnut
Barrel: 16, 18 and 20 in.
Sights: open
Weight: 6.0-7.5 lbs.
Caliber: .38/.357, .44 Mag., .45 Colt, .454 Casull, .480 Ruger

Magazine: full-length tube; capacity varies with barrel length
Features: 18-inch barrel ported; available with 24-inch octagon barrel; HiViz sights; .45 carbine with large-loop lever; stainless and blued finishes available
MSRP: . . . . **from $959**

Les Baer Rifles

AR .223 SUPER VARMINT MODEL

Action: autoloader
Stock: synthetic
Barrel: 18 in. and 24 in.
Sights: none
Weight: 13.0 lbs.

Caliber: .204 Ruger
Magazine: detachable box, 5-rounds
Features: Les Baer 416-R stainless barrel; chromed National Match carrier and extractor; titanium firing pin; aluminum gas block with Picatinny top; match-grade stainless; two-stage,

24-inch Jewell trigger; Picatinny rail; optional Leupold Long Range 8.5-25x50mm Vari-X III package; Versa Pod bipod; all-weather Baer Coat finish; camo finish and special rifling twist available as options
MSRP: . . . . **starting at $2390**

Do most of your live-fire rifle practice with a quality rimfire. It will save money and help overcome flinching.

Lone Star Rifles

ROLLING BLOCK ·

ROLLING BLOCK

Action: single shot
Stock: walnut   **Barrel**: 28-34 in.
Sights: many options
Weight: 6.0-16.0 lbs.
Caliber: .25, .20 WCF, .25-35, .30-30, .30-40, .32-20, .32-40, .38-50, .38-55, .40-50SS, .40-50SBN, .40-70SMB, .40-70SS, .40-82, .40-90SS, .45-70, .45-90, .45-100, .45-110, .45-120, .44-60, .44-77SBN, .44-90SBN, .44-100 Rem. Sp., .50-70, .50-90, .50-140
Magazine: none
Features: true-to-form replicas of post-Civil War Remington rolling blocks; single set or double set triggers; case-colored actions on Silhouette, Creedmoor, Sporting, Deluxe Sporting, Buffalo, Custer Commemorative, #5, #7

Standard:	**Discontinued**
Sporting:	**$2195**
Buffalo Rifle:	**$3200**
#7:	**Discontinued**
Take Down:	**Discontinued**

Magnum Research Rifles

MAGNUMLITE BARRACUDA STOCK

MOUNTAIN EAGLE
MAGNUMLITE GRAPHITE CENTERFIRE

MAGNUMLITE RIMFIRE

Action: autoloading
Stock: composite or laminated
Barrel: graphite sleeved, 16.75 in.
Sights: none
Weight: 5.2 lbs.
Caliber: .22LR, .22 WMR, .17 HMR and .17M2
Magazine: rotary, 9 rounds
Features: Ruger 10/22 action; carbon-fiber barrel with steel liner

With composite stock:	**$599**
.17 M2:	**$599-759**
.17 HMR:	**$709-999**
With laminated stock:	**$759**
Magnum with composite:	**$665**
Magnum with laminated:	**$959**

MOUNTAIN EAGLE MAGNUMLITE GRAPHITE CENTERFIRE

Action: bolt
Stock: composite
Barrel: graphite sleeved, 24 or 26 in.
Sights: none
Weight: 7.8 lbs.
Caliber: .280, .30-06, 7mm Rem. Mag., .300 Win. Mag., 7 WSM, .300 WSM
Magazine: box, 3 or 4 rounds
Features: adjustable trigger, free-floating match-grade barrel; platform bedding; left-hand available

MSRP:	**$2295**

Marlin Rifles

MODEL 60

MODEL 70PSS

MODEL 308MX

MODEL 308MXLR

MODEL 336C

RIFLES

MODEL 60

Action: autoloading
Stock: hardwood
Barrel: 19 in.
Sights: open
Weight: 5.5 lbs.
Caliber: .22 LR
Magazine: under-barrel tube, 14 rounds
Features: last shot hold-open device; stainless, synthetic and laminated stocked versions available; also available with camo-finished stock
Standard: $178
Camo: $210
Stainless: $226
Stainless, synthetic: $283
Stainless,
   laminated two-tone: . . . $165–204

MODEL 70PSS

Action: autoloading
Stock: synthetic
Barrel: 16 in.
Sights: open
Weight: 3.3 lbs.
Caliber: .22 LR
Magazine: detachable box, 7 rounds

Features: take-down rifle; nickel-plated swivel studs; floatable, padded carrying case included
MSRP: $284

MODEL 308MX

Action: lever
Stock: American black walnut
Barrel: 22 in.
Sights: adjustable semi-buckhorn folding rear; ramp front sight with brass bead and Wide-Scan hood
Weight: 7 lbs.
Caliber: .308 Marlin Express
Magazine: 5-shot tubular
Features: traditional blued barrel and receiver; full pistol grip; solid-top receiver tapped for scope mount; offset hammer spur (right or left hand) for scope use; deluxe recoil pad; swivel studs; tough Mar-Shield finish
MSRP: $611

MODEL 308MXLR

Action: lever
Stock: black/gray laminated hardwood
Barrel: 24 in.

Sights: adjustable semi-buckhorn folding rear; ramp front sight with brass bead and Wide-Scan hood
Weight: 7 lbs.
Caliber: .308 Marlin Express
Magazine: 5-shot tubular
Features: stainless-steel barrel and receiver; full pistol grip; Marlin signature solid-top receiver with side-ejection; deluxe recoil pad; nickel plated swivel studs
MSRP: $806

MODEL 336C

Action: lever
Stock: checkered walnut, pistol grip
Barrel: 20 in.
Sights: open
Weight: 7.0 lbs.
Caliber: .30-30 Win., and .35 Rem.
Magazine: tube, 6 rounds
Features: blued; hammer-block safety; offset hammer spur for scope use
Model 336C: $5582
Model 336A, .30-30 only,
   birch stock: . . . . . . **Discontinued**
Model 336W, .30-30 only,
   gold-plated: $455

Marlin Rifles

MODEL 336SS

MODEL 336XLR

MODEL 444

MODEL 717M2

MODEL 336SS
Action: lever
Stock: checkered walnut, pistol grip
Barrel: 20 in.
Sights: open
Weight: 7.0 lbs.
Caliber: .30-30
Magazine: under-barrel tube, 6 rounds
Features: offset hammer spur for scope use; Micro-Groove rifling
MSRP: **$641**

MODEL 336XLR
Action: lever
Stock: laminated
Barrel: 24 in.
Sights: adjustable
Weight: 7.0 lbs.
Caliber: .30/30
Magazine: tube, 5 rounds
Features: 24 in. stainless barrel w/ broached Ballard rifling; stainless solid-top receiver with side-ejection —tapped for scope mount; semi-buckhorn folding rear sight, ramp front sight with Wide-Scan hood; black/gray laminated hardwood pistol grip stock, cut checkering; nickel plated swivel studs; decelerator recoil pad
MSRP: **$806**

MODEL 444
Action: lever
Stock: walnut, pistol grip, fluted comb, checkering
Barrel: 22 in.
Sights: open
Weight: 7.5 lbs.
Caliber: .444 Marlin
Magazine: tube, 5 rounds
Features: blued; hammer-block safety; offset hammer spur for scope use
MSRP: **$611**

MODEL 444XLR
Action: lever
Stock: laminated
Barrel: 24 in.
Sights: adjustable
Weight: 7.5 lbs.
Caliber: .444 Marlin
Magazine: tube, 5 rounds
Features: 24 in. stainless barrel w/ broached Ballard rifling; stainless solid-top receiver with side-ejection —tapped for scope mount; semi-buckhorn folding rear sight, ramp front sight with Wide-Scan hood; black/gray laminated hardwood pistol grip stock; cut checkering; nickel plated swivel studs; decelerator recoil pad
MSRP: **$806**

MODEL 717M2
Action: autoloading
Stock: hardwood
Barrel: 18 in.
Sights: open
Weight: 5.0 lbs.
Caliber: .17 Mach 2
Magazine: detachable box, 7 rounds
Features: Sportster barrel; last-shot bolt hold-open; manual bolt hold-open; cross-bolt safety; adjustable ramp front sight; receiver grooved for scope mount; Monte Carlo walnut-finished laminated hardwood stock with pistol grip; 37 in. overall length
Discontinued

MODEL 917

MODEL 917VSF

MODEL 917VR

MODEL 925C (CAMO)

MODEL 925M

MODEL 917

Action: bolt
Stock: synthetic
Barrel: 22 in.
Sights: adjustable
Weight: 6.0 lbs.
Caliber: .17 HMR
Magazine: clip, 7 rounds
Features: Sporter barrel; adjustable T-900 trigger system; fiberglass-filled synthetic stock with full pistol grip, swivel studs and molded-in checkering; adjustable open rear, ramp front sights
MSRP: $239

MODEL 917V

Action: bolt
Stock: hardwood
Barrel: heavy 22 in.
Sights: none
Weight: 6.0 lbs.

Caliber: .17 HMR
Magazine: detachable box, 7 rounds
Features: T-900 Fire Control System; 1-in. scope mounts provided; also available: 917VS stainless steel with laminated hardwood stock (7 lbs.)
917V: $261
917VS: $374
917 VSF (fluted barrel): $397

MODEL 917VR

Action: bolt
Stock: synthetic
Barrel: 22 in.
Sights: none
Weight: 6.0 lbs.
Caliber: .17 HMR
Magazine: clip, 7 rounds
Features: Varmint barrel; thumb safety; red cocking indicator; receiver is grooved for scope mount; drilled and tapped for scope bases (scope bases

included); fiberglass-filled synthetic stock with full pistol grip, swivel studs and molded-in checkering
MSRP: $251

MODEL 925

Action: bolt
Stock: hardwood
Barrel: 22 in.
Sights: open
Weight: 5.5 lbs.
Caliber: .22 LR
Magazine: detachable box, 7 rounds
Features: T-900 Fire Control System; Micro-Groove rifling; can be ordered with scope; also available with Mossy Oak camo stock finish
925: $205
925 with scope: $235
925C (camo): $238

Marlin Rifles

MODEL 925R

MODEL 981T

MODEL 983T

MODEL 1894

MODEL 1894 COWBOY

MODEL 925R

Action: bolt
Stock: synthetic
Barrel: 22 in.
Sights: adjustable
Weight: 5.5 lbs.
Caliber: .22 LR
Magazine: clip, 7 rounds
Features: Micro-Groove sporter barrel; patented T-900 Fire Control System; black synthetic stock with molded-in checkering and swivel studs; adjustable open rear, ramp front sights
MSRP: $197

MODEL 981T

Action: bolt
Stock: synthetic
Barrel: 22 in.
Sights: open
Weight: 6.0 lbs.
Caliber: .22 L, S or LR
Magazine: under-barrel tube, 17 rounds
Features: Micro-Groove rifling; T-900 Fire Control System
918T: $204

MODEL 983T

Action: bolt
Stock: synthetic
Barrel: 22 in.
Sights: open
Weight: 6.0 lbs.
Caliber: .22 WMR
Magazine: under-barrel tube, 12 rounds
Features: T-900 Fire Control System; Micro-Groove rifling; available as Model 983 with walnut stock or laminated stock and stainless barrel
983T: $244
Model 983:. $306
Model 983S:. $335

MODEL 1894

Action: lever
Stock: checkered American walnut
Barrel: 20 in.
Sights: open
Weight: 6.0 lbs.
Caliber: .44 Rem. Mag./.44 Special
Magazine: tube, 10 rounds
Features: straight grip stock with Mar-Shield finish
MSRP: $591

MODEL 1894CL

Action: lever
Stock: walnut
Barrel: 22 in.
Sights: open
Weight: 6 lbs.
Caliber: .32-20 Win.
Magazine: under-barrel tube, 6 rounds
Features: Micro-Groove finish barrel; solid top receiver; hammer block safety; half-length tube magazine; Marble adjustable semi-buckhorn rear and carbine front sights; straight-grip stock with cut checkering and hard rubber butt pad; 39.5 in. overall length
Discontinued

MODEL 1894 COWBOY

Action: lever
Stock: walnut, straight grip, checkered
Barrel: tapered octagon, 24 in.
Sights: open
Weight: 6.5 lbs.
Caliber: .357 Mag./.38 Special, .44 Mag./.44 Special and .45 Colt
Magazine: tube, 10 rounds
Features: blued finish; hammer-block safety; hard rubber buttplate; Competition model available in .38 Special or .45 Colt with 20 in. barrel
Cowboy in .32 HMR Mag: . . . .
Discontinued
1894 Cowboy: $842

Marlin Rifles

MODEL 1894 COWBOY COMPETITION

MODEL 1894SS

MODEL 1895

MODEL 1895M

MODEL 1895XLR

MODEL 1894 COWBOY COMPETITION

Action: lever
Barrel: 20 in.
Weight: 7.0 lbs.
Caliber: .38 Spl., .45 Long Colt
Magazine: 10 rounds
Features: case-colored receiver
Stock: walnut
Sights: open
Discontinued

MODEL 1894SS

Action: lever
Stock: checkered walnut, straight grip
Barrel: 20 in. **Sights:** open
Weight: 6.0 lbs.
Caliber: .44 Rem. Mag.
Magazine: under-barrel tube, 10 rounds
Features: Micro-groove rifling
1894C (blued): **$591**
1894 SS: **$722**
1894 CL: . . . . **Discontinued**

MODEL 1895

Action: lever
Stock: checkered walnut, pistol grip
Barrel: 22 in. **Sights:** open
Weight: 7.5 lbs.
Caliber: .45-70 Govt.
Magazine: tube, 4 rounds
Features: blued; hammer-block safety, offset hammer spur for scope use; Model 1895G has 18.5 in. barrel and straight grip
1895: **$611**
1895G: **$621**
1895GS in stainless steel: **$742**
1895 Cowboy
(26" octagonbarrel): **$775**

MODEL 1895M

Action: lever
Stock: checkered walnut, straight grip
Barrel: Ballard rifled, 18.5 in.
Sights: open
Weight: 7.0 lbs.
Caliber: .450
Magazine: tube, 4 rounds
Features: blued finish; hammer-block safety; offset hammer spur for scope use
MSRP: **$669**

MODEL 1895MXLR

Action: lever
Stock: laminated
Barrel: 24 in.
Sights: adjustable
Weight: 7.0 lbs.
Caliber: .450 Marlin
Magazine: tube, 4 rounds
Features: 24 in. stainless steel barrel w/ Ballard rifling; stainless solid-top receiver with side-ejection—tapped for scope mount; semi-buckhorn folding rear sight, ramp front sight with brass bead and Wide-Scan hood; black/gray laminated hardwood pistol grip stock, cut checkering; nickel-plated swivel studs; decelerator recoil pad
MSRP: **$806**

MODEL 1895XLR

Action: lever
Stock: laminated
Barrel: 24 in.
Sights: adjustable
Weight: 7.5 lbs.
Caliber: .45/70
Magazine: tube, 4 rounds
Features: 24 in. stainless steel barrel w/ Ballard rifling; stainless solid-top receiver with side-ejection—tapped for scope mount; semi-buckhorn folding rear sight, ramp front sight with brass bead and Wide-Scan hood; black/gray laminated hardwood pistol grip stock with fluted comb, cut checkering; nickel-plated swivel studs; decelerator recoil pad
MSRP: **$806**

Marlin Rifles

MODEL 7000

GOLDEN 39A

MODEL 7000
Action: autoloading
Stock: synthetic
Barrel: target weight, 28 in.
Sights: none
Weight: 5.3 lbs.
Caliber: .22 LR
Magazine: detachable box, 10 rounds
Features: also available as Model 795

and 795 SS, with sights and lighter barrel (weight: 4.5 lbs.)
Model 7000: . . . . **Discontinued**
795: **$158**
795 SS: **$226**

GOLDEN 39A
Action: lever
Stock: checkered walnut, pistol grip

Barrel: 24 in.
Sights: open
Weight: 6.5 lbs.
Caliber: .22 LR
Magazine: under-barrel tube, 19 rounds
Features: Micro-Groove rifling, single-screw take-down; swivel studs
MSRP: **$585**

Merkel Rifles

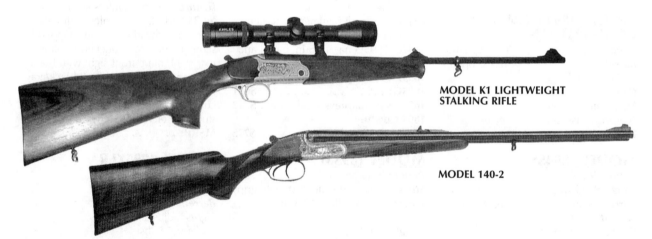

MODEL K1 LIGHTWEIGHT STALKING RIFLE

MODEL 140-2

MODEL K1 LIGHTWEIGHT STALKING RIFLE
Action: hinged breech
Stock: select walnut
Barrel: 24 in.
Sights: open
Weight: 5.6 lbs.
Caliber: .243, .270, 7x57R, 7mm Rem. Mag., .308, .30-06, .300 Win. Mag., 9.3x74R
Magazine: none

Features: single-shot; Franz Jager action; also available: Premium and Hunter grades
MSRP: **$3795**

SAFARI SERIES MODEL 140-2
Action: hinged breech
Stock: select walnut
Barrel: length and contour to order
Sights: open

Weight: 9.0 lbs.
Caliber: .375 H&H, .416 Rigby, .470 N.E.
Magazine: none
Features: Anson & Deely box-lock; double triggers; includes oak and leather luggage case; higher grade available; also Model 141.1, light-weight double in .308, .30-06, 9.3x74R
MSRP: . . . . **from $11995**

RIFLES

Mossberg Rifles

100 ATR SHORT-ACTION
Action: bolt
Stock: hardwood
Barrel: 22 in.
Sights: none
Weight: 7 lbs.
Caliber: .243 Win, .308 Win.

Magazine: internal box, 4 + 1 rounds
Features: free floating matte blued barrel; side-lever safety; factory installed Weaver style scope bases; walnut finished hardwood stock; rubber recoil pad
MSRP: $424–471

Navy Arms Rifles

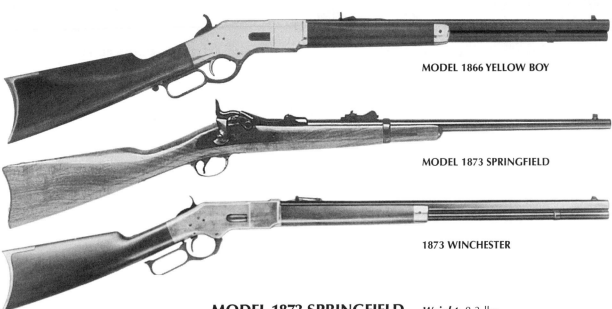

MODEL 1866 YELLOW BOY

MODEL 1873 SPRINGFIELD

1873 WINCHESTER

MODEL 1866 YELLOW BOY
Action: lever
Stock: walnut, straight grip
Barrel: octagon, 20 in.
Sights: open
Weight: 7.5 lbs.
Caliber: .38 Special, .44-40, .45 Colt
Magazine: under-barrel tube, 10 rounds
Features: also available: Yellow Boy with 24 in. barrel (8.3 lbs.)
MSRP: $1015

MODEL 1873 SPRINGFIELD
Action: dropping block
Stock: walnut
Barrel: 22 in.
Sights: open
Weight: 7.0 lbs.
Caliber: .45-70
Magazine: none
Features: "Trapdoor" replica; saddle bar with ring
MSRP: $1475

MODEL 1873 WINCHESTER
Action: lever
Stock: walnut, straight grip
Barrel: 24 in.
Sights: open

Weight: 8.3 lbs.
Caliber: .357 Mag., .44-40, .45 Colt
Magazine: under-barrel tube, 13 rounds
Features: case-colored receiver; also: Carbine, Border, Deluxe (checkered) Border and Sporting models
1873 Winchester: $1132
Carbine: . . . . .Discontinued
Border Model: . . . . . .Discontinued
Sporting Rifle: . . . . . .Discontinued
Deluxe Border Model: $1241

Navy Arms Rifles

MODEL 1874 SHARPS

HENRY

ROLLING BLOCK #2 JOHN BODINE

ROLLING BLOCK BUFFALO RIFLE

SHARPS #2 SPORTING

MODEL 1874 SHARPS
Action: dropping block
Stock: walnut
Barrel: 22 in.
Sights: open   **Weight**: 7.8 lbs.
Caliber: .45-70   **Magazine**: none
Features: also: No. 3 Long Range
Sharps with double set triggers, 34 in.
barrel (10.9 lbs.) and Buffalo Rifle with
double set triggers, 28 in. octagon
barrel (10.6 lbs.)
Carbine: **$1210**
No. 3: **$2479**

HENRY
Action: lever
Stock: walnut, straight grip
Barrel: 24 in.
Sights: open
Weight: 9.0 lbs.
Caliber: .44-40, .45 Colt
Magazine: under-barrel tube,
13 rounds

Features: blued or case-colored
receiver
Military Henry: **$1212**
Henry: **$1212**

ROLLING BLOCK #2 JOHN BODINE
Action: dropping block
Stock: walnut   **Barrel**: 30 in.
Sights: adjustable tang
Weight: 12.0 lbs.
Caliber: .45-70   **Magazine**: none
Features: double set triggers; nickel-
finish breech
MSRP: **$1937**

ROLLING BLOCK BUFFALO RIFLE
Action: dropping block
Stock: walnut
Barrel: 26 in. or 30 in.
Sights: open
Weight: 9.0 lbs.

Caliber: .45-70
Magazine: none
Features: case-colored receiver;
optional brass telescopic sight; drilled
for Creedmoor sight; also checkered
#2 model with tang and globe sights
MSRP: **$910**

MODEL SHARPS #2 SPORTING
Action: dropping block
Stock: walnut
Barrel: 30 in.
Sights: target   **Weight**: 10.0 lbs.
Caliber: .45-70   **Magazine**: none
Features: also #2 Silhouette
Creedmoor and Quigley
(with 34 in. barrel)
Sporting: . . . . **Discontinued**
Silhouette . . . . **Discontinued**
Quigley . . . . **Discontinued**
Creedmoor: **$1844**

New England Firearms Rifles

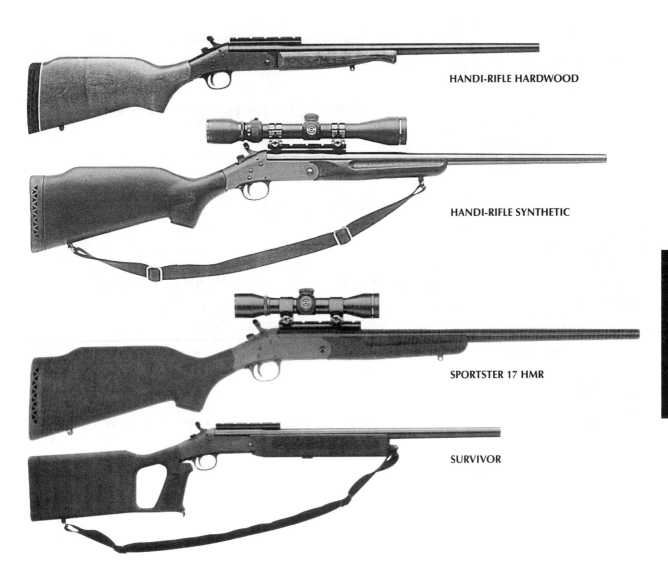

HANDI-RIFLE HARDWOOD

HANDI-RIFLE SYNTHETIC

SPORTSTER 17 HMR

SURVIVOR

HANDI-RIFLE
Action: hinged breech
Stock: Monte Carlo synthetic or hardwood
Barrel: 22 in. or 26 in.
Sights: none
Weight: 7.0 lbs.
Caliber: .223, .22-250, .243, .270, .30-06
Magazine: none
Features: offset hammer; open-sight version of Handi-Rifle in .22 Hornet, .30-30, .357 Mag., .44 Mag., .45-70 Govt.; Youth models in .223, .243 and 7mm-08
Handi-Rifle: **$274**
With hardwood stock: **$250–265**
Synthetic Stainless: . . **Discontinued**
Youth: . . . . **Discontinued**

SPORTSTER 17 HMR & 17 MACH2
Action: hinged breech
Stock: synthetic
Barrel: heavy varmint, 22 in.
Sights: none
Weight: 6.0 lbs.
Caliber: .17 Hornady Magnum Rimfire, .17 MACH 2
Magazine: none
Features: Monte Carlo stock; sling swivel studs; recoil pad; Sportster Youth available with 20 in. barrel (5.5 lbs.), in .22 LR or .22 WMR
Youth: **$175**
Sportster: **$175**

SURVIVOR
Action: hinged breech
Stock: synthetic
Barrel: 22 in. bull
Sights: open
Weight: 6.0 lbs.
Caliber: .223 & .308
Magazine: none
Features: single-shot; recoil pad; hollow synthetic stock with storage compartment; thumbscrew take down
MSRP: **$277**

New Ultra Light Arms Rifles

MODEL 20 MOUNTAIN RIFLE

MODEL 20 RF

MODEL 28

MODEL 20 MOUNTAIN RIFLE

Action: bolt
Stock: Kevlar/graphite composite
Barrel: 22 in.
Sights: none
Weight: 4.75 lbs.
Caliber: short action: 6mm, .17, .22 Hornet, .222, .222 Rem. Mag., .22-250, .223, .243, .250-3000 Savage, .257, .257 Ackley, 7x57, 7x57 Ackley, 7mm-08, .284, .300 Savage, .308, .358
Magazine: box, 4, 5 or 6 rounds
Features: two-position safety; choice of 7 or more stock colors; available in left-hand
Mountain Rifle: **$3000**
Left-hand: **$3100**

MODEL 20 RF

Action: bolt
Stock: composite
Barrel: Douglas Premium #1 Contour, 22 in.
Sights: none
Weight: 5.25 lbs.
Caliber: .22 LR
Magazine: none (or detachable box, 5 rounds)
Features: single-shot or repeater; drilled and tapped for scope; recoil pad, sling swivels; fully adjustable Timney trigger; 3-position safety; color options
Single-shot: **$1300**
Repeater: **$1350**

MODEL 24 AND 28

Action: bolt
Stock: Kevlar composite
Barrel: 22 in.
Sights: none
Weight: 5.25 lbs.
Caliber: long action: .270, .30-06, .25-06, .280, .280 Ackley, .338-06, .35 Whelen; Model 28: .264, 7mm, .300, .338, .300 WSM, .270 WSM, 7mm WSM; Model 40: .300 Wby. and .416 Rigby
Magazine: box, 4 rounds
Features: Model 28 has 24 in. bbl. and weighs 5.5 lbs.; Model 40 has 24 in. bbl. (6.5 lbs.); all available in left-hand versions
Model 24: **$3100**
Model 24, left-hand: **$3200**
Model 28 or Model 40: **$3400**
Model 28 or Model 40,
   left-hand: **$3500**

Nosler Rifles

NOSLER BOLT-ACTION

Action: bolt
Stock: Turkish walnut
Barrel: 24 in.
Sights: optical
Weight: 7.75 lbs.
Caliber: .300 WSM
Magazine: internal box, 3 rounds
Features: hand-lapped, match-grade Wiseman barrel; three-position safety;
Timney trigger; Leupold VX-III 2.5-8x36 scope serial-numbered to the rifle; production limited to 500 units
MSRP: **$2795**

Pedersoli Replica Rifles

.45-70 OFFICER'S MODEL
TRAPDOOR SPRINGFIELD

KODIAK MARK IV DOUBLE

ROLLING BLOCK TARGET

SHARPS 1874 CAVALRY

RIFLES

.45-70 OFFICER'S MODEL TRAPDOOR SPRINGFIELD

Action: single-shot hinged breech
Stock: walnut
Barrel: 26 in.
Sights: Creedmoor style tang
Weight: 7.72 lbs.
Caliber: .45-70
Magazine: none
Features: blued, 26 in. tapered round barrel, precision broach rifled with 6 lands and grooves with a one turn-in-18 inches rifling twist; color case-hardened receiver, breechblock, trigger guard, barrel band, buttplate and lock plate; satin-finished American black walnut stock
MSRP: $1600

KODIAK MARK IV DOUBLE

Action: hinged breech
Stock: walnut
Barrel: 22 in. and 24 in.

Sights: open
Weight: 8.2 lbs.
Caliber: .45-70, 9.3x74R, 8x57JSR
Magazine: none
Features: .45-70 weighs 8.2 lbs.; also available: Kodiak Mark IV with interchangeable 20-gauge barrel
45-70: . . . . **special order only**
8x57, 9.3x74: . . . **special order only**
Kodiak Mark IV: . **special order only**

ROLLING BLOCK TARGET

Action: dropping block
Stock: walnut
Barrel: octagon, 30 in.
Sights: target
Weight: 9.5 lbs.
Caliber: .45-70 and .357 (10 lbs.)
Magazine: none
Features: Creedmoor sights; also available: Buffalo, Big Game, Sporting, Baby Carbine, Custer, Long Range Creedmoor
MSRP: $989

SHARPS 1874 CAVALRY & INFANTRY MODEL

Action: dropping block
Stock: walnut
Barrel: 22 in.
Sights: open
Weight: 8.4 lbs.
Caliber: .45-70
Magazine: none
Features: also available: 1874 Infantry (set trigger, 30 in. bbl.), 1874 Sporting (.40-65 or .45-70, set trigger, 32 in. oct. bbl.), 1874 Long Range (.45-70 and .45-90, .45-120, 34 in. half oct. bbl., target sights)
Cavalry: $1281
Infantry (one trigger): $1561
Infantry (two triggers): $1624
Sporting: $1350
Long Range: $1761
Long Range Big Bore: $1916

PGW Defense Technology Rifles

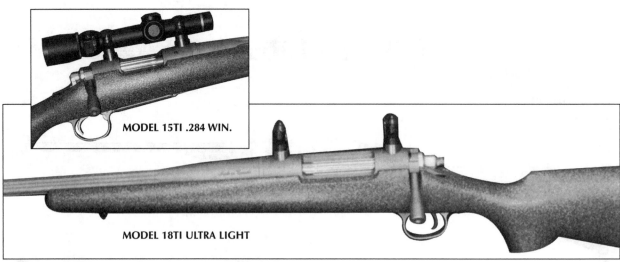

MODEL 15TI .284 WIN.

MODEL 18TI ULTRA LIGHT

MODEL 15TI ULTRA LIGHT
Action: bolt
Stock: composite *Barrel:* 22 in.
Sights: none *Weight:* 5.0 lbs.
Caliber: most short-action calibers
Magazine: box, 5 rounds
Features: Rem. 700 short-action, custom alloy scope mounts; new firing pin and bolt shroud tuned; also: Model 18Ti with long 700 action
Discontinued

TIMBERWOLF
Action: bolt
Stock: McMillan fiberglass
Barrel: fluted, match grade
Sights: none
Caliber: .338 Lapua
Magazine: 5 rounds
Features: stainless receiver; adjustable trigger; 3-position safety, titanium rail with guide rib

Timberwolf: **$6110**
    also available in .408: Discontinued
Coyote in 7.62
    (5 or 10-shot magazine): . . . **$440**
LRT .50 Caliber Take-Down: . . . .
        Discontinued
LRT-2 in .338 or .408 . . **Discontinued**

Purdey Rifles

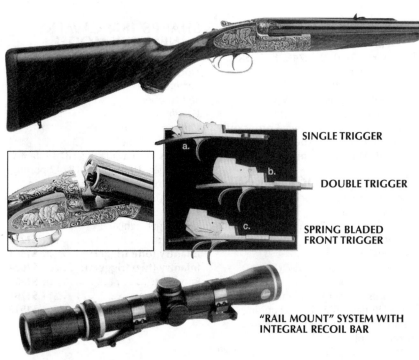

SINGLE TRIGGER

DOUBLE TRIGGER

SPRING BLADED FRONT TRIGGER

"RAIL MOUNT" SYSTEM WITH INTEGRAL RECOIL BAR

DOUBLE BARREL RIFLE .577 NITRO

Purdey's double-barrel Express rifles are built to customer specifications on actions sized to each particular cartridge. Standard chamberings include .375 H&H Magnum and .470, .577 and .600 Nitro Express. The Purdey side-by-side action patented in 1880, designed by Frederick Beesley, retains a portion of the energy in the mainsprings to facilitate the opening of the gun.

The over-under is derived from the Woodward, patented in 1913. The action blocks for all guns are cut from certified forgings, for consistency of grain throughout, and are fitted to the barrels to make an absolute joint. The actioner then fits the fore-part, the locks, the strikers and the safety work before finally detonating the action.

Purdey Rifles

A – SINGLE TRIGGER

The Purdey single trigger works both by inertia and mechanically. It is simple, effective and fast. The firing sequence is fixed, therefore no barrel selection is possible.

B & C – DOUBLE TRIGGERS

The standard double triggers (B) can be augmented with an articulated front trigger (C). This device alleviates damage to the back of the trigger finger on discharge.

Purdey makes its own dedicated actions for bolt rifles in the following calibers: .375 H&H, .416/450 Rigby or other, .500 and .505 Gibbs. The action length is suited to cartridge length in each caliber. Mauser Square Bridge and Mauser '98 actions are available.

RAIL MOUNT SYSTEM

This is Purdey's own system for big bolt rifles. It is very secure and facilitates fast on/off. Rings and mounts are all made with an integral recoil bar from a single piece of steel. This system is recommended for Purdey actions and Mauser Square Bridge actions.

Remington Arms Rifles

RIFLES

MODEL 40-XBBR KS

MODEL 40-XB TACTICAL

MODEL 552 SPEEDMASTER

MODEL 40-XBBR KS

Action: bolt
Stock: fiberglass
Barrel: 24 in.
Sights: none
Weight: 9.75 lbs.
Caliber: .22 LR
Magazine: single shot
Features: benchrest with stainless barrel; Aramid-fiber reinforced Remington green stock
Custom order

MODEL 40-XB TACTICAL

Action: bolt
Stock: black with green fiberglass
Barrel: 27.25 in.
Sights: none
Weight: 10.25 lbs.
Caliber: .308 Win.
Magazine: hinged floorplate, 5 rounds
Features: built to order
Custom order

MODEL 40-X TARGET

Action: bolt
Stock: target, benchrest or tactical
Barrel: 24 in. or 27 in.
Sights: none
Weight: 10.25-11.25 lbs.
Caliber: 18 popular standard and magnum calibers
Magazine: box, 3 or 5 rounds
Features: rimfire and single-shot versions available; walnut, laminated and composite stocks; forend rail, match trigger
40-X: **$2561–3014**
Left-hand: **$1884-2555**
Custom 40-XR Sporter: **$4523**

MODEL 552 BDL DELUXE SPEEDMASTER

Action: autoloading
Stock: walnut
Barrel: 21 in.
Sights: Big Game
Weight: 5.75 lbs.
Caliber: .22 S, .22 L, .22 LR
Magazine: under-barrel tube, 15-20 rounds
Features: classic autoloader made 1966 to date
MSRP: **$593**

Remington Arms Rifles

MODEL 572 FIELDMASTER

MODEL 597

MODEL 700 AFRICAN BIG GAME

MODEL 700 AFRICAN PLAINS RIFLE

MODEL 700 ALASKAN TI

MODEL 572
BDL DELUXE FIELDMASTER
Action: pump
Stock: walnut
Barrel: 21 in.
Sights: Big Game
Weight: 5.5 lbs.
Caliber: .22 S, .22 L, .22 LR
Magazine: under-barrel tube, 15-20 rounds
Features: grooved receiver for scope mounts
MSRP: **$607**

MODEL 597
Action: autoloading
Stock: synthetic or laminated
Barrel: 20 in.
Sights: Big Game
Weight: 5.5-6.5 lbs.
Caliber: .22 LR, .22 WMR, .17 HMR
Magazine: detachable box, 10 rounds (8 in magnums)
Features: magnum version in .22 WMR and .17 HMR (both 6 lbs.); also: heavy-barrel model

Model 597: **$193**
Stainless: . . . . **Discontinued**
Stainless laminated: . . **Discontinued**
22 WMR: **$492**
Magnum (.17 HMR): Discontinued
Heavy-barrel: . . . . **Discontinued**

MODEL 700
AFRICAN BIG GAME
Action: bolt
Stock: laminated
Barrel: 26 in.
Sights: open
Weight: 9.5 lbs.
Caliber: .375 H&H, .375 RUM, .458 Win, .416 Rem.
Magazine: box, 3 rounds
Features: barrel-mounted front swivel
MSRP: **$3241**

MODEL 700
AFRICAN PLAINS RIFLE
Action: bolt
Stock: laminated
Barrel: 26 in.
Sights: none
Weight: 7.75 lbs.
Caliber: 10 offerings from 7mm Rem.

Mag. to .375 RUM
Magazine: box, 3 rounds
Features: epoxy bedded action; machined steel trigger and floor plate.
Discontinued

MODEL 700 ALASKAN TI
Action: bolt; short, long and magnum
Stock: Bell & Carlson carbon fiber synthetic, matte finish, Maxx Guard protective coating
Barrel: 24 in.
Sights: none; drilled and tapped for scope mounts
Weight: 6-6.3 lbs.
Caliber: .270 Win, 7mm-08 Rem, .25-06 Rem, .280 Rem, .30-06 Sprg, 7mm Rem Mag, .270 WSM, .300 WSM, .300 Win Mag
Magazine: hinged floorplate, 4 rounds (short, long action calibers), 3 rounds (magnum)
Features: titanium receiver; spiral flutes on bolt body and handle; 416 stainless steel barrel with Light Varmint style fluting; Remington X-Mark Pro trigger; R3 recoil pad; sling swivel studs
MSRP: **$2225–2349**

RIFLES

MODEL 700 BDL

MODEL 700 CDL

MODEL 700 CDL SF

MODEL 700 CDL
.17 FIREBALL

MODEL 700
BDL CUSTOM DELUXE

Action: bolt
Stock: walnut
Barrel: 22-26 in.
Sights: open   *Weight*: 7.25-7.5 lbs.
Caliber: popular standard calibers from .17 Rem. to .300 RUM
Magazine: box, 3 or 5 rounds
Features: hinged floorplate; sling swivel studs; hooded ramp front & adjustable rear sights
BDL: **$927**
BDL Magnum: **$955**
BDL Ultra-Mags: **$955**

MODEL 700 CDL

Action: bolt
Stock: walnut
Barrel: 24 in. (standard) and 26 in. (magnum, Ultra Mag)
Sights: none (drilled and tapped for scope mounts)
Weight: 7.5 lbs.
Caliber: .243, .25-06 Rem., .35 Whelen, .270, 7mm-08, 7mm Rem.

Mag., 7mm Ultra Mag, .30-06, .300 Win. Mag., .300 Ultra Mag
Magazine: box, 4 rounds (3 in magnums, Ultra Mags)
Features: fully adjustable trigger
Standard: **$959**
Ultra Mag: **$987**
Mag & Ultra Mag, left-hand
  (6 calibers): **$987–1013**

MODEL 700 CDL SF

Action: bolt; short, long and magnum
Stock: American walnut, satin finish
Barrel: 24 in. (short, long, short magnum), 26 in. (magnum)
Sights: none; drilled and tapped for scope mounts
Weight: 7.4-7.6 lbs.
Caliber: .270 Win, 7mm-08 Rem, .30-06 Sprg, 7mm Rem Mag, .270 WSM, .300 WSM
Features: 416 stainless steel fluted barrel; solid steel cylindrical receiver; hammer-forged barrel; Remington X-Mark Pro trigger; jeweled bolt; R3 recoil pad; sling swivel studs
MSRP: **$1100**

MODEL 700
CDL SF LIMITED,
.17 REMINGTON FIREBALL

Action: bolt, short
Stock: American walnut, satin finish
Barrel: 24 in.
Sights: none; drilled and tapped for scope mounts
Weight: 7.6 lbs.
Caliber: .17 Remington Fireball
Magazine: 4 rounds
Features: commemorative engraving on the hinged floorplate denoting the introduction of the .17 Remington Fireball cartridge and "Model 700 Limited" rollmark on the receiver; limited production quantities; right-handed cheek piece; 416 stainless fluted barreled action; hammer-forged barrel; Remington X-Mark Pro trigger; jeweled bolt; R3 recoil pad; sling swivel studs
MSRP: **$1132**

Remington Arms Rifles

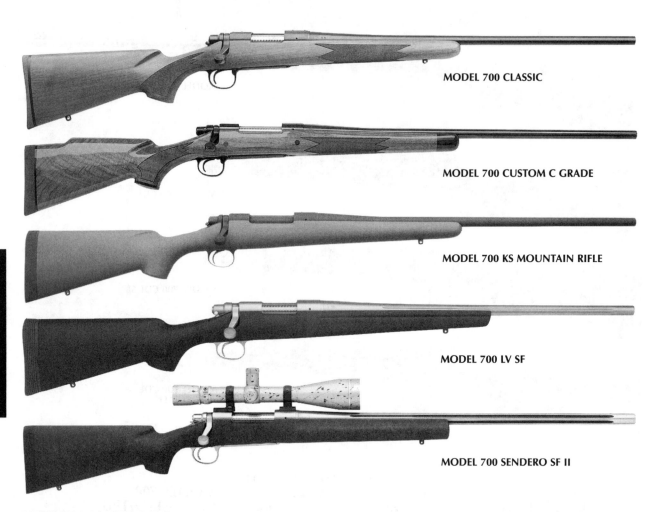

MODEL 700 CLASSIC

MODEL 700 CUSTOM C GRADE

MODEL 700 KS MOUNTAIN RIFLE

MODEL 700 LV SF

MODEL 700 SENDERO SF II

MODEL 700 CLASSIC
Action: bolt
Stock: walnut
Barrel: 24 in.
Sights: none
Weight: 7.25 lbs.
Caliber: .308 Win.
Magazine: box, 5 rounds
Features: one-year run per caliber
Discontinued

MODEL 700 CUSTOM C GRADE
Action: bolt
Stock: fancy American walnut
Barrel: 24 in. (Ultra Mag 26 in.)
Sights: none
Weight: 7.5 lbs.
Caliber: any popular standard or magnum chambering
Magazine: 3-5 rounds
Features: some custom-shop options available
MSRP: **$3236**

MODEL 700 CUSTOM KS MOUNTAIN RIFLE
Action: bolt
Stock: lightweight composite black matte
Barrel: 24 or 26 in., blued or stainless
Sights: none
Weight: 6.5-7.0 lbs. (magnums)
Caliber: 13 choices from .270 to .375 RUM
Magazine: box, 3 or 4 rounds
Discontinued

MODEL 700 LIGHT VARMINT (LV SF)
Action: bolt
Stock: synthetic
Barrel: 22 in., stainless, fluted
Sights: none (drilled and tapped for scope mounts)
Weight: 6.7 lbs.
Caliber: .17 Rem., .204 Ruger, .221 Fireball, .22-250, .223

Magazine: box, 4 or 5 rounds
Features: fully adjustable trigger
Discontinued

MODEL 700 SENDERO SF II
Action: bolt
Stock: composite
Barrel: 26 in.
Weight: 8.5 lbs.
Caliber: .264 Win. Mag., 7mm Rem. Mag., 7mm Rem. Ultra Mag., .300 Win. Mag., .300 Win. Ultra Mag.
Features: heavy-contour (0.820" Muzzle O.D.) polished stainless fluted barrel; full-length aluminum bedding blocks; black with gray webbing H.S. Precision aramid fiber reinforced composite stock with contoured beavertail forend with ambidextrous finger grooves and palm swell; twin front swivel studs for sling and a bipod
MSRP: **$1359**

MODEL 700 SPS

MODEL 700 SPS
BUCKMASTERS

MODEL 700 SPS
BUCKMASTERS
YOUNG BUCKS

MODEL 700 SPS VARMINT

MODEL 700 SPS

Action: bolt
Stock: synthetic
Barrel: 24 in. or 26 in.
Sights: none
Weight: 7.25-7.5 lbs.
Caliber: .204 Ruger to .300 Ultra Mag
Magazine: detachable box, 3-5 rounds
Features: also available in youth models with 20- and 22-inch barrels; chrome-moly or stainless, sporter
MSRP: $639–673

MODEL 700 SPS BUCKMASTERS

Action: bolt; short, long and magnum
Stock: camo-covered synthetic, Realtree Hardwoods HD
Barrel: 24 in. (short and long), 26 in. (magnum)
Sights: none; drilled and tapped for scope mounts
Weight: 7.3-7.6 lbs.
Caliber: .243 Win, 7mm-08, .270

Win, .30-06 Sprg, 7mm Rem Mag, .300 Win Mag
Magazine: hinged floorplate
Features: specially engraved floorplate with Buckmasters logo; fully camouflaged stock; carbon steel barrel with matte blued finish; sling swivel studs, R3 recoil pad
MSRP: $707

MODEL 700 SPS BUCKMASTERS YOUNG BUCKS YOUTH EDITION

Action: bolt; short
Stock: camo-covered synthetic, Realtree Hardwoods HD
Barrel: 20 in.
Sights: none; drilled and tapped for scope mounts
Weight: 6.8 lbs.
Caliber: .243 Win
Magazine: hinged floorplate
Features: specially engraved floorplate with Buckmasters logo; fully camou-

flaged stock; carbon steel barrel with matte blued finish; sling swivel studs, R3 recoil pad
MSRP: $707

MODEL 700 SPS VARMINT

Action: bolt; short
Stock: synthetic, matte black
Barrel: 26 in.
Sights: none; drilled and tapped for scope mounts
Weight: 7.4 lbs.
Caliber: .204 Ruger, .22-250 Rem, .223 Rem, .243 Win, .308 Win, .17 Rem Fireball
Magazine: 4 or 5 rounds, hinged floorplate
Features: carbon steel, heavy varmint-contour barrel with matte blued finish; Remington X-Mark Pro trigger; sling swivel studs
MSRP: $665

Remington Arms Rifles

MODEL 700 VL SS TH

MODEL 700 XCR

MODEL 700 XCR ELK
FOUNDATION

MODEL 700
XCR TACTICAL

MODEL 700 VL SS TH

Action: bolt; short
Stock: satin finish brown laminate; thumbhole style
Barrel: 26 in.
Sights: none; drilled and tapped for scope mounts
Weight: 9.2 lbs.
Caliber: .204 Ruger, .22-250 Rem, .223 Rem
Magazine: 4 rounds, hinged floorplate
Features: cylindrical solid steel receiver; hammer-forged, heavy-contour barrel with satin finish; Remington X-Mark Pro trigger; sling swivel studs
MSRP: $1085

MODEL 700 VSF TARGET

Action: bolt
Stock: composite
Barrel: heavy, 26 in.
Sights: none
Weight: 9.5 lbs.
Caliber: .223, .22-250, .243, .308
Magazine: box, 5 rounds
Features: fluted barrel, stock with beavertail forend, tactical style dual front swivel studs for bi-pod; VSSF II also available in .204 Ruger and .220 Swift

VSF (Desert tan): . . . . Discontinued
VSSF II: $1332
VLS (laminate): $979

MODEL 700 XCR

Action: bolt
Stock: synthetic
Barrel: 24 in. or 26 in.
Sights: none
Weight: 7.5 lbs.
Caliber: 11 chamberings, from .270 to .375 Ultra Mag
Magazine: internal box, 3-5 rounds
Features: stainless barreled action; TriNyte corrosion control coating; Hogue grip panels; stock finish is Realtree Hardwoods Gray HD; R3 recoil pad
MSRP: $1068-1141

MODEL 700 XCR ELK FOUNDATION RIFLE, .300 REM. ULTRA MAG

Action: bolt
Stock: camo-covered synthetic, overmolded, Realtree All-Purpose HD
Barrel: 26 in.
Sights: none; drilled and tapped for scope mounts
Weight: 7.6 lbs.

Caliber: .300 Rem. Ultra Mag
Magazine: hinged floorplate
Features: Rocky Mtn. Elk Foundation logo engraved on the hinged floorplate and stock; stainless-steel barrel with TriNyte Satin finish; sling swivel studs; R3 recoil pad; Remington X-Mark Pro trigger
MSRP: $1199

MODEL 700 XCR TACTICAL LONG RANGE RIFLE

Action: bolt, short and magnum
Stock: Tactical Bell and Carlson; synthetic composite, OD Green/Black Webbed
Barrel: 26 in.
Sights: none; drilled and tapped for scope mounts
Weight: 8.5 lbs.
Caliber: .300 Rem. Ultra Mag
Magazine: 3, 4 or 5 rounds
Features: 416 stainless-steel, varmint-contour, fluted barrel with black TriNyte finish; sling swivel studs; Remington X-Mark Pro trigger; recessed thumb hook behind the pistol grip
MSRP: $1407

Remington Arms Rifles

MODEL 750 WOODMASTER

MODEL 770

MODEL 770
YOUTH

MODEL 750 WOODMASTER

Action: autoloader
Stock: walnut
Barrel: 18.5 (carbines) and 22 in.
Sights: open, adjustable
Weight: 7.25 lbs. and 7.5 lbs.
Caliber: .243 Win., .308 Win., .270 Win., .30-06 Sprng., .35 Whelen, .308 Win. (carbine), .30-06 (carbine), .35 Whelen (carbine)
Features: improved gas system; low-profile design; R3 recoil pad; receiver drilled and tapped for Model 7400 scope mounts; satin finish American walnut forend and stock with machine-cut checkering
MSRP: $879

MODEL 770

Action: bolt; short, long and magnum
Stock: synthetic, matte black
Barrel: 22 or 24 in.
Sights: none; drilled and tapped for scope mounts
Weight: 8.5-8.6 lbs.
Caliber: .243 Win, .270 Win, .30-06 Sprg, 7mm Rem Mag, .300 Win Mag, 7mm-08 Rem, .308 Win
Magazine: 3 or 4 rounds, center-feed steel box
Features: complete with factory-mounted and bore-sighted Bushnell Sharpshooter 3-9x40mm scope; all steel receiver; ordnance-grade steel barrel with six-groove, button-rifling; all steel bolt cams; ergonomically contoured stock; sling swivel studs
MSRP: $540

MODEL 770 YOUTH

Action: bolt; short
Stock: synthetic, matte black
Barrel: 20 in.
Sights: none; drilled and tapped for scope mounts
Weight: 8.5-8.6 lbs.
Caliber: .243 Win
Magazine: 4 rounds, center-feed steel box
Features: $12^{3/8}$ in length of pull (1 in. shorter than standard model); complete with factory-mounted and bore-sighted Bushnell Sharpshooter 3-9x40mm scope; all steel receiver; ordnance-grade steel barrel with six-groove, button-rifling; all steel bolt cams; ergonomically contoured stock; sling swivel studs
MSRP: $460

Remington Arms Rifles

MODEL 798

MODEL 799

MODEL 7400

MODEL 7600

MODEL 7615
CAMO HUNTER

MODELS 798 AND 799

Action: bolt
Stock: laminated
Barrel: 20, 22, 24 in.
Sights: none
Weight: 7.0 lb. (798), 6.75 lbs. (799)
Caliber: .243 Win, .308 Win, .30-06, .270 Win, 7mm Rem. Mag., .300 Win. Mag., .375 H&H Mag., .458 Win. Mag. (Model 798). .22 Hornet, .222 Rem., .22-250 Rem., .223 Rem., 7.62x39mm (Model 799)
Magazine: internal (M-799 .22 Hornet) or detachable box, 5 rounds
Features: Model 98 Mauser action; M-798: 22 in. bl. (standard calibers); 24 in. bl. (long-action magnums); M-799: 20 in. bl.; hinged magazine floorplate; claw extractor; Sporter style 2-position safety; blued barrel and receiver; brown laminated stock; M-799 .22 Hornet utilizes a 5-round detachable box magazine; receivers are drilled and tapped for standard Mauser 98 long- and short-action scope mounts; one-inch rubber butt pad
Discontinued

MODEL 7400

Action: autoloading
Stock: walnut
Barrel: 22 in.
Sights: open
Weight: 7.5 lbs.
Caliber: .243, .270, .308, .30-06
Magazine: detachable box, 4 rounds
Features: also 7400 carbine with 18 in. barrel (7.25 lbs.)
Discontinued

MODEL 7600

Action: pump
Stock: walnut or synthetic
Barrel: 22 in.
Sights: open
Weight: 7.5 lbs.
Caliber: .243, .270, .308, .30-06
Magazine: detachable box, 4 rounds
Features: also 7600 carbine with 18 in. barrel (7.25 lbs.)
Synthetic: $665
Walnut: $792

MODEL 7615 CAMO HUNTER

Action: pump; short
Stock: camo-covered synthetic, Mossy Oak Brush
Barrel: 22 in.
Sights: rifle
Weight: 7.2 lbs.
Caliber: .223 Rem
Magazine: 10 rounds, detachable box
Features: carbon steel barrel and solid-steel receiver fully camouflaged with Mossy Oak Brush pattern; drilled and tapped for scope mounts
Discontinued

Remington Arms Rifles

MODEL 7615
RANCH CARBINE

MODEL 7615 TACTICAL

MODEL FIVE

MODEL SEVEN MAGNUM

MODEL SEVEN XCR CAMO

RIFLES

MODEL 7615 RANCH CARBINE

Action: pump; short
Stock: American walnut, satin finish
Barrel: 18.5 in.
Sights: rifle
Weight: 7 lbs.
Caliber: .223 Rem
Magazine: 10 rounds, detachable box
Features: carbon steel barrel with hardened Parkerized finish; solid-steel receiver; drilled and tapped for scope mounts
Discontinued

MODEL 7615 TACTICAL

Action: pump; short
Stock: synthetic, black matte
Barrel: 16.5 in.
Sights: rifle
Weight: 6.8 lbs.
Caliber: .223 Rem
Magazine: 10 rounds, detachable box
Features: carbon steel barrel with Parkerized finish; solid-steel receiver; Knoxx SpecOps NRS (No Recoil Suppression) stock with convenient adjustable length of pull feature for

proper fit; drilled and tapped for scope mounts; accepts standard M16/AR15-style box magazines
Discontinued

MODEL FIVE

Action: bolt
Stock: laminated
Barrel: 22 in.
Sights: adjustable, open
Weight: 6.75 lbs.
Caliber: .22LR, .22WMR
Magazine: clip, 5 rounds
Features: blued barrel; receiver grooved for scope mounts; walnut finish laminated stock
Discontinued

MODEL SEVEN MAGNUM

Action: bolt
Stock: synthetic or laminate
Barrel: stainless or blued, 22 in.
Sights: open   **Weight**: 7.25 lbs.
Caliber: 7mm SAUM, .300 SAUM
Magazine: box, 3 rounds
Features: also laminated stock versions with chrome-moly steel
Discontinued

MODEL SEVEN XCR CAMO

Action: bolt; short and short magnum
Stock: camo-covered synthetic, Realtree All-Purpose HD
Barrel: 20 or 23 in.
Sights: none; drilled and tapped for scope mounts
Weight: 7.0-7.2 lbs.
Caliber: .243 Win, 7mm-08 Rem, .308 Win, .270 WSM, .300 WSM
Magazine: 3+1 or 4+1, hinged floorplate
Features: 416 stainless steel, fluted barrel with TriNyte coating and matte finish; sling swivel studs; R3 recoil pad; Remington X-Mark Pro trigger
Discontinued

XR-100 RANGEMASTER

Action: bolt
Stock: laminated thumb-hole
Barrel: 26 in.   **Sights**: none
Weight: 9.2 lbs.
Caliber: .204, .223, .22-250
Magazine: none
Features: Varmint-contour heavy chrome-moly barrel; 40-XB target trigger; gray laminate thumbhole stock
Discontinued

Rifles Inc. Rifles

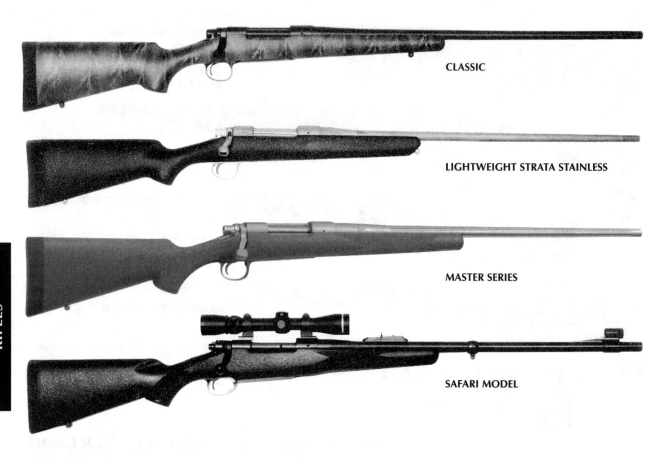

CLASSIC

LIGHTWEIGHT STRATA STAINLESS

MASTER SERIES

SAFARI MODEL

CLASSIC
Action: bolt
Stock: laminated fiberglass
Barrel: stainless steel, match grade 24-26 in.
Sights: none
Weight: 6.5 lbs.
Caliber: all popular chamberings up to .375 H&H
Magazine: box, 3 or 5 rounds
Features: Winchester 70 or Rem. 700 action; lapped bolt; pillar glass bedded stock; adjustable trigger; hinged floor-plate; also 27 in. fluted barrel, synthetic stock in .300 Rem. UM
MSRP: $2300

LIGHTWEIGHT STRATA STAINLESS
Action: bolt
Stock: laminated with textured epoxy
Barrel: stainless match grade 22-25 in.
Sights: none
Weight: 5.0 lbs.
Caliber: all popular chamberings up to .375 H&H
Magazine: box, 3 or 5 rounds
Features: stainless Rem. action, fluted bolt and hollowed-handle; pillar glass bedded stock; stainless metal finish; blind or hinged floorplate; custom Protektor pad; also Lightweight 70 (5.75 lbs.); Lightweight Titanium Strata
Lightweight Strata: $2600
Lightweight 70: $2500
Titanium Strata: $2300

MASTER SERIES
Action: bolt
Stock: laminated fiberglass
Barrel: match grade, 24-27 in.
Sights: none
Weight: 7.75 lbs.
Caliber: all popular chamberings up to .300 Rem. Ultra Mag.
Magazine: box, 3 rounds
Features: Remington 700 action
MSRP: $2750

SAFARI MODEL
Action: bolt
Stock: laminated fiberglass
Barrel: stainless match grade 23-25 in.
Sights: optional Express
Weight: 8.5 lbs.
Caliber: all popular chamberings
Magazine: box, 3 or 5 rounds, optional drop box
Features: Win. Model 70 action; drilled and tapped for 8-40 screws; stainless Quiet Slimbrake; stainless or black Teflon finish; adjustable trigger; hinged floor-plate; barrel band optional
MSRP: $2950

Rogue Rifle Company

CHIPMUNK

Action: bolt
Stock: walnut, laminated black, brown or camo
Barrel: 16 in.
Sights: target

Weight: 2.5 lbs.
Caliber: Sporting rifle in .17 HMR and .17 MACH 2; Target model in .22, .22 LR, .22 WMR
Magazine: none
Features: single-shot; manual-cocking action; receiver-mounted rear sights; Target model weighs 5 lbs. and comes with competition-style receiver sight and globe front and adjustable trigger, extendable buttplate and front rail

Standard:. **$140-200**
Stainless:. **$160-220**
Bull barrel:. **$175-220**
Bull barrel/stainless: **$263–277**
Target with options:. .**Discontinued**

Rossi Rifles

MATCHED PAIR WITH BOTH .22 LONG RIFLE AND .410-BORE SHOTGUN BARRELS

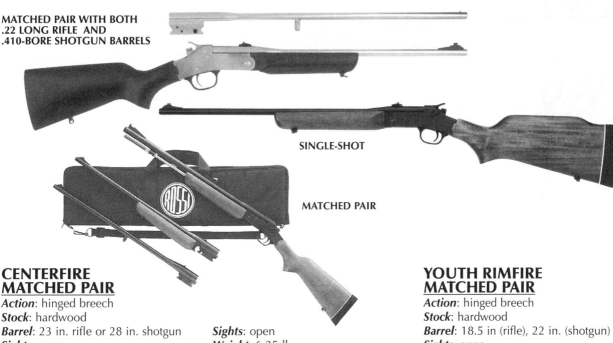

SINGLE-SHOT

MATCHED PAIR

CENTERFIRE MATCHED PAIR

Action: hinged breech
Stock: hardwood
Barrel: 23 in. rifle or 28 in. shotgun
Sights: open
Weight: 5.0-6.0 lbs.
Caliber: 12 or 20 ga. with .223 Rem., .243 Rem., .243 Win., .308, .30-06, .270 and .22-250 (Youth only)
Magazine: none
Features: carry case and sling included; adjustable sights
MSRP: **$299**

SINGLE-SHOT

Action: hinged breech
Stock: hardwood
Barrel: 23 in.

Sights: open
Weight: 6.25 lbs.
Caliber: .17 HMR, .223, 243, .308, .30-06, .270, .22-250 , 7.62x39
Magazine: none
Features: single shot; recoil pad; sling swivels; extra-wide positive-action extractor; good rifle for first time shooters; all calibers except .17 HMR have Monte Carlo stock
.17 HMR blue: **$175**
.17 HMR stainless:. **$221**
Single Shot with heavy barrel (.223, .243, .22-250):. **$272**
Youth model:. **$263**

YOUTH RIMFIRE MATCHED PAIR

Action: hinged breech
Stock: hardwood
Barrel: 18.5 in (rifle), 22. in. (shotgun)
Sights: open
Weight: 4.0-6.0 lbs.
Caliber: 20 ga/.22 LR, .410/.22 LR, .410/.17 HMR
Magazine: none
Features: single shot; blue or stainless steel; single-stage trigger, adjustable sights; full size 12 or 20 gauge with .22 LR, .22 Mag or .17 HMR
Blued: **$164**
Stainless: **$210**
.410 and .17 HMR, blue: **$219**
Stainless: **$210**
Full-size: **$210**

Ruger Rifles

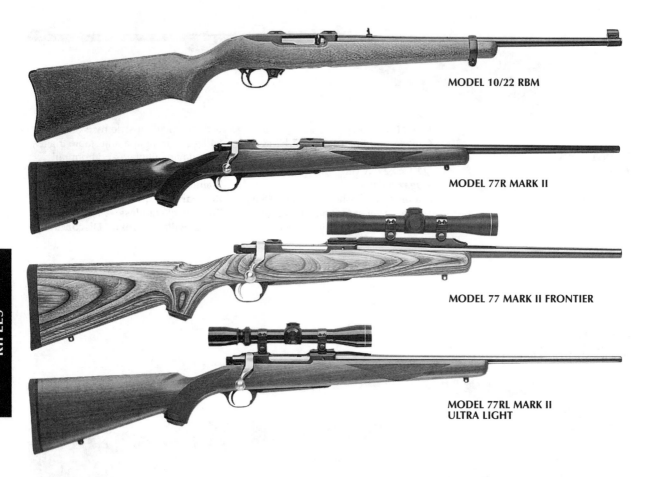

MODEL 10/22 RBM

MODEL 77R MARK II

MODEL 77 MARK II FRONTIER

MODEL 77RL MARK II
ULTRA LIGHT

MODEL 10/22
Action: autoloading
Stock: walnut, birch, synthetic
or laminated
Barrel: 18 in.
Sights: open
Weight: 5.0 lbs.
Caliber: .22 LR
Magazine: rotary, 10 rounds
Features: blowback action; also
International with full-stock, heavy-
barreled Target and stainless steel ver-
sions; Magnum with 9-shot magazine
Model 10/22: $269
Stainless: $318
Walnut: $355
Target: $485
Target stainless, laminated: . . . $533
Magnum:. . . . . Discontinued
.17 HMR: . . . . Discontinued

MODEL 77R MARK II
Action: bolt
Stock: walnut
Barrel: 22 in.
Sights: none
Weight: 7.25-8.25 lbs.
Caliber: most popular standard and
magnum calibers
Magazine: box, 3-5 rounds
Features: scope rings included; RBZ
has stainless steel, laminated stock;
RSBZ with sights
MSRP: $803

MODEL 77 MARK II FRONTIER
Action: bolt
Stock: laminated
Barrel: 16½-in sporter
Sights: none
Weight: 6.75 lbs.
Caliber: .243, 7mm-08, .308,
.300 WSM
Magazine: internal box, 3- or 5-rounds
Features: rib for barrel-mounted scope
Discontinued

MODEL 77 RFP MARK II
Action: bolt
Stock: synthetic
Barrel: 22 in.
Sights: none
Weight: 7.0-8.0 lbs.
Caliber: most popular standard and
magnum calibers
Magazine: box, 3-5 rounds
Features: stainless steel barrel and
action, (magnums with 24 in. barrel);
scope rings included
MSRP: $803

MODEL 77RL MARK II ULTRA LIGHT
Action: bolt
Stock: walnut
Barrel: 20 in.
Sights: none
Weight: 6.25-6.75 lbs.
Caliber: .223, .243, .257, .270, .308
Magazine: box, 4 or 5 rounds
77RL Ultra Light: $862
International Model
(18 in. bbl.):. $939

Ruger Rifles

MODEL M77 RSM

MODEL 77VT MARK II

MODEL 77/17

MODEL 77/22VBZ

MODEL 77 RSM MAGNUM

Action: bolt
Stock: Circassian walnut
Barrel: 23 in. with quarter rib
Sights: open
Weight: 9.5-10.0 lbs.
Caliber: .375 H&H, .416 Rigby
(10.3 lbs.), .458 Lott
Magazine: box, 3 or 4 rounds
Features: barrel-mounted front swivel;
also Express rifle in popular standard
and magnum long-action calibers
MSRP: **$2334**

MODEL 77 VT MARK II

Action: bolt
Stock: brown laminate
Barrel: heavy stainless 26 in.,
target gray finish
Sights: none
Weight: 9.8 lbs.
Caliber: .223, .204, .22-250, .220
Swift, .243, .25-06, .308
Magazine: box, 4 or 5 rounds
MSRP: **$935**

MODEL 77/17

Action: bolt
Stock: walnut, synthetic or laminated
Barrel: 22 in.
Sights: none
Weight: 6.5 lbs.
Caliber: .17 HMR
Magazine: 9 rounds
Features: also stainless (P) and stain-
less varmint with laminated stock
(VMBBZ), 24 in. barrel (6.9 lbs.)
77/17 RM: **$754**
K77/17 VMBBZ: **$836**
77/17 RMP: . . . . **Discontinued**
Also Available:
**.17 MACH2 (20 in. blue or
    stainless blue) . . . . Discontinued**

MODEL 77/22 RIMFIRE RIFLE

Action: bolt
Stock: walnut
Barrel: 20 in.
Sights: none
Weight: 6.0 lbs.
Caliber: .22 LR, .22 Mag., .22 Hornet
Magazine: rotary, 6-10 rounds
Features: also Magnum (M) and
stainless synthetic (P) versions; scope
rings included for all; sights on S
versions; VBZ has 24 in. medium
stainless barrel (6.9 lbs.)
77/22R: **$754**
77/22RM: **$754**
K77/22RP: **$754**
K77/22 RMP: **$754**
77/22RH (.22 Hornet): **$754**
K77/22VBZ: **$836**
K77/22VMBZ: **$836**

Ruger Rifles

MODEL 96

M77 HAWKEYE

M77 HAWKEYE
AFRICAN

M77 HAWKEYE
ALASKAN

MODEL 96
LEVER-ACTION RIFLE
Action: lever
Stock: hardwood
Barrel: 18½ in., blued
Sights: adjustable rear sight
Weight: 5.25 lbs.
Caliber: .17 HMR, .22 WMR,
.44 Mag.
Magazine: rotary magazine, 9 rounds
Features: enclosed short-throw lever
action; cross bolt safety; standard tip-
off scope-mount base
Model 96: $390
.44 Mag. (4-round): $546

M77 HAWKEYE
Action: bolt
Stock: American walnut (Standard
models) or black synthetic (All-
Weather models)
Barrel: 22 or 24 in.
Sights: none
Weight: 8 lbs.

Caliber: .204 Ruger, .22-250 Rem,
.223 Rem, .243 Win, .25-06 Rem,
.270 Win, .280 Rem, .30-06 Sprgfld.,
.300 Win Mag, .308 Win, .338
Federal, .338 Win Mag, .358 Win,
7mm Rem Mag, 7mm-08 Rem
Magazine: 4 rounds
Features: Matte blued or matte stainless
finish; Ruger LC6 trigger; non-rotating,
Mauser-type controlled-feed extractor;
fixed-blade type ejector; hinged steel
floor plate with Ruger logo; scope rings
included; three-position safety
MSRP: $803

M77 HAWKEYE AFRICAN
Action: bolt
Stock: American walnut
Barrel: 23 in.
Sights: front: white bead; rear: shallow
V, windage adjustable
Weight: 7.8 lbs.
Caliber: .375 Ruger
Magazine: 3 rounds

Features: Matte blue finish; Ruger LC6
trigger; non-rotating, Mauser-type controlled-feed extractor; fixed-blade type
ejector; hinged steel floor plate with
Ruger logo; scope rings included;
three-position safety
MSRP: $1079

M77 HAWKEYE ALASKAN
Action: bolt
Stock: Black Hogue rubber overmolded
Barrel: 20 in.
Sights: front: white bead; rear: shallow
V, windage adjustable
Weight: 8 lbs.
Caliber: .375 Ruger
Magazine: 3 rounds
Features: Alaskan Black finish; Ruger
LC6 trigger; non-rotating, Mauser-type
controlled-feed extractor; fixed-blade
type ejector; hinged steel floor plate
with Ruger logo; scope rings included;
three-position safety
MSRP: $1079

Ruger Rifles

NO. 1 SINGLE SHOT

NO. 1 VARMINTER

NO. 1 STAINLESS VARMINTER (.204)

MODEL PC4

NO. 1 SINGLE-SHOT

Action: dropping block
Stock: select checkered walnut
Barrel: 22, 24 or 26 in. (RSI: 20 in.)
Sights: open
Weight: 7.25-8.25 lbs.
Caliber: all popular chamberings in Light Sporter, Medium Sporter, Standard Rifle
Magazine: none
Features: pistol grip; all rifles come with Ruger 1" scope rings; 45-70 is available in stainless; No. 1 Stainless comes in .243, .25-06, 7mm Rem. Mag., .204, .30-06, .270, .300 Win. Mag., .308
No. 1: **$1147**
Stainless steel: . . . . . . **Discontinued**

NO. 1 VARMINTER

Action: dropping block
Stock: select checkered walnut
Barrel: heavy 24 or 26 in. (.220 Swift)
Sights: open
Weight: 8.75 lbs.
Caliber: .22-250, .220 Swift, .223, .25-06
Magazine: box, 5 rounds
Features: Ruger target scope block; stainless available in .22-250; also No. 1H Tropical (heavy 24 in. bbl.) in .375 H&H, .416 Rigby, .458 Lott, .458 Win. Mag., .405; No.1 RSI International (20 in. light bbl. and full-length stock) in .243, .270, .30-06, 7x57
MSRP: **$1147**

MODEL PC4 CARBINE

Action: autoloading
Stock: synthetic
Barrel: 16.25 in.
Sights: open
Weight: 6.3 lbs.
Caliber: 9mm, .40 S&W
Magazine: detachable, 10-15 rounds
Features: delayed blowback action; optional ghost ring sight
Carbine: **$623**
With ghost ring sights: **$647**

Ruger Rifles

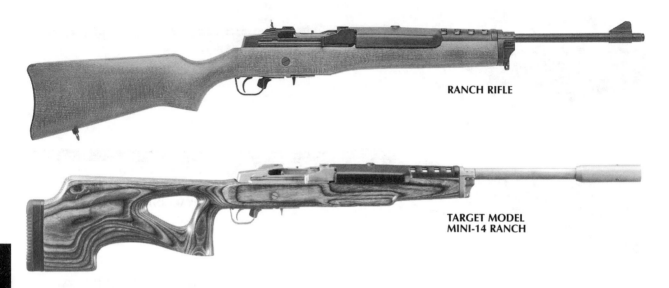

RANCH RIFLE

**TARGET MODEL
MINI-14 RANCH**

RANCH RIFLE
Action: autoloading
Stock: hardwood
Barrel: 18 in.
Sights: target
Weight: 6.5-7.0 lbs.
Caliber: .223
Magazine: detachable box, 5 rounds
Features: also stainless, stainless syn-
thetic versions of Mini-14/5; Ranch
Rifle (with scope mounts) and Mini-
thirty (in 7.62x39)
Deerfield Carbine .44 Mag.: . . $702
Ranch Rifle:. $872

Ranch rifle, stainless: $938
Ranch rifle,
   stainless synthetic: $938
Mini-Thirty,
   stainless synthetic: $921

TARGET MODEL MINI-14 RANCH RIFLE
Action: autoloading
Stock: gray laminated target stock
Barrel: 22 in.
Sights: none; factory set-up for scope use
Weight: 9 lbs.
Caliber: .223 Rem

Magazine: 5 rounds
Features: satin-finished stainless
steel receiver; hammer-forged matte
stainless-steel target barrel with
recessed target crown and adjustable
barrel weight; Garand-style breech
bolt locking system, with a fixed-pistol
gas system and self-cleaning, moving
gas cylinder; ventilated handguard;
stainless-steel Ruger scope rings;
non-slip grooved rubber buttpad;
Garand-type safety
MSRP: $1066

Sako Rifles

MODEL 85 GRAY WOLF
Action: bolt
Stock: laminated
Barrel: 22.25 or 22.75 in.
Sights: none
Weight: 7.75 lbs.
Caliber: .223, .22-05, .260, .270 Win.,

.270 WSM,
Magazine: detachable box, 4-6 rounds
Features: stainless, cold hammer-
forged barrel; four action sizes; gray
laminated stock
MSRP: $1575

Sako Rifles

MODEL 85 HUNTER

MODEL TRG-22

MODEL TRG-22
FOLDING STOCK

MODEL TRG-42
GREEN

MODEL 85 HUNTER

Action: bolt
Stock: walnut or synthetic
Barrel: hammer-forged 22.5 or 24.25 in.
Sights: none
Weight: 7.75 lbs.
Caliber: most popular standard and magnum calibers from .222 Rem. to .270 and 300 WSM and .375 H&H
Magazine: detachable box, 4-5 rounds
Features: barrel length depends on caliber; 4 action lengths; also stainless synthetic and short-barreled Finnlight versions; Deluxe Grade with fancy walnut stock

Hunter: $1626
.270 WSM & .300 WSM: $1626

MODEL TRG-22

Action: bolt
Stock: synthetic
Barrel: 26 in.
Sights: none
Weight: 10.3 lbs.
Caliber: .308
Magazine: detachable box, 10 rounds
Features: 3-lug bolt; fully adjustable trigger; optional bipod, brake; also TRG 42 in .300 Win. Mag. and .338 Lapua (5-round magazine, 27 in. barrel, 11.3 lbs.)

TRG-22: $2850
TRG-22, folding stock: $4560
TRG-42: $2850
TRG-42, green: $2850

Sako Rifles

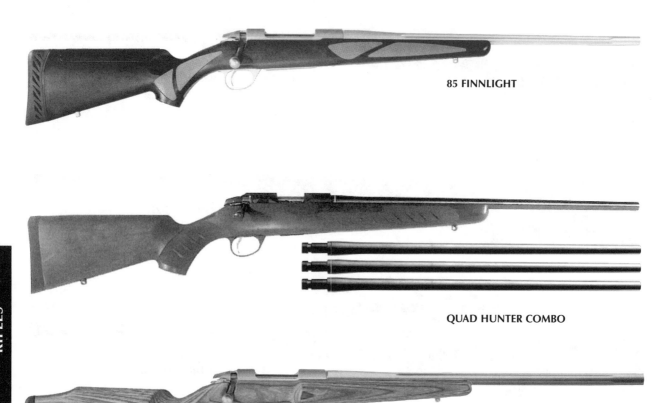

85 FINNLIGHT

QUAD HUNTER COMBO

VARMINT SS LAMINATED

RIFLES

85 FINNLIGHT
Action: bolt
Stock: synthetic
Barrel: 20 or 24 in.
Sights: none
Caliber: .243 Win, 25-06 Rem, .260 Rem, .270 Win, .270 WSM, .30-06 Sprg, .300 Win Mag, .300 WSM, .308 Win, .338 Federal, 6.5x5.5 Swedish Mauser, 7mm Rem Mag, 7mm WSM, 7mm-08 Rem
Magazine: detachable box
Features: stainless-steel barreled action; available in 4 action lengths; stainless inner parts
MSRP: **$1600**

QUAD HUNTER
Action: bolt
Stock: hardwood
Barrel: 22 in.
Sights: none
Caliber: .17 HMR, .17 Mach 2, .22 LR, .22 WMR,
Magazine: box, 5 rounds
Features: Quad barrel system—four interchangeable barrels; stainless-steel barreled action; stainless inner parts; adjustable trigger
Quad Hunter
 Two-Barrel Combo $1870
 (2 barrels; .22 LR & .22 WMR)
Quad Hunter
 Four-Barrel Combo: . . $1739–1798
 (4 barrels; .17 HMR, .17 Mach 2, .22 LR & .22 WMR)

VARMINT SS LAMINATED
Action: bolt
Stock: laminated
Barrel: 23.5 in.
Sights: none
Weight: 7.7 lbs.
Caliber:.204 Ruger, .222 Rem, .223 Rem, .223 Rem, .22-250 Rem, .243 Win. .260 Rem, .7mm-08 Rem, .308 Win, .338 Federal
Features: cold hammer-forged stainless steel, free-floating, heavy fluted barrel (available with short barrel threaded for muzzle brake or suppressor); short & extra short actions available; adjustable trigger; safety allows loading and unloading rifle with safety engaged; extended recoil lug; integral scope mount rail
Laminated SS Varmint: $1950

Sauer Rifles

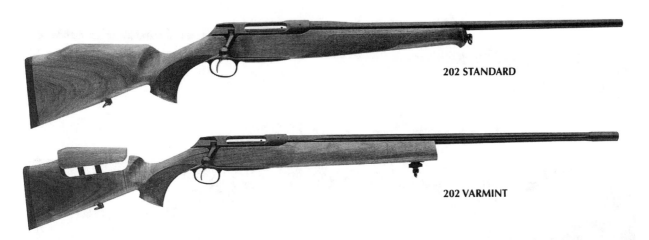

202 STANDARD

202 VARMINT

MODEL 202
Action: bolt
Stock: Claro walnut
Barrel: 24 in.   *Sights:* none
Weight: 7.7 lbs.
Caliber: .243, .25-06, 6.5x55, .270, .308, .30-06

Magazine: detachable box, 5 rounds
Features: adjustable trigger; quick-change barrel; also Supreme Magnum with 26 in. barrel in 7mm Rem., .300 Win., .300 Wby., .375 H&H; Varmint and Tactical versions too
Model 202: **$4250**

Magnum: **$4250**
Synthetic: **$2875**
Lightweight: . . . . **Discontinued**
Varmint: **$3400**
Left-hand (.30-06, walnut): . . . **$3700**
SSG 3000 Tactical: **$2900-5000**

Savage Rifles

MODEL 11G

MODEL 11F
Action: bolt
Stock: synthetic
Barrel: 22.0 in.
Sights: none
Weight: 6.8 lbs.
Caliber: .223, .22-250, .243, 7mm-08, .308, .270 WSM, 7mm WSM, .300 WSM,
Magazine: box, 5 rounds
Features: open sights available; also 11G with walnut stock, 10 GY Youth with short stock in .223, .243 and .308
11F: **$591**
11G: **$618**

MODEL 11/111
Action: bolt
Stock: hardwood or synthetic
Barrel: 24.0 in.
Sights: none
Weight: 7.0 lbs.
Caliber: .270 WSM, 7mm WSM, .300 WSM, 7mm SUM, .300 SUM
Magazine: 3 rounds
Features: top tang safety; adjustable sights available
MSRP: **$591**

MODEL 12, 112 10FP SERIES
Action: bolt
Stock: synthetic or laminated
Barrel: 20.0 in. or 26.0 in.
Sights: none
Weight: 8.3 lbs.
Caliber: .223, .22-250, .243, .25-06, 7mm Rem. Mag., .308, .30-06, .300 WSM, .300 Win. Mag.
Magazine: 3 or 4 rounds
Features: single-shot or box magazine; Savage AccuTrigger
MSRP: **$934**

Savage Rifles

MODEL 12FV

MODEL 12 FVSS

MODEL 114

MODEL 16FSS

MODEL 12FV (SHORT-ACTION)

Action: bolt
Stock: synthetic
Barrel: varmint, 26.0 in.
Sights: none
Weight: 9.0 lbs.
Caliber: .223, .22-250, .243, .308, .300 WSM, .204 Ruger
Magazine: box, 5 rounds
Features: also 12 VSS with fluted stainless barrel, Choate adjustable stock (11.3 lbs.) and V2 BVSS with stainless fluted barrel, laminated or synthetic stock (9.5 lbs.)
FV: **$658**
FVSS: **$815**
BVSS laminated: **$899**

MODEL 14/114

Action: bolt
Stock: checkered walnut
Barrel: 22.0 in. and 24.0 in.
Sights: none
Weight: 7.25 lbs.
Caliber: .223 to .300 Win. Mag.
Magazine: detachable box, 3-5 rounds
Features: AccuTrigger
MSRP: **$826**

MODEL 16FSS (SHORT-ACTION)

Action: bolt
Stock: synthetic
Barrel: stainless, 22 or 24 in.
Sights: none
Weight: 6.0 lbs.
Caliber: .223, .243, .204 Ruger, 7mm WSM, .22-250 REM, 7mm-08, .308, .270 WSM, .300 WSM
Magazine: box, 3 or 4 rounds
Features: also 16BSS with checkered laminated stock in .300 WSM only
MSRP: **$678–705**

.17 SERIES MODEL 93R17BTVS

MODEL 30G

MODEL 40

MODEL 64FSS

.17 SERIES MODEL 93R17BTVS

Action: bolt
Stock: laminated
Barrel: 21 in.
Sights: none
Weight: 6.0 lb.
Caliber: .17 HMR
Magazine: detachable box, 5 rounds
Features: AccuTrigger; stainless steel bolt-action; button-rifled heavy varmint barrel; swivel studs; brown laminated vented thumbhole stock
MSRP: **$448**

MODEL 30

Action: dropping block
Stock: walnut
Barrel: octagon, 21 in.
Sights: open

Weight: 4.3 lbs.
Caliber: .22 LR, .22 WMR, .17 HMR
Magazine: none
Features: re-creation of Steven's Favorite
30G: **$344**
Take-down .22: **$360**
30R 17: . . . . **Discontinued**
Take-down .17: . . . . . **Discontinued**

MODEL 40 W/ ACCUTRIGGER

Action: bolt
Stock: laminated, beavertail, with third swivel stud
Barrel: 24 in., heavy, sleeved, free-floating
Sights: none (drilled and tapped for scope mounts)
Weight: 8.5 lbs.

Caliber: .22 Hornet
Magazine: none
Discontinued

MODEL 64F

Action: autoloading
Stock: synthetic
Barrel: 21 in.
Sights: open
Weight: 5.5 lbs.
Caliber: .22 LR
Magazine: detachable box, 10 rounds
Features: also 64 FSS stainless, 64FV and FVSS heavy barrel, 64G hardwood stock
64F: **$152**
64G: **$187**

Savage Rifles

MODEL 93

MODEL 93G

MODEL 112BVSS

MODEL CFM SIERRA

MODEL 93
Action: bolt
Stock: synthetic, hardwood or laminated
Barrel: 21 in.
Sights: none
Weight: 5.0 lbs.
Caliber: .17 HMR *Magazine*: 5 rounds
Features: scope bases included; eight versions with stainless or C-M steel, different stocks; varmint models weigh 6.0 lbs.
Synthetic F: **$241**
Laminated stainless FVSS: **$347**

MODEL 93G
Action: bolt
Stock: synthetic
Barrel: 21 in.
Sights: open   *Weight*: 5.8 lbs.
Caliber: .22 WMR, .17 HMR
Magazine: detachable box, 5 rounds
Features: 93G with hardwood stock; 93 FSS stainless; 93FVSS with heavy barrel; 93G with hardwood stock
MSRP: **$260**

MODEL 110 LONG RANGE
Action: bolt
Stock: lightweight composite
Barrel: heavy 24 in.

Sights: none   *Weight*: 8.5 lbs.
Caliber: .25-06, 7mm Rem. Mag., .30-06, .300 Win. Mag.
Magazine: box, 4 rounds
Features: also short-action Model 10 in .223, .308
Discontinued

MODEL 112 BVSS (LONG-ACTION)
Action: bolt
Stock: lightweight composite
Barrel: fluted, stainless 26 in.
Sights: none   *Weight*: 10.3 lbs.
Caliber: .25-06, 7mm Rem. Mag., .30-06, .300 Win. Mag.
Magazine: box, 4 rounds
Features: also 112 BVSS with laminated stock
Discontinued

MODEL 116FSS (LONG-ACTION)
Action: bolt
Stock: synthetic
Barrel: stainless 22, 24 or 26 in.
Sights: none   *Weight*: 6.5 lbs.
Caliber: .270, .30-06 (22 in.), 7mm Rem. Mag., .300 Win. Mag., .338

Win. Mag., .300 RUM (26 in.)
Magazine: box, 3 or 4 rounds
Features: also 116BSS with checkered laminated stock
MSRP: **$569**

MODEL 200
Action: bolt
Stock: synthetic
Barrel: 22 in. and 24 in. sporter
Sights: none   *Weight*: 7.5 lbs.
Caliber: 10 chamberings, from .223 to .300 Win. Mag.
Magazine: blind box
Features: pillar-bedded
Discontinued

MODEL CFM SIERRA
Action: bolt
Stock: synthetic
Barrel: 20-in. sporter
Sights: none
Weight: 6.0 lbs.
Caliber: .243, 7mm-08, .308, .270 WSM, .300 WSM
Magazine: detachable box, 3-5 rounds
Features: AccuTrigger
Discontinued

RIFLES

Savage Rifles

MARK I G SINGLE-SHOT

MARK II FSS

MARK II FV HEAVY-BARREL

VARMINTER

MARK I
Action: bolt
Stock: hardwood
Barrel: 19 in. or 21 in.
Sights: open
Weight: 5.5 lbs.
Caliber: .22 S, .22 L, .22 LR
Magazine: none
Features: also MkIG Youth (19 in. barrel), MkILY Youth laminated stock, MIY Youth camo stock
Mark I FVT (with peep sights): . . . . .
                  Discontinued
Mark I G: **$179**
Mark I GSB (.22 LR Short): . . . .
                  Discontinued
G Youth: **$179**

MARK II F
Action: bolt
Stock: synthetic
Barrel: 21 in.
Sights: open
Weight: 5.0 lbs.
Caliber: .22 LR
Magazine: detachable box, 5 rounds
Features: also MkIIG with hardwood stock, MkIIFSS stainless, MkIIGY with short stock and 19 in. barrel
F: **$249–256**
G: **$226**
FSS: **$273**
GY: **$226**
Camo: **$246**

MARK II FV HEAVY-BARREL
Action: bolt
Stock: synthetic
Barrel: heavy 21 in.
Sights: none
Weight: 6.0 lbs.
Caliber: .22 LR
Magazine: detachable box, 5 or 10 rounds
Features: Weaver scope bases included; also MkII LV with laminated stock (6.5 lbs.)
FV: **$278-285**
BV: . . . . **Discontinued**

VARMINTER
Action: bolt   *Stock*: laminated
Barrel: heavy fluted stainless, button-rifled
Sights: none (drilled and tapped for scope mounts)
Weight: 9.0 lbs.
Caliber: .223 and .22-250, .204 Ruger
Magazine: 4-round box or single-shot
Features: fully adjustable AccuTrigger
MSRP: **$991**

Smith & Wesson Rifles

M&P15

M&P15A

M&P15T

M&P15 & M&P15A

Action: autoloader
Stock: synthetic
Barrel: 16 in.
Sights: adjustable
Weight: 6.74 lbs.
Caliber: 5.56/.223 NATO
Magazine: detachable box, 30 rounds
Features: gas-operated semi automatic; 4140 steel barrel; black anodized finish; adjustable post front sight; adjustable dual aperture rear sight; 6-position telescopic black synthetic stock—rifle measures 35 in. long when fully extended and 32 in. with the stock collapsed; M&P15A available with folding rear combat sight in place of the flat-top handle

M&P15: **$1406**
M&P15A: **$1422**

M&P15T

Action: autoloader
Stock: synthetic
Barrel: 16 in.
Sights: adjustable post front sight; adjustable dual aperture rear sight
Weight: 6.85 lbs.
Caliber: 5.56 mm NATO / .223
Magazine: detachable box, 30 rounds (5.56 mm or .223)
Features: gas-operated semi automatic; free floating chrome-lined 4140 steel barrel; black anodized finish; folding front and rear combat sights with four-sided Picatinny fore-end; 6-position telescopic hard coat black anodized synthetic stock—rifle measures 35 in. long when fully extended and 32 in. with stock collapsed; front rail system with Smith & Wesson handrails
MSRP: **$1888**

RIFLES

Springfield Rifles

M1A STANDARD

M1A SCOUT RIFLE

M1 GARAND

M1A
Action: autoloading
Barrel: 22 in.
Weight: 9.2 lbs.
Magazine: detachable box,
5 or 10 rounds
Features: also with fiberglass stock and
M1A/Scout with 18 in. barrel and

Stock: walnut
Sights: target
Caliber: .308

scope mount (9.0 lbs.)
M1A: **$1608**
M1A Scout Rifle: .... **Discontinued**

M1 GARAND
Action: autoloading
Barrel: 24 in.
Weight: 9.5 lbs.

Stock: walnut
Sights: target
Caliber: .30-06, .308

Magazine: clip-fed, 8 rounds
Features: gas-operated; new stock,
receiver, barrel; other parts mil-spec
Discontinued

Steyr Rifles

MANNLICHER CLASSIC

MANNLICHER CLASSIC MOUNTAIN

MANNLICHER CLASSIC
Action: bolt
Stock: European walnut
Barrel: 20 in., 23.6 in. and 25.6 in.
Sights: open
Weight: 7.4 lbs., 7.7 lbs. (magnum)
Caliber: .222, .223, .243, 6.5x55 SE,

6.5x57, 25-06, .270, 7x64, 7mm-08,
308, 30-06, 8x57 JS, 9, 3x62, 7 mm
Rem. Mag., .300 Win. Mag., 7 mm
WSM, .270 WSM, .300 WSM
Magazine: box, 4 rounds
Features: three-position roller tang
safety with front locking lugs and ice/

residue groove; full stock or half stock
models; total length 41.7 in.; set or
direct trigger; sights as optional extras
on half-stock models
Half-stock: **$2799**
Mountain: **$2269**
Classic: **$2999**

Steyr Rifles

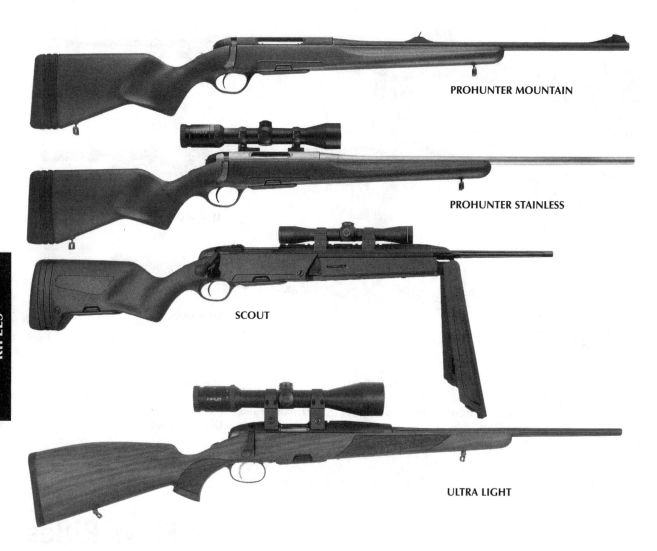

PROHUNTER MOUNTAIN

PROHUNTER STAINLESS

SCOUT

ULTRA LIGHT

PROHUNTER

Action: bolt
Stock: synthetic
Barrel: 20 in. (Mtn.),
23.6 in. and 25.6 in.
Sights: open
Weight: 7.8 lbs. (std.), 8.2 lbs. (mag.),
7.4 lbs. (Mtn.)
Caliber: .222, .223, .243, 6.5x55 SE,
6.5x57, .25-06, .270, 7x64, 7mm-08,
.308, .30-06, 8x57 JS, 9.3x62, 7mm
Rem. Mag., .300 Win. Mag., 7mm
WSM, .270 WSM, .300 WSM
Magazine: detachable box, 5 rounds
Features: high-strength aluminum receiver; SBS safety system; three position roller tang safety; set or direct trigger; charcoal-gray, charcoal-black or Realtree Hardwoods HD stocks; heavy barrel available in .308 or .300 Win. Mag.
ProHunter: $1150

ProHunter Stainless: $1250
ProHunter Mountain: $1150
ProHunter
   Mountain Stainless: $1250

SCOUT

Action: bolt
Stock: synthetic
Barrel: 19 in.
Sights: open   *Weight*: 7.0 lbs.
Caliber: .223, .243, 7mm-08, .308,
.376 Steyr
Magazine: detachable box, 5 rounds
Features: high-strength aluminum receiver; SBS (Safe Bolt System) safety; system; three position roller tang safety full, set or direct trigger; Weaver-type rail; spare magazine in the butt stock; integral folding bipod; matte black finish; total length 38.5 in.
Scout: $2099–2199

ULTRA LIGHT

Action: bolt
Stock: European walnut
Barrel: 19 in.
Sights: none
Weight: 5.9 lbs.
Caliber: .222, .223, .243 Win.,
7mm-08 Rem., .308
Magazine: detachable box, 4 rounds
Features: high-strength aluminum receiver; bolt lugs lock into steel safety bushing; SBS (Safe Bolt System) safety system; three position roller tang safety with front locking lugs and ice/residue groove; set trigger or direct trigger; integral Weaver-type scope mounting rail; total length 38.5 in.
MSRP: 2799

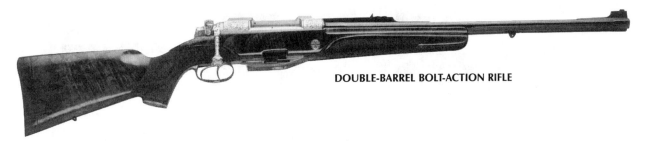

DOUBLE-BARREL BOLT-ACTION RIFLE

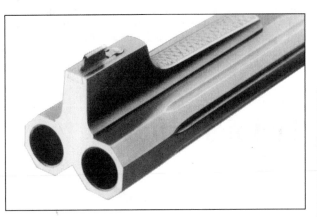

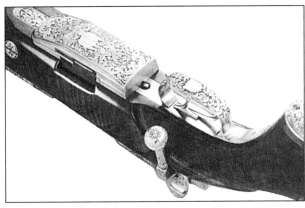

The Szecsei & Fuchs double-barrel bolt-action rifle may be the only one of its kind. Built with great care and much handwork from the finest materials, it follows a design remarkable for its cleverness. While the rifle is not light-weight, it can be aimed quickly and offers more large-caliber firepower than any competitor. The six-shot magazine feeds two rounds simultaneously, both of which can then be fired by two quick pulls of the trigger.

Chamberings: .300 Win, 9.3 x 64, .358 Norma, .375 H&H, .404 Jeff, .416 Rem., .458 Win., .416 Rigby, .450 Rigby, .460 Short A-Square, .470 Capstick, .495 A-Square, .500 Jeffery **Weight**: 14 lbs. with round barrels, 16 with octagon barrels.
Price: **$499**

To help steady a rifle, raise your shooting elbow so it is parallel to the ground or at a 90-degree angle to your body. This pinches the rifle between your shoulder and cheek, providing a rigid shooting platform.

Tactical Rifles

TACTICAL L.R.

Action: bolt, M700 Remington
Stock: thumbhole aluminum, with resin panels, optional adjustable cheekpiece
Barrel: heavy, match-grade, 26 in.

Sights: none (drilled and tapped for scope, supplied with Picatinny rail)
Weight: 13.4 lbs.
Caliber: 7.62 NATO (Magnum version available, in .300 WSM)
Magazine: detachable box, 5 rounds

(10-round boxes available)
Features: adjustable trigger; soft rubber recoil pad, swivel studs; options include stainless fluted barrel
MSRP: **$2450**

Taylor's Rifles

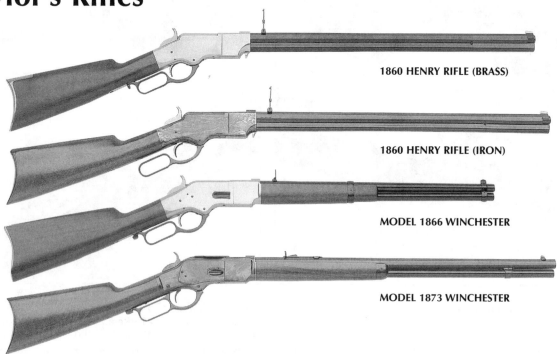

1860 HENRY RIFLE (BRASS)

1860 HENRY RIFLE (IRON)

MODEL 1866 WINCHESTER

MODEL 1873 WINCHESTER

1860 HENRY RIFLE

Action: lever
Stock: walnut
Barrel: 24 in.
Sights: open
Weight: 7.5 lbs.
Caliber: .44-40, .45 Long Colt
Magazine: under-barrel tube, 13 rounds
Features: brass frame; also original-type steel-frame in .44-40 only
MSRP: **$1290–1525**

MODEL 1866 WINCHESTER

Action: lever
Stock: walnut
Barrel: 20 in.
Sights: open
Weight: 6.5 lbs.
Caliber: .38 Spl., .45 Long Colt
Magazine: under-barrel tube, 9 rounds
Features: brass frame, octagon barrel
1866: **$925–1045**

MODEL 1873 WINCHESTER RIFLE

Action: lever
Stock: walnut
Barrel: 24 in.
Sights: open
Weight: 7.5 lbs.
Caliber: .44-40, .45 Long Colt
Magazine: under-barrel tube, 13 rounds
Features: optional front globe and rear tang sights
1873: **$1150–1255**

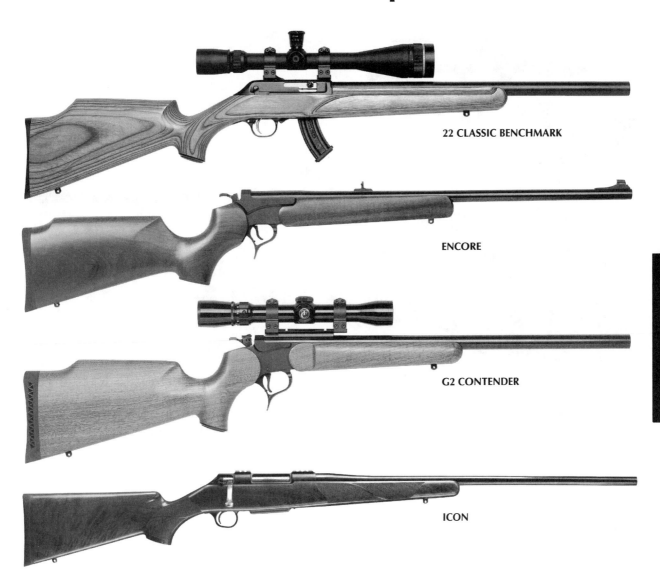

22 CLASSIC BENCHMARK

ENCORE

G2 CONTENDER

ICON

22 CLASSIC BENCHMARK

Action: autoloading
Stock: laminated
Barrel: heavy, 18 in.
Sights: none
Weight: 6.8 lbs.   *Caliber:* .22 LR
Magazine: 10 rounds
Features: target rifle for bench shooting; drilled for scope
MSRP: $481

ENCORE

Action: hinged breech
Stock: walnut
Barrel: 24 and 26 in.
Sights: open
Weight: 6.8 lbs.
Caliber: most popular calibers, from .22 Hornet to .300 Win. Mag. and .45-70

Magazine: none
Features: also synthetic and stainless versions; Hunter package with .308 or .300 includes 3-9x40 T/C scope and hard case
Synthetic: $454
Walnut: $525
Stainless: $375

G2 CONTENDER

Action: hinged breech
Stock: walnut
Barrel: 23 in.
Sights: none
Weight: 5.4 lbs.
Caliber: .17 HMR, .17 MACH 2, .22 LR, .223, 6.8 Rem., .30-30, .204 Ruger, .45/70, .375 JDJ
Magazine: none

Features: recocks without opening rifle
G2 Rifle: $555–600
.50 cal. Muzzleloader: $555–600

ICON

Action: bolt
Stock: high-grade walnut
Barrel: 23.5 in.
Sights: none
Weight: 7.25 to 7.75 lbs.
Caliber: .243, .308, .22-250, .30 TC
Magazine: 3-round removable box
Features: receiver machined from solid steel; button rifled match grade barrel; 3-lug bolt with T-slot extractor; Interlock Bedding Block System; cocking indicator integrated into the bolt sleeve; fully adjustable trigger; two-position safety
MSRP: $800–995

Thompson/Center Rifles

PRO HUNTER RIFLE

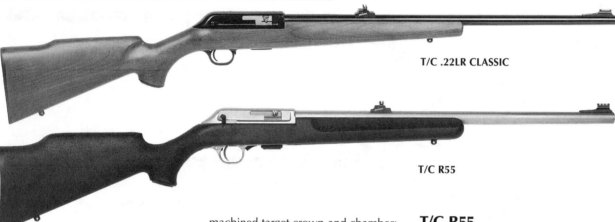

T/C .22LR CLASSIC

T/C R55

PRO HUNTER RIFLE

Action: hinged breech
Stock: synthetic
Barrel: 28 in.
Sights: none
Caliber: .204 Ruger, .22-250 Rem, .223 Rem, .243 Win, .25-06, .270 Win, .30-06, .300 Win, .308 Win, .338 Win, .7mm Mag, 7mm-08
Magazine: none
Features: stainless steel fluted barrel; machined target crown and chamber; Swing Hammer rotating hammer; all-steel one-piece extractor; FlexTech stock system
Pro Hunter: . . . . **.650–750**

T/C.22LR CLASSIC

Action: autoloading
Stock: walnut
Barrel: 22.0 in.
Sights: illuminated
Weight: 5.5 lbs. Caliber: .22 LR
Magazine: detachable box, 8 rounds
MSRP: **$603**

T/C R55

Action: blowback autoloader
Stock: synthetic/stainless or lam./ blued
Barrel: 20.0 in.
Sights: adjustable, with fiber optic inserts
Weight: 5.5 lbs.
Caliber: .17 Mach 2
Magazine: detachable box, 5-rounds
Features: available in blued or stainless steel
Laminated/blued:. **$600-610**
Synthetic/stainless: **$668**

Tikka Rifles

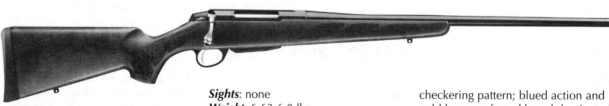

T3 HUNTER

Action: bolt
Stock: walnut, (T3 Lite, synthetic)
Barrel: 22.44, 24.38 in.
Sights: none
Weight: 6.63-6.8 lbs.
Caliber: .22-250 Rem, .223 Rem, .243 Win, .25-06 Rem, .270 Win, .270 WSM, .30-06, .308 Win, 6.5 x 55
Magazine: detachable box, 3 rounds
Features: Walnut stock with distinctive checkering pattern; blued action and cold hammer-forged barrel; laminated stock with stainless action and barrel, 2- to 4-lb. adjustable trigger; integral scope rail, required rings are supplied with each gun
MSRP: **$675**

Tikka Rifles

T3 LITE

T3 LITE STAINLESS

T3 TACTICAL

T3 VARMINT

T3 LITE

Action: bolt
Stock: synthetic
Barrel: 23.0, 24.0 in.
Sights: none
Weight: 6.19-6.38 lbs.
Caliber: 22-250 Rem, .223 Rem, .243 Win, .25-06 Rem, .270 Win, .270 WSM, .30-06 Sprg, .300 Win Mag, .300 WSM, .308 Win, .338 Win Mag, 7mm Rem Mag, 7mm-08 Rem
Magazine: 3 or 4 rounds
Features: blue or stainless; 3-shot 1 in. group at 100 yds. in factory testing
T3 Lite:. $525
Stainless:. $600

T3 TACTICAL

Action: two-lug bolt
Stock: synthetic
Barrel: 20 in.
Sights: none
Weight: 7.25 to 7.75 lbs.
Caliber: .223, .308
Magazine: detachable box, 5 rounds
Features: free-floating, hammer-forged barrel, fully adjustable trigger; Picatinny rail; black phosphate finish, a synthetic varmint-style stock with adjustable cheek piece
Tactical:. $1600

T3 VARMINT

Action: bolt
Stock: synthetic
Barrel: 23.27 in.
Sights: none
Weight: 6.63 lbs.
Caliber: .22-250 Rem, .223 Rem, .308 Win
Magazine: detachable box, 5 rounds
Features: heavy contour, free-floating, varmint type barrel, fully adjustable trigger; blued finish; drilled and tapped for scope mounts
T3 Varmint: $900

Uberti Rifles

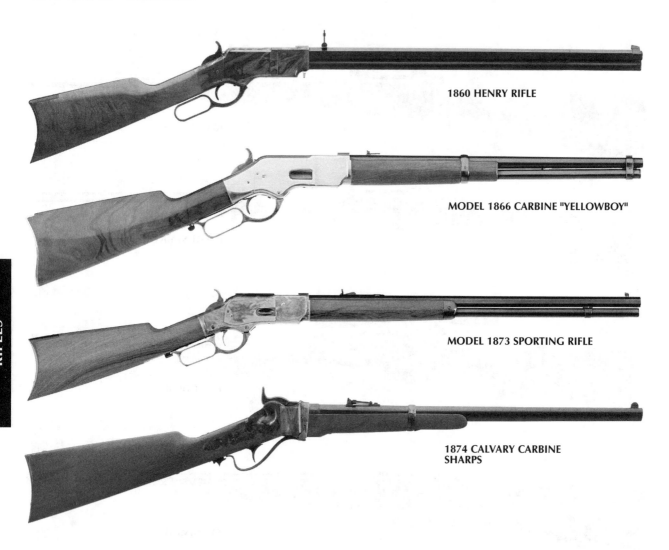

1860 HENRY RIFLE

MODEL 1866 CARBINE "YELLOWBOY"

MODEL 1873 SPORTING RIFLE

1874 CALVARY CARBINE SHARPS

1860 HENRY RIFLE

Action: lever
Stock: walnut
Barrel: 18.5 in. and 24.25 in.
Sights: adjustable
Weight: 9 lbs
Caliber: .44-40, .45 Colt
Magazine: tube, 10 or 13 rounds
Features: octagon barrel; brass or steel frame; lever lock; front loading, under-barrel tube magazine; A-grade straight walnut stock
MSRP: $1329

MODEL 1866 WINCHESTER "YELLOWBOY"

Action: lever
Stock: walnut
Barrel: 19 (Carbine), 20, or 24.25 in.
Sights: adjustable
Weight: 7.4 lbs.
Caliber: .38 Spl., .44-40, .45 Colt
Magazine: tube, 10 or 13 rounds
Features: brass frame; under-barrel tube magazine with loading gate on frame; lever lock; A-grade straight walnut stock
1866 Yellowboy Carbine: $1079
1866 Yellowboy Rifle: $1129

MODEL 1873 WINCHESTER RIFLE

Action: lever
Stock: walnut
Barrel: 19 (Carbine), 20 or 24.25 in.,
Sights: adjustable
Weight: 7.5 lbs.
Caliber: .357 Mag., .44-40, .45 Colt
Magazine: tube, 10 or 13 rounds
Features: Rifle & Special Sporting Rifle with 20 or 24-in. octagonal barrel and color case-hardened frame; Carbine with 19-in. round barrel and blued frame; under-barrel tube magazine with loading gate; lever lock; straight or pistol grip A-grade walnut stock
Carbine: $1199
Rifle: $1249
Special Sporting Rifle: $1379

1874 CALVARY CARBINE SHARPS

Action: falling block
Stock: walnut
Barrel: 22 in.
Weight: 8 lbs.
Caliber: .45-70
Magazine: 1 round
Features: round barrel; color-case-hardened receiver; A-grade walnut stock
MSRP: $1569

1874 SHARPS

1874 SHARPS SPECIAL

1874 BUFFALO HUNTER SHARPS

1874 LONG RANGE SHARPS

1876 "CENTENNIAL"

1885 HIGH WALL CARBINE

1874 SHARPS RIFLE

Action: falling block
Stock: walnut
Barrel: 30, 32 or 34 in.
Sights: adjustable   **Weight:** 10.5 lbs.
Caliber: .45-70   **Magazine**: none
(capacity 1 round)
Features: color case-hardened frame,
buttplate and lever; blued barrel;
Standard: 30-in. round barrel; Special:
32-in. octagonal barrel; Deluxe: 34-in.
octagonal barrel; Down Under: 34 in.
octagonal barrel; Buffalo Hunter:
32-in. octagonal barrel; Long Range:
34-in. half octagonal barrel; adjustable
ladder or Creedmore rear sights
Standard: $1459
Special: $1729
Buffalo Hunter: $2219
Down Under: $2249
Long Range: $2279
Deluxe: $2749

1876 "CENTENNIAL"

Action: lever
Stock: walnut
Barrel: 28 in.
Sights: adjustable buckhorn
Weight: 10 lbs.
Caliber: .40-60, .45-60, .45-75, .50-95
Magazine: 11 + 1 rounds
Features: octagonal, blued barrel;
color case-hardened receiver; A-grade,
oil finished straight walnut stock
MSRP: $1569

1885 HIGH-WALL SINGLE-SHOT

Action: falling block
Stock: walnut
Barrel: 28 in. (carbine), 30 or 32 in.
Sights: adjustable
Weight: 9.5
Caliber: .45-70 (carbine) .45-70,
.45-90, .45-120

Magazine: none (capacity 1 round)
Features: single shot, Special Sporting
rifle with walnut checkered pistol grip
stock; Sporting Rifles with straight
stock; optional Creedmore sights; color
case-hardened frame with blued barrel
1885 Carbine: $969
1885 Sporting: $1029
1885 Special Sporting: $1179

LIGHTNING

Action: pump
Stock: walnut
Barrel: 20 in. and 24.25 in.
Sights: adjustable
Weight: 7.5 lbs
Caliber: .357 mag, .45 Colt
Magazine: 10 + 1 rounds
Features: blued or color case-
hardened finish; straight walnut stock
with checkered forend
MSRP: $1179

Uberti Rifles

LIGHTNING

SHARPS HUNTER

SPRINGFIELD TRAPDOOR CARBINE

SPRINGFIELD TRAPDOOR RIFLE

SHARPS HUNTER
Action: falling block
Stock: walnut
Barrel: 28 in.
Sights: adjustable
Weight: 9.5 lbs.
Caliber: .45-70
Magazine: none (capacity 1 round)
Features: round, matte blued barrel;
color-case-hardened receiver and
buttplate; adjustable fiber optic sights;
A-grade straight walnut stock
MSRP: **$1459**

SPRINGFIELD TRAPDOOR CARBINE
Action: hinged breech
Stock: walnut
Barrel: 22 in.
Sights: adjustable ladder
Weight: 7.2 lbs.
Caliber: .45-70
Magazine: none (capacity 1 round)
Features: ladder 1000-yd rear sight;
carbine ring; blued barrel and action;
case-hardened trapdoor and buttplate
MSRP: **$1429**

SPRINGFIELD TRAPDOOR RIFLE
Action: hinged breech
Stock: walnut
Barrel: 32.5 in.
Sights: adjustable ladder
Weight: 8.8 lbs.
Caliber: .45-70
Magazine: none (capacity 1 round)
Features: rear ladder sight adjustable
up to 1000 yds.; blued barrel and
action; case-hardened trapdoor and
buttplate; cleaning rod
MSRP: **$1669**

Walther Rifles

G22 CARBINE
Action: blowback autoloading
Stock: synthetic
Barrel: 20 in.

Sights: adjustable on handle and front strut
Weight: 6 lbs.
Caliber: .22 LR

Magazine: detachable box
Features: Weaver-style accessory rail; black or green synthetic stock
MSRP: **$493**

Weatherby Rifles

MARK V ACCUMARK

MARK V DELUXE

MARK V FIBERMARK

MARK V ACCUMARK
Action: bolt   **Stock**: composite
Barrel: 26 in. and 28 in.
Sights: none
Weight: 7.0 lbs.
Caliber: Wby. Magnums: .257, .270, 7mm, .300, .340, .30-378, .338-378 and .300 Win. Mag., 7mm Rem. Mag.
Magazine: box, 3 or 5 rounds
Features: weight depends on caliber; hand-laminated; raised comb, Pachmayr recoil pad
Magnums: **$1879**
With Accubrake: **$1939**

MARK V DELUXE
Action: bolt
Stock: Claro walnut
Barrel: 26 in. and 28 in.
Sights: none
Weight: 8.5 lbs.
Caliber: .257 Wby. Mag to .460 Wby. Mag.
Magazine: box, 3 or 5 rounds
Features: 26 in. barrels for most magnum calibers; 28 in. barrel for .378, .416, .460
With Accubrake: **$2279**
.378, .416 with Accubrake: . . . **$2679**
.460: **$3149**

MARK V FIBERMARK
Action: bolt   **Stock**: synthetic
Barrel: 24 in. and 26 in.
Sights: none   **Weight**: 8.0 lbs.
Caliber: popular magnum chamberings from .257 Wby. Mag. to .375 H&H Mag.
Magazine: box, 3-5 rounds
Features: Krieger Criterion barrel; one-piece forged fluted bolt with three gas ports; hand-laminated, raised comb, pillar-bedded Monte Carlo composite stock; adjustable trigger; Pachmayr Decelerator recoil pad
Magnum: **$1449**
With Accubrake: **$1739**

Weatherby Rifles

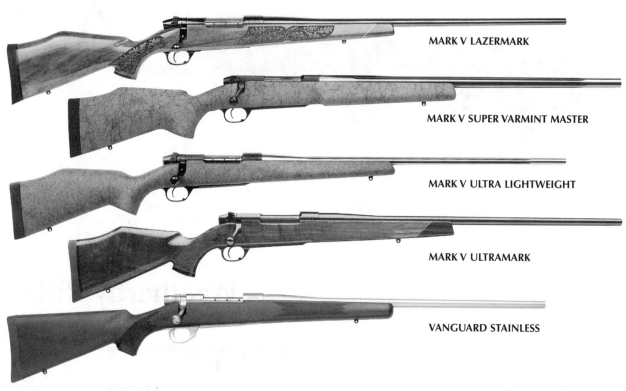

MARK V LAZERMARK

MARK V SUPER VARMINT MASTER

MARK V ULTRA LIGHTWEIGHT

MARK V ULTRAMARK

VANGUARD STAINLESS

MARK V LAZERMARK
Action: bolt
Stock: walnut   **Barrel**: 26 in.
Sights: none   **Weight**: 8.5 lbs.
Caliber: Wby. Magnums from
.257 to .340
Magazine: box, 3 rounds
Features: laser-carved stock; button
rifled Krieger barrel
MSRP: **$2479**

MARK V SPORTER
Action: bolt
Stock: walnut
Barrel: 24 and 26 in.
Sights: none   **Weight**: 8.0 lbs.
Caliber: popular magnum chamber-
ings from .257 Wby. Mag. to .340
Wby. Mag.
Magazine: box, 3 or 5 rounds
Features: checkered grip and forend
MSRP: **$1499**

MARK V SUPER VARMINT MASTER
Action: bolt
Stock: composite   **Barrel**: 26 in.
Sights: none   **Weight**: 8.5 lbs.
Caliber: .223, .22-250, .220 Swift, .243
Magazine: box, 5 rounds
Features: Super Varmint Master has

heavy 26 in., fluted stainless barrel,
flat-bottomed stock
MSRP: **$1959**

MARK V SYNTHETIC
Action: bolt
Stock: synthetic
Barrel: 24, 26 and 28 in.
Sights: none
Weight: 8.5 lbs.
Caliber: popular standard and mag-
num calibers from .22-250 to .257
Wby. Mag.
Magazine: box, 3 or 5 rounds
Features: also stainless version
Mark V Synthetic: **$1209**
Magnum: **$1279**
With Accubrake: **$1509**

MARK V ULTRA LIGHTWEIGHT
Action: bolt
Stock: composite
Barrel: 24 in. and 26 in.
Sights: none
Weight: 6.0 lbs.
Caliber: .243, .240 Wby., .25-06,
.270, 7mm-08, .280, 7mm Rem. Mag.,
.308, .30-06, .300 Win. Mag., Wby.
Magnums: .257, .270, 7mm, .300
Magazine: box, 3 or 5 rounds

Features: lightweight action; 6-lug bolt
Ultra Lightweight: **$1879**
Magnums: **$1979**

MARK V ULTRAMARK
Action: bolt   **Stock**: walnut
Barrel: 26 in.   **Weight**: 8.5 lbs.
Caliber: .257 Weatherby Magnum,
.300 Weatherby Magnum
Magazine: box, 3 + 1 rounds
Features: six locking lugs for a
54-degree bolt lift; high gloss, raised
comb Monte Carlo stock from hand-
selected highly figured, exhibition
grade walnut
MSRP: **$2979**

VANGUARD
Action: bolt
Stock: composite   **Barrel**: 24 in.
Sights: none   **Weight**: 7.8 lbs.
Caliber: .223, .22-250, .243, .270,
.308, .30-06, .257 Wby. Mag., 7mm
Rem. Mag., .300 Win. Mag., .300
WSM, .270 WSM, .300 Wby. Mag.,
.338 Win. Mag.
Magazine: internal box, 3-5 rounds
Features: 2-lug action; made in Japan;
1½-inch guarantee for 3-shot group
Synthetic: **$399**
Stainless: **$709**

RIFLES

Weatherby Rifles

VANGUARD COMPACT

VANGUARD SPORTER

VANGUARD COMPACT
Action: bolt
Stock: synthetic
Barrel: 20 in. sporter
Sights: none
Weight: 6.75 lbs.
Caliber: .22-250, .243, .308
Magazine: internal box, 5 rounds
Features: Chrome-moly or stainless steel barrel
MSRP: **$649**

VANGUARD SPORTER
Action: bolt
Stock: checkered walnut
Barrel: 24 in.
Sights: none
Weight: 7.75 lbs.
Caliber: 13 chamberings, from .223 to .338 Win. Mag.
Magazine: internal box, 3-5 rounds
Features: Chrome-moly or stainless steel barrel; pillar-bedded composite

stock with Aramid, fiberglass and graphite components.
Blue: **$719**
Stainless: **$869**

Wild West Guns

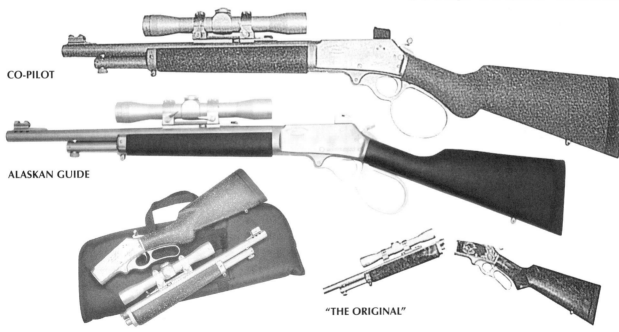

CO-PILOT

ALASKAN GUIDE

"THE ORIGINAL"

CO-PILOT
Action: lever
Stock: walnut
Barrel: 16, 18 or 20 in.
Sights: illuminated
Weight: 7.0 lbs.
Caliber: .45-70, .457 Magnum, .50 Alaskan

Magazine: under-barrel tube
Features: 1895 Marlin action; ported barrels; take-down feature; Alaskan Guide similar, not take-down
.50 Alaskan conversion: **$250**
Alaskan on supplied 1895:
    Marlin: **$935**

Alaskan Guide: **$1320**
Take-Down on supplied:
    1895G: **$1595**
    Master Guide Take-Down: . **$1895**
    Co-Pilot: **$1995**

Winchester Rifles

SUPER X RIFLE-SXR

SXR GRADE II

WILDCAT BOLT-ACTION .22

WILDCAT TARGET/VARMINT .22

SUPER X RIFLE-SXR
Action: autoloader
Stock: walnut
Barrel: 22-24 in.
Sights: none
Weight: 7.0-7.25 lbs.
Caliber: .30-06, .300 Win Mag, .300 WSM, .270 WSM
Magazine: 4 rounds (.30-06); 3 rounds (other calibers), detachable box
Features: Rotary bolt semi-auto, center-fire system; crossbolt safety; single-stage trigger w/ enlarged trigger guard; Pachmayr Decelerator recoil pad; sling swivel studs
.30-06: $949
.300 WSM, .270 WSM,
   .300 Win Mag: $979

SXR GRADE II
Action: autoloader
Stock: grade II walnut
Barrel: 22 or 24 in.
Sights: none
Weight: 7.2 lbs.
Caliber: .270 WSM, .30-06 Sprgfld., .300 Win. Mag., .300 WSM
Features: gas-operated action; adjustable ergonomic stock
Discontinued

WILDCAT BOLT-ACTION .22
Action: bolt
Stock: checkered hardwood
Barrel: 21 in.
Sights: none
Weight: 6.5 lbs.
Caliber: .22
Magazine: one 5-round and three 10-round magazines

Features: checkered black synthetic Winchester buttplate; Schnabel fore-end; steel sling swivel studs
MSRP: $289

WILDCAT TARGET/ VARMINT .22
Action: bolt
Stock: checkered hardwood
Barrel: 21 in.
Sights: none
Weight: 6.5 lbs.
Caliber: .22
Magazine: one 5-round and three 10-round magazines
Features: heavy .866 in. diameter bull barrel; adjustable trigger; receiver drilled and tapped for bases, as well as grooved for mounting a scope; dual front steel swivel studs; scope not included
MSRP: $309

RIFLES

Anschütz Air Rifles

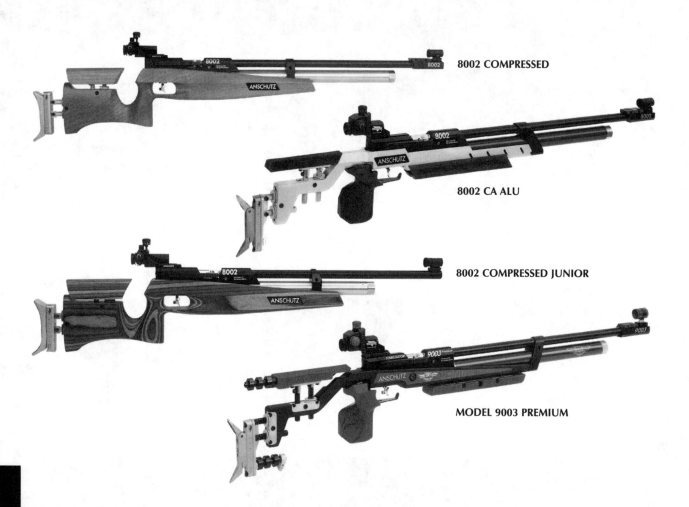

8002 COMPRESSED

8002 CA ALU

8002 COMPRESSED JUNIOR

MODEL 9003 PREMIUM

8002 COMPRESSED AIR RIFLE
Power: compressed air
Stock: walnut
Barrel: 26.2 in.
Sights: none
Weight: 10.36 lbs
Caliber: .177
Features: Single loader; vibration free shot release; carrier with special aluminum regulation valve; capacity for compressed air cylinder appr. 300 shots; adjustable cheek piece and buttplate
MSRP: $220–2780

8002 CA ALU METAL STOCK
Power: compressed air
Stock: aluminum
Barrel: 25.2 in.
Sights: none
Weight: 10.8 lbs.

Caliber: .177
Features: Single loader; recoil & vibration free barreled action; compressed air cylinder with monometer (max 200 bar filling pressure); capacity for filled compressed air cylinder appr. 350 shots; special aluminum regulation valve; barrel weights & weight rings
MSRP: $2100–2740

8002 COMPRESSED AIR RIFLE JUNIOR
Power: compressed air
Stock: laminated
Barrel: 23.2
Sights: none
Weight: 9.9 lbs.
Caliber: .177 cal
Features: Single loader; vibration free shot release; carrier with special aluminum regulation valve; capacity for compressed air cylinder appr. 280

shots; adjustable cheek piece and buttplate; stock can be lengthened by spacers; right & left hand cheek piece
MSRP: $1965

MODEL 9003 PREMIUM
Power: compressed air
Stock: aluminum
Sights: none
Weight: 9.92 lbs
Length: 42.52 in.
Caliber: .177
Features: single shot; vibration damping barrel/stock connection; adjustable match trigger and trigger blade; cocking lever mountable left and right; soft link shock absorber; adjustable pistol grip; fully adjustable fore-end; exchangeable compressed air cylinder; air filter with manometer; filling adapter with air release screw
MSRP: $2900–3780

Beeman Air Rifles

MODEL 1024 COMBO

MODEL 1072 DUAL CALIBER SS1000-S

MODEL 1082 SS1000-H

MODEL 1024 COMBO

Power: break barrel/spring piston
Stock: hardwood
Sights: tapped for scope
Weight: 10.0 lbs
Caliber: .177
Length: 45.5 in.
Features: Velocity 550 fps; removable barrel; all-steel receiver; raised cheek piece; comes with 4x20 wide-angle scope
MSRP: $70

MODEL 1072 DUAL CALIBER SS1000-S

Power: break barrel/spring piston
Stock: hardwood
Sights: adjustable, tapped for scope
Weight: 10.0 lbs
Caliber: .177, .22
Length: 45.5 in.
Features: Velocity 1000 fps (850 fps .22); two removable barrels; all-steel receiver; two-stage adjustable trigger; blued finish; raised cheek piece
Discontinued

MODEL 1082 SS1000-H

Power: break barrel/spring piston
Stock: hardwood
Sights: adjustable
Weight: 7.9 lbs.
Caliber: .177, .22
Length: 46.5 in
Features: velocity: 1000fps, 850 (.22); rifled steel barrel; ported muzzlebrake; blued finish; automatic safety; two-stage adjustable trigger; Monte Carlo cheek piece; rubber pad buttplate; 3-9x32 AO scope
MSRP: $179

MDEL FWB 603 MATCH

Power: side lever/ single stroke pneumatic
Stock: laminated hardwood
Sights: none
Weight: 10.8 lbs.
Caliber: .177
Length: 43 in.
Features: Velocity 570 fps; 25-in. barrel shroud with 16.6-in. rifled inner barrel; single-stroke pneumatic cocking lever; precision adjustable trigger; laminated hardwood/hard rubber stock; adjustable cheek piece and buttplate
Discontinued

MODEL HW77 MKII

Power: under lever/spring piston
Stock: hardwood
Sights: none
Weight: 8.7 lbs.
Caliber: .177
Length: 39.7 in.
Features: Velocity 930 fps; two-stage adjustable trigger; automatic safety; receiver grooved to except 11mm ring or one-piece mounts; beech sporter stock, with tapered forend, hand-cut checkering on the pistol grip, high comb with raised cheek piece
MSRP: $710

MODEL HW97 MK III

Power: under lever/spring piston
Stock: hardwood
Sights: none
Weight: 9.2 lbs.
Caliber: .177, .20
Length: 44.1 in.
Features: Velocity 930 fps; two-stage adjustable trigger; automatic safety; receiver grooved to except 11mm ring or one-piece mounts; beech sporter stock, with tapered forend, hand-cut checkering on the pistol grip, high comb with raised cheek piece
MSRP: $695–720

AIR RIFLES

Beeman Air Rifles

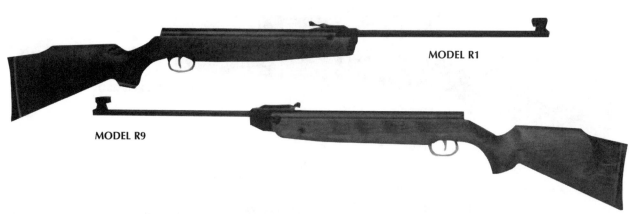

MODEL R1

MODEL R9

MODEL R1, R1 CARBINE
Power: break barrel/spring piston
Stock: hardwood
Sights: adjustable
Weight: 8.8 lbs.
Caliber: .177, .20
Length: 45.2 in., 42.0 in. (Carbine)
Features: 14.23 fp muzzle energy; 950 fps velocity; (.22 cal. — muzzle energy16.4 fps, 765 fps velocity); automatic safety; two-stage adjustable trigger; beech stained hardwood stock
MSRP: **$730–750**

MODEL R9
Power: break barrel/spring piston
Stock: hardwood
Sights: adjustable
Weight: 7.3 to 7.5 lbs.
Caliber: .177, .20
Length: 43 in.
Features: Velocity 930 fps (.177), 800 fps. (.20);
R9: **$500–525**

MODEL R11 MK II
Power: break barrel/spring piston
Stock: hardwood
Sights: none
Weight: 8.6 lbs.
Caliber: .177
Length: 43.5 in.
Features: Velocity: 925 fps; blued, all-steel barrel sleeve; two-stage adjustable trigger; automatic safety; adjustable cheek piece and buttplate assembly; stippled forestock and palm swell
Discontinued

Crosman Air Rifles

MODEL 664SB

MODEL 760XLS

MODEL 664SB POWERMASTER
Power: pneumatic pump
Stock: synthetic
Sights: adjustable
Weight: 2 lbs. 15 oz.
Caliber: .177
Length: 38.5 in.
Features: Velocity: BB: up to 690 fps (210.3 m/s) Pellet: up to 645 fps (196.5 m/s); rifled steel barrel; five-shot manual-feed clip; reservoir: 200 BBs, magazine: 18 Bbs; Monte Carlo cheekpiece
Discontinued

MODEL 760 PUMPMASTER
Power: pneumatic pump
Stock: synthetic
Sights: adjustable
Weight: 3.69 lbs
Caliber: .177
Length: 33.5 in.

Features: Velocity: BB: up to 625 fps (190.5 m/s) Pellet: up to 600 fps (182.8 m/s); smooth bore steel barrel; reservoir: 200 BBs, magazine: 18 BBs; Model 760 XLS with hardwood stock, variable power short-stroke pump action, optional BB repetition or single-shot pellet fire
Model 760:. **$44**
Model 760XLS:. **$76**

AIR RIFLES

Crosman Air Rifles

MODEL 781AK

MODEL 1077

MODEL 2100B

MODEL 2250B

MODEL 2260

MODEL 764SB
Power: pneumatic pump
Stock: synthetic
Sights: adjustable
Weight: 2.69 lbs.
Caliber: .177
Length: 33.5 in.
Features: Velocity: BB: up to 625 fps
(190.5 m/s) Pellet: up to 600 fps
(182.9m/s); smooth bore steel barrel;
reservoir: 200 BBs, magazine: 18 BBs;
available with 4-power precision scope
MSRP: **$90**

MODEL 781
Power: pneumatic pump
Stock: synthetic
Sights: adjustable
Weight: 2 lbs. 14 oz.
Caliber: .177
Length: 35in.
Features: Velocity: 440 fps; reservoir:
195 BBs, magazine: 21 BBs
Discontinued

MODEL 795 SPRING MASTER
Power: break barrel/spring piston

Stock: synthetic
Sights: adjustable
Weight: 4 lbs. 6 oz.
Caliber: .177
Length: 42 in.
Features: Velocity: 600 fps; Rifled steel
Barrel; Single shot
Discontinued

MODEL 1077
Power: CO2
Stock: synthetic
Sights: adjustable
Weight: 3 lbs. 11 oz.
Caliber: .177
Length: 36.88 in.
Features: Velocity: 625 fps; rifled steel
barrel; 12-shot rotary clip; Model
1077W with hardwood stock
Model 1077: **$120**
Model 1077W: . . . . . . **Discontinued**

MODEL 2100
Power: pneumatic pump
Stock: synthetic
Sights: adjustable
Weight: 4 lbs. 13 oz.
Caliber: .177

Length: 39.75 in.
Features: Velocity: BB: up to 755
fps(230.2 m/s) Pellet: up to 725
fps(221.1 m/s); rifled steel barrel; reservoir: 200 BBs, magazine: 17 BBs
MSRP: **$113**

MODEL 2250B
Power: CO_2
Stock: synthetic
Sights: adjustable
Weight: 3 lbs. 6 oz.
Caliber: .22
Length: 30.25 in.
Features: Velocity: 550 fps; rifled steel
barrel; single shot; 4-power scope
MSRP: **$111**

MODEL 2260
Power: CO_2
Stock: hardwood
Sights: adjustable
Weight: 4 lbs. 12 oz.
Caliber: .22
Length: 39.75 in.
Features: Velocity: 600 fps; rifled steel
barrel; single shot
MSRP: **$142**

Crosman Air Rifles

CHALLENGER CH 2000

TAC 1 EXTREME

CHALLENGER CH 2000

Power: CO^2
Stock: synthetic
Sights: adjustable
Weight: 6 lbs. 15.2 oz.
Caliber: .177
Length: 36.25 in.
Features: Velocity: 485 fps; single shot; rifled steel barrel; ambidextrous steel straight pull bolt; trigger over-travel screw; adjustable stock, buttplate and cheek piece; molded pistol-style grip, available with hooded front aperture sight and fully adjustable rear sight
MSRP: $813

PHANTOM 1000

Power: break barrel/spring piston
Stock: synthetic
Sights: adjustable
Weight: 6.02 lbs.

Caliber: .177
Length: 44.5 in.
Features: Velocity: 1,000 fps; rifled steel barrel; two-stage, adjustable trigger; fiber optic front sight, micro-adjustable fiber optic rear sight; checkered grip and forearm
MSRP: $179

TAC 1 EXTREME

Power: break barrel/spring piston
Stock: synthetic

Sights: optical or red dot
Weight: 6.02 lbs.
Length: 44.5 in.
Caliber: .22
Features: Velocity: 800 fps; single shot; rifled steel barrel; two-stage adjustable trigger; totally ambidextrous; all-weather synthetic stock with pistol grip; contoured forearm; TAC 1 comes with a 3-9X32mm scope, flashlight, bipod and red dot sight.
MSRP: $510

Daisy Air Rifles

MODEL 880

MODEL 853 LEGEND

Power: pneumatic pump
Stock: hardwood
Sights: adjustable
Weight: 5.50 lbs.
Length: 38.5 in.
Caliber: .177
Features: Velocity: 510 fps., 490 fps. (853C Legend EX); single-shot, straight pull-bolt; diecast receiver; Lothar Walther rifled steel barrel; manual

crossbolt trigger block safety; hooded front sight, micrometer adjustable rear sight; sporter-style hardwood stock
Model 853 Legend: $432
Model 853C Legend EX: $432

MODEL 880

Power: pneumatic pump
Stock: synthetic
Sights: adjustable
Weight: 3.70 lbs.

Length: 37.6 in.
Caliber: .177
Features: Velocity:750 fps/BB; 665 fps/pellet; capacity:50 shot/BB; single shot/pellet; resin receiver with dovetail mount for scope; crossbolt trigger block safety; Truglo fiber optic front, adjustable rear sights; woodgrain Monte Carlo stock and forearm
MSRP: $72

Daisy Air Rifles

MODEL 887 AVANTI MEDALIST

MODEL 1000

POWERLINE 800

MODEL 887 AVANTI MEDALIST
Power: CO^2
Stock: laminated
Sights: target
Weight: 6.90 lbs.
Length: 38.5 in.
Caliber: .177
Features: Velocity: 500 fps; single-shot bolt action; Lothar Walther rifled steel crowned, barrel; manual, crossbolt trigger block safety; refillable 2.5 oz. CO2 cylinder; hooded front sight, micrometer adjustable rear peep sight; rail adapter; sporter-style multicolored laminated hardwood stock
MSRP: **$599**

MODEL 1000
Power: break barrel/spring piston
Stock: synthetic or walnut (1000X)
Sights: adjustable
Weight: 6.60 lbs.
Length: 44.5 in.
Caliber: .177
Features: Velocity: 1000 fps; rifle steel barrel; rear button safety; fiber optic hooded front and micro adjustable rear sight; available with Winchester 3-9X 32 scope; sporter-style black composite stock; 1000X with solid steel barrel shroud, auto rear button safety and sporter-style select walnut stock
Model 1000: **$232**
Model 1000X: . . . . **Discontinued**

POWERLINE 800
Power: break barrel/spring piston
Stock: synthetic
Sights: adjustable
Weight: 5.70 lbs.
Length: 45.7 in.
Caliber: .177
Features: Velocity: 800 fps; rifled steel barrel, grooved to accept optics; rear button safety; micro-adjustable rear sight; sporter style black composite stock; Model 800X with sporter-style select walnut stock
MSRP: **$121**

POWERLINE 900
Power: break barrel/spring piston
Stock: synthetic
Sights: adjustable
Weight: 5.70 lbs.
Length: 45.7 in.
Caliber: .177
Features: Velocity: 800 fps; single shot; rifled steel barrel; rear button safety; micro-adjustable rear sight; grooved to accept optics; black composite stock
Discontinued

POWERLINE 901
Power: pneumatic pump
Stock: synthetic
Sights: adjustable, open
Weight: 3.70 lbs.
Length: 37.5 in.
Caliber: .177
Features: Velocity: 750 fps. (BB); shoots either BBs or pellets - 50 shot BB, single shot pellet; composite receiver with dovetail mounts for optics; rifled steel barrel; crossbolt trigger block safety; TruGlo fiber optic front sight; black composite stock and forearm
MSRP: **$84**

RWS Air Rifles

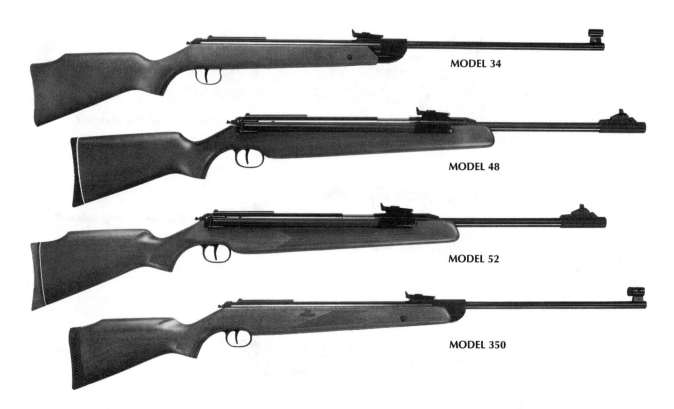

MODEL 34

MODEL 48

MODEL 52

MODEL 350

MODEL 24 RIFLE AND CARBINE

Power: break barrel/spring piston
Stock: hardwood
Barrel: 17 in. (13.5 in. carbine)
Sights: adjustable
Weight: 6 lbs. (5 lbs. Carbine)
Caliber: .177, .22
Features: Velocity: .177/700 fps,
.22/400 fps, Carbine: .177/700 fps;
rifled barrel; automatic safety; scope rail
Model 24 Rifle: **$196–220**
Model 24 Carbine: **$196–220**

MODEL 34 RIFLE AND CARBINE

Power: break barrel/spring piston
Stock: synthetic
Barrel: 19 in. (15.5 in. Carbine)
Sights: adjustable
Weight: 7.5 lbs. (7 lbs. Carbine)
Caliber: .177, .22
Features: Velocity: .177/1000 fps;
.22/800 fps; rifled barrel, adjustable
trigger; automatic safety; blued finish
Model 34: **$258–318**
Model 34N (nickel): . . .**Discontinued**
Model 34BC (matte black): $305–515
Carbine: **$203–290**
Model 36 Rifle: **$435–450**
Model 36 Carbine: **$435–451**

MODEL 45

Power: side lever/spring piston
Stock: hardwood
Barrel: 19 in.
Sights: adjustable
Weight: 8 lbs.
Caliber: .177
Features: Velocity: .177 1000 fps;
automatic safety; two stage adjustable
trigger; scope rail
MSRP: **$397**

MODEL 48

Power: side lever/spring piston
Stock: hardwood
Barrel: 17 in.
Sights: adjustable
Weight: 8.5 lbs.
Caliber: .177, .22, .25
Features: Velocity: .177 1100 fps/.22
900 fps; fixed rifled barrel with sliding
breech opening; automatic safety;
adjustable trigger
Model 48, .177: **$472**
Model 48, .22: **$472**
Model 48, .25: . . . . . . **Discontinued**

MODEL 52

Power: side lever/spring piston
Stock: walnut or rosewood
Barrel: 17 in.
Sights: adjustable
Weight: 8.5 lbs.
Caliber: .177, .22, .25
Features: Velocity: .177 1100 fps; .22
900 fps; Monte Carlo stock, sculpted
cheek piece with checkering on wrist
and forearm; Deluxe version with
select walnut stock, rosewood forearm
cap, pistol grip caps, palm swell, and
hand cut checkering
Model 52, .177: **$525**
Model 52, .22: **$581**
Model 52, .25: . . . . . .**Discontinued**
Model 52 Deluxe, .177: . . . .
Discontinued

MODEL 350

Power: break barrel/spring piston
Stock: hardwood
Barrel: 18 in.
Sights: adjustable
Weight: 8.2 lbs.
Caliber: .177, .22
Features: Velocity: .177 1250 fps; .22
1050 fps.; Monte Carlo stock w/ cheek
piece and checkering
MSRP: **$452**

AYA Shotguns

MODEL 4/53
Action: side-by-side
Stock: walnut, straight grip
Barrel: 26, 27 or 28 in.
Chokes: improved cylinder, modified, full
Weight: 7.0 lbs.

Bore/Gauge: 12, 16, 20, 28, .410
Magazine: none
Features: boxlock; chopper lump barrels; bushed firing pins, automatic safety and ejectors
MSRP: $3500

Benelli Shotguns

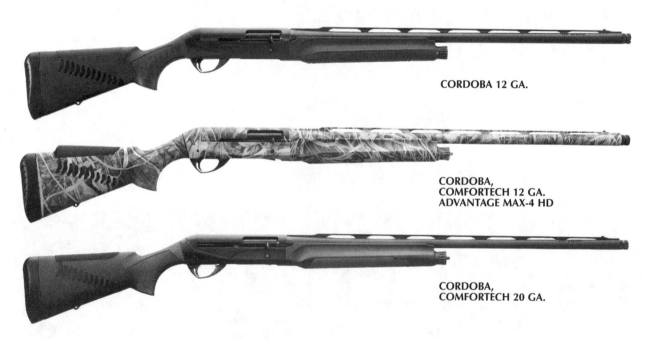

CORDOBA 12 GA.

CORDOBA, COMFORTECH 12 GA. ADVANTAGE MAX-4 HD

CORDOBA, COMFORTECH 20 GA.

CORDOBA
Action: inertia operated semi-auto
Stock: synthetic with Grip-Tight surface coating
Barrel: 28 or 30 in.
Chokes: 5 extended Crio screw-in tubes
Weight: 7.85 lbs. (12)
Bore/Gauge: 12
Magazine: 4 + 1 rounds
Features: Comfortech recoil reduction system; ported Crio barrel; inertia operated; 3 in. chamber
MSRP: $2470–2600

CORDOBA COMFORTECH 12-GA. ADVANTAGE MAX-4 HD
Action: inertia operated semi-auto
Stock: synthetic (Advantage Max-4 HD)
Barrel: 28 in.
Chokes: 5 extended Crio screw-in tubes
Weight: 7.9 lbs. (12)
Bore/Gauge: 12
Magazine: 4 + 1 rounds
Features: Comfortech recoil reduction system; ported Crio barrel; 3 in. chamber; optional gel-combs
MSRP: $2039

CORDOBA COMFORTECH 20-GA.
Action: inertia operated semi-auto
Stock: black synthetic with GripTight surface coating.
Barrel: 28 in.
Chokes: 5 extended Crio screw-in tubes
Weight: 6.3 lbs.
Bore/Gauge: 20
Magazine: 4 + 1 rounds
Features: Comfortech recoil reduction; ported Crio barrel; inertia operated; 3 in. chamber; shell view magazine
MSRP: $2470–2600

SHOTGUNS

Benelli Shotguns

LEGACY

M2 FIELD 12 GA., WALNUT STOCK

M2 FIELD REALTREE APG HD STEADY GRIP

M-2 FIELD, 20 GA. COMFORTECH

M2 FIELD, 20 GA. REALTREE APG HD COMFORTECH

LEGACY

Action: inertia operated semi-auto
Stock: Select AA grade walnut
Barrel: 24, 26 or 28 in.
Chokes: screw-in crio tubes
Weight: 7.5 lbs. (12); 5.8lbs (20)
Bore/Gauge: 12, 20
Magazine: 4 + 1 rounds
Features: 3 in. chambers; inertia operated; rotating bolt with dual lugs; two-toned receiver with engraved game scenes.
MSRP: **$1689**

M2 FIELD - 12 GA.

Action: inertia operated semi-auto
Stock: synthetic, satin walnut, APG or Max 4
Barrel: 21, 24, 26 or 28 in.
Chokes: screw-in crio tube
Weight: 6.9-7.1 lbs.
Bore/Gauge: 12
Magazine: 3 + 1 rounds
Features: Comfortech recoil reduction; inertia operated; 3 in. chamber; dual lug rotating bolt
Walnut: **$1170**
Synthetic: **$1319**
Camo: **$1210–1336**
Steady Grip **$1429**

M2 FIELD - 20 GA.

Action: inertia operated semi-auto
Stock: synthetic or Realtree APG HD
Barrel: 24 and 26 in.
Chokes: screw-in crio tube
Weight: 5.7-5.5 lbs.
Bore/Gauge: 20
Magazine: 3 + 1 rounds
Features: Comfortech recoil reduction system; Inertia operated; 3 in. chamber; optional Comfortech gel recoil pads to adjust LOP
Black synthetic: **$1319**
APG: **$1429**
Rifled slug: . . . . **Discontinued**

SHOTGUNS

Benelli Shotguns

NOVA BLACK 12 GA.
SYNTHETIC

NOVA PUMP
REALTREE APG HD

NOVA PUMP YOUTH, 20 GA.
SHORT STOCK, SYNTHETIC

NOVA H$_2$O PUMP

NOVA - 12 GA.
Action: pump
Stock: synthetic or camo
Barrel: 24, 26 or 28 in.
Chokes: screw-in tubes
Weight: 8.1 lbs
Bore/Gauge: 12
Magazine: 4 rounds
Features: 3.5-inch magnum chamber; molded polymer (steel reinforced) one-piece stock and receiver; rotating bolt locks into steel barrel extension; screw-in choke tubes (IC, M, F); available in Max-4 HD or APG HD camo
Synthetic: **$409**
Camo: **$499**

NOVA - 20 GA.
Action: pump
Stock: synthetic or APG Realtree
Barrel: 24 or 26 in.
Chokes: screw-in tubes
Weight: 6.6 lbs
Bore/Gauge: 20
Magazine: 4 rounds
Features: 3-inch magnum chamber; molded polymer (steel reinforced) one-piece stock and receiver; rotating steel bolt locks into steel barrel extension; screw-in choke tubes (IC, M, F)
Synthetic: **$429**
Realtree APG HD: **$529**
Youth: **$429**

NOVA H$_2$O PUMP
Action: pump
Stock: synthetic
Barrel: 18.5 in.
Chokes: cylinder, fixed
Weight: 7.2 lbs.
Bore/Gauge: 12
Magazine: 4 + 1 rounds
Features: matte nickel finish; open rifle sights
MSRP: **$599**

Benelli Shotguns

SPORT II

SUPER BLACK EAGLE II WITH SCOPE
STEADYGRIP, APG

SUPER BLACK EAGLE II MAX-4

SUPER BLACK EAGLE II, 12 GA.
COMFORTECH, APG, SLUG

SPORT II
Action: inertia operated semi-auto
Stock: select walnut, with spacers to adjust drop, cast
Barrel: 28 or 30 in.
Sights: red bar on tapered stepped rib
Chokes: screw-in extended crio tubes
Weight: 7.5 lbs. (12 ga.) 6.3 (20 ga.)
Bore/Gauge: 12, 20
Magazine: 4+1 rounds
Features: ultra-reliable operating system; hammer-forged, ported, cryo barrel; light and heavy loads interchangeably without adjustment; extended screw-in crio tubes (C, IC, M, IM, F); select walnut stock with spacers to adjust drop & cast; red bar sight
MSRP: **$1699**

SUPER BLACK EAGLE II
Action: inertia operated semi-auto
Stock: synthetic, walnut, APG or Max-4
Barrel: 24, 26 or 28 in.
Chokes: screw-in Crio tubes
Weight: 7.2 lbs.
Bore/Gauge: 12
Magazine: 3+1 rounds
Features: Comfortech recoil reduction system; Crio barrel; 3½ in. chamber; drilled & tapped receiver; SteadyGrip stock option for one-hand control
Walnut: **$1549**
Synthetic Comfortech: **$1649**
APG, MAX-4: **$1759**
Steady Grip: **$1680**

SUPER BLACK EAGLE II, COMFORTECH SLUG GUN
Action: inertia operated semi-auto
Stock: synthetic or APG
Barrel: 24 in.
Chokes: none
Weight: 7.4 lbs. (slug);
Bore/Gauge: 12
Magazine: 3+1 rounds
Features: available with fully rifled slug barrel with 3in. chamber; drilled and tapped receiver; Comfortech recoil reduction system; inertia-operated; adjustable sights; optional high comb; stock in Realtree APG HD camo
Rifled: **$1730**

Benelli Shotguns

SUPERNOVA FIELD MAX-4 HD
COMFORTECH

SUPERNOVA
RIFLED SLUG, COMFORTECH

SUPERVOVA TACTICAL
PISTOL GRIP, DESERT CAMO

SUPERVOVA TACTICAL
PISTOL GRIP, SYNTHETIC

SUPERNOVA FIELD

Action: pump
Stock: synthetic
Barrel: 24, 26 or 28 in.
Chokes: screw-in tubes
Weight: 7.8-8.0 lbs.
Bore/Gauge: 12
Magazine: 4+1 rounds
Features: two-lug rotary bolt; light-weight steel skeleton frame over-molded with high-tech polymer; dual-action bars; 2 ¾, 3 and 3 ½-in. chambers; Comfortech recoil reduction system; optional SteadyGrip stock; stock available in Realtree APG HD, Advantage Max-4 HD camo. screw-in choke tubes (IC, M, F)

SuperNova ComforTech: $499
SuperNova ComforTech
Camo (APG or Max-4): $599
SuperNova SteadyGrip: $499
SuperNova Rifled Slug: Discontinued
SuperNova SteadyGrip,
   APG HD: $619

SUPERNOVA TACTICAL

Action: pump
Stock: synthetic
Barrel: 18 in.
Chokes: fixed cyl.
Weight: 7.8 lbs.
Bore/Gauge: 12
Magazine: 4+1 rounds
Features: rotary bolt; 2¾, 3 and 3½-in.

chambers; open rifle sights or ghost ring rear sight with optional 3-dot tritium inserts; receiver drilled and tapped for scope mounting; stock available with ComforTech and pistol grip in black synthetic or Desert Camo.

Supernova Tactical,
   Comfortech: $459
Supernova Tactical,
   Pistol Grip: $499
Supernova Tactical,
   Desert Camo: $589

Benelli Shotguns

SUPER SPORT

SUPER SPORT

Action: inertia operated semi-auto
Stock: synthetic
Barrel: 28 or 30 in.
Chokes: screw-in extended crio tubes
Weight: 7.2 lbs. (12) 6.4 (20)
Bore/Gauge: 12, 20

Magazine: 4 rounds
Features: Comfortech recoil reduction system; ported Crio barrel; inertia operated; 3 in. chamber; rotating bolt with dual lugs; Carbon Fiber synthetic stock application; Shellview in 20 ga.
MSRP: **$1979**

Beretta Shotguns

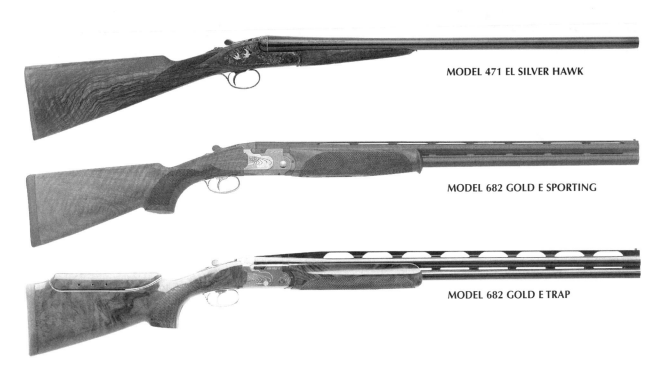

MODEL 471 EL SILVER HAWK

MODEL 682 GOLD E SPORTING

MODEL 682 GOLD E TRAP

MODELS 471 & 471 EL SILVER HAWK

Action: side-by-side
Stock: walnut
Barrel: 26 or 28 in.
Chokes: 12 Gauge Optima Chokes, 20 Gauge Mobilechokes or fixed chokes
Weight: 6.5 lbs. (5.9 lbs. 20 ga.)
Bore/Gauge: 12, 20
Magazine: none
Features: boxlock; satin chromed or case-colored receiver; single selective trigger or double triggers; automatic ejectors; EL has case-colored receiver; gold inlay; straight or pistol grips
Model 471: **$3750**
Model 471 EL: **$8350**

MODEL 682 GOLD E

Action: over/under
Stock: walnut
Barrel: 28, 30 or 32 in.
Chokes: screw-in tubes
Weight: 7.5-8.8 lbs.
Bore/Gauge: 12
Magazine: none
Features: boxlock; single selective adjustable trigger; automatic ejectors; adjustable combs on Skeet and Trap models
Combo Trap Top Single:Discontinued
Sporting: **$4075**
Skeet: **$5575**
Trap: **$5575**

Beretta Shotguns

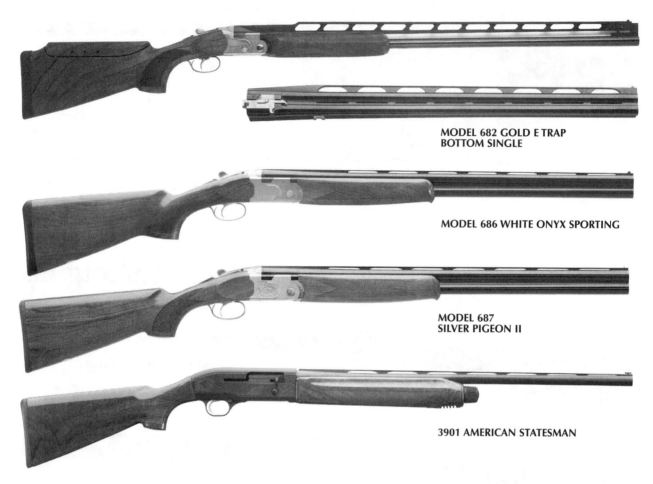

MODEL 682 GOLD E TRAP
BOTTOM SINGLE

MODEL 686 WHITE ONYX SPORTING

MODEL 687
SILVER PIGEON II

3901 AMERICAN STATESMAN

MODEL 682 GOLD E TRAP BOTTOM SINGLE

Action: over/under
Stock: walnut
Barrel: 30, 34 or 32 in.
Chokes: screw-in tubes
Weight: 6.5 lbs.
Bore/Gauge: 12
Magazine: none
Features: boxlock; single selective adjustable trigger; automatic ejectors; fully adjustable unsingle rib; combo versions available with 34 in. unsingle w/ 30 in. O/U and 34 in. unsingle w/ 32 in. O/U barrels; adjustable comb

Bottom Single: **$5575**
Bottom Single
    Combo 30/34: **$5575**
Bottom Single
    Combo 32/34: **$5575**

MODEL 686 ONYX SERIES

Action: over/under
Stock: walnut

Barrel: 26, 28 or 30 in.
Chokes: screw-in tubes
Weight: 6.8-7.7lbs. (12 ga.)
Bore/Gauge: 12, 20, 28, .410
Magazine: none
Features: boxlock; 3 in. chambers; single selective trigger; automatic ejectors; 3.5 has 3½ in. chambers
White Onyx: . . . . . . **Discontinued**
White Onyx Sporting: . . **$1700–1900**

MODEL 687 PIGEON SERIES

Action: over/under
Stock: walnut
Barrel: 26, 28, 30 in.
Chokes: screw-in tubes
Weight: 6.8 lbs. (12 ga.)
Bore/Gauge: 12, 20, 20/28 & 28/.410 Combo
Magazine: none
Features: boxlock; 3-inch chambers; single selective trigger; automatic ejectors;
Silver Pigeon S: . . . . . **Discontinued**
Silver Pigeon II: **$3150**

Silver Pigeon III: **$3425**
Silver Pigeon IV: . . . . **Discontinued**
Silver Pigeon V: . . . . . **Discontinued**
EELL Diamond Pigeon: **$7000**

3901 AMERICAN SERIES

Action: autoloader
Stock: walnut or synthetic
Barrel: 24 (rifled),26 or 28 in.
Chokes: screw-in tubes
Weight: 6.6 (20 ga.); 7.4 - 7.6 lbs.
Bore/Gauge: 12, 20
Magazine: 3 rounds
Features: steel alloy, hammer forged barrel; self-compensating gas operation; 3-in. chamber; Gel-Tek & Tru-Glo sights (Ambassador); adjustable comb (Target RL only); Mobil-choke (F, M. IC); stock shim
Citizen: **$875**
Rifled Slug: **$850**
Statesman: **$975**
Target RL: **$1000**

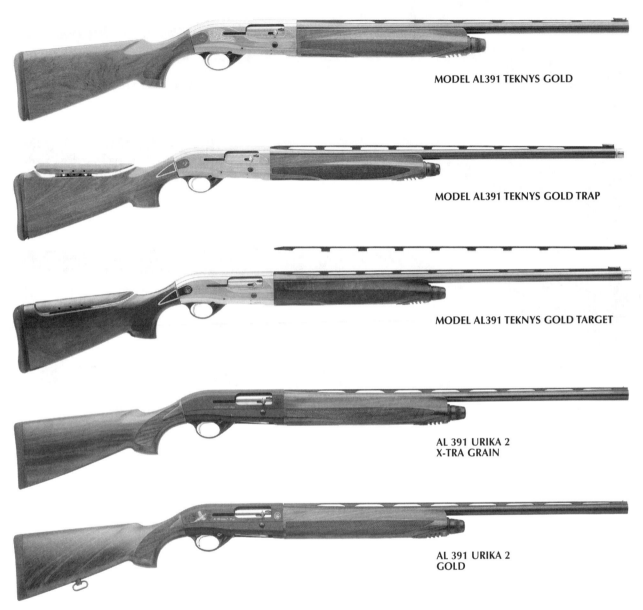

MODEL AL391 TEKNYS GOLD

MODEL AL391 TEKNYS GOLD TRAP

MODEL AL391 TEKNYS GOLD TARGET

AL 391 URIKA 2
X-TRA GRAIN

AL 391 URIKA 2
GOLD

MODEL AL391 TEKNYS

Action: autoloader
Stock: walnut
Barrel: 26, 28, 30 or 32 in.
Chokes: screw-in tubes
Weight: 7.3 lbs. (12 ga.), 5.9 lbs. (20 ga.)
Bore/Gauge: 12, 20
Magazine: 3 rounds
Features: self-compensating gas system; reversible cross-bolt safety; Optima-Bore overbored barrels (12 ga.); Optima Choke flush tubes; Gold target model with additional stepped rib
AL391 Teknys Gold: **$1926**
AL391 Teknys Gold Sporting: . . . . . .
Discontinued

AL391 Teknys Gold Trap: . . . .
Discontinued
AL391 Teknys Gold Target: . . . .
Discontinued

AL 391 URIKA 2

Action: autoloader
Stock: X-tra Grain wood finish
Barrel: 22, 24, 26, 28 or 30 in.
Chokes: Mobilchoke, Optimachoke and/or Cylinder choke
Weight: 5.7-6.6 lbs.
Bore/Gauge: 12 or 20
Magazine: 3 rounds
Features: gas operation system with self-cleaning and self-compensating valve; 3 in. chamber; receivers of

Urika 2 Gold models engraved with "gold" game scenes; Classic and Gold models available with slug barrel, short rib with ramp, V-shape rear sight and anti-glare front sight
Urika 2 Classic: **$1300-1350**
Urika 2 Gold: **$1550**

Beretta Shotguns

MODEL AL391 XTREMA2 CAMO

MODEL DT 10 TRIDENT

KING RANCH SILVER PIGEON IV

ULTRALIGHT DELUXE

MODEL A391 XTREMA2
Action: autoloader
Stock: synthetic
Barrel: 26, 28 in.
Chokes: screw-in tubes
Weight: 7.8 lbs.
Bore/Gauge: 12
Magazine: 3 + 1 rounds
Features: 3½ in. chambers; self-cleaning gas system; Kick-Off recoil reduction; spring/mass recoil reducer; Gel-Tek; Aqua Technology; stock adjustment shims; quick-detach sling swivel
Synthetic: **$1100**
Camo: **$1100**

MODEL DT 10 TRIDENT
Action: over/under
Stock: walnut
Barrel: 28, 30, 32 or 34 in.
Chokes: screw-in tubes
Weight: 8 - 8.8 lbs.
Bore/Gauge: 12
Magazine: none
Features: boxlock; single selective trig-

ger; automatic ejectors; Skeet, Trap and Sporting models are Beretta's best competition guns; combo with top single or bottom single; Trap versions available
Sporting: **$7500**
Trap: . . . . **Discontinued**
Trap, Bottom Single: **$8500**
Trap, Combo Top Single: . . . .
                            Discontinued

KING RANCH SERIES
Action: over/under
Stock: walnut, oil finish
Barrel: 26, 28 in.
Chokes: Mobilchoke
Weight: various
Bore/Gauge: 12, 20, 28
Magazine: 2 rounds
Features: engraving motifs derived from King Ranch executed on popular Beretta models; Limited Editions
686 Silver Pigeon S: **$2450**
687 Silver Pigeon IV: **$3375**
687 Diamond Pigeon EELL: . . **$7500**

ULTRALIGHT SERIES
Action: O/U, improved box lock
Stock: select walnut
Barrel: 28 in.
Chokes: screw-in tubes (Mobilchoke)
Weight: 5.75 lbs.
Bore/Gauge: 12
Magazine: none
Features: aluminum, titanium-reinforced frame; single selective trigger; automatic safety; 2¾ in. chamber; Schnabel fore-end; checkered stock; gold inlay
Ultralight: **$2075**
Ultralight Deluxe: **$2450**

Bernardelli Shotguns

HEMINGWAY DELUXE

OVER/UNDER SERIES

PLATINUM SERIES

SEMI-AUTOMATIC SERIES

SLUG SERIES

HEMINGWAY DELUXE

Action: side-by-side
Stock: walnut, straight grip
Barrel: 26 in.
Chokes: modified, improved modified, full
Weight: 6.25 lbs.
Bore/Gauge: 16, 20, 28
Magazine: none
Features: boxlock double; single or double trigger; automatic ejectors
MSRP: . . . .**price on request**

OVER/UNDER SERIES

Action: over/under
Stock: walnut, pistol grip
Barrel: 26 or 28 in.
Chokes: modified, improved modified, full, screw-in tubes
Weight: 7.2 lbs.
Bore/Gauge: 12, 20
Magazine: none
Features: boxlock over/under; single or double triggers; vent rib, various grades
MSRP: . . . .**price on request**

PLATINUM SERIES

Action: side-by-side
Stock: walnut, straight or pistol grip
Barrel: 26 or 28 in.
Chokes: modified, improved modified, full
Weight: 6.5 lbs.
Bore/Gauge: 12
Magazine: none
Features: sidelock double; articulated single selective or double trigger; triple-lug Purdey breeching automatic ejectors; various grades
MSRP: . . . .**price on request**

SEMI-AUTOMATIC SERIES

Action: autoloader
Stock: walnut, synthetic or camo
Barrel: 24, 26 or 28 in.
Chokes: screw-in tubes
Weight: 6.7 lbs.
Bore/Gauge: 12
Magazine: 5 rounds
Features: gas-operated; concave top rib; ABS case included
MSRP: . . . .**price on request**

SLUG SERIES

Action: side-by-side
Stock: walnut, pistol grip
Barrel: 24 in.
Chokes: modified, improved modified, full
Weight: 7.0 lbs.
Bore/Gauge: 12
Magazine: none
Features: boxlock double; single or double trigger; automatic ejectors; rifle sights
MSRP: . . . .**price on request**

Browning Shotguns

MODEL BPS 3.5 MAGNUM

MODEL BPS RIFLED DEER, 20- GAUGE, MOSSY OAK

MODEL BPS TRAP

MODEL BT-99

MODEL BPS

Action: pump
Stock: walnut or synthetic
Barrel: 20, 22, 24, 26, 28 or 30 in.
Chokes: screw-in tubes
Weight: 8.0 lbs.
Bore/Gauge: 10, 12, 20, 28, .410
Magazine: 4 rounds
Features: Both 10 and 12 ga. available with 3 in. chambers; Upland Special has short barrel, straight grip; Deer Special has rifled barrel; Micro BPS has short barrel, stock

Stalker (synthetic): **$559**
Hunter (walnut): **$569–609**
Magnum (3.5-inch): . . **Discontinued**
Camo Synthetic: . . . . **Discontinued**
Magnum camo: . . . . . **Discontinued**
Upland Special: **$569–609**
Micro (20): **$569**
Rifled Deer (12): **$719**

MODEL BPS RIFLED DEER, 20-GA.

Action: bottom-ejection pump
Stock: satin finish walnut or composite
Barrel: 22 in.; rifled
Chokes: none
Weight: 7.3 lbs.
Bore/Gauge: 20
Magazine: 2¾ in: 4+1;
3 and 3½ in.: 3+1
Features: Satin wood or Mossy Oak New Break-Up camo finish with Dura-Touch armor coating. Included is a cantilever scope base for consistent accuracy, even if the barrel is removed and reinstalled.

Mossy Oak: **$839**
Satin Wood: . . . . **Discontinued**

MODEL BPS TRAP

Action: bottom-ejection pump
Stock: satin finish walnut
Barrel: 30 in.
Chokes: 3 Invector-Plus choke tubes
Weight: 8.1 lbs.

Bore/Gauge: 12
Magazine: 2¾in: 4+1;
3 and 3½ in.: 3+1
Features: bottom feed, bottom eject system; magazine cut-off; HiViz TriComp fiber optic sight; top tang safety; available in standard and youth models.
MSRP: **$729**

MODEL BT-99

Action: hinged single-shot
Stock: walnut, trap-style
Barrel: 30, 32 or 34 in.
Chokes: screw-in tubes
Weight: 8.0 lbs.
Bore/Gauge: 12   *Magazine:* none
Features: boxlock single-shot competition gun with high-post rib
BT-99: **$1529**
With adjustable comb: **$1839**
Micro: **$1549**
Golden Clays
  with adjustable comb: **$3989**

www.skyhorsepublishing.com

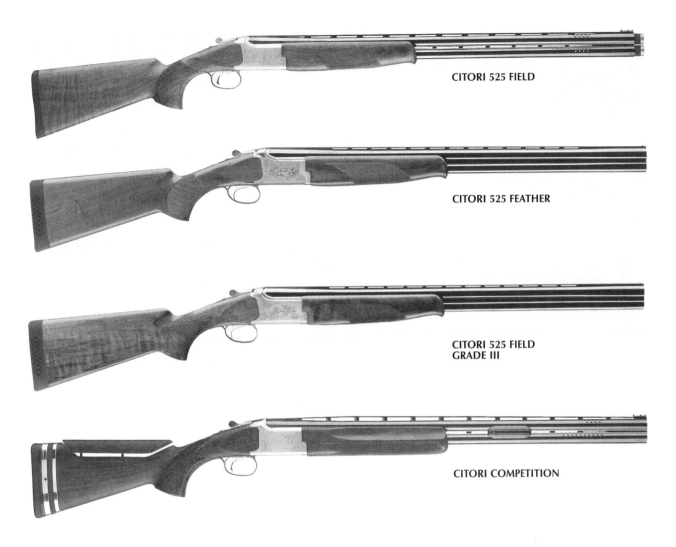

CITORI 525 FIELD

CITORI 525 FEATHER

CITORI 525 FIELD
GRADE III

CITORI COMPETITION

CITORI 525

Action: over/under   **Stock:** walnut
Barrel: 26, 28, 30 or 32 in.
Chokes: screw-in tubes
Weight: 7.3 lbs.
Bore/Gauge: 12, 20, 28, .410
Magazine: none
Features: boxlock; European-style stock; pronounced pistol grip; floating top and side ribs; Golden Clays has gold inlays
Discontinued

CITORI 525 FEATHER

Action: over/under
Stock: oil finished grade II / III walnut
Barrel: 26 or 28 in.
Chokes: 3 Invector-Plus choke tubes
Weight: 6.1 or 6.3 lbs.
Bore/Gauge: 12
Magazine: none

Features: lightweight alloy receiver with steel breech face and hinge pin, high relief engraving
Discontinued

CITORI 525
FIELD GRADE III

Action: over/under
Stock: oil finished grade III / IV walnut
Barrel: 26 or 28 in.
Chokes: 3 Invector-Plus choke tubes
Weight: 8.2 lbs.
Bore/Gauge: 12
Magazine: none
Features: steel/nitride receiver, high relief engraving
Discontinued

CITORI COMPETITION

Action: over/under
Stock: walnut

Barrel: 26, 28 or 30 in.
Chokes: screw-in tubes
Weight: 8.0 lbs.
Bore/Gauge: 12
Magazine: none
Features: boxlock; XS Pro-Comp has ported barrels, adjustable stock comb, GraCoil recoil reducer; Trap and Skeet Models are stocked and barreled accordingly
XT Trap: $2749
XT Trap
   with adjustable comb: $3079
XT Trap Gold
   with adjustable comb: $3079
XS Skeet: $2939
XS Skeet
   with adjustable comb: $3269

Browning Shotguns

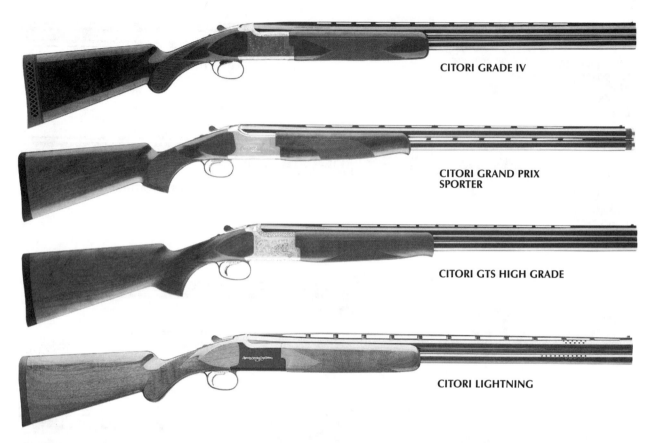

CITORI GRADE IV

CITORI GRAND PRIX SPORTER

CITORI GTS HIGH GRADE

CITORI LIGHTNING

CITORI GRADE IV AND VII LIGHTNING

Action: over/under
Stock: select walnut
Barrel: 26 and 28 in., back-bored, 3 in. chambers in 12, 20 and .410
Chokes: screw-in tubes
Weight: 6.5-8.0 lbs.
Bore/Gauge: 12, 20, 28 and .410
Magazine: none
Features: Boxlock action with automatic ejectors; engraved receivers
12, 20 Grade IV: **$3119**
28, .410 Grade IV: **$3489**
12, 20 Grade VII: **$4959**
28, .410 Grade VII: **$5339**

CITORI GRAND PRIX SPORTER

Action: over/under
Stock: oil finish walnut
Barrel: 28, 30 or 32 in.
Chokes: 5 Invector-Plus Midas Grade choke tubes
Weight: 8.1-8.5 lbs.
Bore/Gauge: 12
Magazine: none
Features: steel receiver with silver nitride finish; Browning's exclusive Selection Ejection System; lightweight, back-bored barrels; gold enhancements
MSRP: **$3439**

CITORI GTS GRADE I

Action: over/under
Stock: oil finish grade II/III walnut
Barrel: 28 or 30 in.
Chokes: 5 Invector-Plus choke tubes
Weight: 8.1-8.3 lbs.
Bore/Gauge: 12
Magazine: none
Features: 3 in. chambers; steel receiver with silver nitride finish; engraving of a game bird transforming into a clay target; Triple Trigger System; HiViz Pro-Comp fiber-optic sight; ABS case included
MSRP: **$2349**

CITORI GTS HIGH GRADE

Action: over/under
Stock: oil finish grade III/IV walnut
Barrel: 28 or 30 in.
Chokes: 5 Invector-Plus choke tubes
Weight: 8.1-8.3 lbs.
Bore/Gauge: 12
Magazine: none
Features: 3 in. chambers; steel receiver with silver nitride finish; gold engraving of a game bird transforming into a clay target; Triple Trigger System; HiViz Pro-Comp fiber-optic sight; ABS case included
MSRP: **$4309**

CITORI LIGHTNING

Action: over/under
Stock: walnut
Barrel: 26 or 28 in.
Chokes: screw-in tubes
Weight: 6.3-8.0 lbs.
Bore/Gauge: 12, 20, 28, .410
Magazine: none
Features: boxlock; single selective trigger, automatic ejectors; higher grades available; ported barrels optional
Citori Lightning: **$1949**
28 & .410: **$2029**
Citori White Lightning: **$2029**
28 & .410: **$2119**
Citori Lightning Feather: **$3629**
Citori Superlight Feather: . . . **$2319**

Browning Shotguns

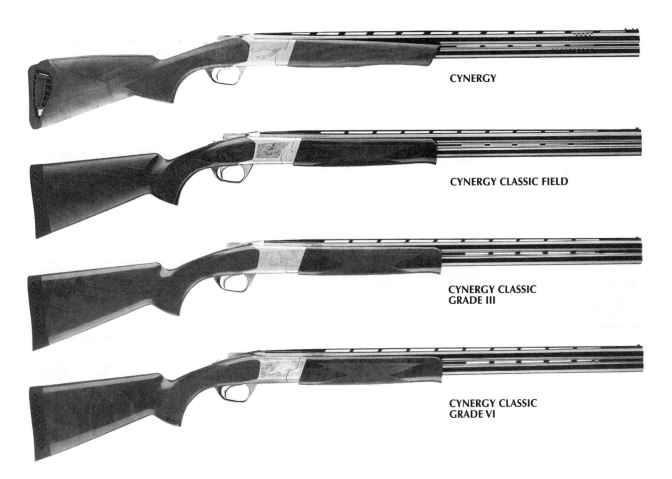

CYNERGY

CYNERGY CLASSIC FIELD

CYNERGY CLASSIC GRADE III

CYNERGY CLASSIC GRADE VI

CYNERGY
Action: box-lock over/under, with reverse striker firing mechanism
Stock: walnut, oil-finished and checkered, or composite, both with black recoil pad
Barrel: 26, 28, 30 or 32 in., fitted with removable choke tubes
Sights: double beads on tapered rib
Chokes: screw-in tubes (three provided)
Weight: 7.7 lbs.
Bore/Gauge: 12
Magazine: none
Features: single selective trigger; manual safety; selective ejectors
Cynergy: $2489
Also available:
20 & 28 ga.: $2509

CYNERGY CLASSIC FIELD
Action: over/under
Stock: walnut
Barrel: 26 or 28 in.
Chokes: screw-in tubes
Weight: 7.69-7.8 lbs
Bore/Gauge: 12

Magazine: none
Features: back-bored barrels; silver nitride receiver; impact ejectors; low profile Monolock hinge; mechanical triggers; Inflex recoil pad; conventional butt stock configuration; satin finish walnut stock; three Invector-Plus choke tubes
MSRP: $2489

CYNERGY CLASSIC GRADE III
Action: over/under
Stock: gloss finish grade III/IV walnut
Barrel: 26 or 28 in.
Chokes: 3 Invector-Plus choke tubes
Weight: 6.5-8.1 lbs.
Bore/Gauge: 20 and 12
Magazine: none
Features: steel receiver with silver nitride finish; Reverse Striker ignition system; impact ejectors. Full receiver coverage with high-relief engraving. The 12 gauge depicts pheasants on the left side and mallards on the right, while the 20 gauge highlights teal on the left and partridge on the right side of the receiver.

Recoil pad on the 12 ga. model.
Grade III, 12 ga.: $3639
Grade III, 20 ga.: $3679

CYNERGY CLASSIC GRADE VI
Action: over/under
Stock: gloss finish grade V/VI walnut
Barrel: 26 or 28 in.
Chokes: 3 Invector-Plus choke tubes
Weight: 6.5-8.1 lbs.
Bore/Gauge: 20 and 12
Magazine: none
Features: steel receiver with silver nitride finish; Reverse Striker ignition system; impact ejectors; ultra-low profile. Full coverage high-relief engraving is gold enhanced and includes the trigger guard, tang and lever. 12 ga. models illustrate pheasants on the right, mallards on the left. 20 ga. models feature quail and grouse. Recoil pad on the 12 ga. model.
Grade VI, 12 ga.: $5439
Grade VI, 20 ga.: $5459

SHOTGUNS

Browning Shotguns

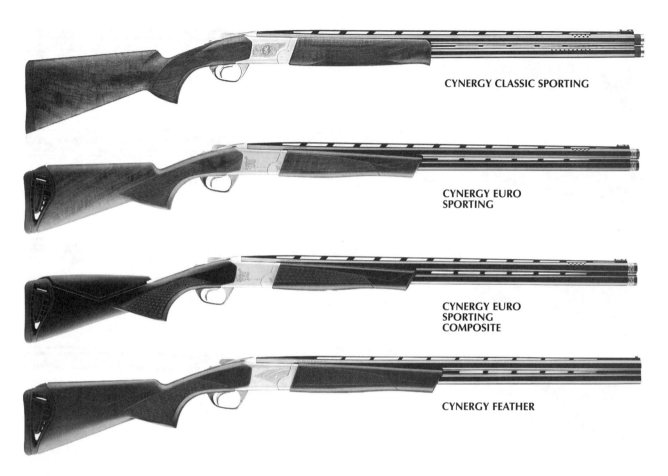

CYNERGY CLASSIC SPORTING

CYNERGY EURO SPORTING

CYNERGY EURO SPORTING COMPOSITE

CYNERGY FEATHER

CYNERGY CLASSIC SPORTING

Action: over/under
Stock: walnut
Barrel: 28, 30 or 32 in.
Chokes: screw-in tubes
Weight: 7.69-7.94 lbs.
Bore/Gauge: 12
Magazine: none
Features: steel, silver nitride receiver; ultra-low profile; MonoLock Hinge; grade III/IV walnut stock; 3 Invector-Plus Midas Grade choke tubes
MSRP: **$3639**

CYNERGY CLASSIC TRAP

Action: over/under
Stock: gloss finish Monte Carlo walnut
Barrel: 30 or 32 in.
Chokes: 3 Invector-Plus Midas Grade choke tubes
Weight: 8.7 lbs.
Bore/Gauge: 12
Magazine: none
Features: steel receiver with silver nitride finish; monolock hinge;

mechanical triggers; chrome chambers; Reverse Striker ignition system; impact ejectors; ultra-low profile; modified semi-beavertail forearm with finger grooves; Inflex Recoil Pad System; HiViz Pro-Comp fiber-optic sight. Available in Monte Carlo or adjustable comb configurations.
Monte Carlo: **$3679**
Adjustable: **$3999**

CYNERGY EURO SPORTING

Action: over/under
Stock: oil finish walnut or black composite
Barrel: 28, 30 or 32 in.
Chokes: 3 Invector-Plus Diana Grade choke tubes
Weight: 7.5-8.0 lbs.
Bore/Gauge: 12
Magazine: none
Features: steel receiver with silver nitride finish; gold enhanced engraving; Reverse Striker ignition system; impact ejectors; ultra-low profile;

Inflex Recoil Pad System; HiViz Pro-Comp fiber-optic sight. Adjustable model has comb adjustment for cast and drop. Available in three models.
Sporting: **$3859**
Sporting Adjustable: **$4239**
Sporting Composite: **$3639**

CYNERGY FEATHER

Action: over/under
Stock: satin finish walnut or black composite
Barrel: 26 or 28 in.
Chokes: 3 Invector-Plus choke tubes
Weight: 6.5-6.7 lbs.
Bore/Gauge: 12
Magazine: none
Features: lightweight alloy receiver with steel breech face; gold enhanced grayed finish; ultra-low profile; MonoLock Hinge; Inflex Recoil Pad System
Feather: **$2679**
Feather Composite: **$2609**

SHOTGUNS

Browning Shotguns

CYNERGY SMALL GAUGE

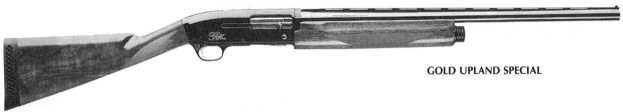

GOLD UPLAND SPECIAL

GOLD SUPERLITE FLD HUNTER

CYNERGY SMALL GAUGE

Action: over/under
Stock: walnut
Barrel: 26 or 28 in. (Field),
30 or 32 in. (Sporting)
Chokes: screw-in tubes
Weight: 6.25-6.5 lbs
Bore/Gauge: 20 and 28
Magazine: none
Features: Boxlock action; 20 ga.
comes with ported barrels; mechanical
single trigger
Field: $1900–2100
Sporting: $2800–3000

GOLD

Action: autoloader
Stock: walnut (Hunter) or syn. (Stalker)
Barrel: 24, 26, 28 or 30 in.
Chokes: screw-in tubes
Weight: 8.0 lbs.
Bore/Gauge: 10, 12, 20
Magazine: 3 rounds
Features: gas-operated, 3½ in. cham-
bers on 10 and one 12 ga. version;
Youth and Ladies' versions available
Stalker: $679
Hunter: $700
Micro: $700

Upland Special: $700
Camo: $112–1320
Gold Light (10 ga.): $1509
Gold Fusion HighGrade: $1652
Rifled Deer Stalker (22 in. bbl): . . . .
. . . . Discontinued
Sporting Clays: . . . . . Discontinued
Gold Fusion: . . . . Discontinued
Rifled Deer Hunter: . . Discontinued
31D: . . . . Discontinued

GOLD SUPERLITE

Features: gas-operated, 3½ in. cham-
bers on 10 and one 12 ga. version;
Youth and Ladies' versions available
Stalker: $900–1000
Hunter: $1161
Micro: $1161
Upland Special: $1161
Camo: $1200–1400
Gold Light (10 ga.): $1200–1400
Rifled Deer Stalker (22 in. bbl): . . . .
. . . . Discontinued
Sporting Clays: . . . . . Discontinued
Gold Fusion: . . . . Discontinued
Rifled Deer Hunter: . . Discontinued
3 1/2 in. Hunter: . Rifled Deer Stalker
(22 in. bbl): . . . . Discontinued

Sporting Clays: . . . . . Discontinued
Gold Fusion: . . . . Discontinued
Rifled Deer Hunter: . . Discontinued
Gold Light: . Rifled Deer Stalker (22
in. bbl): . . . . Discontinued
Sporting Clays: . . . . . Discontinued
Gold Fusion: . . . . Discontinued
Rifled Deer Hunter: . . Discontinued
Gold Fusion High Grade: . . . .
. . . . Discontinued

GOLD SUPERLITE FLD HUNTER

Action: autoloader
Stock: walnut
Barrel: 26 or 28 in.
Chokes: screw-in tubes
Weight: 6.4 -7 lbs.
Bore/Gauge: 20, 12
Magazine: 3 rounds
Features: aluminum alloy receiver;
semi humpback design; 3 in. chamber;
lightweight alloy magazine tube; shim-
adjustable satin finish walnut stock
with ¼ in. adjustment range; three
Invector-Plus choke tubes
MSRP: $800–1000

Browning Shotguns

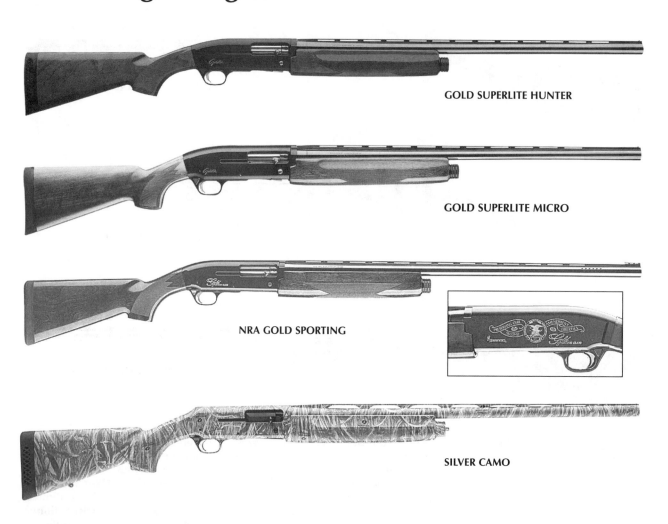

GOLD SUPERLITE HUNTER

GOLD SUPERLITE MICRO

NRA GOLD SPORTING

SILVER CAMO

GOLD SUPERLITE HUNTER

Action: autoloader
Stock: walnut
Barrel: 26 or 28 in.
Chokes: screw-in tubes
Weight: 6.32-7.13 lbs.
Bore/Gauge: 12, 20
Magazine: 3 rounds
Features: aluminum alloy receiver;
lightweight alloy magazine tube; gloss
finish walnut stock; three Invector-Plus
choke tubes
Gold Superlite Hunter
(3 in.): $950–1150
Gold Superlite Hunter
(3½ in.): $1050–1250

GOLD SUPERLITE MICRO

Action: autoloader
Stock: walnut
Barrel: 26 in.
Chokes: screw-in tube

Weight: 9.6 lbs.
Bore/Gauge: 20, 12
Magazine: 3 rounds
Features: Aluminum alloy receiver; 3
in. chamber lightweight alloy maga-
zine tube; magazine cut-off; compact,
gloss finish walnut stock; three
Invector-Plus choke tubes.
MSRP: $1105

NRA GOLD SPORTING

Action: autoloader
Stock: walnut
Barrel: 28 and 30 in.
Chokes: screw-in tubes
Weight: 7.75-7.8 lbs.
Bore/Gauge: 12
Magazine: 4 rounds
Features: limited edition with gold-
filled NRA Heritage mark and motto
on the receiver; 2¾ in. chamber;
HiViz TriComp front sight; gloss finish

walnut, shim adjustable stock with ¼
in. adjustment range; three Invector-
Plus choke tubes; donation to the NRA
Basic Firearms Training Program for
every gun sold
MSRP: $900–1200

SILVER CAMO

Action: autoloader
Stock: composite
Barrel: 26 or 28 in.
Chokes: screw-in tube
Weight: 7.5-7.88 lbs.
Bore/Gauge: 12   **Magazine**: 3 rounds
Features: 3 or 3½ in. chamber; Mossy
Oak New Break-Up and Mossy Oak
New Shadow Grass finish, Dura-Touch
armor coating; F, M and IC Invector-
PlusT choke tubes
Silver Camo 3 in.: $900–1000
Silver Camo 3½ in.: $1000–1100

Browning Shotguns

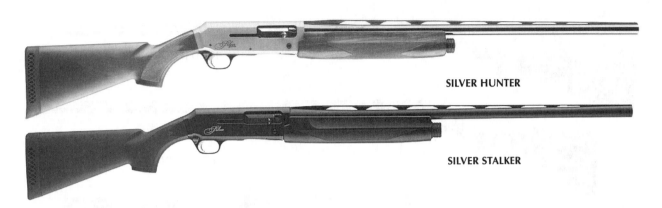

SILVER HUNTER

SILVER STALKER

SILVER HUNTER
Action: autoloader
Stock: checkered satin finish walnut
Barrel: 26, 28 and 30 in.
Chokes: screw-in tubes
Weight: 7.25-7.56 lbs.
Bore/Gauge: 12
Magazine: 3 rounds
Features: Silver finish aluminum alloy receiver; hump back configuration;

available with 3 or 3½ in. chambers; interchangeable F, M and IC Invector-PlusT tubes
Silver Hunter 3 in.: **$1079**
Silver Hunter 3½ in.: **$1239**

SILVER STALKER
Action: autoloader
Stock: composite
Barrel: 26 or 28 in.

Chokes: screw-in tube
Weight: 7.5-7.56 lbs.
Bore/Gauge: 12
Magazine: 3 rounds
Features: black matte finish, 3 or 3½ in. chamber; Dura-Touch armor coating; interchangeable F, M and IC Invector-PlusT tubes
Silver Stalker 3½ in.: **$1179**

Charles Daly Shotguns

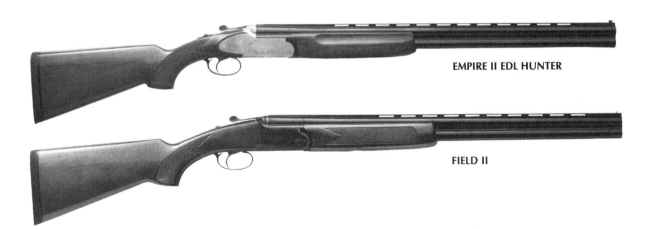

EMPIRE II EDL HUNTER

FIELD II

EMPIRE II EDL HUNTER
Action: over/under
Stock: walnut
Barrel: 26 or 28 in.
Chokes: screw-in tubes
Weight: 7.2 lbs.
Bore/Gauge: 12, 20, 28, .410
Magazine: none
Features: boxlock; single selective trig-

ger; automatic safety; automatic ejectors
28 ga.: **$1560**
.410: **$1560**
12 or 20 ga.: **$1560**
Trap: .... **Discontinued**

FIELD II
Action: over/under
Stock: walnut

Barrel: 26 or 28 in.
Chokes: mod/full (28 in.), imp.cyl/mod (26 in.), full/full (.410)
Weight: 7.2 lbs.
Bore/Gauge: 12, 16, 20, 28, .410
Magazine: none
Features: boxlock; single selective trigger; automatic safety
Field II: **$959-1219**

Charles Daly Shotguns

FIELD II HUNTER SXS

FIELD HUNTER CAMO

FIELD II ULTRA-LIGHT

FIELD HUNTER PUMP

SUPERIOR COMBINATION GUN

FIELD II HUNTER SXS

Action: side-by-side
Stock: walnut
Barrel: 26, 28 or 30 in.
Chokes: imp.cyl/mod (26 in.), mod/full (28, 30 in.), full/full (.410)
Weight: 10.0 lbs.
Bore/Gauge: 12, 16, 20, 28, .410
Magazine: none
Features: boxlock; single selective trigger; automatic safety
12 or 20 ga.: **$1100**
16, 28 ga. or .410: **$1100**
Superior Grade: . . . . . **Discontinued**
Empire Grade: . . . . . . **Discontinued**

FIELD HUNTER AUTOLOADER

Action: autoloader
Stock: synthetic
Barrel: 22, 24, 26, 28 or 30 in.
Chokes: screw-in tubes

Weight: 7.5 lbs.
Bore/Gauge: 12, 20, 28
Magazine: 4 rounds
Features: ventilated rib; Superior II Grade has walnut stock, ported barrel
12 or 20 ga.: **$489**
28 ga.: **$509**
Camo: **$509**
3.5-in. magnum synthetic: **$499**
3.5-in. magnum camo: **$574**
Superior Hunter: **$574**
Superior Trap: **$574**

FIELD HUNTER PUMP

Action: pump
Stock: synthetic
Barrel: 26 or 28 in.
Chokes: screw-in tubes
Weight: 7.0 lbs.
Bore/Gauge: 12, 20
Magazine: 4 rounds
Features: ventilated rib

Field Hunter: **$289**
Camo: **$364**
3.5-in. magnum synthetic: **$329**
3.5-in. magnum camo: **$399**

SUPERIOR COMBINATION GUN

Action: over/under
Stock: walnut
Barrel: 24 in.
Chokes: improved cylinder
Weight: 7.5 lbs.
Bore/Gauge: 12
Magazine: none
Features: boxlock drilling; 12 ga. over .22 Hornet, .223 or .30-06 rifle; double triggers; sling swivels
Discontinued

SHOTGUNS

DURANGO

RINGNECK

DURANGO

Action: side-by-side
Stock: walnut
Barrel: 20 in.
Weight: 6.0 lbs.
Bore/Gauge: 20, 12
Magazine: none
Features: Color case-hardened receiver; trigger guard and forend; single trigger (Durango); double trigger (Amarillo); hand checkered walnut stock with round knob pistol grip; overall length: 37½ in.; 14½ in. LOP
Discontinued

BOBWHITE AND RINGNECK

Action: side-by-side
Stock: Turkish walnut   *Barrel:* 26 in.
Chokes: Screw-in chokes (12 & 20); fixed chokes in .410. (IC & Mod)
Weight: 5.2 lbs.
Bore/Gauge: 20, 28, 12, .410
Magazine: none
Features: Color case-hardened finish and hand engraving; 20 and 28 ga. built on appropriate size frame; straight English-style grip and double triggers (Bobwhite); American pistol grip with a single trigger (Ringneck); hand checkered; overall length 43 in.; 14½ in. LOP
Bobwhite: **$789–987**
Ringneck: **$1036–1244**

HAMMER COACH SHOTGUN

Action: side-by-side
Stock: walnut
Barrel: 20 in.
Chokes: IC and Mod
Weight: 6.7 lbs.
Bore/Gauge: 12
Magazine: none
Features: chambered for shells up to 3 in.; external hammers; double triggers
MSRP: **$940**

Flodman Shotguns

FLODMAN SHOTGUN

Action: over/under
Stock: walnut, fitted to customer
Barrel: any standard length
Chokes: improved cylinder, modified, full
Weight: 7.0 lbs.
Bore/Gauge: 12, 20
Magazine: none
Features: boxlock offered in any standard ga. or rifle/shotgun combination; true hammerless firing mechanism; single selective trigger; automatic ejector
Flodman shotgun: **$9500–15000**

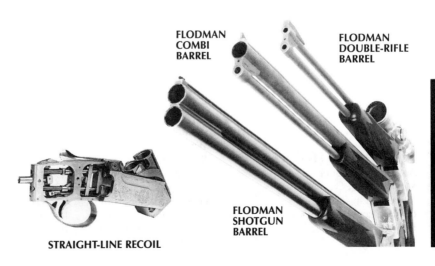

FLODMAN COMBI BARREL

FLODMAN DOUBLE-RIFLE BARREL

FLODMAN SHOTGUN BARREL

STRAIGHT-LINE RECOIL

SHOTGUNS

Franchi Shotguns

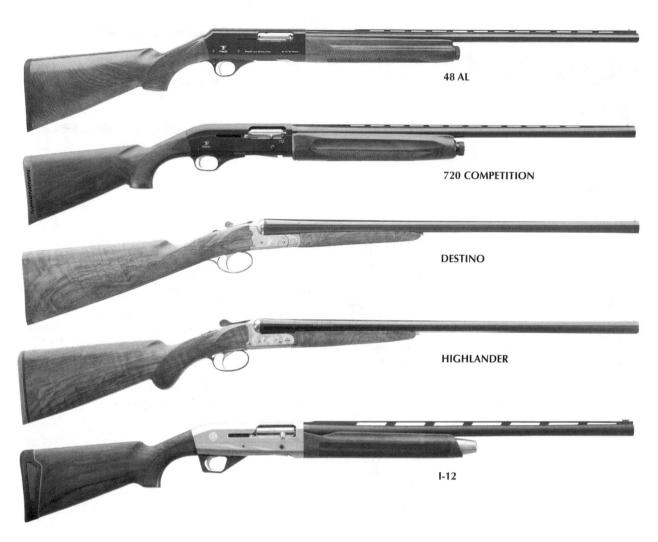

48 AL

720 COMPETITION

DESTINO

HIGHLANDER

I-12

48 AL
Action: autoloader
Stock: walnut
Barrel: 24, 26 or 28 in.
Chokes: screw-in tubes
Weight: 5.6 lbs.
Bore/Gauge: 20, 28
Magazine: 4 rounds
Features: long recoil action; pistol grip
20 ga.: $839
28 ga.: $999
Deluxe 20: $1099
Deluxe 28: $1199

720 COMPETITION
Action: autoloader
Stock: walnut
Barrel: 28 in.
Chokes: screw-in tubes
Weight: 6.25 lbs.
Bore/Gauge: 20

Magazine: 4 rounds
Features: ported barrel; rotary bolt; satin nickel receiver finish; accepts 2½ and 3 in. shells; screw-in extended chokes (C, IC, M); walnut stock with with WeatherCoat protection
MSRP: $1149

DESTINO
Action: side-by-side
Stock: walnut
Barrel: 26 in.
Chokes: standard (F, IM, M, IC, C)
Weight: 5.9 lbs.
Bore/Gauge: 20
Magazine: none
Features: production limited to 250 guns; CNC machined steel receiver; single, selectable trigger; automatic safety & extractors; gold embellished game scenes on silver-sided receiver;

screw-in choke tubes (C, IC, M, IM, F) English style, AAA select, oil-finished walnut stock; traditional checkered wood buttplate; fitted rubber butt pad
Discontinued

HIGHLANDER
Action: side-by-side
Stock: walnut
Barrel: 26 in. (20 ga.), 28 in. (12 ga.)
Chokes: screw-in tubes
Weight: 6.2 lbs. (20 ga.), 6.8 lbs. (12 ga.)
Bore/Gauge: 20, 12
Magazine: none
Features: nickel/steel alloy receiver with upland scenes; single trigger; ejectors; automatic safety screw-in choke tubes (IC, M); select grade, oil-finished walnut stock with Prince of Wales stock grip with cut checking;
Discontinued

Franchi Shotguns

I-12 LIMITED

RENAISSANCE CLASSIC 12-GAUGE

RENAISSANCE ELITE 20-GAUGE

RENAISSANCE FIELD 12-GAUGE

RENAISSANCE CLASSIC SPORTING 12-GAUGE

I-12
Action: inertia operated semi-auto
Stock: walnut or synthetic
Barrel: 24, 26, or 28 in.
Chokes: screw-in tubes
Weight: 7.5 lbs.
Bore/Gauge: 12
Magazine: 4 + 1 rounds
Features: inertia-recoil; lightweight aluminum alloy receiver with steel inserts; rotary bolt; TSA recoil reduction; available with walnut Weathercoat or black or camo synthetic stocks; screw-in extended choke tubes (C, IC, M, IM, F)
MSRP: **$949**

I-12 LIMITED
Action: inertia operated semi-auto
Stock: walnut
Barrel: 28 in.
Chokes: screw-in tubes
Weight: 7.7 lbs.
Bore/Gauge: 12
Magazine: 4 + 1 rounds
Features: chambered for 3 in.; nickel receiver accented with white gold game birds; Inertia Driven operating system; Twin Shock Absorber recoil pad with gel insert; oil finished AA-grade figured walnut stock w/ cut checkering; screw-in chokes (C, IC, M, IM, F); shim kit to adjust drop
MSRP: **$1699**

RENAISSANCE SERIES FIELD, CLASSIC, CLASSIC SPORTING AND ELITE MODELS
Action: over/under
Stock: walnut
Barrel: 26 and 28 in. (20, 12 ga.); 26 in. (28 ga.)
Chokes: screw-in tubes
Weight: 6.0 lbs.
Bore/Gauge: 20, 28 and 12
Magazine: none
Features: lightweight aluminum alloy receiver; Twin Shock Absorber recoil pad with gel insert; oil finish select walnut stock with Prince of Wales pistol grips, cut checkering; screw-in choke tubes (C, IC, M, IM, F)
MSRP: **$1729–2399**

Franchi Shotguns

RENAISSANCE SERIES SPORTING

RENAISSANCE SERIES SPORTING
Action: over/under
Stock: walnut
Barrel: 30 in.

Chokes: screw-in tubes
Weight: 8 lbs.
Bore/Gauge: 12
Magazine: none
Features: ported barrel; stainless, box-lock action; lengthened forcing cones;

engraving and gold embellishments on receiver; oil finished, select A grade walnut stock w/ adjustable comb & cut checkering; Twin Shock Absorber system; screw-in extended choke tubes
MSRP: **$2249**

Harrington & Richardson Shotguns

EXCELL SYNTHETIC

EXCELL TURKEY

EXCELL WALNUT

EXCELL WATERFOWL

EXCELL AUTO
Action: autoloader
Stock: synthetic
Barrel: 28 in. (Synthetic, Walnut, Waterfowl); 22 in. (Turkey); 28 in. w/ ventilated rib, 24 in. rifled barrel (Combo)
Chokes: screw-in tubes

Weight: 7.0 lbs.
Bore/Gauge: 12
Magazine: 5 rounds
Features: vent rib barrels (except slug barrel); 3 in. magnum capability; magazine cut-off; ventilated recoil pads; stock available in black, American walnut, Real Tree Advantage Wetlands

or Real Tree Advantage Hardwoods; 4 screw-in tube chokes IC,M,IM,F
Synthetic: $376–515
Walnut: **$406**
Waterfowl: **$459**
Turkey: **$459**
Combo: **$515**

SHOTGUNS

Harrington & Richardson Shotguns

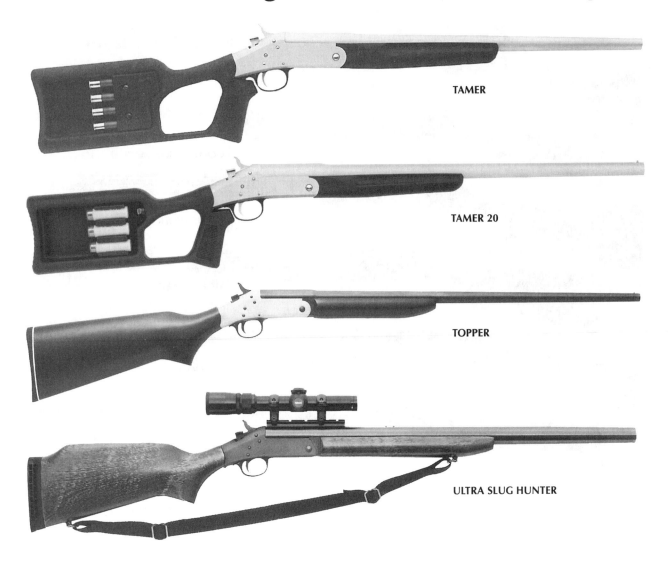

TAMER

TAMER 20

TOPPER

ULTRA SLUG HUNTER

TAMER
Action: hinged single-shot
Stock: synthetic
Barrel: 19 in.
Chokes: full
Weight: 6 lbs.
Bore/Gauge: .410
Magazine: none
Features: thumbhole stock with recessed cavity for ammo storage
MSRP: $158

TAMER 20
Action: hinged single-shot
Stock: high-density polymer
Barrel: 20 in.
Chokes: full
Weight: 6 lbs.
Bore/Gauge: 20
Magazine: none
Features: weather-resistant nickel-plated receiver and barrel; black matte finish pistol grip stock; thumbhole design with storage compartment; automatic shell ejection; Transfer Bar System to prevent accidental firing; locking system for safe storage
MSRP: $158

TOPPER
Action: hinged single-shot
Stock: hardwood
Barrel: 26 or 28 in.
Chokes: screw-in tubes
Weight: 6.0 lbs.
Bore/Gauge: 12, 20, 28, .410
Magazine: none
Features: hinged-breech with side lever release; automatic ejection
Topper: $140
12 ga. 3.5-inch: $164
Junior with walnut stock: $147
Deluxe Classic: $164–206

ULTRA SLUG HUNTER
Action: hinged single-shot
Stock: hardwood
Barrel: 24 in., rifled
Chokes: none
Weight: 7.5 lbs.
Bore/Gauge: 12, 20
Magazine: none
Features: factory-mounted Weaver scope base, swivels and sling
Ultra Slug Hunter: $247
Youth: . . . . Discontinued
With camo laminated wood: . . . $341

HK Fabarm Shotguns

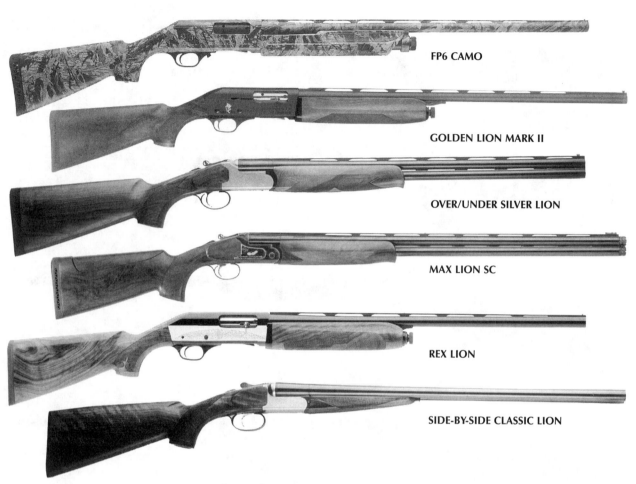

FP6 CAMO

GOLDEN LION MARK II

OVER/UNDER SILVER LION

MAX LION SC

REX LION

SIDE-BY-SIDE CLASSIC LION

MODEL FP6
Action: pump
Stock: walnut
Barrel: 26 or 28 in.
Chokes: screw-in tubes
Weight: 7.0 lbs.
Bore/Gauge: 12 **Magazine:** 4 rounds
Features: back-bored barrel
Discontinued

GOLDEN LION MARK II
Action: autoloader
Stock: walnut or synthetic
Barrel: 24, 26 or 28 in.
Chokes: screw-in tubes
Weight: 7.0 lbs.
Bore/Gauge: 12 **Magazine:** 4 rounds
Features: gas-operated actions; shim-adjustable buttstock
Discontinued

OVER/UNDER
Action: over/under
Stock: walnut   **Barrel:** 26 or 28 in.
Chokes: screw-in tubes
Weight: 7.0 lbs.
Bore/Gauge: 12, 20 **Magazine:** none
Features: boxlock; back-bored barrels; single selective trigger
Discontinued

PARADOX LION
Action: over/under
Stock: walnut   **Barrel:** 24 in.
Chokes: screw-in tubes
Weight: 7.6 lbs.
Bore/Gauge: 12, 20 **Magazine:** none
Features: boxlock; choke tube on top barrel and rifled below; case-colored receiver; 6.6 lbs. for 20 ga.; new Max Lion Sporting Clays w/adjustable stock and 32 in. tube-choked barrels (7.9 lbs.)
Discontinued

REX LION AND GOLD LION
Action: autoloader
Stock: walnut   **Barrel:** 26 or 28 in.
Chokes: screw-in tubes
Weight: 7.7 lbs.
Bore/Gauge: 12 **Magazine:** 2 rounds
Features: gas operated; Turkish walnut stock; chrome-lined barrel
Discontinued

SIDE-BY-SIDE
Action: side-by-side   **Stock:** walnut
Barrel: 26 or 28 in.
Chokes: screw-in tubes
Weight: 7.0 lbs.
Bore/Gauge: 12 **Magazine:** none
Features: boxlock; back-bore barrels; single selective trigger
Discontinued

SHOTGUNS

Ithaca Shotguns

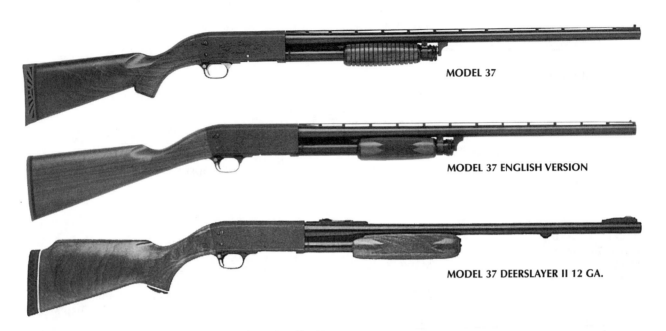

MODEL 37

MODEL 37 ENGLISH VERSION

MODEL 37 DEERSLAYER II 12 GA.

MODEL 37

Action: pump
Stock: walnut or synthetic
Barrel: 20, 22, 24, 26 or 28 in.
Chokes: screw-in tubes
Weight: 7.0 lbs.
Bore/Gauge: 12, 16, 20
Magazine: 4 rounds
Features: bottom ejection
**M37 Guide Series slug gun,
   12 or 20:. . . . . Discontinued**

Turkey Slayer Guide: **$600**
Deluxe vent rib:. **$627**
Classic: **$812**
Ultralight 20 ga.: **$834**
English straight-grip: **$647**
**Trap or Sporting Clays with
   Briley tubes, starting: $1495**

MODEL 37 DEERSLAYER II

Action: pump
Stock: walnut

Barrel: 20 or 25 in., rifled or smoothbore
Weight: 7.0 lbs.
Bore/Gauge: 12, 16, 20   **Magazine**: 4
Features: open sights; receiver fitted with Weaver-style scope base; also available: Deerslayer III with 26-in. heavy rifled barrel and Turkeyslayer (12 or 20) with 22 in. barrel, extra-full tube
Deerslayer: . . . . Discontinued
Deerslayer II:. $899

Kimber Shotguns

VALIER

Action: side-by-side, sidelock
Stock: Turkish walnut
Barrel: 26 or 28-in.
Chokes: IC & Mod.
Bore/Gauge: 20

Features: Chrome lined barrels; chambered for 3 in. shells; hand engraved, case-colored receivers and furniture; hinged forward trigger; gold line cocking indicators; straight grip, Turkish walnut stock; 14¾ in. length-of-pull;

finished in niter and rust blue; Valier Grade I with extractors; Grade II features tuned ejectors
Discontinued

Krieghoff Shotguns

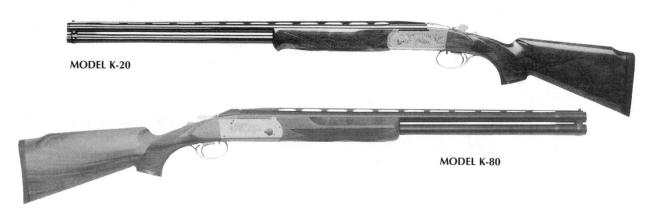

MODEL K-20

MODEL K-80

MODEL K-20
Action: over/under
Stock: walnut
Barrel: 28 or 30 in.
Chokes: screw-in tubes
Weight: 7.2 lbs.
Bore/Gauge: 20, 28, .410
Magazine: none
Features: boxlock; single selective trigger, automatic ejectors; tapered rib;

choice of receiver finish; fitted aluminum case
MSRP: $10965

MODEL K-80
Action: over/under
Stock: walnut
Barrel: 28 or 30 in.
Chokes: screw-in tubes
Weight: 8.0 lbs.

Bore/Gauge: 12
Magazine: none
Features: boxlock; single selective trigger, automatic ejectors; tapered rib, choice of receiver finish; (Sporting Clays, Live Bird, Trap and Skeet models available)
MSRP: $9470–10695

L.C. Smith Shotguns

MODEL LC28-DB

MODEL LC410-DB

MODEL LC28-DB
Action: side-by-side
Stock: checkered walnut
Barrel: 26 in. with solid rib
Chokes: 3 tubes (IC, M, F)
Weight: 6.5 lbs.
Bore/Gauge: 28
Magazine: none
Features: 2¾ in. chamber; color case hardened receiver with gold game bird decorations on sides and bottom; sin-

gle selective trigger; selective automatic ejectors; chrome-lined barrels with solid rib; bead front sight
MSRP: $1464

MODEL LC410-DB
Action: side-by-side
Stock: checkered walnut
Barrel: 26 in. with solid rib
Chokes: 3 tubes (IC, M, F)
Weight: 6.5 lbs.

Bore/Gauge: .410
Magazine: none
Features: 3 in. chamber; color case hardened receiver with gold game bird decorations on sides and bottom; single selective trigger; selective automatic ejectors; chrome-lined barrels with solid rib; bead front sight
MSRP: $1464

SHOTGUNS

Legacy Sports Shotguns

ESCORT PUMP FIELD HUNTER

ESCORT SEMI-AUTO PS AIM GUARD

ESCORT PUMP-ACTION SHOTGUN

Action: pump
Stock: black or chrome polymer
Barrel: 18, 22, 26 or 28 in.
Sights: Hi Viz
Chokes: IC, M, F
Weight: 6.4-7.0 lbs.
Bore/Gauge: 12, 20
Magazine: 5-shot with cut-off button
Features: alloy receiver with 3/8 in. milled dovetail for sight mounting; black chrome or camp finish; black chrome bolt; trigger guard safety; 5-shot magazine with cut-off button; two stock adjustment shims; three choke tubes: IC, M, F (except AimGuard); 24 in. Bbl comes with extra turkey choke tube and HI Viz TriViz sight combo.

Aim Guard, 18 in. bbl.: $289
Field Hunter, black: $389
Field Hunter Camo: $439
Field Hunter slug, black: $425
Combo .20-28 in. barrel: ....
                   Discontinued
Field Hunter, camo, TriViz Sights: ..
                   Discontinued
Field Hunter Slug combo: ....
                   Discontinued

ESCORT SEMI-AUTOMATIC SHOTGUN

Action: autoloader
Stock: polymer or walnut
Barrel: 18, 22, 26 & 28 in.
Sights: HiViz
Weight: 6.4-7.8 lbs.
Bore/Gauge: 12, 20
Magazine: 5 rounds
Features: gas operated and chambered for 2¾ or 3in. shells; barrels are nickel-chromium-molybdenum steel with additional chrome plating internally and a ventilated anti-glare checkered rib; bolts are chrome plated; extras include three chokes, a migratory plug and two spacers to adjust the slope of the stock; camo waterfowl and turkey combo available with Hi Viz sights, 28 in. barrel; hard case.

AS walnut: $479
AS Youth walnut: $479
PS polymer: $425
PS Aim Guard: ...... **Discontinued**
PS Slug, black: $479
PS Camo, Spark sights: $499
PS blue, 3.5 mag.: $589
PS Waterfowl & Turkey: $659
Combo, Waterfowler/Turkey
   24-28 in. bbl., TriViz Sights,
   Turkey choke: $659

Ljutic Shotguns

MONO GUN

Action: single barrel
Stock: AAA English walnut
Barrel: 32-34 in.
Chokes: Fixed, Ljutic SIC, Briley SIC
Weight: 10 lbs.
Bore/Gauge: 740 bore, 12 gauge
MSRP: **$7495**

Ljutic Shotguns

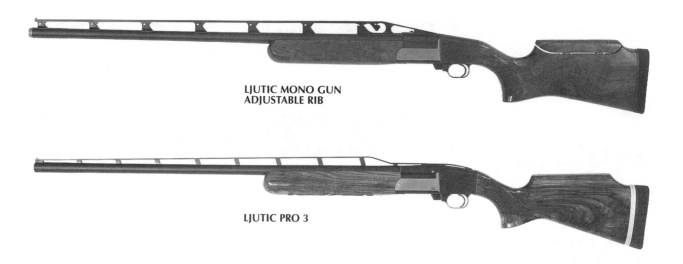

LJUTIC MONO GUN
ADJUSTABLE RIB

LJUTIC PRO 3

MONO GUN, ADJUSTABLE RIB

Action: single barrel
Stock: AAA English walnut
Barrel: 34 in.
Chokes: Fixed or Ljutic SIC
Weight: 10 lbs.
Bore/Gauge: 740 bore, 12 gauge
Features: adjustable "One Touch" impact from 60 to 100%, adjustable comb, adjustable base plate
MSRP: **$7995**

MONO GUN, ADJUSTABLE RIB, STAINLESS STEEL

Action: single barrel
Stock: AAA English walnut
Barrel: 34 in.
Chokes: Fixed or Ljutic SIC
Weight: 10 lbs.
Bore/Gauge: 740 bore, 12 gauge
Features: adjustable "One Touch" impact from 60 to 100%, adjustable comb, adjustable base plate
MSRP: **$8995**

MONO GUN, STAINLESS STEEL

Action: single barrel
Stock: AAA English walnut
Barrel: 32-34 in.
Chokes: Fixed, Ljutic SIC, Briley SIC
Weight: 10 lbs.
Bore/Gauge: 740 bore, 12 gauge
MSRP: **$8495**

PRO 3

Action: single barrel
Stock: high quality English walnut and checkering
Barrel: 34 in.
Chokes: Fixed, Ljutic Extended Chokes or Ljutic Internal Flush Mount
Weight: 9 lbs.
Bore/Gauge: Special bore, 12 gauge
Features: adjustable Comb, adjustable Aluminum Base Plate with 2 pad system
MSRP: **$8995**

PRO 3, ADJUSTABLE RIB

Action: single barrel
Stock: high quality English walnut and checkering
Barrel: 34 in.
Chokes: Fixed or Ljutic SIC
Weight: 9 lbs.
Bore/Gauge: 740 bore, 12 gauge
Features: adjustable "One Touch" impact from 60 to 100%, adjustable comb, adjustable base plate with 2 pad system
MSRP: **$8,995**

PRO 3 STAINLESS STEEL

Action: single barrel
Stock: high quality English walnut and checkering
Barrel: 34 in.
Chokes: Fixed, Ljutic Extended Chokes or Ljutic Internal Flush Mount
Weight: 9 lbs.
Bore/Gauge: Special bore, 12 gauge
Features: adjustable comb, adjustable aluminum base plate with 2 pad system
MSRP: **$9995**

PRO 3 STAINLESS STEEL, ADJUSTABLE RIB

Action: single barrel
Stock: high quality English walnut and checkering
Barrel: 34 in.
Chokes: Fixed or Ljutic SIC
Weight: 9 lbs.
Bore/Gauge: 740 bore, 12 gauge
Features: adjustable "One Touch" impact from 60 to 100%, adjustable comb, adjustable base plate with 2 pad system
MSRP: **$9995**

SLE PRO

Action: single barrel
Stock: AAA English walnut
Barrel: 32-34 in.
Chokes: Fixed, Ljutic SIC, Briley SIC
Weight: 10 lbs.
Bore/Gauge: Special bore, 12 gauge
Features: adjustable comb, adjustable aluminum base plate, SLE forearm
MSRP: **$8495**

SLE PRO STAINLESS STEEL

Action: single barrel
Stock: AAA English walnut
Barrel: 32-34 in.
Chokes: Fixed, Ljutic SIC, Briley SIC
Weight: 10 lbs.
Bore/Gauge: Special bore, 12 gauge
Features: adjustable comb, adjustable aluminum base plate, SLE forearm
MSRP: **$8995**

Marlin Shotguns

L.C. SMITH 12 GAUGE O/U

L.C. SMITH 12 GAUGE S/S

L.C. SMITH
Action: side-by-side and over/under
Stock: checkered walnut
Barrel: 26 and 28 in.
Chokes: screw-in tubes
Weight: 6.0 lbs. (20 ga. side-by-side),
to 7.75 lbs (12 ga. O/U)
Bore/Gauge: 12, 20
Magazine: no magazine
Features: automatic ejectors; 3 in.
chamber
Discontinued

Marocchi Shotguns

MODEL 99
Action: over/under   *Stock:* walnut
Barrel: back-bored 28, 29, 30 or 32 in.
Chokes: screw-in tubes
Weight: 8.0 lbs.   *Bore/Gauge:* 12
Magazine: none
Features: boxlock; single adjustable
trigger, BOSS locking system
Model 99: **$2750**
Grade III: . . . . **Discontinued**

*"Shotgun technique is directly opposite that
of a rifle. With a rifle, you place your single
bullet with perfect aiming and slow precision trigger squeezing. With a shotgun,
you 'throw' a cloud of shot with lightning
reaction." —John Cartier*

Merkel Shotguns

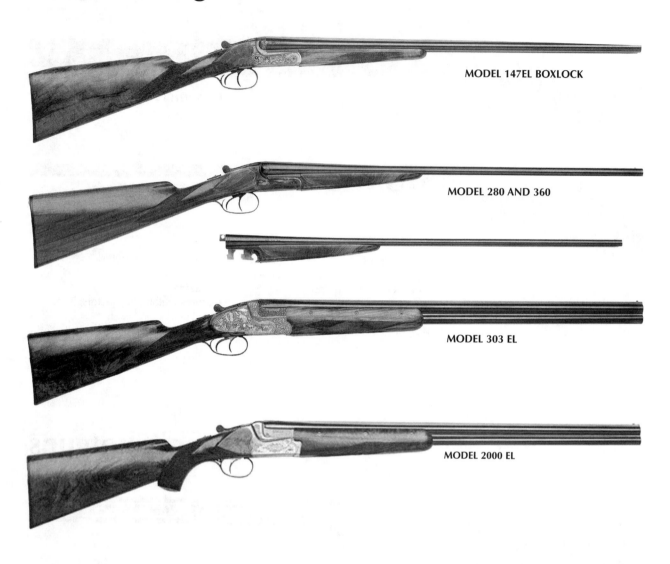

MODEL 147EL BOXLOCK

MODEL 280 AND 360

MODEL 303 EL

MODEL 2000 EL

MODEL 147E

Action: side-by-side
Stock: walnut, straight or pistol grip
Barrel: 27 or 28 in.
Chokes: imp.cyl/mod or mod/full
Weight: 7.2 lbs.
Bore/Gauge: 12, 20
Magazine: none
Features: boxlock; single selective or double triggers; automatic ejectors; fitted luggage case
47E: $4595–5795
147E (deluxe): $5795
147EL (super deluxe): $7195

MODEL 280 AND 360

Action: side-by-side
Stock: walnut, straight grip
Barrel: 28 in.
Chokes: imp.cyl/mod (28 ga.),
mod/full (.410)
Weight: 6.0 lbs.
Bore/Gauge: 28, .410
Magazine: none
Features: boxlock; double triggers, automatic ejectors; fitted luggage case (Model 280: 28 ga. and Model 360: .410)
Model 280 or Model 360: $4995
two-barrel sets: $7695
S models
with sidelocks: . . . $10995–11595

MODEL 303 EL

Action: over/under
Stock: walnut, straight or pistol grip
Barrel: 27 or 28 in.
Chokes: improved cylinder, modified, full
Weight: 7.3 lbs.
Bore/Gauge: 16, 20, 28

Magazine: none
Features: sidelock; automatic ejectors; special-order features
MSRP: $24995

MODEL 2000 CL

Action: over/under
Stock: walnut, straight or pistol grip
Barrel: 27 or 28 in.
Chokes: improved cylinder, modified, full
Weight: 7.3 lbs.
Bore/Gauge: 12, 20, 28
Magazine: none
Features: boxlock; single selective or double trigger; three-piece forend, automatic ejectors
MSRP: $8495

Mossberg Shotguns

MODEL 500 SPORTING

MODEL 835 PUMP ULTI-MAG CAMO

MODEL 835 ULTI-MAG

MODEL 835 ULTI-MAG COMBO

MODEL 500

Action: pump
Stock: wood or synthetic
Barrel: 18, 22, 24, 26 or 28 in.
Chokes: screw-in tubes
Weight: 7.5 lbs.
Bore/Gauge: 12, 20, .410
Magazine: 5 rounds
Features: barrels mostly vent rib, some ported; top tang safety; camouflage stock finish options; 10-year warranty

Model 500: $354–456
Camo: $422
Bantam: . . . . Discontinued
Two–Barrel: . . . . Discontinued
Super Bantam: . . . . . . Discontinued

MODEL 835 ULTI-MAG

Action: pump
Stock: synthetic or camo
Barrel: 24 or 28 in.
Chokes: full

Weight: 7.0 lbs.
Bore/Gauge: 12
Magazine: 4 rounds
Features: barrel ported, back-bored with vent rib; 3½ in. chamber; top tang safety; rifled slug barrel and combination sets available; 10-year warranty
Model 835: $437–674
Model 835, camo: $510–522
Combo: $559

"You will never attain maximum shotgunning potential if you hold your shotgun as if you're choking it. Relax your grip. Caress the pistol grip and forearm with gentle but confident hands. Holding them too firmly will tighten up the muscles in your arms and, shoulders, making a smooth, flowing swing virtually impossible. Golfers grip the club as if it were a tiny bird, tightly enough to prevent escape, but not enough to cause harm. Try the same with your shotgun."
—Grits Gresham

New England Arms/FAIR Shotguns

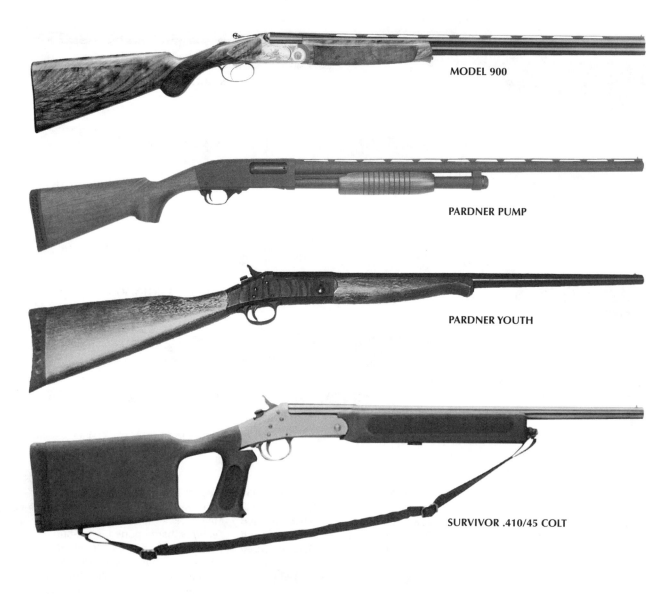

MODEL 900

PARDNER PUMP

PARDNER YOUTH

SURVIVOR .410/45 COLT

MODEL 900

Action: over/under
Stock: walnut, straight or pistol grip
Barrel: all standard lengths
Chokes: screw-in tubes
Weight: 7.5 lbs.
Bore/Gauge: 12, 16, 20, 28, .410
Magazine: none
Features: boxlock; single selective trigger, automatic safety, automatic ejector; .410 has fixed choke
Discontinued

PARDNER PUMP SHOTGUN

Action: hammerless pump
Stock: walnut, synthetic or camo
Barrel: 28 in., with vent rib, screw-in choke tube; 22 in. Turkey model; combo comes with 22 in. rifled slug barrel
Sights: gold bead front, TruGlo front & rear on Turkey model
Chokes: screw-in Browning/ Winchester/ Mossberg tubes (one provided), turkey choke
Weight: 7.5 lbs.   *Bore/Gauge*: 12
Magazine: 5-shot tube, with 2-shot plug provided
Features: twin action bars; easy take-down
MSRP: $205-305

SURVIVOR AND PARDNER

Action: hinged single-shot
Stock: synthetic
Barrel: 22, 26, 28 or 32 in.
Chokes: modified, full *Weight:* 6.0 lbs.
Bore/Gauge: 12, 16, 20, 28, .410
Magazine: none
Features: Youth and camo-finish Turkey models available; Survivor has hollow pistol-grip buttstock for storage; chambers .410/.45 Colt
Pardner:. $129–137
Pardner Youth: $180–195
Pardner Turkey (3 1/2 in.,
**   10 and 12 ga.): . . . . Discontinued**
Pardner
**   Turkey Camo Youth: . . .$180–195**
Survivor blue or silver: . . .$286–288

New England Firearms Shotguns

TRACKER II RIFLED SLUG GUN

TURKEY & SPECIAL PURPOSE

TRACKER II RIFLED SLUG GUN
Action: hinged single-shot
Stock: hardwood
Barrel: rifled 24 in.
Chokes: none
Weight: 6.0 lbs.
Bore/Gauge: 12, 20
Magazine: none
Features: adjustable rifle sights; swivel studs standard
MSRP: **$193**

TURKEY & SPECIAL PURPOSE
Action: hinged single-shot
Stock: hardwood
Barrel: 24 in. (Turkey) or 28 in. (Waterfowl)
Chokes: full, screw-in tubes
Weight: 9.5 lbs.
Bore/Gauge: 10, 12
Magazine: none
Features: Turkey and Waterfowl models available with camo finish; swivel

studs standard (Turkey Gun)
Turkey Gun
   (black, tubes): **$175**
   (camo, full choke): **$185**
Special Purpose Waterfowl
   10 ga.: **$227**
With 28 in. barrel, walnut: **$206**

Perazzi Shotguns

MX8 SPORTING

MODEL MX15

MODEL MX8
Action: over/under
Stock: walnut
Barrel: 28 or 34 in.
Chokes: screw-in tubes
Weight: 7.3 lbs.
Bore/Gauge: 12, 20
Magazine: none

Features: hinged-breech action; double triggers or single selective or non-selective trigger; Sporting, Skeet and Trap models and 28 ga. and .410 also available
MX8: **$7999–11999**

MODEL MX15
Action: hinged single-shot
Stock: walnut, adjustable comb
Barrel: 32 or 35 in.   *Chokes*: full
Weight: 8.4 lbs.   *Bore/Gauge*: 12
Magazine: none
Features: high trap rib
MX15: . . . . **from $8140**

Purdey Shotguns

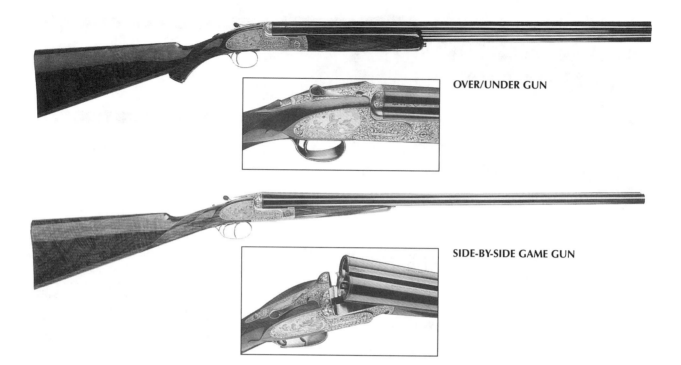

OVER/UNDER GUN

SIDE-BY-SIDE GAME GUN

OVER/UNDER GUN

The over/under gun is available in 12, 16, 20, 28 and .410, with each bore made on a dedicated action size. As with side-by-side, the shape of the action has an effect on the weight of the gun. Conventionally, the Purdey over-under will shoot the lower barrel first, but can be made to shoot the top barrel first if required. The standard for regulating and patterning the shooting of a gun is the percentage of the shot charge, which is evenly concentrated in a circle of 30 in. diameter at a range of 40 yards.
MSRP: . . . . **from $94757**

SIDE-BY-SIDE GAME GUN

Purdey easy opening action: All side-by-side guns are built on the easy opening system invented by Frederick Beesley. This system is incorporated in guns built from 1880 onwards.

Purdey offers dedicated action sizes for each of the bores 10, 12, 20, 28 & .410 cores. An extra pair of barrels can be ordered, even if you want a barrel set one ga. smaller. For example, you can have fitted 28 ga. barrels on a 20 ga., and .410 on a 28 ga. These guns are made with a single forend for both bores. All Purdey barrels, both SxS and O/U, are of chopper lump construction. Each individual tube is hand filled and then

"struck up" using striking files. This gives the tube the correct Purdey profile.

Once polished, the individual tubes are joined at the breech using silver solder. The loop iron is similarly fixed. Once together, the rough chokes can be cut and the internal bores finished using a traditional lead lapping technique.

Ribs are hand-filed to suit the barrel contour exactly, and then soft-soldered in place, using pine resin as the fluxing agent. Pine resin provides extra water resistance to the surfaces enclosed by the ribs.
MSRP: . . . . **from $80683**

The world's largest annual shooting tournament is the Grand American World Trapshooting Championships conducted by the Amateur Trapshooting Association. At this competition, 100 trap fields set side by side stretch for 1.75 miles. Several thousand competitors (ages 8 to 80) shoot as many as 5 million clay targets during the 10-day event. Since the first Grand American in 1900, many famous shooters have participated, including Annie Oakley, John Philip Sousa and Roy Rogers.

MODEL 11-87 DEER GUN

MODEL 11-87 SPS

MODEL 11-87 AUTO SPS SUPER MAGNUM

11-87 SPS SUPER MAGNUM WATERFOWL

MODEL 11-87 AUTOLOADERS

Action: autoloader
Stock: walnut or synthetic
Barrel: 21, 23, 26, 28 or 30 in.
Chokes: screw-in tubes
Weight: 6.25-8.25 lbs.
Bore/Gauge: 12, 20
Magazine: 5 rounds
Features: gas-operated, handles 2¾ and 3 in. shells interchangeably; deer gun has cantilever scope mount, rifled bore; Upland Special has straight grip; Super Magnum chambers 3½ in. shells
Discontinued

MODEL 11-87 SPS SUPER MAGNUM WATERFOWL

Action: autoloader
Stock: camo-covered synthetic, Mossy Oak Duck Blind
Barrel: 30 in.
Chokes: 3 Rem Choke tubes
Weight: 8.3 lbs.
Bore/Gauge: 12
Magazine: 4 rounds (2¾ or 3 in.) or 3 rounds (3½ in.)
Features: gas-operated system; SpeedFeed I shell holder stock; fully camouflaged with Mossy Oak Duck Blind pattern; HiViz Fiber Optic sight system; vent rib Rem Choke barrel; rear swivel studs; black padded sling; R3 recoil pad
Discontinued

SHOTGUNS

Remington Shotguns

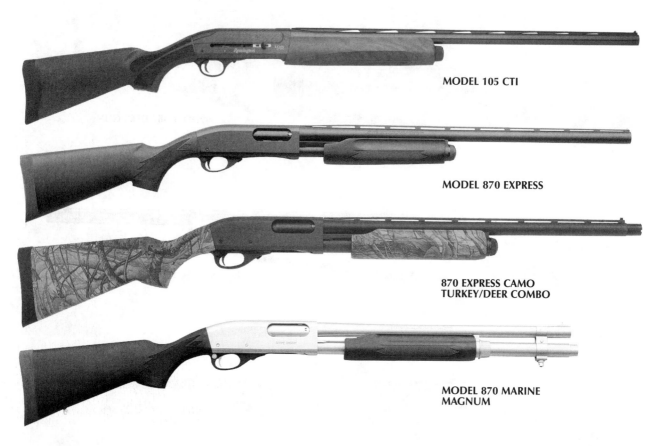

MODEL 105 CTI

MODEL 870 EXPRESS

870 EXPRESS CAMO TURKEY/DEER COMBO

MODEL 870 MARINE MAGNUM

MODEL 105 CTI

Action: autoloader
Stock: walnut
Barrel: 26 or 28 in.
Chokes: screw-in tubes
Weight: 7.0 lb.
Bore/Gauge: 12
Magazine: 5 rounds
Features: bottom-eject, titanium/carbon-fiber receiver; 3 in. chamber; optimized gas operation; "Double-Down" bottom feed and eject system; R3 recoil pad; FAA approved lockable hard case; 3 choke tubes, IC, M, F
MSRP: **$1599**

MODEL 870 EXPRESS

Action: pump
Stock: synthetic, hardwood or camo
Barrel: 18-28 in.
Chokes: screw-in tubes
Weight: 6.0-7.5 lbs.
Bore/Gauge: 12, 16, 20, 28, .410
Magazine: 5 rounds
Features: Super Magnum chambered for 3½ in. shells; deer gun has rifled barrel, open sights

Express: **$383**
Express Deer w/RS: **$383**
Express Youth 16 & 20 ga.: **$385**
Express Turkey: **$445**
Express Deer FR: **$425**
Express Super Magnum: **$431**
Express Super Mag. Turkey: . . . .
                        Discontinued
Youth Turkey: . . . . **Discontinued**
Express LH: **$401**
Turkey camo: **$445**
Express Deer w/cantilever: **$532**
**Combo with Rem choke
  barrel and slug barrel:** **$612**
**Express Super Mag. Turkey,
  camo:** **$564**
**Express Super Mag. Combo
  with deer barrel:** **$577**
JR NWTF: . . . . **Discontinued**
Super Mag., camo: . . **Discontinued**

870 EXPRESS CAMO TURKEY/DEER COMBO

Action: pump
Stock: synthetic, Mossy Oak Break-Up
Barrel: 21 in. (turkey), 23 in. (deer)
Chokes: vent rib Rem Choke (turkey),

Fully Rifled (deer)
Weight: 7.3 lbs. (turkey), 7.4 lbs. (deer)
Bore/Gauge: 12
Magazine: 4 rounds (3 in.)
Features: switch barrels to hunt turkeys with tight, dense shot loads or deer with slug loads; solid-steel receiver; twin action bar design; carbon steel, hammer-forged barrels with non-reflective matte black finish twin bead sights for turkey, cantilever scope mount for deer
Discontinued

MODEL 870 MARINE MAGNUM

Action: pump
Stock: synthetic
Barrel: 18 in.
Chokes: none, cylinder bore
Weight: 7.5 lbs.
Bore/Gauge: 12
Magazine: 7 rounds
Features: nickel-plated exterior metal; R3 recoil pad
MSRP: **$772**

Remington Shotguns

MODEL 870 SPS

870 SPS SUPER MAGNUM MAX GOBBLER

MODEL 870 WINGMASTER

870 XCS MARINE MAGNUM

MODEL 870 SPS

Action: pump
Stock: camo   Barrel: 20-28 in.
Chokes: screw-in tubes
Weight: 6.25-7.5 lbs.
Bore/Gauge: 12 & 20
Magazine: 4 (3: 3½ in.) rounds
Features: turkey models available; R3 recoil pad
Super Magnum:..... Discontinued
   with thumbhole: .. Discontinued
Turkey:................... $625

870 SPS SUPER MAGNUM MAX GOBBLER

Action: pump
Stock: Knoxx SpecOps synthetic, Realtree All-Purpose Green HD
Barrel: 23 in.
Chokes: Rem Choke, Super Full Turkey Choke Tube

Weight: 8 lbs.
Bore/Gauge: 12
Magazine: 4 rounds (2¾ or 3 in.) or 3 rounds (3½ in.)
Features: solid steel milled receiver drilled and tapped for Weaver-style rail mount; twin-action bar design; recoil compensating system; pistol grip design; Williams FireSights fiber optic sight system; padded sling
Discontinued

MODEL 870 WINGMASTER

Action: pump
Stock: walnut
Barrel: 25-30 in.
Chokes: screw-in tubes
Weight: 6.5-7.5 lbs.
Bore/Gauge: 12, 16, 20, 28 & .410
Magazine: 3-4 rounds
Features: machine-cut checkering; blued receiver

3 in.: $785
Classic Trap:.............. $1039
LW-20 (3 in.): $785
LW-Small Bore: $839–892

870 XCS MARINE MAGNUM

Action: pump
Stock: synthetic, black matte
Barrel: 18 in.
Chokes: fixed cylinder choke
Weight: 7.5 lbs.
Bore/Gauge: 12
Magazine: 6+1 rounds (3 in.)
Features: carbon steel receiver; hammer-forged, smoothbore barrel; Black TriNyte metal finish; single bead sights; SpeedFeed I shell holder stock can hold up to 4 additional 2¾ in. shells; R3 recoil pad, sling swivel studs; padded sling
Discontinued

Remington Shotguns

MODEL 1100 G3

PREMIER COMPETITION STS

PREMIER FIELD GRADE

PREMIER UPLAND GRADE

SP-10 MAGNUM WATERFOWL

MODEL 1100 G3

Action: autoloader
Stock: laminated
Barrel: 26 or 28 in.
Chokes: screw-in tubes
Weight: 6.75 lbs.
Bore/Gauge: 20, 12
Features: pressure compensated barrel; solid carbon steel receiver; honed operating parts w/ nickel-plated, Teflon coating; Titanium PVD (Physical Vapor Deposition) coating; R3 Recoil Pad; Realwood carbon reinforced walnut laminate stock; 5 choke tubes, Skeet, IC, LM, M, Full ProBore on 12 ga.; IC, LM, M, IM and Full Rem Choke on 20 ga.
Discontinued

PREMIER COMPETITION STS

Action: over/under
Stock: walnut   **Barrel**: 28 or 30 in.
Chokes: screw-in tubes
Weight: 7½-7¾ lbs.
Bore/Gauge: 12
Magazine: none
Features: Titanium PVD-finished receiver; gold trigger and engraved receiver;

right-hand palm swell and target Schnabel forend; 10mm target-style rib; ivory front bead and steel midpost; gloss finish figured walnut stock; 5 extended ProBore tubes with knurled extensions: Skeet, IC, LM, M, F
Discontinued

PREMIER FIELD GRADE AND PREMIER UPLAND GRADE

Action: over/under
Stock: walnut
Barrel: 26 or 28 in.
Chokes: screw-in tubes
Weight: 6.5-7.75 lbs.
Bore/Gauge: 20, 28, 12
Magazine: none
Features: Field w/ nickel-finished receiver; Upland w/ case-colored receiver; 7mm rib; ivory front bead and steel midpost; traditional Schnabel forend; satin-finished premium walnut stock (Field); oil finished walnut stock (Upland); 5 flush mount ProBore tubes; 28 ga. w/3 flush mount ProBore tubes
Discontinued

MODEL SP-10

Action: autoloader
Stock: walnut, synthetic or camo
Barrel: 26 or 30 in.
Chokes: screw-in tubes
Weight: 10.75-11.0 lbs.
Bore/Gauge: 10
Magazine: 2 rounds
Features: the only gas-operated 10 ga. made; stainless piston and sleeve; R3 recoil pad on synthetic
SP-10:. **$1722**
Camo: **$1932**

SP-10 MAGNUM WATERFOWL

Action: autoloader
Stock: camo-covered synthetic, Mossy Oak Duck Blind
Barrel: 26 in.
Chokes: 3 Briley Waterfowl tubes
Weight: 10.8 lbs.
Bore/Gauge: 10
Magazine: 2 rounds 3½ in. mag.
Features: soft-recoiling, gas-operating system; fully camouflaged with Mossy Oak Duck Blind pattern; HiViz Fiber Optic front sight; vent rib Rem Choke barrel; rear swivel studs; black padded sling; R3 recoil pad.
MSRP: **$1945**

SHOTGUNS

Remington Shotguns

SP-10 MAGNUM THUMBHOLE CAMO

SP-10 MAGNUM

SPARTAN 210

SPARTAN O/U

SPORTSMAN 11-87

SPR 453 AUTOLOADER

SP-10 MAGNUM THUMBHOLE CAMO

Action: autoloader
Stock: camo-covered synthetic/laminate, Mossy Oak Obsession
Barrel: 23 in.
Chokes: Briley straight-rifled ported turkey choke tube
Weight: 10.8 lbs.
Bore/Gauge: 10
Magazine: 2 rounds 3½ in. mag.
Features: laminated thumbhole stock; soft-recoiling, gas-operating system; Limbsaver recoil reducing technology; fully camouflaged with Mossy Oak Obsession pattern; fiber optic sights; Rem Choke rifle-sighted barrel; R3 recoil pad
MSRP: $2052

SPARTAN SXS AND O/U SHOTGUNS

Action: hinged breech
Stock: walnut
Barrel: 26 or 28 in.
(also, 20 in. Coach Gun)
Chokes: screw-in tubes
(fixed chokes in 28 and .410)
Weight: 6.25-7.0 lbs. (SxS) and 7.5 lbs. (O/U)
Bore/Gauge: 12, 20, 28 and .410 (16 in O/U)
Magazine: none
Features: chrome-lined barrels; all-steel breech; single selective trigger and selective ejectors; automatic safety; (SXS and O/U), single or double triggers
Discontinued

SPORTSMAN 11-87

Action: autoloading
Stock: synthetic
Barrel: 26 and 28 in.
(21 in. on Slug and Youth guns)
Chokes: RemChoke tubes
Weight: 7.75-8.5 lbs (6.5 lbs. Youth)
Bore/Gauge: 12 and 20
(12 Slug, 20 Youth)
Magazine: 4 rounds
Discontinued

SPR 453 AUTOLOADER

Action: autoloader
Stock: synthetic
Barrel: 24, 26 and 28 in. vent rib
Chokes: screw-in tubes
Weight: 8.0-8.5 lbs.
Bore/Gauge: 12
Magazine: 4 + 1 rounds
Features: matte finished vent rib barrel and receiver; tunable gas system; dual extractors; chambers 2¾ field loads to 3½ magnums; black synthetic or Mossy Oak Break-Up stock; four extended screw-in SPR choke tubes- IC, M, F and Super-Full Turkey
Discontinued

Renato Gamba Shotguns

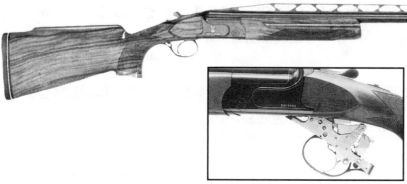

DAYTONA MONO TRAP

DETACHABLE TRIGGER
GROUP WITH
GUIDE-PROTECTED
COIL SPRINGS

THE DAYTONA SHOTGUN

The Daytona shotgun is available in several styles oriented specifically to American Trap, International Trap, American Skeet, International Skeet and Sporting Clays. The Daytona SL, (the side plate model), and the Daytona SLHH, (the side lock model), are the top of the Daytona line. All employ the Boss locking system in a breech milled from one massive block of steel.

The trigger group: The trigger group is detachable and is removable without the use of tools. The frame that contains the hammers, sears and springs is milled from a single block of special steel and jeweled for oil retention. On special order, an adjustable trigger may be produced with one inch of movement that can accommodate shooters with exceptionally large or small hands. Internally, the hammer springs are constructed from coils that are contained in steel sleeves placed directly behind the hammers. With the fail safe capsule surrounding the springs, the shotgun will fire even if breakage occurs.

Hunter O/U: . . . . . . .Discontinued
Le Mans: . . . . .Discontinued
Concorde o/u: $5500–6100
Daytona 2K o/u: $5500–7600

Rossi Shotguns

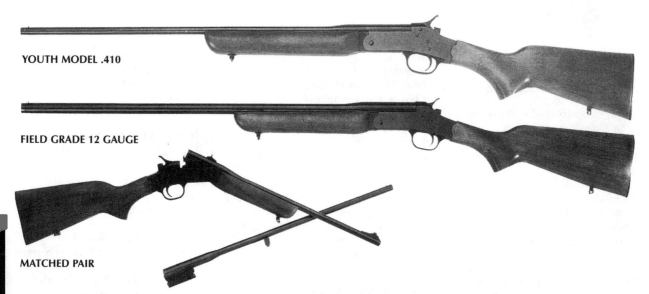

YOUTH MODEL .410

FIELD GRADE 12 GAUGE

MATCHED PAIR

SINGLE BARREL SHOTGUNS

Action: hinged single-shot
Stock: hardwood
Barrel: 28 in.
Chokes: modified, full

Weight: 5.3 lbs.
Bore/Gauge: 12, 20, .410
Magazine: none
Features: exposed-hammer, transfer-bar action; Youth model available; rifle barrels have open sights

Single-Shot: $117
Youth, 22 in. barrel: $117
Rifled barrel slug gun
    (23 in. bbl., 12 or 20 ga.): . . . $203
Matched Pair
    (.50 cal/12 ga. rifled slug): . . $329

SHOTGUNS

Rossi Shotguns

TURKEY GUN

TURKEY GUN
Action: hinged single-shot
Stock: satin, oil-finished exotic hardwood
Barrel: 24 in.
Chokes: removable Briley Extended Turkey Choke

Bore/Gauge: 12
Magazine: none
Features: 3½ in. chamber; fiber optic sights; drilled and tapped barrel; spur hammer with an integral linkage system that prevents the action from opening or closing when the hammer

is cocked; pistol grip; ambidextrous operation; installed sling swivels; Taurus Security System utilizes a key to lock the firearm
MSRP: **$187**

Ruger Shotguns

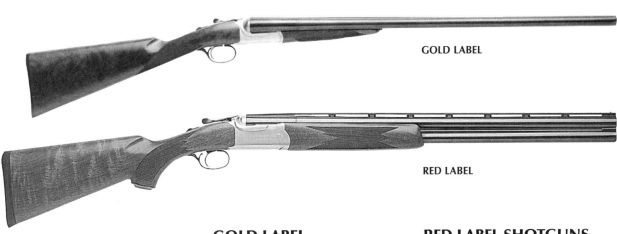

GOLD LABEL

RED LABEL

GOLD LABEL
Action: over/under
Stock: walnut, straight or pistol grip
Barrel: 28 in.
Chokes: screw-in tubes
Weight: 6.5 lbs.
Bore/Gauge: 12
Magazine: none
Features: boxlock; round stainless frame
Discontinued

RED LABEL SHOTGUNS
Action: over/under
Stock: walnut or synthetic, straight or pistol grip
Barrel: 26, 28, 30 in.
Chokes: screw-in tubes
Weight: 6.0-8.0 lbs.
Bore/Gauge: 12, 20, 28
Magazine: none
Features: boxlock; All-Weather version has stainless steel, synthetic stock; 28 ga. only available in 26 or 28 in. barrel
Standard or All-Weather: **$1956**
Engraved: **$2180**

SHOTGUNS

Savage Shotguns

MODEL 24F COMBINATION RIFLE/SHOTGUN

MODEL 210F SLUG WARRIOR

MILANO

MODEL 24F

Action: hinged single-shot
Stock: synthetic
Barrel: rifle over shotgun, 24 in.
Chokes: none
Weight: 8.0 lbs.
Bore/Gauge: 12, 20
Magazine: none
Features: open sights; hammer-mounted barrel selector; available in 20 ga./.22LR, 20/.22 Hornet, 20/.223, 12 ga./.22 Hornet, 12/.223, 12/.30-30
Discontinued

MODEL 210F SLUG WARRIOR

Action: bolt
Stock: synthetic
Barrel: rifled, 24 in.
Chokes: none
Weight: 7.5 lbs.
Bore/Gauge: 12
Magazine: 2 rounds
Features: top tang safety; no sights; new camo version available
210F: **$634**
Camo: **$555**

MILANO

Action: over/under
Stock: walnut
Barrel: 28 in.
Chokes: screw-in tubes
Weight: 6.25-7.5 lbs.
Bore/Gauge: .410, 20, 28, 12
Magazine: none
Features: chrome-lined barrel w/ elongated forcing cone; automatic ejectors; single selective trigger; fiber optic front sight with brass mid-rib bead; satin finish Turkish walnut stock; F, M, IC included; .410 chokes: M, IC
MSRP: **$1714**

High-visibility, fiber-optic front sights are an accessory every shotgun shooter should consider using. Usually seen in orange or yellow-green, these little beauties collect and concentrate ambient light (diffused light that's already there). They can help your shooting by catching the shooting eye so you are instantly aware of the gun and its muzzle orientation and can immediately start focusing on and tracking the target as you should.

Silma Shotguns

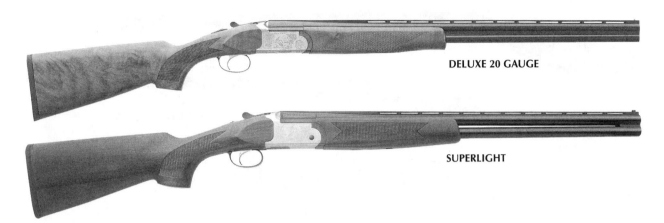

DELUXE 20 GAUGE

SUPERLIGHT

MODEL 70 EJ DELUXE

Action: box lock
Stock: walnut
Barrel: 28 in.
Bore/Gauge: 12, 20 (Standard); 12, 20, 28, .410 bore (Deluxe); 12, 20 (Superlight); 12 (Superlight deluxe); 12, 20 (Clays)
Magazine: none

Features: all 12 ga. models, except Superlight, come with 3½ in. chambers; high grade steel barrels; proofed for steel shot; all models come with single selective trigger; automatic safety; automatic ejectors; ventilated rib; recoil pad; gold plated.
Discontinued

SKB Shotguns

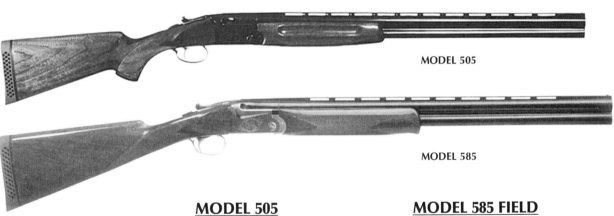

MODEL 505

MODEL 585

MODEL 505

Action: over/under
Stock: walnut
Barrel: 26 or 28 in.
Chokes: screw-in tubes
Weight: 8.4 lbs.
Bore/Gauge: 12, 20
Magazine: none
Features: boxlock; ventilated rib, automatic ejectors
MSRP: $1429

MODEL 585 FIELD

Action: over/under
Stock: walnut, straight or pistol grip
Barrel: 26 or 28 in.
Chokes: screw-in tubes
Weight: 9.0 lbs.
Bore/Gauge: 12, 20, 28, .410
Magazine: none
Features: boxlock; Field, Upland and Youth; Silver and Gold series available
Discontinued

SHOTGUNS

Smith & Wesson Shotguns

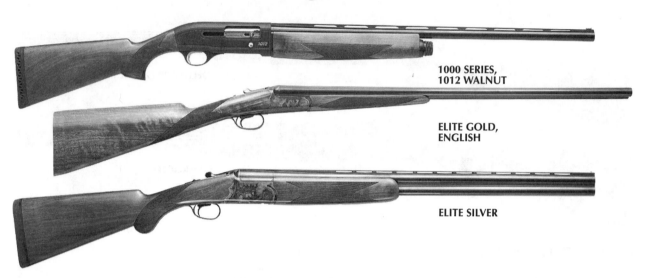

1000 SERIES,
1012 WALNUT

ELITE GOLD,
ENGLISH

ELITE SILVER

1000 SERIES

Action: autoloader
Stock: walnut or synthetic (satin, black, Realtree MAX-4 and Realtree APG)
Barrel: 24 to 30 in.
Chokes: 5 choke tubes
Weight: 6.5 lbs.
Bore/Gauge: 20 or 12
Magazine: 3+1 or 4+1
Features: offered in 29 configurations; chrome-lined barrel; 4-piece shim kit for stock adjustments; TRUGLO fiber-optic sights; dual-piston feature allows shooting heavy or standard loads
MSRP: **$623–882**

ELITE GOLD SERIES, GRADE 1

Action: side-by-side
Stock: grade III Turkish walnut
Barrel: 26 or 28 in.
Chokes: 5 English-Teague choke tubes
Weight: 6.5 lbs.
Bore/Gauge: 20
Magazine: none
Features: hand-engraved receiver with bone-charcoal case hardening and triggerplate round body action; rust-blued, chopper-lump barrels; Prince of Wales pistol grip or straight English style grips; white front bead sight; brass mid-bead sight
MSRP: **$2380**

ELITE SILVER SERIES, GRADE 1

Action: over/under
Stock: grade III Turkish walnut with proprietary catalytic finish
Barrel: 26, 28 or 30 in.
Chokes: 5 English-Teague style choke tubes
Weight: 7.7-7.9 lbs.
Bore/Gauge: 12
Magazine: none
Features: receiver with bone-charcoal case hardening and triggerplate round body action; rust-blued, chopper-lump barrels; Prince of Wales pistol grip; white front bead sight; brass mid-bead sight; solid rubber recoil pad
MSRP: **$2380**

Stoeger Shotguns

MODEL 2000 REALTREE APG HD

Action: inertia operated semi-auto
Stock: synthetic
Barrel: 24, 26 and 28 in.
Chokes: screw-in tubes
Weight: 6.7-6.8 lbs.
Bore/Gauge: 12
Magazine: 4+1 rounds
Features: inertia operating system; bolt assembly with inertia spring and rotating locking head; cavity in buttstock accommodates 13 oz. mercury-filled recoil reducer (synthetic stock; wood stock 11 oz.); fires 2¾ and 3 in. ammunition; screw-in choke tubes (C, IC, M, F, XF); Red Bar front sight; synthetic, pistol grip stock in Realtree APG HD camo
MSRP: **$549**

SHOTGUNS

Stoeger Shotguns

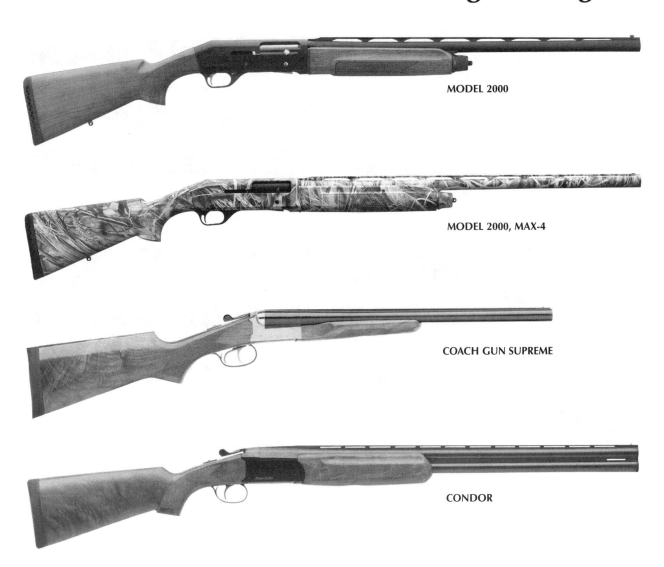

MODEL 2000

MODEL 2000, MAX-4

COACH GUN SUPREME

CONDOR

MODEL 2000 WALNUT, SYNTHETIC, APG, MAX-4
Action: inertia operated semi-auto
Stock: synthetic or walnut
Barrel: 18.5(Defense), 24, 26 or 28 in.
Chokes: screw-in tubes
Weight: 6.5-7.2 lbs.
Bore/Gauge: 12
Magazine: 4+1 rounds
Features: inertia-recoil system; ventilated rib; recoil reducers; 2¾ and 3 in. shells; barrels: Max-4 (26 or 28 in.), walnut (26, 28 or 30 in.); chokes (C, IC, M, F, XF); Defense: fixed cylinder
Max 4 Camo: $549
Walnut: $499
Black synthetic: $499
Defense: $499
APG $549

COACH GUN
Action: side-by-side
Stock: walnut
Barrel: 20 in.
Chokes: screw-in or fixed (.410)
Weight: 6.4-6.5 lbs.
Bore/Gauge: 12, 20, .410
Magazine: none
Features: boxlock, double triggers; automatic safety; flush & extended screw-in and fixed chokes (IC & M); available w/ stainless receiver and blued or polished nickel finish; walnut or black hardwood stocks
Coach Gun: $369
Nickel Coach Gun: $469
Silverado Coach Gun: $469
Silverado Coach Gun
   w/English stock: $469

CONDOR
Action: over/under
Stock: American Walnut
Barrel: 26, 28 in.
Chokes: screw-in or fixed
Weight: 6.7 to 7.4 lbs., 5.5 lbs. (Youth)
Bore/Gauge: 12, 20, 16 & .410
Magazine: none
Features: single trigger; 2¾ and 3 in. shells; 16-gauge w/ 2¾ in.; Standard and Supreme grades; Supreme available with 24 in. barrel; screw-in (IC & M) and fixed chokes (M & F), .410 (F & F); American walnut stock
Condor: $399
Condor Supreme: $599
Condor Youth: $399

Stoeger Shotguns

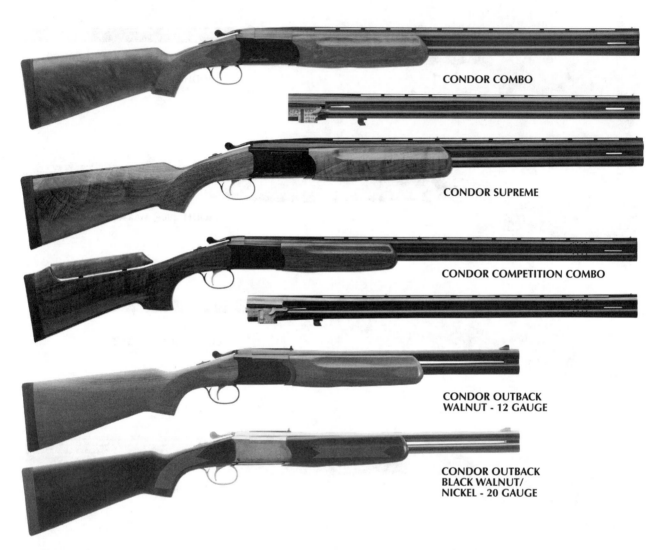

CONDOR COMBO

CONDOR SUPREME

CONDOR COMPETITION COMBO

**CONDOR OUTBACK
WALNUT - 12 GAUGE**

**CONDOR OUTBACK
BLACK WALNUT/
NICKEL - 20 GAUGE**

CONDOR COMBO
Action: over/under
Stock: walnut   **Barrel**: 28/26 in.
Chokes: screw-in
Weight: 7.4 /6.8-lbs.
Bore/Gauge: 12, 20   **Magazine:** none
Features: boxlock; single trigger; screw-in chokes (I & M); 2 barrel sets (12 and 20 ga.); A-grade (Condor) or AA-grade (Supreme) American walnut stocks; ejectors (Supreme only)
Condor: **$549**
Condor Supreme: **$719**

CONDOR COMPETITION
Action: over/under
Stock: walnut   **Barrel:** 30 in.
Chokes: screw in
Weight: 7.8 (12 ga.), 7.3 (20 ga.)
Bore/Gauge: 12, 20   **Magazine:** none
Features: single trigger; ported barrels;

barrel selector and ejectors; screw-in chokes (IC, M, F; brass bead front & silver bead mid sights; right- and left-hand models w/ palm swell; adjustable comb; AA-grade American walnut stocks
MSRP: **$599**

CONDOR COMPETITION COMBO 12 GA./20 GA.
Action: over/under
Stock: walnut   **Barrel:** 30/30 in.
Chokes: screw in
Weight: 7.8/7.3
Bore/Gauge: 12/20   **Magazine:** none
Features: single trigger; ported barrels; barrel selector and ejectors; screw-in chokes (IC, M, F); brass bead front & silver bead mid sights; right- and left-hand models w/ palm swell; adjustable comb; AA-grade walnut stocks
MSRP: **$829**

CONDOR OUTBACK
Action: over/under
Stock: walnut; black hardwood
Barrel: 20 in.
Chokes: screw-in tubes
Weight: 6.5 to 7.0 lbs.
Bore/Gauge: 12, 20
Magazine: none
Features: box-lock action; single trigger; extractors; 3 in. chambers; notched rear and fixed blade front sights; screw-in tube chokes (IC & M) optional flush & extended screw-in tubes (C, IC, M, F); A-grade walnut or black finished hardwood stocks
Walnut/high polish blue: **$369**
**Black hardwood/polished
   nickel:** **$449**

P350 APG, 12-GA.

P350 APG, 12-GA.
STEADYGRIP

P-350 MAX4, 12-GA.

P-350 SYNTHETIC, 12-GA.

P-350 SYNTHETIC DEFENSE

P350 PUMP

Action: pump
Stock: synthetic
Barrel: 24, 26 and 28 in. 18.5 in. (Defense)
Chokes: screw-in
Weight: 6.4 to 6.9 lbs
Bore/Gauge: 12
Magazine: 4 + 1 rounds
Features: bolt with rotating lugs; raised rib; fires all types of 12-gauge ammunition — accepts 2¾ in., 3 in., 3½ in. Magnum (target loads, steel shot, lead shot and slugs); available with optional 13-oz. mercury filled recoil reducer; screw-in choke tubes (C, IC, M, F, XF turkey); stocks available in black synthetic, Advantage Max-4 HD or synthetic available in pistol grip, Max-4 HD & APG HD available in Steady Grip configuration; red bar front and metal bead mid sights; Defense model with black synthetic pistol-grip stocks, 3½-in. chamber, blade front sight, fixed cylinder choke

Synthetic: $329
Synthetic Pistol Grip: $329
APG HD Camo: $429
Max 4 Camo: $429
APG HD Steady Grip: $429
Timber HD Steady Grip: $429
Defense: $329

SHOTGUNS

Stoeger Shotguns

UPLANDER

UPLANDER SUPREME

UPLANDER
Action: side-by-side
Stock: walnut
Barrel: 22 (youth), 24, 26 and 28 in.
Chokes: screw-in and fixed
Weight: 7 to 7.5 lbs, 6.5 to 6.8 (Youth)

Bore/Gauge: 12, 20, 16, 28 and .410
Magazine: none
Features: single selective trigger; tang-mounted automatic safety; extractors; brass bead front sight; 2¾ and 3-in. chambers (16- and 28-ga. in 2¾ in. chambers only); screw-in chokes 12 & 20 ga. (IC & M), fixed chokes 16, 28 ga. and .410 bore (F&F); optional flush and extended screw-in choke tubes

available for 12 & 20 ga. (C, IC, M, IM, F); A-grade satin walnut stocks; Youth model 20 ga. or .410 with 13-in. length-of-pull and 22-in. barrel; Combo sets available in 12/20 or 20/28-ga. configurations
Uplander: $369
Uplander Combo: $649
Uplander Supreme: $489
Uplander Youth: $369

Tristar Sporting Arms Shotguns

BASQUE BRITTANY

MAROCCHI DIANA SYNTHETIC AND SYNTHETIC MAGNUM

BASQUE SERIES
Action: side-by-side
Stock: walnut, straight or pistol grip
Barrel: 26 or 28 in.
Chokes: screw-in tubes
Weight: 6.8 lbs.
Bore/Gauge: 12, 16, 20, 28, .410
Magazine: none
Features: boxlock; single selective trig-

ger; automatic ejectors; chromed bores; also: 20 in. Coach gun; chokes in 16 ga.: M/F and IC/M in 28 ga. and .410.
Discontinued

MAROCCHI DIANA
Action: autoloader
Stock: walnut, synthetic or camo
Barrel: 24, 26, 28 or 30 in.

Chokes: screw-in tubes
Weight: 7.0 lbs.
Bore/Gauge: 12, 20, 28
Magazine: 4 rounds
Features: gas-operated; stock shims; slug model has sights; scope mount on rifled barrel
Discontinued

SHOTGUNS

Verona Shotguns

LX 1001-308/20 EXPRESS

LX 1001-20 GA OVER/UNDER BARREL SET

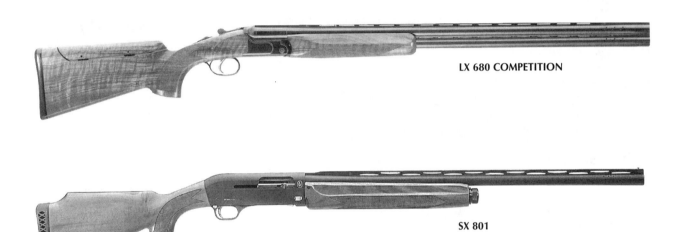

LX 680 COMPETITION

SX 801

SX 405

MODEL LX EXPRESS
Action: over/under
Stock: Turkish walnut
Barrel: 28 in.
Chokes: screw-in tubes
Weight: 8.0 lbs.
Bore/Gauge: .223, .243, .270, .308 or .30-06 over 20 ga.
Magazine: none
Features: single selective trigger; automatic ejectors
Express Combo with Express and 20 ga. over/under set: $2599

MODEL LX 680 COMPETITION SERIES
Action: over/under
Stock: Turkish walnut
Barrel: 30 in. (32 in. on Trap Model)
Chokes: screw-in tubes
Weight: 7.5 lbs.   *Bore/Gauge:* 12
Magazine: none
Features: boxlock; removable competition trigger; ported barrels; deluxe case; also multiple-barrel sets
Discontinued

MODEL SX 801
Action: autoloader
Stock: walnut
Barrel: 28 or 30 in.
Chokes: screw-in tubes
Weight: 6.8 lbs.   *Bore/Gauge:* 12
Magazine: 3 rounds
Features: gas-operated, alloy receiver; sporting and competition models available; also model SX405: synthetic or camo, 22 in. slug or 26 in. field
Discontinued

Weatherby Shotguns

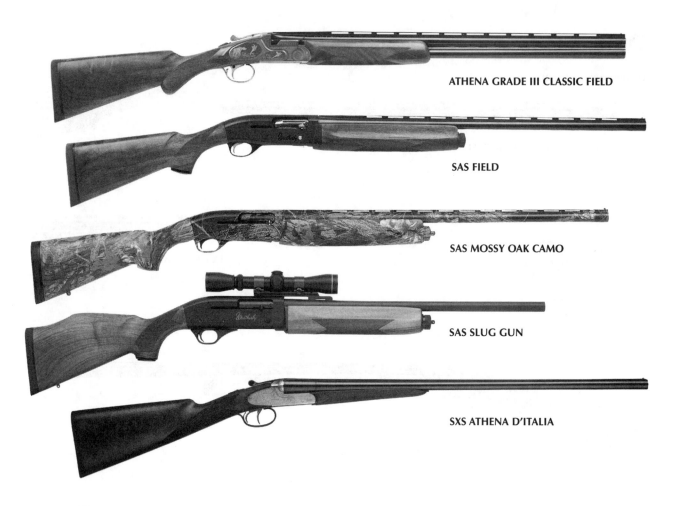

ATHENA GRADE III CLASSIC FIELD

SAS FIELD

SAS MOSSY OAK CAMO

SAS SLUG GUN

SXS ATHENA D'ITALIA

ATHENA

Action: over/under
Stock: walnut
Barrel: 26 or 28 in.
Chokes: screw-in tubes
Weight: 8.0 lbs.
Bore/Gauge: 12, 20, 28
Magazine: none
Features: boxlock; single selective
mechanical trigger, automatic ejectors
Grade III Classic Field:. **$2599**
Grade V Classic Field: **$3999**

ORION

Action: over/under
Stock: walnut, straight or pistol grip
Barrel: 26, 28, 30 or 32 in.
Chokes: screw-in tubes
Weight: 8.0 lbs.
Bore/Gauge: 12, 20 or 28
Magazine: none
Features: boxlock; single selective trigger, automatic ejectors
Upland: **$1364**

Grade II: **$1899**
Super Sporting Clays: **$2599**
Grade III: **$2199**

SAS

Action: autoloader
Stock: walnut, synthetic or camo
Barrel: 24, 26, 28 or 30 in., vent rib
Chokes: screw-in tubes
Weight: 7.8 lbs.
Bore/Gauge: 12
Magazine: 4 rounds
Features: gas-operated; 3 in. chamber;
magazine cutoff
Discontinued

SAS SLUG GUN

Action: autoloader
Stock: walnut
Barrel: 22 in. rifled
Chokes: none
Weight: 7.3 lbs.
Bore/Gauge: 12

Magazine: 4 rounds
Features: self-compensating gas system;
cantilever scope base included; "smart"
follower, magazine cutoff, stock has
shims to alter drop, pitch, cast-off
Discontinued

SXS ATHENA DÍITALIA

Action: side-by-side
Stock: Turkish walnut
Barrel: 26 or 28 in.
Chokes: screw-in tubes
(fixed chokes in 28 ga.)
Weight: 6.75-7.25 lbs.
Bore/Gauge: 12, 20, 28
Magazine: none
Features: chrome-lined and back-
bored barrels; Anson and Deeley
boxlock mechanism; automatic
ejectors; engraved sideplates; double
triggers and a straight grip, IC and
M chokes in 28 ga.
MSRP: **$3799–3929**

Winchester Shotguns

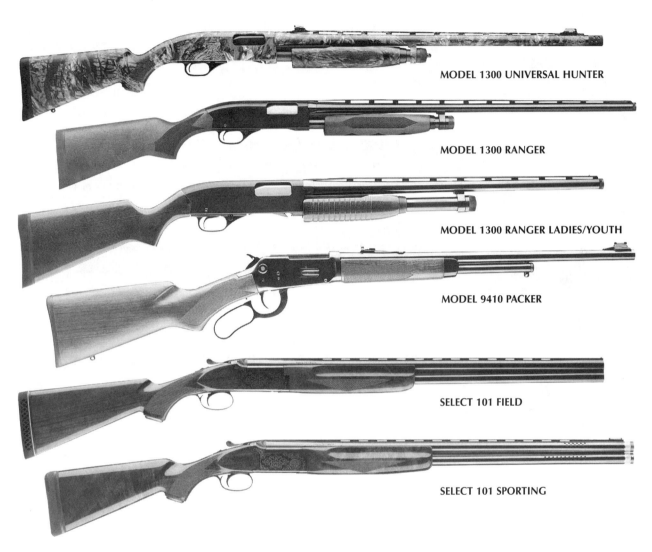

MODEL 1300 UNIVERSAL HUNTER

MODEL 1300 RANGER

MODEL 1300 RANGER LADIES/YOUTH

MODEL 9410 PACKER

SELECT 101 FIELD

SELECT 101 SPORTING

MODEL 1300

Action: pump
Stock: walnut or synthetic
Barrel: 18, 22, 24, 26 or 28 in.
Chokes: screw-in tubes
Weight: 7.5 lbs.
Bore/Gauge: 12, 20
Magazine: 4 rounds
Features: Deer versions feature either smooth or rifled 22 in. barrels, rifle sights

Black Shadow:	$357
Buck & Tom:	$556
NRA Defender, 8-shot:	$414
Ranger Deer:	$396
Ranger Gloss Compact:	$391
Short Turkey:	$514
Sporting Field:	$444
Sporting Field Compact:	$444
Universal Hunter:	$517
Upland Special Field:	$444
Walnut Field:	$409

MODEL 9410

Action: lever
Stock: walnut
Barrel: 20 or 24 in.
Chokes: full
Weight: 7.0 lbs.
Bore/Gauge: .410
Magazine: 9 rounds
Features: 2½ in. chamber; Truglo front sight, shallow V rear

9410:	$579–626
Packer with 20-inch barrel:	$583–647
Packer w/ TruGlo sights (no choke):	$789
M9410 Ranger, hardwood:	$532

SELECT 101

Action: over/under
Stock: high gloss grade II/III walnut
Barrel: 26 or 28 (Field model); 28, 30 or 32 in. (Sporting)
Chokes: Invector-Plus with three tubes (Field model) or five Signature extended tubes (Sporting model)
Weight: 7.0-7.7 lbs.
Bore/Gauge: 12
Magazine: none
Features: blued receiver with deep-relief engraving; lightweight ported barrels; Pachmayr Decelerator sporting pad control recoil; 10mm runway rib and white mid-bead; TRUGLO front sight round

101 Field:	$1739
101 Sporting:	$2579

SHOTGUNS

Winchester Shotguns

SUPER X2 UNIVERSAL HUNTER

SUPER X2 SPORTING CLAYS 3"

SUPER X2 PRACTICAL MK II

SUPER X2 MAGNUM
STANDARD COMPOSITE

SUPER X2 MAGNUM
UNIVERSAL HUNTER

SUPER X2 SIGNATURE RED

SUPER X2
Action: autoloader
Stock: walnut or synthetic
Barrel: 22, 24, 26, 28 or 30 in.
Chokes: screw-in tubes
Weight: 8.0 lbs.
Bore/Gauge: 12
Magazine: 4 rounds
Features: gas-operated mechanism, back-bored barrels; all with

Dura-Touch finish, some with Tru-Glo sights
Sporting Clays: **$1459**
NWTI Turkey: . . . . **Discontinued**
Universal Hunter: . . . **Discontinued**
Practical MKI: . . . . . . **Discontinued**

SUPER X2 SIGNATURE RED
Action: autoloader
Stock: hardwood, Dura-Touch finish

Barrel: 28 or 30 in.
Chokes: screw-in tubes
Weight: 8.0 lbs.
Bore/Gauge: 12
Magazine: 4 rounds
Features: shims adjust buttstock; backbored barrel; Dura-Touch armor coating now available on many other Winchesters
Discontinued

Winchester Shotguns

SUPER X3 CAMO FIELD

SUPER X3 COMPOSITE

SUPER X3 FIELD

SUPER X3 RIFLED CANTILEVER DEER

SUPER X3 CAMO FIELD

Action: autoloader
Stock: composite
Barrel: 26 or 28 in.
Chokes: screw-in tubes
Weight: 7.5 lbs.
Bore/Gauge: 12
Magazine: 4 rounds
Features: Mossy Oak New Break-Up finish; composite stock w/ shims and Dura-Touch Armor Coating finish; Invector-Plus choke tube system
MSRP: **$1439**

SUPER X3 COMPOSITE

Action: autoloader
Stock: composite
Barrel: 26 or 28 in.
Chokes: screw-in tubes
Weight: 7.5 lbs.
Bore/Gauge: 12
Magazine: 4 rounds
Features: slim barrel with machined rib; lightweight alloy receiver; lightweight alloy magazine tube and recoil spring system; self-adjusting Active Valve gas system; Pachmayr Decelerator recoil pad; composite stock w/ Dura-Touch Armor Coating finish; Invector-Plus choke tube system
Super X3 Composite 3 in.: . . . **$1119**
Super X3 Composite 3¾ in.: . . . **$1239**

SUPER X3 FIELD

Action: autoloader
Stock: walnut
Barrel: 26 or 28 in.
Chokes: screw-in tubes
Weight: 7.0 lbs.
Bore/Gauge: 12
Magazine: 4 rounds
Features: lightweight back-bored (.742 in.) barrel; machined rib; self-adjusting Active Valve gas system; chambered for 3 in.; ultralight alloy magazine tube and recoil spring; gunmetal gray Perma-Cote finish; Pachmayr Decelerator recoil pad; Invector-Plus choke tube system
Discontinued

SUPER X3 RIFLED CANTILEVER DEER

Action: autoloader
Stock: composite
Barrel: 22 in.
Chokes: none
Weight: 7.0 lb.
Bore/Gauge: 12
Magazine: 4 rounds
Features: fully rifled barrel; cantilever scope base mount and rifle style sights; lengthwise groove in the cantilever; TruGlo fiber-optic front sight; Weaver-style rail on the cantilever; composite stock w/ Dura-Touch armor coating
MSRP: **$1179**

Winchester Shotguns

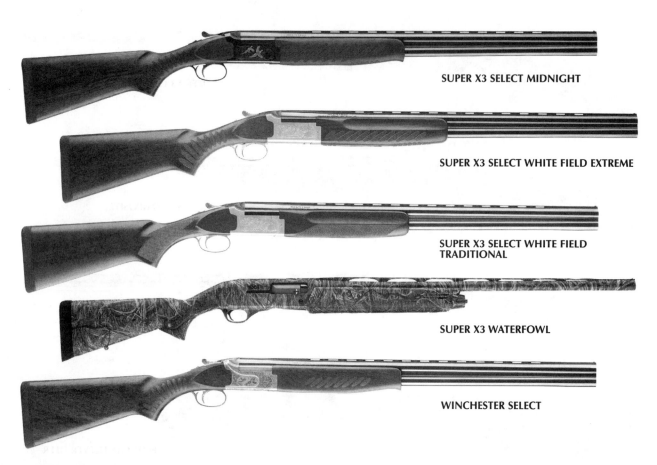

SUPER X3 SELECT MIDNIGHT

SUPER X3 SELECT WHITE FIELD EXTREME

SUPER X3 SELECT WHITE FIELD TRADITIONAL

SUPER X3 WATERFOWL

WINCHESTER SELECT

SUPER X3 SELECT MIDNIGHT
Action: over/under **Stock:** walnut
Barrel: 26 or 28 in.
Chokes: screw-in tubes
Weight: 7.0-7.25 lbs.
Bore/Gauge: 12 **Magazine:** none
Features: lightweight barrels; low-profile receiver with gold accented game birds and extensive engraving; high-gloss bluing on receiver and barrels; satin finished grade II/III walnut stock with oval checkering on grip; deluxe recoil pad; Invector-Plus choke system with three choke tubes–F, M, IC
Discontinued

SUPER X3 SELECT WHITE FIELD EXTREME
Action: over/under **Stock:** walnut
Barrel: 26 or 28 in.
Chokes: screw-in tubes
Weight: 7.0-7.25 lbs.
Bore/Gauge: 12 **Magazine:** none
Features: lightweight profile barrels; 3 in. chamber; low-profile engraved silver nitride receiver; walnut stock with oval-style checkering; Invector-Plus choke system with three choke tubes supplied–F, M, IC
Discontinued

SUPER X3 SELECT WHITE FIELD TRADITIONAL
Action: over/under
Stock: walnut **Barrel:** 26 or 28 in.
Chokes: screw-in tubes
Weight: 7.0-7.25 lbs.
Bore/Gauge: 12 **Magazine:** none
Features: engraved receiver; walnut stock with traditional cut checkering; Invector-Plus choke system with three choke tubes–F, M, IC
Discontinued

SUPER X3 WATERFOWL
Action: autoloader **Stock:** composite
Barrel: 26 or 28 in.
Chokes: screw-in tubes
Weight: 7.5 lb. **Bore/Gauge:** 12
Magazine: 4 rounds
Features: barrel with improved ventilated rib design; Active Valve system; weather-resistant composite stock and forearm with Dura-Touch Armor Coating finish; available in Mossy Oak New Shadow Grass finish; stock shims for cast and comb height adjustability; sling swivel studs are included; Invector-Plus choke tube system
MSRP: **$1439**

WINCHESTER SELECT
Action: boxlock over/under with low-profile breech
Stock: checkered walnut (adjustable comb available on target models, standard with palm swell)
Barrel: 26, 28 in. (field), 28, 30, 32 in. (target) threaded for Invector Plus choke tubes
Sights: bead front (TruGlo on target)
Weight: 7.0-7.3 lbs. (field), 7.5-7.8 lbs. (target)
Bore/Gauge: 12 **Magazine:** none
Features: 3 in. chambers on field guns; ventilated middle rib on target guns
Discontinued

Accu-Tek Handguns

AT-380 II
Action: autoloader
Grips: composite
Barrel: 2.8 in.
Sights: target
Weight: 23.5 oz
Caliber: 380 ACP
Capacity: 6 + 1 rounds
Features: exposed hammer; one-hand manual safety; European type magazine release on bottom of grip; adjustable rear sight; stainless steel magazine
MSRP: **$262**

American Derringer Handguns

MODEL 4

MODEL 1
Action: hinged breech
Grips: rosewood or stag
Barrel: 3 in.   *Sights:* fixed open
Weight: 15.0 oz.
Caliber: .45 Colt/.410
Capacity: 2 rounds
Features: single-action; automatic barrel selection; manually operated hammer-block type safety
MSRP: **$705**

MODEL 4
Action: hinged breech
Grips: rosewood or stag
Barrel: 4.1 in., 6 in. (Alaskan Survival)
Sights: fixed open   *Weight:* 16.5 oz.
Caliber: .32 H&R, .357 Mag., .357 Max., .44 Mag., .45 Colt/.410, .45-70
Capacity: 2 rounds

Features: satin or high polish stainless steel finish; single-action; automatic barrel selection; manually operated hammer-block type safety
.357 Mag.: **$760**
.357 Max.: **$760**
.44 Mag.: **$815**
Alaskan Survival
  (.45 Colt/.410): **$815**

MODEL 6
Action: hinged breech
Grips: rosewood, walnut, black
Barrel: 6 in.
Sights: fixed open
Weight: 21.0 oz.
Caliber: .357 Mag; .45 Auto; .45 Colt/.410
Capacity: 2 rounds
Features: satin or high polish stainless

steel finish; single-action; automatic barrel selection; manually operated hammer-block type safety
MSRP: **$860**

MODEL 7 LIGHTWEIGHT & ULTRA LIGHTWEIGHT
Action: hinged breech
Grips: blackwood
Barrel: 3 in.
Sights: fixed open
Weight: 7.5 oz.
Caliber: .22LR; .22 Mag;.32 Mag/.32 S&W Long; .380 Auto;.38 Special; .44 Special
Capacity: 2 rounds
Features: gray matte finish; single-action; automatic barrel selection; manually operated hammer-block type safety
MSRP: **$705**

American Derringer Handguns

MODEL 8

Action: hinged breech
Grips: rosewood, walnut, black
Barrel: 8 in.
Sights: red-dot scope
Weight: 24.0 oz.
Caliber: .357 Mag; .45 Auto; .45 Colt/.410
Capacity: 2 rounds
Features: satin or high polish stainless steel finish; single-action; automatic barrel selection; manually operated hammer-block type safety—automatically disengages when the hammer is cocked
.357 Mag.: $910
.45 Auto: $910
.45 Colt/.410: $910

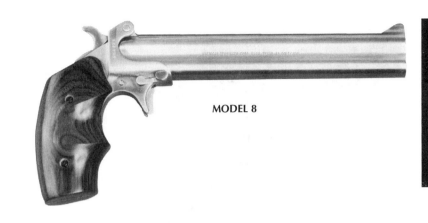

MODEL 8

Auto-Ordnance Handguns

MODEL 1911A1

Action: autoloader
Grips: plastic
Barrel: 5 in.
Sights: fixed open
Weight: 39.0 oz.
Caliber: .45 ACP
Capacity: 7 + 1 rounds
Features: single-action 1911 Colt design; Deluxe version has rubber wrap-around grips, 3-dot sights; Thompson 1911C stainless; 1911 SE in blued finish
1911 SE Standard: . . . Discontinued
Deluxe: . . . . Discontinued
WWII Parkerized: $627

MODEL 1911A1

1911WGSE
DELUXE

Beretta Handguns

MODEL 21 BOBCAT

MODEL 84 CHEETAH

MODEL 85 CHEETAH

MODEL 87 TARGET

MODEL 21 BOBCAT
Action: autoloader
Grips: plastic or walnut
Barrel: 2.4 in.
Sights: fixed open
Weight: 11.5 oz.
Caliber: .22 LR, .25 Auto
Capacity: 7 (.22) or 8 (.25) rounds
Features: double-action; tip-up barrel; alloy frame; walnut grips extra
Matte: **$335**
Stainless: **$420**

MODEL 84 CHEETAH
Action: autoloader
Grips: plastic or wood
Barrel: 3.8 in.
Sights: fixed open
Weight: 23.3 oz.
Caliber: .380 Auto
Capacity: 13 + 1 rounds

(10+1 restricted capacity)
Features: double-action; ambidextrous safety
Cheetah 84: **$755**
Cheetah 84 nickel: **$805**

MODEL 85 CHEETAH
Action: autoloader
Grips: plastic or wood
Barrel: 3.8 in.
Sights: fixed open
Weight: 23.3 oz.
Caliber: .380 Auto
Capacity: 8 + 1 rounds
Features: double-action; ambidextrous safety; single stacked magazine
Cheetah 85: **$755**
Cheetah 85 nickel: **$805**

MODEL 87 CHEETAH
Action: autoloader
Grips: wood
Barrel: 3.8 in.   *Sights:* fixed open
Weight: 23.3 oz.
Caliber: .22LR
Capacity: 7 + 1 rounds
Features: double-action; ambidextrous safety
MSRP: **$830**

MODEL 87 TARGET
Action: autoloader
Grips: plastic or wood
Barrel: 5.9 in.   *Sights:* fixed open
Weight: 20.1 oz.
Caliber: .22 LR
Capacity: 10 + 1 rounds
Features: blowback design; Target weighs 40.9 oz. with target sights
MSRP: **$725**

Beretta Handguns

90-TWO

MODEL 92

92FS INOX

MODEL 3032 TOMCAT

90-TWO

Action: autoloader
Grips: technopolymer single-piece wraparound, standard or slim size
Barrel: 4.9 in.
Sights: Super-LumiNova
Weight: 32.5 oz.
Caliber: 9mm, .40 S&W
Capacity: 10, 12 or 17 rounds
Features: aluminum frame with Beretta's exclusive Bruniton non-reflective matte black finish; short recoil, delayed blow-back system; front accessory rail with removable cover; internal recoil buffer
MSRP: **$725**

MODEL 92/96 SERIES

Action: autoloader
Grips: plastic
Barrel: 4.7 to 4.9 in. *Sights:* 3-dot
Weight: 34.4-41.0 oz.
Caliber: 9mm
Capacity: 15+ 1 rounds (10 + 1 restricted capacity)
Features: chrome-lined bore; double-action tritium sights available; reversible magazine catch; manual safety doubles as de-cocking lever; visible/touch sensitive loaded chamber indicator
Model 92FS:.............. **$650**
Model 92FS Inox:.......... **$750**

MODEL 3032 TOMCAT

Action: autoloader
Grips: plastic
Barrel: 2.5 in.
Sights: fixed open
Weight: 14.5 oz.
Caliber: .32 Auto
Capacity: 7 + 1 rounds
Features: double-action; tip-up barrel
Matte: **$435**
Stainless: **$555**
Tritium: ....**Discontinued**
Tritium with laser grip: **$555**

Beretta Handguns

MODEL M9

MODEL PX4

PX4 STORM .45

MODEL M9

Action: autoloader
Grips: plastic
Barrel: 4.9 in.
Sights: dot and post, low profile, windage adjustable rear
Weight: 34.4 oz.
Caliber: 9mm
Capacity: 15 + 1 rounds (10 + 1 restricted capacity)
Features: chrome-lined bore; double-action; reversible magazine release; short recoil, delayed locking block system; lightweight forged aluminum alloy frame w/ combat-style trigger guard, manual safety doubles as decocking lever; visible/touch sensitive loaded chamber indicator; open slide design; automatic firing pin block; ambidextrous manual safety; disassembly latch
MSRP: **$650**

MODEL M9A1

Action: autoloader
Grips: plastic
Barrel: 4.9 in.
Sights: post and dot, low profile, windage adjustable rear

Weight: 34.4 oz.
Caliber: 9mm
Capacity: 15+ 1 rounds (10 + 1 restricted capacity)
Features: chrome-lined bore; double-action; reversible magazine release button; sand resistant magazine; short recoil; delayed locking block system; lightweight forged aluminum alloy frame w/ combat-style trigger guard and integral MIL-STD-1913 "Picatinny" rail; checkered front and back strap; manual safety doubles as decocking lever; visible/touch sensitive loaded chamber indicator; open slide design, automatic firing pin block; ambidextrous manual safety; disassembly latch
MSRP: **$750**

MODEL PX4

Action: autoloader
Grips: 3 sizes, interchangeable polymer
Barrel: 4 in.
Sights: Super-LumiNova
Weight: 27.7 oz
Caliber: 9mm and .40 S&W
Capacity: 9mm: 17 + 1 rounds (10 + 1 restricted capacity) 40 S&W: 14 + 1

rounds (10 + 1 restricted capacity)
Features: double-action; cold hammer forged barrel; chrome-lined bore and chamber; MIL-STD -1913 "Picatinny" accessory rail for laser sight; flashlight; interchangeable/ambidextrous magazine release buttons; interchangeable backstraps; Night sights available as option
MSRP: **$600**

PX4 STORM .45

Action: autoloader
Grips: synthetic
Barrel: 4 in.
Sights: 3-dot dovetail
Weight: 27.7 oz.
Caliber: .45 ACP
Capacity: 10 rounds
Features: locked breech rotating barrel system; ambidextrous manual safety; reversible magazine release button; interchangeable slide catch; Picatinny rail; interchangeable backstraps
MSRP: **$650**

PX4 STORM .45 SD

Beretta Handguns

PX4 STORM .45
SPECIAL DUTY

PX4 STORM SUBCOMPACT

STAMPEDE
MARSHALL

(SPECIAL DUTY)
Action: autoloader
Grips: synthetic
Barrel: 4.5 in.
Sights: 3-dot dovetail
Weight: 27.7 oz.
Caliber: .45 ACP
Capacity: 10 rounds
Features: locked breech rotating barrel system; ambidextrous manual safety; reversible magazine release button; interchangeable slide catch; Picatinny rail; interchangeable backstraps. Package includes: 9-round magazine, two 10-round magazines, spare medium and high magazine release buttons, lanyard loop, hammer spring cap without lanyard loop, Teflon oil bottle, deluxe heavy-duty waterproof carrying case.
Discontinued

PX4 STORM SUBCOMPACT
Action: autoloader
Grips: synthetic
Sights: 3-dot dovetail with Super-LumiNova
Caliber: 9mm, .40 S&W
Capacity: 10 rounds (40 S&W), 13 rounds (9mm)
Features: locked breech and tilt barrel system; stainless-steel barrel; interchangeable backstraps; ambidextrous manual safety lever; reversible magazine release button; interchangeable slide catch can be replaced with an optional low profile configuration; standard Picatinny Rail (MIL-STD-1913); SnapGrip Magazine Extender flips down easily, maximizing the grip for larger hands
Discontinued

STAMPEDE
Action: revolver
Grips: polymer, plastic or Walnut
Barrel: 4.75-7.5 in.
Sights: fixed, open
Weight: 36.8-38.4 oz.
Caliber: .45 Colt, .357 Mag.
Capacity: 6 rounds
Features: single-action; color case-hardened frame; blue, charcoal blue, Inox, or Old West finish
Bisley: . . . . **Discontinued**
Blued: **$575**
Deluxe: **$675**
Old West: **$650**
Marshall: **$575**
Old West Marshall: **$650**

Beretta Handguns

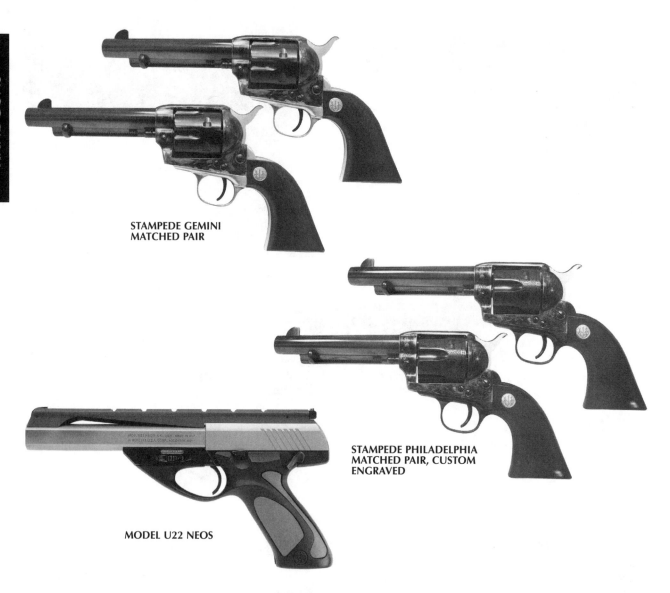

STAMPEDE GEMINI
MATCHED PAIR

STAMPEDE PHILADELPHIA
MATCHED PAIR, CUSTOM
ENGRAVED

MODEL U22 NEOS

STAMPEDE GEMINI, MATCHED PAIR

Action: revolver
Grips: oil finished, hand rubbed walnut fitted with a gold Beretta medallion
Barrel: 5.5 in.
Sights: open, fixed
Caliber: .45 LC
Capacity: 6 rounds
Features: German silver trigger guards and backstraps; matching paired serial numbers; "UGB" inspector cartouche stamped on outside panel of each grip; optional custom fitted deluxe wood case
Stampede Gemini:..... $1350 pair, $675 each

STAMPEDE PHILADELPHIA, MATCHED PAIR, CUSTOM ENGRAVED

Action: revolver
Grips: walnut with checkering and inlaid gold Beretta medallions
Barrel: 5.5 in.
Sights: open, fixed
Caliber: .45 LC
Capacity: 6 rounds
Features: inspired by the limited edition Philadelphia Centennial engraving (1876); laser engraved then hand finished on the receiver cylinder and barrel; gold-filled "1" and "2" on top of backstrap; paired serial numbers
Stampede Philadelphia:. .$2100 pair, $1050 each

MODEL U22 NEOS

Action: autoloader
Grips: plastic
Barrel: 4.5 in. or 6 in.
Sights: target
Weight: 31.7 oz.
Caliber: .22 LR
Capacity: 10 + 1 rounds
Features: single-action; removable colored grip inserts; model with 6 in. barrel weighs 36.2 oz.; Deluxe model features adjustable trigger, replaceable sights; optional 7.5 in. barrel
U22 Neos: $275
Inox: $375

Bersa Handguns

**THUNDER 9
ULTRA COMPACT**

THUNDER 40

**THUNDER 45
ULTRA COMPACT**

THUNDER 380

THUNDER 9
ULTRA COMPACT

Action: autoloader
Grips: black polymer
Barrel: 3.5 in.
Sights: target
Weight: 24.5 oz.
Caliber: .9mm
Capacity: 10 + 1 rounds
Features: double-action; manual and firing pin safeties; anatomically designed grips
Matte: $402
Satin Nickel: $371
Thunder 9 High Capacity: . . . . **Discontinued**

THUNDER 40

Action: autoloader
Grips: black polymer
Barrel: 4.2 in.
Sights: target
Weight: 28 oz.
Caliber: .40 ACP

Capacity: 16 + 1 rounds
Features: double-action; manual and firing pin safeties; anatomically designed grips
Matte: $409
Satin Nickel: $419
Thunder 40: . . . . **Discontinued**

THUNDER 45
ULTRA COMPACT

Action: autoloader
Grips: black polymer
Barrel: 3.6 in.
Sights: target
Weight: 27 oz.
Caliber: .45 ACP
Capacity: 7 + 1 rounds
Features: double-action; manual and firing pin safeties; anatomically designed grips
Matte: $345
Stainless: $480
Duotone: $402

THUNDER 380

Action: autoloader
Grips: black polymer
Barrel: 3 in.
Sights: fixed open
Weight: 19.75 oz.
Caliber: .380 ACP
Capacity: 7 + 1 rounds
Features: double-action; safeties: integral locking system, manual, firing pin
Deluxe Blue: $332
Matte: $310
Matte CC: $315
Satin nickel: $316

HANDGUNS

Bond Arms Handguns

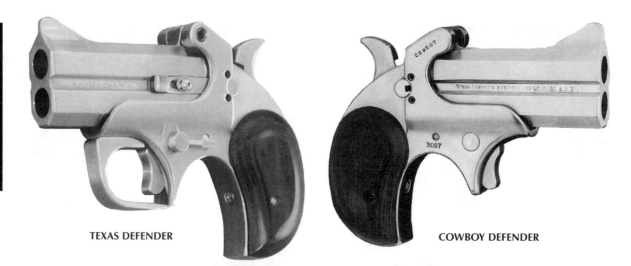

TEXAS DEFENDER

COWBOY DEFENDER

SNAKE SLAYER IV

CENTURY 2000

Action: single-action
Grips: laminated
Barrel: 3.5 in.
Sights: fixed, open
Weight: 21 oz.
Caliber: .410/45LC
Capacity: 2 rounds
Features: interchangeable barrels; automatic extractor; rebounding hammer; crossbolt safety; stainless steel with satin polish finish; black ash or rosewood laminated grips
MSRP: $420

DEFENDER

Action: single-action
Grips: laminated
Barrel: 3 or 5 in.
Sights: fixed, open
Weight: 19 oz., 20 oz.

Caliber: .22 LR, 9 mm, 32 H & R Mag, .357 Mag/.38 Spl., .357 Max., 10 mm, .40 S&W, .45 LC; .45 ACP, .45 Glock; .44 Sp., .44-40 Win., .45 Colt/.410 Shot Shell (rifled)
Capacity: 2 rounds
Features: interchangeable barrels; automatic extractor; rebounding hammer; crossbolt safety; stainless steel with satin polish finish; black ash or rosewood laminated grips
Texas Defender:. $399
Cowboy Defender: $399

SNAKE SLAYER

Action: single-action
Grips: rosewood
Barrel: 3.5 in.
Sights: fixed, open
Weight: 22 oz.
Caliber: .410/45LC

Capacity: 2 rounds
Features: interchangeable barrels; automatic extractor; rebounding hammer; crossbolt safety; stainless steel with satin polish finish; extended grips
MSRP: $469

SNAKE SLAYER IV

Action: hinged breech
Grips: rosewood
Barrel: 4.25 in.
Sights: blade front, fixed rear
Weight: 23.5 oz.
Caliber: .410/45LC with 3 in. chambers
Capacity: 2 rounds
Features: stainless steel double barrel; automatic extractor; rebounding hammer; retracting firing pins; crossbolt safety; extended custom rosewood grips
MSRP: $499

Browning Handguns

**BUCK MARK STANDARD
(5.5" BARREL)**

**BUCK MARK
5.5 TARGET**

BUCK MARK HUNTER

**BUCK MARK PLUS UDX
WALNUT**

**BUCK MARK PLUS UDX
ROSEWOOD**

**BUCK MARK PLUS UDX
BLACK LAMINTED, STAINLESS**

BUCK MARK

Action: autoloader
Grips: composite, laminated or wood
Barrel: 4, 5.5 or 7.5 in.
Sights: target
Weight: 34 oz.
Caliber: .22 LR
Capacity: 10 + 1 rounds
Features: standard, camper, target, bullseye models available with various grips, barrel contours; Plus with adjustable rear and Truglo/Marble fiber-optic front sights; FLD Plus with rosewood grips and adjustable rear and Truglo/Marble fiber-optic front sights
Buck Mark: **$579**

Camper: **$329**
Stainless: **$323**
Field: **$579**
Hunter (7.5 in. bbl): **$429**
Micro (4 in. bl.): **$399**
Stainless: **$359**
Plus: **$469**
Nickel: . . . . **Discontinued**
FLD: **$449–469**
Target: **$579**

BUCK MARK PLUS UDX

Action: autoloader
Grips: walnut, black laminated or rosewood Ultragrip DX ambidextrous
Barrel: 5.5 in.
Sights: adjustable Pro-Target rear sight; Truglo/Marble's fiber-optic front sight
Weight: 34 oz.
Caliber: .22 L.R.
Capacity: 15 rounds (9mm), 10 rounds (.40 S&W)
Features: alloy receiver; stainless slab-side barrel; single-action trigger
Walnut: **$469**
Rosewood: **$469**
Black laminated, stainless: **$509**

Browning Handguns

HI-POWER

PRO-9

HI-POWER
Action: autoloader
Grips: walnut, rubber or composite
Barrel: 4.74 in.
Sights: fixed or adjustable
Weight: 33 oz.; 35 oz. (.40 S&W)
Caliber: 9mm, .40 S&W
Capacity: 10+1 rounds
Features: single-action; locked breech action; ambidextrous thumb safety;

polished blued finish on slide
MSRP: **$999**

PRO-9 & PRO-40
Action: autoloader
Grips: polymer
Barrel: 4 in.
Sights: fixed
Weight: 30-35 oz.
Caliber: 9mm, .40 S& W

Capacity: 10 rounds
Features: Pro-9 (9mm only) polymer receiver; has stainless steel slide and replaceable backstrap inserts; double-action; polymer receiver; stainless steel slide; under-barrel accessory rail; ambidextrous safety/decocker; inter-changeable backstrap inserts
Pro-9:. **$628**
Pro-40:. **$628**

Charles Daly Handguns

MODEL 1911

**MODEL 1911
TARGET STAINLESS**

MODEL 1911 A-1
Action: autoloader
Grips: walnut
Barrel: 3.5, 4 or 5 in.
Sights: target
Weight: 34, 38 or 39.5 oz.
Caliber: .45 ACP
Capacity: 6+1 (ECS), 8 + 1 rounds
Features: extended hi-rise beavertail

grip safety; combat trigger; combat hammer; beveled magazine well; flared and lowered ejection port; dovetailed front and low profile rear sights; ECS series with contoured left hand safety
Model 1911 A-1:. . . . . **Discontinued**
G-4 Series. **$819**
Modell 1911: . . . . **Discontinued**

A-1 Empier Stainless: . **Discontinued**
(ECS&EMS): . . . . **Discontinued**
Target: . . . . **Discontinued**
Target Stainless:. . . . . **Discontinued**
Target Custom: . . . . . **Discontinued**

Charles Daly Handguns

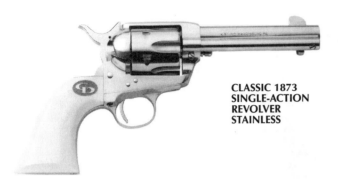

CLASSIC 1873
SINGLE-ACTION
REVOLVER
STAINLESS

M-5 COMMANDER

CLASSIC 1873 SINGLE-ACTION REVOLVER
Action: single-action revolver
Grips: walnut
Barrel: 4.75, 5.5, 7.5 in.
Sights: fixed open
Caliber: .45 LC, .357 mag.
Capacity: 6 rounds
Features: stainless steel or color case-hardened finish; available in civilian, cavalry and artillery models; brass or steel backstrap and trigger guard
Discontinued

HI-POWER
Action: autoloader
Grips: polymer
Barrel: 4.8 in.
Sights: X/S Sight System
Weight: 34.5 oz.
Caliber: 9mm
Capacity: 13 rounds
Features: single-action; carbon steel frame; thumb safety; x/s sight system; matte blue finish
Discontinued

MODEL M-5
Action: autoloader
Grips: walnut, rubber or composite

Barrel: 3.1, 4.4 in., 5 in.
Sights: fixed or adjustable
Weight: 28 oz., 30.5 oz., 33.5 oz.
Caliber: 9mm (Compact), .40 S&W, .45 ACP
Capacity: 10+1 rounds
Features: single-action; polymer frame; tapered bull barrel and full-length guide rod; stainless steel beaver-tail grip safeties; grip with raised contact pad with serrations
M-5: **$759**
M-5 Commander: **$759**
M-5 Ultra X Compact: **$759**

Cimarron Handguns

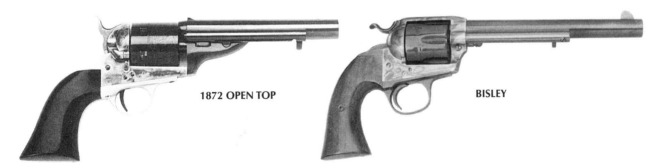

1872 OPEN TOP

BISLEY

MODEL 1872 OPEN TOP
Action: single-action revolver
Grips: walnut
Barrel: 5.5 and 7.5 in.
Sights: fixed open
Weight: 40.0 oz.
Caliber: .38 Spec, .44 Colt and .45 S&W
Capacity: 6 rounds

Features: forged, color case-hardened frame; blue, charcoal blue or nickel finish; weight varies up to 46 oz.
1872: **$508**
1872 Navy grip: **$467**

BISLEY
Action: single-action revolver
Grips: walnut
Barrel: 4.75, 5.5 & 7.5 in.

Sights: open, fixed
Weight: 40.3, 40.6, 44.0 (.357 Mag.) oz.
Caliber: .357, .45LC, .44 Sp., .44 WCF
Capacity: 6 rounds
Features: reproduction of the original Colt Bisley; forged, color case-hardened frame; blue, charcoal blue, nickel finish
MSRP: **$574**

Cimarron Handguns

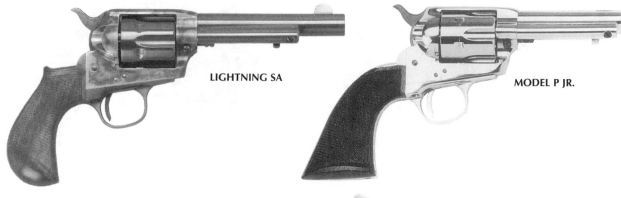

LIGHTNING SA

MODEL P JR.

THUNDERER

GEORGE ARMSTRONG CUSTER 7TH U.S. CAVALRY MODEL

Action: single-action revolver
Grips: walnut
Barrel: 7.5 in.
Sights: open, fixed
Weight: 40.4 oz.
Caliber: .45 LC.
Capacity: 6 rounds
Features: forged, color case-hardened frame; blue, charcoal blue or US Armory finish
MSRP: $548

LIGHTNING SA

Action: single-action revolver
Grips: walnut
Barrel: 3.5, 4.75 or 5.5 in.
Sights: open, fixed
Weight: 28.5, 29.5, 30.75 (.38 Colt) oz.
Caliber: .38 Colt and .38 Special
Capacity: 6 rounds
Features: forged, color case-hardened frame; blue, charcoal blue or nickel finish
MSRP: $508

MODEL P 1873

Action: single-action revolver
Grips: walnut, hard rubber, ivory
Barrel: 4.75, 5.5 and 7.5 in.
Sights: none
Weight: 44.0 oz.
Caliber: .32 WCP, .357, .38 WCF, 45 ACP, .45 LC, .45 Schofield, .38 WCF, .32 WCF, .44 WCF.
Capacity: 6 rounds
Features: fashioned after the 1873 Colt SAA but 20% smaller
MSRP: $508

MODEL P JR.

Action: single-action revolver
Grips: walnut
Barrel: 3.5, 4.75 and 5.5 in.
Sights: open
Weight: 35.2 oz.
Caliber: .38 Special
Capacity: 6 rounds
Features: fashioned on the 1873 Colt SAA but 20% smaller; color case-hardened frame; blue, charcoal blue or nickel finish
MSRP: $494

NEW SHERIFF'S MODEL

Action: single-action revolver
Grips: walnut, black hard rubber
Barrel: 3.5 in.
Sights: open fixed
Weight: 33.5 oz.

Caliber: .45 Colt, 44 WCF
Capacity: 6 rounds
Features: forged, color case-hardened frame; blue, charcoal blue, nickel finish
MSRP: $494

THUNDERER

Action: single-action revolver
Grips: walnut, ivory, mother of pearl or black hard rubber
Barrel: 3.5 w/ejector, 4 .75, 5.5 or 7.5 in.
Sights: open, fixed
Weight: 38, 40, 40.75, 43.60 (.357 Mag.) oz.
Caliber: .357 Mag., .44 SP, .44 WCF, .45 ACP, .45 Colt
Capacity: 6 rounds
Features: forged, color case-hardened frame; blue, charcoal blue or nickel finish
MSRP: $534

U.S.V. ARTILLERY MODEL

Action: single-action revolver
Grips: walnut
Barrel: 5.5 in.
Sights: open, fixed
Weight: 40 oz.
Caliber: .45 LC.
Capacity: 6 rounds
Features: forged, color case-hardened frame; blue, charcoal blue or US Armory finish
MSRP: $548

Colt Handguns

.38 SUPER

1991

DEFENDER

GOLD CUP

.38 SUPER

Action: autoloader
Grips: rosewood or composite
Barrel: 5 in.
Sights: fixed open
Weight: 39.0 oz.
Caliber: .38 Super
Capacity: 9 + 1 rounds
Features: M1911 stainless models
available; aluminum trigger
Blue: **$837**
Stainless: **$866**
Bright stainless: **$1090**

1991 SERIES

Action: autoloader
Grips: rosewood or composite
Barrel: 5 in.

Sights: fixed open
Weight: 39.0 oz.
Caliber: .45 ACP
Capacity: 7 + 1 rounds
Features: M1911 Commander with 4.3
in. barrel available; both versions in
stainless or chrome moly
1991: **$786**
Stainless: **$839**

DEFENDER

Action: autoloader
Grips: rubber finger-grooved
Barrel: 3 in.
Sights: 3-dot
Weight: 30.0 oz.
Caliber: .45 ACP
Capacity: 7 + 1 rounds

Features: stainless M1911; extended
safety; upswept beavertail; beveled
magazine well
MSRP: **$885**

GOLD CUP

Action: autoloader
Grips: black composite
Barrel: 5 in.
Sights: target
Weight: 39.0 oz.
Caliber: .45 ACP
Capacity: 8 + 1 rounds
Features: stainless or chrome-moly;
Bo-Mar or Eliason sights
Gold Cup, blue: **$1022**
Stainless: **$1071**

When shooting a handgun, accuracy walks hand-in-hand with consistency. Be as consistent as possible with things such as how you raise the gun to the target, how you establish your sight picture, and how long it takes to settle and discharge the shot. Also try to keep physical conditions constant, such as barrel temperature (this is controlled to some extent by the time between shots) and ammunition type.

Colt Handguns

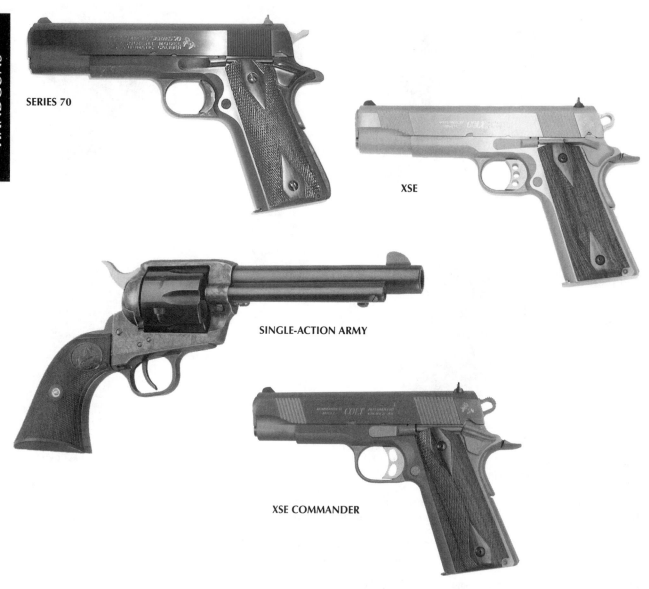

SERIES 70

XSE

SINGLE-ACTION ARMY

XSE COMMANDER

SERIES 70

Action: autoloader
Grips: walnut
Barrel: 5 in.
Sights: fixed open
Weight: 39.0 oz.
Caliber: .45 ACP
Capacity: 7 + 1 rounds
Features: single-action M1911 design
Series 70: **$919–990**

SINGLE-ACTION ARMY

Action: single-action revolver
Grips: composite
Barrel: 4.3, 5.5 or 7.5 in.
Sights: fixed open
Weight: 46.0 oz.
Caliber: .32/20, .357 Mag., .38 Spl.,
.44-40, .45 Colt, .38/40
Capacity: 6 rounds
Features: case-colored frame; transfer
bar; weight for .44-40, 48 oz. and 50
oz. for .45 Colt
Single-Action Army: **$1290**
Nickel: **$1350**

MODEL XSE

Action: autoloader
Grips: rosewood
Barrel: 5 in.
Sights: 3-dot
Weight: 39.0 oz.
Caliber: .45 ACP
Capacity: 8 + 1 rounds
Features: stainless; M1911 with
extended ambidextrous safety;
upswept beavertail; slotted hammer
and trigger; also available as 4.3 in.
barrel Commander
MSRP: **$944–1055**

MODEL 75

MODEL 75 CHAMPION

MODEL 75 COMPACT
.40 S&W

MODEL 75 KADET

THE KADET ADAPTER IN ITS REAR (COCKED) POSITION

MODEL 83

MODEL 75

Action: autoloader
Grips: composite
Barrel: 4.7 in.
Sights: 3-dot
Weight: 35.0 oz.
Caliber: 9mm or .40 S&W
Capacity: 10 + 1 rounds
Features: single- or double-action
9mm: **$597–756**
.40 S&W: **$615–669**

MODEL 75 CHAMPION

Action: autoloader
Grips: composite
Barrel: 4.5 in.
Sights: target
Weight: 35.0 oz.
Caliber: 9mm or .40 S&W
Capacity: 10 + 1 rounds

Features: also available: IPSC version with 5.4 in. barrel
Champion: **$1739**
IPSC: . . . . **Discontinued**

MODEL 75 COMPACT

Action: autoloader
Grips: composite
Barrel: 3.9 in.
Sights: fixed open
Weight: 32.0, 37.8 (40 S&W) oz.
Caliber: 9mm or .40 S&W
Capacity: 10 rounds
Features: single- or double-action; ambidextrous safety
Compact: **$631–651**
Compact .40 S&W: **$672**

MODEL 75 KADET

Action: autoloader   *Grips:* composite
Barrel: 4.9 in.
Sights: target
Weight: 38.0 oz.
Caliber: .22 LR
Capacity: 10 + 1 rounds
Features: single- or double-action
Kadet: **$689**
.22 conversion kit: . . . **Discontinued**

MODEL 83

Action: autoloader
Grips: composite
Barrel: 3.8 in.   *Sights:* fixed open
Weight: 26.0 oz.
Caliber: 9mm
Capacity: 10 + 1 rounds
Features: single- or double-action
MSRP: **$495–522**

CZ Handguns

MODEL 85 COMBAT

MODEL 97

MODEL 100

2075 RAMI

MODEL 85 COMBAT
Action: autoloader
Grips: composite
Barrel: 4.7 in.
Sights: target
Weight: 35.0 oz.
Caliber: 9mm
Capacity: 10 + 1 rounds
Features: single- or double-action
MSRP: $702–732

MODEL 97
Action: autoloader
Grips: composite
Barrel: 4.8 in.
Sights: fixed open
Weight: 41.0 oz.
Caliber: .45 ACP
Capacity: 10 + 1 rounds
Features: single- or double-action
MSRP: $779–799

MODEL 100
Action: autoloader
Grips: polymer
Barrel: 3.9 in.
Sights: adjustable
Weight: 24.0 oz.
Caliber: 9mm, .40 S&W
Capacity: 12 rounds
Features: DAO-type trigger mechanism; firing pin safety and loaded chamber indicator
Discontinued

2075 RAMI
Action: single- and double-action autoloader
Grips: lack composite
Barrel: 3 in.
Sights: blade front, shrouded rear
Weight: 25.0 oz.
Caliber: 9mm Luger, .40 S&W

Capacity: 10 rounds (9mm), 8 rounds (.40 S&W)
Features: firing pin block; manual safety; double-stack magazine
MSRP: $612

MODEL P-01
Action: autoloader
Grips: rubber
Barrel: 3.8 in.
Sights: 3-dot
Weight: 27.3 oz.
Caliber: 9mm
Capacity: 13 + 1 rounds
Features: single- or double-action; decocking lever; safety stop on hammer; firing pin safety
MSRP: $672

Dan Wesson Handguns

**ALASKAN GUIDE
SPECIAL (7445-AGS)**

**PATRIOT COMMANDER
CLASSIC BOBTAIL**

POINTMAN

RAZORBACK

ALASKAN GUIDE SPECIAL (7445-AGS)

Action: double-action revolver
Barrel: 4 in.
Sights: adjustable
Weight: 52.8 oz.
Caliber: .445 Supermag
Capacity: 6 rounds
Features: stainless frame; chambered for the .445 SuperMag cartridge, will also allow chambering of standard .44 magnum variants (.44 Magnum, .44 Special and .445 SuperMag); black matte "Yukon Coat" finish
Discontinued

PATRIOT COMMANDER CLASSIC BOBTAIL

Action: autoloader
Grips: cocobolo wood
Barrel: 4.74 in.
Sights: fixed open
Weight: 34.08 oz.
Caliber: 10mm, .45 ACP
Capacity: 8 rounds (10mm), 7 rounds (.45 ACP)

Features: series 70 stainless steel frame; forged stainless steel slide; forged one-piece stainless steel match barrel; high ride beavertail grip safety; extended thumb safety; lowered and relieved ejection port
MSRP: **$1191–1223**

POINTMAN

Action: autoloader
Grips: exotic wood
Barrel: 5 in.
Sights: open fixed
Weight: 38.4 oz. (10mm), 38.08 oz. (.45 ACP)
Caliber: 10mm, .45 ACP
Capacity: 8 rounds (10mm), 7 rounds (.45 ACP)
Features: series 70 stainless frame; stainless slide; forged one-piece stainless match barrel; match grade trigger and sear; extended thumb safety; stainless high ride beavertail grip safety
MSRP: **$1191–1391**

RAZORBACK

Action: autoloader
Grips: black rubber
Barrel: 5 in.
Sights: target
Weight: 38.4 oz.
Caliber: 10 mm
Capacity: 8 rounds
Features: Series 70 stainless frame; forged stainless slide; forged one-piece stainless match barrel; solid match trigger; extended thumb safety; stainless high ride beavertail grip safety
Discontinued

Downsizer Handguns

WSP (WORLD'S SMALLEST PISTOL)
Action: tip-up hinged breech
Grips: composite
Barrel: 2.1 in.
Sights: none

Weight: 11.0 oz.
Caliber: .357 Mag., .38 SP, .45 ACP
Capacity: 1 round
Features: double-action; stainless steel frame & barrel; internal firing pin block
MSRP: **$499**

Ed Brown Handguns

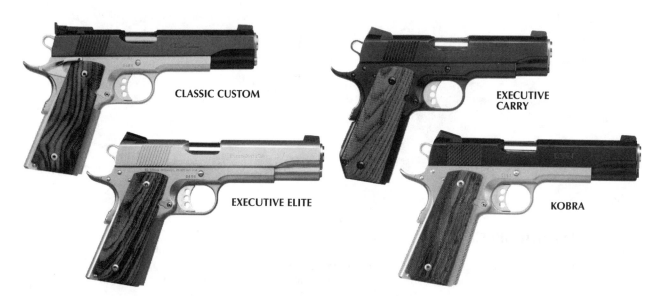

CLASSIC CUSTOM

EXECUTIVE CARRY

EXECUTIVE ELITE

KOBRA

CLASSIC CUSTOM
Action: autoloader
Grips: cocobolo wood
Barrel: 5 in. *Sights*: target
Weight: 37.0 oz.
Caliber: .45 ACP
Capacity: 7 + 1 rounds
Features: single-action, M1911 Colt design; Bo-Mar sights; checkered forestrap; ambidextrous safety; stainless
Classic Custom: **$3155**
Stainless/blue: **$3155**
Stainless: **$3155**

EXECUTIVE CARRY
Action: autoloader
Grips: checkered cocobolo wood
Barrel: 4.25 in.
Sights: low-profile combat
Weight: 33.0 oz.

Caliber: .45 ACP
Capacity: 7 + 1 rounds
Features: Bob-tail butt; checkered forestrap; stainless optional
Commander Bobtail: . Discontinued
Executive Carry: **$2645**
Stainless/blue: **$2645**
Stainless: **$2645**

EXECUTIVE ELITE
Action: autoloader
Grips: checkered cocobolo wood
Barrel: 5 in. *Sights*: to order
Weight: 36.0 oz.
Caliber: .45 ACP
Capacity: 7 + 1 rounds
Features: custom-grade M1911 Colt
Elite: **$2395**
Stainless/blue: **$2395**
Stainless: **$2395**

KOBRA
Action: autoloader
Grips: cocobolo wood
Barrel: 4.3 (Kobra Carry) or .5 in.
Sights: low-profile combat
Weight: 36.0 oz.
Caliber: .45 ACP
Capacity: 7 + 1 rounds
Features: single-action M1911 Colt design; matte finish with Snakeskin treatment on forestrap; mainspring housing and rear of slide; stainless models
Kobra: **$2195**
Stainless/blue: **$2195**
Stainless: **$2195**
Kobra Carry: **$2445**
Stainless/blue: **$2445**
Stainless: **$2445**

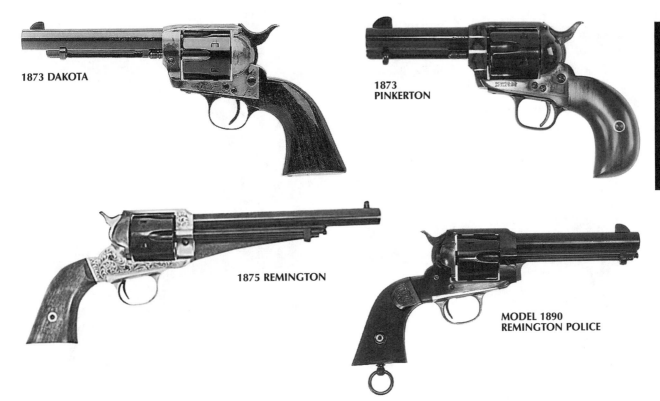

1873 DAKOTA

1873 PINKERTON

1875 REMINGTON

MODEL 1890 REMINGTON POLICE

1873 HARTFORD
Action: single-action revolver
Grips: walnut
Barrel: 4, 4.75, 5.5, 7.5 in.
Sights: fixed open
Weight: 46.0 oz.
Caliber: 32/20, 38/40, 44/40, 44SP, 45LC, .357.
Capacity: 6 rounds
Features: Birdshead grip; steel back-strap and trigger guard; Great Western II features various combinations of deluxe nickel, satin nickel, casehardened or blue finish with bone, ultra stag or ultra ivory grips
1873 Hartford: . . . . . . Discontinued
Dakota: . . . . Discontinued
Great Western II: $520
Great Western II Californian
   (walnut grips): $520

1873 HARTFORD STALLION
Action: single-action revolver
Grips: walnut
Barrel: 3.5, 4.75, 5.5 in.
Sights: fixed open
Weight: 46.0 oz.
Caliber: 32/20, 38/40, 44/40, 44SP, 45LC, .357.

Capacity: 6 rounds
Features: Birdshead grip; steel back-strap and trigger guard
Discontinued

1873 PINKERTON
Action: single-action revolver
Grips: walnut, birds-head
Barrel: 4 or 4.75 in.
Sights: fixed open
Weight: 44.0 oz.
Caliber: .357, .45 Colt, .45LC
Capacity: 6 rounds
Features: case-colored frame
Discontinued

1875 REMINGTON
Action: single-action revolver
Grips: walnut
Barrel: 5.5 or 7.5 in.
Sights: fixed open
Weight: 48.0 oz.
Caliber: .357 Mag., .44/40, .45 LC
Capacity: 6 rounds
Features: case-hardened colored steel frame
Model 1875: $424
Engraved: $659
Nickel: $599

1890 REMINGTON POLICE
Action: single-action revolver
Grips: walnut
Barrel: 5.8 in.
Sights: fixed open
Weight: 48.0 oz.
Caliber: .357 Mag., .44-40, .45 Colt
Capacity: 6 rounds
Features: lanyard loop; case-colored frame
Model 1890: $450
Nickel: $675

1894 BISLEY
Action: single-action revolver
Grips: walnut
Barrel: 5.5 or 7.5 in.
Sights: fixed open
Weight: 48.0 oz.
Caliber: .45LC
Capacity: 6 rounds
Features: forged color case-hardened steel frame; Bisley grip; steel backstrap and trigger guard
Discontinued

Entréprise Arms Handguns

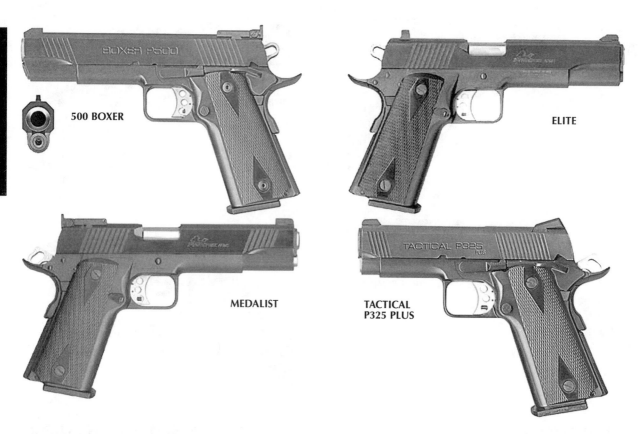

500 BOXER

ELITE

MEDALIST

TACTICAL P325 PLUS

MODEL 500 BOXER

Action: autoloader
Grips: composite
Barrel: 5 in.
Sights: target
Weight: 44.0 oz.
Caliber: .40 S&W, .45 ACP
Capacity: 10 + 1 rounds
Features: match-grade components and fitting; stainless one-piece guide rod; lapped slide; flared ejection port
.45 ACP: **$1399**
.40 S&W: **$1499**

ELITE

Action: autoloader
Grips: composite
Barrel: 3.25, 4.25 or 5 in.
Sights: adjustable

Weight: 38, 40.0 oz.
Caliber: .45 ACP
Capacity: 10 + 1 rounds
Features: lowered and flared ejection port; reinforced dustcover; bolstered front strap; high grip cut; high-ride beavertail grip safety; steel flat mainspring housing; extended thumb lock; adjustable rear sights
MSRP: **$699**

MEDALIST

Action: autoloader
Grips: composite
Barrel: 5 in. *Sights*: target
Weight: 44.0 oz.
Caliber: .40 S&W, .45 ACP
Capacity: 10 + 1 rounds
Features: up-turned beavertail, stain-

less hammer and sear; flared ejection port; match trigger, lapped slide
.45: **$979**
.40 S&W: **$1099**

TACTICAL P325 PLUS

Action: autoloader
Grips: composite
Barrel: 3.3 in.
Sights: low-profile combat
Weight: 37.0 oz.
Caliber: .45 ACP
Capacity: 10 + 1 rounds
Features: extended ambidextrous safety; lapped slide; up-turned beavertail; skeleton trigger and hammer; Tactical Ghost Ring or Novak sights; (also available with 4.3 and 5.0 in. barrels)
MSRP: **$979**

"Handgun shooting is widely considered to be the most difficult of the shooting arts. Pistols are relatively light, hard to hold steady and, unlike rifles and shotguns, not supported against the shooter's body when fired. Concentration and self-discipline are required to reliably hit the target with a handgun. Even after a satisfactory level of skill is acquired, regular practice is necessary to maintain that skill. Continuing practice is far more important with a handgun than it is with a rifle." —Chuck Hawks

European American Armory Handguns

BIG BORE BOUNTY HUNTER

SMALL BORE BOUNTY HUNTER

WITNESS

WITNESS P COMPACT

BOUNTY HUNTER

Action: single-action revolver
Grips: walnut
Barrel: 4.5 or 7.5 in.
Sights: fixed open
Weight: 39.0-41.0 oz.
Caliber: .357 Mag., .44 Mag., .45 Colt
Capacity: 6 rounds
Features: case-colored or blued or nickel frame; version with 7.5 in. barrel weighs 42 oz.

Bounty Hunter: **$391**
Nickel: **$432**
Case color: **$391**
Also available:
Small Bore Bounty Hunter
  (.22 LR or .22 WMR): **$292**
  Nickel: **$324**

WITNESS

Action: autoloader
Grips: rubber
Barrel: 4.5 in.
Sights: 3-dot
Weight: 33.0 oz.
Caliber: 9mm, .38 Super, .40 S&W, 10 mm, .45 ACP
Capacity: 10 + 1 rounds
Features: double-action; polymer frame available

Steel: **$514**
Polymer: **$478**
"Wonder" finish: **$512**
Gold Team: **$1902**

WITNESS COMPACT

Action: autoloader
Grips: rubber
Barrel: 3.6 in.
Sights: 3-dot
Weight: 29.0 oz.
Caliber: 9mm, .40 S&W, .45 ACP
Capacity: 10 + 1 rounds
Features: double-action; polymer frame and ported barrels available

Steel: **$514**
Polymer: **$478**
Witness P Carry: **$598**

WITNESS S/A HUNTER

Action: autoloader
Grips: rubber
Barrel: 6 in.
Sights: adjustable
Weight: 41.0 oz.
Caliber: 10mm, .45 ACP
Capacity: 10+1 rounds
Features: single-action; auto firing pin block; drilled & tapped for scope mount

Hunter Pro 10: **$930**
Hunter Pro 45: **$930**

Firestorm Handguns

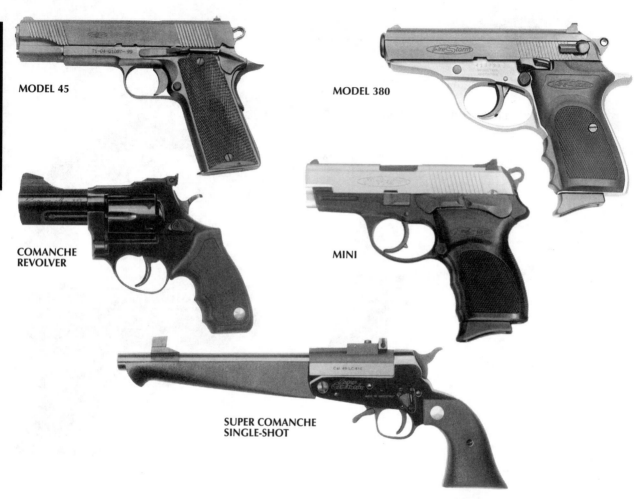

MODEL 45

MODEL 380

COMANCHE REVOLVER

MINI

SUPER COMANCHE SINGLE-SHOT

MODEL 45
Action: autoloader
Grips: rubber
Barrel: 4.3 or 5.2 in.   *Sights:* 3-dot
Weight: 34.0 oz.
Caliber: .45 ACP
Capacity: 7 + 1 rounds
Features: single-action; 1911 Colt design; from cocking grooves
Model 45: $415
Duotone:. $410

MODEL 380
Action: autoloader
Grips: rubber   *Barrel*: 3.5 in.
Sights: 3-dot   *Weight:* 23.0 oz.
Caliber: .380
Capacity: 7 + 1 rounds
Features: double-action; also available in .22 LR; 10-shot magazine
Model 380:. $312
Duotone:. $320
22 LR:. $310

COMANCHE REVOLVER
Action: double-action revolver
Grips: rubber
Barrel: 3 or 6 in.   *Sights:* target
Weight: 22.0 oz.
Caliber: .38 Spl. (also in .22, .357)
Capacity: 6 rounds
Features: adjustable sights; stainless or blue finish
Comanche I (.22, 6 in.) blue:. . $237
Comanche I (.22, 6 in.) SS: . . . $259
Comanche II (.38 Spl., 3or 4 in.) blue: $220
Comanche II (.38 Spl., 3or 4 in.) SS:. $237
Comanche III(.357, 3, 4 or 6 in.) blue: $254
Comanche III (.357, 3, 4 or 6 in.) SS:. $275

MINI
Action: autoloader
Grips: polymer

Barrel: 3.5 in.   *Sights:* target
Weight: 24.5 oz.
Caliber: 9mm, .40 S&W, .45 ACP
Capacity: 10 + 1 rounds (7 + 1 in .45)
Features: double-action
Mini: $395
Duotone:. $402
Duotone .45: $410
Nickel:. $410
.45 nickel: $415

SUPER COMANCHE
Action: hinged breech
Grips: composite
Barrel: 10 in.   *Sights:* target
Weight: 47.0 oz.
Caliber: .45 LC/.410
Capacity: 1 round
Features: adjustable sight; accepts 2.5 or 3 in. shells; rifled slugs or buck-shot(.410); blue or satin nickel finish
Nickel:. $192
Blue: $175

FNH USA Handguns

FIVE-SEVEN USG

FNP 40

FIVE-SEVEN USG

Action: autoloader **Grips**: plastic
Barrel: 4.75 in. **Sights**: fixed, open
Weight: 19.2 oz.
Caliber: 5.7 x 28mm
Capacity: 10 +1 rounds
Features: single-action; forged barrel with hard chrome finish; polymer frame and slide cover; reversible magazine release
MSRP: $1238

FNP 9

Action: autoloader **Grips:** plastic
Barrel: 4.75in. **Sights**: fixed, open
Weight: 25.2 oz. (24.8 Compact)
Caliber: 9mm **Capacity:** 10 +1 rounds
Features: double/single-action; polymer frame w/tactical accessory rail; ambidextrous de-cocking levers and reversible magazine release
MSRP: $720–770

FNP 40

Action: autoloader **Grips:** plastic
Barrel: 4 in. **Sights**: fixed, open
Weight: 26.7 oz. **Caliber**: .40 S&W
Capacity: 10 + 1 rounds
Features: double/single-action operation; molded polymer frame w/ tactical accessory rail; ambidextrous de-cocking levers and reversible magazine release; numerous sight configurations available
MSRP: $720–770

Freedom Arms Handguns

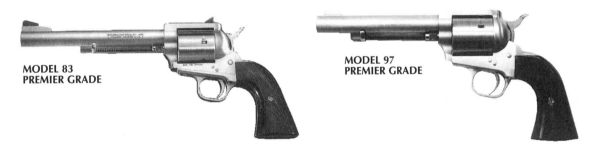

MODEL 83
PREMIER GRADE

MODEL 97
PREMIER GRADE

MODEL 83 PREMIER GRADE

Action: single-action revolver with manual safety bar
Grips: hardwood or optional Micarta
Barrel: 4.75, 6, 7.5, 9 or 10 in.
Sights: fixed or adjustable
Weight: 52.5 oz.
Caliber: .357 Mag., .41 Mag., .44 Mag., .454 Casull, .475 Linebaugh
Capacity: 5 rounds
Features: sights, scope mounts and extra cylinders optional
MSRP: $2099–2186

MODEL 83 RIMFIRE FIELD GRADE

Action: single-action revolver
Grips: Pachmyr or optional hardwood or Micarta
Barrel: 4.75, 6, 7.5, 9 or 10 in.
Sights: adjustable
Weight: 55.5 oz.
Caliber: .22 LR, .357 Mag., .41 mag., .44 Mag., .454 Casull, .475 Linebaugh
Capacity: 5 rounds
Features: sights, scope mounts and extra cylinders optional
MSRP: $1979

MODEL 97 PREMIER GRADE

Action: single-action revolver with automatic transfer bar safety
Grips: hardwood or optional Micarta
Barrel: 4.5, 5.5, 7.5 or 10 in.
Sights: fixed or adjustable
Weight: 39.0 oz.
Caliber: .17 HMR, .22 LR, .32 H&R Mag., .357 Mag., .41 Mag., .44 Spl., .45 Colt
Capacity: 5 rounds for .41 and bigger, 6 rounds for smaller calibers
Features: sights; scope mounts and extra cylinders optional
MSRP: $1772–1840

Glock Handguns

HANDGUNS

MODEL G19

MODEL G23

MODEL G17

MODEL G20

MODEL G22

MODEL G26

MODEL G27

MODEL G29

MODEL G30

MODEL G33

GLOCK HANDGUNS COMPACT PISTOLS G-19, G-23, G-25, G-38, G-32

Action: autoloader
Grips: composite
Barrel: 4.0 and 6.0 in.
Sights: fixed open
Weight: 20.19 to 24.16 oz.
Caliber: 9mm, .40 S&W, .357 Mag., 10mm, .45 ACP
Capacity: 9, 10, 13, 15 rounds
Features: trigger safety; double-action
MSRP: $624

STANDARD PISTOLS G-17, G-20, G-21, G-22, G-37

Action: autoloader
Grips: composite
Barrel: 4.5 in.
Sights: fixed open
Weight: 22.4 to 27.68 oz.
Caliber: 9mm, .40 S&W, .357 Mag., 10mm, .45 ACP
Capacity: 10, 13, 15, 17 rounds
Features: trigger safety; double-action
MSRP: $662

SUBCOMPACT PISTOLS G-26, G-27, G-29, G-39, G-30, G-28, G-33

Action: autoloader
Grips: composite
Barrel: 5.67 in.
Sights: fixed open
Weight: 18.66 to 24.69 oz.
Caliber: 9mm, .40 S&W, .357, .45
Capacity: 9, 10, 6 rounds
Features: trigger safety; double-action
MSRP: $624–639

Glock Handguns

MODEL G34

MODEL G35

G-36 SLIMLINE

COMPETITION G-34, G-35

Action: autoloader
Grips: synthetic
Barrel: 5.32 in.
Sights: fixed open
Weight: 22.9 oz.
Caliber: 9x19
Capacity: 17 + 1 rounds
Features: extended barrel; 7.56-in. line of sight; right hand, hexagonal barrel rifling, 9.84-in. length-of-twist; Glock safe action system
MSRP: **$704**

G-36 SLIMLINE

Action: autoloader
Grips: synthetic
Barrel: 3.8 in.
Sights: fixed open
Weight: 21.0 oz.
Caliber: .45 ACP
Capacity: 6 + 1 rounds
Features: single-stack magazine for thinner grip
MSRP: **$662**

Hämmerli Handguns

SP20

X-ESSE .22 L.R. WITH LONG BARREL

X-ESSE .22 L.R. WITH SHORT BARREL

MODEL SP20

Action: autoloader
Grips: synthetic
Barrel: 4.6 in.
Sights: target
Weight: 40.0 oz.
Caliber: .22 LR, .32 S&W
Capacity: 5 rounds
Features: front-end magazine
.22: **$1774**
.32: **$1924**

MODEL X-ESSE SPORT

Action: autoloader
Grips: composite
Barrel: 4.5 or 5.5 in.
Sights: target
Weight: 36.0 oz.
Caliber: .22 LR
Capacity: 10 rounds
Features: single-action
MSRP: **$725**

Heckler & Koch Handguns

COLOR FRAME PISTOLS

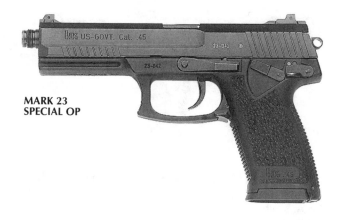

MARK 23
SPECIAL OP

P2000

USP 9

COLOR FRAME PISTOLS

Heckler & Koch is offering a limited edition run of color frame versions of its most popular pistol models. These guns are functionally identical to their black-framed counterparts but are unique alternatives with molded-in colors especially suited for desert, jungle or urban environments.

Offered in select models of HK's USP, USP Compact, USP Tactical and Mark 23 pistols, Desert Tan, Green and Gray frame variations feature a tough, matte black corrosion resistant finish on all metal parts. Each color frame model comes with two magazines, a cleaning kit and nylon carry case.

Heckler & Koch color frames are available in: Gray (USP 45 & USP 40 Compact); Green (USP 45, USP 40, USP 40 Compact & USP 45 Tactical); Desert Tan (USP 45, USP 40, USP 40 Compact,

USP 45 Tactical and Mark 23).
Suggested retail prices for the color frame models are the same as for the black frame variation.

MARK 23 SPECIAL OP
Action: autoloader
Grips: polymer
Barrel: 5.9 in.
Sights: 3-dot
Weight: 42.0 oz.
Caliber: .45 ACP
Capacity: 10 + 1 rounds
Features: military version of USP
MSRP: **$2310**

P2000 AND P2000 SK
Action: autoloader
Grips: polymer
Barrel: 3.6 in. (2000) and 2.5 in. (2000 SK)
Sights: 3-dot

Weight: 24 oz. (2000) and 22 oz. (2000 SK)
Caliber: 9mm, .357 SIG, .40 S&W
Capacity: 9-13 rounds
Features: double-action; pre-cock hammer; ambidextrous magazine releases and interchangeable grip straps; mounting rail for lights and lasers
P2000: **$941**
P2000 SK: **$983**

USP 9 & 40
Action: autoloader
Grips: polymer
Barrel: 4.25 in. Sights: 3-dot
Weight: 27.0 oz.
Caliber: 9mm, .40 S&W
Capacity: 13 rounds
Features: short-recoil action; also in kit form
MSRP: **$902**

Heckler & Koch Handguns

USP 40 COMPACT LEM

Action: autoloader
Grips: composite
Barrel: 3.6 in.
Sights: fixed open
Weight: 24.0 oz.
Caliber: .40 S&W
Capacity: 12 rounds
Features: double-action only with improved trigger pull; also in 9mm
MSRP: **$991**

USP 45

Action: autoloader
Grips: polymer
Barrel: 4.4 in.
Sights: 3-dot
Weight: 30.0 oz.
Caliber: .45 ACP
Capacity: 12 rounds
Features: short-recoil action
MSRP: **$983**

USP 40
COMPACT LEM

USP 45

Heritage Handguns

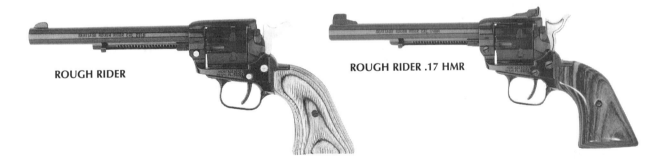

ROUGH RIDER

ROUGH RIDER .17 HMR

ROUGH RIDER

Action: single-action revolver
Grips: hardwood, regular or birdshead
Barrel: 3.5, 4.75, 6.5, 9 in.
Sights: fixed open
Weight: 31.0 oz.
Caliber: .22, .22 LR (.22 WMR cylinder available)
Capacity: 6 rounds
Features: action on Colt 1873 pattern; transfer bar; satin or blued finish; weight to 38 oz. dependent on barrel length

Rough Rider: $138–320
With WMR cylinder: $183
Satin, with WMR cylinder:. . . . $171
Satin, adjustable sights,
   WMR cylinder: $229
Bird's head grip: $185

ROUGH RIDER IN .17 HMR

Action: single-action revolver
Grips: laminated camo
Barrel: 6.5 or 9 in.
Sights: adjustable
Weight: 38.0 oz.
Caliber: .17 HMR
Capacity: 6 rounds
Features: Williams Fire Red ramp front sight and Millet rear
MSRP: **$244**

High Standard Handguns

SUPERMATIC CITATION MS

OLYMPIC

SUPERMATIC TROPHY

M1911 TARGET PISTOLS

Action: autoloader
Grips: walnut
Barrel: 5 in. (6 in. Supermatic)
Sights: fixed or target
Weight: 40 oz.
Caliber: .45 ACP
Capacity: 7 + 1 rounds
Features: Mil spec. slide; mil. spec. barrel and bushing; flared ejection port; beveled magazine well; match trigger with overtravel stop; 4-pound trigger pull; stippled front grip; available in stainless steel, blued or Parkerized finish
Camp Perry Model
Fixed sights: $825
Adjustable sights:...................$895
Supermatic Tournament: $795

CRUSADER COMBAT

Action: autoloader
Grips: cocobolo wood
Barrel: 4.5 in. *Sights*: fixed open
Weight: 38 oz.
Caliber: .45 ACP
Capacity: 7+1 rounds
Features: precision fitted frame and slide; flared ejection port; lightweight long trigger with over-travel stop; trigger pull tuned at 5-6 lbs.; extended slide stop and safety; wide beavertail grip safety; available in stainless steel, blued or Parkerized finish
MSRP: $825

CRUSADER M1911 A-1

Action: autoloader
Grips: cocobolo wood
Barrel: 5 in.
Sights: fixed open
Weight: 40 oz.
Caliber: .38 Super, .45 ACP
Capacity: 7+1 (.38 Super),
9 + 1 rounds
Features: precision fitted frame and slide; flared ejection port; lightweight long trigger with over-travel stop; trigger pull tuned at 5-6 lbs.; extended slide stop and safety; wide beavertail grip safety; available in stainless steel, blued or Parkerized finish
MSRP: $860

G-MAN MODEL

Action: autoloader
Grips: cocobolo wood
Barrel: 5 in.
Sights: fixed open
Weight: 39 oz.
Caliber: .45 ACP
Capacity: 8+1 rounds
Features: custom-fit match grade stainless barrel and National Match bushing; polished feed ramp; throated barrel; lightweight trigger with over-travel stop; flared ejection port; wide, beavertail grip and ambidextrous thumb safeties; black Teflon finish
MSRP: $1395

OLYMPIC

Action: autoloader
Grips: walnut
Barrel: 5.5 in.
Sights: target
Weight: 44.0 oz.
Caliber: .22 Short
Capacity: 10 + 1 rounds
Features: single-action, blowback mechanism
MSRP: $795

SUPERMATIC CITATION

Action: autoloader
Grips: walnut
Barrel: 10 in.
Sights: target
Weight: 54.0 oz.
Caliber: .22 LR
Capacity: 10 + 1 rounds
Features: optional scope mount; slide conversion kit for .22 short
MSRP: $845

SUPERMATIC TROPHY

Action: autoloader
Grips: walnut
Barrel: 5.5 (bull) or 7.3 (fluted) in.
Sights: target
Weight: 44.0 oz.
Caliber: .22 LR
Capacity: 10 + 1 rounds
Features: left-hand grip optional
5.5 in. barrel: $795
7.3 in barrel (46 oz.): $845

High Standard Handguns

VICTOR

Action: autoloader
Grips: walnut   **Barrel**: 4.5 or 5.5 in.
Sights: target   **Weight**: 45.0 oz.
Caliber: .22 LR
Capacity: 10 + 1 rounds
Features: optional slide conversion kit
for .22 Short
4.5 in. barrel: **$795**
5.5 in. barrel (46 oz.): **$795**
4.5 in. barrel with
  universal scope base: **$745**
5.5 in. barrel with universal
  scope base: **$745**

VICTOR

Hi-Point Handguns

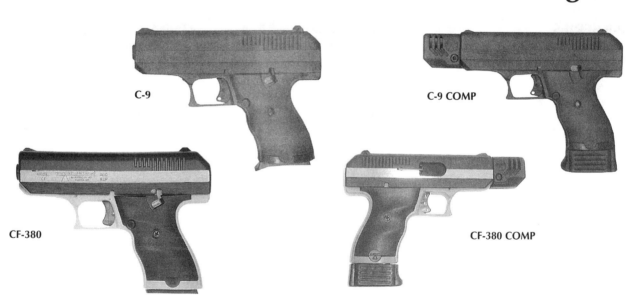

C-9

C-9 COMP

CF-380

CF-380 COMP

MODEL 40S&W/POLY & .45 ACP

Action: autoloader
Grips: polymer
Barrel: 4.5 in.
Sights: 3-dot adjustable
Weight: 32 oz.
Caliber: .40 S&W, .45 ACP
Capacity: 9 + 1 rounds (10 round
magazine available for COMP)
Features: high-impact polymer frame;
last-round lock-open; quick on-and-off
thumb safety; magazine disconnect
safety; powder coat black finish
MSRP: **$186**

MODEL C-9 AND C-9 COMP

Action: autoloader
Grips: polymer
Barrel: 3.5 in.
Sights: 3-dot
Weight: 25.0, 30.0 (COMP) oz.
Caliber: 9mm
Capacity: 8 + 1 rounds (10 round
magazine available for COMP)
Features: high-impact polymer frame;
COMP models feature a compensator,
last-round lock-open
MSRP: **$155**

MODEL CF-380 AND 380 COMP

Action: autoloader
Grips: polymer
Barrel: 3.5 or 4 in. (COMP)
Sights: 3-dot adjustable
Weight: 25.0, 30.0 (COMP) oz.
Caliber: .380 ACP
Capacity: 8 + 1 rounds (10 round
magazine available for COMP)
Features: high-impact polymer frame;
last-round lock-open; COMP models
feature a compensator; powder coat
black finish with chrome rail
CF-380: **$135**
380 COMP: **$135**

Kahr Handguns

MODEL P-9

MODEL P-40

MODEL P-45

KP4544

P-9 SERIES
Action: autoloader
Grips: polymer or wood
Barrel: 3.5, and 4.0 in.
Sights: fixed or adjustable
Weight: 15-26 oz.   **Caliber**: 9mm
Capacity: 6 + 1 to 8 + 1 rounds
Features: trigger cocking DAO; lock breech; "Browning-type" recoil lug; passive striker block; no magazine disconnect; black polymer frame
CW9093, polymer, matte stainless slide (3.5 in. bl, 15.8 oz.): . . $549
KT9093, Hogue grips, matte stainless (4.0 in. bl, 26.0 oz.): $831
KT9093-Novak, Hogue grips, Novak sights, matte stainless: $968
KP9093, polymer frame, matte stainless slide (3.5 in. bl, 15.8 oz.):. $739
KP9094, polymer frame, blackened stainless slide w/Tungsten DLC: $786
PM9093, polymer frame, matte stainless slide (3 in. bl, 14.0 oz.): $786
PM9094 polymer frame, blackened stainless steel slide w/Tungsten DLC: $837
K9093, matte stainless steel (3.5 in. bl, 23.1 oz.):. $855
K9094, matte blackened stainless w/Tungsten DLC:. . $891
K9098 K9 Elite 2003, stainless: $932
M9093 matte stainless (4 in. bl, 22.1 oz.): $855

M9093-BOX, matte stainless frame, matte black slide (3 in. bl, 22.1 oz.): $475
M9098 Elite 2003, stainless steel: $932

P-40 SERIES
Action: autoloader
Grips: polymer or wood
Barrel: 3.5-4 in.
Sights: target or adjustable
Weight: 15.0-22.1 oz.
Caliber: .40 S&W
Capacity: 5+1 (Covert) to 7+1 rounds
Features: trigger cocking DAO; lock breech; "Browning-type" recoil lug; passive striker block; no magazine disconnect; black polymer frame
KT4043 4-in. barrel, Hogue grips, matte stainless (4-in. bl): . . . $831
KT4043-Novak, Hogue grips, Novak sights, matte stainless (4-in. bl): $838
KP4043 polymer frame, matte stainless slide (3.08-in. bl): . $739
KP4044 polymer frame, blackened stainless slide w/Tungsten DLC (3.5-in. bl): $786
KPS4043 Covert, polymer frame w/shortened grip, matte stainless slide (3.5-in.): $697
PM4043 polymer frame, matte stainless slide (3.08-in. bl): . $786
PM4044 polymer frame, blackened stainless slide w/Tungsten DLC (3.08-in.): $837
K4043 matte stainless steel

(3.5-in.):. $855
K4044 matte blackened stainless w/ Tungsten DLC (3.5-in. bl.): $891
K4048 Elite, stainless steel (3.5-in.):. $932
M4043 matte stainless steel (3-in.): $855
M4048 Elite, stainless steel (3-in.): $932

P-45 SERIES KP4543
Action: autoloader
Grips: polymer   **Barrel**: 3.54 in.
Sights: target or adjustable
Weight: 18.5 oz.   **Caliber**: .45 ACP
Capacity: 6 + 1 rounds
Features: trigger cocking DAO; lock breech; "Browning-type" recoil lug; passive striker block; no magazine disconnect; polymer frame; matte stainless slide
P45: $805
Matte stainless slide with night sights:. $921

KP4544
Action: autoloader   **Grips**: polymer
Barrel: 3.54 in.   **Sights**: bar-dot
Weight: 18.5 oz.
Caliber: .45 ACP   **Capacity**: 6 rounds
Features: black textured polymer frame; matte blackened stainless steel slide; drift-adjustable, white bar-dot combat sights (tritium night sights optional); textured polymer grips
MSRP: $855

P-3AT

P-11

P-32

PF-9

SUB RIFLE 2000

SUB RIFLE 2000 (READY TO FIRE)

P-3AT

Action: autoloader
Grips: polymer
Barrel: 2.8 in.
Sights: fixed open
Weight: 7.3 oz.
Caliber: .380
Capacity: 6 + 1 rounds
Features: locked-breech mechanism
P-3AT: $324
Parkerized: $366
Chrome: $382

P-11

Action: autoloader
Grips: polymer
Barrel: 3.1 in.
Sights: fixed open
Weight: 14.4 oz.
Caliber: 9mm
Capacity: 10 + 1 rounds
Features: locked-breech mechanism
P-11: $333

Parkerized: $377
Chrome: $390

P-32

Action: autoloader
Grips: polymer
Barrel: 2.7 in.
Sights: fixed open
Weight: 6.6 oz.
Caliber: .32 Auto
Capacity: 7 + 1 rounds
Features: locked-breech mechanism
P-32: $318
Parkerized: $341
Chrome: $377

PF-9

Action: autoloader
Grips: plastic
Barrel: 3.1 in.
Sights: open, adjustable
Weight: 12.7 oz.
Caliber: 9mm Luger

Capacity: 7+1 rounds
Features: firing mechanism, double-action only with automatic hammer-block safety; available in blued, Parkerized, and hard chrome finishes; single stack magazine; black, gray or olive drab grips
Blued: $333
Parkerized: $377
Hard chrome: $390

SUB RIFLE 2000

Action: autoloader
Grips: polymer
Barrel: 16 in.
Sights: target
Weight: 64.0 oz.
Caliber: 9mm and .40 S&W
Capacity: 10 + 1 rounds
Features: take-down, uses pistol magazines
Sub Rifle: $406
SU-16 in .223: $374–665

Kimber Handguns

CUSTOM CDP II

COMPACT II

CUSTOM TARGET II

DESERT WARRIOR

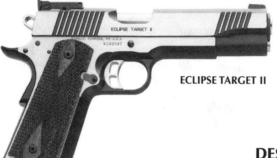

ECLIPSE TARGET II

CDP II SERIES
Action: autoloader
Grips: rosewood
Barrel: 3, 4, or 5 in.
Sights: low-profile night
Weight: 25.0-31.0 oz.
Caliber: .45 ACP
Capacity: 7 + 1 rounds
Features: alloy frame, stainless slide; also in 4 in. (Pro Carry and Compact) and 3 in. (Ultra) configurations
MSRP: **$1318**

COMPACT II
Action: autoloader
Grips: synthetic   **Barrel:** 4 in.
Sights: low-profile combat
Weight: 34.0 oz.
Caliber: .45 ACP, .40 S&W
Capacity: 7 + 1 rounds
Features: shortened single-action 1911; also Pro Carry with alloy frame at 28 oz.; match-grade bushingless bull barrel

Compact II stainless: $1099
Pro Carry II: $888
Pro Carry II stainless: $979
Pro Carry HD II: $1088

CUSTOM II
Action: autoloader
Grips: synthetic or rosewood
Barrel: 5 in.
Sights: target or fixed
Weight: 38.0 oz.
Caliber: .38 Super, .40 S&W, .45 ACP, 10mm, 9mm
Capacity: 7 + 1 rounds
Features: single-action; 1911 Colt design; front cocking serrations; skeleton trigger and hammer
Custom II: $828
Stainless II: $964
Target II: . . . . Discontinued
Stainless Target II: $1068

DESERT WARRIOR .45ACP
Action: autoloader   **Grips:** synthetic
Barrel: 5 in.
Sights: Tactical wedge
Weight: 39 oz.
Caliber: .45 ACP
Capacity: 7 + 1 rounds
Features: match grade solid steel barrel; ambidextrous thumb safety; bumped and grooved beavertail grip safety and bumper pad on the magazine; integral Tactical Rail; G-10 Tactical Grips; Tactical Wedge Tritium low profile night sights; KimPro II Dark Earth finish; lanyard loop
MSRP: **$1458**

ECLIPSE II
Action: autoloader
Grips: laminated
Barrel: 5 in.   **Sights:** 3-dot night
Weight: 38.0 oz.
Caliber: .45 ACP, 10mm
Capacity: 7 + 1 rounds

Kimber Handguns

GOLD MATCH II

GOLD MATCH II STAINLESS

PRO TLE II (LG)

ULTRA CARRY II STAINLESS

Features: matte-black oxide finish over stainless, polished bright on flats; also 3-in. Ultra and 4 in. Pro Carry versions; sights also available in low profile combat or target

Eclipse II: . . . . Discontinued
Target II: **$1345**
Ultra II: **$888**
Pro II: **$888**
Pro Target II: **$1345**

GOLD MATCH II

Action: autoloader
Grips: rosewood
Barrel: 5 in.
Sights: adjustable target
Weight: 38.0 oz.
Caliber: .45 ACP
Capacity: 7 + 1 rounds
Features: single-action 1911 Colt design; match components; ambidextrous safety

Gold Match II: **$1345**
Stainless: **$1519**
Stainless in .40 S&W: Discontinued
Team Match II: **$1535**

PRO TLE II (LG) .45 ACP

Action: autoloader
Barrel: 4 in.
Sights: 3 dot
Weight: 36 oz.
Caliber: .45 ACP
Capacity: 7 + 1 rounds
Features: bushingless match grade bull barrel; steel frame; Crimson Trace Lasergrips (normal grip pressure activates a laser mounted in a grip panel); Meprolight Tritium 3 dot night sights
MSRP: **$1102**

TEN II HIGH CAPACITY

Action: autoloader
Grips: polymer
Barrel: 5 in.
Sights: low-profile combat

Weight: 34.0 oz.
Caliber: .45 ACP
Capacity: 10 + 1 rounds
Features: double-stack magazine; polymer frame; also in 4 in. (Pro Carry) configuration, from 32 oz.
Discontinued

ULTRA CARRY II

Action: autoloader
Grips: synthetic
Barrel: 3 in.
Sights: low-profile combat
Weight: 25.0 oz.
Caliber: .40 S&W, .45 ACP
Capacity: 7 + 1 rounds
Features: smallest commercial 1911-style pistol
Ultra Carry II: **$888**
Stainless II: **$964**

Magnum Research Handguns

BABY EAGLE

BABY EAGLE

Action: autoloader
Grips: plastic composite
Barrel: 3.5, 4, 4.5 in.
Sights: 3-dot combat
Weight: 26.8-39.8 oz.
Caliber: 9mm, .40 S&W, .45 ACP
Capacity: 10 rounds (15 for 9mm)
Features: squared, serrated trigger guard
MSRP: $549

BFR (BIGGEST FINEST REVOLVER)

Action: single-action revolver
Grips: rubber
Barrel: 6.5, 7.5 or 10 in.
Sights: open adjustable
Weight: 50.0-67.3 oz.
Caliber: .45/70, .444, .450, .500 S&W, .30-30 Win. (long cylinder), .480 Ruger, .475 Linbaugh, .22 Hornet, .45 Colt/.410, .50 AE (short cylinder)
Capacity: 5 rounds
Features: both short and long-cylinder models entirely of stainless steel
MSRP: $1050

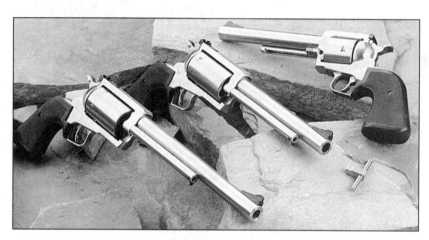

BFR

MARK XIX DESERT EAGLE

Action: autoloader
Grips: plastic composite
Barrel: 6 or 10 in.
Sights: fixed combat
Weight: 70.2 oz.
Caliber: .357 Mag., .44 Mag., .50 AE
Capacity: 9 + 1 rounds, 8 + 1 rounds, 7 + 1 rounds
Features: gas operated; all with polygonal rifling, integral scope bases
Desert Eagle, 6 in. barrel: . . . $1563
10 in. barrel (79 oz.): $1650
6 in. chrome or nickel: $1838
6 in. Titanium Gold: $2055

MARK XIX DESERT EAGLE
.50 MAGNUM TITANIUM FINISH

MOA Handguns

MAXIMUM

Action: hinged breech
Grips: walnut
Barrel: 8.5, 10.5 or 14 in.
Sights: target   *Weight:* 56.0 oz.
Caliber: most rifle chamberings from
.22 Hornet to .375 H&H
Features: stainless breech; Douglas
barrel; extra barrels; muzzle brake
available
Maximum: $823
With stainless barrel: $919

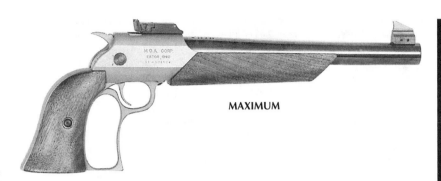

MAXIMUM

Navy Arms Handguns

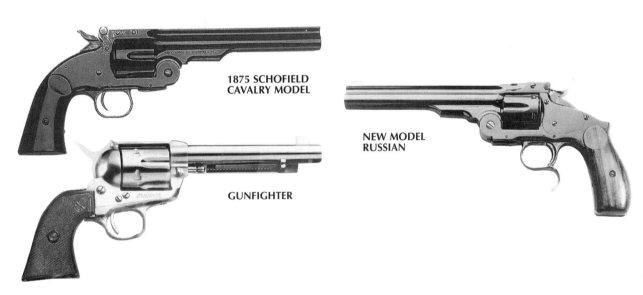

1875 SCHOFIELD
CAVALRY MODEL

NEW MODEL
RUSSIAN

GUNFIGHTER

MODEL 1875 SCHOFIELD CAVALRY MODEL

Action: single-action revolver
Grips: walnut
Barrel: 3.5, 5.0 or 7.0 in.
Sights: fixed open
Weight: 35.0 oz.
Caliber: .38 Spl.,. 44-40, .45 Colt,
Capacity: 6 rounds
Features: top-break action, automatic
ejectors; 5 in. barrel (37 oz.) and 7 in.
barrel (39 oz.)
.38 Spl.: $899
44-40: $899
.45 Colt: $899

BISLEY

Action: single-action revolver
Grips: walnut
Barrel: 4.8, 5.5 or 7.5 in.
Sights: fixed open   *Weight:* 45.0 oz.
Caliber: .44-40, .45 Colt
Capacity: 6 rounds
Features: Bisley grip case-colored
frame; weight to 48 oz.
MSRP: $532

GUNFIGHTER SERIES

Action: single-action revolver
Grips: walnut
Barrel: 4.8, 5.5, 7.5 in.
Sights: fixed open
Weight: 47.0 oz.
Caliber: .357, .44-40, .45 Colt
Capacity: 6 rounds

Features: case-colored frames, after
1873 Colt design
Gunfighter: $585
Stainless: $591

NEW MODEL RUSSIAN

Action: single-action revolver
Grips: walnut
Barrel: 6.5 in.
Sights: fixed open
Weight: 40.0 oz.
Caliber: .44 Russian
Capacity: 6 rounds
Features: top-break action
Discontinued

Nighthawk Custom Handguns

10-8 GUN
Action: autoloader
Grips: VZ Diamondback, green or black linen micarta accented with the 10-8 logo
Barrel: 5 in.
Sights: 10-8 Performance rear sight, serrated front sights with a tritium insert
Caliber: .45 ACP
Features: long, solid trigger with a hidden fixed overtravel stop designed by Hilton Yam; front and rear cocking serrations on the slide; strong-side-only safety; 25-lpi checkered front strap; lanyard loop mainspring housing; black Perma Kote finish; low-profile Dawson Light Speed rail for easy attachment of Surefire X200 Series lights for use at night
MSRP: **$2620**

North American Arms Handguns

GUARDIAN .32

GUARDIAN .380

GUARDIAN .32
Action: autoloader
Grips: polymer
Barrel: 2.5 in.
Sights: fixed open
Weight: 12.0 oz.
Caliber: .32 ACP or .25 NAA
Capacity: 6 + 1 rounds
Features: stainless, double-action
MSRP: **$402**

GUARDIAN .380
Action: autoloader
Grips: composite
Barrel: 2.5 in.
Sights: fixed open
Weight: 18.8 oz.
Caliber: .380 ACP or .32 NAA
Capacity: 6 rounds
Features: stainless, double-action
MSRP: **$449**

North American Arms Handguns

MINI MASTER

MINI REVOLVER
W/HOLSTER GRIP

MINI MASTER SERIES REVOLVER

Action: single-action revolver
Grips: rubber
Barrel: 2 or 4 in.
Sights: fixed or adjustable
Weight: 8.8 oz. (2 in.) or 10.7 oz. (4 in.)
Caliber: .22LR or .22 Mag.,
.17 MACH 2, .17 HMR
Capacity: 5 rounds
Features: conversion cylinder or
adjustable sights available

.22 Mag, LR (2 in.), .17 MACH2 or
   .17 HMR: $269
.22 Mag w/conversion
   .22 LR (2 in.): $334
.22 Mag or LR (4 in.): $284
.22 Mag w/conversion
   .22 LR (4 in.) or .17 HMR with
   .17 MACH2 conversion: $349

MINI REVOLVER

Action: single-action revolver
Grips: laminated rosewood

Barrel: 1.2 in.
Sights: fixed open
Weight: 5.0 oz.
Caliber: .22 Short, .22 LR, .22 WMR,
.17 MACH 2, .17 HMR
Capacity: 5 rounds
Features: holster grip
.22 Short, .22 LR, .17 MACH2: . $215
With holster grip: $244
.22 Magnum, .17 HMR: $244
.22 Magnum with holster grip: . . $319

Olympic Arms Handguns

COHORT

Action: autoloader
Grips: walnut
Barrel: 4 in. bull   **Sights:** target
Weight: 38.0 oz.
Caliber: .45 ACP
Capacity: 7 + 1 rounds
Features: single-action on 1911 Colt
design; extended beavertail; stainless
or parkerized
MSRP: $974

COHORT

ENFORCER

ENFORCER

Action: autoloader
Grips: walnut
Barrel: 4 in. bull
Sights: low-profile combat
Weight: 36.0 oz.
Caliber: .45 ACP
Capacity: 6 + 1 rounds
Features: single-action on 1911 Colt
design; extended beavertail; stainless
or parkerized
MSRP: $1034

Olympic Arms Handguns

MATCHMASTER

Action: autoloader
Grips: walnut
Barrel: 5 or 6 in.   *Sights:* target
Weight: 40.0-44.0 oz.
Caliber: .45 ACP
Capacity: 7 + 1 rounds
Features: single-action on 1911 Colt design; extended beavertail; stainless or parkerized
Matchmaster 5 in.: **$903**
6 in. barrel (44 oz.): **$973**
RS (40 oz.): **$899**

WESTERNER

Action: autoloader
Grips: walnut
Barrel: 4, 5, or 6 in. *Sights:* target
Weight: 35-43 oz.   *Caliber*: .45 ACP
Capacity: 7 + 1 rounds

Features: single-action; matched frames and slides; fitted and head-spaced barrels; complete ramp and throat jobs; lowered and widened ejection ports; beveled mag wells; hand-stoned-to-match hammers and sears; adjusted triggers; extended thumb safeties; wide beavertail grip safeties; adjustable rear sights; dovetail front sights
Westerner: **$1034**
Trail Boss (6 in. bbl): **$1014**
Constable (4 in. bbl): **$1164**

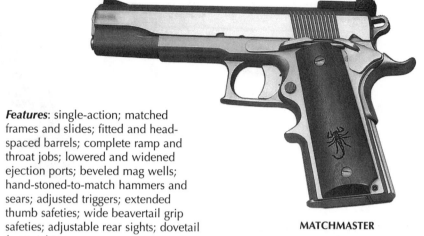

MATCHMASTER

Para Ordnance Handguns

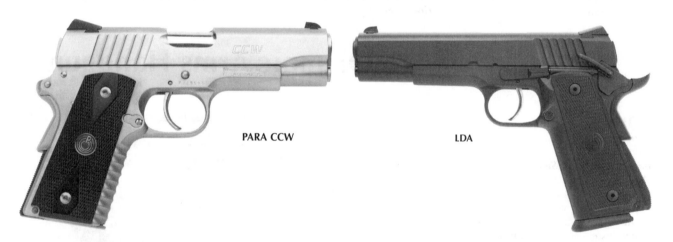

PARA CCW   LDA

CCW AND COMPANION CARRY

Action: double-action autoloader
Grips: cocobolo
Barrel: 2.5, 3.5 or 4.1 in.
Sights: low-profile combat
Weight: 32.0-34.0 oz.
Caliber: .45 ACP
Capacity: 7 + 1 rounds
Features: double-action; stainless; Tritium night sights available
4.25 in. CCW: **$1129**
3.5 in. Companion Carry: . . . **$1129**

LDA HIGH CAPACITY

Action: autoloader
Grips: composite
Barrel: 4.25 or 5.0 in. ramped
Sights: target
Weight: 37.0-40.0 oz.
Caliber: 9mm, .40 S&W or .45 ACP
Capacity: 14 + 1 rounds, 16 + 1 rounds, 18 + 1 rounds
Features: double-action, double-stack magazine; stainless
LDA: **$999-1269**
Carry option, 3.5 in. barrel: . . **$1199**

LDA SINGLE STACK

Action: double-action autoloader
Grips: composite
Barrel: 3.5, 4.25 or 5 in.
Sights: target
Weight: 32.0-40.0 oz.
Caliber: .45 ACP
Capacity: 7 + 1 rounds
Features: ramped, stainless barrel
MSRP: **$999-1269**

Para Ordnance Handguns

**MODEL P12•45 ACP
(3.5" BARREL, STAINLESS)**

PXT 1911

**PXT 14•45 HIGH
CAPACITY LIMITED**

PXT WARTHOG

TAC-FOUR

P-SERIES
Action: single-action autoloader
Grips: composite
Barrel: 3.0, 3.5, 4.25 or 5.0 in.
Sights: fixed open
Weight: 24.0-40.0 oz.
Caliber: 9mm, .45 ACP
Capacity: 10 + 1 to 18 + 1 rounds
Features: customized 1911 Colt
design; beveled magazine well; polymer
magazine; also available with 3-dot or
low-profile combat sights; stainless
MSRP: **$855-995**

PXT 1911 PISTOLS
Action: autoloading
Grips: cocobolo wood with gold
medallion and beavertail extension
Barrel: 3.5, 4.25 and 5 in.
Sights: blade front, white
3 dot rear
Weight: 32.0-39.0 oz.
Caliber: .45 ACP

Capacity: 7+1 rounds
Features: single-action match trigger;
extended slide lock; Para Kote Regal
finish; stainless competition hammer;
ramped stainless barrel
MSRP: **$959–1149**

PXT 14•45 HIGH CAPACITY LIMITED
Action: autoloader
Grips: polymer
Barrel: 5 in.
Sights: adjustable
Weight: 40.0 oz.
Caliber: .45 ACP
Capacity: 14 + 1 rounds
Features: stainless receiver: sterling
finish
MSRP: **$1259**

PXT WARTHOG
Action: autoloader
Grips: black plastic

Barrel: 3 in.
Sights: 3 dot
Weight: 24 oz.
Caliber: .45 ACP
Capacity: 10 + 1 rounds
Features: single-action; ramped barrel;
alloy receiver; spurred hammer
Warthog: **$959**
Nite Hawg: **$1099**

TAC-FOUR
Action: double-action autoloader
Grips: black polymer
Barrel: 4.25 in.
Sights: low-profile combat
Weight: 36.0 oz.
Caliber: .45 ACP
Capacity: 13 + 1 rounds
Features: double-action; stainless;
flush hammer; bobbed beavertail
MSRP: **$1099**

Rossi Handguns

HANDGUNS

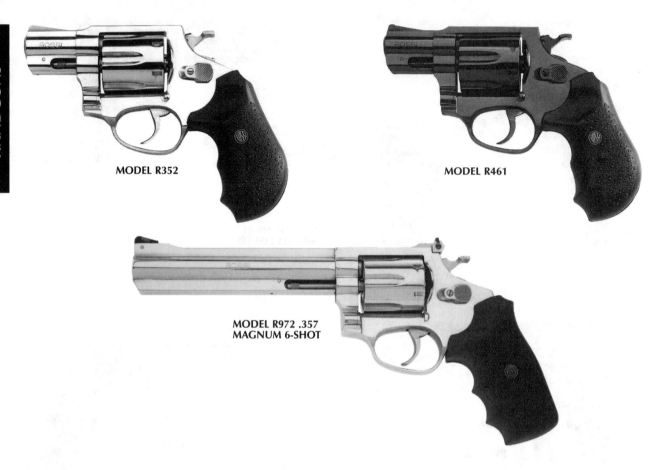

MODEL R352

MODEL R461

MODEL R972 .357
MAGNUM 6-SHOT

MODEL R351 AND R352
Action: double-action revolver
Grips: rubber
Barrel: 2 in.
Sights: fixed open
Weight: 24.0 oz.
Caliber: .38 Spl.
Capacity: 6 rounds
Features: stainless; R351 chrome-moly also available
R35202 stainless: **$406**
R35102 blue: **$352**

MODEL R462 & R461
Action: double-action revolver
Grips: rubber
Barrel: 2 in.
Sights: fixed open
Weight: 26.0 oz.
Caliber: .357 Mag.
Capacity: 6 rounds
Features: stainless; R461 chrome-moly also available
R462 stainless: **$406**
R461 blue: **$352**

MODEL R851
Action: double-action revolver
Grips: rubber
Barrel: 4 in.
Sights: adjustable
Weight: 32.0 oz.
Caliber: .38 Spl.
Capacity: 6 rounds
Features: adjustable rear sight; blue finish
R85104: **$352**

MODEL R972
Action: double-action revolver
Grips: rubber
Barrel: 6 in.
Sights: target
Weight: 34.0 oz.
Caliber: .357 Mag.
Capacity: 6 rounds
Features: stainless after S&W M19 pattern; also R971 chrome-moly with 4 in. barrel
R972 stainless: **$460**
R971 blue: **$406**

BISLEY SINGLE-ACTION TARGET

GP-100 .357 MAGNUM 6" HEAVY BARREL

MARK III HUNTER

BIRD'S HEAD VAQUERO

Action: single-action revolver
Grips: black micarta or simulated ivory
Barrel: 3.75 or 4.6 in.
Sights: fixed open
Weight: 40.0-45.0 oz.
Caliber: .45 Colt or .357
Capacity: 6 rounds
Features: gloss stainless or color case; reverse indexing pawl; bird's head grip
Discontinued

BISLEY

Action: single-action revolver
Grips: walnut
Barrel: 6.5 (.22 LR) or 7.5 in.
Sights: target
Weight: 43.0-50.0 oz.
Caliber: .22 LR, .357 Mag., .44 Mag., .45 Colt
Capacity: 6 rounds
Features: rimfire and centerfire (48 oz.); low-profile hammer
.22LR: . . . .**Discontinued**
.357, .44, .45: **$683**

BISLEY VAQUERO

Action: single-action revolver
Grips: rosewood
Barrel: 4.6, 5.5 in.
Sights: fixed open
Weight: 43.5-44.0 oz.
Caliber: .45 Colt or .44 Rem. Mag

Capacity: 6 rounds
Features: stainless or color case blued; transfer bar operating mechanism/ loading gate interlock
Blued: . . . .**Discontinued**
Stainless: **$729**

MODEL GP100

Action: double-action revolver
Grips: rubber with rosewood insert
Barrel: 4.3 or 6 in.
Sights: fixed open
Weight: 38.0-46.0 oz.
Caliber: .38 Spl. or .357
Capacity: 6 rounds
Features: chrome-moly or stainless; weight to 46 oz. depending on barrel length
Blued: **$616**
Stainless: **$659–680**

MARK II

Action: autoloader
Grips: synthetic or rosewood
Barrel: 4 in., 4 in. Bull, 6.7 in. Bull
Sights: open, fixed or adjustable
Caliber: .22 LR
Capacity: 10 rounds
Features: slab bull barrel; manual safety; loaded chamber indicator; magazine disconnect; adjustable rear sight; blued finish

4 in. Bull (Limited Edition rosewood grips): . . . .**price on request**
6.7 in. Bull: **$535**
6.7 in slab Bull: **$555**

MARK III

Action: autoloader
Grips: black synthetic or wood
Barrel: 5.5 in. Bull or 6.7 in. Bull
Sights: open, adjustable
Weight: 41 oz.
Caliber: .22 LR
Capacity: 10 rounds
Features: Bull barrel; contoured ejection port and tapered bolt ears; manual safety; loaded chamber indicator; magazine disconnect; adjustable rear sight; stainless finish; drilled and tapped for a Weaver-type scope base adapter
Stainless, 5.5 in. Bull bl.: **$417**
Stainless, 6.7 in. bl.: **$532**
Stainless, 6.7 in. slab Bull bl.: **$606**
Blue, 4.75 in. bl.: **$352**
Blue, 6 in. bl.: **$352**
22/45 Mark III (4-in slab bull bl.): **$326**

Ruger Handguns

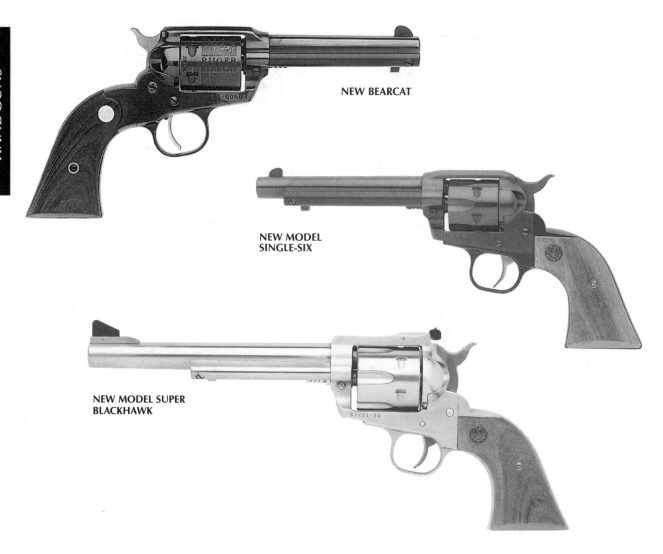

NEW BEARCAT

NEW MODEL SINGLE-SIX

NEW MODEL SUPER BLACKHAWK

NEW BEARCAT

Action: single-action revolver
Grips: rosewood
Barrel: 4 in.
Sights: fixed open
Weight: 24.0 oz.
Caliber: .22 LR
Capacity: 6 rounds
Features: transfer bar
New Bearcat: **$501**
Stainless: **$540**

NEW MODEL SINGLE SIX

Action: single-action revolver
Grips: rosewood or Micarta
Barrel: 4.6, 5.5, 6.5 or 9.5 in.
Sights: fixed open
Weight: 33.0-45.0 oz.
Caliber: .22 LR, .22 WMR, .17 HMR,
.17 MACH 2
Capacity: 6 rounds
Features: adjustable sights available;
weight to 38 oz. depending on barrel
length
Single Six: **$519**
Stainless: **$584–732**
32 H&R: . . . .**Discontinued**
17 HMR: **$519**

NEW MODEL SUPER BLACKHAWK

Action: single-action revolver
Grips: walnut
Barrel: 4.6, 5.5, 7.5 or 10.5 in.
Sights: target
Weight: 45.0-55.0 oz.
Caliber: .41 Rem Mag, .44 Rem Mag
.45 Colt
Capacity: 6 rounds
Features: weight to 51 oz. depending
on barrel length; also available: Super
Black-hawk Hunter, stainless with 7.5
in. barrel, black laminated grips, rib,
scope rings
Blue: **$650**
Stainless: **$667–781**

NEW VAQUERO

Action: single-action revolver
Grips: black, checkered
Barrel: 4.6, 5.5 or 7.5 in.
Sights: fixed open
Weight: 37.0-41.0 oz.
Caliber: .45 Colt or .357
Capacity: 6 rounds
Features: gloss stainless or color case, reverse indexing pawl
Vaquero: **$659**
Engraved: . . . . **Discontinued**

NEW VAQUERO

P-SERIES

Action: autoloader
Grips: polymer
Barrel: 3.9 or 4.5 in.
Sights: fixed open
Weight: 30.0 oz.
Caliber: 9mm, .40 S&W, .45 Auto
Capacity: 10 + 1 rounds (8 + 1 in .45, 15 + 1 in 9mm)
Features: double-action; ambidextrous grip safety; decocker on some models; manual safety on others (9mm)

KP95PR Stainless 3.9 in. bl.: $424
P95PR Blued 3.9 in. bl.: **$393**
KP89 Stainless 4.5 in. bl.: . . . **$525**
KP94 Stainless 4.1 in. bl.: . . . **$628**
KP95 Stainless 3.9 in. bl.: . . . **$424**
P89 Blued 4.5 in. bl.: **$475**
P95 Blued 3.9 in. bl.: **$425**
(.40 S&W)
KP94 Stainless 4.1 in. bl.: . . . **$628**
P94 .40 S&W
Blued 4.1 in. bl.: **$541**
(.45 ACP)
KP345 Stainless 4.5 in. bl.: . . . **$540**
KP345PR 4.25 in. bl.: **$599**
P345PR Blued 4.25 in. bl.: . . **$561**
KP90 Stainless 4.5 in. bl.: . . . **$617**
P90 Blued 4.5 in. bl.: **$574**

MODEL P94

P345

A semi-auto pistol is designed to operate as the slide moves against the abutment of a firmly held frame. A low grasp allows the muzzle to whipsaw upward from recoil as the mechanism is automatically cycling, diverting momentum from the slide through the frame. Now the slide can run out of momentum before it has completed its work. This is why holding a pistol too low can cause it to jam.

Ruger Handguns

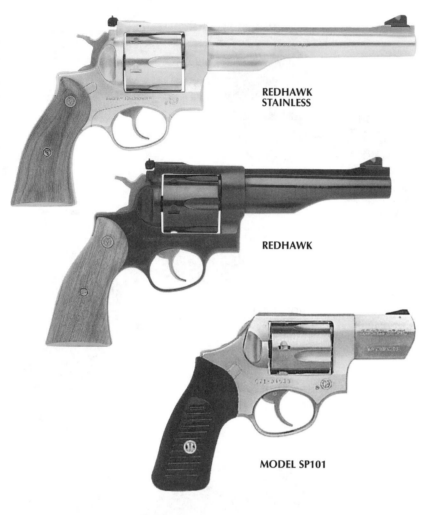

REDHAWK STAINLESS

REDHAWK

MODEL SP101

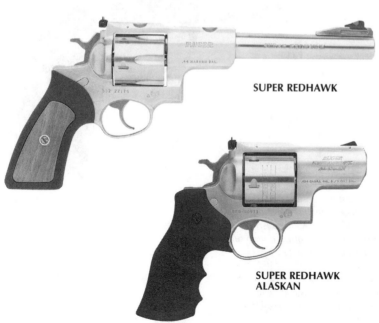

SUPER REDHAWK

SUPER REDHAWK ALASKAN

REDHAWK

Action: double-action revolver
Grips: rosewood
Barrel: 5.5 or 7.5 in.
Sights: target
Weight: 49.0 oz.
Caliber: .44 Rem Mag.
Capacity: 6 rounds
Features: stainless model available; 7.5 in. version weighs 54 oz.; scope rings available
Redhawk: ....Discontinued
Stainless: $861
Stainless with rings:.........$915

MODEL SP101

Action: double-action revolver
Grips: rubber with synthetic insert
Barrel: 2.3, 3.0 or 4.0 in.
Sights: fixed open (adjustable on .32 H&R)
Weight: 25.0-30.0 oz.
Caliber: .22 LR, .32 H&R, 9mm, .38 Spl., .357
Capacity: 5 or 6 rounds
Features: chrome-moly or stainless; weight to 30 oz. depending on barrel length
Stainless 2.25 in. bl.: $589–839
Stainless 3.1 in. bl.: $589
.22LR: ....Discontinued

SUPER REDHAWK

Action: double-action revolver
Grips: rubber/black laminate
Barrel: 7.5 or 9.5 in. (2.25 Alaskan)
Sights: target
Weight: 53.0 oz.
Caliber: .44 Mag., .454 Casull, .480 Ruger
Capacity: 6 rounds
Features: stainless or low glare stainless finish; 9.5 in. version weighs 58 oz.
.44 Magnum: $915
.454, .480 Ruger: $992
Alaskan:................$963–992

Sig Sauer Handguns

MODEL P220

Action: autoloader
Grips: polymer or laminated
Barrel: 4.4 in., 3.9 in. (Carry)
Sights: adjustable
Weight: 27.8 oz., 30.84 oz. (Carry), 31.2 (Compact)
Caliber: .45 ACP
Capacity: 8 rounds, 6 rounds (Compact)
Features: DA/SA; de-cocking lever; automatic firing pin safety block; Nitron or two-tone finish; Picatinny rail; available with SIGLITE Night Sights
Nitron:. **$975**
Two-tone: **$1110**
Elite: **$1200**
Carry Nitron: **$975**
Carry Two-tone:. **$1100**
Carry Elite:. **$1200**
Carry Elite Two-tone: **$1107**
Compact Nitron: **$1050**
Compact Two-tone: **$1110**

MODEL P226

Action: autoloader
Grips: polymer or laminated hardwood
Barrel: 4.4 in.
Sights: adjustable
Weight: 34 to 34.2 oz w/ mag.
Caliber: 9mm; 357 SIG, 40 S&W
Capacity: 10 or 5 rounds (9mm), 10 or 12 + 1 rounds (357 SIG, 40 S&W)
Features: DA/SA; de-cocking lever; automatic firing pin safety block; reversible magazine release; Picatinny rail; available with SIGLITE Night Sights
Nitron:. **$975**
Two-tone: **$1110**
Elite: **$1200**
Elite two-tone: **$1200**
Elite stainless: **$1350**

MODEL P229

Action: autoloader
Grips: polymer or laminated wood
Barrel: 3.9 in.
Sights: fixed open
Weight: 32 to 32.4 oz. w/ mag.
Caliber: 9mm, .357 SIG, .40 S&W
Capacity: 10 + 1 rounds
Features: DA/SA; de-cocking lever; automatic firing pin safety block; available with SIGLITE Night Sights
MSRP: **$975**

MODEL P226

MODEL P229

SIG CLASSIC
COMPACT P229 ST

Sig Sauer Handguns

MODEL SP2022

MODEL P232

MODEL P239

MOSQUITO

MODEL SP2022
Action: autoloader **Grips:** polymer
Barrel: 3.6 in. **Sights:** fixed open
Weight: 30.2 oz.
Caliber: 9mm, .357 SIG, .40 S&W
Capacity: 7 + 1 rounds
Features: DA/SA; Nitron coated stainless slide, polymer frame; can be converted from DA to SA.
MSRP: $613

MODEL P232
Action: autoloader **Grips:** polymer
Barrel: 3.6 in.
Sights: fixed open
Weight: 16.2 oz.
Caliber: .380
Capacity: 7 + 1 rounds
Features: double-action; Picatinny rail; available with SIGLITE Night Sights
Blued: $660
Two-tone: $755
Stainless: $825

MODEL P239
Action: autoloader
Grips: polymer
Barrel: 3.6 in.
Sights: fixed open
Weight: 27.0 oz.
Caliber: 9mm, .357 Sig, .40 S&W
Capacity: 7 + 1 rounds
Features: DA/SA; lightweight alloy frame
Nitron: $840
Two-tone: $975

MOSQUITO
Action: autoloader
Grips: polymer, composite
Barrel: 4 in. **Sights:** adjustable
Weight: 24.6 oz. w/ mag.
Caliber: .22 LR
Capacity: 10 rounds
Features: DA/SA; polymer frame; Picatinny rail; slide mounted ambidextrous safety; internal locking device
Blued: $390
Two-tone: $404

REVOLUTION 1911
Action: autoloader
Grips: custom hardwood
Barrel: 5 in.
Sights: foxed open or target
Weight: 30.3 to 40.3 oz.
Caliber: .45 ACP
Capacity: 8+1 rounds
Features: 1911 series pistol; SA; hand-fitted stainless steel frame and slide available in black Nitron finish; match grade barrel; available with 4¼ in. barrel (Compact); hammer/sear set and trigger; beavertail grip safety; firing pin safety and hammer intercept notch; available with Novak night sights
Nitron: $1200
Stainless: $1170
Stainless Carry: $1170
Compact Nitron: $1200
Compact Stainless: $1170

Smith & Wesson Handguns

MODEL 10
HEAVY BARREL

MODEL 21
CLASSIC

MODEL 22A
SPORT

MODEL 22 CLASSIC

MODEL 22 OF
1917 CLASSIC

MODEL 10
Action: double-action revolver
Grips: Uncle Mike's Combat
Barrel: 4.0 in. heavy
Sights: fixed open
Weight: 33.5 oz.
Caliber: .38 Spl.
Capacity: 6 rounds
Features: "military and police" model;
also in stainless, K-frame
Model 10: $758

MODEL 21 CLASSIC
Action: revolver
Grips: Altamont walnut
Barrel: 4 in.
Sights: front: pinned half moon ser-
vice; rear: service
Weight: 37 oz.
Caliber: .44 SP
Capacity: 6 rounds
Features: carbon steel frame and cylin-
der; blue, color case or nickel finish;
square butt; serrated trigger
MSRP: $924

MODEL 22A SPORT
Action: autoloader
Grips: polymer
Barrel: 4, 5.5 or 7 in.
Sights: target
Weight: 28.0 oz.
Caliber: .22 LR
Capacity: 10 + 1 rounds
Features: scope mounting rib; 5½ in.
bull barrel available
4 in.: $324
5.5 in. (31 oz.): $356
5.5 in. bull: $356
5.5 in. bull, Hi-Viz sights: $356
7 in. (33 oz.): $324
5.5 in. stainless: $356

MODEL 22 CLASSIC
Action: revolver
Grips: Altamont walnut
Barrel: 4 in.
Sights: front: pinned half moon ser-
vice; rear: service
Weight: 36.8 oz.
Caliber: .45 ACP

Capacity: 6 rounds
Features: carbon steel frame and cylinder; blue, color case or nickel finish;
comes with two six-shot full-moon
clips
MSRP: $1059

MODEL 22 OF 1917 CLASSIC
Action: revolver
Grips: Altamont walnut
Barrel: 5.5 in.
Sights: front: pinned half moon ser-
vice; rear: service
Weight: 37.2 oz.
Caliber: .45 ACP
Capacity: 6 rounds
Features: carbon steel frame and cylin-
der; blue, color case or nickel finish;
comes with two six-shot full-moon
clips
MSRP: $1098

Smith & Wesson Handguns

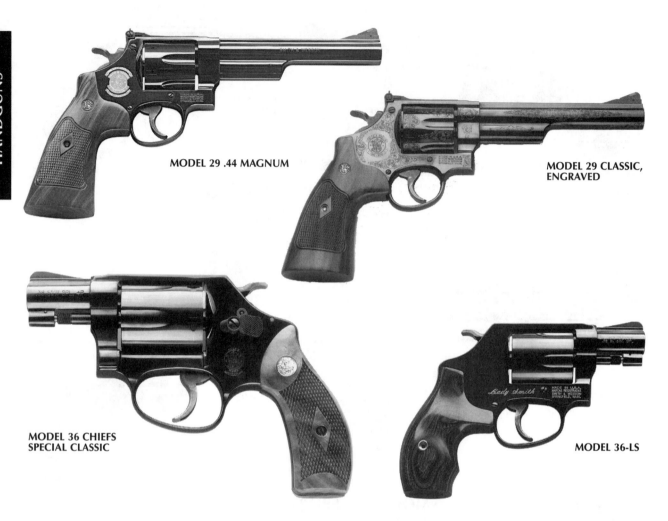

MODEL 29 .44 MAGNUM

MODEL 29 CLASSIC, ENGRAVED

MODEL 36 CHIEFS SPECIAL CLASSIC

MODEL 36-LS

MODEL 29 .44 MAGNUM 50TH ANNIVERSARY EDITION

Action: double-action revolver
Grips: African cocobolo wood
Barrel: 6.5 in.
Sights: target
Weight: 48.5 oz.
Caliber: .44 MAG
Capacity: 6 rounds
Features: 24kt gold-plated anniversary logo on the frame; red ramp front sight, adjustable white outline rear sight; shipped with a mahogany presentation case and a Smith & Wesson cleaning kit with screwdriver
Discontinued

MODEL 29 CLASSIC, ENGRAVED

Action: revolver
Grips: African cocobolo wood

Barrel: 6.5 in.
Sights: front: red ramp; rear: adjustable white outline
Weight: 48.5 oz.
Caliber: .44 Magnum
Capacity: 6 rounds
Features: carbon steel frame and cylinder; blue or nickel finish; square butt frame; serrated trigger; Smith & Wesson logo engraved on the four-screw side plate and decorative scrolling down the length of the barrel; shipped in a glass-top wooden presentation case, with a traditional cleaning rod, brush and replica screwdriver
MSRP: . . . . **Custom**

MODEL 36 CHIEFS SPECIAL CLASSIC

Action: revolver
Grips: Altamont walnut
Barrel: 1-1/8 in.

Sights: front: integral; rear: fixed
Weight: 20.4 oz.
Caliber: .38 Spl.+P
Capacity: 5 rounds
Features: carbon steel J frame; blue, color case or nickel finish
MSRP: **$822**

MODEL 36-LS

Action: double-action revolver
Grips: laminated rosewood, round butt
Barrel: 1.8, 2.2, 3 in.
Sights: fixed open
Weight: 20.0 oz.
Caliber: .38 Spl.
Capacity: 5 rounds
Features: weight to 24 oz. depending on barrel length; stainless version in .357 Mag. available (60 LS)
Model 36 LS: . . . . **Discontinued**
60 LS: **$798**

Smith & Wesson Handguns

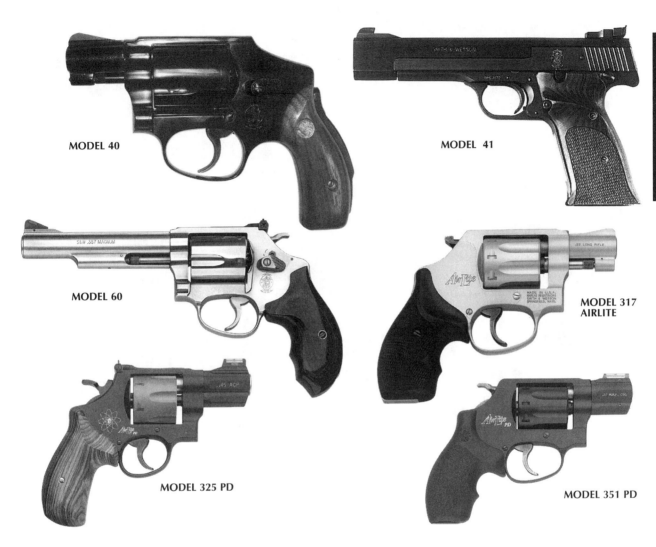

MODEL 40

MODEL 41

MODEL 60

MODEL 317
AIRLITE

MODEL 325 PD

MODEL 351 PD

MODEL 40

Action: hammerless revolver
Grips: Altamont walnut
Barrel: 1-7/8 in.
Sights: front: integral; rear: fixed
Weight: 20.4 oz.
Caliber: .38 Spl.+P
Capacity: 5 rounds
Features: carbon steel construction;
safety hammerless design; grip safety;
blue, color case or nickel finish
MSRP: $853

MODEL 41

Action: autoloader
Grips: walnut
Barrel: 5.5 or 7 in.
Sights: target
Weight: 41.0 oz.
Caliber: .22 LR
Capacity: 12 + 1 rounds

Features: adjustable trigger;
7 in. barrel: 44 oz.
MSRP: $1288

MODEL 60

Action: double-action revolver
Grips: wood
Barrel: 5 in.
Sights: adjustable open
Weight: 30.5 oz.
Caliber: .357
Capacity: 5 rounds
Features: stainless frame
MSRP: $830

MODEL 317

Action: double-action revolver
Grips: rubber
Barrel: 1.8 or 3 in.
Sights: fixed open
Weight: 10.5 oz.

Caliber: .22 LR
Capacity: 8 rounds
Features: alloy frame
1.8 in.: $766
3 in.: $830

MODELS 325 PD AND 351 PD REVOLVER

Action: double-action revolver
Grips: wood (.45), rubber (.22)
Barrel: 2¾ in. (.45), 1⅞ in. (.22)
Sights: adjustable rear, HiViz front
(.45), fixed rear, red ramp front (.22)
Weight: 21.5 oz. (.45), 10.6 oz. (.22)
Caliber: .45 ACP (Model 325), .22
WMR (Model 351)
Capacity: 6 (.45), 7 (.22) rounds
.22: $1153
.45: $1153

Smith & Wesson Handguns

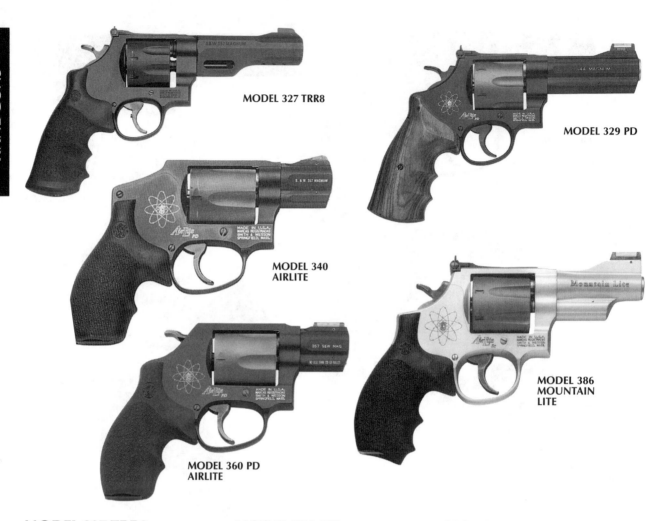

MODEL 327 TRR8

MODEL 329 PD

MODEL 340 AIRLITE

MODEL 386 MOUNTAIN LITE

MODEL 360 PD AIRLITE

MODEL 327 TRR8

Action: double-action revolver
Grips: rubber
Barrel: 5 in., two-piece shrouded steel
Sights: interchangeable front sight, adjustable rear sight
Weight: 35.3 oz.
Caliber: .357 Magnum, .38 S&W Special
Capacity: 8 rounds
Features: precision barrel forcing cone, optimum barrel and cylinder gap; ball and detent cylinder lockup and chamfered charge holes; wide range of options for mounting optics, lights, laser aiming devices and other tactical equipment
MSRP: **$1414**

MODEL 329 PD

Action: double-action revolver
Grips: wood
Barrel: 4 in.
Sights: adjustable fiber optic
Weight: 27.0 oz.
Caliber: .44 Mag.
Capacity: 6 rounds
Features: scandium frame, titanium cylinder
MSRP: **$1264**

MODEL 340

Action: double-action revolver
Grips: rubber
Barrel: 1.8 in.
Sights: fixed open
Weight: 12.0 oz.
Caliber: .357 Mag.
Capacity: 5 rounds
Features: Scandium alloy frame, titanium cylinder
MSRP: **$1122**

MODEL 360

Action: double-action revolver
Grips: rubber
Barrel: 1.8 in.
Sights: fixed open
Weight: 12.0 oz.
Caliber: .357 Mag.
Capacity: 5 rounds
Features: Scandium alloy frame, titanium cylinder
Discontinued

MODEL 386

Action: double-action revolver
Grips: rubber
Barrel: 3.2 in.
Sights: low-profile combat
Weight: 18.5 oz.
Caliber: .357 Mag.
Capacity: 7 rounds
Features: scandium alloy frame; titanium cylinder
Model 386: **$1074**

Smith & Wesson Handguns

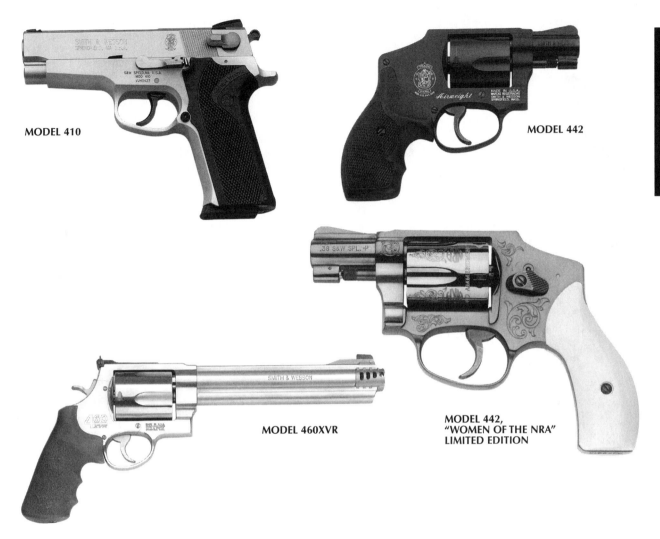

MODEL 410

MODEL 442

MODEL 460XVR

MODEL 442,
"WOMEN OF THE NRA"
LIMITED EDITION

MODELS 410, 457 & 910

Action: autoloader
Grips: rubber
Barrel: 4 in.
Sights: 3 dot
Weight: 28.5 oz.
Caliber: 9mm, .40 S&W
Capacity: 10 + 1 rounds
Features: alloy frame, chrome-moly slide, decocking lever; also M457 in .45 ACP, 7 + 1 rounds capacity; Hi-Viz sights extra
Discontinued

MODEL 442

Action: double-action revolver
Grips: rubber
Barrel: 1.8 in.
Sights: fixed open
Weight: 15.0 oz.
Caliber: .38 Spl.
Capacity: 5 rounds
Features: concealed-hammer, double-action only
Model 442:. **$600**

MODEL 442, "WOMEN OF THE NRA" LIMITED EDITION

Action: hammerless revolver
Grips: synthetic ivory
Barrel: 1-7/8 in.
Sights: front: black blade; rear: fixed
Weight: 15 oz.
Caliber: .38 Spl.
Capacity: 5 rounds
Features: limited edition; aluminum alloy frame with blue finish; machined-engraved NRA logo; inscription on the carbon steel cylinder reads "Original Defender of Freedom 2nd Amendment" and an inscription on the backstrap reads "Women of the NRA"; decorative engraving along the barrel; special serial numbers starting with NRA0001; glass-top, wooden presentation case
MSRP: **$995**

MODEL 460XVR

Action: double-action revolver
Grips: stippled rubber
Barrel: 8.375 in., stainless
Sights: adjustable open
Weight: 72 oz.
Caliber: .460 S&W
Capacity: 5 rounds
Features: ported barrel also fires .454 Casull and .45 Colt
MSRP: **$1446**

Smith & Wesson Handguns

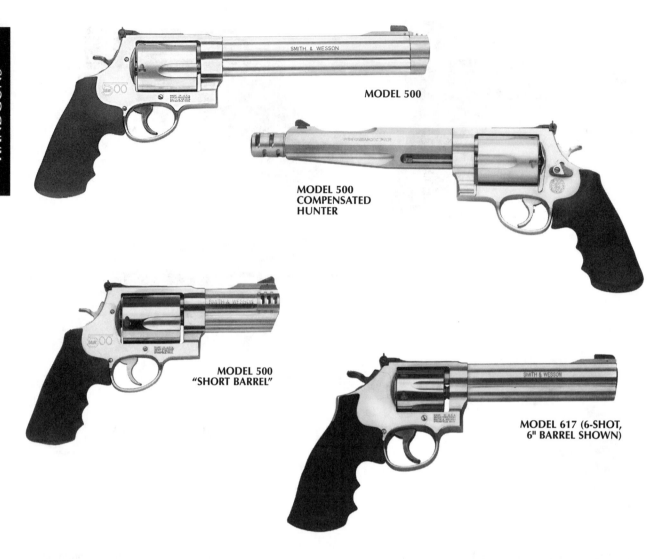

MODEL 500

MODEL 500
COMPENSATED
HUNTER

MODEL 500
"SHORT BARREL"

MODEL 617 (6-SHOT,
6" BARREL SHOWN)

MODEL 500

Action: double-action revolver
Grips: Hogue Sorbathane
Barrel: ported 8.4 in.
Sights: target
Weight: 72.5 oz.
Caliber: .500 S&W
Capacity: 5 rounds
Features: X-Frame, double-action stainless revolver
Model 500:. **$300**
Model 460:. . . . . **Discontinued**

MODEL 500
COMPENSATED HUNTER

Action: revolver
Grips: synthetic Hogue Dual Density Monogrips
Barrel: 7.5 in.
Sights: front: orange ramp dovetail;

rear: adjustable black blade
Weight: 71 oz.
Caliber: .500
Capacity: 5 rounds
Features: stainless-steel frame and cylinder; 360-degree muzzle compensator; two-piece barrel with button rifling and removable scope mount; precision-crowned muzzle; flashed-chromed forged hammer and trigger; ball and detent cylinder lock up; solid ejector rod
MSRP: **$1375**

MODEL 500
"SHORT BARREL"

Action: double-action revolver
Grips: rubber
Barrel: 4 in., sleeved, with brake
Sights: adjustable rear, red ramp front
Weight: 56 oz.

Caliber: .500 S&W
Capacity: 5
Features: double-action; Hogue grip; comes with 2 mukkle compensators
MSRP: **$1446**

MODEL 617

Action: double-action revolver
Grips: Hogue rubber
Barrel: 4.0, 6.0, 8.4 in.
Sights: target
Weight: 42.0 oz.
Caliber: .22 LR
Capacity: 6 rounds
Features: stainless; target hammer and trigger; K-frame; weight to 54 oz. depending on barrel length
4 in.: **$916**
6 in.: **$916**
6 in., 10-shot:. **$916**

Smith & Wesson Handguns

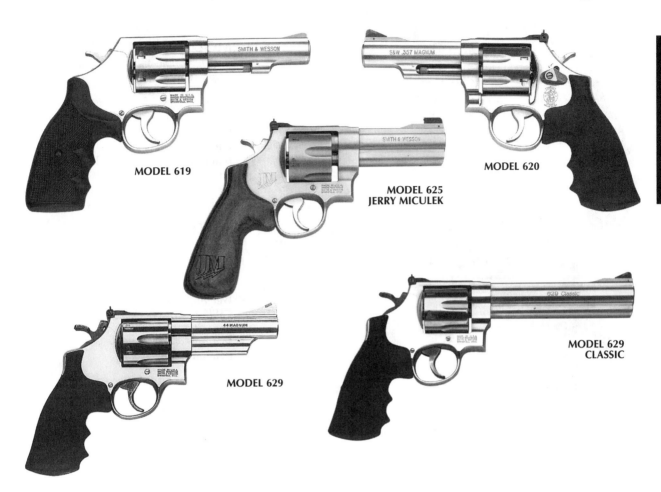

MODEL 619

MODEL 620

MODEL 625
JERRY MICULEK

MODEL 629

MODEL 629
CLASSIC

MODELS 619 AND 620

Action: double-action revolver
Grips: checkered rubber
Barrel: 4 in.
Sights: adjustable open (M620) and fixed (M619)
Weight: 38 oz.
Caliber: .357 Mag.
Capacity: 7 rounds
Features: stainless; semi-lug barrel
Model 619:. **$711**
Model 620:. **$893**

MODEL 625

Action: double-action revolver
Grips: Hogue rubber, round butt
Barrel: 4 or 5 in.
Sights: target
Weight: 49.0 oz.
Caliber: .45 ACP
Capacity: 6 rounds
Features: N-frame, stainless; also in Model 610 10mm with 4 in. barrel; 5 in. barrel 51 oz.
Model 625:. **$1074**

MODEL 625 JERRY MICULEK PROFESSIONAL SERIES REVOLVER

Action: double-action revolver
Grips: wood
Barrel: 4 in.
Sights: adjustable open, removable front bead
Weight: 43 oz.
Caliber: .45 ACP
Capacity: 6 rounds
Features: wide trigger; smooth wood grip; gold bead front sight on a removable blade; comes with five full-moon clips for fast loading
MSRP: **$1074**

MODEL 629

Action: double-action revolver
Grips: Hogue rubber
Barrel: 4 or 6 in.
Sights: target
Weight: 44.0 oz.
Caliber: .44 Mag.
Capacity: 6 rounds
Features: N-frame, stainless; 6 in. weighs 47 oz.
4 in.: **$1035**
6 in.: **$1035**

MODEL 629 CLASSIC

Action: double-action revolver
Grips: Hogue rubber
Barrel: 5, 6.5 or 8.4 in.
Sights: target
Weight: 51.0 oz.
Caliber: .44 Mag.
Capacity: 6 rounds
Features: N-frame, stainless, full lug; weight to 54 oz. depending on barrel length
MSRP: **$1082**

Smith & Wesson Handguns

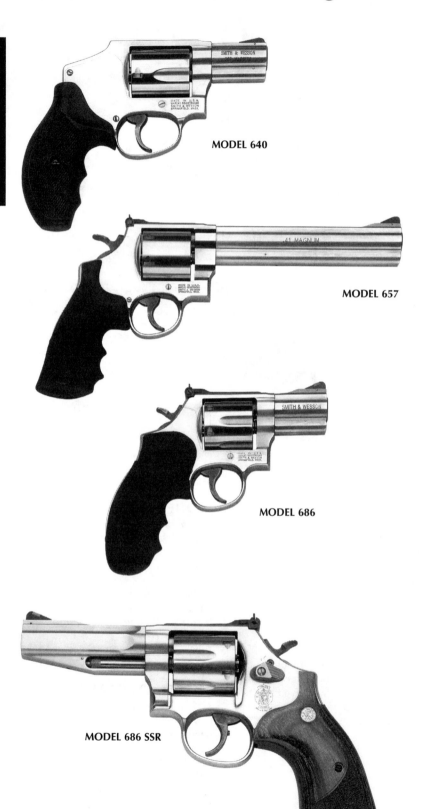

MODEL 640

MODEL 657

MODEL 686

MODEL 686 SSR

MODEL 640 CENTENNIAL

Action: double-action revolver
Grips: rubber
Barrel: 2.2 in.
Sights: fixed open
Weight: 23.0 oz.
Caliber: .357
Capacity: 5 rounds
Features: stainless; concealed-hammer; double-action-only; also M649 Bodyguard single- or double-action
MSRP: **$798**

MODEL 657

Action: double-action revolver
Grips: Hogue rubber
Barrel: 7.5 in.
Sights: target
Weight: 52.0 oz.
Caliber: .41 Mag.
Capacity: 6 rounds
Features: N-frame stainless
Discontinued

MODEL 686

Action: double-action revolver
Grips: combat or target
Barrel: 2.5, 4, 6 in.
Sights: target
Weight: 34.5 oz.
Caliber: .357 Mag.
Capacity: 6 rounds
Features: stainless; K-frame 686 Plus holds 7 rounds; to 48 oz. depending on barrel length
MSRP.:. **$909**

MODEL 686 SSR

Action: double-action revolver
Grips: wood laminate
Barrel: 4 in.
Sights: front: interchangeable; rear: micro adjustable
Weight: 38.3 oz.
Caliber: 357 MAG, .38+P
Capacity: 6 rounds
Features: stainless-steel frame and cylinder; satin stainless finish; forged hammer and trigger; chamfered charge holes; bossed mainsprings; "SSR" inscription on butt
MSRP: **$1059**

Smith & Wesson Handguns

MODEL 945

MODEL 3913 LADYSMITH

MODEL 3913TSW

MODEL 4013TSW

MODEL 945

Action: autoloader
Grips: Hogue black/silver checkered laminate
Barrel: 5 in.
Sights: front: dovetail black blade; rear: adjustable Wilson Combat
Weight: 40.5 oz.
Caliber: .45 ACP
Capacity: 8 + 1 rounds
Features: stainless-steel frame and slide; hand-polished and fitted spherical barrel bushing and feed ramp; competition-grade serrated hammer and match trigger with overtravel stop; 3.5 to 4-pound trigger pull; ambidextrous frame-mounted thumb safety; beveled magazine; aluminum carry case
MSRP: **$2338**

MODEL 3913 LADYSMITH

Action: autoloader
Grips: Hogue rubber
Barrel: 3.5 in.
Sights: low-profile combat
Weight: 24.8 oz.
Caliber: 9mm
Capacity: 8 + 1 rounds
Features: double-action; stainless
MSRP: **$909**

MODEL 3913TSW (TACTICAL SERIES)

Action: autoloader
Grips: rubber
Barrel: 3.5 in.
Sights: 3 dot
Weight: 24.8 oz.
Caliber: 9mm
Capacity: 8 + 1 rounds
Features: alloy frame, stainless slide; also: 3953TSW double-action-only
MSRP: **$924**

MODEL 4013TSW

Action: autoloader
Grips: rubber
Barrel: 3.5 in.
Sights: 3 dot
Weight: 26.8 oz.
Caliber: .40 S&W
Capacity: 9 + 1 rounds
Features: alloy frame; stainless slide; ambidextrous safety; also: 4053TSW double-action only
Discontinued

Smith & Wesson Handguns

CS 9

CS 45

M&P 9MM

M&P9 COMPACT

MODEL CS9 AND CS45 (CHIEF'S SPECIAL)

Action: autoloader
Grips: rubber
Barrel: 3 or 3.25 in.
Sights: 3 dot
Weight: 20.8-24.0 oz.
Caliber: 9mm, .45 ACP
Capacity: 7 + 1 rounds (9mm) and 6 + 1 (.40 S&W)
Features: lightweight; compact
CS 9: **$782**
CS 45: **$830**

MODELS M&P 9MM, M&P .40 AND M&P .357 SIG

Action: autoloader
Barrel: 4.25 in.
Sights: fixed open
Weight: 24 oz. (empty)
Caliber: 9mm, .40, .357 SIG
Capacity: 17 + 1 rounds (9mm),15 + 1 rounds (.40 and.357 SIG)
Features: part of the Smith & Wesson Military & Police Pistol Series; Zytel polymer frame reinforced with a ridged steel chassis; thru-hardened black melonite stainless steel barrel and slide; dovetail-mount steel ramp front sight; steel Novak Lo-mount carry rear sight; optional Tritium sights
MSRP: **$719**

M&P9 COMPACT

Action: autoloader
Grips: 3 interchangeable grip sizes
Barrel: 3.5 in.
Sights: front: steel dovetail mount; rear: steel Novak Lo-Mount carry (Tritium sights available)
Weight: 21.7 oz.
Caliber: 9mm
Capacity: 10+1 or 12+1 rounds
Features: Zytel polymer frame reinforced with a rigid stainless steel chassis and through-hardened black Melonite finished stainless steel barrel and slide; passive trigger safety; sear lever release; loaded chamber indicator on top of the slide; internal lock system; ambidextrous slide stop; reversible magazine release; enlarged trigger guard
MSRP: **$719**

Smith & Wesson Handguns

M&P45 FULL SIZE

M&PR8

MODEL SW9 VE

MODEL 99OL .40

M&P45 FULL SIZE

Action: autoloader
Grips: 3 interchangeable grip sizes
Barrel: 4.5 in.
Sights: front: steel dovetail mount; rear: steel Novak Lo-Mount carry (Tritium sights available)
Weight: 29.6 oz.
Caliber: .45ACP
Capacity: 10+1 or optional 14+1 rounds
Features: Zytel polymer frame reinforced with a rigid stainless steel chassis and through-hardened black Melonite finished stainless steel barrel and slide; offered with a traditional black frame or bi-tone, dark earth brown frame; frame-mounted thumb safety on the bi-tone model; universal Picatinny-style equipment rail for tactical lights and lasers; passive trigger safety; sear lever release; loaded chamber indicator on top of the slide; internallock system; ambidextrous slide stop; reversible magazine release; enlarged trigger guard
MSRP: **$719**

M&PR8

Action: revolver
Grips: rubber
Barrel: 5 in. 2-piece
Sights: front: Interchangeable Partridge White Dot; rear: adjustable V-notch
Weight: 36.3 oz.
Caliber: 357MAG, .38+P
Capacity: 8 rounds
Features: integral accessory Picatinny style rail for lights or lasers; removable Picatinny-style mount for optics; crisp single action; smooth double action with wolff mainspring and traditional sear; polished button polygonal rifling; precision barrel forcing cone; optimum barrel cylinder gap; 2 full moon clips; chamfered charge holes; ball detent lock-up; aluminum gun case
MSRP: **$1414**

MODEL SW9 VE

Action: autoloader
Grips: polymer
Barrel: 4 in.
Sights: 3 dot
Weight: 24.7 oz.
Caliber: 9mm
Capacity: 10 + 1 rounds
Features: double-action; stainless slide; polymer frame; finish options
SW9 VE: **$482**

MODEL SW990L

Action: autoloader
Grips: polymer
Barrel: 3.5, 4 or 5 in.
Sights: low-profile combat
Weight: 22.5-25.0 oz.
Caliber: .40 S&W, 9mm
Capacity: 8-16 rounds
Features: double-action pistol made in collaboration with Walther
MSRP: **$751**

Smith & Wesson Handguns

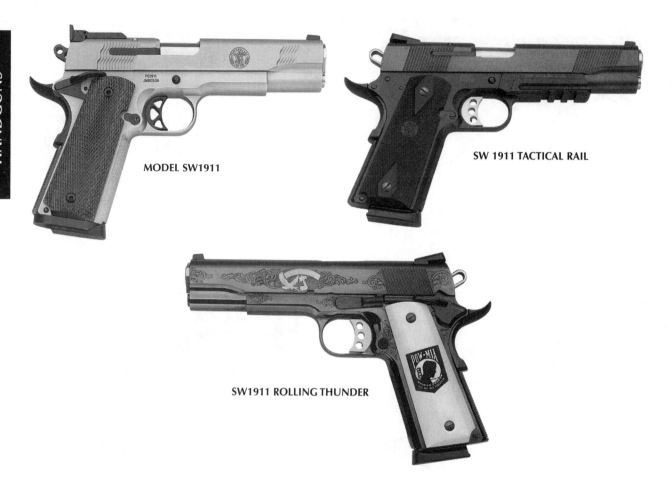

MODEL SW1911

SW 1911 TACTICAL RAIL

SW1911 ROLLING THUNDER

MODEL SW1911

Action: autoloader
Grips: checkered composite, checkered wood
Barrel: 5 in. (4 in. for Model 945)
Sights: adjustable open
Weight: 28-41 oz.
Caliber: .45 ACP (.38 Super in SW1911DK)
Capacity: 8+1 rounds (10 in SW1911DK)
Features: single-action; extended beavertail; match trigger
MSRP: **$1130–2599**

MODELS SW1911PD AND SW1911 TACTICAL RAIL SERIES

Action: autoloader
Barrel: 5 in.
Sights: fixed open
Weight: 32 oz. (1911PD), 39 oz. (1911)
Caliber: .45 ACP
Capacity: 8 + 1 rounds
Features: Model SW1911 stainless steel slide w/ melonite finish; black anodized Scandium Alloy frame; non-reflective matte gray finish; white dot front sight and Novak Lo Mount Carry rear sight; Picatinny-style rail with standard 1911 configuration
1911PD: **$1057-1120**

MODEL SW1911, ROLLING THUNDER COMMEMORATIVE

With the SW1011 Rolling Thunder Commemorative, Smith & Wesson, in conjunction with Rolling Thunder Inc., commemorates the lives of America's men and women who have become prisoners of war or are missing in action.
Action: autoloader
Grips: ivory (imitation)
Barrel: 5 in.
Sights: fixed open
Weight: 38.5 oz.
Caliber: .45 ACP
Capacity: 8 + 1 Rounds
Features: limited edition Model SW1911; machine engraving on frame with 24kt gold plated Rolling Thunder logo; white dot front sight, Novak Lo Mount Carry rear; glass top presentation case; special serial range starting with RTS0001; imitation ivory grips
Discontinued

Springfield Armory Handguns

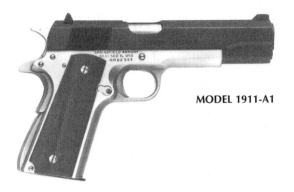

MODEL 1911-A1

MODEL 1911-A1
CHAMPION

1911-A1
ULTRA-COMPACT

1911-A1
MICRO
COMPACT

1911-A1

Action: autoloader
Grips: cocobolo
Barrel: 5 in.
Sights: fixed or adjustable
Weight: 38.0 oz.
Caliber: 9mm, .45 ACP
Capacity: 7 + 1 rounds
Features: steel or lightweight aluminum frames; stainless, blued and parkerized finishes; V-12 barrel porting; fixed combat or fully adjustable rear sights

Black stainless: **$1219**
Stainless: **$979**
Parkerized: . . . . **Discontinued**
Black Stainless: . . . . . **Discontinued**
Bo Mar Rear: . . . . **Discontinued**
9MM Service: . . . . . . **Discontinued**
Lightweight: . . . . **Discontinued**
Bi Tone: . . . . **Discontinued**
MC Operation: . . . . . **Discontinued**
(42 oz.): . . . . **Discontinued**

MODEL 1911 A-1 CHAMPION

Action: autoloader
Grips: walnut
Barrel: 4 in.
Sights: fixed open
Weight: 28.0, 34.0 oz.
Caliber: .45 ACP
Capacity: 7 + 1 rounds
Features: fully supported ramped bull barrel; Novak sights; stainless Bi-Tone finish option
Discontinued

1911-A1 COMPACT MODELS

Action: autoloader
Grips: plastic or cocobolo
Barrel: 3 (Micro-Compact) or 3.5 in.
Sights: Fixed, open
Weight: 32.0 oz.
Caliber: .45 ACP
Capacity: 6+1 rounds
Features: forged aluminum anodized alloy frame; forged steel slide; ambidextrous thumb safety
Ultra-Compact: **$1031**
Micro-Compact: **$1323**

1911-A1 LONG SLIDE

Action: autoloader
Grips: walnut
Barrel: 6 in.
Sights: target
Weight: 41.0 oz.
Caliber: .45 ACP
Capacity: 7 + 1 rounds
Features: slide is 1 in. longer than full-size 1911-A1
Discontinued

Springfield Armory Handguns

**MODEL 1911-A1
TROPHY MATCH**

MODEL XD SERVICE

**XD SUB-COMPACT
W/LIGHT**

1911-A1 MIL-SPEC

Action: autoloader
Grips: plastic   *Barrel*: 5 in.
Sights: fixed open
Weight: 35.6-39.0 oz.
Caliber: .38 Super, .45 ACP
Capacity: 7 + 1 rounds
Features: traditional M1911 A-1
Parkerized: **$737**
Stainless Steel:. **$809**
.38 Super: **$682**

MODEL 1911 A-1 TROPHY MATCH

Action: autoloader
Grips: cocobolo
Barrel: 5 in.   *Sights*: target
Weight: 38.0 oz.
Caliber: .45 ACP
Capacity: 7 + 1 rounds
Features: match barrel and bushing;
Videcki speed trigger; serrated front
strap; stainless
MSRP: **$1573**

MODEL XD SERVICE

Action: autoloader   *Grips*: walnut
Barrel: 4 or 5 in.   *Sights*: fixed open
Weight: 22.8-27.0 oz.
Caliber: 9mm, .357 Sig, .40 S&W,
.45 GAP
Capacity: 10 + 1 rounds
Features: single-action; short recoil;
black or OD green
XD: **$536**
W/ Tritium sights: **$633**
V-10 Ported:. **$573**
XD Tactical (5 in. bl.): **$588–666**
Bi-Tone (.45 GAP only): **$605**
Trijicon Sights:. **$683–725**
W/ Tritium Sights: **$633**

MODEL XD SUB COMPACTS

Action: autoloader
Grips: black composite
Barrel: 3.1 in.   *Sights*: fixed, open
Weight: 20.5 oz.
Caliber: 9mm, .357 SIG, .40, .45 GAP
Capacity: 10+1 rounds
Features: cold hammer forged barrel;
polymer frame with heat-treated steel
slide and rails; short-recoil, locked-
breech action; dual recoil springs;
three safeties; cocking indicator; light
rail (Mini Light optional); 3-dot sights;
black or OD green finish
MSRP: **$543–605**

STI International Inc. Handguns

EAGLE

EDGE

EXECUTIVE

LSA LAWMAN

LS

EAGLE

Action: autoloader
Grips: polymer   **Barrel**: 5 or 6 in.
Sights: target (5 in.), open fixed (6 in.)
Weight: 34.5oz. (5 in.), 40 oz. (6 in.)
Caliber: 9mm, 9X21, .38 Super, .40 S&W, .45 ACP
Capacity: 10+1 rounds
Features: modular steel frame; classic slide; long curved trigger; fully supported, ramped bull barrel; stainless STI grip and ambidextrous thumb safeties; blue finish
Eagle (5 in.): **$1940**
Eagle (6 in.): **$2050**

EDGE

Action: autoloader
Grips: polymer   **Sights**: target
Weight: 39 oz.
Caliber: 9mm, .40 S&W, 10mm, .45 ACP
Capacity: 6+1 rounds
Features: modular steel; long wide frame; overall length 8⅝ in.; fully supported, ramped bull barrel; long curved trigger; stainless STI grip and ambidextrous thumb safeties; blue finish
MSRP: **$1994**

EXECUTIVE

Action: autoloader
Grips: polymer
Barrel: 5 in.
Sights: target
Weight: 39 oz.
Caliber: .40 S&W
Capacity: 10+1 rounds
Features: modular steel; long wide frame; overall length 8⅝ in.; fully supported, ramped bull barrel; long curved trigger; stainless STI grip and ambidextrous thumb safeties
MSRP: **$2464**

LAWMAN

Action: autoloader
Grips: rosewood
Barrel: 5 in.
Sights: fixed open
Weight: 40 oz.
Caliber: .45 ACP
Capacity: 6+1 rounds
Features: forged steel government-length frame; overall length 8½ in.; 1911 style slide; fully supported, ramped barrel with match bushing; STI aluminum trigger; STI grip and single sided thumb STI high rise beavertail

safeties; two tone polymer finish (light brown over olive drab)
MSRP: **$1420**

LS

Action: autoloader
Grips: rosewood
Barrel: 3.4 in.
Sights: fixed open
Weight: 28 oz.
Caliber: 9mm, .40 S&W
Capacity: 7+1 rounds (9mm), 6+1 rounds (.40 S&W)
Features: Government size steel frame with full size grip; fully supported, ramped bull barrel; undercut trigger guard and front strap; long curved trigger; STI grip and single-sided thumb safeties; integral front sight with Heinie low-mount rear sight; flat blue finish; slide does not lock back after last round is fired
MSRP: **$899**

STI International Inc. Handguns

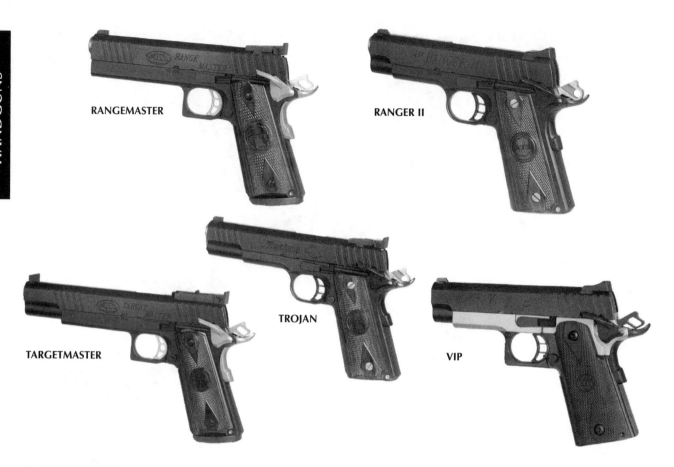

RANGEMASTER

RANGER II

TARGETMASTER

TROJAN

VIP

RANGEMASTER

Action: autoloader
Grips: rosewood
Barrel: 5 in. *Sights*: target
Weight: 38 oz.
Caliber: 9mm, .45 ACP
Features: single stack government
length steel frame; flat top slide; full
length dust cover; fully supported,
ramped bull barrel; aluminum long
curved trigger; polished stainless grip
and ambidextrous thumb safeties; overall length 8.5 in.; polished blue finish
MSRP: **$1521**

RANGER II

Action: autoloader
Grips: rosewood
Barrel: 4.15 in. *Sights*: fixed open
Weight: 30 oz.
Caliber: .45 ACP
Capacity: 7+1 rounds
Features: commander size with full
length 1911-style frame and fully sup-
ported barrel; hi-rise trigger guard;
1911-style flat topped slide; long
curved trigger with stainless bow;

hi-rise grip and single sided thumb
safeties; blue finish
MSRP: **$1110**

TARGETMASTER

Action: autoloader
Grips: rosewood
Barrel: 6 in.
Sights: target
Weight: 40 oz.
Caliber: 9mm, .45 ACP
Features: single stack government
length frame; classic flat top slide;
fully supported ramped match bull
barrel; overall length 9½ in.; tri-level
adjustable sights; aluminum long
curved trigger; STI stainless grip and
ambidextrous thumb safeties; polished
blue finish
MSRP: **$1695**

TROJAN

Action: autoloader
Grips: rosewood
Barrel: 5 or 6 in.
Sights: target
Weight: 36 oz. (5 in.); 38 oz. (6 in.)

Caliber: 9mm, .38 Super, .40 S&W,
.45 ACP
Features: single stack government size
frame; 5 in. or 6 in. classic flat top
slide; fully supported match barrel;
high rise grip safety, STI long curved
polymer trigger and undercut trigger
guard; flat blue finish
Trojan (5 in.): **$1110**
Trojan (6 in.): **$1420**

VIP

Action: Autoloader (SA)
Grips: polymer
Barrel: 3.9 in.
Sights: fixed open
Weight: 25 oz.
Caliber: 9mm, .38 Super, 9X21, .40
S&W,.45 ACP
Capacity: 10 + 1 rounds
Features: modular aluminum frame;
overall length 7½ in.; classic flat top
slide; fully supported, ramped bull
barrel; STI long curved trigger; STI
stainless grip and single-sided thumb
safeties
MSRP: **$1646**

Stoeger Handguns

COUGAR 8000

Action: double/single
Grips: black plastic
Barrel: 3.6 in.
Sights: fixed
Weight: 32.6 oz.
Caliber: 9mm Parabellum, .40 S&W
Capacity: 15 rounds (9mm),
11 rounds (.40 S&W)
Features: cold hammer-forged barrel;
rotary lock action; chrome-lined bore;
ambidextrous safety; combat-style trigger
guard; fixed 3-Dot dovetail rear and
removable blade front sights;
matte black finish
MSRP: **$469**

COUGAR 8000

Swiss Arms Handguns

MODEL P210 SPORT

Action: autoloader
Grips: wood
Barrel: 4.8 in.
Sights: target
Weight: 24.0 oz.
Caliber: 9mm
Capacity: 8 + 1 rounds
Features: chrome-moly, single-action
Swiss Army: . . . . **Discontinued**
Target Grade: . . . . **Discontinued**
P210 . . . . **$1680**

P210 SPORT

*One of the most fantastic firearms ever created is a work-
ing, scaled-up copy of a Remington 1859 revolver built by
Ryszard Tobys of Czempin, Poland. Listed by the Guinness
Book of World Records as the world's largest revolver, this
99.2-pound, 4-foot-long gun holds six bullets, each weighing more than a quarter of a pound. In 2002, the gigantic
revolver was used in a shooting competition between
NATO Reserve Forces from Great Britain, Denmark, the
Czech Republic, Germany and Poland. The Czechs won.*

Taurus Handguns

MODEL 24/7

24/7 OSS

MODEL 44

MODEL 82

MODEL 24/7

Action: autoloader
Grips: polymer with rubber overlay
Barrel: 6 in.
Sights: 3 dot
Weight: 32.0 oz.
Caliber: .40 S&W
Capacity: 15 rounds
Features: double-action; reversible magazine release; Picatinny rail
MSRP: **$475**

24/7 OSS

Action: autoloader
Grips: checkered polymer
Barrel: 5.25 in.
Sights: Heinie 1-dot (front), Heinie Straight Eight (rear)
Weight: 31.4-32.5 oz.
Caliber: .45ACP, .40 S&W, 9mm
Capacity: 12 + 1, 15 + 1 or 17 +1 rounds
Features: Single Action/Double Action trigger system; checkered grip; combat-necessary ambidextrous decock/safety

levers that allow for "cocked and locked" and/or double-action carry; an SA/DA indicator on the rear of the slide that shows whether the pistol is in cocked or decocked mode; reversible magazine release; 18.5-lb. recoil spring that cycles the slide faster; stainless-steel guide rod adds just the right amount of front-end weight for improved recoil control and rapid fire accuracy
MSRP: **$686**

MODEL 44

Action: double-action revolver
Grips: rubber
Barrel: 4, 6.5 or 8.4 in.
Sights: target
Weight: 44.0 oz.
Caliber: .44 Mag.
Capacity: 6 rounds
Features: vent rib, porting; weight to 57 oz. depending on barrel length
Stainless, 4 in.: **$674**
Stainless, 6.5 in.: **$674**
Stainless, 8.4 in.: **$674**

MODEL 82

Action: double-action revolver
Grips: rubber
Barrel: 4 in.
Sights: fixed open
Weight: 36.5 oz.
Caliber: .38 Spl. +P
Capacity: 6 rounds
Features: also, 21-ounce model 85 in .38 Spl, with 2 in. barrel, grip options
Model 82, blue: **$482**
Model 82, stainless: **$472**
Model 85, blue: **$433**
Model 85, stainless: **$480**

1911

Action: autoloader
Grips: checkered black
Barrel: 5 in.
Sights: Heinie "Straight Eight" 2-dot
Weight: 32-38 oz.
Caliber: .45 ACP
Capacity: 8 + 1 rounds
Features: forged frame, slide and barrel; ambidextrous safety; skeletonized trigger; target hammer; serrated slide; checkered trigger guard; mainspring housing and front strap; polished feed ramp; lowered and flared ejection port; custom internal extractor; beavertail grip safety with memory pad; extended magazine release; two 8-round magazines with bumper pads; finishes and variations include matte blue steel, matte blue steel with integral accessory rail, two-tone matte/high polished blue steel, stainless steel, stainless steel with rail and an Ultra-Lite model with forged alloy frame
MSRP: **$757–905**

1911

JUDGE .45/.410

Action: double-action revolver
Grips: ergonomic Ribber Grips
Barrel: 3.0 or 6.5 in.
Sights: fixed rear, fiber optic front
Caliber: 410 bore, 2.5-in., .45 Colt,
Capacity: 5 rounds
Features: capable of chambering both .410 bore shotgun shells and .45 Colt ammunition; Taurus Security System allows users to securely lock the gun using an inconspicuous key-lock system; several models and variations, including blue, blue steel, stainless steel and titanium
MSRP: **$556–652**

JUDGE .45/.410

PROTECTOR

Action: double-action revolver
Grips: rubber
Barrel: 2 in.
Sights: fixed open
Weight: 24.5 oz.
Caliber: .357 Mag. or .38 Spl.
Capacity: 5 rounds
Features: shrouded but accessible hammer; also Titanium and UltraLight versions to 17 oz.
Blue: **$433**
Stainless: **$480**
Shadow Gray Titanium: **$650**

Ed McGivern of Montana was one of the most incredible handgun shooters who ever lived. At South Dakota's Lead Club Range on August 20, 1932, he shot a .45-caliber revolver five times from 15 feet into an area with a diameter of 1.1875 inches. He accomplished this in 45/100s of a second and did it twice that same day.

Taurus Handguns

MODEL 92

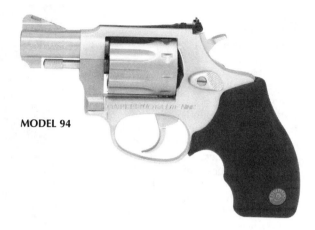

MODEL 94

MODEL 444
ULTRALITE

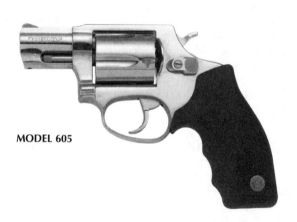

MODEL 605

MODEL 92

Action: autoloader
Grips: rosewood or rubber
Barrel: 5 in.
Sights: fixed open   **Weight**: 34.0 oz.
Caliber: 9mm
Capacity: 10 + 1 rounds or 17 + 1
Features: double-action; also PT99
with adjustable sights
Blue: **$571**
Stainless: **$589**
Stainless gold,
   Mother of Pearl: **$663**

MODEL 94/941

Action: double-action revolver
Grips: hardwood
Barrel: 2, 4 or 5 in.
Sights: target
Weight: 18.5-27.5 oz.
Caliber: .22 LR, .22 Mag.
Capacity: 8-9 rounds
Features: small frame, solid rib

Blue: **$389**
Magnum, blue: **$406**
Stainless: **$436**
Magnum, stainless: **$453**
.22 LR, Ultralite: **$441**
.22 Mag., Ultralite: **$472**

MODEL 444 ULTRALITE

Action: double-action revolver
Grips: rubber
Barrel: 4 in.
Sights: adjustable with fiber optic
insert
Weight: 28 oz.
Caliber: .44 Mag.
Capacity: 6 rounds
Features: alloy frame, titanium cylinder
Blued: **$701**
Stainless: **$764**

MODEL 605

Action: double-action revolver
Grips: rubber
Barrel: 2 in.
Sights: fixed open
Weight: 24.5 oz.
Caliber: .357 Mag.
Capacity: 5 rounds
Features: small frame, transfer bar;
porting optional
Model 605: **$424**
Titanium (16 oz.): **$472**
Stainless: **$472**

MODEL 608

Action: double-action revolver
Grips: rubber
Barrel: 4, 6.5 or 8.4 in., ported
Sights: target   **Weight**: 49.0 oz.
Caliber: .357 Mag.
Capacity: 8 rounds
Features: large frame; transfer bar;
weight to 53 oz. depending on barrel
length
Stainless, 4 in.: **$615**
Stainless, 6.5 or 8.4 in.: **$641**

MODEL 905

Action: double-action revolver
Grips: rubber
Barrel: 2 in.   **Sights**: fixed open
Weight: 21.0 oz.
Caliber: 9mm, .40 S&W, .45 ACP 9
with 2, 4 or 6.5 in. barrel
Capacity: 5 rounds
Features: stellar clips furnished;
UltraLite weighs 17 oz.
Blue: **$433**
Stainless: **$480**
.32 Mag.: **$433**

MODEL M17C

Action: double-action revolver
Grips: rubber
Barrel: 2, 4, 5, 6.5 or 12 in.
Sights: target
Weight: 18.5-26.0 oz.
Caliber: .17 HMR
Capacity: 8 rounds
Features: 8 models available in blued
and stainless steel; weight varies with
barrel length
Discontinued

MODEL 22B

Action: autoloader
Grips: rosewood
Barrel: 2.8 in.   **Sights**: fixed open
Weight: 12.3 oz.
Caliber: .22 LR
Capacity: 8 + 1 rounds
Features: double-action only; blue,
nickel or DuoTone finish;
also in .25 ACP (PT25)
Blued: **$262**
With checkered wood: **$262**
With gold trim: **$280**
With Mother of Pearl grips: . . . **$280**

MODEL 608

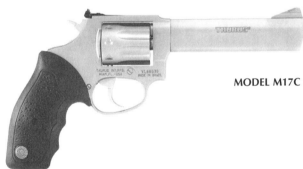

MODEL 905

MODEL M17C

MODEL 22B

Taurus Handguns

MODEL PT945

GAUCHO

MILLENNIUM PRO

MODEL 911B

Action: autoloader
Grips: checkered rubber
Barrel: 4 in.
Sights: 3 dot
Weight: 28.2 oz.
Caliber: 9mm
Capacity: 10 + 1 rounds or 15 + 1
Features: double-action only; ambi-
dextrous decocker
Blued: **$615**
Stainless: **$633**

MODEL 945

Action: autoloader
Grips: checkered rubber, rosewood or
Mother of Pearl
Barrel: 4.3 in.
Sights: 3 dot
Weight: 29.5 oz.
Caliber: .45 ACP, .38 Super
Capacity: 8 + 1 rounds (.38: 10 + 1)
Features: double-action; also PT38 in
.38 Super

Blued: **$658**
Stainless: **$674**
Stainless, gold,
Mother of Pearl: **$743**
Stainless rosewood: **$727**
Model 940 blue: **$615**
Model 940 stainless: **$633**

GAUCHO

Action: single-action revolver
Grips: hard rubber
Barrel: 5.5 in.
Sights: fixed
Weight: 37 oz.
Caliber: .45 Colt
Capacity: 6 rounds
Features: single-action; transfer bar
safety
Blued: **$520**
Stainless or blued with
case-colored frame: **$536**

MILLENNIUM PRO

Action: autoloader
Grips: polymer
Barrel: 3.25 in.   *Sights*: 3 dot
Weight: 18.7 oz.
Caliber: 9mm, .40 S&W, .45 ACP, .32
ACP, .380 ACP
Capacity: 10 + 1 rounds
Features: double-action; polymer
frame; also comes with night sights
(BL or SS), add $78
.40 blue: **$441**
.40 stainless: **$459**
.45 blue/composite: **$441**
.45 stainless/composite: **$459**
9mm, .32 or .380 BL: **$441**
9mm, .32 or .380 SS: **$459**
9mm Titanium: **$623**

**RAGING BULL
.500 S&W**

NINE BY SEVENTEEN

Action: autoloader
Grips: hard rubber
Barrel: 4 in.
Sights: 3 dot
Weight: 26 oz.
Caliber: 9mm
Capacity: 17 rounds
Features: double-action with de-cocker
Blued: **$571**
Stainless: **$589**

RAGING BULL

Action: double-action revolver
Grips: rubber
Barrel: 5, 6.5 or 8.3 in.
Sights: target
Weight: 53.0-63.0 oz.
Caliber: .41 Mag., .44 Mag., .480
Ruger, .454 Casull
Capacity: 6 rounds
Features: stainless vent rib, ported;
also 72 oz. 5 round Raging Bull in
.500 Mag with 10 in. barrel
.41: **$743**
.44 Mag, blue: **$674**
stainless .44 & .480 Ruger: .$674–722
454 Casull, blue: **$923–992**
454 Casull, stainless: **$992**
.500 Mag: . . . . **Discontinued**

**RAGING BULL
454 CASULL**

TRACKER

Action: double-action revolver
Grips: rubber with ribs
Barrel: 4 or 6.5 in.   *Sights:* target
Weight: 24.0-45.0 oz.
Caliber: .22 LR, .41 Mag., .357 Mag.,
.44 Mag., .17 HMR, .500 S&W
Capacity: 5-7 rounds (full-moon clips)
Features: ported barrel on .44 Mag.,
.357 and .41 Mag.; available in
Titanium
.17 HMR: **$477**
.22 LR: **$472**
.357 Mag.: **$600**
.357 Mag. (Shadow Gray): **$688**
.41 Mag., stainless: **$597**
.41 Mag. (Shadow Gray): . . . .
Discontinued
.44 Mag., blue: **$581**
.44 Mag., stainless: **$632**
.500 S&W: **$899**

**TRACKER
TITANIUM**

Thompson/Center Handguns

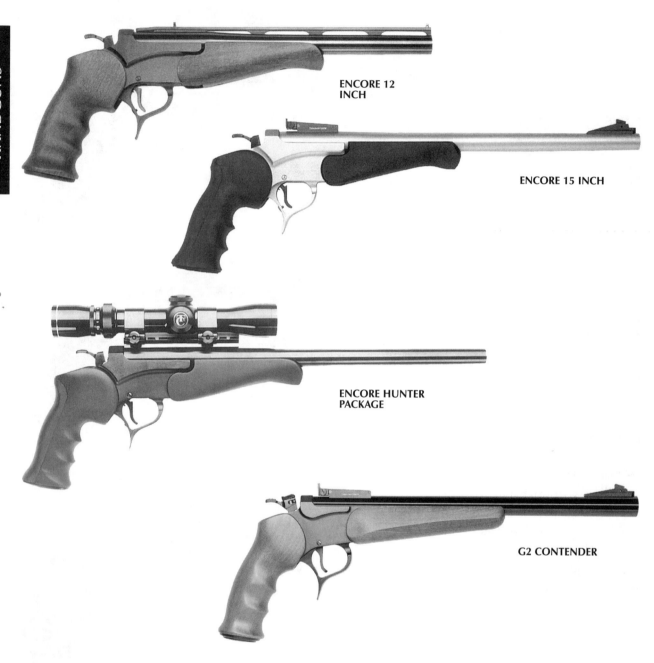

ENCORE 12
INCH

ENCORE 15 INCH

ENCORE HUNTER
PACKAGE

G2 CONTENDER

ENCORE

Action: hinged breech
Grips: walnut or rubber
Barrel: 12 or 15 in.
Sights: target
Weight: 68.0 oz.
Caliber: many popular rifle and big-bore pistol rounds, from the .22 Hornet to the .30-06 and .45-70, the .454 Casull and .480 Ruger
Capacity: 1 round
Features: also in package with 2-7x

scope, carry case; prices vary with caliber, options
12 in.: $753
15 in. (72 oz.): $730
.45/.410 with rib: $730
Stainless with rubber grips: . . . $753

G2 CONTENDER

Action: hinged breech
Grips: walnut
Barrel: 12 or 14 in.
Sights: target

Weight: 60.0 oz.
Caliber: .22 LR, .22 Hornet, .357 Mag., .17 MACH 2, 6.8 Rem SPC, .44 Mag., .45/.410 (12 in.), .17 HMR, .22 LR, .22 Hornet, .223, 7-30, .30-30, .44 Mag., .45/.410, .45-70 (15 in.), .204 Ruger, .375 JDJ
Capacity: 1 round
Features: improved, stronger version of Contender
12 in.: $555–600
14 in. (64 oz.): $555–600

1851 NAVY CONVERSION

Action: single-action revolver
Grips: walnut
Barrel: 4.75, 5.5 and 7.5 in.
Sights: fixed, open
Weight: 41.6 oz.
Caliber: .38 Special
Capacity: 6 rounds
Features: engraved cylinder; frame retro-fitted with loading gate to accommodate cartridges, just like original; fitted with ejector rod for removing casings from cylinder; brass backstrap and trigger guard
MSRP: $519

1851 NAVY
CONVERSION

1860 ARMY CONVERSION

Action: single-action revolver
Grips: walnut
Barrel: 4.75, 5.5 and 8 in.
(.38 Special); 5.5 and 8 in. (.45 Colt)
Sights: fixed, open
Weight: 41.6 oz.
Caliber: .38 Special, .45 Colt
Capacity: 6 rounds
Features: cylinder adapted for center-fire metalic cartridges; frame retro-fitted with loading gate; engraved cylinder; ejector rod; blued steel backstrap and trigger guard
MSRP: $549

1860 ARMY
CONVERSION

1871-1872 OPEN-TOP

Action: single-action revolver
Grips: walnut
Barrel: 4.75, 5.5 and 7.5 in. (1871 Open-Top); 7.5 in. (1872 Open-Top)
Sights: fixed, open
Weight: 41.6 oz.
Caliber: .38, .45 Colt
Capacity: 6 rounds
Features: cylinder adapted for center-fire metalic cartridges; engraved cylinder; 1871 Model with frame and cylinder designed for cartridges, brass backstrap and trigger guard; 1872 Model with blued steel backstrap and trigger guard; both models fitted with ejector rods
1871 Open-Top: $499
1872 Open-Top: $519

1871 OPEN-TOP
(EARLY MODEL)

1872 OPEN-TOP
(LATE MODEL)

Uberti Handguns

HANDGUNS

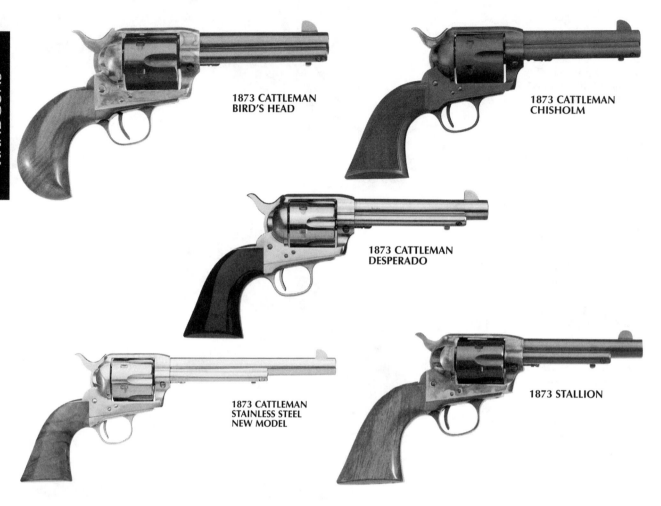

1873 CATTLEMAN BIRD'S HEAD

1873 CATTLEMAN CHISHOLM

1873 CATTLEMAN DESPERADO

1873 CATTLEMAN STAINLESS STEEL NEW MODEL

1873 STALLION

1873 CATTLEMAN BIRD'S HEAD

Action: single-action revolver
Grips: walnut
Barrel: 3.5, 4, 4.5 or 5.5 in.
Sights: fixed, open **Weight**: 36.8 oz.
Caliber: .357 Mag., .45 LC
Capacity: 6 rounds
Features: fluted cylinder; round barrel; forged steel; color case-hardened frame; curved grip frame and grip
MSRP: **$539**

1873 CATTLEMAN CHISHOLM

Action: single-action revolver
Grips: walnut
Barrel: 4.75, 5.75 or 7.5 in.
Sights: fixed, open
Weight: 35 oz.
Caliber: .45 Colt **Capacity**: 6 rounds
Features: 6-shot fluted cylinder; checkered walnut grip; matte blue finish
MSRP: **$539**

1873 CATTLEMAN DESPERADO

Action: single-action revolver
Grips: black horn
Barrel: 4.75, 5.5 or 7.5 in.
Sights: fixed, open
Weight: 35 oz.
Caliber: .45 Colt **Capacity**: 6 rounds
Features: 6-shot fluted cylinder; nickel finish; black bison horn style grips
MSRP: **$789**

1873 SINGLE-ACTION CATTLEMAN

Action: single-action revolver
Grips: walnut
Barrel: 4.75, 5.5, 7.5 or 18 in.
Sights: fixed, open
Weight: 37 oz.
Caliber: .357 Mag., .44-40, .45 Colt
Capacity: 6 rounds
Features: 6-shot fluted cylinder; color case-hardened frame; more than 100 configurations available

1873: **$489**
Nickel finish: **$609**
Old West antique finish: **$629**
Matte black Hombre: **$429**
Charcoal blue: **$579**
Stainless New Model: **$649**
Buntline: **$639**

1873 STALLION

Action: single-action revolver
Grips: walnut
Barrel: 5.5 in.
Sights: fixed, open or target
Weight: 22.3 oz.
Caliber: .22 LR, .38 SP
Capacity: 6 rounds
Features: color case-hardened frame; fluted cylinder, brass or steel backstrap & trigger guard; optional target sights
MSRP: **$429–539**

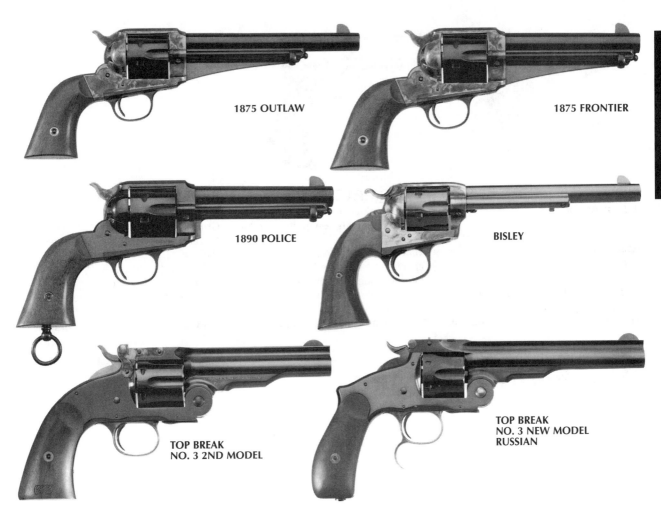

1875 OUTLAW

1875 FRONTIER

1890 POLICE

BISLEY

TOP BREAK
NO. 3 2ND MODEL

TOP BREAK
NO. 3 NEW MODEL
RUSSIAN

1875 OUTLAW & FRONTIER

Action: single-action revolver
Grips: walnut
Barrel: 7.5 in. (5.5 Frontier)
Sights: fixed, open
Weight: 44.8 oz. (40 oz. Frontier)
Caliber: .45 Colt
Capacity: 6 rounds
Features: color case-hardened frame with blued barrel; fluted cylinder
Outlaw: **$539**
Outlaw, Nickel: **$629**
Frontier: **$539**

1890 POLICE REVOLVER

Action: single-action revolver
Grips: walnut
Barrel: 5.5 in.
Sights: fixed, open
Weight: 41.6 oz.
Caliber: .357 Mag., .45 Colt,
Capacity: 6 rounds

Features: fluted cylinder; blued finish; lanyard loop
MSRP: **$549**

BISLEY

Action: single-action revolver
Grips: walnut
Barrel: 4.75, 5.5, 7.5 in.
Sights: fixed, open
Weight: 40.2 oz.
Caliber: .357 Mag., .45 LC
Capacity: 6 rounds
Features: Bisley style grip; color case-hardened frame; fluted cylinder
MSRP: **$569**

TOP BREAK REVOLVERS

Action: single-action revolver
Grips: walnut
Barrel: 3.5, 5, 7 in.
Sights: fixed open
Weight: 36 oz.
Caliber: .38 sp., .44/40, .45 Colt,

Capacity: 6 rounds
Features: top break action; blue finish; fluted cylinder
No. 3 2nd Model: **$999**
No. 3 2nd Model, Nickel, mother of pearl grips: **$1369**

NEW MODEL RUSSIAN REVOLVER

Action: single-action revolver
Grips: walnut
Barrel: 6.5 in.
Sights: fixed, open
Weight: 40 oz.
Caliber: 44 Russian, .45 Colt
Capacity: 6 rounds
Features: improved top latch, 6-shot fluted cylinder; blued frame, barrel and backstrap; color case-hardened trigger guard with spur; lanyard loop
New Model Russian: **$1049**
New Model Russian Nickel, mother of pearl grips: **$1399**

Walther Handguns

P99 COMPACT

PPK/S

P22
Action: autoloader
Grips: polymer
Barrel: 3.4 or 5 in.   **Sights**: 3 dot
Weight: 19.6 oz.
Caliber: .22 LR
Capacity: 10 + 1 rounds
Features: double-action; 20.3 oz. 5 in. barrel
MSRP: $362–456

P99 COMPACT
Action: autoloader   **Grips**: polymer
Barrel: 4 in. **Sights**: low-profile combat
Weight: 25.0 oz.
Caliber: 9mm, .40 S&W
Capacity: 10 + 1 rounds
Features: double-action; ambidextrous magazine release; high-capacity magazines available
P99 Compact: $799

PPK AND PPK/S
Action: autoloader
Grips: polymer
Barrel: 3.4 in.   **Sights**: fixed open
Weight: 22.0 oz.
Caliber: .380 and .32 ACP
Capacity: 7 + 1 rounds
Features: double-action; blue or stainless; decocker
MSRP: $605

Weatherby Handguns

MARK V CFP
Action: bolt
Grips: ambidextrous; Fibermark composite
Barrel: 16 in.
Weight: 84 oz.
Caliber: .223 Rem., .22-250 Rem.,
.243 Win., 7mm-08 Rem.
Capacity: 5 + 1 rounds
Features: Button-rifled, #2 contour, chrome moly (4140 steel) barrel; one-piece forged and fluted bolt; cocking indicator; adjustable trigger
MSRP: $1689

Wildey Handguns

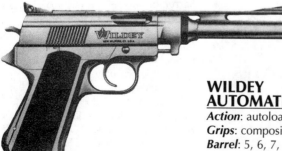

WILDEY AUTOMATIC PISTOL
Action: autoloader
Grips: composite
Barrel: 5, 6, 7, 8, 10, 12 or 14 in.
Sights: target   **Weight**: 64.0 oz.
Caliber: .45 Win. Mag., .44 Auto Mag., .45 and .475 Wildey
Capacity: 7 + 1 rounds
Features: gas operated; ribbed barrel
MSRP: $1571–2149
Silhouette: . . . .**Discontinued**

Cabela's Black Powder

BLUE RIDGE FLINTLOCK RIFLE

TRADITIONAL HAWKEN RIFLE

KODIAK EXPRESS DOUBLE RIFLE

BLUE RIDGE FLINTLOCK RIFLE

Lock: side-hammer caplock
Stock: walnut
Barrel: 39 in., 1:48 twist
Sights: none
Weight: 7.75 lbs. (7.25 lbs., .45, .50, .54 cal.)
Bore/Caliber: .32, .36, .45, .50 and .54
Features: double set triggers; case-colored locks
MSRP: $599

DOUBLE SHOTGUN

Lock: traditional caplock
Stock: walnut
Barrel: 27, 28 or 30 in.
Sights: none
Weight: 7.0 lbs. (6.5 20 ga.)
Bore/Caliber: 20, 12 or 10 ga.
Features: screw-in choke tubes: X-Full, Mod, IC; double triggers; weight to 10 lbs. depending on ga.
MSRP: $750–940

HAWKEN

Lock: traditional cap or flint
Stock: walnut
Barrel: 29 in., 1:48 twist
Sights: adjustable open
Weight: 9.0 lbs.
Bore/Caliber: .50 or .54
Features: brass furniture; double-set trigger
**Traditional percussion
   (right or left-hand)**: $370
**Sporterized percussion
   (28-in. bl.)**: $440

KODIAK EXPRESS DOUBLE RIFLE

Lock: traditional caplock
Stock: walnut, pistol grip
Barrel: 28 in., 1:48 twist
Sights: folding leaf
Weight: 9.3 lbs.
Bore/Caliber: .50, .54, .58 and .72
Features: double triggers
MSRP: $1000–1100

1849 POCKET REVOLVER

Lock: caplock revolver
Grips: walnut
Barrel: 4 in.
Sights: fixed
Weight: 1.5 lbs.
Bore/Caliber: .31
Features: case-colored frame
Discontinued

1851 NAVY

Lock: caplock revolver
Grips: walnut
Barrel: 7.5 in.
Sights: fixed
Weight: 2.5 lbs.
Bore/Caliber: .36
Features: case-colored frame
Discontinued

1860 ARMY

Lock: caplock revolver
Grips: walnut
Barrel: 8 in.
Sights: fixed
Weight: 2.6 lbs.
Bore/Caliber: .44
Features: case-colored frame, hammer, plunger; also with fluted cylinder and adapted for shoulder stock
Discontinued

1861 NAVY

Lock: caplock revolver
Grips: walnut
Barrel: 7.5 in.
Sights: fixed
Weight: 2.6 lbs.
Bore/Caliber: .36
Features: revolver with case-colored frame, hammer, lever, plunger
Discontinued

Use only powders specific to each particular muzzleloader and recommended by that firearms manufacturer. To do otherwise can cause damage to the firearm and may cause serious injury, and even death, to the shooter and/or spectators.

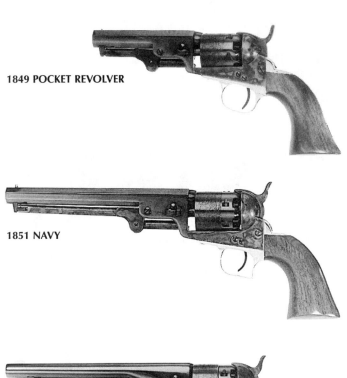

1849 POCKET REVOLVER

1851 NAVY

1860 ARMY

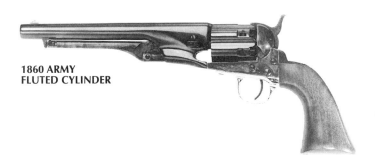

1860 ARMY
FLUTED CYLINDER

1861 NAVY

BLACK POWDER

Colt Black Powder

1861 RIFLE

THIRD MODEL
DRAGOON

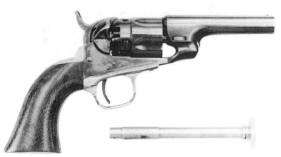

TRAPPER
1862 POCKET POLICE

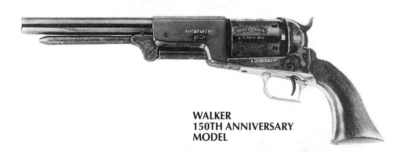

WALKER
150TH ANNIVERSARY
MODEL

1861 RIFLE
Lock: traditional caplock
Stock: walnut
Barrel: 40 in.
Sights: folding leaf
Weight: 9.2 lbs.
Bore/Caliber: .58
Features: authentic reproduction of
1861 Springfield
Discontinued

THIRD MODEL DRAGOON
Lock: caplock revolver
Grips: walnut
Barrel: 7.5 in.
Sights: fixed
Weight: 4.1 lbs.
Bore/Caliber: .44
Features: case-colored frame, hammer,
lever, plunger
Discontinued

TRAPPER 1862 POCKET POLICE
Lock: caplock revolver
Grips: walnut
Barrel: 3.5 in.
Sights: fixed
Weight: 1.25 lbs.
Bore/Caliber: .36
Features: revolver with case-colored
frame; separate brass ramrod
Discontinued

WALKER
Lock: caplock revolver
Grips: walnut
Barrel: 9 in.
Sights: fixed
Weight: 4.6 lbs.
Bore/Caliber: .44
Features: case-colored frame; authen-
tic remake of 1847 Walker
Discontinued

Colt Black Powder

BUCK HORN 209 MAGNUM

ELKHORN 209 MAGNUM

KODIAK 209 MAGNUM

KODIAK PRO 209 MAGNUM

BUCK HORN 209 MAGNUM

Lock: in-line
Stock: synthetic
Barrel: 24 in., 1:28 twist
Sights: fiber optic
Weight: 6.3 lbs.
Bore/Caliber: .50
Features: in-line action; thumb-actuated safety; blued barrel; stainless steel 209 ignition; Illuminator fiber optic sights; solid composite stock with molded-in grip panels and sling swivel studs; drilled and tapped for scope mounts.
Discontinued

ELKHORN 209 MAGNUM

Lock: in-line, bolt-action
Stock: synthetic or camo
Barrel: 26 in. fluted, 1:28 twist
Sights: adjustable fiber optic
Weight: 7.0 lbs.

Bore/Caliber: .45 or .50
Features: 3-way ignition with primer ejecting bolt face; DuraBright fiber optic sights; aluminum loading rod; composite stock in Realtree Camo or Black Fleck
Discontinued

KODIAK 209 MAGNUM

Lock: in-line
Stock: synthetic
Barrel: 28 in.
Sights: fiber optic
Weight: 7.5 lbs.
Bore/Caliber: .50
Features: in-line action; stainless steel 209 breech plug; ambidextrous solid stock in black or Mossy Oak Camo
Discontinued

KODIAK PRO 209 MAGNUM

Lock: pivot block
Stock: composite or laminated
Barrel: 29 in.
Sights: DuraBright fiber optic
Weight: 7.5 lb.
Bore/Caliber: .45, .50
Features: fluted blue or stainless barrel; all metal DuraBright fiber optic sights; thumbhole or standard composite or laminated wood stock in camo or black finish; semi-solid stock comes with a Quake Claw sling and a CrushZone recoil pad
Discontinued

CVA Black Powder

ELECTRA
STAINLESS STEEL, BLACK FIBERGRIP

ELECTRA
STAINLESS STEEL, REALTREE

OPTIMA 209 SYNTHETIC/BLUE

OPTIMA 209 CAMO/BLUE

OPTIMA 209 CAMO/NICKEL

ELECTRA

Lock: in-line
Stock: composite; RealTree HD camo or Black FiberGrip; ambidextrous
Barrel: 26-in. Bergara Barrel, stainless steel or blued steel; 1:28 twist
Sights: DuraSight Fiber Optic
Weight: 7.5 lbs.
Bore/Caliber: .50
Features: world's first electronic ignition muzzleloader; Electronic ARC Ignition (completely sealed from the elements) eliminates the need for 209 primers; when the trigger is pulled, ignition is instantaneous; powered by a 9-volt lithium battery, which will reliably fire the gun up to 500 times; when the system is activated, the gun is ready to fire in approximately 20 seconds; Quake Claw Sling; Crush-Zone recoil pad; DuraSight rail scope mount

Stainless Steel/Realtree HD: . . $519
Stainless Steel/Black FiberGrip: $461
Blued/Black FiberGrip: $404

OPTIMA 209 AND OPTIMA PRO 209

Lock: in-line
Stock: synthetic or camo
Barrel: 26 in. (Pro: 29 in.), 1:28 twist
Sights: adjustable fiber optic
Weight: 8.2 lbs. (Pro: 8.8 lbs.)
Bore/Caliber: .45 or .50
Features: stainless steel 209 breech plug, ambidextrous stock

Optima, synthetic/blue: $230
Camo blue: . . . . Discontinued
Camo/nickel: $323
Optima Pro:. . . . . Discontinued

OPTIMA ELITE 209

OPTIMA ELITE 209 FIBER GRIP

OPTIMA ELITE 209 REALTREE HD

OPTIMA PRO 209 SHOTGUN

OPTIMA ELITE 209 MAGNUM BREAK-ACTION

Lock: in-line
Stock: composite
Barrel: 29 in. blued or stainless fluted
Sights: DuraBright adjustable fiber optic
Weight: 8.8 lb.
Bore/Caliber: .45 and .50
Features: Bergara button rifled barrel with bullet guiding muzzle (Optima Pro and Optima barrels cannot be installed on the Optima Elite frame); stainless 209 breech plug; reversible cocking spur available; extendable loading rod; ambidextrous solid composite stock in standard or thumbhole design in Realtree HD or Black FiberGrip; CrushZone recoil pad; Quake Claw sling
MSRP: **$346**

OPTIMA ELITE COMPACT 209 MAGNUM

Lock: in-line, break-action
Stock: synthetic or camo
Barrel: 24 in., 1:28 twist
Sights: adjustable fiber optic
Weight: 6.0 lbs.
Bore/Caliber: .45 or .50
Features: in-line break-action; available with Bergara muzzleloading barrel; ambidextrous solid composite stock; adjustable fiber optic sights; drilled and tapped for scope mounts
MSRP: **$311**

OPTIMA PRO 209 SHOTGUN

Lock: in-line
Stock: composite
Barrel: 26 in.
Sights: DuraBright fiber optic
Weight: 7.5 lbs.
Choke: screw-in tube
Bore/Caliber: 12
Features: barrel finished in Mossy Oak New Breakup camo or Matte Blue; removable, stainless steel breech plug; closed-breech receiver; extendable aluminum loading rod; includes powder measure and shot cups; ambidextrous deep-grip, solid composite stock in Mossy Oak New Breakup Camo; DuraBright sights and the integral Weaver style rail; screw in extra full choke tube
Discontinued

Dixie Black Powder

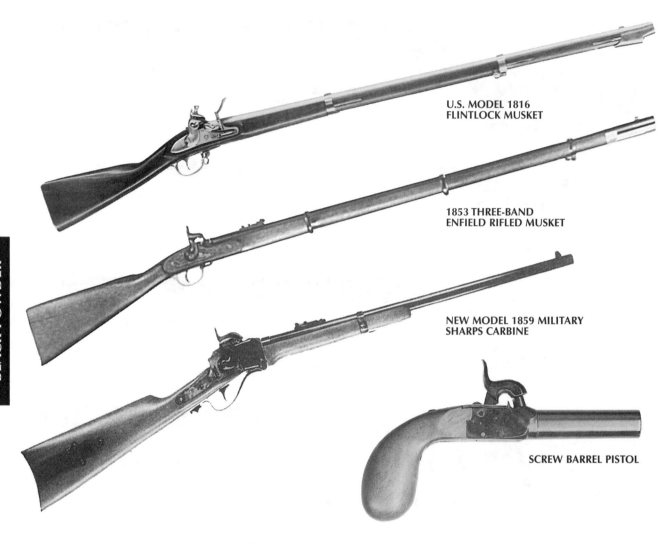

U.S. MODEL 1816
FLINTLOCK MUSKET

1853 THREE-BAND
ENFIELD RIFLED MUSKET

NEW MODEL 1859 MILITARY
SHARPS CARBINE

SCREW BARREL PISTOL

MODEL U.S. 1816 FLINTLOCK MUSKET

Lock: traditional flintlock
Stock: walnut
Barrel: 42 in. smoothbore
Sights: fixed
Weight: 9.8 lbs.
Bore/Caliber: .69
Features: most common military flintlock from U.S. armories, complete with bayonet lug and swivels
MSRP: **$1200**

1853 THREE-BAND ENFIELD

Lock: traditional caplock
Stock: walnut *Barrel*: 39 in.
Sights: fixed
Weight: 10.5 lbs.
Bore/Caliber: .58

Features: case-colored lock, brass furniture; also 1858 two-band Enfield with 33 in. barrel
Three-band: **$715**
Unfinished kit: . . . . . **Discontinued**
Two-band: **$650**

NEW MODEL 1859 MILITARY SHARPS CARBINE

Lock: dropping block
Stock: walnut *Barrel:* 22 in.
Sights: adjustable open
Weight: 7.8 lbs.
Bore/Caliber: .54
Features: case-colored furniture, including saddle ring; also 1859 military rifle with 30 in. barrel (9 lbs.); both by Pedersoli
MSRP: **$925**

SCREW BARREL PISTOL

Lock: traditional caplock
Grips: hardwood
Barrel: 3 in.
Sights: none
Weight: 0.75 lbs.
Bore/Caliber: .445
Features: barrel detaches for loading; folding trigger
MSRP: **$185**

EMF Hartford Black Powder

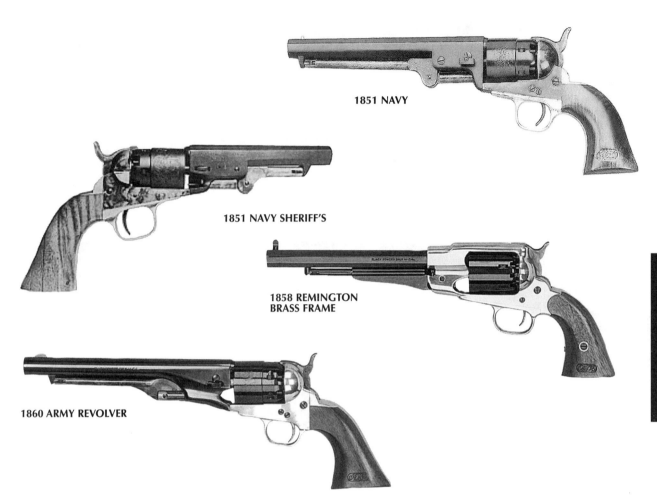

1851 NAVY

1851 NAVY SHERIFF'S

1858 REMINGTON BRASS FRAME

1860 ARMY REVOLVER

1851 NAVY

Lock: caplock revolver
Grips: walnut
Barrel: 7.5 in.
Sights: fixed
Weight: 2.5 lbs.
Bore/Caliber: .36 or .44
Features: octagonal barrel; brass or steel frame
Brass frame:. $200
Case-hardened steel frame:. . . $215

1851 NAVY SHERIFF'S

Lock: caplock revolver
Grips: walnut
Barrel: 5.5 in.
Sights: none
Weight: 2 lbs.
Bore/Caliber: .44
Features: brass guard; strap
MSRP: $215

1858 REMINGTON ARMY REVOLVER

Lock: caplock revolver
Grips: walnut
Barrel: 8 in.
Sights: fixed
Weight: 2.5 lbs.
Bore/Caliber: .44
Features: brass or stainless steel frame
Brass frame:. $210
Blued steel frame: $260
Stainless frame: $390

1860 ARMY REVOLVER

Lock: caplock revolver
Stock: walnut
Barrel: 8 in.
Sights: fixed
Weight: 2.6 lbs.
Bore/Caliber: .44
Features: case-colored frame; brass guard; strap
MSRP: $215

1863 SHARPS MILITARY CARBINE

Lock: dropping block
Stock: walnut
Barrel: 22 in.
Sights: adjustable open
Weight: 7.5 lbs.
Bore/Caliber: .54
Features: blued barrel; case-hardened frame; adjustable rear sight
Discontinued

1863 SHARPS SPORTING RIFLE

Lock: dropping block
Stock: walnut
Barrel: 28 in.
Sights: adjustable open
Weight: 8.6 lbs.
Bore/Caliber: .54
Features: blued octagon barrel; adjustable rear sight
Discontinued

Euroarms of America Black Powder

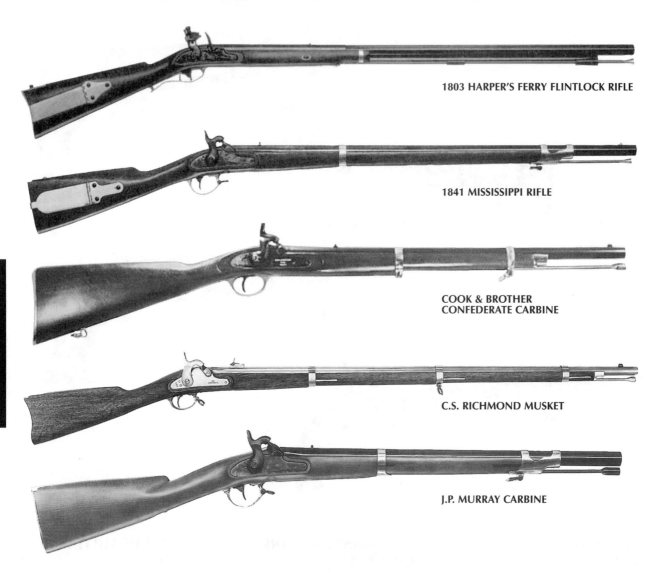

1803 HARPER'S FERRY FLINTLOCK RIFLE

1841 MISSISSIPPI RIFLE

COOK & BROTHER
CONFEDERATE CARBINE

C.S. RICHMOND MUSKET

J.P. MURRAY CARBINE

1803 HARPER'S FERRY FLINTLOCK
Lock: traditional flintlock
Stock: walnut
Barrel: 35 in.
Sights: fixed
Weight: 10.0 lbs.
Bore/Caliber: .54
Features: half-stock, browned steel
MSRP: $809

1841 MISSISSIPPI RIFLE
Lock: traditional caplock
Stock: walnut
Barrel: 33 in.
Sights: fixed
Weight: 9.5 lbs.
Bore/Caliber: .54 or .58
Features: brass furniture
MSRP: $631

COOK & BROTHER CONFEDERATE CARBINE
Lock: traditional caplock
Stock: walnut
Barrel: 24 in.
Sights: fixed
Weight: 7.9 lbs.
Bore/Caliber: .577
Features: carbine; also rifle with 33 in. barrel
Carbine: . . . . Discontinued
Rifle: $606

C.S. RICHMOND MUSKET
Lock: traditional caplock
Stock: walnut   *Barrel*: 40 in.
Sights: fixed
Weight: 9.0 lbs.
Bore/Caliber: .58
Features: 3-band furniture; swivels
MSRP: $730

J.P. MURRAY CARBINE
Lock: traditional caplock
Stock: walnut
Barrel: 23 in.
Sights: fixed
Weight: 7.5 lbs.
Bore/Caliber: .58
Features: brass furniture; replica of rare Confederate Cavalry Carbine
MSRP: $573

Euroarms of America Black Powder

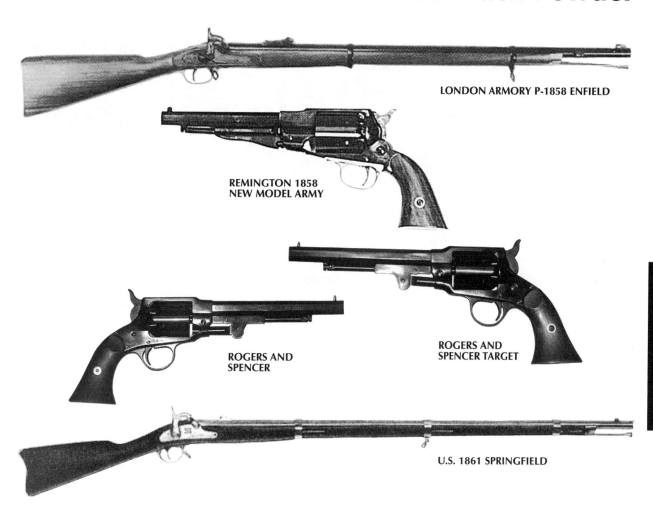

LONDON ARMORY P-1858 ENFIELD

REMINGTON 1858
NEW MODEL ARMY

ROGERS AND SPENCER TARGET

ROGERS AND SPENCER

U.S. 1861 SPRINGFIELD

LONDON ARMORY P-1858 ENFIELD
Lock: traditional caplock
Stock: walnut
Barrel: 33 in.
Sights: adjustable open
Weight: 8.8 lbs.
Bore/Caliber: .58
Features: steel ramrod; 2-band
1861 London Enfield: $521
P-1858 Enfield: $563
1853 rifled musket: $606

REMINGTON 1858 NEW MODEL ARMY
Lock: caplock revolver
Grips: walnut
Barrel: 8 in.
Sights: fixed
Weight: 2.5 lbs.
Bore/Caliber: .44
Features: brass guard; engraved version
New Model Army: $242
Engraved: $332

ROGERS AND SPENCER
Lock: caplock revolver
Grips: walnut
Barrel: 7.5 in.
Sights: fixed
Weight: 2.9 lbs.
Bore/Caliber: .44
Features: recommended ball diameter .451; also target model with adjustable sight
Rogers and Spencer: $340
London gray finish: $370
Target: $360

U.S. 1841 MISSISSIPPI RIFLE
Lock: traditional caplock
Stock: walnut
Barrel: 33 in.
Sights: fixed
Weight: 9.5 lbs.
Bore/Caliber: .54 or .58
Features: brass furniture
Mississippi: $631

U.S. 1861 SPRINGFIELD
Lock: traditional caplock
Stock: walnut
Barrel: 40 in.
Sights: fixed
Weight: 10.0 lbs.
Bore/Caliber: .58
Features: sling swivels; also London P-1852 rifled musket; London Enfield P-1861 (7.5 lbs.)
MSRP: $730

Green Mountain Black Powder

LIMITED EDITION .32-CALIBER SMALL GAME RIFLE

Lock: in-line
Stock: brown laminated
Barrel: 22.5 in., Green Mountain octagonal, blue-black finish
Sights: none; Redfield scope bases and rings provided
Weight: 5.8 lbs.
Bore/Caliber: .32
Features: Knight DISC Extreme action; limited edition with a production of 250 rifles, with its own exclusive serial number range; one-piece receiver; custom jeweled bolt, raised cheekpiece on stock
MSRP: $500

Knight Rifles Black Powder

BIGHORN

DISC EXTREME

BIGHORN

Lock: in-line
Stock: synthetic
Barrel: 26 in.
Sights: fiber optic or adjustable open
Weight: 7.6 lbs.
Bore/Caliber: .50
Features: 3 ignition systems: #11 nipple, musket nipple and the 209 Extreme shotgun primer system; full set of non-fiber optic sights
Discontinued

DISC EXTREME

Lock: in-line
Stock: synthetic or laminated
Barrel: 26 in.
Sights: fiber optic
Weight: 7.8 lbs.
Bore/Caliber: .45, .50, .52
Features: Green Mountain action and barrel; full plastic jacket ignition system; quick-release bolt system
Discontinued

Knight Rifles Black Powder

KP1 MAGNUM

KP1 WHITETAIL

ROLLING BLOCK

LONG RANGE HUNTER

KP1 MAGNUM

Lock: in-line & single shot
Stock: synthetic
Length: 43.5 in.
Sights: adjustable
Weight: 8 lbs.
Bore/Caliber: .50
Features: Blued, stainless steel barrel; blued or stainless barrel; 209 primer ignition system; removable and non-adjustable trigger; metallic fiber-optic sights; composite or laminate wood stock; recoil pad; sling swivel studs
Discontinued

KP1 WHITETAIL

Lock: in-line & single shot
Stock: synthetic
Length: 43.5 in. (muzzleloader); 39.5 in. (centerfire)
Sights: adjustable
Weight: 8 lbs. (muzzleloader); 7.8 lbs. (centerfire)
Bore/Caliber: .50 (muzzleloader), 17 HMR .22 LR, .223 Rem., .243 Win., .270 Win., .30-06, .300 Win.
Features: Interchangable stainless steel barrel combination package with muzzleloader—rimfire/centerfire options; blued or stainless barrel; 209 primer ignition system; removable and non-adjustable trigger; metallic fiber-optic sights; black synthetic or Next G-1 Camo stock; recoil pad; sling swivel studs
Discontinued

KNIGHT ROLLING BLOCK

Lock: in-line
Stock: composite
Barrel: Green Mountain; Length: 43 in.
Sights: fully adjustable
Weight: 8 lbs.
Bore/Caliber: .50
Features: rolling-block action with bare 209 primer ignition; metallic fiber-optic sights; easy access to the breech plug and interior for cleaning; removable and non-adjustable trigger; versions available: blued/composite, stainless and black, stainless steel/Next G-1 Green Camo, all Next G-1 Green Camo; recoil pad; sling swivel studs
Discontinued

LONG RANGE HUNTER

Lock: in-line
Stock: laminated
Barrel: 27 in.
Sights: adjustable
Weight: 8.25 lbs.
Bore/Caliber: .50, .52
Features: spiral custom-fluted, stainless free floated barrel; adjustable target trigger; metallic fiber optic sights; cast-off stock for right- and left-handed shooters w/ vent slots in forest green laminated wood or sand stone
Discontinued

Knight Rifles Black Powder

MASTER HUNTER DISC EXTREME,
STAINLESS, LAMINATED

MASTER HUNTER DISC EXTREME

REVOLUTION

REVOLUTION II

MASTER HUNTER DISC EXTREME
Lock: in-line
Stock: synthetic
Barrel: 26 in.
Sights: fiber optic
Weight: 7.8 lbs.
Bore/Caliber: .45, .50, .52
Features: Green Mountain action and cryogenically accurized barrel; full plastic jacket ignition system; quick-release bolt system
Discontinued

REVOLUTION
Lock: in-line
Stock: synthetic
Barrel: 27 in.
Sights: fiber optic
Weight: 7.14 lbs.
Bore/Caliber: .50, .52
Features: 209 full plastic jacket ignition system; sling swivel studs; stainless w/laminate, blued w/black, Realtree camo available
Discontinued

REVOLUTION II
Lock: pivot-block drop action
Stock: composite or laminate
Barrel: 27 in.
Sights: adjustable
Weight: 7.45 lbs.
Bore/Caliber: .50, .52
Features: stainless steel barrel; quick detachable action; drilled and tapped for scope; metallic fiber optic sights; two-piece black composite, camouflage composite and wood laminate stock
Discontinued

Knight Rifles Black Powder

WOLVERINE 209

VISION
Lock: in-line
Stock: synthetic
Barrel: 26 in.
Sights: adjustable fixed
Weight: 7.9 lbs.
Bore/Caliber: .50
Features: Green Mountain barrel; overmolded composite polymer coated stainless steel receiver break-open action; full plastic primer jackets; quick detachable trigger mechanism; cross bolt safety; available in Mossy Oak Break-Up or RealTree Hardwoods HD-Green
Discontinued

WOLVERINE 209
Lock: in-line
Stock: synthetic or camo
Barrel: 22 in., 1:28 twist
Sights: fiber optic
Weight: 7.0 lbs.
Bore/Caliber: .50
Features: full plastic jacket ignition
Discontinued

Lenartz Black Powder

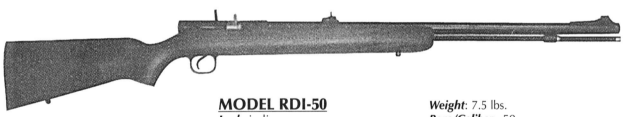

MODEL RDI-50
Lock: in-line
Stock: walnut
Barrel: 26 in., 1:28 twist
Sights: adjustable open
Weight: 7.5 lbs.
Bore/Caliber: .50
Features: adjustable trigger; uses 209 primers, converts to #11
MSRP: . . . . **price on request**

A short-started (unseated) load in your black-powder gun can cause big problems. This happens when the bullet is not firmly seated on the powder. Though the phenomenon is not well understood, it appears that the air space created by an unseated load causes the powder to detonate rather than burn. That is not good. For safety's sake, make certain every powder/projectile combination is seated correctly.

Lyman Black Powder

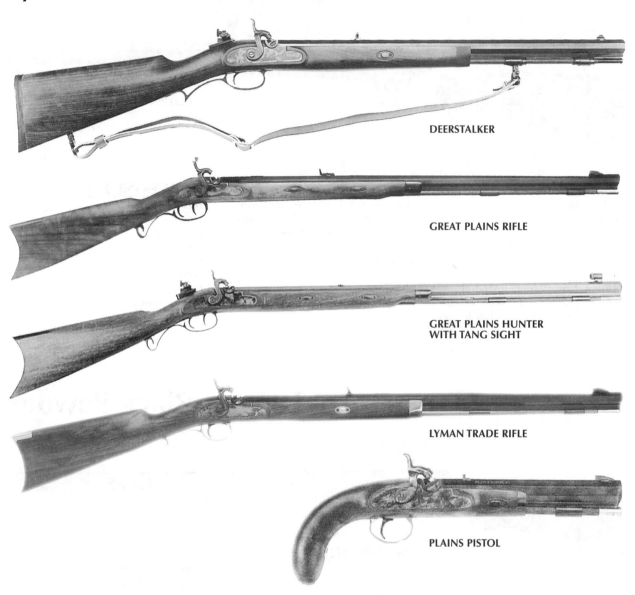

DEERSTALKER

GREAT PLAINS RIFLE

GREAT PLAINS HUNTER WITH TANG SIGHT

LYMAN TRADE RIFLE

PLAINS PISTOL

DEERSTALKER
Lock: traditional cap or flint
Stock: walnut
Barrel: 24 in.
Sights: aperture
Weight: 7.5 lbs.
Bore/Caliber: .50 or .54
Features: left-hand models available
Caplock: **$488**
Left-hand: **$510**
Flintlock: **$530**
Left-hand: **$570**
Stainless caplock: **$610**

GREAT PLAINS RIFLE
Lock: traditional cap or flint
Stock: walnut

Barrel: 32 in., 1:66 twist
Sights: adjustable open
Weight: 8.0 lbs.
Bore/Caliber: .50 or .54
Features: double set triggers, left-hand models available; also Great Plains Hunter with 1:32 twist
Caplock: **$655**
Kit: . . . . **Discontinued**
Flintlock: **$700**
Kit: . . . . **Discontinued**
Hunter: . . . . **Discontinued**

LYMAN TRADE RIFLE
Lock: traditional cap or flint
Stock: walnut
Barrel: 28 in., 1:48 twist

Sights: adjustable open
Weight: 8.0 lbs.
Bore/Caliber: .50 or .54
Features: brass furniture
Caplock: **$475**
Flint: **$500**

PLAINS PISTOL
Lock: traditional caplock
Stock: walnut
Barrel: 6 in.
Sights: fixed
Weight: 2.2 lbs.
Bore/Caliber: .50 or .54
Features: iron furniture
Plains Pistol: **$350**
Kit: **$290**

Markesbery Black Powder

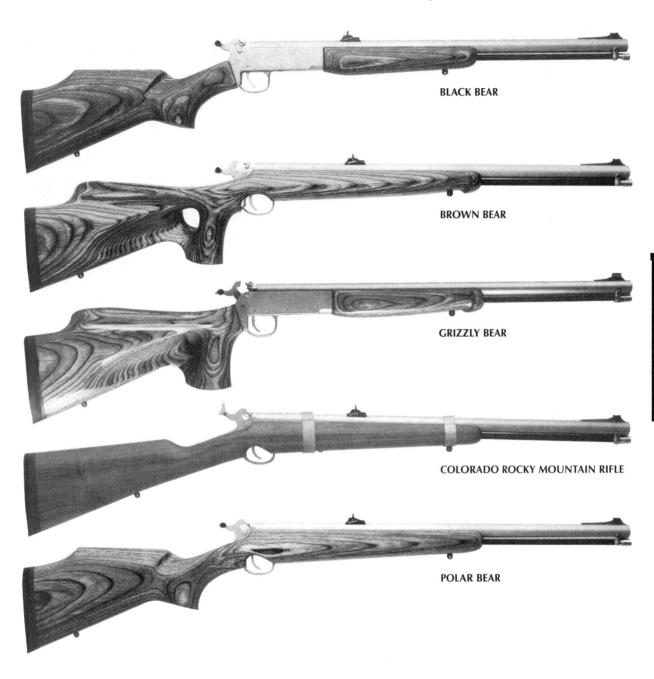

BLACK BEAR

BROWN BEAR

GRIZZLY BEAR

COLORADO ROCKY MOUNTAIN RIFLE

POLAR BEAR

BLACK BEAR
Lock: in-line
Stock: two-piece walnut, synthetic or laminated
Barrel: 24 in., 1:26 twist
Sights: adjustable open
Weight: 6.5 lbs.
Bore/Caliber: .36, .45, .50, .54
Features: also Grizzly Bear with thumbhole stock, Brown Bear with one-piece thumbhole stock, both checkered, aluminum ramrod

Black Bear:. **$498–549**
Brown Bear:. **$649–680**
Grizzly Bear: **$649–680**

COLORADO ROCKY MOUNTAIN RIFLE
Lock: in-line
Stock: walnut, laminated
Barrel: 24 in., 1:26 twist
Sights: adjustable open
Weight: 7.0 lbs.
Bore/Caliber: .36, .45, .50, .54

Features: #11 or magnum ignition
MSRP: **$498–549**

POLAR BEAR
Lock: in-line
Stock: laminated
Barrel: 24 in., 1:26 twist
Sights: adjustable open
Weight: 7.8 lbs.
Bore/Caliber: .36, .45, .50, .54
Features: one-piece stock
MSRP: **$498–549**

Navy Arms Black Powder

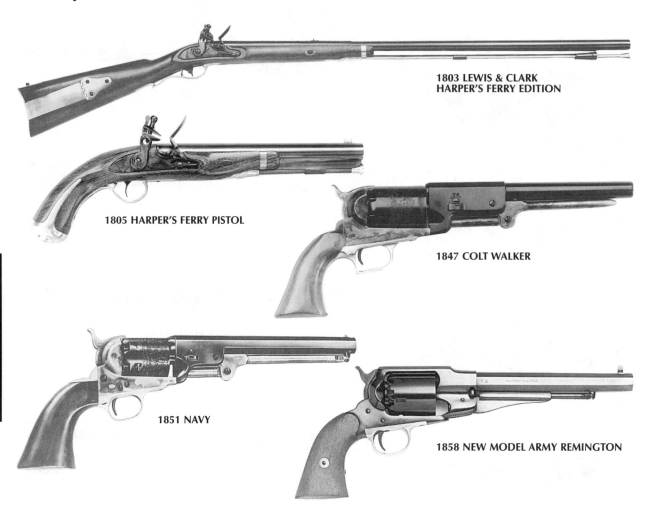

1803 LEWIS & CLARK HARPER'S FERRY EDITION

1805 HARPER'S FERRY PISTOL

1847 COLT WALKER

1851 NAVY

1858 NEW MODEL ARMY REMINGTON

1763 CHARLEVILLE MUSKET
Lock: traditional flintlock
Stock: walnut
Barrel: 44.75 in.
Sights: fixed
Weight: 9.8 lbs.
Bore/Caliber: .69
Features: full stock; polished steel barrel and furniture
Discontinued

1803 LEWIS & CLARK HARPER'S FERRY EDITION
Lock: traditional flintlock
Stock: walnut
Barrel: 35 in.
Sights: fixed
Weight: 8.5 lbs.
Bore/Caliber: .54
Features: case-colored lock; brass patch box
Discontinued

1805 HARPER'S FERRY PISTOL
Lock: traditional flintlock
Stock: walnut
Barrel: 10 in.
Sights: fixed
Weight: 2.75 lbs.
Bore/Caliber: .58
Features: browned rifled barrel; case-hardened lock
MSRP: **$495**

1847 COLT WALKER
Lock: caplock revolver
Grips: walnut
Barrel: 9 in.
Sights: fixed
Weight: 4.5 lbs.
Bore/Caliber: .44
Features: case-colored frame; brass guard
Discontinued

1851 NAVY
Lock: caplock revolver
Grips: walnut
Barrel: 7.5 in.
Sights: fixed
Weight: 2.7 lbs.
Bore/Caliber: .36 and .44
Features: brass guard and strap
Discontinued

1858 NEW MODEL ARMY REMINGTON
Lock: caplock revolver
Grips: walnut
Barrel: 8 in.
Sights: fixed
Weight: 2.5 lbs.
Bore/Caliber: .44
Features: brass guard; steel frame with top strap
Discontinued

Navy Arms Black Powder

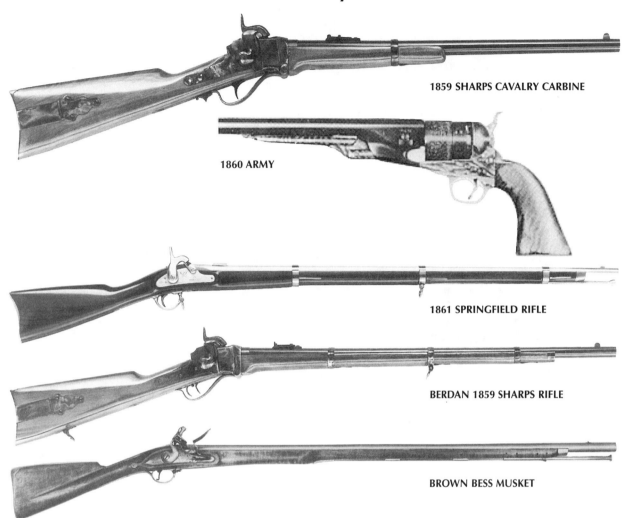

1859 SHARPS CAVALRY CARBINE

1860 ARMY

1861 SPRINGFIELD RIFLE

BERDAN 1859 SHARPS RIFLE

BROWN BESS MUSKET

BLACK POWDER

1859 SHARPS CAVALRY CARBINE

Lock: percussion, dropping block
Stock: walnut
Barrel: 22 in.
Sights: adjustable open
Weight: 7.8 lbs.
Bore/Caliber: .54
Features: blued steel barrel; color case-hardened frame; saddle bar with ring
Discontinued

1860 ARMY

Lock: caplock revolver
Grips: walnut
Barrel: 8 in.
Sights: fixed
Weight: 2.6 lbs.
Bore/Caliber: .44
Features: brass guard; steel backstrap
Discontinued

1861 SPRINGFIELD RIFLE MUSKET

Lock: traditional caplock
Stock: walnut
Barrel: 40 in.   *Sights*: fixed
Weight: 10.0 lbs.
Bore/Caliber: .58
Features: three-band furniture polished bright
Discontinued

BERDAN 1859 SHARPS RIFLE

Lock: traditional caplock
Stock: walnut   *Barrel:* 30 in.
Sights: adjustable open
Weight: 8.5 lbs.
Bore/Caliber: .54
Features: case-colored receiver; double set trigger
Discontinued

BROWN BESS MUSKET

Lock: traditional flintlock
Stock: walnut
Barrel: 42 in.
Sights: fixed
Weight: 9.5 lbs.
Bore/Caliber: .75
Features: full stock without bands
MSRP: $1100

Navy Arms Black Powder

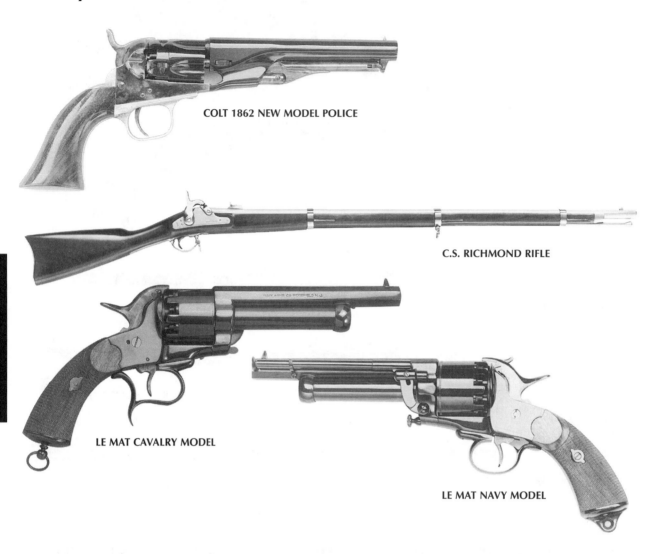

COLT 1862 NEW MODEL POLICE

C.S. RICHMOND RIFLE

LE MAT CAVALRY MODEL

LE MAT NAVY MODEL

COLT 1862 NEW MODEL POLICE
Lock: caplock revolver
Grips: walnut
Barrel: 5.5 in.
Sights: fixed
Weight: 2.7 lbs.
Bore/Caliber: .36
Features: last of the percussion Colts; has brass guard; case-colored frame
MSRP: **$278**

C.S. RICHMOND RIFLE
Lock: traditional caplock
Stock: walnut
Barrel: 40 in.
Sights: fixed
Weight: 10.0 lbs.
Bore/Caliber: .58
Features: polished furniture
MSRP: **$976**

HARPER'S FERRY FLINTLOCK PISTOL
Lock: traditional flintlock
Grips: walnut
Barrel: 10 in.
Sights: fixed
Weight: 2.6 lbs.
Bore/Caliber: .58
Features: case-colored lock; brass furniture; browned barrel
MSRP: **$455**

J. P. MURRAY CARBINE
Lock: traditional caplock
Stock: walnut
Barrel: 23.5 in.   *Sights*: fixed
Weight: 7.5 lbs.
Bore/Caliber: .58
Features: color case hardened lock; brass furniture
MSRP: **$748**

LE MAT REVOLVER
Lock: caplock revolver
Grips: walnut
Barrel: 7.6 in.
Sights: fixed
Weight: 3.4 lbs.
Bore/Caliber: .44
Features: 9-shot cylinder; Navy, Cavalry, Army models available
MSRP: **$748**

Navy Arms Black Powder

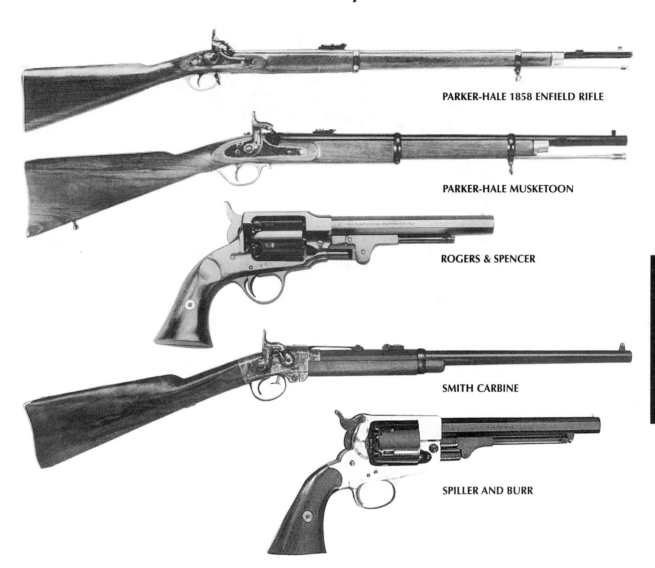

PARKER-HALE 1858 ENFIELD RIFLE

PARKER-HALE MUSKETOON

ROGERS & SPENCER

SMITH CARBINE

SPILLER AND BURR

BLACK POWDER

PARKER-HALE 1858 ENFIELD RIFLE
Lock: traditional caplock
Stock: walnut
Barrel: 39 in. (2-band 33 in.)
Sights: adjustable open
Weight: 9.6 lbs. (2-band 8.50 lbs.)
Bore/Caliber: .58
Features: brass furniture
Parker-Hale Enfield: **$848**
1858 Two band Enfield: **$819**

PARKER-HALE MUSKETOON
Lock: traditional caplock
Stock: walnut
Barrel: 24 in.
Sights: adjustable open
Weight: 7.5 lbs.

Bore/Caliber: .58
Features: brass furniture
MSRP: **$734**

ROGERS AND SPENCER
Lock: caplock revolver
Grips: walnut
Barrel: 7.5 in.
Sights: fixed
Weight: 3.0 lbs.
Bore/Caliber: .44
Features: octagonal barrel;
6-shot cylinder
MSRP: **$363**

SMITH CARBINE
Lock: traditional caplock
Stock: walnut
Barrel: 22 in.

Sights: adjustable open
Weight: 7.8 lbs.
Bore/Caliber: .50
Features: cavalry and artillery models
available
MSRP: **$791**

SPILLER AND BURR
Lock: caplock revolver
Grips: walnut
Barrel: 7 in.
Sights: fixed
Weight: 2.6 lbs.
Bore/Caliber: .36
Features: brass frame
MSRP: **$196**

Pedersoli Black Powder

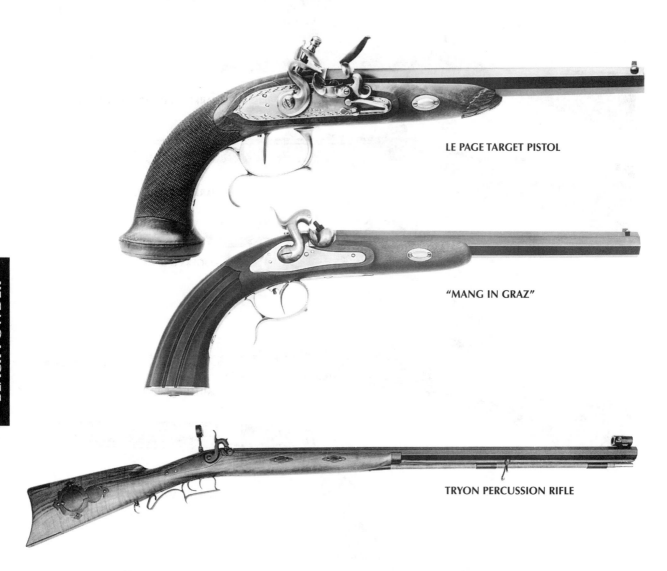

LE PAGE TARGET PISTOL

"MANG IN GRAZ"

TRYON PERCUSSION RIFLE

LEPAGE TARGET PISTOL
Lock: traditional flintlock
Grips: walnut
Barrel: 10.5 in., 1:18 twist
Sights: fixed
Weight: 2.5 lbs.
Bore/Caliber: .44 or .45
Features: smoothbore .45 available
LePage flintlock: **$1005**
Percussion in .36, .38, .44: **$753**

"MANG IN GRAZ"
Lock: traditional caplock
Grips: walnut
Barrel: 11 in., 1:15 or 1:18 (.44) twist
Sights: fixed
Weight: 2.5 lbs.
Bore/Caliber: .38 or .44
Features: grooved butt
MSRP: **$1375**

MORTIMER TARGET RIFLE
Lock: flintlock
Stock: English-style European walnut
Barrel: octagon to round 36 in.
Sights: target
Weight: 8.8 lbs.
Bore/Caliber: .54
Features: case-colored lock; stock has cheek piece and hand checkering; 7-groove barrel
MSRP: **$1384**

TRYON PERCUSSION RIFLE
Lock: traditional caplock
Stock: walnut
Barrel: 32 in., 1:48 or 1:66 (.54) twist
Sights: adjustable open
Weight: 9.5 lbs.
Bore/Caliber: .45, .50, .54
Features: Creedmoor version with aperture sight available
Tryon Percussion: **$869**
Creedmoor: **$1200**

Remington Black Powder

GENESIS ML CAMO

GENESIS ML SF THUMBHOLE

GENESIS ML SYNTHETIC

GENESIS ML SF BUCKMASTERS EDITION

GENESIS
Lock: in-line
Stock: synthetic or laminate
Barrel: 28 in.
Sights: fiber-optic
Weight: 7.5-8.0 lbs.
Bore/Caliber: .50
Features: 1:28 twist barrel; ultra-compact TorchCam breech; 209 primer system; Carbon Blue Matte and Camo (ML line) barrel; stainless steel (MLS and ML SF Thumbhole lines); drilled and tapped for scope mounts; over-travel hammer w/ ambidextrous

Hammer Spur; crossbolt safety; aluminum anodized ramrod; Williams fiber-optic sights; Black Synthetic, Mossy Oak New Break-Up (ML, MLS and ML SF Thumbhole stock lines); Gray Laminate (ML SF Thumbhole line)
Discontinued

GENESIS ML SF BUCKMASTERS EDITION
Lock: in-line
Stock: camo-covered synthetic, Realtree Hardwoods HD
Barrel: 28 in.

Sights: fiber-optic
Weight: 7.5 lbs.
Bore/Caliber: .50
Features: Buckmasters logo laser engraved on the left receiver panel; fluted, stainless-steel barrel with satin finish; ultra-compact TorchCam breech; 209 primer ignition; over-travel hammer w/ ambidextrous Hammer Spur; crossbolt safety; aluminum anodized ramrod; Williams fiber-optic sights
Discontinued

OLD ARMY CAP AND BALL
Lock: caplock revolver
Grips: walnut
Barrel: 5.5 or 7.5 in.
Sights: fixed
Weight: 3.0 lbs.
Bore/Caliber: .45
Features: Civil War-era reproduction in modern steel, music wire springs
Discontinued

Ruger Black Powder

Savage Black Powder

MODEL 10ML-11

MODEL 10ML-11
STAINLESS LAMINATED

MODEL 10ML-11 MUZZLELOADER

Lock: in-line
Stock: synthetic, camo or laminated
Barrel: 24 in.

Sights: adjustable fiber optic
Weight: 8.0 lbs.
Bore/Caliber: .50
Features: bolt-action mechanism; 209 priming

Blue synthetic:. $660
Stainless:. $738
Blue camo:. $711
Stainless camo:. $787
Stainless laminated:. $888

Shiloh Black Powder

1863 SHARPS

1874 CREEDMOOR TARGET RIFLE
(WITHOUT SIGHTS)

1874 SPORTER

MODEL 1863 SHARPS

Lock: traditional caplock
Stock: walnut   **Barrel**: 30 in.
Sights: adjustable open
Weight: 9.5 lbs.
Bore/Caliber: .50 or .54
Features: sporting model with half-stock; double set trigger military model with 3-band full stock; also car-bine with 22 in. barrel (7.5 lbs.)

Sporting rifle and carbine: . . $1800
Military rifle: $2092

MODEL 1874 CREEDMOOR TARGET

Lock: black powder cartridge
Stock: walnut
Barrel: 32 in. half octagon

Sights: none
Weight: 9.0 lbs.
Bore/Caliber: all popular black powder cartridges from .38-55 to .50-90
Features: shotgun buttstock, pistol grip; single trigger; fancy walnut, pewter tip
MSRP: $2743
#2 Creedmoor Silhouette (30 in. round, tapered barrel): . . . $2743

BLACK POWDER

Thompson/Center Black Powder

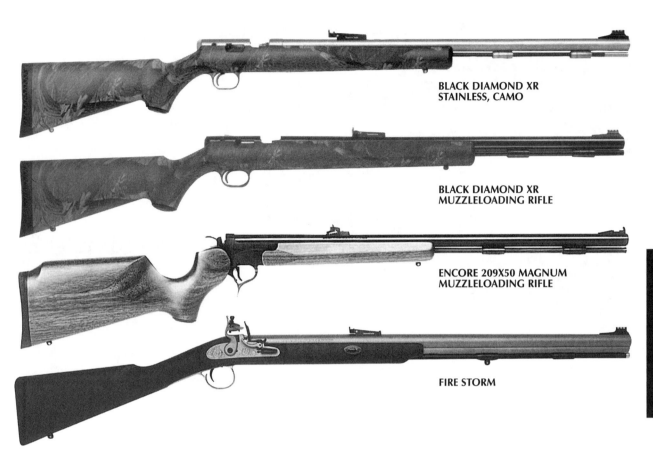

BLACK DIAMOND XR STAINLESS, CAMO

BLACK DIAMOND XR MUZZLELOADING RIFLE

ENCORE 209X50 MAGNUM MUZZLELOADING RIFLE

FIRE STORM

BLACK POWDER

BLACK DIAMOND RIFLE XR

Lock: in-line
Stock: walnut or synthetic
Barrel: 26 in., 1:28 twist
Sights: adjustable fiber optic
Weight: 6.6 lbs.
Bore/Caliber: .50
Features: musket; cap or no. 11 nipple
Blue synthetic: **$337–440**
Stainless camo: **$337–440**

ENCORE 209X50 RIFLE

Lock: in-line
Stock: walnut or synthetic
Barrel: 26 in., 1:28 twist
Sights: adjustable fiber optic
Weight: 7.0 lbs.
Bore/Caliber: .50
Features: automatic safety; interchangeable barrel with Encore centerfire barrels; also available 209x45 9.45
Blue synthetic: **$637**
Blue walnut: **$678**
Blue walnut .45: . . . . . **Discontinued**
Blue camo: **$877**
Stainless synthetic: **$852**
Stainless synthetic .45: **Discontinued**
Camo: . . . . **Discontinued**

FIRE STORM

Lock: traditional cap or flint
Stock: synthetic
Barrel: 26 in., 1:48 twist
Sights: adjustable fiber optic
Weight: 7.0 lbs.
Bore/Caliber: .50
Features: aluminum ramrod
Blue: **$474**
Stainless: **$474**

Always use the right muzzleloading projectile. A heavy, round-nosed bullet might drop 2 feet at 200 yards, while a lighter, sleeker, saboted bullet will only drop a foot. Guess which one is easier to connect with when that buck steps clear at 200 yards?

Thompson/Center Black Powder

PRO HUNTER 209 X 50
MUZZLELOADER

TRIUMPH BLUED COMPOSITE

TRIUMPH CAMO COMPOSITE

TRIUMPH WEATHERSHIELD
COMPOSITE

PRO HUNTER 209 X 50 MUZZLELOADER

Lock: in-line
Stock: FlexTech composite
Barrel: 28 in., stainless, fluted; interchangeable with shotgun and rifle barrels
Sights: fiber-optic
Weight: N/A
Bore/Caliber: .50
Features: stainless, fluted precision barrel—interchangeable with shotgun and rifle barrels; Swing Hammer design; engraved receiver; FlexTech

(recoil system) composite stock in black or Realtree Hardwoods camo with or without thumbhole
Black:.................... $710
Realtree
   Hardwoods camo:.... $830–898

TRIUMPH

Lock: in-line
Stock: composite, black or Realtree AP HD camo
Barrel: Weather Shield metal coating with QLA
Sights: none; Redfield scope bases and

rings provided
Bore/Caliber: .50
Features: only four moving parts so there's no need to remove the trigger group, disassemble or use tools to clean the rifle; alloy receiver; tip-up barrel with Toggle Lock action; solid aluminum ramrod; SIMS Limbsaver recoil pad; sling swivel studs; breech plug (Speed Breech XT) can be removed by hand; Set trigger with automatic hammer block safety
MSRP: . . . . $457 to $575

Traditions Black Powder

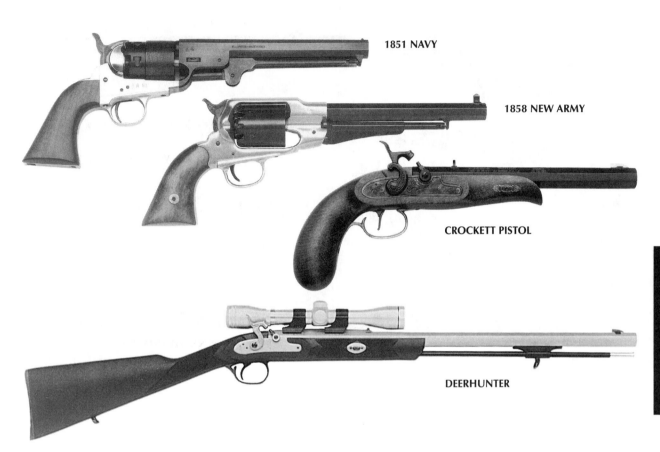

1851 NAVY

1858 NEW ARMY

CROCKETT PISTOL

DEERHUNTER

1851 NAVY REVOLVER

Lock: caplock
Grips: walnut
Barrel: 7.5 in.
Sights: fixed
Weight: 2.7 lbs.
Bore/Caliber: .36
Features: blued, octagon barrel; steel or brass frame
Brass frame: **$190**
Steel frame: **$249**
**1851 Navy U.S. Marshall
    (old silver, 5 in. bbl.):** **$367**
**1851 Navy Old Silver
    (7.5 in. bbl.):** **$315**

1858 NEW ARMY REVOLVER

Lock: caplock
Grips: walnut
Barrel: 8 in.
Sights: fixed
Weight: 2.6 lbs.
Bore/Caliber: .44
Features: octagon barrel; steel frame
1858 New Army (brass): **$250**
1858 New Army (steel): **$308**
1858 New Army (stainless): . . . **$514**

1860 ARMY REVOLVER

Lock: caplock
Grips: walnut
Barrel: 8 in.
Sights: fixed
Weight: 2.8 lbs.
Bore/Caliber: .44
Features: blued; round barrel; steel or brass frame
Brass frame: **$260**
Steel frame: **$287**
Nickel: **$342**

BUCKSKINNER FLINTLOCK CARBINE

Lock: traditional flintlock
Grips: synthetic or laminate
Barrel: 21 in., 1:48 twist
Sights: adjustable
Weight: 6.0 lbs.
Bore/Caliber: .50
Features: fully adjustable TruGlo fiber optic sights; Monte Carlo stock; hooked breech for easy barrel removal; synthetic ramrod
Discontinued

CROCKETT PISTOL

Lock: traditional caplock
Grips: hardwood
Barrel: 10 in.
Sights: fixed
Weight: 2.0 lbs.
Bore/Caliber: .32 caplock
Features: blued, octagon barrel
MSRP: **$214**

DEERHUNTER RIFLE

Lock: traditional cap or flint
Stock: hardwood, synthetic or camo
Barrel: 24 in., 1:48 twist
Sights: fixed
Weight: 6.0 lbs.
Bore/Caliber: .32, .50, .54
Features: blackened furniture; also economy-model Panther, 24 in .50 or .54
Cap, nickel, synthetic: **$228**
Flint, blue, synthetic: **$256**
Flint, nickel, synthetic: **$278**
Cap, blue, hardwood: **$264**
Flint, blue, hardwood: **$315**
Flint, nickel, camo: . . **Discontinued**

Traditions Black Powder

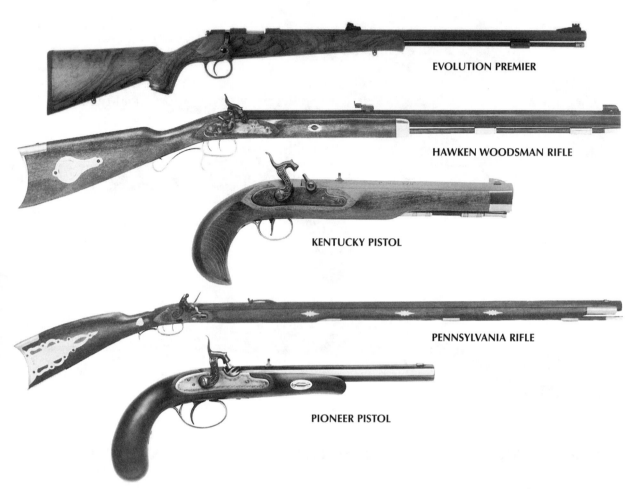

EVOLUTION PREMIER

HAWKEN WOODSMAN RIFLE

KENTUCKY PISTOL

PENNSYLVANIA RIFLE

PIONEER PISTOL

EVOLUTION
Lock: bolt
Stock: synthetic, laminated or camo
Barrel: 26 in.
Sights: fiber optics
Weight: 7.0 lbs.
Bore/Caliber: .50
Features: fluted, tapered barrel, drilled & tapped for scope; 209 ignition; swivel studs, rubber butt pad; LD model in .45 or .50 has Tru-Glo sights.
LD blue:. . . . . Discontinued
LD nickel synthetic:. $314
LD blue camo:. . . . . . Discontinued
LD nickel camo:. $370
Premier, blue: . . . . . . Discontinued
Premier stainless, camo: . . . .
. . . . Discontinued
Premier stainless: . . . Discontinued

EXPRESS DOUBLE OVER & UNDER MUZZLELOADER
Lock: 209 primer top break
Stock: synthetic   **Barrel**: 24 in.
Sights: adjustable   **Weight**: 12.5 lbs.

Bore/Caliber: .50
Features: double barrel over/under; 209-ignition system; blued barrels; double trigger, top tang safety; fiber optic sights; drilled & tapped for a scope
MSRP: $1599–1766
Close-out $799

HAWKEN WOODSMAN RIFLE
Lock: traditional cap or flint
Stock: beech
Barrel: 28 in., 1:48 twist
Sights: adjustable open
Weight: 7.7 lbs.
Bore/Caliber: .50 or .54
Features: brass furniture
Caplock: $396
Left-hand caplock:. $415
Flintlock: $434
Crockett: . . . . Discontinued

KENTUCKY PISTOL
Lock: traditional caplock
Grips: beech   **Barrel**: 10 in.

Sights: fixed   **Weight**: 2.5 lbs.
Bore/Caliber: .50
Features: brass furniture
MSRP: $175

PENNSYLVANIA RIFLE
Lock: traditional cap or flint
Stock: walnut
Barrel: 20 in., 1:66 twist
Sights: adjustable open
Weight: 8.5 lbs.
Bore/Caliber: .50
Features: brass furniture
MSRP: $664–720

PIONEER PISTOL
Lock: traditional caplock
Grips: walnut
Barrel: 9.6 in.
Sights: fixed
Weight: 1.9 lbs.
Bore/Caliber: .45
Features: German silver furniture
Discontinued

Traditions Black Powder

SHENANDOAH RIFLE

THUNDER BOLT

TRACKER 209

TRAPPER PISTOL

WILLIAM PARKER PISTOL

PURSUIT LT BREAK OPEN

Lock: break-open, 209 ignition system
Grips: synthetic
Barrel: 28 in.   *Sights*: adjustable
Weight: 8.25 lbs.
Bore/Caliber: .45
Features: 209-ignition; fluted barrel; cross block trigger safety; fiber optic sights
Blued/black:. . . . . . . **Discontinued**
Nickel/black: **$284**
Realtree Hardwoods/blue:. . . . **$320**
Realtree nickel: . . . . . **Discontinued**

SHENANDOAH RIFLE

Lock: traditional cap or flint
Stock: beech
Barrel: 33 in., 1:66 twist
Sights: fixed
Weight: 7.2 lbs.
Bore/Caliber: .50
Features: brass furniture; squirrel rifle in .36
Caplock: **$551**
Flintlock: **$588**
Caplock .36:. **$558**

Flintlock .36: **$618**
Kentucky,
    flint or caplock: **$364**

THUNDER BOLT

Lock: bolt
Stock: synthetic
Barrel: 24 in. (21 in. youth)
Sights: adjustable
Weight: 7.0 lbs.
Bore/Caliber: .45 or. 50
Features: 209-ignition; checkered stock; sling swivels; rubber butt pad; drilled & tapped for scope
Youth: . . . . **Discontinued**
Blue synthetic:. **$150**
Nickel: . . . . **Discontinued**
Blue camo: **$150**
Nickel camo: **$312**

TRACKER 209

Lock: in-line
Stock: synthetic or camo
Barrel: 22 in., 1:28 twist (1:24 .45)
Sights: fiber optic
Weight: 6.5 lbs.

Bore/Caliber: .45 or .50
Features: 209 primer ignition
Blue synthetic:. **$161**
Nickel synthetic: **$184**
Nickel camo: . . . . **Discontinued**

TRAPPER PISTOL

Lock: traditional cap or flint
Grips: beech
Barrel: 9.8 in.
Sights: adjustable open
Weight: 2.9 lbs.
Bore/Caliber: .50
Features: brass furniture
Trapper: **$286**
Flintlock: **$312**

WILLIAM PARKER PISTOL

Lock: traditional caplock
Grips: walnut
Barrel: 10.4 in.
Sights: fixed
Weight: 2.3 lbs.
Bore/Caliber: .50
Features: checkered with brass furniture
MSRP: **$381**

Uberti Black Powder

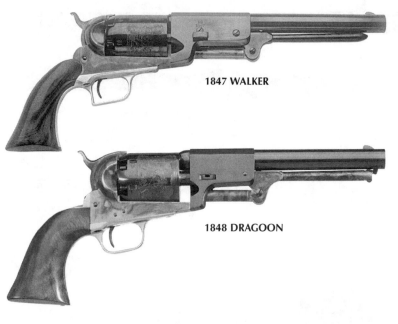

1847 WALKER

1848 DRAGOON

1848 WHITENEYVILLE DRAGOON

1851 NAVY REVOLVER

1858 REMINGTON NEW ARMY

WALKER

Lock: caplock revolver
Grips: walnut grips
Barrel: 9 in.
Sights: fixed, open
Weight: 71.2 oz.
Bore/Caliber: .44
Features: color case-hardened frame;
brass trigger guard
MSRP: **$429**

1848 DRAGOON

Lock: caplock revolver
Grips: walnut
Barrel: 7.5 in.
Sights: fixed, open
Weight: 64.9 oz.
Bore/Caliber: .44
Features: comes in 1st, 2nd and 3rd
models; color case-hardened frame;
brass trigger guard
1848 Dragoon: **$409**
1848 Whiteneyville Dragoon: . . **$429**

1851 NAVY REVOLVER

Lock: caplock revolver
Grips: walnut
Barrel: 7.5 in.
Sights: fixed, open
Weight: 44.8 oz.
Bore/Caliber: .36
Features: color case-hardened frame;
brass round or square trigger-guard
MSRP: **$329**

1858 REMINGTON NEW ARMY

Lock: caplock revolver
Grips: walnut
Barrel: 8 in.
Sights: fixed, open
Weight: 44.8 oz.
Bore/Caliber: .44
Features: octagonal barrel;
brass trigger guard, blue finish
New Army: **$349**
Stainless: **$429**
18 in. barrel, carbine: **$549**

BLACK POWDER

Uberti Black Powder

1860 ARMY REVOLVER

Lock: caplock revolver
Grips: walnut
Barrel: 8 in.
Sights: fixed, open
Weight: 41.6 oz.
Bore/Caliber: .44
Features: color case-hardened frame
1860 Army: **$339**
Fluted cylinder: **$349**

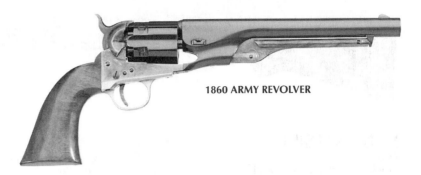

1860 ARMY REVOLVER

1861 NAVY REVOLVER

Lock: caplock revolver
Grips: walnut
Barrel: 7.5 in.   **Sights**: fixed, open
Weight: 44.8 oz.
Bore/Caliber: .36
Features: color case-hardened frame; brass or steel trigger-guard
MSRP: **$349**

1861 NAVY REVOLVER

1862 POCKET NAVY

Lock: caplock revolver
Grips: walnut
Barrel: 5.5 or 6.5 in.
Sights: fixed, open
Weight: 26.9 oz.
Bore/Caliber: .36
Features: color case-hardened frame; 6-shot cylinder; forged steel barrel, brass backstrap and trigger guard.
MSRP: **$349**

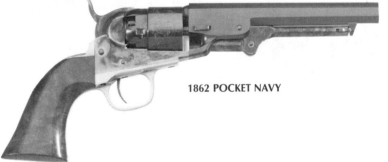

1862 POCKET NAVY

1862 POLICE

Lock: caplock revolver
Grips: walnut
Barrel: 5.5 or 6.5 in.
Sights: fixed, open
Weight: 26.9 oz.
Bore/Caliber: .36
Features: color case-hardened frame; 6-shot cylinder; forged steel barrel; brass backstrap and trigger guard.
MSRP: **$349**

1862 POLICE

1848-1849 POCKET REVOLVERS

Lock: caplock revolver
Grips: walnut
Barrel: 4 in.
Sights: fixed, open
Weight: 23.8 - 24.9 oz.
Bore/Caliber: .31
Features: color case-hardened frame; 5-shot cylinders; forged steel barrel, brass backstrap and trigger guard.
1849 Wells Fargo: **$339**
1849 Pocket: **$339**

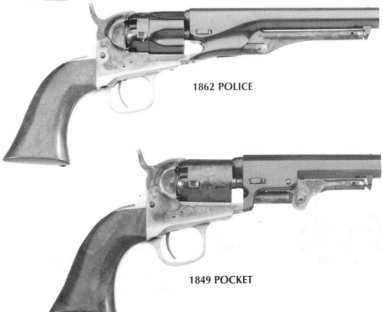

1849 POCKET

White Rifles Black Powder

THUNDERBOLT

HUNTER SERIES
Lock: in-line
Stock: synthetic or laminated
Barrel: stainless, 22 in. (24 in. Elite)
Sights: fiber-optic
Weight: 7.7 lbs.

Bore/Caliber: .45 or .50
Features: Elite weighs 8.6 lbs.; aluminum ramrod with bullet extractor; also: Thunderbolt bolt action with 209-ignition, 26 in. barrel

Whitetail: **$399**
Blacktail and Elite: **$499**
Thunderbolt: **$699**
Odyssey (ss/laminated thumbhole stock): **$1299**

Winchester Black Powder

APEX STAINLESS SYNTHETIC

MODEL X-150

APEX MUZZLELOADER
Lock: in-line
Stock: synthetic or camo
Barrel: 28 in., 1:28 twist
Sights: fiber optic
Weight: 7.2 lbs.
Bore/Caliber: .45 or .50
Features: "swing-action" breech
Discontinued

MODEL X-150 MUZZLELOADING RIFLE
Lock: in-line
Stock: synthetic or camo
Barrel: 26 in. fluted, 1:28 twist
Sights: fiber optic
Weight: 7.9 lbs.
Bore/Caliber: .45 or .50
Features: 209 primer ignition; stainless bolt action
Discontinued

BLACK POWDER

Alpen Optics Scopes

APEX 3.5-10x50

KODIAK 4-12

APEX AND KODIAK SCOPES

Alpen Optics offers two lines of riflescopes, comprising 11 models. Apex variables feature fully multi-coated lens systems, plus resettable finger-adjustable windage and elevation adjustments with 1/4-min. clicks. Kodiak scopes are fully waterproof and fogproof.

APEX SCOPES				
MAGNIFICATION (X OBJ. DIA.)	FIELD OF VIEW (FT., 100 YDS)	DIA./LENGTH (IN.)	WEIGHT (OZ.)	MSRP
3-9x42	40/14	1/12.5	17	$319
3.5-10x50	28-10	1/12.8	17	$254
4-16x50	23.6/-62	1/14.8	23	$269
6-24x50	15-4	1/16	16	$292

KODIAK SCOPES				
MAGNIFICATION (X OBJ. DIA.)	FIELD OF VIEW (FT., 100 YDS)	DIA./LENGTH (IN.)	WEIGHT (OZ.)	MSRP
4x32	34	1/12.3	12	$52
1.5-4.5x32	50-21	1/11.7	14	$64.99
3-9x32	37-14	1/12	12	$54
3-9x40	42-14	1/13	13	$95
2.5-10x44	42-12	1/13	20	$129
3.5-10x50	35-12	1/13.2	21	$132
4-12x40	32-11	1/13.4	16	$129
6-24x50	18-6	1/16.2	26	$152

Browning Scopes

RIFLESCOPES

Browning's line consists of scopes featuring a fast-focus eyepiece, 1/4-min. click adjustments and a one-piece water- and fogproof tube. Eye relief is 3½ in. The lenses are all multi-coated. **Discontinued**

BSA Scopes

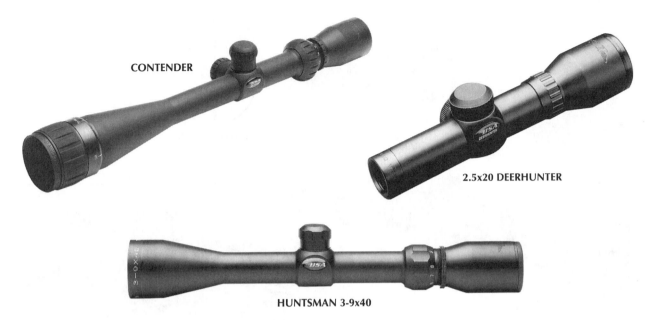

CONTENDER

2.5x20 DEERHUNTER

HUNTSMAN 3-9x40

CATSEYE SCOPES

Catseye scopes have multi-coated lenses and European-style reticles; the PowerBright's reticle lights up against dark backgrounds; the Big Cat has long eye relief

1.5-4.5x32 European Reticle: .... Discontinued
1.5-4.5x32 Illum. Reticle: .... Discontinued
3-10x44: ....Discontinued
3-10x44 illum: ....Discontinued
3-12x44: $229.95
3-10x44: ....Discontinued
3-10x44 Illum. Reticle: Discontinued
3.5-10x50: $219.95
3.5-10x50 Illum. Reticle: $239.95
4-16x50 AO: $229.95
6-24x50: $239.95

CONTENDER SCOPES

Feature multicoated lenses; eyepiece focusing from -4 to +4 diopter for duplex reticle; focusing for 10 yds. & 300 yds.; power ring & turret caps; finger adjustable windage & elevation

3-12x40 A/O TT: $129.95
3-12x50: ....Discontinued
4-16x40 A/O TT: $132
6-24x40mm A/O TT: $150
8-32x40 A/O TT: ....Discontinued

DEERHUNTER SCOPES

Deerhunter Scopes are nitrogen gas filled and feature a one piece, 1 in. tube; camera quality lenses; black textured finish; easy focus eyepiece

1.5-4.5x32mm: $80
2.5-10x44mm: $110
2.5x20mm (Shotgun): $49.95
3-9x40mm: .... : $69.95
3-9x40mm Illuminated Reticle: .$130
3-9x40mm: $100
3-9x50mm: $89.95

HUNTSMAN SCOPES

The Huntsman series features multicoated lenses, finger-adjustable windage and elevation and generous eye relief; warranted waterproof, fogproof and shockproof

1.5-4.5x32mm, Deer/Turkey Reticle: Discontinued
3-12x50mm: $119.95
3-9x40mm: $109.95
3-9x44mm: ....Discontinued
4-16x40mm: $114.95
4x32mm, Deer/Turkey Reticle: .... Discontinued
18x40mmAO: $129.95

MIL-DOT SCOPES

Mil-Dot scopes have multicoated objective & ocular lenses; eyepiece focusing from -4 to +4 diopter for dupleX reticle; finger adjustable windage & elevation knobs

4-16x40: $99.95
6-24x40: $149.95
8-32x40: ....Discontinued
6-24x40 Illum.: $179.95
4-16x40 Illum.: $159.95

PANTHER ALL-WEATHER SCOPES

Feature BSA Standard Reticles; fully multicoated camera quality glass lenses; ocular speed focus; European style eyeball; finger adjustable windage and elevation with "push/pull" locking system

3-10x40: ....Discontinued
2.5-10x44: $99.95
3.5-10x50: ....Discontinued
6.5-20x44: ....Discontinued

PLATINUM TARGET SCOPES

Platinum target scopes are fitted with finger-adjustable windage and elevation dials; these scopes have a threepiece objective lens systems

PT 6-24x44 AO: $149.95–179.95
PT 8-32x44 AO: $149.95–179.95
PT 6-24x44 AO Mildot Reticle: $149.95–179.95
PT 8-32x44 AO Mildot Reticle: $149.95–179.95

SWEET 17 SCOPES

Designed for the .17 HMR, these scopes feature a 1-in. mounting tube; fully-coated optics; finger-adjustable windage and elevation

2-7x32 A/O: $99.95
3-12x40: $129.95
4-12x40: ....Discontinued
6-18x40: $169.95

Burris Scopes

4X-16X BLACK DIAMOND

BALLISTIC MIL-DOT

EURO DIAMOND 3 -10x40

3X-12X-50MM

LASERSCOPE

BLACK DIAMOND RIFLESCOPES

Features a 50mm objective and heavy 30mm matte finish tube. The Black Diamond line includes three models of a 30mm main tube with various finishes, reticles and adjustment knobs. These scopes have rubber-armored parallax-adjust rings, an adjustable and resettable adjustment dial and an internal focusing eyepiece. Available with BallPlex, Ballistic Mildot, BallM-Dot/PosiLock reticles. Black Diamond Titanium scopes are made of solid titanium, coated with molecularly bonded aluminum titanium nitride. Black Diamond Titanium scope lenses have a scratch-proof T-Plate coating applied to the objective and eyepiece lenses.

EURO DIAMOND SCOPES

All Euro Diamond scopes come in matte black finish, with fully multi-

coated lenses and ¼-min. clicks on resettable dials. Eye relief is 3½ to 4 in. The eyepiece and power ring are integrated and the scopes have a helical rear ocular ring. Options include: ballistic Plex or German 3P#4 reticle and PosiLock or illuminated.

FULLFIELD II VARIABLE SCOPES

Feature one piece main tubes; multi-coated lenses; one-piece power ring/eyepiece; soft rubber eyeguard; double integral springs; available with Ballistic Plex, Ballistic Mildot, Fine Plex reticles; finished in matte, silver or black; nitrogen filled with special quad seals.

LASERSCOPE

Burris' LaserScope is the successful integration of a laser rangefinder and a quality riflescope into an affordable package that stands up under severe

recoil and with a moderate size and weight. The Burris Ballistic Plex reticle incorporated in the LaserScope lets you quickly range the target, hold dead on and squeeze off your shot without losing sight of your target. Although fully functional as a self-contained single unit, the LaserScope also comes with a remote activation switch that straps to the forearm of a rifle to allow more convenient and steady operation of the laser.

LIGHTED RETICLE SCOPES

The Burris Electro-Dot adds a bright pinpoint aiming spot to the center of the crosshair. Available with Ballistic Plex or Fast Plex reticles. Battery Life: Medium Power—50-60 hrs; High Power—40-50 hrs.

Burris Scopes

2.75X SCOUT

3-9X SHORT MAG SCOPE

4.5-14X SHORT MAG SCOPE

1.5-6X SIG LRS

3x10 SIG LRS

SCOUT SCOPES

For hunters who need a 7- to 14-in. eye relief for mounting in front of the ejection port; this scope allows you to shoot with both eyes open. The 15-ft. field of view and 2.75X magnification are ideal for brush guns and shotgunners.

SHORT MAG SCOPES

Short Mag riflescopes feature top grade optical glass and index-matched HiLume lens multicoatings; generous 3½-5 in. eye relief; re-settable windage and elevation dials. Lens system formulation combines edge-to-edge clarity with 3½-5 in. of light rifle magnum eye relief. Each variable power Short Mag features a Ballistic Plex reticle.

SIGNATURE SCOPES

Features include premium quality lenses with Hi-Lume multi-coat; large internal lenses; deep relief grooves on the power ring and parallax adjust ring and centrally located adjustment turret; shooter-viewable, easy-to-grip power ring integrated with the eyepiece; non-slip ring of rubber on the internally focusable eyepiece ring. Available with Ball Plex, Ball Plex/PosiLock, Ballistic MilDot and 3P#4/PossiLock reticles.

Burris Scopes

Item	Model	Reticle	Finish	Features	List
BLACK DIAMOND T-PLATES SCOPES (30MM)					
200929	4X-16X-50mm	Ballistic MDot	mat	PA	$1212
BLACK DIAMOND SCOPES (30MM)					
200954	4X-16X-50mm	Plex	mat	Side PA	discontinued
200955	4X-16X-50mm	Ballistic MDot	mat	Side PA	$1212
200958	4X-16X-50mm	Ballistic MDot	mat	PLOCK/ SideP 1,202	discontinued
200926	4X-16X-50mm	Ballistic Plex	mat	—	$1130
200933	6X-24X-50mm	Fine Plex	mat	Tar-Side /PA	$1224
200934	6X-24X-50mm	Ballistic MDot	mat	Tar-Side /PA	$1339
200942	8X-32X-50mm	Fine Plex	mat	Tar-Side /PA	$1226
200943	8X-32X-50mm	Ballistic MDot	mat	Tar-Side /PA	$1416
EURO DIAMOND SCOPES					
200960	1.5X-6X-40mm	German 3P#4	mat	Posi-Lock	$835
200961	1.5X-6X-40mm	German 3P#4	mat	Illuminated	discontinued
200965	3X-10X-40mm	German 3P#4	mat	Posi-Lock	discontinued
200967	3X-10X-40mm	German 3P#4	mat	Illuminated	discontinued
200966	3X-10X-40mm	Ballistic Plex	mat	—	$862
200919	2.5X-10X-44mm	German 3P#4	mat	Posi-Lock	discontinued
200918	2.5X-10X-44mm	Ballistic Plex	mat	—	$888
200914	3X-12X-50mm	German 3P#4	mat	Posi-Lock	discontinued
200915	3X-12X-50mm	German 3P#4	mat	Illuminated	$1108
200916	3X-12X-50mm	Ballistic Plex	mat	—	$955
FULLFIELD II SCOPES					
200052	6X-40mm	Plex	mat	—	$397
200057	6X-32mm HBRII	Superfine XHr	mat	Target /PA	discontinued
200056	6X-32mm HBRII	.375 Dot	mat	Target /PA	discontinued
200153	3X-9X-50mm	Plex	mat	—	discontinued
200154	3X-9X-50mm	Ballistic Plex	mat	—	$524
200089	1.75-5X-20mmPlex	—	camo	—	discontinued
200087	1.75-5X-20mmPlex	—	mat	—	discontinued
200160	3X-9X-40mm	Plex	blk	—	$331
200161	3X-9X-40mm	Plex	mat	—	$331
200162	3X-9X-40mm	Ballistic Plex	mat	—	$349

Item	Model	Reticle	Finish	Features	List
200163	3X-9X-40mm	Plex	nic	—	$384
200164	3X-9X-40mm	German 3P#4	mat	—	discontinued
200166	3X-9X-40mm	Ballistic Plex	blk	—	discontinued
200169	3X-9X-40mm	Ballistic Plex	nic	—	$384
200174	3.5X-10X-50mm	3P#4	blk	—	discontinued
200171	3.5X-10X-50mm	Plex	mat	—	discontinued
200172	3.5X-10X-50mm	Ballistic Plex	mat	—	$608
200180	4.5X-14X	Plex	blk	PA	$611
200181	4.5X-14X	Plex	mat	PA	$611
200183	4.5X-14X-42mm	Ballistic Plex	mat	PA	discontinued
200184	4.5X-14X-42	German 3P#4	mat	PA	discontinued
200191	6.5X-20X-50mm	Fine Plex	mat	PA	$731
200192	6.5X-20X-50mm	Fine Plex	mat	Target /PA	discontinued
200193	6.5X-20X-50mm	Ballistic MDot	mat	PA	$856
200413	2.5X shotgun	Plex	mat	—	discontinued
LASERSCOPES					
200111	4-12x42mm	XTR Ballistic Mil-Dot	mat	Remote activation	$1176
LRS LIGHTED RETICLE SCOPES					
200167	3X-9X Fullfield II	Electro-Dot	mat	—	discontinued
200168	3X-9X FFII LRS	LRS Ball Plex	mat	—	discontinued
200173	3.5X-10X-50 FFII LRS	LRS Ball Plex	mat	—	discontinued
200710	1.75X-5X Sig LRS	LRS Fast Plex	mat	—	discontinued
200179	3-9X-40 Fullfield II	Plex	mat	—	discontinued
200175	3-10X-50 FFII	Plex	mat	—	discontinued
200185	4.5X-14X-42 FFII	Ballistic Plex	mat	—	discontinued
200186	4.5X-14X-42 FFII	Plex	mat	—	discontinued
200719	1.5X-6X-40 Sig Select	Electro-Dot	mat	—	$667
200565	3X-10X-40 Sig Select	Electro-Dot	mat	—	discontinued
200566	3X-10X-40 Sig Select	Ballistic Plex	mat	—	discontinued
200567	3X-10X-40 Sig Select	Ballistic Plex	mat	Posi-Lock	discontinued
200771	4X-16X-44 Sig Select	Electro-Dot	mat	PA	discontinued

SCOPES

ITEM	MODEL	RETICLE	FINISH	FEATURES	LIST
200772	4X-16X-44 Sig Select	Ballistic Plex	mat	PA	$1078
200773	4X-16X-44 Sig Select	Ballistic Plex	mat	Posi-Lock/ PA	discontinued
SCOUT SCOPES					
200424	1X XER	Plex	mat	—	discontinued
200269	2.75X	Heavy Plex	mat	—	$391
SHORT MAG SCOPES					
200424	1X XER	Plex	mat	—	discontinued
201310	4X	Plex	blk	—	discontinued
201311	4X	Plex	mat	—	discontinued
201320	2X-7X	Plex	mat	—	discontinued
201321	2X-7X	Ballistic PlexTM	mat	—	discontinued
201330	3X-9X	Plex	mat	—	discontinued
201331	3X-9X	Ballistic PlexTM	mat	—	discontinued
201340	4.5X-14X	Plex	mat	PA	discontinued
201341	4.5X-14X	Ballistic PlexTM	mat	PA	discontinued
SIGNATURE SERIES SCOPES					
200707	1.75X-5X-32 Safari	Taper Plex	mat	—	discontinued
200708	1.75X-5X-32 Safari	Taper Plex	mat	Posi-Lock	discontinued
200713	1.75X-5X-32 Safari	German 3P#4	mat	Posi-Lock	discontinued

ITEM	MODEL	RETICLE	FINISH	FEATURES	LIST
200717	1.5X-6X-40mm	Taper Plex	mat	—	$667
200718	1.5X-6x-40mm	Taper Plex	mat	Posi-Lock	discontinued
200560	3X-10X-40mm	Ballistic Plex	mat	—	$738
200562	3X-10X-40mm	Plex	mat	—	discontinued
200561	3X-10X-40mm	Ballistic Plex	mat	Posi-Lock	discontinued
200616	3X-12X-44mm	Ballistic Plex	mat	—	$778
200617	3X-12X-44mm	Ballistic Plex	mat	Posi-Lock	$831
200768	4X-16X-44mm	Ballistic Plex	mat	PA	$844
200769	4X-16X-44mm	Ballistic Mdot	mat	PA	$937
200770	4X-16X-44mm	Ballistic Plex	mat	Posi-Lock/ PA	$1078
200822	6X-24X-44mm	Plex	mat	PA	discontinued
200823	6X-24X-44mm	Fine Plex	mat	Target/PA	$912
200824	6X-24X-44mm	Ballistic MDot	mat	Target/PA	$1031
200867	8X-32X	Fine Plex	mat	Target/PA	$922
200868	8X-32X	Ballistic MDot	mat	Target/PA	$1039

Bushnell Riflescopes

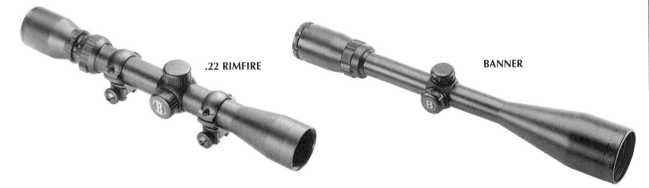

.22 RIMFIRE

BANNER

.22 RIMFIRE RIFLESCOPES

Bushnell .22 Rimfire scopes are designed with a 50-yd parallax setting and fully coated optics. The one-piece 1 in. tube is waterproof and fogproof; ¼ MOA windage and elevation adjustments are fingertip-easy to turn. Scopes come with rings for grooved receivers.

BANNER RIFLESCOPES

Banner Dusk & Dawn riflescopes feature DDB multi-coated lenses to maximize dusk and dawn brightness for clarity in low and full light. A fast-focus eyepiece and wide-angle field of view complement a one-piece tube and ¼ in. MOA resettable windage and elevation adjustments. An easy-trip power change ring allows fast power changes. This scope is waterproof, fogproof and shockproof.

SCOPES

Bushnell Riflescopes

ELITE 3200 4-12

**ELITE 4200
2.5-10X40**

ELITE 2.5-10x50

ELITE 3-9x40

**ELITE 4200
1.5-4X24**

ELITE 3200 RIFLESCOPES

Riflescopes are made with multi-coated optics and a patented Rainguard lens coating that reduces large water drops to near-microscopic specks. Bushnell's FireFly reticle is available on several 3200 models, illuminating the crosshairs. The FireFly reticle glows green after a 10-second flashlight charge. Elite 3200 riflescopes are dry-nitrogen filled and feature a one-piece hammer-forged aluminum tube, 1/4 MOA fingertip, audible/resettable windage and elevation adjustment and are waterproof, fogproof, and shockproof.

ELITE 4200 RIFLESCOPES

Riflescopes feature 95% light transmission at 550mm. 4200s have multi-coated optics with hydrophobic Rainguard lens coating. These scopes feature hammer-forged one-piece aluminum/ titanium alloy dry-nitrogen filled tubes, 1/4 MOA fingertip, audible/resettable windage and elevation adjustment; and are waterproof, fog-proof and shockproof. 4200 scopes are available with Bushnell's FireFly reticle.

ELITE 4200 1.25-4X24

To better address the needs of the tactical and law enforcement market, Bushnell has added a 1.25-4x24mm model to its Elite 4200 line of precision riflescopes. It is equipped with a European reticle with an illuminated 1 MOA mil dot for quicker target acquisition and precise aiming. It has fingertip adjustments for windage and elevation with audible clicks, plus a Fast Focus eyepiece and fully multi-coated optics. It is nitrogen-purged and O-ring sealed, making it waterproof and fog proof inside and out. RainGuard, a permanent water repellent coating, is applied to the objective and ocular lenses to prevent fogging from rain, snow or sudden temperature changes. All Elite 4200 series riflescopes are constructed with titanium-reinforced tubes and recoil tested to 10,000 rounds of a .375 H&H.

Bushnell Riflescopes

SPORTSMAN RIFLESCOPES
Featuring multi-coated optics and a fast-focus eyepiece, easy-grip power change ring and 1/4 MOA fingertip windage and elevation adjustments. The rigid one-piece 1 in. tube is waterproof, fogproof and shockproof.

TROPHY RIFLESCOPES
Riflescopes feature multi-coated optics, Amber-Bright high contrast lens coating, one-piece dry-nitrogen filled tube construction, 1/4 MOA fingertip, audible/resettable windage and elevation adjustment, a fast-focus eyepiece and are waterproof, fogproof and shockproof.

TROPHY 1X28MM RED DOT WITH AUTO ON/OFF
Bushnell's Trophy 1x28mm Red Dot scope features an automatic On/Off switch that conserves battery life by automatically turning the batteries on when the gun is raised to a shooting position and then off when the gun is on its side. It also has a manual override so that the sight can be switched to ALWAYS ON and ALWAYS OFF by hand. Shooters can choose any of four reticle options — 3 MOA dot, 10 MOA dot crosshair, and circle with dot in center— with just a simple twist of the reticle selector knob. The scope is constructed with a one-piece body tube that is dry nitrogen purged and then sealed with an "O" ring to protect the optics against moisture and fog.
MSRP $116.49

TROPHY 1X32MM MP RED DOT RIFLESCOPE
This scope, used on tactical firearms, has integrated Weaver style mounts, and its bright optics, low magnification and T-Dot reticle make for fast target acquisition. The Trophy MP Red Dot offers a choice between a green T-Dot for low-light conditions and a red T-Dot reticle under brighter conditions. It features unlimited eye relief and is dry nitrogen purged and sealed with an o-ring to protect the optics against moisture and fog. Windage and elevation adjustments are 1/4 MOA It comes in a matte black finish.
MSRP: $223.49

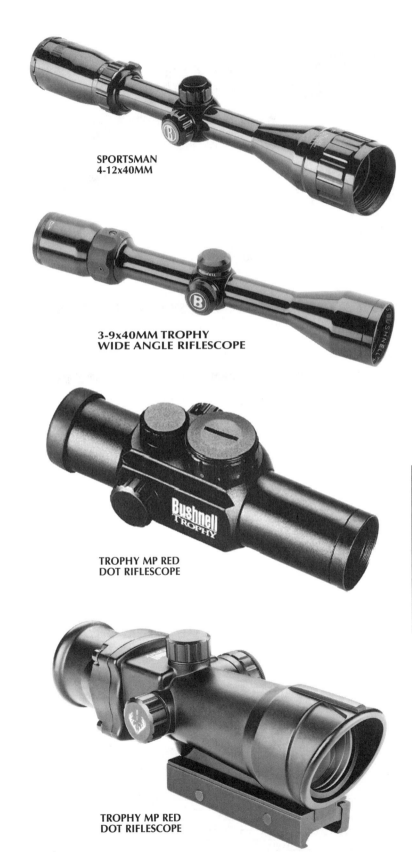

SPORTSMAN
4-12x40MM

3-9x40MM TROPHY
WIDE ANGLE RIFLESCOPE

TROPHY MP RED
DOT RIFLESCOPE

TROPHY MP RED
DOT RIFLESCOPE

SCOPES

Bushnell Riflescopes

YARDAGE PRO LASER RANGEFINDER RIFLESCOPE

This new riflescope combines premium, fully multi-coated optics with a laser rangefinder that accurately ranges targets from 30 to 800 yds. with Bullet Drop Compensator turrets that quickly and easily adjust elevation to the displayed range. The scope comes with five Bullet Drop Compensator (BDC) turrets calibrated to match the most popular calibers and bullet weights. In the field or at the range, the shooter uses a wireless trigger pad to activate the laser rangefinder. Once the distance is displayed in the scope, the BDC turret is adjusted to match the range, eliminating the need for hold-over. Once the shooter knows the range, the Mil Dot reticle can be used to compensate for windage and elevation. Other features include fully multi-coated optics, and waterproof/fog proof construction. Eye relief is set at 3½ in. It is compact in design and weighs just 25.3 oz.

MSRP: **$989.99**

.22 RIMFIRE

Model	Finish	Power / Obj. Lens (mm)	Reticle	Field-of-View (ft@100yds)	Weight (oz)	Length (in)	Eye Relief (in)	Exit Pupil (mm)	Click Value (in@100yds)	Adj. Range (in@100yds)	Suggested Retail
76-2239	Matte	3–9x32	Multi-X®	40–13	11.2	11.75	3.0	10.6–3.6	.25	40	53.99
76-2239S	Silver	3–9x32	Multi-X®	40–13	11.2	11.75	3.0	10.6–3.6	.25	40	53.99
76-2243	Matte	4x32	Multi-X®	30 / 10@4x	10	11.5	3.0	8	.25	40	46.99

BANNER DUSK & DAWN

Model	Finish	Power / Obj. Lens (mm)	Reticle	Field-of-View (ft@100yds)	Weight (oz)	Length (in)	Eye Relief (in)	Exit Pupil (mm)	Click Value (in@100yds)	Adj. Range (in@100yds)	Suggested Retail
71-0432	Matte	4x32	Circle-X®	31.5–10.5@4x	11.1	11.3	3.3	8@4x	.25	50	discontinued
71-1432	Matte	1–4x32	Circle-X®	78.5–24.9	12.2	10.5	4.3	16.9@1x / 8@4x	.25	50	discontinued
71-1436	Matte	1.75–4x32	Circle-X®	35–16	12.1	10.8	6	18.3@1.75x –6.4@4x	.25	100	discontinued
71-1545	Matte	1.5–4.5x32	Multi-X®	67v23	10.5	10.5	4.0	17@1.5x / 7@4.5x	.25	60	discontinued
71-3510	Matte	3.5-10x36	Multi-X®	30-10.4 15.0	12.5	3.4		10.3@ 3.5/3.6 @10	.25	85	129.99
71-3944	Matte	3–9x40	Circle-X®	36–13	12.5	11.5	4.0	13@3x / 4.4@9x	.25	60	178.49
71-3944MO	MosOak	3–9x40	Circle-X®	36/12@3x–12/4.3@9x	12.5	11.5	4.0	13@3x / 4.4@9x	.25	60	discontinued
71-3946	Matte	3–9x40	Multi-X®	40–14	13	12	4.0	13@3x / 4.4@9x	.25	60	60
71-3947	Matte	3–9x40	Multi-X®	40–13.6	13	12	3.3	13@3x / 4.4@9x	.25	60	107.99
71-3948	Matte	3–9x40	Multi-X®	40–14	13	12	3.3	13.3@3x / 4.4@9x	.25	60	101.99
71-3949I	Matte	3–9x40	R/G illuminated	40/13.6@3x–14/4.7@9x	13	12	3.3	13.3@3x / 4.4@9x	.25	60	129.99
71-3950	Matte	3–9x50	Multi-X®	26–12	19	16	3.8	16@3x / 5.6@9x	.25	50	158.49
71-3951	Matte	3–9x50	3-2-1 Low Light™	26–12	19	16	3.8	16@3x / 5.6@9x	.25	50	discontinued
71-3959I	Matte	3–9x50	R/G illuminated	36/12@3x–12/4@9x	20	16	3.8	16@3x / 5.6@9x	.25	50	168.49
71-4124	Matte	4–12x40	Multi-X®	29–11	15	12	3.3	10@4x / 3.3@12x	.25	60	138.95
71-4164I	Matte	4–16x40	illuminated	22/7@4x–6/2@16x	16	14	3.3	10@4x / 2.5@16x	.25	70	discontinued
71-6185	Matte	6–18x50	Multi-X®	17–6	18	16	3.5	8.3@6x / 2.8@18x	.25	40	178.49
71-6244	Matte	6–24x40	Mil Dot	17–5	19.6	16.1	3.4	6.7@6x / 1.7@24x	.25	36	178.49

ELITE 3200

Model	Finish	Power / Obj. Lens (mm)	Reticle	Field-of-View (ft@100yds)	Weight (oz)	Length (in)	Eye Relief (in)	Exit Pupil (mm)	Click Value (in@100yds)	Adj. Range (in@100yds)	Suggested Retail
32-1040M	Matte	10x40	Mil Dot	11	15.5	11.7	3.5	4.0	.25	100	discontinued
32-1546M	Matte	1.5–4.5x32	FireFly™	63/21@1.5x	13	12.5	3.6	21–7.6	.25	100	discontinued
32-2632M	Matte	2–6x32	Multi-X®	10/3@2x	10	9	20	16–5.3	.25	50	discontinued
32-2632S	Silver	2–6x32	Multi-X®	10/3@2x	10	9	20	16–5.3	.25	50	discontinued
*32-2636M	Matte	2–6x32	FireFly™	10/3@2x	10	9	20	16–5.3	.25	50	discontinued
32-2732M	Matte	2–7x32	Multi-X®	44.6/15@2x	12	11.6	3.0	12.2–4.6	.25	50	221.99
32-3104M	Matte	3-10 x40	Multi-X®	35.5/11.8 03x	14.5	11	3.7	13.1-4	.25	85	255.49
32-3940G	Gloss	3–9x40	Multi-X®	33.8/11@3x	13	12.6	3.3	13.3–4.4	.25	50	223.99
32-3940S	Silver	3–9x40	Multi-X®	33.8/11@3x	13	12.6	3.3	13.3–4.4	.25	50	223.99
32-3944B	Matte	3–9x40	Ballistic	9.8@3x	13	12.6	3.3	13.3–4.4	.25	50	discontinued
32-3944M	Matte	3–9x40	Multi-X®	33.8/11@3x	13	12.6	3.3	13.3–4.4	.25	50	223.99
32-3946M	Matte	3–9x40	FireFly™	33.8/11@3x	13	12.6	3.3	13.3–4.4	.25	50	discontinued
32-3954M	Matte	3–9x50	Multi-X®	31.5/10@3x	19	15.7	3.3	16–5.6	.25	50	287.49
32-3955E	Matte	3–9x50	European	31.5/10@3x	22	15.6	3.3	16–5.6	.36	70	discontinued
32-3956M	Matte	3–9x50	FireFly™	31.5/1.50@3x	19	15.7	3.3	16.7–5.6	.25	50	364.49
32-3957M	Matte	3–9x50	FireFly™	31.5/10.5@3x	22	15.6	3.3	16.7–5.6	.25	70	discontinued
32-4124A	Matte	4–12x40	Multi-X®	26.9/9@4x	15	13.2	3.3	10–3.33	.25	50	351.49
32-4124B	Matte	4–12x40	Ballistic	26.9/9@4x	15	13.2	3.3	10–3.33	.25	50	discontinued
32-5154M	Matte	5–15x40	Multi-X®	21/7@5x	19	14.5	4.3	9–2.7	.25	50	376.99
32-5155M	Matte	5–15x50	Multi-X®	21/7@5x	24	15.9	3.4	10–3.3	.25	40	395.99
*32-5156M	Matte	5–15x40	FireFly™	21/7@5x	19	14.5	4.3	9–2.7	.25	50	discontinued
32-7214M	Matte	7-21x40	MilDot	13.5/4.5@7x	15	12.8	3.3	14.6-6	.25	40	470.49

Bushnell Riflescopes

ELITE 4200

MODEL	FINISH	POWER / OBJ. LENS (MM)	RETICLE	FIELD-OF-VIEW (FT@100YDS)	WEIGHT (OZ)	LENGTH (IN)	EYE RELIEF (IN)	EXIT PUPIL (MM)	CLICK VALUE (IN@100YDS)	ADJ. RANGE (IN@100YDS)	SUGGESTED RETAIL
42-1636M	Matte	1.5–6x36	Multi-X®	61.8/20.6@1.5x	15.4	12.8	3.3	14.6–6	.25	60	discontinued
42-1637M	Matte	1.5–6x36	FireFly™	61.8/20.6 @65x	15.4	12.8	3.3	14.6–6	.25	60	discontinued
42-2104M	Matte	2.5–10x40	Multi-X®	41.5/13.8@2.5x	16	13.5	3.3	15.6–4	.25	50	$469.99
42-2104G	Gloss	2.5–10x40	Multi-X®	41.5/13.8@2.5x	16	13.5	3.3	15.6–4	.25	50	discontinued
42-2104S	Silver	2.5–10x40	Multi-X®	41.5/13.8@2.5x	16	13.5	3.3	15.6–4	.25	50	discontinued
42-2105M	Matte	2.5–10x50	Multi-X®	40.3/13.4@2.5x	18	14.3	3.3	15–5	.25	50	$611.99
42-2106M	Matte	2.5–10x50	FireFly™	40.3/13.4 @25x	18	14.3	3.3	15–5	.25	50	discontinued
42-2146M	Matte	2.5–10x40	FireFly™	41.5/13.8@2.5x	16	13.5	3.3	15.6–4	.25	50	discontinued
42-2151M	Matte	2.5–10x50	4A w/1 M.O.A Dot	40/13.3@2.5x	22	14.5	3.3	5–15	.25	60	discontinued
42-2152M	Matte	2.5–10x50	4A w/1 MOA illumated Dot	12@2.5x	22	14.5	3.3	15–5	.25	60	discontinued
42-4164M	Matte	4–16x40	Multi-X®	26/8.7@4x	18.6	14.4	3.3	10–25	.125	40	discontinued
42-4165M	Matte	4–16x50	Multi-X®	26/9@4x	22	15.6	3.3	12.5–3.1	.125	50	discontinued
42-6242M	Matte	6–24x40	Mil Dot	18/6@6x	20.2	16.9	3.3	6.7–1.7	.125	26	$603.49
42-6243A	Matte	6–24x40	¼ MOA Dot	18/6@6x	20.2	16.9	3.3	6.7–1.7	.125	26	$584.99
42-6244M	Matte	6–24x40	Multi-X®	18/4.5@6x	20.2	16.9	3.3	6.7–1.7	.125	26	$584.99
42-8324M	Matte	8–32x40	Multi-X®	14/4.7@8x	22	18	3.3	5–1.25	.125	20	$643.99

SPORTSMAN® RIFLESCOPES

MODEL	FINISH	POWER / OBJ. LENS (MM)	RETICLE	FIELD-OF-VIEW (FT@100YDS)	WEIGHT (OZ)	LENGTH (IN)	EYE RELIEF (IN)	EXIT PUPIL (MM)	CLICK VALUE (IN@100YDS)	ADJ. RANGE (IN@100YDS)	SUGGESTED RETAIL
*72-0038	Matte	3–9x32	Multi-X®	37–14	13.5	12	3.5	10.6–3.6	.25	100	discontinued
**72-0039	Gloss	3–9x32	Multi-X®	40 13.1	163	12.2	430	3.6–11	.25	100	$100.99
72-0130	Matte	1x23	6 MOA Red Dot	60	4.9	5.5	Unlimited	2.3	.5	50	discontinued
72-1393	Gloss	3–9x32	Multi-X®	37–14	13.5	12	3.5	10–3.6	.25	100	discontinued
72-1393S	Silver	3–9x32	Multi-X®	37–14	13.5	12	3.5	10–3.6	.25	100	$59.49
72-1398	Matte	3–9x32	Multi-X®	37–14	13.5	12	3.5	10–3.6	.25	100	$59.49
72-1403	Matte	4x32	Multi-X®	29	11	11.7	3.4	8	.25	110	$50.49
72-1545	Matte	1.5–4.5x21	Multi-X®	24–69	11.7	10.1	3.3	10–3.6	.25	210	discontinued
72-1548R	Camo	1.5–4.5x32	Circle-X®	46.2–19.3	13.5	11.7	4.3	21–7.1	.25	100	discontinued
72-3940M	Matte	3–9x40	Multi-X®	37–12	15	13	3.5	13–4.4	.25	100	discontinued
72-3943	Matte	3–9x40	Lowlight	37–12	15	13	3.5	13–4.4	.25	100	discontinued

*Airgun scope   **Target Airgun scope

TROPHY® RIFLESCOPES

MODEL	FINISH	POWER / OBJ. LENS (MM)	RETICLE	FIELD-OF-VIEW (FT@100YDS)	WEIGHT (OZ)	LENGTH (IN)	EYE RELIEF (IN)	EXIT PUPIL (MM)	CLICK VALUE (IN@100YDS)	ADJ. RANGE (IN@100YDS)	SUGGESTED RETAIL
73-0131	Matte	1x28	6 MOA Red Dot	68–22.6	6	5.5	Unlimited	28	.5	50	$87.49
73-0132A	Matte	1x28	5 MOA Red Dot	68–22.6	7.0	5.5	Unlimited	28	3.3	50	$153.99
73-0132P	Matte	1x32	Red/Green T- dot	44	15.6	13.7	3.3	32	.25	70	$223.45
73-0134	Matte	1x28	4 Dial-In Electronic	68–22.6	6	5.5	Unlimited	28	.5	50	$116.49
73-0135	Matte	1x30	4 Dial-Fn	68–22.6	6	5.5	Unlimited	28	.5	50	$127.49
73-0232S	Silver	2x32	Multi-X®	20–7	7.7	8.7	18	16	.25	90	discontinued
73-1421	Matte	1.75–4x32	Circle-X®	73–30	10.9	10.8	4.1	18@1.75x / 8@4x	.25	120	discontinued
73-1422AP	Camo	1.75–4x32	Circle-X®	73–30	10.9	10.8	4.1	18@1.75x / 8@4x	.25	120	$158.49
73-1500	Gloss	1.75–5x32	Multi-X®	68–23	12.3	10.8	4.1	18.3@1.75x / 6.4@5x	.25	120	discontinued
73-2632	Matte	2–6x32	Multi-X®	11–4	10.9	9.1	9–26	16@2x / 5.3@6x	.25	50	$213.99
73-2632S	Silver	2–6x32	Multi-X®	11–4	10.9	9.1	9–26	16@2x / 5.3@6x	.25	50	$243.99
73-3940	Gloss	3–9x40	Multi-X®	42–14	13.2	11.7	3.4	13.3@3x / 4.4@9x	.25	60	$130.49
73-3940S	Silver	3–9x40	Multi-X®	42–14	13.2	11.7	3.4	13.3@3x / 4.4@9x	.25	60	$130.49
73-3946	Matte	3–9x40	Mil Dot	42–14	13.2	11.7	3.4	13.3@3x / 4.4@9x	.25	60	$144.99
73-3948	Matte	3–9x40	Multi-X®	42–14	13.2	11.7	3.4	13.3@3x / 4.4@9x	.25	60	$129.99
73-39481	Matte	3–9x40	TRX	42–14	13.2	11.7	3.4	13.3 @3x/4.4 @9x	.25	60	discontinued
73-3949	Matte	3–9x40	Circle-X®	42–14	13.2	11.7	3.4	13.3@3x / 4.4@9x	.25	60	$144.99
73-4124	Gloss	4–12x40	Multi-X®	32–11	16.1	12.6	3.4	10@4x / 3.3@12x	.25	60	discontinued
73-4124M	Matte	4–12x40	Multi-X®	32–11	16.1	12.6	3.4	10@4x / 3.3@12x	.25	60	$215.49
73-6184	Matte	6–18 x 40	Multi-X®	17.3–6	17.9	14.8	3.0	6.6@6x / 2.2@18x	.125	40	$321.49

YARDAGE

MODEL	RANGE (YARDS)	MAGNIFICATION	OBJ. LENS	FIELD OF VIEW FT.@100 YDS. M@100M	EYE RELIEF	LENGTH (IN / MM)	WEIGHT (OZ. / G)	BATTERY TYPE	SCAN	TREE (YARDS)	DEER (YARDS)	ACCURACY (YARDS)	PRICE
20-4124	30-800	4–12x	42mm	26@4x / 8.7@4x 8.5@12x / 2.8@12x	3.5 / 8.7	13 / 330	24 / 680	3-volt	Yes	800	550	+/-1	discontinued

"Bring a spare scope. A rifle that's put out of commission can often be fixed, but if your scope is damaged, it's time to pee on the fire and call in the dogs, because the hunt is over." —David E. Petzal

Cabela's Scopes

PINE RIDGE								
POWER	FINISH	RETICLE	OBJECTIVE DIAMETER (MM)	EYE RELIEF (IN.)	LENGTH (IN.)	WEIGHT (OZ.)	FOV 100 YARDS (FT)	PRICE
2-7	Matte	MX(5-4)	32	4.1	12.2	16	47-15	$99–179
3-9	Matte	MX(5-7)	40	4.3	13.3	17.6	39-13	$99–179
3-12SF	Matte	MX(5-7)	40	3.3	13.1	17.1	36-9	$99–179
6-18SF	Matte	MX(5-7)	40	3.4	15.7	18.6	17-6	$99–179

PINE RIDGE .17 TACTICAL RIFLESCOPES

Cabela's scopes are specially engineered for rifles in the .17 HMR caliber. The Pine Ridge .17 Tactical Riflescopes are incrementally calibrated to adjust for bullet drop out to 300 yds. Waterproof, fogproof and shockproof, these scopes have fully coated optics. Mounting tube is 1 in., and eye relief is 3 in. The scopes also have finger-adjustable windage and elevation with trajectory compensation turret and parallax adjustment. The 3-12x40 and 6-18x40 feature side-focus parallax adjustment. These scopes have all the quality features and high-performance optics of the regular .17 Tactical Scopes above, but by repositioning the parallax setting knob location on the scope, Cabela's has enabled the user to keep the target in sight while making adjustments from 50 to 300 yds. and beyond. Side-focus models also have a larger field of view for quicker target acquisition.

Docter Sports Optics Scopes

3-10x40MM

DESCRIPTION	MAGNIFICATION	OBJECTIVE LENS DIA.	COLOR	RETICLE	PRICE
ONE-INCH TUBE SCOPES					
3-9x40 Variable	3x to 9x	40mm	Matte Black	Plex	$599–999
3-9x40 Variable	3x to 9x	40mm	Matte Black	German #4	$599–999
3-10x40 Variable	3x to 10x	40mm	Matte Black	Plex	$599–999
3-10x40 Variable	3x to 10x	40mm	Matte Black	German #4	$599–999
4.5-14x40 Variable	4.5x to 14x	40mm	Matte Black	Plex	$599–999
4.5-14x40 Variable	4.5x to 14x	40mm	Matte Black	Dot	$599–999
8-25x50 Variable	8x to 25x	50mm	Matte Black	Dot	$599–999
8-25x50 Variable	8x to 25x	50mm	Matte Black	Plex	$599–999
30mm TUBE SCOPES					
1.5-6x42 Variable	1.5x to 6x	42mm	Matte Black	Plex	$899
1.5-6x42 Variable	1.5x to 6x	42mm	Matte Black	German #4	discontinued
1.5-6x42 Var., Aspherical Lens	1.5x to 6x	42mm	Matte Black	Plex	discontinued
1.5-6x42 Var., Aspherical Lens	1.5x to 6x	42mm	Matte Black	German #4	discontinued
2.5-10x48 Variable	2.5x to 10x	48mm	Matte Black	Plex	$899
2.5-10x48 Variable	2.5x to 10x	48mm	Matte Black	German #4	$899
2.5-10x48 Var., Aspherical Lens	2.5x to 10x	48mm	Matte Black	Plex	discontinued
2.5-10x48 Var., Aspherical Lens	2.5x to 10x	48mm	Matte Black	German #4	discontinued
3-12x56 Variable	3x to 12x	56mm	Matte Black	Plex	$989
3-12x56 Variable	3x to 12x	56mm	Matte Black	German #4	discontinued
3-12x56 Var., Aspherical Lens	3x to 12x	56mm	Matte Black	Plex	$989
3-12x56 Var., Aspherical Lens	3x to 12x	56mm	Matte Black	German #4	$989

RIFLE SCOPES

Features: High strength, one-piece tube; high grade multi-coating; joints sealed with statically and dynamically loaded ring gaskets; diopter focus; precise click-stop adjustments of 1/4 in. at 100 yds. for windage and elevation; more than 3 in. of eye relief; wide rubber ring on the eye-piece; wide range of adjustment (50 in.) for easier mounting error compensation.

**HELIA CL 1-IN.
3-9x42**

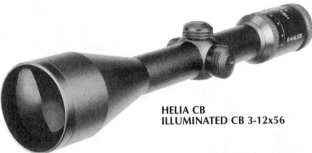

**HELIA CB
ILLUMINATED CB 3-12x56**

HELIA COMPACT C 1,1-4x24

HELIA CSX 1.5-6x42

HELIA CL 1-INCH RIFLESCOPES

Features of Helia CL 1-in. scopes include the Kahles multizero system, a revolutionary "micro-mechanic" ballistic system that will allow users to pre-set up to five different sight settings on the scope; third turret parallax; enhanced AMV Lens Coating technology on all air-to-glass surfaces which now maximizes low light performance by transmitting a higher percentage of the visible light spectrum; waterproof submersible turrets even when protective caps are removed; expanded point-of-impact total range of adjustment; and an 18% larger ocular diameter which has expanded the eye relief, expanded the field-of-view, fast focus ocular dial and enhanced the edge-to-edge resolution.

All Kahles CL riflescopes have the reticle located in the (non-magnifying) second image focal plane that maintains its size throughout the magnification range, come standard with a technologically advanced, scratch-resistant matte finish.

HELIA COMPACT

Kahles AMV-multi-coatings transmit up to 99.5% per air-to-glass surface. This ensures optimum use of incident light, especially in low light level conditions or at twilight. These 30mm Kahles rifle scopes are shockproof, waterproof and fogproof, nitrogen purged several times to assure the elimination of any moisture.

HELIA CB ILLUMINATED

Adjustable for illumination, and minimizes stray light. Battery life: 110 hrs.

HELIA CL RIFLESCOPES						
Model	Power/Obj. Lens (mm)	Field of View (ft/100yds)	Eye Relief (in.)	Click Value (in.@100yds)	Length (in.)	Weight (oz.)	Price
CL 2-7x36	2-7x36	48-17	3.6	.36	11	13.6	$999
CL 3-9x42	3-9x42	39-13.5	3.6	.36	12.1	14.1	$769
CL 3-10x50	3-10x50	34-12	3.6	.36	12.1	14.1	$799
4-12x52	4-12x52	29-10	3.6	.25	13.9	18.0	$899

HELIA COMPACT RIFLESCOPES						
Model	Power/Obj. Lens (mm)	Field of View (ft/100yds)	Eye Relief (in.)	Click Value (in.@100yds)	Length (in.)	Weight (oz.)	Price
C 1.1-4x24	1.1-4x24	118.8-32	3.6	.54	10.8	14.6-21.5	$1467
C 1.5-6x42	1.5-6x42	75.5-21.5	3.6	.36	12.0	16.4-24.2	$1027.97
C 2.5-10x50	2.5-10x50	45.3-13	3.6	.36	12.8	17.3-25.4	$1644
C 3-12x56	3-12x56	37.8-10.9	3.6	.36	14.0	19.4-28.5	$1727
C 4x36	4x36	35	3.6	.36	11.4	12.7	$658
C 6x42	6x42	23.6	3.6	.36	12.6	14.5-21.2	$845

HELIA CB ILLUMINATED						
Model	Power/Obj. Lens (mm)	Field of View (ft/100yds)	Eye Relief (in.)	Click Value (in.@100yds)	Length (in.)	Weight (oz.)	Price
CBX 2.5-10X50	2.5-10X50	45.3-13	3.5	.36	12.8	18.3-19.4	$1779
CBX 3-12x56	3-12x56	37.8-10.9	3.5	.36	14.0	20.5-21.5	$1728
CSX 1.5-6x42	1.5-6x42	81.5-21.5	3.6	.36	12.0	17.3-18.3	$1627
CSX 2.5-10x50	2.5-10x50	43.8-12.7	3.6	.36	12.8	18.3-19.4	$1826.59

Kaps Optics Scopes

Kap scopes feature high-quality glass and state-of-the-art coatings, illuminated reticles, 30mm alloy tubes, satin finish.

KAPS				
MAGNIFICATION x OBJ. DIA.	FIELD OF VIEW (FT., 100 YDS.)	DIA./LENGTH (IN.)	WEIGHT (OZ.)	MSRP
4x36	32.8	1.18/12.8	14.1	$699
6x42	20.3	1.18/12.8	15.9	$799
8x56	18	1.18/14.2	20.8	$899
10x50	13.8	1.18/14.1	20.6	$999
1-4x22	98-33	1.18/14.2	20.6	$899
1.5-6x42	62-23	1.18/12.4	17.3	$999
2-8x42	57-17	1.18/13.2	17.3	$1099
2.5-10x50	40.7-13.8	1.18/14.1	20.6	$1199
2.5-10x56	40.7-13.8	1.18/14.6	20.6	$1199

Konus USA Scopes

PRO SHOTGUN/BLACKPOWDER

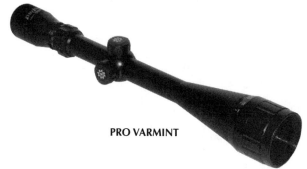

PRO VARMINT

PRO SHOTGUN/ BLACKPOWDER SCOPE

Two new KonusPro scopes in a fixed 2.5X32mm and a variable 1.5X-5X32mm configuration, both with etched reticles, are available for shotgun and blackpowder applications. Other features include long-eye relief, Aim-Pro reticle design (circle/diamond pattern), multi-coated optical glass for increased light transmission and a nitrogen purged tube assembly for 100% waterproof and fogproof integrity.

2.5X32mm: $83.99
1.5X-5X32mm: $99.99

PRO VARMINT SCOPE

The KonusPro 6X-24X44mm Varmint Scope features an etched reticle and adjustable objective. It also includes finger-adjustable windage and elevation controls, multi-coated glass optics, nitrogen purged tube assembly and a tapered 30/30 styled reticle. The KonusPro rifle scope line all contain a glass engraved/laser etched reticle system. The reticle is etched on to precision glass rather than using a thin wire. The etched reticle system is extremely rugged and eliminates the chances of breaking or becoming misaligned. **Discontinued**

KONUS USA PRO SHOTGUN/BLACKPOWDER SCOPE							
MODEL	POWER/OBJ. LENS (MM)	FIELD OF VIEW (FT/100YDS)	EYE RELIEF (IN.)	RETICLE TYPE	LENGTH (IN.)	WEIGHT (OZ.)	PRICE
7248	2.5x32	37	5	Grabada Aim-Pro	10.9	11.6	$83.99

KONUS USA PRO VARMINT SCOPE							
MODEL	POWER/OBJ. LENS (MM)	FIELD OF VIEW (FT/100YDS)	EYE RELIEF (IN.)	RETICLE TYPE	LENGTH (IN.)	WEIGHT (OZ.)	PRICE
7258	6-24x44	16.5-4.1	3.6	Grabada 30/30	15.5	21.3	discontinued

Leatherwood/Hi-Lux Scopes

SHORT MALCOLM SCOPE

Leatherwood/Hi-Lux Optics' shorter 17-in. version of the original Wm. Malcolm scopes can be used on a wide range of vintage-style breech-loading rifle models dating from the 1880s into the first half of the 20th Century. The ¾ in. diameter, blued-steel scope comes standard with Unertl-style mounting blocks, requiring gunsmith installation (two holes drilled and tapped for each block) on many rifles. Optional "no gunsmithing" mounts now also make it easy for the Winchester Model 1873 and Model 1876 rifle owner to off-set mount this scope, utilizing the rear sight dovetail and raised dust-cover rail of the receiver. The mounts move the scope just enough to the left to permit top-ejected cases to clear. Leatherwood/Hi-Lux Optics also offers specialty mounts to fit a variety of other current production rifles, such as the Henry Repeating Arms lever-actions, the Marlin Model 1895 Cowboy, Sharps 1874 side-hammer rifles and the break-open H&R Buffalo Classic and Model .38-55 Target rifles.

The company chose to produce this scope in 3x, making it an ideal hunting scope. The caged rear mount is easily adjusted for windage and elevation, making sighting in a snap. Like the originals, this scope does not offer microme-ter click adjustment. Instead, the shooter unlocks a collar under the adjustment

SHORT MALCOLM SCOPE

screw (with either windage or elevation). Then, once an adjustment has been made, the lock collar is turned to lock that adjustment in place. When the scope is fully adjusted, the lock collars for both adjustments can be snugged tight and the scope will hold that setting. The scope has super bright, sharp and crisp multi-coated lenses.
MSRP: **$278.99**

"WM. MALCOLM" SCOPE AND MOUNTS

The Wm. Malcolm scope offers authentic 1870s looks and styling, but has been built with the benefits of modern scope-making technology. Unlike the originals used on Sharps, Winchester High Wall and Remington Rolling Block black powder cartridge rifles, this 6X long tube-type scope is built with light gathering full multi-coated lenses. This scope is built with a nitro-

"WM. MALCOLM" SCOPE AND MOUNTS

gen-filled ¾ in. tube for fog-free service. The scope can be mounted on old-style rifles with barrel lengths from 28 to 34 in. using the factory cut front and rear sight dovetails. Comes with fully adjustable external mounts.
MSRP: **$399.99**

Legacy Sports International

DIAMOND SPORTSMAN

DIAMOND SPORTSMAN RIFLESCOPES

Legacy scopes made by Nikko Stirling are immersion- and shock-tested at the factory and nitrogen filled to eliminate fogging. The N-S Diamond series features first-quality, Diamond-Bright multi-coated lenses sealed in a one-piece air-craft aluminum tube with an adjustable neoprene padded eyepiece. The Diamond Sportsman riflescopes offer adjustable parallax settings from 10 yds. to infinity. All other Nikko-Stirling scopes, including the Gold Crown series, are parallax set to 100 yds., effectively providing no discernible parallax between 75 yds. to infinity.
Discontinued

Legacy Sports International

GOLD CROWN

GOLD CROWN RIFLESCOPES
1.5-6X42: . . . . Discontinued
3-9X42 NO AO: . . . . . Discontinued
4.5-14X50 AO: . . . . . . Discontinued
4-12X42 AO: . . . . Discontinued
4X32: . . . . Discontinued
4X42: . . . . Discontinued
6X42: . . . . Discontinued

PLATINUM EUROHUNTER (30MM TUBE)
1.5-6X44 #4: . . . . Discontinued
1.5-6X44 IR #4: . . . . . Discontinued
3-12X56 IR #4: . . . . . Discontinued
3-12X56 #4: . . . . Discontinued

PLATINUM NIGHTEATER HUNTING (1-IN. TUBE)
1.5-6X36 #: . . . . Discontinued
3.5-10X42 #4: . . . . . . Discontinued
4-16X44 #4: . . . . Discontinued
6-24X44 MD: . . . . Discontinued
8-32X44 MD: . . . . Discontinued
6X36 #4: . . . . Discontinued
12X44 #4: . . . . Discontinued

PLATINUM NIGHTEATER RIFLESCOPES (30MM TUBE)
4-16X50 MD: . . . . Discontinued
6-24X56 MD: . . . . Discontinued
6-24X56 MD: . . . . Discontinued
6-24X56 IR MD: . . . . . Discontinued
12X50 MD: . . . . Discontinued

Leupold Scopes

COMPETITION SERIES 45X45MM

FX-II 12x40MM STANDARD

FX-II 2.5x28

FX-II 6x36

FX-II 6x42

FX-II 4X33

FX-II 2.2x20MM COMPACT

COMPETITION SERIES SCOPES
Leupold's new Competition series offer a bright, crisp sight picture with outstanding contrast. The side-focus parallax adjustment knob allows you to adjust your scope to be parallax-free at distances from 40 yds. to infinity. Available in matte finish with target dot or target crosshair reticle.

FX-II (FIXED POWER) SCOPES
Features: Multicoat 4 lens system; _ MOA click windage and elevation dials; special 9 in. eye relief; available in matte or gloss finish; duplex or wide duplex reticles; Leupold full lifetime guarantee.

Leupold Scopes

HANDGUN SCOPES

Features: Compact scope for handguns; multicoat 4 lens system; ¼ MOA click windage and elevation dials; special 9 in. eye relief; available in matte or gloss finish; duplex or wide duplex reticles; Leupold full lifetime guarantee.

LPS PREMIERE SCOPES

Leupold's Premiere Scope (LPS) line features 30mm tubes, fast-focus eyepieces, armored power selector dials that can be read from the shooting position, 4 in. constant eye relief, Diamondcoat lenses for increased light transmission, scratch resistance, and finger-adjustable, low-profile elevation and windage adjustments.

MARK 2 TACTICAL RIFLESCOPES

Leupold's new Mark 2 tactical riflescopes include the 1.5-4x20mm, 3-9x40mm Hunter, 3-9x40mm T2, 4-12x40mm Adjustable Objective T2 and 6-18x40mm Adjustable Objective T1. Each riflescope in the series is completely waterproof and features Leupold's Multicoat 4 lens coating for superior clarity and brightness, edge-to-edge sharpness across the visual field and optimal contrast for easy target identification in virtually any light or atmospheric condition. Additionally, the riflescopes also feature lockable, fast-focus eyepieces and tactile power indicators.

MARK 4 TACTICAL SCOPES

Fixed and variable power. ¼ MOA audible click windage and elevation adjustments (Except M-3s). Duplex or MilDot reticle. Waterproof. Leupold Long Range/Tactical optics feature: 30mm (1.18 in.) main tubes–increased windage and elevation adjustment; index matched lens system; finger-adjustable dials. Fully illuminated Mil Dot, Duplex or TMR reticles available in select models. Front Focal model with the reticle in the front focal plane of the scope increases in magnification along with the image.

LPS 3.5-14x50MM SIDE FOCUS (SATIN FINISH)

MARK 2 TACTICAL

MARK 4 3.5-10x40 LRT M1

MARK 4 2.5-8x36

MARK 4 16x40MM

Leupold Scopes

MARK 4 8.5-25x50MM ER/T M1

VX-1 2-7x28
RIMFIRE

3-9x40MM DUPLEX

6-18x40MM

MARK 4 8.5-25X50MM ER/T M1 RIFLESCOPE

Engineered with its reticles in the front focal plane, Leupold's 8.5-25x50mm Mark 4 Extended Range/Tactical ER/T M1 riflescope allows tactical shooters to range targets at all magnifications. The front focal design allows a shooter to increase the riflescope's magnification, as well as the magnification of the reticle. By doing so, shooters maintain the versatility of a variable magnification optic as well as the ability to use the Mil Dot or TMR reticle to engage a target at any magnification setting. Designed for the U.S. Marine Corps, the Mil Dot reticle features a series of dots in one milliradian increments on the crosshair. Bracketing the target between dots allows the shooter to estimate range. The TMR expands on the Mil Dot principle incorporating a series of various sized and spaced hash marks for increased ranging precision and more accurate shot placement. The ER/T M1 also features Leupold's Index Matched Lens System for maximum light transmission and clarity, as well as reduced glare. Additionally, the lockable, fast-focus eyepiece delivers long eye relief to provide the shooter with nearly instant target acquisition and protection from the hardest recoiling extreme range firearms such as the .50 BMG and .338 Lapua.

RIMFIRE SCOPES

Adapted to the unique requirements of rimfire shooting. Features: Standard multicoat lens system; micro-friction windage and elevation dials; 60 yds. parallax correction distance; Leupold full lifetime guarantee.

SHOTGUN & MUZZLELOADERS SCOPES

Leupold shotgun scopes are parallax-adjusted to deliver precise focusing at 75 yds. Each scope features a special Heavy Duplex reticle that is more effective against heavy, brushy backgrounds. All scopes have matte finish and Multicoat 4 lens coating.

Leupold Scopes

TACTICAL PRISMATIC 1X14MM RIFLESCOPE

With an etched-glass reticle that is always crisp, and provides military and law enforcement professionals with unmatched reliability, the Leupold 1x14mm Tactical Prismatic separates itself from red dot sights by remaining functional if the batteries die.

The Leupold Tactical Prismatic features a unique, removable Illuminated Module which illuminates the circle dot reticle in red. The riflescope also allows instant target acquisition by virtue of its wide field of view and one true power magnification that allows sighting with both eyes open. In addition, shooters experience no need to change focus from the target to the sight. The sight features a focusing eyepiece, allowing the Tactical Prismatic to be easily adjusted, and is compatible with A.R.M.S. #22-34mm throw-lever rings base and spacer system as well as the conventional 30mm ring. Different height mounting spacers are included, and DiamondCoat 2 lens coatings exceed the military's durability standard with 500 rub performance.

ULTRALIGHT SCOPES

Ultralight riflescopes have about 17% less weight than their full-size counterparts, but retain all of the features of the larger scopes. Ultralight scopes have a Multicoat 4 lens system, are waterproof and are covered by the Leupold Full Lifetime Guarantee. They are available in matte finish with Duplex or Heavy Duplex reticles.

VX-I SCOPES

A tough, gloss black finish and Duplex reticle.

TACTICAL PRISMATIC 1x14MM

ULTRALIGHT VX-II 3-9x33

VX-I 1-4x20MM SHOTGUN/ MUZZLELOADER

VX-I 3-9x40MM

SCOPES

If a scope is mounted too far to the rear, the eyepiece can injure the shooter's brow. Shooting at an uphill angle also increases this hazard because it shortens the distance between the brow and the rear of the scope. Therefore, when mounting your scope, position it as far forward in the mounts as possible to take full advantage of the scope's eye relief.

Leupold Scopes

VX III

VX-III 4.5-14x40

VX-II SCOPES

The VX-II line offers Multi-Coated 4 lens coatings for improved light transmission; ¼ MOA click adjustments; a locking eyepiece for reliable ocular adjustment; a sealed, nitrogen-filled interior for fog-free sighting.

VX-III SCOPES

The VX-III scopes, which replace the Vari-X III line, feature new lens coatings and the Index Matched Lens System (IMLS). The IMLS matches coatings to the different types of glass used in a scope's lens system. Other refinements include finger-adjustable dials with resettable pointers to indicate zero, a fast-focus, lockable eyepiece and a 30mm main tube for scopes with side-mounted focus (parallax correction) dials.

ULTRALIGHT SCOPES

Magnification (x obj. dia.)	Field of View (ft., 100 yds)	Dia./Length (in.)	Weight (oz.)	MSRP
VX-II 2-7x28mm	41.7(2x) 16.5(7x)	1/9.9	8.2	$359
VX-II 3-9x33mm	34.0(3x) 13.5(9)	1/10.96	8.8	$379
VX-II 3-9x33mm EFR	34.0(3x) 13.50(9x)	1/11.32	11.0	$399

COMPETITION SERIES SCOPES

Magnification (x obj. dia.)	Field of View (ft., 100 yds)	Dia./Length (in.)	Weight (oz.)	MSRP
35x45mm	3.3	1/15.9	20.3	$1046
40x45mm	2.7	1/15.9	20.3	$1046
45x45mm	2.5	1/15.9	20.3	$1046

FX-II (FIXED POWER)

Magnification (x obj. dia.)	Field of View (ft., 100 yds)	Dia./Length (in.)	Weight (oz.)	MSRP
2.5x28mm Scout	22.0	1/10.10	7.5	$279
4x33mm	24.0	1/10.47	9.3	$263
6x36mm	17.7	1/11.35	10.0	$309
6x42mm	17.0	1/11.90	11.3	discontinued
12x40mm Adj. Obj. Target	9.10	1/13.0	13.5	discontinued

HANDGUN SCOPES

Magnification (x obj. dia.)	Field of View (ft., 100 yds)	Dia./Length (in.)	Weight (oz.)	MSRP
FX-II 2x20mm	21.20	1/8.0	6.0	$349
FX-II 4x28mm	9.0	1/8.43	7.0	$349

LPS SCOPES

Magnification (x obj. dia.)	Field of View (ft., 100 yds)	Dia./Length (in.)	Weight (oz.)	MSRP
2.5-10x45mm	37.2(2.5x) 9.9(10x)	1/11.80	17.2	$1449
3.5-14x50mm Side Focus	27.2(3.5X) 7.1(14X)	1/13.5	19.5	$1549

RIMFIRE SCOPES

Magnification (x obj. dia.)	Field of View (ft., 100 yds)	Dia./Length (in.)	Weight (oz.)	MSRP
FX-I 4x28mm	25.5	1/9.2	7.5	$219
VX-I 2-7x28mm	41.7(2x) 16.5(7x)	1/9.9	8.2	$219
X-II 3-9x33mm EFR	34.0(3x) 13.50(9x)	1/11.32	11.0	$349

MUZZLELOADER

Magnification (x obj. dia.)	Field of View (ft., 100 yds)	Dia./Length (in.)	Weight (oz.)	MSRP
VX-I 1-4x20mm	75.0(1x) 28.5(4x)	1/9.2	9.0	$219
VX-I 2-7x33mm	42.5(2x) 17.8(7x)	1/11.0	10.5	$209
VX-I 3-9x40mm	32.9(3x) 13.1(9x)	1/12.2	12.0	$229

MARK 2 TACTICAL SCOPES

Magnification (x obj. dia.)	Field of View (ft., 100 yds)	Dia./Length (in.)	Weight (oz.)	MSRP
1.5-4x20mm	28.5-75.0	1.0/9.2	9.5	$429
3-9x40mm T2	14.0-32.3	1.0/12.4	12.5	$549
3-9x40mm Tactical Hunter	14.0-32.3	1.0/12.4	12.5	$619
4-12x40mm Adj. Obj. T2	11.2-22.8	1.0/12.4	14.5	$579
6-18x40mm Adj. Obj. T1	6.6-14.5	1.0/13.5	14.5	$649

MARK 4 TACTICAL SCOPES

Magnification (x obj. dia.)	Field of View (ft., 100 yds)	Dia./Length (in.)	Weight (oz.)	MSRP
10x40mm LR/T M1	11.1	1.18/13.10	21.0	discontinued
10x40mm LR/T M3	3.7	1.18/13.10	21.0	discontinued
16x40mm LR/T M1	6.8	1.18/12.90	22.5	discontinued
4 3.5-10x40mm LR/T M3	29.9(3.5x) 11.0(10x)	1.18/13.50	19.5	discontinued
2.5-8x36	37-13.5	1.7/11.3	16	discontinued
4.5-14x50mm LR/T M1	14.3(6.5x) 5.5(20x)	1.18/14.5	22.0	$1329
8.5-25x50mm	4.4-11.2	1.2/14.5	22.5	$1579

TACTICAL PRISMATIC SCOPES

Magnification (x obj. dia.)	Field of View (ft., 100 yds)	Dia./Length (in.)	Weight (oz.)	MSRP
1x14mm	83.0	1.2/4.5	12.0	$516

VX-I SCOPES

Magnification (x obj. dia.)	Field of View (ft., 100 yds)	Dia./Length (in.)	Weight (oz.)	MSRP
3-9x40mm	32.9(3x) 13.1(9x)	1/12.2	12	$254
3-9x50mm	33.0(3x) 13.1(9x)	1/12.4	14.1	$319
4-12x40mm	19.9(4x) 9.4(12x)	1/12.2	13	$249

VX-II SCOPES

Magnification (x obj. dia.)	Field of View (ft., 100 yds)	Dia./Length (in.)	Weight (oz.)	MSRP
2-7x33mm	42.5(2x) 17.8(7x)	1/11.0	10.5	$329
3-9x40mm	32.3(3x) 14.0(9x)	1/12.4	12	$359
3-9x50mm	32.3(3x) 14.0(9x)	1/12.1	13.7	$429
4-12x40mm Adj. Obj.	22.8(4x) 11.0(12x)	1/12.4	14	$479
4-12x50mm	33.0(4x) 13.1(12x)	1/12.2	14.5	$529
6-18x40mm Adj. Obj.	14.5(6x) 6.6(18x)	1/13.5	15.8	$599

VX-III SCOPES

Magnification (x obj. dia.)	Field of View (ft., 100 yds)	Dia./Length (in.)	Weight (oz.)	MSRP
1.5-5x20mm	65.7(1.5x) 23.7(5x)	1/9.4	9.7 oz.	$339
1.75-6x32mm	17.0(1.75x) 6.4(6x)	1/11.23	11.2	$399
2.5-8x36mm	37.3(2.5x) 13.7(8x)	1/11.4	11.2	$479
3.5-10x40mm	29.7(3.5x) 11.0(10x)	1/12.6	13.0	$479
3.5-10x50mm	29.8(3.5x) 11.0(10x)	1/12.2	15.1	$549
4.5-14x40mm	19.9(4.5x) 7.4(14x)	1/12.6	13.2	$599
4.5-14x40mm Adj. Obj.	20.8-7.4	1/12.5	15	$679
6.5-20x40mm EFR Target	14.3(6.5x) 5.6(20x)	1/14.4	19.0	$649

SCOPES

Nikon Scopes

BUCKMASTER
MODEL 6415

BUCKMASTER
MODEL 6435

MODEL 6595

BUCKMASTER
MODEL 6466

SCOPES

BUCKMASTER SCOPES

Nikon Buckmaster scopes integrate shockproof, fogproof and waterproof construction. Nikon's Brightvue™ anti-reflective system of multicoated lenses provides over 93% anti-reflection capability for high levels of light transmission. These riflescopes are parallax-adjusted at 100 yds. and have durable matte finishes that reduce glare. They also feature positive steel-to-brass, ¼-min.-click windage and elevation adjustments for instant, repeatable accuracy and a Nikoplex reticle for quick target acquisition.

Model 6465 1x20: . . . . **Discontinued**
Model 6405 4x40: . . . . **Discontinued**

Model 6425 3-9x40
   Black Matte: . . . . . **Discontinued**
Model 6415 3-9x40 Silver: . . . .
                   Discontinued
Model 6435 3-9x50: **$219**
Model 6450 4.5-14x40 AO
   Black Matte: **$229**
Model 6455 4.5-14x40 AO
   Silver: . . . . **Discontinued**
Model 6466 4.5-14X40AO
   Matte Adj. Mildot: . **Discontinued**
Model 6440 4-12x50 AO Matte: . . . . .
                   Discontinued

HANDGUN AND SHOTGUN SCOPES

Model 6560 2x20 EER
   Black Lustre: . . . . . **Discontinued**
Model 6562 2x20 EER Matte: . . . . . .
                   Discontinued
Model 6565 2x20 EER Silver: . . . .
                   Discontinued
Model 6590 1.5-4.5x20 Shotgun
Black Matte: . . . . **Discontinued**
Model 6595 1.5-4.5x20 Sabot/Slug
   Black Matte: . . . . . **Discontinued**

ILLUMINATED SCOPES

3.5-10x50 (Nikoplex or Mildot): . . . .
                   Discontinued
6.5-20x44 (Nikoplex or Mildot): . . . .
                   Discontinued

Nikon Scopes

LASER IRT

MODEL 6510

MODEL 6556

MODEL 6630

LASER IRT RIFLESCOPE

The Laser IRT riflescope system combines Nikon's BDC (Bullet Drop Compensating) reticle with an integral Laser Rangefinder. The rangefinder and reticle work together to provide hunters precise distance measurement, proper aiming point and speed for immediate shot placement. The riflescope is also available with Nikon's Nikoplex reticle.

The patent-pending IRT technology returns precise and continuous distance readings for 12 seconds, allowing the hunter time to range the animal and select the appropriate aiming circle. When the animal is spotted, simply hit the button and settle in for the shot. The IRT keeps the hunter current on the range as the animal moves. The one-touch rangefinding capabilities also can be operated using the included remote control switch, which can be attached to the rifle with a Velcro strap. O-ring sealed and nitrogen-filled for true waterproof, fogproof and shockproof performance.

The scope operates on a 3-volt CR-2 battery, ranges up to 766 yds. and has a bright, 3-digit electroluminescent display that measures in yds. or meters.

MONARCH RIFLE SCOPES

Monarch Rifle Scopes feature multi-coated Ultra ClearCoat optical system; ¼ min. positive click windage and elevation; one-piece aluminum tube construction. All Monarch scopes are shockproof, waterproof and fogproof. The Monarch series includes scopes specifically designed for use with blackpowder rifles shooting sabots or shotguns shooting sabot-style slugs. Available in matte or lustre finish.

Model 6500 4x40 Lustre: $180
Model 6505 4x40 Matte: $264
Model 6506 6x42 Lustre: $236
Model 6508 6x42 Matte: $499
Model 6510 2-7x32 Lustre: $268
Model 6515 2-7x32 Matte: $268
Model 6520 3-9x40 Lustre: $229
Model 6525 3-9x40 Matte: $229
Model 6528 3-9x40 Silver Matte: $285
Model 6530 3.5-10x50 Lustre: . . $399
Model 6535 3.5-10x50 Matte: . . $439
Model 6537 3.3-10x44 AO
    Lustre: $369

Model 6538 3.3-10x44 AO
    Matte (Mildot): $369
Model 6539 3.3-10x44 AO
    Matte: $369
Model 6540 4-12x40 AO
    Lustre: $359
Model 6545 4-12x40 AO
    Matte: $379
Model 6580 5.5-16.5x44 AO
    Black Lustre: $431
Model 6585 5.5-16.5x44 AO
    Black Matte: $399
Model 6550 6.5-20x44 AO
    Lustre: . . . . Discontinued
Model 6555 6.5-20x44 AO
    Matte: . . . . Discontinued
Model 6570 6.5-20x44 HV: . . . .
    Discontinued
Model 6575 6.5-20x44 HV: . . . .
    Discontinued
Model 6556 6.5-20x44 AO
    Lustre target Dot: Discontinued
Model 6558 6.5-20x44 AO
    Matte target Dot: . Discontinued
Model 6630 3.3-10x44 AO
    (Titanium): $574
Model 6680 5.5-16.5x44
    AO (Titanium): $578

SCOPES

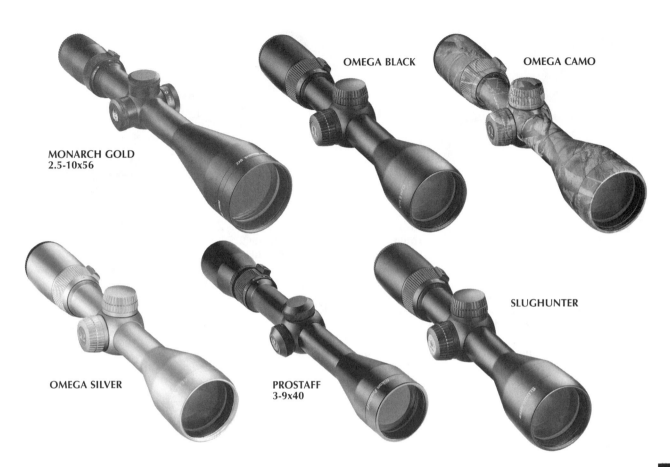

MONARCH GOLD
2.5-10x56

OMEGA BLACK

OMEGA CAMO

OMEGA SILVER

PROSTAFF
3-9x40

SLUGHUNTER

MONARCH GOLD

1.5-6x42: **$599**
2.5-10x50: **$699**
2.5-10x56: **$799**

OMEGA MUZZLELOADING RIFLESCOPE

The Nikon Omega 3-9x40 with BDC-250 reticle was created to help shooters take advantage of the full accuracy potential of their muzzleloaders. The Omega offers a bullet drop compensating reticle designed specifically for muzzleloading loads and ranges and was designed to utilize .50 caliber muzzleloading loads –150 grains of Pyrodex (pellets or powder), 250-grain bullets and ranges (out to 250-yds).

The BDC-250 is a trajectory-compensating reticle designed and calibrated to provide fast, simple aiming points for various shot distances. This unique system integrates a series of small "ballistic circles"—each subtending 2 in. @ 100 yds.—allowing an unimpeded view of the target. (At 200 yds., the circles are 4 in.; at 250 yds., they are 5 in.) The reti-

cle is designed to be sighted-in at 100 yds., with aiming-point circles at 150, 200, 225 and 250 yds. A generous 25.2 8.4-foot field-of-view also makes getting on a trophy animal a breeze. The Omega Riflescope is equipped with precise, ¼-MOA click reticle adjustments. Available in Matte, Silver and Realtree Hardwoods Green HD finishes.

PROSTAFF RIFLESCOPES

Nikon's Prostaff line includes the 4x32, 2-7x32 and 3-9x40 scopes. The 4x is parallax-corrected at 50 yds.. It measures 11.2 in. long and weighs just 11.6 ounces, in silver, matte black or Realtree camo finish. The 2-7x, parallax-free at 75 yds., is a 12-ounce scope available in matte black or camo. The 13-ounce 3-9x is available in all three finishes. The Prostaff scopes have multicoated lenses and ¼-min. adjustments and are waterproof, and fogproof.

4x32 Rimfire Classic: **$119**
2-7x32: **$139**
3-9x40: **$159**
3-9x40 Realtree Nikoplex: **$189**

SLUGHUNTER

Nikon's 3-9x40 SlugHunter is the first scope dedicated to the slug gun. It's designed around Nikon's BDC 200, a trajectory compensating reticle that provides fast, simple aiming points for various shot distances. Calibrated to be sighted in on the crosshair at 50 yds., the BDC 200 has two ballistic circles that represent 100-yard and 150-yard aiming points. For exceptionally accurate gun and load combinations, the lower reticle post becomes a 200-yard aiming point as well. Multicoated optics produce crisp, clear images, while 92 percent light transmission keeps the hunter in the field when the game is moving. Waterproof, fogproof and shockproof.

Nikon Scopes

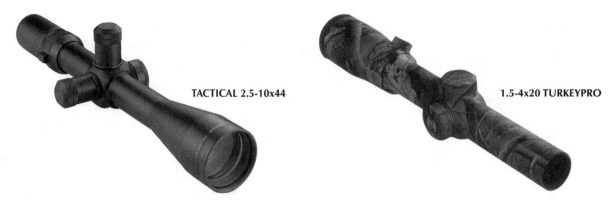

TACTICAL 2.5-10x44

1.5-4x20 TURKEYPRO

TACTICAL RIFLESCOPES

Nikon's Tactical Riflescopes are available in 2.5-10x44 and 4-16x50. The 2.5-10x44 features a choice of reticles: Nikoplex, Mildot, and Dual Illuminated Mildot. The 4-16 is offered with Nikoplex or Mildot. Both are equipped with turret mounted parallax adjustment knobs, have a tough, black-anodized matte finish and have easy-to-grip windage and elevation knobs for accurate field adjustments.

Tactical 2.5-10x44
 (Mildot or Nikoplex):. . $828–1099
  With Illuminated Mildot:$828–1099
Tactical 4-16x50
 (Mildot or Nikoplex):. . $828–1099

1.5-4.5X20 TURKEYPRO

Available in Realtree Hardwoods camo, the 1.5-4x20 Monarch TurkeyPro is parallax-free at 50 yds..
MSRP: $259

2.5-8X28 EER HANDGUN SCOPE

Nikon's 2.5-8x28 EER (Extended Eye Relief) has a wide field of view at low power, but a twist of the power ring instantly supplies 8x magnification for long shots.
MSRP: $289

MONARCH UCC RIFLESCOPE									
MODEL	**4x40**	**1.5-4.5x20**	**2-7x32**	**3-9x40**	**3.5-10x50**	**4-12x40AO**	**5.5-16.5x44AO**	**6.5-20x44AO**	**2x20EER**
Lustre	6500	N/A	6510	6520	6530	6540	6580	6550/6556	6560
Matte	6505	6595	6515	6525	6535	6545	6585	6555/6558	6562
Silver	N/A	N/A	N/A	6528	N/A	N/A	N/A	N/A	6565
Actual Magnification	4x	1.5x-4.5x	2x-7x	3x-9x	3.5x-10x	4x-12x	5.5x-16.5x	6.5x-19.46x	1.75x
Objective Diameter (mm)	40	20	32	40	50	40	44	44	20
Exit Pupil (mm)	10	13.3-4.4	16-4.6	13.3-4.4	14.3-5	10-3.3	8-2.7	6.7-2.2	11.4
Eye Relief (in)	3.5	3.7-3.5	3.9-3.6	3.6-3.5	3.9-3.8	3.6-3.4	3.2-3.0	3.5-3.1	26.4-10.5
FOV @ 100 yds (ft)	26.9	50.3-16.7*	44.5-12.7	33.8-11.3	25.5-8.9	25.6-8.5	19.1-6.4	16.1-5.4	22
Tube Diameter (in.)	1	1	1	1	1	1	1	1	1
Objective Tube(mm/in)	47.3-1.86	25.4/1	39.3-1.5	47.3-1.86	57.3-2.2	53.1-2.09	54-2.13	54-2.13	25, 4/1
Eyepiece O.D. (mm)	38	38	38	38	38	38	38	38	38
Length (in)	11.7	10	11.1	12.3	13.7	13.7	13.4	14.6	8.1
Weight (oz)	11.2	9.3	11.2	12.6	15.5	16.9	18.4	20.1	6.6
Adjustment Gradation	¼ MOA	¼ MOA	¼ MOA	¼ MOA	¼ MOA	¼ MOA	¼ MOA	1/8 MOA	¼ MOA
Max Internal Adjustment	120 MOA	120 MOA	70 MOA	55 MOA	45 MOA	45 MOA	40 MOA	38 MOA	120 MOA
Parallax Setting (yds)	100	75	100	100	100	50 to ∞	50 to ∞	50 to ∞	100

BUCKMASTER SCOPES					
MODEL	**1x20**	**4x40**	**3-9x40**	**3-9x50**	**4.5-14x40AO**
Matte	6465	6405	6425	6435	6450
Silver	N/A	N/A	6415	N/A	6455
Actual Magnification	1x	4x	3.3-8.5x	3.3-8.5x	4.5-13.5x
Objective Diameter (mm)	20	40	40	50	40
Exit Pupil (mm)	20	10	12.1-4.7	15.1-5.9	8.9-2.9
Eye Relief (in)	4.3-13.0	3.5	3.5-3.4	3.5-3.4	3.6-3.4
FOV @ 100 yds (ft)	52.5	30.6	33.9-12.9	33.9-12.9	22.5-7.5
Tube Diameter (in.)	1	1	1	1	1
Objective Tube (mm/in)	27/1.06	47.3/1.86	47.3/1.86	58.7/2.3	53/2.1
Eyepiece O.D. (mm)	37	42.5	42.5	42.5	38
Length (in)	8.8	12.7	12.7	12.9	14.8
Weight (oz)	9.2	11.8	13.4	18.2	18.7
Adjustment Gradation	¼: 1 click	¼: 1 click	¼: 1 click	¼: 1 click	—
Max Internal Adjustment	50	80	80	70	40
Parallax Setting (yds)	75	100	100	100	50 to ∞

OMEGA 3-9X40 MUZZLELOADING RIFLESCOPE						
POWER/OBJ. LENS (MM)	**FIELD OF VIEW (FT/100YDS)**	**EYE RELIEF (IN.)**	**TUBE DIAMETER (IN.)**	**LENGTH (IN.)**	**WEIGHT (OZ.)**	**PRICE**
3-9x40	25.2-8.4	5	1	11.3	13.7	$349

LASER IRT SCOPES						
POWER/OBJ. LENS (MM)	**FIELD OF VIEW (FT/100YDS)**	**EYE RELIEF (IN.)**	**TUBE DIAMETER (IN.)**	**LENGTH (IN.)**	**WEIGHT (OZ.)**	**PRICE**
4-12X42	24.9-8.3	3		13.1	26	$899

SLUGHUNTER SCOPES						
POWER/OBJ. LENS (MM)	**FIELD OF VIEW (FT/100YDS)**	**EYE RELIEF (IN.)**	**TUBE DIAMETER (IN.)**	**LENGTH (IN.)**	**WEIGHT (OZ.)**	**PRICE**
3-9X40	25.2-9.4	5.0		11.3	13.7	$269

SCOPES

Pentax Scopes

4X-16XAO LIGHTSEEKER 30

8.5X-32XAO LIGHTSEEKER 30

6X-24XAO LIGHTSEEKER 30

**LIGHTSEEKER 2.5xSG PLUS
MOSSY OAK BREAK-UP**

LIGHTSEEKER-XL 3-9x50

LIGHTSEEKER 1.75X-6X

GAMESEEKER

WHITETAILS UNLIMITED

SCOPES

GAMESEEKER

Featuring one in., one-piece tube construction, Pentax Gameseeker riflescopes are extremely durable and fully waterproof for the most extreme hunting situations. Each scope is nitrogen filled to prevent internal fogging of optical elements, and the fully-multi-coated optics with PentaBright technology help increase light transmission to deliver sharp, clear images. Every Gameseeker includes the new bullet drop compensating Precision Plex reticle.

LIGHTSEEKER

The Lightseeker features a scratch-resistant outer tube. High Quality cam zoom tube made of a bearing-type brass with precision machined cam slots. The zoom control screws are precision-ground to ½ of one thousandth tolerance. Power rings are sealed on a separate precision-machined seal tube. The scopes are filled with nitrogen and double-sealed with heavy-duty "O" rings, making them leakproof and fogproof.

Lightseeker optics are multi-coated. The Lightseeker-30 has the same features as the Lightseeker II, but with a 30mm tube. Ballistic Plex reticles are available on the 3X-9X and 6.5X-20X Whitetails Unlimited Scopes.

Pentax Scopes

Model	Tube Diameter (in)	Objective Diameter (mm)	Eyepiece Diameter (mm)	Exit Pupil (mm)	Eye Relief (in)	Field of View (ft@ 100 yd)	Adj. Grad. (in@ 100 yd)	Max. Adjust. (in@ 100 yd)	Length (in)	Weight (oz)	Reticle	Price
RIFLE SCOPES												
Lightseeker 3X - 9X	1	40	39	12.0-5.0	3.5-4.0	36-14	¼	50	12.7	15	P, MD	$400
Lightseeker 3X - 9X	1	50	39	16.1-5.6	3.5-4.0	35-12	¼	50	13.0	19	TW, BP	$499
Lightseeker 2.5X - 10X	1	50	39	16.3-4.6	4.2-4.7	35-10	¼	100	14.1	23	TW	$549
Lightseeker 4X - 16X	1	44	36	10.4-2.8	3.5-4.0	33-9	¼	35	15.4	23.7	BP	$569
Lightseeker 2.5X SG Plus	1	25	39	7.0	3.5-4.0	55	½	60	10.0	9	DW	discontinued
LIGHTSEEKER-30												
3X-10X AO	30mm	40	35	13.3-4.4	3.5-4.0	34-14	¼	90	13.1	20.0	BP	$519
4X-16X AO	30mm	50	42	12-3.1	3.3-3.8	27-7.5	¼	74	15.2	23	TW, MD	$619
6X-24X AO	30mm	50	42	7.6-2.1	3.2-3.7	18-5	1/8	52	16.9	27	MD, FP	$832
8.5X-32X AO	30mm	50	42	6.2-1.7	3.0-3.5	14-4	1/8	39	18.0	27	MD, FP	$729
WHITETAILS UNLIMITED												
2X-5X WTU	1	20	39	11.1-4.2	3.1-3.8	65-23	½	70	10.7	10	TW	$279
3X-9X WTU	1	40	39	12.9-4.7	3.1-3.8	31-13	¼	50	12.4	13	TW	$299
3.5X-10X WTU	1	50	39	13-5.1	3.1-3.8	28-11	¼	50	13.1	15	LBP	$489
3.7X-11X WTU	1	42	39	13-5.1	3.1-3.8	28-11	¼	50	13.1	15	TW	$302
4.5X-14X WTU	1	42	39	9.3-3.0	3.7-4.2	23-8	¼	52	12.9	17	BP	$370
6.5X-20X WTU	1	50	39	7.6-2.6	3.1-3.6	17-6	¼	30	14.6	19	BP	discontinued
3X-9X WTU	1	50	39	16.0-5.3	3.1-3.8	32-13	¼	50	13.2	17	BP	discontinued

Scopes are available in high gloss black, matte black, or camouflage, depending on model.
P=Penta-Plex, FP=Fine-Plex, DW=Deepwoods Plex, MD=Mil-Dot, CP=Comp-Plex, TW=Twilight Plex, BP=Ballistic Plex, LBP=Laser Ballistic Plex

GAMESEEKER						
Power/Obj. Lens (mm)	Field of View (ft/100yds)	Eye Relief (in.)	Adj. Gradation (in.@100yds)	Length (in.)	Weight (oz.)	Price
3-9x40	38-13.1	3	.25	12.3	14.2	$109
3-9x50	33-12.1	3	.25	13.1	18.2	$129
1.75-5x20	64-21.6	3	.50	10	11.8	discontinued
1.5-6x40	56-15.7	3-3.6	.25	11.9	13.5	$129
4-12x40	27.3-10-5	3	.25	13.0	14.8	$139
2.5-10x56	34.6-8.9	3-3.4	.25	13.7	22.1	$159
4-16x50	24.0-6.2	3-3.4	.25	13.9	18.8	$136
3.5-10x50	28.6-9.4	3	.25	13.0	18.8	$129

Redfield Optics Scopes

3-15x52

RIFLESCOPES

Redfield's scopes feature ED glass objective lenses; one-piece aluminum tubes; water resistant lens coating; TrueZero windage and elevation dials; 3-cam 5X zoom system; side focus adjustments (on select models); black matte finish.

REDFIELD RIFLESCOPES						
Model	Power/Obj. Lens (mm)	Field of View (ft/100yds)	Eye Relief (in.)	Length (in.)	Weight (oz.)	Price
475201	5-25x52	18.8-3.8	4	13.75	21.5	discontinued
475200	3-15x52	31.5-6.3	4	13.75	20.0	discontinued
475102	6-30x56	15.8-3	4	15.3	25	discontinued
475101	4-20x56	23.6-4.8	4	14.8	24.7	discontinued

Schmidt & Bender Scopes

2.5-10x56 VARIABLE HUNTING SCOPE

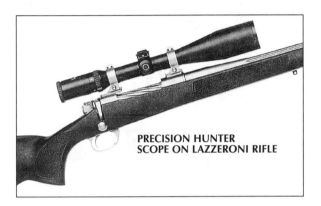

PRECISION HUNTER SCOPE ON LAZZERONI RIFLE

ILLUMINATED 1.25-4x20

ZENITH 1.5-6x42

RIFLESCOPES

Redfield's scopes feature ED glass objective lenses; one-piece aluminum tubes; water resistant lens coating; TrueZero windage and elevation dials; 3-cam 5X zoom system; side focus adjustments (on select models); black matte finish.

This German firm manufactures carriage-class optics for discriminating sportsmen and tactical shooters. Variable scopes have 30mm and 34mm tubes. Note: All variable power scopes have glass reticles and aluminum tubes.

FIXED POWER SCOPES

4x36:	. . . .$979–1389.70
6x42:	. . . . $1069–1545
8x56:	. . . . $1229–1619
10x42:	. . . . $1129

ILLUMINATED SCOPES

Designed for use on magnum rifles and for quick shots at dangerous game. Long eye relief, and a wide field of view (31.5 yds. at 200 yds.) speed your aim. The Flash Dot reticle shows up bright against the target at the center of the crosswire. Illuminated scopes feature illuminated reticles; hard multi-coating on lenses; 30mm tubes

1.25-4x20:	. . . . $1299–1819
1.5-6x42:	. . . . $1343–1869
2.5-10x56:	. . . . $1539–2089
3-12x50:	. . . . $1459–2059
3-12x42:	. . . . Discontinued

PRECISION HUNTER

Precision Hunter scopes combine the optical quality of S&B hunting scopes, with a sophisticated mil-dot reticle (developed by the U.S. Marine Corps) with a bullet drop compensator to give shooters the ability and confidence to place an accurate shot at up to 500 yds.

2.5-10x56 with #9 Reticle:	. . . . $2089
3-12x42 with P3 Reticle:	. . . $3118.70
3-12x50 with P3 Reticle:	. . . $3118.70
4-16x50 with P3 Reticle:	. . . $3573.70

PRECISION HUNTER WITH PARALLAX ADJUSTMENT

3-12x50 Parallax:	. . . . $3508.70
4-16x50 Parallax:	. . . . $4093.70

VARIABLE HUNTING SCOPES

1.5-6x42:	. . . . Discontinued
2.5-10x56:	. . . . $1659–1879
3-12x42:	. . . . $1629–1959
3-12x50:	. . . . $1629–1879
3-12x50:	. . . . Discontinued
4-16x50:	. . . . $1979–2399

ZENITH SERIES SCOPES

1.1-4x24:	. . . . $1439–1730
1.1-4x24:	. . . . $1869–2289
1.5-6x42:	. . . . $1499–1819
1.5-6x42:	. . . . $1929–2369
2.5-10x56:	. . . . $1759–2119
2.5-10x56:	. . . . $2189–2579
3-12x50 h:	. . . . $1759–2119

Sightron Scopes

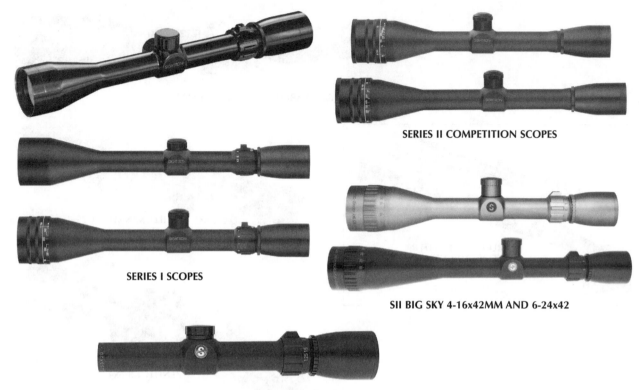

SERIES II COMPETITION SCOPES

SERIES I SCOPES

SII BIG SKY 4-16x42MM AND 6-24x42

SII BIG SKY 1.25-5x20MM BIG GAME SCOPE

SERIES I SCOPES

Series I scopes include multi-coated objective and ocular lenses; finger adjustable windage and elevation; scopes are shockproof, waterproof.

1x20:	$168.99
2.5-10x44:	$175.99
2.5x32:	$118.37
3-9x32RF:	$162.99
3-9x40ST:	$146.25
3-9x40GL:	$146.25
3-9x40MD:	$154.38
3.5-10x50:	$250

SERIES II SCOPES

Series II riflescopes feature the ExacTrack windage and elevation system; one piece body tube; multi-coated optics. SII Series scopes are waterproof, shockproof, fogproof and nitrogen filled. Available in stainless with a wide choice of reticles from plex and double diamond to mildot.

SII BIG SKY 4-16X42MM AND 6-24X42

Three new rifle scopes in Sightron's SII Big Sky line have been designed and built to meet the demanding needs of competitive shooters and hunters who shoot long range.

The three scopes include two 4-16x42mm models, one with a satin black finish and the other stainless, plus one 6-24x42 satin black model. All three scopes incorporate a mil-dot reticle that makes adjustments for wind and elevation simple. This reticle has proven itself in both military and civilian applications.

Each Sightron SII Big Sky scope starts with a one-piece mono-tube design, crafted from a bar of aluminum that is 400 times stronger than jointed scopes that may have several pieces in the tube.

Features on all three models include a one-piece tube, ExacTrack adjustment system and Zact-7 Climate Control Coatings. Each scope has target knobs and an adjustable objective lens. Eye relief is between 3.7 and 4 in.

The scopes come with a Lifetime Replacement Warranty. Should a Sightron product ever fail, consumers can return the product to Sightron or a participating dealer for replacement.
MSRP: **$767.84**

SII BIG SKY 1.25-5X20MM BIG GAME SCOPE

With big dangerous game in mind, Sightron has added a compact 1.25-5x20mm scope to their SII Big Sky line. This scope is built with a one-piece, mono-tube design to give it maximum strength. Lenses are precision ground and multi-coated with Sightron's Zact-7 multi-layer coating with Climate Control Coatings. These coatings will disperse moisture on the outside lens in rainy and foggy hunting conditions. Mounting surface is a consideration when scopes of these designs have to be mounted on magnum rifle actions. The SII Big Sky 1.25x5 scope has a 6.18 inch maximum mounting length between rings, one of the longest in the industry.
MSRP: **$505.69**

SII BIG SKY 36x42MM TARGET RIFLE SCOPE

SERIES III SCOPES

SERIES II COMPACT RIFLE SCOPE

SII BIG SKY 36X42MM TARGET RIFLE SCOPE

Sightron's new 36-power rifle scope is sure to catch the eye of avid benchrest target shooters. This addition to the SII Big Sky line of scopes has several features that serious benchrest shooters look for in a quality scope. It's built around a one-piece mono-tube, the perfect platform for a large scope, giving it strength and durability. The glass lenses are precision ground and hand-fitted. Outside lens surfaces are multi-coated with Zact-7, Revcoat with Climate Control Coating. These lenses will enable the shooters to see clearly in all types of weather, including rain.

The SII Big Sky 36x42mm scope uses Sightron's enhanced ExacTrack adjustment system with 1/8 MOA target knobs. By loosening three set screws on the turret, the scope can be reset to zero. The scope also incorporates a 1/8 MOA dot reticle. Focus goes all the way down to 10 yds.. Each scope comes with a sunshade and lens covers.
MSRP: **$806.28**

SII COMPACT SCOPES
2.5-7x32: . . . . Discontinued
2.5-10x32: $306.49
4x32: $241.69
6x42: $364.54

SII SHOTGUN SCOPE
SII shotgun 2.5-7x32: Discontinued

SII SIDE FOCUS RIFLE SCOPES
3.5-10x44: $567.69
4.5-14x44: $607.29
6.5-20x50: $623.99

SII VARIABLE POWER RIFLE SCOPES
1.5-6x42: . . . . Discontinued
3-12x42: . . . . Discontinued
3-12x50: . . . . Discontinued
3.5-10x42: $381.29
3.5-10x50: . . . . Discontinued
3-9x36: $340.64
3-9x42ST: $414.79

COMPETITION SCOPES
3-6x42: $612.89
4-16x42: $583.69
4-16x42 dot: . . . . .Discontinued
6-24x42: $601.29
6-24x42 dot: . . . . .Discontinued
6x42 HBRD: . . . . .Discontinued
6-24x42: $586

SERIES III SCOPES
Series III scopes feature one-piece aluminum main tubes; multi-coated objective and ocular lenses; windage and elevation adjustment; side focus; fast-focus eyepiece. SIII scopes are waterproof, shockproof, fogproof and nitrogen charged.
624x50 . . . .$1030.55
624x50MD $935.99
3.510x44MD $936.38
1.56x50 . . . .$788.69

SCOPES

Sightron Scopes

RETICLE DIMENSION REFERENCES

Plex Reticle

Dot Reticle

Mil Dot Reticle

Crosshair (CH) Reticle

Double Diamond Reticle

German 4A Reticle

Magnification	Objective Diameter (mm)	Field of View (ft@ 100 yd)	Eye Relief (in)	Recticle Type	Reticle Subtension Min. Power A/B/C/D/E (in.@100 yds)	Reticle Subtension Max. Power A/B/C/D/E (in.@100 yds)	Click Value	Windage Elevation Travel (in)	Tube (Dia.)	Weight (oz)	Finish
SERIES II BIG SKY RIFLESCOPES											
4-16X	42	26-7	3.6	Plex			1/8 MOA	56		16	Satin Black
6-24X	42	15.7-4.4	4.0-3.7	Mil-Dot			1/8 MOA	55		17.6	Satin Black
1.5-5X	20	79.0-19.2	4.0-3.8	Duplex			1/2 MOA	100		10.1	Satin Black
36X	42	4.4	3.7	Dot			1/8 MOA	40		17.3	Satin Black
SERIES II RIFLESCOPES – Side Focus											
3.5-10X	44	25.4-8.9	4.7-3.7	Plex	102.6/10.26/3.25/2.2/.69	36/3.6/1.15/.8/.23	1/4 MOA	80	1.0 in.	19.0	Satin Black
4.5-14X	44	20.5-6.8	4.7-3.7	Plex	79.0/1.33/5.32	19.8/.33/1.32	1/4 MOA	70	1.0 in.	19.80	Satin Black
6.5-20X	50	14.9-4.0	4.3-3.4	Plex	79.0/1.33/5.32	19.8/.33/1.32	1/4 MOA	45	1.0 in.	20.50	Satin Black
SERIES II RIFLESCOPES – Variable Power											
1.5-6X	42	50-15	4.0-3.8	Plex	79.0/1.33/5.32	19.8/.33/1.32	1/4 MOA	70	1.0 in.	14.00	Satin Black
2.5-8X	42	36-12	3.6-4.2	Plex	48.0/.80/3.20	15.0/.25/1.0	1/4 MOA	90	1.0 in.	12.82	Satin Black
3-9X	42	34-12	3.6-4.2	Plex	39.9/.66/2.66	13.2/.22/.88	1/4 MOA	95	1.0 in.	13.22	Satin Black
3-9X	42	34-12	3.6-4.2	Plex	39.9/.66/2.66	13.2/.22/.88	1/4 MOA	95	1.0 in.	13.22	Stainless
3-9X	42	34-12	3.6-4.2	Dot	4/.66	1.3/.22	1/4 MOA	95	1.0 in.	13.22	Satin Black
3-12X	42	32-9	3.6-4.2	Plex	39.9/.66/2.66	9.9/.16/.66	1/4 MOA	80	1.0 in.	12.99	Satin Black
3.5-10X	42	32-11	3.6	Plex	34.2/.57/2.28	12.0/.20/.80	1/4 MOA	60	1.0 in.	13.80	Satin Black
4.5-14X	42	22-7.9	3.6	Plex	26.4/.44/1.76	8.5/.14/.56	1/4 MOA	50	1.0 in.	16.07	Satin Black
3-9X	50	34-12	4.2-3.6	Plex	39.9/.66/2.66	13.2/.22/.88	1/4 MOA	*	1.0 in.	15.40	Satin Black
3-12X	50	34-8.5	4.5-3.7	Plex	39.9/.66/2.66	9.9/.16/.66	1/4 MOA	*	1.0 in.	16.30	Satin Black
3.5-10X	50	30-10	4.0-3.4	Plex	34.2/.57/2.28	12.0/.20/.80	1/4 MOA	50	1.0 in.	15.10	Satin Black
4.5-14X	50	23-8	3.9-3.25	Plex	26.4/.44/1.76	8.4/.14/.56	1/4 MOA	60	1.0 in.	15.20	Satin Black
SERIES II RIFLESCOPES –Variable Power Target Scopes											
4-16X	42	26-7	3.6	Plex	30/.50/2.0	7.5/.125/.50	1/8 MOA	56	1.0 in.	16.00	Satin Black
4-16X	42	26-7	3.6	Plex	30/.50/2.0	7.5/.125/.50	1/8 MOA	56	1.0 in.	16.00	Stainless
4-16X	42	26-7	3.6	Dot	1.7/.10	.425/.025	1/8 MOA	56	1.0 in.	16.00	Satin Black
4-16X	42	26-7	3.6	Dot	1.7/.10	.425/.025	1/8 MOA	56	1.0 in.	16.00	Stainless
6-24X	42	15.7-4.4	3.6	Plex	19.8/.33/1.32	4.8/.08/.32	1/8 MOA	40	1.0 in.	18.70	Satin Black
6-24X	42	15.7-4.4	3.6	Plex	19.8/.33/1.32	4.8/.08/.32	1/8 MOA	40	1.0 in.	18.70	Stainless
6-24X	42	15.7-4.4	3.6	Dot	1.12/.066	.27/.016	1/8 MOA	40	1.0 in.	18.70	Satin Black
6-24X	42	15.7-4.4	3.6	Dot	1.12/.066	.27/.016	1/8 MOA	40	1.0 in.	18.70	Stainless
3-12X	42	32-9	3.6-4.2	Mil-Dot	144/14/4.7/3.1/.7	36/3.6/1.2/.79/.1	1/4 MOA	80	1.0 in.	12.99	Satin Black
4-16X	42	26-7	3.6	Mil-Dot	144/14/4.7/3.1/.6	36/3.6/1.2/.79/.1	1/8 MOA	56	1.0 in.	16.00	Satin Black
4-16X	42	26-7	3.6	Mil-Dot	144/14/4.7/3.1/.6	36/3.6/1.2/.79/.1	1/8 MOA	56	1.0 in.	16.00	Stainless
6-24X	42	15.7-4.4	3.6	Mil-Dot	144/14/4.7/3.1/.4	36/3.6/1.2/.79/.1	1/8 MOA	40	1.0 in.	18.70	Satin Black
6-24X	42	15.7-4.4	3.6	Mil-Dot	144/14/4.7/3.1/.4	36/3.6/1.2/.79/.1	1/8 MOA	40	1.0 in.	18.70	Stainless
24X	44	4.4	4.33	Dot	.27/.016	.27/.016	1/8 MOA	60	1.0 in.	15.87	Satin Black
6X	42	20	4.00	Dot	.375/.070	.375/.070	1/8 MOA	100	1.0 in.	16.00	Satin Black
SERIES II RIFLESCOPES-Compact Scopes											
4X	32	25	4.52	Plex	30/.50/2.0	30/.50/2.0	1/4 MOA	120	1.0 in.	9.80	Satin Black
2.5-7X	32	41-11.8	3.8-3.2	Plex	48/.80/3.20	17.2/.29/1.2	1/4 MOA	120	1.0 in.	11.60	Satin Black
2.5-10X	32	41-10.5	3.8-3.5	Plex	48/.80/3.20	12/.20/.80	1/4 MOA	120	1.0 in.	10.93	Satin Black
6X	42	20	3.60	Plex	19.8/.33/1.32	19.8/.33/1.32	1/4 MOA	100	1.0 in.	12.69	Satin Black
SERIES II SHOTGUN SCOPES											
2.5X	20	41	4.33	Plex	48.0/.80/3.20 1/4 MOA	48.0/.80/3.20	1/4 MOA	160.	1.0 in.	9.00	Satin Black
2.5-7X	32	41-11.8	3.8-3.2	DD	48/24/.60	17/8.5/.26	1/4 MOA	120	1.0 in.	11.60	Satin Black

*Specifications not available at press time

Simmons Scopes

AETEC 2.8-10x44

AETEC RIFLESCOPES

Features TrueZero flex erector system; Quick Target Acquisition eyepiece, with constant minimum 3½ in. of eye relief; one-piece tube construction; aspherical lens technology and fully multi-coated optics; HydroShield lens coating; SureGrip rubber surfaces on all eyepieces and side-focus parallax adjustments.

SCOPES

Simmons Scopes

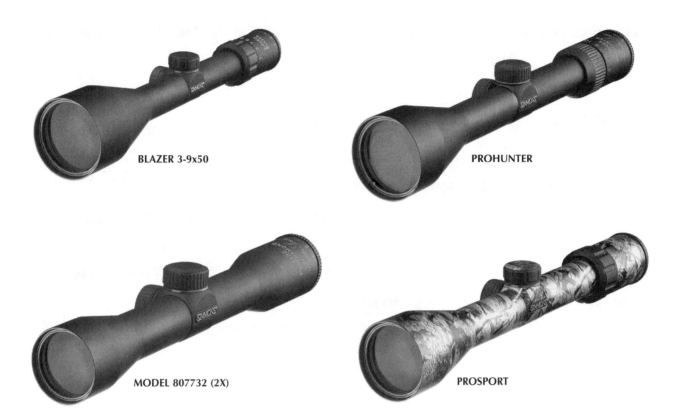

BLAZER 3-9x50

PROHUNTER

MODEL 807732 (2X)

PROSPORT

BLAZER RIFLESCOPES

The Blazer line of riflescopes feature the TrueZero adjustment system; QTA eyepiece; high-quality optical glass and fully coated optics; HydroShield lens coating SureGrip rubber surfaces.

PRODIAMOND SHOTGUN SCOPES

Master Series ProDiamond shotgun scopes feature TrueZero adjustment system QTA eyepiece; up to 5½ in. of eye relief; ProDiamond reticle; one-piece tube construction; high–quality optical glass and multi-coated optics; HydroShield lens coating; SureGrip rubber surfaces on power change rings and eyepieces.

PROHUNTER HANDGUN SCOPES

ProHunter handgun scopes feature long eye relief, ½ and ¼ MOA adjustments, and are waterproof, fogproof and shockproof. Available in black and silver matte finishes.

PROHUNTER RIFLESCOPES

Master Series ProHunter rifle and shotgun scopes feature the TrueZero adjustment system; QTA eyepiece; one-piece tube construction; high-quality optical glass and multi-coated optics; HydroShield lens coating; SureGrip rubber surfaces and side-focus parallax adjustments.

PROSPORT SCOPES

Master Series ProSport scopes feature TrueZero adjustment system and QTA eyepiece with up to 5½ in. of eye relief; one-piece tube construction; high-quality optical glass and fully coated optics; HydroShield lens coating; SureGrip rubber surfaces.

RIMFIRE RIFLESCOPES

The Rimfire collection is scaled down in size with ¾ in. tubes for smaller rifles. All are calibrated parallax free at 50 yds. for shorter rimfire ranges. They come complete with a set of rings ready to be mounted on your favorite rimfire rifle.

22 MAG RIMFIRE SCOPES

Featuring TrueZero adjustment system; QTA quick target acquisition eyepiece; high-quality optical glass and fully coated optics; HydroShield lens coating; SureGrip rubber surfaces; scopes come with a set of rimfire rings. Scopes come in gloss or matte finish.

RED DOT SCOPES

Simmons Red Dot scopes work great on handguns, crossbows, shotguns and paintball guns with rapid target acquisition. Click type, 1 MOA windage and elevation adjustments.

Simmons Scopes

AETEC RIFLESCOPES

Magnification (x obj. dia.)	Field of View (ft., 100 yds)	Dia./Length (in.)	Weight (oz.)	MSRP
2.8-10 x 44 Gloss	43.5/11.5	na	13.8	$234
2.8-10 x 44 Matte	43.5/11.5	na	13.8	$234
2.8-10 x 44 Silver	43.5/11.5	na	13.8	$234
2.8-10 x 44 Ill. Ret.	43.5/11.5	na	12.3	$254
4-14 x 44 SF Matte	29.3/8.2	na	15	$266
4-14 x 44 SF	Ill. Ret. 29.3/8.2	na	15.5	$266

BLAZER RIFLESCOPES

Magnification (x obj. dia.)	Field of View (ft., 100 yds)	Dia./Length (in.)	Weight (oz.)	MSRP
3-9 x 32	31.4/10.5	na	9.6	$44
3-9 x 40	31.4/10.5	na	10.8	$52
3-9 x 50	31.4/10	na	13.2	$64
4 x 32	23.6	na	8.8	$40

PRO-DIAMOND SHOTGUN SCOPES

Magnification (x obj. dia.)	Field of View (ft., 100 yds)	Dia./Length (in.)	Weight (oz.)	MSRP
1.5-5 x 32 illum.	63/20	na	9.3.	$200
1 x 20	85	na	8.4	$68.99–79.99
2 x 32 (ProDiamond reticle)	31.4	na	8.4	discontinued
1.5-5 x 20 (ProDiamond reticle)	67/20	na	9.3	discontinued
1.5-5 x 32 (Camo Pro Diamond)	67/20	na	9.3	$120
4X32	17	1/8.5	9.1	$90

PROHUNTER HANDGUN SCOPES

Magnification (x obj. dia.)	Field of View (ft., 100 yds)	Dia./Length (in.)	Weight (oz.)	MSRP
2-6 x 32	14/4.5	na	9.7	$180
2 x 20	21.5	8.75	6.75	discontinued
4 x 32	15	9	8	$124

PROHUNTER RIFLESCOPES

Magnification (x obj. dia.)	Field of View (ft., 100 yds)	Dia./Length (in.)	Weight (oz.)	MSRP
2 - 7 x 32	47.2	1/12.3	9.8	discontinued
3 - 9 x 40	31.4	1/11	10.8	$164
3–10.5 x 44	33	1/9.4	11.3	$220
4-12 x 44 SF	23.8	1/8.2	13.3	$260
6-18 x 40 SF	16	1/5.3	13	$124.95
6-24 x 44 SF	16	¼	13	discontinued
6-21 x 44 SF	16	¼.6	13.3	discontinued

PROSPORT SCOPES

Magnification (x obj. dia.)	Field of View (ft., 100 yds)	Dia./Length (in.)	Weight (oz.)	MSRP
3-9 x 32	31.4/10.5	na	9.6	$58
3-9 x 40	31.4/10.5	na	10.8	$90
3-9 x 50	31.4/10.5	na	13.2	$110
4-32	23.6	na	8.4	$70
4-12 x 40 AO	24.8/8.1	na	13.8	$136
6-18 x 50 A/O	14.7/5.3	na	8.3	$160

RIMFIRE RIFLESCOPES

Magnification (x obj. dia.)	Field of View (ft., 100 yds)	Dia./Length (in.)	Weight (oz.)	MSRP
4 x 15	18.5	¾/na	3.25	discontinued
4 x 20	19	¾/na	3.25	discontinued
3 - 7 x 20	21.75 - 9.5	¾/na	4.75	discontinued

22 MAG RIMFIRE SCOPES

Magnification (x obj. dia.)	Field of View (ft., 100 yds)	Dia./Length (in.)	Weight (oz.)	MSRP
3 - 9 x 32	31.4/10.5	na	9.6	$58
3 - 9 x 32 A/O	31.4/10.5	na	10.8	$88
4 x 32	21	na	8.8	$50

RED DOT SCOPES

Description	Field of View	Eye Relief	Weight (oz.)	Reticle	MSRP
30mm	Variable	Unlimited	6.5	4 MOA Dot	$68
30mm	Variable	Unlimited	5.6	Multi Reticle	$68
42mm	Variable	Unlimited	8.25	4 MOA Dot	$68

Swarovski Scopes

3-10x42

6-18x50

4-12x50

3-9x36

AV SERIES SCOPES

AV scopes are lightweight 1-in. scopes featuring constant-size reticles, lightweight alloy tubes and satin finish. Totally waterproof even with caps removed, these scopes have fully multi-coated lenses.

3-10x42 4A Reticle AV: $1099
3-10x42 RAIL 4A Reticle AV: . . . . Discontinued
3-10x42 PLEx Reticle AV: $1099

3-10x42 TDS Plex Reticle AV: . . $1177
3-9x36 4A Reticle AV: $988
3-9x36 PLEx Reticle AV: $988
3-9x36 TDS Reticle AV: Discontinued
4-12x50 4A Reticle AV: Discontinued
4-12x50 RAIL 4A Reticle AV: . . $1177
4-12x50 RAIL TDS Plex Reticle AV: $1288
4-12x50 TDS Plex Reticle AV: $1254
4-12x50 PLEx Reticle AV: $1177

4-12x50 RAIL PLEx Reticle AV: . . . . Discontinued
6-18x50 TDS Plex Reticle AV: $1388
6-18x50 4A Reticle AV: $1288
6-18x50 PLEX Reticle AV: $1288

PV-S
6-24x50P

SR RAIL MOUNT

PF / PF-N SERIES

PF fixed magnification rifle scopes feature less weight, an extra wide field of view and a telescopic damp-ening system for the eyecup. They also feature a scratchproof surface. The Habicht PF-N versions come with an illuminated reticle.

PF 6x42 1 In. w/4A
Reticle: .... Discontinued
PF 8x50 30mm w/4A
Reticle: $1100
PF 8x56 30mm w/4A
Reticle: .... Discontinued
PF 8x56 30mm w/PLEXN Illum.
Reticle: .... Discontinued

SR RAIL PH SERIES

The Swarovski SR line uses an integral toothed rail on PH scopes that makes the tube stronger while eliminating the ring/tube juncture that can fail during heavy recoil.

1.25-4x24 RAIL Series #24
Reticle: .... Discontinued
1.5-6x42 RAIL Series #4A
Reticle: $1599

2.5-10x56 RAIL Series #4
Reticle PH: $1966
3-12x50 RAIL Series #4A
Reticle PH: .... Discontinued
3-12x50 RAIL Series TDS PLEx
Reticle: $1866
3-12x50 RAIL Series Illum. #4AN
Reticle PH: .... Discontinued
3-12x50 RAIL Series Illum. #4NK
Reticle: .... Discontinued

AV LIGHTWEIGHT	3-9x36	3-10x42	4-12x50	6-18x50
Magnification	3-9x	3.3-10x	4-12x	6-18x
Objective lens diameter (mm)	36	42	50	50
Objective lens diameter (in.)	1.42	1.55	1.97	1.97
Exit pupil, diameter (mm)	12-4	12.6-4.2	12.5-4.2	8.3-2.8
Eye relief (in.)	3.5	3.5	3.5	3.5
Field of view, real (m/100m)	13-4.5	11-3.9	9.7-3.3	17.4-6.5
Field of view, real (ft./100yds.)	39-13.5	33-11.7	29.1-9.9	17.4-6.5
Diopter compensation (dpt)	± 2.6	± 2.5	± 2.5	± 2.5
Transission (%)	94	94	94	92
Twilight factor (DIN 58388)	9-18	9-21	11-25	17-30
Impact Point correction per click (in./100yds.)	0.25	0.25	0.25	0.25
Max. elevation/windage adjustment range (ft./100yds.)	4.8	4.2	3.6	3.9
Length, approx (in.)	11.8	12.44	13.5	14.85
Weight, approx (oz.): L	11.6	12.7	13.9	20.3
LS	–	13.6	15.2	–

L=light alloy • LS=light alloy with rail

PF & PV	PF 6x42	PF/PF-N 8X50	PF/PF-N 8x56	PV/PV-1 1.25-4X24	PV 1.5-6x42	PV/PV-N 2.5-10X42	PV/PV-N 2.5-10X56	PV/PV-N 3-1-1X50	PV 4-16X50P	PV 6-24X50P	PV-S 6-24X50P
Magnification	6x	8x	8x	1.25-4x	1.5-6x	2.5-10x	2.5-10x	3-12x	4-16x	6-24x	6-24x
Objective lens diameter (mm)	42	50	56	17-24	20-42	33-42	33-56	39-50	50	50	50
Objective lens diameter (in.)	1.65	1.97	2.20	0.67-0.94	0.79-1.65	1.3-1.65	1.3-2.20	1.54-1.97	1.97	1.97	1.97
Exit pupil, diameter (mm)	7	6.25	7	12.5-6	13.1-7	13.1-4.2	13.1-5.6	13.1-4.2	12.5-3.1	8.3-2.1	8.3-2.1
Eye relief (in.)	3.15	3.15	3.15	3.15	3.15	3.15	3.15	3.15	3.15	3.15	3.15
Field of view, real (m/100m)	7	5.2	5	32.8-10.4	21.8-7	13.2-4.2	13.2-4.1	11-3.5	9.1-2.6	6.2-1.8	6.2-1.8
Field of view, real (ft./100yds.)	21	15.6	15.6	98.4-31.2	65.4-21	39.6-12.6	39.6-12.3	33-10.5	27.3-7.8	18.6-5.4	18.6-5.4
Diopter compensation (dpt)	+2. -3	+2. -3	+2. -3	+2. -3	+2. -3	+2. -3	+2. -3	+2. -3	+2. -3	+2. -3	+2. -3
Transission (%)	94	94/92	93/91	93/91	93	94/92	93/91	94/92	90	90	90
Twilight factor (DIN 58388)	16	20	21	4-10	4-16	7-21	7-24	9-25	11-28	17-35	17-35
Impact Point correction per click (in./100yds.)	0.36	0.36	0.36	0.54	0.36	0.36	0.36	0.36	0.18	0.18	0.17
Max. elevation/windage adjustment range (ft./100yds.)	3.9	3.3	3.9	9.9	6.6	3.9	3.9	3.3	E:5.4/W:3	E:3.6/W:2.1	E:3.6/W:2.1
Length, approx (in.)	12.83	13.94	13.27	10.63	12.99	13.23	13.62	14.33	14.21	15.43	15.43
Weight, approx (oz.): L	12.0	14.8	15.9	12.7	16.2	15.2	18.0	16.9	22.2	23.6	24.5
LS	13.4	15.9	16.9	13.8	17.5	16.4	19.0	18.3	—	—	—

L=light alloy • LS=light alloy with rail

SCOPES

Swift Scopes

688M 6-18x44

688M 6-18x44

685M 3-9x40

Swift Premier line features include full saddle construction; Speed Focus; fully multi-coated optics; clear dust caps; scopes are constructed to withstand the severe reverse recoil. Elevation and windage adjustments are mounted full saddle on hard anodized 1 in. tubes. Available in matte and silver finish.

PISTOL SCOPES				
MAGNIFICATION (X OBJ. DIA.)	**FIELD OF VIEW (FT., 100 YDS)**	**DIA./LENGTH (IN.)**	**WEIGHT (OZ.)**	**MSRP**
2-6x32	14' @ 2x, 4.5' @ 6x	1/5.5	10.6	$170–240
4x32	6.6	1/9.4	9.9	$130
PREMIER RIFLESCOPES				
MAGNIFICATION (X OBJ. DIA.)	**FIELD OF VIEW (FT., 100 YDS)**	**DIA./LENGTH (IN.)**	**WEIGHT (OZ.)**	**MSRP**
1.5-4.5x32	71 @ 1.5x, 25 @ 4.5x	1/10.41	12.7	$157–239
2-7x40	60 @ 2x, 17 @ 7x	1/12.2	14.8	$157–230
3-9x40	40 @ 3x, 14.2 @ 9x	1/12	13.1	$180–250
3.5-10x44	35 @ 3.5x, 11 @ 10x	1/12.6	15.2	$260
4-12x50	29.5' @ 4x, 9.5 @ 12x	1/13.8	15.8	$290
4-12x40	29.5' @ 4x, 11 @ 12x	1/12.4	15.4	$160–240
6-18x44	19.5' @ 6x, 7 @ 18x	1/15.4	22.6	$240
6-18x50	19' @ 6x, 6.7 @ 18x	1/15.8	20.9	$220–340
STANDARD RIFLESCOPES				
MAGNIFICATION (X OBJ. DIA.)	**FIELD OF VIEW (FT., 100 YDS)**	**DIA./LENGTH (IN.)**	**WEIGHT (OZ.)**	**MSRP**
3-9x32	38 @ 3x, 12 @ 9x	1/12	9.5	discontinued
3-9x40	40 @ 3x,14 @ 9x	1/12.6	12.2	$140
4x32	25	1/10	8.9	$120
4x40	35	1/12.2	11.4	$100
6x40	23 @ 100 yrds	1/12.6	10.4	discontinued

Tasco Scopes

2.5-10x42 VARMINT

3-9X40 WORLD CLASS 40

3-12X40 WORLD CLASS .22

GOLDEN ANTLER
Golden Antler riflescopes are engineered with 1 in. advanced construction for durability and feature HDC (High Definition Coating) on lens surfaces in addition to fully coated optics. Golden Antler scopes are waterproof/fogproof/shockproof. Backed by a Limited Lifetime Warranty.

PRONGHORN RIFLESCOPES
Wide view Pronghorn scopes feature magenta multi-coating on the objective and ocular lenses for increased

light transmission and are waterproof, fogproof and shockproof.

RIMFIRE SCOPES
Tasco Rimfire scopes are designed for either .22 rifles or quality air guns, and feature lenses calibrated for short ranges and coated optics for a bright image. Rimfire scopes fit .22 and airgun receivers.

TARGET & VARMINT SCOPES
Tasco Target and Varmint riflescopes share high-quality, multi-coated optics

and large objective lenses along with ¼ or ⅛ min. click windage and elevation adjustments. Target and Varmint scopes are waterproof, fogproof and shockproof.

TITAN SERIES
Titan riflescopes are waterproof, fogproof and shockproof with premium, multi-coated, SuperCon optics and finger-adjustable windage and elevation controls.

WORLD CLASS RIFLESCOPES
World Class riflescopes feature Tasco

Tasco Scopes

SuperCon multi-layered coating on the objective and ocular lenses and fully coated optics. Models feature either ProShot, 30/30 or True MilDot reticles and are waterproof, fogproof and shockproof. The scopes are built with monotube construction and carry a Limited Lifetime Warranty.

22 RIFLESCOPES
Tailor-made for .22 rimfire rifles, featuring full-sized, 1 in. Advanced Monotube Construction; 50 yd. parallax setting and rings to fit standard .22 bases; magenta multi-layered lens coatings and fully coated optics; waterproof and fogproof construction.

GOLDEN ANTLER			
Magnification (x obj. dia.)	Field of View (ft., 100 yds)	Dia./Length (in.)	Weight (oz.)
4x32mm	32	1/12.75	11
3-9x32mm	39-13	1/13.25	12.2
2.5x32mm	43	1/11.4	10.1
3-9x40mm	41-15	1/12.75	13
TARGET & VARMINT SCOPES			
Magnification (x obj. dia.)	Field of View (ft., 100 yds)	Dia./Length (in.)	Weight (oz.)
2.5-10x42	35-9	1/14	19.1
6-24x40	17-4	1/16	19.1
6-24x42	13-3.7	1/16	19.6
10-40x50	11-2.5	1/15.5	25.5
TITAN SERIES			
Magnification (x obj. dia.)	Field of View (ft., 100 yds)	Dia./Length (in.)	Weight (oz.)
3.5-10x50	30-10.5	1/13	17.1
3-9x44	39-14	1/12.75	16.5
3-12x30	27-10	1/14	20.7
1.5-6x42	59 20	1/12	16.5
PROPOINT SIGHTS			
Magnification (x obj. dia.)	Field of View (ft., 100 yds)	Dia./Length (in.)	Weight (oz.)
1x25mm	40	1.18/5	5.5
1x30mm	68	1.18/4.75	5.4

WORLD CLASS RIFLESCOPES			
Magnification (x obj. dia.)	Field of View (ft., 100 yds)	Dia./Length (in.)	Weight (oz.)
3-9x40mm IR	34.50-10.50	1/12.50	16.26
1.5-4.5x32mm	77-23	1/11.25	12
2-8x32mm	50-17	1/10.5	12.5
3-9x40mm	41-15	1/12.75	13
PRONGHORN RIFLESCOPES			
Magnification (x obj. dia.)	Field of View (ft., 100 yds)	Dia./Length (in.)	Weight (oz.)
2.5x32	43	1/11.4	10.1
3-9x32	39-13	1/12	11
3-9x40	39-13	1/13	12.1
4x32	32	1/12	11
22 RIFLESCOPES			
Magnification (x obj. dia.)	Field of View (ft., 100 yds)	Dia./Length (in.)	Weight (oz.)
3-9x32	17.75-6	1/12.75	11.3
4x32	13.5	1/12.25	12.1
RIMFIRE SCOPES			
Magnification (x obj. dia.)	Field of View (ft., 100 yds)	Dia./Length (in.)	Weight (oz.)
4x20mm	23	¾/10.5	3.8
3-7x20mm	24-11	¾/11.5	5.7
4x15mm	20.5	¾/11	4

Trijicon Scopes

ACCUPOINT SCOPE

ACCUPOINT 3-9x40

ACCUPOINT SCOPES
AccuPoint's features a dual-illuminated aiming point—reticle illumination is supplied by advanced fiber optics or, in low-light conditions, by a self-contained tritium lamp. The AccuPoint scopes feature quick-focus eyepiece; water-resistant and nitrogen filled, multi-layer coated lenses; scope body crafted of hard anodized aluminum; manual brightness adjustment override; fiber-optic light collector. Choice of amber or red aiming point illuminated by a special tritium lamp.

ACCUPOINT 3–9X40 RIFLESCOPE
Utilizing Trijicon's exclusive battery-free, dual-illumination technology, and a fiber optic collector that automatically adjusts the brightness of the aiming point, the Trijicon AccuPoint 3–9x40 Riflescope has a super-precise, tritium-illuminated, amber-colored reticle to help ensure optimum clarity, regardless of the available light. This scope also fea-

tures the revolutionary Bindon Aiming Concept, a both-eyes-open aiming method using telescopic magnification that allows a shooter to lock onto a moving target more quickly than with a traditional riflescope. Features include multi-layer coated lenses for excellent light transmission with no distortion; quick-focus eyepiece; long eye relief of 3.6 to 3.2 in.; manual brightness adjustment override; 1/4 MOA windage and elevation adjustments. The weather-resistant, nitrogen-filled scope body is crafted of aircraft-quality, hard anodized aluminum for maximum durability, and its black matte finish eliminates glare and helps to conceal the shooter's presence. Offered with either an amber or red reticle.

ACCUPOINT SCOPES				
Magnification (x obj. dia.)	Field of View (ft., 100 yds)	Dia./Length (in.)	Weight (oz.)	MSRP
3-9x40	33.8-11.3	1.18/12.2	13.4	$799
1.25-4x24	61.6-20.5	1.18/10.2	11.4	$799
2.5-10x56	37.6-10.1	1.18/13.8	22.1	$950

Vortex Scopes

DIAMONDBACK SCOPES

Every glass surface of the Diamondback is fully multi-coated. By transmitting 91 percent of the light, you'll see the brightly detailed views you need when taking aim. Fast focus eyepiece is quick and easy to use. Pop-up dials let you easily set elevation and windage back to zero. Audible clicks are easily count-

ed for fast, precise adjustment of elevation and windage. Zero reset accuracy. Machined for durability. Rugged one-

piece tube, constructed of 6061 T6 aircraft-grade aluminum. Argon gas eliminates internal fogging.

Model	Field of view (ft/100yds)	Eye relief (in)	Click value (in@100yd)	Length (in)	Weight (oz.)	MSRP
2-7x35	64.3-19.3	3.5-3.1	1/4 MOA	11.6	14.2	$249
3.5-10x50	35.8-13.5	3.6-3.3	1/4 MOA	12.6	16.6	$299
1.75-5x32	68.3-23.1	3.7-3.5	1/4 MOA	10.3	12.8	$239
3-9x40	44.6-14.8	3.5-3.3	1/4 MOA	11.8	14.8	$259
4-12x40	32.4-11.3	3.4-3.1	1/4 MOA	12.1	14.8	$269

Weaver Scopes

K-6

CLASSIC HANDGUN 1.5-4X20

RIMFIRE RV-7

CLASSIC HANDGUN & SHOTGUN SCOPES

Fixed-power scopes include 2x28 and 4x28 scopes in gloss black or silver. Variables in 1.5-4x20 and 2.5-8x28 come with a gloss black finish. Features: one-piece tubes, multi-coated lenses and generous eye relief.

2x28 Gloss Black or Silver: **$226**
4x28 Gloss Black or Silver: **$245**
1.5-4x20 Gloss Black: **$300**
2.5-8x28 Gloss Black or Silver: . **$319**
2.5-8x28 Matte: **$319**
Also available:
  Classic shotgun 4x32: **$246**
  1.5-5x32: **$260**

CLASSIC K SERIES

Classic American scopes, the K2.5, K4 and K6 now have a sleeker look,

weigh less but deliver brighter images. K scopes–including the target model, KT-15–have one-piece tubes.

K-2.5 (2.5x20 Gloss): **$172**
K-4 (Gloss): **$195**
K-4 (Matte): **$195**
K-6 (Gloss): **$208**
K-6 (Matte): **$208**
K-6 (Matte, LER): **$250**
KT-15 (15x42 Gloss): **$380**

CLASSIC RIMFIRE RV4, RV-7 AND RV-9

Rimfire scopes are well suited .22s and airguns. They are designed with a sturdy one-piece aluminum housing and are waterproof and fogproof with fully multi-coated, nonglare lenses and 28mm objective lenses. Available in fixed or variable power.

4x28 Rimfire Matte Black: **$178**
2.5-7x28 Rimfire Matte
  Black or Silver: **$208**
3-9x32 AO Matte:...................**$338**

GRAND SLAM SCOPES

The Grand Slam series features an advanced one-piece tube design with a "sure-grip" power ring and AO adjustment. An offset parallax indicator lets you remain in shooting position while adjusting the scope. The eyepiece has a fast-focus adjustment ring. Grand Slam configurations include: 4.75x40mm, a fixed-power scope; 1.5-5x32mm, the ideal scope for short-range rifles; 3.5-10x40mm, the traditional choice of big-game hunters; 3.5-10x50mm, which provides the brightest view in low-light

SCOPES

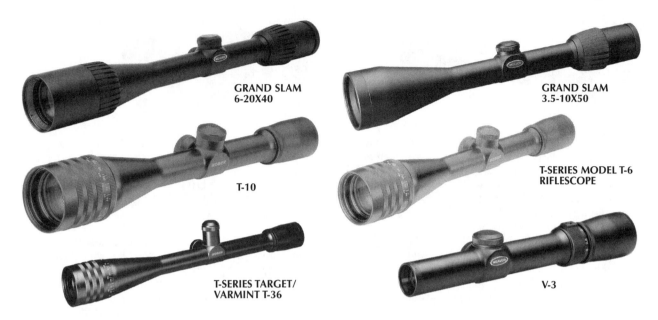

**GRAND SLAM
6-20X40**

**GRAND SLAM
3.5-10X50**

T-10

**T-SERIES MODEL T-6
RIFLESCOPE**

**T-SERIES TARGET/
VARMINT T-36**

V-3

situations; 4.5-14x40mm AO, possibly the most versatile Grand Slam; and 6-20x40mm AO, target/varminter model. Windage and elevation knobs have target-type finger adjustments. Grand Slam scopes are also equipped with Micro-Trac, Weaver's four-point adjustment system. All Grand Slam scopes are offered with a plex reticle. The scopes have a non-glare black matte or silver and black finish.

6-20x40 AO Black or Silver: . . . **$580**
4.5-14x40 AO Black or Silver: . . **$570**
3.5-10x50 Black or Silver: **$520**
3-10x40 Black or Silver: **$430**
1.5-5x32 Black: **$480**
4.75x40 Black: **$400**

T-10 AND T-24 TARGET

The T-10 target model (no AO) has ¼-min. click adjustments and a ⅛ min. dot reticle. It weighs just 1 lb., has a 40mm objective lens and comes in black satin finish. The T-24 also has a 40mm front end. The parallax (AO) adjustment is the traditional forward ring. Weight 17 oz. Choose a ⅛ min. dot or a ½ min. dot.

T-10: **$598**
T-24: **$638**

T-SERIES MODEL T-6 RIFLESCOPE

Weaver's T-6 competition 6x scope is only 12.7 in. long and weighs less than 15 oz. All optical surfaces are fully multi-coated for maximum clarity

and light transmission. The T-6 features Weaver's Micro-Trac precision adjustments in ⅛ min. clicks to ensure parallel tracking. The protected target-style turrets are a low-profile configuration combining ease of adjustment with weight reduction. A 40mm adjustable objective permits parallax correction from 50 ft. to infinity without shifting the point of impact. A special AO lock ring eliminates bell vibration or shift. The T-6 comes with screw-in metal lens caps and features a competition matte black finish.
Reticles: dot, Fine Crosshair
6x40 Satin Black: **$407**

T-SERIES TARGET/VARMINT T-36

Weaver's 36x features patented Micro-Trac adjustments in a dual-spring, four-bearing housing that allows independent movement of windage and elevation. Optics are fully multi-coated and an adjustable objective allows for parallax zero from 50 ft. to infinity. Choice of fine crosshair or dot reticles. Scopes come with sunshade, an extra pair of oversize benchrest adjustment knobs, and screw-in metal lens caps.
Magnification/Objective: 36X40mm
Field of View: 3.0 ft.
Eye Relief: 3.0 in.
Length: 15.1 in.
Weight: 16.7 oz.
Reticle: 1/8 MOA Dot, Fine Crosshair
Finish: Matte black or silver

Matte: **$679**
Silver: **$679**
Matte Dot: **$679**
Silver Dot: **$732**

V-3

Magnification/Objective: 1-3x20
Field of View: 100x34
Eye Relief: 3.5 in.
Length: 9 in.
Weight: 9.0 oz.
Finish: Matte black
Matte Black: **$267**

V-9

Magnification/Objective: 3-9x38
Field of View: 34-11 ft.
Eye Relief: 3.5 in.
Length: 12 in.
Weight: 11.0 oz.
Finish: Matte black, gloss
Matte Black or Gloss: **$315**
3-9x50 Matte: **$296**

V-10

Magnification/Objective: 2-10x38mm
Field of View: 38.5-9.5
Eye Relief: 3.5 in.
Length: 12.2 in.
Weight: 11.2 oz.
Reticle: Dual-X
Finish: Matte black, silver
**Matte Black, Silver or
    Gloss Black:** $274
V-10 2-10x50 Matte: $386

SCOPES

Weaver Scopes

V16

SURE GRIP
WINDAGE
ADJUSTABLE
RINGS

V-16 AND V-24

The V16 is popular for a variety of shooting applications, from close shots that require a wide field of view to long-range varmint or benchrest shooting. Adjustable objective allows a parallax-free view from 30 ft. to infinity. Features one-piece tube for strength and moisture resistance and multi-coated lenses for clear, crisp images. Two finishes and three reticle options.
Magnification/Objective: 4-16x42mm
Field of View: 26.8-6.8
Eye Relief: 3.1 in.
Length: 13.9 in.
Weight: 16.5 oz.

Reticle: Choice of Dual-X, ¼ MOA Dot, or Fine Crosshair
Finish: Matte black
V-16 4-16x42:.........................**$458**
V-24 6-24x42 Black Matte:.........**$534**
V-24 6-24x42 With Mil Dot:.......**$554**

QUAD LOCK RINGS

All Quad-Lock rings utilize four straps per set for added gripping strength. These rings mount to all Weaver Top Mount Bases and their all-aluminum construction offers hunters a lightweight, sturdy option. The silver or matte Tip-Off Quad Lock rings fit a ³/₈ in. dovetail receiver and three Quad

Locks sets are available in silver (medium, high and high extension).

SURE GRIP WINDAGE ADJUSTABLE RINGS

With the Sure Grip Windage Adjustable Rings, hunters and shooters can rest assured that these rings will handle any recoil thrown at them. The four-screw system and steel cap offer shot-of-a-lifetime dependability. The windage adjustable models ensure zeroing in your scope to the critical optical clarity zone is certain.

CLASSIC HANDGUN SCOPES (VARIABLE)								
Model	Magnification Power, Objective	Finish	Exit Pupil (mm)	Field of View (ft. @ 1000 yds.)	Eye Relief (in.)	Overall Length (in.)	Weight (oz.)	Reticle
849427	1.5-4x20mm	Gloss Black	13.33-5.5	15.5-6.5	4	9	8.2	Duplex
849428	2.5-8x28mm	Gloss Black	11.2-3.5	12.22-3.93	4	9.375	9.1	Duplex
849429	2.5-8x28mm	Matte Black	11.2-3.5	12.22-3.93	4	9.375	9.1	Duplex

CLASSIC HANDGUN SCOPES (FIXED)								
Model	Magnification Power, Objective	Finish	Exit Pupil (mm)	Field of View (ft. @ 1000 yds.)	Eye Relief (in.)	Overall Length (in.)	Weight (oz.)	Reticle
849423	2x28mm	Gloss Black	16	21	4.29	8.375	6.7	Duplex
849424	2x28mm	Silver	16	21	4.29	8.375	6.7	Duplex
849425	4x28mm	Matte Black	7	8.29	12-8	8.5	6.4	Duplex
849426	4x28mm	Silver	7	8.29	12-8	8.5	6.4	Duplex

CLASSIC SHOTGUN SCOPES								
Model	Magnification Power, Objective	Finish	Exit Pupil (mm)	Field of View (ft. @ 1000 yds.)	Eye Relief (in.)	Overall Length (in.)	Weight (oz.)	Reticle
849421	4x32mm	Matte Black	8	22.25	3.5	9.5	8.7	Duplex
849422	1.5-5x32	Matte Black	16-6.4	62-18.5	4.25-3.375	10.375	10	Diamond

CLASSIC K SERIES								
Model	Magnification Power, Objective	Finish	Exit Pupil (mm)	Field of View (ft. @ 1000 yds.)	Eye Relief (in.)	Overall Length (in.)	Weight (oz.)	Reticle
849417	15x40mm AO	Gloss Black	2.8	7.4	3	13.25	14.8	Duplex
849416	6x38mm	Gloss Black	6.3	18.4	3.25	11.625	9.8	Duplex
849418	6x38mm	Matte Black	6.3	18.4	3.25	11.625	9.8	Duplex
849414	4x38mm	Gloss Black	9.5	23.1	3.3	11.5	9.9	Duplex
849415	4x38mm	Matte Black	9.5	23.1	3.3	11.5	9.9	Duplex
849413	2.5x20mm	Gloss Black	8	36.8	4	9.625	7.1	Duplex

SCOPES

CLASSIC RIMFIRE								
Model	Magnification Power, Objective	Finish	Exit Pupil (mm)	Field of View (ft. @ 1000 yds.)	Eye Relief (in.)	Overall Length (in.)	Weight (oz.)	Reticle
849431	2.5-7x28mm	Matte Black	11.2-4	41.25-15.7	3.5	11.5	9.75	Duplex
849432	2.5-7x28mm	Silver	11.2-4	41.25-15.7	3.7-3.3	11.5	9.75	Duplex
849430	4x28mm	Matte Black	7	21.8	3.25	10.25	8.5	Duplex

GRAND SLAM								
Model	Magnification Power, Objective	Finish	Exit Pupil (mm)	Field of View (ft. @ 1000 yds.)	Eye Relief (in.)	Overall Length (in.)	Weight (oz.)	Reticle
800469	6-20x40	Matte Black	6.6-2	16.5-5.25	3-2.75	14.25	1lb 1.75oz	Duplex Dot
800471	1.5-5x32	Matte Black	17.4-6.2	71-21	3.25-3.25	10.25	11.5	Duplex
800472	4.75x40	Matte Black	7.7	20	3.25	11	10.75	Duplex
800473	3-10x40	Matte Black	12.6-4	35-11.3	3.5-3	11.875	13	Duplex
800474	3.5-10x50	Matte Black	11.5-4.5	23.6-10.91	3.12-3	12.75	1lb 0.3oz	Duplex
800475	4.5-14x40	Matte Black	8.8-2.6	22.5-10.5	3.5-3	14.25	1lb 1.5oz	Duplex
800476	6-20x40	Matte Black	6.6-2	16.5-5.25	3-2.75	14.25	1lb 1.75oz	Fine Crosshair Dot
800588	3-10x40	Matte Black	2.6-4	35-11.3	3.5-3	11.875	13	Duplex
800589	3.5-10x50	Silver Matte	11.5-4.5	23.6-10.91	3.12-3	12.75	1lb 0.3oz	Duplex
800590	4.5-14x40 AO	Silver Matte	8.8-2.6	22.5-10.5	3.5-3	14.25	1lb 1.5oz	Duplex
800591	6-20x40 AO	Silver Matte	6.6-2	16.5-5.25	3-2.75	14.25	1lb 1.75oz	Duplex Dot
800592	6-20x40 AO	Silver Matte	6.6-2	16.5-5.25	3-2.75	14.25	1lb 1.75oz	Fine Crosshair Dot

T SERIES								
Model	Magnification Power, Objective	Finish	Exit Pupil (mm)	Field of View (ft. @ 1000 yds.)	Eye Relief (in.)	Overall Length (in.)	Weight (oz.)	Reticle
849970	36x40 AO	Matte Black	1.16	3	3	15.125	17	Fine Crosshair Dot
849981	36x40 AO	Silver	1.16	3	3	15.125	17	Fine Crosshair Dot
849974	36x40 AO	Matte Black	1.16	3	3	15.125	17	1/8 MOA Dot
849969	36x40 AO	Silver	1.16	3	3	15.125	17	1/8 MOA Dot
849976	24x40mm	Black Satin	1.6	4.4	3	15.1	16.7	Fine Crosshair Dot
849811	10x40mm	Black Satin	4	9.3	3	15.1	16.7	Fine Crosshair Dot
849995	6x40mm	Black Satin	6	17	3	12.75	15	Fine Crosshair Dot

V SERIES								
Model	Magnification Power, Objective	Finish	Exit Pupil (mm)	Field of View (ft. @ 1000 yds.)	Eye Relief (in.)	Overall Length (in.)	Weight (oz.)	Reticle
V24 (849411)	6-24x42mm AO	Matte Black	7-1.175	15.7-4.36	3.25-3	14.125	1lb .75oz	Duplex Dot
V24 (849402)	3-9x38mm	Matte Black	12.67-4.2	34-11.35	3.25-3	12.25	11.25	Mil-Dot
V16 (849408)	4-16x42mm AO	Matte Black	10.5-2.63	24.4-6.98	3.13-3	14	1lb .75oz	Duplex
V16 (849409)	4-16x42mm AO	Matte Black	10.5-2.63	24.4-6.98	3.13-3	14	1lb .75oz	FC
V16 (849410)	4-16x42mm AO	Matte Black	10.5-2.63	24.4-6.98	3.13-3	14	1lb .75oz	FCD
V10 (849404)	2-10x38mm	Gloss Black	19-3.8	38-9.6	3.25-3	12.5	11	Duplex
V10 (849405)	2-10x38mm	Matte Black	19-3.8	38-9.6	3.25-3	12.5	11	Duplex
V10 (849406)	2-10x38mm	Silver	19-3.8	38-9.6	3.25-3	12.5	11	Duplex
V10 (849407)	2-10x50mm	Matte Black	12-5.0	37.4-9.1	3.25-3	13.75	15.5	Duplex
V9 (849401)	3-9x38mm	Gloss Black	12.67-4.2	34-11.35	3.25-3	12.25	11.25	Duplex
V9 (849402)	3-9x38mm	Matte Black	12.67-4.2	34-11.35	3.25-3	12.25	11.25	Duplex
V9 (849403)	3-9x50mm	Matte Black	10.5-5	28.5-9.75	3.25-3	132.5	15.5	Duplex
V3 (849400)	1-3x20mm	Matte Black	15-6.6	87-30.75	3.12-3.12	9.125	8.5	Duplex

Zeiss Scopes

CONQUEST 3-9X50

**CONQUEST 3.5-10x44
STAINLESS STEEL FINISH**

CONQUEST 3-9x40

DIAVARI VM/V 3-9x42T

DIAVARI 1.1-4x24 T

DIAVARI 1.5-6x42 T

DIAVARI 2.5-10x50 T

DIAVARI VM/V 5-15x42T

**VICTORY DIARANGE
3 - 12x56 T WITH LASER
RANGEFINDER**

CONQUEST RIFLESCOPES

The Conquest series features MC anti-reflective coating, excellent low-light performance; arsenic/lead-free glass technology; Zeiss MC multicoating; Lifetime Transferable Warranty. Conquest scopes are waterproof and fogproof.

DIAVARI RIFLESCOPES

Light, compact riflescope available with illuminated vari-point reticle and wide field of view. The Diviari features easy-grip adjustment knobs and is available with bullet drop compensator.

VARIPOINT RIFLESCOPES

Compact scopes with the widest field-of-view offered by Zeiss (108 ft. at 100 yds.). The dot reticle is in the second image plane, so it's large and visible at low powers, small but distinct at high powers. The unilluminated reticle is highly visible.

VICTORY DIARANGE 3 - 12 X 56 T WITH LASER RANGEFINDER

The Victory Diarange 3-12x56 T with integrated laser range-finder is a new riflescope that delivers excellent optical per-formance and mechanical sturdiness, and the precise range to the target at the push of a button. Measures range up to 999 yds. High mechanical sturdiness as well as recoil proof, waterproof, nitrogen filled. Four different illuminated reticles for use in low-light conditions. Fast and comfortable mounting with Zeiss rail.

CONQUEST				
MAGNIFICATION (X OBJ. DIA.)	**FIELD OF VIEW (FT., 100 YDS)**	**DIA./LENGTH (IN.)**	**WEIGHT (OZ.)**	**MSRP**
3-9x40 MC black	33.90-11.01	1/12.99	15.17	$556–639
3-9x40 MC stainless	33.90-11.01	1/12.99	15.17	$611–694
3-9x50 MC	37.5-12.9	1/12.36	16.58	$667–750
3-9x50 MC ss	37.5-12.9	1/12.36	16.58	$778–861
3.5-10x44 MC black	35.1-11.70	1/12.68	15.87	$778–861
3.5-10x44 MC silver	35.1-11.70	1/12.68	15.87	$833–917
3.5-10x50 MC	35.1-11.7	1/13.15	17.11	$833–972
3-12x56 MC black	27.6-9.9	1/15.3	25.8	$1111
3-12x56 MC stainless	27.6-9.9	1/15.3	25.8	$1176
4.5-14x50 MC	25.5-8.84	1/14.02	19.75	$944–1083
4.5-14x44 AO MC black	24.9-8.4	1/13.86	17.11	$889–972
4.5-14x44 AO MC silver	24.9-8.4	1/13.86	17.11	$944–1028
6.5-20x50 AO MC black	17.7-5.7	1/15.59	21.83	$1111–1194
6.5-20x50 AO MC silver	17.7-5.7	1/15.59	21.83	$1167–1250

DIAVARI				
MAGNIFICATION (X OBJ. DIA.)	**FIELD OF VIEW (FT., 100 YDS)**	**DIA./LENGTH (IN.)**	**WEIGHT (OZ.)**	**MSRP**
V 6-24x56T	18.6-5.10	1.18/14.84	28.40	$2444–2667
VM/V 1.5-6x42 T	72-20.7	1.18/12.3	15	$1833
VM/V 2.5-10x50 T	43.5-12	1.18/12.5	15.9	$2000
VM/V 2.5-10x50 T w/ Illum Reticle	43.5-12	1.18/12.5	15.9	$2444
VM/V 3-12x56 T	37.5-10.5	1.18/13.54	18.38	$2111–2222

VARIPOINT				
MAGNIFICATION (X OBJ. DIA.)	**FIELD OF VIEW (FT., 100 YDS)**	**DIA./LENGTH (IN.)**	**WEIGHT (OZ.)**	**MSRP**
1.1-4x24 T VM/V	108-30.75	1.18/11.8	15.3	$2444
1.5-6x42 T VM/V	72-20.7	1.18/12.80	15	$2444
2.5-10x50 T VM/V w/ Illum	43.5-12	1.18/12.80	20.4	$2556
VICTORY DIARANGE WITH LASER RANGERFINDER				
MAGNIFICATION (X OBJ. DIA.)	**FIELD OF VIEW (FT., 100 YDS)**	**DIA./LENGTH (IN.)**	**WEIGHT (OZ.)**	**MSRP**
3-12X56	7.5-10.5	-/14.2	32	$4444

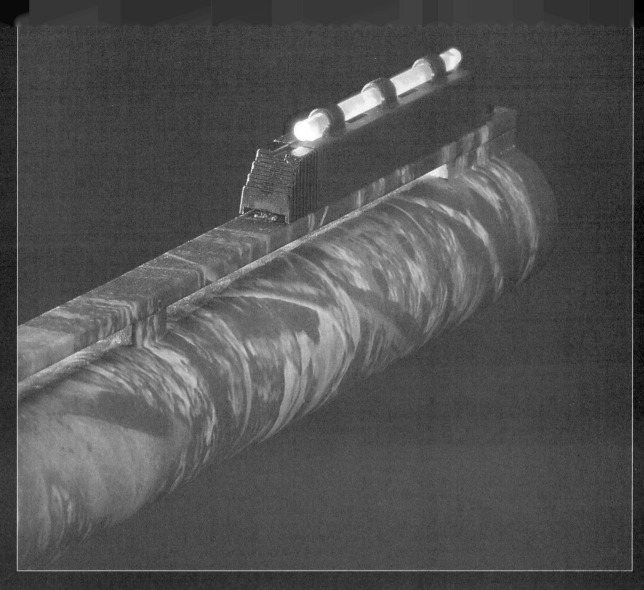

Aimpoint Sights

9000

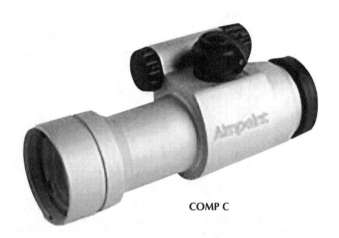

COMP C

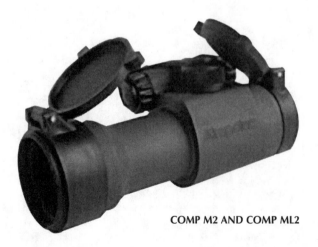

COMP M2 AND COMP ML2

9000

System: Passive Red Dot Collimator Reflex Sight
Optical: anti-reflex coated lens
Adjustment: 1 click = 10mm at 80 meters = 13mm at 100 meters = ½ in. at 100 yds
Length: 7.9 inches
Weight: 8.1 oz.
Objective diameter: 36mm
Diameter of dot: 2 MOA
Mounting system: 30mm ring
Magnification: 1X
Material: extruded aluminum; black finish
9000L: **$400**
9000SC: **$400**

COMP C13

System: 100% Parallax free
Optics: anti-reflex coated lenses
Eye relief: Unlimited
Batteries: 3V Lithium
Adjustment: 1 click = ½ in. at 100 yards
Length: 4¾ in.
Weight: 6.5 oz.
Objective diameter: 36mm
Dot diameter: 4 MOA
Mounting system: 30mm ring
Magnification: 1X
Material: Black or stainless finish
MSRP: **$432**
CompC SM
    (7 MOA silver metallic): **$387**
        Anodized, graphic gray: . . . .
                            Discontinued

COMP ML2

System: Parallax free
Optical: Anti-reflex coated lens
Adjustment: 1 click = ½ in. at 100 yards
Length: 4.7 in.
Weight: 6.5 oz.
Objective diameter: 36mm
Diameter of dot: 2 MOA
Mounting system: 30mm ring
Magnification: 2X fixed
Material: anodized aluminum; black finish
Comp ML2: **$596**
Comp M2: **$510**
    now only in 4 MOA

Browning Sport Optics Sights

HIVIZ BIRD BUSTER MAGNETIC SHOTGUN SIGHT

HIVIZ BUCK MARK PISTOL SIGHT

HIVIZ COMP SIGHT

HIVIZ FLASH POINT SIGHT

HIVIZ MAGNI-OPTIC SIGHT

HIVIZ MID BRIGHT SIGHT

HIVIZ SPARK SIGHT

HIVIZ TRI-COMP SIGHT

HIVIZ TRIVIZ TURKEY SIGHT

HIVIZ BIRD BUSTER MAGNETIC SHOTGUN SIGHTS

Available with four interchangeable LitePipes. Fits all Browning shotguns and includes three sizes of magnetic bases. Comes in red, green or yellow.
MSRP: **$19.99**

HIVIZ BUCK MARK PISTOL SIGHT

Includes six LitePipes. Easy to install, replaces factory sight with single screw. Fits Browning Buck Mark Plus, Camper, Standard and Micro models.
MSRP: **$39.99**

HIVIZ COMP SIGHT

Interchangeable LitePipes—includes eight LitePipes of different diameters and colors. Base threads directly into shotgun bead.
MSRP: **$39.99**

HIVIZ FLASH POINT SIGHT

Mounts with single screw in front bead hole of any shotgun. Includes LitePipes in various heights and colors.
MSRP: **$24–27**

HIVIZ MAGNI-OPTIC SIGHT

Enables any shotgunner to shoot with both eyes open for improved target acquisition and better hand/eye coordination.
MSRP: **$39.99**

HIVIZ MID BRIGHT SIGHT

Replaces the mid bead on many shotguns. Works well with Comp Sight, TriComp or Magnetic HiViz sights. Ensures proper barrel alignment and sight picture. Available in green or red.
MSRP: **$8.95–12.45**

HIVIZ SPARK SIGHT

Bright green fiber optic. Replaces factory bead. Thread sizes for most major shotguns.
MSRP: **$6.95**

HIVIZ TRI-COMP SIGHT

Solid steel construction with interchangeable triangular and round LitePipes.
MSRP: **$34.99–39.95**

HIVIZ TRIVIZ TURKEY SIGHT

Injection-molded optical-grade resin rear sight—fully adjustable for windage. Includes four green front sight LitePipes in different heights. Mounts on all common vent rib sizes.
MSRP: **$33.50–36**

MAGNETIC SHOTGUN SIGHTS

Available with four interchangeable LitePipes of different diameters for different light conditions. HiViz sights fit all Browning shotguns.

M2000
Beretta S686 Silver Essential, S686 Ultralight, S686 Silver Pigeon Field, S687 Silver Pigeon, S687 Gold Pigeon, AL-390 series, A304 series. Sig Arms SA-S Upland Hunter.

M3000
All Benelli shotgun models, Beretta S682 Gold Skeet and Gold Trap, Silver Pigeon Skeet, ASE models, Pintail, A303 Youth, SOS Sporting. Ithaca Model 37, Model 51. Krieghoff K-80. All Remington shotguns except 396 Sporting and 296 Skeet. Ruger Red Label. Weatherby Athena, Orion. Winchester Model 12 and Model 101. Perazzi all game models.

M4000
Fits Beretta S682 Gold Competition and Trap, ASE Gold Trap. Marocchi Conquista. All Mossberg shotgun models. Remington 396 Sporting and Skeet. SKB 505 and 585 Field. Winchester M 1300, M 1400 and Super X2.
MSRP: **$22.00–27.95**

SIGHTS

BSA Sights

RED DOT SIGHTS

Perfect sight for pistols and shotguns; a small bright red dot appears in the center; available in BSA's Shadow Black rubber; choose either a push-button control, or 11-position click rheostat

PD30BK—30mm with rings: . . $89.95
PD30SIL—30mm with rings,
   Silver: $46
RD30—30mm Red Dot Sight: . . . $50
RD30SB—30mm Red Dot Sight in
   Shadow Black Finish: $50

RD30SIL—30mm Red Dot Sight in
   Matte Silver: $50
RD42SB—42mm Red Dot Sight in
   Shadow Black Finish: $109
   RD50SB—50mm Red Dot Sight in
   Shadow Black Finish: $129.95
MR30BK—30mm: $58.99–72.24
RD42CP—RD Red Dot Series: . . $50

Burris Sights

FASTFIRE RED DOT REFLEX SIGHT

Originally developed for semi-automatic handguns as a sight that could withstand the abuse of slide mounting, this tiny but tough, non-magnifying, reflex type red dot sight has proven to be a terrific fast target acquisition sight for turkey shotguns, deer slug guns, tactical and close range hunting carbines, muzzleloaders, paintball guns, home defense shotguns and even upland and waterfowl shotguns.

FastFire weighs just 2 ounces, and shrugs off recoil forces up to 1000 Gs. A target-directed light sensor automatically adjusts and controls the brightness of the 4MOA red dot for maximum visibility based on the ambient light conditions. Multicoating is sandwiched between two highly polished, optical quality glass lenses for protection from scratches and abrasion. Power is provided by a supplied standard lithium Type CR 2032 3-volt battery, and each FastFire sight is supplied with a mount for attachment to any Weaver-style or Picatinny-style base. In addition, 10 affordable handgun mounts are available.

MSRP: $313

Bushnell Sights

HOLOSIGHT XLP

HOLOSIGHT

Projects the appearance of an illuminated crosshair 50 yards in front of your gun with no projected forward light. Shockproof, waterproof and fogproof with unlimited field of view and eye relief. Fits handguns, shotguns and rifles with a standard Weaver style mount. Available in two battery styles—N cell or AAA.

MSRP: $450–460

HOLO SIGHT									
MODEL	RETICLE	MAG. @ 100 YDS.	FIELD OF VIEW FT. @ 100 YDS.	WEIGHT	LENGTH	EYE RELIEF	BATTERIES	BRIGHTNESS ADJ.	PRICE
51-0021	Holographic	1x	Unlimited	6.4 oz.	4.12 in.	½-in.-10'	2 Type N	20 Levels	$389.95
53-0021	Holographic	1x	Unlimited	12 oz.	6 in.	Unlimited	AAA	20 Levels	249
53-0027	Holographic	1x	Unlimited	12 oz.	6 in.	Unlimited	AAA	20 Levels	259

SIGHTS

CenterPoint Precision Optics Sights

1X34MM
COMPACT RED DOT

1X25MM
COMPACT RED DOT

1X34MM, 1X25MM COMPACT RED DOT SIGHTS

CenterPoint's Red Dot sights offer a versatile dot sight for a wide range of pistols, shotguns and rifles. They are precision machined to exact tolerances from aircraft-grade aluminum alloy and feature all-weather, angled objectives for built-in rain protection and sunshield. Their 30mm tubes provide maximum light transmission, as well as wider windage and elevation adjustment. These sights also offer a Red/Green Dot with various brightness settings to account for changing light conditions and backgrounds, and feature finger adjustable windage and elevation dials. They come standard with lens covers and a Weaver/Picatinny low profile mount.

List Prices
1x25mm Compact:. $79.99
1x34mm: $79.99

Docter Sports Optics Sights

RED DOT SIGHT

Weighing just one ounce, it is not much bulkier than a standard rear aperture. There is no battery switch; batteries last up to five years without rest. Available in 3.5 or 7 M.D.A.
MSRP: $398

LaserLyte Sights

SUB-COMPACT LASER SIGHT

LaserLyte's FSL-0650-140, Sub-Compact Laser Sight is for owners of virtually all pistols and long guns with Picatinny, Weaver and Tactical rails. This ultra low-profile laser sight utilizes digital circuitry with a 650nm Hi-Definition laser module, wireless compression switch and adjustments for windage and elevation. With a range of up to 500 yds. at night, the Sub-Compact Laser Sight is set to become the standard. Miniature in size and weighing less than 1 ounce with batteries, the sight won't affect the firearm's ergonomics and adapts to many standard holsters. The sight incorporates a visible low battery indicator. When batteries are low the laser dot pulses, allowing the operator to use the laser for target acquisition. This extends the battery life by approximately 2.5 hours. The FSL sight offers 4 hours total run time with average use and 1.5 hours with continuous use before the low battery indicator alerts the user. The claw-type mounting system securely attaches the laser to the pistol's rails or onto LaserLyte's Rail Adapters for S&W Sigma VE, HK USP and USP Compact, Bersa and Hi-Point series. The Sub-Compact Laser Sight is precision CNC-machined from aerospace-grade aluminum.
MSRP: $150

SUBCOMPACT LASER ON SW HANDGUN

SIGHTS

Lyman Sights

20 MJT-20 LJT GLOBE

57 AND 66 RECEIVER "PEEP" SIGHT

66 WB RECEIVER SIGHT FOR 1886

93 MATCH GLOBE FRONT SIGHT

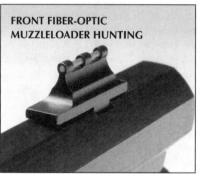

FRONT FIBER-OPTIC MUZZLELOADER HUNTING

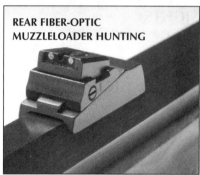

REAR FIBER-OPTIC MUZZLELOADER HUNTING

20 MJT-20 LJT GLOBE FRONT SIGHTS

The 20 MJT-20 LJT – 7/8 in. diameter Globe Front Sights are machined from one solid piece of steel designed to be mounted in a 3/8 in. barrel dovetail or dovetail base. 20 MJT height .700 in., 20 LJT height 7/8 in. from the bottom of dovetail to the aperture center supplied with seven Anschutz size steel apertures.
MSRP: $42.95

57 AND 66 RECEIVER "PEEP" SIGHTS

For flat receivers, such as lever action rifles or modern shotguns. Features include ¼ minute audible click micrometer adjustments for elevation and windage, quick-release slide, coin-slotted "stayset" knobs and two interchangeable aperture discs (large hunting aperture and small target aperture). Weight: 4 oz.
MSRP: $89.95

66 WB RECEIVER SIGHT FOR 1886

Features semi-target knobs and ¼ minute audible clicks for windage and elevation. Supplied with hunting and target aperture disks and quick release slide.
MSRP: $77

90 MJT TARGET RECEIVER SIGHT

Designed to mount on Lyman and other mounting bases. Adjustable zero scales and elevation stop screw permit instantaneous return to zero. Quick release slide with release button. Large 7/8 in. non glare .040 aperture. Elevation adjustable from 1.060 to 1.560 above bore centerline.
MSRP: $89.95

93 MATCH GLOBE FRONT SIGHT

Designed to fit any rifle, the 93 match sight (7/8 in. diameter) mounts on a standard dovetail base. Supplied with seven Anschutz size inserts. The sight height is .550 from the top of the dovetail to the center of the aperture.
MSRP: $55

FIBER-OPTIC MUZZLELOADER HUNTING SIGHTS

Lyman Products offers a new set of fiber-optic hunting sights for Lyman and many other muzzleloading rifles. Black-powder hunters can update their rifles with state-of-the-art fiber-optic technology. These bright, light-gathering sights let hunters take advantage of every minute in the field. They are especially helpful during the very productive dawn and dusk periods when game is most active. Designed to fit the Lyman Great Plains, Trade and Deerstalker Rifles, these state-of-the-art sights will also fit most other European-made black powder rifles, including Cabela's Hawken.
MSRP: $35

#37 HUNTING FRONT SIGHT

HUNTING FRONT SIGHTS

The #3 and #28 are designed to be mounted into the barrel dovetail. The #31 and #37 are designed to mount on ramps. #3 and #31 have 1/16 in. bead. #28 and #37 have 3/32 in. bead availability in ivory or gold.
MSRP: $10.75

SIGHTS

Lyman Sights

NO. 2 TANG SIGHT

The No. 2 Tang will fit most new and old 94 models plus Winchester Models 1885, 1887, 1890 and 1894. (The No. 2 will also fit other models when adjusted to full height).
A version is available for Marlin Models 336, 1894, 1895 and 30 series lever action-rifles. Marlin version includes adapter base. The No. 2 is all steel construction and features height index marks on the aperture post, with a maximum elevation of .800. It includes both a .093 quick sighting hunting aperture and a .040 Large Disk Target Aperture.

MSRP: **$86.50**

NO. 2 TANG SIGHT 1886

The Lyman No. 2 Tang Sight is now available for the Winchester 1886 lever action rifle. It fits the original Winchester Model 1886 and Browning replicas. Features include height index marks on the aperture post and an .800 maximum elevation adjustment. Also included is a .093 x ½ in. quick-sighting aperture and .040 x ⅝ in. target disk. Note: does not fit new rifles with Tang safety.

MSRP: **$86.50**

NO. 16 FOLDING LEAF SIGHT

This open rear sight with adjustable elevation blade is the perfect auxiliary sight for scope-mounted rifles. Folds close to the barrel when not in use. Designed to fit ⅜ in. dovetail slots.

MSRP: **$15.50**

NO. 2 TANG SIGHT

NO. 2 TANG SIGHT 1886

17 A TARGET FRONT SIGHT

SHOTGUN SIGHT

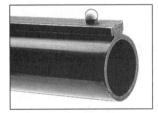

SERIES 17A TARGET FRONT SIGHTS

Machined from solid steel and designed to be mounted in ⅜ in. dovetail slots. Supplied with eight interchangeable inserts. Sight Heights (bottom of dovetail to center of aperture): 17 AHB .404; 17AMI .494; 17AUG .584

MSRP: **$33.95**

SHOTGUN SIGHTS

Oversized ivory-like beads—easy to see under any light conditions. No. 10 Front Sights (press fit) for use on double barrel, or ribbed single barrel guns. No. 10D Front Sights (screw fit) for use on non-ribbed single barrel guns. No. 11 Middle Sight (press fit) small middle sight for use on double and ribbed single barrel guns.

MSRP: **$6.50**

Marble Arms Sights

CONTOUR FRONT SIGHTS

Marble's Contour Front Sights are strong, stable and give your rifle a true traditional look. Available in various widths and heights from .260 inches to .570 in. Choose a gold, ivory or fiber optic bead.

MSRP: $13–16

PEEP TANG SIGHTS

The Marble's Peep Tang Sight is adjustable for windage and elevation. The adjustments are micrometer precise. Each firm detent click equals four-tenths of an inch movement at 100 yards. Each sight includes three apertures and mounting screws.

MSRP: **$119.95–125**

UNIVERSAL REAR SIGHTS

The #20 Universal Rear Sight system combines a strong uni-base with both peep and U-shaped semi-buckhorn uprights. All components are machined from solid steel. Marble's barrel-mounted fiber optic rear sights can be used on modern rifles, slug shotguns and muzzleloaders. Available in all standard barrel contours and a variety of heights.

MSRP: **$26.95**

SIGHTS

Nikon Sights

MONARCH DOT

MONARCH VSD BLACK

MONARCH VSD SILVER

MONARCH
VSD REALTREE

MONARCH DOT SIGHT

The Monarch Dot is waterproof, fog-proof and shockproof. Objective and ocular lenses are 30mm diameter and fully multi-coated. Nikon Dot sights have zero magnification, providing unlimited eye relief and a 47.2' field of view at 100 yds. Brightness is controlled by a lithium battery. The standard Monarch Dot Sight has a 6 MOA dot and is available in silver, black and Realtree camouflage.

Standard: . . . . **Discontinued**
VSD: **$249.95**
VSD in Camo: **$279.95**

MONARCH VARIABLE SIZE DOT SIGHT (VSD)

Waterproof, fogproof and shockproof construction of the Monarch 1x30mm VSD helps it handle the abuse of a magnum-shooting turkey gun or large caliber handgun. Select any of the five dot sizes—1, 4, 6, 8 or 10 MOA—with the simple twist of a knob. An 11-position rheostat allows almost limitless reticle brightness adjustment and guarantees performance in weak dawn light or bright mid-day sun. A large field-of-view—47½ ft. at 100 yds.—and fully multi-coated lenses work together to provide sharp, crystal clear images. The unlimited eye relief means that even the sneaky tom trying to slip in from behind is in serious trouble. A mounting system is included that works with any Weaver-style mount base. Adjustments are ½ MOA per click and the parallax is set at 50 yds. Available in Matte, Silver and Realtree APG HD. The Dot Sight measures 3.76 in. in length and runs on a single lithium battery that is included.

Matte and Silver: **$250**
Realtree APG: **$280**

Pachmayr Sights

ACCU-SET PISTOL SIGHTS

Low-profile, adjustable sights function properly with factory front sights. Constructed of carbon steel and available in blued finish. Available in plain black, white outline, or 3-dot. Micro-adjustable windage and elevation click screw for precise adjustments. Dovetail design slips easily into the factory dovetail groove and is held in place by a locking Allen screw.

MSRP: **$45**

SIGHTS

Pentax Sights

GAMESEEKER DOT SIGHTS

Each of Pentax's Gameseeker Dot Sights features a 4 MOA dot, an ideal size for most shooters, as well as 11 brightness settings for various shooting conditions and a battery that provides 72 hours of continuous use. Also featuring PentaBright Technology, each Gameseeker dot sight offers a sharp, clear image that is parallax free for accurate target acquisition.

Gameseeker Dot Sights: . . . $67–80

Phoenix Precision Sights

PREMIUM TARGET SIGHTS

CNC machined aircraft aluminum; Zero-able, ¼ min click numbered knobs; 70 min elevation adjustment; 60 min windage adjustment; adjustable scales engraved in 3 min increments; oil impregnated bronze guide and thread bushings.

AR-15 Flat Top 1-Piece
   Mount Rear Sight: $380
Standard Right Hand
   Rear Sight: $355

AR-15 FLAT TOP
REAR SIGHT

STANDARD
RIGHT HAND
REAR SIGHT

Tasco Sights

PROPOINT
SIGHT

SOLAR POWERED
RED DOT SCOPE

TS RED DOT SCOPE

PROPOINT SIGHTS

ProPoint Sights are designed for competitive pistol and revolver shooters, turkey hunters and slug gun hunters. ProPoints deliver pinpoint accuracy with a rheostat-controlled illuminated red dot, unlimited eye relief and a clear field-of-view. ProPoints are powered by lithium batteries.

Propoint Sights: $117.95-122.95

SOLAR POWERED RED DOT SCOPE

The Solar Cell Red Dot scope solar cell technology is available in a 1x30mm. For use during low light early morning or late afternoon hours, it can be switched from solar power to a back up battery. Standard features include fully coated lenses; an illuminated 5 MOA red dot reticle; Tasco Rubicon lens coating and unlimited eye relief. A rheostat lets the user dial in the brightness of the red dot to match hunting or shooting conditions.

MSRP: $97

TS RED DOT SCOPE

The TS Red Dot 1x32mm scope will function as well on the range as it will in the field. With a new single mounting ring design it mounts easily on rifles, shotguns or pistols. It is also the ideal scope for use on tactical firearms. Other key features include fully coated lenses; flip-up caps on the objective and ocular lenses; an illuminated 5 MOA red dot reticle and unlimited eye relief. The intensity of the red dot can be adjusted with an 11 position rheostat. It is covered by a lifetime limited warranty.

TS Red Dot Scope: $135–181

Trijicon Sights

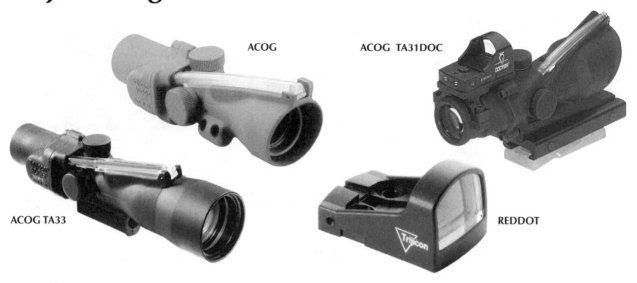

ACOG   ACOG TA31DOC

ACOG TA33

REDDOT

ACOG

The ACOGs are internally-adjustable, compact telescopic sights with tritium illuminated reticle patterns for use in low light or at night. Many models are dual-illuminated, featuring fiber optics which collect ambient light for maximum brightness in day-time shooting. The ACOGs combine traditional, precise distance marksmanship with close-in aiming speed.

MSRP: **$1090-2600**
Compact ACOG: . . . . **Discontinued**

ACOG TA31DOC

The TA31DOC combines the technology of the battle-tested Trijicon ACOG (4x32) gun sight with the Docter Optic Red Dot sight. The Trijicon ACOG model TA31DOC is an internally adjustable telescopic sight powered by Trijicon fiber optics and tritium-based technology. It's dual-illuminated reticle is designed to hold zero under the most extreme conditions and present a bright aiming point in all lighting conditions—providing excellent long-range precision targeting or even faster short range target selection using the Bindon Aiming Concept (BAC). With the field-proven Docter Optic 1x red dot sight mounted on top of the Trijicon ACOG TA31DOC, this innovative sighting system provides the user with lightening fast target acquisition in CQB situations while allowing for excellent situational awareness.

MSRP: **$1850**

ACOG TA33

The new Trijicon ACOG TA33 is a 3x30mm model designed for law enforcement and military applications where the combination of ample magnification, low light capability and long eye relief are needed. This aiming system is available with Bullet Drop Compensated reticles calibrated to the trajectory of the .223 and .308 cartridges and provides precision aiming for targets out to 600 meters. The extended eye relief allows the TA33 to be mounted on larger caliber weapons, giving the marksman ample eye relief for all shooting positions. The TA33 uses Trijicon's patented fiber optics and tritium-based technology, providing a dual illuminated reticle. It's totally battery-free, featuring a red or amber chevron aiming point. The TA33 also takes advantage of the innovative Bindon Aiming Concept. In tandem with scope magnification, this revolutionary both-eyes-open aiming method provides the shooter with "instinctive" target acquisition and increased hit potential. A forged, 7075-T6 aluminum alloy housing gives it durability, and multi-coated lenses provide maximum optical performance in any light. The unit is waterproof to 328 ft. and nitrogen-filled to eliminate fogging.

MSRP: **$1090**

NIGHT SIGHTS

Trijicon's self-luminous iron sights give shooters five times greater night fire accuracy. The light is provided by glowing tritium gas-filled lamps which are fully warranted up to twelve years for the green or yellow rear dots and up to five years for the orange dots. Trijicon night sights also feature a white outline around the glowing dots for the highest possible daylight visibility. The tritium lamps are protected by aluminum sleeves and polished synthetic sapphire windows. In addition a silicone rubber cushion helps protect the glass lamp within the aluminum sleeve. The metal body is manufactured for specific handgun makes and models. Night Sights are available for the following pistols, revolvers and rifles: Beretta, Browning, Colt, CZ, Desert Eagle, Firestar, Glock, H&K, Kimber, Remington, Ruger, SIG, Smith & Wesson, Walther, Taurus.

MSRP: **$50-155**

REDDOT SIGHT

Developed for quick target acquisition, the Trijicon RedDot Sight is designed for mounting atop the Trijicon ACOG (Advanced Combat Optical Gunsight). The sight features an innovative LED (light emitting diode) insert to sense the target's light level and control the light output of the LED. This technology ensures optimum visibility of the red dot against the target. Power is provided by a long-life lithium battery. Accuracy is enhanced with adjustments for windage and elevation. And, performance is assured with a stronger-than-aluminum, polymer alloy body. Tough, yet smaller and lighter than any alternative, the Trijicon RedDot Sight is suitable for all military and law enforcement applications.

MSRP: **$425**

Trijicon Sights

REFLEX

TRIPOWER

REFLEX SIGHTS

The dual-illuminated, Trijicon Reflex sight gives shooters next-generation technology for super-fast, any-light aiming without batteries. The Reflex sight features an amber aiming dot or triangle that is illuminated both by light from the target area and from a tritium lamp. Bright aiming point in low light, no light or bright light; quick target acquisition; big sight picture and realistic color.

MSRP: **$425-655**

TRIPOWER

The TriPower features a durable body forged in hard-anodized aircraft aluminum alloy, a sleek scope design and upgraded lens coatings. The Trijicon TriPower provides a quick and bright hunting optic. In tactical users, it provides clearly visible aiming point for the varied lighting conditions experienced in CQB (close-quarter battle).

MSRP: **$700**

Uberti Sights

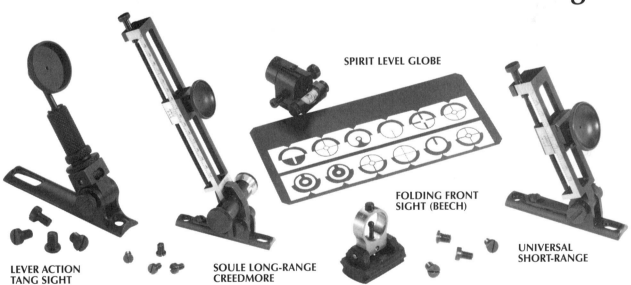

SPIRIT LEVEL GLOBE

FOLDING FRONT SIGHT (BEECH)

LEVER ACTION TANG SIGHT

SOULE LONG-RANGE CREEDMORE

UNIVERSAL SHORT-RANGE

CREEDMORE TANG SIGHTS

For Sharps rifles in three heights— short-range sight good to 300 yards, mid-range to about 600 yards and long-range, about 1,200 yards. Front globe sight fitted with spirit level to level the rifle.

Soule Type Long-Range
  Creedmore: $299
Soule Type Mid-Range
  Creedmore: $289
Universal Long-Range
  Creedmore: $189
Universal Short-Range
  Creedmore: $169
Lever Action Tang Sight: $119

Spirit Level Globe Sight
  with 12 Inserts: $169
Globe Front Sight
  with 12 Inserts: $49-59
Folding Front Sight (Beech): ... $79
Hadley Style Eyepiece: $99
Spirit Level Insert: $35
Glass Bubble Inserts (6): $35

SIGHTS

Williams Sights

5D SERIES

FP-GR-TK ON REMINGTON 581

FP-94 SE ON WINCHESTER 94 SIDE EJECT

FP MINI-14-TK WITH SUB-BASE

FP-KNIGHT-TK SILVER ON MK-85

FP-AG-TK ON BEEMAN AIR RIFLE

FP RECEIVER SIGHT OPTIONS

STANDARD

TARGET KNOBS (TK)

SHOTGUN/BIG GAME APERTURE

BLADE

5D SERIES

5D models are available for most popular rifles and shotguns. These sights have the strength, light weight, and neat appearance of the FP, without the micrometer adjustments. 5D sights offer unobstructed vision with no knobs or side plates to blot out shooter's field of vision. Wherever possible, the manufacturers' mounting screw holes in the receivers of the guns have been utilized for easy installation. The upper staff of the Williams 5D sight is readily detachable. A set screw is provided as a stop screw so that the sight will return to absolute zero after reattaching. The Williams 5D sight is made of high grade alloy.

Most 5D models: **$39.95**
Target—FP (high)
Adjustable From 1.250 in. to 1.750 in. above centerline of bore.
MSRP: **$79.95**

TARGET - FP (HIGH)

TARGET - FP (LOW)

FP SERIES

The "Foolproof" series of aperture sights have internal micrometer adjustments with positive internal locks. The alloy used to manufacture this sight has a tensile strength of 85,000 pounds. Yet, the FP is light and compact, weighing only 1½ oz. Target knobs are available on all models.

For most models: **$72.95**
With target knobs: **$84.50**

TARGET FP-ANSCHUTZ

Designed to fit many of the Anschutz Lightweight .22 Cal. Target and Sporter Models. No drilling and tapping required.
MSRP: **$83.95**

TARGET—FP (LOW)

Adjustable from ¾-1¼ in. above centerline of bore.
MSRP: **$79.95**

SIGHTS

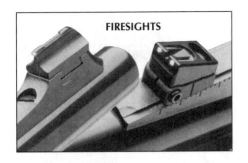

FIRESIGHTS

WGOS

WGRS-CVA ON CVA APOLLLO

WILLIAMS

.22 OR MUZZLELOADER FRONT FIRESIGHT BEAD

Wide steel front bead machined to accept a FireSights fiberoptic light gathering rod. Fits all standard $^3/_8$ in. dovetails in a variety of heights.
MSRP: **$18.95**

AR -15 STYLE FIRESIGHT

Front metallic sight that is fully adjustable for elevation. No gunsmithing required.
MSRP: **$45.95**

BROWNING BLR FIRESIGHT SET

Replaces rear sight and front sight bead. Fully adjustable metallic sights. No gunsmithing required.
MSRP: **$38**

DOVETAIL FIRESIGHT SET

Light gathering fiber optics for most lever-action rifles with ramped front sights. Fully adjustable rear metallic FireSight fits all standard $^3/_8$ in. dovetails on most Marlin and Winchester models. Front FireSight steel bead replaces existing factory bead.
Marlin 25N & 25MN: **$30**
Dovetail Fire Sight Set: **$36.95**

FIRESIGHTS

Steel front dovetail sight beads machined to accept FireSight light gathering rod. A must for all shooters in low-light situations. Comes in a variety of heights. CNC machined steel beads (not plastic).
MSRP: **$18.95**

LEVER ACTION FIRESIGHT PEEP SET

FireSight Steel bead and Williams FP94/36 micro adjustable peep sight for Winchester or Marlin centerfire lever action rifles. (Fits: Win94 top eject, 55, 63, 64, 65, 94-22; Marlin 36, 336, 1894, 1895SS, 1895G, 444SS, 444P)
MSRP: **$82.95**

MILITARY SIGHTS

Open and aperture for: SKS (no drilling required); AK47 (no drilling required)
MSRP: **$20-26**

RIFLE FIRESIGHT PEEP SETS

FireSight steel front bead and Williams WGRS rifle peep sight. Fully adjustable—no drilling and tapping required. Available for Ruger .22, Ruger 99/44, Marlin .336 and Ruger 96/22 and 96/22 Mag.
MSRP: **$49.95**

RUGER 10/22 FIRESIGHT SET

Customize your 10/22 with front and rear fiber optic FireSights. The front steel sight and the fully adjustable metallic rear sight are CNC machined for a perfect fit.
MSRP: **$25.95**

SKS RIFLE FIRESIGHT BEAD

Fiber optic, light gathering metallic front SKS sight. No gunsmithing required.
MSRP: **$20.95**

SKS RIFLE FIRESIGHT SET

Combines the FireSight Front bead with Williams fully adjustable metallic rear sight for an incredible sight picture. No gunsmithing required.
SKS Rifle FireSight Set: **$40**
Front sight: **$20.95**

WGOS SERIES

Made from high tensile strength aluminum. Will not rust. All parts milled— no stampings. Streamlined and lightweight with tough anodized finish. Dovetailed windage and elevation. Easy to adjust, positive locks. Interchangeable blades available in four heights and four styles.
MSRP: **$24.95**

WGRS SERIES

Compact low profile; lightweight, strong, rustproof; positive windage and elevation locks in most cases these sights utilize dovetail or existing screws on top of the receiver for installation. They are made from an aluminum alloy that is stronger than many steels. Williams quality throughout.
Most models: **$37.95**

SIGHTS

XS Sight Systems

SMLE SCOUT
SCOPE MOUNT

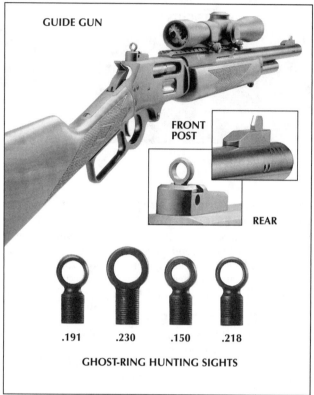

GUIDE GUN

FRONT POST

REAR

.191 .230 .150 .218

GHOST-RING HUNTING SIGHTS

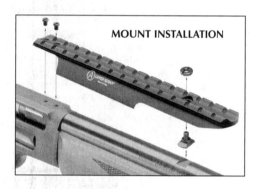

MOUNT INSTALLATION

GHOST-RING SIGHTS & LEVER SCOUT MOUNTS

Scout Scope Mount with 8 in. long Weaver-style rail and cross slots on ½ in. centers. Scope mounts ⅛ in. lower than previously possible on Marlin Lever Guns. Drop-in installation, no gunsmithing required. Installs using existing rear dovetail & front two screw holes on receiver. Allows fast target acquisition with both eyes open—better peripheral vision. Affords use of Ghost-Ring Sights with scope dismounted. Recoil tested for even the stout .45/70 and .450 Loads. Available for Marlin Lever Models: 1895 Guide Series, new .450, .444P, the .336 and 1894.

MSRP: **$50**
XS Lever Scout Mount
    for Win 94: **$55**

GHOST-RING HUNTING SIGHTS

Fully adjustable for windage & elevation. Available for most rifles, including blackpowder. Minimum gun-

smithing for most installations; matches most existing mounting holes. Compact design, CNC machined from steel and heat treated. Perfect for low light hunting conditions and brush/timer hunting, offers minimal target obstruction.

MSRP: . . . . **$90 for most**

SMLE SCOUT SCOPE MOUNTS

Offers Scout Scope Mount with 7 in. long Weaver style rail. Requires no machining of barrel to fit—no drilling or tapping. Tapered counter bore for snug fit of SMLE Barrels. Circular Mount is final filled with Brownells Acraglass.

MSRP: **$60**

XS 24/7 TRITIUM EXPRESS SIGHTS

The original fast acquisition sight. Now enhanced with new 24/7 tritium sight. These sights are the finest sights made for fast sight acquisition under any light conditions. Light or dark, just "dot the i"

and put the dot on the target. Enhances low-light sight acquisition; Improves low-light accuracy; low profile, snag free design. Available for most pistols.

MSRP: **$90-120**

XS ADJUSTABLE EXPRESS SIGHT SETS

Incorporates Adjustable Rear Express Sight with a white stripe rear, or Pro Express Rear with a Vertical Tritium Bar; fits Bomar style cut, LPA style cut, or a Kimber Target cut rear sight. Affords same Express Sight principles as fixed sight models.

Adjustable Express w/White Stripe
    Rear and Big Dot Front
    or Standard Dot Front: **$120**
Adjustable Express w/White Stripe
    Rear and Big Dot Tritium
    or Standard Dot
    Tritium Front: **$150**
Adjustable Pro Express w/Tritium
    Rear and Big Dot Tritium
    or Standard Dot
    Tritium Front: **$150**

SIGHTS

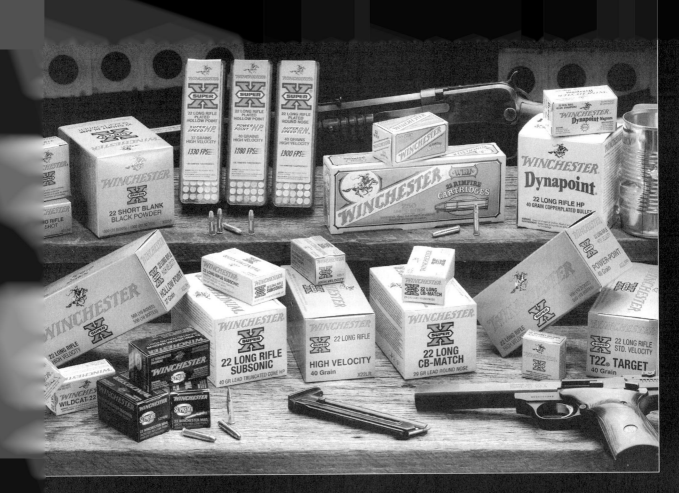

Black Hills Ammunition

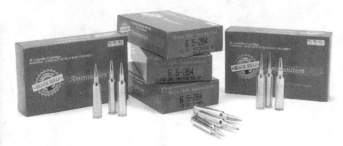

COWBOY ACTION HANDGUN AMMUNITION

Features: Carefully designed to meet the needs of cowboy-action shooters, this ammunition is made of new virgin brass and premium-quality hard-cast bullets. Velocities are moderate to provide low recoil and excellent accuracy.
Available in: .38-40, .44-40, .44 Russian, .44 Colt, .44 Special, .45 Schofield, .45 Colt, .45-70, .32 H&R, .32-20, .38 Long Colt, .38 Special, .38-55, .357 Mag.

FACTORY-NEW HANDGUN AMMUNITION

Features: Black Hills handgun ammunition combines the best of both worlds: quality and affordability. The choice of law-enforcement agencies due to its high level of consistency and dependability, and the affordable price accommodates the large volume of practice needed to achieve precision marksmanship.
Available in: .32 H&R Mag, .380 Auto, .45 ACP, 9mm Luger, .45 Auto Rim, .44 Mag, .40 S&W, .38 Special, .357 Mag

RIFLE AMMUNITION

FACTORY-NEW RIFLE AMMUNITION

Features: This high-performance ammunition is designed to deliver power and performance in several calibers.
Available in: .223 Rem, .308 Win Match, .300 Win Mag, .338 Lapua

BLACK HILLS GOLD

Features: Coupling the finest components with bullets by manufacturers such as Hornady, Barnes and Nosler, these rounds set a high standard for high-performance hunting ammunition.
Available in: .22-250, .243 Win, .25-06 Rem, .270 Win, .270 Win Short Mag, .300 Win Short Mag, .308 Win, .30-06 Sprfd., .300 Win Mag, 7mm Rem Mag.

Brenneke USA Ammunition

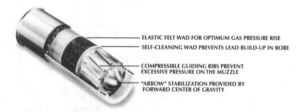

ELASTIC FELT WAD FOR OPTIMUM GAS PRESSURE RISE
SELF-CLEANING WAD PREVENTS LEAD BUILD-UP IN BORE
COMPRESSIBLE GUIDING RIBS PREVENT EXCESSIVE PRESSURE ON THE MUZZLE
"ARROW" STABILIZATION PROVIDED BY FORWARD CENTER OF GRAVITY

SHOTGUN AMMUNITION

BLACK MAGIC MAGNUM AND SHORT MAGNUM SLUGS

Features: 1 oz. (short mag) and 1 3/8 oz.; patented B.E.T. wad; CleanSpeed Coating reduces lead fouling inside the barrel; 3 inch is one of the heaviest slugs on the market ; for all barrel types; range 60 yds. (short mags) to 100 yds. (mag)
Available in: 12 ga., 2¾ and 3 in.

CLASSIC MAGNUM SLUGS

Features: 1 1/8 oz. original slug with felt wad, traditional since 1898; for all barrel types; range 70 yds.
Available in: 12 ga., 2¾ in.

GOLD MAGNUM SLUGS

Features: 1 3/8 oz.; original "Gold" slug with patented B.E.T. wad; special coating reduces lead fouling inside the barrel; for rifled barrels only; range 100+ yds.
Available in: 12 ga., 3 in.

HEAVY FIELD SHORT MAGNUM SLUGS

Features: 1 oz. (20 ga.) to 1 ¼ oz. (12 ga.) original "Emerald" slug with patented B.E.T. wad; for all barrel types; range 60 yds. (20 ga.) to 100 yds. (12 ga.)
Available in: 12 and 20 ga., 2¾ in.

K.O. SABOT

Features: 1 oz.; .63 diameter slug with red plastic wad; 58% more frontal area than standard .50 cal sabots; expansion up to .9 in.; for all barrel types; range 80 yds. (2¾ in.) to 100 yds. (3 in.)
Available in: 12 ga., 2¾ and 3 in.

K.O. SLUG

Features: 1 oz. improved Foster type slug; for all barrel types; range up to 60 yds.
Available in: 12 ga., 2¾ in.

SUPERSABOT

Features: 1 1/8 oz, lead-free slug; expansion up to 1 in.; for rifled barrels only; range 80 yds. (2¾ in.) to 100+ yds. (3 in.)
Available in: 12 ga., 2¾ and 3 in.

TACTICAL HOME DEFENSE

Features: 1 oz.; original "Bronze" slug with patented B.E.T. wad; for urban use; controlled penetration, low risk of dangerous exiting; for all barrel types; range CQB up to 35 yds.
Available in: 12 ga., 2¾ in.

CCI Ammunition

RIMFIRE AMMUNITION

GREEN TAG

Features: Our first and still most popular match rimfire product. Tight manufacturing and accuracy specs mean you get the consistency and accuracy that the unforgiving field of competition demands. And we load our rimfire match ammo to leave the muzzle subsonic. That means no buffeting in the transonic zone. Clean-burning propellants keep actions cleaner. Sure-fire CCI priming. Reusable plastic box with dispenser lid.
Available in: . 22 LR 40 grain lead round nose

HMR TNT

Features: CCI extends the usefulness of the exciting 17 Hornady Magnum Rimfire by offering the first hollow point loading. A 17 grain Speer® TNT hollow point answers requests from varmint hunters and gives explosive performance over the 17's effective range. Clean-burning propellants keep actions cleaner. Sure-fire CCI priming. Reusable plastic box with dispenser lid.
Available in: 17 HMR 17 grain TNT hollow point

LONG HV AND SHORT HV

Features: Designed for rimfire guns that require .22 Long or .22 short ammunition. Clean-burning propellants keep actions cleaner. Sure-fire CCI priming. Reusable plastic box with dispenser lid.
Available in: . 22 Short 29 gr solid lead bullet; .22 Short 27 gr hollow point bullet; .22 Long 29 gr solid lead bullet

MAXI-MAG

Features: CCI has built 22 Magnum RF ammo for over 30 years and is recognized as the technology leader in the specialized skills required to build the long RF Magnum case. MAXI-MAG offers a great power and range increase over the 22 Long Rifle and has become a favorite of varmint shooters everywhere.
Available in: .22 Mag RF

MINI-MAG HV

Features: CCI'S first rimfire product and still most popular. Mini-Mag and Mini-Mag hollow points are high-velocity products and offer excellent all-around performance for small game and varmints. Clean-burning propellants keep actions cleaner. Sure-fire CCI priming. Reusable plastic box with dispenser lid.
Available in: .22 LR—40 grain gilded lead round nose, 36 grain gilded lead hollow point

PISTOL MATCH

Features: Designed expressly for high-end semi-auto match pistols. Single-die tooling and great care in assembly lets you wring the last bit of accuracy from your precision pistol. Clean-burning propellants keep actions cleaner. Sure-fire CCI priming. Reusable plastic box with dispenser lid.
Available in: .22 LR 40 grain lead round nose

SELECT .22LR

Features: The 22 Long Rifle Select is built for semi-automatic competition. Reliable operation, accuracy and consistency make Select an ideal choice for competition shooters.
Available in: .22 LR

STANDARD VELOCITY

Features: Loaded to the same velocity as Green Tag and Pistol Match but priced less, this is the perfect practice load. Clean-burning propellants keep actions cleaner. Sure-fire CCI priming. Reusable plastic box with dispenser lid.
Available in: .22 LR 40 grain lead round nose

V-MAX 17 MACH 2

Features: The 17 Mach 2 is a 22 LR CCI Stinger case necked down to hold a 17 caliber bullet. CCI loads a super-accurate 17-grain polymer-tipped bullet, and drives it 60 percent faster than a 22 Long Rifle 40-grain hollow-point. The loaded cartridge is no longer than a 22 Long rifle, greatly expanding the gun actions that can accommodate 17 caliber rimfire cartridges. Reusable 50-count plastic box that protects and dispenses five cartridges at one time
Available in: 17 Mach 2 (V-Max also available in 17 HMR and 22 Mag RF)

Federal Ammunition

HYDRA-SHOCK　　　　**BARNES TRIPLE SHOCK X**　　　　**ULTRA-SHOCK HEAVYWEIGHT**　　　　**POWER-SHOK RIFLED SLUG**

HANDGUN AMMUNITION

CASTCORE
Features: Heavyweight, flat-nosed, hard cast-lead bullet that smashes through bone.
Available in: 357 Mag, 41 Rem Mag, 44 Rem Mag (Premium Vital-Shok)

EXPANDING FULL METAL JACKET
Features: Barrier-penetrating design combines a scored metal nose over an internal rubber tip that collapses on impact.
Available in: 40 S&W, 45 Auto, 9mm Luger (Premium Personal Defense)

FULL METAL JACKET
Features: Good choice for range practice and reducing lead fouling in the barrel. Jacket extends from the nose to the base, preventing bullet expansion and barrel leading. Primarily as military ammunition and for recreational shooting.
Available in: 10mm Auto, 25 Auto, 32 Auto, 357 Sig, 38 Special, 38 Super +P, 380 Auto, 40 S&W, 45 Auto, 45 G.A.P., 9mm Luger, 9mm Makarov (American Eagle)

HYDRA-SHOK
Features: Unique center-post design delivers controlled expansion, and the notched jacket provides efficient energy transfer to penetrate barriers while retaining stopping power. Deep penetration satisfies even the FBI's stringent testing requirements.
Available in: 10mm Auto, 32 Auto, 357 Mag, 38 Special, 380 Auto, 40 S&W, 44 Rem Mag, 45 Auto, 45 G.A.P., 9mm Luger, 38 Special +P (Premium Personal Defense)

JACKETED HOLLOW POINT
Features: Ideal personal defense round in revolvers and semi-autos. Quick, positive expansion. Jacket ensures smooth feeding into autoloading firearms.
Available in: 357 Sig (Premium Personal Defense); 32 H&R Mag, 357 Mag, 40 S&W, 45 Auto, 9mm Luger (Personal Defense Handgun); 357 Mag, 41 Rem Mag, 44 Rem Mag (Power-Shok Handgun Hunting); 44 Rem Mag (American Eagle)

LEAD ROUND NOSE
Features: Great training round for practicing at the range. 100 lead with no jacket. Excellent accuracy and is very economical.
Available in: 32 S&W Long (Champion Handgun); 38 Special (American Eagle)

LEAD SEMI-WADCUTTER
Features: Most popular all-around choice for target and personal defense, a versatile design which cuts clean holes in targets and efficiently transfers energy.
Available in: 32 H&R Mag (Champion Handgun)

SEMI-WADCUTTER HOLLOW POINT
Features: For both small game and personal defense. Hollow point design promotes uniform expansion.
Available in: 44 Special, 45 Colt (Champion Handgun)

RIFLE AMMUNITION

BARNES TRIPLE SHOCK X-BULLET (TSX)
Features: Superior expansion and deep penetration. The all-copper design provides high weight retention.
Available in: .243 Win., 25-06 Rem., 270 Win., 270 Win. Short Mag, 280 Rem, 300 H&H Mag, 300 Rem. Ultra Mag, 300 Weatherby Mag, 300 Win Mag, 300 Win Short Mag, 30-06 Spring., 308 Win, 338 Win Mag, 7mm Rem Mag, 7mm-08 Rem, 338 Fed (Premium Vital-Shok). 375 H&H Mag, 416 Rem Mag, 416 Rigby, 458 Win Mag (Premium Cape-Shok)

FULL METAL JACKET BOAT-TAIL
Features: Accurate, non-expanding bullets. Flat shooting trajectory, leave a small exit hole in game, and put clean holes in paper. Smooth, reliable feeding into semi-automatics too.
Available in: 223 Rem (Power-Shok); 223 Rem, 30-06 Spring., 308 Win (American Eagle)

FUSION LITE
Features: Provides terminal energy with 50% less recoil. Jacket application process completely eliminates core-jacket separation and makes for high weight retention. Lower velocities. Slower speeds, holds nearly 100% of its weight.
Available in: .270 Win Mag 145-grain at 2200 fps; .30-06 Spring 170-grain at 2000 fps; .308 Win 170-grain at 2000 fps.

NOSLER ACCUBOND
Features: Combines the terminal performance of a bonded bullet with the accuracy and retained energy of a Ballistic Tip.
Available in: 25-06 Rem., 260 Rem, 270 Weatherby Mag, 270 Win, 270 Win. Short Mag, 280 Rem, 300 Win Mag, 300 Win Short Mag, 30-06 Spring., 308 Win, 338 Rem, 338 Win Mag, 375 H&H Mag, 7mm Rem Mag, 7mm STW, 7mm Weatherby Mag, 7mm Win Short Mag, 7mm-08 Rem, 338 Fed (Premium Vital-Shok)

AMMUNITION

Federal Ammunition

NOSLER BALLISTIC TIP

Features: Fast, flat-shooting wind-defying performance. Long-range shots at varmints, predators and small to medium game. Color-coded polycarbonate tip provides easy identification, prevents deformation in the magazine and drives back on impact for expansion. *Available in*: .243 Win., 25-06 Rem., 260 Rem, 270 Win., 270 Win. Short Mag, 280 Rem, 300 Win Short Mag, 30-06 Spring., 308 Win, 7mm Rem Mag, 7mm Win Short Mag, 7mm-08 Rem (Premium Vital-Shok). 222 Rem., 22-250 Rem., 243 Win., 25-06 Rem., 204 Ruger (Premium V-Shok)

NOSLER PARTITION

Features: Proven choice for medium to large game animals. Partitioned copper jacket allows the front half of the bullet to mushroom, while the rear core remains intact, driving forward for deep penetration and stopping power. *Available in*: 223 Rem., 243 Win., 25-06 Rem., 257 Roberts, 270 Win., 270 Win. Short Mag, 280 Rem., 300 H&H Mag, 300 Rem. Ultra Mag, 300 Weatherby Mag, 300 Win. Mag, 300 Win. Short Mag, 30-06 Spring., 30-30 Win., 308 Win., 338 Rem. Ultra Mag, 338 Win. Mag, 6mm Rem., 7mm Mauser, 7mm Rem. Mag, 7mm Win. Short Mag, 7mm-08 Rem., 338 Fed (Premium Vital-Shok). 375 H&H Mag (Premium Cape-Shok)

SIERRA GAMEKING BOAT-TAIL

Features: Long ranges are its specialty. Excellent choice for everything from varmints to big game animals. Tapered, boat-tail design provides extremely flat trajectories. Higher downrange velocity for more energy at the point of impact. Reduced wind drift. *Available in*: 243 Win, 25-06 Rem, 260 Rem, 270 Win, 30-06 Spring., 308 Win, 7mm Rem. Mag (Premium Vital-Shok solid point); 243 Win (Premium Vital-Shok hollow point); 22-250 Rem, 223 Rem (Premium V-Shok)

SOFT POINT

Feature: Proven performer on small game and thin-skinned medium game. Aerodynamic tip for a flat trajectory. Exposed soft point expands rapidly for hard hits, even as velocity slows at longer ranges.
Available in: 222 Rem, 22-250 Rem, 223 Rem, 223 Rem, 243 Win, 270 Win, 270 Win Short Mag, 280 Rem, 300 Savage, 300 Win Short Mag, 30-06 Spring., 303 British, 308 Win, 375 H&H Mag, 6.5x55 Swedish, 6mm Rem, 7.62x39mm Soviet, 7mm Rem Mag, 7mm Win Short Mag, 8mm Mauser (Power-Shok)

SOFT POINT FLAT NOSE

Features: Great for thick cover, it expands reliably and penetrates deep on light to medium game. The flat nose prevents accidental discharge. *Available in*: 30-30 Win, 32 Win Special (Power-Shok)

SOFT POINT ROUND NOSE

Features: The choice in heavy cover. Large exposed tip, good weight retention and specially tapered jacket provide controlled expansion.
Available in: 270 Win, 30 Carbine, 30-30 Win, 35 Rem, 7mm Mauser (Power-Shok)

TROPHY BONDED BEAR CLAW

Features: Ideal for medium to large dangerous game. The jacket and core are 100% fusion-bonded for reliable bullet expansion from 25 yards to extreme ranges. Bullet retains 95% of its weight for deep penetration. Hard solid copper base tapering to a soft, copper nose section for controlled expansion.
Available in: 270 Weatherby Mag, 270 Win, 270 Win Short Mag, 300 Rem Ultra Mag, 300 Weatherby Mag, 300 Win Mag, 300 Win. Short Mag, 30-06 Spring., 308 Win, 338 Win Mag, 35 Whelen, 375 H&H Mag, 7mm Rem Mag, 7mm Weatherby Mag (Premium Vital-Shok); 375 H&H Mag, 416 Rem Mag, 416 Rigby, 458 Win Mag, 470 Nitro Express, 458 Lott (Premium Cape-Shok)

TROPHY BONDED SLEDGEHAMMER

Features: Use it on the largest, most dangerous game in the world. Jack Carter design maximizes stopping power. Bonded bronze solid with a flat nose that minimizes deflection off bone and muscle for a deep, straight wound channel. *Available in*: 375 H&H Mag, 416 Rem Mag, 416 Rigby, 458 Win Mag, 470 Nitro Express, 458 Lott (Premium Cape-Shok)

WOODLEIGH WELDCORE

Features: Respected by Safari hunters. Superb accuracy and excellent stopping power. Special heavy jacket provides 80-85% weight retention. Bullets are favored for large or dangerous game. *Available in*: 470 Nitro Express (Premium Cape-Shok)

SHOTGUN AMMUNITION

GAME-SHOK FIELD TRIAL TRAINING LOAD

Available in: 12 ga.; 2¾ in.; BLANKS

GAME-SHOK GAME LOAD

Available in: 12, 16, 20 ga.; 2¾ in.; shot sizes 6, 7½, 8

GAME-SHOK HEAVY FIELD

Available in: 12, 20 ga.; 2¾ in.; shot sizes 4, 5, 6, 7½, 8

GAME-SHOK HI-BRASS

Available in: 12, 16, 20, 410 ga.; 2½, 2¾, 3 in.; shot sizes 4, 5, 6, 7½, 8

PREMIUM BLACK CLOUD STEEL

Available in: 12 ga.; 3, 3½ in.; shot sizes 2, BB, BBB

PREMIUM GOLD MEDAL TARGET—EXTRA-LITE PAPER (LR)

Available in: 12 ga.; 2¾ in.; shot sizes 7½, 8

PREMIUM GOLD MEDAL TARGET—EXTRA-LITE PLASTIC (LR)

Available in: 12 ga.; 2¾ in.; shot sizes 7½, 8

PREMIUM GOLD MEDAL TARGET—HANDICAP PAPER HV

Available in: 12 ga.; 2¾ in.; shot sizes 7½, 8

Federal Ammunition

PREMIUM GOLD MEDAL TARGET—HANDICAP PLASTIC HV
Available in: 12 ga.; 2¾ in.; shot sizes 7½, 8

PREMIUM GOLD MEDAL TARGET—INTERNATIONAL PAPER
Available in: 12 ga.; 2¾ in.; shot sizes 7½

PREMIUM GOLD MEDAL TARGET—INTERNATIONAL PLASTIC
Available in: 12 ga.; 2¾ in.; shot sizes 7½, 8½

PREMIUM GOLD MEDAL TARGET—PAPER
Available in: 12 ga.; 2¾ in.; shot sizes 7½, 8, 9

PREMIUM GOLD MEDAL TARGET—PLASTIC
Available in: 12, 20, 28, 410 ga.; 2½, 2¾ in.; shot sizes 7½, 8, 8½, 9

PREMIUM GOLD MEDAL TARGET—SPORTING CLAYS
Available in: 12 ga.; 2¾ in.; shot sizes 7½, 8, 8½

PREMIUM MAG-SHOK—HEAVYWEIGHT TURKEY
Available in: 12 ga.; 3, 3½ in.; shot sizes 5, 6, 7

PREMIUM MAG-SHOK HIGH VELOCITY LEAD
Available in: 10, 20 ga.; 3, 3½ in.; shot sizes 4, 5, 6

PREMIUM MAG-SHOK LEAD WITH FLITECONTROL
Available in: 12 ga.; 3, 3½ in.; shot sizes 4, 5, 6

PREMIUM MAG-SHOK LEAD WITH FLITECONTROL HIGH VELOCITY
Available in: 12 ga.; 2¾, 3, 3½ in.; shot sizes 4, 5, 6

PREMIUM ULTRA-SHOK HEAVY HIGH VELOCITY STEEL
Available in: 10, 12 ga.; 2¾, 3, 3½ in.; shot sizes 1, 2, 3, 4, BB, BBB, T

PREMIUM ULTRA-SHOK HEAVYWEIGHT
Available in: 12 ga.; 3, 3½ in.; shot sizes 2, 4, 6

PREMIUM ULTRA-SHOK HIGH DENSITY WATERFOWL
Available in: 10, 12, 20 ga.; 3, 3½ in.; shot sizes 2, 4, BB

PREMIUM ULTRA-SHOK HIGH VELOCITY STEEL
Available in: 12, 16, 20 ga.; 2¾, 3, 3½ in.; shot sizes 1, 2, 3, 4, 6, BB, BBB, T

PREMIUM ULTRA-SHOK SUBSONIC HIGH DENSITY
Available in: 12 ga.; 2¾ in.; shot sizes BB

PREMIUM WING-SHOK FLYER LOADS
Available in: 12 ga.; 2¾ in.; shot sizes 7½

PREMIUM WING-SHOK HIGH BRASS
Available in: 28 ga.; 2¾ in.; shot sizes 6, 7½, 8

PREMIUM WING-SHOK HIGH VELOCITY
Available in: 12 ga.; 2¾, 3 in.; shot sizes 4, 5, 6, 7½

PREMIUM WING-SHOK HIGH VELOCITY—PHEASANT
Available in: 12, 20 ga.; 2¾ in.; shot sizes 4, 5, 6, 7½

PREMIUM WING-SHOK HIGH VELOCITY—QUAIL FOREVER
Available in: 12, 20 ga.; 2¾ in.; shot sizes 7½, 8

PREMIUM WING-SHOK MAGNUM
Available in: 10, 12, 16, 20 ga.; 2¾, 3, 3½ in.; shot sizes 2, 4, 5, 6, BB

SPEED-SHOK STEEL
Available in: 12, 20 ga.; 2¾, 3, 3½ in.; shot sizes 2, 3, 4, 6, 7, BB

STRUT-SHOK
Available in: 12 ga.; 3, 3½ in.; shot sizes 2, 3, 4, 6, 7, BB

TOP GUN SUBSONIC TARGET
Available in: 12 ga.; 2¾ in.; shot sizes 7½

TOP GUN TARGET
Available in: 12, 20 ga.; 2¾ in.; shot sizes 7, 7½, 8, 9

TOP GUN TARGET STEEL
Available in: 20 ga.; 2¾ in.; shot sizes 7

SHOTGUN AMMUNITION (SLUGS)

FUSION SABOT SLUGS
Features: Electro-chemical process applies a copper jacket to the lead core one molecule at a time. Yields a perfectly uniform jacket.
Available in: 20-gauge, 3 in., 5/8 oz. loads; 2¾ in., _ oz. and 3 in., _ oz. 12 ga. loads

POWER-SHOK RIFLED SLUG
Features: Hollow point slug type
Available in: 10, 12, 16, 20, 410 ga.; 2½, 2¾, 3, 3½ in.; ¼, ¾, 7/8, 1, 1 ¼, 1¾ oz. slug wt.

POWER-SHOK SABOT SLUG
Features: Sabot hollow point slug type
Available in: 12 ga.; 2¾ in.; 1 oz. slug wt.

PREMIUM VITAL-SHOK BARNES EXPANDER
Features: Barnes Sabot slug type
Available in: 12, 20 ga.; 2¾, 3 in.; 5/8, ¾, 1 oz. slug wt.

PREMIUM VITAL-SHOK TRUBALL RIFLED SLUG
Features: Truball rifled slug type
Available in: 12, 20 ga.; 2¾ in.; ¾, 1 oz. slug wt.

Fiocchi Ammunition

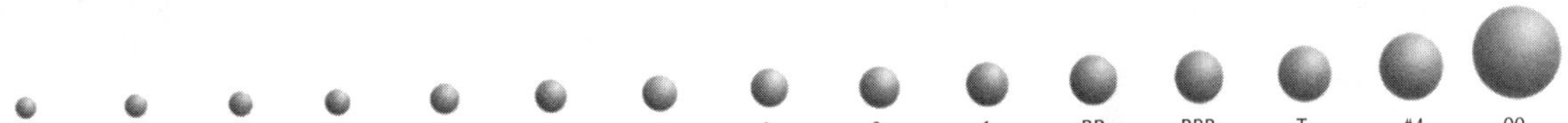

AMMUNITION

Size #	9	8½	8	7½	6	5	4	3	2	1	BB	BBB	T	#4	00
Dia.In.	.08	.085	.09	.095	.11	.12	.13	.14	.15	.16	.18	.19	.20	.24	.33
Dia.MM	2.03	2.16	2.29	2.41	2.79	3.05	3.30	3.56	3.81	4.06	4.57	4.83	5.08	6.10	8.38

HANDGUN AMMUNITION

7.63 MAUSER PISTOL CARTRIDGE

Features: The 7.63 Mauser cartridge was first introduced by the Waffenfabrik Mauser, Orbendorf, Germany in 1896 in the famous C-96 "Broomhandle" Mauser pistol. The C-96 was the first semi-automatic pistol to see wide spread military use in World War I, World War II, the Second Boer War, the Spanish Civil War and the Chinese Civil War. Such notables as Winston Churchill armed himself with the C-96 in 7.63 Mauser as his personal weapon in the Second Boer War. The unique shape of the C-96 pistol makes it one of the most recognizable pistols of our time; it's truly a classic pistol and cartridge combination. Fiocchi Ammunition USA now offers owners of these historic handguns new, high quality 7.63 Mauser ammunition.
Available in: 88-grain Full Metal Jacket (FMJ) with a muzzle velocity of 1425 feet per second (FPS) and 400 foot pounds of energy at the muzzle.

RIFLE AMMUNITION

EXTREMA 223 REM. HVA

Features: Fiocchi now offers the extremely popular 223 Remington cartridge loaded with super accurate and deadly Hornady V-Max 50-grain bullets in Fiocchi's Extrema rifle ammunition line. Extrema 223 Remington HVA has unmatched terminal ballistics that will make the cartridge a favorite of both the Western prairie dog and Eastern ground hog hunter.
Available in: 223 Rem, 50 grain

SHOTGUN AMMUNITION

PREMIUM NICKEL PLATED HUNTING LOADS

Features: Fiocchi offers the hunter a wide selection of hunting loads that incorporate nickel plated shot to help make hunting more successful. Nickel plated shot gives the hunter such benefits as denser, more consistent patterns with fewer stray pellets and increased range and penetration than non-plated shot.
Available in: 1 1/4 oz. Helice Loads (12 ga., 2¾ in., shot sizes 7, 7½, 8); 1½, 1¾ and 2 3/8 oz. Turkey Loads (12 ga., 2¾, 3 and 3½ in., shot sizes 4, 5, 6); ⅞ to 1¾ oz. Golden Pheasant Loads (12, 20, 16, 28 ga., 2¾ and 3 in., shot sizes 4, 5, 6, 7½, 8); and Buckshot Loads (12 ga., 2¾ in., shot sizes 00 Buck, 4 Buck)

PREMIUM TARGET LOADS

Features: Specifically for competitive shooters. Our Target Load Line is the offspring of a 50 year tradition of supporting the world of trap, skeet and now sporting clays, FITASC and Compaq.
Available in: 1 and 1 1/8 oz. Paper Target Loads (12 ga., 2¾ in., shot sizes 7½, 8, 8½); ⅞ oz, 1 1/8 oz. and 1 oz. Premium Target Loads (12, 20, 28, 410 ga., 2½ and 2¾ in., shot sizes 7½, 8, 8½, 9); 1 and 1 1/8 oz. Multi-sport Loads (12 ga., 2¾ in., shot sizes 7½, 8, 9); 1 1/4 oz. Helice Loads (12 ga., 2¾ in., shot sizes 7, 7½, 8); 1 1/8 oz. Power Spreaders (12 ga., 2¾ in., shot sizes 8, 8½); 1 oz. Interceptor Spreaders (12 ga., 2¾ in., shot sizes 8, 8½); ⅞ and 1 oz. Steel Target Loads (12, 20 ga., 2¾ in., shot sizes 7); and¾ and ⅞ oz. Ultra Low Recoil Training Loads (12, 20 ga., 2¾ in., shot sizes 7½, 8)

STEEL HUNTING LOADS

Features: Fiocchi Steel shot hunting loads are manufactured with a combination of treated steel shot, protective wads and the appropriate powders to deliver a consistent dense pattern that is easy on your gun barrel but hard on your target.
Available in: 1 1/8 to 1 5/8 oz., 2¾ to 3½ in. 12 ga. loads in shot sizes 1, 2, 3, 4, BB, BBB, T; ⅞ oz., 3 in. 20 ga. loads in shot sizes 2, 3, 4

UPLAND GAME AND FIELD LOADS

Features: Fiocchi offers a full line of lead hunting loads from Dove Loads to powerful Hi Brass Loads.
Available in: ¾ to 1¾ oz. High Velocity Loads (12, 20, 16, 28, 410 ga., 2¾ and 3 in., shot sizes 4, 5, 6, 7½, 8, 9); 1 to 1 ¼ oz. Field Loads (12, 20, 16 ga., 2¾ in., shot sizes 4, 5, 6, 7½, 8, 9);½ to 1 1/8 oz. Dove Loads (12, 20, 16, 28, 410 ga., 2 to 3 ¼ oz., shot sizes 6, 7½, 8, 9); and ¼ to 1 1/16 oz. Specialty Shotshell Loads (Flobert 9 Rimfire, 24, 32 ga., 1¾ and 2½ in., shot sizes 6, 7½, 8, 9)

WHITE RHINO SHOTSHELLS

Features: Fiocchi's White Rhino uses B&P (Baschieri & Pellagri) wads and 5-percent antimony lead shot. Its additional 50 feet per second velocity over standard trap loads make it a favorite for "handicap trap" and those long distance shots on the sporting clays course. The B&P shot cup, with its softer plastic and better sealing ability, means there's less gas escaping around the wad ensuring higher velocity.
Available in: 12 ga.

Ammunition • 469

Hornady Ammunition

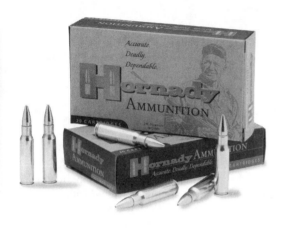
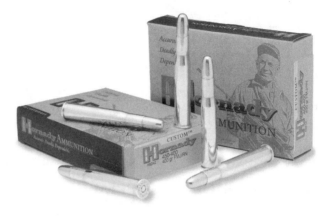

HANDGUN AMMUNITION

500 SMITH & WESSON

Features: Packs a 350 gr. Hornady XTP Mag bullet, one of the most accurate and deadly projectiles. The XTP Mag delivers dead-on, accuracy and reliable expansion for deep, terminal penetration at a wide range of velocities.

RIFLE AMMUNITION

6.8MM SPC

Features: Developed at the request of the U.S. Special Forces. Perfect sporting cartridge for game up to the size of whitetail and mule deer. Same power class as the .300 Savage, but delivers a flatter trajectory and less recoil. Features either a 110 gr. BTHP bullet, specifically designed for the cartridge, or a proven 110 gr. V-MAX bullet. 110 gr. BTHP delivers excellent expansion and maximum energy transfer at all velocities, while the 110 gr. VMAX has all the characteristics of our Varmint Express ammo—flat trajectories and rapid, violent expansion.

9.3 X 74R

Features: Originally designed in Germany during the early 1900s. Offers a 286-grain Spire Point Recoil-Proof bullet loaded to factory specifications and designed to deliver controlled expansion and devastating terminal performance on big game from a double rifle, while regulating. High-tech propellant. Provides maximum case fill for consistent ignition while providing temperature sensitivity in extreme climates.

17HMR XTP

Features: Delivers deeper penetration, less pelt damage and a quick kill. This new XTP bullet was purposed and designed as a hunting load. It's a great choice for small game and varmint hunting where salvaging the pelt is important. Has a 20-gr. XTP bullet.

17 HORNADY MACH 2

Features: Provides target-erasing accuracy and a frozen clothesline trajectory — nearly seven inches flatter at 150 yards than a standard High Velocity 22 Long Rifle cartridge. Delivers 2,100 fps, far outperforming a standard High Velocity 22 Long Rifle's 1,255 fps velocity at the muzzle.

.30 T/C

Features: Designed for Thompson Center's Icon bolt-action rifle. Hornady perfected the balance between case volume, bore volume and burn rates for both the 150- and 165-grain offerings. Slightly smaller in capacity than the 308 Winchester, but delivers ballistic performance exceeding the 30-06. With a muzzle velocity of 3000 fps, the 150-grain load outperforms the 308 Win by 180 fps and outperforms the 30-06 by nearly 100 fps. Provides a 15% reduction in perceived recoil, ultra-smooth feeding, full magazine capacity, a short bolt throw, longer barrel life and delivers full ballistic potential in a short action case. Packaged in boxes of 20.

204 RUGER, 45-GR. SP

Features: Designed to provide controlled expansion for deeper penetration on larger varmints. Built around Hornady's proven Spire Point design, the 204 45 gr SP cartridge provides flat trajectories, enhanced penetration and a new dimension to the 204 Ruger's personality.

.375 RUGER

Features: Delivers performance that exceeds the .375 H&H. Designed to provide greater knockdown power with a shorter cartridge from a standard action and a 20 in. barrel. Improves on the velocity of the .375 H&H by 150 fps. Three different loads, including a 270-grain Spire Point Recoil-Proof, 300-grain Round Nose and a 300-grain Solid. Spire Point Recoil-Proof bullet. Longer ogive and less exposed lead which helps protect the bullet from deformation under recoil in rifle magazines.

405 WINCHESTER 300-GR. SP

Features: When Theodore Roosevelt picked the 405 almost a century ago, he was looking for the perfect big game gun. The "modern" 405 delivers performance Roosevelt never even dreamed of. Two new No. 1H Tropical Single Shot Rifles chambered for this world-class big game load. The most powerful rimmed cartridge ever developed for the lever action rifle.

450 BUSHMASTER

Features: Fires Hornady's 0.452-in., 250 gr. SST with Flex Tip technology. Overall cartridge matches the 223 Remington at 2.250 inch. Flat trajectories and tremendous downrange energy. Soft polymer tipped SST bullet eliminates tip deformation and also initiates expansion over a wide range of impact velocities.

Hornady Ammunition

450/400
NITRO EXPRESS 3-IN.
Features: Comes loaded with either a 400-grain RN expanding bullet or FMJ-RN Solid. Regulate in double rifles. Ideal ammo for hunting hippo, buffalo and other thick-skinned game. Also features cutting-edge propellant technology ensuring consistent performance in all weather types.

LEVEREVOLUTION AMMUNITION
Features: Feature elastomer Flex Tip Technology that is safe in your tubular magazine. Flatter trajectories for fantastic downrange energy. Provides up to 250 feet-per-second faster muzzle velocity than conventional lever gun loads; exceptional accuracy and overwhelming downrange terminal performance; up to 40% more energy.
Available in: .30-30 Win., .308 Marlin Express, .35 Rem., .444 Marlin, .45-70 Gov't., .450 Marlin.

SHOTGUN AMMUNITION

SST SHOTGUN SLUG
Features: Delivers sub-2-in. groups at 100 yards. Flattest trajectory on the market. The polymer tip slices through the air, minimizing drop and wind drift. The tip initiates violent expansion, transferring its energy payload to the target. For use only in fully rifled barrels.
Available in: 12 and 20 ga.

Jarrett Rifles Ammunition

RIFLE AMMUNITION
Features: Jarrett's high-performance cartridges are in 10-round boxes. The cases are from Norma with Jarrett's headstamp.
Available in: 243 Win 85gr. Nosler Partition; 243 Win 85gr. Sierra HPBT; 270 Win 140gr. Nosler Accubond; 270 Win 150gr. Swift A Frame; 300 Jarrett 165gr. Nosler Ballistic Tip; 300 Jarrett 180gr. Nosler Accubond; 300 Jarrett 200gr. Nosler Partition; 300 WM 165gr. HPBT; 300 WM 180gr. Nosler Accubond; 300 WM 200gr. Nosler Partition; 30-06 Sprg. 165gr. Nosler Ballistic Tip; 30-06 Sprg. 180gr. Swift Scirocco; 375 H&H 300gr. Swift A Frame; 375 H&H 300gr. TCCI Solid; 416 Rem Mag 400gr. Swift A Frame; 416 Rem Mag 400gr. TCCI Solid; 7mm Rem Mag 140gr. Nosler Ballistic Tip; 7mm Rem Mag 160gr. Nosler Accubond; 7mm Rem Mag 175gr. Swift A Frame

Kynoch Ammunition

RIFLE AMMUNITION
Features: To reproduce the renowned quality of the nitro express cartridges, painstaking care has been taken to duplicate the original loads. Modern powder has been blended and tested with a wide range of boxer primers to obtain both the correct internal and external ballistics. This work has been meticulously conducted in conjunction with the Proof House, and all new Kynoch ammunition carries Birmingham Proof House CIP approval. This approval conforms to the specifications of the original loadings as proofed in Birmingham. Load development was conducted simultaneously with extensive testing at the firing range. The new Kynoch loads have been test fired in back to back comparison with the original IMI produced Kynoch ammunition of the 1960s. The choice of bullets for these loads has been the subject of extensive testing for both the external and terminal ballistic performance. Additional accommodations were made for dimensional variations from published nominal standards in the bore and rifling, which can frequently occur in older rifles. Kynoch ammunition is now standardized on Woodleigh Weldcore Softnose and Solid bullets. Woodleigh bullets are recognized worldwide as the most reliable big game bullets currently manufactured.
Available in: .700 Nitro Express, 1000 grains; .600 Nitro Express, 900 grains ; .577 Nitro Express, 750 grains; .500 Nitro Express, 570 grains; .500 Jeffery, 535 grains; .505 Gibbs, 525 grains; .476 Westley Richards, 520 grains; .475 No. 2 Jeffery, 500 grains; .475 No. 2 Eley, 480 grains; .500/.465 Nitro Express, 480 grains; .577/.450 Martini Henry, 480 grains; .450 Rigby, 480 grains; .450 No. 2 Nitro Express, 480 grains; .450 Nitro Express, 480 grains; .425 Westley Richards, 410 grains; .404 Jeffery, 400 grains; .416 Rigby, 410 grains; .450/.400 3 ¼ inch, 400 grains; .450/.400 3 inch, 400 grains; .405 Winchester, 300 grains; .400 Purdey, 230 grains; .375 Flanged, 235, 270, 300 grains; .375 Flanged 2½ inch, 270 grains; .400/.360 Westley Richards, 285 grains; .350 Rigby, 225 grains;9.5x57 Mannlicher (.375 rimless), 270 grains; .318 Westley Richards (Box of 10), 187, 250 grains; .303 British, 215 grains; .300 Flanged, 180, 220 grains

Magtech Ammunition

SOLID COPPER HOLLOWPOINT

FIRST DEFENSE

500 S&W

HANDGUN AMMUNITION

CLEANRANGE

Features: CleanRange loads are specially designed to eliminate airborne lead and the need for lead retrieval at indoor ranges. That means an overall cleaner shooting environment and lower maintenance costs for trap owners, as well as cleaner guns and brass casings for shooters. CleanRange ammunition was developed using a state-of-the-art combination of high-tech, lead-free primers and specially designed Fully Encapsulated Bullets. This unique mix of components eliminates lead and heavy metal exposure at the firing point. No more lead in the air.
Available in: .38 SPL, .380 Auto, 9mm Luger, .40 S&W, .45 Auto

COWBOY ACTION

Features: "Old West" Cowboy Action Loads were developed specifically for cowboy action shooting enthusiasts. These flat-nose bullets deliver reliable knockdown power that puts steel targets down on the first shot. Superior components and construction assure trouble-free performance in both single-action revolvers and lever-action rifles.
Available in: .38 SPL, .357 Mag, .44 SPL, .45 Colt, .44-40 Win

FIRST DEFENSE

Features: First Defense rounds are designed with a 100% solid copper bullet, unlike traditional hollow points that contain a lead core covered by a copper jacket. Copper jackets could tear away when fired, causing a loss of weight and a corresponding loss of power. However, Magtech First Defense solid copper bullets have no jacket to split or tear away, ensuring every round you fire meets its target with maximum impact and effectiveness.
Available in: 9mm Luger, .38 SPL+P, .380 Auto, .357 Mag, .40 S&W, .45 Auto+P

GUARDIAN GOLD

Features: Thanks to its tremendous stopping power, deep penetration, awesome expansion and dead-on accuracy, Guardian Gold is fast becoming a favorite among those seeking reliable, affordable personal protection. Simply put, Guardian Gold gives you the advantage against those who may seek to do harm to you or your family. Every round of Guardian Gold undergoes an extensive quality control process before it ever leaves the factory. After passing initial inspection, each case is primed with reliable ignition primers, loaded with the finest clean-burning propellants and assembled with the specified bullet. Only after passing each and every stage is the loaded round approved for final packaging.
Available in: 9mm Luger, 9mm Luger+P, 38 SPL+P, .380 Auto+P, .357 Mag, .40 S&W, .45 Auto+P

SPORT SHOOTING

Features: Magtech pistol and revolver ammunition is ideal for all of your recreational shooting needs. Each cartridge is assembled using only the highest quality components and rigorous quality control is exercised in every stage of the manufacturing process. Originally designed to be the ultimate high performance law enforcement and self-defense handgun bullet, the 100% solid copper hollow-point projectile also meets the critical requirement of stopping power for hand-gun hunting applications. The 100% solid copper bullet features a six-petal hollow-point specifically designed to deliver tight groups, superior expansion, and increased penetration over jacketed lead-core bullets. The one piece design of the solid copper bullet delivers virtually 100% weight retention, even through some of the toughest bone and tissue structure of your favorite thin skinned, big game animal.
Available in: .25 Auto FMJ, .32 Auto FMJ, .32 Auto JHP, .32 Auto LRN, .38 Super Auto+P FMJ, .380 Auto FMJ, .380 Auto JHP, .380 Auto LRN, 9mm Luger FMJ, 9mm Luger JHP, 9mm Luger JSP Flat, 9mm Luger LRN, 9mm Luger JSP Flat w/o grooves, 9mm Luger FMJ Flat Sub, 9mm Luger+P+ JHP, 9mm Luger JHP Sub, 9mm Luger JSP, 9x21mm FMJ, 9x21mm LRN, .40 S&W JHP,.40 S&W FMJ Flat, .40 S&W LSWC, .40 S&W JHP, .40 S&W FMJ Flat, .45 G.A.P. FMJ, .45 Auto FMJ, .45 Auto FMJ-SWC, .45 Auto LSWC (Pistol Cartridges); .32 S&W LRN, .32 S&W Long LRN, .32 S&W Long LWC, .32 S&W Long SJHP, .38 S&W LRN, .38 SPL LRN, .38 SPL LWC, .38 SPL SJSP Flat, .38 SPL+P SJSP Flat, .38 SPL SJHP, .38 SPL+P SJHP, .38 SPL-Short LRN, .38 SPL+P SJHP, .38 SPL LSWC, .38 SPL+P SJSP Flat, .38 SPL FMJ Flat, .38 SPL FMJ Flat, .38 SPL FMJ, .357 Mag SJSP Flat w/ nickel, .357 Mag SJHP, .357 Mag LSWC, .357 Mag FMJ Flat, .357 Mag SJSP Flat w/o nickel, .357 Mag FMJ Flat, .44 Rem Mag SJSP Flat, .44 Rem Mag FMJ Flat, .44 Rem Mag SCHP, .454 Casull SJSP Flat,.454 Casull FMJ Flat, .454 Casull SCHP, .454 Casull SJSP Flat, .500 S&W SJSP Flat, .500 S&W SCHP, .500 S&W FMJ Flat, .500 S&W SJSP-Flat Light (Revolver Cartridges)

Nosler Ammunition

Features: For over 50 years, the professionals at Nosler have been making precision bullets for competition shooters, varmint hunters and big game hunters. Now they've taken Nosler premium hunting bullet technology and created a Custom line of premium Nosler ammunition. Available in over 120 loads, this Nosler ammunition is only sold direct from Nosler and MidwayUSA (www.midwayusa.com).

Available in: 6.5mm, 22 Hornet, 204, 221 Rem Fireball, 222 Rem, 220 Swift, 240 Weatherby Mag, 257 Roberts +P, 257 Weatherby Mag, 260 Rem, 6.5mm - 284 Norma, 264 Win Mag, 270, 270 Weatherby Mag, 280 Rem, 7mm Rem Mag, 7mm Rem Short Action Ultra Mag, 7mm Weatherby Mag, 7mm STW, 308 Win, 30-06 Spring., 300 Rem Short Action Ultra Mag, 300 H&H Mag, 300 Win Mag, 300 Weatherby Mag, 300 Rem Ultra Mag, 30-378 Weatherby Mag, 8x57mm Mauser (8mm Mauser), 8mm Rem Mag, 338-06 A-Square, 338 Win Mag, 338 Rem Ultra Mag, 338 Lapua Mag, 338-378 Weatherby Mag, 340 Weatherby Mag, 35 Whelen, 350 Rem Mag, 9.3mm, 9.3x62mm Mauser, 9.3x74mm Rimmed, 375 H&H Mag, 375 Weatherby Mag, 375 Rem Ultra Mag, 378 Weatherby Mag.

PMC Ammunition

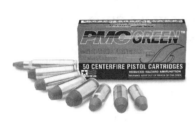

GREEN PISTOL

GOLD HANDGUN

SILVER RIFLE

HANDGUN AMMUNITION

BRONZE LINE

Features: The same quality and dependability built into PMC's Starfire ammunition is incorporated throughout its extensive line of training ammunition and standard hollow point or soft point ammunition. All PMC cartridges pass through the rigorous inspection of the company's electronic powder check station. This station accurately measures the propellant charge in each round. If the propellant in any cartridge varies by a tiny amoun—just two tenths of one grain—the system stops and that cartridge is discarded. No other ammunition manufacturer can truthfully assure you greater uniformity and reliability.
Available in: Variety of bullet types in .25 Auto, .32 Auto, .380 Auto, .38 SPL, .38 Super+P, 9mm Luger, .357 Mag, 10mm Auto, .40 S&W, .44 S&W Special, .44 Rem Mag, .45 Auto.

GOLD LINE, STARFIRE

Features: The secret of Starfire's impressive performance lies in a unique, patented rib-and-flute hollow point cavity design that is like no other. Upon impact, the pre-notched jacket mouth begins to peel back, separating into five uniform copper petals and allowing expansion to begin. Pressure from incoming material creates lateral pressure on the ribs in the cavity wall, forcing them apart and allowing nearly instantaneous expansion of the lead core to the depth of the deep hollow point cavity. The sharp ribs are then exposed and form the leading edge of the expanded bullet, helping it cut its way through. The result is broad temporary and permanent wound cavities and impressive stopping power.
Available in: .380 Auto, .38 SPL+P, .38 SPL, .357 Mag, 9mm Luger, .40 S&W, .44 Rem Mag, .45 Auto.

SILVER LINE, ERANGE

Features: PMC's eRange environmentally friendly ammunition utilizes a reduced hazard primer that is the first of this type in the industry, an encapsulated metal jacket (EMJ) bullet that completely encloses the surface of the bullet core with precision made copper alloy, and powder with clean burning characteristics and smooth fire for increased barrel life.
Available in: .380 Auto, .38 SPL+P, .357 Mag, 9mm Luger, .40 S&W, .44 Rem .45 Auto.

RIFLE AMMUNITION

BRONZE LINE

Features: For shooters and hunters who appreciate affordable quality ammunition, the PMC Bronze Line offers reliable performance for every shooting application, from target shooting to hunting. This long-popular ammunition line makes it possible for hunters and riflemen to enjoy high volume shooting without emptying their wallets.
Available in: Full Metal Jacket (FMJ) bullet types in .223 Rem, .30 Carbine, .308 Win and .50 cal. in commercial and military packaging.

Remington Ammunition

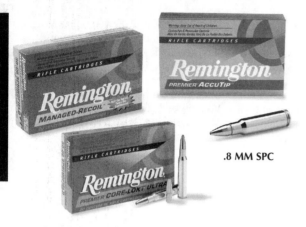

.8 MM SPC

RIMFIRE AMMUNITION

REMINGTON-ELEY
COMPETITION

HANDGUN
AMMUNITION

CENTERFIRE RIFLE AMMUNITION

.17 REMINGTON FIREBALL

Extremely well-balanced cartridge that provides flat trajectory, with match grade accuracy. When loaded with Remington's accurate 20-grain AccuTip-V bullet, the .17 Remington Fireball has a muzzle velocity of 4000 fps. The cartridge uses 50 percent less powder and generates 86 percent less recoil than the .22-250. The Remington .17 Fireball is well suited to short action firearms with 223 Remington bolt dimensions.

MANAGED-RECOIL

Features: Managed-Recoil ammunition delivers Remington field proven hunting performance out to 200 yards with half the recoil. Bullets provide 2x expansion with over 75% weight retention on shots inside 50 yards and out to 200 yards.
Available in: .270 Win., 7mm Remington Mag., .30-30 Win., .30-06 Springfield, .308 Win., .300 Win Mag.

PREMIER ACCUTIP

Features: Featuring precision-engineered polymer tip bullets designed for match-grade accuracy (sub minute-of-angle), Premier AccuTip offers an unprecedented combination of super-flat trajectory and deadly down-range performance.
Available in: .243 Win., .260 Remington, .270 Win., .280 Remington, 7mm-08 Remington, 7mm Remington Mag., .30-06, .300 Win Mag., .308 Win.

PREMIER A-FRAME

Features: Loaded with dual-core A-Frame bullets for reliable expansion at long-range decreased velocities, but without over-expansion at short-range high velocities.
Available in: .270 Win., 7mm Remington Mag., 7mm STW, 7mm Remington Ultra Mag., .30-06, .300 Win Mag., 8mm Remington Mag., .338 Win Mag., .338 Remington Ultra Mag., .375 H&H Mag., .375 Remington Ultra Mag., .416 Remington Mag.

PREMIER CORE-LOKT ULTRA BONDED

Features: The bonded bullet retains up to 95% of its original weight with maximum penetration and energy transfer. Featuring a progressively tapered jacket design, the Core-Lokt Ultra Bonded bullet initiates and controls expansion nearly 2x.
Available in: .243 Win., .25-06 Remington, .260 Remington, 6.8mm Remington SPC, .270 Win., 7mm Remington Mag., 7mm Rem SA Ultra Mag., 7mm Rem Ultra Mag., .30-06, .300 Win Mag., .308 Win., .300 Rem SA Ultra Mag., .300 Rem Ultra Mag., .338 Win Mag.

PREMIER MATCH

Features: Loaded with match-grade bullets, this ammunition employs special loading practices to ensure world-class performance and accuracy with every shot.
Available in: .223 Remington, 6.8mm Rem. SPC, .300 Rem. SA Ultra Mag., .300 Win Mag., .308 Win.

PREMIER SCIROCCO BONDED

Features: The Swift Scirocco Bonded bullet combines polymer tip ballistics with weight retention. The expansion-generating polymer tip and the boat tail base defy air resistance at the front end, and reduce drag at the back.
Available in: .243 Win., .270 Win., 7mm Remington Mag., .30-06, .300 Win Mag., .308 Win., .300 Rem Ultra Mag., .300 WSM

HANDGUN AMMUNITION

CORE-LOKT HIGH-PERFORMANCE

Features: The Core-Lokt Ultra bullet features bonded bullet construction, patented spiral nose cuts jacket taper and patented driving band that initiates precise bore alignment for match-grade accuracy.
Available in: .357 Mag, 165 gr.

EXPRESS HANDGUN AMMUNITION

Features: Remington's exceptionally broad line of handgun ammunition covers a comprehensive range of calibers, bullet weights and bullet styles. Available styles include: Full Metal Case, Lead Round Nose, Jacketed Hollow Point, Lead Hollow Point, Semi-Jacketed Hollow Point, Semi-Wadcutter Lead, Soft Point and Wadcutter Match.

Remington Ammunition

Available in: .25 (6.35mm) Auto., .32 S&W, .32 S&W Long, .32 (7.65mm) Auto., .357 Mag, 9mm Luger, 9mm Luger (+P), 9mm Luger (Subsonic), .380 Auto, .38 S&W, .38 Special, .38 Short Colt, .357 Sig, .40 S&W, .44 Remington Magnum, .44 S&W Special, .45 Colt, .45 Automatic

GOLDEN SABER HPJ

Features: A unique "Driving Band" makes the difference on the Golden Saber HPJ. The bullet diameter directly ahead of the Driving Band is reduced from groove to bore diameter, so the bullet is precisely aligned before the driving band engages the rifling. The result: match-grade accuracy and reduced barrel friction that conserves velocity. In addition, the Driving Band locks the jacket and core together for maximum weight retention and core/jacket integrity.
Available in: .357 Mag., 9mm Luger, .380 Auto, .38 Special (+P), .40 S&W, .45 Auto., .45 Auto+P

RIMFIRE AMMUNITION

.22 RIMFIRE

Features: Whether it's getting young shooters started, practice plinking, small-game hunting or keeping match shooters scoring high, Remington's rimfire quality stands tall. As in their centerfire ammo, they put the maximum level of quality into their .22s so you can get the maximum performance out of them.
Available in: Subsonic (22 Subsonic Long Rifle Hollow Point); Standard Velocity/Target (22 Long Rifle Lead Round Nose); High Velocity Golden Bullet (22 Long Rifle Plated Lead Round Nose, 22 Long Rifle Plated Hollow Point, 22 Short Plated Lead Round Nose); Hyper Velocity (22 Yellow Jacket LR Truncated Cone Hollow Point, 22 Viper LR Truncated Cone Solid); Hi-Speed (22 Thunderbolt LR Lead Round Nose, 22 Cyclone LR Hollow Point, 22 Game Loads Hollow Point)

PREMIER GOLD BOX RIMFIRE

Features: This ammunition uses the AccuTip-V bullet with precision-engineered polymer tip for match-type

accuracy, high on-game energy and rapid expansion.
Available in: .17 HMR, .17 Mach 2, .22 Win Mag.

MAGNUM RIMFIRE

Features: Premier Gold Box Rimfire ammunition features AccuTip-V bullets. Choice of Jacketed Hollow Point or Pointed Soft Point.
Available in: .17 HMR or .22 Win Mag.

REMINGTON-ELEY COMPETITION RIMFIRE

Features: Building on the rimfire expertise of Eley, Ltd., and its reputation among dedicated rimfire shooters as the world's most accurate and reliable ammunition, Remington and Eley offer three grades of their premier 22 Long Rifle ammunition: Target Rifle, Club Xtra and Match EPS.
Available in: .22 LR only

SHOTGUN AMMUNITION

EXPRESS EXTRA LONG RANGE UPLAND LOADS

Features: The hunter's choice for a wide variety of game-bird applications, available in an exceptionally broad selection of loadings, from 12-gauge to .410 bore, with shot size options ranging from BB's all the way down to 9s - suitable for everything from quail to farm predators.
Available in: 12, 16, 20, 28, .410 ga.; 2½, 2¾, 3 in.; shot sizes BB, 2, 4, 5, 6, 7½, 9

GUN CLUB TARGET LOADS

Features: Excellent choice for economical shooting. Loaded with Gun Club Grade Shot, Premier STS Primers, and Power Piston One-Piece Wads, these high-quality shells receive the same care in loading as top-of-the-line Premier STS and Nitro 27 shells. Many shooters are discovering that they can get acceptable reloading life while stretching their shooting dollar.
Available in: 12, 20 ga.; 2¾ in.; shot sizes 7½, 8, 9

LEAD GAME LOADS

Features: For a wide variety of field gaming, these budget-stretching loads include the same quality components as other

Remington shotshells, and are available in four different gauges to match up with your favorite upland shotguns.
Available in: 12, 16, 20, .410 ga.; 2½, 2¾ in.; shot sizes 6, 7½, 8

MANAGED RECOIL STS TARGET LOADS

Features: Managed-Recoil STS target loads offer dramatically reduced recoil—40% less in the 12-ga. load—with target-grinding STS consistency and pattern density. Ideal for new shooters and high-volume practice.
Available in: 12, 20 ga.; 2¾ in.; shot sizes 8½

NITRO BUFFERED TURKEY LOADS

Features: Contain Nitro Mag extra-hard lead shot that is as hard and round as copper-plated shot. Nitro Turkey Magnums will pattern as well as other copper-plated, buffered loads without the higher cost. Utilizing a specially blended powder recipe and Remington's advanced Power Piston® one-piece wad, the loads delivers a full 1 7/8 oz. payload at 1210 fps while delivering 80% pattern densities with outstanding knockdown power.
Available in: 12 ga.; 3, 3½ in.; shot sizes 2, 4, 6

NITRO-MAG BUFFERED MAGNUM TURKEY LOADS

Features: The original buffered magnum shotshells from Remington. The shot charge is packed with a generous amount of shock-absorbing polymer buffering and surrounded by our patented Power Piston wad to protect the specially hardened shot all the way down the barrel for dense, even patterns and uniform shot strings.
Available in: 12, 20 ga.; 2¾, 3 in.; shot sizes 2, 4, 6

NITRO PHEASANT LOADS

Features: Uses Remington's own Copper-Lokt® copper-plated lead shot with high antimony content. Hard shot stays rounder for truer flight, tighter patterns, and greater penetration. Available in both high-velocity and magnum loadings.
Available in: 12, 20 ga.; 2¾, 3 in.; shot sizes 4, 5, 6

Remington Ammunition

WATERFOWL LOADS

UPLAND LOADS

WINGMASTER HD SHOTSHELLS

SLUGS

NITRO-STEEL HIGH VELOCITY MAGNUM WATERFOWL LOADS

Features: Greater hull capacity means heavier charges and larger pellets, which makes these loads ideal for large waterfowl. Nitro-Steel™ delivers denser patterns for greater lethality and is zinc-plated to prevent corrosion.
Available in: 10, 12, 16, 20 ga.; 2¾, 3, 3½ in.; shot sizes T, BBB, BB, 1, 2, 3, 4

PHEASANT LOADS

Features: For the broadest selection in game-specific upland lead shotshells, Remington Pheasant Loads are the perfect choice. Their high-velocity and long-range performance are just right for any pheasant hunting situation. Standard high-base payloads feature Power Piston® one-piece wads.
Available in: 12, 16, 20 ga.; 2¾ in.; shot sizes 4, 5, 6, 7½

PREMIER DUPLEX MAGNUM TURKEY LOADS

Features: Premier Duplex has No. 4 size shot carefully layered on top of No. 6 shot. When ranges vary, they combine retained energy and penetration from the larger pellets with pattern density from the smaller ones. Duplex patterns are extremely well balanced.
Available in: 12 ga.; 2¾, 3½ in.; shot sizes 4x6

PREMIER HIGH-VELOCITY MAGNUM TURKEY LOADS

Features: Utilizing a specially blended powder recipe, Remington's advanced Power Piston one piece wad and hardened copper plated shot, these new high velocity loads result in extremely dense patterns and outstanding knockdown power at effective ranges.

Available in: 12 ga.; 3, 3½ in.; shot sizes 4, 5, 6

PREMIER MAGNUM TURKEY LOADS

Features: Premier® Magnum Turkey Loads provide that extra edge to reach out with penetrating power and dense, concentrated patterns. Its magnum-grade, Copper-Lokt shot is protected by our Power Piston® wad and cushioned with special polymer buffering. Available with some of the heaviest payloads of 4s, 5s, and 6s on the market.
Available in: 10, 12, 20 ga.; 2¾, 3, 3½ in. ; shot sizes 4, 5, 6

PREMIER NITRO 27 HANDICAP TRAP LOADS

Features: Designed specifically for back-fence trap and long-range sporting clays. Delivers consistent handicap velocity and pattern uniformity. New, improved powder loading significantly reduces felt recoil while retaining high velocity - both factors allow avid trap shooters to stay fresh for the shootoff. They score just as high on fast-moving doves.
Available in: 12 ga.; 2¾ in.; shot sizes 7½, 8

PREMIER NITRO GOLD SPORTING CLAYS TARGET LOADS

Features: To meet the special demands of avid sporting clays shooters, we developed a new Premier Nitro Gold Sporting Clays target load. At 1300 fps, the extra velocity gives you an added advantage for those long crossers—making target leads closer to normal for ultimate target-crushing satisfaction. Also makes a great high-velocity dove load.
Available in: 12 ga.; 2¾ in.; shot sizes 7½, 8

PREMIER STS TARGET LOADS

Features: STS Target Loads have taken shot-to-shot consistency to a new performance level, setting the standard at all major skeet, trap, and sporting clays shoots across the country, while providing handloaders with unmatched reloading ease and hull longevity. Available in most gauges, our Premier STS shells are the most reliable, consistent and most reloadable shells you can shoot.
Available in: 12, 20, 28, .410 ga.; 2½, 2¾, 3, 3¼ in.; shot sizes 7½, 8, 8½, 9

SHURSHOT HEAVY FIELD AND HEAVY DOVE LOADS

Features: A sure bet for all kinds of upland game, ShurShot loads have earned the reputation as one of the best-balanced, best-patterning upland field loads available. And for good reason. These shells combine an ideal balance of powder charge and shot payload to deliver effective velocities and near-perfect patterns with mild recoil for high-volume upland hunting situations.
Available in: 12, 20 ga.; 2¾ in.; shot sizes 6, 7½, 8

SHURSHOT HIGH BASE PHEASANT LOADS

Features: The ShurShot High Base Pheasant loads deliver an ideal combination of velocity and payload. Loaded with our reliable Power Piston® Wad and hard lead shot.
Available in: 12 ga.; 2¾ in.; shot sizes 4, 5

SPORT LOADS

Features: Remington Sport Loads are an economical, multi-purpose utility load for a variety of shotgunning

needs. Loaded with Power Piston wads, and plastic Unibody hulls, these shells perform effectively for skeet, trap and sporting clays, as well as quail, doves, and woodcock.
Available in: 12, 20 ga.; 2¾ in.; shot sizes 8

SPORTSMAN HI-SPEED STEEL WATERFOWL LOADS

Features: Sportsman Hi-Speed Steel's sealed primer, high quality steel shot, and consistent muzzle velocities combine to provide reliability in adverse weather, while delivering exceptional pattern density and retained energy. A high-speed steel load that is ideal for short-range high-volume shooting during early duck seasons, or over decoys.
Available in: 10, 12, 20 ga.; 2¾, 3, 3½ in.; shot sizes BB, 1, 2, 3, 4, 6, 7

WINGMASTER HD TURKEY LOADS

Comprised of tungsten, bronze and iron, Wingmaster HD pellets are specifically engineered with a density of 12 grams/cc, 10 percent denser than lead. Wingmaster HD loads also feature a precise balance of payload and velocity that provide turkey hunters with a shotshell that generates nearly 200 ft.-lbs. more energy at 40 yds. than competitive tungsten based shot. This results in deeper penetrating pellets.
Available in: 12 ga. 3½ in., 1⅞ oz.; 12 ga. 3 in., 1⅝ oz.; or 20 ga. 3 in., 1¼ oz. Size 4 or 6 shot.

WINGMASTER HD WATERFOWL LOADS

Features: Wingmaster HD nontoxic shot stretches the kill zone with an ultra-tuned combination of density, shape and energy. At 12.0 grams/cc, it's 10% denser than lead and the scientifically proven optimum density for pellet count and pattern density. Plus, its smooth, round shape delivers awesome aerodynamics and sustained payload energy. Wingmaster HD is also 16% softer than Premier Hevi-Shot, which makes it easier on your barrel. And it's more responsive to chokes, allowing you to open up the pattern for close-range hunting or stretch shotgun range to its farthest reaches. Also available in Turkey and Predator Loads.
Available in: 10, 12, 20 ga.; 2¾, 3, 3½ in.; shot sizes BB, 2, 4, 6

SHOTGUN AMMUNITION (BUCKSHOT)

EXPRESS BUCKSHOT AND EXPRESS MAGNUM BUCKSHOT

Features: A combination of heavy cushioning behind the shot column and a granulated polymer buffering helps maintain pellet roundness for tight, even patterns. Packed in 5-round boxes.
Available in: 12, 20 ga.; 2¾, 3, 3½ in.; shot sizes 0, 00, 000, 1, 3, 4

MANAGED-RECOIL EXPRESS BUCKSHOT

Features: With less felt recoil than full velocity loads, Express Managed-Recoil Buckshot is an ideal close-range performer. Less recoil means second shot recovery is quicker, allowing the user to get back on target more easily. These loads are buffered for dense patterns, allowing for highly effective performance at up to 40 yards.
Available in: 12 ga.; 2¾ in.; shot sizes 00

SHOTGUN AMMUNITION (SLUGS)

BUCKHAMMER LEAD SLUGS

Features: Specifically designed for rifled barrels and rifled choke tubes, these high-performance slugs are capable of producing 3-inch or better groups at 100-yards with nearly 100% weight retention and controlled expansion to nearly one-inch in diameter. Unlike traditional sabot slugs, the BuckHammer's unique attached stabilizer allows for a full bore diameter lead slug that delivers devastating terminal performance with unsurpassed accuracy.
Available in: 12, 20 ga.; 2¾, 3 in.; 1, 1¼, 1⅜ oz.

MANAGED-RECOIL BUCKHAMMER LEAD SLUGS

Features: BuckHammer lead slugs generate 40% less felt-recoil without sacrificing its devastating on-game performance. Specially designed for fully rifled barrels and rifled choke tubes, these lower-recoil slugs still deliver the same outstanding accuracy as our standard BuckHammer loads with near 100% weight retention and controlled expansion to nearly 1-inch in diameter. For use at the range or in the field the Managed Recoil BuckHammer slug maintains an impressive 1032 ft-lbs of deer stopping energy at 100-yards.
Available in: 12, 20 ga.; 2¾.; 7/8, 1⅛ oz.

MANAGED-RECOIL COPPER SOLID SABOT SLUGS

Features: With 40% less recoil, these slugs are perfect for anyone who wants outstanding on-game results without the rearward punch. Or, use them to sight-in, then step up to full loads. There's no finer slug load for young or recoil-sensitive hunters.
Available in: 12 ga.; 2¾ in.; 1 oz.

PREMIER COPPER SOLID SABOT SLUGS

Features: Coupling the angled petal score design of the Copper Solid Muzzleloader bullet with the ballistic coefficient of a deep penetrating slug round, the 12 and 20-gauge Copper Solid Sabot Slugs deliver maximum performance: 100-percent weight retention, 2X controlled expansion and super accuracy.
Available in: 12, 20 ga.; 2¾, 3 in.; 5/8, 1 oz.

PREMIER CORE-LOKT ULTRA BONDED SABOT SLUGS

Features: Ultra-high velocities deliver devastating on-game performance and the tightest groups—1.8"—of any shotgun slug with ultra-flat trajectories. Remington® patented spiral nose cuts ensure consistent 2x expansion over a wide range of terminal velocities, while the sleek, ogive nose delivers high down-range energy retention. The 385-grain bonded bullet yields near 100% weight retention. Flattest shooting slug in existence—10% better than the nearest competition. Designed for use in fully rifled barrels only.
Available in: 12, 20 ga.; 2¾, 3 in.; 260, 385 gr..

Remington Ammunition

SLUGGER HIGH VELOCITY SLUGS

Features: This is the first high-velocity Foster-style lead slug. This higher velocity slug exits the barrel at 1800 fps, 13% faster than standard 1 oz. slugs. The 7/8 oz. Slugger High Velocity delivers 200 ft-lbs more energy at 50 yards with flatter trajectory on deer than standard 1 oz. slugs. Designed for the avid deer hunter using smooth bore guns.
Available in: 12, 20 ga.; 2¾, 3 in.; ½, ⅞ oz.

SLUGGER MANAGED-RECOIL RIFLED SLUGS

Features: Slugger Managed-Recoil Rifled Slugs offer remarkably effective performance but with 45% less felt recoil than full velocity Sluggers. With effective energy out to 80 yards, these 1-ounce slugs easily handle the majority of shotgun deer hunting ranges.
Available in: 12 ga.; 2¾ in.; 1 oz.

SLUGGER RIFLED SLUGS

Features: Remington redesigned their 12-gauge Slugger Rifled Slug for a 25% improvement in accuracy. Also, at 1760 fps muzzle velocity, the 3 in. 12-ga. Magnum slugs shoot 25% flatter than regular 12-ga. slugs. Packed in convenient, easy-carrying 5-round boxes. Also available in a reduced recoil loading.
Available in: 12, 16, 20, .410 ga.; 2¾, 3 in.; ⅕, ⅘, ⅝, 1 oz.

RWS Ammunition

RIMFIRE AMMUNITION

RWS .22 L.R. HV HOLLOW POINT

Features: This higher velocity hollow point offers the shooter greater shocking power in game. Suitable for both small game and vermin.

RWS .22 L.R. RIFLE MATCH

Features: Perfect for the club level target competitor. Accurate and affordable.

RWS .22 L.R. SUBSONIC HOLLOW POINT

Features: Subsonic ammunition is a favorite ammunition of shooters whose shooting range is limited to where the noise of a conventional cartridge would be a problem.

RWS .22 L.R. TARGET RIFLE

Features: An ideal training and field cartridge, the .22 Long Rifle Target also excels in informal competitions. The target .22 provides the casual shooter with accuracy at an economical price.

RWS .22 MAGNUM FULL JACKET

Features: Outstanding penetration characteristics of this cartridge allow the shooter to easily tackle game where penetration is necessary.

RWS .22 MAGNUM HOLLOW POINT

Features: The soft point allows good expansion on impact, while preserving the penetration characteristics necessary for larger vermin and game.

RWS .22 R50

Features: For competitive shooters demanding the ultimate in precision. This cartridge has been used to establish several world records and is used by Olympic Gold Medalists.

RWS .22 SHORT R25

Features: Designed for world class Rapid Fire Pistol events, this cartridge provides the shooter with outstanding accuracy and minimal recoil. Manufactured to exacting standards, so the shooter can be assured of consistent performance.

Winchester Ammunition

HANDGUN AMMUNITION

COWBOY LOADS LEAD

Features: Designed for cowboy action shooters who need high accuracy and consistent performance.
Available in: 38 SPL, 44-40 Win, 44 S&W SPL, 45 Colt

SUPER-CLEAN NT (TIN)

Features: Specially designed jacketed soft point tin core bullet shoots and performs like lead. Meets the totally non-toxic needs of indoor ranges.
Available in: 40 S&W, 9mm Luger

SUPER-X FULL METAL JACKET

Available in : 30 Luger

SUPER-X JHP

Available in: 357 Magnum, 38 Special +P, 454 Casull, 45 Winchester Magnum, 460 S&W Magnum

SUPER-X BLANK - BLACK POWDER

Available in: 32 S&W

SUPER-X BLANK - SMOKELESS

Available in: 38 Special

SUPER-X EXPANDING POINT

Available in: 25 Auto

SUPER-X HOLLOW SOFT POINT

Available in: 30 Carbine, 44 Rem-Mag

SUPER-X JACKETED SOFT POINT

Available in: 357 Mag

SUPER-X LEAD ROUND NOSE

Available in: 32 Short Colt, 32 S&W, 32 S&W Long, 38 Special, 38 S&W, 44 S&W Special, 45 Colt

SUPER-X LEAD SEMI-WAD CUTTER

Available in: 38 Special

SUPER-X LEAD SEMI-WAD CUTTER HP

Available in: 38 Special+P

SUPER-X MATCH

Available in: 38 Special Super Match

SUPER-SILVERTIP HOLLOW POINT

Available in: 10mm Auto, 32 Auto, 357 Mag, 380 Auto, 38 Super Auto +P, 38 Special +P, 38 Special, 40 S&W, 41 Rem Mag, 44 S&W Special , 45 Auto, 45 Colt, 45 G.A.P., 9x23 Winchester, 9mm Luger

SUPER-X JACKETED HOLLOW POINT

Available in: 500 S&W

SUPER-X LEAD FLATNOSE

Available in: 45 Colt

SUPREME PARTITION GOLD

Features: Proven partition technology, consistent, dramatic bullet expansion, deep penetration regardless of barrel length, maximum weight retention
Available in: 357 Mag, 44 Rem Mag, 454 Casull, 460 S&W Mag

SUPREME PLATINUM TIP HOLLOW POINT

Features: Patented notched reverse taper bullet jacket, plated heavy wall jacket and two-part hollow point cavity for uniform bullet expansion, massive energy depot
Available in: 41 Rem Mag, 44 Rem Mag, 454 Casull, 500 S&W

SUPREME T-SERIES

Features: Reverse Taper Jacket design; consistent, reliable bullet expansion through common barrier test events; excellent accuracy; positive functioning
Available in: 380 Auto, 38 Special +P, 38 Special, 40 S&W, 45 Auto, 9mm Luger

WINCLEAN

Features: The patented lead and heavy-metal free primers, Brass Enclosed Base bullets and clean-burning propellants not only eliminate airborne lead at the firing point, they also generate less barrel, action and shell case residue.
Available in: Brass Enclosed Base (357 Sig WinClean, 380 Auto, 40 S&W, 45 Auto, 45 GAP, 9mm Luger, 9mm Luger WinClean), Jacketed Soft Point (357 Mag, 38 Special)

RIFLE AMMUNITION

SUPER-X FLAT POINT

Available in: 405 Winchester

SUPER-X HOLLOW POINT

Available in: 204 Ruger, 218 Bee, 22 Hornet, 30-30 Win

Winchester Ammunition

SUPER-X HOLLOW SOFT POINT
Available in: 30 Carbine, 44 Rem Mag

SUPER-X JACKETED SOFT POINT
Available in: 357 Mag

SUPER-X JHP
Available in: 45-70 Gov't

SUPER-X LEAD
Available in: 32-20 Win

SUPER-X POSITIVE EXPANDING POINT
Available in: 25-06 Rem, 25 WSSM

SUPER-X POWER POINT
Available in: 22-250 Remington, 223 Remington, 223 WSSM, 243 Winchester, 243 WSSM, 257 Roberts + P, 264 Winchester Magnum, 270 Winchester, 270 Winchester, 270 WSM, 284 Winchester, 300 Savage, 30-06 Springfield, 30-06 Springfield, 300 WSM, 300 WSM Winchester Short Mag, 30-30 Winchester, 30-30 Winchester, 30-30 Win, 303 British, 30-40 Krag, 307 Winchester, 308 Winchester, 308 Winchester, 300 Winchester Magnum, 300 Winchester Magnum, 325 Winchester Short Magnum, 32 Winchester Special, 338 Winchester Magnum, 356 Winchester, 35 Remington, 375 Winchester, 6mm Remington, 7mm-08 Remington, 7mm Mauser (7 x 57), 7mm Remington Magnum, 7mm Remington Magnum, 7mm WSM, 8mm Mauser (8 x 57)

SUPER-X SILVERTIP
Available in: 250 Savage, 270 Winchester, 30-06 Springfield, 30-30 Winchester, 308 Winchester, 348 Winchester, 358 Winchester

SUPER-X SILVERTIP HOLLOW POINT
Available in: 44 Rem Mag

SUPER-X SOFT POINT
Available in: 22 Hornet, 25-20 Winchester, 25-35 Winchester, 38-40 Winchester, 38-55 Winchester, 44-40 Winchester, 458 Winchester, 6.5x55 Swedish, 7.62x39mm Russian

SUPER-X SUPER CLEAN NT TIN
Available in: 5.56mm

SUPREME ACCUBOND CT
Features: Fully bonded lead alloy core, high weight retention, pinpoint accuracy, boattail design, Lubalox coating/red polymer tip
Available in: 25-06 Remington, 25 WSSM, 270 Winchester, 270 WSM, 30-06 Springfield, 300 Winchester Magnum, 300 WSM, 325 Winchester Short Magnum, 338 Winchester Magnum, 7mm Remington Magnum, 7mm WSM

SUPREME BALLISTIC SILVERTIP
Features: Solid based boat tail design delivers excellent long range accuracy. In .22 calibers, the Ballistic plastic polycarbonate Silvertip bullet initiates rapid fragmentation. In medium to larger calibers special jacket contours extend range and reduce cross-wind drift. Harder lead core ensures proper bullet expansion.
Available in: 204 Ruger, 22-250 Remington, 223 Remington, 223 WSSM, 243 Winchester, 243 WSSM, 25-06 Remington, 25 WSSM, 270 Winchester, 270 WSM, 280 Remington, 300 Winchester Magnum, 30-06 Springfield, 300 WSM, 30-30 Winchester, 308 Winchester, 325 Winchester Short Magnum, 338 Winchester Magnum, 7mm Remington Magnum, 7mm-08 Remington, 7mm Remington Magnum, 7mm WSM

SUPREME E-TIP
Available in: 30-06 Springfield, 300 Winchester Magnum, 300 WSM, 308 Winchester

SUPREME NOSLER PARTITION AND NOSLER SOLID
Available in: 375 H&H, 416 Rigby, 416 Rem Mag, 458 Win Mag

SUPREME HOLLOWPOINT BOATTAIL MATCH
Available in: 300 Winchester Match

SUPREME PARTITION GOLD
Features: Proven partition technology, consistent, dramatic bullet expansion, deep penetration regardless of barrel length, maximum weight retention
Available in: 45-70 Government

SUPREME ELITE XP3
Features: The XP3 bullet starts with a 2-stage expansion design, then combines all the best-known bullet technology into one bullet. It delivers precision accuracy, awesome knockdown power, and deep penetration all in one package—and it's as effective on thin-skinned game, like deer and antelope, as it is on tough game, like elk, moose, bear, and African animals, at short and long ranges.
Available in: 243 Winchester, 243 WSSM, 270 WSM, 270 Winchester, 30-06 Springfield, 3000 WSM, 300 Winchester Magnum, 308 Winchester, 325 WSM, 7mm Rem Magnum, 7mm WSM

RIMFIRE AMMUNITION

DYNAPOINT
Available in: 22 LR

SUPREME JHP AND SUPREME V-MAX
Available in: 17HMR, 22 Win Mag

SUPER-X #12 SHOT
Available in: 17HMR, 22 Short, 22 Long, 22 LR, 22 Win Mag

SUPER-X BLANK
Available in: 17HMR, 22 Short, 22 Long, 22 LR, 22 Win Mag

SUPER-X FULL METAL JACKET
Available in: 17HMR, 22 Short, 22 Long, 22 LR, 22 Win Mag

SUPER-X JHP
Available in: 17HMR, 22 Short, 22 Long, 22 LR, 22 Win Mag

SUPER-X LEAD HOLLOW POINT
Available in: 17HMR, 22 Short, 22 Long, 22 LR, 22 Win Mag

Winchester Ammunition

SUPER-X LEAD ROUND NOSE
Available in: 17HMR, 22 Short, 22 Long, 22 LR, 22 Win Mag

SUPER-X LEAD ROUND NOSE, STANDARD VELOCITY
Available in: 17HMR, 22 Short, 22 Long, 22 LR, 22 Win Mag

SUPER-X POWER-POINT
Available in: 17HMR, 22 Short, 22 Long, 22 LR, 22 Win Mag

SUPER-X POWER-POINT, LEAD HOLLOW POINT
Available in: 17HMR, 22 Short, 22 Long, 22 LR, 22 Win Mag

XPERT LEAD HOLLOW POINT
Available in: 22 LR

WILDCAT DYNAPOINT PLATED
Available in: 22 LR, 22 Win Mag, 22 WRF

WILDCAT LEAD FLAT NOSE
Available in: 22 LR, 22 Win Mag, 22 WRF

WILDCAT LEAD ROUND NOSE
Available in: 22 LR, 22 Win Mag, 22 WRF

SHOTGUN AMMUNITION

AA TARGET LOADS
Features: The hunter's choice for a wide variety of game-bird applications, available in an exceptionally broad selection of loadings, from 12-gauge to .410 bore, with shot size options ranging from BB's all the way down to 9s—suitable for everything from quail to farm predators.
Available in: 12, 20, 28, .410 ga.; 2½, 2¾; shot sizes 7½, 8, 8½, 9

SUPER-TARGET TARGET LOADS
Available in: 12, 20 ga.; 2¾ in.; shot sizes 7, 7½, 8

SUPER-X GAME AND FIELD LOADS
Available in: 12, 16, 20, 28, .410 ga.; 2½, 2¾, 3 in.; shot sizes 4, 5, 6, 7½, 8, 9

SUPER-X SUPER PHEASANT LOADS
Available in: 12, 20 ga.; 2¾, 3 in.; shot sizes 4, 5, 6

SUPER-X SUPER PHEASANT STEEL LOADS
Available in: 12 ga.; 3 in.; shot sizes 4

SUPER-X TRIALS AND BLANKS
Available in: 10, 12 ga.; 2¾, 2 7/8 in.; shot sizes (blank)

SUPER-X TURKEY LOADS
Available in: 12 ga.; 2¾, 3 in.; shot sizes 4, 5, 6

SUPER-X WATERFOWL LOADS
Available in: 10, 12, 20 ga.; 2¾, 3, 3 ½ in.; shot sizes T, BBB, BB, 1, 2, 3, 4

SUPREME GAME AND FIELD LOADS
Available in: 12, 20 ga.; 2¾, 3 in.; shot sizes 4, 5, 6

SUPREME TURKEY LOADS
Available in: 10, 12 20 ga.; 2¾, 3, 3 ½ in.; shot sizes 4, 5, 6

SUPREME WATERFOWL LOADS
Available in: 10, 12 ga.; 3, 3 ½ in.; shot sizes BBB, BB, 2, 3, 4

SUPREME ELITE XTENDED RANGE HD COYOTE
Available in: 12 ga.; 3 in.; shot sizes B

SUPREME ELITE XTENDED RANGE HD TURKEY
Available in: 12, 20 ga.; 2¾, 3, 3 ½ in.; shot sizes 4, 5, 6

SUPREME ELITE XTENDED RANGE HD WATERFOWL
Available in: 12, 20 ga.; 2¾, 3, 3 ½ in.; shot sizes B, 2, 4

WINLITE LOW RECOIL, LOW NOISE TARGET LOADS
Available in: 12, 20 ga.; 2¾ in.; shot sizes 8

XPERT HI-VELOCITY STEEL LOADS
Available in: 12, 16, 20, 28, .410 ga.; 2¾, 3, 3 ½ in.; shot sizes BB, 1, 2, 3, 4

XPERT STEEL LOADS
Available in: 12, 20 ga.; 2¾ in.; shot sizes 6, 7

SHOTGUN AMMUNITION (BUCKSHOT)

SUPER-X BUCKSHOT
Available in: 12, 16, 20, .410 ga.; 2½, 2¾, 3, 3 ½ in.; shot sizes 4, 3, 1, 00, 000

SUPREME BUCKSHOT
Available in: 12 ga.; 2¾, 3, 3 ½ in.; shot sizes 4, 00

WINLITE LOW RECOIL BUCKSHOT
Available in: 12 ga.; 2¾ in.

SHOTGUN AMMUNITION (SLUGS)

SUPER-X SLUGS
Available in: 12, 16, 20, .410 ga.; 2½, 2¾, 3 in.; 1/5, ¼, 5/8, ¾, 1 oz.

SUPREME ELITE XP3 SABOT SHOTGUN SLUGS
Available in: 12 ga.; 2¾, 3 in.; 300 gr.

SUPREME PLATINUM TIP HOLLOW POINT SLUGS
Available in: 12, 20, ga.; 2¾, 3 in.; 260 or 400 gr.

SUPREME RACKMASTER RIFLED SLUGS
Available in: 12 ga.; 2¾, 3 in.; 1 1/8 oz.

SUPREME WINCHESTER SLUGS
Available in: 12, 20, ga.; 2¾, 3 in.; 260 or 385 gr.

WINLITE LOW RECOIL SLUGS
Available in: 12 ga.; 2¾ in.; 1 oz. or 400 gr.

Barnes Bullets MUZZLELOADING AMMUNITION

EXPANDER MZ MUZZLELOADER BULLETS AND ALIGNERS
Features: Semi-spitzer ogive, boat-tail base. Six copper petals w/ double-diameter expansion. Full weight retention.
Available in: .50 Caliber (245, 285 gr.)

SPIT-FIRE MZ
Features: Semi-spitzer ogive, boattail base. Six copper petals with double-diameter expansion. Full weight retention.
Available in: .50 Caliber (245, 285 gr.)

SPIT-FIRE TMZ
Features: Boattail, All copper with polymer tip. Expands at 1050 fps.; remains intact at extreme velocities.
Available in: .50 Caliber (250, 290 gr.)

Buffalo Bullets

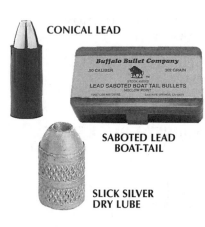

CONICAL LEAD

SABOTED LEAD BOAT-TAIL

SLICK SILVER DRY LUBE

CONICAL LEAD BULLETS
Features: Cold-formed pure lead. Pre-Lubed, hollow point or round nose with double gas seals.
Available in: .45 caliber (285 gr. 325 gr.); .50 (350,385 gr.); .54 390 , 410, 425,. 435, 525 gr.)

SABOTED LEAD BOAT-TAIL BULLETS
Features: Pure lead with truncated cone and large hollow point. Buffalo Buster sabots are color coded as to caliber. Sabots are designed for copper jacketed or lead bullets.
Available in: .45 caliber (145, 435, 225, 240, 252 , 302, 375 gr.); .54 (225, 240 gr.)

SLICK SILVER DRY LUBE BULLETS
Features: Pressure formed Pure lead pre-lubed with Slick Silver dry lubricant.
Available in: .50 caliber (385 gr.); .54 caliber (425 gr.)

CVA

POWERBELT COPPER
Features: Thin copper plating reduces bore friction while allowing for optimal bullet expansion. Available in four tip designs: Hollow Point, AeroTip, Flat Point and Steel Tip.
Available in: .45 caliber (175,195, 195, 225, 225, 275, 275 gr.); 50 caliber (223, 245, 295, 348, 405 gr.); .54 caliber (295, 348, 405, 444 gr.)

POWERBELT PLATINUM AEROTIP
Features: Proprietary hard plating and aggressive bullet taper design for improved ballistic coefficient. A large size fluted gas check produces higher and more consistent pressures.
Available in: .45 caliber (223, 300 gr.); .50 caliber (270, 300, 338 gr.)

POWERBELT PURE LEAD
Pure lead, available in four different grain weights in Hollow Point and 444 in Flat Point.
Available in: .50 caliber (295, 348, 405 gr.); .54 caliber (295, 348 , 405 gr.)

Federal Ammunition

FUSION MUZZLELOADER SLUGS
Features: The Fusion bullet process now is available for hunters using .50-caliber muzzleloaders. A .45-caliber slug is offered in three grain weights paired with a .50-cal crush rib sabot. The Fusion bullet is deep penetrating, with high weight retention at 95 percent and high accuracy. In addition, the crush rib sabot reduces loading friction up to 50 percent.
Available in: .50 caliber in 240, 260 and 300 grain

Harvester

SCORPION

SABER TOOTH BELTED BULLETS

Features: Copper-Clad belted bullet in Harvester Crush Rib Sabot.
Available in: .50 cal. (250, 270, 300 gr.)

SCORPION

Features: Electroplated copper plating does not separate from lead core. Loaded in Harvester Crush Rib Sabots.
Available in: Funnel Point Mag. and Polymer Ballistic Tip—.50 caliber (240, 260, 300 gr.); .54 caliber (240, 260, 300 gr.)

SABOER TOOTH BELTED BULLETS

Hornady Mfg. Co.

GREAT PLAINS MAXI HOLLOW BASE HOLLOW POINTS

Features: Pre-scored hollow points, a short ogive and three diameter bearing surface.
Available in: .45 caliber (285 gr.); .50 caliber (385, 410 gr.); .54 caliber (390, 425, 525 gr.)

HP/XTP BULLET/SABOT

Features: Hornady XTP bullet/sabot combination with controlled expansion XTP bullet.
Available in: .45 caliber (180 gr.); .50 caliber (180, 240, 300 gr.); .54 caliber (300 gr.)

GREAT PLAINS MAXI HOLLOW BASE HOLLOW POINTS

HP/XTP BULLET/SABOT

Knight Rifles

JACKETED BULLETS WITH SABOTS

Features: Copper jacketed, hollow point bullet with sabot.
Available in: .50 cal. (240, 260, 300 gr.)

LEAD BULLETS WITH SABOTS

Features: Pure lead bullet with sabot.
Available in: .50 caliber (260, 310 gr.)

RED HOT BULLETS

Features: Saboted Barnes solid copper bullet with superior expansion.
Available in: .45 caliber (175, 195 gr.); .50 caliber (250, 300, 250, 250 gr.); .52 caliber (275 grain, 350, 375 gr.)

ULTIMATE SLAM HYDRA-CON

Features: Pure lead bullet.
Available in: .50 caliber (440 gr.); .52 caliber (530 gr.)

ULTIMATE SLAM PBT (POLYMER BOAT TAIL)

Features: Sabot with all copper polymer tip bullet; expands into six razor-sharp copper petals while retaining 100 percent of original weight.
Available in: .50 caliber (250, 250, 290 gr.)

ULTIMATE SLAM SPITZER BOAT TAIL

Features: Sabot loaded with Barnes Spitzer Boat tail bullet.
Available in: .50 caliber (245, 285 gr.)

Nosler

BLACK POWDER PARTITION-HG SABOT

Features: HG Sabot with Nosler Partition jacketed hollow point bullet.
Available in: .50 cal. (250, 260, 300 gr.)

Remington

XBLS MUZZLELOADING SABOTS

Features: Remington Expander-LT bullets with sealed hydraulic chamber in the nose to ensure expansion.
Available in: .50 caliber (275, 300 gr.)

Thompson/Center Arms

BONE CRUSHER SABOT

MAXIBALL

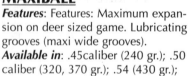

MAXI HUNTER   SHOCK WAVE

BONE CRUSHER SABOT

Features: .458 diameter solid projectile for 50 caliber muzzleloaders
Available in: .50 caliber (400 gr.)

MAGNUM EXPRESS SABOTS

Features: Mag express sabots separate from the projectile quickly. Sabots are available preassembled with XTP bullets.
Available in: .50 caliber (300 gr.); .54 caliber (250 gr.)

MAXIBALL

Features: Features: Maximum expansion on deer sized game. Lubricating grooves (maxi wide grooves).
Available in: .45caliber (240 gr.); .50 caliber (320, 370 gr.); .54 (430 gr.); .58 caliber (555 gr.)

MAXI-HUNTER

Features: Maximum expansion on deer sized game. Lubricating grooves (maxi hunter multiple grooves).
Available in: .45 caliber (255 gr.); .50 caliber (275, 350 gr.); .54 caliber (435 gr.); .58 caliber (560 gr.)

SHOCK WAVE

Features: Polymer tip spire point bullet with sabot. Incorporates harder lead core with walls interlocked with the jacket for maximum weight retention and expansion. Available with spire point or bonded bullets
Available in: .45 caliber (200, 245 gr.); .50 caliber (200, 250, 250, 370, 300 gr.)

Winchester

BLACK POWDER PARTITION GOLD & SUPREME PLATINUM TIP

Features: Sabot loaded with Supreme Platinum Tip Hollow Point Bullets or Partition Gold bullet.
Available in: .50 caliber (260, 400 gr.)

Barnes Bullets

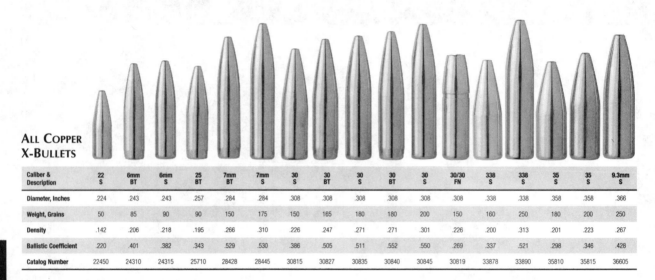

ALL COPPER X-BULLETS

Caliber & Description	22 S	6mm BT	6mm S	25 BT	7mm BT	7mm S	30 S	30 BT	30 S	30 BT	30 S	30/30 FN	338 S	338 S	35 S	35 S	9.3mm S
Diameter, Inches	.224	.243	.243	.257	.284	.284	.308	.308	.308	.308	.308	.308	.338	.338	.358	.358	.366
Weight, Grains	50	85	90	90	150	175	150	165	180	180	200	150	160	250	180	200	250
Density	.142	.206	.218	.195	.266	.310	.226	.247	.271	.271	.301	.226	.200	.313	.201	.223	.267
Ballistic Coefficient	.220	.401	.382	.343	.529	.530	.386	.505	.511	.552	.550	.269	.337	.521	.298	.346	.428
Catalog Number	22450	24310	24315	25710	28428	28445	30815	30827	30835	30840	30845	30819	33878	33890	35810	35815	36605

Caliber & Description	9.3mm S	375 S	405 Win S	416 S	458 S	458 Mag S	45/70 FN	45/70 FN	50 BT
Diameter, Inches	.366	.375	.411	.416	.284	.458	.458	.458	.510
Weight, Grains	286	210	300	300	300	350	250	300	647
Density	.305	.213	.254	.247	.204	.283	.170	.206	.355
Ballistic Coefficient	.468	.341	.313	.394	.340	.402	.172	.204	.592
Catalog Number	36615	37575	41178	41680	45802	45805	45831	45832	51064

LEGEND
BMG	– Browning Machinegun
BT	– Boattail
FB	– Flat Base
FMJ	– Full Metal Jacket
FN	– Flat Nose
RN	– Round Nose
S	– Spitzer
SP	– Soft Point

TRIPLE-SHOCK X-BULLET

Caliber & Description	22 FB	6mm BT	25 BT	25 FB	6.5mm FB	270 BT	270 BT	7mm BT	7mm FB	30 BT	30 BT	30 BT	30 FB	338 BT	338 FB
Diameter, Inches	.224	.243	.257	.257	.264	.277	.277	.284	.308	.308	.308	.308	.308	.338	.338
Weight, Grains	53	85	100	115	130	130	140	140	160	180	168	180	200	185	225
Density	.151	.206	.216	.249	.266	.242	.261	.248	.283	.226	.253	.271	.301	.231	.281
Ballistic Coefficient	.231	.333	.420	.429	.479	.466	.497	.5477	.508	.428	.476	.552	.550	.437	.482
Catalog Number	22443	24341	25742	25743	26442	27742	27744	28444	28446	30841	30844	30846	30848	33843	33846

HANDLOADING

Barnes Bullets

XLC COATED XBULLETS

Caliber & Description	22 HORNET BT	22 S	6mm S	25 BT	6.5mm S	6.5mm S	270 BT	7mm BT	7mm S	30 BT
Diameter, Inches	.224	.224	.243	.257	.4264	.264	.277	.284	.284	.308
Weight, Grains	45	53	95	100	120	140	130	140	160	130
Density	.128	.151	.230	.216	.246	.287	.242	.248	.283	.196
Ballistic Coefficient	.203	.231	.398	.420	.441	.522	.466	.477	.508	.374
Catalog Number	22452	22455	24355	25754	26451	26453	27754	28455	28458	30851

LEGEND
BMG	– Browning Machinegun
BT	– Boattail
FB	– Flat Base
FMJ	– Full Metal Jacket
FN	– Flat Nose
RN	– Round Nose
S	– Spitzer
SP	– Soft Point

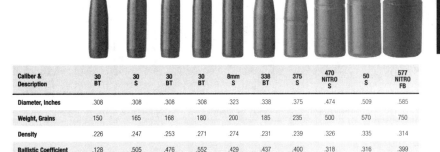

Caliber & Description	30 BT	30 S	30 BT	30 BT	8mm S	338 BT	375 S	470 NITRO S	50 S	577 NITRO FB
Diameter, Inches	.308	.308	.308	.308	.323	.338	.375	.474	.509	.585
Weight, Grains	150	165	168	180	200	185	235	500	570	750
Density	.226	.247	.253	.271	.274	.231	.239	.326	.335	.314
Ballistic Coefficient	.128	.505	.476	.552	.429	.437	.400	.318	.316	.399
Catalog Number	30854	30857	30856	30859	32312	33854	37553	47550	50957	58475

BURNER VARMIN-A-TOR BULLETS

Caliber & Description	22	22	6mm	6mm
Diameter, Inches	.224	.224	.243	.243
Weight, Grains	40	50	58	72
Density	.114	.142	.139	.174
Ballistic Coefficient	.175	.217	.191	.244
Catalog Number	22429	22439	24329	24339

Rather than loading everything at home before going to the range, build a loading box for your scale, powder measure and an inexpensive press. Then take some sized and primed brass, powder and bullets to the range for initial load development. This way you can throw charges and seat bullets as needed. No more pulling bullets from loads that did not work or shooting up loads made at home just to get rid of them.

Barnes Bullets

Copper-Jacket/Lead Core Original

Caliber & Description	6mm RNSP	348 WIN FNSP	348 WIN FNSP	357 WIN FNSP	38/55 FNSP	38/55 FNSP	401 WIN RNSP	40/65 WIN FNSP	45/70 SSP	45/70 FNSP	45/70 SSP	45/70 FNSP	458 MAG RNSP	50/110 WIN FNSP	50/110 WIN FNSP
Diameter, Inches	.243	.348	.348	.375	.375	.377	.406	.406	.458	.458	.458	.458	.458	.510	.510
Jacket, Inches	.030	.032	.032	.032	.032	.032	.032	.032	.032	.032	.032	.032	.049	.032	.032
Weight, Grains	115	220	250	255	255	255	250	250	300	300	400	400	600	300	450
Density	.290	.260	.295	.259	.259	.256	.217	.217	.204	.204	.272	.272	.409	.165	.247
Ballistic Coefficient	.322	.301	.327	.290	.290	.290	.241	.231	.291	.227	.389	.302	.454	.183	.274
Catalog Number	24330	34805	34810	375W20	38/5510	38/5520	40610	40611	457010	457020	457030	457040	45860	5011010	5011020

Solids

Caliber & Description	22 FB	22 FB	6mm BT	25 BT	7mm BT	7mm FB	30 FB	30 BT	30 FB	338 BT	9.3mm S	577 NITRO FN	50 BMG BT	50 BMG BT	50 BMG BT	50 BMG BT	600 NITRO FB
Diameter, Inches	.224	.224	.243	.257	.284	.284	.308	.308	.308	.338	.366	.585	.510	.510	.510	.510	.620
Weight, Grains	45	50	75	90	150	100	125	165	220	250	286	750	750	750	750	800	900
Density	.128	.142	.181	.195	.266	.177	.188	.248	.331	.313	.305	.313	.412	.412	.412	.439	.334
Ballistic Coefficient	.212	.235	.330	.324	.529	.343	.372	.481	.305	.326	.342	.351	1.070	—	—	1.095	.380
Catalog Number	22401	22402	24301	25720	28428	28401	30812	30822	30842	33825	36612	58520	510750A	510750	510750T	510800A	62020

HANDGUN BULLETS

XPB Pistol Bullets

Caliber & Description	9mm XPB	40 S&W XPB	44 MAG XPB	44 MAG XPB	45 LONG COLT XPB	44 ACP XPB	454 CASULL XPB	480 RUGER 475 LINBAUGH XPB	50 XPB	50 XPB	50 XPB
Diameter, Inches	.355	.400	.429	.429	.451	.451	.451	.475	.500	.500	.500
Weight, Grains	115	155	200	225	225	185	250	275	275	325	375
Density	.130	.138	.155	.175	.158	.130	.176	.174	.157	.186	.214
Ballistic Coefficient	.167	.189	.172	.195	.146	.167	.141	.155	.141	.228	.261
Catalog Number	35515	40055	42920	42922	45120	45185	45123	48010	50025	50026	50028

LEGEND

BMG	– Browning Machinegun
BT	– Boattail
FB	– Flat Base
FMJ	– Full Metal Jacket
FN	– Flat Nose
RN	– Round Nose
S	– Spitzer
SP	– Soft Point

HANDLOADING

Berger Bullets

Famous for their superior performance in benchrest matches, Berger bullets also include hunting designs. From .17 to .30, all Bergers feature 14 jackets with wall concentricity tolerance of .0003. Lead cores are 99.9% pure and swaged in dies to within .0001 of round. Berger's line includes several profiles: Low Drag, Very Low Drag, Length Tolerant and Maximum-Expansion, besides standard flat-base and standard boat-tail.

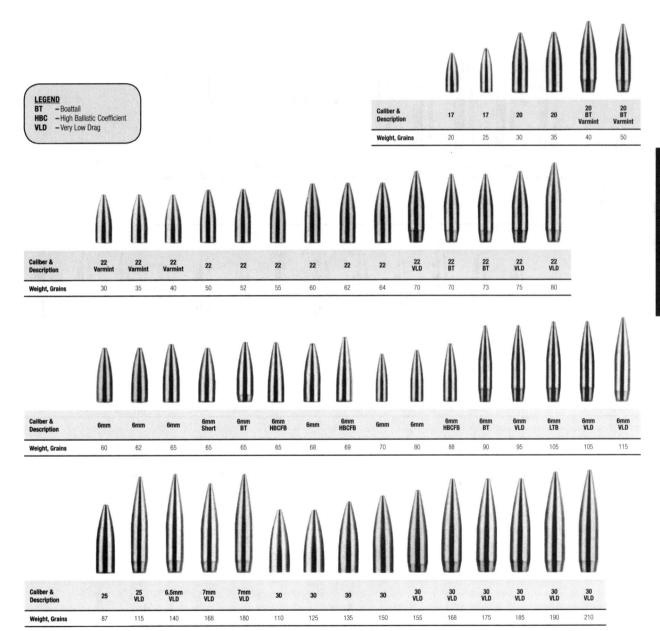

Caliber & Description	17	17	20	20	20 BT Varmint	20 BT Varmint
Weight, Grains	20	25	30	35	40	50

Caliber & Description	22 Varmint	22 Varmint	22 Varmint	22	22	22	22	22	22	22 VLD	22 BT	22 BT	22 VLD	22 VLD
Weight, Grains	30	35	40	50	52	55	60	62	64	70	70	73	75	80

Caliber & Description	6mm	6mm	6mm	6mm Short	6mm BT	6mm HBCFB	6mm	6mm HBCFB	6mm	6mm	6mm HBCFB	6mm BT	6mm VLD	6mm LTB	6mm VLD	6mm VLD
Weight, Grains	60	62	65	65	65	65	68	69	70	80	88	90	95	105	105	115

Caliber & Description	25	25 VLD	6.5mm VLD	7mm VLD	7mm VLD	30	30	30	30	30 VLD	30 VLD	30 VLD	30 VLD	30 VLD	30 VLD
Weight, Grains	87	115	140	168	180	110	125	135	150	155	168	175	185	190	210

Empty glucose test-strip containers are great for storing and organizing handloading items. They have a handy flip lid, and they're just right for small parts. You can label with a Sharpie or print a laser label for each one so it doesn't smear.

HANDLOADING

Hornady Bullets

The 200-grain .40 and 250- and 300-grain .45 bullets are meant for use in sabot sleeves. They feature a jacketed lead core with the signature red polymer tip. The SST has led also to Hornady's newest big game bullet, the Interbond. Essentially, it's an SST with a thicker jacket that has an inner "expansion control ring" near the front of the shank. Jacket and core are also bonded to ensure deep penetration and high weight retention. Though it typically opens to double its initial diameter, the Interbond bullet can be expected to hold 90 percent of its weight in the animal.

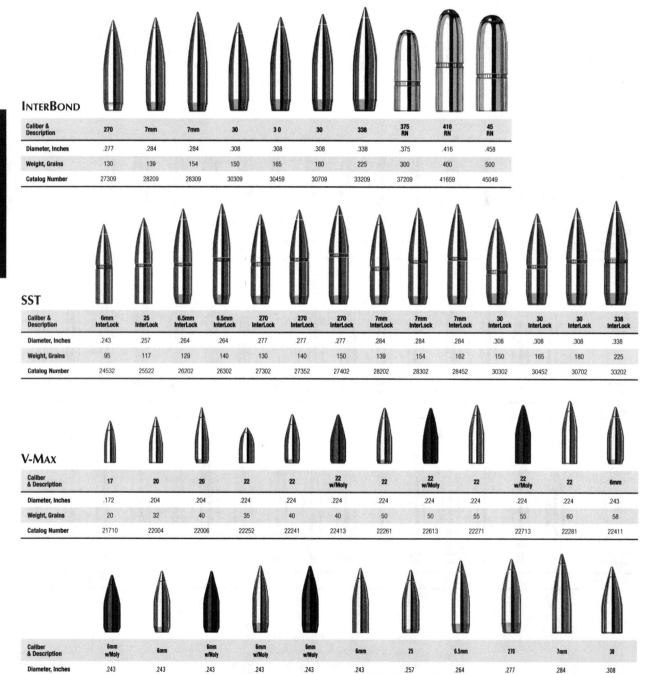

InterBond

Caliber & Description	270	7mm	7mm	30	3 0	30	338	375 RN	416 RN	45 RN
Diameter, Inches	.277	.284	.284	.308	.308	.308	.338	.375	.416	.458
Weight, Grains	130	139	154	150	165	180	225	300	400	500
Catalog Number	27309	28209	28309	30309	30459	30709	33209	37209	41659	45049

SST

Caliber & Description	6mm InterLock	25 InterLock	6.5mm InterLock	6.5mm InterLock	270 InterLock	270 InterLock	270 InterLock	7mm InterLock	7mm InterLock	7mm InterLock	30 InterLock	30 InterLock	30 InterLock	338 InterLock
Diameter, Inches	.243	.257	.264	.264	.277	.277	.277	.284	.284	.284	.308	.308	.308	.338
Weight, Grains	95	117	129	140	130	140	150	139	154	162	150	165	180	225
Catalog Number	24532	25522	26202	26302	27302	27352	27402	28202	28302	28452	30302	30452	30702	33202

V-Max

Caliber & Description	17	20	20	22	22	22 w/Moly	22	22 w/Moly	22	22 w/Moly	22	6mm
Diameter, Inches	.172	.204	.204	.224	.224	.224	.224	.224	.224	.224	.224	.243
Weight, Grains	20	32	40	35	40	40	50	50	55	55	60	58
Catalog Number	21710	22004	22006	22252	22241	22413	22261	22613	22271	22713	22281	22411

Caliber & Description	6mm w/Moly	6mm	6mm w/Moly	6mm w/Moly	6mm w/Moly	6mm	25	6.5mm	270	7mm	30
Diameter, Inches	.243	.243	.243	.243	.243	.243	.257	.264	.277	.284	.308
Weight, Grains	58	65	65	75	75	87	75	95	110	120	110
Catalog Number	24113	22415	24154	22420	24204	22440	22520	22601	22720	22810	23010

Hornady Bullets

Traditional Varmint

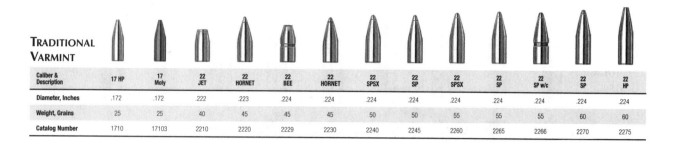

Caliber & Description	17 HP	17 Moly	22 JET	22 HORNET	22 BEE	22 HORNET	22 SPSX	22 SP	22 SPSX	22 SP	22 SP w/c	22 SP	22 HP
Diameter, Inches	.172	.172	.222	.223	.224	.224	.224	.224	.224	.224	.224	.224	.224
Weight, Grains	25	25	40	45	45	45	50	50	55	55	55	60	60
Catalog Number	1710	17103	2210	2220	2229	2230	2240	2245	2260	2265	2266	2270	2275

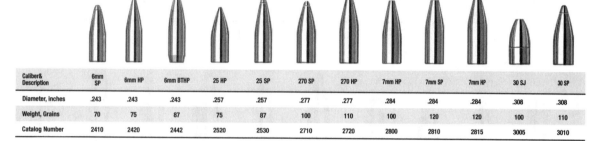

Caliber & Description	6mm SP	6mm HP	6mm BTHP	25 HP	25 SP	270 SP	270 HP	7mm HP	7mm SP	7mm HP	30 SJ	30 SP
Diameter, inches	.243	.243	.243	.257	.257	.277	.277	.284	.284	.284	.308	.308
Weight, Grains	70	75	87	75	87	100	110	100	120	120	100	110
Catalog Number	2410	2420	2442	2520	2530	2710	2720	2800	2810	2815	3005	3010

Traditional Hunting

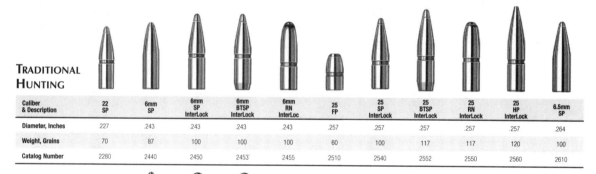

Caliber & Description	22 SP	6mm SP	6mm SP InterLock	6mm BTSP InterLock	6mm RN InterLoc	25 FP	25 SP InterLock	25 BTSP InterLock	25 RN InterLock	25 HP InterLock	6.5mm SP
Diameter, Inches	.227	.243	.243	.243	.243	.257	.257	.257	.257	.257	.264
Weight, Grains	70	87	100	100	100	60	100	117	117	120	100
Catalog Number	2280	2440	2450	2453	2455	2510	2540	2552	2550	2560	2610

Caliber & Description	6.5mm SP InterLock	6.5mm RN InterLock	6.5mm RN InterLock	6.5mm RN Carcano	270 SP InterLock	270 BTSP InterLock	270 SP InterLock	270 RN InterLock	7mm SP InterLock	7mm BTSP InterLock
Diameter, Inches	.264	.264	.264	.267	.277	.277	.277	.277	.284	.284
Weight, Grains	129	140	160	160	130	140	150	150	139	139
Catalog Number	2620	2630	2640	2645	2730	2735	2740	2745	2820	2825

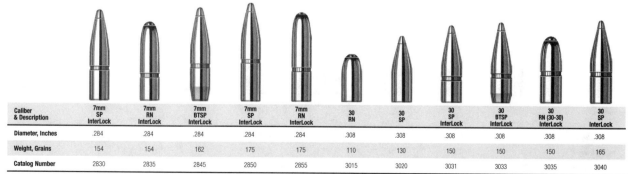

Caliber & Description	7mm SP InterLock	7mm RN InterLock	7mm BTSP InterLock	7mm SP InterLock	7mm RN InterLock	30 RN	30 SP	30 SP InterLock	30 BTSP InterLock	30 RN (30-30) InterLock	30 SP InterLock
Diameter, Inches	.284	.284	.284	.284	.284	.308	.308	.308	.308	.308	.308
Weight, Grains	154	154	162	175	175	110	130	150	150	150	165
Catalog Number	2830	2835	2845	2850	2855	3015	3020	3031	3033	3035	3040

Hornady Bullets

Traditional Hunting (CONT.)

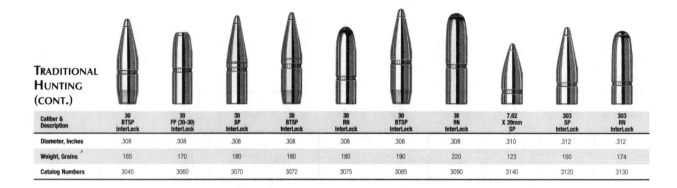

Caliber & Description	30 BTSP InterLock	30 FP (30-30) InterLock	30 SP InterLock	30 BTSP InterLock	30 RN InterLock	30 BTSP InterLock	30 RN InterLock	7.62 X 39mm SP	303 SP InterLock	303 RN InterLock
Diameter, Inches	.308	.308	.308	.308	.308	.308	.308	.310	.312	.312
Weight, Grains	165	170	180	180	180	190	220	123	150	174
Catalog Numbers	3045	3060	3070	3072	3075	3085	3090	3140	3120	3130

Caliber & Description	32 FP InterLock	8mm SP InterLock	8mm SP InterLock	8mm RN InterLock	8mm SP InterLock	338 SP InterLock	338 SP InterLock	338 SP InterLock	338RN InterLock	348 FP InterLock
Diameter, Inches	.321	.323	.323	.323	.323	.338	.338	.338	.338	.348
Weight, Grains	170	125	150	170	195	200	225	250	250	200
Catalog Number	3210	3230	3232	3235	3236	3310	3320	3335	3330	3410

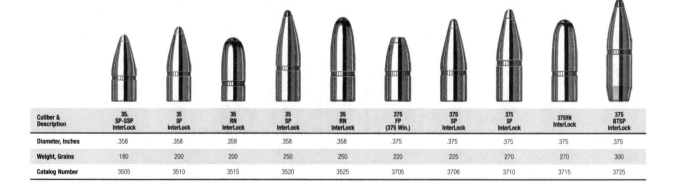

Caliber & Description	35. SP-SSP InterLock	35 SP InterLock	35 RN InterLock	35 SP InterLock	35 RN InterLock	375 FP (375 Win.)	375 SP InterLock	375 SP InterLock	375RN InterLock	375 BTSP InterLock
Diameter, Inches	.358	.358	.358	.358	.358	.375	.375	.375	.375	.375
Weight, Grains	180	200	200	250	250	220	225	270	270	300
Catalog Number	3505	3510	3515	3520	3525	3705	3706	3710	3715	3725

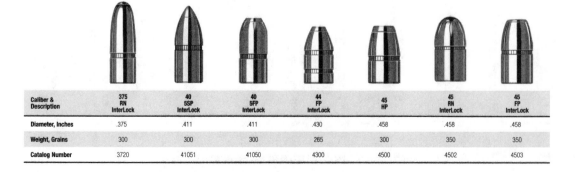

Caliber & Description	375 RN InterLock	40 5SP InterLock	40 5FP InterLock	44 FP InterLock	45 HP	45 RN InterLock	45 FP InterLock
Diameter, Inches	.375	.411	.411	.430	.458	.458	.458
Weight, Grains	300	300	300	265	300	350	350
Catalog Number	3720	41051	41050	4300	4500	4502	4503

Hornady Bullets

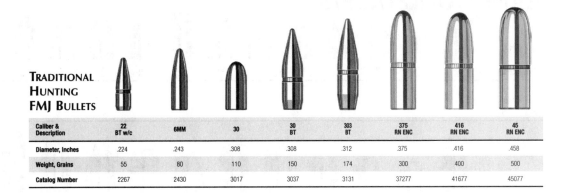

TRADITIONAL HUNTING FMJ BULLETS

Caliber & Description	22 BT w/c	6MM	30	30 BT	303 BT	375 RN ENC	416 RN ENC	45 RN ENC
Diameter, Inches	.224	.243	.308	.308	.312	.375	.416	.458
Weight, Grains	55	80	110	150	174	300	400	500
Catalog Number	2267	2430	3017	3037	3131	37277	41677	45077

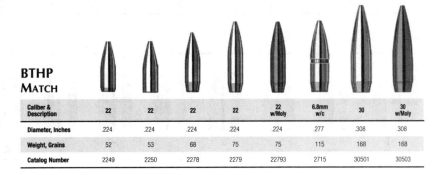

BTHP MATCH

Caliber & Description	22	22	22	22	22 w/Moly	6.8mm w/c	30	30 w/Moly
Diameter, Inches	.224	.224	.224	.224	.224	.277	.308	.308
Weight, Grains	52	53	68	75	75	115	168	168
Catalog Number	2249	2250	2278	2279	22793	2715	30501	30503

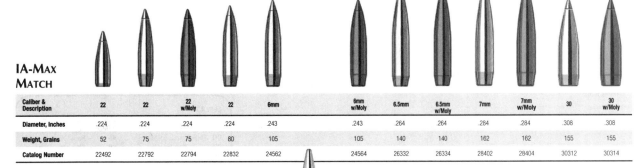

IA-MAX MATCH

Caliber & Description	22	22	22 w/Moly	22	6mm	6mm w/Moly	6.5mm	6.5mm w/Moly	7mm	7mm w/Moly	30	30 w/Moly
Diameter, Inches	.224	.224	.224	.224	.243	.243	.264	.264	.284	.284	.308	.308
Weight, Grains	52	75	75	80	105	105	140	140	162	162	155	155
Catalog Number	22492	22792	22794	22832	24562	24564	26332	26334	28402	28404	30312	30314

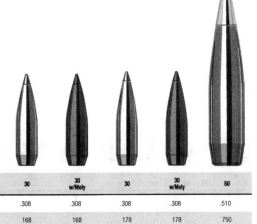

Caliber & Description	30	30 w/Moly	30	30 w/Moly	50
Diameter, Inches	.308	.308	.308	.308	.510
Weight, Grains	168	168	178	178	750
Catalog Number	30502	30504	30712	30714	5165

LEGEND

B	– Bulk	**LRN**	– Lead Round Nose
BT	– Boattail	**w/Moly**	– Moly-Coated
C/T	– Combat Target	**RN**	– Round Nose
CL	– Crimp Lock™	**SIL**	– Silhouette
ENC	– Encapsulated	**SJ**	– Short Jacket
FMJ	– Full Metal Jacket	**SP**	– Spire Point
FP	– Flat Point	**SST**	– Super Shock Tipped™
HBWC	– Hollow Base Wadcutter	**SSP**	– Single Shot Pistol
HP	– Hollow Point	**SWC**	– Semi-Wadcutter
HM	– Heavy Magnum™	**SX**	– Super Explosive
I	– InterLock™ Bullet	**VX**	– Varmint Express™
IB	– InterBond™ Bullet	**XTP**	– Extreme Terminal Performance™
JFP	– Jacketed Flat Point		
L	– Swaged Lead Bullet	**+P**	– Plus Pressure
LM	– Light Magnum™		

Hornady Bullets

HANDGUN BULLETS

XTP Bullets

Caliber & Description	30 HP	32 HP	32 HP	32 HP	9mm HP	9mm HP	9mm HP	9mm BTHP	38 HP	38 HP	38 FP	38 HP	38 HP	38 FP
Diameter, Inches	.308	.312	.312	.312	.355	.355	.355	.355	.357	.357	.357	.357	.357	.357
Weight, Grains	90	60	85	100	90	115	124	147	110	125	125	140	158	158
Catalog Number	31000	32010	32050	32070	35500	35540	35571	35580	35700	35710	35730	35740	35750	35780

Caliber & Description	38 HP	9 X 18mm HP	10mm HP	10mm HP	10mm HP	41 HP	44 HP	44 HP	44 HP	44 CL-SIL	44 HP	45 HP
Diameter, Inches	.357	.365	.400	.400	.400	.410	.430	.430	.430	.430	.430	.451
Weight, Grains	180	95	155	180	200	210	180	200	240	240	300	185
Catalog Number	35771	36500	40000	40040	40060	41000	44050	44100	44200	4425	44280	45100

Caliber & Description	45 HP	45 HP	45 MAG	45 HP	45 MAG	45 HP	475 MAG	475 MAG	50 MAG	50 FP
Diameter, Inches	.451	.451	.452	.452	.452	.452	.475	.475	.500	.500
Weight, Grains	200	230	240	250	300	300	325	400	350	500
Catalog Number	45140	45160	45220	45200	45235	45230	47500	47550	50100	50105

FMJ Bullets

Caliber & Description	9mm RN-ENC	9mm FP-ENC	9mm RN-ENC	45 SWC-ENC	45 CT-ENC	45 RN-ENC	45 FP-ENC
Diameter, Inches	.355	.355	.355	.451	.451	.451	.451
Weight, Grains	115	124	124	185	200	230	230
Catalog Number	35557	35567	35577	45137	45157	45177	45187

HAP Bullets

Caliber & Description	9mm	9mm	10mm	10mm	45
Diameter, Inches	.356	.356	.400	.400	.451
Weight, Grains	121	125	180	200	230
Catalog Number	35530B	35572B	40042B	40061B	45161B

LEGEND

B	– Bulk	LRN	– Lead Round Nose
BT	– Boattail	w/Moly	– Moly-Coated
C/T	– Combat Target	RN	– Round Nose
CL	– Crimp Lock™	SIL	– Silhouette
ENC	– Encapsulated	SJ	– Short Jacket
FMJ	– Full Metal Jacket	SP	– Spire Point
FP	– Flat Point	SST	– Super Shock Tipped™
HBWC	– Hollow Base Wadcutter	SSP	– Single Shot Pistol
HP	– Hollow Point	SWC	– Semi-Wadcutter
HM	– Heavy Magnum™	SX	– Super Explosive
I	– InterLock™ Bullet	VX	– Varmint Express™
IB	– InterBond™ Bullet	XTP	– Extreme Terminal Performance™
JFP	– Jacketed Flat Point		
L	– Swaged Lead Bullet	+P	– Plus Pressure
LM	– Light Magnum™		

Frontier/Lead Bullets

Caliber & Description	32 SWC	32 HBWC	38 FP Cowboy	38 HBWC	38 SWC	38 HP-SWC	38 LRN	44 FP Cowboy	44 FP Cowboy	44 SWC	44 HP-SWC	45 SWC	45 L-C/T	45 LRN	45 FP Cowboy
Diameter, Inches	.314	.314	.358	.358	.358	.358	.358	.427	.430	.430	.430	.452	.452	.452	.454
Weight, Grains	90	90	140	148	158	158	158	205	180	240	240	200	200	230	255
Catalog Number	10008	10028	10078	10208	10408	10428	10508	11208	11058	11108	11118	12108	12208	12308	12458

HANDLOADING

Lapua Bullets

Lapua precision bullets are made from the best raw materials and meet the toughest precision specifications. Each bullet is subject to visual inspection and tested with advanced measurement devices.

D46
The D46 bullet is manufactured to the strictest tolerances for concentricity and uniformity of shape and weight.

D166
The Lapua's unique D166 construction has remained the same since the late 1930s: superb accurate FMJBT bullet for 7.62x53R and 7.62x54R cartridges.

FMJ SPITZER
The FMJ S is exceptionally accurate. Ten rounds (S374 in .308 Win) from 100 meters easily achieve groupings less than 30 mm.

HOLLOW POINT
This HPCE bullet cuts a clean and easily distinguishable hole in your target. With ten rounds (G477 in .308 Win) fired at 100 meters, this bullet typically achieves groupings of under 25 mm— sometimes even less than 15 mm.

LOCK BASE
The construction of the Lock Base bullet makes it possible to use maximum pressures and achieve higher velocities without damaging the base of the bullet. FMJBT configuration reduces drag and provides a flatter trajectory.

MEGA
Mega is a soft-point bullet with a protective copper jacket with quadruple expansion on impact, which causes rapid energy transfer. Mega's lead alloy core achieves up to 97% weight retention.

SCENAR
The Scenar hollow-point, boat-tail bullet provides low drag and a superb ballistic coefficient. These bullets deliver superb performance at long ranges and benchrest shooting. All Scenar bullets are also available in a coated Silver Jacket version.

D46

D166

FMJ S

HOLLOW POINT

LOCK BASE

MEGA

SCENAR

HANDLOADING

Nosler Bullets

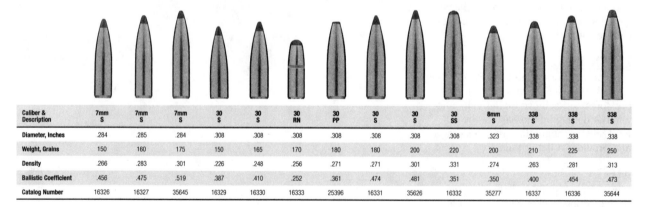

CUSTOM COMPETITION

Caliber & Description	22 HPBT	22 HPBT	22 HPBT	22 HPBT	6.5mm HPBT	30 HPBT	30 HPBT	45 JHP
Diameter, Inches	.220	.224	.224	.224	.264	.308	.308	.451
Weight, Grains	52	69	77	80	140	155	168	185
Density	.148	.196	.219	.228	.287	233	.253	.130
Ballistic Coefficient	.220	.305	.340	.415	.529	.450	.462	.142
Catalog Number	53294	17101 53065	22421 53064	25116 53080	26725	53155 53169	53164 53168	44847

PARTITION

Caliber & Description	22 S	6mm S	6mm S	6mm S	25 S	25 S	25 S	6.5mm S	6.5mm S	6.5mm S	270 S	270 S	270 S	270 SS
Diameter, Inches	.220	.243	.243	.243	.257	.257	.257	.264	.264	.264	.277	.277	.277	.277
Weight, Grains	60	85	95	100	100	115	20	100	125	140	130	140	150	160
Density	.171	.206	.230	.242	.216	.249	.260	.205	.256	.287	.242	.261	.279	.298
Ballistic Coefficient	.228	.315	.365	.384	.377	.389	.391	.326	.449	.490	.416	.432	.465	.434
Catalog Number	16316	16314	16315	35642	16317	16318	35643	16319	16320	16321	16322	35200	16323	16324

Caliber & Description	7mm S	7mm S	7mm S	30 S	30 S	30 RN	30 PP	30 S	30 S	30 SS	8mm S	338 S	338 S	338 S
Diameter, Inches	.284	.285	.284	.308	.308	.308	.308	.308	.308	.308	.323	.338	.338	.338
Weight, Grains	150	160	175	150	165	170	180	180	200	220	200	210	225	250
Density	.266	.283	.301	.226	.248	.256	.271	.271	.301	.331	.274	.263	.281	.313
Ballistic Coefficient	.456	.475	.519	.387	.410	.252	.361	.474	.481	.351	.350	.400	.454	.473
Catalog Number	16326	16327	35645	16329	16330	16333	25396	16331	35626	16332	35277	16337	16336	35644

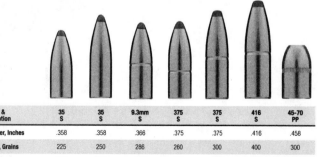

Caliber & Description	35 S	35 S	9.3mm S	375 S	375 S	416 S	45-70 PP
Diameter, Inches	.358	.358	.366	.375	.375	.416	.458
Weight, Grains	225	250	286	260	300	400	300
Density	.251	.279	.307	.264	.305	.330	.204
Ballistic Coefficient	.430	.446	.482	.314	.398	.390	.199
Catalog Number	44800	44801	44750	44850	44845	45200	45325

LEGEND

Type of Bullet		Type of Tip	
BT	– Boat Tail	PT	– Purple Tip
HP	– Hollow Point	BT	– Blue Tip
J	– Jacketed	BrT	– Brown Tip
PP	– Protected Point	BuT	– Buckskin Tip
RN	– Round Nose	GT	– Green Tip
S	– Spitzer	GuT	– Gunmetal Tip
SS	– Semi Spitzer	MT	– Maroon Tip
W	– Whelen	OT	– Olive Tip
		RT	– Red Tip
		SLT	– Soft Lead Tip
		YT	– Yellow Tip

Nosler Bullets

BALLISTIC TIP HUNTING

Caliber & Description	6mm SPT	6mm SPT	25 SBT	25 SBT	6.5mm SBrT	6.5mm SBrT	270 SYT	270 SYT	270 SYT	7mm SRT
Diameter, inches	.243	.243	.257	.257	.264	.264	.277	.277	.284	.284
Weight, Grains	90	95	100	115	100	120	130	140	150	120
Density	.218	.230	.216	.249	.205	.246	.242	.261	.279	.213
Ballistic Coefficient	.365	.379	.393	.453	.350	.458	.433	.456	.496	.417
Catalog Number	24090	24095	25100	25115	26100	26120	27130	27140	27150	28120

Caliber & Description	7mm SRT	7mm SRT	30 SRT	30 SRT	30 SRT	30 SRT	8mm SGuT	338 SMT	338 SMT	35 WBu	9.3mm SOT
Diameter, inches	.284	.284	.308	.308	.308	.308	.323	.338	.338	.358	.366
Weight, Grains	140	150	125	150	165	180	180	180	200	225	250
.248	.248	.266	.188	.226	.248	.271	.247	.225	.250	.251	.267
Ballistic Coefficient	.485	.493	.366	.435	.475	.507	.357	.372	.414	.421	.494
Catalog Number	28140	28150	30125	30150	30165	30180	32180	33180	33200	35225	36250

BALLISTIC TIP VARMINT

Caliber & Description	20 SRT	22 SOT	22 SOT	22 SOT	22 SOT	22 SOT	6mm SPT	6mm SPT	6mm SPT	25 SBT
Diameter, inches	.204	.224	.224	.227	.224	.224	.243	.243	.243	.257
Weight, Grains	32	40	40	45	50	55	55	70	80	85
Density	.110	.137	.114	.128	.142	.157	.133	.169	.194	.183
Ballistic Coefficient	.206	.239	.221	.144	.238	.267	.276	.310	.329	.329
Catalog Number	35216	52111	39510 39555	35487	39522 39557	39526 39560	24055 39565	39532 39570	24080	43004

CT BALLISTIC SILVERTIP HUNTING

Caliber & Description	6mm S	25 S	25 S	270 S	270 S	7mm S	7mm S	30 S	30 S	30 S	338 S
Diameter, inches	.243	.257	.257	.277	.277	.284	.284	.308	.308	.308	.338
Weight, Grains	95	85	115	130	150	140	150	150	168	180	200
Density	.230	.183	.249	.242	.279	.248	.266	.226	.253	.271	.250
Ballistic Coefficient	.379	.329	.453	.433	.496	.485	.493	.435	.490	.507	.414
Catalog Number	51040	51045	51050	51075	51100	51105	51110	51150	51160	51170	51200

Nosler Bullets

CT FAIL SAFE

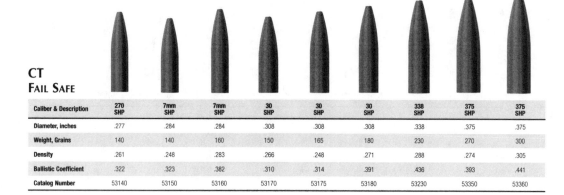

Caliber & Description	270 SHP	7mm SHP	7mm SHP	30 SHP	30 SHP	30 SHP	338 SHP	375 SHP	375 SHP
Diameter, inches	.277	.284	.284	.308	.308	.308	.338	.375	.375
Weight, Grains	140	140	160	150	165	180	230	270	300
Density	.261	.248	.283	.266	.248	.271	.288	.274	.305
Ballistic Coefficient	.322	.323	.382	.310	.314	.391	.436	.393	.441
Catalog Number	53140	53150	53160	53170	53175	53180	53230	53350	53360

ACCUBOND

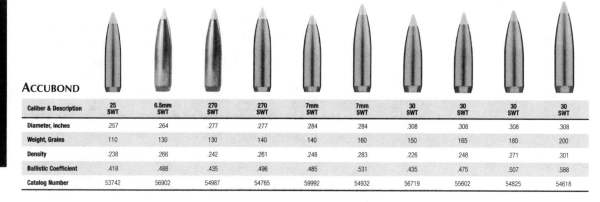

Caliber & Description	25 SWT	6.5mm SWT	270 SWT	270 SWT	7mm SWT	7mm SWT	30 SWT	30 SWT	30 SWT	30 SWT
Diameter, inches	.257	.264	.277	.277	.284	.284	.308	.308	.308	.308
Weight, Grains	110	130	130	140	140	160	150	165	180	200
Density	.238	.266	.242	.261	.248	.283	.226	.248	.271	.301
Ballistic Coefficient	.418	.488	.435	.496	.485	.531	.435	.475	.507	.588
Catalog Number	53742	56902	54987	54765	59992	54932	56719	55602	54825	54618

Caliber & Description	8mm SWT	338 SWT	338 SWT	338 SWT	35 SWT	9.3mm SWT	357 SWT
Diameter, inches	.323	.338	.338	.338	.358	.366	.375
Weight, Grains	200	180	200	225	225	250	260
Density	.274	.225	.250	.281	.251	.267	.264
Ballistic Coefficient	.379	.372	.414	.550	.423	.496	.473
Catalog Number	54374	57625	56382	54357	50712	59756	54413

LEGEND

Type of Bullet		Type of Tip	
BT	– Boat Tail	PT	– Purple Tip
HP	– Hollow Point	BT	– Blue Tip
J	– Jacketed	BrT	– Brown Tip
PP	– Protected Point	BuT	– Buckskin Tip
RN	– Round Nose	GT	– Green Tip
S	– Spitzer	GuT	– Gunmetal Tip
SS	– Semi Spitzer	MT	– Maroon Tip
W	– Whelen	OT	– Olive Tip
		RT	– Red Tip
		SLT	– Soft Lead Tip
		YT	– Yellow Tip

CT BALLISTIC SILVERTIP VARMINT

Caliber & Description	22 S	22 S	22 S	6mm S
Diameter, inches	.224	.224	.224	.243
Weight, Grains	40	50	55	55
Density	.114	.142	.157	.133
Ballistic Coefficient	.221	.238	.267	.276
Catalog Number	51005	51010	51031	51030

PARTITION-HG

Caliber & Description	38 HP	44 HP	45 HP	45 PP
Diameter, inches	.357	.429	.451	.451
Weight, Grains	180	250	260	300
Density	.202	.194	.182	.211
Ballistic Coefficient	.201	.200	.174	.199
Catalog Number	35180	44250	45260	45350

HANDLOADING

Nosler Bullets

HANDGUN BULLETS

SPORTING HANDGUN

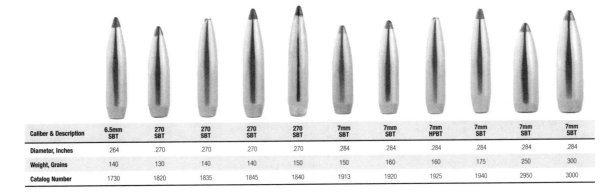

Caliber & Description	9mm JHP	38 JHP	10mm JHP	10mm JHP	41 JHP	44 JHP	44 JHP	44 JHP	44 JHP	44 Colt JHP
Diameter, Inches	.355	.357	.400	.400	.410	.429	.429	.429	.429	.451
Weight, Grains	115	158	135	150	210	200	240	240	300	250
Density	.130	.177	.121	.134	.178	.155	.186	.186	.233	.176
Ballistic Coefficient	.109	.182	.093	.106	.170	.151	.173	.177	.206	.177
Catalog Number	44848	44841	44852	44860	43012	44846	44842	44868	42069	43013

Sierra Bullets

BLITZ

Caliber & Description	204 Hornet	204 Hornet
Diameter, Inches	.200	.200
Weight, Grains	32	39
Catalog Number	1032	1039

BLITZKING

Caliber & Description	22 Hornet	22 Hornet	22 Hornet	6mm Hornet	6mm Hornet
Diameter, Inches	.224	.224	.224	.243	.243
Weight, Grains	40	50	55	55	70
Catalog Number	1440	1450	1455	1502	1507

GAMEKING

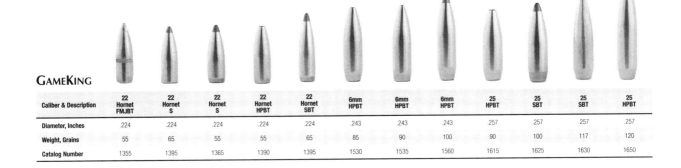

Caliber & Description	22 Hornet FMJBT	22 Hornet S	22 Hornet S	22 Hornet HPBT	22 Hornet SBT	6mm HPBT	6mm HPBT	6mm HPBT	25 HPBT	25 SBT	25 SBT	25 HPBT
Diameter, Inches	.224	.224	.224	.224	.224	.243	.243	.243	.257	.257	.257	.257
Weight, Grains	55	65	55	55	65	85	90	100	90	100	117	120
Catalog Number	1355	1395	1365	1390	1395	1530	1535	1560	1615	1625	1630	1650

Caliber & Description	6.5mm SBT	270 SBT	270 SBT	270 SBT	270 SBT	7mm SBT	7mm SBT	7mm HPBT	7mm SBT	7mm SBT	7mm SBT
Diameter, Inches	.264	.270	.270	.270	.270	.284	.284	.284	.284	.284	.284
Weight, Grains	140	130	140	140	150	150	160	160	175	250	300
Catalog Number	1730	1820	1835	1845	1840	1913	1920	1925	1940	2950	3000

Sierra Bullets

GameKing (cont.)

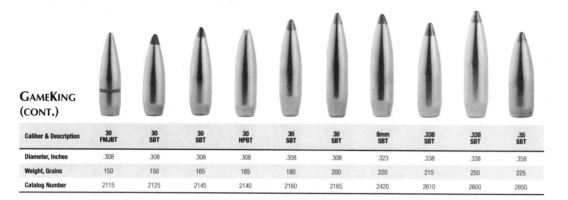

Caliber & Description	30 FMJBT	30 SBT	30 SBT	30 HPBT	30 SBT	30 SBT	8mm SBT	.338 SBT	.338 SBT	.35 SBT
Diameter, Inches	.308	.308	.308	.308	.308	.308	.323	.338	.338	.358
Weight, Grains	150	150	165	165	180	200	220	215	250	225
Catalog Number	2115	2125	2145	2140	2160	2165	2420	2610	2600	2850

MatchKing

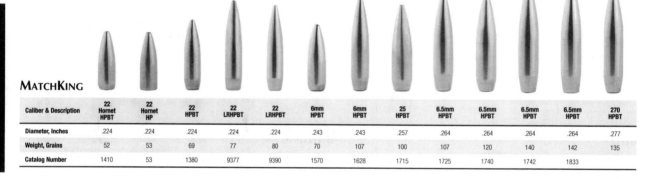

Caliber & Description	22 Hornet HPBT	22 Hornet HP	22 HPBT	22 LRHPBT	22 LRHPBT	6mm HPBT	6mm HPBT	25 HPBT	6.5mm HPBT	6.5mm HPBT	6.5mm HPBT	6.5mm HPBT	270 HPBT
Diameter, Inches	.224	.224	.224	.224	.224	.243	.243	.257	.264	.264	.264	.264	.277
Weight, Grains	52	53	69	77	80	70	107	100	107	120	140	142	135
Catalog Number	1410	53	1380	9377	9390	1570	1628	1715	1725	1740	1742	1833	

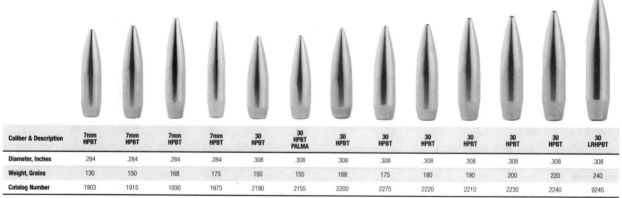

Caliber & Description	7mm HPBT	7mm HPBT	7mm HPBT	7mm HPBT	30 HPBT	30 HPBT PALMA	30 HPBT	30 HPBT	30 HPBT	30 HPBT	30 HPBT	30 HPBT	30 LRHPBT
Diameter, Inches	.284	.284	.284	.284	.308	.308	.308	.308	.308	.308	.308	.308	.308
Weight, Grains	130	150	168	175	150	155	168	175	180	190	200	220	240
Catalog Number	1903	1915	1930	1975	2190	2155	2200	2275	2220	2210	2230	2240	9245

Caliber & Description	303 S	8mm HPBT	338 HBPT	338 LRHPBT
Diameter, Inches	.308	.308	.308	.308
Weight, Grains	174	200	200	300
Catalog Number	2315	2415	2145	9300

LEGEND
BT	– Boattail
FMJ	– Full Metal Jacket
FN	– Flat Nose
FPJ	– Full Profile Jacket
HP	– Hollow Point
JFP	– Jacketed Flat Point
JHC	– Jacketed Hollow Cavity
JHP	– Jacketed Hollow Point
JSP	– Jacketed Soft Point
RN	– Round Nose
S	– Spitzer
SMP	– Semi-Pointed
SSP	– Single Shot Pistol

Sierra Bullets

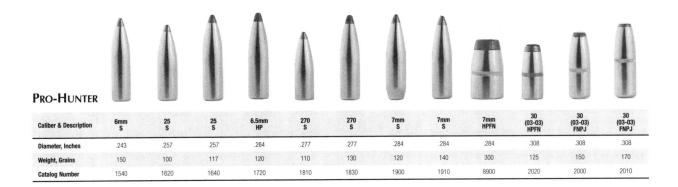

PRO-HUNTER

Caliber & Description	6mm S	25 S	25 S	6.5mm HP	270 S	270 S	7mm S	7mm S	7mm HPFN	30 (03-03) HPFN	30 (03-03) FNPJ	30 (03-03) FNPJ
Diameter, Inches	.243	.257	.257	.264	.277	.277	.284	.284	.284	.308	.308	.308
Weight, Grains	150	100	117	120	110	130	120	140	300	125	150	170
Catalog Number	1540	1620	1640	1720	1810	1830	1900	1910	8900	2020	2000	2010

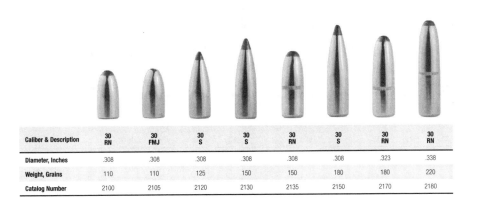

Caliber & Description	30 S	30 FMJ	30 S	30 S	30 RN	30 S	30 RN	30 RN
Diameter, Inches	.308	.308	.308	.308	.308	.308	.323	.338
Weight, Grains	110	110	125	150	150	180	180	220
Catalog Number	2100	2105	2120	2130	2135	2150	2170	2180

LEGEND
BT	– Boattail
FMJ	– Full Metal Jacket
FN	– Flat Nose
FPJ	– Full Profile Jacket
HP	– Hollow Point
JFP	– Jacketed Flat Point
JHC	– Jacketed Hollow Cavity
JHP	– Jacketed Hollow Point
JSP	– Jacketed Soft Point
RN	– Round Nose
S	– Spitzer
SMP	– Semi-Pointed
SSP	– Single Shot Pistol

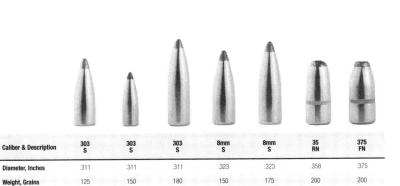

Caliber & Description	303 S	303 S	303 S	8mm S	8mm S	35 RN	375 FN
Diameter, Inches	.311	.311	.311	.323	.323	.358	.375
Weight, Grains	125	150	180	150	175	200	200
Catalog Number	2305	2300	2310	2400	2410	2800	2900l

VARMINTER

Caliber & Description	22 Hornet	22 Hornet	22 Hornet	22 Hornet
Diameter, Inches	.223	.223	.223	.223
Weight, Grains	40	45	40	45
Catalog Number	1100	1110	1200	1210

VARMINTER (CONT.)

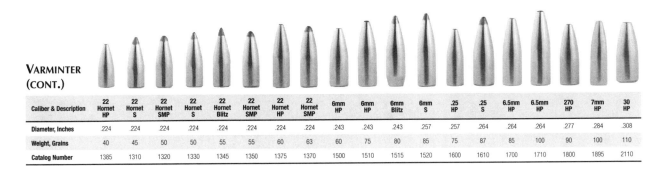

Caliber & Description	22 Hornet HP	22 Hornet S	22 Hornet SMP	22 Hornet S	22 Hornet Blitz	22 Hornet SMP	22 Hornet HP	22 Hornet SMP	6mm HP	6mm HP	6mm Blitz	6mm S	.25 HP	.25 S	6.5mm HP	6.5mm HP	270 HP	7mm HP	30 HP
Diameter, Inches	.224	.224	.224	.224	.224	.224	.224	.224	.243	.243	.243	.257	.257	.264	.264	.264	.277	.284	.308
Weight, Grains	40	45	50	50	55	55	60	63	60	75	80	85	75	87	85	100	90	100	110
Catalog Number	1385	1310	1320	1330	1345	1350	1375	1370	1500	1510	1515	1520	1600	1610	1700	1710	1800	1895	2110

Sierra Bullets

HANDGUN BULLETS

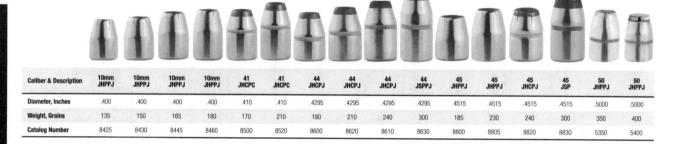

SPORTS MASTER

Caliber & Description	30 RN	32 JHCPJ	9mm JHPPJ	9mm JHPPJ	9mm JHPPJ	38 Blitz JHCPJ	38 JSP	38 JHCPJ	38 JHCPJ	38 JSP	38 JHCPJ	38 JHCPJ
Diameter, Inches	.224	.224	.224	.224	.224	.243	.243	.257	.264	.264	.264	.264
Weight, Grains	52	53	69	77	80	70	107	100	107	120	140	142
Catalog Number	1410	53	1380	9377	9390	1570	1628	1715	1725	1740	1742	1833

Caliber & Description	10mm JHPPJ	10mm JHPPJ	10mm JHPPJ	10mm JHPPJ	41 JHCPC	41 JHCPC	44 JHCPJ	44 JHCPJ	44 JHCPJ	44 JSPPJ	45 JHPPJ	45 JHPPJ	45 JHCPJ	45 JSP	50 JHPPJ	50 JHPPJ
Diameter, Inches	.400	.400	.400	.400	.410	.410	.4295	.4295	.4295	.4295	.4515	.4515	.4515	.4515	.5000	.5000
Weight, Grains	135	150	165	180	170	210	180	210	240	300	185	230	240	300	350	400
Catalog Number	8425	8430	8445	8460	8500	8520	8600	8620	8610	8630	8800	8805	8820	8830	5350	5400

TOURNAMENT MASTER

Caliber & Description	25 FMJ	32 FMJ	9mm FMJ	9mm FMJ	9mm FMJ	38 Match FMJ	9mm Makarov FPJ	10mm FPJ	44 Match FPJ	44 Match FPJ	45 Match FPJ	45 Match FPJ	45 Match FMJ
Diameter, Inches	.251	.312	.355	.355	.355	.357	.363	.400	.4295	.4295	.4515	.4515	.4515
Weight, Grains	50	71	95	115	125	180	100	190	220	250	185	200	230
Catalog Number	8000	8010	8105	8115	8120	8370	8210	8480	8605	8615	8810	8825	8815

SINGLE SHOT PISTOL

Caliber & Description	6mm SPT	7mm SPT
Diameter, Inches	.243	.284
Weight, Grains	80	130
7150	7150	7250

LEGEND
- **BT** – Boattail
- **FMJ** – Full Metal Jacket
- **FN** – Flat Nose
- **FPJ** – Full Profile Jacket
- **HP** – Hollow Point
- **JFP** – Jacketed Flat Point
- **JHC** – Jacketed Hollow Cavity
- **JHP** – Jacketed Hollow Point
- **JSP** – Jacketed Soft Point
- **RN** – Round Nose
- **S** – Spitzer
- **SMP** – Semi-Pointed
- **SSP** – Single Shot Pistol

Speer Bullets

BOAT TAIL BULLETS

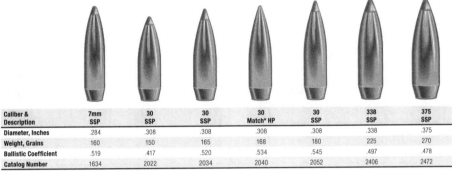

Caliber & Description	22 Match* HP	6mm SSP	6mm S SP	25 SHP	25 SSP	270 SSP	270 SSP	7mm SSP	7mm SSP	7mm Match* HP
Diameter, Inches	.224	.243	.243	.257	.257	.277	.277	.284	.284	.284
Weight, Grains	52	85	100	100	120	130	150	130	145	145
Ballistic Coefficient	.230	.380	.446	.393	.480	.412	.489	.424	.472	.468
Catalog Number	1036	1213	1220	1408	1410	1458	1604	1624	1628	1631

*Match bullets are not recommended for use on game animals.

Caliber & Description	7mm SSP	30 SSP	30 SSP	30 Match* HP	30 SSP	338 SSP	375 SSP
Diameter, Inches	.284	.308	.308	.308	.308	.338	.375
Weight, Grains	160	150	165	168	180	225	270
Ballistic Coefficient	.519	.417	.520	.534	.545	.497	.478
Catalog Number	1634	2022	2034	2040	2052	2406	2472

*Match bullets are not recommended for use on game animals.

GRAND SLAM

Caliber & Description	6mm SP	25 HCSP	6.5mm HCSP	270 HCSP	270 HCSP	7mm HCSP	7mm HCSP	7mm HCSP	30 HCSP	30 HCSP
Diameter, Inches	.243	.257	.264	.277	.277	.284	.284	.284	.308	.308
Weight, grains	100	120	140	130	150	145	160	175	150	165
BC	.327	.356	.385	.332	.378	.353	.389	.436	.295	.354
Part Number	1222	1415	1444	1465	1608	1632	1638	1643	2026	2038

Caliber & Description	30 HCSP	30 HCSP	30 HCSP	30 HCSP	30 HCSP	30 HCSP
Diameter, Inches	.308	.308	.338	.338	.358	.375
Weight, grains	180	200	225	250	250	285
BC	.374	.453	.382	.436	.353	.354
Part Number	2063	2212	2407	2408	2455	2473

Speer Bullets

HOT-COR BULLETS*

Caliber & Description	6mm SSP	6mm SSP	6mm SSP	25 SSP	25 SSP	25 SSP	6.5mm SSP	6.5mm SSP	270 SSP	270 SSP	7mm SSP	7mm SSP	7mm S SP	7mm Mag-Tip™ SP	7mm Mag-Tip™ SP
Diameter, Inches	.243	.243	.243	.257	.257	.257	.264	.264	.277	.277	.284	.284	.284	.284	.284
Weight, grains	80	90	105	87	100	120	120	140	130	150	130	145	160	160	175
BC	.325	.365	.424	.300	.334	.405	.392	.498	.383	.455	.368	.416	.504	.340	.382
Part Number	1211	1217	1229	1241	1405	1411	1435	1441	1459	1605	1623	1629	1635	1637	1641
Bullets/box	100	100	100	100	100	100	100	100	100	100	100	100	100	100	100
Bullet Construction	HC	HC	HC	HC	HC	HC	HC	HC	HC	HC	HC	HC	HC	HC	HC

Not recommended for lever-action rifles.

Caliber & Description	30 Carbine SP	30 Spire SP	30 FNSP	30 FNSP	30 RNSP	30 SSP	30 Mag-Tip™ SP	30 SSP	30 FNSP	30 RNSP	30 SSP	30 Mag-Tip™ SP	30 SSP	7.62x39 S SP
Diameter, Inches	.308	.308	.308	.308	.308	.308	.308	.308	.308	.308	.308	.308	.308	.310
Weight, Grains	110	110	130	150	150	150	150	165	170	180	180	180	200	123
Ballistic Coefficient	.136	.245	.213	.255	.235	.377	.278	.444	.298	.312	.441	.349	.478	.283
Catalog Number	1845	1855	2007	2011	2017	2023	2025	2035	2041	2047	2053	2059	2211	2213

Not recommended for lever-action rifles.

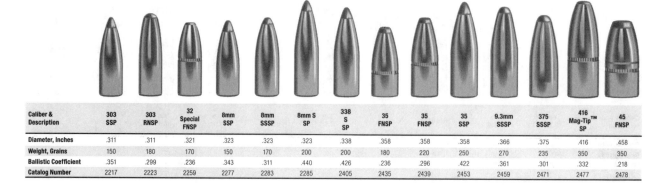

Caliber & Description	303 SSP	303 RNSP	32 Special FNSP	8mm SSP	8mm SSSP	8mm S SP	338 S SP	35 FNSP	35 FNSP	35 SSP	9.3mm SSSP	375 SSSP	416 Mag-Tip™ SP	45 FNSP
Diameter, Inches	.311	.311	.321	.323	.323	.323	.338	.358	.358	.358	.366	.375	.416	.458
Weight, Grains	150	180	170	150	170	200	200	180	220	250	270	235	350	350
Ballistic Coefficient	.351	.299	.236	.343	.311	.440	.426	.236	.296	.422	.361	.301	.332	.218
Catalog Number	2217	2223	2259	2277	2283	2285	2405	2435	2439	2453	2459	2471	2477	2478

JACKETED BULLETS

Caliber & Description	22 Spire SP	22 SSP	22 SSP	22 HP	22 SSP	22 SSP (cann)	22 SSSP	6mm HP	25 HP	270 HP	7mm HP	30 Plinker® SP	30 HP	30 HP	45 FNSP
Diameter, Inches	.224	.224	.224	.224	.224	.224	.224	.243	.257	.277	.284	.308	.308	.308	.458
Weight, Grains	40	45	50	52	55	55	70	75	100	100	115	100	110	130	400
Ballistic Coefficient	.144	.143	.207	.168	.212	.212	.219	.192	.263	.201	.250	.144	.128	.244	.259
Catalog Number	1017	1023	1029	1035	1047	1049	1053	1205	1407	1447	1617	1805	1835	2005	2479

HANDLOADING

Speer Bullets

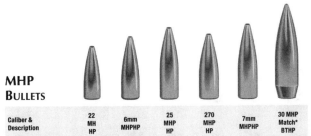

MHP BULLETS

Caliber & Description	22 MH HP	6mm MHPHP	25 MHP HP	270 MHP HP	7mm MHPHP	30 MHP Match* BTHP
Diameter, Inches	.224	.243	.257	.277	.284	.308
Weight, grains	50	70	87	90	110	168
Ballistic Coefficient	.234	.296	.344	.310	.398	.541
Catalog Number	1031	1207	1247	1457	1615	2039

TNT BULLETS

Caliber & Description	22 Hornet TNT	22 TNT HP	22 TNT HP Hi-Vel.	6mm TNT HP	25 TNT HP	6.5mm TNT HP	270 TNT HP	7mm TNT HP	30 TNT HP
Diameter, Inches	.224	.224	.224	.243	.257	.264	.277	.284	.308
Weight, grains	33	50	55	70	87	90	90	110	125
Ballistic Coefficient	.080	.228	.233	.279	.337	.281	.303	.384	.341
Catalog Number	1014	1030	1032	1206	1246	1445	1446	1616	1986

SPECIAL PURPOSE BULLETS*

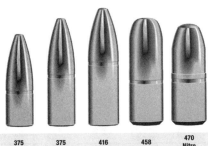

Caliber & Description	218 Bee FNSP	22 FMJ BT	22 FMJ BT	25-20 Win FNSP	7-30 Waters FNSP	30 Carbine TMJ	30 FMJ BT	32-20 Win FNHP	45 UCHP
Diameter, Inches	.224	.224	.224	.257	.284	.308	.308	.312	.458
Weight, grains	46	55	62	75	130	110	150	100	300
Ballistic Coefficient	.087	.269	.307	.135	.257	.179	.425	.167	.206
Catalog Number	1024	1044	1050	1237	1625	1846	2018	3981	2482

Recommended for twist rates of 1 in 10" or faster.

TROPHY BONDED BEAR CLAW

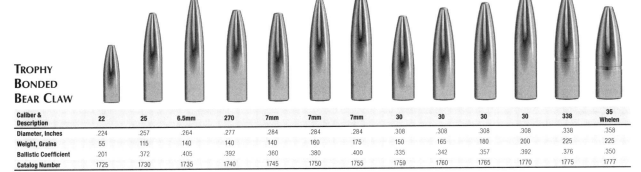

Caliber & Description	22	25	6.5mm	270	7mm	7mm	7mm	30	30	30	30	338	35 Whelen
Diameter, Inches	.224	.257	.264	.277	.284	.284	.284	.308	.308	.308	.308	.338	.358
Weight, Grains	55	115	140	140	140	160	175	150	165	180	200	225	225
Ballistic Coefficient	.201	.372	.405	.392	.360	.380	.400	.335	.342	.357	.392	.376	.350
Catalog Number	1725	1730	1735	1740	1745	1750	1755	1759	1760	1765	1770	1775	1777

Caliber & Description	375 TBBC	375 TBBC	416 TBBC	458 TBBC	470 Nitro Express TBBC
Diameter, Inches	.375	.375	.416	.458	.474
Weight, Grains	250	300	400	500	500
Ballistic Coefficient	.286	.336	.374	.340	.330
Catalog Number	1778	1780	1785	1790	1795

LEGEND

BT	— Boat Tail	S	— Spitzer
FB	— Fusion Bonded	SS	— Semi-Spitzer
FMJ	— Full Metal Jacket	SB™	— For Short-Barrel Firearms
FN	— Flat Nose	SP	— Soft Point
GD	— Gold Dot®	TMJ®	— Encased-Core Full Jacket
HC	— Hot-Cor®	RN	— Round Nose
HP	— Hollow Point	SWC	— Semi-Wadcutter
L	— Lead	UC	— Uni-Cor®
MHP™	— Molybdenum Disulfide Impregnated	WC	— Wadcutter

Speer Bullets

HANDGUN BULLETS

GOLD DOT BULLETS

Caliber & Description	25 Auto HP	32 Auto HP	380 Auto HP	9mm Luger HP	9mm Luger HP	9mm Luger HPSB	9mm Luger HP	357 SIG/38 Super HP	38 Special HPSB	38 Spl 357 Mag HPSB	38 Spl 357 Mag HPSB	357 Mag HP	357 Mag HP	357 Mag SP
Diameter, Inches	.251	.312	.355	.355	.355	.355	.355	.355	.357	.357	.357	.357	.357	.357
Weight, Grains	35	60	90	115	124	124	147	125	110	135	147	125	158	170
Ballistic Coefficient	.091	.118	.101	.125	.134	—	.164	.141	.117	.141	.153	.140	.168	.185
Catalog Number	3985	3986	3992	3994	3998	4000	4002	4360	4009	4014	4016	4012	4215	4230

Caliber & Description	9x18mm Makarov HP	40/10mm HP	40/10mm HP	40/10mm HP	41 Mag HP	44 Special HP	44 Mag HP	44 Mag HP	44 Mag SP	44 Mag SP
Diameter, Inches	.364	.400	.400	.400	.410	.429	.429	.429	.429	.429
Weight, Grains	90	155	165	180	210	200	210	240	240	270
Ballistic Coefficient	.107	.123	.138	.143	.183	.145	.154	.175	.175	.193
Catalog Number	3999	4400	4397	4406	4430	4427	4428	4455	4456	4461

Caliber & Description	45 Auto Gold Dot HP	45 Auto Gold Dot HP	45 Auto Gold Dot HP	45 Auto Gold Dot HP SB	45 Colt Gold Dot HP	454 Casull Gold Dot HP	480 Ruger Gold Dot HP	480 Ruger Gold Dot SP	475 Linebaugh® Gold Dot SP†	50 Action Express Gold Dot HP
Diameter, Inches	.451	.451	.451	.451	.452	.452	.475	.475	.475	.500
Weight, Grains	185	200	230	230	250	300	275	325	400	300
Ballistic Coefficient	.109	.138	.143	—	.165	.233	.162	.191	.242	.155
Catalog Number	4470	4478	4483	—	4484	3974	3973	3978	3976	4493

†=475 Linebaugh is a registered trademark of Timothy B. Sundles

JACKETED BULLETS

Caliber & Description	32 Revolver JHP	32 Revolver JHP	38 Spl 357 Magnum SWC-JHP	41 Magnum SWC-JHP	41 Magnum SWC-JSP	44 Magnum JHP	44 Magnum SWC-JHP	44 Magnum SWC-JSP	44 Magnum JHP	44 Magnum JSP	45 Colt JHP	45 Colt JHP
Diameter, Inches	.312	.312	.357	.410	.410	.429	.429	.429	.429	.429	.451	.451
Weight, grains	85	100	146	200	220	200	225	240	240	240	225	260
BC	.121	.167	.159	.113	.137	.122	.146	.157	.165	.164	.169	.183
Part Number	3987	3981	4205	4405	4417	4425	4435	4447	4453	4457	4479	4481
Bullets/box	100	100	100	100	100	100	100	100	100	100	100	100
Bullet Construction	C	C	C	C	C	C	C	C	C	C	C	C

HANDLOADING

Uni-Cor Bullets

Caliber & Description	25 Auto TMJ	380 Auto TMJ	9mm Luger TMJ	9mm Luger UCSP	9mm Luger TMJ Match	9mm Luger TMJ	357 SIG 38 Super TMJ	38 Spl 357 Magnum UCHP	38 Spl 357 Magnum UCSP	38 Spl 357 Magnum UCHP	38 Spl 357 Magnum TMJ	38 Spl 357 Magnum UCHP	357 Magnum UCHP	357 Magnum UCSP	357 Magnum TMJ	357 Magnum Sil. Match TMJ	357 Magnum Sil. Match TMJ
Diameter, Inches	.251	.355	.355	.355	.355	.355	.355	.357	.357	.357	.357	.357	.357	.357	.357	.357	.357
Weight, grains	50	95	115	124	130	147	125	110	125	125	140	125	158	158	158	180	200
BC	.110	.131	.151	.115	.165	.188	.147	.113	.129	.129	.146	.145	.163	.164	.173	.230	.236
Part Number	3982	4001	3995	3997	4010	4006	4362	4007	4011	4013	4015	4203	4211	4217	4207	4229	4231
Bullets/box	100	100	100	100	100	100	100	100	100	100	100	100	100	100	100	100	100
Bullet Construction	UC	UC	UC	UC	UC	UC	UC	UC	UC	UC	UC	UC	UC	UC	UC	UC	UC

Caliber & Description	9x18 Makarov TMJ	40/10mm TMJ	40/10mm TMJ	40/10mm TMJ	40/10mm TMJ	44 Magnum Sil. Match TMJ	44 Magnum UCSP	45 Auto SWC Match TMJ	45 Auto FN TMJ	45 Auto SWC Match TMJ	45 Auto FN TMJ	45 Auto RN TMJ	45 Colt UCSP	50 Action Express FN TMJ	50 Action Express UCHP
Diameter	.364	.400	.400	.400	.400	.429	.429	.451	.451	.451	.451	.451	.451	.500	.500
Weight	95	155	165	180	200	240	300	185	185	200	200	230	300	300	325
BC	.127	.125	.135	.143	.168	.206	.213	.090	.094	.128	.102	.153	.199	.157	.169
Part No	4375	4399	4410	4402	4403	4459	4463	4473	4476	4475	4471	4480	4485	4490	4495
Bullets/box	100	100	100	100	100	100	50	100	100	100	100	100	100	50	50
Construction	UC	UC	UC	UC	UC	UC	UC	UC	UC	UC	UC	UC	UC	UC	UC

Lead Handgun Bullets

Caliber & Description	32 S&W HBWC	9mm Luger RN	38 Bevel-Base WC	38 Double-Ended WC	38 Hollow-Base WC	38 SWC	38 SWC HP	38 RN	44 SWC	45 Auto SWC	45 Auto RN	45 Colt SWC
Diameter, Inches	.314	.356	.358	.358	.358	.358	.358	.358	.430	.452	.452	.452
Weight, grains	98	125	148	148	148	158	158	158	240	200	230	250
Part No	–	4601	4605	–	4617	4623	4627	4647	4660	4677	4690	4683
Box Count	–	100	100	–	100	100	100	100	100	100	100	100
Bulk Part No.	4600	4602	4606	4611	4618	4624	4628	4648	4661	4678	4691	4684
Bulk Count	1000	500	500	500	500	500	500	500	500	500	500	500

LEGEND

BT	— Boat Tail	S	— Spitzer
FB	— Fusion Bonded	SS	— Semi-Spitzer
FMJ	— Full Metal Jacket	SB™	— For Short-Barrel Firearms
FN	— Flat Nose	SP	— Soft Point
GD	— Gold Dot®	TMJ®	— Encased-Core Full Jacket
HC	— Hot-Cor®	RN	— Round Nose
HP	— Hollow Point	SWC	— Semi-Wadcutter
L	— Lead	UC	— Uni-Cor®
MHP™	— Molybdenum Disulfide Impregnated	WC	— Wadcutter

Swift Bullets

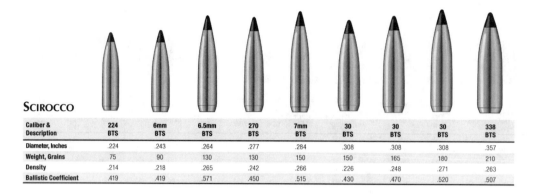

SCIROCCO

Caliber & Description	224 BTS	6mm BTS	6.5mm BTS	270 BTS	7mm BTS	30 BTS	30 BTS	30 BTS	338 BTS
Diameter, Inches	.224	.243	.264	.277	.284	.308	.308	.308	.357
Weight, Grains	75	90	130	130	150	150	165	180	210
Density	.214	.218	.265	.242	.266	.226	.248	.271	.263
Ballistic Coefficient	.419	.419	.571	.450	.515	.430	.470	.520	.507

A-FRAME

Caliber & Description	25 SS	25 SS	6.5mm SS	6.5mm SS	270 SS	270 SS	270 SS	7mm SS	7mm SS	7mm SS	30 SS	30 SS	30 SS
Diameter, Inches	.257	.257	.264	.264	.277	.277	.277	.284	.284	.284	.308	.308	.308
Weight, Grains	100	120	120	140	130	140	150	140	160	175	165	180	200
Density	.216	.260	.246	.287	.242	.261	.279	.248	.283	.310	.248	.271	.301
Ballistic Coefficient	.318	.382	.344	.401	.323	.414	.444	.335	.450	.493	.367	.400	.444

THE SWIFT BULLET COMPANY

The Scirocco rifle bullet starts with a tough, pointed polymer tip that reduces air resistance, prevents tip deformation, and blends into the radius of its secant ogive nose section. A moderate 15-degree boat-tail base reduces drag and eases seating. The thick base prevents bullet deformation during launch. Scirocco's shape creates two other significant advantages. One is an extremely high ballistic coefficient. The other, derived from the secant ogive nose, is a comparatively long bearing surface for a sharply pointed bullet, a feature that improves rotational stability.

Inside, the Scirocco has a bonded-core construction with a pure lead core encased in a tapered, progressively thickening jacket of pure copper. Pure copper was selected because it is more malleable and less brittle than less expensive gilding metal. Both jacket and core are bonded by Swift's proprietary process so that the bullet expands without break-up as if the two parts were the same metal. In tests, the bullet mushroomed effectively at velocities as low as 1440 fps, yet stayed together at velocities in excess of 3,000 fps, with over 70 percent weight retention.

Swift A-Frame bullet, with its midsection wall of copper, is still earning praise for its deep-driving dependability in tough game. Less aerodynamic than the Scirocco, it produces a broad mushroom while carrying almost all its weight through muscle and bone. Available in a wide range of weights and diameters, it is also a bonded-core bullet.

HANDLOADING

Swift Bullets

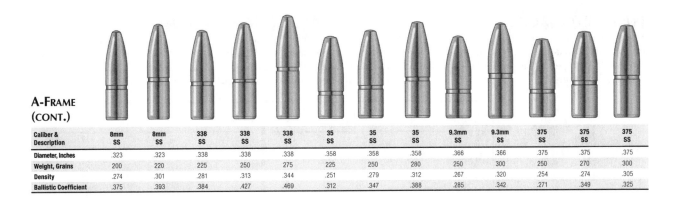

A-FRAME (CONT.)

Caliber & Description	8mm SS	8mm SS	338 SS	338 SS	338 SS	35 SS	35 SS	35 SS	9.3mm SS	9.3mm SS	375 SS	375 SS	375 SS
Diameter, Inches	.323	.323	.338	.338	.338	.358	.358	.358	.366	.366	.375	.375	.375
Weight, Grains	200	220	225	250	275	225	250	280	250	300	250	270	300
Density	.274	.301	.281	.313	.344	.251	.279	.312	.267	.320	.254	.274	.305
Ballistic Coefficient	.375	.393	.384	.427	.469	.312	.347	.388	.285	.342	.271	.349	.325

Caliber & Description	416 SS	416 SS	404 SS	458 FN	458 FN	458 SS	458 SS	470 AFRN
Diameter, Inches	.416	.416	.423	.458	.458	.458	.458	.475
Weight, Grains	350	400	400	350	400	450	500	500
Density	.289	.330	.319	.238	.72	.307	.341	.329
Ballistic Coefficient	.321	.367	.375	.170	.258	.325	.361	.364

LEGEND
BT – Boattail
FN – Flat Nose
HP – Hollow Point
RN – Round Nose
S – Spitzer
SS – Semi-Spitzer

HANDGUN BULLETS

A-FRAME

Caliber & Description	44 HP	444 HP	44 HP	45 HP	45 HP	45 HP
Diameter, Inches	.416	.416	.423	.458	.458	.458
Weight, Grains	350	400	400	350	400	450
Density	.289	.330	.319	.238	.72	.307
Ballistic Coefficient	.321	.367	.375	.170	.258	.325

After charging cases with powder, it's a good idea to check all powder levels to be sure you have not double-charged a case or missed charging a case.

Woodleigh Premium Bullets

FULL METAL JACKET

Fashioned from gilding metal-clad steel 2mm thick, jackets on FMJ bullets are heavy at the nose for extra impact resistance. The jacket then tapers toward the base to assist rifling engraving.

WELDCORE SOFT NOSE

A product of Australia, Woodleigh Weldcore Soft Nose bullets are made from 90/100 gilding metal (90% copper; 10% zinc) 1.6 mm thick. Maximum retained weight is obtained by fusing the pure lead to the gilding metal jacket.

**98% & 95%
RETAINED WEIGHT
300 WIN MAG 180GR PP**

**458 X 500GN SN
RECOVERED FROM BUFFALO**

**270 WIN 150GN PP
86% RETAINED WEIGHT**

**94% RETAINED WEIGHT
300 WIN MAG 180GR PP**

**500/465 RECOVERED
FROM BUFFALO**

Caliber Diameter	Type	Weight Grain	SD	BC
700 Nitro	SN	1000	.292	.340
.700"	FMJ	1000	.292	.340
600 Nitro	SN	900	.334	.371
.620"	FMJ	900	.334	.334
577 Nitro	SN	750	.313	.346
.585"	FMJ	750	.313	.351
	SN	650	.271	.292
	FMJ	650	.271	.292
577 B.P. .585"	SN	650	.271	.320
500 Nitro	SN	570	.313	.474
.510"	FMJ	570	.313	.434
500 B.P. .510"	SN	440	.242	.336
500	PP	535	.304	.460
Jeffery	SN	535	.304	.460
.510"	FMJ	535	.304	.422
505	PP	600	.336	.450
Gibbs	SN	525	.294	.445
.505"	FMJ	525	.294	.408
	FMJ	600	.366	.450
475 No2	SN	500	.300	.420
Jeffery .488"	FMJ	500	.300	.416
475 No2	SN	480	.303	.400
.483"	FMJ	480	.303	.410
476 W.R.	SN	520	.328	.420
.476"	FMJ	520	.328	.455
475 Nitro	SN	480	.227	.307
.476"	FMJ	480	.227	.257
470 Nitro	SN	500	.318	.411
.474"	FMJ	500	.318	.410
465 Nitro	SN	480	.318	.410
.468"	FMJ	480	.318	.407
450 Nitro	SN	480	.327	.419
.458"	FMJ	480	.327	.410
458 Mag.	SN	500	.341	.430
.458"	SN	550	.375	.480
	FMJ	500	.341	.405
	FMJ	550	.375	.426
	PP	400	.272	.420
	RN	350	.238	.305
45/70 .458"	FN	405	.276	.250
11.3x62 Schuler .440"	SN	401	.296	.411
425 W.R.	SN	410	.310	.344
.435"	FMJ	410	.310	.336
404	SN	400	.319	.354
Jeffery	FMJ	400	.319	.358
.423"	SN	350	.279	.357
10.75x68mm	SN	347	.277	.355
.423"	FMJ	347	.277	.307
416	SN	410	.338	.375
Rigby	FMJ	410	.338	.341
.416"	PP	340	.281	.425
	SN	450	.372	.402
450/400	SN	400	.338	.384
Nitro .411" or .408"	FMJ	400	.338	.433
.408	SN	400	.338	.384
.408	FMJ	400	.338	.433

Caliber Diameter	Type	Weight Grain	SD	BC
375 Mag.	PP	235	.239	.331
.375"	RN	270	.275	.305
	SP	270	.275	.380
	PP	270	.275	.352
	RN	300	.305	.340
	SP	300	.305	.425
	PP	300	.305	.420
	FMJ	300	.305	.307
	RN	350	.354	.354
	PP	350	.354	.440
	FMJ	350	.354	.372
405 Win., .411"	SN	300	.254	.194
9.3mm	SN	286	.305	.331
.366"	PP	286	.305	.381
	FMJ	286	.305	.324
	SN	250	.267	.296
360 No2	SN	320	.341	.378
.366"	FMJ	320	.341	.362
	PP	320	.343	.428
358 Cal	SN	225	.250	.277
.358"	FMJ	225	.250	.298
	SN	250	.285	.365
	SN	310	.346	.400
	FMJ	310	.346	.378
338 Mag	PP	225	.281	.425
.338"	SN	250	.313	.332
	PP	250	.313	.470
	FMJ	250	.313	.326
	SN	300	.375	.416
	FMJ	300	.375	.398
333	SN	250	.328	.400
Jeffery	SN	300	.386	.428
.333"	FMJ	300	.386	.419
318 W.R.	SN	250	.328	.420
.330"	FMJ	250	.328	.364
8mm	SN	196	.268	.370
.323"	SN	220	.302	.363
	SN	250	.343	.389
8X57	SN	200	.282	.370
303	SN	174	.257	.342
British .312	PP	215	.316	.359
308 Cal	FMJ	220	.331	.359
.308"	RN	220	.331	.367
	PP	180	.273	.376
	PP	165	.250	.320
	PP	150	.226	.301
Win Mag.	PP	180	.273	.435
	PP	200	.301	.450
275 H&H	PP	160	.275	.474
.287"	PP	175	.301	.518
7mm	PP	140	.247	.436
.284"	PP	160	.282	.486
	PP	175	.312	.530
270 Win	PP	130	.241	.409
.277"	PP	150	.278	.463

SP = Semi-point
PP = Protected Point
FN = Flat Nose
RN = Round Nose
FMJ = Full Metal Jacket
All PP, FN, RN, SP, SN bullets are Weldcore Softnose

Accurate Powder

	NG*	Avgerage Length/Thickness in./mm.	Avgerage Diameter inches	Avgerage Diameter millimeters	Bulk Density gram/cc	VMD cc/grain	Comparative Powders*** Ball	Comparative Powders*** Extruded
BALL PROPELLANTS - Handguns/Shotshell								
No. 2 Imp.	14.0	—	0.018	0.457	0.650	0.100	WIN 231	Bullseye
No. 5	18.0	—	0.027	0.686	0.950	0.068	WIN 540	—
No. 7	12.0	—	0.012	0.305	0.985	0.066	WIN 630	—
No. 9	10.0	—	1.015	0.381	0.935	0.069	WIN 296	—
1680	10.0	—	0.014	0.356	0.950	0.068	WIN 680	—
Solo 4100	10.0	—	0.011	0.279	0.960	0.068	WIN 296	—
BALL PROPELLANTS - Rifle								
2230	10.0	—	0.022	0.559	0.980	0.066	BL C2, WIN 748	—
2460	10.0	—	0.022	0.559	0.990	0.065	BL C2, WIN 748	—
2520	10.0	—	0.022	0.559	0.970	0.067	—	—
2700	10.0	—	0.022	0.559	0.960	0.068	WIN 760	—
MAGPRO	9.0	—	0.030	0.762	0.970	0.067	—	—
8700	10.0	—	0.030	0.762	0.960	0.068	H870	—
EXTRUDED PROPELLANTS - Shotshell/Handguns								
Nirto 100	21.0	0.010/ 0.254	0.058	1.473	0.505	0.128	—	700X, Red Dot
Solo 1000	—	0.010/ 0.254	0.052	1.321	0.510	0.127	—	Green Dot
Solo 1250	—	0.013/ 0.033	0.051	1.295	0.550	0.118	—	PB
EXTRUDED PROPELLANTS - Rifle/handgun								
5744	20.00	0.048/ 1.219	0.033	0.838	0.880	0.074	—	—
EXTRUDED PROPELLANTS - Rifle								
2015	—	0.039/ 0.991	0.031	0.787	0.880	0.074	—	H322,N201 IMR 4198
2495	—	0.068/ 1.727	0.029	0.737	0.880	0.074	—	IMR 4895
4064	—	0.050/ 1.270	0.035	0.889	0.890	0.072	—	IMR 4064
4350	—	0.083/ 0.038	0.038	0.965	0.890	0.072	—	IMR 4350
3100	—	0.083/ 0.038	0.038	0.965	0.920	0.070	—	IMR 4831

*NG-NItroglycerin ***For comparison only, not a loading recommendation

Alliant Smokeless Powders

410
Cleanest .410 bore powder on the market.

2400
Legendary for its performance in .44 magnum and other magnum pistol loads. Originally developed for the .22 Hornet, it's also the shooter's choice for .410 bore. *Available in 8 lb., 4 lb. and 1 lb. canisters.*

AMERICAN SELECT
This ultra-clean burning premium powder makes a versatile target load and superior 1 oz. load for improved clay target scores. Great for Cowboy Action handgun loading, too. *Available in 8 lb., 4 lb. and 1 lb. canisters.*

BLUE DOT
The powder of choice for magnum lead shotshell loads. 10, 12, 16 and 20 ga. Consistent and accurate. Doubles as magnum handgun powder. *Available in 5 lb. and 1 lb. canisters.*

BULLSEYE
America's best known pistol powder. Unsurpassed for .45 ACP target loads. *Available in 8 lb., 4 lb. and 1 lb. canisters.*

E^3
The first of a new generation of high performance powders.

GREEN DOT
It delivers precise burn rates for uniformly tight patterns, and you'll appreciate the lower felt recoil. Versatile for target and field. *Available in 8 lb., 4 lb. and 1 lb. canisters.*

HERCO
Since 1920, a proven powder for heavy shotshell loads, including 10, 12, 16, 20 and 28 ga. target loads. The ultimate in 12 ga., 1¼ oz. upland game loads. *Available in 8 lb., 4 lb. and 1 lb. canisters.*

POWER PISTOL
Designed for high performance in semi-automatic pistols (9mm, .40 S&W and .357 SIG). *Available in 4 lb. and 1 lb. canisters.*

Alliant Shotshell Powders

RED DOT
America's #1 choice for clay target loads, now 50% cleaner. Since 1932, more 100 straights than any other powder. *Available in 8 lb., 4 lb. and 1 lb. canisters.*

RELODER 7
Designed for small-caliber varmint loads, it meters consistently and meets the needs of the most demanding bench rest shooter. Great in .45-70 and .450 Marlin. *Available in 5 lb. and 1 lb. canisters.*

RELODER 10X
Best choice for light bullet applications in .222 Rem, .223 Rem, .22-250 Rem and key bench rest calibers. Also great in light bullet .308 Win. loads. *Available in 5 lb. and 1 lb. canisters*

RELODER 15
An all-around medium speed rifle powder. It provides excellent .223 and .308 cal. performance. Selected as the powder for U.S. Military's M118 Special Ball Long Range Sniper Round. *Available in 5 lb. and 1 lb. canisters.*

RELODER 19
Provides superb accuracy in most medium and heavy rifle loads and is the powder of choice for 30-06 and .338 calibers. *Available in 5 lb. and 1 lb. canisters.*

RELODER 22
This top performing powder for big-game loads provides excellent metering and is the powder of choice for .270, 7mm magnum and .300 Win. magnum. *Available in 5 lb. and 1 lb. canisters.*

RELODER 25
This powder for big-game hunting features improved slower burning and delivers the high-energy heavy magnum loads needed. *Available in 5 lb. and 1 lb. canisters.*

STEEL
Designed for waterfowl shotshells. Gives steel shot high velocity within safe pressure limits for 10 and 12 ga. loads. *Available in 4 lb. and 1 lb. canisters.*

UNIQUE
Shotgun/handgun powder for 12, 16, 20 and 28 ga. loads. Use with most hulls, primers and wads. *Available in 8 lb., 4 lb. and 1 lb. canisters.*

When handloading, spilled powder should never be picked up with a vacuum cleaner. Use only a brush and pan and dispose of the powder in a safe manner.

Hodgdon Smokeless Powder

CLAYS
Tailored for use in 12 ga., 7/8 oz., 1 oz. and 1 1/8 oz. loads. Performs well in many handgun applications, including .38 Special, .40 S&W and 45 ACP. Perfect for 1 1/8 oz. and 1 oz. loads.

CLAYS, INTERNATIONAL
Ideal for 12 and 20 ga. autoloaders who want reduced recoil.

CLAYS, UNIVERSAL
Loads nearly all of the straight-wall pistol cartridges as well as 12 ga. 1 1/4 oz. thru 28 ga. 3/4 oz. target loads.

EXTREME BENCHMARK
A fine choice for small rifle cases like the .223 Rem and PPC competition rounds. Appropriate also for the 300-30 and 7x57.

EXTREME H50 BMG
Designed for the 50 Browning Machine Gun cartridge. Highly insensitive to extreme temperature changes.

EXTREME H322
This powder fills the gap between H4198 and BL-C9(2). Performs best in small to medium capacity cases.

EXTREME H1000 EXTRUDED POWDER
Fills the gap between H4831 and H870. Works especially well in overbore capacity cartridges (1,000-yard shooters take note).

EXTREME H4198
H4198 was developed especially for small and medium capacity cartridges.

EXTREME H4350
Gives superb accuracy at optimum velocity for many large capacity metallic rifle cartridges.

EXTREME H4831
Outstanding performance with medium and heavy bullets in the 6mm's, 25/06, 270 and Magnum calibers. Also available with shortened grains (H4831SC) for easy metering.

EXTREME H4895
4895 gives desirable performance in almost all cases from 222 Rem. to 458 Win. Reduced loads, to as low as 3/5 maximum, still give target accuracy.

EXTREME VARGET
Features small extruded grain powder for uniform metering, plus higher velocities/normal pressures in such calibers as .223, 22-250, 306, 30-06, 375 H&H.

H110
A spherical powder made especially for the 30 M1 carbine. H110 also does very well in 357, 44 spec., 44 Mag. or 410 ga. shotshell. Recommended for consistent ignition.

H4227
An extruded powder similar to H110, recommended for the 22 Hornet and some specialized loading in the 45-70 caliber. Excellent in magnum pistol and .410 shotgun.

HP38
A fast pistol powder for most pistol loading. Especially recommended for mid-range 38 specials.

HS-6 AND HS-7
HS-6 and HS-7 for Magnum field loads are unsurpassed. Deliver uniform charges and are dense to allow sufficient wad column for best patterns.

LIL' GUN
Developed specifically for the .410 shotgun but works very well in rifle cartridges like the .22 Hornet and in the .44 magnum.

LONGSHOT
Spherical powder for heavy shotgun loads.

PYRODEX PELLETS
Both rifle and pistol pellets eliminate powder measures, speeds shooting for black powder enthusiasts.

RETUMBO
Designed for such cartridges as the 300 Rem. Ultra Mag., 30-378 Weatherby, the 7mm STW and other cases with large capacities and small bores. Expect up to 40-100 feet per second more velocity than other magnum powders.

SPHERICAL BL-C2
Best performance is in the 222, .308 other cases smaller than 30/06.

SPHERICAL H335
Similar to BL-C(2), H335 is popular for its performance in medium capacity cases, especially in 222 and 308 Winchester.

SPHERICAL H380
Fills a gap between 4320 and 4350. It is excellent in 22/250, 220 Swift, the 6mm's, 257 and 30/06.

SPHERICAL H414
In many popular medium to medium-large calibers, pressure velocity relationship is better.

TITEGROUP
Excellent for most straight-walled pistol cartridges, incl. 38 Spec., 44 Spec., 45 ACP. Low charge weights, clean burning; position insensitive and flawless ignition.

TITEWAD
This 12 ga. flattened spherical shotgun powder is ideal for 7/8 oz., 1 oz. and 1 1/8 oz. loads, with minimum recoil and mild muzzle report. The fastest fuel in Hodgdon's line.

TRIPLE SEVEN
Hodgdon Powder Company offers its sulfur-free Triple Seven powder in 50-grain pellets. Formulated for use with 209 shotshell primers, Triple Seven leaves no rotten egg smell, and the residue is easy to clean from the bore with water only. The pellets are sized for 50-caliber muzzleloaders and can be used singly (for target shooting or small game) as well as two at a time.

RIFLE POWDERS

IMR 3031—A propellant with many uses, IMR 3031 is a favorite of 308 match shooters using 168 grain match bullets. It is equally effective in small-capacity varmint cartridges from .223 Remington to .22-250 Remington and a great .30-30 Winchester powder.

IMR 4060—The most versatile propellant in the IMR spectrum. .223 Remington, .22-250 Remington, .220 Swift, 6mm Remington, .243 Winchester Super Short Magnum, .308 Winchester, .338 Winchester Magnum, etc.

IMR 4198—This fast-burning rifle powder gives outstanding performance in cartridges like the .222 Remington, 221 Fireball, .45-70 and .450 Marlin.

IMR 4227—The choice for true magnum velocities and performance. In rifles, this powder delivers excellent velocity and accuracy in such cartridges as the .22 Hornet and .221 Fireball.

IMR 4320—Short granulation, easy metering and perfect for the .223 Remington, .22-250 Remington, .250 Savage and other medium burn rate cartridges. It has long been a top choice for the vintage .300 Savage cartridge.

IMR 4350—The number one choice for the new short magnums, both Remington and Winchester versions. For magnums with light to medium bullet weights, IMR 4350 is the best choice.

IMR 4832—Slightly slower in burn speed than IMR 4350, IMR 4832 gives top velocities and performance with heavier bullets in medium sized magnums.

IMR 4895—Originally a military powder featured in the .30-06, IMR 4895 is extremely versatile. From .17 Remington to the .243 Winchester to the .375 H&H Magnum, accuracy and performance are excellent. In addition, it is a long-time favorite of match shooters.

IMR 7828—The big magnum powder. This slow burner gives real magnum performance to the large overbored magnums, such as the .300 Remington Ultra Mag, the .30-378 Weatherby Magnum and 7mm Remington Ultra Magnum.

HANDGUN & SHOTGUN POWDERS

"Hi Skor" 700-X—This extruded flake-type powder is ideally suited for shotshells in 12 and 16 ga. where clay target and light field loads are the norm. It doubles as an excellent pistol target powder for such cartridges as the .38 Special, .45 ACP and many more.

"Hi Skor" 800-X—This large-grained flake powder is at its best when used in heavy field loads from 10 ga. to 28 ga. In handgun cartridges, 800-X performs superbly in cartridges such as the 10mm Auto, .357 Magnum and .44 Remington Magnum.

PB—Named for the porous base structure of its grains by which the burning rate is controlled, PB is an extremely clean-burning, single-base powder. It gives very low pressure in 12 and 20 ga. shotshell target loads and performs well in a wide variety of handgun loads.

SR 4756—This fine-grained, easy-metering propellant has long been a favorite of upland and waterfowl handloaders. SR4756 performs extremely well in the big handgun cartridges.

SR 4759—This bulky handgun powder works great in the magnums, but really shines as a reduced load propellant for rifle cartridges. Its large-grain size gives good loading density for reduced loads, enhancing velocity uniformity.

SR 7625—SR7625 covers the wide range of shotshells from 10 ga. to 28 ga. in both target and field loadings. This versatile powder is equally useful in a large array of handgun cartridges for target, self-defense and hunting loads.

Word Play: The word "bullet" is sometimes erroneously used to refer to the combination of bullet, case, gunpowder and primer more properly known as a "cartridge" or "round."

Ramshot Powders

Ramshot (Western Powders, Inc.) powders are all double-base propellants, meaning they contain nitrocellulose and nitroglycerine. While some spherical or ball powders are known for leaving plenty of residue in barrels, these fuels burn very clean. They meter easily, as do all ball powders. Plastic canisters are designed for spill-proof use and include basic loading data on the labels.

RAMSHOT BIG GAME is a versatile propellant for cartridges as diverse as the .30-06 and the .338 Winchester, and for light-bullet loads in small-bore magnums.

RAMSHOT COMPETITION is for the clay target shooter. A fast-burning powder comparable to 700-X or Red Dot, it performs well in a variety of 12 ga. target loads, offering low recoil, consistent pressures and clean combustion.

RAMSHOT ENFORCER is a match for high-performance handgun hulls like the .40 Smith & Wesson. It is designed for full-power loading and high velocities. Ramshot X-Terminator, a fast-burning rifle powder, excels in small-caliber, medium-capacity cartridges. It has the versatility to serve in both target and high-performance varmint loads.

RAMSHOT MAGNUM is the slowest powder of the Western line, and does its best work in cartridges with lots of case volume and small to medium bullet diameter. It is the powder of choice in 7mm and .30 Magnums.

RAMSHOT SILHOUETTE is ideal for the 9mm handgun cartridge, from light to heavy loads. It also works well in the .40 Smith & Wesson and combat loads for the .45 Auto.

RAMSHOT TAC was formulated for tactical rifle cartridges, specifically the .223 and .308. It has produced exceptional accuracy with a variety of bullets and charge weights.

RAMSHOT TRUE BLUE was designed for small- to medium-size handgun cartridges. Similar to Winchester 231 and Hodgdon HP-38, it has enough bulk to nearly fill most cases, thereby better positioning the powder for ignition.

RAMSHOT X-TERMINATOR is a clean burning powder designed for the .222 Rem., 223 Rem. and .22 Benchrest calibers.

RAMSHOT ZIP, a fast-burning target powder for cartridges like the .38 Special and .45 ACP, gives competitors uniform velocities.

VihtaVuori

N110—A very fast-burning propellant that can be used in applications that previously used Hercules 2400, Hodgdon H110 or Winchester 296. Typical applications include: .22 Hornet, .25-20 Winchester, .357 S&W Magnum, .357 Maximum, .44 Magnum and .45 Winchester Magnum.

N120—A limited application propellant. This speed develops higher pressure than N110 in order to optimize burning. Burning rate falls near the various 4227s. It works well with light bullets in .22 caliber cartridges.

N130—Burning rate is between IMR 4227 and the discontinued Winchester 680. This is the powder used in factory-loaded .22 and 6mm PPC.

N133—This powder's speed is very close to IMR 4198 in quickness. Thus, it is ideal for the .222 Remington, .223 Remington, .45-70 Government and other applications where a relatively fast-burning rifle propellant is needed.

N135—This is a moderate-burning propellant. It will fit applications similar to Hercules Reloader 12, IMR-4895 or IMR 4064. Applications range from the .17 Remington to the .458 Winchester.

N140—This powder can usually be used in place of Hercules Reloader 15, IMR 4320 and Hodgdon H380. Applications include: .222 Remington Magnum, .22-250 Remington (factory powder), .30-.30 Winchester, .308 Winchester, .30-06 Springfield, .375 H&H Magnum and so on.

N150—This is a moderately slow powder that can help refine rifle cartridge ballistics when N140 is too fast and N160 is too slow. Works well in many applications previously filled by 760, H414 and IMR 4350.

N160—A relatively slow powder ideally suited to many magnum and standard rounds requiring a slow propellant. It has characteristics that make it work well for applications previously using various 4350s, Hercules Reloader 19 and the various 4831s. For example, some ideal applications are: .243 Winchester, .25-06 Remington, .264 Winchester Magnum, .270 Winchester (factory load), 7mm Remington Magnum, .30-06 Springfield, .300 Winchester Magnum, .338 Winchester Magnum, .375 H&H Magnum, etc.

N165—A very slow-burning magnum propellant for use with heavy bullets. Applications begin with heavy bullets in the .30-06, and include the .338 Winchester Magnum.

N170—VihtaVuori's slowest speed propellant and the slowest canister reloading powder generally available from any manufacturer.

N500 Series
VihtaVuori calls powders that have nitroglycerol added (maximum 25%) producing the high energy NC-powders that form the N500 series. Geometrically the powders in the N500 series are equal to the N100 series. Although these powders have a higher energy content, they do not cause greater wear to the gun. This is because the surface of the powder has been treated with an agent designed to reduce barrel wear. N500 series powders work well at different temperatures.

N530—Burning rate close to N135. Especially for .223 Remington. Excellent also for .45-70 Government.

N540—Burning rate like N140. Especially for the .308 Winchester.

N550—Burning rate like N150. Especially for the .308 Winchester and .30-06 Springfield.

N560—Burning rate like N160. Especially for .270 Winchester and 6.5 x 55 Swedish Mauser.

Battenfeld Technologies

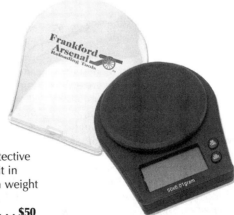

FRANKFORD ARSENAL MICRO RELOADING SCALE
The Micro Reloading Scale is the perfect accessory for reloaders who want a light, accurate, portable scale. The unit is suitable for use on the reloading bench, yet is at home on the shooting range or in the field. The Micro Reloading Scale weighs objects up to 750 grains. It is accurate within ± .1 grains. The digital scale can be set to read in grains, grams, ounces, ct, dwt or ozt. It comes with a protective sleeve and is small enough to fit in your shirt pocket. A calibration weight and batteries are also included.
MSRP: **$50**

Dillon Precision Reloaders

MODEL RL550B

MODEL SL900

RL550B PROGRESSIVE LOADER

- Accommodates over 120 calibers
- Interchangeable toolhead assembly
- Auto/Powder priming systems
- Uses standard ⁷/₈" x 14" dies
- Loading rate: 500-600 rounds per hour

MSRP: **$406.95**

SL900R

Based on Dillon's proven XL 650 O-frame design, the SL 900 progressive press features an automatic case insert system, an electric case collator, adjustable case-activated shot and powder bars. Should the operator forget to insert a wad during the reloading process, the SL 900 will not dispense shot into the powder-charged hull. Both powder and shot systems are based on Dillon's adjustable pow-

der bar design, which is accurate to within a few tenths of a grain. Simply adjust the measures to dispense the exact charges required.

An interchangeable tool-head makes it quick and easy to change from one gauge to another using a collet-type sizing die that re-forms the base of the shotshell to factory specifications. The SL 900 also has an extra large, remote shot hopper that holds an entire 25-pound bag of shot, making it easy to fill with a funnel. The shot reservoir/dispenser helps ensure that a consistent volume of shot is delivered to each shell. The heat-treated steel crimp-die forms and folds the hull before the final taper crimp die radiuses and blends the end of the hull and locks the crimp into place.

MSRP: **$819.95**

Dillon Precision Reloaders

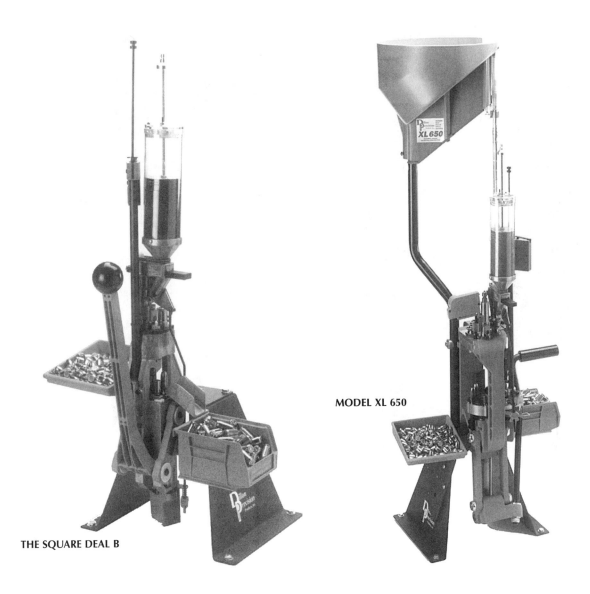

MODEL XL 650

THE SQUARE DEAL B

THE SQUARE DEAL B

Designed to produce up to 400 or 500 handgun rounds per hour. The Square Deal B comes with a factory adjusted carbide die set. Square Deal B is available in all popular handgun calibers and you can change from one caliber to another in minutes with a Square Deal B caliber conversion kit. Features: Automatic indexing; auto powder/priming systems; available in 14 handgun calibers; loading dies standard.
MSRP: **$349.95**

MODEL XL 650

The XL 650 loads virtually every popular pistol and rifle cartridge utilizing standard dies. The optional powder charge check die on the third station sounds an alarm if the powder charge in a round is out of limits either high or low. An exclusive primer system uses a rotary indexing plate that positively controls each primer and keeps a steel shield between the primers and the operator. Features: Automatic indexing; five-station interchangeable tool-head; auto powder / priming systems; uses standard 7/8" x 14" dies rotary indexing plate for primers.
MSRP: **$529.95**

Forster Reloading

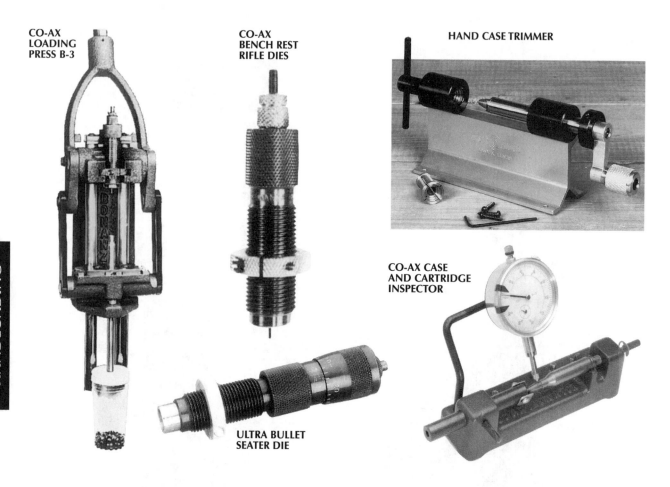

CO-AX
LOADING
PRESS B-3

CO-AX
BENCH REST
RIFLE DIES

HAND CASE TRIMMER

CO-AX CASE
AND CARTRIDGE
INSPECTOR

ULTRA BULLET
SEATER DIE

CO-AX LOADING PRESS MODEL B-3

Designed to make reloading easier and more accurate, this press offers the following features: Snap-in and snap-out die change; positive spent primer catcher; automatic self-acting shell holder; floating guide rods; top priming device seats primers to factory specifications; uses any standard 7/8" x 14" dies.
MSRP: **$378**

CO-AX BENCH REST RIFLE DIES

Bench Rest Rifle Dies are glass-hard and polished mirror-smooth with special attention given to headspace, tapers and diameters. Sizing die has an elevated expander button to ensure better alignment of case and neck.
Bench Rest Die Set: **$92**
Bench Rest Seating Die: **$56**
Ultra Bench Rest Die Set: **$129**
Full Length Sizer: **$44**

ULTRA BULLET SEATER DIE

The micrometer-style Ultra Die is available in 61 calibers. Adjustment is identical to that of a precision micrometer—the head is graduated to .001" increments with .025" bullet movement per revolution. The cartridge case, bullet and seating stem are completely supported and perfectly aligned in a close-fitting chamber before and during the bullet seating operation.
MSRP: **$89.60**

CASE PREPARATION

Handles more than 100 different big bore calibers–500 Nitro Express, 416 Rigby, 50 Sharps, 475 H&H, etc. Also available: .50 BMG Case Trimmer, designed specifically for reloading needs of .50 Cal. BMG shooters.
"Classic 50" Case Trimmer: . . . **$112**
.50 BMG Case Trimmer: **$117**

HAND CASE TRIMMER

Shell holder is a Brown & Sharpe-type collet. Case and cartridge conditioning accessories include inside neck reamer, outside neck turner, deburring tool, hollow pointer and primer pocket cleaners. The case trimmer trims all cases, ranging from .17 to .458 Winchester caliber.
MSRP: **$78**

CO-AX CASE AND CARTRIDGE INSPECTOR

Provides the ability to ensure uniformity by measuring three critical dimensions: neck wall thickness; case neck concentricity; bullet run-out. Measurements are in increments of one-thousandth of an inch. The Inspector checks both the bullet and case alignment in relation to the centerline (axis) of the entire cartridge or case.
MSRP: **$104**

Forster Reloading

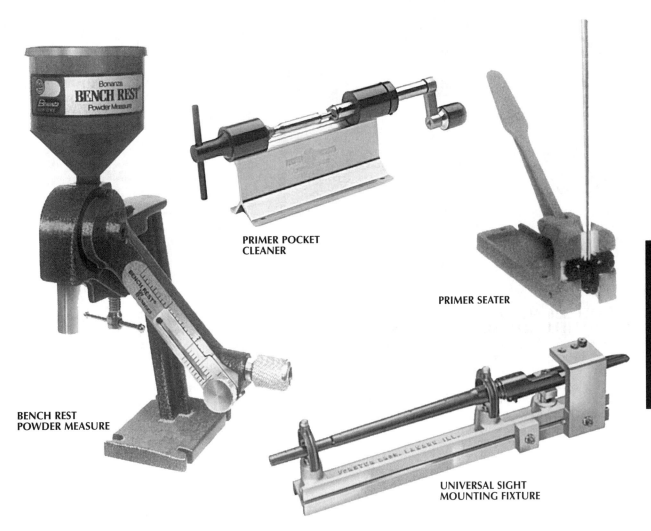

PRIMER POCKET CLEANER

PRIMER SEATER

BENCH REST POWDER MEASURE

UNIVERSAL SIGHT MOUNTING FIXTURE

BENCH REST POWDER MEASURE

When operated uniformly, this measure will throw uniform charges from 2½-grains Bullseye to 95-grains #4320. No extra drums are needed. Powder is metered from the charge arm, allowing a flow of powder without extremes in variation while minimizing powder shearing. Powder flows through its own built-in baffle, entering the charge arm uniformly.
MSRP: **$140**

PRIMER POCKET CLEANER

The Primer Pocket Cleaner helps ensure consistent ignition and reduce the incidence of misfires by removing powder and primer residue from the primer pockets of your cases. This tool is easy to use by holding the case

mouth over the Primer Pocket Center with one hand while you quickly and easily clean the primer pockets by turning the Case Trimmer Handle.
MSRP: **$9.20**

PRIMER SEATER

Designed so that primers are seated co-axially (primer in line with primer pocket). Mechanical leverage allows primers to be seated fully without crushing. With the addition of one extra set of disc shell holders and one extra Primer Unit, all modern cases, rim or rimless, from .222 up to .458 Magnum, can be primed. Shell holders are easily adjusted to any case by rotating to contact rim or cannelure of the case.
MSRP: **$90**

UNIVERSAL SIGHT MOUNTING FIXTURE

The fixture handles any single-barrel gun—bolt-action, lever-action or pump-action—as long as the barrel can be laid into the "V" blocks of the fixture. Rifles with tube magazines are drilled in the same manner by removing the magazine tube. The fixture's main body is made of aluminum casting. The two "V" blocks are adjustable for height and are made of hardened steel ground accurately on the "V" as well as the shaft.
MSRP: **$444**

Hornady

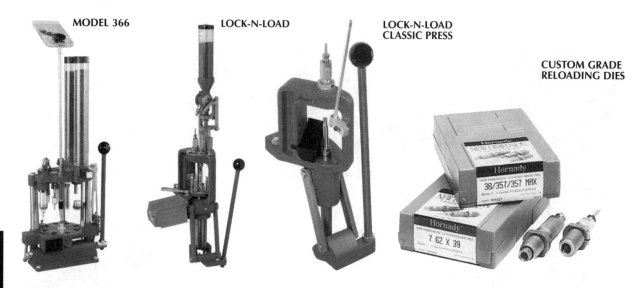

MODEL 366   LOCK-N-LOAD   LOCK-N-LOAD CLASSIC PRESS   CUSTOM GRADE RELOADING DIES

MODEL 366 AUTO SHOTSHELL RELOADER

The 366 Auto features full-length resizing with each stroke, automatic primer feed, swing-out wad guide, three-state crimping featuring Taper-Loc for factory tapered crimp, automatic advance to the next station and automatic ejection. The turntable holds 8 shells for 8 operations with each stroke. Automatic charge bar loads shot and powder, dies and crimp starters for 6 point, 8 point and paper crimps.

12, 20, 28 ga.: **$670**
.410: **$790**

LOCK-N-LOAD AUTO PROGRESSIVE PRESS

The Lock-N-Load Automatic Progressive reloading press features the Lock-N-Load bushing system. Dies and powder measure are inserted into Lock-N-Load die bushings. The bushings remain with the die and powder measure and can be removed in seconds. Other features include: deluxe powder measure, automatic indexing, off-set handle, power-pac linkage, case ejector, five die bushings, shellplate, primer catcher, Positive Priming System, powder drop, Deluxe Powder Measure, automatic primer feed.

MSRP: **$490**

LOCK-N-LOAD CLASSIC PRESS

Lock-N-Load is available on Hornady's single stage and progressive reloader models. This bushing system locks the die into the press like a rifle bolt. Instead of threading dies in and out of the press, you simply lock and unlock them with a slight twist. Dies are held firmly in a die bushing that stays with the die and retains the die setting. Features: Easy-grip handle; O-style high-strength alloy frame; positive priming system.

MSRP: **$145**
Lock-N-Load Classic
  Press Kit: **$383**
Also Available:
Lock-N-Load 50 Cal.
  BMG Press: **$329**
Lock-N-Load 50 Cal.
  BMG Press Kit: **$605**

CUSTOM GRADE RELOADING DIES

An Elliptical Expander in Hornady dies minimizes friction and reduces case neck stretch. Other design features include a hardened steel decap pin and a bullet seater alignment sleeve. Dimension Reloading Dies include: collar and collar lock to center expander precisely; one-piece expander spindle with tapered bottom for easy cartridge insertion; wrench flats on die body; Sure-Loc lock rings and collar lock for easy tightening; and built-in crimper. The new Zip Spindle design features a series of light threads cut on the spindle and spindle collet. This design elimi-

nates spindle slippage and takes the knucklebusting out of tightening the spindle lock while making spindle adjustments a snap.

Series I: **$39**
Series II Three-die Rifle Set: . . . **$45**
Series III: **$45**
Match Grade: **$50**

HANDHELD PRIMING TOOL

Hornady's handheld priming tool features a one-piece primer tray with an improved retaining system for the lid. It also sports integral molded bushings for ultra reliable function. The new primer tray also eliminates the need for separate bushings. The system comes with an additional tray designed for use with RCBS shell holders. The body has been modified for easier change-over, and the seater punch and spring are captured inside the body, allowing shell holders and primer trays to be changed without removing them.

MSRP: **$45.48**

UNIVERSAL SHELL HOLDERS

Shell Holders for the single stage press have been improved. The mouth of the shell holder has been widened with a radius to allow easier case insertion while maintaining maximum contact area once the case is in the shell holder. Made for use in any tool designed to use a shell holder.

MSRP: **$8.17**

Lyman Reloading Tools

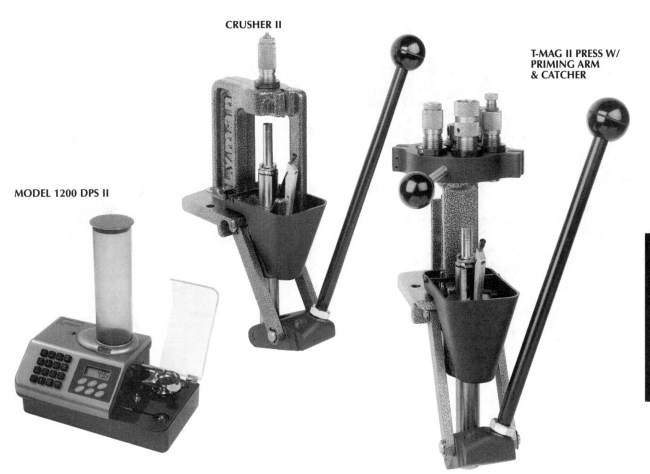

CRUSHER II

T-MAG II PRESS W/
PRIMING ARM
& CATCHER

MODEL 1200 DPS II

MODEL 1200 DPS II (DIGITAL POWDER SYSTEM)

The 1200 DPS dispenses powder quickly, with .1-grain precision. The 4500 Lube sizer, with a one-piece base casting and a built-in heating element (choose 110 or 220 volt). The long ball-knob handle offers the leverage for sizing and lubricating big bullets. It comes with a gas check seater.

1200 DPS:. $385–395
4500 Lube sizer:. $182.95

CRUSHER II RELOADING PRESS

The only press for rifle or pistol cartridges that offers the advantage of powerful compound leverage combined with a true Magnum press opening. A unique handle design transfers power easily to the center of the ram. A 4½ in. press opening accommodates even the largest cartridges.

MSRP: $154.95

CRUSHER II PRO KIT

Includes press, loading block, case lube kit, primer tray, Model 500 Pro scale, powder funnel and Lyman Reloading Handbook.

MSRP: $224.95

T-MAG II TURRET RELOADING PRESS

With the T-Mag II, up to six different reloading dies can be mounted on one turret—dies can be precisely mounted, locked in and ready to reload at all times. The T-Mag works with all ⁷⁄₈″ x 14″ dies. The T-Mag II turret with quick-disconnect release system is held in alignment by a ¾ in. steel stud. The T-Mag II features Lyman's Crusher II compound leverage system.

MSRP: $214.95
Extra Turret Head: $49.95

Also available:
Expert Kit: (T-MAG II Press, Universal Case Trimmer and pilot Multi-Pak, Model 500 powder scale and Model 50 powder measure, plus accessories. Available in calibers .30-06, .270 and .308

MSRP: $454.95

Lyman Reloading Tools

CLASSIC DIE SETS

DIE SET, 5.7X28MM

3-DIE CARBIDE PISTOL DIE SETS

Lyman originated the Tungsten Carbide (T-C) sizing die and the addition of extra seating screws for pistol die sets and the two step neck expanding die. Multi-Deluxe Die sets offer these features; a one-piece hardened steel decapping rod and extra seating screws for all popular bullet nose shapes; all-steel construction.
MSRP: **$59.95**

CLASSIC DIE SETS

Lyman Products offers new reloading dies sets for .40-60 Win, .45-65 Win and .45-75 Win cartridges. These cartridges have become popular with the introduction of the new '76 Winchester lever action reproductions. Most importantly, these new dies have been carefully engineered to modern standards to provide precise reloads with either black or smokeless powder.
MSRP: **$59.95**

DIE SET FOR 5.7X28MM FN PISTOL CARTRIDGE

Lyman has added a new die set for the 5.7x28mm FN pistol cartridge. Offered for those shooters who want to enjoy the economy and accuracy advantages of reloading this unique new pistol round, these new dies are precisely dimensioned to load ammo that will provide accurate and reliable function in autoloaders.
MSRP: **$57.50**

RIFLE DIE SETS

Lyman precision rifle dies feature fine adjustment threads on the bullet seating stem to allow for precision adjustments of bullet seating depth. Lyman dies fit all popular presses using industry standard $7/8"$ x 14" threads, including RCBS, Lee, Hornady, Dillon, Redding and others. Each sizing die for bottle-necked rifle cartridges is carefully vented. This vent hole is precisely placed to prevent air traps that can damage cartridge cases. Each sizing die is polished and heat-treated for toughness.

RIFLE 2-DIE SETS

Set consists of a full-length resizing die with de-capping stem and neck expanding button and a bullet-seating die for loading jacketed bullets in bottlenecked rifle cases. For those who load cast bullets, use a neck-expanding die, available separately.
MSRP: **$38.50**

RIFLE 3-DIE SETS

Straight wall rifle cases require these three die sets consisting of a full length resizing die with decapping stem, a two step neck expanding (M) die and a bullet seating die. These sets are ideal for loading cast bullets due to the inclusion of the neck-expanding die.
MSRP: **$50.50**
Classic Calibers: **$59.95**
Classic Neck Size Dies: **$27.50**

PREMIUM CARBIDE 4-DIE SETS FOR PISTOLS

Lyman 4-Die Sets feature a separate taper crimp die and powder charge/expanding die. The powder charge/expand die has a special hollow 2-step neck expanding plug which allows powder to flow through the die from a powder measure directly into the case. The powder charge/expanding die has a standard $7/8"$ x 14" thread and will accept Lyman's 55 Powder Measure, or most other powder measures.
MSRP: **$74.95**

Lyman Reloading Tools

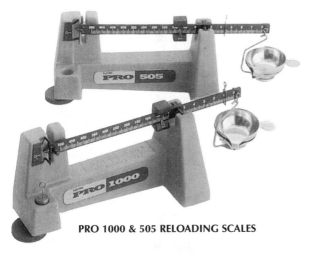

PRO 1000 & 505 RELOADING SCALES

POWER CASE TRIMMER

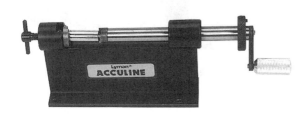

ACCU-TRIMMER

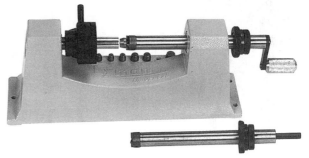

UNIVERSAL TRIMMER WITH
NINE PILOT MULTI-PACK
WITH POWER ADAPTER

PRO 1000 & 505 RELOADING SCALES

Features include improved platform system; hi-tech base design of high-impact styrene; extra-large, smooth leveling wheel; dual agate bearings; larger damper for fast zeroing; built-in counter weight compartment; easy-to-read beam.

Pro 1000 scale:. $75.95
Pro 500 scale:. $59.95
Metric scale: $62

ACCU-TRIMMER

Lyman's Accu-Trimmer can be used for all rifle and pistol cases from .22 to .458 Winchester Magnum. Standard shellholders are used to position the case, and the trimmer incorporates standard Lyman cutter heads and pilots. Mounting options include bolting to a bench, C-clamp or vise.

Accu Trimmer w/ 9-pilot
  Multi-Pak: $58.25

POWER CASE TRIMMER

The Lyman Power Trimmer is powered by a fan-cooled electric motor designed to withstand the severe demands of case trimming. The unit, which features the Universal Chuckhead, allows cases to be positioned for trimming or easy removal. The Power Trimmer package includes Nine-Pilot Multi-Pack, two cutter heads and a pair of wire end brushes for cleaning primer pockets. Other features include safety guards, on-off rocker switch, heavy cast base with receptacles for nine pilots and bolt holes for mounting on a work bench. Power Trimmer is available for 110 or 220 volt systems.

110 V Model: $284.95
220 V Model: $290

UNIVERSAL TRIMMER

This trimmer with patented chuckhead accepts all metallic rifle or pistol cases, regardless of rim thickness. To change calibers, simply change the case head pilot. Other features include coarse and fine cutter adjustments, an oil-impregnated bronze bearing, and a rugged cast base to assure precision alignment. Optional carbide cutter available.

Trimmer Multi-Pack (9 pilots: 22, 24,
  27, 28/7mm, 30, 9mm, 35,
  44 and 4A):. $91.50
Universal Trimmer
  Power Adapter: $23.25
Power Trimmer—115 V.:. . . .$284.95

Lyman Reloading Tools

TURBO TWIN TUMBLER

MODEL 2500
PRO MAGNUM TUMBLER

.40-60 WINCHESTER
BULLET MOLD

55 CLASSIC
BLACK POWDER MEASURE

MODEL 1200 CLASSIC TURBO TUMBLER

This case tumbler features an improved base and drive system, plus a stronger suspension system and built-in exciters for better tumbling action and faster cleaning.

Model 1200 Classic: . . . **$103–112.50**
Model 1200 Auto-Flo: . . **$103.95–116**
Also available:
Model 600: **$72.95**
Model 2200 Auto-Flo: **$150**

MODEL 2500 PRO MAGNUM TUMBLER

The Lyman 2500 Pro Magnum tumbler handles up to 900 .38 Special cartridges at once.

2500 Pro Magnum Tumbler: . . . .
$100–108
W/ Auto Flow feature: **$137.50–140**

TURBO TWIN TUMBLER

The Twin features Lyman 1200 Pro Tumbler with an extra 600 bowl system. Reloaders may use each bowl interchangeably for small or large capacity loads. 1200 Pro Bowl System has a built-in sifter lid for easy sifting of cases and media at the end of the polishing cycle. The Twin Tumbler features the Lyman Hi-Profile base design with built-in exciters and anti-rotation pads for faster, more consistent tumbling action.

MSRP: **$86–90**

.40-60 WINCHESTER BULLET MOLD

The .40-60 Winchester cartridge has become popular with the introduction of the '76 Winchester lever action reproductions. The mold is a proven ideal design that was popular back when these big-bore, lever-action rifles were originally introduced. It has been carefully updated and dimensioned to modern standards for precise reloads with either black or smokeless powder.

MSRP: **$76.50**

55 CLASSIC BLACK POWDER MEASURE

Lyman's 55 Classic Powder Measure is ideal for the Cowboy Action Competition or black powder cartridge shooters. The one-pound-capacity aluminum reservoir and brass powder meter eliminate static. The internal powder baffle assures highly accurate and consistent charges. The 24" powder compacting drop tube allows the maximum charge in each cartridge. Drop tube works on calibers 38 through 50 and mounts easily to the bottom of the measure.

55 Classic Powder Measure
(std model-no tubes): . . . **$137.50**
55 Classic Powder Measure
(with drop tubes): **$154.95**
Powder Drop Tubes only: **$32**

Lyman Reloading Tools

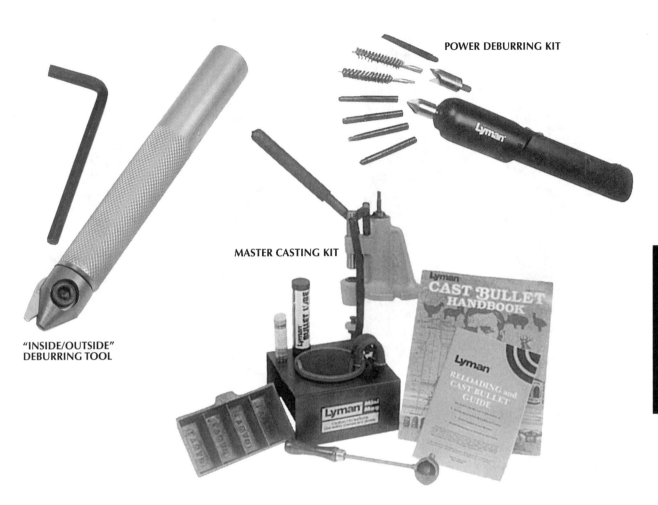

POWER DEBURRING KIT

MASTER CASTING KIT

"INSIDE/OUTSIDE" DEBURRING TOOL

ACCULINE OUTSIDE NECK TURNER

To obtain perfectly concentric case necks, Lyman's Outside Neck Turner assures reloaders of uniform neck wall thickness and outside neck diameter. The unit fits Lyman's Universal Trimmer and AccuTrimmer. Rate of feed is adjustable and a mechanical stop controls length of cut. Mandrels are available for calibers from .17 to .375; cutter blade can be adjusted for any diameter from .195" to .405."

Outside Neck Turner w/extra blade, 6 mandrels: **$36.25**
Individual Mandrels: **$4.25**

"INSIDE/OUTSIDE" DEBURRING TOOL

This tool features an adjustable cutting blade that adapts easily to the mouth of any rifle or pistol case from .22 to .45 caliber with a simple hex wrench

adjustment. Inside deburring is completed by a conical internal section with slotted cutting edges, thus providing uniform inside and outside deburring in one simple operation. The deburring tool is mounted on an anodized aluminum handle that is machine-knurled for a sure grip.
MSRP: **$16.50**

MASTER CASTING KIT

Designed especially to meet the needs of blackpowder shooters, this kit features Lyman's combination round ball and maxi ball mould blocks. It also contains a combination double cavity mould, mould handle, mini-mag furnace, lead dipper, bullet lube, a user's manual and a cast bullet guide. Kits are available in .45, .50 and .54 caliber.
MSRP: **$220**

POWER DEBURRING KIT

Features a high torque, rechargeable power driver plus a complete set of accessories, including inside and outside deburr tools, large and small reamers and cleaners and case neck brushes. No threading or chucking required. Set also includes battery recharger and standard flat and Phillips driver bits.
MSRP: **$58.95**

MEC Reloading

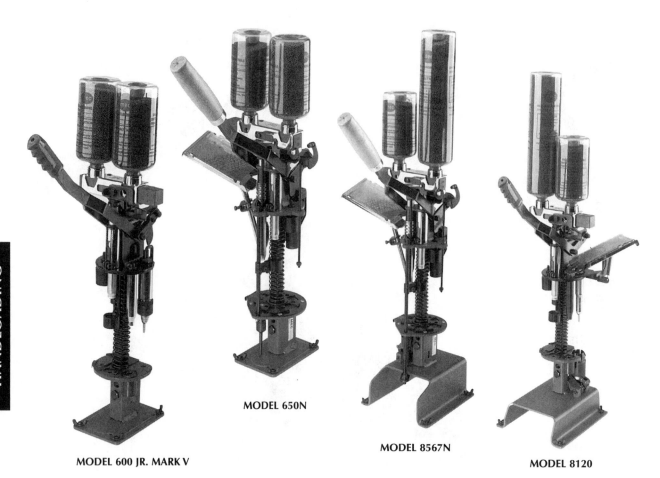

MODEL 600 JR. MARK V

MODEL 650N

MODEL 8567N

MODEL 8120

MODEL 600 JR. MARK V

This single-stage reloader features a cam-action crimp die to ensure that each shell returns to its original condition. MEC's 600 Jr. Mark 5 can load 6 to 8 boxes per hour and can be updated with the 285 CA primer feed. Press is adjustable for 3 in. shells.
MSRP: **$153–167**

MODEL 650N

This reloader works on 6 shells at once. A reloaded shell is completed with every stroke. The MEC 650 does not resize except as a separate operation. Automatic primer feed is standard. Simply fill it with a full box of primers and it will do the rest. Reloader has 3 crimping stations: the first one starts the crimp, the second closes the crimp and the third places a taper on the shell. Available in 12, 16, 20 and 28 ga. and .410 bore. No die sets available.
MSRP: **$305–334**

MODEL 8567N GRABBER

This reloader features 12 different operations at all 6 stations, producing finished shells with each stroke of the handle. It includes a fully automatic primer feed and Auto-Cycle charging, plus MEC's exclusive 3-stage crimp. The "Power Ring" resizer ensures consistent, accurately sized shells without interrupting the reloading sequence. Simply put in the wads and shell casings, then remove the loaded shells with each pull of the handle. Optional kits to load 3 in. shells and steel shot make this reloader tops in its field. Resizes high and low base shells. Available in 12, 16, 20, 28 ga. and .410 bore.
MSRP: **$429–470**

MODEL 8120 SIZEMASTER

Sizemaster's "Power Ring" collet resizer returns each base to factory specifications. This resizing station handles brass or steel heads, both high and low base. An 8-fingered collet squeezes the base back to original dimensions, then opens up to release the shell easily. The E-Z Prime auto primer feed is standard equipment (not offered in .410 bore). Press is adjustable for 3 in. shells and is available in 10, 12, 16, 20, 28 ga. and .410 bore. Die sets are available at: $88.67 ($104.06 in 10 ga.).
MSRP: **$231–253**

MEC Reloading

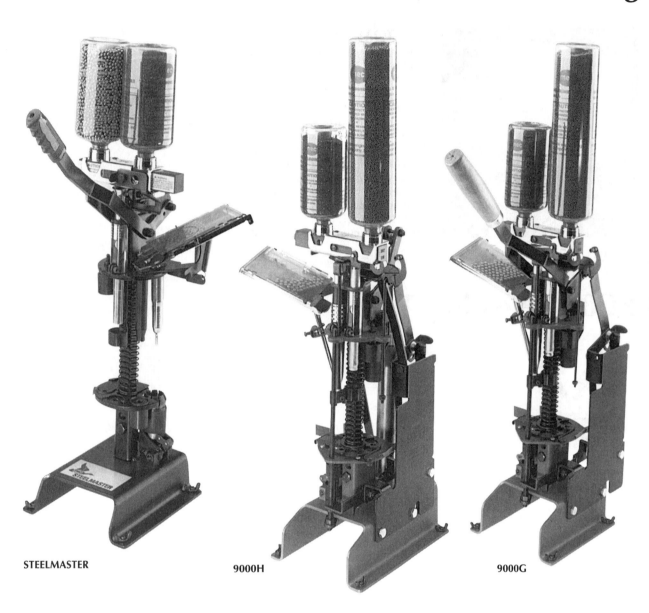

STEELMASTER

9000H

9000G

HANDLOADING

STEELMASTER SINGLE STATE

Equipped to load steel shotshells as well as lead ones. Every base is resized to factory specs by a precision "power ring" collet. Handles brass or steel heads in high or low base. The E-Z prime auto primer feed dispenses primers automatically and is standard equipment. Separate presses are available for 12 ga. 2¾", 3", 3½" and 10 ga.

8639 Steelmaster 10 & 12 ga.: . . . . . .
                       $262–274

8755 Steelmaster
   12 ga. 3½" only: **$274**

9000 SERIES SHOTSHELL RELOADER

MEC's 9000 Series features automatic indexing and finished shell ejection for quicker and easier reloading. The factory set speed provides uniform movement through every reloading stage. Dropping the primer into the reprime station no longer requires operator "feel." The reloader requires only a minimal adjustment from low to high brass domestic shells, any one of which can be removed for inspection from any station. Can be set up for automat-

ic or manual indexing. Available in 12, 16, 20 and 28 ga. and .410 bore. No die sets are available.

MEC 9000HN: **$1056–1650**
MEC 9001HN without pump: . . . . . .
                          $578–634
MEC 9000GN Series: **$517–566**
MEC Super Sizer: **$87–95**

Nosler Reloading

CUSTOM BRASS

Nosler offers cartridge brass in .260 Remington, .280 Ackley Improved, .300 H&H Magnum and .300 Short Action Ultra Mag. The cartridge brass is made to exact dimensional standards and tolerances for maximum accuracy/consistency and long case life. Flash holes are deburred, and necks are deburred and chamfered. Packaged in custom boxes of 50.

260 Rem: **$50.95**
.280 Ackley: **$60.95**
.300 H&H Mag: **$50.95**
.300 Short Action: **$58.95**

HANDLOADING

RCBS Reloading Tools

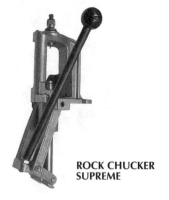

ROCK CHUCKER SUPREME

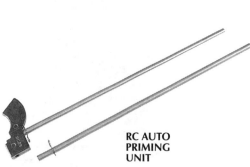

RC AUTO PRIMING UNIT

AMMOMASTER-2 SINGLE STAGE

PRESSES

ROCK CHUCKER SUPREME PRESS

With its easy operation, outstanding strength and versatility, a Rock Chucker Supreme press serves beginner and pro alike. It can also be upgraded to a progressive press with an optional Piggyback conversion unit.

- Heavy-duty cast iron for easy case-resizing
- Larger window opening to accommodate longer cartridges
- 1" ram held in place by 12½ sq. in. of rambearing surface
- Ambidextrous handle
- Compound leverage system
- ⁷/₈" x 14" thread for all standard reloading dies and accessories

MSRP: **$184.95**

ROCK CHUCKER SUPREME AUTO PRIMING UNIT

RCBS's Rock Chucker Supreme Auto Priming Unit will allow the users of the current single stage model to advance to a tube-fed auto priming system. The new auto-priming option will expand the capabilities of one of the most popular reloading presses. It eliminates the need to handle primers and boasts a 100 primer capacity. The new feature is easy to install to existing presses, as the RC Supreme Auto Prime body attaches to the same place as the standard priming arm. The upgraded unit is operated with a push bar, and comes with a large and small primer pick up, feed tubes and primer seat plugs.

MSRP: **$47.95**

AMMOMASTER-2 RELOADING SYSTEM

The AmmoMaster offers handloaders the freedom to configure a press to particular needs and preferences. It covers the complete spectrum of reloading, from single stage through fully automatic progressive reloading, from .25 Auto to .50 caliber. The AmmoMaster Auto has all the features of a five-station press.

MSRP: **$331.95**

RCBS Reloading Tools

GRAND SHOTSHELL PRESS

MINI-GRAND SHOTSHELL PRESS

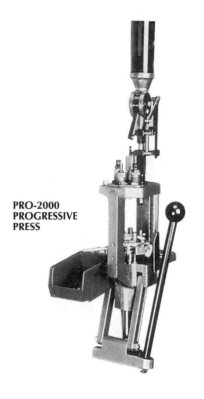

PRO-2000 PROGRESSIVE PRESS

.50 BMG PACK

The Pack includes the press, dies and accessory items needed, all in one box. The press is the Ammo Master Single Stage rigged for 1½″ dies. It has a 1½″ solid steel ram and plenty of height for the big .50. The kit also has a set of RCBS .50 BMG, 1½″ reloading dies, including both full-length sizer and seater. Other items are a shell holder, ram priming unit and a trim die.
MSRP: **$721.95**

GRAND SHOTSHELL PRESS

Features: The combination of the Powder system and shot system and Case Holders allows the user to reload shells without fear of spillage. The powder system is case-actuated: no hull, no powder. Cases are easily removed with universal 12 and 20 ga. case holders allowing cases to be sized down to the rim. Priming system: Only one primer feeds at a time. Steel size ring: Provides complete resizing of high and low base hulls. Holds 25 lbs. of shot and 1½ lbs. of powder. Lifetime warranty.
MSRP: **$966.95**
Grand Conversion kit: **$461.95**

MINI-GRAND SHOTSHELL PRESS

The Mini-Grand shotgun press, a seven-station single-stage press, loads 12 and 20 ga. hulls, from 2¾ to 3½ in. in length. It utilizes RCBS, Hornady and Ponsness Warren powder and shot bushings, with a half-pound capacity powder hopper and 12½ lb. capacity shot hopper. The machine will load both lead and steel shot.
MSRP: **$159.95**

ROCK CHUCKER SUPREME MASTER RELOADING KIT

The Rock Chucker Master Reloading Kit includes all the tools and accessories needed to start handloading: Rock Chucker Press; RCBS 505 Reloading Scale; Speer Manual #13; Uniflow Powder Measure; deburring tool; case loading block; Primer Tray-2; Hand priming tool; powder funnel; case lube pad; case neck brushes; fold-up hex key set; Trim Pro Manual Case Trimmer Kit.
MSRP: **$432.95**

PARTNER PRESS

Easy-to-use, durable press in a compact package. Features compound linkage, durable steel links, priming arm. Reloads most standard calibers.
MSRP: **$88.95**
Partner Press Reloading Kit: $222.95

PRO-2000 PROGRESSIVE PRESS

Constructed of cast iron, the Pro-2000 features five reloading stations. The case-actuated powder measure assures repeatability of dispensing powder. A Micrometer Adjustment Screw allows precise return to previously recorded charges. All dies are standard ⅞″ x 14″, including the Expander Die. The press incorporates the APS Priming System. Allows full-length sizing in calibers from .32 Auto to .460 Weatherby Mag.
MSRP: **$635.95**
Deluxe Reloading Kit: **$1142.95**

RCBS Reloading Tools

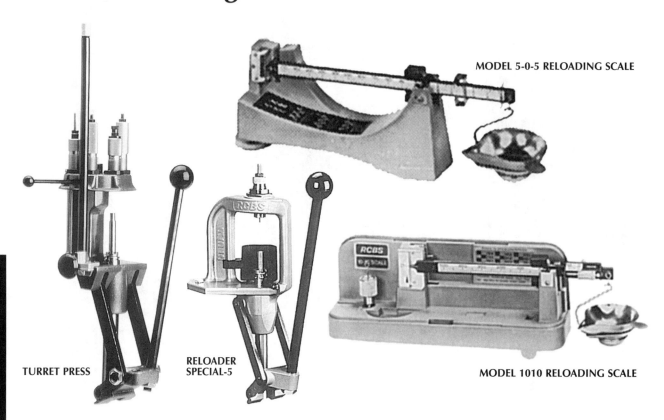

MODEL 5-0-5 RELOADING SCALE

TURRET PRESS

RELOADER SPECIAL-5

MODEL 1010 RELOADING SCALE

TURRET PRESS

With pre-set dies in the six-station turret head, the Turret Press can increase production from 50 to 200 rounds per hour. The frame, links, and toggle block are constructed of cast iron and the handle offers compound leverage for full-length sizing of any caliber from .25 ACP to .460 Weatherby Magnum. Six stations allow for custom set-up. The quick-change turret head makes caliber changes fast and easy. This press accepts all standard 7/8" x 14" dies and shell holders.
MSRP: **$263.95**
Turret Deluxe Reloading Kit: $517.95

RELOADER SPECIAL-5 PRESS

The Reloader Special press features a ball handle and primer arm so that cases can be primed and resized at the same time. Other features include a compound leverage system; solid aluminum "O" frame offset; corrosion-resistant baked-powder finish; 7/8" x 14" thread for all standard reloading dies and accessories; optional Piggyback II conversion unit.
MSRP: **$151.95**
Reloading Starter Kit: **$343.95**

PIGGYBACK III CONVERSION KIT

The Piggyback III conversion unit moves from single-stage reloading to 5-station, manual-indexing, progressive reloading in one step. The Piggyback III will work with the RCBS Rock Chucker, Reloader Special-3 and Reloader Special-5.
MSRP: **$479.95**

RELOADING SCALES

MODEL 5-0-5 RELOADING SCALE

This 511-grain capacity scale has a three-poise system with widely spaced, deep beam notches. Two smaller poises on right side adjust from 0.1 to 10 grains, larger one on left side adjusts in full 10-grain steps. The scale uses magnetic dampening to eliminate beam oscillation. The 5-0-5 also has a sturdy die-cast base with large leveling legs. Self-aligning agate bearings support the hardened steel beam pivots for a guaranteed sensitivity to 0.1 grains.
MSRP: **$109.95**

MODEL 1010 RELOADING SCALE

Normal capacity is 510 grains, which can be increased without loss of sensitivity by attaching the included extra weight up to 1010 grains. Features include micrometer poise for quick, precise weighing, special approach-to-weight indicator, easy-to-read graduation, magnetic dampener, agate bearings, anti-tip pan and a dustproof lid snaps on to cover scale for storage. Sensitivity is guaranteed to 0.1 grains.
MSRP: **$183.95**

RCBS Reloading Tools

CHARGEMASTER 1500

RANGEMASTER 750

APS PRIMER STRIP LOADER

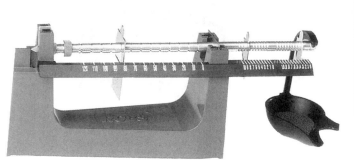

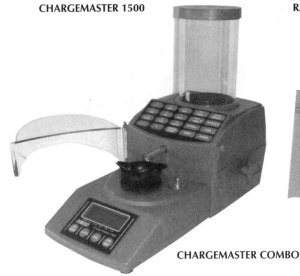

RC-130 MECHANICAL SCALE

CHARGEMASTER COMBO

CHARGEMASTER 1500 SCALE

High performance reloading scale with 1500-grain capacity. Scale reads in grains or grams; calibration weights included. Available in 110 or 220 volt—AC adaptor included. Can be upgraded to an automatic dispensing system with the RCBS ChargeMaster.
MSRP: **$232.95**

CHARGEMASTER COMBO

Performs as a scale or as a complete powder dispensing system. Scale can be removed and used separately. Dispenses from 2.0 to 300 grains. Reads and dispenses in grains or grams. Stores up to 30 charges in memory for quick recall of favorite

loads. 110 volt or 220 volt adaptor included.
MSRP: **$443.95**

RANGEMASTER 750 SCALE

Compact, lightweight and portable with 750-grain capacity. Scale reads in grams or grains; calibration weights included. Accurate to ± 0.1 of a grain; fast calibration; Powered by AC or 9 volt battery—AC adaptor included. 110 or 220 volt model available.
MSRP: **$147.95**

RC-130 MECHANICAL SCALE

The RC130 features a 130-grain capacity and maintenance-free movement, plus a magnetic dampening sys-

tem for fast readings. A 3-poise design incorporates easy adjustments with a beam that is graduated in increments of 10 grains and 1 grain. A micrometer poise measures in 0.1-grain increments with accuracy to ±0.1 grain.
MSRP: **$54.95**

HANDLOADING ACCESSORIES

APS PRIMER STRIP LOADER

For those who keep a supply of CCI primers in conventional packaging, the APS primer strip loader allows quick filling of empty strips. Each push of the handle seats 25 primers.
MSRP: **$36.95**

RCBS Reloading Tools

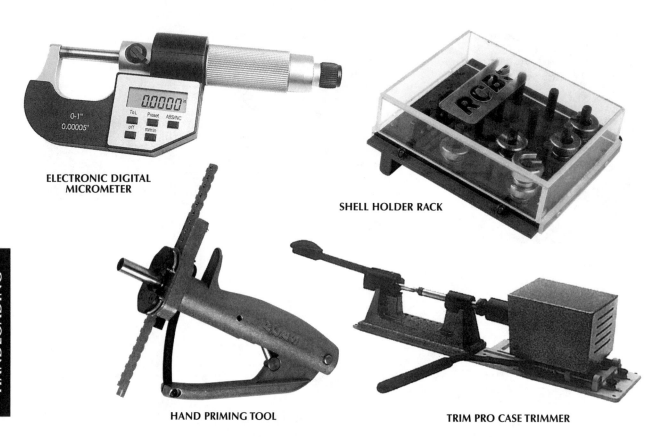

ELECTRONIC DIGITAL MICROMETER

SHELL HOLDER RACK

HAND PRIMING TOOL

TRIM PRO CASE TRIMMER

ELECTRONIC DIGITAL MICROMETER

Instant reading; large, easy to read numbers for error reduction with instant inch/millimeter conversion; zero adjust at any position; thimble lock for measuring like objects; replaceable silver oxide cell—1.55 Volt; auto off after 5 minutes for longer battery life; adjustment wrench included; fitted wooden storage cases.
MSRP: $147.95

HAND PRIMING TOOL

A patented safety mechanism separates the seating operation from the primer supply, virtually eliminating the possibility of tray detonation. Fits in your hand for portable primer seating. Primer tray installation requires no contact with the primers. Uses the same RCBS shell holders as RCBS presses. Made of cast metal.
MSRP: $46.95

SHELL HOLDER RACK

RCBS has developed the Shell Holder Rack to give reloaders another unique way to stay organized. This item allows shooters quick and easy access to all shell holders, and eliminates digging through several loose holders to find the right one. The Shell Holder Rack has twelve positions that hold two shell holders on each post. There is also room to store six Trim Pro Shell Holders as well. Its clear cover keeps out the dust and dirt while allowing you to see what is stored in the rack. This rack can also be mounted on the wall or used on the bench. The wall mount spacing allows it to be hung off of standard 1-in. pegboard hooks as well. The support legs angle the bottom out for wall mounting or the top up for bench use. Several Shell Holder Racks can be snapped together if more shell holder storage is needed, and stickers are included to label shell holder posts.
MSRP: $18.95

POW'R PULL BULLET PULLER

The RCBS Pow'r Pull bullet puller features a three-jaw chuck that grips the case rim—just rap it on any solid surface like a hammer, and powder and bullet drop into the main chamber for re-use. A soft cushion protects bullets from damage. Works with most centerfire cartridges from .22 to .45 (not for use with rimfire cartridges).
MSRP: $18.95

TRIM PRO CASE TRIMMER

Cases are trimmed quickly and easily. The lever-type handle is more accurate to use than draw collet systems. A flat plate shell holder keeps cases locked in place and aligned. A micrometer fine adjustment bushing offers trimming accuracy to within .001 in. Made of die-cast metal with hardened cutting blades.
Power 120 Vac Kit: $337.95
Manual Kit: $121.95
Trim Pro Case
    Trimmer Stand: $24.95

Redding Reloading Tools

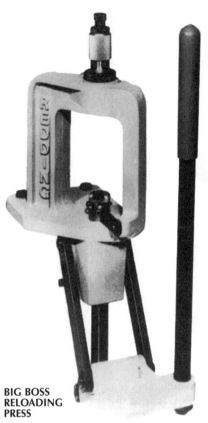

BIG BOSS RELOADING PRESS

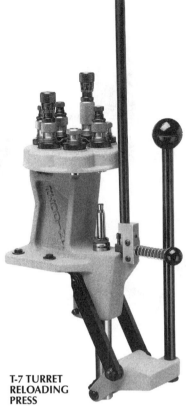

T-7 TURRET RELOADING PRESS

ULTRAMAG RELOADING PRESS

HANDLOADING

HANDLOADING PRESSES

BOSS RELOADING PRESS

This "O" type reloading press features a rigid cast iron frame whose 36 degree offset provides the best visibility and access of comparable presses. Its "Smart" primer arm moves in and out of position automatically with ram travel. The priming arm is positioned at the bottom of ram travel for lowest leverage and best feel. Model 721 accepts all standard $7/8$" x 14" threaded dies and universal shell holders.

MSRP: **$186**
W/ Shellholder and 10A Dies: . . . . .
. . . . **$241.50**
Boss Pro-Pak Reloading Kit: $469.50
W/o dies and shellholder: **$414**

BIG BOSS RELOADING PRESS

A larger version of the Boss reloading press built on a heavier frame with a longer ram stroke for reloading magnum cartridges. It features a 1 in. diameter ram with over 3.8 inches of

stroke; Smart primer arm; offset ball handle; heavy duty cast iron frame; heavy duty compound linkage; steel adapter bushing accepts all standard $7/8$" x 14" threaded dies.
MSRP: **$262.50**

T-7 TURRET RELOADING PRESS

Features 7 station turret head, heavy duty cast iron frame, 1 in. diameter ram, optional "Slide Bar Automatic Primer Feeder System." This feeder eliminates handling of primers during sizing and speeds up reloading operations.

T-7 Turret Press: **$408**
Kit (press, shellholder and
. . . **10A dies):** **$463.50**
Slide Bar Automatic
. . . **Primer Feeder System:** **$60**

ULTRAMAG RELOADING PRESS

The Ultramag's compound leverage system is connected at the top of the press frame. This allows the reloader to develop tons of pressure without the

usual concern of press frame deflection. Huge frame opening will handle 50 x 3¼-inch Sharps with ease.
MSRP: **$424.50**
Kit, includes shell holder
. . . **and one set of 10A dies:** . . . **$480**

DIES & BUSHINGS

BODY DIES

Designed to full-length resize the case body and bump the shoulder position for proper chambering without disturbing the case neck. They are intended for use only to resize cases that have become increasingly difficult to chamber after repeated firing and neck sizing. Small Base Body Dies are available in .223 Rem, 6mm P.P.C, 6mm B. R. Rem, 6mm/284 Win, .260 Rem, 6.5mm/284 Win, .284 Win, .308 Win, .30-06.
Category I: **$337.80**
Category II: **$46.80**
Category III: **$57.60**
Small Base Body Dies: **$47.10**

Redding Reloading Dies

COMPETITION BULLET
SEATING DIE

FORM & TRIM
DIES

NECK SIZING
DIES

NECK SIZING
BUSHINGS

COMPETITION
BUSHING STYLE - NECK
SIZING DIE

PISTOL TRIM
DIES

HANDLOADING

COMPETITION BULLET SEATING DIE FOR HANDGUN & STRAIGHT-WALL RIFLE CARTRIDGES

The precision seating stem moves well down into the die chamber to accomplish early bullet contact. The seating stem's spring loading provides positive alignment bias between the tapered nose and the bullet ogive. Thus spring loading and bullet alignment are maintained as the bullet and cartridge case move upward until the actual seating of the bullet begins. The Competition Bullet Seating Die features dial-in micrometer adjustment calibrated in .001-in. increments, is infinitely adjustable and has a "zero" set feature that allows setting desired load to zero. The die is compatible with all progressive reloading presses and has industry standard 7/8" x 14" threaded extended die bodies. An oversize bell-mouth chamfer with smooth radius has been added to the bottom of the die.
MSRP: **$108.60**

COMPETITION BUSHING-STYLE NECK SIZING DIE

This die allows you to fit the neck of your case perfectly in the chamber. As in the Competition Seating Die, the cartridge case is completely supported and aligned with the sizing bushing and remains supported in the sliding sleeve as it moves upward while the resizing bushing self-centers on the case neck. The micrometer adjustment of the bushing position delivers precise control to the desired neck length. All dies are supplied without bushings.
Category I: **$144.60**
Category II: **$172.50**
Category III: **$213**

FORM & TRIM DIES

Redding trim dies file trim cases without unnecessary resizing because they are made to chamber dimensions. For case forming and necking brass down from another caliber, Redding trim dies can be the perfect intermediate step before full length resizing.
Series A: **$37.80**
Series B: **$52.50**
Series C: **$64.20**
Series D: **$70.80**

NECK SIZING BUSHINGS

Redding Neck Sizing Bushings are available in two styles. Both share the same external dimensions (½" O.D. x 3/8" long) and freely interchange in all

Redding Bushing style Neck Sizing Dies. They are available in .001" size increments throughout the range of .185" thru .365", covering all calibers from .17 to .338.
MSRP: **$18.30**
Heat treated steel bushings: .**$32.40**

NECK SIZING DIES

These dies size only the necks of bottleneck cases to prolong brass life and improve accuracy. These dies size only the neck and not the shoulder or body, fired cases should not be interchanged between rifles of the same caliber. Available individually or in Deluxe Die Sets.
Series A: **$42.60**
Series B: **$57.60**
Series C: **$72.90**
Series D: **$82.20**

PISTOL TRIM DIES

Redding trim dies for pistol calibers allow trimming cases without excessive resizing. Pistol trim dies require extended shellholders.
Series A: **$37.80**
Series B: **$52.50**
Series C: **$64.20**
Series D: **$70.80**

Redding Reloading Tools

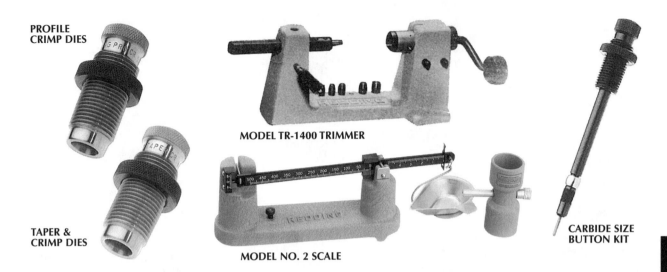

PROFILE CRIMP DIES

MODEL TR-1400 TRIMMER

TAPER & CRIMP DIES

MODEL NO. 2 SCALE

CARBIDE SIZE BUTTON KIT

PROFILE CRIMP DIES

For handgun cartridges which do not head-space on the case mouth. These dies were designed for those who want the best possible crimp. Profile crimp dies provide a tighter, more uniform roll type crimp, and require the bullet to be seated to the correct depth in a previous operation.

Series A: $33.90
Series B: $42
Series C: $51
Series D: $57.60

TAPER & CRIMP DIES

Designed for handgun cartridges which headspace on the case mouth where conventional roll crimping is undesirable. Also available for some revolver cartridges, for those who prefer the uniformity of a taper crimp. Available in the following rifle calibers: .223 Rem., 7.62MM x 39, .30-30, .308 Win, .30-06, .300, Win Mag.

Series A: $33.90
Series B: $42
Series C: $51
Series D: $57.60

TYPE S–BUSHING STYLE DIES

The new Type S - Bushing Style Neck Sizing Die provides reloaders with a simple means to precisely control case neck size and tension. The Type-S features: interchangeable sizing bushings available in .001 in. increments; adjustable decapping rod with standard size button; self-centering resizing bushing; decapping pin retainer. All dies are supplied without bushings.

Category I:. $75
Category II: $91.50
Category III: $112.50

CASE TRIMMERS

MASTER CASE TRIMMER MODEL TR-1400

This unit features a universal collet that accepts all rifle and pistol cases. The frame is cast iron with storage holes in the base for extra pilots. Coarse and fine adjustments are provided for case length. The Master Case Trimmer also features: six pilots (.22, 6mm, .25, .270, 7mm and .30 cal.); universal collet; two neck cleaning brushes (.22 through .30 cal.); two primer pocket cleaners (large and small); tin coated replaceable cutter; accessory power screwdriver adaptor.

Master Case Trimmer: $132
Pilots: $5.70

POWDER SCALES

MODEL NO. 2 MASTER POWDER AND BULLET SCALE

Model No. 2 features 505-grain capacity and .1-grain accuracy, a dampened beam and hardened knife edges and milled stainless bearing seats for smooth, consistent operation and a high level of durability.

MSRP: $118.50

HANDLOADING ACCESSORIES

CARBIDE SIZE BUTTON KITS

Make inside neck sizing smoother and easier without lubrication. Now die sets can be upgraded with a carbide size button kit. Available for bottleneck cartridges .22 thru .338 cal. The carbide size button is free-floating on the decap rod, allowing it to self-center in the case neck. Kits contain: carbide size button, retainer and spare decapping pin. These kits also fit all Type-S dies.

MSRP: $36

MODEL 3 POWDER MEASURE

The Model 3 has a micrometer metering chamber in front for easy setting and reading. The frame is precision machined cast iron with hand honed fit between the frame and hard surfaced drum to easily cut and meter powders. The Model 3 features a large capacity clear powder reservoir; see-through drop tube; body w/ standard $7/8$" x 14" thread to fit mounting bracket and optional bench stand; cast mounting bracket included.

Powder Measure 3 with universal metering chamber: $178.50
Powder Measure 3K, w/ two metering chambers: $216.60
Handgun Metering Chamber: $49.50

Redding Reloading Tools

EZ FEED SHELL HOLDERS

HEADSPACE & BULLET COMPARATOR

MODEL 10X-PISTOL AND SMALL RIFLE MEASURE

MODEL BR-30 MEASURE

EXTENDED SHELL HOLDERS

COMPETITION MODEL 10X-PISTOL AND SMALL RIFLE POWDER MEASURE

Combines all of the features of Competition Model BR-30, with a drum and metering unit designed to provide uniform metering of small charge weights. To achieve the best metering possible at the targeted charge weight of approximately 10 grains, the diameter of the metering cavity is reduced and the metering plunger is given a hemispherical shape. Charge range: 1 to 25 grains. Drum assembly easily changed from right to left-handed operation.
MSRP: $267

COMPETITION MODEL BR-30 POWDER MEASURE

This powder measure features a drum and micrometer that limit the overall charging range from a low of 10 grains to a maximum of 50 grains. The diameter of Model 3BR's metering cavity has been reduced, and the metering plunger has a unique hemispherical shape, creating a powder cavity that resembles the bottom of a test tube. The result: irregular powder settling is alleviated and charge-to-charge uniformity is enhanced.
MSRP: $267

MATCH-GRADE POWDER MEASURE MODEL 3BR

Interchange Universal- or pistol-metering chambers. Measures charges up to 100 grains. Unit is fitted with lock ring for fast dump with large clear plastic reservoir. See-through drop tube accepts all calibers from .22 to .600. Precision-fitted rotating drum is critically honed to prevent powder escape. Knife-edged powder chamber shears coarse-grained powders with ease, ensuring accurate charges.
Match Grade 3BR measure: . . $225
3BR Kit, with both
    chambers: $279
Pistol Metering chamber
    (0-10 grains): $68.40

SHELLHOLDERS

EZ FEED SHELLHOLDERS

Redding shellholders are of a Universal "snap-in" design recommended for use with all Redding dies and presses, as well as all other popular brands. They are precision machined to very close tolerances and heat treated to fit cases and eliminate potential resizing problems. The outside knurling makes them easier to handle and change.
MSRP: $11.70

EXTENDED SHELL HOLDERS

Extended shellholders are required when trimming short cases under 1½ in. O.A.L. They are machined to the same tolerances as standard shellholders, except they're longer.
MSRP: $18.60

HANDLOADING TOOLS

INSTANT INDICATOR HEADSPACE & BULLET COMPARATOR

The Instant Indicator checks the headspace from the case shoulder to the base. Bullet seating depths can be compared and bullets can be sorted by checking the base of bullets to give dimension. Case length can be measured. Available for 33 cartridges from .222 Rem to .338 Win. Mag., including new WSSM cartridges.
W/ Dial Indicator: $162.60
W/o Dial Indicator: $125.70

540 CENTERFIRE RIFLE BALLISTICS TABLES FOR SPORTING RIFLE CARTRIDGES

572 CENTERFIRE HANDGUN BALLISTICS TABLES

Centerfire Rifle Ballistics

Comprehensive Ballistics Tables for Currently Manufactured Sporting Rifle Cartridges

No more collecting catalogs and peering at microscopic print to find out what ammunition is offered for a cartridge, and how it performs relative to other factory loads! *Shooter's Bible* has assembled the data for you, in easy-to-read tables, by cartridge. Of course, this section will be updated every year to bring you the latest information.

Data is taken from manufacturers' charts; your chronograph readings may vary. Listings are current as of February the year *Shooter's Bible* appears (not the cover year). Listings are not intended as recommendations. For example, the data for the .44 Magnum at 400 yards shows its effective range is much shorter. The lack of data for a 285-grain .375 H&H bullet beyond 300 yards does not mean the bullet has no authority farther out. Besides ammunition, the rifle, sights, conditions and shooter ability all must be considered when contemplating a long shot. Accuracy and bullet energy both matter when big game is in the offing.

Barrel length affects velocity, and at various rates depending on the load. As a rule, figure 50 fps per inch of barrel, plus or minus, if your barrel is longer or shorter than 22 inches.

Bullets are given by make, weight (in grains) and type. Most type abbreviations are self-explanatory: BT=Boat-Tail, FMJ=Full Metal Jacket, HP=Hollow Point, SP=Soft Point—except in Hornady listings, where SP is the firm's Spire Point. TNT and TXP are trademarked designations of Speer and Norma. XLC identifies a coated Barnes X bullet. HE indicates a Federal High Energy load, similar to the Hornady LM (Light Magnum) and HM (Heavy Magnum) cartridges.

Arc (trajectory) is based on a zero range published by the manufacturer, from 100 to 300 yards. If a zero does not fall in a yardage column, it lies halfway between—at 150 yards, for example, if the bullet's strike is "+" at 100 yards and "-" at 200.

.17 REMINGTON TO .221 REMINGTON FIREBALL

CARTRIDGE BULLET	RANGE, YARDS:	0	100	200	300	400
.17 REMINGTON						
Rem. 20 AccuTip BT	velocity, fps:	4250	3594	3028	2529	2081
	energy, ft-lb:	802	574	407	284	192
	arc, inches:		+1.3	+1.3	-2.5	-11.8
Rem. 20 Fireball	velocity, fps	4000	3380	2840	2360	1930
	energy, ft-lb:	710	507	358	247	165
	arc, inches		+1.6	+1.5	-2.8	-13.5
Rem. 25 HP Power-Lokt	velocity, fps:	4040	3284	2644	2086	1606
	energy, ft-lb:	906	599	388	242	143
	arc, inches:		+1.8	0	-3.3	-16.6
.204 RUGER						
Federal 32 Nosler Ballistic Tip	velocity, fps	4030	3465	2968	2523	2119
	arc, inches		+0.7	0	-4.7	-14.9
Hornady 32 V-Max	velocity, fps:	4225	3632	3114	2652	2234
	energy, ft-lb:	1268	937	689	500	355
	arc, inches:		+0.6	0	-4.2	-13.4
Hornady 40 V-Max	velocity, fps:	3900	3451	3046	2677	2335
	energy, ft-lb:	1351	1058	824	636	485
	arc, inches:		+0.7	0	-4.5	-13.9
Rem. 32 AccuTip	velocity, fps:	4225	3632	3114	2652	2234
	Energy, ft-lb:	1268	937	689	500	355
	Arc, inches:		+0.6	0	-4.1	-13.1
Rem. 40 AccuTip	velocity, fps:	3900	3451	3046	2677	2336
	energy, ft-lb:	1351	1058	824	636	485
	arc, inches:		+0.7	0	-4.3	-13.2
Win. 32 Ballistic Silver Tip	velocity, fps	4050	3482	2984	2537	2132
	energy, ft-lb	1165	862	632	457	323
	arc, inches		+0.7	0	-4.6	-14.7
Win. 34 HP	velocity, fps:	4025	3339	2751	2232	1775
	energy, ft-lb:	1223	842	571	376	238
	arc, inches:		+0.8	0	-5.5	-18.1

CARTRIDGE BULLET	RANGE, YARDS:	0	100	200	300	400
.218 BEE						
Win. 46 Hollow Point	velocity, fps:	2760	2102	1550	1155	961
	energy, ft-lb:	778	451	245	136	94
	arc, inches:		0	-7.2	-29.4	
.22 HORNET						
Hornady 35 V-Max	velocity, fps:	3100	2278	1601	1135	929
	energy, ft-lb:	747	403	199	100	67
	arc, inches:		+2.8	0	-16.9	-60.4
Rem. 35 AccuTip	velocity, fps:	3100	2271	1591	1127	924
	energy, ft-lb:	747	401	197	99	66
	arc, inches:		+1.5	-3.5	-22.3	-68.4
Rem. 45 Pointed Soft Point	velocity, fps:	2690	2042	1502	1128	948
	energy, ft-lb:	723	417	225	127	90
	arc, inches:		0	-7.1	-30.0	
Rem. 45 Hollow Point	velocity, fps:	2690	2042	1502	1128	948
	energy, ft-lb:	723	417	225	127	90
	arc, inches:		0	-7.1	-30.0	
Win. 34 Jacketed HP	velocity, fps:	3050	2132	1415	1017	852
	energy, ft-lb:	700	343	151	78	55.
	arc, inches:		0	-6.6	-29.9	
Win. 45 Soft Point	velocity, fps:	2690	2042	1502	1128	948.
	energy, ft-lb:	723	417	225	127	90
	arc, inches:		0	-7.7	-31.3	
Win. 46 Hollow Point	velocity, fps:	2690	2042	1502	1128	948.
	energy, ft-lb:	739	426	230	130	92
	arc, inches:		0	-7.7	-31.3	
.221 REMINGTON FIREBALL						
Rem. 50 AccuTip BT	velocity, fps:	2995	2605	2247	1918	1622
	energy, ft-lb:	996	753	560	408	292
	arc, inches:		+1.8	0	-8.8	-27.1

.222 REMINGTON

CARTRIDGE BULLET	RANGE, YARDS:	0	100	200	300	400
Federal 50 Hi-Shok	velocity, fps:	3140	2600	2120	1700	1350
	energy, ft-lb:	1095	750	500	320	200
	arc, inches:		+1.9	0	-9.7	-31.6
Federal 55 FMJ boat-tail	velocity, fps:	3020	2740	2480	2230	1990
	energy, ft-lb:	1115	915	750	610	484.
	arc, inches:		+1.6	0	-7.3	-21.5
Hornady 40 V-Max	velocity, fps:	3600	3117	2673	2269	1911
	energy, ft-lb:	1151	863	634	457	324
	arc, inches:		+1.1	0	-6.1	-18.9
Hornady 50 V-Max	velocity, fps:	3140	2729	2352	2008	1710.
	energy, ft-lb:	1094	827	614	448	325
	arc, inches:		+1.7	0	-7.9	-24.4
Norma 50 Soft Point	velocity, fps:	3199	2667	2193	1771	
	energy, ft-lb:	1136	790	534	348	
	arc, inches:		+1.7	0	-9.1	
Norma 50 FMJ	velocity, fps:	2789	2326	1910	1547	
	energy, ft-lb:	864	601	405	266	
	arc, inches:		+2.5	0	-12.2	
Norma 62 Soft Point	velocity, fps:	2887	2457	2067	1716	
	energy, ft-lb:	1148	831	588	405	
	arc, inches:		+2.1	0	-10.4	
PMC 50 Pointed Soft Point	velocity, fps:	3044	2727	2354	2012	1651
	energy, ft-lb:	1131	908	677	494	333
	arc, inches:		+1.6	0	-7.9	-24.5
PMC 55 Pointed Soft Point	velocity, fps:	2950	2594	2266	1966	1693
	energy, ft-lb:	1063	822	627	472	350
	arc, inches:		+1.9	0	-8.7	-26.3
Rem. 50 Pointed Soft Point	velocity, fps:	3140	2602	2123	1700	1350.
	energy, ft-lb:	1094	752	500	321	202
	arc, inches:		+1.9	0	-9.7	-31.7
Rem. 50 HP Power-Lokt	velocity, fps:	3140	2635	2182	1777	1432.
	energy, ft-lb:	1094	771	529	351	228
	arc, inches:		+1.8	0	-9.2	-29.6
Rem. 50 AccuTip BT	velocity, fps:	3140	2744	2380	2045	1740
	energy, ft-lb:	1094	836	629	464	336.
	arc, inches:		+1.6	0	-7.8	-23.9
Win. 40 Ballistic Silvertip	velocity, fps:	3370	2915	2503	2127	1786
	energy, ft-lb:	1009	755	556	402	283
	arc, inches:		+1.3	0	-6.9	-21.5
Win. 50 Pointed Soft Point	velocity, fps:	3140	2602	2123	1700	1350
	energy, ft-lb:	1094	752	500	321	202
	arc, inches:		+2.2	0	-10.0	-32.3

.223 REMINGTON

CARTRIDGE BULLET	RANGE, YARDS:	0	100	200	300	400
Black Hills 40 Nosler B. Tip	velocity, fps:	3600				
	energy, ft-lb:	1150				
	arc, inches:					
Black Hills 50 V-Max	velocity, fps:	3300				
	energy, ft-lb:	1209				
	arc, inches:					
Black Hills 52 Match HP	velocity, fps:	3300				
	energy, ft-lb:	1237				
	arc, inches:					
Black Hills 55 Softpoint	velocity, fps:	3250				
	energy, ft-lb:	1270				
	arc, inches:					
Black Hills 60 SP or V-Max	velocity, fps:	3150				
	energy, ft-lb:	1322				
	arc, inches:					
Black Hills 60 Partition	velocity, fps:	3150				
	energy, ft-lb:	1322				
	arc, inches:					
Black Hills 68 Heavy Match	velocity, fps:	2850				
	energy, ft-lb:	1227				
	arc, inches:					
Black Hills 69 Sierra MK	velocity, fps:	2850				
	energy, ft-lb:	1245				
	arc, inches:					
Black Hills 73 Berger BTHP	velocity, fps:	2750				
	energy, ft-lb:	1226				
	arc, inches:					
Black Hills 75 Heavy Match	velocity, fps:	2750				
	energy, ft-lb:	1259				
	arc, inches:					
Black Hills 77 Sierra MKing	velocity, fps:	2750				
	energy, ft-lb:	1293				
	arc, inches:					
Federal 50 Jacketed HP	velocity, fps:	3400	2910	2460	2060	1700
	energy, ft-lb:	1285	940	675	470	320
	arc, inches:		+1.3	0	-7.1	-22.7
Federal 50 Speer TNT HP	velocity, fps:	3300	2860	2450	2080	1750
	energy, ft-lb:	1210	905	670	480	340
	arc, inches:		+1.4	0	-7.3	-22.6
Federal 52 Sierra MatchKing BTHP	velocity, fps:	3300	2860	2460	2090	1760
	energy, ft-lb:	1255	945	700	505	360
	arc, inches:		+1.4	0	-7.2	-22.4
Federal 55 Hi-Shok	velocity, fps:	3240	2750	2300	1910	1550
	energy, ft-lb:	1280	920	650	445	295
	arc, inches:		+1.6	0	-8.2	-26.1
Federal 55 FMJ boat-tail	velocity, fps:	3240	2950	2670	2410	2170
	energy, ft-lb:	1280	1060	875	710	575
	arc, inches:		+1.3	0	-6.1	-18.3
Federal 55 Sierra GameKing BTHP	velocity, fps:	3240	2770	2340	1950	1610
	energy, ft-lb:	1280	935	670	465	315
	arc, inches:		+1.5	0	-8.0	-25.3
Federal 55 Trophy Bonded	velocity, fps:	3100	2630	2210	1830	1500.
	energy, ft-lb:	1175	845	595	410	275
	arc, inches:		+1.8	0	-8.9	-28.7
Federal 55 Nosler Bal. Tip	velocity, fps:	3240	2870	2530	2220	1920
	energy, ft-lb:	1280	1005	780	600	450
	arc, inches:		+1.4	0	-6.8	-20.8
Federal 55 Sierra BlitzKing	velocity, fps:	3240	2870	2520	2200	1910
	energy, ft-lb:	1280	1005	775	590	445
	arc, inches:		+-1.4	0	-6.9	-20.9
Federal 62 FMJ	velocity, fps:	3020	2650	2310	2000	1710
	energy, ft-lb:	1225	970	735	550	405
	arc, inches:		+1.7	0	-8.4	-25.5
Federal 64 Hi-Shok SP	velocity, fps:	3090	2690	2325	1990	1680
	energy, ft-lb:	1360	1030	770	560	400
	arc, inches:		+1.7	0	-8.2	-25.2
Federal 69 Sierra MatchKing BTHP	velocity, fps:	3000	2720	2460	2210	1980
	energy, ft-lb:	1380	1135	925	750	600
	arc, inches:		+1.6	0	-7.4	-21.9
Hornady 40 V-Max	velocity, fps:	3800	3305	2845	2424	2044
	energy, ft-lb:	1282	970	719	522	371
	arc, inches:		+0.8	0	-5.3	-16.6
Hornady 53 Hollow Point	velocity, fps:	3330	2882	2477	2106	1710
	energy, ft-lb:	1305	978	722	522	369
	arc, inches:		+1.7	0	-7.4	-22.7
Hornady 55 V-Max	velocity, fps:	3240	2859	2507	2181	1891.
	energy, ft-lb:	1282	998	767	581	437
	arc, inches:		+1.4	0	-7.1	-21.4
Hornady 55 TAP-FPD	velocity, fps:	3240	2854	2500	2172	1871
	energy, ft-lb:	1282	995	763	576	427

Centerfire Rifle Ballistics

.223 REMINGTON TO .22-250 REMINGTON

CARTRIDGE BULLET	RANGE, YARDS:	0	100	200	300	400
Hornady 55 Urban Tactical	arc, inches:		+1.4	0	-7.0	-21.4
	velocity, fps:	2970	2626	2307	2011	1739
	energy, ft-lb:	1077	842	650	494	369
Hornady 60 Soft Point	arc, inches:		+1.5	0	-8.1	-24.9
	velocity, fps:	3150	2782	2442	2127	1837.
	energy, ft-lb:	1322	1031	795	603	450
Hornady 60 TAP-FPD	arc, inches:		+1.6	0	-7.5	-22.5
	velocity, fps:	3115	2754	2420	2110	1824
	energy, ft-lb:	1293	1010	780	593	443
Hornady 60 Urban Tactical	arc, inches:		+1.6	0	-7.5	-22.9
	velocity, fps:	2950	2619	2312	2025	1762
	energy, ft-lb:	1160	914	712	546	413
Hornady 75 BTHP Match	arc, inches:		+1.6	0	-8.1	-24.7
	velocity, fps:	2790	2554	2330	2119	1926
	energy, ft-lb:	1296	1086	904	747	617
Hornacy 75 TAP-FPD	arc, inches:		+2.4	0	-8.8	-25.1
	velocity, fps:	2790	2582	2383	2193	2012
	energy, ft-lb:	1296	1110	946	801	674
Hornady 75 BTHP Tactical	arc, inches:		+1.9	0	-8.0	-23.2
	velocity, fps:	2630	2409	2199	2000	1814
	energy, ft-lb:	1152	966	805	666	548
PMC 40 non-toxic	arc, inches:		+2.0	0	-9.2	-25.9
	velocity, fps:	3500	2606	1871	1315	
	energy, ft-lb:	1088	603	311	154	
PMC 50 Sierra BlitzKing	arc, inches:		+2.6	0	-12.8	
	velocity, fps:	3300	2874	2484	2130	1809
	energy, ft-lb:	1209	917	685	504	363
PMC 52 Sierra HPBT Match	arc, inches:		+1.4	0	-7.1	-21.8
	velocity, fps:	3200	2808	2447	2117	1817
	energy, ft-lb:	1182	910	691	517	381
PMC 53 Barnes XLC	arc, inches:		+1.5	0	-7.3	-22.5.
	velocity, fps:	3200	2815	2461	2136	1840
	energy, ft-lb:	1205	933	713	537	398.
PMC 55 HP boat-tail	arc, inches:		+1.5	0	-7.2	-22.2
	velocity, fps:	3240	2717	2250	1832	1473
	energy, ft-lb:	1282	901	618	410	265
PMC 55 FMJ boat-tail	arc, inches:		+1.6	0	-8.6	-27.7
	velocity, fps:	3195	2882	2525	2169	1843
	energy, ft-lb:	1246	1014	779	574	415
PMC 55 Pointed Soft Point	arc, inches:		+1.4	0	-6.8	-21.1
	velocity, fps:	3112	2767	2421	2100	1806
	energy, ft-lb:	1182	935	715	539	398
PMC 64 Pointed Soft Point	arc, inches:		+1.5	0	-7.5	-22.9
	velocity, fps:	2775	2511	2261	2026	1806.
	energy, ft-lb:	1094	896	726	583	464
PMC 69 Sierra BTHP Match	arc, inches:		+2.0	0	-8.8	-26.1
	velocity, fps:	2900	2591	2304	2038	1791
	energy, ft-lb:	1288	1029	813	636	492
Rem. 50 AccuTip BT	arc, inches:		+1.9	0	-8.4	-25.3
	velocity, fps:	3300	2889	2514	2168	1851
	energy, ft-lb:	1209	927	701	522	380
Rem. 55 Pointed Soft Point	arc, inches:		+1.4	0	-6.9	-21.2
	velocity, fps:	3240	2747	2304	1905	1554
	energy, ft-lb:	1282	921	648	443	295
Rem. 55 HP Power-Lokt	arc, inches:		+1.6	0	-8.2	-26.2
	velocity, fps:	3240	2773	2352	1969	1627
	energy, ft-lb:	1282	939	675	473	323
Rem. 55 AccuTip BT	arc, inches:		+1.5	0	-7.9	-24.8
	velocity, fps:	3240	2854	2500	2172	1871
	energy, ft-lb:	1282	995	763	576	427
Rem. 55 Metal Case	arc, inches:		+1.5	0	-7.1	-21.7
	velocity, fps:	3240	2759	2326	1933	1587
	energy, ft-lb:	1282	929	660	456	307

CARTRIDGE BULLET	RANGE, YARDS:	0	100	200	300	400
Rem. 62 HP Match	arc, inches:		+1.6	0	-8.1	-25.5
	velocity, fps:	3025	2572	2162	1792	1471
	energy, ft-lb:	1260	911	643	442	298
Rem. 69 BTHP Match	arc, inches:		+1.9	0	-9.4	-29.9
	velocity, fps:	3000	2720	2457	2209	1975
	energy, ft-lb:	1379	1133	925	747	598
Win. 40 Ballistic Silvertip	arc, inches:		+1.6	0	-7.4	-21.9
	velocity, fps:	3700	3166	2693	2265	1879.
	energy, ft-lb:	1216	891	644	456	314
Win. 45 JHP	arc, inches:		+1.0	0	-5.8	-18.4
	velocity, fps:	3600				
	energy, ft-lb:	1295				
Win. 50 Ballistic Silvertip	arc, inches:		+1.2	0	-6.4	-19.8
	velocity, fps:	3410	2982	2593	2235	1907.
	energy, ft-lb:	1291	987	746	555	404
Win. 53 Hollow Point	arc, inches:		+1.7	0	-7.4	-22.7
	velocity, fps:	3330	2882	2477	2106	1770
	energy, ft-lb:	1305	978	722	522	369
Win. 55 Pointed Soft Point	arc, inches:		+1.9	0	-8.5	-26.7
	velocity, fps:	3240	2747	2304	1905	1554.
	energy, ft-lb:	1282	921	648	443	295
Win. 55 Super Clean NT	arc, inches:		+2.8	0	-11.9	-38.9
	velocity, fps:	3150	2520	1970	1505	1165
	energy, ft-lb:	1212	776	474	277	166
Win. 55 FMJ	arc, inches:					
	velocity, fps:	3240	2854			
	energy, ft-lb:	1282	995			
Win. 55 Ballistic Silvertip	arc, inches:		+1.4	0	-6.8	-20.8
	velocity, fps:	3240	2871	2531	2215	1923
	energy, ft-lb:	1282	1006	782	599	451
Win. 64 Power-Point	arc, inches:		+1.7	0	-8.2	-25.1
	velocity, fps:	3020	2656	2320	2009	1724
	energy, ft-lb:	1296	1003	765	574	423
Win. 64 Power-Point Plus	arc, inches:		+1.7	0	-8.2	-25.4
	velocity, fps:	3090	2684	2312	1971	1664
	energy, ft-lb:	1357	1024	760	552	393

.5.6 X 52 R

Norma 71 Soft Point	velocity, fps:	2789	2446	2128	1835	
	energy, ft-lb:	1227	944	714	531	
	arc, inches:		+2.1	0	-9.9	

.22 PPC

A-Square 52 Berger	velocity, fps:	3300	2952	2629	2329	2049
	energy, ft-lb:	1257	1006	798	626	485
	arc, inches:		+1.3	0	-6.3	-19.1

.225 WINCHESTER

Win. 55 Pointed Soft Point	velocity, fps:	3570	3066	2616	2208	1838.
	energy, ft-lb:	1556	1148	836	595	412
	arc, inches:		+2.4	+2.0	-3.5	-16.3

.224 WEATHERBY MAGNUM

Wby. 55 Pointed Expanding	velocity, fps:	3650	3192	2780	2403	2056
	energy, ft-lb:	1627	1244	944	705	516
	arc, inches:		+2.8	+3.7	0	-9.8

.22-250 REMINGTON

Black Hills 50 Nos. Bal. Tip	velocity, fps:	3700				
	energy, ft-lb:	1520				
	arc, inches:					
Black Hills 60 Nos. Partition	velocity, fps:	3550				
	energy, ft-lb:	1679				
	arc, inches:					

Centerfire Rifle Ballistics

CARTRIDGE BULLET	RANGE, YARDS:	0	100	200	300	400
Federal 40 Nos. Bal. Tip	velocity, fps:	4150	3610	3130	2700	2300
	energy, ft-lb:	1530	1155	870	645	470
	arc, inches:		+0.6	0	-4.2	-13.2
Federal 40 Sierra Varminter	velocity, fps:	4000	3320	2720	2200	1740
	energy, ft-lb:	1420	980	660	430	265
	arc, inches:		+0.8	0	-5.6	-18.4
Federal 55 Hi-Shok	velocity, fps:	3680	3140	2660	2220	1830
	energy, ft-lb:	1655	1200	860	605	410
	arc, inches:		+1.0	0	-6.0	-19.1
Federal 55 Sierra BlitzKing	velocity, fps:	3680	3270	2890	2540	2220
	energy, ft-lb:	1655	1300	1020	790	605
	arc, inches:		+0.9	0	-5.1	-15.6
Federal 55 Sierra GameKing BTHP	velocity, fps:	3680	3280	2920	2590	2280
	energy, ft-lb:	1655	1315	1040	815	630
	arc, inches:		+0.9	0	-5.0	-15.1
Federal 55 Trophy Bonded	velocity, fps:	3600	3080	2610	2190	1810.
	energy, ft-lb:	1585	1155	835	590	400.
	arc, inches:		+1.1	0	-6.2	-19.8
Hornady 40 V-Max	velocity, fps:	4150	3631	3147	2699	2293
	energy, ft-lb:	1529	1171	879	647	467
	arc, inches:		+0.5	0	-4.2	-13.3
Hornady 50 V-Max	velocity, fps:	3800	3349	2925	2535	2178
	energy, ft-lb:	1603	1245	950	713	527
	arc, inches:		+0.8	0	-5.0	-15.6
Hornady 53 Hollow Point	velocity, fps:	3680	3185	2743	2341	1974.
	energy, ft-lb:	1594	1194	886	645	459
	arc, inches:		+1.0	0	-5.7	-17.8
Hornady 55 V-Max	velocity, fps:	3680	3265	2876	2517	2183
	energy, ft-lb:	1654	1302	1010	772	582
	arc, inches:		+0.9	0	-5.3	-16.1
Hornady 60 Soft Point	velocity, fps:	3600	3195	2826	2485	2169
	energy, ft-lb:	1727	1360	1064	823	627
	arc, inches:		+1.0	0	-5.4	-16.3
Norma 53 Soft Point	velocity, fps:	3707	3234	2809	1716	
	energy, ft-lb:	1618	1231	928	690	
	arc, inches:		+0.9	0	-5.3	
PMC 50 Sierra BlitzKing	velocity, fps:	3725	3264	2641	2455	2103
	energy, ft-lb:	1540	1183	896	669	491
	arc, inches:		+0.9	0	-5.2	-16.2
PMC 50 Barnes XLC	velocity, fps:	3725	3280	2871	2495	2152
	energy, ft-lb:	1540	1195	915	691	514.
	arc, inches:		+0.9	0	-5.1	-15.9.
PMC 55 HP boat-tail	velocity, fps:	3680	3104	2596	2141	1737
	energy, ft-lb:	1654	1176	823	560	368
	arc, inches:		+1.1	0	-6.3	-20.2
PMC 55 Pointed Soft Point	velocity, fps:	3586	3203	2852	2505	2178
	energy, ft-lb:	1570	1253	993	766	579
	arc, inches:		+1.0	0	-5.2	-16.0
Rem. 50 AccuTip BT (also in EtronX)	velocity, fps:	3725	3272	2864	2491	2147
	energy, ft-lb:	1540	1188	910	689	512
	arc, inches:		+1.7	+1.6	-2.8	-12.8
Rem. 55 Pointed Soft Point	velocity, fps:	3680	3137	2656	2222	1832
	energy, ft-lb:	1654	1201	861	603	410
	arc, inches:		+1.9	+1.8	-3.3	-15.5
Rem. 55 HP Power-Lokt	velocity, fps:	3680	3209	2785	2400	2046.
	energy, ft-lb:	1654	1257	947	703	511
	arc, inches:		+1.8	+1.7	-3.0	-13.7
Rem. 60 Nosler Partition (also in EtronX)	velocity, fps:	3500	3045	2634	2258	1914
	energy, ft-lb:	1632	1235	924	679	488
	arc, inches:		+2.1	+1.9	-3.4	-15.5
Win. 40 Ballistic Silvertip	velocity, fps:	4150	3591	3099	2658	2257
	energy, ft-lb:	1530	1146	853	628	453
	arc, inches:		+0.6	0	-4.2	-13.4

CARTRIDGE BULLET	RANGE, YARDS:	0	100	200	300	400
Win. 50 Ballistic Silvertip	velocity, fps:	3810	3341	2919	2536	2182
	energy, ft-lb:	1611	1239	946	714	529.
	arc, inches:		+0.8	0	-4.9	-15.2
Win. 55 Pointed Soft Point	velocity, fps:	3680	3137	2656	2222	1832
	energy, ft-lb:	1654	1201	861	603	410
	arc, inches:		+2.3	+1.9	-3.4	-15.9
Win. 55 Ballistic Silvertip	velocity, fps:	3680	3272	2900	2558	2240
	energy, ft-lb:	1654	1307	1027	799	613
	arc, inches:		+0.9	0	-5.0	-15.4
Win. 64 Power-Point	velocity, fps:	3500	3086	2708	2360	2038
	energy, ft-lb:	1741	1353	1042	791	590
	arc, inches:		+1.1	0	-5.9	-18.0

.220 SWIFT

CARTRIDGE BULLET	RANGE, YARDS:	0	100	200	300	400
Federal 52 Sierra MatchKing BTHP	velocity, fps:	3830	3370	2960	2600	2230
	energy, ft-lb:	1690	1310	1010	770	575
	arc, inches:		+0.8	0	-4.8	-14.9
Federal 55 Sierra BlitzKing	velocity, fps:	3800	3370	2990	2630	2310.
	energy, ft-lb:	1765	1390	1090	850	650
	arc, inches:		+0.8	0	-4.7	-14.4
Federal 55 Trophy Bonded	velocity, fps:	3700	3170	2690	2270	1880
	energy, ft-lb:	1670	1225	885	625	430
	arc, inches:		+1.0	0	-5.8	-18.5
Hornady 40 V-Max	velocity, fps:	4200	3678	3190	2739	2329
	energy, ft-lb:	1566	1201	904	666	482
	arc, inches:		+0.5	0	-4.0	-12.9
Hornady 50 V-Max	velocity, fps:	3850	3396	2970	2576	2215.
	energy, ft-lb:	1645	1280	979	736	545
	arc, inches:		+0.7	0	-4.8	-15.1
Hornady 50 SP	velocity, fps:	3850	3327	2862	2442	2060.
	energy, ft-lb:	1645	1228	909	662	471
	arc, inches:		+0.8	0	-5.1	-16.1
Hornady 55 V-Max	velocity, fps:	3680	3265	2876	2517	2183
	energy, ft-lb:	1654	1302	1010	772	582
	arc, inches:		+0.9	0	-5.3	-16.1
Hornady 60 Hollow Point	velocity, fps:	3600	3199	2824	2475	2156
	energy, ft-lb:	1727	1364	1063	816	619
	arc, inches:		+1.0	0	-5.4	-16.3
Norma 50 Soft Point	velocity, fps:	4019	3380	2826	2335	
	energy, ft-lb:	1794	1268	887	605	
	arc, inches:		+0.7	0	-5.1	
Rem. 50 Pointed Soft Point	velocity, fps:	3780	3158	2617	2135	1710
	energy, ft-lb:	1586	1107	760	505	325
	arc, inches:		+0.3	-1.4	-8.2	
Rem. 50 V-Max boat-tail (also in EtronX)	velocity, fps:	3780	3321	2908	2532	2185
	energy, ft-lb:	1586	1224	939	711	530
	arc, inches:		+0.8	0	-5.0	-15.4
Win. 40 Ballistic Silvertip	velocity, fps:	4050	3518	3048	2624	2238.
	energy, ft-lb:	1457	1099	825	611	445
	arc, inches:		+0.7	0	-4.4	-13.9
Win. 50 Pointed Soft Point	velocity, fps:	3870	3310	2816	2373	1972
	energy, ft-lb:	1663	1226	881	625	432
	arc, inches:		+0.8	0	-5.2	-16.7

.223 WSSM

CARTRIDGE BULLET	RANGE, YARDS:	0	100	200	300	400
Win. 55 Ballistic Silvertip	velocity, fps:	3850	3438	3064	2721	2402
	energy, ft-lb:	1810	1444	1147	904	704
	arc, inches:		+0.7	0	-4.4	-13.6
Win. 55 Pointed Softpoint	velocity, fps:	3850	3367	2934	2541	2181
	energy, ft-lb:	1810	1384	1051	789	581
	arc, inches:		+0.8	0	-4.9	-15.1
Win. 64 Power-Point	velocity, fps:	3600	3144	2732	2356	2011
	energy, ft-lb:	1841	1404	1061	789	574
	arc, inches:		+1.0	0	-5.7	-17.7

BALLISTICS

Centerfire Rifle Ballistics

6MM PPC TO .243 WINCHESTER

6MM PPC

CARTRIDGE BULLET	RANGE, YARDS:	0	100	200	300	400
A-Square 68 Berger	velocity, fps:	3100	2751	2428	2128	1850
	energy, ft-lb:	1451	1143	890	684	516
	arc, inches:		+1.5	0	-7.5	-22.6

6x70 R

CARTRIDGE BULLET	RANGE, YARDS:	0	100	200	300	400
Norma 95 Nosler Bal. Tip	velocity, fps:	2461	2231	2013	1809	
	energy, ft-lb:	1211	995	810	654	
	arc, inches:		+2.7	0	-11.3	

6.8MM SPC

CARTRIDGE BULLET	RANGE, YARDS:	0	100	200	300	400
Hornady 110 V-Max	velocity, fps:	2550	2319	2100	1893	1700
	energy, ft-lb:	1588	1313	1077	875	706
	arc, inches:		+2.5	0	-10.4	-30.6

.243 WINCHESTER

CARTRIDGE BULLET	RANGE, YARDS:	0	100	200	300	400
Black Hills 55 Nosler B. Tip	velocity, fps:	3800				
	energy, ft-lb:	1763				
	arc, inches:					
Black Hills 95 Nosler B. Tip	velocity, fps:	2950				
	energy, ft-lb:	1836				
	arc, inches:					
Federal 70 Nosler Bal. Tip	velocity, fps:	3400	3070	2760	2470	2200
	energy, ft-lb:	1795	1465	1185	950	755.
	arc, inches:		+1.1	0	-5.7	-17.1
Federal 70 Speer TNT HP	velocity, fps:	3400	3040	2700	2390	2100
	energy, ft-lb:	1795	1435	1135	890	685
	arc, inches:		+1.1	0	-5.9	-18.0
Federal 80 Sierra Pro-Hunter	velocity, fps:	3350	2960	2590	2260	1950
	energy, ft-lb:	1995	1550	1195	905	675
	arc, inches:		+1.3	0	-6.4	-19.7
Federal 85 Sierra GameKing BTHP	velocity, fps:	3320	3070	2830	2600	2380
	energy, ft-lb:	2080	1770	1510	1280	1070
	arc, inches:		+1.1	0	-5.5	-16.1
Federal 90 Trophy Bonded	velocity, fps:	3100	2850	2610	2380	2160.
	energy, ft-lb:	1920	1620	1360	1130	935
	arc, inches:		+1.4	0	-6.1	-19.2
Federal 100 Hi-Shok	velocity, fps:	2960	2700	2450	2220	1990
	energy, ft-lb:	1945	1615	1330	1090	880
	arc, inches:		+1.6	0	-7.5	-22.0
Federal 100 Sierra GameKing BTSP	velocity, fps:	2960	2760	2570	2380	2210
	energy, ft-lb:	1950	1690	1460	1260	1080
	arc, inches:		+1.5	0	-6.8	-19.8
Federal 100 Nosler Partition	velocity, fps:	2960	2730	2510	2300	2100
	energy, ft-lb:	1945	1650	1395	1170	975.
	arc, inches:		+1.6	0	-7.1	-20.9
Hornady 58 V-Max	velocity, fps:	3750	3319	2913	2539	2195
	energy, ft-lb:	1811	1418	1093	830	620
	arc, inches:		+1.2	0	-5.5	-16.4
Hornady 75 Hollow Point	velocity, fps:	3400	2970	2578	2219	1890
	energy, ft-lb:	1926	1469	1107	820	595
	arc, inches:		+1.2	0	-6.5	-20.3
Hornady 100 BTSP	velocity, fps:	2960	2728	2508	2299	2099
	energy, ft-lb:	1945	1653	1397	1174	979
	arc, inches:		+1.6	0	-7.2	-21.0
Hornady 100 BTSP LM	velocity, fps:	3100	2839	2592	2358	2138
	energy, ft-lb:	2133	1790	1491	1235	1014
	arc, inches:		+1.5	0	-6.8	-19.8
Norma 80 FMJ	velocity, fps:	3117	2750	2412	2098	
	energy, ft-lb:	1726	1344	1034	782	
	arc, inches:		+1.5	0	-7.5	
Norma 100 FMJ	velocity, fps:	3018	2747	2493	2252	
	energy, ft-lb:	2023	1677	1380	1126	
	arc, inches:		+1.5	0	-7.1	
Norma 100 Soft Point	velocity, fps:	3018	2748	2493	2252	
	energy, ft-lb:	2023	1677	1380	1126	
	arc, inches:		+1.5	0	-7.1	
Norma 100 Oryx	velocity, fps:	3018	2653	2316	2004	
	energy, ft-lb:	2023	1563	1191	892	
	arc, inches:		+1.7	0	-8.3	
PMC 80 Pointed Soft Point	velocity, fps:	2940	2684	2444	2215	1999
	energy, ft-lb:	1535	1280	1060	871	709
	arc, inches:		+1.7	0	-7.5	-22.1
PMC 85 Barnes XLC	velocity, fps:	3250	3022	2805	2598	2401
	energy, ft-lb:	1993	1724	1485	1274	1088
	arc, inches:		+1.6	0	-5.6	16.3
PMC 85 HP boat-tail	velocity, fps:	3275	2922	2596	2292	2009
	energy, ft-lb:	2024	1611	1272	991	761
	arc, inches:		+1.3	0	-6.5	-19.7
PMC 100 Pointed Soft Point	velocity, fps:	2743	2507	2283	2070	1869
	energy, ft-lb:	1670	1395	1157	951	776
	arc, inches:		+2.0	0	-8.7	-25.5
PMC 100 SP boat-tail	velocity, fps:	2960	2742	2534	2335	2144
	energy, ft-lb:	1945	1669	1425	1210	1021
	arc, inches:		+1.6	0	-7.0	-20.5
Rem. 75 AccuTip BT	velocity, fps:	3375	3065	2775	2504	2248
	energy, ft-lb:	1897	1564	1282	1044	842
	arc, inches:		+2.0	+1.8	-3.0	-13.3
Rem. 80 Pointed Soft Point	velocity, fps:	3350	2955	2593	2259	1951
	energy, ft-lb:	1993	1551	1194	906	676
	arc, inches:		+2.2	+2.0	-3.5	-15.8
Rem. 80 HP Power-Lokt	velocity, fps:	3350	2955	2593	2259	1951
	energy, ft-lb:	1993	1551	1194	906	676
	arc, inches:		+2.2	+2.0	-3.5	-15.8
Rem. 90 Nosler Bal. Tip (also in EtronX) or Scirocco	velocity, fps:	3120	2871	2635	2411	2199
	energy, ft-lb:	1946	1647	1388	1162	966
	arc, inches:		+1.4	0	-6.4	-18.8
Rem. 95 AccuTip	velocity, fps:	3120	2847	2590	2347	2118
	energy, ft-lb:	2053	1710	1415	1162	946
	arc, inches:		+1.5	0	-6.6	-19.5
Rem. 100 PSP Core-Lokt (also in EtronX)	velocity, fps:	2960	2697	2449	2215	1993
	energy, ft-lb:	1945	1615	1332	1089	882
	arc, inches:		+1.6	0	-7.5	-22.1
Rem. 100 PSP boat-tail	velocity, fps:	2960	2720	2492	2275	2069
	energy, ft-lb:	1945	1642	1378	1149	950
	arc, inches:		+2.8	+2.3	-3.8	-16.6
Speer 100 Grand Slam	velocity, fps:	2950	2684	2434	2197	
	energy, ft-lb:	1932	1600	1315	1072	
	arc, inches:		+1.7	0	-7.6	-22.4
Win. 55 Ballistic Silvertip	velocity, fps:	4025	3597	3209	2853	2525
	energy, ft-lb:	1978	1579	1257	994	779
	arc, inches:		+0.6	0	-4.0	-12.2
Win. 80 Pointed Soft Point	velocity, fps:	3350	2955	2593	2259	1951.
	energy, ft-lb:	1993	1551	1194	906	676
	arc, inches:		+2.6	+2.1	-3.6	-16.2
Win. 95 Ballistic Silvertip	velocity, fps:	3100	2854	2626	2410	2203
	energy, ft-lb:	2021	1719	1455	1225	1024
	arc, inches:		+1.4	0	-6.4	-18.9
Win. 95 Supreme Elite XP3	velocity, fps	3100	2864	2641	2428	2225
	energy, ft-lb	2027	1730	1471	1243	1044
	a rc, inches:		+1.4	0	-6.4	-18.7
Win. 100 Power-Point	velocity, fps:	2960	2697	2449	2215	1993
	energy, ft-lb:	1945	1615	1332	1089	882
	arc, inches:		+1.9	0	-7.8	-22.6.
Win. 100 Power-Point Plus	velocity, fps:	3090	2818	2562	2321	2092
	energy, ft-lb:	2121	1764	1458	1196	972
	arc, inches:		+1.4	0	-6.7	-20.0

CARTRIDGE BULLET	RANGE, YARDS:	0	100	200	300	400

6MM REMINGTON

CARTRIDGE BULLET		0	100	200	300	400
Federal 80 Sierra Pro-Hunter	velocity, fps:	3470	3060	2690	2350	2040
	energy, ft-lb:	2140	1665	1290	980	735
	arc, inches:		+1.1	0	-5.9	-18.2
Federal 100 Hi-Shok	velocity, fps:	3100	2830	2570	2330	2100
	energy, ft-lb:	2135	1775	1470	1205	985
	arc, inches:		+1.4	0	-6.7	-19.8
Federal 100 Nos. Partition	velocity, fps:	3100	2860	2640	2420	2220
	energy, ft-lb:	2135	1820	1545	1300	1090
	arc, inches:		+1.4	0	-6.3	-18.7
Hornady 100 SP boat-tail	velocity, fps:	3100	2861	2634	2419	2231
	energy, ft-lb:	2134	1818	1541	1300	1088
	arc, inches:		+1.3	0	-6.5	-18.9
Hornady 100 SPBT LM	velocity, fps:	3250	2997	2756	2528	2311
	energy, ft-lb:	2345	1995	1687	1418	1186
	arc, inches:		+1.6	0	-6.3	-18.2
Rem. 75 V-Max boat-tail	velocity, fps:	3400	3088	2797	2524	2267
	energy, ft-lb:	1925	1587	1303	1061	856
	arc, inches:		+1.9	+1.7	-3.0	-13.1
Rem. 100 PSP Core-Lokt	velocity, fps:	3100	2829	2573	2332	2104.
	energy, ft-lb:	2133	1777	1470	1207	983
	arc, inches:		+1.4	0	-6.7	-19.8
Rem. 100 PSP boat-tail	velocity, fps:	3100	2852	2617	2394	2183.
	energy, ft-lb:	2134	1806	1521	1273	1058
	arc, inches:		+1.4	0	-6.5	-19.1
Win. 100 Power-Point	velocity, fps:	3100	2829	2573	2332	2104
	energy, ft-lb:	2133	1777	1470	1207	983
	arc, inches:		+1.7	0	-7.0	-20.4

.243 WSSM

CARTRIDGE BULLET		0	100	200	300	400
Win. 55 Ballistic Silvertip	velocity, fps:	4060	3628	3237	2880	2550
	energy, ft-lb:	2013	1607	1280	1013	794
	arc, inches:		+0.6	0	-3.9	-12.0
Win. 95 Ballistic Silvertip	velocity, fps:	3250	3000	2763	2538	2325
	energy, ft-lb:	2258	1898	1610	1359	1140
	arc, inches:		+1.2	0	5.7	16.9
Win. 95 Supreme Elite XP3	velocity, fps	3150	2912	2686	2471	2266
	energy, ft-lb	2093	1788	1521	1287	1083
	arc, inches		+1.3	0	-6.1	-18.0
Win. 100 Power Point	velocity, fps:	3110	2838	2583	2341	2112
	energy, ft-lb:	2147	1789	1481	1217	991
	arc, inches:		+1.4	0	-6.6	-19.7

.240 WEATHERBY MAGNUM

CARTRIDGE BULLET		0	100	200	300	400
Wby. 87 Pointed Expanding	velocity, fps:	3523	3199	2898	2617	2352
	energy, ft-lb:	2397	1977	1622	1323	1069
	arc, inches:		+2.7	+3.4	0	-8.4
Wby. 90 Barnes-X	velocity, fps:	3500	3222	2962	2717	2484
	energy, ft-lb:	2448	2075	1753	1475	1233
	arc, inches:		+2.6	+3.3	0	-8.0
Wby. 95 Nosler Bal. Tip	velocity, fps:	3420	3146	2888	2645	2414
	energy, ft-lb:	2467	2087	1759	1475	1229
	arc, inches:		+2.7	+3.5	0	-8.4
Wby. 100 Pointed Expanding	velocity, fps:	3406	3134	2878	2637	2408
	energy, ft-lb:	2576	2180	1839	1544	1287
	arc, inches:		+2.8	+3.5	0	-8.4
Wby. 100 Partition	velocity, fps:	3406	3136	2882	2642	2415
	energy, ft-lb:	2576	2183	1844	1550	1294
	arc, inches:		+2.8	+3.5	0	-8.4

.25-20 WINCHESTER

CARTRIDGE BULLET		0	100	200	300	400
Rem. 86 Soft Point	velocity, fps:	1460	1194	1030	931	858
	energy, ft-lb:	407	272	203	165	141
	arc, inches:		0	-22.9	-78.9	-173.0

CARTRIDGE BULLET	RANGE, YARDS:	0	100	200	300	400
Win. 86 Soft Point	velocity, fps:	1460	1194	1030	931	858.
	energy, ft-lb:	407	272	203	165	141
	arc, inches:		0	-23.5	-79.6	-175.9

.25-35 WINCHESTER

CARTRIDGE BULLET		0	100	200	300	400
Win. 117 Soft Point	velocity, fps:	2230	1866	1545	1282	1097
	energy, ft-lb:	1292	904	620	427	313
	arc, inches:		+2.1	-5.1	-27.0	-70.1

.250 SAVAGE

CARTRIDGE BULLET		0	100	200	300	400
Rem. 100 Pointed SP	velocity, fps:	2820	2504	2210	1936	1684.
	energy, ft-lb:	1765	1392	1084	832	630
	arc, inches:		+2.0	0	-9.2	-27.7
Win. 100 Silvertip	velocity, fps:	2820	2467	2140	1839	1569
	energy, ft-lb:	1765	1351	1017	751	547
	arc, inches:		+2.4	0	-10.1	-30.5

.257 ROBERTS

CARTRIDGE BULLET		0	100	200	300	400
Federal 120 Nosler Partition	velocity, fps:	2780	2560	2360	2160	1970
	energy, ft-lb:	2060	1750	1480	1240	1030
	arc, inches:		+1.9	0	-8.2	-24.0
Hornady 117 SP boat-tail	velocity, fps:	2780	2550	2331	2122	1925
	energy, ft-lb:	2007	1689	1411	1170	963
	arc, inches:		+1.9	0	-8.3	-24.4
Hornady 117 SP boat-tail LM	velocity, fps:	2940	2694	2460	2240	2031
	energy, ft-lb:	2245	1885	1572	1303	1071
	arc, inches:		+1.7	0	-7.6	-21.8
Rem. 117 SP Core-Lokt	velocity, fps:	2650	2291	1961	1663	1404
	energy, ft-lb:	1824	1363	999	718	512
	arc, inches:		+2.6	0	-11.7	-36.1
Win. 117 Power-Point	velocity, fps:	2780	2411	2071	1761	1488
	energy, ft-lb:	2009	1511	1115	806	576.
	arc, inches:		+2.6	0	-10.8	-33.0

.25-06 REMINGTON

CARTRIDGE BULLET		0	100	200	300	400
Black Hills 100 Nos. Bal. Tip	velocity, fps:	3200				
	energy, ft-lb:	2273				
	arc, inches:					
Black Hills 100 Barnes XLC	velocity, fps:	3200				
	energy, ft-lb:	2273				
	arc, inches:					
Black Hills 115 Barnes X	velocity, fps:	2975				
	energy, ft-lb:	2259				
	arc, inches:					
Federal 90 Sierra Varminter	velocity, fps:	3440	3040	2680	2340	2030
	energy, ft-lb:	2365	1850	1435	1100	825
	arc, inches:		+1.1	0	-6.0	-18.3
Federal 100 Barnes XLC	velocity, fps:	3210	2970	2750	2540	2330
	energy, ft-lb:	2290	1965	1680	1430	1205
	arc, inches:		+1.2	0	-5.8	-17.0
Federal 100 Nosler Bal. Tip	velocity, fps:	3210	2960	2720	2490	2280
	energy, ft-lb:	2290	1940	1640	1380	1150.
	arc, inches:		+1.2	0	-6.0	-17.5
Federal 115 Nosler Partition	velocity, fps:	2990	2750	2520	2300	2100
	energy, ft-lb:	2285	1930	1620	1350	1120
	arc, inches:		+1.6	0	-7.0	-20.8
Federal 115 Trophy Bonded	velocity, fps:	2990	2740	2500	2270	2050
	energy, ft-lb:	2285	1910	1590	1310	1075
	arc, inches:		+1.6	0	-7.2	-21.1
Federal 117 Sierra Pro Hunt.	velocity, fps:	2990	2730	2480	2250	2030
	energy, ft-lb:	2320	1985	1645	1350	1100
	arc, inches:		+1.6	0	-7.2	-21.4
Federal 117 Sierra GameKing BTSP	velocity, fps:	2990	2770	2570	2370	2190
	energy, ft-lb:	2320	2000	1715	1465	1240
	arc, inches:		+1.5	0	-6.8	-19.9

BALLISTICS

Centerfire Rifle Ballistics

.25-06 REMINGTON TO 6.5X55 SWEDISH

CARTRIDGE BULLET	RANGE, YARDS:	0	100	200	300	400
Hornady 117 SP boat-tail	velocity, fps:	2990	2749	2520	2302	2096
	energy, ft-lb:	2322	1962	1649	1377	1141
	arc, inches:		+1.6	0	-7.0	-20.7
Hornady 117 SP boat-tail LM	velocity, fps:	3110	2855	2613	2384	2168
	energy, ft-lb:	2512	2117	1774	1476	1220
	arc, inches:		+1.8	0	-7.1	-20.3
PMC 100 SPBT	velocity, fps:	3200	2925	2650	2395	2145
	energy, ft-lb:	2273	1895	1561	1268	1019
	arc, inches:		+1.3	0	-6.3	-18.6
PMC 117 PSP	velocity, fps:	2950	2706	2472	2253	2047
	energy, ft-lb:	2261	1900	1588	1319	1088
	arc, inches:		+1.6	0	-7.3	-21.5
Rem. 100 PSP Core-Lokt	velocity, fps:	3230	2893	2580	2287	2014
	energy, ft-lb:	2316	1858	1478	1161	901
	arc, inches:		+1.3	0	-6.6	-19.8
Rem. 115 Core-Lokt Ultra	velocity, fps:	3000	2751	2516	2293	2081
	energy, ft-lb:	2298	1933	1616	1342	1106
	arc, inches:		+1.6	0	-7.1	-20.7
Rem. 120 PSP Core-Lokt	velocity, fps:	2990	2730	2484	2252	2032
	energy, ft-lb:	2382	1985	1644	1351	1100
	arc, inches:		+1.6	0	-7.2	-21.4
Speer 120 Grand Slam	velocity, fps:	3130	2835	2558	2298	
	energy, ft-lb:	2610	2141	1743	1407	
	arc, inches:		+1.4	0	-6.8	-20.1
Win. 85 Ballistic Silvertip	velocity, fps	3470	3156	2863	2589	2331
	energy, ft-lb:	2273	1880	1548	1266	1026
	arc, inches:		+1.0	0	-5.2	-15.7
Win. 90 Pos. Exp. Point	velocity, fps:	3440	3043	2680	2344	2034
	energy, ft-lb:	2364	1850	1435	1098	827
	arc, inches:		+2.4	+2.0	-3.4	-15.0
Win. 110 AccuBond CT	velocity, fps:	3100	2870	2651	2442	2243
	energy, ft-lb:	2347	2011	1716	1456	1228
	arc, inches:		+1.4	0	-6.3	-18.5
Win. 115 Ballistic Silvertip	velocity, fps:	3060	2825	2603	2390	2188
	energy, ft-lb:	2391	2038	1729	1459	1223
	arc, inches:		+1.4	0	-6.6	-19.2
Win. 120 Pos. Pt. Exp.	velocity, fps:	2990	2717	2459	2216	1987
	energy, ft-lb:	2382	1967	1612	1309	1053
	arc, inches:		+1.6	0	-7.4	-21.8

.25 WINCHESTER SUPER SHORT MAGNUM

CARTRIDGE BULLET	RANGE, YARDS:	0	100	200	300	400
Win. 85 Ballistic Silvertip	velocity, fps:	3470	3156	2863	2589	2331
	energy, ft-lb:	2273	1880	1548	1266	1026
	arc, inches:		+1.0	0	-5.2	-15.7
Win. 110 AccuBond CT	velocity, fps:	3100	2870	2651	2442	2243.
	energy, ft-lb:	2347	2011	1716	1456	1228
	arc, inches:		+1.4	0	-6.3	-18.5
Win. 115 Ballistic Silvertip	velocity, fps:	3060	2844	2639	2442	2254
	energy, ft-lb:	2392	2066	1778	1523	1298
	arc, inches:		+1.4	0	-6.4	-18.6
Win. 120 Pos. Pt. Exp.	velocity, fps:	2990	2717	2459	2216	1987
	energy, ft-lb:	2383	1967	1612	1309	1053
	arc, inches:		+1.6	0	-7.4	-21.8

.257 WEATHERBY MAGNUM

CARTRIDGE BULLET	RANGE, YARDS:	0	100	200	300	400
Federal 115 Nosler Partition	velocity, fps:	3150	2900	2660	2440	2220.
	energy, ft-lb:	2535	2145	1810	1515	1260
	arc, inches:		+1.3	0	-6.2	-18.4
Federal 115 Trophy Bonded	velocity, fps:	3150	2890	2640	2400	2180
	energy, ft-lb:	2535	2125	1775	1470	1210
	arc, inches:		+1.4	0	-6.3	-18.8
Wby. 87 Pointed Expanding	velocity, fps:	3825	3472	3147	2845	2563
	energy, ft-lb:	2826	2328	1913	1563	1269
	arc, inches:		+2.1	+2.8	0	-7.1

CARTRIDGE BULLET	RANGE, YARDS:	0	100	200	300	400
Wby. 100 Pointed Expanding	velocity, fps:	3602	3298	3016	2750	2500
	energy, ft-lb:	2881	2416	2019	1680	1388
	arc, inches:		+2.4	+3.1	0	-7.7
Wby. 115 Nosler Bal. Tip	velocity, fps:	3400	3170	2952	2745	2547
	energy, ft-lb:	2952	2566	2226	1924	1656.
	arc, inches:		+3.0	+3.5	0	-7.9
Wby. 115 Barnes X	velocity, fps:	3400	3158	2929	2711	2504
	energy, ft-lb:	2952	2546	2190	1877	1601
	arc, inches:		+2.7	+3.4	0	-8.1
Wby. 117 RN Expanding	velocity, fps:	3402	2984	2595	2240	1921
	energy, ft-lb:	3007	2320	1742	1302	956
	arc, inches:		+3.4	+4.31	0	-11.1
Wby. 120 Nosler Partition	velocity, fps:	3305	3046	2801	2570	2350
	energy, ft-lb:	2910	2472	2091	1760	1471
	arc, inches:		+3.0	+3.7	0	-8.9

6.53 (.257) SCRAMJET

CARTRIDGE BULLET	RANGE, YARDS:	0	100	200	300	400
Lazzeroni 85 Nosler Bal. Tip	velocity, fps:	3960	3652	3365	3096	2844
	energy, ft-lb:	2961	2517	2137	1810	1526
	arc, inches:		+1.7	+2.4	0	-6.0
Lazzeroni 100 Nosler Part.	velocity, fps:	3740	3465	3208	2965	2735
	energy, ft-lb:	3106	2667	2285	1953	1661.
	arc, inches:		+2.1	+2.7	0	-6.7

6.5x50 JAPANESE

CARTRIDGE BULLET	RANGE, YARDS:	0	100	200	300	400
Norma 156 Alaska	velocity, fps:	2067	1832	1615	1423	
	energy, ft-lb:	1480	1162	904	701	
	arc, inches:		+4.4	0	-17.8	

6.5x52 CARCANO

CARTRIDGE BULLET	RANGE, YARDS:	0	100	200	300	400
Norma 156 Alaska	velocity, fps:	2428	2169	1926	1702	
	energy, ft-lb:	2043	1630	1286	1004	
	arc, inches:		+2.9	0	-12.3	

6.5x55 SWEDISH

CARTRIDGE BULLET	RANGE, YARDS:	0	100	200	300	400
Federal 140 Hi-Shok	velocity, fps:	2600	2400	2220	2040	1860
	energy, ft-lb:	2100	1795	1525	1285	1080
	arc, inches:		+2.3	0	-9.4	-27.2
Federal 140 Trophy Bonded	velocity, fps:	2550	2350	2160	1980	1810
	energy, ft-lb:	2020	1720	1450	1220	1015
	arc, inches:		+2.4	0	-9.8	-28.4
Federal 140 Sierra MatchKg. BTHP	velocity, fps:	2630	2460	2300	2140	2000
	energy, ft-lb:	2140	1880	1640	1430	1235
	arc, inches:		+16.4	+28.8	+33.9	+31.8
Hornady 129 SP LM	velocity, fps:	2770	2561	2361	2171	1994
	energy, ft-lb:	2197	1878	1597	1350	1138
	arc, inches:		+2.0	0	-8.2	-23.2
Hornady 140 SP Interlock	velocity, fps	2525	2341	2165	1996	1836
	energy, ft-lb:	1982	1704	1457	1239	1048
	arc, inches:		+2.4	0	-9.9	-28.5
Hornady140 SP LM	velocity, fps:	2740	2541	2351	2169	1999
	energy, ft-lb:	2333	2006	1717	1463	1242
	arc, inches:		+2.4	0	-8.7	-24.0
Norma 120 Nosler Bal. Tip	velocity, fps:	2822	2609	2407	2213	
	energy, ft-lb:	2123	1815	1544	1305	
	arc, inches:		+1.8	0	-7.8	
Norma 139 Vulkan	velocity, fps:	2854	2569	2302	2051	
	energy, ft-lb:	2515	2038	1636	1298	
	arc, inches:		+1.8	0	-8.4	
Norma 140 Nosler Partition	velocity, fps:	2789	2592	2403	2223	
	energy, ft-lb:	2419	2089	1796	1536	
	arc, inches:		+1.8	0	-7.8	
Norma 156 TXP Swift A-Fr.	velocity, fps:	2526	2276	2040	1818	
	energy, ft-lb:	2196	1782	1432	1138	

BALLISTICS

CARTRIDGE BULLET	RANGE, YARDS:	0	100	200	300	400
	arc, inches:		+2.6	0	-10.9	
Norma 156 Alaska	velocity, fps:	2559	2245	1953	1687	
	energy, ft-lb:	2269	1746	1322	986	
	arc, inches:		+2.7	0	-11.9	
Norma 156 Vulkan	velocity, fps:	2644	2395	2159	1937	
	energy, ft-lb:	2422	1987	1616	1301	
	arc, inches:		+2.2	0	-9.7	
Norma 156 Oryx	velocity, fps:	2559	2308	2070	1848	
	energy, ft-lb:	2269	1845	1485	1183	
	arc, inches:		+2.5	0	-10.6	
PMC 139 Pointed Soft Point	velocity, fps:	2850	2560	2290	2030	1790
	energy, ft-lb:	2515	2025	1615	1270	985
	arc, inches:		+2.2	0	-8.9	-26.3
PMC 140 HP boat-tail	velocity, fps:	2560	2398	2243	2093	1949
	energy, ft-lb:	2037	1788	1563	1361	1181
	arc, inches:		+2.3	0	-9.2	-26.4
PMC 140 SP boat-tail	velocity, fps:	2560	2386	2218	2057	1903
	energy, ft-lb:	2037	1769	1529	1315	1126
	arc, inches:		+2.3	0	-9.4	-27.1
PMC 144 FMJ	velocity, fps:	2650	2370	2110	1870	1650
	energy, ft-lb:	2425	1950	1550	1215	945
	arc, inches:		+2.7	0	-10.5	-30.9
Rem. 140 PSP Core-Lokt	velocity, fps:	2550	2353	2164	1984	1814
	energy, ft-lb:	2021	1720	1456	1224	1023
	arc, inches:		+2.4	0	-9.8	-27.0
Speer 140 Grand Slam	velocity, fps:	2550	2318	2099	1892	
	energy, ft-lb:	2021	1670	1369	1112	
	arc, inches:		+2.5	0	-10.4	-30.6
Win. 140 Soft Point	velocity, fps:	2550	2359	2176	2002	1836
	energy, ft-lb:	2022	1731	1473	1246	1048.
	arc, inches:		+2.4	0	-9.7	-28.1

.260 REMINGTON

CARTRIDGE BULLET	RANGE, YARDS:	0	100	200	300	400
Federal 140 Sierra GameKing	velocity, fps:	2750	2570	2390	2220	2060
BTSP	energy, ft-lb:	2350	2045	1775	1535	1315
	arc, inches:		+1.9	0	-8.0	-23.1
Federal 140 Trophy Bonded	velocity, fps:	2750	2540	2340	2150	1970
	energy, ft-lb:	2350	2010	1705	1440	1210
arc, inches:		+1.9	0	-8.4	-24.1	
Rem. 120 Nosler Bal. Tip	velocity, fps:	2890	2688	2494	2309	2131
	energy, ft-lb:	2226	1924	1657	1420	1210
	arc, inches:		+1.7	0	-7.3	-21.1
Rem. 120 AccuTip	velocity, fps:	2890	2697	2512	2334	2163
	energy, ft-lb:	2392	2083	1807	1560	1340
	arc, inches:		+1.6	0	-7.2	-20.7
Rem. 125 Nosler Partition	velocity, fps:	2875	2669	2473	2285	2105.
	energy, ft-lb:	2294	1977	1697	1449	1230
arc, inches:		+1.71	0	-7.4	-21.4	
Rem. 140 PSP Core-Lokt	velocity, fps:	2750	2544	2347	2158	1979
(and C-L Ultra)	energy, ft-lb:	2351	2011	1712	1448	1217
	arc, inches:		+1.9	0	-8.3	-24.0
Speer 140 Grand Slam	velocity, fps:	2750	2518	2297	2087	
	energy, ft-lb:	2351	1970	1640	1354	
	arc, inches:		+2.3	0	-8.9	-25.8

6.5/284

CARTRIDGE BULLET	RANGE, YARDS:	0	100	200	300	400
Norma 120 Nosler Bal. Tip	velocity, fps:	3117	2890	2674	2469	
	energy, ft-lb:	2589	2226	1906	1624	
	arc, inches:		+1.3	0	-6.2	
Norma 140 Nosler Part.	velocity, fps:	2953	2750	2557	2371	
	energy, ft-lb:	2712	2352	2032	1748	

CARTRIDGE BULLET	RANGE, YARDS:	0	100	200	300	400
	arc, inches:		+1.5	0	-6.8	

6.5 REMINGTON MAGNUM

CARTRIDGE BULLET	RANGE, YARDS:	0	100	200	300	400
Rem. 120 Core-Lokt PSP	velocity, fps:	3210	2905	2621	2353	2102
	energy, ft-lb:	2745	2248	1830	1475	1177
	arc, inches:		+2.7	+2.1	-3.5	-15.5

.264 WINCHESTER MAGNUM

CARTRIDGE BULLET	RANGE, YARDS:	0	100	200	300	400
Rem. 140 PSP Core-Lokt	velocity, fps:	3030	2782	2548	2326	2114
	energy, ft-lb:	2854	2406	2018	1682	1389
	arc, inches:		+1.5	0	-6.9	-20.2
Win. 140 Power-Point	velocity, fps:	3030	2782	2548	2326	2114.
	energy, ft-lb:	2854	2406	2018	1682	1389
	arc, inches:		+1.8	0	-7.2	-20.8

6.8MM REMINGTON SPC

CARTRIDGE BULLET	RANGE, YARDS:	0	100	200	300	400
Rem. 115 Open Tip Match	velocity, fps:	2800	2535	2285	2049	1828
(and HPBT Match)	energy, ft-lb:	2002	1641	1333	1072	853
	arc, inches:		+2.0	0	-8.8	-26.2
Rem. 115 Metal Case	velocity, fps:	2800	2523	2262	2017	1789
	energy, ft-lb:	2002	1625	1307	1039	817
	arc, inches:		+2.0	0	-8.8	-26.2
Rem. 115 Sierra HPBT	velocity, fps:	2775	2511	2263	2028	1809
(2005; all vel. @ 2775)	energy, ft-lb:	1966	1610	1307	1050	835
	arc, inches:		+2.0	0	-8.8	-26.2.
Rem. 115 CL Ultra	velocity, fps:	2775	2472	2190	1926	1683
	energy, ft-lb:	1966	1561	1224	947	723
	arc, inches:		+2.1	0	-9.4	-28.2

.270 WINCHESTER

CARTRIDGE BULLET	RANGE, YARDS:	0	100	200	300	400
Black Hills 130 Nos. Bal. T.	velocity, fps:	2950				
	energy, ft-lb:	2512				
	arc, inches:					
Black Hills 130 Barnes XLC	velocity, ft-lb:	2950				
	energy, ft-lb:	2512				
	arc, inches:					
Federal 130 Hi-Shok	velocity, fps:	3060	2800	2560	2330	2110
	energy, ft-lb:	2700	2265	1890	1565	1285
	arc, inches:		+1.5	0	-6.8	-20.0
Federal 130 Sierra Pro-Hunt.	velocity, fps:	3060	2830	2600	2390	2190
	energy, ft-lb:	2705	2305	1960	1655	1390
	arc, inches:		+1.4	0	-6.4	-19.0
Federal 130 Sierra GameKing	velocity, fps:	3060	2830	2620	2410	2220.
	energy, ft-lb:	2700	2320	1980	1680	1420
	arc, inches:		+1.4	0	-6.5	-19.0
Federal 130 Nosler Bal. Tip	velocity, fps:	3060	2840	2630	2430	2230
	energy, ft-lb:	2700	2325	1990	1700	1440
	arc, inches:		+1.4	0	-6.5	-18.8
Federal 130 Nos. Partition	velocity, fps:	3060	2830	2610	2400	2200
And Solid Base	energy, ft-lb:	2705	2310	1965	1665	1400
	arc, inches:		+1.4	0	-6.5	-19.1.
Federal 130 Barnes XLC	velocity, fps:	3060	2840	2620	2420	2220
And Triple Shock	energy, ft-lb:	2705	2320	1985	1690	1425
	arc, inches:		+1.4	0	-6.4	-18.9
Federal 130 Trophy Bonded	velocity, fps:	3060	2810	2570	2340	2130
	energy, ft-lb:	2705	2275	1905	1585	1310
	arc, inches:		+1.5	0	-6.7	-19.8
Federal 140 Trophy Bonded	velocity, fps:	2940	2700	2480	2260	2060
	energy, ft-lb:	2685	2270	1905	1590	1315
	arc, inches:		+1.6	0	-7.3	-21.5
Federal 140 Tr. Bonded HE	velocity, fps:	3100	2860	2620	2400	2200.
	energy, ft-lb:	2990	2535	2140	1795	1500

Centerfire Rifle Ballistics

.270 WINCHESTER TO .270 WINCHESTER

CARTRIDGE BULLET	RANGE, YARDS:	0	100	200	300	400
Federal 140 Nos. AccuBond	arc, inches:		+1.4	0	-6.4	-18.9
	velocity, fps:	2950	2760	2580	2400	2230.
	energy, ft-lb:	2705	2365	2060	1790	1545
Federal 150 Hi-Shok RN	arc, inches:		+1.5	0	-6.7	-19.6
	velocity, fps:	2850	2500	2180	1890	1620
	energy, ft-lb:	2705	2085	1585	1185	870
Federal 150 Sierra GameKing	arc, inches:		+2.0	0	-9.4	-28.6
	velocity, fps:	2850	2660	2480	2300	2130
	energy, ft-lb:	2705	2355	2040	1760	1510
Federal 150 Sierra GameKing HE	arc, inches:		+1.7	0	-7.4	-21.4
	velocity, fps:	3000	2800	2620	2430	2260
	energy, ft-lb:	2995	2615	2275	1975	1700
Federal 150 Nosler Partition	arc, inches:		+1.5	0	-6.5	-18.9
	velocity, fps:	2850	2590	2340	2100	1880.
	energy, ft-lb:	2705	2225	1815	1470	1175
Hornady 130 SST (or Interbond)	arc, inches:		+1.9	0	-8.3	-24.4
	velocity, fps:	3060	2845	2639	2442	2254
	energy, ft-lb:	2700	2335	2009	1721	1467
Hornady 130 SST LM (or Interbond)	arc, inches:		+1.4	0	-6.6	-19.1
	velocity, fps:	3215	2998	2790	2590	2400
	energy, ft-lb:	2983	2594	2246	1936	1662
Hornady 140 SP boat-tail	arc, inches:		+1.2	0	-5.8	-17.0
	velocity, fps:	2940	2747	2562	2385	2214
	energy, ft-lb:	2688	2346	2041	1769	1524
Hornady 140 SP boat-tail LM	arc, inches:		+1.6	0	-7.0	-20.2
	velocity, fps:	3100	2894	2697	2508	2327.
	energy, ft-lb:	2987	2604	2261	1955	1684
Hornady 150 SP	arc, inches:		+1.4	0	6.3	-18.3
	velocity, fps:	2800	2684	2478	2284	2100
	energy, ft-lb:	2802	2400	2046	1737	1469
Norma 130 SP	arc, inches:		+1.3	0	-6.5	
	velocity, fps:	3140	2862	2601	2354	
	energy, ft-lb:	2847	2365	1953	1600	
Norma 130 FMJ	arc, inches:		+1.8	0	-7.8	
	velocity, fps:	2887	2634	2395	2169	
	energy, ft-lb:					
Norma 150 SP	arc, inches:		+1.9	0	-8.3	
	velocity, fps:	2799	2555	2323	2104	
	energy, ft-lb:	2610	2175	1798	1475	
Norma 150 Oryx	arc, inches:		+1.8	0	-8.0	
	velocity, fps:	2854	2608	2376	2155	
	energy, ft-lb:	2714	2267	1880	1547	
PMC 130 Barnes X	arc, inches:		+1.6	0	-7.1	-20.4
	velocity, fps:	2910	2717	2533	2356	2186
	energy, ft-lb:	2444	2131	1852	1602	1379
PMC 130 SP boat-tail	arc, inches:		+1.5	0	-6.5	-19.0
	velocity, fps:	3050	2830	2620	2421	2229
	energy, ft-lb:	2685	2312	1982	1691	1435
PMC 130 Pointed Soft Point	arc, inches:		+1.6	0	-7.5	-22.1
	velocity, fps:	2950	2691	2447	2217	2001
	energy, ft-lb:	2512	2090	1728	1419	1156
PMC 150 Barnes X	arc, inches:		+2.0	0	-8.1	-23.1
	velocity, fps:	2700	2541	2387	2238	2095
	energy, ft-lb:	2428	2150	1897	1668	1461
PMC 150 SP boat-tail	arc, inches:		+1.7	0	-7.4	-21.4
	velocity, fps:	2850	2660	2477	2302	2134
	energy, ft-lb:	2705	2355	2043	1765	1516.
PMC 150 Pointed Soft Point	arc, inches:		+2.0	0	-8.4	-24.6
	velocity, fps:	2750	2530	2321	2123	1936
	energy, ft-lb:	2519	2131	1794	1501	1248
Rem. 100 Pointed Soft Point	velocity, fps:	3320	2924	2561	2225	1916
	energy, ft-lb:	2448	1898	1456	1099	815

CARTRIDGE BULLET	RANGE, YARDS:	0	100	200	300	400
Rem. 115 PSP Core-Lokt mr	arc, inches:		+2.3	+2.0	-3.6	-16.2
	velocity, fps:	2710	2412	2133	1873	1636
	energy, ft-lb:	1875	1485	1161	896	683
Rem. 130 PSP Core-Lokt	arc, inches:		+1.0	-2.7	-14.2	-35.6
	velocity, fps:	3060	2776	2510	2259	2022
	energy, ft-lb:	2702	2225	1818	1472	1180
Rem. 130 Bronze Point	arc, inches:		+1.5	0	-7.0	-20.9
	velocity, fps:	3060	2802	2559	2329	2110
	energy, ft-lb:	2702	2267	1890	1565	1285
Rem. 130 Swift Scirocco	arc, inches:		+1.5	0	-6.8	-20.0
	velocity, fps:	3060	2838	2677	2425	2232
	energy, ft-lb:	2702	2325	1991	1697	1438
Rem. 130 AccuTip BT	arc, inches:		+1.4	0	-6.5	-18.8
	velocity, fps:	3060	2845	2639	2442	2254
	energy, ft-lb:	2702	2336	2009	1721	1467
Rem. 140 Swift A-Frame	arc, inches:		+1.4	0	-6.4	-18.6
	velocity, fps:	2925	2652	2394	2152	1923
	energy, ft-lb:	2659	2186	1782	1439	1150
Rem. 140 PSP boat-tail	arc, inches:		+1.7	0	-7.8	-23.2
	velocity, fps:	2960	2749	2548	2355	2171
	energy, ft-lb:	2723	2349	2018	1724	1465
Rem. 140 Nosler Bal. Tip	arc, inches:		+1.6	0	-6.9	-20.1
	velocity, fps:	2960	2754	2557	2366	2187
	energy, ft-lb:	2724	2358	2032	1743	1487
Rem. 140 PSP C-L Ultra	arc, inches:		+1.6	0	-6.9	-20.0
	velocity, fps:	2925	2667	2424	2193	1975
	energy, ft-lb:	2659	2211	1826	1495	1212
Rem. 150 SP Core-Lokt	arc, inches:		+1.7	0	-7.6	-22.5
	velocity, fps:	2850	2504	2183	1886	1618
	energy, ft-lb:	2705	2087	1587	1185	872
Rem. 150 Nosler Partition	arc, inches:		+2.0	0	-9.4	-28.6
	velocity, fps:	2850	2652	2463	2282	2108
	energy, ft-lb:	2705	2343	2021	1734	1480
Speer 130 Grand Slam	arc, inches:		+1.7	0	-7.5	-21.6
	velocity, fps:	3050	2774	2514	2269	
	energy, ft-lb:	2685	2221	1824	1485	
Speer 150 Grand Slam	arc, inches:		+1.5	0	-7.0	-20.9
	velocity, fps:	2830	2594	2369	2156	
	energy, ft-lb:	2667	2240	1869	1548	
Win. 130 Power-Point	arc, inches:		+1.8	0	-8.1	-23.6
	velocity, fps:	3060	2802	2559	2329	2110
	energy, ft-lb:	2702	2267	1890	1565	1285.
Win. 130 Power-Point Plus	arc, inches:		+1.8	0	-7.1	-20.6
	velocity, fps:	3150	2881	2628	2388	2161
	energy, ft-lb:	2865	2396	1993	1646	1348
Win. 130 Silvertip	arc, inches:		+1.3	0	-6.4	-18.9
	velocity, fps:	3060	2776	2510	2259	2022.
	energy, ft-lb:	2702	2225	1818	1472	1180
Win. 130 Ballistic Silvertip	arc, inches:		+1.8	0	-7.4	-21.6
	velocity, fps:	3050	2828	2618	2416	2224
	energy, ft-lb:	2685	2309	1978	1685	1428
Win. 140 AccuBond	arc, inches:		+1.4	0	-6.5	-18.9
	velocity, fps:	2950	2751	2560	2378	2203
	energy, ft-lb:	2705	2352	2038	1757	1508
Win. 140 Fail Safe	arc, inches:		+1.6	0	-6.9	-19.9
	velocity, fps:	2920	2671	2435	2211	1999
	energy, ft-lb:	2651	2218	1843	1519	1242
Win. 150 Power-Point	arc, inches:		+1.7	0	-7.6	-22.3
	velocity, fps:	2850	2585	2336	2100	1879
	energy, ft-lb:	2705	2226	1817	1468	1175
Win. 150 Power-Point Plus	arc, inches:		+2.2	0	-8.6	-25.0
	velocity, fps:	2950	2679	2425	2184	1957
	energy, ft-lb:	2900	2391	1959	1589	1276

BALLISTICS

.270 Winchester (continued)

CARTRIDGE BULLET	RANGE, YARDS:	0	100	200	300	400
	arc, inches:		+1.7	0	-7.6	-22.6
Win. 150 Partition Gold	velocity, fps:	2930	2693	2468	2254	2051
	energy, ft-lb:	2860	2416	2030	1693	1402
	arc, inches:		+1.7	0	-7.4	-21.6
Win. 150 Supreme Elite XP3	velocity, fps:	2950	2763	2583	2411	2245
	energy, ft-lb:	2898	2542	2223	1936	1679
	arc, inches:		+1.5	0	-6.9	-15.5

.270 WINCHESTER SHORT MAGNUM

CARTRIDGE BULLET	RANGE, YARDS:	0	100	200	300	400
Black Hills 140 AccuBond	velocity, fps:	3100				
	energy, ft-lb:	2987				
	arc, inches:					
Federal 130 Nos. Bal. Tip	velocity, fps:	3300	3070	2840	2630	2430
	energy, ft-lb:	3145	2710	2335	2000	1705
	arc, inches:		+1.1	0	-5.4	-15.8
Federal 130 Nos. Partition	velocity, fps:	3280	3040	2810	2590	2380
And Nos. Solid Base	energy, ft-lb:	3105	2665	2275	1935	1635
And Barnes TS	arc, inches:		+1.1	0	-5.6	-16.3
Federal 140 Nos. AccuBond	velocity, fps	3200	3000	2810	2630	2450
	energy, ft-lb:	3185	2795	2455	2145	1865
	arc, inches:		+1.2	0	-5.6	-16.2
Federal 140 Trophy Bonded	velocity, fps:	3130	2870	2640	2410	2200
	energy, ft-lb:	3035	2570	2160	1810	1500
	arc, inches:		+1.4	0	-6.3	18.7
Federal 150 Nos. Partition	velocity, fps:	3160	2950	2750	2550	2370
	energy, ft-lb:	3325	2895	2515	2175	1870
	arc, inches:		+1.3	0	-5.9	-17.0
Norma 130 FMJ	velocity, fps:	3150	2882	2630	2391	
	energy, ft-lb:					
	arc, inches:		+1.5	0	-6.4	
Norma 130 Ballistic ST	velocity, fps:	3281	3047	2825	2614	
	energy, ft-lb:	3108	2681	2305	1973	
	arc, inches:		+1.1	0	-5.5	
Norma 140 Barnes X TS	velocity, fps:	3150	2952	2762	2580	
	energy, ft-lb:	3085	2709	2372	2070	
	arc, inches:		+1.3	0	-5.8	
Norma 150 Nosler Bal. Tip	velocity, fps:	3280	3046	2824	2613	
	energy, ft-lb:	3106	2679	2303	1972	
	arc, inches:		+1.1	0	-5.4	
Norma 150 Oryx	velocity, fps:	3117	2856	2611	2378	
	energy, ft-lb:	3237	2718	2271	1884	
	arc, inches:		+1.4	0	-6.5	
Win. 130 Bal. Silvertip	velocity, fps:	3275	3041	2820	2609	2408
	energy, ft-lb:	3096	2669	2295	1964	1673
	arc, inches:		+1.1	0	-5.5	-16.1
Win. 140 AccuBond	velocity, fps:	3200	2989	2789	2597	2413
	energy, ft-lb:	3184	2779	2418	2097	1810
	arc, inches:		+1.2	0	-5.7	-16.5
Win. 140 Fail Safe	velocity, fps:	3125	2865	2619	2386	2165
	energy, ft-lb:	3035	2550	2132	1769	1457
	arc, inches:		+1.4	0	-6.5	-19.0
Win. 150 Ballistic Silvertip	velocity, fps:	3120	2923	2734	2554	2380.
	energy, ft-lb:	3242	2845	2490	2172	1886.
	arc, inches:		+1.3	0	-5.9	-17.2
Win. 150 Power Point	velocity, fps:	3150	2867	2601	2350	2113
	energy, ft-lb:	3304	2737	2252	1839	1487
	arc, inches:		+1.4	0	-6.5	-19.4
Win. 150 Supreme Elite XP3	velocity, fps:	3120	2926	2740	2561	2389
	energy, ft-lb:	3242	2850	2499	2184	1901
	arc, inches:		+1.3	0	-5.9	-17.1

.270 WEATHERBY MAGNUM

CARTRIDGE BULLET	RANGE, YARDS:	0	100	200	300	400
Federal 130 Nosler Partition	velocity, fps:	3200	2960	2740	2520	2320
	energy, ft-lb:	2955	2530	2160	1835	1550

.270 Weatherby Magnum (continued)

CARTRIDGE BULLET	RANGE, YARDS:	0	100	200	300	400
	arc, inches:		+1.2	0	-5.9	-17.3
Federal 130 Sierra GameKing	velocity, fps:	3200	2980	2780	2580	2400
BTSP	energy, ft-lb:	2955	2570	2230	1925	1655
	arc, inches:		+1.2	0	-5.7	-16.6
Federal 140 Trophy Bonded	velocity, fps:	3100	2840	2600	2370	2150.
	energy, ft-lb:	2990	2510	2100	1745	1440
	arc, inches:		+1.4	0	-6.6	-19.3
Wby. 100 Pointed Expanding	velocity, fps:	3760	3396	3061	2751	2462
	energy, ft-lb:	3139	2560	2081	1681	1346
	arc, inches:		+2.3	+3.0	0	-7.6
Wby. 130 Pointed Expanding	velocity, fps:	3375	3123	2885	2659	2444
	energy, ft-lb:	3288	2815	2402	2041	1724
	arc, inches:		+2.8	+3.5	0	-8.4
Wby. 130 Nosler Partition	velocity, fps:	3375	3127	2892	2670	2458.
	energy, ft-lb:	3288	2822	2415	2058	1744
	arc, inches:		+2.8	+3.5	0	-8.3
Wby. 140 Nosler Bal. Tip	velocity, fps:	3300	3077	2865	2663	2470.
	energy, ft-lb:	3385	2943	2551	2204	1896
	arc, inches:		+2.9	+3.6	0	-8.4
Wby. 140 Barnes X	velocity, fps:	3250	3032	2825	2628	2438
	energy, ft-lb:	3283	2858	2481	2146	1848
	arc, inches:		+3.0	+3.7	0	-8.7
Wby. 150 Pointed Expanding	velocity, fps:	3245	3028	2821	2623	2434
	energy, ft-lb:	3507	3053	2650	2292	1973
	arc, inches:		+3.0	+3.7	0	-8.7
Wby. 150 Nosler Partition	velocity, fps:	3245	3029	2823	2627	2439.
	energy, ft-lb:	3507	3055	2655	2298	1981
	arc, inches:		+3.0	+3.7	0	-8.

7-30 WATERS

CARTRIDGE BULLET	RANGE, YARDS:	0	100	200	300	400
Federal 120 Sierra GameKing	velocity, fps:	2700	2300	1930	1600	1330.
BTSP	energy, ft-lb:	1940	1405	990	685	470
	arc, inches:		+2.6	0	-12.0	-37.6

7MM MAUSER (7X57)

CARTRIDGE BULLET	RANGE, YARDS:	0	100	200	300	400
Federal 140 Sierra Pro-Hunt.	velocity, fps:	2660	2450	2260	2070	1890.
	energy, ft-lb:	2200	1865	1585	1330	1110
	arc, inches:		+2.1	0	-9.0	-26.1
Federal 140 Nosler Partition	velocity, fps:	2660	2450	2260	2070	1890.
	energy, ft-lb:	2200	1865	1585	1330	1110
	arc, inches:		+2.1	0	-9.0	-26.1
Federal 175 Hi-Shok RN	velocity, fps:	2440	2140	1860	1600	1380
	energy, ft-lb:	2315	1775	1340	1000	740
	arc, inches:		+3.1	0	-13.3	-40.1
Hornady 139 SP boat-tail	velocity, fps:	2700	2504	2316	2137	1965
	energy, ft-lb:	2251	1936	1656	1410	1192
	arc, inches:		+2.0	0	-8.5	-24.9
Hornady 139 SP Interlock	velocity, fps:	2680	2455	2241	2038	1846
	energy, ft-lb:	2216	1860	1550	1282	1052
	arc, inches:		+2.1	0	-9.1	-26.6
Hornady 139 SP boat-tail LM	velocity, fps:	2830	2620	2450	2250	2070
	energy, ft-lb:	2475	2135	1835	1565	1330
	arc, inches:		+1.8	0	-7.6	-22.1
Hornady 139 SP LM	velocity, fps:	2950	2736	2532	2337	2152.
	energy, ft-lb:	2686	2310	1978	1686	1429
	arc, inches:		+2.0	0	-7.6	-21.5
Norma 150 Soft Point	velocity, fps:	2690	2479	2278	2087	
	energy, ft-lb:	2411	2048	1729	1450	
	arc, inches:		+2.0	0	-8.8	
PMC 140 Pointed Soft Point	velocity, fps:	2660	2450	2260	2070	1890
	energy, ft-lb:	2200	1865	1585	1330	1110.
	arc, inches:		+2.4	0	-9.6	-27.3
PMC 175 Soft Point	velocity, fps:	2440	2140	1860	1600	1380
	energy, ft-lb:	2315	1775	1340	1000	740

BALLISTICS

Centerfire Rifle Ballistics

7MM MAUSER TO 7X65 R

CARTRIDGE BULLET	RANGE, YARDS:	0	100	200	300	400
	arc, inches:		+1.5	-3.6	-18.6	-46.8
Rem. 140 PSP Core-Lokt	velocity, fps:	2660	2435	2221	2018	1827
	energy, ft-lb:	2199	1843	1533	1266	1037
	arc, inches:		+2.2	0	-9.2	-27.4
Win. 145 Power-Point	velocity, fps:	2660	2413	2180	1959	1754
	energy, ft-lb:	2279	1875	1530	1236	990
	arc, inches:		+1.1	-2.8	-14.1	-34.4

7x57 R

CARTRIDGE BULLET	RANGE, YARDS:	0	100	200	300	400
Norma 150 FMJ	velocity, fps:	2690	2489	2296	2112	
	energy, ft-lb:	2411	2063	1756	1486	
	arc, inches:		+2.0	0	-8.6	
Norma 154 Soft Point	velocity, fps:	2625	2417	2219	2030	
	energy, ft-lb:	2357	1999	1684	1410	
	arc, inches:		+2.2	0	-9.3	
Norma 156 Oryx	velocity, fps:	2608	2346	2099	1867	
	energy, ft-lb:	2357	1906	1526	1208	
	arc, inches:		+2.4	0	-10.3	

7MM-08 REMINGTON

CARTRIDGE BULLET	RANGE, YARDS:	0	100	200	300	400
Black Hills 140 AccuBond	velocity, fps:	2700				
	energy, ft-lb:					
	arc, inches:					
Federal 140 Nosler Partition	velocity, fps:	2800	2590	2390	2200	2020
	energy, ft-lb:	2435	2085	1775	1500	1265
	arc, inches:		+1.8	0	-8.0	-23.1
Federal 140 Nosler Bal. Tip And AccuBond	velocity, fps:	2800	2610	2430	2260	2100
	energy, ft-lb:	2440	2135	1840	1590	1360.
	arc, inches:		+1.8	0	-7.7	-22.3
Federal 140 Tr. Bonded HE	velocity, fps:	2950	2660	2390	2140	1900
	energy, ft-lb:	2705	2205	1780	1420	1120
	arc, inches:		+1.7	0	-7.9	-23.2
Federal 150 Sierra Pro-Hunt.	velocity, fps:	2650	2440	2230	2040	1860
	energy, ft-lb:	2340	1980	1660	1390	1150
	arc, inches:		+2.2	0	-9.2	-26.7
Hornady 139 SP boat-tail LM	velocity, fps:	3000	2790	2590	2399	2216
	energy, ft-lb:	2777	2403	2071	1776	1515
	arc, inches:		+1.5	0	-6.7	-19.4
Norma 140 Ballistic ST	velocity, fps:	2822	2633	2452	2278	
	energy, ft-lb:	2476	2156	1870	1614	
	arc, inches:		+1.8	0	-7.6	
PMC 139 PSP	velocity, fps:	2850	2610	2384	2170	1969
	energy, ft-lb:	2507	2103	1754	1454	1197
	arc, inches:		+1.8	0	-7.9	-23.3
Rem. 120 Hollow Point	velocity, fps:	3000	2725	2467	2223	1992
	energy, ft-lb:	2398	1979	1621	1316	1058
	arc, inches:		+1.6	0	-7.3	-21.7
Rem. 140 PSP Core-Lokt	velocity, fps:	2860	2625	2402	2189	1988
	energy, ft-lb:	2542	2142	1793	1490	1228
	arc, inches:		+1.8	0	-7.8	-22.9
Rem. 140 PSP boat-tail	velocity, fps:	2860	2656	2460	2273	2094
	energy, ft-lb:	2542	2192	1881	1606	1363
	arc, inches:		+1.7	0	-7.5	-21.7
Rem. 140 AccuTip BT	velocity, fps:	2860	2670	2488	2313	2145
	energy, ft-lb:	2543	2217	1925	1663	1431
	arc, inches:		+1.7	0	-7.3	-21.2
Rem. 140 Nosler Partition	velocity, fps:	2860	2648	2446	2253	2068
	energy, ft-lb:	2542	2180	1860	1577	1330
	arc, inches:		+1.7	0	-7.6	-22.0
Speer 145 Grand Slam	velocity, fps:	2845	2567	2305	2059	
	energy, ft-lb:	2606	2121	1711	1365	
	arc, inches:		+1.9	0	-8.4	-25.5
Win. 140 Power-Point	velocity, fps:	2800	2523	2268	2027	1802.
	energy, ft-lb:	2429	1980	1599	1277	1010

CARTRIDGE BULLET	RANGE, YARDS:	0	100	200	300	400
	arc, inches:		+2.0	0	-8.8	-26.0
Win. 140 Power-Point Plus	velocity, fps:	2875	2597	2336	2090	1859
	energy, ft-lb:	2570	1997	1697	1358	1075
	arc, inches:		+2.0	0	-8.8	26.0
Win. 140 Fail Safe	velocity, fps:	2760	2506	2271	2048	1839
	energy, ft-lb:	2360	1953	1603	1304	1051
	arc, inches:		+2.0	0	-8.8	-25.9
Win. 140 Ballistic Silvertip	velocity, fps:	2770	2572	2382	2200	2026
	energy, ft-lb:	2386	2056	1764	1504	1276
	arc, inches:		+1.9	0	-8.0	-23.8

7x64 BRENNEKE

CARTRIDGE BULLET	RANGE, YARDS:	0	100	200	300	400
Federal 160 Nosler Partition	velocity, fps:	2650	2480	2310	2150	2000
	energy, ft-lb:	2495	2180	1895	1640	1415
	arc, inches:		+2.1	0	-8.7	-24.9
Norma 140 AccuBond	velocity, fps:	2953	2759	2572	2394	
	energy, ft-lb:	2712	2366	2058	1782	
	arc, inches:		+1.5	0	-6.8	
Norma 154 Soft Point	velocity, fps:	2821	2605	2399	2203	
	energy, ft-lb:	2722	2321	1969	1660	
	arc, inches:		+1.8	0	-7.8	
Norma 156 Oryx	velocity, fps:	2789	2516	2259	2017	
	energy, ft-lb:	2695	2193	1768	1410	
	arc, inches:		+2.0	0	-8.8	
Norma 170 Vulkan	velocity, fps:	2756	2501	2259	2031	
	energy, ft-lb:	2868	2361	1927	1558	
	arc, inches:		+2.0	0	-8.8	
Norma 170 Oryx	velocity, fps:	2756	2481	2222	1979	
	energy, ft-lb:	2868	2324	1864	1478	
	arc, inches:		+2.1	0	-9.2	
Norma 170 Plastic Point	velocity, fps:	2756	2519	2294	2081	
	energy, ft-lb:	2868	2396	1987	1635	
	arc, inches:		+2.0	0	-8.6	
PMC 170 Pointed Soft Point	velocity, fps:	2625	2401	2189	1989	1801
	energy, ft lb:	2601	2175	1808	1493	1224
	arc, inches:		+2.3	0	-9.6	-27.9
Rem. 175 PSP Core-Lokt	velocity, fps:	2650	2445	2248	2061	1883
	energy, ft-lb:	2728	2322	1964	1650	1378
	arc, inches:		+2.2	0	-9.1	-26.4
Speer 160 Grand Slam	velocity, fps:	2600	2376	2164	1962	
	energy, ft-lb:	2401	2006	1663	1368	
	arc, inches:		+2.3	0	-9.8	-28.6
Speer 175 Grand Slam	velocity, fps:	2650	2461	2280	2106	
	energy, ft-lb:	2728	2353	2019	1723	
	arc, inches:		+2.4	0	-9.2	-26.2

7x65 R

CARTRIDGE BULLET	RANGE, YARDS:	0	100	200	300	400
Norma 150 FMJ	velocity, fps:	2756	2552	2357	2170	
	energy, ft-lb:	2530	2169	1850	1569	
	arc, inches:		+1.9	0	-8.2	
Norma 156 Oryx	velocity, fps:	2723	2454	2200	1962	
	energy, ft-lb:	2569	2086	1678	1334	
	arc, inches:		+2.1	0	-9.3	
Norma 170 Plastic Point	velocity, fps:	2625	2390	2167	1956	
	energy, ft-lb:	2602	2157	1773	1445	
	arc, inches:		+2.3	0	-9.7	
Norma 170 Vulkan	velocity, fps:	2657	2392	2143	1909	
	energy, ft-lb:	2666	2161	1734	1377	
	arc, inches:		+2.3	0	-9.9	
Norma 170 Oryx	velocity, fps:	2657	2378	2115	1871	
	energy, ft-lb:	2666	2135	1690	1321	
	arc, inches:		+2.3	0	-10.1	

CARTRIDGE BULLET	RANGE, YARDS:	0	100	200	300	400

.284 WINCHESTER

CARTRIDGE BULLET	RANGE, YARDS:	0	100	200	300	400
Win. 150 Power-Point	velocity, fps:	2860	2595	2344	2108	1886
	energy, ft-lb:	2724	2243	1830	1480	1185
	arc, inches:		+2.1	0	-8.5	-24.8

.280 REMINGTON

CARTRIDGE BULLET	RANGE, YARDS:	0	100	200	300	400
Federal 140 Sierra Pro-Hunt.	velocity, fps:	2990	2740	2500	2270	2060
	energy, ft-lb:	2770	2325	1940	1605	1320
	arc, inches:		+1.6	0	-7.0	-20.8
Federal 140 Trophy Bonded	velocity, fps:	2990	2630	2310	2040	1730
	energy, ft-lb:	2770	2155	1655	1250	925
	arc, inches:		+1.6	0	-8.4	-25.4
Federal 140 Tr. Bonded HE	velocity, fps:	3150	2850	2570	2300	2050
	energy, ft-lb:	3085	2520	2050	1650	1310
	arc, inches:		+1.4	0	-6.7	-20.0
Federal 140 Nos. AccuBond And Bal. Tip And Solid Base	velocity, fps:	3000	2800	2620	2440	2260
	energy, ft-lb:	2800	2445	2130	1845	1590
	arc, inches:		+1.5	0	-6.5	-18.9
Federal 150 Hi-Shok	velocity, fps:	2890	2670	2460	2260	2060
	energy, ft-lb:	2780	2370	2015	1695	1420
	arc, inches:		+1.7	0	-7.5	-21.8
Federal 150 Nosler Partition	velocity, fps:	2890	2690	2490	2310	2130
	energy, ft-lb:	2780	2405	2070	1770	1510.
	arc, inches:		+1.7	0	-7.2	-21.1
Federal 150 Nos. AccuBond	velocity, fps	2800	2630	2460	2300	2150
	energy, ft-lb:	2785	2455	2155	1885	1645
	arc, inches:		+1.8	0	-7.5	-21.5
Federal 160 Trophy Bonded	velocity, fps:	2800	2570	2350	2140	1940
	energy, ft-lb:	2785	2345	1960	1625	1340
	arc, inches:		+1.9	0	-8.3	-24.0
Hornady 139 SPBT LMmoly	velocity, fps:	3110	2888	2675	2473	2280.
	energy, ft-lb:	2985	2573	2209	1887	1604
	arc, inches:		+1.4	0	-6.5	-18.6
Norma 156 Oryx	velocity, fps:	2789	2516	2259	2017	
	energy, ft-lb:	2695	2193	1768	1410	
	arc, inches:		+2.0	0	-8.8	
Norma 170 Plastic Point	velocity, fps:	2707	2468	2241	2026	
	energy, ft-lb:	2767	2299	1896	1550	
	arc, inches:		+2.1	0	-9.1	
Norma 170 Vulkan	velocity, fps:	2592	2346	2113	1894	
	energy, ft-lb:	2537	2078	1686	1354	
	arc, inches:		+2.4	0	-10.2	
Norma 170 Oryx	velocity, fps:	2690	2416	2159	1918	
	energy, ft-lb:	2732	2204	1760	1389	
	arc, inches:		+2.2	0	-9.7	
Rem. 140 PSP Core-Lokt	velocity, fps:	3000	2758	2528	2309	2102
	energy, ft-lb:	2797	2363	1986	1657	1373
	arc, inches:		+1.5	0	-7.0	-20.5
Rem. 140 PSP boat-tail	velocity, fps:	2860	2656	2460	2273	2094
	energy, ft-lb:	2542	2192	1881	1606	1363
	arc, inches:		+1.7	0	-7.5	-21.7
Rem. 140 Nosler Bal. Tip	velocity, fps:	3000	2804	2616	2436	2263
	energy, ft-lb:	2799	2445	2128	1848	1593
	arc, inches:		+1.5	0	-6.8	-19.0
Rem. 140 AccuTip	velocity, fps:	3000	2804	2617	2437	2265
	energy, ft-lb:	2797	2444	2129	1846	1594
	arc, inches:		+1.5	0	-6.8	-19.0
Rem. 150 PSP Core-Lokt	velocity, fps:	2890	2624	2373	2135	1912
	energy, ft-lb:	2781	2293	1875	1518	1217
	arc, inches:		+1.8	0	-8.0	-23.6
Rem. 165 SP Core-Lokt	velocity, fps:	2820	2510	2220	1950	1701
	energy, ft-lb:	2913	2308	1805	1393	1060.

CARTRIDGE BULLET	RANGE, YARDS:	0	100	200	300	400
Speer 145 Grand Slam	arc, inches:		+2.0	0	-9.1	-27.4
	velocity, fps:	2900	2619	2354	2105	
	energy, ft-lb:	2707	2207	1784	1426	
Speer 160 Grand Slam	arc, inches:		+2.1	0	-8.4	-24.7
	velocity, fps:	2890	2652	2425	2210	
	energy, ft-lb:	2967	2497	2089	1735	
Win. 140 Fail Safe	arc, inches:		+1.7	0	-7.7	-22.4
	velocity, fps:	3050	2756	2480	2221	1977
	energy, ft-lb:	2893	2362	1913	1533	1216
Win. 140 Ballistic Silvertip	arc, inches:		+1.5	0	-7.2	-21.5
	velocity, fps:	3040	2842	2653	2471	2297
	energy, ft-lb:	2872	2511	2187	1898	1640
	arc, inches:		+1.4	0	-6.3	-18.4

7MM REMINGTON MAGNUM

CARTRIDGE BULLET	RANGE, YARDS:	0	100	200	300	400
A-Square 175 Monolithic Solid	velocity, fps:	2860	2557	2273	2008	1771
	energy, ft-lb:	3178	2540	2008	1567	1219
	arc, inches:		+1.92	0	-8.7	-25.9
Black Hills 140 Nos. Bal. Tip	velocity, fps:	3150				
	energy, ft-lb:	3084				
	arc, inches:					
Black Hills 140 Barnes XLC	velocity, fps:	3150				
	energy, ft-lb:	3084				
	arc, inches:					
Black Hills 140 Nos. Partition	velocity, fps:	3150				
	energy, ft-lb:	3084				
	arc, inches:					
Federal 140 Nosler Bal. Tip And AccuBond	velocity, fps:	3110	2910	2720	2530	2360.
	energy, ft-lb:	3005	2630	2295	1995	1725
	arc, inches:		+1.3	0	-6.0	-17.4
Federal 140 Nosler Partition	velocity, fps:	3150	2930	2710	2510	2320
	energy, ft-lb:	3085	2660	2290	1960	1670
	arc, inches:		+1.3	0	-6.0	-17.5
Federal 140 Trophy Bonded	velocity, fps:	3150	2910	2680	2460	2250.
	energy, ft-lb:	3085	2630	2230	1880	1575
	arc, inches:		+1.3	0	-6.1	-18.1
Federal 150 Hi-Shok	velocity, fps:	3110	2830	2570	2320	2090
	energy, ft-lb:	3220	2670	2200	1790	1450
	arc, inches:		+1.4	0	-6.7	-19.9
Federal 150 Sierra GameKing BTSP	velocity, fps:	3110	2920	2750	2580	2410
	energy, ft-lb:	3220	2850	2510	2210	1930
	arc, inches:		+1.3	0	-5.9	-17.0
Federal 150 Nosler Bal. Tip	velocity, fps:	3110	2910	2720	2540	2370
	energy, ft-lb:	3220	2825	2470	2150	1865
	arc, inches:		+1.3	0	-6.0	-17.4
Federal 150 Nos. Solid Base	velocity, fps:	3100	2890	2690	2500	2310
	energy, ft-lb:	3200	2780	2405	2075	1775
	arc, inches:		+1.3	0	-6.2	-17.8
Federal 160 Barnes XLC	velocity, fps:	2940	2760	2580	2410	2240
	energy, ft-lb:	3070	2695	2360	2060	1785
	arc, inches:		+1.5	0	-6.8	-19.6
Federal 160 Sierra Pro-Hunt.	velocity, fps:	2940	2730	2520	2320	2140
	energy, ft-lb:	3070	2640	2260	1920	1620
	arc, inches:		+1.6	0	-7.1	-20.6
Federal 160 Nosler Partition	velocity, fps:	2950	2770	2590	2420	2250.
	energy, ft-lb:	3090	2715	2375	2075	1800
	arc, inches:		+1.5	0	-6.7	-19.4
Federal 160 Nos. AccuBond	velocity, fps:	2950	2770	2600	2440	2280.
	energy, ft-lb:	3090	2730	2405	2110	1845
	arc, inches:		+1.5	0	-6.6	-19.1
Federal 160 Trophy Bonded	velocity, fps:	2940	2660	2390	2140	1900
	energy, ft-lb:	3070	2505	2025	1620	1280.
	arc, inches:		+1.7	0	-7.9	-23.3

Centerfire Rifle Ballistics

7MM REMINGTON MAGNUM TO 7MM REMINGTON MAGNUM

CARTRIDGE BULLET	RANGE, YARDS:	0	100	200	300	400
Federal 165 Sierra GameKing BTSP	velocity, fps:	2950	2800	2650	2510	2370.
	energy, ft-lb:	3190	2865	2570	2300	2050
	arc, inches:		+1.5	0	-6.4	-18.4
Federal 175 Hi-Shok	velocity, fps:	2860	2650	2440	2240	2060
	energy, ft-lb:	3180	2720	2310	1960	1640
	arc, inches:		+1.7	0	-7.6	-22.1
Federal 175 Trophy Bonded	velocity, fps:	2860	2600	2350	2120	1900
	energy, ft-lb:	3180	2625	2150	1745	1400
	arc, inches:		+1.8	0	-8.2	-24.0
Hornady 139 SPBT	velocity, fps:	3150	2933	2727	2530	2341
	energy, ft-lb:	3063	2656	2296	1976	1692
	arc, inches:		+1.2	0	-6.1	-17.7
Hornady 139 SST (or Interbond)	velocity, fps:	3150	2948	2754	2569	2391
	energy, ft-lb:	3062	2681	2341	2037	1764
	arc, inches:		+1.1	0	-5.7	-16.7
Hornady 139 SST LM (or Interbond)	velocity, fps:	3250	3044	2847	2657	2475
	energy, ft-lb:	3259	2860	2501	2178	1890
	arc, inches:		+1.1	0	-5.5	-16.2
Hornady 139 SPBT HMmoly	velocity, fps:	3250	3041	2822	2613	2413
	energy, ft-lb:	3300	2854	2458	2106	1797.
	arc, inches:		+1.1	0	-5.7	-16.6
Hornady 154 Soft Point	velocity, fps:	3035	2814	2604	2404	2212
	energy, ft-lb:	3151	2708	2319	1977	1674
	arc, inches:		+1.3	0	-6.7	-19.3
Hornady 154 SST (or Interbond)	velocity, fps:	3035	2850	2672	2501	2337
	energy, ft-lb:	3149	2777	2441	2139	1867
	arc, inches:		+1.4	0	-6.5	-18.7
Hornady 162 SP boat-tail	velocity, fps:	2940	2757	2582	2413	2251
	energy, ft-lb:	3110	2735	2399	2095	1823
	arc, inches:		+1.6	0	-6.7	-19.7
Hornady 175 SP	velocity, fps:	2860	2650	2440	2240	2060.
	energy, ft-lb:	3180	2720	2310	1960	1640
	arc, inches:		+2.0	0	-7.9	-22.7
Norma 140 Nosler Bal. Tip	velocity, fps:	3150	2936	2732	2537	
	energy, ft-lb:	3085	2680	2320	2001	
	arc, inches:		+1.2	0	-5.9	
Norma 140 Barnes X TS	velocity, fps:	3117	2912	2716	2529	
	energy, ft-lb:	3021	2637	2294	1988	
	arch, inches:		+1.3	0	-6.0	
Norma 150 Scirocco	velocity, fps:	3117	2934	2758	2589	
	energy, ft-lb:	3237	2869	2535	2234	
	arc, inches:		+1.2	0	-5.8	
Norma 156 Oryx	velocity, fps:	2953	2670	2404	2153	
	energy, ft-lb:	3021	2470	2002	1607	
	arc, inches:		+1.7	0	-7.7	
Norma 170 Vulkan	velocity, fps:	3018	2747	2493	2252	
	energy, ft-lb:	3439	2850	2346	1914	
	arc, inches:		+1.5	0	-2.8	
Norma 170 Oryx	velocity, fps:	2887	2601	2333	2080	
	energy, ft-lb:	3147	2555	2055	1634	
	arc, inches:		+1.8	0	-8.2	
Norma 170 Plastic Point	velocity, fps:	3018	2762	2519	2290	
	energy, ft-lb:	3439	2880	2394	1980	
	arc, inches:		+1.5	0	-7.0	
PMC 140 Barnes X	velocity, fps:	3000	2808	2624	2448	2279
	energy, ft-lb:	2797	2451	2141	1863	1614
	arc, inches:		+1.5	0	-6.6	18.9
PMC 140 Pointed Soft Point	velocity, fps:	3099	2878	2668	2469	2279
	energy, ft-lb:	2984	2574	2212	1895	1614
	arc, inches:		+1.4	0	-6.2	-18.1
PMC 140 SP boat-tail	velocity, fps:	3125	2891	2669	2457	2255
	energy, ft-lb:	3035	2597	2213	1877	1580
	arc, inches:		+1.4	0	-6.3	-18.4

CARTRIDGE BULLET	RANGE, YARDS:	0	100	200	300	400
PMC 160 Barnes X	velocity, fps:	2800	2639	2484	2334	2189
	energy, ft-lb:	2785	2474	2192	1935	1703
	arc, inches:		+1.8	0	-7.4	-21.2
PMC 160 Pointed Soft Point	velocity, fps:	2914	2748	2586	2428	2276
	energy, ft-lb:	3016	2682	2375	2095	1840
	arc, inches:		+1.6	0	-6.7	-19.4
PMC 160 SP boat-tail	velocity, fps:	2900	2696	2501	2314	2135
	energy, ft-lb:	2987	2582	2222	1903	1620
	arc, inches:		+1.7	0	-7.2	-21.0
PMC 175 Pointed Soft Point	velocity, fps:	2860	2645	2442	2244	2957
	energy, ft-lb:	3178	2718	2313	1956	1644
	arc, inches:		+2.0	0	-7.9	-22.7
Rem. 140 PSP Core-Lokt mr	velocity, fps:	2710	2482	2265	2059	1865
	energy, ft-lb:	2283	1915	1595	1318	1081
	arc, inches:		+1.0	-2.5	-12.8	-31.3
Rem. 140 PSP Core-Lokt	velocity, fps:	3175	2923	2684	2458	2243
	energy, ft-lb:	3133	2655	2240	1878	1564
	arc, inches:		+2.2	+1.9	-3.2	-14.2
Rem. 140 PSP boat-tail	velocity, fps:	3175	2956	2747	2547	2356
	energy, ft-lb:	3133	2715	2345	2017	1726
	arc, inches:		+2.2	+1.6	-3.1	-13.4
Rem. 150 AccuTip	velocity, fps:	3110	2926	2749	2579	2415
	energy, ft-lb:	3221	2850	2516	2215	1943
	arc, inches:		+1.3	0	-5.9	-17.0
Rem. 150 PSP Core-Lokt	velocity, fps:	3110	2830	2568	2320	2085
	energy, ft-lb:	3221	2667	2196	1792	1448
	arc, inches:		+1.3	0	-6.6	-20.2
Rem. 150 Nosler Bal. Tip	velocity, fps:	3110	2912	2723	2542	2367
	energy, ft-lb:	3222	2825	2470	2152	1867
	arc, inches:		+1.2	0	-5.9	-17.3
Rem. 150 Swift Scirocco	velocity, fps:	3110	2927	2751	2582	2419
	energy, ft-lb:	3221	2852	2520	2220	1948
	arc, inches:		+1.3	0	-5.9	-17.0
Rem. 160 Swift A-Frame	velocity, fps:	2900	2659	2430	2212	2006
	energy, ft-lb:	2987	2511	2097	1739	1430
	arc, inches:		+1.7	0	-7.6	-22.4
Rem. 160 Nosler Partition	velocity, fps:	2950	2752	2563	2381	2207
	energy, ft-lb:	3091	2690	2333	2014	1730
	arc, inches:		+0.6	-1.9	-9.6	-23.6
Rem. 175 PSP Core-Lokt	velocity, fps:	2860	2645	2440	2244	2057
	energy, ft-lb:	3178	2718	2313	1956	1644
	arc, inches:		+1.7	0	-7.6	-22.1
Speer 145 Grand Slam	velocity, fps:	3140	2843	2565	2304	
	energy, ft-lb:	3174	2602	2118	1708	
	arc, inches:		+1.4	0	-6.7	
Speer 175 Grand Slam	velocity, fps:	2850	2653	2463	2282	
	energy, ft-lb:	3156	2734	2358	2023	
	arc, inches:		+1.7	0	-7.5	-21.7
Win. 140 Fail Safe	velocity, fps:	3150	2861	2589	2333	2092
	energy, ft-lb:	3085	2544	2085	1693	1361
	arc, inches:		+1.4	0	-6.6	-19.5
Win. 140 Ballistic Silvertip	velocity, fps:	3100	2889	2687	2494	2310
	energy, ft-lb:	2988	2595	2245	1934	1659.
	arc, inches:		+1.3	0	-6.2	-17.9
Win. 140 AccuBond CT	velocity, fps:	3180	2965	2760	2565	2377
	energy, ft-lb:	3143	2733	2368	2044	1756
	arc, inches:		+1.2	0	-5.8	-16.9
Win. 150 Power-Point	velocity, fps:	3090	2812	2551	2304	2071
	energy, ft-lb:	3181	2634	2167	1768	1429
	arc, inches:		+1.5	0	-6.8	-20.2
Win. 150 Power-Point Plus	velocity, fps:	3130	2849	2586	2337	2102
	energy, ft-lb:	3264	2705	2227	1819	1472
	arc, inches:		+1.4	0	-6.6	-19.6

BALLISTICS

Centerfire Rifle Ballistics

CARTRIDGE BULLET	RANGE, YARDS:	0	100	200	300	400
Win. 150 Ballistic Silvertip	velocity, fps:	3100	2903	2714	2533	2359
	energy, ft-lb:	3200	2806	2453	2136	1853
	arc, inches:		+1.3	0	-6.0	-17.5
Win. 160 AccuBond	velocity, fps:	2950	2766	2590	2420	2257
	energy, ft-lb:	3091	2718	2382	2080	1809
	arc, inches:		+1.5	0	-6.7	-19.4
Win. 160 Partition Gold	velocity, fps:	2950	2743	2546	2357	2176
	energy, ft-lb:	3093	2674	2303	1974	1682
	arc, inches:		+1.6	0	-6.9	-20.1
Win. 160 Fail Safe	velocity, fps:	2920	2678	2449	2331	2025
	energy, ft-lb:	3030	2549	2131	1769	1457
	arc, inches:		+1.7	0	-7.5	-22.0
Win. 175 Power-Point	velocity, fps:	2860	2645	2440	2244	2057
	energy, ft-lb:	3178	2718	2313	1956	1644
	arc, inches:		+2.0	0	-7.9	-22.7

7MM REMINGTON SHORT ULTRA MAGNUM

CARTRIDGE BULLET	RANGE, YARDS:	0	100	200	300	400
Rem. 140 PSP C-L Ultra	velocity, fps:	3175	2934	2707	2490	2283
	energy, ft-lb:	3133	2676	2277	1927	1620.
	arc, inches:		+1.3	0	-6.0	-17.7
Rem. 150 PSP Core-Lokt	velocity, fps:	3110	2828	2563	2313	2077
	energy, ft-lb:	3221	2663	2188	1782	1437
	arc, inches:		+2.5	+2.1	-3.6	-15.8
Rem. 160 Partition	velocity, fps:	2960	2762	2572	2390	2215
	energy, ft-lb:	3112	2709	2350	2029	1744
	arc, inches:		+2.6	+2.2	-3.6	-15.4
Rem. 160 PSP C-L Ultra	velocity, fps:	2960	2733	2518	2313	2117
	energy, ft-lb:	3112	2654	2252	1900	1592
	arc, inches:		+2.7	+2.2	-3.7	-16.2

7MM WINCHESTER SHORT MAGNUM

CARTRIDGE BULLET	RANGE, YARDS:	0	100	200	300	400
Federal 140 Nos. AccuBond	velocity, fps:	3250	3040	2840	2660	2470
	energy, ft-lb:	3285	2875	2515	2190	1900
	arc, inches:		+1.1	0	-5.5	-15.8
Federal 140 Nos. Bal. Tip	velocity, fps:	3310	3100	2900	2700	2520
	energy, ft-lb:	3405	2985	2610	2270	1975
	arc, inches:		+1.1	0	-5.2	15.2
Federal 150 Nos. Solid Base	velocity, fps:	3230	3010	2800	2600	2410
	energy, ft-lb:	3475	3015	2615	2255	1935
	arc, inches:		+1.3	0	-5.6	-16.3
Federal 160 Nos. AccuBond	velocity, fps:	3120	2940	2760	2590	2430
	energy, ft-lb:	3460	3065	2710	2390	2095
	arc, inches:		+1.3	0	-5.9	-16.8
Federal 160 Nos. Partition	velocity, fps:	3160	2950	2750	2560	2380.
	energy, ft-lb:	3545	3095	2690	2335	2015.
	arc, inches:		+1.2	0	-5.9	-16.9
Federal 160 Barnes TS	velocity, fps:	2990	2780	2590	2400	2220
	energy, ft-lb:	3175	2755	2380	2045	1750
	arc, inches:		+1.5	0	-6.6	-19.4
Federal 160 Trophy Bonded	velocity, fps:	3120	2880	2650	2440	2230
	energy, ft-lb:	3460	2945	2500	2105	1765
	arc, inches:		+1.4	0	-6.3	-18.5
Win. 140 Bal. Silvertip	velocity, fps:	3225	3008	2801	2603	2414
	energy, ft-lb:	3233	2812	2438	2106	1812
	arc, inches:		+1.2	0	-5.6	-16.4
Win. 140 AccuBond CT	velocity, fps:	3225	3008	2801	2604	2415
	energy, ft-lb:	3233	2812	2439	2107	1812
	arc, inches:		+1.2	0	-5.6	-16.4
Win. 150 Power Point	velocity, fps:	3200	2915	2648	2396	2157
	energy, ft-lb:	3410	2830	2335	1911	1550
	arc, inches:		+1.3	0	-6.3	-18.6
Win. 160 AccuBond	velocity, fps:	3050	2862	2682	2509	2342
	energy, ft-lb:	3306	2911	2556	2237	1950
	arc, inches:		1.4	0	-6.2	-17.9

CARTRIDGE BULLET	RANGE, YARDS:	0	100	200	300	400
Win. 160 Fail Safe	velocity, fps:	2990	2744	2512	2291	2081
	energy, ft-lb:	3176	2675	2241	1864	1538
	arc, inches:		+1.6	0	-7.1	-20.8

7MM WEATHERBY MAGNUM

CARTRIDGE BULLET	RANGE, YARDS:	0	100	200	300	400
Federal 160 Nosler Partition	velocity, fps:	3050	2850	2650	2470	2290
	energy, ft-lb:	3305	2880	2505	2165	1865
	arc, inches:		+1.4	0	-6.3	-18.4
Federal 160 Sierra GameKing BTSP	velocity, fps:	3050	2880	2710	2560	2400
	energy, ft-lb:	3305	2945	2615	2320	2050
	arc, inches:		+1.4	0	-6.1	-17.4
Federal 160 Trophy Bonded	velocity, fps:	3050	2730	2420	2140	1880.
	energy, ft-lb:	3305	2640	2085	1630	1255
	arc, inches:		+1.6	0	-7.6	-22.7
Hornady 154 Soft Point	velocity, fps:	3200	2971	2753	2546	2348.
	energy, ft-lb:	3501	3017	2592	2216	1885
	arc, inches:		+1.2	0	-5.8	-17.0
Hornady 154 SST (or Interbond)	velocity, fps:	3200	3009	2825	2648	2478
	energy, ft-lb:	3501	3096	2729	2398	2100
	arc, inches:		+1.2	0	-5.7	-16.5
Hornady 175 Soft Point	velocity, fps:	2910	2709	2516	2331	2154
	energy, ft-lb:	3290	2850	2459	2111	1803
	arc, inches:		+1.6	0	-7.1	-20.6
Wby. 139 Pointed Expanding	velocity, fps:	3340	3079	2834	2601	2380.
	energy, ft-lb:	3443	2926	2478	2088	1748
	arc, inches:		+2.9	+3.6	0	-8.7
Wby. 140 Nosler Partition	velocity, fps:	3303	3069	2847	2636	2434
	energy, ft-lb:	3391	2927	2519	2159	1841
	arc, inches:		+2.9	+3.6	0	-8.5
Wby. 150 Nosler Bal. Tip	velocity, fps:	3300	3093	2896	2708	2527
	energy, ft-lb:	3627	3187	2793	2442	2127
	arc, inches:		+2.8	+3.5	0	-8.2
Wby. 150 Barnes X	veloctiy, fps:	3100	2901	2710	2527	2352
	energy, ft-lb:	3200	2802	2446	2127	1842
	arc, inches:		+3.3	+4.0	0	-9.4
Wby. 154 Pointed Expanding	velocity, fps:	3260	3028	2807	2597	2397
	energy, ft-lb:	3634	3134	2694	2307	1964
	arc, inches:		+3.0	+3.7	0	-8.8
Wby. 160 Nosler Partition	velocity, fps:	3200	2991	2791	2600	2417
	energy, ft-lb:	3638	3177	2767	2401	2075.
	arc, inches:		+3.1	+3.8	0	-8.9
Wby. 175 Pointed Expanding	velocity, fps:	3070	2861	2662	2471	2288
	energy, ft-lb:	3662	3181	2753	2373	2034
	arc, inches:		+3.5	+4.2	0	-9.9

7MM DAKOTA

CARTRIDGE BULLET	RANGE, YARDS:	0	100	200	300	400
Dakota 140 Barnes X	velocity, fps:	3500	3253	3019	2798	2587
	energy, ft-lb:	3807	3288	2833	2433	2081
	arc, inches:		+2.0	+2.1	-1.5	-9.6
Dakota 160 Barnes X	velocity, fps:	3200	3001	2811	2630	2455
	energy, ft-lb:	3637	3200	2808	2456	2140
	arc, inches:		+2.1	+1.9	-2.8	-12.5

7MM STW

CARTRIDGE BULLET	RANGE, YARDS:	0	100	200	300	400
A-Square 140 Nos. Bal. Tip	velocity, fps:	3450	3254	3067	2888	2715
	energy, ft-lb:	3700	3291	2924	2592	2292
	arc, inches:		+2.2	+3.0	0	-7.3
A-Square 160 Nosler Part.	velocity, fps:	3250	3071	2900	2735	2576.
	energy, ft-lb:	3752	3351	2987	2657	2357
	arc, inches:		+2.8	+3.5	0	-8.2
A-Square 160 SP boat-tail	velocity, fps:	3250	3087	2930	2778	2631
	energy, ft-lb:	3752	3385	3049	2741	2460
	arc, inches:		+2.8	+3.4	0	-8.0

Centerfire Rifle Ballistics

7MM STW TO .30-30 WINCHESTER

CARTRIDGE BULLET	RANGE, YARDS:	0	100	200	300	400
Federal 140 Trophy Bonded	velocity, fps	3330	3080	2850	2630	2420
	energy, ft-lb:	3435	2950	2520	2145	1815
	arc, inches:		+1.1	0	-5.4	-15.8
Federal 150 Trophy Bonded	velocity, fps	3250	3010	2770	2560	2350.
	energy, ft-lb:	3520	3010	2565	2175	1830
	arc, inches:		+1.2	0	-5.7	-16.7
Federal 160 Sierra GameKing BTSP	velocity, fps	3200	3020	2850	2670	2530.
	energy, ft-lb:	3640	3245	2890	2570	2275
	arc, inches:		+1.1	0	-5.5	-15.7
Rem. 140 PSP Core-Lokt	velocity, fps	3325	3064	2818	2585	2364
	energy, ft-lb:	3436	2918	2468	2077	1737
	arc, inches:		+2.0	+1.7	-2.9	-12.8
Rem. 140 Swift A-Frame	velocity, fps	3325	3020	2735	2467	2215
	energy, ft-lb:	3436	2834	2324	1892	1525
	arc, inches:		+2.1	+1.8	-3.1	-13.8
Speer 145 Grand Slam	velocity, fps	3300	2992	2075	2435	
	energy, ft-lb:	3506	2882	2355	1909	
	arc, inches:		+1.2	0	-6.0	-17.8
Win. 140 Ballistic Silvertip	velocity, fps	3320	3100	2890	2690	2499
	energy, ft-lb:	3427	2982	2597	2250	1941
	arc, inches:		+1.1	0	-5.2	-15.2
Win. 150 Power-Point	velocity, fps	3250	2957	2683	2424	2181
	energy, ft-lb:	3519	2913	2398	1958	1584
	arc, inches:		+1.2	0	-6.1	-18.1
Win. 160 Fail Safe	velocity, fps	3150	2894	2652	2422	2204
	energy, ft-lb:	3526	2976	2499	2085	1727
	arc, inches:		+1.3	0	-6.3	-18.5

7MM REMINGTON ULTRA MAGNUM

CARTRIDGE BULLET	RANGE, YARDS:	0	100	200	300	400
Rem. 140 PSP Core-Lokt	velocity, fps	3425	3158	2907	2669	2444
	energy, ft-lb:	3646	3099	2626	2214	1856
	arc, inches:		+1.8	+1.6	-2.7	-11.9
Rem. 140 Nosler Partition	velocity, fps	3425	3184	2956	2740	2534
	energy, ft-lb:	3646	3151	2715	2333	1995
	arc, inches:		+1.7	+1.6	-2.6	-11.4
Rem. 160 Nosler Partition	velocity, fps	3200	2991	2791	2600	2417
	energy, ft-lb:	3637	3177	2767	2401	2075
	arc, inches:		+2.1	+1.8	-3.0	-12.9

7.21 (.284) FIREHAWK

CARTRIDGE BULLET	RANGE, YARDS:	0	100	200	300	400
Lazzeroni 140 Nosler Part.	velocity, fps	3580	3349	3130	2923	2724
	energy, ft-lb:	3985	3488	3048	2656	2308
	arc, inches:		+2.2	+2.9	0	-7.0
Lazzeroni 160 Swift A-Fr.	velocity, fps	3385	3167	2961	2763	2574
	energy, ft-lb:	4072	3565	3115	2713	2354
	arc, inches:		+2.6	+3.3	0	-7.8

7.5x55 SWISS

CARTRIDGE BULLET	RANGE, YARDS:	0	100	200	300	400
Norma 180 Soft Point	velocity, fps	2651	2432	2223	2025	
	energy, ft-lb:	2810	2364	1976	1639	
	arc, inches:		+2.2	0	-9.3	
Norma 180 Oryx	velocity, fps	2493	2222	1968	1734	
	energy, ft-lb:	2485	1974	1549	1201	
	arc, inches:		+2.7	0	-11.8	

7.62x39 RUSSIAN

CARTRIDGE BULLET	RANGE, YARDS:	0	100	200	300	400
Federal 123 Hi-Shok	velocity, fps	2300	2030	1780	1550	1350
	energy, ft-lb:	1445	1125	860	655	500.
	arc, inches:		0	-7.0	-25.1	
Federal 124 FMJ	velocity, fps	2300	2030	1780	1560	1360
	energy, ft-lb:	1455	1135	875	670	510
	arc, inches:		+3.5	0	-14.6	-43.5
PMC 123 FMJ	velocity, fps	2350	2072	1817	1583	1368
	energy, ft-lb:	1495	1162	894	678	507
	arc, inches:		0	-5.0	-26.4	-67.8

CARTRIDGE BULLET	RANGE, YARDS:	0	100	200	300	400
PMC 125 Pointed Soft Point	velocity, fps	2320	2046	1794	1563	1350
	energy, ft-lb:	1493	1161	893	678	505.
	arc, inches:		0	-5.2	-27.5	-70.6
Rem. 125 Pointed Soft Point	velocity, fps	2365	2062	1783	1533	1320
	energy, ft-lb:	1552	1180	882	652	483
	arc, inches:		0	-6.7	-24.5	
Win. 123 Soft Point	velocity, fps	2365	2033	1731	1465	1248
	energy, ft-lb:	1527	1129	818	586	425
	arc, inches:		+3.8	0	-15.4	-46.3

.30 CARBINE

CARTRIDGE BULLET	RANGE, YARDS:	0	100	200	300	400
Federal 110 Hi-Shok RN	velocity, fps	1990	1570	1240	1040	920
	energy, ft-lb:	965	600	375	260	210
	arc, inches:		0	-12.8	-46.9	
Federal 110 FMJ	velocity, fps	1990	1570	1240	1040	920
	energy, ft-lb:	965	600	375	260	210
	arc, inches:		0	-12.8	-46.9	
Magtech 110 FMC	velocity, fps	1990	1654			
	energy, ft-lb:	965	668			
	arc, inches:		0			
PMC 110 FMJ	(and RNSP)velocity, fps:	1927	1548	1248		
	energy, ft-lb:	906	585	380		
	arc, inches:		0	-14.2		
Rem. 110 Soft Point	velocity, fps	1990	1567	1236	1035	923
	energy, ft-lb:	967	600	373	262	208
	arc, inches:		0	-12.9	-48.6	
Win. 110 Hollow Soft Point	velocity, fps	1990	1567	1236	1035	923
	energy, ft-lb:	967	600	373	262	208
	arc, inches:		0	-13.5	-49.9	

.30 T/C HORNADAY

CARTRIDGE BULLET	RANGE, YARDS:	0	100	200	300	400
Hornady 150	velocity, fps	3000	2772	2555	2348	
	energy, ft-lb	2997	2558	2176	1836	
	arc, inches	-1.5	+1.5	0	-6.9	
Hornady 165	velocity, fps	2850	2644	2447	2258	
	energy, ft-lb	2975	2560	2193	1868	
	arc, inches	-1.5	+1.7	0	-7.6	

.30-30 WINCHESTER

CARTRIDGE BULLET	RANGE, YARDS:	0	100	200	300	400
Federal 125 Hi-Shok HP	velocity, fps	2570	2090	1660	1320	1080
	energy, ft-lb:	1830	1210	770	480	320
	arc, inches:		+3.3	0	-16.0	-50.9
Federal 150 Hi-Shok FN	velocity, fps	2390	2020	1680	1400	1180
	energy, ft-lb:	1900	1355	945	650	460
	arc, inches:		+3.6	0	-15.9	-49.1
Federal 170 Hi-Shok RN	velocity, fps	2200	1900	1620	1380	1190
	energy, ft-lb:	1830	1355	990	720	535
	arc, inches:		+4.1	0	-17.4	-52.4
Federal 170 Sierra Pro-Hunt.	velocity, fps	2200	1820	1500	1240	1060
	energy, ft-lb:	1830	1255	845	575	425
	arc, inches:		+4.5	0	-20.0	-63.5
Federal 170 Nosler Partition	velocity, fps	2200	1900	1620	1380	1190
	energy, ft-lb:	1830	1355	990	720	535
	arc, inches:		+4.1	0	-17.4	-52.4
Hornady 150 Round Nose	velocity, fps	2390	1973	1605	1303	1095
	energy, ft-lb:	1902	1296	858	565	399
	arc, inches:		0	-8.2	-30.0	
Hornady 160 Evolution	velocity, fps	2400	2150	1916	1699	
	energy, ft-lb:	2046	1643	1304	1025	
	arc, inches:		+3.0	0.2	-12.1	
Hornady 170 Flat Point	velocity, fps	2200	1895	1619	1381	1191
	energy, ft-lb:	1827	1355	989	720	535
	arc, inches:		0	-8.9	-31.1	

CARTRIDGE BULLET	RANGE, YARDS:	0	100	200	300	400
Norma 150 Soft Point	velocity, fps	2329	2008	1716	1459	
	energy, ft-lb:	1807	1344	981	709	
	arc, inches:		+3.6	0	-15.5	
PMC 150 Starfire HP	velocity, fps	2100	1769	1478		
	energy, ft-lb:	1469	1042	728		
	arc, inches:		0	-10.8		
PMC 150 Flat Nose	velocity, fps	2300	1943	1627		
	energy, ft-lb:	1762	1257	881		
	arc, inches:		0	-7.8		
PMC 170 Flat Nose	velocity, fps	2150	1840	1566		
	energy, ft-lb:	1745	1277	926		
	arc, inches:		0	-8.9		
Rem. 55 PSP (sabot) "Accelerator"	velocity, fps	3400	2693	2085	1570	1187
	energy, ft-lb:	1412	886	521	301	172
	arc, inches:		+1.7	0	-9.9	-34.3
Rem. 150 SP Core-Lokt	velocity, fps	2390	1973	1605	1303	1095
	energy, ft-lb:	1902	1296	858	565	399
	arc, inches:		0	-7.6	-28.8	
Rem. 170 SP Core-Lokt	velocity, fps	2200	1895	1619	1381	1191
	energy, ft-lb:	1827	1355	989	720	535
	arc, inches:		0	-8.3	-29.9	
Rem. 170 HP Core-Lokt	velocity, fps	2200	1895	1619	1381	1191.
	energy, ft-lb:	1827	1355	989	720	535
	arc, inches:		0	-8.3	-29.9	
Speer 150 Flat Nose	velocity, fps	2370	2067	1788	1538	
	energy, ft-lb:	1870	1423	1065	788	
	arc, inches:		+3.3	0	-14.4	-43.7
Win. 150 Hollow Point	velocity, fps	2390	2018	1684	1398	1177
	energy, ft-lb:	1902	1356	944	651	461
	arc, inches:		0	-7.7	-27.9	
Win. 150 Power-Point	velocity, fps	2390	2018	1684	1398	1177
	energy, ft-lb:	1902	1356	944	651	461
	arc, inches:		0	-7.7	-27.9	
Win. 150 Silvertip	velocity,fps:	2390	2018	1684	1398	1177
	energy, ft-lb:	1902	1356	944	651	461
	arc, inches:		0	-7.7	-27.9	
Win. 150 Power-Point Plus	velocity, fps:	2480	2095	1747	1446	1209
	energy, ft-lb:	2049	1462	1017	697	487
	arc, inches:		0	-6.5	-24.5	
Win. 170 Power-Point	velocity, fps:	2200	1895	1619	1381	1191
	energy, ft-lb:	1827	1355	989	720	535.
	arc, inches:		0	-8.9	-31.1	
Win. 170 Silvertip	velocity, fps:	2200	1895	1619	1381	1191
	energy, ft-lb:	1827	1355	989	720	535
	arc, inches:		0	-8.9	-31.1	

.300 SAVAGE

CARTRIDGE BULLET	RANGE, YARDS:	0	100	200	300	400
Federal 150 Hi-Shok	velocity, fps:	2630	2350	2100	1850	1630
	energy, ft-lb:	2305	1845	1460	1145	885
	arc, inches:		+2.4	0	-10.4	-30.9
Federal 180 Hi-Shok	velocity, fps:	2350	2140	1940	1750	1570
	energy, ft-lb:	2205	1825	1495	1215	985
	arc, inches:		+3.1	0	-12.4	-36.1
Rem. 150 PSP Core-Lokt	velocity, fps:	2630	2354	2095	1853	1631
	energy, ft-lb:	2303	1845	1462	1143	806.
	arc, inches:		+2.4	0	-10.4	-30.9
Rem. 180 SP Core-Lokt	velocity, fps:	2350	2025	1728	1467	1252
	energy, ft-lb:	2207	1639	1193	860	626
	arc, inches:		+2.9	0	-7.1	-25.9
Win. 150 Power-Point	velocity, fps:	2630	2311	2015	1743	1500
	energy, ft-lb:	2303	1779	1352	1012	749
	arc, inches:		+2.8	0	-11.5	-34.4

.307 WINCHESTER

CARTRIDGE BULLET	RANGE, YARDS:	0	100	200	300	400
Win. 180 Power-Point	velocity, fps:	2510	2179	1874	1599	1362
	energy, ft-lb:	2519	1898	1404	1022	742
	arc, inches:		+1.5	-3.6	-18.6	-47.1

.30-40 KRAG

CARTRIDGE BULLET	RANGE, YARDS:	0	100	200	300	400
Rem. 180 PSP Core-Lokt	velocity, fps:	2430	2213	2007	1813	1632.
	energy, ft-lb:	2360	1957	1610	1314	1064
	arc, inches, s:		0	-5.6	-18.6	
Win. 180 Power-Point	velocity, fps:	2430	2099	1795	1525	1298
	energy, ft-lb:	2360	1761	1288	929	673
	arc, inches, s:		0	-7.1	-25.0	

7.62x54R RUSSIAN

CARTRIDGE BULLET	RANGE, YARDS:	0	100	200	300	400
Norma 150 Soft Point	velocity, fps:	2953	2622	2314	2028	
	energy, ft-lb:	2905	2291	1784	1370	.
	arc, inches:		+1.8	0	-8.3	
Norma 180 Alaska	velocity, fps:	2575	2362	2159	1967	
	energy, ft-lb:	2651	2231	1864	1546	
	arc, inches:		+2.9	0	-12.9	

.308 MARLIN EXPRESS

CARTRIDGE BULLET	RANGE, YARDS:	0	100	200	300	400
Hornady 160	velocity, fps	2660	2438	2226	2026	1836
	energy, ft-lb	2513	2111	1761	1457	1197
	arc, inches	-1.5	+3.0	+1.7	-6.7	-23.5

.308 WINCHESTER

CARTRIDGE BULLET	RANGE, YARDS:	0	100	200	300	400
Black Hills 150 Nosler B. Tip	velocity, fps:	2800				
	energy, ft-lb:	2611				
	arc, inches:					
Black Hills 165 Nosler B. Tip (and SP)	velocity, fps:	2650				
	energy, ft-lb:	2573				
	arc, inches:					
Black Hills 168 Barnes X (and Match)	velocity, fps:	2650				
	energy, ft-lb:	2620				
	arc, inches:					
Black Hills 175 Match	velocity, fps:	2600				
	energy, ft-lb:	2657				
	arc, inches:					
Black Hills 180 AccuBond	velocity, fps:	2600				
	energy, ft-lb:	2701				
	arc, inches:					
Federal 150 Hi-Shok	velocity, fps:	2820	2530	2260	2010	1770
	energy, ft-lb:	2650	2140	1705	1345	1050
	arc, inches:		+2.0	0	-8.8	-26.3
Federal 150 Nosler Bal. Tip.	velocity, fps:	2820	2610	2410	2220	2040
	energy, ft-lb:	2650	2270	1935	1640	1380
	arc, inches:		+1.8	0	-7.8	-22.7
Federal 150 FMJ boat-tail	velocity, fps:	2820	2620	2430	2250	2070
	energy, ft-lb:	2650	2285	1965	1680	1430
	arc, inches:		+1.8	0	-7.7	-22.4
Federal 150 Barnes XLC	velocity, fps:	2820	2610	2400	2210	2030
	energy, ft-lb:	2650	2265	1925	1630	1370
	arc, inches:		+1.8	0	-7.8	-22.9
Federal 155 Sierra MatchKg. BTHP	velocity, fps:	2950	2740	2540	2350	2170
	energy, ft-lb:	2995	2585	2225	1905	1620
	arc, inches:		+1.9	0	-8.9	-22.6
Federal 165 Sierra GameKing BTSP	velocity, fps:	2700	2520	2330	2160	1990
	energy, ft-lb:	2670	2310	1990	1700	1450
	arc, inches:		+2.0	0	-8.4	-24.3
Federal 165 Trophy Bonded	velocity, fps:	2700	2440	2200	1970	1760
	energy, ft-lb:	2670	2185	1775	1425	1135
	arc, inches:		+2.2	0	-9.4	-27.7

BALLISTICS

Centerfire Rifle Ballistics

.308 WINCHESTER TO .308 WINCHESTER

CARTRIDGE BULLET	RANGE, YARDS:	0	100	200	300	400
Federal 165 Tr. Bonded HE	velocity, fps:	2870	2600	2350	2120	1890
	energy, ft-lb:	3020	2485	2030	1640	1310
	arc, inches:		+1.8	0	-8.2	-24.0
Federal 168 Sierra MatchKg. BTHP	velocity, fps:	2600	2410	2230	2060	1890
	energy, ft-lb:	2520	2170	1855	1580	1340.
	arc, inches:		+2.1	0	+8.9	+25.9
Federal 180 Hi-Shok	velocity, fps:	2620	2390	2180	1970	1780
	energy, ft-lb:	2745	2290	1895	1555	1270
	arc, inches:		+2.3	0	-9.7	-28.3
Federal 180 Sierra Pro-Hunt.	velocity, fps:	2620	2410	2200	2010	1820
	energy, ft-lb:	2745	2315	1940	1610	1330
	arc, inches:		+2.3	0	-9.3	-27.1
Federal 180 Nosler Partition	velocity, fps:	2620	2430	2240	2060	1890
	energy, ft-lb:	2745	2355	2005	1700	1430.
	arc, inches:		+2.2	0	-9.2	-26.5
Federal 180 Nosler Part. HE	velocity, fps:	2740	2550	2370	2200	2030
	energy, ft-lb:	3000	2600	2245	1925	1645
	arc, inches:		+1.9	0	-8.2	-23.5
Hornady 110 TAP-FPD	velocity, fps:	3165	2830	2519	2228	1957
	energy, ft-lb:	2446	1956	1649	1212	935
	arc, inches:		+1.4	0	-6.9	-20.9
Hornady 110 Urban Tactical	velocity, fps:	3170	2825	2504	2206	1937
	energy, ft-lb:	2454	1950	1532	1189	916
	arc, inches:		+1.5	0	-7.2	-21.2
Hornady 150 SP boat-tail	velocity, fps:	2820	2560	2315	2084	1866
	energy, ft-lb:	2648	2183	1785	1447	1160
	arc, inches:		+2.0	0	-8.5	-25.2
Hornady 150 SST (or Interbond)	velocity, fps:	2820	2593	2378	2174	1984
	energy, ft-lb:	2648	2240	1884	1574	1311
	arc, inches:		+1.9	0	-8.1	-22.9
Hornady 150 SST LM (or Interbond)	velocity, fps:	3000	2765	2541	2328	2127
	energy, ft-lb:	2997	2545	2150	1805	1506.
	arc, inches:		+1.5	0	-7.1	-20.6
Hornady 150 SP LM	velocity, fps:	2980	2703	2442	2195	1964
	energy, ft-lb:	2959	2433	1986	1606	1285
	arc, inches:		+1.6	0	-7.5	-22.2
Hornady 155 A-Max	velocity, fps:	2815	2610	2415	2229	2051
	energy, ft-lb:	2727	2345	2007	1709	1448
	arc, inches:		+1.9	0	-7.9	-22.6
Hornady 155 TAP-FPD	velocity, fps:	2785	2577	2379	2189	2008
	energy, ft-lb:	2669	2285	1947	1649	1387
	arc, inches:		+1.9	0	-8.0	-23.3
Hornady 165 SP boat-tail	velocity, fps:	2700	2496	2301	2115	1937
	energy, ft-lb:	2670	2283	1940	1639	1375
	arc, inches:		+2.0	0	-8.7	-25.2
Hornady 165 SPBT LM	velocity, fps:	2870	2658	2456	2283	2078
	energy, ft-lb:	3019	2589	2211	1877	1583
	arc, inches:		+1.7	0	-7.5	-21.8
Hornady 165 SST LM (or Interbond)	velocity, fps:	2880	2672	2474	2284	2103
	energy, ft-lb:	3038	2616	2242	1911	1620
	arc, inches:		+1.6	0	-7.3	-21.2
Hornady 168 BTHP Match	velocity, fps:	2700	2524	2354	2191	2035.
	energy, ft-lb:	2720	2377	2068	1791	1545
	arc, inches:		+2.0	0	-8.4	-23.9
Hornady 168 BTHP Match LM	velocity, fps:	2640	2630	2429	2238	2056
	energy, ft-lb:	3008	2579	2201	1868	1577
	arc, inches:		+1.8	0	-7.8	-22.4
Hornady 168 A-Max Match	velocity, fps:	2620	2446	2280	2120	1972
	energy, ft-lb:	2560	2232	1939	1677	1450
	arc, inches:		+2.6	0	-9.2	-25.6
Hornady 168 A-Max	velocity, fps:	2700	2491	2292	2102	1921
	energy, ft-lb:	2719	2315	1959	1648	1377
	arc, inches:		+2.4	0	-9.0	-25.9

CARTRIDGE BULLET	RANGE, YARDS:	0	100	200	300	400
Hornady 168 TAP-FPD	velocity, fps:	2700	2513	2333	2161	1996
	energy, ft-lb:	2719	2355	2030	1742	1486
	arc, inches:		+2.0	0	-8.4	-24.3
Hornady 178 A-Max	velocity, fps:	2965	2778	2598	2425	2259
	energy, ft-lb:	3474	3049	2666	2323	2017
	arc, inches:		+1.6	0	-6.9	-19.8
Hornady 180 A-Max Match	velocity, fps:	2550	2397	2249	2106	1974
	energy, ft-lb:	2598	2295	2021	1773	1557
	arc, inches:		+2.7	0	-9.5	-26.2
Norma 150 Nosler Bal. Tip	velocity, fps:	2822	2588	2365	2154	
	energy, ft-lb:	2653	2231	1864	1545	
	arc, inches:		+1.6	0	-7.1	
Norma 150 Soft Point	velocity, fps:	2861	2537	2235	1954	
	energy, ft-lb:	2727	2144	1664	1272	
	arc, inches:		+2.0	0	-9.0	
Norma 165 TXP Swift A-Fr.	velocity, fps:	2700	2459	2231	2015	
	energy, ft-lb:	2672	2216	1824	1488	
	arc, inches:		+2.1	0	-9.1	
Norma 180 Plastic Point	velocity, fps:	2612	2365	2131	1911	
	energy, ft-lb:	2728	2235	1815	1460	
	arc, inches:		+2.4	0	-10.1	
Norma 180 Nosler Partition	velocity, fps:	2612	2414	2225	2044	
	energy, ft-lb:	2728	2330	1979	1670	
	arc, inches:		+2.2	0	-9.3	
Norma 180 Alaska	velocity, fps:	2612	2269	1953	1667	
	energy, ft-lb:	2728	2059	1526	1111	
	arc, inches:		+2.7	0	-11.9	
Norma 180 Vulkan	velocity, fps:	2612	2325	2056	1806	
	energy, ft-lb:	2728	2161	1690	1304	
	arc, inches:		+2.5	0	-10.8	
Norma 180 Oryx	velocity, fps:	2612	2305	2019	1755	
	energy, ft-lb:	2728	2124	1629	1232	
	arc, inches:		+2.5	0	-11.1	
Norma 200 Vulkan	velocity, fps:	2461	2215	1983	1767	
	energy, ft-lb:	2690	2179	1747	1387	
	arc, inches:		+2.8	0	-11.7	
PMC 147 FMJ boat-tail	velocity, fps:	2751	2473	2257	2052	1859
	energy, ft-lb:	2428	2037	1697	1403	1150
	arc, inches:		+2.3	0	-9.3	-27.3
PMC 150 Barnes X	velocity, fps:	2700	2504	2316	2135	1964
	energy, ft-lb:	2428	2087	1786	1518	1284
	arc, inches:		+2.0	0	-8.6	-24.7
PMC 150 Pointed Soft Point	velocity, fps:	2750	2478	2224	1987	1766
	energy, ft-lb:	2519	2045	1647	1315	1039
	arc, inches:		+2.1	0	-9.2	-27.1
PMC 150 SP boat-tail	velocity, fps:	2820	2581	2354	2139	1935
	energy, ft-lb:	2648	2218	1846	1523	1247.
	arc, inches:		+1.9	0	-8.2	-24.0
PMC 168 Barnes X	velocity, fps:	2600	2425	2256	2095	1940
	energy, ft-lb:	2476	2154	1865	1608	1379
	arc, inches:		+2.2	0	-9.0	-26.0
PMC 168 HP boat-tail	velocity, fps:	2650	2460	2278	2103	1936
	energy, ft-lb:	2619	2257	1935	1649	1399
	arc, inches:		+2.1	0	-8.8	-25.6
PMC 168 Pointed Soft Point	velocity, fps:	2559	2354	2160	1976	1803
	energy, ft-lb:	2443	2067	1740	1457	1212
	arc, inches:		+2.4	0	-9.9	-28.7
PMC 168 Pointed Soft Point	velocity, fps:	2600	2404	2216	2037	1866
	energy, ft-lb:	2476	2064	1709	1403	1142
	arc, inches:		+2.3	0	-9.8	-28.7
PMC 180 Pointed Soft Point	velocity, fps:	2550	2335	2132	1940	1760
	energy, ft-lb:	2599	2179	1816	1504	1238.
	arc, inches:		+2.5	0	-10.1	-29.5

CARTRIDGE BULLET	RANGE, YARDS:	0	100	200	300	400
PMC 180 SP boat-tail	velocity, fps:	2620	2446	2278	2117	1962
	energy, ft-lb:	2743	2391	2074	1790	1538
	arc, inches:		+2.2	0	-8.9	-25.4
Rem. 125 PSP C-L MR	velocity, fps:	2660	2348	2057	1788	1546
	energy, ft-lb:	1964	1529	1174	887	663
	arc, inches:		+1.1	-2.7	-14.3	-35.8
Rem. 150 PSP Core-Lokt	velocity, fps:	2820	2533	2263	2009	1774
	energy, ft-lb:	2648	2137	1705	1344	1048
	arc, inches:		+2.0	0	-8.8	-26.2
Rem. 150 PSP C-L Ultra	velocity, fps:	2620	2404	2198	2002	1818
	energy, ft-lb:	2743	2309	1930	1601	1320
	arc, inches:		+2.3	0	-9.5	-26.4
Rem. 150 Swift Scirocco	velocity, fps:	2820	2611	2410	2219	2037
	energy, ft-lb:	2648	2269	1935	1640	1381
	arc, inches:		+1.8	0	-7.8	-22.7
Rem. 165 AccuTip	velocity, fps:	2700	2501	2311	2129	1958.
	energy, ft-lb:	2670	2292	1957	1861	1401.
	arc, inches:		+2.0	0	-8.6	-24.8
Rem. 165 PSP boat-tail	velocity, fps:	2700	2497	2303	2117	1941.
	energy, ft-lb:	2670	2284	1942	1642	1379
	arc, inches:		+2.0	0	-8.6	-25.0
Rem. 165 Nosler Bal. Tip	velocity, fps:	2700	2613	2333	2161	1996
	energy, ft-lb:	2672	2314	1995	1711	1460
	arc, inches:		+2.0	0	-8.4	-24.3
Rem. 165 Swift Scirocco	velocity, fps:	2700	2513	2233	2161	1996
	energy, fps:	2670	2313	1994	1711	1459
	arc, inches:		+2.0	0	-8.4	-24.3
Rem. 168 HPBT Match	velocity, fps:	2680	2493	2314	2143	1979
	energy, ft-lb:	2678	2318	1998	1713	1460
	arc, inches:		+2.1	0	-8.6	-24.7
Rem. 180 SP Core-Lokt	velocity, fps:	2620	2274	1955	1666	1414
	energy, ft-lb:	2743	2066	1527	1109	799
	arc, inches:		+2.6	0	-11.8	-36.3
Rem. 180 PSP Core-Lokt	velocity, fps:	2620	2393	2178	1974	1782
	energy, ft-lb:	2743	2288	1896	1557	1269
	arc, inches:		+2.3	0	-9.7	-28.3
Rem. 180 Nosler Partition	velocity, fps:	2620	2436	2259	2089	1927.
	energy, ft-lb:	2743	2371	2039	1774	1485
	arc, inches:		+2.2	0	-9.0	-26.0
Speer 150 Grand Slam	velocity, fps:	2900	2599	2317	2053	
	energy, ft-lb:	2800	2249	1788	1404	
	arc, inches:		+2.1	0	-8.6	-24.8
Speer 165 Grand Slam	velocity, fps:	2700	2475	2261	2057	
	energy, ft-lb:	2670	2243	1872	1550	
	arc, inches:		+2.1	0	-8.9	-25.9
Speer 180 Grand Slam	velocity, fps:	2620	2420	2229	2046	
	energy, ft-lb:	2743	2340	1985	1674	
	arc, inches:		+2.2	0	-9.2	-26.6
Win. 150 Power-Point	velocity, fps:	2820	2488	2179	1893	1633
	energy, ft-lb:	2648	2061	1581	1193	888
	arc, inches:		+2.4	0	-9.8	-29.3
Win. 150 Power-Point Plus	velocity, fps:	2900	2558	2241	1946	1678
	energy, ft-lb:	2802	2180	1672	1262	938
	arc, inches:		+1.9	0	-8.9	-27.0
Win. 150 Partition Gold	velocity, fps:	2900	2645	2405	2177	1962
	energy, ft-lb:	2802	2332	1927	1579	1282.
	arc, inches:		+1.7	0	-7.8	-22.9
Win. 150 Ballistic Silvertip	velocity, fps:	2810	2601	2401	2211	2028
	energy, ft-lb:	2629	2253	1920	1627	1370.
	arc, inches:		+1.8	0	-7.8	-22.8
Win. 150 Fail Safe	velocity, fps:	2820	2533	2263	2010	1775
	energy, ft-lb:	2649	2137	1706	1346	1049
	arc, inches:		+2.0	0	-8.8	-26.2

CARTRIDGE BULLET	RANGE, YARDS:	0	100	200	300	400
Win. 150 Supreme Elite XP3	velocity, fps:	2825	2616	2417	2226	2044
	energy, ft-lb:	2658	2279	1945	1650	1392
	arc, inches:		+1.8	0	-7.8	-22.6
Win. 168 Ballistic Silvertip	velocity, fps:	2670	2484	2306	2134	1971
	energy, ft-lb:	2659	2301	1983	1699	1449
	arc, inches:		+2.1	0	-8.6	-24.8
Win. 168 HP boat-tail Match	velocity, fps:	2680	2485	2297	2118	1948
	energy, ft-lb:	2680	2303	1970	1674	1415
	arc, inches:		+2.1	0	-8.7	-25.1
Win. 180 Power-Point	velocity, fps:	2620	2274	1955	1666	1414
	energy, ft-lb:	2743	2066	1527	1109	799
	arc, inches:		+2.9	0	-12.1	-36.9
Win. 180 Silvertip	velocity, fps:	2620	2393	2178	1974	1782
	energy, ft-lb:	2743	2288	1896	1557	1269
	arc, inches:		+2.6	0	-9.9	-28.9

.30-06 SPRINGFIELD

CARTRIDGE BULLET	RANGE, YARDS:	0	100	200	300	400
A-Square 180 M & D-T	velocity, fps:	2700	2365	2054	1769	1524
	energy, ft-lb:	2913	2235	1687	1251	928
	arc, inches:		+2.4	0	-10.6	-32.4
A-Square 220 Monolythic Solid	velocity, fps:	2380	2108	1854	1623	1424
	energy, ft-lb:	2767	2171	1679	1287	990
	arc, inches:		+3.1	0	-13.6	-39.9
Black Hills 150 Nosler B. Tip	velocity, fps:	2900				
	energy, ft-lb:	2770				
	arc, inches:					
Black Hills 165 Nosler B. Tip	velocity, fps:	2750				
	energy, ft-lb:	2770				
	arc, inches:					
Black Hills 168 Hor. Match	velocity, fps:	2700				
	energy, ft-lb:	2718				
	arc, inches:					
Black Hills 180 Barnes X	velocity, fps:	2650				
	energy, ft-lb:	2806				
	arc, inches:					
Black Hills 180 AccuBond	velocity, ft-lb:	2700				
	energy, ft-lb:					
	arc, inches:					
Federal 125 Sierra Pro-Hunt.	velocity, fps:	3140	2780	2450	2140	1850
	energy, ft-lb:	2735	2145	1660	1270	955
	arc, inches:		+1.5	0	-7.3	-22.3
Federal 150 Hi-Shok	velocity, fps:	2910	2620	2340	2080	1840
	energy, ft-lb:	2820	2280	1825	1445	1130
	arc, inches:		+1.8	0	-8.2	-24.4
Federal 150 Sierra Pro-Hunt.	velocity, fps:	2910	2640	2380	2130	1900
	energy, ft-lb:	2820	2315	1880	1515	1205
	arc, inches:		+1.7	0	-7.9	-23.3
Federal 150 Sierra GameKing BTSP	velocity, fps:	2910	2690	2480	2270	2070
	energy, ft-lb:	2820	2420	2040	1710	1430
	arc, inches:		+1.7	0	-7.4	-21.5
Federal 150 Nosler Bal. Tip	velocity, fps:	2910	2700	2490	2300	2110
	energy, ft-lb:	2820	2420	2070	1760	1485
	arc, inches:		+1.6	0	-7.3	-21.1
Federal 150 FMJ boat-tail	velocity, fps:	2910	2710	2510	2320	2150
	energy, ft-lb:	2820	2440	2100	1800	1535
	arc, inches:		+1.6	0	-7.1	-20.8
Federal 165 Sierra Pro-Hunt.	velocity, fps:	2800	2560	2340	2130	1920
	energy, ft-lb:	2875	2410	2005	1655	1360
	arc, inches:		+1.9	0	-8.3	-24.3
Federal 165 Sierra GameKing BTSP	velocity, fps:	2800	2610	2420	2240	2070.
	energy, ft-lb:	2870	2490	2150	1840	1580
	arc, inches:		+1.8	0	-7.8	-22.4

Centerfire Rifle Ballistics

.30-06 SPRINGFIELD TO .30-06 SPRINGFIELD

CARTRIDGE BULLET	RANGE, YARDS:	0	100	200	300	400
Federal 165 Sierra GameKing HE	velocity, fps:	3140	2900	2670	2450	2240.
	energy, ft-lb:	3610	3075	2610	2200	1845
	arc, inches:		+1.5	0	-6.9	-20.4
Federal 165 Nosler Bal. Tip	velocity, fps:	2800	2610	2430	2250	2080
	energy, ft-lb:	2870	2495	2155	1855	1585
	arc, inches:		+1.8	0	-7.7	-22.3
Federal 165 Trophy Bonded	velocity, fps:	2800	2540	2290	2050	1830
	energy, ft-lb:	2870	2360	1915	1545	1230
	arc, inches:		+2.0	0	-8.7	-25.4
Federal 165 Tr. Bonded HE	velocity, fps:	3140	2860	2590	2340	2100
	energy, ft-lb:	3610	2990	2460	2010	1625.
	arc, inches:		+1.6	0	-7.4	-21.9
Federal 168 Sierra MatchKg. BTHP	velocity, fps:	2700	2510	2320	2150	1980
	energy, ft-lb:	2720	2350	2010	1720	1460
	arc, inches:		+16.2	+28.4	+34.1	+32.3
Federal 180 Hi-Shok	velocity, fps:	2700	2470	2250	2040	1850
	energy, ft-lb:	2915	2435	2025	1665	1360
	arc, inches:		+2.1	0	-9.0	-26.4
Federal 180 Sierra Pro-Hunt. RN	velocity, fps:	2700	2350	2020	1730	1470
	energy, ft-lb:	2915	2200	1630	1190	860
	arc, inches:		+2.4	0	-11.0	-33.6
Federal 180 Nosler Partition	velocity, fps:	2700	2500	2320	2140	1970
	energy, ft-lb:	2915	2510	2150	1830	1550
	arc, inches:		+2.0	0	-8.6	-24.6
Federal 180 Nosler Part. HE	velocity, fps:	2880	2690	2500	2320	2150
	energy, ft-lb:	3315	2880	2495	2150	1845
	arc, inches:		+1.7	0	-7.2	-21.0
Federal 180 Sierra GameKing BTSP	velocity, fps:	2700	2540	2380	2220	2080
	energy, ft-lb:	2915	2570	2260	1975	1720
	arc, inches:		+1.9	0	-8.1	-23.1
Federal 180 Barnes XLC	velocity, fps:	2700	2530	2360	2200	2040.
	energy, ft-lb:	2915	2550	2220	1930	1670
	arc, inches:		+2.0	0	-8.3	-23.8
Federal 180 Trophy Bonded	velocity, fps:	2700	2460	2220	2000	1800
	energy, ft-lb:	2915	2410	1975	1605	1290
	arc, inches:		+2.2	0	-9.2	-27.0
Federal 180 Tr. Bonded HE	velocity, fps:	2880	2630	2380	2160	1940
	energy, ft-lb:	3315	2755	2270	1855	1505
	arc, inches:		+1.8	0	-8.0	-23.3
Federal 220 Sierra Pro-Hunt. RN	velocity, fps:	2410	2130	1870	1630	1420
	energy, ft-lb:	2835	2215	1705	1300	985
	arc, inches:		+3.1	0	-13.1	-39.3
Hornady 150 SP	velocity, fps:	2910	2617	2342	2083	1843
	energy, ft-lb:	2820	2281	1827	1445	1131
	arc, inches:		+2.1	0	-8.5	-25.0
Hornady 150 SP LM	velocity, fps:	3100	2815	2548	2295	2058
	energy, ft-lb:	3200	2639	2161	1755	1410
	arc, inches:		+1.4	0	-6.8	-20.3
Hornady 150 SP boat-tail	velocity, fps:	2910	2683	2467	2262	2066.
	energy, ft-lb:	2820	2397	2027	1706	1421
	arc, inches:		+2.0	0	-7.7	-22.2
Hornady 150 SST (or Interbond)	velocity, fps:	2910	2802	2599	2405	2219
	energy, ft-lb:	3330	2876	2474	2118	1803
	arc, inches:		+1.5	0	-6.6	-19.3
Hornady 150 SST LM	velocity, fps:	3100	2860	2631	2414	2208
	energy, ft-lb:	3200	2724	2306	1941	1624
	arc, inches:		+1.4	0	-6.6	-19.2
Hornady 165 SP boat-tail	velocity, fps:	2800	2591	2392	2202	2020
	energy, ft-lb:	2873	2460	2097	1777	1495
	arc, inches:		+1.8	0	-8.0	-23.3
Hornady 165 SPBT LM	velocity, fps:	3015	2790	2575	2370	2176
	energy, ft-lb:	3330	2850	2428	2058	1734
	arc, inches:		+1.6	0	-7.0	-20.1

CARTRIDGE BULLET	RANGE, YARDS:	0	100	200	300	400
Hornady 165 SST (or Interbond)	velocity, fps:	2800	2598	2405	2221	2046
	energy, ft-lb:	2872	2473	2119	1808	1534
	arc, inches:		+1.9	0	-8.0	-22.8
Hornady 165 SST LM	velocity, fps:	3015	2802	2599	2405	2219
	energy, ft-lb:	3330	2878	2474	2118	1803.
	arc, inches:		+1.5	0	-6.5	-19.3
Hornady 168 HPBT Match	velocity, fps:	2790	2620	2447	2280	2120.
	energy, ft-lb:	2925	2561	2234	1940	1677.
	arc, inches:		+1.7	0	-7.7	-22.2
Hornady 180 SP	velocity, fps:	2700	2469	2258	2042	1846
	energy, ft-lb:	2913	2436	2023	1666	1362
	arc, inches:		+2.4	0	-9.3	-27.0
Hornady 180 SPBT LM	velocity, fps:	2880	2676	2480	2293	2114
	energy, ft-lb:	3316	2862	2459	2102	1786
	arc, inches:		+1.7	0	-7.3	-21.3
Norma 150 Nosler Bal. Tip	velocity, fps:	2936	2713	2502	2300	
	energy, ft-lb:	2872	2453	2085	1762	
	arc, inches:		+1.6	0	-7.1	
Norma 150 Soft Point	velocity, fps:	2972	2640	2331	2043	
	energy, ft-lb:	2943	2321	1810	1390	
	arc, inches:		+1.8	0	-8.2	
Norma 180 Alaska	velocity, fps:	2700	2351	2028	1734	
	energy, ft-lb:	2914	2209	1645	1202	
	arc, inches:		+2.4	0	-11.0	
Norma 180 Nosler Partition	velocity, fps:	2700	2494	2297	2108	
	energy, ft-lb:	2914	2486	2108	1777	
	arc, inches:		+2.1	0	-8.7	
Norma 180 Plastic Point	velocity, fps:	2700	2455	2222	2003	
	energy, ft-lb:	2914	2409	1974	1603	
	arc, inches:		+2.1	0	-9.2	
Norma 180 Vulkan	velocity, fps:	2700	2416	2150	1901	
	energy, ft-lb:	2914	2334	1848	1445	
	arc, inches:		+2.2	0	-9.8	
Norma 180 Oryx	velocity, fps:	2700	2387	2095	1825	
	energy, ft-lb:	2914	2278	1755	1332	
	arc, inches:		+2.3	0	-10.2	
Norma 180 TXP Swift A-Fr.	velocity, fps:	2700	2479	2268	2067	
	energy, ft-lb:	2914	2456	2056	1708	
	arc, inches:		+2.0	0	-8.8	
Norma 180 AccuBond	velocity, fps:	2674	2499	2331	2169	
	energy, ft-lb:	2859	2497	2172	1881	
	arc, inches:		+2.0	0	-8.5	
Norma 200 Vulkan	velocity, fps:	2641	2385	2143	1916	
	energy, ft-lb:	3098	2527	2040	1631	
	arc, inches:		+2.3	0	-9.9	
Norma 200 Oryx	velocity, fps:	2625	2362	2115	1883	
	energy, ft-lb:	3061	2479	1987	1575	
	arc, inches:		+2.3	0	-10.1	
PMC 150 X-Bullet	velocity, fps:	2750	2552	2361	2179	2005
	energy, ft-lb:	2518	2168	1857	1582	1339
	arc, inches:		+2.0	0	-8.2	-23.7
PMC 150 Pointed Soft Point	velocity, fps:	2773	2542	2322	2113	1916
	energy, ft-lb:	2560	2152	1796	1487	1222.
	arc, inches:		+1.9	0	-8.4	-24.6
PMC 150 SP boat-tail	velocity, fps:	2900	2657	2427	2208	2000
	energy, ft-lb:	2801	2351	1961	1623	1332
	arc, inches:		+1.7	0	-7.7	-22.5
PMC 150 FMJ	velocity, fps:	2773	2542	2322	2113	1916
	energy, ft-lb:	2560	2152	1796	1487	1222
	arc, inches:		+1.9	0	-8.4	-24.6
PMC 168 Barnes X	velocity, fps:	2750	2569	2395	2228	2067
	energy, ft-lb:	2770	2418	2101	1818	1565
	arc, inches:		+1.9	0	-8.0	-23.0

BALLISTICS

CARTRIDGE BULLET	RANGE, YARDS:	0	100	200	300	400
PMC 180 Barnes X	velocity, fps:	2650	2487	2331	2179	2034
	energy, ft-lb:	2806	2472	2171	1898	1652
	arc, inches:		+2.1	0	-8.5	-24.3
PMC 180 Pointed Soft Point	velocity, fps:	2650	2430	2221	2024	1839
	energy, ft-lb:	2807	2359	1972	1638	1351
	arc, inches:		+2.2	0	-9.3	-27.0
PMC 180 SP boat-tail	velocity, fps:	2700	2523	2352	2188	2030
	energy, ft-lb:	2913	2543	2210	1913	1646
	arc, inches:		+2.0	0	-8.3	-23.9
PMC 180 HPBT Match	velocity, fps:	2800	2622	2456	2302	2158
	energy, ft-lb:	3133	2747	2411	2118	1861
	arc, inches:		+1.8	0	-7.6	-21.7
Rem. 55 PSP (sabot) "Accelerator"	velocity, fps:	4080	3484	2964	2499	2080
	energy, ft-lb:	2033	1482	1073	763	528.
	arc, inches:		+1.4	+1.4	-2.6	-12.2
Rem. 125 PSP C-L MR	velocity, fps:	2660	2335	2034	1757	1509
	energy, ft-lb:	1964	1513	1148	856	632
	arc, inches:		+1.1	-3.0	-15.5	-37.4
Rem. 125 Pointed Soft Point	velocity, fps:	3140	2780	2447	2138	1853
	energy, ft-lb:	2736	2145	1662	1269	953.
	arc, inches:		+1.5	0	-7.4	-22.4
Rem. 150 AccuTip	velocity, fps:	2910	2686	2473	2270	2077
	energy, ft-lb:	2820	2403	2037	1716	1436
	arc, inches:		+1.8	0	-7.4	-21.5
Rem. 150 PSP Core-Lokt	velocity, fps:	2910	2617	2342	2083	1843
	energy, ft-lb:	2820	2281	1827	1445	1131
	arc, inches:		+1.8	0	-8.2	-24.4
Rem. 150 Bronze Point	velocity, fps:	2910	2656	2416	2189	1974
	energy, ft-lb:	2820	2349	1944	1596	1298
	arc, inches:		+1.7	0	-7.7	-22.7
Rem. 150 Nosler Bal. Tip	velocity, fps:	2910	2696	2492	2298	2112.
	energy, ft-lb:	2821	2422	2070	1769	1485
	arc, inches:		+1.6	0	-7.3	-21.1
Rem. 150 Swift Scirocco	velocity, fps:	2910	2696	2492	2298	2111
	energy, ft-lb:	2820	2421	2069	1758	1485
	arc, inches:		+1.6	0	-7.3	-21.1
Rem. 165 AccuTip	velocity, fps:	2800	2597	2403	2217	2039
	energy, ft-lb:	2872	2470	2115	1800	1523
	arc, inches:		+1.8	0	-7.9	-22.8
Rem. 165 PSP Core-Lokt	velocity, fps:	2800	2534	2283	2047	1825.
	energy, ft-lb:	2872	2352	1909	1534	1220
	arc, inches:		+2.0	0	-8.7	-25.9
Rem. 165 PSP boat-tail	velocity, fps:	2800	2592	2394	2204	2023
	energy, ft-lb:	2872	2462	2100	1780	1500
	arc, inches:		+1.8	0	-7.9	-23.0
Rem. 165 Nosler Bal. Tip	velocity, fps:	2800	2609	2426	2249	2080.
	energy, ft-lb:	2873	2494	2155	1854	1588
	arc, inches:		+1.8	0	-7.7	-22.3
Rem. 168 PSP C-L Ultra	velocity, fps:	2800	2546	2306	2079	1866
	energy, ft-lb:	2924	2418	1984	1613	1299
	arc, inches:		+1.9	0	-8.5	-25.1
Rem. 180 SP Core-Lokt	velocity, fps:	2700	2348	2023	1727	1466
	energy, ft-lb:	2913	2203	1635	1192	859
	arc, inches:		+2.4	0	-11.0	-33.8
Rem. 180 PSP Core-Lokt	velocity, fps:	2700	2469	2250	2042	1846
	energy, ft-lb:	2913	2436	2023	1666	1362
	arc, inches:		+2.1	0	-9.0	-26.3
Rem. 180 PSP C-L Ultra	velocity, fps:	2700	2480	2270	2070	1882
	energy, ft-lb:	2913	2457	2059	1713	1415
	arc, inches:		+2.1	0	-8.9	-25.8
Rem. 180 Bronze Point	velocity, fps:	2700	2485	2280	2084	1899.
	energy, ft-lb:	2913	2468	2077	1736	1441
	arc, inches:		+2.1	0	-8.8	-25.5
Rem. 180 Swift A-Frame	velocity, fps:	2700	2465	2243	2032	1833
	energy, ft-lb:	2913	2429	2010	1650	1343
	arc, inches:		+2.1	0	-9.1	-26.6
Rem. 180 Nosler Partition	velocity, fps:	2700	2512	2332	2160	1995
	energy, ft-lb:	2913	2522	2174	1864	1590
	arc, inches:		+2.0	0	-8.4	-24.3
Rem. 220 SP Core-Lokt	velocity, fps:	2410	2130	1870	1632	1422
	energy, ft-lb:	2837	2216	1708	1301	988
	arc, inches, s:		0	-6.2	-22.4	
Speer 150 Grand Slam	velocity, fps:	2975	2669	2383	2114	
	energy, ft-lb:	2947	2372	1891	1489	
	arc, inches:		+2.0	0	-8.1	-24.1
Speer 165 Grand Slam	velocity, fps:	2790	2560	2342	2134	
	energy, ft-lb:	2851	2401	2009	1669	
	arc, inches:		+1.9	0	-8.3	-24.1
Speer 180 Grand Slam	velocity, fps:	2690	2487	2293	2108	
	energy, ft-lb:	2892	2472	2101	1775	
	arc, inches:		+2.1	0	-8.8	-25.1
Win. 125 Pointed Soft Point	velocity, fps:	3140	2780	2447	2138	1853
	energy, ft-lb:	2736	2145	1662	1269	953
	arc, inches:		+1.8	0	-7.7	-23.0
Win. 150 Power-Point	velocity, fps:	2920	2580	2265	1972	1704
	energy, ft-lb:	2839	2217	1708	1295	967
	arc, inches:		+2.2	0	-9.0	-27.0
Win. 150 Power-Point Plus	velocity, fps:	3050	2685	2352	2043	1760
	energy, ft-lb:	3089	2402	1843	1391	1032
	arc, inches:		+1.7	0	-8.0	-24.3
Win. 150 Silvertip	velocity, fps:	2910	2617	2342	2083	1843
	energy, ft-lb:	2820	2281	1827	1445	1131
	arc, inches:		+2.1	0	-8.5	-25.0
Win. 150 Partition Gold	velocity, fps:	2960	2705	2464	2235	2019
	energy, ft-lb:	2919	2437	2022	1664	1358.
	arc, inches:		+1.6	0	-7.4	-21.7
Win. 150 Ballistic Silvertip	velocity, fps:	2900	2687	2483	2289	2103
	energy, ft-lb:	2801	2404	2054	1745	1473
	arc, inches:		+1.7	0	-7.3	-21.2
Win. 150 Fail Safe	velocity, fps:	2920	2625	2349	2089	1848
	energy, ft-lb:	2841	2296	1838	1455	1137
	arc, inches:		+1.8	0	-8.1	-24.3
Win. 165 Pointed Soft Point	velocity, fps:	2800	2573	2357	2151	1956
	energy, ft-lb:	2873	2426	2036	1696	1402
	arc, inches:		+2.2	0	-8.4	-24.4
Win. 165 Fail Safe	velocity, fps:	2800	2540	2295	2063	1846
	energy, ft-lb:	2873	2365	1930	1560	1249
	arc, inches:		+2.0	0	-8.6	-25.3
Win. 168 Ballistic Silvertip	velocity, fps:	2790	2599	2416	2240	2072
	energy, ft-lb:	2903	2520	2177	1872	1601
	arc, inches:		+1.8	0	-7.8	-22.5
Win. 180 Ballistic Silvertip	velocity, fps:	2750	2572	2402	2237	2080
	energy, ft-lb:	3022	2644	2305	2001	1728
	arc, inches:		+1.9	0	-7.9	-22.8
Win. 180 Power-Point	velocity, fps:	2700	2348	2023	1727	1466
	energy, ft-lb:	2913	2203	1635	1192	859
	arc, inches:		+2.7	0	-11.3	-34.4
Win. 180 Power-Point Plus	velocity, fps:	2770	2563	2366	2177	1997
	energy, ft-lb:	3068	2627	2237	1894	1594
	arc, inches:		+1.9	0	-8.1	-23.6
Win. 180 Silvertip	velocity, fps:	2700	2469	2250	2042	1846
	energy, ft-lb:	2913	2436	2023	1666	1362
	arc, inches:		+2.4	0	-9.3	-27.0
Win. 180 AccuBond	velocity, fps:	2750	2573	2403	2239	2082
	energy, ft-lb:	3022	2646	2308	2004	1732
	arc, inches:		+1.9	0	-7.9	-22.8

Centerfire Rifle Ballistics

.30-06 SPRINGFIELD TO .300 WINCHESTER MAGNUM

CARTRIDGE BULLET	RANGE, YARDS:	0	100	200	300	400
Win. 180 Partition Gold	velocity, fps:	2790	2581	2382	2192	2010
	energy, ft-lb:	3112	2664	2269	1920	1615
	arc, inches:		+1.9	0	-8.0	-23.2
Win. 180 Fail Safe	velocity, fps:	2700	2486	2283	2089	1904
	energy, ft-lb:	2914	2472	2083	1744	1450
	arc, inches:		+2.1	0	-8.7	-25.5
Win. 150 Supreme Elite XP3	velocity, fps:	2925	2712	2508	2313	2127
	energy, ft-lb:	2849	2448	2095	1782	1507
	arc, inches:		+1.6	0	-7.2	-20.8
Win. 180 Supreme Elite XP3	velocity, fps:	2750	2579	2414	2256	2103
	energy, ft-lb:	3022	2658	2330	2034	1768
	arc, inches:		+1.9	0	-7.8	-22.5

.300 H&H MAGNUM

CARTRIDGE BULLET	RANGE, YARDS:	0	100	200	300	400
Federal 180 Nosler Partition	velocity, fps:	2880	2620	2380	2150	1930
	energy, ft-lb:	3315	2750	2260	1840	1480
	arc, inches:		+1.8	0	-8.0	-23.4
Win. 180 Fail Safe	velocity, fps:	2880	2628	2390	2165	1952
	energy, ft-lb:	3316	2762	2284	1873	1523
	arc, inches:		+1.8	0	-7.9	-23.2

.308 NORMA MAGNUM

CARTRIDGE BULLET	RANGE, YARDS:	0	100	200	300	400
Norma 180 TXP Swift A-Fr.	velocity, fps:	2953	2704	2469	2245	
	energy, ft-lb:	3486	2924	2437	2016	
	arc, inches:		+1.6	0	-7.3	
Norma 180 Oryx	velocity, fps:	2953	2630	2330	2049	
	energy, ft-lb:	3486	2766	2170	1679	
	arc, inches:		+1.8	0	-8.2	
Norma 200 Vulkan	velocity, fps:	2903	2624	2361	2114	
	energy, ft-lb:	3744	3058	2476	1985	
	arc, inches:	0	+1.8	0	-8.0	

.300 WINCHESTER MAGNUM

CARTRIDGE BULLET	RANGE, YARDS:	0	100	200	300	400
A-Square 180 Dead Tough	velocity, fps:	3120	2756	2420	2108	1820
	energy, ft-lb:	3890	3035	2340	1776	1324
	arc, inches:		+1.6	0	-7.6	-22.9
Black Hills 180 Nos. Bal. Tip	velocity, fps:	3100				
	energy, ft-lb:	3498				
	arc, inches:					
Black Hills 180 Barnes X	velocity, fps:	2950				
	energy, ft-lb:	3498				
	arc, inches:					
Black Hills 180 AccuBond	velocity, fps:	3000				
	energy, ft-lb:	3597				
	arc, inches:					
Black Hills 190 Match	velocity, fps:	2950				
	energy, ft-lb:	3672				
	arc, inches:					
Federal 150 Sierra Pro Hunt.	velocity, fps:	3280	3030	2800	2570	2360.
	energy, ft-lb:	3570	3055	2600	2205	1860
	arc, inches:		+1.1	0	-5.6	-16.4
Federal 150 Trophy Bonded	velocity, fps:	3280	2980	2700	2430	2190
	energy, ft-lb:	3570	2450	2420	1970	1590
	arc, inches:		+1.2	0	-6.0	-17.9
Federal 180 Sierra Pro Hunt.	velocity, fps:	2960	2750	2540	2340	2160
	energy, ft-lb:	3500	3010	2580	2195	1860
	arc, inches:		+1.6	0	-7.0	-20.3
Federal 180 Barnes XLC	velocity, fps:	2960	2780	2600	2430	2260
	energy, ft-lb:	3500	3080	2700	2355	2050
	arc, inches:		+1.5	0	-6.6	-19.2
Federal 180 Trophy Bonded	velocity, fps:	2960	2700	2460	2220	2000
	energy, ft-lb:	3500	2915	2410	1975	1605
	arc, inches:		+1.6	0	-7.4	-21.9

CARTRIDGE BULLET	RANGE, YARDS:	0	100	200	300	400
Federal 180 Tr. Bonded HE	velocity, fps:	3100	2830	2580	2340	2110
	energy, ft-lb:	3840	3205	2660	2190	1790
	arc, inches:		+1.4	0	-6.6	-19.7
Federal 180 Nosler Partition	velocity, fps:	2960	2700	2450	2210	1990
	energy, ft-lb:	3500	2905	2395	1955	1585
	arc, inches:		+1.6	0	-7.5	-22.1
Federal 190 Sierra MatchKg. BTHP	velocity, fps:	2900	2730	2560	2400	2240
	energy, ft-lb:	3550	3135	2760	2420	2115
	arc, inches:		+12.9	+22.5	+26.9	+25.1
Federal 200 Sierra GameKing BTSP	velocity, fps:	2830	2680	2530	2380	2240
	energy, ft-lb:	3560	3180	2830	2520	2230
	arc, inches:		+1.7	0	-7.1	-20.4
Federal 200 Nosler Part. HE	velocity, fps:	2930	2740	2550	2370	2200
	energy, ft-lb:	3810	3325	2885	2495	2145
	arc, inches:		+1.6	0	-6.9	-20.1
Federal 200 Trophy Bonded	velocity, fps:	2800	2570	2350	2150	1950
	energy, ft-lb:	3480	2935	2460	2050	1690
	arc, inches:		+1.9	0	-8.2	-23.9
Hornady 150 SP boat-tail	velocity, fps:	3275	2988	2718	2464	2224
	energy, ft-lb:	3573	2974	2461	2023	1648
	arc, inches:		+1.2	0	-6.0	-17.8
Hornady 150 SST (and Interbond)	velocity, fps:	3275	3027	2791	2565	2352
	energy, ft-lb:	3572	3052	2593	2192	1842
	arc, inches:		+1.2	0	-5.8	-17.0
Hornady 165 SP boat-tail	velocity, fps:	3100	2877	2665	2462	2269.
	energy, ft-lb:	3522	3033	2603	2221	1887
	arc, inches:		+1.3	0	-6.5	-18.5
Hornady 165 SST	velocity, fps:	3100	2885	2680	2483	2296
	energy, ft-lb:	3520	3049	2630	2259	1930
	arc, inches:		+1.4	0	-6.4	-18.6
Hornady 180 SP boat-tail	velocity, fps:	2960	2745	2540	2344	2157
	energy, ft-lb:	3501	3011	2578	2196	1859
	arc, inches:		+1.9	0	-7.3	-20.9
Hornady 180 SST	velocity, fps:	2960	2764	2575	2395	2222
	energy, ft-lb:	3501	3052	2650	2292	1974
	arc, inches:		+1.6	0	-7.0	-20.1.
Hornady 180 SPBT HM	velocity, fps:	3100	2879	2668	2467	2275
	energy, ft-lb:	3840	3313	2845	2431	2068
	arc, inches:		+1.4	0	-6.4	-18.7
Hornady 190 SP boat-tail	velocity, fps:	2900	2711	2529	2355	2187
	energy, ft-lb:	3549	3101	2699	2340	2018
	arc, inches:		+1.6	0	-7.1	-20.4
Norma 150 Nosler Bal. Tip	velocity, fps:	3250	3014	2791	2578	
	energy, ft-lb:	3519	3027	2595	2215	
	arc, inches:		+1.1	0	-5.6	
Norma 150 Barnes TS	velocity, fps:	3215	2982	2761	2550	
	energy, ft-lb:	3444	2962	2539	2167	
	arc, inches:		+1.2	0	-5.8	
Norma 165 Scirocco	velocity, fps:	3117	2921	2734	2554	
	energy, ft-lb:	3561	3127	2738	2390	
	arc, inches:		+1.2	0	-5.9	
Norma 180 Soft Point	velocity, fps:	3018	2780	2555	2341	
	energy, ft-lb:	3641	3091	2610	2190	
	arc, inches:		+1.5	0	-7.0	
Norma 180 Plastic Point	velocity, fps:	3018	2755	2506	2271	
	energy, ft-lb:	3641	3034	2512	2062	
	arc, inches:		+1.6	0	-7.1	
Norma 180 TXP Swift A-Fr.	velocity, fps:	2920	2688	2467	2256	
	energy, ft-lb:	3409	2888	2432	2035	
	arc, inches:		+1.7	0	-7.4	
Norma 180 AccuBond	velocity, fps:	2953	2767	2588	2417	
	energy, ft-lb:	3486	3061	2678	2335	
	arc, inches:		+1.5	0	-6.7	

.300 WINCHESTER MAGNUM TO .300 WINCHESTER SHORT MAGNUM

CARTRIDGE BULLET	RANGE, YARDS:	0	100	200	300	400
Norma 180 Oryx	velocity, fps:	2920	2600	2301	2023	
	energy, ft-lb:	3409	2702	2117	1636	
	arc, inches:		+1.8	0	-8.4	
Norma 200 Vulkan	velocity, fps:	2887	2609	2347	2100	
	energy, ft-lb:	3702	3023	2447	1960	
	arc, inches:		+1.8	0	-8.2	
Norma 200 Oryx	velocity, fps:	2789	2510	2248	2002	
	energy, ft-lb:	3455	2799	2245	1780	
	arc, inches:		+2.0	0	-8.9	
PMC 150 Barnes X	velocity, fps:	3135	2918	2712	2515	2327
	energy, ft-lb:	3273	2836	2449	2107	1803
	arc, inches:		+1.3	0	-6.1	-17.7
PMC 150 Pointed Soft Point	velocity, fps:	3150	2902	2665	2438	2222
	energy, ft-lb:	3304	2804	2364	1979	1644.
	arc, inches:		+1.3	0	-6.2	-18.3
PMC 150 SP boat-tail	velocity, fps:	3250	2987	2739	2504	2281
	energy, ft-lb:	3517	2970	2498	2088	1733
	arc, inches:		+1.2	0	-6.0	-17.4
PMC 180 Barnes X	velocity, fps:	2910	2738	2572	2412	2258
	energy, ft-lb:	3384	2995	2644	2325	2037
	arc, inches:		+1.6	0	-6.9	-19.8
PMC 180 Pointed Soft Point	velocity, fps:	2853	2643	2446	2258	2077
	energy, ft-lb:	3252	2792	2391	2037	1724
	arc, inches:		+1.7	0	-7.5	-21.9
PMC 180 SP boat-tail	velocity, fps:	2900	2714	2536	2365	2200
	energy, ft-lb:	3361	2944	2571	2235	1935
	arc, inches:		+1.6	0	-7.1	-20.3
PMC 180 HPBT Match	velocity, fps:	2950	2755	2568	2390	2219
	energy, ft-lb:	3478	3033	2636	2283	1968
	arc, inches:		+1.5	0	-6.8	-19.7
Rem. 150 PSP Core-Lokt	velocity, fps:	3290	2951	2636	2342	2068
	energy, ft-lb:	3605	2900	2314	1827	1859
	arc, inches:		+1.6	0	-7.0	-20.2
Rem. 150 PSP C-L MR	velocity, fps:	2650	2373	2113	1870	1646
	energy, ft-lb:	2339	1875	1486	1164	902
	arc, inches:		+1.0	-2.7	-14.3	-35.8
Rem. 150 PSP C-L Ultra	velocity, fps:	3290	2967	2666	2384	2120
	energy, ft-lb:	3065	2931	2366	1893	1496
	arc, inches:		+1.2	0	-6.1	-18.4
Rem. 180 AccuTip	velocity, fps:	2960	2764	2577	2397	2224
	energy, ft-lb:	3501	3053	2653	2295	1976
	arc, inches:		+1.5	0	-6.8	-19.6
Rem. 180 PSP Core-Lokt	velocity, fps:	2960	2745	2540	2344	2157
	energy, ft-lb:	3501	3011	2578	2196	1424
	arc, inches:		+2.2	+1.9	-3.4	-15.0
Rem. 180 PSP C-L Ultra	velocity, fps:	2960	2727	2505	2294	2093
	energy, ft-lb:	3501	2971	2508	2103	1751
	arc, inches:		+2.7	+2.2	-3.8	-16.4
Rem. 180 Nosler Partition	velocity, fps:	2960	2725	2503	2291	2089
	energy, ft-lb:	3501	2968	2503	2087	1744
	arc, inches:		+1.6	0	-7.2	-20.9
Rem. 180 Nosler Bal. Tip	velocity, fps:	2960	2774	2595	2424	2259.
	energy, ft-lb:	3501	3075	2692	2348	2039
	arc, inches:		+1.5	0	-6.7	-19.3
Rem. 180 Swift Scirocco	velocity, fps:	2960	2774	2595	2424	2259
	energy, ft-lb:	3501	3075	2692	2348	2039
	arc, inches:		+1.5	0	-6.7	-19.3
Rem. 190 PSP boat-tail	velocity, fps:	2885	2691	2506	2327	2156
	energy, ft-lb:	3511	3055	2648	2285	1961
	arc, inches:		+1.6	0	-7.2	-20.8
Rem. 190 HPBT Match	velocity, fps:	2900	2725	2557	2395	2239
	energy, ft-lb:	3547	3133	2758	2420	2115
	arc, inches:		+1.6	0	-6.9	-19.9

CARTRIDGE BULLET	RANGE, YARDS:	0	100	200	300	400
Rem. 200 Swift A-Frame	velocity, fps:	2825	2595	2376	2167	1970
	energy, ft-lb:	3544	2989	2506	2086	1722
	arc, inches:		+1.8	0	-8.0	-23.5
Speer 180 Grand Slam	velocity, fps:	2950	2735	2530	2334	
	energy, ft-lb:	3478	2989	2558	2176	
	arc, inches:		+1.6	0	-7.0	-20.5
Speer 200 Grand Slam	velocity, fps:	2800	2597	2404	2218	
	energy, ft-lb:	3481	2996	2565	2185	
	arc, inches:		+1.8	0	-7.9	-22.9
Win. 150 Power-Point	velocity, fps:	3290	2951	2636	2342	2068.
	energy, ft-lb:	3605	2900	2314	1827	1424
	arc, inches:		+2.6	+2.1	-3.5	-15.4
Win. 150 Fail Safe	velocity, fps:	3260	2943	2647	2370	2110
	energy, ft-lb:	3539	2884	2334	1871	1483
	arc, inches:		+1.3	0	-6.2	-18.7
Win. 165 Fail Safe	velocity, fps:	3120	2807	2515	2242	1985
	energy, ft-lb:	3567	2888	2319	1842	1445
	arc, inches:		+1.5	0	-7.0	-20.0
Win. 180 Power-Point	velocity, fps:	2960	2745	2540	2344	2157
	energy, ft-lb:	3501	3011	2578	2196	1859
	arc, inches:		+1.9	0	-7.3	-20.9
Win. 180 Power-Point Plus	velocity, fps:	3070	2846	2633	2430	2236
	energy, ft-lb:	3768	3239	2772	2361	1999
	arc, inches:		+1.4	0	-6.4	-18.7
Win. 180 Ballistic Silvertip	velocity, fps:	2950	2764	2586	2415	2250
	energy, ft-lb:	3478	3054	2673	2331	2023
	arc, inches:		+1.5	0	-6.7	-19.4
Win. 180 AccuBond	velocity, fps:	2950	2765	2588	2417	2253
	energy, ft-lb:	3478	3055	2676	2334	2028
	arc, inches:		+1.5	0	-6.7	-19.4
Win. 180 Fail Safe	velocity, fps:	2960	2732	2514	2307	2110
	energy, ft-lb:	3503	2983	2528	2129	1780
	arc, inches:		+1.6	0	-7.1	-20.7
Win. 180 Partition Gold	velocity, fps:	3070	2859	2657	2464	2280
	energy, ft-lb:	3768	3267	2823	2428	2078
	arc, inches:		+1.4	0	-6.3	-18.3
Win. 150 Supreme Elite XP3	velocity, fps:	3260	3030	2811	2603	2404
	energy, ft-lb:	3539	3057	2632	2256	1925
	arc, inches:		+1.1	0	-5.6	-16.2
Win. 180 Supreme Elite XP3	velocity, fps:	3000	2819	2646	2479	2318
	energy, ft-lb:	3597	3176	2797	2455	2147
	arc, inches:		+1.4	0	-6.4	-18.5

.300 REMINGTON SHORT ULTRA MAGNUM

CARTRIDGE BULLET	RANGE, YARDS:	0	100	200	300	400
Rem. 150 PSP C-L Ultra	velocity, fps:	3200	2901	2672	2359	2112
	energy, ft-lb:	3410	2803	2290	1854	1485
	arc, inches:		+1.3	0	-6.4	-19.l
Rem. 165 PSP Core-Lokt	velocity, fps:	3075	2792	2527	2276	2040
	energy, ft-lb:	3464	2856	2339	1828	1525
	arc, inches:		+1.5	0	-7.0	-20.7
Rem. 180 Partition	velocity, fps:	2960	2761	2571	2389	2214
	energy, ft-lb:	3501	3047	2642	2280	1959
	arc, inches:		+1.5	0	-6.8	-19.7
Rem. 180 PSP C-L Ultra	velocity, fps:	2960	2727	2506	2295	2094
	energy, ft-lb:	3501	2972	2509	2105	1753
	arc, inches:		+1.6	0	-7.1	-20.9
Rem. 190 HPBT Match	velocity, fps:	2900	2725	2557	2395	2239
	energy, ft-lb:	3547	3133	2758	2420	2115
	arc, inches:		+1.6	0	-6.9	-19.9

.300 WINCHESTER SHORT MAGNUM

CARTRIDGE BULLET	RANGE, YARDS:	0	100	200	300	400
Black Hills 175 Sierra MKing	velocity, fps:	2950				
	energy, ft-lb:	3381				
	arc, inches:					

Centerfire Rifle Ballistics

.300 WINCHESTER SHORT MAGNUM TO .300 WEATHERBY MAGNUM

CARTRIDGE BULLET	RANGE, YARDS:	0	100	200	300	400
Black Hills 180 AccuBond	velocity, fps:	2950				
	energy, ft-lb:	3478				
	arc, inches:					
Federal 150 Nosler Bal. Tip	velocity, fps:	3200	2970	2755	2545	2345
	energy, ft-lb:	3410	2940	2520	2155	1830.
	arc, inches:		+1.2	0	-5.8	-17.0
Federal 165 Nos. Partition	velocity, fps:	3130	2890	2670	2450	2250
	energy, ft-lb:	3590	3065	2605	2205	1855.
	arc, inches:		+1.3	0	-6.2	-18.2
Federal 165 Nos. Solid Base	velocity, fps:	3130	2900	2690	2490	2290
	energy, ft-lb:	3590	3090	2650	2265	1920
	arc, inches:		+1.3	0	-6.1	-17.8
Federal 180 Barnes TS And Nos. Solid Base	velocity, fps:	2980	2780	2580	2400	2220
	energy, ft-lbs:	3550	3085	2670	2300	1970
	arc, inches:		+1.5	0	-6.7	-19.5
Federal 180 Grand Slam	velocity, fps:	2970	2740	2530	2320	2130
	energy, ft-lb:	3525	3010	2555	2155	1810
	arc, inches:		+1.5	0	-7.0	-20.5
Federal 180 Trophy Bonded	velocity, fps:	2970	2730	2500	2280	2080
	energy, ft-lb:	3525	2975	2500	2085	1725
	arc, inches:		+1.5	0	-7.2	-21.0
Federal 180 Nosler Partition	velocity, fps:	2975	2750	2535	2290	2126
	energy, ft-lb:	3540	3025	2570	2175	1825
	arc, inches:		+1.5	0	-7.0	-20.3
Federal 180 Nos. AccuBond	velocity, fps:	2960	2780	2610	2440	2280
	energy, ft-lb:	3500	3090	2715	2380	2075
	arc, inches:		+1.5	0	-6.6	-19.0
Federal 180 Hi-Shok SP	velocity, fps:	2970	2520	2115	1750	1430
	energy, ft-lb:	3525	2540	1785	1220	820
	arc, inches:		+2.2	0	-9.9	-31.4
Norma 150 FMJ	velocity, fps:	2953	2731	2519	2318	
	energy, ft-lb:					
	arc, inches:		+1.6	0	-7.1	
Norma 150 Barnes X TS	velocity, fps:	3215	2982	2761	2550	
	energy, ft-lb:	3444	2962	2539	2167	
	arc, inches:		+1.2	0	-5.7	
Norma 180 Nosler Bal. Tip	velocity, fps:	3215	2985	2767	2560	
	energy, ft-lb:	3437	2963	2547	2179	
	arc, inches:		+1.2	0	-5.7	
Norma 180 Oryx	velocity, fps:	2936	2542	2180	1849	
	energy, ft-lb:	3446	2583	1900	1368	
	arc, inches:		+1.9	0	-8.9	
Win. 150 Power-Point	velocity, fps:	3270	2903	2565	2250	1958
	energy, ft-lb:	3561	2807	2190	1686	1277
	arc, inches:		+1.3	0	-6.6	-20.2
Win. 150 Ballistic Silvertip	velocity, fps:	3300	3061	2834	2619	2414
	energy, ft-lb:	3628	3121	2676	2285	1941
	arc, inches:		+1.1	0	-5.4	-15.9
Win. 165 Fail Safe	velocity, fps:	3125	2846	2584	2336	2102
	energy, ft-lb:	3577	2967	2446	1999	1619
	arc, inches:		+1.4	0	-6.6	-19.6
Win. 180 Ballistic Silvertip	velocity, fps:	3010	2822	2641	2468	2301.
	energy, ft-lb:	3621	3182	2788	2434	2116
	arc, inches:		+1.4	0	-6.4	-18.6
Win. 180 AccuBond	velocity, fps:	3010	2822	2643	2470	2304
	energy, ft-lb:	3622	3185	2792	2439	2121
	arc, inches:		+1.4	0	-6.4	-18.5
Win. 180 Fail Safe	velocity, fps:	2970	2741	2524	2317	2120
	energy, ft-lb:	3526	3005	2547	2147	1797
	arc, inches:		+1.6	0	-7.0	-20.5
Win. 180 Power Point	velocity, fps:	2970	2755	2549	2353	2166
	energy, ft-lb:	3526	3034	2598	2214	1875
	arc, inches:		+1.5	0	-6.9	-20.1

CARTRIDGE BULLET	RANGE, YARDS:	0	100	200	300	400
Win. 150 Supreme Elite XP3	velocity, fps:	3300	3068	2847	2637	2437
	energy, ft-lb:	3626	3134	2699	2316	1978
	arc, inches:		+1.1	0	-5.4	-15.8
Win. 180 Supreme Elite XP3	velocity, fps:	3010	2829	2655	2488	2326
	energy, ft-lb:	3621	3198	2817	2473	2162
	arc, inches:		+1.4	0	-6.4	-18.3

.300 WEATHERBY MAGNUM

CARTRIDGE BULLET	RANGE, YARDS:	0	100	200	300	400
A-Square 180 Dead Tough	velocity, fps:	3180	2811	2471	2155	1863.
	energy, ft-lb:	4041	3158	2440	1856	1387
	arc, inches:		+1.5	0	-7.2	-21.8
A-Square 220 Monolithic Solid	velocity, fps:	2700	2407	2133	1877	1653
	energy, ft-lb:	3561	2830	2223	1721	1334
	arc, inches:		+2.3	0	-9.8	-29.7
Federal 180 Sierra GameKing BTSP	velocity, fps:	3190	3010	2830	2660	2490
	energy, ft-lb:	4065	3610	3195	2820	2480
	arc, inches:		+1.2	0	-5.6	-16.0
Federal 180 Trophy Bonded	velocity, fps:	3190	2950	2720	2500	2290
	energy, ft-lb:	4065	3475	2955	2500	2105
	arc, inches:		+1.3	0	-5.9	-17.5
Federal 180 Tr. Bonded HE	velocity, fps:	3330	3080	2850	2750	2410
	energy, ft-lb:	4430	3795	3235	2750	2320
	arc, inches:		+1.1	0	-5.4	-15.8
Federal 180 Nosler Partition	velocity, fps:	3190	2980	2780	2590	2400
	energy, ft-lb:	4055	3540	3080	2670	2305
	arc, inches:		+1.2	0	-5.7	-16.7
Federal 180 Nosler Part. HE	velocity, fps:	3330	3110	2810	2710	2520
	energy, ft-lb:	4430	3875	3375	2935	2540
	arc, inches:		+1.0	0	-5.2	-15.1
Federal 200 Trophy Bonded	velocity, fps:	2900	2670	2440	2230	2030
	energy, ft-lb:	3735	3150	2645	2200	1820
	arc, inches:		+1.7	0	-7.6	-22.2
Hornady 150 SST (or Interbond)	velocity, fps:	3375	3123	2882	2652	2434
	energy, ft-lb:	3793	3248	2766	2343	1973
	arc, inches:		+1.0	0	-5.4	-15.8
Hornady 180 SP	velocity, fps:	3120	2891	2673	2466	2268.
	energy, ft-lb:	3890	3340	2856	2430	2055
	arc, inches:		+1.3	0	-6.2	-18.1
Hornady 180 SST	velocity, fps:	3120	2911	2711	2519	2335
	energy, ft-lb:	3890	3386	2936	2535	2180
	arc, inches:		+1.3	0	-6.2	-18.1
Rem. 180 PSP Core-Lokt	velocity, fps:	3120	2866	2627	2400	2184
	energy, ft-lb:	3890	3284	2758	2301	1905
	arc, inches:		+2.4	+2.0	-3.4	-14.9
Rem. 190 PSP boat-tail	velocity, fps:	3030	2830	2638	2455	2279
	energy, ft-lb:	3873	3378	2936	2542	2190.
	arc, inches:		+1.4	0	-6.4	-18.6
Rem. 200 Swift A-Frame	velocity, fps:	2925	2690	2467	2254	2052
	energy, ft-lb:	3799	3213	2701	2256	1870
	arc, inches:		+2.8	+2.3	-3.9	-17.0
Speer 180 Grand Slam	velocity, fps:	3185	2948	2722	2508	
	energy, ft-lb:	4054	3472	2962	2514	
	arc, inches:		+1.3	0	-5.9	-17.4
Wby. 150 Pointed Expanding	velocity, fps:	3540	3225	2932	2657	2399
	energy, ft-lb:	4173	3462	2862	2351	1916
	arc, inches:		+2.6	+3.3	0	-8.2
Wby. 150 Nosler Partition	velocity, fps:	3540	3263	3004	2759	2528
	energy, ft-lb:	4173	3547	3005	2536	2128
	arc, inches:		+2.5	+3.2	0	-7.7
Wby. 165 Pointed Expanding	velocity, fps:	3390	3123	2872	2634	2409
	energy, ft-lb:	4210	3573	3021	2542	2126
	arc, inches:		+2.8	+3.5	0	-8.5

Centerfire Rifle Ballistics

.300 WEATHERBY MAGNUM TO 7.7X58 JAPANESE ARISAKA

CARTRIDGE BULLET	RANGE, YARDS:	0	100	200	300	400
Wby. 165 Nosler Bal. Tip	velocity, fps:	3350	3133	2927	2730	2542
	energy, ft-lb:	4111	3596	3138	2730	2367
	arc, inches:		+2.7	+3.4	0	-8.1
Wby. 180 Pointed Expanding	velocity, fps:	3240	3004	2781	2569	2366
	energy, ft-lb:	4195	3607	3091	2637	2237
	arc, inches:		+3.1	+3.8	0	-9.0
Wby. 180 Barnes X	velocity, fps:	3190	2995	2809	2631	2459
	energy, ft-lb:	4067	3586	3154	2766	2417
	arc, inches:		+3.1	+3.8	0	-8.7
Wby. 180 Bal. Tip	velocity, fps:	3250	3051	2806	2676	2503
	energy, ft-lb:	4223	3721	3271	2867	2504
	arc, inches:		+2.8	+3.6	0	-8.4
Wby. 180 Nosler Partition	velocity, fps:	3240	3028	2826	2634	2449
	energy, ft-lb:	4195	3665	3193	2772	2396
	arc, inches:		+3.0	+3.7	0	-8.6
Wby. 200 Nosler Partition	velocity, fps:	3060	2860	2668	2485	2308
	energy, ft-lb:	4158	3631	3161	2741	2366
	arc, inches:		+3.5	+4.2	0	-9.8
Wby. 220 RN Expanding	velocity, fps:	2845	2543	2260	1996	1751.
	energy, ft-lb:	3954	3158	2495	1946	1497
	arc, inches:		+4.9	+5.9	0	-14.6

.300 DAKOTA

CARTRIDGE BULLET	RANGE, YARDS:	0	100	200	300	400
Dakota 165 Barnes X	velocity, fps:	3200	2979	2769	2569	2377
	energy, ft-lb:	3751	3251	2809	2417	2070
	arc, inches:		+2.1	+1.8	-3.0	-13.2
Dakota 200 Barnes X	velocity, fps:	3000	2824	2656	2493	2336
	energy, ft-lb:	3996	3542	3131	2760	2423
	arc, inches:		+2.2	+1.5	-4.0	-15.2

.300 PEGASUS

CARTRIDGE BULLET	RANGE, YARDS:	0	100	200	300	400
A-Square 180 SP boat-tail	velocity, fps:	3500	3319	3145	2978	2817
	energy, ft-lb:	4896	4401	3953	3544	3172
	arc, inches:		+2.3	+2.9	0	-6.8
A-Square 180 Nosler Part.	velocity, fps:	3500	3295	3100	2913	2734
	energy, ft-lb:	4896	4339	3840	3392	2988
	arc, inches:		+2.3	+3.0	0	-7.1
A-Square 180 Dead Tough	velocity, fps:	3500	3103	2740	2405	2095
	energy, ft-lb:	4896	3848	3001	2312	1753
	arc, inches:		+1.1	0	-5.7	-17.5

.300 REMINGTON ULTRA MAGNUM

CARTRIDGE BULLET	RANGE, YARDS:	0	100	200	300	400
Federal 180 Trophy Bonded	velocity, fps:	3250	3000	2770	2550	2340
	energy, ft-lb:	4220	3605	3065	2590	2180
	arc, inches:		+1.2	0	-5.7	-16.8
Rem. 150 Swift Scirocco	velocity, fps:	3450	3208	2980	2762	2556
	energy, ft-lb:	3964	3427	2956	2541	2175
	arc, inches:		+1.7	+1.5	-2.6	-11.2
Rem. 180 Nosler Partition	velocity, fps:	3250	3037	2834	2640	2454
	energy, ft-lb:	4221	3686	3201	2786	2407
	arc, inches:		+2.4	+1.8	-3.0	-12.7
Rem. 180 Swift Scirocco	velocity, fps:	3250	3048	2856	2672	2495
	energy, ft-lb:	4221	3714	3260	2853	2487
	arc, inches:		+2.0	+1.7	-2.8	-12.3
Rem. 180 PSP Core-Lokt	velocity, fps:	3250	2988	2742	2508	2287
	energy, ft-lb:	3517	2974	2503	2095	1741
	arc, inches:		+2.1	+1.8	-3.1	-13.6
Rem. 200 Nosler Partition	velocity, fps:	3025	2826	2636	2454	2279
	energy, ft-lb:	4063	3547	3086	2673	2308
	arc, inches:		+2.4	+2.0	-3.4	-14.6

.30-378 WEATHERBY MAGNUM

CARTRIDGE BULLET	RANGE, YARDS:	0	100	200	300	400
Wby. 165 Nosler Bal. Tip	velocity, fps:	3500	3275	3062	2859	2665
	energy, ft-lb:	4488	3930	3435	2995	2603
	arc, inches:		+2.4	+3.0	0	-7.4

CARTRIDGE BULLET	RANGE, YARDS:	0	100	200	300	400
Wby. 180 Nosler Bal. Tip	velocity, fps:	3420	3213	3015	2826	2645
	energy, ft-lb:	4676	4126	3634	3193	2797
	arc, inches:		+2.5	+3.1	0	-7.5
Wby. 180 Barnes X	velocity, fps:	3450	3243	3046	2858	2678.
	energy, ft-lb:	4757	4204	3709	3264	2865
	arc, inches:		+2.4	+3.1	0	-7.4
Wby. 200 Nosler Partition	velocity, fps:	3160	2955	2759	2572	2392.
	energy, ft-lb:	4434	3877	3381	2938	2541
	arc, inches:		+3.2	+3.9	0	-9.1

7.82 (.308) WARBIRD

CARTRIDGE BULLET	RANGE, YARDS:	0	100	200	300	400
Lazzeroni 150 Nosler Part.	velocity, fps:	3680	3432	3197	2975	2764
	energy, ft-lb:	4512	3923	3406	2949	2546.
	arc, inches:		+2.1	+2.7	0	-6.6
Lazzeroni 180 Nosler Part.	velocity, fps:	3425	3220	3026	2839	2661
	energy, ft-lb:	4689	4147	3661	3224	2831
	arc, inches:		+2.5	+3.2	0	-7.5
Lazzeroni 200 Swift A-Fr.	velocity, fps:	3290	3105	2928	2758	2594.
	energy, ft-lb:	4808	4283	3808	3378	2988
	arc, inches:		+2.7	+3.4	0	-7.9

7.65x53 ARGENTINE

CARTRIDGE BULLET	RANGE, YARDS:	0	100	200	300	400
Norma 174 Soft Point	velocity, fps:	2493	2173	1878	1611	
	energy, ft-lb:	2402	1825	1363	1003	
	arc, inches:		+2.0	0	-9.5	
Norma 180 Soft Point	velocity, fps:	2592	2386	2189	2002	
	energy, ft-lb:	2686	2276	1916	1602	
	arc, inches:		+2.3	0	-9.6	

.303 BRITISH

CARTRIDGE BULLET	RANGE, YARDS:	0	100	200	300	400
Federal 150 Hi-Shok	velocity, fps:	2690	2440	2210	1980	1780
	energy, ft-lb:	2400	1980	1620	1310	1055
	arc, inches:		+2.2	0	-9.4	-27.6
Federal 180 Sierra Pro-Hunt.	velocity, fps:	2460	2230	2020	1820	1630
	energy, ft-lb:	2420	1995	1625	1315	1060
	arc, inches:		+2.8	0	-11.3	-33.2
Federal 180 Tr. Bonded HE	velocity, fps:	2590	2350	2120	1900	1700
	energy, ft-lb:	2680	2205	1795	1445	1160
	arc, inches:		+2.4	0	-10.0	-30.0
Hornady 150 Soft Point	velocity, fps:	2685	2441	2210	1992	1787
	energy, ft-lb:	2401	1984	1627	1321	1064
	arc, inches:		+2.2	0	-9.3	-27.4
Hornady 150 SP LM	velocity, fps:	2830	2570	2325	2094	1884.
	energy, ft-lb:	2667	2199	1800	1461	1185
	arc, inches:		+2.0	0	-8.4	-24.6
Norma 150 Soft Point	velocity, fps:	2723	2438	2170	1920	
	energy, ft-lb:	2470	1980	1569	1228	
	arc, inches:		+2.2	0	-9.6	
PMC 174 FMJ (and HPBT)	velocity, fps:	2400	2216	2042	1876	1720
	energy, ft-lb:	2225	1898	1611	1360	1143
	arc, inches:		+2.8	0	-11.2	-32.2
PMC 180 SP boat-tail	velocity, fps:	2450	2276	2110	1951	1799
	energy, ft-lb:	2399	2071	1779	1521	1294
	arc, inches:		+2.6	0	-10.4	-30.1
Rem. 180 SP Core-Lokt	velocity, fps:	2460	2124	1817	1542	1311
	energy, ft-lb:	2418	1803	1319	950	687
	arc, inches, s:		0	-5.8	-23.3	
Win. 180 Power-Point	velocity, fps:	2460	2233	2018	1816	1629
	energy, ft-lb:	2418	1993	1627	1318	1060
	arc, inches, s:		0	-6.1	-20.8	

7.7x58 JAPANESE ARISAKA

CARTRIDGE BULLET	RANGE, YARDS:	0	100	200	300	400
Norma 174 Soft Point	velocity, fps:	2493	2173	1878	1611	
	energy, ft-lb:	2402	1825	1363	1003	
	arc, inches:		+2.0	0	-9.5	

7.7X58 JAPANESE ARISAKA TO .338 WINCHESTER MAGNUM

CARTRIDGE BULLET	RANGE, YARDS:	0	100	200	300	400
Norma 180 Soft Point	velocity, fps:	2493	2291	2099	1916	
	energy, ft-lb:	2485	2099	1761	1468	
	arc, inches:		+2.6	0	-10.5	

.32-20 WINCHESTER

CARTRIDGE BULLET	RANGE, YARDS:	0	100	200	300	400
Rem. 100 Lead	velocity, fps:	1210	1021	913	834	769
	energy, ft-lb:	325	231	185	154	131
	arc, inches:		0	-31.6	-104.7	
Win. 100 Lead	velocity, fps:	1210	1021	913	834	769
	energy, ft-lb:	325	231	185	154	131
	arc, inches:		0	-32.3	-106.3	

.32 WINCHESTER SPECIAL

CARTRIDGE BULLET	RANGE, YARDS:	0	100	200	300	400
Federal 170 Hi-Shok	velocity, fps:	2250	1920	1630	1370	1180
	energy, ft-lb:	1910	1395	1000	710	520
	arc, inches:		0	-8.0	-29.2	
Rem. 170 SP Core-Lokt	velocity, fps:	2250	1921	1626	1372	1175
	energy, ft-lb:	1911	1393	998	710	521
	arc, inches:		0	-8.0	-29.3	
Win. 170 Power-Point	velocity, fps:	2250	1870	1537	1267	1082
	energy, ft-lb:	1911	1320	892	606	442
	arc, inches:		0	-9.2	-33.2	

8MM MAUSER (8X57)

CARTRIDGE BULLET	RANGE, YARDS:	0	100	200	300	400
Federal 170 Hi-Shok	velocity, fps:	2360	1970	1620	1330	1120
	energy, ft-lb:	2100	1465	995	670	475
	arc, inches:		0	-7.6	-28.5	
Hornady 195 SP	velocity, fps:	2550	2343	2146	1959	1782
	energy, ft-lb:	2815	2377	1994	1861	1375
	arc, inches:		+2.3	0	-9.9	-28.8.
Hornady 195 SP (2005)	velocity, fps:	2475	2269	2074	1888	1714
	energy, ft-lb:	2652	2230	1861	1543	1271
	arc, inches:		+2.6	0	-10.7	-31.3
Norma 123 FMJ	velocity, fps:	2559	2121	1729	1398	
	energy, ft-lb:	1789	1228	817	534	
	arc, inches:		+3.2	0	-15.0	
Norma 196 Oryx	velocity, fps:	2395	2146	1912	1695	
	energy, ft-lb:	2497	2004	1591	1251	
	arc, inches:		+3	0	-12.6	
Norma 196 Vulkan	velocity, fps:	2395	2156	1930	1720	
	energy, ft-lb:	2497	2023	1622	1289	
	arc, inches:		3.0	0	-12.3	
Norma 196 Alaska	velocity, fps:	2395	2112	1850	1611	
	energy, ft-lb:	2714	2190	1754	1399	
	arc, inches:		0	-6.3	-22.9	
Norma 196 Soft Point (JS)	velocity, fps:	2526	2244	1981	1737	
	energy, ft-lb:	2778	2192	1708	1314	
	arc, inches:		+2.7	0	-11.6	
Norma 196 Alaska (JS)	velocity, fps:	2526	2248	1988	1747	
	energy, ft-lb:	2778	2200	1720	1328	
	arc, inches:		+2.7	0	-11.5	
Norma 196 Vulkan (JS)	velocity, fps:	2526	2276	2041	1821	
	energy, ft-lb:	2778	2256	1813	1443	
	arc, inches:		+2.6	0	-11.0	
Norma 196 Oryx (JS)	velocity, fps:	2526	2269	2027	1802	
	energy, ft-lb:	2778	2241	1789	1413	
	arc, inches:		+2.6	0	-11.1	
PMC 170 Pointed Soft Point	velocity, fps:	2360	1969	1622	1333	1123
	energy, ft-lb:	2102	1463	993	671	476
	arc, inches:		+1.8	-4.5	-24.3	-63.8
Rem. 170 SP Core-Lokt	velocity, fps:	2360	1969	1622	1333	1123
	energy, ft-lb:	2102	1463	993	671	476
	arc, inches:		+1.8	-4.5	-24.3	-63.8.

CARTRIDGE BULLET	RANGE, YARDS:	0	100	200	300	400
Win. 170 Power-Point	velocity, fps:	2360	1969	1622	1333	1123
	energy, ft-lb:	2102	1463	993	671	476
	arc, inches:		+1.8	-4.5	-24.3	-63.8

.325 WSM

CARTRIDGE BULLET	RANGE, YARDS:	0	100	200	300	400
Win. 180 Ballistic ST	velocity, fps:	3060	2841	2632	2432	2242
	energy, ft-lb:	3743	3226	2769	2365	2009
	arc, inches:		+1.4	0	-6.4	-18.7
Win. 200 AccuBond CT	velocity, fps:	2950	2753	2565	2384	2210
	energy, ft-lb:	3866	3367	2922	2524	2170
	arc, inches:		+1.5	0	-6.8	-19.8
Win. 220 Power-Point	velocity, fps:	2840	2605	2382	2169	1968
	energy, ft-lb:	3941	3316	2772	2300	1893
	arc, inches:		+1.8	0	-8.0	-23.3

8MM REMINGTON MAGNUM

CARTRIDGE BULLET	RANGE, YARDS:	0	100	200	300	400
A-Square 220 Monolythic Solid	velocity, fps:	2800	2501	2221	1959	1718
	energy, ft-lb:	3829	3055	2409	1875	1442
	arc, inches:		+2.1	0	-9.1	-27.6
Rem. 200 Swift A-Frame	velocity, fps:	2900	2623	2361	2115	1885
	energy, ft-lb:	3734	3054	2476	1987	1577
	arc, inches:		+1.8	0	-8.0	-23.9

.338-06

CARTRIDGE BULLET	RANGE, YARDS:	0	100	200	300	400
A-Square 200 Nos. Bal. Tip	velocity, fps:	2750	2553	2364	2184	2011
	energy, ft-lb:	3358	2894	2482	2118	1796
	arc, inches:		+1.9	0	-8.2	-23.6
A-Square 250 SP boat-tail	velocity, fps:	2500	2374	2252	2134	2019
	energy, ft-lb:	3496	3129	2816	2528	2263
	arc, inches:		+2.4	0	-9.3	-26.0
A-Square 250 Dead Tough	velocity, fps:	2500	2222	1963	1724	1507
	energy, ft-lb:	3496	2742	2139	1649	1261
	arc, inches:		+2.8	0	-11.9	-35.5
Wby. 210 Nosler Part.	velocity, fps:	2750	2526	2312	2109	1916
	energy, ft-lb:	3527	2975	2403	2074	1712
	arc, inches:		+4.8	+5.7	0	-13.5

.338 WINCHESTER MAGNUM

CARTRIDGE BULLET	RANGE, YARDS:	0	100	200	300	400
A-Square 250 SP boat-tail	velocity, fps:	2700	2568	2439	2314	2193
	energy, ft-lb:	4046	3659	3302	2972	2669
	arc, inches:		+4.4	+5.2	0	-11.7
A-Square 250 Triad	velocity, fps:	2700	2407	2133	1877	1653
	energy, ft-lb:	4046	3216	2526	1956	1516
	arc, inches:		+2.3	0	-9.8	-29.8
Federal 210 Nosler Partition	velocity, fps:	2830	2600	2390	2180	1980
	energy, ft-lb:	3735	3160	2655	2215	1835
	arc, inches:		+1.8	0	-8.0	-23.3
Federal 225 Sierra Pro-Hunt.	velocity, fps:	2780	2570	2360	2170	1980
	energy, ft-lb:	3860	3290	2780	2340	1960
	arc, inches:		+1.9	0	-8.2	-23.7
Federal 225 Trophy Bonded	velocity, fps:	2800	2560	2330	2110	1900
	energy, ft-lb:	3915	3265	2700	2220	1800
	arc, inches:		+1.9	0	-8.4	-24.5
Federal 225 Tr. Bonded HE	velocity, fps:	2940	2690	2450	2230	2010
	energy, ft-lb:	4320	3610	3000	2475	2025
	arc, inches:		+1.7	0	-7.5	-22.0
Federal 225 Barnes XLC	velocity, fps:	2800	2610	2430	2260	2090
	energy, ft-lb:	3915	3405	2950	2545	2190
	arc, inches:		+1.8	0	-7.7	-22.2
Federal 250 Nosler Partition	velocity, fps:	2660	2470	2300	2130	1960
	energy, ft-lb:	3925	3395	2925	2505	2130.
	arc, inches:		+2.1	0	-8.8	-25.1

BALLISTICS

.338 WINCHESTER MAGNUM TO .338-378 WEATHERBY MAGNUM

CARTRIDGE BULLET	RANGE, YARDS:	0	100	200	300	400
Federal 250 Nosler Part HE	velocity, fps:	2800	2610	2420	2250	2080
	energy, ft-lb:	4350	3775	3260	2805	2395
	arc, inches:		+1.8	0	-7.8	-22.5
Hornady 225 Soft Point HM	velocity, fps:	2920	2678	2449	2232	2027
	energy, ft-lb:	4259	3583	2996	2489	2053
	arc, inches:		+1.8	0	-7.6	-22.0
Norma 225 TXP Swift A-Fr.	velocity, fps:	2740	2507	2286	2075	
	energy, ft-lb:	3752	3141	2611	2153	
	arc, inches:		+2.0	0	-8.7	
Norma 230 Oryx	velocity, fps:	2756	2514	2284	2066	
	energy, ft-lb:	3880	3228	2665	2181	
	arc, inches:		+2.0	0	-8.7	
Norma 250 Nosler Partition	velocity, fps:	2657	2470	2290	2118	
	energy, ft-lb:	3920	3387	2912	2490	
	arc, inches:		+2.1	0	-8.7	
PMC 225 Barnes X	velocity, fps:	2780	2619	2464	2313	2168
	energy, ft-lb:	3860	3426	3032	2673	2348.
	arc, inches:		+1.8	0	-7.6	-21.6
Rem. 200 Nosler Bal. Tip	velocity, fps:	2950	2724	2509	2303	2108
	energy, ft-lb:	3866	3295	2795	2357	1973
	arc, inches:		+1.6	0	-7.1	-20.8
Rem. 210 Nosler Partition	velocity, fps:	2830	2602	2385	2179	1983
	energy, ft-lb:	3734	3157	2653	2214	1834
	arc, inches:		+1.8	0	-7.9	-23.2
Rem. 225 PSP Core-Lokt	velocity, fps:	2780	2572	2374	2184	2003
	energy, ft-lb:	3860	3305	2815	2383	2004
	arc, inches:		+1.9	0	-8.1	-23.4
Rem. 225 PSP C-L Ultra	velocity, fps:	2780	2582	2392	2210	2036
	energy, ft-lb:	3860	3329	2858	2440	2071
	arc, inches:		+1.9	0	-7.9	-23.0
Rem. 225 Swift A-Frame	velocity, fps:	2785	2517	2266	2029	1808
	energy, ft-lb:	3871	3165	2565	2057	1633
	arc, inches:		+2.0	0	-8.8	-25.2
Rem. 250 PSP Core-Lokt	velocity, fps:	2660	2456	2261	2075	1898
	energy, ft-lb:	3927	3348	2837	2389	1999
	arc, inches:		+2.1	0	-8.9	-26.0
Speer 250 Grand Slam	velocity, fps:	2645	2442	2247	2062	
	energy, ft-lb:	3883	3309	2803	2360	
	arc, inches:		+2.2	0	-9.1	-26.2
Win. 200 Power-Point	velocity, fps:	2960	2658	2375	2110	1862
	energy, ft-lb:	3890	3137	2505	1977	1539
	arc, inches:		+2.0	0	-8.2	-24.3
Win. 200 Ballistic Silvertip	velocity, fps:	2950	2724	2509	2303	2108
	energy, ft-lb:	3864	3294	2794	2355	1972
	arc, inches:		+1.6	0	-7.1	-20.8
Win. 225 AccuBond	velocity, fps:	2800	2634	2474	2319	2170
	energy, ft-lb:	3918	3467	3058	2688	2353
	arc, inches:		+1.8	0	-7.4	-21.3
Win. 230 Fail Safe	velocity, fps:	2780	2573	2375	2186	2005
	energy, ft-lb:	3948	3382	2881	2441	2054
	arc, inches:		+1.9	0	-8.1	-23.4
Win. 250 Partition Gold	velocity, fps:	2650	2467	2291	2122	1960
	energy, ft-lb:	3899	3378	2914	2520	2134
	arc, inches:		+2.1	0	-8.7	-25.2

.340 WEATHERBY MAGNUM

CARTRIDGE BULLET	RANGE, YARDS:	0	100	200	300	400
A-Square 250 SP boat-tail	velocity, fps:	2820	2684	2552	2424	2299
	energy, ft-lb:	4414	3999	3615	3261	2935
	arc, inches:		+4.0	+4.6	0	-10.6
A-Square 250 Triad	velocity, fps:	2820	2520	2238	1976	1741
	energy, ft-lb:	4414	3524	2781	2166	1683
	arc, inches:		+2.0	0	-9.0	-26.8

CARTRIDGE BULLET	RANGE, YARDS:	0	100	200	300	400
Federal 225 Trophy Bonded	velocity, fps:	3100	2840	2600	2370	2150
	energy, ft-lb:	4800	4035	3375	2800	2310
	arc, inches:		+1.4	0	-6.5	-19.4
Wby. 200 Pointed Expanding	velocity, fps:	3221	2946	2688	2444	2213
	energy, ft-lb:	4607	3854	3208	2652	2174
	arc, inches:		+3.3	+4.0	0	-9.9
Wby. 200 Nosler Bal. Tip	velocity, fps:	3221	2980	2753	2536	2329
	energy, ft-lb:	4607	3944	3364	2856	2409
	arc, inches:		+3.1	+3.9	0	-9.2
Wby. 210 Nosler Partition	velocity, fps:	3211	2963	2728	2505	2293
	energy, ft-lb:	4807	4093	3470	2927	2452
	arc, inches:		+3.2	+3.9	0	-9.5
Wby. 225 Pointed Expanding	velocity, fps:	3066	2824	2595	2377	2170
	energy, ft-lb:	4696	3984	3364	2822	2352
	arc, inches:		+3.6	+4.4	0	-10.7
Wby. 225 Barnes X	velocity, fps:	3001	2804	2615	2434	2260
	energy, ft-lb:	4499	3927	3416	2959	2551
	arc, inches:		+3.6	+4.3	0	-10.3
Wby. 250 Pointed Expanding	velocity, fps:	2963	2745	2537	2338	2149
	energy, ft-lb:	4873	4182	3572	3035	2563
	arc, inches:		+3.9	+4.6	0	-11.1
Wby. 250 Nosler Partition	velocity, fps:	2941	2743	2553	2371	2197
	energy, ft-lb:	4801	4176	3618	3120	2678
	arc, inches:		+3.9	+4.6	0	-10.9

.330 DAKOTA

CARTRIDGE BULLET	RANGE, YARDS:	0	100	200	300	400
Dakota 200 Barnes X	velocity, fps:	3200	2971	2754	2548	2350
	energy, ft-lb:	4547	3920	3369	2882	2452
	arc, inches:		+2.1	+1.8	-3.1	-13.4
Dakota 250 Barnes X	velocity, fps:	2900	2719	2545	2378	2217
	energy, ft-lb:	4668	4103	3595	3138	2727
	arc, inches:		+2.3	+1.3	-5.0	-17.5

.338 REMINGTON ULTRA MAGNUM

CARTRIDGE BULLET	RANGE, YARDS:	0	100	200	300	400
Federal 210 Nosler Partition	velocity, fps:	3025	2800	2585	2385	2190
	energy, ft-lb:	4270	3655	3120	2645	2230
	arc, inches:		+1.5	0	-6.7	-19.5
Federal 250 Trophy Bonded	velocity, fps:	2860	2630	2420	2220	2020
	energy, ft-lb:	4540	3850	3245	2715	2260.
	arc, inches:		+0.8	0	-7.7	-22.6
Rem. 250 Swift A-Frame	velocity, fps:	2860	2645	2440	2244	2057
	energy, ft-lb:	4540	3882	3303	2794	2347
	arc, inches:		+1.7	0	-7.6	-22.1
Rem. 250 PSP Core-Lokt	velocity, fps:	2860	2647	2443	2249	2064
	energy, ft-lb:	4540	3888	3314	2807	2363
	arc, inches:		+1.7	0	-7.6	-22.0

.338 LAPUA

CARTRIDGE BULLET	RANGE, YARDS:	0	100	200	300	400
Black Hills 250 Sierra MKing	velocity, fps:	2950				
	energy, ft-lb:	4831				
	arc, inches:					
Black Hills 300 Sierra MKing	velocity, fps:	2800				
	energy, ft-lb:	5223				
	arc, inches:					

.338-378 WEATHERBY MAGNUM

CARTRIDGE BULLET	RANGE, YARDS:	0	100	200	300	400
Wby. 200 Nosler Bal. Tip	velocity, fps:	3350	3102	2868	2646	2434
	energy, ft-lb:	4983	4273	3652	3109	2631
	arc, inches:	0	+2.8	+3.5	0	-8.4
Wby. 225 Barnes X	velocity, fps:	3180	2974	2778	2591	2410.
	energy, ft-lb:	5052	4420	3856	3353	2902
	arc, inches:	0	+3.1	+3.8	0	-8.9

Centerfire Rifle Ballistics

.338-378 WEATHERBY MAGNUM TO 9.3X62

CARTRIDGE BULLET	RANGE, YARDS:	0	100	200	300	400
Wby. 250 Nosler Partition	velocity, fps:	3060	2856	2662	2475	2297
	energy, ft-lb:	5197	4528	3933	3401	2927
	arc, inches:	0	+3.5	+4.2	0	-9.8

8.59 (.338) TITAN

CARTRIDGE BULLET	RANGE, YARDS:	0	100	200	300	400
Lazzeroni 200 Nos. Bal. Tip	velocity, fps:	3430	3211	3002	2803	2613
	energy, ft-lb:	5226	4579	4004	3491	3033
	arc, inches:		+2.5	+3.2	0	-7.6
Lazzeroni 225 Nos. Partition	velocity, fps:	3235	3031	2836	2650	2471
	energy, ft-lb:	5229	4591	4021	3510	3052
	arc, inches:		+3.0	+3.6	0	-8.6
Lazzeroni 250 Swift A-Fr.	velocity, fps:	3100	2908	2725	2549	2379
	energy, ft-lb:	5336	4697	4123	3607	3143
	arc, inches:		+3.3	+4.0	0	-9.3

.338 A-SQUARE

CARTRIDGE BULLET	RANGE, YARDS:	0	100	200	300	400
A-Square 200 Nos. Bal. Tip	velocity, fps:	3500	3266	3045	2835	2634
	energy, ft-lb:	5440	4737	4117	3568	3081
	arc, inches:		+2.4	+3.1	0	-7.5
A-Square 250 SP boat-tail	velocity, fps:	3120	2974	2834	2697	2565.
	energy, ft-lb:	5403	4911	4457	4038	3652
	arc, inches:		+3.1	+3.7	0	-8.5
A-Square 250 Triad	velocity, fps:	3120	2799	2500	2220	1958
	energy, ft-lb:	5403	4348	3469	2736	2128
	arc, inches:		+1.5	0	-7.1	-20.4.

.338 EXCALIBER

CARTRIDGE BULLET	RANGE, YARDS:	0	100	200	300	400
A-Square 200 Nos. Bal. Tip	velocity, fps:	3600	3361	3134	2920	2715
	energy, ft-lb:	5755	5015	4363	3785	3274
	arc, inches:		+2.2	+2.9	0	-6.7
A-Square 250 SP boat-tail	velocity, fps:	3250	3101	2958	2684	2553
	energy, ft-lb:	5863	5339	4855	4410	3998
	arc, inches:		+2.7	+3.4	0	-7.8
A-Square 250 Triad	velocity, fps:	3250	2922	2618	2333	2066
	energy, ft-lb:	5863	4740	3804	3021	2370
	arc, inches:		+1.3	0	-6.4	-19.2

.348 WINCHESTER

CARTRIDGE BULLET	RANGE, YARDS:	0	100	200	300	400
Win. 200 Silvertip	velocity, fps:	2520	2215	1931	1672	1443.
	energy, ft-lb:	2820	2178	1656	1241	925
	arc, inches:		0	-6.2	-21.9	

.357 MAGNUM

CARTRIDGE BULLET	RANGE, YARDS:	0	100	200	300	400
Federal 180 Hi-Shok HP Hollow Point	velocity, fps:	1550	1160	980	860	770
	energy, ft-lb:	960	535	385	295	235
	arc, inches:		0	-22.8	-77.9	-173.8
Win. 158 Jacketed SP	velocity, fps:	1830	1427	1138	980	883
	energy, ft-lb:	1175	715	454	337	274
	arc, inches:		0	-16.2	-57.0	-128.3

.35 REMINGTON

CARTRIDGE BULLET	RANGE, YARDS:	0	100	200	300	400
Federal 200 Hi-Shok	velocity, fps:	2080	1700	1380	1140	1000
	energy, ft-lb:	1920	1280	840	575	445
	arc, inches:		0	-10.7	-39.3	
Hornady 200 Evolution	velocity, fps:	2225	1963	1721	1503	
	energy, ft-lb:	2198	1711	1315	1003	
	arc, inches:		+3.0	-1.3	-17.5	
Rem. 150 PSP Core-Lokt	velocity, fps:	2300	1874	1506	1218	1039
	energy, ft-lb:	1762	1169	755	494	359
	arc, inches:		0	-8.6	-32.6	
Rem. 200 SP Core-Lokt	velocity, fps:	2080	1698	1376	1140	1001
	energy, ft-lb:	1921	1280	841	577	445
	arc, inches:		0	-10.7	-40.1	

CARTRIDGE BULLET	RANGE, YARDS:	0	100	200	300	400
Win. 200 Power-Point	velocity, fps:	2020	1646	1335	1114	985
	energy, ft-lb:	1812	1203	791	551	431
	arc, inches:		0	-12.1	-43.9	

.356 WINCHESTER

CARTRIDGE BULLET	RANGE, YARDS:	0	100	200	300	400
Win. 200 Power-Point	velocity, fps:	2460	2114	1797	1517	1284
	energy, ft-lb:	2688	1985	1434	1022	732
	arc, inches:		+1.6	-3.8	-20.1	-51.2

.358 WINCHESTER

CARTRIDGE BULLET	RANGE, YARDS:	0	100	200	300	400
Win. 200 Silvertip	velocity, fps:	2490	2171	1876	1610	1379
	energy, ft-lb:	2753	2093	1563	1151	844
	arc, inches:		+1.5	-3.6	-18.6	-47.2

.35 WHELEN

CARTRIDGE BULLET	RANGE, YARDS:	0	100	200	300	400
Federal 225 Trophy Bonded	velocity, fps:	2600	2400	2200	2020	1840
	energy, ft-lb:	3375	2865	2520	2030	1690.
	arc, inches:		+2.3	0	-9.4	-27.3
Rem. 200 Pointed Soft Point	velocity, fps:	2675	2378	2100	1842	1606
	energy, ft-lb:	3177	2510	1958	1506	1145
	arc, inches:		+2.3	0	-10.3	-30.8
Rem. 250 Pointed Soft Point	velocity, fps:	2400	2197	2005	1823	1652
	energy, ft-lb:	3197	2680	2230	1844	1515
	arc, inches:		+1.3	-3.2	-16.6	-40.0

.358 NORMA MAGNUM

CARTRIDGE BULLET	RANGE, YARDS:	0	100	200	300	400
A-Square 275 Triad	velocity, fps:	2700	2394	2108	1842	1653
	energy, ft-lb:	4451	3498	2713	2072	1668
	arc, inches:		+2.3	0	-10.1	-29.8
Norma 250 TXP Swift A-Fr.	velocity, fps:	2723	2467	2225	1996	
	energy, ft-lb:	4117	3379	2748	2213	
	arc, inches:		+2.1	0	-9.1	
Norma 250 Woodleigh	velocity, fps:	2799	2442	2112	1810	
	energy, ft-lb:	4350	3312	2478	1819	
	arc, inches:		+2.2	0	-10.0	
Norma 250 Oryx	velocity, fps:	2756	2493	2245	2011	
	energy, ft-lb:	4217	3451	2798	2245	
	arc, inches:		+2.1	0	-9.0	

.358 STA

CARTRIDGE BULLET	RANGE, YARDS:	0	100	200	300	400
A-Square 275 Triad	velocity, fps:	2850	2562	2292	2039	1764
	energy, ft-lb:	4959	4009	3208	2539	1899.
	arc, inches:		+1.9	0	-8.6	-26.1

9.3x57

CARTRIDGE BULLET	RANGE, YARDS:	0	100	200	300	400
Norma 232 Vulkan	velocity, fps:	2329	2031	1757	1512	
	energy, ft-lb:	2795	2126	1591	1178	
	arc, inches:		+3.5	0	-14.9	
Norma 232 Oryx	velocity, fps:	2362	2058	1778	1528	
	energy, ft-lb:	2875	2182	1630	1203	
	arc, inches:		+3.4	0	-14.5	
Norma 285 Oryx	velocity, fps:	2067	1859	1666	1490	
	energy, ft-lb:	2704	2188	1756	1404	
	arc, inches:		+4.3	0	-16.8	
Norma 286 Alaska	velocity, fps:	2067	1857	1662	1484	
	energy, ft-lb:	2714	2190	1754	1399	
	arc, inches:		+4.3	0	-17.0	

9.3x62

CARTRIDGE BULLET	RANGE, YARDS:	0	100	200	300	400
A-Square 286 Triad	velocity, fps:	2360	2089	1844	1623	1369
	energy, ft-lb:	3538	2771	2157	1670	1189
	arc, inches:		+3.0	0	-13.1	-42.2
Norma 232 Vulkan	velocity, fps:	2625	2327	2049	1792	
	energy, ft-lb:	3551	2791	2164	1655	
	arc, inches:		+2.5	0	-10.8	

BALLISTICS

Centerfire Rifle Ballistics

CARTRIDGE BULLET	RANGE, YARDS:	0	100	200	300	400
Norma 232 Oryx	velocity, fps:	2625	2294	1988	1708	
	energy, ft-lb:	3535	2700	2028	1497	
	arc, inches:		+2.5	0	-11.4	
Norma 250 A-Frame	velocity, fps:	2625	2322	2039	1778	
	energy, ft-lb:	3826	2993	2309	1755	
	arc, inches:		+2.5	0	-10.9	
Norma 286 Plastic Point	velocity, fps:	2362	2141	1931	1736	
	energy, ft-lb:	3544	2911	2370	1914	
	arc, inches:		+3.1	0	-12.4	
Norma 286 Alaska	velocity, fps:	2362	2135	1920	1720	
	energy, ft-lb:	3544	2894	2342	1879	
	arc, inches:		+3.1	0	-12.5	

9.3x64

CARTRIDGE BULLET	RANGE, YARDS:	0	100	200	300	400
A-Square 286 Triad	velocity, fps:	2700	2391	2103	1835	1602
	energy, ft-lb:	4629	3630	2808	2139	1631
	arc, inches:		+2.3	0	-10.1	-30.8

9.3x74 R

CARTRIDGE BULLET	RANGE, YARDS:	0	100	200	300	400
A-Square 286 Triad	velocity, fps:	2360	2089	1844	1623	
	energy, ft-lb:	3538	2771	2157	1670	
	arc, inches:		+3.6	0	-14.0	
Hornady 286	velocity, fps:	2360	2136	1924	1727	1545
	energy, ft-lb	3536	2896	2351	1893	1516
	arc, inches	-1.5	0	-6.1	-21.7	-49.0
Norma 232 Vulkan	velocity, fps:	2625	2327	2049	1792	
	energy, ft-lb:	3551	2791	2164	1655	
	arc, inches:		+2.5	0	-10.8	
Norma 232 Oryx	velocity, fps:	2526	2191	1883	1605	
	energy, ft-lb:	3274	2463	1819	1322	
	arc, inches:		+2.9	0	-12.8	
Norma 285 Oryx	velocity, fps:	2362	2114	1881	1667	
	energy, ft-lb:	3532	2829	2241	1758	
	arc, inches:		+3.1	0	-13.0	
Norma 286 Alaska	velocity, fps:	2362	2135	1920	1720	
	energy, ft-lb:	3544	2894	2342	1879	
	arc, inches:		+3.1	0	-12.5	
Norma 286 Plastic Point	velocity, fps:	2362	2135	1920	1720	
	energy, ft-lb:	3544	2894	2342	1879	
	arc, inches:		+3.1	0	-12.5	

.375 WINCHESTER

CARTRIDGE BULLET	RANGE, YARDS:	0	100	200	300	400
Win. 200 Power-Point	velocity, fps:	2200	1841	1526	1268	1089
	energy, ft-lb:	2150	1506	1034	714	
	arc, inches:		0	-9.5	-33.8	

.375 H&H MAGNUM

CARTRIDGE BULLET	RANGE, YARDS:	0	100	200	300	400
A-Square 300 SP boat-tail	velocity, fps:	2550	2415	2284	2157	2034
	energy, ft-lb:	4331	3884	3474	3098	2755
	arc, inches:		+5.2	+6.0	0	-13.3
A-Square 300 Triad	velocity, fps:	2550	2251	1973	1717	1496
	energy, ft-lb:	4331	3375	2592	1964	1491
	arc, inches:		+2.7	0	-11.7	-35.1
Federal 250 Trophy Bonded	velocity, fps:	2670	2360	2080	1820	1580
	energy, ft-lb:	3955	3100	2400	1830	1380
	arc, inches:		+2.4	0	-10.4	-31.7
Federal 270 Hi-Shok	velocity, fps:	2690	2420	2170	1920	1700
	energy, ft-lb:	4340	3510	2810	2220	1740
	arc, inches:		+2.4	0	-10.9	-33.3
Federal 300 Hi-Shok	velocity, fps:	2530	2270	2020	1790	1580
	energy, ft-lb:	4265	3425	2720	2135	1665
	arc, inches:		+2.6	0	-11.2	-33.3

CARTRIDGE BULLET	RANGE, YARDS:	0	100	200	300	400
Federal 300 Nosler Partition	velocity, fps:	2530	2320	2120	1930	1750
	energy, ft-lb:	4265	3585	2995	2475	2040
	arc, inches:		+2.5	0	-10.3	-29.9
Federal 300 Trophy Bonded	velocity, fps:	2530	2280	2040	1810	1610
	energy, ft-lb:	4265	3450	2765	2190	1725
	arc, inches:		+2.6	0	-10.9	-32.8
Federal 300 Tr. Bonded HE	velocity, fps:	2700	2440	2190	1960	1740
	energy, ft-lb:	4855	3960	3195	2550	2020
	arc, inches:		+2.2	0	-9.4	-28.0
Federal 300 Trophy Bonded Sledgehammer Solid	velocity, fps:	2530	2160	1820	1520	1280.
	energy, ft-lb:	4265	3105	2210	1550	1090
	arc, inches, s:		0	-6.0	-22.7	-54.6
Hornady 270 SP HM	velocity, fps:	2870	2620	2385	2162	1957
	energy, ft-lb:	4937	4116	3408	2802	2296
	arc, inches:		+2.2	0	-8.4	-23.9
Hornady 300 FMJ RN HM	velocity, fps:	2705	2376	2072	1804	1560
	energy, ft-lb:	4873	3760	2861	2167	1621
	arc, inches:		+2.7	0	-10.8	-32.1
Norma 300 Soft Point	velocity, fps:	2549	2211	1900	1619	
	energy, ft-lb:	4329	3258	2406	1747	
	arc, inches:		+2.8	0	-12.6	
Norma 300 TXP Swift A-Fr.	velocity, fps:	2559	2296	2049	1818	
	energy, ft-lb:	4363	3513	2798	2203	
	arc, inches:		+2.6	0	-10.9	
Norma 300 Oryx	velocity, fps:	2559	2292	2041	1807	
	energy, ft-lb:	4363	3500	2775	2176	
	arc, inches:		+2.6	0	-11.0	
Norma 300 Barnes Solid	velocity, fps:	2493	2061	1677	1356	
	energy, ft-lb:	4141	2829	1873	1234	
	arc, inches:		+3.4	0	-16.0	
PMC 270 PSP	velocity, fps:					
	energy, ft-lb:					
	arc, inches:					
PMC 270 Barnes X	velocity, fps:	2690	2528	2372	2221	2076
	energy, ft-lb:	4337	3831	3371	2957	2582
	arc, inches:		+2.0	0	-8.2	-23.4
PMC 300 Barnes X	velocity, fps:	2530	2389	2252	2120	1993
	energy, ft-lb:	4263	3801	3378	2994	2644
	arc, inches:		+2.3	0	-9.2	-26.1
Rem. 270 Soft Point	velocity, fps:	2690	2420	2166	1928	1707
	energy, ft-lb:	4337	3510	2812	2228	1747
	arc, inches:		+2.2	0	-9.7	-28.7
Rem. 300 Swift A-Frame	velocity, fps:	2530	2245	1979	1733	1512
	energy, ft-lb:	4262	3357	2608	2001	1523
	arc, inches:		+2.7	0	-11.7	-35.0
Speer 285 Grand Slam	velocity, fps:	2610	2365	2134	1916	
	energy, ft-lb:	4310	3540	2883	2323	
	arc, inches:		+2.4	0	-9.9	
Speer 300 African GS Tungsten Solid	velocity, fps:	2609	2277	1970	1690	
	energy, ft-lb:	4534	3453	2585	1903	
	arc, inches:		+2.6	0	-11.7	-35.6
Win. 270 Fail Safe	velocity, fps:	2670	2447	2234	2033	1842
	energy, ft-lb:	4275	3590	2994	2478	2035
	arc, inches:		+2.2	0	-9.1	-28.7
Win. 300 Fail Safe	velocity, fps:	2530	2336	2151	1974	1806
	energy, ft-lb:	4265	3636	3082	2596	2173
	arc, inches:		+2.4	0	-10.0	-26.9

.375 DAKOTA

CARTRIDGE BULLET	RANGE, YARDS:	0	100	200	300	400
Dakota 270 Barnes X	velocity, fps:	2800	2617	2441	2272	2109
	energy, ft-lb:	4699	4104	3571	3093	2666
	arc, inches:		+2.3	+1.0	-6.1	-19.9

BALLISTICS

Centerfire Rifle Ballistics

.375 DAKOTA TO .416 HOFFMAN

CARTRIDGE BULLET	RANGE, YARDS:	0	100	200	300	400
Dakota 300 Barnes X	velocity, fps:	2600	2316	2051	1804	1579
	energy, ft-lb:	4502	3573	2800	2167	1661
	arc, inches:		+2.4	-0.1	-11.0	-32.7

.375 RUGER

Hornady 300 Solid	velocity, fps	2660	2344	2050	1780	1536
	energy, ft-lb	4713	3660	2800	2110	1572
	arc, inches:	-1.5	+2.4	0	-10.8	-32.6

.375 WEATHERBY MAGNUM

A-Square 300 SP boat-tail	velocity, fps:	2700	2560	2425	2293	2166
	energy, ft-lb:	4856	4366	3916	3503	3125
	arc, inches:		+4.5	+5.2	0	-11.9
A-Square 300 Triad	velocity, fps:	2700	2391	2103	1835	1602
	energy, ft-lb:	4856	3808	2946	2243	1710
	arc, inches:		+2.3	0	-10.1	-30.8
Wby. 300 Nosler Part.	velocity, fps:	2800	2572	2366	2140	1963
	energy, ft-lb:	5224	4408	3696	3076	2541
	arc, inches:		+1.9	0	-8.2	-23.9

.375 JRS

A-Square 300 SP boat-tail	velocity, fps:	2700	2560	2425	2293	2166.
	energy, ft-lb:	4856	4366	3916	3503	3125
	arc, inches:		+4.5	+5.2	0	-11.9
A-Square 300 Triad	velocity, fps:	2700	2391	2103	1835	1602
	energy, ft-lb:	4856	3808	2946	2243	1710
	arc, inches:		+2.3	0	-10.1	-30.8

.375 REMINGTON ULTRA MAGNUM

Rem. 270 Soft Point	velocity, fps:	2900	2558	2241	1947	1678
	energy, fps:	5041	3922	3010	2272	1689
	arc, inches:		+1.9	0	-9.2	-27.8
Rem. 300 Swift A-Frame	velocity, fps:	2760	2505	2263	2035	1822
	energy, fps:	5073	4178	3412	2759	2210
	arc, inches:		+2.0	0	-8.8	-26.1

.375 A-SQUARE

A-Square 300 SP boat-tail	velocity, fps:	2920	2773	2631	2494	2360
	energy, ft-lb:	5679	5123	4611	4142	3710
	arc, inches:		+3.7	+4.4	0	-9.8
A-Square 300 Triad	velocity, fps:	2920	2596	2294	2012	1762
	energy, ft-lb:	5679	4488	3505	2698	2068
	arc, inches:		+1.8	0	-8.5	-25.5

.376 STEYR

Hornady 225 SP	velocity, fps:	2600	2331	2078	1842	1625
	energy, ft-lb:	3377	2714	2157	1694	1319
	arc, inches:		+2.5	0	-10.6	-31.4
Hornady 270 SP	velocity, fps:	2600	2372	2156	1951	1759
	energy, ft-lb:	4052	3373	2787	2283	1855
	arc, inches:		+2.3	0	-9.9	-28.9

.378 WEATHERBY MAGNUM

A-Square 300 SP boat-tail	velocity, fps:	2900	2754	2612	2475	2342
	energy, ft-lb:	5602	5051	4546	4081	3655
	arc, inches:		+3.8	+4.4	0	-10.0
A-Square 300 Triad	velocity, fps:	2900	2577	2276	1997	1747
	energy, ft-lb:	5602	4424	3452	2656	2034
	arc, inches:		+1.9	0	-8.7	-25.9
Wby. 270 Pointed Expanding	velocity, fps:	3180	2921	2677	2445	2225
	energy, ft-lb:	6062	5115	4295	3583	2968
	arc, inches:		+1.3	0	-6.1	-18.1

CARTRIDGE BULLET	RANGE, YARDS:	0	100	200	300	400
Wby. 270 Barnes X	velocity, fps:	3150	2954	2767	2587	2415
	energy, ft-lb:	5948	5232	4589	4013	3495
	arc, inches:		+1.2	0	-5.8	-16.7
Wby. 300 RN Expanding	velocity, fps:	2925	2558	2220	1908	1627.
	energy, ft-lb:	5699	4360	3283	2424	1764
	arc, inches:		+1.9	0	-9.0	-27.8
Wby. 300 FMJ	velocity, fps:	2925	2591	2280	1991	1725
	energy, ft-lb:	5699	4470	3461	2640	1983
	arc, inches:		+1.8	0	-8.6	-26.1

.38-40 WINCHESTER

Win. 180 Soft Point	velocity, fps:	1160	999	901	827	
	energy, ft-lb:	538	399	324	273	
	arc, inches:		0	-23.4	-75.2	

.38-55 WINCHESTER

Black Hills 255 FN Lead	velocity, fps:	1250				
	energy, ft-lb:	925				
	arc, inches:					
Win. 255 Soft Point	velocity, fps:	1320	1190	1091	1018	
	energy, ft-lb:	987	802	674	587	
	arc, inches:		0	-33.9	-110.6	

.41 MAGNUM

Win. 240 Platinum Tip	velocity, fps:	1830	1488	1220	1048	
	energy, ft-lb:	1784	1180	792	585	
	arc inches:		0	-15.0	-53.4	

.450/.400 (3")

A-Square 400 Triad	velocity, fps:	2150	1910	1690	1490	
	energy, ft-lb:	4105	3241	2537	1972	
	arc, inches:		+4.4	0	-16.5	

.450/.400 (3 L/4")

A-Square 400 Triad	velocity, fps:	2150	1910	1690	1490	
	energy, ft-lb:	4105	3241	2537	1972	
	arc, inches:		+4.4	0	-16.5	

.450/.400 NITRO EXPRESS

Hornady 400 RN	velocity, fps	2050	1815	1595	1402	
	energy, ft-lb	3732	2924	2259	1746	
	arc, inches:	-1.5	0	-10.0	-33.4	

.404 JEFFERY

A-Square 400 Triad	velocity, fps:	2150	1901	1674	1468	1299
	energy, ft-lb:	4105	3211	2489	1915	1499
	arc, inches:		+4.1	0	-16.4	-49.1

.405 WINCHESTER

Hornady 300 Flatpoint	velocity, fps:	2200	1851	1545	1296	
	energy, ft-lb:	3224	2282	1589	1119	
	arc, inches:		0	-8.7	-31.9	
Hornady 300 SP Interlock	velocity, fps:	2200	1890	1610	1370	
	energy, ft-lb:	3224	2379	1727	1250	
	arc, inches:		0	-8.3	-30.2	

.416 TAYLOR

A-Square 400 Triad	velocity, fps:	2350	2093	1853	1634	1443
	energy, ft-lb:	4905	3892	3049	2371	1849
	arc, inches:		+3.2	0	-13.6	-39.8

.416 HOFFMAN

A-Square 400 Triad	velocity, fps:	2380	2122	1879	1658	1464
	energy, ft-lb:	5031	3998	3136	2440	1903
	arc, inches:		+3.1	0	-13.1	-38.7

.416 REMINGTON MAGNUM

CARTRIDGE BULLET	RANGE, YARDS:	0	100	200	300	400
A-Square 400 Triad	velocity, fps:	2380	2122	1879	1658	1464
	energy, ft-lb:	5031	3998	3136	2440	1903
	arc, inches:		+3.1	0	-13.2	-38.7
Federal 400 Trophy Bonded	velocity, fps:	2400	2150	1920	1700	1500
Sledgehammer Solid	energy, ft-lb:	5115	4110	3260	2565	2005
	arc, inches:		0	-6.0	-21.6	-49.2
Federal 400 Trophy Bonded	velocity, fps:	2400	2180	1970	1770	1590
	energy, ft-lb:	5115	4215	3440	2785	2245
	arc, inches:		0	-5.8	-20.6	-46.9
Rem. 400 Swift A-Frame	velocity, fps:	2400	2175	1962	1763	1579
	energy, ft-lb:	5115	4201	3419	2760	2214
	arc, inches:		0	-5.9	-20.8	

.416 RIGBY

CARTRIDGE BULLET	RANGE, YARDS:	0	100	200	300	400
A-Square 400 Triad	velocity, fps:	2400	2140	1897	1673	1478
	energy, ft-lb:	5115	4069	3194	2487	1940
	arc, inches:		+3.0	0	-12.9	-38.0
Federal 400 Trophy Bonded	velocity, fps:	2370	2150	1940	1750	1570
	energy, ft-lb:	4990	4110	3350	2715	2190
	arc, inches:		0	-6.0	-21.3	-48.1
Federal 400 Trophy Bonded	velocity, fps:	2370	2120	1890	1660	1460
Sledgehammer Solid	energy, ft-lb:	4990	3975	3130	2440	1895
	arc, inches:		0	-6.3	-22.5	-51.5
Federal 410 Woodleigh	velocity, fps:	2370	2110	1870	1640	1440
Weldcore	energy, ft-lb:	5115	4050	3165	2455	1895
	arc, inches:		0	-7.4	-24.8	-55.0
Federal 410 Solid	velocity, fps:	2370	2110	2870	1640	1440
	energy, ft-lb:	5115	4050	3165	2455	1895
	arc, inches:		0	-7.4	-24.8	-55.0
Norma 400 TXP Swift A-Fr.	velocity, fps:	2350	2127	1917	1721	
	energy, ft-lb:	4906	4021	3266	2632	
	arc, inches:		+3.1	0	-12.5	
Norma 400 Barnes Solid	velocity, fps:	2297	1930	1604	1330	
	energy, ft-lb:	4687	3310	2284	1571	
	arc, inches:		+3.9	0	-17.7	

.416 RIMMED

CARTRIDGE BULLET	RANGE, YARDS:	0	100	200	300	400
A-Square 400 Triad	velocity, fps:	2400	2140	1897	1673	
	energy, ft-lb:	5115	4069	3194	2487	
	arc, inches:		+3.3	0	-13.2	

.416 DAKOTA

CARTRIDGE BULLET	RANGE, YARDS:	0	100	200	300	400
Dakota 400 Barnes X	velocity, fps:	2450	2294	2143	1998	1859
	energy, ft-lb:	5330	4671	4077	3544	3068
	arc, inches:		+2.5	-0.2	-10.5	-29.4

.416 WEATHERBY

CARTRIDGE BULLET	RANGE, YARDS:	0	100	200	300	400
A-Square 400 Triad	velocity, fps:	2600	2328	2073	1834	1624
	energy, ft-lb:	6004	4813	3816	2986	2343
	arc, inches:		+2.5	0	-10.5	-31.6
Wby. 350 Barnes X	velocity, fps:	2850	2673	2503	2340	2182
	energy, ft-lb:	6312	5553	4870	4253	3700
	arc, inches:		+1.7	0	-7.2	-20.9
Wby. 400 Swift A-Fr.	velocity, fps:	2650	2426	2213	2011	1820
	energy, ft-lb:	6237	5227	4350	3592	2941
	arc, inches:		+2.2	0	-9.3	-27.1
Wby. 400 RN Expanding	velocity, fps:	2700	2417	2152	1903	1676
	energy, ft-lb:	6474	5189	4113	3216	2493
	arc, inches:		+2.3	0	-9.7	-29.3
Wby. 400 Monolithic Solid	velocity, fps:	2700	2411	2140	1887	1656
	energy, ft-lb:	6474	5162	4068	3161	2435
	arc, inches:		+2.3	0	-9.8	-29.7

10.57 (.416) METEOR

CARTRIDGE BULLET	RANGE, YARDS:	0	100	200	300	400
Lazzeroni 400 Swift A-Fr.	velocity, fps:	2730	2532	2342	2161	1987
	energy, ft-lb:	6621	5695	4874	4147	3508
	arc, inches:		+1.9	0	-8.3	-24.0

.425 EXPRESS

CARTRIDGE BULLET	RANGE, YARDS:	0	100	200	300	400
A-Square 400 Triad	velocity, fps:	2400	2136	1888	1662	1465
	energy, ft-lb:	5115	4052	3167	2454	1906
	arc, inches:		+3.0	0	-13.1	-38.3

.44-40 WINCHESTER

CARTRIDGE BULLET	RANGE, YARDS:	0	100	200	300	400
Rem. 200 Soft Point	velocity, fps:	1190	1006	900	822	756
	energy, ft-lb:	629	449	360	300	254
	arc, inches:		0	-33.1	-108.7	-235.2
Win. 200 Soft Point	velocity, fps:	1190	1006	900	822	756
	energy, ft-lb:	629	449	360	300	254
	arc, inches:		0	-33.3	-109.5	-237.4

.44 REMINGTON MAGNUM

CARTRIDGE BULLET	RANGE, YARDS:	0	100	200	300	400
Federal 240 Hi-Shok HP	velocity, fps:	1760	1380	1090	950	860
	energy, ft-lb:	1650	1015	640	485	395
	arc, inches:		0	-17.4	-60.7	-136.0
Rem. 210 Semi-Jacketed HP	velocity, fps:	1920	1477	1155	982	880
	energy, ft-lb:	1719	1017	622	450	361
	arc, inches:		0	-14.7	-55.5	-131.3
Rem. 240 Soft Point	velocity, fps:	1760	1380	1114	970	878
	energy, ft-lb:	1650	1015	661	501	411
	arc, inches:		0	-17.0	-61.4	-143.0
Rem. 240 Semi-Jacketed	velocity, fps:	1760	1380	1114	970	878
Hollow Point	energy, ft-lb:	1650	1015	661	501	411
	arc, inches:		0	-17.0	-61.4	-143.0
Rem. 275 JHP Core-Lokt	velocity, fps:	1580	1293	1093	976	896
	energy, ft-lb:	1524	1020	730	582	490
	arc, inches:		0	-19.4	-67.5	-210.8
Win. 210 Silvertip HP	velocity, fps:	1580	1198	993	879	795
	energy, ft-lb:	1164	670	460	361	295
	arc, inches:		0	-22.4	-76.1	-168.0
Win. 240 Hollow Soft Point	velocity, fps:	1760	1362	1094	953	861
	energy, ft-lb:	1650	988	638	484	395
	arc, inches:		0	-18.1	-65.1	-150.3
Win. 250 Platinum Tip	velocity, fps:	1830	1475	1201	1032	931
	energy, ft-lb:	1859	1208	801	591	481
	arc, inches:		0	-15.3	-54.7	-126.6.

.444 MARLIN

CARTRIDGE BULLET	RANGE, YARDS:	0	100	200	300	400
Rem. 240 Soft Point	velocity, fps:	2350	1815	1377	1087	941
	energy, ft-lb:	2942	1755	1010	630	472
	arc, inches:		+2.2	-5.4	-31.4	-86.7
Hornady 265 Evolution	velocity, fps:	2325	1971	1652	1380	
	energy, ft-lb:	3180	2285	1606	1120	
	arc, inches:		+3.0	-1.4	-18.6	
Hornady 265 FP LM	velocity, fps:	2335	1913	1551	1266	
	energy, ft-lb:	3208	2153	1415	943	
	arc, inches:		+ 2.0	-4.9	-26.5	

.45-70 GOVERNMENT

CARTRIDGE BULLET	RANGE, YARDS:	0	100	200	300	400
Black Hills 405 FPL	velocity, fps:	1250				
	energy, ft-lb:					
	arc, inches:					
Federal 300 Sierra Pro-Hunt.	velocity, fps:	1880	1650	1430	1240	1110
HP FN	energy, ft-lb:	2355	1815	1355	1015	810
	arc, inches:		0	-11.5	-39.7	-89.1
PMC 350 FNSP	velocity, fps:					
	energy, ft-lb:					
	arc, inches:					

BALLISTICS

Centerfire Rifle Ballistics

.45-70 GOVERNMENT TO .500/.465

CARTRIDGE BULLET	RANGE, YARDS:	0	100	200	300	400
Rem. 300 Jacketed HP	velocity, fps	1810	1497	1244	1073	969
	energy, ft-lb	2182	1492	1031	767	625
	arc, inches:		0	-13.8	-50.1	-115.7
Rem. 405 Soft Point	velocity, fps	1330	1168	1055	977	918
	energy, ft-lb	1590	1227	1001	858	758
	arc, inches:		0	-24.0	-78.6	-169.4
Win. 300 Jacketed HP	velocity, fps	1880	1650	1425	1235	1105
	energy, ft-lb	2355	1815	1355	1015	810
	arc, inches:		0	-12.8	-44.3	-95.5
Win. 300 Partition Gold	velocity, fps	1880	1558	1292	1103	988
	energy, ft-lb	2355	1616	1112	811	651
	arc, inches:		0	-12.9	-46.0	-104.9.

.450 BUSHMASTER

CARTRIDGE BULLET	RANGE, YARDS:	0	100	200	300	400
Hornady 250 SST-ML	velocity, fps	2200	1840	1524	1268	
	energy, ft-lb	2686	1879	1289	893	
	arc, inches	-2.0	+2.5	-3.5	-24.5	

.450 MARLIN

CARTRIDGE BULLET	RANGE, YARDS:	0	100	200	300	400
Hornady 350 FP	velocity, fps	2100	1720	1397	1156	
	energy, ft-lb	3427	2298	1516	1039	
	arc, inches:		0	-10.4	-38.9	

.450 NITRO EXPRESS (3¼")

CARTRIDGE BULLET	RANGE, YARDS:	0	100	200	300	400
A-Square 465 Triad	velocity, fps	2190	1970	1765	1577	
	energy, ft-lb	4952	4009	3216	2567	
	arc, inches:		+4.3	0	-15.4	

.450 #2

CARTRIDGE BULLET	RANGE, YARDS:	0	100	200	300	400
A-Square 465 Triad	velocity, fps	2190	1970	1765	1577	
	energy, ft-lb	4952	4009	3216	2567	
	arc, inches:		+4.3	0	-15.4	

.458 WINCHESTER MAGNUM

CARTRIDGE BULLET	RANGE, YARDS:	0	100	200	300	400
A-Square 465 Triad	velocity, fps	2220	1999	1791	1601	1433
	energy, ft-lb	5088	4127	3312	2646	2121
	arc, inches:		+3.6	0	-14.7	-42.5
Federal 350 Soft Point	velocity, fps	2470	1990	1570	1250	1060
	energy, ft-lb	4740	3065	1915	1205	870
	arc, inches:		0	-7.5	-29.1	-71.1
Federal 400 Trophy Bonded	velocity, fps	2380	2170	1960	1770	1590
	energy, ft-lb	5030	4165	3415	2785	2255
	arc, inches:		0	-5.9	-20.9	-47.1
Federal 500 Solid	velocity, fps	2090	1870	1670	1480	1320
	energy, ft-lb	4850	3880	3085	2440	1945
	arc, inches:		0	-8.5	-29.5	-66.2
Federal 500 Trophy Bonded	velocity, fps	2090	1870	1660	1480	1310
	energy, ft-lb	4850	3870	3065	2420	1915
	arc, inches:		0	-8.5	-29.7	-66.8
Federal 500 Trophy Bonded Sledgehammer Solid	velocity, fps	2090	1860	1650	1460	1300
	energy, ft-lb	4850	3845	3025	2365	1865
	arc, inches:		0	-8.6	-30.0	-67.8
Federal 510 Soft Point	velocity, fps	2090	1820	1570	1360	1190
	energy, ft-lb	4945	3730	2790	2080	1605
	arc, inches:		0	-9.1	-32.3	-73.9
Hornady 500 FMJ-RN HM	velocity, fps	2260	1984	1735	1512	
	energy, ft-lb	5670	4368	3341	2538	
	arc, inches:		0	-7.4	-26.4	
Norma 500 TXP Swift A-Fr.	velocity, fps	2116	1903	1705	1524	
	energy, ft-lb	4972	4023	3228	2578	
	arc, inches:		+4.1	0	-16.1	
Norma 500 Barnes Solid	velocity, fps	2067	1750	1472	1245	
	energy, ft-lb	4745	3401	2405	1721	
	arc, inches:		+4.9	0	-21.2	

CARTRIDGE BULLET	RANGE, YARDS:	0	100	200	300	400
Rem. 450 Swift A-Frame PSP	velocity, fps	2150	1901	1671	1465	1289
	energy, ft-lb	4618	3609	2789	2144	1659
	arc, inches:		0	-8.2	-28.9	
Speer 500 African GS Tungsten Solid	velocity, fps	2120	1845	1596	1379	
	energy, ft-lb	4989	3780	2828	2111	
	arc, inches:		0	-8.8	-31.3	
Speer African Grand Slam	velocity, fps	2120	1853	1609	1396	
	energy, ft-lb	4989	3810	2875	2163	
	arc, inches:		0	-8.7	-30.8	
Win. 510 Soft Point	velocity, fps	2040	1770	1527	1319	1157
	energy, ft-lb	4712	3547	2640	1970	1516
	arc, inches:		0	-10.3	-35.6	

.458 LOTT

CARTRIDGE BULLET	RANGE, YARDS:	0	100	200	300	400
A-Square 465 Triad	velocity, fps	2380	2150	1932	1730	1551
	energy, ft-lb	5848	4773	3855	3091	2485
	arc, inches:		+3.0	0	-12.5	-36.4
Hornady 500 RNSP or solid	velocity, fps	2300	2022	1776	1551	
	energy, ft-lb	5872	4537	3502	2671	
	arc, inches:		+3.4	0	-14.3	
Hornady 500 InterBond	velocity, fps	2300	2028	1777	1549	
	energy, ft-lb	5872	4535	3453	2604	
	arc, inches:		0	-7.0	-25.1	

.450 ACKLEY

CARTRIDGE BULLET	RANGE, YARDS:	0	100	200	300	400
A-Square 465 Triad	velocity, fps	2400	2169	1950	1747	1567
	energy, ft-lb	5947	4857	3927	3150	2534
	arc, inches:		+2.9	0	-12.2	-35.8

.460 SHORT A-SQUARE

CARTRIDGE BULLET	RANGE, YARDS:	0	100	200	300	400
A-Square 500 Triad	velocity, fps	2420	2198	1987	1789	1613
	energy, ft-lb	6501	5362	4385	3553	2890
	arc, inches:		+2.9	0	-11.6	-34.2

.450 DAKOTA

CARTRIDGE BULLET	RANGE, YARDS:	0	100	200	300	400
Dakota 500 Barnes Solid	velocity, fps	2450	2235	2030	1838	1658
	energy, ft-lb	6663	5544	4576	3748	3051
	arc, inches:		+2.5	-0.6	-12.0	-33.8

.460 WEATHERBY MAGNUM

CARTRIDGE BULLET	RANGE, YARDS:	0	100	200	300	400
A-Square 500 Triad	velocity, fps	2580	2349	2131	1923	1737
	energy, ft-lb	7389	6126	5040	4107	3351
	arc, inches:		+2.4	0	-10.0	-29.4
Wby. 450 Barnes X	velocity, fps	2700	2518	2343	2175	2013
	energy, ft-lb	7284	6333	5482	4725	4050
	arc, inches:		+2.0	0	-8.4	-24.1
Wby. 500 RN Expanding	velocity, fps	2600	2301	2022	1764	1533.
	energy, ft-lb	7504	5877	4539	3456	2608
	arc, inches:		+2.6	0	-11.1	-33.5
Wby. 500 FMJ	velocity, fps	2600	2309	2037	1784	1557
	energy, ft-lb	7504	5917	4605	3534	2690
	arc, inches:		+2.5	0	-10.9	-33.0

.500/.465

CARTRIDGE BULLET	RANGE, YARDS:	0	100	200	300	400
A-Square 480 Triad	velocity, fps	2150	1928	1722	1533	
	energy, ft-lb	4926	3960	3160	2505	
	arc, inches:		+4.3	0	-16.0	

Centerfire Rifle Ballistics

.470 NITRO EXPRESS TO .700 NITRO EXPRESS

CARTRIDGE BULLET	RANGE, YARDS:	0	100	200	300	400
.470 NITRO EXPRESS						
A-Square 500 Triad	velocity, fps:	2150	1912	1693	1494	
	energy, ft-lb:	5132	4058	3182	2478	
	arc, inches:		+4.4	0	-16.5	
Federal 500 Woodleigh Weldcore	velocity, fps:	2150	1890	1650	1440	1270
	energy, ft-lb:	5130	3965	3040	2310	1790
	arc, inches:		0	-9.3	-31.3	-69.7
Federal 500 Woodleigh Weldcore Solid	velocity, fps:	2150	1890	1650	1440	1270.
	energy, ft-lb:	5130	3965	3040	2310	1790
	arc, inches:		0	-9.3	-31.3	-69.7
Federal 500 Trophy Bonded	velocity, fps:	2150	1940	1740	1560	1400
	energy, ft-lb:	5130	4170	3360	2695	2160
	arc, inches:		0	-7.8	-27.1	-60.8
Federal 500 Trophy Bonded Sledgehammer Solid	velocity, fps:	2150	1940	1740	1560	1400
	energy, ft-lb:	5130	4170	3360	2695	2160
	arc, inches:		0	-7.8	-27.1	-60.8
Norma 500 Woodleigh SP	velocity, fps:	2165	1975	1795	1627	
	energy, ft-lb:	5205	4330	3577	2940	
	arc, inches:		0	-7.4	-25.7	
Norma 500 Woodleigh FJ	velocity, fps:	2165	1974	1794	1626	
	energy, ft-lb:	5205	4328	3574	2936	
	arc, inches:		0	-7.5	-25.7	
.470 CAPSTICK						
A-Square 500 Triad	velocity, fps:	2400	2172	1958	1761	1553
	energy, ft-lb:	6394	5236	4255	3445	2678
	arc, inches:		+2.9	0	-11.9	-36.1
.475 #2						
A-Square 480 Triad	velocity, fps:	2200	1964	1744	1544	
	energy, ft-lb:	5158	4109	3240	2539	
	arc, inches:		+4.1	0	-15.6	
.475 #2 JEFFERY						
A-Square 500 Triad	velocity, fps:	2200	1966	1748	1550	
	energy, ft-lb:	5373	4291	3392	2666	
	arc, inches:		+4.1	0	-15.6	

CARTRIDGE BULLET	RANGE, YARDS:	0	100	200	300	400
.495 A-SQUARE						
A-Square 570 Triad	velocity, fps:	2350	2117	1896	1693	1513
	energy, ft-lb:	6989	5671	4552	3629	2899
	arc, inches:		+3.1	0	-13.0	-37.8
.500 NITRO EXPRESS (3")						
A-Square 570 Triad	velocity, fps:	2150	1928	1722	1533	
	energy, ft-lb:	5850	4703	3752	2975	
	arc, inches:		+4.3	0	-16.1	
.500 A-SQUARE						
A-Square 600 Triad	velocity, fps:	2470	2235	2013	1804	1620
	energy, ft-lb:	8127	6654	5397	4336	3495
	arc, inches:		+2.7	0	-11.3	-33.5
.505 GIBBS						
A-Square 525 Triad	velocity, fps:	2300	2063	1840	1637	
	energy, ft-lb:	6166	4962	3948	3122	
	arc, inches:		+3.6	0	-14.2	
.577 NITRO EXPRESS						
A-Square 750 Triad	velocity, fps:	2050	1811	1595	1401	
	energy, ft-lb:	6998	5463	4234	3267	
	arc, inches:		+4.9	0	-18.5	
.577 TYRANNOSAUR						
A-Square 750 Triad	velocity, fps:	2460	2197	1950	1723	1516
	energy, ft-lb:	10077	8039	6335	4941	3825
	arc, inches:		+2.8	0	-12.1	-36.0
.600 NITRO EXPRESS						
A-Square 900 Triad	velocity, fps:	1950	1680	1452	1336	
	energy, ft-lb:	7596	5634	4212	3564	
	arc, inches:		+5.6	0	-20.7	
.700 NITRO EXPRESS						
A-Square 1000 Monolithic Solid	velocity, fps:	1900	1669	1461	1288	
	energy, ft-lb:	8015	6188	4740	3685	
	arc, inches:		+5.8	0	-22.2	

BALLISTICS

Centerfire Handgun Ballistics

Data shown here is taken from manufacturers' charts; your chronograph readings may vary. Barrel lengths for pistol data vary, and depend in part on which pistols are typically chambered in a given cartridge. Velocity variations due to barrel length depend on the baseline bullet speed and the load. Velocity for the .30 Carbine, normally a rifle cartridge, was determined in a pistol barrel.

Listings are current as of February the year *Shooter's Bible* appears (not the cover year). Listings are not intended as recommendations. For example, the data for the .25 Auto gives velocity and energy readings to 100 yards. Few handgunners would call the little .25 a 100-yard cartridge.

Abbreviations: Bullets are designated by loading company, weight (in grains) and type, with these abbreviations for shape and construction: BJHP=brass-jacketed hollowpoint; FN=Flat Nose; FMC=Full Metal Case; FMJ=Full Metal Jacket; HP=Hollowpoint; L=Lead; LF=Lead-Free; +P=a more powerful load than traditionally manufactured for that round; RN=Round Nose; SFHP=Starfire (PMC) Hollowpoint; SP=Softpoint; SWC=Semi Wadcutter; TMJ=Total Metal Jacket; WC=Wadcutter; CEPP, SXT and XTP are trademarked designations of Lapua, Winchester and Hornady, respectively.

.25 AUTO TO .32 S&W LONG

CARTRIDGE BULLET	RANGE, YARDS:	0	25	50	75	100
.25 AUTO						
Federal 50 FMJ	velocity, fps:	760	750	730	720	700
	energy, ft-lb:	65	60	60	55	55
Hornady 35 JHP/XTP	velocity, fps:	900		813		742
	energy, ft-lb:	63		51		43
Magtech 50 FMC	velocity, fps:	760		707		659
	energy, ft-lb:	64		56		48
PMC 50 FMJ	velocity, fps:	754	730	707	685	663
	energy, ft-lb:	62				
Rem. 50 Metal Case	velocity, fps:	760		707		659
	energy, ft-lb:	64		56		48
Speer 35 Gold Dot	velocity, fps:	900		816		747
	energy, ft-lb:	63		52		43
Speer 50 TMJ (and Blazer)	velocity, fps:	760		717		677
	energy, ft-lb:	64		57		51
Win. 45 Expanding Point	velocity, fps:	815		729		655
	energy, ft-lb	66		53		42
Win. 50 FMJ	velocity, fps:	760		707		
	energy, ft-lb	64		56		
.30 LUGER						
Win. 93 FMJ	velocity, fps:	1220		1110		1040
	energy, ft-lb	305		255		225
7.62x25 TOKAREV						
PMC 93 FMJ	velocity and energy figures not available					
.30 CARBINE						
Win. 110 Hollow SP	velocity, fps:	1790		1601		1430
	energy, ft-lb	783		626		500
.32 AUTO						
Federal 65 Hydra-Shok JHP	velocity, fps:	950	920	890	860	830
	energy, ft-lb:	130	120	115	105	100
Federal 71 FMJ	velocity, fps:	910	880	860	830	810
	energy, ft-lb:	130	120	115	110	105
Hornady 60 JHP/XTP	velocity, fps:	1000		917		849
	energy, ft-lb:	133		112		96
Hornady 71 FMJ-RN	velocity, fps:	900		845		797
	energy, ft-lb:	128		112		100

CARTRIDGE BULLET	RANGE, YARDS:	0	25	50	75	100
Magtech 71 FMC	velocity, fps:	905		855		810
	energy, ft-lb:	129		115		103
Magtech 71 JHP	velocity, fps:	905		855		810
	energy, ft-lb:	129		115		103
PMC 60 JHP	velocity, fps:	980	849	820	791	763
	energy, ft-lb:	117				
PMC 70 SFHP	velocity, fps:	velocity and energy figures not available				
PMC 71 FMJ	velocity, fps:	870	841	814	791	763
	energy, ft-lb:	119				
Rem. 71 Metal Case	velocity, fps:	905		855		810
	energy, ft-lb:	129		115		97
Speer 60 Gold Dot	velocity, fps:	960		868		796
	energy, ft-lb:	123		100		84
Speer 71 TMJ (and Blazer)	velocity, fps:	900		855		810
	energy, ft-lb:	129		115		97
Win. 60 Silvertip HP	velocity, fps:	970		895		835
	energy, ft-lb	125		107		93
Win. 71 FMJ	velocity, fps:	905		855		
	energy, ft-lb	129		115		
.32 S&W						
Rem. 88 LRN	velocity, fps:	680		645		610
	energy, ft-lb:	90		81		73
Win. 85 LRN	velocity, fps:	680		645		610
	energy, ft-lb	90		81		73
.32 S&W LONG						
Federal 98 LWC	velocity, fps:	780	700	630	560	500
	energy, ft-lb:	130	105	85	70	55
Federal 98 LRN	velocity, fps:	710	690	670	650	640
	energy, ft-lb:	115	105	100	95	90
Lapua 83 LWC	velocity, fps:	240		189*		149*
	energy, ft-lb:	154		95*		59*
Lapua 98 LWC	velocity, fps:	240		202*		171*
	energy, ft-lb:	183		130*		93*
Magtech 98 LRN	velocity, fps:	705		670		635
	energy, ft-lb:	108		98		88
Magtech 98 LWC	velocity, fps:	682		579		491
	energy, ft-lb:	102		73		52
Norma 98 LWC	velocity, fps:	787	759	732		683
	energy, ft-lb:	136	126	118		102

Centerfire Handgun Ballistics

CARTRIDGE BULLET	RANGE, YARDS:	0	25	50	75	100
PMC 98 LRN	velocity, fps:	789	770	751	733	716
	energy, ft-lb:	135				
PMC 100 LWC	velocity, fps:	683	652	623	595	569
	energy, ft-lb:	102				
Rem. 98 LRN	velocity, fps:	705		670		635
	energy, ft-lb:	115		98		88
Win. 98 LRN	velocity, fps:	705		670		635
	energy, ft-lb:	115		98		88

.32 Short Colt

CARTRIDGE BULLET	RANGE, YARDS:	0	25	50	75	100
Win. 80 LRN	velocity, fps:	745		665		590
	energy, ft-lb	100		79		62

.32-20

CARTRIDGE BULLET	RANGE, YARDS:	0	25	50	75	100
Black Hills 115 FPL	velocity, fps:	800				
	energy, ft-lb:					

.32 H&R Mag

CARTRIDGE BULLET	RANGE, YARDS:	0	25	50	75	100
Black Hills 85 JHP	velocity, fps	1100				
	energy, ft-lb	228				
Black Hills 90 FPL	velocity, fps	750				
	energy, ft-lb					
Black Hills 115 FPL	velocity, fps	800				
	energy, ft-lb					
Federal 85 Hi-Shok JHP	velocity, fps:	1100	1050	1020	970	930
	energy, ft-lb:	230	210	195	175	165
Federal 95 LSWC	velocity, fps:	1030	1000	940	930	900
	energy, ft-lb:	225	210	195	185	170

9mm Makarov

CARTRIDGE BULLET	RANGE, YARDS:	0	25	50	75	100
Federal 90 Hi-Shok JHP	velocity, fps:	990	950	910	880	850
	energy, ft-lb:	195	180	165	155	145
Federal 90 FMJ	velocity, fps:	990	960	920	900	870
	energy, ft-lb:	205	190	180	170	160
Hornady 95 JHP/XTP	velocity, fps:	1000		930		874
	energy, ft-lb:	211		182		161
PMC 100 FMJ-TC	velocity, fps:	velocity and energy figures not available				
Speer 95 TMJ Blazer	velocity, fps:	1000		928		872
	energy, ft-lb:	211		182		161

9x21 IMI

CARTRIDGE BULLET	RANGE, YARDS:	0	25	50	75	100
PMC 123 FMJ	velocity, fps:	1150	1093	1046	1007	973
	energy, ft-lb:	364				

9mm Luger

CARTRIDGE BULLET	RANGE, YARDS:	0	25	50	75	100
Black Hills 115 JHP	velocity, fps:	1150				
	energy, ft-lb:	336				
Black Hills 115 FMJ	velocity, fps:	1150				
	energy, ft-lb:	336				
Black Hills 115 JHP +P	velocity, fps:	1300				
	energy, ft-lb:	431				
Black Hills 115 EXP JHP	velocity, fps:	1250				
	energy, ft-lb:	400				
Black Hills 124 JHP +P	velocity, fps:	1250				
	energy, ft-lb:	430				
Black Hills 124 JHP	velocity, fps:	1150				
	energy, ft-lb:	363				
Black Hills 124 FMJ	velocity, fps:	1150				
	energy, ft-lb:	363				
Black Hills 147 JHP subsonic	velocity, fps:	975				
	energy, ft-lb:	309				
Black Hills 147 FMJ subsonic	velocity, fps:	975				
	energy, ft-lb:	309				
Federal 105 EFMJ	velocity, fps:	1225	1160	1105	1060	1025
	energy, ft-lb:	350	315	285	265	245

CARTRIDGE BULLET	RANGE, YARDS:	0	25	50	75	100
Federal 115 Hi-Shok JHP	velocity, fps:	1160	1100	1060	1020	990
	energy, ft-lb:	345	310	285	270	250
Federal 115 FMJ	velocity, fps:	1160	1100	1060	1020	990
	energy, ft-lb:	345	310	285	270	250
Federal 124 FMJ	velocity, fps:	1120	1070	1030	990	960
	energy, ft-lb:	345	315	290	270	255
Federal 124 Hydra-Shok JHP	velocity, fps:	1120	1070	1030	990	960
	energy, ft-lb:	345	315	290	270	255
Federal 124 TMJ TMF Primer	velocity, fps:	1120	1070	1030	990	960
	energy, ft-lb:	345	315	290	270	255
Federal 124 Truncated FMJ Match	velocity, fps:	1120	1070	1030	990	960
	energy, ft-lb:	345	315	290	270	255
Federal 124 Nyclad HP	velocity, fps:	1120	1070	1030	990	960
	energy, ft-lb:	345	315	290	270	255
Federal 124 FMJ +P	velocity, fps:	1120	1070	1030	990	960
	energy, ft-lb:	345	315	290	270	255
Federal 135 Hydra-Shok JHP	velocity, fps:	1050	1030	1010	980	970
	energy, ft-lb:	330	315	300	290	280
Federal 147 Hydra-Shok JHP	velocity, fps:	1000	960	920	890	860
	energy, ft-lb:	325	300	275	260	240
Federal 147 Hi-Shok JHP	velocity, fps:	980	950	930	900	880
	energy, ft-lb:	310	295	285	265	255
Federal 147 FMJ FN	velocity, fps:	960	930	910	890	870
	energy, ft-lb:	295	280	270	260	250
Federal 147 TMJ TMF Primer	velocity, fps:	960	940	910	890	870
	energy, ft-lb:	300	285	270	260	245
Hornady 115 JHP/XTP	velocity, fps:	1155		1047		971
	energy, ft-lb:	341		280		241
Hornady 124 JHP/XTP	velocity, fps:	1110		1030		971
	energy, ft-lb:	339		292		259
Hornady 124 TAP-FPD	velocity, fps:	1100		1028		967
	energy, ft-lb:	339		291		257
Hornady 147 JHP/XTP	velocity, fps:	975		935		899
	energy, ft-lb:	310		285		264
Hornady 147 TAP-FPD	velocity, fps:	975		935		899
	energy, ft-lb:	310		285		264
Lapua 116 FMJ	velocity, fps:	365		319*		290*
	energy, ft-lb:	500		381*		315*
Lapua 120 FMJ CEPP Super	velocity, fps:	360		316*		288*
	energy, ft-lb:	505		390*		324*
Lapua 120 FMJ CEPP Extra	velocity, fps:	360		316*		288*
	energy, ft-lb:	505		390*		324*
Lapua 123 HP Megashock	velocity, fps:	355		311*		284*
	energy, ft-lb:	504		388*		322*
Lapua 123 FMJ	velocity, fps:	320		292*		272*
	energy, ft-lb:	410		342*		295*
Lapua 123 FMJ Combat	velocity, fps:	355		315*		289*
	energy, ft-lb:	504		397*		333*
Magtech 115 JHP +P	velocity, fps:	1246		1137		1056
	energy, ft-lb:	397		330		285
Magtech 115 FMC	velocity, fps:	1135		1027		961
	energy, ft-lb:	330		270		235
Magtech 115 JHP	velocity, fps:	1155		1047		971
	energy, ft-lb:	340		280		240
Magtech 124 FMC	velocity, fps:	1109		1030		971
	energy, ft-lb:	339		292		259
Norma 84 Lead Free Frangible (Geco brand)	velocity, fps:	1411				
	energy, ft-lb:	371				
Norma 124 FMJ (Geco brand)	velocity, fps:	1120				
	energy, fps:	341				
Norma 123 FMJ	velocity, fps:	1099	1032	980		899
	energy, ft-lb:	331	292	263		221

BALLISTICS

Centerfire Handgun Ballistics

9MM LUGER TO .380 AUTO

CARTRIDGE BULLET	RANGE, YARDS:	0	25	50	75	100
Norma 123 FMJ	velocity, fps:	1280	1170	1086		972
	energy, ft-lb:	449	375	323		259
PMC 75 Non-Toxic Frangible	velocity, fps:	1350	1240	1154	1088	1035
	energy, ft-lb:	303				
PMC 95 SFHP	velocity, fps:	1250	1239	1228	1217	1207
	energy, ft-lb:	330				
PMC 115 FMJ	velocity, fps:	1157	1100	1053	1013	979
	energy, ft-lb:	344				
PMC 115 JHP	velocity, fps:	1167	1098	1044	999	961
	energy, ft-lb:	350				
PMC 124 SFHP	velocity, fps:	1090	1043	1003	969	939
	energy, ft-lb:	327				
PMC 124 FMJ	velocity, fps:	1110	1059	1017	980	949
	energy, ft-lb:	339				
PMC 124 LRN	velocity, fps:	1050	1006	969	937	908
	energy, ft-lb:	304				
PMC 147 FMJ	velocity, fps:	980	965	941	919	900
	enerby, ft-lb:	310				
PMC 147 SFHP	velocity, fps:	velocity and energy figures not available				
Rem. 101 Lead Free Frangible	velocity, fps:	1220		1092		1004
	energy, ft-lb:	334		267		226
Rem. 115 FN Enclosed Base	velocity, fps:	1135		1041		973
	energy, ft-lb:	329		277		242
Rem. 115 Metal Case	velocity, fps:	1135		1041		973
	energy, ft-lb:	329		277		242
Rem. 115 JHP	velocity, fps:	1155		1047		971
	energy, ft-lb:	341		280		241
Rem. 115 JHP +P	velocity, fps:	1250		1113		1019
	energy, ft-lb:	399		316		265
Rem. 124 JHP	velocity, fps:	1120		1028		960
	energy, ft-lb:	346		291		254
Rem. 124 FNEB	velocity, fps:	1100		1030		971
	energy, ft-lb:	339		292		252
Rem. 124 BJHP	velocity, fps:	1125		1031		963
	energy, ft-lb:	349		293		255
Rem. 124 BJHP +P	velocity, fps:	1180		1089		1021
	energy, ft-lb:	384		327		287
Rem. 124 Metal Case	velocity, fps:	1110		1030		971
	energy, ft-lb:	339		292		259
Rem. 147 JHP subsonic	velocity, fps:	990		941		900
	energy, ft-lb:	320		289		264
Rem. 147 BJHP	velocity, fps:	990		941		900
	energy, ft-lb:	320		289		264
Speer 90 Frangible	velocity, fps:	1350		1132		1001
	energy, ft-lb:	364		256		200
Speer 115 JHP Blazer	velocity, fps:	1145		1024		943
	energy, ft-lb:	335		268		227
Speer 115 FMJ Blazer	velocity, fps:	1145		1047		971
	energy, ft-lb:	341		280		241
Speer 115 FMJ	velocity, fps:	1200		1060		970
	energy, ft-lb:	368		287		240
Speer 115 Gold Dot HP	velocity, fps:	1200		1047		971
	energy, ft-lb:	341		280		241
Speer 124 FMJ Blazer	velocity, fps:	1090		989		917
	energy, ft-lb:	327		269		231
Speer 124 FMJ	velocity, fps:	1090		987		913
	energy, ft-lb:	327		268		230
Speer 124 TMJ-CF (and Blazer)	velocity, fps:	1090		989		917
	energy, ft-lb:	327		269		231
Speer 124 Gold Dot HP	velocity, fps:	1150		1030		948
	energy, ft-lb:	367		292		247
Speer 124 Gold Dot HP+P	velocity, ft-lb:	1220		1085		996
	energy, ft-lb:	410		324		273

CARTRIDGE BULLET	RANGE, YARDS:	0	25	50	75	100
Speer 147 TMJ Blazer	velocity, fps:	950		912		879
	energy, ft-lb:	295		272		252
Speer 147 TMJ	velocity, fps:	985		943		906
	energy, ft-lb:	317		290		268
Speer 147 TMJ-CF (and Blazer)	velocity, fps:	985		960		924
	energy, ft-lb:	326		300		279
Speer 147 Gold Dot	velocity, fps:	985		960		924
	energy, ft-lb:	326		300		279
Win. 105 Jacketed FP	velocity, fps:	1200		1074		989
	energy, ft-lb:	336		269		228
Win. 115 Silvertip HP	velocity, fps:	1225		1095		1007
	energy, ft-lb:	383		306		259
Win. 115 Jacketed HP	velocity, fps:	1225		1095		
	energy, ft-lb:	383		306		
Win. 115 FMJ	velocity, fps:	1190		1071		
	energy, ft-lb:	362		293		
Win. 115 EB WinClean	velocity, fps:	1190		1088		
	energy, ft-lb:	362		302		
Win. 124 FMJ	velocity, fps:	1140		1050		
	energy, ft-lb:	358		303		
Win. 124 EB WinClean	velocity, fps:	1130		1049		
	energy, ft-lb:	352		303		
Win. 147 FMJ FN	velocity, fps:	990		945		
	energy, ft-lb:	320		292		
Win. 147 SXT	velocity, fps:	990		947		909
	energy, ft-lb:	320		293		270
Win. 147 Silvertip HP	velocity, fps:	1010		962		921
	energy, ft-lb:	333		302		277
Win. 147 JHP	velocity, fps:	990		945		
	energy, ft-lb:	320		291		
Win. 147 EB WinClean	velocity, fps:	990		945		
	energy, ft-lb:	320		291		

9 x 23 WINCHESTER

CARTRIDGE BULLET	RANGE, YARDS:	0	25	50	75	100
Win. 124 Jacketed FP	velocity, fps:	1460		1308		
	energy, ft-lb:	587		471		
Win. 125 Silvertip HP	velocity, fps:	1450		1249		1103
	energy, ft-lb:	583		433		338

.38 S&W

CARTRIDGE BULLET	RANGE, YARDS:	0	25	50	75	100
Rem. 146 LRN	velocity, fps:	685		650		620
	energy, ft-lb:	150		135		125
Win. 145 LRN	velocity, fps:	685		650		620
	energy, ft-lb:	150		135		125

.38 SHORT COLT

CARTRIDGE BULLET	RANGE, YARDS:	0	25	50	75	100
Rem. 125 LRN	velocity, fps:	730		685		645
	energy, ft-lb:	150		130		115

.38 LONG COLT

CARTRIDGE BULLET	RANGE, YARDS:	0	25	50	75	100
Black Hills 158 RNL	velocity, fps:	650				
	energy, ft-lb:					

.380 AUTO

CARTRIDGE BULLET	RANGE, YARDS:	0	25	50	75	100
Black Hills 90 JHP	velocity, fps:	1000				
	energy, ft-lb:	200				
Black Hills 95 FMJ	velocity, fps:	950				
	energy, ft-lb:	190				
Federal 90 Hi-Shok JHP	velocity, fps:	1000	940	890	840	800
	energy, ft-lb:	200	175	160	140	130
Federal 90 Hydra-Shok JHP	velocity, fps:	1000	940	890	840	800
	energy, ft-lb:	200	175	160	140	130
Federal 95 FMJ	velocity, fps:	960	910	870	830	790
	energy, ft-lb:	190	175	160	145	130

CARTRIDGE BULLET	RANGE, YARDS:	0	25	50	75	100
Hornady 90 JHP/XTP	velocity, fps:	1000		902		823
	energy, ft-lb:	200		163		135
Magtech 85 JHP + P	velocity, fps:	1082		999		936
	energy, ft-lb:	221		188		166
Magtech 95 FMC	velocity, fps:	951		861		781
	energy, ft-lb:	190		156		128
Magtech 95 JHP	velocity, fps:	951		861		781
	energy, ft-lb:	190		156		128
PMC 77 NT/FR	velocity, fps:	1200	1095	1012	932	874
	energy, ft-lb:	223				
PMC 90 FMJ	velocity, fps:	910	872	838	807	778
	energy, ft-lb:	165				
PMC 90 JHP	velocity, fps:	917	878	844	812	782
	energy, ft-lb:	168				
PMC 95 SFHP	velocity, fps:	925	884	847	813	783
	energy, ft-lb:	180				
Rem. 88 JHP	velocity, fps:	990		920		868
	energy, ft-lb:	191		165		146
Rem. 95 FNEB	velocity, fps:	955		865		785
	energy, ft-lb:	190		160		130
Rem. 95 Metal Case	velocity, fps:	955		865		785
	energy, ft-lb:	190		160		130
Rem. 102 BJHP	velocity, fps:	940		901		866
	energy, ft-lb:	200		184		170
Speer 88 JHP Blazer	velocity, fps:	950		920		870
	energy, ft-lb:	195		164		148
Speer 90 Gold Dot	velocity, fps:	990		907		842
	energy, ft-lb:	196		164		142
Speer 95 TMJ Blazer	velocity, fps:	945		865		785
	energy, ft-lb:	190		160		130
Speer 95 TMJ	velocity, fps:	950		877		817
	energy, ft-lb:	180		154		133
Win. 85 Silvertip HP	velocity, fps:	1000		921		860
	energy, ft-lb:	189		160		140
Win. 95 SXT	velocity, fps:	955		889		835
	energy, ft-lb:	192		167		147
Win. 95 FMJ	velocity, fps:	955		865		
	energy, ft-lb:	190		160		
Win. 95 EB WinClean	velocity, fps:	955		881		
	energy, ft-lb:	192		164		

.38 SPECIAL

CARTRIDGE BULLET	RANGE, YARDS:	0	25	50	75	100
Black Hills 125 JHP +P	velocity, fps:	1050				
	energy, ft-lb:	306				
Black Hills 148 HBWC	velocity, fps:	700				
	energy, ft-lb:					
Black Hills 158 SWC	velocity, fps:	850				
	energy, ft-lb:					
Black Hills 158 CNL	velocity, fps:	800				
	energy, ft-lb:					
Federal 110 Hydra-Shok JHP	velocity, fps:	1000	970	930	910	880
	energy, ft-lb:	245	225	215	200	190
Federal 110 Hi-Shok JHP +P	velocity, fps:	1000	960	930	900	870
	energy, ft-lb:	240	225	210	195	185
Federal 125 Nyclad HP	velocity, fps:	830	780	730	690	650
	energy, ft-lb:	190	170	150	130	115
Federal 125 Hi-Shok JSP +P	velocity, fps:	950	920	900	880	860
	energy, ft-lb:	250	235	225	215	205
Federal 125 Hi-Shok JHP +P	velocity, fps:	950	920	900	880	860
	energy, ft-lb:	250	235	225	215	205
Federal 125 Nyclad HP +P	velocity, fps:	950	920	900	880	860
	energy, ft-lb:	250	235	225	215	205
Federal 129 Hydra-Shok JHP+P	velocity, fps:	950	930	910	890	870
	energy, ft-lb:	255	245	235	225	215

CARTRIDGE BULLET	RANGE, YARDS:	0	25	50	75	100
Federal 130 FMJ	velocity, fps:	950	920	890	870	840
	energy, ft-lb:	260	245	230	215	205
Federal 148 LWC Match	velocity, fps:	710	670	630	600	560
	energy, ft-lb:	165	150	130	115	105
Federal 158 LRN	velocity, fps:	760	740	720	710	690
	energy, ft-lb:	200	190	185	175	170
Federal 158 LSWC	velocity, fps:	760	740	720	710	690
	energy, ft-lb:	200	190	185	175	170
Federal 158 Nyclad RN	velocity, fps:	760	740	720	710	690
	energy, ft-lb:	200	190	185	175	170
Federal 158 SWC HP +P	velocity, fps:	890	870	860	840	820
	energy, ft-lb:	280	265	260	245	235
Federal 158 LSWC +P	velocity, fps:	890	870	860	840	820
	energy, ft-lb:	270	265	260	245	235
Federal 158 Nyclad SWC-HP+P	velocity, fps:	890	870	860	840	820
	energy, ft-lb:	270	265	260	245	235
Hornady 125 JHP/XTP	velocity, fps:	900		856		817
	energy, ft-lb:	225		203		185
Hornady 140 JHP/XTP	velocity, fps:	825		790		757
	energy, ft-lb:	212		194		178
Hornady 140 Cowboy	velocity, fps:	800		767		735
	energy, ft-lb:	199		183		168
Hornady 148 HBWC	velocity, fps:	800		697		610
	energy, ft-lb:	210		160		122
Hornady 158 JHP/XPT	velocity, fps:	800		765		731
	energy, ft-lb:	225		205		188
Lapua 123 HP Megashock	velocity, fps:	355		311*		284*
	energy, ft-lb:	504		388*		322*
Lapua 148 LWC	velocity, fps:	230		203*		181*
	energy, ft-lb:	254		199*		157*
Lapua 150 SJFN	velocity, fps:	325		301*		283*
	energy, ft-lb:	512		439*		388*
Lapua 158 FMJLF	velocity, fps:	255		243*		232*
	energy, ft-lb:	332		301*		275*
Lapua 158 LRN	velocity, fps:	255		243*		232*
	energy, ft-lb:	332		301*		275*
Magtech 125 JHP +P	velocity, fps:	1017		971		931
	energy, ft-lb:	287		262		241
Magtech 148 LWC	velocity, fps:	710		634		566
	energy, ft-lb:	166		132		105
Magtech 158 LRN	velocity, fps:	755		728		693
	energy, ft-lb:	200		183		168
Magtech 158 LFN	velocity, fps:	800		776		753
	energy, ft-lb:	225		211		199
Magtech 158 SJHP	velocity, fps:	807		779		753
	energy, ft-lb:	230		213		199
Magtech 158 LSWC	velocity, fps:	755		721		689
	energy, ft-lb:	200		182		167
Magtech 158 FMC-Flat	velocity, fps:	807		779		753
	energy, ft-lb:	230		213		199
PMC 85 Non-Toxic Frangible	velocity, fps:	1275	1181	1109	1052	1006
	energy, ft-lb:	307				
PMC 110 SFHP +P	velocity, fps:	velocity and energy figures not available				
PMC 125 SFHP +P	velocity, fps:	950	918	889	863	838
	energy, ft-lb:	251				
PMC 125 JHP +P	velocity, fps:	974	938	906	878	851
	energy, ft-lb:	266				
PMC 132 FMJ	velocity, fps:	841	820	799	780	761
	energy, ft-lb:	206				
PMC 148 LWC	velocity, fps:	728	694	662	631	602
	energy, ft-lb:	175				
PMC 158 LRN	velocity, fps:	820	801	783	765	749
	energy, ft-lb:	235				

BALLISTICS

Centerfire Handgun Ballistics

.38 SPECIAL TO .357 MAGNUM

CARTRIDGE BULLET	RANGE, YARDS:	0	25	50	75	100
PMC 158 JSP	velocity, fps:	835	816	797	779	762
	energy, ft-lb:	245				
PMC 158 LFP	velocity, fps:	800		761		725
	energy, ft-lb:	225		203		185
Rem. 101 Lead Free Frangible	velocity, fps:	950		896		850
	energy, ft-lb:	202		180		162
Rem. 110 SJHP	velocity, fps:	950		890		840
	energy, ft-lb:	220		194		172
Rem. 110 SJHP +P	velocity, fps:	995		926		871
	energy, ft-lb:	242		210		185
Rem. 125 SJHP +P	velocity, ft-lb:	945		898		858
	energy, ft-lb:	248		224		204
Rem. 125 BJHP	velocity, fps:	975		929		885
	energy, ft-lb:	264		238		218
Rem. 125 FNEB	velocity, fps:	850		822		796
	energy, ft-lb:	201		188		176
Rem. 125 FNEB +P	velocity, fps:	975		935		899
	energy, ft-lb:	264		242		224
Rem. 130 Metal Case	velocity, fps:	950		913		879
	energy, ft-lb:	261		240		223
Rem. 148 LWC Match	velocity, fps:	710		634		566
	energy, ft-lb:	166		132		105
Rem. 158 LRN	velocity, fps:	755		723		692
	energy, ft-lb:	200		183		168
Rem. 158 SWC +P	velocity, fps:	890		855		823
	energy, ft-lb:	278		257		238
Rem. 158 SWC	velocity, fps:	755		723		692
	energy, ft-lb:	200		183		168
Rem. 158 LHP +P	velocity, fps:	890		855		823
	energy, ft-lb:	278		257		238
Speer 125 JHP +P Blazer	velocity, fps:	945		898		858
	energy, ft-lb:	248		224		204
Speer 125 Gold Dot +P	velocity, fps:	945		898		858
	energy, ft-lb:	248		224		204
Speer 158 TMJ +P (and Blazer)	velocity, fps:	900		852		818
	energy, ft-lb:	278		255		235
Speer 158 LRN Blazer	velocity, fps:	755		723		692
	energy, ft-lb:	200		183		168
Speer 158 Trail Blazer LFN	velocity, fps:	800		761		725
	energy, ft-lb:	225		203		184
Speer 158 TMJ-CF +P (and Blazer)	velocity, fps:	900		852		818
	energy, ft-lb:	278		255		235
Win. 110 Silvertip HP	velocity, fps:	945		894		850
	energy, ft-lb:	218		195		176
Win. 110 Jacketed FP	velocity, fps:	975		906		849
	energy, ft-lb:	232		201		176
Win. 125 Jacketed HP	velocity, fps:	945		898		
	energy, ft-lb:	248		224		
Win. 125 Jacketed HP +P	velocity, fps:	945		898		858
	energy, ft-lb:	248		224		204
Win. 125 Jacketed FP	velocity, fps:	850		804		
	energy, ft-lb:	201		179		
Win. 125 Silvertip HP + P	velocity, fps:	945		898		858
	energy, ft-lb:	248		224		204
Win. 125 JFP WinClean	velocity, fps:	775		742		
	energy, ft-lb:	167		153		
Win. 130 FMJ	velocity, fps:	800		765		
	energy, ft-lb:	185		169		
Win. 130 SXT +P	velocity, fps:	925		887		852
	energy, ft-lb:	247		227		210
Win. 148 LWC Super Match	velocity, fps:	710		634		566
	energy, ft-lb:	166		132		105
Win. 150 Lead	velocity, fps:	845		812		
	energy, ft-lb:	238		219		

CARTRIDGE BULLET	RANGE, YARDS:	0	25	50	75	100
Win. 158 Lead	velocity, fps:	800		761		725
	energy, ft-lb:	225		203		185
Win. 158 LRN	velocity, fps:	755		723		693
	energy, ft-lb:	200		183		168
Win. 158 LSWC	velocity, fps:	755		721		689
	energy, ft-lb:	200		182		167
Win. 158 LSWC HP +P	velocity, fps:	890		855		823
	energy, ft-lb:	278		257		238

.38-40

CARTRIDGE BULLET	RANGE, YARDS:	0	25	50	75	100
Black Hills 180 FPL	velocity, fps:	800				
	energy, ft-lb:					

.38 SUPER

CARTRIDGE BULLET	RANGE, YARDS:	0	25	50	75	100
Federal 130 FMJ +P	velocity, fps:	1200	1140	1100	1050	1020
	energy, ft-lb:	415	380	350	320	300
PMC 115 JHP	velocity, fps:	1116	1052	1001	959	923
	energy, ft-lb:	318				
PMC 130 FMJ	velocity, fps:	1092	1038	994	957	924
	energy, ft-lb:	348				
Rem. 130 Metal Case	velocity, fps:	1215		1099		1017
	energy, ft-lb:	426		348		298
Win. 125 Silvertip HP +P	velocity, fps:	1240		1130		1050
	energy, ft-lb:	427		354		306
Win. 130 FMJ +P	velocity, fps:	1215		1099		
	energy, ft-lb:	426		348		

.357 SIG

CARTRIDGE BULLET	RANGE, YARDS:	0	25	50	75	100
Federal 125 FMJ	velocity, fps:	1350	1270	1190	1130	1080
	energy, ft-lb:	510	445	395	355	325
Federal 125 JHP	velocity, fps:	1350	1270	1190	1130	1080
	energy, ft-lb:	510	445	395	355	325
Federal 150 JHP	velocity, fps:	1130	1080	1030	1000	970
	energy, ft-lb:	420	385	355	330	310
Hornady 124 JHP/XTP	velocity, fps:	1350		1208		1108
	energy, ft-lb:	502		405		338
Hornady 147 JHP/XTP	velocity, fps:	1225		1138		1072
	energy, ft-lb:	490		422		375
PMC 85 Non-Toxic Frangible	velocity, fps:	1480	1356	1245	1158	1092
	energy, ft-lb:	413				
PMC 124 SFHP	velocity, fps:	1350	1263	1190	1132	1083
	energy, ft-lb:	502				
PMC 124 FMJ/FP	velocity, fps:	1350	1242	1158	1093	1040
	energy, ft-lb:	512				
Rem. 104 Lead Free Frangible	velocity, fps:	1400		1223		1094
	energy, ft-lb:	453		345		276
Rem. 125 Metal Case	velocity, fps:	1350		1146		1018
	energy, ft-lb:	506		422		359
Rem. 125 JHP	velocity, fps:	1350		1157		1032
	energy, ft-lb:	506		372		296
Speer 125 TMJ (and Blazer)	velocity, fps:	1350		1177		1057
	energy, ft-lb:	502		381		307
Speer 125 TMJ-CF	velocity, fps:	1350		1177		1057
	energy, ft-lb:	502		381		307
Speer 125 Gold Dot	velocity, fps:	1375		1203		1079
	energy, ft-lb:	525		402		323
Win. 105 JFP	velocity, fps:	1370		1179		1050
	energy, ft-lb	438		324		257
Win. 125 FMJ FN	velocity, fps:	1350		1185		
	energy, ft-lb	506		390		

.357 MAGNUM

CARTRIDGE BULLET	RANGE, YARDS:	0	25	50	75	100
Black Hills 125 JHP	velocity, fps:	1500				
	energy, ft-lb:	625				
Black Hills 158 CNL	velocity, fps:	800				

BALLISTICS

Centerfire Handgun Ballistics

CARTRIDGE BULLET	RANGE, YARDS:	0	25	50	75	100
Black Hills 158 SWC	energy, ft-lb:					
	velocity, fps:	1050				
Black Hills 158 JHP	energy, ft-lb:					
	velocity, fps:	1250				
Federal 110 Hi-Shok JHP	velocity, fps:	1300	1180	1090	1040	990
	energy, ft-lb:	410	340	290	260	235
Federal 125 Hi-Shok JHP	velocity, fps:	1450	1350	1240	1160	1100
	energy, ft-lb:	580	495	430	370	335
Federal 130 Hydra-Shok JHP	velocity, fps:	1300	1210	1130	1070	1020
	energy, ft-lb:	490	420	370	330	300
Federal 158 Hi-Shok JSP	velocity, fps:	1240	1160	1100	1060	1020
	energy, ft-lb:	535	475	430	395	365
Federal 158 JSP	velocity, fps:	1240	1160	1100	1060	1020
	energy, ft-lb:	535	475	430	395	365
Federal 158 LSWC	velocity, fps:	1240	1160	1100	1060	1020
	energy, ft-lb:	535	475	430	395	365
Federal 158 Hi-Shok JHP	velocity, fps:	1240	1160	1100	1060	1020
	energy, ft-lb:	535	475	430	395	365
Federal 158 Hydra-Shok JHP	velocity, fps:	1240	1160	1100	1060	1020
	energy, ft-lb:	535	475	430	395	365
Federal 180 Hi-Shok JHP	velocity, fps:	1090	1030	980	930	890
	energy, ft-lb:	475	425	385	350	320
Federal 180 Castcore	velocity, fps:	1250	1200	1160	1120	1080
	energy, ft-lb:	625	575	535	495	465
Hornady 125 JHP/XTP	velocity, fps:	1500		1314		1166
	energy, ft-lb:	624		479		377
Hornady 125 JFP/XTP	velocity, fps:	1500		1311		1161
	energy, ft-lb:	624		477		374
Hornady 140 Cowboy	velocity, fps:	800		767		735
	energy, ft-lb:	199		183		168
Hornady 140 JHP/XTP	velocity, fps:	1400		1249		1130
	energy, ft-lb:	609		485		397
Hornady 158 JHP/XTP	velocity, fps:	1250		1150		1073
	energy, ft-lb:	548		464		404
Hornady 158 JFP/XTP	velocity, fps:	1250		1147		1068
	energy, ft-lb:	548		461		400
Lapua 150 FMJ CEPP Super	velocity, fps:	370		527*		303*
	energy, ft-lb:	664		527*		445*
Lapua 150 SJFN	velocity, fps:	385		342*		313*
	energy, ft-lb:	719		569*		476*
Lapua 158 SJHP	velocity, fps:	470		408*		359*
	energy, ft-lb:	1127		850*		657*
Magtech 158 SJSP	velocity, fps:	1235		1104		1015
	energy, ft-lb:	535		428		361
Magtech 158 SJHP	velocity, fps:	1235		1104		1015
	energy, ft-lb:	535		428		361
PMC 85 Non-Toxic Frangible	velocity, fps:	1325	1219	1139	1076	1025
	energy, ft-lb:	331				
PMC 125 JHP	velocity, fps:	1194	1117	1057	1008	967
	energy, ft-lb:	399				
PMC 150 JHP	velocity, fps:	1234	1156	1093	1042	1000
	energy, ft-lb:	512				
PMC 150 SFHP	velocity, fps:	1205	1129	1069	1020	980
	energy, ft-lb:	484				
PMC 158 JSP	velocity, fps:	1194	1122	1063	1016	977
	energy, ft-lb:	504				
PMC 158 LFP	velocity, fps:	800		761		725
	energy, ft-lb:	225		203		185
Rem. 110 SJHP	velocity, fps:	1295		1094		975
	energy, ft-lb:	410		292		232
Rem. 125 SJHP	velocity, fps:	1450		1240		1090
	energy, ft-lb:	583		427		330

CARTRIDGE BULLET	RANGE, YARDS:	0	25	50	75	100
Rem. 125 BJHP	velocity, fps:	1220		1095		1009
	energy, ft-lb:	413		333		283
Rem. 125 FNEB	velocity, fps:	1450		1240		1090
	energy, ft-lb:	583		427		330
Rem. 158 SJHP	velocity, fps:	1235		1104		1015
	energy, ft-lb:	535		428		361
Rem. 158 SP	velocity, fps:	1235		1104		1015
	energy, ft-lb:	535		428		361
Rem. 158 SWC	velocity, fps:	1235		1104		1015
	energy, ft-lb:	535		428		361
Rem. 165 JHP Core-Lokt	velocity, fps:	1290		1189		1108
	energy, ft-lb:	610		518		450
Rem. 180 SJHP	velocity, fps:	1145		1053		985
	energy, ft-lb:	542		443		388
Speer 125 Gold Dot	velocity, fps:	1450		1240		1090
	energy, ft-lb:	583		427		330
Speer 158 JHP Blazer	velocity, fps:	1150		1104		1015
	energy, ft-lb:	535		428		361
Speer 158 Gold Dot	velocity, fps:	1235		1104		1015
	energy, ft-lb:	535		428		361
Speer 170 Gold Dot SP	velocity, fps:	1180		1089		1019
	energy, ft-lb:	525		447		392
Win. 110 JFP	velocity, fps:	1275		1105		998
	energy, ft-lb:	397		298		243
Win. 110 JHP	velocity, fps:	1295		1095		
	energy, ft-lb:	410		292		
Win. 125 JFP WinClean	velocity, fps:	1370		1183		
	energy, ft-lb:	521		389		
Win. 145 Silvertip HP	velocity, fps:	1290		1155		1060
	energy, ft-lb:	535		428		361
Win. 158 JHP	velocity, fps:	1235		1104		1015
	energy, ft-lb:	535		428		361
Win. 158 JSP	velocity, fps:	1235		1104		1015
	energy, ft-lb:	535		428		361
Win. 180 Partition Gold	velocity, fps:	1180		1088		1020
	energy, ft-lb:	557		473		416

.40 S&W

CARTRIDGE BULLET	RANGE, YARDS:	0	25	50	75	100
Black Hills 155 JHP	velocity, fps:	1150				
	energy, ft-lb:	450				
Black Hills 165 EXP JHP	velocity, fps:	1150 (2005: 1100)				
	energy, ft-lb:	483				
Black Hills 180 JHP	velocity, fps:	1000				
	energy, ft-lb:	400				
Black Hills 180 JHP	velocity, fps:	1000				
	energy, ft-lb:	400				
Federal 135 Hydra-Shok JHP	velocity, fps:	1190	1050	970	900	850
	energy, ft-lb:	420	330	280	245	215
Federal 155 FMJ Ball	velocity, fps:	1140	1080	1030	990	960
	energy, ft-lb:	445	400	365	335	315
Federal 155 Hi-Shok JHP	velocity, fps:	1140	1080	1030	990	950
	energy, ft-lb:	445	400	365	335	315
Federal 155 Hydra-Shok JHP	velocity, fps:	1140	1080	1030	990	950
	energy, ft-lb:	445	400	365	335	315
Federal 165 EFMJ	velocity, fps:	1190	1060	970	905	850
	energy, ft-lb:	520	410	345	300	265
Federal 165 FMJ	velocity, fps:	1050	1020	990	960	935
	energy, ft-lb:	405	380	355	335	320
Federal 165 FMJ Ball	velocity, fps:	980	950	920	900	880
	energy, ft-lb:	350	330	310	295	280
Federal 165 Hydra-Shok JHP	velocity, fps:	980	950	930	910	890
	energy, ft-lb:	350	330	315	300	290
Federal 180 High Antim. Lead	velocity, fps:	990	960	930	910	890
	energy, ft-lb:	390	365	345	330	315

BALLISTICS

Centerfire Handgun Ballistics

.40 S&W TO .41 REMINGTON MAGNUM

CARTRIDGE BULLET	RANGE, YARDS:	0	25	50	75	100
Federal 180 TMJ TMF Primer	velocity, fps:	990	960	940	910	890
	energy, ft-lb:	390	370	350	330	315
Federal 180 FMJ Ball	velocity, fps:	990	960	940	910	890
	energy, ft-lb:	390	370	350	330	315
Federal 180 Hi-Shok JHP	velocity, fps:	990	960	930	910	890
	energy, ft-lb:	390	365	345	330	315
Federal 180 Hydra-Shok JHP	velocity, fps:	990	960	930	910	890
	energy, ft-lb:	390	365	345	330	315
Hornady 155 JHP/XTP	velocity, fps:	1180		1061		980
	energy, ft-lb:	479		387		331
Hornady 155 TAP-FPD	velocity, fps:	1180		1061		980
	energy, ft-lb:	470		387		331
Hornady 180 JHP/XTP	velocity, fps:	950		903		862
	energy, ft-lb:	361		326		297
Hornady 180 TAP-FPD	velocity, fps:	950		903		862
	energy, ft-lb:	361		326		297
Magtech 155 JHP	velocity, fps:	1025		1118		1052
	energy, ft-lb:	500		430		381
Magtech 180 JHP	velocity, fps:	990		933		886
	energy, ft-lb:	390		348		314
Magtech 180 FMC	velocity, fps:	990		933		886
	energy, ft-lb:	390		348		314
PMC 115 Non-Toxic Frangible	velocity, fps:	1350	1240	1154	1088	1035
	energy, ft-lb:	465				
PMC 155 SFHP	velocity, fps:	1160	1092	1039	994	957
	energy, ft-lb:	463				
PMC 165 JHP	velocity, fps:	1040	1002	970	941	915
	energy, ft-lb:	396				
PMC 165 FMJ	velocity, fps:	1010	977	948	922	899
	energy, ft-lb:	374				
PMC 180 FMJ/FP	velocity, fps:	985	957	931	908	885
	energy, ft-lb:	388				
PMC 180 SFHP	velocity, fps:	985	958	933	910	889
	energy, ft-lb:	388				
Rem. 141 Lead Free Frangible	velocity, fps:	1135		1056		996
	energy, ft-lb:	403		349		311
Rem. 155 JHP	velocity, fps:	1205		1095		1017
	energy, ft-lb:	499		413		356
Rem. 165 BJHP	velocity, fps:	1150		1040		964
	energy, ft-lb:	485		396		340
Rem. 180 JHP	velocity, fps:	1015		960		914
	energy, ft-lb:	412		368		334
Rem. 180 FN Enclosed Base	velocity, fps:	985		936		893
	energy, ft-lb:	388		350		319
Rem. 180 Metal Case	velocity, fps:	985		936		893
	energy, ft-lb:	388		350		319
Rem. 180 BJHP	velocity, fps:	1015		960		914
	energy, ft-lb:	412		368		334
Speer 105 Frangible	velocity, fps:	1380		1128		985
	energy, ft-lb:	444		297		226
Speer 155 TMJ Blazer	velocity, fps:	1175		1047		963
	energy, ft-lb:	475		377		319
Speer 155 TMJ	velocity, fps:	1200		1065		976
	energy, ft-lb:	496		390		328
Speer 155 Gold Dot	velocity, fps:	1200		1063		974
	energy, ft-lb:	496		389		326
Speer 165 TMJ Blazer	velocity, fps:	1100		1006		938
	energy, ft-lb:	443		371		321
Speer 165 TMJ	velocity, fps:	1150		1040		964
	energy, ft-lb:	484		396		340
Speer 165 Gold Dot	velocity, fps:	1150		1043		966
	energy, ft-lb:	485		399		342
Speer 180 HP Blazer	velocity, fps:	985		951		909
	energy, ft-lb:	400		361		330

CARTRIDGE BULLET	RANGE, YARDS:	0	25	50	75	100
Speer 180 FMJ Blazer	velocity, fps:	1000		937		886
	energy, ft-lb:	400		351		313
Speer 180 FMJ	velocity, fps:	1000		951		909
	energy, ft-lb:	400		361		330
Speer 180 TMJ-CF (and Blazer)	velocity, fps:	1000		951		909
	energy, ft-lb:	400		361		330
Speer 180 Gold Dot	velocity, fps:	1025		957		902
	energy, ft-lb:	420		366		325
Win. 140 JFP	velocity, fps:	1155		1039		960
	energy, ft-lb:	415		336		286
Win. 155 Silvertip HP	velocity, fps:	1205		1096		1018
	energy, ft-lb	500		414		357
Win. 165 SXT	velocity, fps:	1130		1041		977
	energy, ft-lb:	468		397		349
Win. 165 FMJ FN	velocity, fps:	1060		1001		
	energy, ft-lb:	412		367		
Win. 165 EB WinClean	velocity, fps:	1130		1054		
	energy, ft-lb:	468		407		
Win. 180 JHP	velocity, fps:	1010		954		
	energy, ft-lb:	408		364		
Win. 180 FMJ	velocity, fps:	990		936		
	energy, ft-lb:	390		350		
Win. 180 SXT	velocity, fps:	1010		954		909
	energy, ft-lb:	408		364		330
Win. 180 EB WinClean	velocity, fps:	990		943		
	energy, ft-lb:	392		356		

10 MM AUTO

CARTRIDGE BULLET	RANGE, YARDS:	0	25	50	75	100
Federal 155 Hi-Shok JHP	velocity, fps:	1330	1230	1140	1080	1030
	energy, ft-lb:	605	515	450	400	360
Federal 180 Hi-Shok JHP	velocity, fps:	1030	1000	970	950	920
	energy, ft-lb:	425	400	375	355	340
Federal 180 Hydra-Shok JHP	velocity, fps:	1030	1000	970	950	920
	energy, ft-lb:	425	400	375	355	340
Federal 180 High Antim. Lead	velocity, fps:	1030	1000	970	950	920
	energy, ft-lb:	425	400	375	355	340
Federal 180 FMJ	velocity, fps:	1060	1025	990	965	940
	energy, ft-lb:	400	370	350	330	310
Hornady 155 JHP/XTP	velocity, fps:	1265		1119		1020
	energy, ft-lb:	551		431		358
Hornady 180 JHP/XTP	velocity, fps:	1180		1077		1004
	energy, ft-lb:	556		464		403
Hornady 200 JHP/XTP	velocity, fps:	1050		994		948
	energy, ft-lb:	490		439		399
PMC 115 Non-Toxic Frangible	velocity, fps:	1350	1240	1154	1088	1035
	energy, ft-lb:	465				
PMC 170 JHP	velocity, fps:	1200	1117	1052	1000	958
	energy, ft-lb:	543				
PMC 180 SFHP	velocity, fps:	950	926	903	882	862
	energy, ft-lb:	361				
PMC 200 TC-FMJ	velocity, fps:	1050	1008	972	941	912
	energy, ft-lb:	490				
Rem. 180 Metal Case	velocity, fps:	1150		1063		998
	energy, ft-lb:	529		452		398
Speer 200 TMJ Blazer	velocity, fps:	1050		966		952
	energy, ft-lb:	490		440		402
Win. 175 Silvertip HP	velocity, fps:	1290		1141		1037
	energy, ft-lb:	649		506		418

.41 REMINGTON MAGNUM

CARTRIDGE BULLET	RANGE, YARDS:	0	25	50	75	100
Federal 210 Hi-Shok JHP	velocity, fps:	1300	1210	1130	1070	1030
	energy, ft-lb:	790	680	595	540	495
PMC 210 TCSP	velocity, fps:	1290	1201	1128	1069	1021
	energy, ft-lb:	774				

BALLISTICS

.41 REMINGTON MAGNUM TO .45 AUTOMATIC (ACP)

CARTRIDGE BULLET	RANGE, YARDS:	0	25	50	75	100
PMC 210 JHP	velocity, fps:	1289	1200	1127	1068	1020
	energy, ft-lb:	774				
Rem. 210 SP	velocity, fps:	1300		1162		1062
	energy, ft-lb:	788		630		526
Win. 175 Silvertip HP	velocity, fps:	1250		1120		1029
	energy, ft-lb:	607		488		412
Win. 240 Platinum Tip	velocity, ft-lb:	1250		1151		1075
	energy, ft-lb:	833		706		616

.44 COLT

Black Hills 230 FPL	velocity, fps:	730				
	energy, ft-lb:					

.44 RUSSIAN

Black Hills 210 FPL	velocity, fps:	650				
	energy, ft-lb:					

.44 SPECIAL

Black Hills 210 FPL	velocity, fps:	700				
	energy, ft-lb:					
Federal 200 SWC HP	velocity, fps:	900	860	830	800	770
	energy, ft-lb:	360	330	305	285	260
Federal 250 CastCore	velocity, fps:	1250	1200	1150	1110	1080
	energy, ft-lb:	865	795	735	685	645
Hornady 180 JHP/XTP	velocity, fps:	1000		935		882
	energy, ft-lb:	400		350		311
Magtech 240 LFN	velocity, fps:	750		722		696
	energy, ft-lb:	300		278		258
PMC 180 JHP	velocity, fps:	980	938	902	869	839
	energy, ft-lb:	383				
PMC 240 SWC-CP	velocity, fps:	764	744	724	706	687
	energy, ft-lb:	311				
PMC 240 LFP	velocity, fps:	750		719		690
	energy, ft-lb:	300		275		253
Rem. 246 LRN	velocity, fps:	755		725		695
	energy, ft-lb:	310		285		265
Speer 200 HP Blazer	velocity, fps:	875		825		780
	energy, ft-lb:	340		302		270
Speer 200 Trail Blazer LFN	velocity, fps:	750		714		680
	energy, ft-lb:	250		226		205
Speer 200 Gold Dot	velocity, fps:	875		825		780
	energy, ft-lb:	340		302		270
Win. 200 Silvertip HP	velocity, fps:	900		860		822
	energy, ft-lb:	360		328		300
Win. 240 Lead	velocity, fps:	750		719		690
	energy, ft-lb	300		275		253
Win. 246 LRN	velocity, fps:	755		725		695
	energy, ft-lb:	310		285		265

.44 REMINGTON MAGNUM

Black Hills 240 JHP	velocity, fps:	1260				
	energy, ft-lb:	848				
Black Hills 300 JHP	velocity, fps:	1150				
	energy, ft-lb:	879				
Federal 180 Hi-Shok JHP	velocity, fps:	1610	1480	1370	1270	1180
	energy, ft-lb:	1035	875	750	640	555
Federal 240 Hi-Shok JHP	velocity, fps:	1180	1130	1080	1050	1010
	energy, ft-lb:	740	675	625	580	550
Federal 240 Hydra-Shok JHP	velocity, fps:	1180	1130	1080	1050	1010
	energy, ft-lb:	740	675	625	580	550
Federal 240 JHP	velocity, fps:	1180	1130	1080	1050	1010
	energy, ft-lb:	740	675	625	580	550
Federal 300 CastCore	velocity, fps:	1250	1200	1160	1120	1080
	energy, ft-lb:	1040	960	885	825	775

CARTRIDGE BULLET	RANGE, YARDS:	0	25	50	75	100
Hornady 180 JHP/XTP	velocity, fps:	1550		1340		1173
	energy, ft-lb:	960		717		550
Hornady 200 JHP/XTP	velocity, fps:	1500		1284		1128
	energy, ft-lb:	999		732		565
Hornady 240 JHP/XTP	velocity, fps:	1350		1188		1078
	energy, ft-lb:	971		753		619
Hornady 300 JHP/XTP	velocity, fps:	1150		1084		1031
	energy, ft-lb:	881		782		708
Magtech 240 SJSP	velocity, fps:	1180		1081		1010
	energy, ft-lb:	741		632		623
PMC 180 JHP	velocity, fps:	1392	1263	1157	1076	1015
	energy, ft-lb:	772				
PMC 240 JHP	velocity, fps:	1301	1218	1147	1088	1041
	energy, ft-lb:	900				
PMC 240 TC-SP	velocity, fps:	1300	1216	1144	1086	1038
	energy, ft-lb:	900				
PMC 240 SFHP	velocity, fps:	1300	1212	1138	1079	1030
	energy, ft-lb:	900				
PMC 240 LSWC-GCK	velocity, fps:	1225	1143	1077	1025	982
	energy, ft-lb:	806				
Rem. 180 JSP	velocity, fps:	1610		1365		1175
	energy, ft-lb:	1036		745		551
Rem. 210 Gold Dot HP	velocity, fps:	1450		1276		1140
	energy, ft-lb:	980		759		606
Rem. 240 SP	velocity, fps:	1180		1081		1010
	energy, ft-lb:	721		623		543
Rem. 240 SJHP	velocity, fps:	1180		1081		1010
	energy, ft-lb:	721		623		543
Rem. 275 JHP Core-Lokt	velocity, fps:	1235		1142		1070
	energy, ft-lb:	931		797		699
Speer 240 JHP Blazer	velocity, fps:	1200		1092		1015
	energy, ft-lb:	767		636		549
Speer 240 Gold Dot HP	velocity, fps:	1400		1255		1139
	energy, ft-lb:	1044		839		691
Speer 270 Gold Dot SP	velocity, fps:	1250		1142		1060
	energy, ft-lb:	937		781		674
Win. 210 Silvertip HP	velocity, fps:	1250		1106		1010
	energy, ft-lb:	729		570		475
Win. 240 Hollow SP	velocity, fps:	1180		1081		1010
	energy, ft-lb:	741		623		543
Win. 240 JSP	velocity, fps:	1180		1081		
	energy, ft-lb:	741		623		
Win. 250 Partition Gold	velocity, fps:	1230		1132		1057
	energy, ft-lb:	840		711		620
Win. 250 Platinum Tip	velocity, fps:	1250		1148		1070
	energy, ft-lb:	867		732		635

.44-40

Black Hills 200 RNFP	velocity, fps:	800				
	energy, ft-lb:					
Hornady 205 Cowboy	velocity, fps:	725		697		670
	energy, ft-lb:	239		221		204
Magtech 225 LFN	velocity, fps:	725		703		681
	energy, ft-lb:	281		247		232
PMC 225 LFP	velocity, fps:	725		723		695
	energy, ft-lb:	281		261		242
Win. 225 Lead	velocity, fps:	750		723		695
	energy, ft-lb:	281		261		242

.45 AUTOMATIC (ACP)

Black Hills 185 JHP	velocity, fps:	1000				
	energy, ft-lb:	411				

.45 AUTOMATIC (ACP) TO .45 GAP

CARTRIDGE BULLET	RANGE, YARDS:	0	25	50	75	100
Black Hills 200 Match SWC	velocity, fps:	875				
	energy, ft-lb:	340				
Black Hills 230 FMJ	velocity, fps:	850				
	energy, ft-lb:	368				
Black Hills 230 JHP	velocity, fps:	850				
	energy, ft-lb:	368				
Black Hills 230 JHP +P	velocity, fps:	950				
	energy, ft-lb:	460				
Federal 165 Hydra-Shok JHP	velocity, fps:	1060	1020	980	950	920
	energy, ft-lb:	410	375	350	330	310
Federal 165 EFMJ	velocity, fps:	1090	1045	1005	975	942
	energy, ft-lb:	435	400	370	345	325
Federal 185 Hi-Shok JHP	velocity, fps:	950	920	900	880	860
	energy, ft-lb:	370	350	335	315	300
Federal 185 FMJ-SWC Match	velocity, fps:	780	730	700	660	620
	energy, ft-lb:	245	220	200	175	160
Federal 200 Exp. FMJ	velocity, fps:	1030	1000	970	940	920
	energy, ft-lb:	470	440	415	395	375
Federal 230 FMJ	velocity, fps:	850	830	810	790	770
	energy, ft-lb:	370	350	335	320	305
Federal 230 FMJ Match	velocity, fps:	855	835	815	795	775
	energy, ft-lb:	375	355	340	325	305
Federal 230 Hi-Shok JHP	velocity, fps:	850	830	810	790	770
	energy, ft-lb:	370	350	335	320	300
Federal 230 Hydra-Shok JHP	velocity, fps:	850	830	810	790	770
	energy, ft-lb:	370	350	335	320	305
Federal 230 FMJ	velocity, fps:	850	830	810	790	770
	energy, ft-lb:	370	350	335	320	305
Federal 230 TMJ TMF Primer	velocity, fps:	850	830	810	790	770
	energy, ft-lb:	370	350	335	315	305
Hornady 185 JHP/XTP	velocity, fps:	950		880		819
	energy, ft-lb:	371		318		276
Hornady 200 JHP/XTP	velocity, fps:	900		855		815
	energy, ft-lb:	358		325		295
Hornady 200 HP/XTP +P	velocity, fps:	1055		982		925
	energy, ft-lb:	494		428		380
Hornady 200 TAP-FPD	velocity, fps:	1055		982		926
	energy, ft-lbs:	494		428		380
Hornady 230 FMJ/RN	velocity, fps:	850		809		771
	energy, ft-lb:	369		334		304
Hornady 230 FMJ/FP	velocity, fps:	850		809		771
	energy, ft-lb:	369		334		304
Hornady 230 HP/XTP +P	velocity, fps:	950		904		865
	energy, ft-lb:	462		418		382
Hornady 230 TAP-FPD	velocity, fps:	950		908		872
	energy, ft-lb:	461		421		388
Magtech 185 JHP +P	velocity, fps:	1148		1066		1055
	energy, ft-lb:	540		467		415
Magtech 200 LSWC	velocity, fps:	950		910		874
	energy, ft-lb:	401		368		339
Magtech 230 FMC	veloctiy, fps:	837		800		767
	energy, ft-lb:	356		326		300
Magtech 230 FMC-SWC	velocity, fps:	780		720		660
	energy, ft-lb:	310		265		222
PMC 145 Non-Toxic Frangible	velocity, fps:	1100	1045	999	961	928
	energy, ft-lb:	390				
PMC 185 JHP	velocity, fps:	903	870	839	811	785
	energy, ft-lb:	339				
PMC 200 FMJ-SWC	velocity, fps:	850	818	788	761	734
	energy, ft-lb:	321				
PMC 230 SFHP	velocity, fps:	850	830	811	792	775
	energy, ft-lb:	369				
PMC 230 FMJ	velocity, fps:	830	809	789	769	749
	energy, ft-lb:	352				
Rem. 175 Lead Free Frangible	velocity, fps:	1020		923		851
	energy, ft-lb:	404		331		281
Rem. 185 JHP	velocity, fps:	1000		939		889
	energy, ft-lb:	411		362		324
Rem. 185 BJHP	velocity, fps:	1015		951		899
	energy, ft-lb:	423		372		332
Rem. 185 BJHP +P	velocity, fps:	1140		1042		971
	energy, ft-lb:	534		446		388
Rem. 185 MC	velocity, fps:	1015		955		907
	energy, ft-lb:	423		375		338
Rem. 230 FN Enclosed Base	velocity, fps:	835		800		767
	energy, ft-lb:	356		326		300
Rem. 230 Metal Case	velocity, fps:	835		800		767
	energy, ft-lb:	356		326		300
Rem. 230 JHP	velocity, fps:	835		800		767
	energy, ft-lb:	356		326		300
Rem. 230 BJHP	velocity, fps:	875		833		795
	energy, ft-lb:	391		355		323
Speer 140 Frangible	velocity, fps:	1200		1029		928
	energy, ft-lb:	448		329		268
Speer 185 Gold Dot	velocity, fps:	1050		956		886
	energy, ft-lb:	453		375		322
Speer 185 TMJ/FN	velocity, fps:	1000		909		839
	energy, ft-lb:	411		339		289
Speer 200 JHP Blazer	velocity, fps:	975		917		860
	energy, ft-lb:	421		372		328
Speer 200 Gold Dot +P	velocity, fps:	1080		994		930
	energy, ft-lb:	518		439		384
Speer 200 TMJ/FN	velocity, fps:	975		897		834
	energy, ft-lb:	422		357		309
Speer 230 FMJ (and Blazer)	velocity, fps:	845		804		775
	energy, ft-lb:	363		329		304
Speer 230 TMJ-CF (and Blazer)	velocity, fps:	845		804		775
	energy, ft-lb:	363		329		304
Speer 230 Gold Dot	velocity, fps:	890		845		805
	energy, ft-lb:	405		365		331
Win. 170 JFP	velocity, fps:	1050		982		928
	energy, ft-lb:	416		364		325
Win. 185 Silvertip HP	velocity, fps:	1000		938		888
	energy, ft-lb:	411		362		324
Win. 185 FMJ FN	velocity, fps:	910		861		
	energy, ft-lb:	340		304		
Win. 185 EB WinClean	velocity, fps:	910		835		
	energy, ft-lb:	340		286		
Win. 230 JHP	velocity, fps:	880		842		
	energy, ft-lb:	396		363		
Win. 230 FMJ	velocity, fps:	835		800		
	energy, ft-lb:	356		326		
Win. 230 SXT	velocity, fps:	880		846		816
	energy, ft-lb:	396		366		340
Win. 230 JHP subsonic	velocity, fps:	880		842		808
	energy, ft-lb:	396		363		334
Win. 230 EB WinClean	velocity, fps:	835		802		
	energy, ft-lb:	356		329		

.45 GAP

CARTRIDGE BULLET	RANGE, YARDS:	0	25	50	75	100
Federal 185 Hydra-Shok JHP And Federal TMJ	velocity, fps:	1090	1020	970	920	890
	energy, ft-lb:	490	430	385	350	320
Federal 230 Hydra-Shok And Federal FMJ	velocity, fps:	880	870	850	840	820
	energy, ft-lb:	395	380	3760	355	345

BALLISTICS

Centerfire Handgun Ballistics

CARTRIDGE BULLET	RANGE, YARDS:	0	25	50	75	100
Win. 185 STHP	velocity, fps:	1000		938		887
	energy, ft-lb:	411		361		323
Win. 230 JHP	velocity, fps:	880		842		
	energy, ft-lb:	396		363		
Win. 230 EB WinClean	velocity, fps:	875		840		
	energy, ft-lb:	391		360		
Win. 230 FMJ	velocity, fps:	850		814		
	energy, ft-lb:	369		338		

.45 WINCHESTER MAGNUM

CARTRIDGE BULLET	RANGE, YARDS:	0	25	50	75	100
Win. 260 Partition Gold	velocity, fps:	1200		1105		1033
	energy, ft-lb:	832		705		616
Win. 260 JHP	velocity, fps:	1200		1099		1026
	energy, ft-lb:	831		698		607

.45 SCHOFIELD

CARTRIDGE BULLET	RANGE, YARDS:	0	25	50	75	100
Black Hills 180 FNL	velocity, fps:	730				
	energy, ft-lb:					
Black Hills 230 RNFP	velocity, fps:	730				
	energy, ft-lb:					

.45 COLT

CARTRIDGE BULLET	RANGE, YARDS:	0	25	50	75	100
Black Hills 250 RNFP	velocity, fps:	725				
	energy, ft-lb:					
Federal 225 SWC HP	velocity, fps:	900	880	860	840	820
	energy, ft-lb:	405	385	370	355	340
Hornady 255 Cowboy	velocity, fps:	725		692		660
	energy, ft-lb:	298		271		247
Magtech 250 LFN	velocity, fps:	750		726		702
	energy, ft-lb:	312		293		274
PMC 250 LFP	velocity, fps:	800		767		736
	energy, ft-lb:	355		331		309
PMC 300 +P+	velocity, fps:	1250	1192	1144	1102	1066
	energy, ft-lb:	1041				
Rem. 225 SWC	velocity, fps:	960		890		832
	energy, ft-lb:	460		395		346
Rem. 250 RLN	velocity, fps:	860		820		780
	energy, ft-lb:	410		375		340
Speer 200 FMJ Blazer	velocity, fps:	1000		938		889
	energy, ft-lb:	444		391		351
Speer 230 Trail Blazer LFN	velocity, fps:	750		716		684
	energy, ft-lb:	287		262		239
Speer 250 Gold Dot	velocity, fps:	900		860		823
	energy, ft-lb:	450		410		376
Win. 225 Silvertip HP	velocity, fps:	920		877		839
	energy, ft-lb:	423		384		352
Win. 255 LRN	velocity, fps:	860		820		780
	energy, ft-lb:	420		380		345
Win. 250 Lead	velocity, fps:	750		720		692
	energy, ft-lb:	312		288		266

.454 CASULL

CARTRIDGE BULLET	RANGE, YARDS:	0	25	50	75	100
Federal 300 Trophy Bonded	velocity, fps:	1630	1540	1450	1380	1300
	energy, ft-lb:	1760	1570	1405	1260	1130
Federal 360 CastCore	velocity, fps:	1500	1435	1370	1310	1255
	energy, ft-lb:	1800	1640	1500	1310	1260
Hornady 240 XTP-MAG	velocity, fps:	1900		1679		1483
	energy, ft-lb:	1923		1502		1172
Hornady 300 XTP-MAG	velocity, fps:	1650		1478		1328
	energy, ft-lb:	1813		1455		1175
Magtech 260 SJSP	velocity, fps:	1800		1577		1383
	energy, ft-lb:	1871		1437		1104
Rem. 300 Core-Lokt Ultra	velocity, fps:	1625		1472		1335
	energy, ft-lb:	1759		1442		1187

CARTRIDGE BULLET	RANGE, YARDS:	0	25	50	75	100
Speer 300 Gold Dot HP	velocity, fps:	1625		1477		1343
	energy, ft-lb:	1758		1452		1201
Win. 250 JHP	velocity, fps:	1300		1151		1047
	energy, ft-lb:	938		735		608
Win. 260 Partition Gold	velocity, fps:	1800		1605		1427
	energy, ft-lb:	1871		1485		1176
Win. 260 Platinum Tip	velocity, fps:	1800		1596		1414
	eneryg, ft-lb:	1870		1470		1154
Win. 300 JFP	velocity, fps:	1625		1451		1308
	energy, ft-lb:	1759		1413		1141

.460 SMITH & WESSON

CARTRIDGE BULLET	RANGE, YARDS:	0	25	50	75	100
Hornady 200 SST	velocity, fps:	2250		2003		1772
	energy, ft-lb:	2248		1395		1081
Win. 260 Supreme Part. Gold	velocity, fps	2000		1788		1592
	energy, ft-lb	2309		1845		2012

.475 LINEBAUGH

CARTRIDGE BULLET	RANGE, YARDS:	0	25	50	75	100
Hornady 400 XTP-MAG	velocity, fps:	1300		1179		1093
	energy, ft-lb:	1501		1235		1060

.480 RUGER

CARTRIDGE BULLET	RANGE, YARDS:	0	25	50	75	100
Hornady 325 XTP-MAG	velocity, fps:	1350		1191		1076
	energy, ft-lb:	1315		1023		835
Hornady 400 XTP-MAG	velocity, fps:	1100		1027		971
	energy, ft-lb:	1075		937		838
Speer 275 Gold Dot HP	velocity, fps:	1450		1284		1152
	energy, ft-lb:	1284		1007		810
Speer 325 SP	velocity, fps:	1350		1224		1124
	energy, ft-lb:	1315		1082		912

.50 ACTION EXPRESS

CARTRIDGE BULLET	RANGE, YARDS:	0	25	50	75	100
Speer 300 Gold Dot HP	velocity, fps:	1550		1361		1207
	energy, ft-lb:	1600		1234		970
Speer 325 UCHP	velocity, fps:	1400		1232		1106
	energy, ft-lb:	1414		1095		883

.500 SMITH & WESSON

CARTRIDGE BULLET	RANGE, YARDS:	0	25	50	75	100
Hornady 350 XTP Mag	velocity, fps:	1900		1656		1439
	energy, ft-lb:	2805		2131		1610
Hornady 500 FP-XTP	velocity, fps:	1425		1281		1164
	energy, ft-lb:	2254		1823		1505
Win. 350 Super-X	velocity, fps	1400		1231		1106
	energy, ft-lb	1523		1178		951
Win. 400 Platinum Tip	velocity, fps:	1800		1647		1505
	energy, ft-lb:	2877		2409		2012

BALLISTICS

Directory of Manufacturers & Suppliers

Accurate Arms Co., Inc.
c/o Western Powders, Inc.
P.O. Box 158
Miles City, MT 59301
Phone: 406-234-0422
http://www.accuratepowder.com

Accu-Tek Firearms
EXCEL INDUSTRIES, INC.
4510 Carter Court
Chino, CA 91710
Phone: 909-627-2404
http://www.accu-tekfirearms
.com

Aimpoint, Inc.
14103 Mariah Ct.
Chantilly, VA 20151
Phone: 703-263-9795
http://www.aimpoint.com

Alliant Powder
P.O. Box 6
Radford, VA 24143-0006
Phone: 800-276-9337
http://www.alliantpowder.com

Alpen Outdoors Corp.
10329 Dorset Street, Rancho
Cucamonga, CA 91730
Phone: 909-987-8370
http://www.alpenoutdoor.com

American Derringer Corp.
127 North Lacy Drive
Waco, TX 76715-4640
Phone: 254-799-9111
http://www.amderringer.com

J. G. Anschutz Co.
http://www.anschuetz-sport
.com
See Tristar Sporting Arms

Armalite, Inc.
P.O. Box 299
Geneseo, Il. 61254
Phone: 309-944-6939
Toll Free: 800-336-0184
http://www.armalite.com

ArmsCo
1247 Rand Rd
Des Plaines, IL 60016 US
Phone: 847-768-1000

Austin & Halleck
2150 South 950 East
Provo UT 84606
Phone: 877-543-3256
          801-371-0412
http://www.topratedadventures.com

Barnes Bullets
P.O. Box 620
Mona, UT 84645
Phone: 800-574-9200
http://www.barnesbullets.com

Barrett Firearms Mfg.
P.O. Box 1077
Murfreesboro, TN 37133
Phone: 615-896-2938
http://www.barrettrifles.com

B. C. Outdoors
Eldorado Cartridge Corporation
P.O. Box 62173
Boulder City, NV 89006-2173
Phone: 702-293-6285
http://www.pmcammo.com

Berger Bullets, Inc.
4275 N. Palm St.
Fullerton, CA 92835
Phone: 714-447-5456
http://www.bergerbullets.com

Black Hills Ammunition
P.O. Box 3090
Rapid City, SD 57709-3090
Phone: 605-348-5150
http://www.black-hills.com

Bond Arms, Inc.
P.O. Box 1296
Granbury, TX 76048
Phone: 817-573-4445
http://www.bondarms.com

Brenneke of America Ltd.
P.O. Box 1481
Clinton, IA 52733-1481
Phone: 800-753-9733
http://www.brennekeusa.com

Ed. Brown Products, Inc.
P.O. Box 492,
Perry, MO 63462
Phone: 573-565-3261
http://www.edbrown.com

Browning
One Browning Place
Morgan, UT 84050
Phone: 800-333-3288
http://www.browning.com

Brown Precision, Inc.
P.O. Box 270 W.,
Los Molinos, CA 96055
Phone: 530-384-2506
http://www.brownprecision.com

Brunton
620 East Monroe Avenue
Riverton, WY 82501
Phone: 307-856-6559
http://www.brunton.com

BSA Optics, Inc.
3911 SW 47th Avenue, Suite
914
Fort Lauderdale, FL 33314
Phone: 954-581-2144
http://www.bsaoptics.com

Burris Company, Inc.
331 East 8th Street
P.O. Box 1747
Greeley, CO 80631
Phone: 970-356-1670
http://www.burrisoptics.com

**Bushmaster Firearms
International, LLC**
P.O. Box 1479
Windham, ME 04062
Phone: 800-998-7928
http://www.bushmaster.com

Bushnell Outdoors Products
9200 Cody
Overland Park, KS 66214-1734
Phone: 800-423-3537
http://www.bushnell.com

Cabela's, Inc.
One Cabela Drive
Sidney, NE 69160
Phone: 800-331-3454
http://www.cabelas.com

Cci/Speer-Blount, Inc.
2299 Snake River Avenue
Lewiston, ID 83501
Phone: 800-627-3640
http://www.speer-bullets.com

CheyTac Associates Ltd.
363 Sunset Dr.
P.O. Box 822
Arco, ID 83213
Phone: 800-CHEYTAC (800-
243-9822)
http://www.cheytac.com

Christensen Arms
192 E. 100 N
Fayettet, UT 84630
Phone: 888-517-8855
http://www.christensenarms.com

Cimarron Firearms Co., Inc.
105 Winding Oak Road
Fredericksburg, TX 78624
Phone: 830-997-9090
http://www.cimarron-firearms.com

Colt Blackpowder Arms Co.
110 8th St.
Brooklyn, NY 11215
Phone: 718-499-4678
http://www.gzanders.com

**Colt's Manufacturing Company
LLC**
545 New Park Avenue
West Hartford, CT 06110 USA
Phone: 860-236-6311
http://www.coltsmfg.com

Cooper Arms, Inc.
P.O. Box 114
Stevensville, MT 59870
Phone: 406-777-0373
http://cooperfirearms.com

COR-BON/Glaser
P.O. Box 369
Sturgis, SD 57785
Phone: 800-626-7266
http://www.dakotaammo.net

Connecticut Valley Arms
5988 Peachtree Corners East
Norcross, GA 30071
Phone: 770-449-4687
http://www.cva.com

CZ-USA
P.O. Box 171073
Kansas City, KS 66117-0073
Phone: 800-955-4486
http://cz-usa.com

Dakota Arms
1310 Industry Road
Sturgis, SD 57785
Phone: 605-347-4686
http://www.dakotaarms.com

Dillon Precision Products, Inc.
8009 East Dillon's Way
Scottsdale, AZ 85260
Phone: 800-223-4570
http://www.dillonprecision.com

Dixie Gun Works
P.O. Box 130
Union City, TN 38281
Phone: 800-238-6785
http://www.dixiegunworks.com

Directory of Manufacturers & Suppliers

Downsizer Corporation
P.O. Box 710316
Santee, CA 92072-0316
Phone: 619-448-5510

Dynamit Nobel/RWS
81 Ruckman Road
Closter, NJ 07624
Phone: 201-767-1995
http://www.rwsairguns.com

Eagle Imports, Inc.
1750 Brielle Ave. Unit B-1
Wanamassa, NJ 07712
Phone: 732-493-0333
http://www.bersafirearmsusa.com

E.D.M. Arms
2410 West 350 North
Hurricane, UT 84737
Phone: 435-635-5233
http://www.edmarms.com

Entreprise Arms
5321 Irwindale Ave
Irwindale, CA 91706
Phone: 626-962-8712
http://www.entreprise.com

Euroarms of America, Inc.
P.O. BOX 3277
Winchester, VA 22601
Phone: 540-662-1863
http://www.euroarms.net

European American Armory Corp.
P.O. Box 560746
Rockledge, FL 32956-0746
Phone: 321-639-4842
http://www.eaacorp.com

Federal Cartridge Co.
900 Ehlen Dr
Anoka, MN 55303-1778
Phone: 763-421-7100
http://www.federalpremium.com

Skullman Enterprise AB
Flodman Guns
S - 647 95 Akers styckebruk
Jarsta, Sweden
Phone: +46-159-30861
http://www.flodman.com

Fiocchi of America
6930 N. Fremont Road
Ozark, MO 65721
Phone: 417-725-4118
http://www.fiocchiusa.com

FNH USA, Inc.
P.O. Box 697
McLean, VA 22101
Phone: 703-288-1292
http://www.fnhusa.com

Forster Products
310 East Lanark Avenue
Lanark, IL 61046
Phone: 815-493-6360
http://www.forsterproducts.com

Freedom Arms
314 Highway 239
P.O. Box 150
Freedom, WY 83120
Phone: 307-883-2468
http://www.freedomarms.com

Glock, Inc.
6000 Highlands Parkway
Smyrna, GA 30082
Phone: 770-432-1202
http://www.glock.com

Gonic Arms
134 Flagg Rd.
Gonic, NH 03839
Phone: 603-332-8456

Harrington & Richardson
H&R 1871, LLC
P.O. Box 1871
Madison, NC 27025
Phone: 866-776-9292
http://www.hr1871.com

H-S Precision
1301 Turbine Dr.,
Rapid City, SD 57703
Phone: 605-341-3006
http://www.hsprecision.com

Hammerli USA
Larry's Guns
56 West Gray Road
Gray, ME 04039
Phone: 207-657-4559
http://www.larrysguns.com

Heckler & Koch
7661 Commerce Ln.
Trussville, AL 35173
Phone: 706-568-1906
http://www.hk-usa.com

Henry Repeating Arms Co.
59 East 1st Street
Bayonne, NJ 07002
Phone: 201-858-4400
http://www.henryrepeating.com

Heritage Manufacturing
4600 NW 135th St.
Opa Locka, FL 33054
Phone: 305-685-5966
http://www.heritagemfg.com

High Standard Mfg. Co.
5200 Mitchelldale, Suite E-17
Houston, TX 77092
Phone: 800-272-7816
http://www.highstandard.com

Hodgdon Powder Co., Inc.
6231 Robinson
P.O. Box 2932
Shawnee Mission, KS 66202
Phone: 913-362-9455
http://www.hodgdon.com

Hornady Mfg. Co.
3625 Old Potash Hwy
P.O. Box 1848
Grand Island, NE 68802-1848
Phone: 800-338-3220
http://www.hornady.com

Ithaca Gun Co.
420 N. Warpole Street
Upper Sandusky, OH 43351
Phone: 877-6-ITHACA (877-648-4222)
http://www.ithacagun.com

Jarrett Rifles, Inc.
383 Brown Road
Jackson, SC 29831
Phone: 803-471-3616
http://www.jarrettrifles.com

Kahles
P.O. Box 21004
Cranston, RI 02920-1004
Phone: 866-606-8779
http://www.kahlesoptik.com

Kahr Arms
P.O. Box 220
Blauvelt, NY 10913
Phone: 845-652-8535
http://www.kahr.com

Kel-Tec Cnc
P.O. Box 236009
Cocoa, FL 32926
Phone: 321-631-0068
http://www.kel-tec-cnc.com

Kimber Manufacturing, Inc.
1 Lawton Street
Yonkers, NY 10705
Phone: 914-964-0771 Ext: 350
http://www.kimberamerica.com

Knight Rifles
21852 Hwy J46
Centerville, IA 52544
Phone: 641-856-2626
http://www.knightrifles.com

Krieghoff International, Inc.
P.O. Box 549
Ottsville, PA 18942
Phone: 610-847-5173
http://www.krieghoff.com

L.A.R. Manufacturing, Inc.
4133 West Farm Road
West Jordan, UT 84088-4997
Phone: 801-280-3505
http://www.largrizzly.com

Lazzeroni Arms Co.
P.O. Box 26696
Tucson, AZ 85726-6696
Phone: 888-492-7247
http://www.lazzeroni.com

Legacy Sports Intl.
4750 Longley Lane, Suite 208
Reno, NV 89502
Phone: 775-828-0555
http://www.legacysports.com

Lenartz Muzzleloading
8001 Whitneyville Rd SE
Alto, MI 49302
Phone: 616-891-0372
http://www.lenartztravel.com

Leupold & Stevens, Inc.
14400 NW Greenbrier Parkway
Beaverton, OR 97006-5790
Phone: 800-LEUP.O.LD (800-538-7653)
http://www.leupold.com

Lone Star Rifle Co., Inc.
11231 Rose Road
Conroe, Texas 77303
Phone: 936-228-2448
http://www.lonestarrifle.com

Lyman Products Corp.
475 Smith Street
Middletown, CT 06457
Phone: 800-225-9626
     800-423-9704
     860-632-2020
http://www.lymanproducts.com

Magnum Research, Inc.
7110 University Avenue N.E.
Minneapolis, MN 55432
Phone: 800-772-6168
http://www.magnumresearch.com

Magtech Ammunition Co., Inc
248 Apollo Drive, Suite 180
Lino Lakes, MN 55014
Phone: 800-466-7191
http://www.magtechammunition.com

Markesbery Muzzleloaders, Inc.
7065 Production Court
Florence, KY 41042
Phone: 859-534-5630
http://www.markesbery.com

MANUFACTURERS

Directory of Manufacturers & Suppliers

Marlin Firearms Co.
100 Kenna Drive
P.O. Box 248
North Haven, CT 06473-0905
Phone: 203-239-5621
        800-544-8892
http://www.marlinfirearms.com

O.F. Mossberg & Sons, Inc.
7 Grasso Ave.
North Haven, CT 06473
Phone: 203-230-5300
http://www.mossberg.com

Navy Arms Company, Inc.
219 Lawn St
Martinsburg, WV 25405-5009
Phone: 304-262-1651
http://www.navyarms.com

New England Arms Corp.
P.O. Box 278
Kittery Point, ME 03905
Phone: 207-439-0593
http://www.newenglandarms.com

New England Firearms Co., Inc.
H&R 1871, LLC
P.O. Box 1871
Madison, NC 27025
Phone: 866-776-9292
http://www.hr1871.com

New Ultra Light Arms
P.O. Box 340
214 Price Street (Shipping)
Granville, WV 26534
Phone: 304-292-0600
http://www.newultralight.com

Nikon, Inc.
1300 Walt Whitman Rd.
Melville, NY 11747
Phone: 631-271-2145
http://www.nikon.com

North America Arms
2150 South 950 East
Provo, UT 84606
Phone: 800-821-5783
http://www.naaminis.com

Nosler, Inc.
P.O. Box 671
Bend, OR 97709
Phone: 800-285-3701
http://www.nosler.com

Olympic Arms, Inc.
624 Old Pacific Hwy. SE
Olympia, WA 98513
Phone: 800-228-3471
http://www.olyarms.com

Para-Ordnance Mfg, Inc.
980 Tapscott Road,
Toronto, ON M1X 1C3
Canada
Phone: 416-297-7855
http://www.paraord.com

Pentax Imaging Co.
600 12th St
Golden, CO 80401
Phone: 303-728-0230
http://www.pentaximaging.com

Perazzi USA
1010 W. Tenth St.
Azusa, Ca. 91702
Phone: 626-334-1234
http://www.perazzi.com

Pgw Defense Technologies
1-761 Marion St.
Winnipeg, Manitoba
Canada R2J0K6

RCBS
605 Oro Dam Blvd
Oroville, CA 95965
Phone: 800-533-5000
http://www.rcbs.com

Redding Reloading Equipment
1089 Starr Rd.
Cortland, NY 13045
Phone: 607-753-3331
http://www.redding-reloading
.com

Redfield USA
201 Plantation Oak Drive
Thomasville, GA 31792
Phone: 800-323-3191
http://www.redfieldoptics.co.uk

Remington Arms Company, Inc.
870 Remington Drive
P.O. Box 700
Madison, NC 27025-0700
Phone: 800-243-9700
http://www.remington.com

Rifles, Inc.
3580 Leal Road
Pleasanton, TX 78064
Phone: 830-569-2055
http://www.riflesinc.com

Rizzini
100 Burritt Street
New Britain, CT 06053
Phone: 860-225-6581
http://www.rizziniusa.com

Rogue Rifle Co.
1114 Birch Ave
Lewiston, ID 83501-5517
Phone: 208-746-5401

Rossi Firearms
BrazTech Intl.
16175 NW 49 Avenue
Miami, FL 33014
Phone: 305-474-0401
http://www.rossiusa.com

Sauer
SIG SAUER Inc.
Customer Service Dept.
18 Industrial Drive
Exeter, NH 03833-4557
Phone: 603-772-2302 (press #3
for Customer Service)
http://www.sigsauer.com

Savage Arms, Inc.
100 Springdale Road,
Westfield, MA 01085
Phone: 413-568-7001
http://www.savagearms.com

Shiloh Rifle Mfg.
P.O. Box 279
201 Centennial Drive
Big Timber, MT 59011
Phone: 406-932-4266
        406-932-4454
http://www.shilohrifle.com

Sierra Bullets
1400 West Henry Street
Sedalia, MO 65301
Phone: 660-827-6300
http://www.sierrabullets.com

Sigarms, Inc.
SIG SAUER Inc.
Customer Service Dept.
18 Industrial Drive
Exeter, NH 03833-4557
Phone: 603-772-2302 (press #3
for Customer Service)
http://www.sigsauer.com

Sightron, Inc.
100 Jeffrey Way Suite A
Youngsville, NC 27596
Phone: 919-562-3000
http://www.sightron.com

Simmons Outdoor Corp.
9200 Cody
Overland Park, KS 66214-1734
Phone: 888-276-5945
http://www.simmonsoptics.com

SKB Shotguns
GU, Inc. / SKB Shotguns
4441 S 134th St
Omaha, NE 68137-1107
Phone: 800-752-2767
http://www.skbshotguns.com

Smith & Wesson
2100 Roosevelt Avenue
Springfield, MA 01104
Phone: 800-331-0852
http://smith-wesson.com

Springfield Armory
420 W. Main St.
Geneseo, IL 61254
Phone: 800-680-6866
http://www.springfield-armory.com

Sturm, Ruger & Company, Inc.
1 Lacey Pl
Southport, CT 06890-1207
Phone: 203-259-7843
http://www.ruger-firearms.com

Swarovski Optik, NA
2 Slater Rd
Cranston, RI 02920-4468
Phone: 401-734-1800
http://www.swarovskioptik.us

Swift Bullet Co.
One Thousand One Swift
Avenue
P.O. Box 27
Quinter, KS 67752
Phone: 785-754-3959
http://www.swiftbullets.com

Swift Optics
2055 Gateway Pl
Suite 500
San Jose, CA 95110-1082
Phone: 408-293-2380

Szecsei & Fuchs
North American Office
450 Charles St.
Windsor, ON Canada
N8X 371
Phone: 519-966-1234
http://www.szecseidoublebol-
trepeater.ca

Tactical Rifles – Dow Arms
38439 5th Ave #186
Zephyrhills, FL 33542-4328
Phone: 877-811-GUNS (877-
811-4867)
http://www.tacticalrifles.net

Taurus Intl., Inc.
16175 NW 49 Avenue
Miami, FL 33014
Phone: 305-624-1115
http://www.taurususa.com

Directory of Manufacturers & Suppliers

Thompson/Center Arms
P.O. Box 5002
Rochester, NH 03866
Phone: 603-330-5659
http://www.tcarms.com

Traditions Firearms
1375 Boston Post Road
P.O. Box 776
Old Saybrook, CT 06475
Phone: 860-388-4656
http://www.traditionsfirearms.com

Trijicon
49385 Shafer Avenue
P.O. Box 930059
Wixom, MI 48393
Phone: 248-960-7700
http://www.trijicon.com

Tristar Sporting Arms, Ltd.
1816 Linn Street
North Kansas City, MO 64116
Phone: 816-421-1400
http://www.tristarsportingarms.com

U.S. Repeating Arms Co.
275 Winchester Ave.
Morgan, UT 84050
Phone: 800-333-3288
       801.876.2711
http://www.winchesterguns.com

Vihtavuori/Lapua
1241 Ellis Street
Bensenville, IL 60106
Phone: 630-350-1116
http://www.vihtavuori-lapua.com

Walther
2100 Roosevelt Avenue
Springfield, MA 01104
Phone: 800-372-6454
http://www.waltheramerica.com

Weatherby, Inc.
1605 Commerce Way
Paso Robles, CA 93446
Phone: 805-227-2600
http://www.weatherby.com

Western Powders
P.O. Box 158
Miles City, MT 59301
Phone: 406-234-0422
http://www.accuratearms.com

White Rifles
P.O. Box 1044
Orem, UT 84059-1044
http://www.whiterifles.com

Wildey, Inc.
45 Angevine Rd
Warren, CT 06754
Phone: 860-355-9000
http://www.wildeyguns.com

Wild West Guns, Inc.
7100 Homer Drive
Anchorage, AK 99518
Phone: 800-992-4570
http://www.wildwestguns.com

Williams Gun Sight Co.
7389 Lapeer Rd.
Davison, MI 48423
Phone: 800-530-9028
http://www.williamsgunsight
.com

Winchester
427 N Shamrock St
East Alton, IL 62024-1174
Phone: 618-258-2000
http://www.winchester.com

XS Sight Systems
2401 Ludelle
Fort Worth, TX 76105
Phone: 888-744-4880
http://www.xssights.com

Zeiss Sports Optics
13005 North Kingston Avenue
Chester, VA 23836-8333
Phone: 800-441-3005
http://www.zeiss.com

Z-Hat Custom Dies
1991 Lilac St.
Casper, WY 82604
http://www.z-hat.com

To help you find the model of your choice, the following index includes every firearm found in this edition of *Shooter's Bible*, listed by type of gun.

Gunfinder Index

Gunfinder Index